Handbook of Parenting

Volume 3
Being and Becoming a Parent

Handbook of Parenting

Second Edition

Volume 3
Being and Becoming a Parent

Edited by
Marc H. Bornstein

National Institute of Child Health and Human Development

 LAWRENCE ERLBAUM ASSOCIATES, PUBLISHERS
2002   Mahwah, New Jersey   London

Editor:	Bill Webber
Editorial Assistant:	Erica Kica
Cover Design:	Kathryn Houghtaling Lacey
Textbook Production Manager:	Paul Smolenski
Full-Service Compositor:	TechBooks
Text and Cover Printer:	Hamilton Printing Company

This book was typeset in 10/11.5 pt. Times, Italic, Bold, Bold Italic.
The heads were typeset in Helvetica, Italic, Bold, Bold Italic.

Lawrence Erlbaum Associates, Inc., Publishers
10 Industrial Avenue
Mahwah, New Jersey 07430

Library of Congress Cataloging-in-Publication Data

Handbook of parenting / edited by Marc H. Bornstein.—2nd ed.
    p. cm.
    Includes bibliographical references and indexes.
    Contents: v. 1. Children and parenting—v. 2. Biology and ecology of parenting—v. 3. Being
and becoming a parent—v. 4. Social conditions and applied parenting—v. 5. practical issues
in parenting.
    ISBN 0-8058-3778-7 (hc : v. 1 : alk. paper)—ISBN 0-8058-3779-5 (hc : v. 2 : alk. paper)—
ISBN 0-8058-3780-9 (hc : v. 3 : alk. paper)—ISBN 0-8058-3781-7 (hc : v. 4 : alk. paper)—
ISBN 0-8058-3782-5 (hc : v. 5 : alk. paper)
    1. Parenting. 2. Parents. I. Bornstein, Marc H.

HQ755.8.H357 2002
649′.1—dc21
                                            2001058458

Printed in the United States of America
10 9 8 7 6 5 4 3 2

For *Marian* and *Harold Sackrowitz*

Contents of Volume 3:
Being and Becoming a Parent

Preface

This new edition of the *Handbook of Parenting* appears at a time that is momentous in the history of parenting. The family generally, and parenting specifically, are today in a greater state of flux, question, and redefinition than perhaps ever before. We are witnessing the emergence of striking permutations on the theme of parenting: blended families, lesbian and gay parents, teen versus fifties first-time moms and dads. One cannot but be awed on the biological front by technology that now renders postmenopausal women capable of childbearing and with the possibility of designing babies. Similarly, on the sociological front, single parenthood is a modern-day fact of life, adult–child dependency is on the rise, and parents are ever less certain of their roles, even in the face of rising environmental and institutional demands that they take increasing responsibility for their offspring. The *Handbook of Parenting* is concerned with all facets of parenting.

Despite the fact that most people become parents and everyone who has ever lived has had parents, parenting remains a most mystifying subject. Who is ultimately responsible for parenting? Does parenting come naturally, or must we learn how to parent? How do parents conceive of parenting? Of childhood? What does it mean to parent a preterm baby, twins, or a child with a disability? To be a younger or an older parent, or one who is divorced, disabled, or drug abusing? What do theories in psychology (psychoanalysis, personality theory, and behavior genetics, for example) contribute to our understanding of parenting? What are the goals parents have for themselves? For their children? What are the functions of parents' beliefs? Of parents' behaviors? What accounts for parents' believing or behaving in similar ways? What accounts for all the attitudes and actions of parents that differ? How do children influence their parents? How do personality, knowledge, and world view affect parenting? How do social status, culture, and history shape parenthood? How can parents effectively relate to schools, daycare, their children's pediatricians?

These are some of the questions addressed in this second edition of the *Handbook of Parenting* ... for this is a book on *how to parent* as much as it is one on *what being a parent is all about*.

Put succinctly, parents create people. It is the entrusted and abiding task of parents to prepare their offspring for the physical, psychosocial, and economic conditions in which they will eventually fare and, it is hoped, flourish. Amidst the many influences on child development, parents are the "final common pathway" to children's development and stature, adjustment and success. Human social inquiry—at least since Athenian interest in Spartan childrearing practices—has always, as a matter of course, included reports of parenting. Yet Freud opined that childrearing is one of three "impossible professions"—the other two being governing nations and psychoanalysis. And one encounters as many views as the number of people one asks about the relative merits of being an at-home or a working mother, about whether daycare, family care, or parent care is best for a child, about whether good parenting reflects intuition or experience.

The *Handbook of Parenting* concerns itself with different types of parents—mothers and fathers, single, adolescent, and adoptive parents; with basic characteristics of parenting—behaviors, knowledge, beliefs, and expectations about parenting; with forces that shape parenting—employment, social status, culture, environment, and history; with problems faced by parents—handicaps, marital difficulties, drug addiction; and with practical concerns of parenting—how to promote children's health, foster social adjustment and cognitive competence, and interact with school, legal, and public officials. Contributors to the *Handbook of Parenting* have worked in different ways toward understanding all these diverse aspects of parenting, and all look to the most recent research and thinking in the field to shed light on many topics every parent wonders about.

Parenthood is a job whose primary object of attention and action is the child. But parenting also has consequences for parents. Parenthood is giving and responsibility, but parenting has its own intrinsic pleasures, privileges, and profits as well as frustrations, fears, and failures. Parenthood can enhance psychological development, self-confidence, and sense of well-being, and parenthood also affords opportunities to confront new challenges and to test and display diverse competencies. Parents can derive considerable and continuing pleasure in their relationships and activities with their children. But parenting is also fraught with small and large stresses and disappointments. The transition to parenting is formidable; the onrush of new stages of parenthood is relentless. In the final analysis, however, parents receive a great deal "in kind" for the hard work of parenting—they are often recipients of unconditional love, they gain skills, and they even pretend to immortality. This edition of the *Handbook of Parenting* presents the many positives that accompany parenting and offers solutions for the many challenges.

The *Handbook of Parenting* encompasses the broad themes of who are parents, whom parents parent, the scope of parenting and its many effects, the determinants of parenting, and the nature, structure, and meaning of parenthood for parents. This second edition of the *Handbook of Parenting* is divided into five volumes, each with two parts:

Volume 1 concerns CHILDREN AND PARENTING. Parenthood is, perhaps first and foremost, a functional status in the life cycle: Parents issue as well as protect, care for, and represent their progeny. But human development is too subtle, dynamic, and intricate to admit that parental caregiving alone determines the developmental course and outcome of ontogeny. Volume 1 of the *Handbook of Parenting* begins with chapters concerned with how children influence parenting. The origins of parenting are, of course, complex, but certain factors are of obvious importance. First, children affect parenting: Notable are their more obvious characteristics, like age or developmental stage; but more subtle ones, like gender, physical state, temperament, mental ability, and other individual-differences factors, are also instrumental. The chapters in Part I, on Parenting Children and Older People, discuss the unique rewards and special demands of parenting children of different ages—infants, toddlers, youngsters in middle childhood, and adolescents—as well as the modern notion of parent–child relationships in adulthood and later years. The chapters in Part II, on Parenting Children of Varying Status, discuss the common matters of parenting siblings and girls versus boys as well as more unique situations of parenting twins, adopted and foster children, and children with special needs, such as those born preterm, with mental retardation, or aggressive and withdrawn disorders.

Volume 2 concerns the BIOLOGY AND ECOLOGY OF PARENTING. For parenting to be understood as a whole, psychophysiological and sociological determinants of parenting need to be brought into the picture. Volume 2 of the *Handbook* relates parenting to its biological roots and sets parenting within its ecological framework. Some aspects of parenting are influenced by the biological makeup of human beings, and the chapters in Part I, on the Biology of Parenting, examine the evolution of parenting, hormonal and psychobiological determinants of parenting in nonhumans and in human beings, parenting in primates, and intuitive universals in human parenting. A deep understanding of what it means to parent also depends on the ecologies in which parenting takes place. Beyond the nuclear family, parents are embedded in, influence, and are themselves affected by larger social systems. The chapters in Part II, on the Social Ecology of Parenting, examine employment status and parenting, the socioeconomic, cultural, environmental, and historical contexts of parenting, and provide an overarching developmental contextual perspective on parenting.

Volume 3 concerns BEING AND BECOMING A PARENT. A large cast of characters is responsible for parenting, each has her or his own customs and agenda, and the psychological makeups and social interests of those individuals are revealing of what parenting is. Chapters in Part I, on The Parent, show how rich and multifaceted is the constellation of children's caregivers. Considered successively are mothers, fathers, coparenting, single parenthood, grandparenthood, adolescent parenthood, nonparental caregiving, sibling caregivers, parenting in divorced and remarried families, lesbian and gay parents, and the role of contemporary reproductive technologies in parenting. Parenting also draws on transient and enduring physical, personality, and intellectual characteristics of the individual. The chapters in Part II, on Becoming and Being a Parent, consider the transition to parenting, stages of parental development, personality and parenting, parents' knowledge of, beliefs in, cognitions about, attributions for, and attitudes toward childrearing, as well as relations between psychoanalysis and parenthood. Such parental cognitions serve many functions: They generate and shape parental behaviors, mediate the effectiveness of parenting, and help to organize parenting.

Volume 4 concerns SOCIAL CONDITIONS AND APPLIED PARENTING. Parenting is not uniform in all communities, groups, or cultures; rather, parenting is subject to wide variation. Volume 4 of the *Handbook* describes socially defined groups of parents and social conditions that promote variation in parenting. The chapters in Part I, on Social Conditions of Parenting, include ethnic and minority parenting in general and parenting among Latino, African American, and Asian populations, in particular, as well as parents in poverty and parenting and social networks. Parents are ordinarily the most consistent and caring people in the lives of children. In everyday life, however, parenting does not always go right or well. Information, education, and support programs can remedy these ills. The chapters in Part II, on Applied Issues in Parenting, explore parenting competence, maternal deprivation, marital relationships and conflict, parenting with a sensory or physical disability, parental psychopathology, substance-abusing parents, parental child maltreatment, and parent education.

Volume 5 concerns PRACTICAL ISSUES IN PARENTING. Parents meet the biological, physical, and health requirements of children. Parents interact with children socially. Parents stimulate children to engage and understand the environment and to enter the world of learning. Parents provision, organize, and arrange children's home and local environments and the media to which children are exposed. Parents also manage child development vis-à-vis childcare, school, the worlds of medicine and law, as well as other social institutions through their active citizenship. Volume 5 of the *Handbook* describes the nuts and bolts of parenting as well as the promotion of positive parenting practices. The chapters in Part I, on Practical Parenting, review the ethics of parenting, parenting and attachment, child compliance, the development of children's self-regulation, children's prosocial and moral development, socialization and children's values, maximizing children's cognitive abilities, parenting talented children, play in parent–child interactions, everyday stresses and parenting, parents and children's peer relationships, and health promotion. Such caregiving principles and practices have direct effects on children. Parents indirectly influence children as well, for example, through their relationships with each other and their local or larger community. The chapters in Part II, on Parents and Social Institutions, explore parents and their children's childcare, schools, media, and doctors and delve into relations between parenthood and the law and public policy.

Each chapter in the second edition of the *Handbook of Parenting* addresses a different but central topic in parenting; each is rooted in current thinking and theory as well as in classical and modern research in that topic; each has been written to be read and absorbed in a single sitting. Each chapter in this new *Handbook* follows a standard organization, including an introduction to the chapter as a whole, followed by historical considerations of the topic, a discussion of central issues and theory, a review of classical and modern research, forecasts of future directions of theory and research, and a set of conclusions. Of course, each chapter considers the contributors' own convictions and research, but contributions to this new edition of the *Handbook of Parenting* present all major points of view and central lines of inquiry and interpret them broadly. The *Handbook of Parenting* is intended to be both comprehensive and state of the art. To assert that parenting is complex is to understate the obvious. As the expanded scope of this second edition of the *Handbook of Parenting* amply shows, parenting is naturally and closely allied with many other fields.

The *Handbook of Parenting* is concerned with child outcomes of parenting but also with the nature and dimensions of variations in parenting per se. Beyond an impressive range of information, readers will find *passim* critical discussions of typologies of parenting (e.g., authoritarian–autocratic, indulgent–permissive, indifferent–uninvolved, authoritative–reciprocal), theories of parenting (e.g., ecological, psychoanalytic, behavior genetic, ethological, behavioral, sociobiological), conditions of parenting (e.g., mother versus father, cross cultural, situation-by-age-by-style), recurrent themes in parenting studies (e.g., attachment, transaction, systems), and even aphorisms (e.g., "A child should have strict discipline in order to develop a fine, strong character," "The child is father to the man").

In the course of editing this new edition of the *Handbook*, I set about to extract central messages and critical perspectives expressed in each chapter, fully intending to construct a comprehensive Introduction to these volumes. In the end, I took away two significant impressions from my own efforts and the texts of my many collaborators in this work. First, my notes cumulated to a monograph on parenting . . . clearly inappropriate for an Introduction. Second, when all was written and done, I found the chorus of contributors to this new edition of the *Handbook* more eloquent and compelling than one lone voice could ever be. Each chapter in the *Handbook of Parenting* begins with an articulate and persuasive Introduction that lays out, in a clarity, expressiveness, and force (I frankly envy), the meanings and implications of that contribution and that perspective to parenting. In lieu of one Introduction, readers are urged to browse the many Introductions that will lead their way into the *Handbook of Parenting*.

Once upon a time, parenting was a seemingly simple thing: Mothers mothered; Fathers fathered. Today, parenting has many motives, many meanings, and many manifestations. Contemporary parenting is viewed as immensely time consuming and effortful. The perfect mother or father or family is a figment of past imagination. Modern society recognizes "subdivisions" of the call: genetic mother, gestational mother, biological mother, birth mother, social mother. For some, the individual sacrifices that mark parenting arise for the sole and selfish purpose of passing one's genes on to succeeding generations. For others, a second child is conceived to save the life of a first child. A multitude of factors influence the unrelenting advance of events and decisions that surround parenting—biopsychological, dyadic, contextual, historical. Recognizing this complexity is important to informing people's thinking about parenting, especially information-hungry parents themselves. This second edition of the *Handbook of Parenting* explores all these motives, meanings, and manifestations of parenting.

Each day more than three fourths of a million adults around the world experience the rewards and the challenges as well as the joys and the heartaches of becoming parents. The human race succeeds because of parenting. From the start, parenting is a "24/7" job. Parenting formally begins during or before pregnancy and can continue throughout the lifespan: Practically speaking for most, *once a parent, always a parent*. But parenting is a subject about which people hold strong opinions and about which too little solid information or considered reflection exists. Parenting has never come with a *Handbook* . . . until now.

ACKNOWLEDGMENTS

I would like to express my sincere gratitude to the staffs at Lawrence Erlbaum Associates, Publishers, and TechBooks who perfectly parented production of the *Handbook of Parenting*: Victoria Danahy, Susan Detwiler, Sheila Johnston, Arthur M. Lizza, Paul Smolenski, and Christopher Thornton.

—Marc H. Bornstein

Contents of Volume 1: Children and Parenting

Contents of Volume 2: Biology and Ecology of Parenting

PART II: SOCIAL ECOLOGY OF PARENTING

Contents of Volume 4:
Social Conditions and Applied Parenting

PART II: APPLIED ISSUES IN PARENTING

Contents of Volume 5:
Practical Issues in Parenting

About the Authors in Volume 3

VIRGINIA D. ALLHUSEN is a Research Associate in the Department of Psychology and Social Behavior, School of Social Ecology, the University of California at Irvine. She earned a B.S. at Duke University and a M.A. and Ph.D. at Cornell University. She is a Co-Principal Investigator on the NICHD Study of Early Child Care and Youth Development. She is a member of the American Psychological Association, the Society for Research in Child Development, and the National Association for the Education of Young Children. Allhusen's research interests include children's attachment relationships with parents and other care providers, daycare quality and its effects on social development, and the social networks of young children and their families.

* * *

NAOMI BARENDS is a doctoral student in child clinical psychology at the Pennsylvania State University. She is a graduate of Brown University (B.A.), and she received her M.Sc. at the Pennsylvania State University. She is a student affiliate of the Society for Research in Child Development and the American Psychological Association. Her professional interests include the effects of personality disorders and normal personality on parenting and child development as well as clinical work with both children and adults.

* * *

KATHRYN E. BARNARD is Professor of Nursing and Adjunct Professor of Psychology and Affiliate of the Center for Human Development and Disability at the University of Washington. She received her B.S. in Nursing from the University of Nebraska and her M.S. in Maternal Child Nursing from Boston University; she earned her Ph.D. in the Ecology of Early Development at the University of Washington. The theme of Barnard's research has been on parenting and child outcomes. She is the author of the NCAST scales to evaluate parent-child interaction. She has served on numerous boards including Zero to Three: The National Center for Infants and Children, The Carnegie Task Force on Meeting the Needs of Young Children; the Department of Health and Human Services' Secretary's Committee on the Design of Early Head Start, the Washington Governor's Commission on Early Learning, and the Washington Foundation for Early Learning. She has served on the Advisory Board of the *Infant Mental Health Journal* and the *Journal of Scholarly Nursing Practice*.

* * *

JAY BELSKY, Director of the Institute for the Study of Children, Families and Social Issues and Professor of Psychology, Birkbeck University of London, received his B.A. from Vassar College and his M.S. and Ph.D. in Human Development and Family Studies from Cornell University. He was previously on the faculty of the Pennsylvania State University. Belsky's interests focus on the intersection of child development, family relationships, and the broader ecology of human development. He is involved in the NICHD Study of Early Child Care and Youth Development and the Dunedin (New Zealand) Multidisciplinary Longitudinal Study of Health and Development. Belsky is the author of *The Transition to Parenthood: How a First Child Changes a Marriage.*

* * *

JEANNE BROOKS-GUNN is the Virginia and Leonard Marx Professor of Child Development and Education at Teachers College, Columbia University, and Director of the Center for Children and Families. She received her B.A. from Connecticut College, E.M. from Harvard University, and Ph.D. from the University of Pennsylvania. Formerly, she was a Senior Research Scientist at Educational Testing Service and Visiting Scholar at the Russell Sage Foundation. Brooks-Gunn is a member of the Roundtable on Children at the Brookings Institute, the MacArthur Network on the Family and the Economy, and the NICHD Research Network on Child and Family Well-Being. She has served on three National Academy of Science Panels. She is past president of the Society for Research on Adolescence and is a Fellow in the American Psychological Association and the American Psychological Society. She received the Vice President's National Performance Review Hammer Award, the Nicholas Hobbs Award from the American Psychological, and the John B. Hill Award from the Society for Research on Adolescence. Brooks-Gunn's specialty is policy-oriented research focusing on family and community influences on the development of children, youth, and families. Her research centers around designing and evaluating interventions aimed at enhancing the well-being of children living in poverty and associated conditions. She is author of over 300 published articles and 15 books, including *Adolescent Mothers in Later Life* and *He and She: How Children Develop Their Sex Role Identity* as well as several edited volumes, including, *Consequences of Growing up Poor, Escape from Poverty: What Makes a Difference for Children?, Neighborhood Poverty: Context and Consequences for Children, Volume 1. Policy Implications in Studying Neighborhoods, Volume 2., Social Cognition and the Acquisition of Self, Girls at Puberty: Biological and Psychosocial Perspectives, Encyclopedia of Adolescence, Transitions Through Adolescence: Interpersonal Domains and Context,* and *Conflict and Cohesion in Families: Causes and Consequences.*

* * *

M. JEANELL BUCK is a graduate student in the Department of Psychology at the University of Texas at Austin. She received her B.S. from the University of Texas at El Paso. She has participated in research investigating possible problems associated with the child interviewing in the McMartin preschool case, the Kelly Michael's case, and numerous CPS cases. Her research interests include parent–child relationships, especially discipline, and the processes that underlie family violence.

* * *

DAPHNE B. BUGENTAL is Professor of Psychology in the Department of Psychology and Co-Director of the Interdisciplinary Program in Human Development, at the University of California, Santa Barbara. She received her B.A. and Ph.D. at the University of California, Los Angeles. She was a Fellow in the University of Iowa Social Psychophysiology Program. Bugental is a Fellow in the American Psychological Association, the American Psychological Society, and the Society for the Psychological Study of Social Issues. She is a member of the Society for Research in Child Development, the International Society for Research on Emotion, the Society for Experimental Social Psychology, Society for Personality and Social Psychology, and the Society for Psychophysiological Research. She is past Associate Editor of *Personality and Social Psychology Bulletin.* Her research has tested a bio–social–cognitive model of parent–child relationships.

* * *

K. ALISON CLARKE-STEWART is Professor in the Department of Psychology and Social Behavior and Associate Dean for Research, School of Social Ecology, at the University of California-Irvine. She received her education at the University of British Columbia (B.A., M.A.) and Yale University (Ph.D.). She was previously at the University of Chicago in the Department of Education and the Committee on Human Development. Clarke-Stewart is a fellow of the American Psychological Association and the American Psychological Society and a member of the Society for Research in Child Development and the International Society for Infant Studies. Her research interests include the study of family interactions, daycare, divorce and custody, and children's eyewitness testimony. She is a Principal Investigator in the NICHD Study of Early Child Care and Youth Development. She has written *Daycare* and *Children at Home and in Daycare*.

* * *

BERTRAM J. COHLER is William Rainey Harper Professor of the Social Sciences, The College and The Committee on Human Development, The Departments of Psychology and Psychiatry, and The Committee on General Studies in the Humanities, The University of Chicago. He received his education at The University of Chicago (B.A.) and Harvard University (Ph.D). He received his psychoanalytic education at The Institute for Psychoanalysis (Chicago) in clinical and theoretical aspects of psychoanalysis. He is a Fellow of the American Psychological Association, The Gerontological Society, and past President of the American Orthopsychiatric Association. He has been editor of *Psychoanalytic Psychology*. His research interests include parenthood and intergenerational relations, the study of parents with chronic psychiatric illness and their offspring, and narrative methods and study of the life-history. He is coauthor of two books on parenting, *Mentally Ill Mothers and Their Children* and *Mothers, Grandmothers and Daughters: Personality and Child Care in Three Generation Families*, as well as coauthor of *the Essential Other* and *The Course of Gay and Lesbian Lives*, and coeditor of *the Psychoanalytic Study of Lives over Time*.

* * *

ANN C. CROUTER is Professor of Human Development in the Department of Human Development and Family Studies, College of Health and Human Development, at the Pennsylvania State University. She received her B.A. from Stanford University and Ph.D. from Cornell University. She serves on the Executive Council of the Society for Research in Adolescence and is a member of the Society for Research in Child Development, the National Council on Family Relations, the International Society for the Study of Behavioral Development, and the American Psychological Society. She currently serves as Deputy Editor of the *Journal of Marriage and the Family*. Her research interests focus on the implications of mothers' and fathers' employment circumstances for family dynamics, including parents' knowledge about their children's and adolescents' daily experiences, for the development of school-age children and adolescents.

* * *

WENDY DECOURCEY is a doctoral candidate in the Clinical Psychology program at Clark University.

* * *

JACK DEMICK is the Research Director of the Center for Adoption Research and an affiliate Professor in the Department of Psychiatry at the University of Massachusetts Medical School. Demick was educated at Yale University (A.B.) and Clark University (M.A. and Ph.D.). He was professor at Suffolk University in Boston. Demick's theoretical interests are in a holistic, developmental, systems-oriented approach to person-in-environment functioning across the lifespan, and his research interests include the study of cognitive and social development. He serves as the editor of the *Journal of Adult Development*.

* * *

LINDA M. DREW is a Post Doctoral Research Fellow at the Andrus Gerontology Center, University of Southern California. She completed her Ph.D. at Goldsmiths College, University of London. Her research interests are in family relationships, gerontology, and bereavement.

* * *

PAULINE I. ERERA is Associate Professor at the University of Washington School of Social Work. She received her BSW and MSW from the University of Haifa and her Ph.D. from Cornell University. Her research focus is on family diversity. Her publications include articles on stepfamilies, foster families, lesbian families, and noncustodial fathers. She wrote, *Family Diversity: Continuity and Change in the Contemporary Family.*

* * *

SUSAN GOLOMBOK is Professor of Psychology and Director of the Family & Child Psychology Research Centre at City University, London. She was educated at the University of Glasgow where she graduated with a B.Sc., London University Institute of Education where she obtained a M.Sc., and London University Institute of Psychiatry where she was awarded a Ph.D. The main focus of the Family & Child Psychology Research Centre is the investigation of the effects of nontraditional families on parenting and child development. Her research examines the impact on children's social, emotional and identity development, and on parent–child relationships, of being reared in new family forms, including lesbian mother families, solo mother families, and families created by contemporary reproductive technologies (IVF, donor insemination, egg donation, and surrogacy). Golombok co-authored *Bottling It Up, Gender Development, Growing up in a Lesbian Family, Modern Psychometrics,* and *Parenting: What Really Counts?*

* * *

JACQUELINE JARRETT GOODNOW is a Professorial Research Fellow at Macquarie University, Sydney. She obtained her B.A. from the University of Sydney and her Ph.D. from Harvard. Her previous positions were at the University of Sydney, Harvard, the Walter Reed Institute of Research, and George Washington University. Her work is concerned with the way people frame tasks and perceive options and with the influence of social contexts (familial or cultural) on these aspects of behavior. Goodnow received the G. Stanley Hall Distinguished Scientist Award and an Award for Distinguished Contributions to Research from the Society for Research in Child Development. She is coauthor or coeditor of *A Study of Thinking, Children Drawing, Children and Families in Australia, Women, Social Science and Social Policy, Home and School: Child's Eye Views, Development According to Parents, Parental Belief Systems, Men, Women, And Household Work,* and *Cultural Practices as Contexts for Development.*

* * *

MARCY B. GRINGLAS is a Clinical Assistant Professor of Pediatrics at Thomas Jefferson University Hospital in Philadelphia. She received her B.A. from Indiana University in Bloomington, her M.A. from Columbia University, and her Ph.D. from Temple University. Her research includes longitudinal follow-up of high-risk infants and early childhood development. Gringlas is a member of the American Psychological Association, the Society for Research in Child Development, the World Association for Infant Mental Health, and the National Center for Clinical Infant Programs.

* * *

KEITH R. HAPPANEY is a Postdoctoral Fellow in the Department of Psychology at the University of Toronto. He received his education at Lehman College of the City University of New York (B.A.) and the University of California, Santa Barbara (M.A., Ph.D.). Happaney is a member of the American Psychological

Society, the Society for Research in Child Development, and the Society for Personality and Social Psychology. His research concerns the effects of social context on children's emerging theory of mind.

* * *

MELISSA R. HEAD is a doctoral candidate in the Department of Human Development and Family Studies, College of Health and Human Development, at the Pennsylvania State University. She received her B.A. from Transylvania University in Lexington, KY, and her M.S. from the Pennsylvania State University. She is a member of the Society for Research in Child Development, Society for Research in Adolescence, National Council on Family Relations, International Network on Personal Relationships, and the International Society for the Study of Personal Relationships. Her research interests include the study of parent–adolescent relationships and parental development.

* * *

CHRISTOPH M. HEINICKE is a Professor in the Department of Psychiatry and Biobehavioral Sciences and Director of the Family Development Project at the University of California, Los Angeles. Heinicke received his Ph.D. from Harvard University. His clinical training began at the Anna Freud Hampstead Clinic, London, where he collaborated with Bowlby in the study of the effects of mother–child separation. Heinicke has studied child outcomes of psychotherapy; how casework combines with individualized daycare to affect child development; prebirth parent personality and marital characteristics that have an impact on early family development; and optimal conditions of home interventions to enhance family development of first-time mothers identified as being at risk for neglecting and abusing children. Heinicke's book *Brief Separation* was awarded the Lester Hoffheimer Prize for research in psychiatry.

* * *

E. MAVIS HETHERINGTON is Emerita Professor in the Department of Psychology at the University of Virginia. She received her education at the University of British Columbia (B.A., M.A.) and at the University of California at Berkeley (Ph.D.) and previously was on the faculty at Rutgers University at Newark and the University of Wisconsin at Madison. She is a past President of Division 7 of the American Psychological Association, the Society for Research in Adolescence, and the Society for Research in Child Development. Among her awards are Distinguished Scientists Awards from the American Psychological Society, the National Council on Family Relations, the Society for Research in Child Development, the Society for Research in Adolescence, Division 7 of the American Psychological Association, the American Association for Marriage and Family Therapy and the American Family Therapy Association. In addition, she has received the University of Virginia Jefferson Award, the State of the Virginia Professor of the Year Award, and the American Psychological Association Teaching Award. She has been associate editor of *Developmental Psychology* and editor of *Child Development*. Among her books, authored, coauthored, or edited, are *Coping With Divorce, Single Parenting and Remarriage; Family Transitions; Child Development: A Contemporary Viewpoint; The Relationship Code and Advances in Family Research;* and *Stress, Coping and Resiliency in Children and Families.*

* * *

GEORGE W. HOLDEN is Professor and Associate Chair of the Psychology Department at the University of Texas at Austin. He received his B.A. from Yale University and his M.A. and Ph.D. from the University of North Carolina at Chapel Hill. He is a fellow of the American Psychological Society and a member of the Society for Research in Child Development and the American Professional Society on the Abuse of Children. His research interests include parent–child relationships, parental social cognition, and the problem of family violence. He is currently on the editorial boards of *Developmental Psychology* and the *Journal of Emotional Abuse*. Holden is the author of *Parents and the Dynamics of Child Rearing* and coeditor of *Children Exposed to Marital Violence* and *The Handbook of Family Measurement Techniques,* Volumes 2 and 3.

* * *

DANIELLE LYNN HORVATH is a doctoral candidate in the Developmental Psychology Program at Temple University. She received her B.A. from The Pennsylvania State University. She is assistant to the editor of *Monographs of the Society for Research in Child Development* and a Research Assistant in the NICHD Study of Early Childcare and Youth Development. Her research interests include contextual and indigenous influences on maternal sensitivity, attachment during middle childhood, childhood psychopathology, and familial influences on child development.

* * *

INNA KHAZAN is a doctoral candidate in the Clinical Psychology program at Clark University.

* * *

KATHLEEN KOSTELNY is a Research Associate at the Erikson Institute for Advanced Study in Child Development. She received her her B.A. from Bethel College, her M.A. from the University of Chicago, and her Ph.D. from Erikson Institute/Loyola University. Kostelny's research interests pertain to the protection of children and families in dangerous enviornments. She is coauthor of *Children in Danger: Coping with the Consequence of Community Violence* and *No Place to Be a Child: Growing Up in a War Zone.*

* * *

ANN V. McGILLICUDDY-DE LISI is the Marshall R. Metzgar Professor of Psychology at Lafayette College. She was educated at the University of Rochester (B.A.) and the Catholic University of America (M.A., Ph.D.). She was a Research Scientist at the Educational Testing Service and has served on the editorial boards of *Child Development* and the *Journal of Applied Developmental Psychology.* McGillicuddy-De Lisi is a member of the American Psychological Association, the Jean Piaget Society, and the Society for Research in Child Development. Her research interests include the study of families as learning environments for children and parents, the development of spatial knowledge, children's moral reasoning, and the development of sex differences in mathematical and spatial performance. She is coeditor of *Biology, Society, and Behavior: The Development of Sex Differences in Cognition* as well as *Parental Belief Systems: The Psychological Consequences for Children.*

* * *

JAMES P. McHALE is Associate Professor and Director of Clinical Training in the Department of Psychology, Clark University. He received his education at the University of South Florida (B.S.), Tulane University (M.S.), and the University of California at Berkeley (Ph.D.). His research has examined the nature of interadult parenting support, coordination, and distress in families of young children, and the effect of different coparental dynamics on children's socioemotional development. He is a member of the Society for Research in Child Development, the International Council for Infant Studies, the World Association for Infant Mental Health, and the National Council on Family Relations. He is editor of *Retrospect and Prospect in the Psychological Study of Families* and *Understanding How Family-Level Dynamics Affect Children's Development.*

* * *

MELANIE McCONNELL is a doctoral candidate in the Clinical Psychology program at Clark University.

* * *

MIGNON R. MOORE is Assistant Professor of Sociology at Columbia University, where she also directs the Undergraduate Program in African American Studies. Moore received the B.A. from Columbia and M.A. and Ph.D. from the University of Chicago in the Department of Sociology. She has been a postdoctoral Fellow at the Poverty Research and Training Program at the University of Michigan and a Ford Foundation Dissertation

Fellow. Her research interests are in family structure, parent–child relationships, adolescent sexuality and well-being, urban poverty, and racial and ethnic identity. Much of her research focuses on the effects of family environment and community context on adolescent outcomes, particularly for disadvantaged and African American youth.

* * *

ROSS D. PARKE is Distinguished Professor of Psychology and Director of the Center for Family Studies at the University of California, Riverside. Parke was educated at the Universities of Toronto and Waterloo and previously was affiliated with the Universities of Wisconsin and Illinois and the Fels Research Institute. He is a past President of Division 7, the Developmental Psychology Division of the American Psychological Association, and is President-Elect of the Society for Research in Child Development. His interests include the relations between families and peers, ethnic variation in families, and the impact of new reproductive technologies on families. He has been editor of *Developmental Psychology* and associate editor of *Child Development*, and is currently editor of the *Journal of Family Psychology*. Parke is the author of *Fathers* and *Fatherhood* and coauthor of *Child Psychology* and *Throwaway Dads*.

* * *

CHARLOTTE J. PATTERSON is a Professor in the Department of Psychology and the Center for Children, Families, and the Law at the University of Virginia. She received her B.A. at Pomona College and her M.A. and Ph.D. at Stanford University. She is a Fellow of the American Psychological Association and a member of the Society for Research in Child Development, the American Psychological Society, and the National Council on Family Relations. Patterson won the Outstanding Achievement Award of the American Psychological Association's Committee on Lesbian, Gay and Bisexual Concerns and the Distinguished Scientific Contribution Award from Division 44 of the American Psychological Association. Her research interests focus on social and personality development of children and adolescents in the context of family, peer, and school environments; on child development in lesbian- and gay-parented families; and on the role of sexual orientation in human development. She is the coeditor of *Lesbian, Gay and Bisexual Identities Over the Lifespan*, *Lesbian, Gay and Bisexual Identities in Families*, and *Lesbian, Gay and Bisexual Identities Among Youth*.

* * *

SUSAN PAUL is a doctoral candidate in the Committee on Human Development, The University of Chicago. She received her education at Beloit College (B.A.) and The School of Social Service Administration of The University of Chicago (M.A.).

* * *

TAMIR ROTMAN is a doctoral candidate in the Clinical Psychology program at Clark University.

* * *

IRVING E. SIGEL is Distinguished Research Scientist (Emeritus) at Educational Testing Service. He received his B.A. at Clark University and his M.A. and Ph.D. at the University of Chicago and Hon. Doctor of Science at Clark University. He was previously associated with Smith College, Michigan State University, the Merrill-Palmer Institute, and SUNY, Buffalo. Sigel is a Fellow of the American Psychological Association, a member of the Society for Research in Child Development, and a member of the Jean Piaget Society. His research interests are in socialization of cognitive development, especially in the context of the family. He is the founding editor of the *Journal of Applied Developmental Psychology*, editor of the series, *Advances in Applied Developmental Psychology*, as well coeditor of *Parental Belief Systems*.

* * *

PETER K. SMITH is Professor of Psychology and Head of the Unit for School and Family Studies at Goldsmiths College, University of London. He received his B.Sc. at the University of Oxford and his Ph.D. from the University of Sheffield. Smith is a Fellow of the British Psychological Society. Smith is on the editorial board of *Social Development, Children & Society*, and *Evolution and Human Behavior*. His research interests are in social development, grandparenting, play, bullying, and evolutionary theory. He is editor of *The Psychology of Grandparenthood*, coauthor of *Understanding Children's Development*, and coeditor of *Theories of Theories of Mind* and *The Nature of School Bullying*.

* * *

JOANNE E. SOLCHANY is an Assistant Professor in the Department of Family and Child Nursing, School of Nursing, at the University of Washington, in Seattle. She holds degrees from Western Washington University in Bellingham, WA (B.A.), University of Alaska, Anchorage (B.S.N.), University of California, San Francisco (M.S.N.), and the University of Washington in Seattle (Ph.D.). She is a clinical specialist, nurse practitioner, and psychotherapist in Infant, Child, and Adolescent Psychiatric and Mental Health Nursing. Solchany is currently a Solnit Fellow with Zero to Three, The National Center for Clinical Infant Studies. Her research interests are in adoption, attachment, maternal deprivation, infant mental health, prenatal mental health, and intervention development. She has recently written *Working with Women in Pregnancy: Theory, Practice, and Intervention*.

* * *

MARGARET M. STANLEY-HAGEN was Associate Professor of Psychology at the University of North Carolina, Charlotte. She completed her Ph.D. at the University of Virginia. Her research focused on individual differences in coping with life stresses and the personal, family, and community factors that facilitate or impede coping. She studied relationships and adjustment in families experiencing marital transitions and published on family relationships within divorced and remarried families. Stanley-Hagen worked with a Charlotte-based intervention program that coordinates community-based services to improve the family and community lives of poor preschool children who are at risk for school failure.

* * *

MARSHA WEINRAUB is the Laura H. Carnell Professor of Psychology at Temple University, Director of the Laboratory for Personality and Social Development, and Chair of the Developmental Program in the Psychology Department. She received her education at Brandeis University (B.A.) and the University of Michigan (Ph.D). Weinraub was at Virginia Polytechnic Institute and State University. She is a fellow of the American Psychological Association and the American Psychological Society, a member of the Society for Research in Child Development and the International Society for Infant Studies, and a recipient of the Lindback Award for Distinguished Teaching at Temple University. She has served on the editorial boards of *Child Development* and the *Psychology of Women*. Her research interests include the study of early personality development, parent–child interactions, childcare, maternal employment, and single parenting.

* * *

PATRICIA ZUKOW-GOLDRING is Research Associate Professor in the Department of Linguistics at the University of Southern California, and she was Research Scholar at the Center for the Study of Women at the University of California, Los Angeles. She received her education at the University of California, Los Angeles (B.A., M.A., and Ph.D.) and has held academic positions in Psychology at the Universidad Anahuac in Mexico

City and at UCLA and in the School of Social Ecology at the University of California, Irvine. She has received an individual NIMH Fellowship, A. W. Mellon Fellow in Literacy, and a Visiting Fellowship from the British Psychological Society. Her research explores how children come to notice, participate in, and communicate within daily activities at home and at school. Zukow-Goldring has conducted studies among rural and urban families in Central Mexico and among Latino blue-collar and European American middle-socioeconomic families in the Western United States. Zukow-Goldring edited *Sibling Interaction Across Cultures: Methodological and Theoretical Issues* and served as coeditor of *Evolving Explanations of Development: Ecological Approaches to Organism-Environment Systems.*

* * *

Handbook of Parenting

Volume 3
Being and Becoming a Parent

PART I

THE PARENT

1

Mothering

Kathryn E. Barnard
JoAnne E. Solchany
University of Washington

INTRODUCTION

Think about the word "mother." Close your eyes and allow the images evoked by this word to come into focus. What comes to your mind? Images of a woman with a child? Images of your idea of an ideal mother? Images of your mother? Maybe the image you have is of a special person who mothered you at different times in your life? Regardless of the image you create in your mind, it is most likely a powerful image, spawning intense feelings of love, adoration, fear, sadness, or even rage. Continue to hold the image in your mind. What else do you see? A child? Someone you knew? A sad, withering child who is in need of mothering? A happy, robust child who is in the arms of a loving mother? The child that was once you? Do these images jog your memory? What comes to mind? A quiet moment over homework? An outing? Sitting down to a meal? Being held as you cried over your skinned knee? Being punished? Or perhaps, the sight of your mother walking away from you on that first day of school?

There is nothing small about a mother; she evokes powerful images, feelings, and memories. Throughout history mothers have been revered just as often as they have been feared. Even death does not alter the power of mothers. Folktales and traditional beliefs of several cultures maintain that the power and influence mothers have in the lives of their children and their children's children transcends death and remains strong. Scandinavian folklore includes the story of the passing of wisdom from one generation to the next through grandmothers, mothers, and daughters (Paxson, 1998). Paxson tells of the young girl who sets herself down on her grandmother's grave in order to learn from her teachings. Through the night the girl experiences a dreamlike phenomenon within which her kerchief-wearing grandmother appears with a plate of strudel. Come morning, the girl awakens to find herself still on the grave of her grandmother. She also finds the taste of sugar on her lips and the teachings of her grandmother in her mind. The maternal power has been passed on to her, adding maternal strength to her family. Mothers transcend boundaries to share wisdom. In other cultural tales, mothers transcend human boundaries to protect their children in times of danger (Paxson, 1998). Some have the ability to foresee the future, predicting the fate of a child.

The concept of mother connotes an interesting dichotomy between an altruistic, benevolent, wise, mystical goddess holding the power of fertility and birth and the awesome, secretive, merciless, devouring goddess holding the power of fate. Jung (1959) simply referred to this dichotomous archetyping of mothers as "the loving and the terrible mother." Mothers have the power to give life and sustain it through their motherly love and actions, just as they have the power to end life or condemn it through the abandonment and refusal to bestow their motherly love and actions.

Historically, mothers have consistently filled both the "loving" and the "terrible" roles. In fact, van der Heever (1990), in an exploration of several studies, found that the further one goes back in history, the lower the quality of childcare and the more children were likely to be abandoned, beaten, terrorized, and sexually abused (French, in Vol. 2 of this *Handbook*). Examining the relationships between parents and their children reveals an indifference to infants and small children, by mothers, fathers and society as a whole. Badinter (1981) characterized motherhood in eighteenth century France, where infants were routinely abandoned or left to the care of wet-nurses or surrogate mothers (often women of the lower, poverty class). van der Heever elaborated on this concept, suggesting that these children, even those from well-to-do families, received the poorest of care as women of poverty would often feed and care for their own children first, providing for the surrogate child only as time and resources allowed. Motherhood and caring for one's infant were not seen as loving roles or behaviors, but instead were something to be passed on to the "peasants."

The turn of the twentieth century brought with it the beginning of a shift in how mothers and children were seen (Cohler and Paul, in Vol. 3 of this *Handbook*). It was around this time that Sigmund Freud (1913/1955) made the claim that there was no love like a mother's. He stated that this relationship was the strongest of all relationships, enduring for a lifetime, and the root of one's future intimate relationships. His ideas gained momentum over the years, strengthening the beliefs that mothers were crucial to the development of an emotionally stable and successful adult. The acceptance and support of this belief came by way of a difficult scientific journey, which has taken over 100 years. Two separate but interconnected trails led to this understanding: maternal deprivation and maternal impact.

In this chapter we begin with a discussion of these two trails, maternal deprivation and the maternal impact. The meaning of motherhood in the context of becoming a woman is then explored in the section on becoming a mother. Next, the preparation for motherhood is examined within the pregnancy and postpartum periods in subsections on processes in pregnancy and processes in the postpartum period. A discussion on the capacity for mothering is presented, followed by a discussion on mothering from the context of a holding environment for the child. In this latter section we focus on three important functions of mothering: monitoring and surveillance, expected nurturing, and the responsive caregiving–social partner role. Finally, maternal responsibilities during interaction, developmentally based mothering, and challenges in mothering are explored.

MATERNAL DEPRIVATION

Eight hundred years ago, Fredrick II, who was the Emperor of the Holy Roman Empire, created an experiment in which he wanted to find out which language children would speak "naturally" or on their own (Stone and Church, 1957). He ordered that a group of babies be taken from their mothers and cared for by foster mothers and nurses. These caregivers were told to feed, bathe, and see to the needs of these children, but no one was to speak to these children at all, in any language. He apparently wondered which of the great languages the babies would naturally speak: Hebrew, Greek, Latin, Arabic, or the language of their parents to whom they were born. Of course, Frederick never found out which language the children would have spoken. Sadly, his experiment resulted in the death of all the babies—because of the lack of appropriate mothering. The babies were not able to live without being touched, seeing smiles and changes of emotion, and hearing the loving, soothing words of a mother. The babies became withdrawn, depressed, and died (Stone and Church, 1957).

At the turn of the twentieth century, it was not uncommon for children to be placed in state-run institutions or foundling homes. During the early 1900s, several medical doctors looked into the extreme death rates, between 90% and 100% in some of these institutions. They found that even the few children who survived early childhood in these homes developed delays and disturbances in the normal course of development. Rene Spitz (1945, p. 54) described these child survivors of institutions as "asocial, delinquent, feeble-minded, psychotic, or problem children ... practically without exception," and he related these findings to the lack of maternal nurturance. Wanting to understand what effects the lack of mothering would have on a baby, Spitz (1946) observed and recorded what happened to a group of 123 infants who were deprived of emotional and physical contact with others by nature of their institutional environment. This environment provided these motherless babies with basic care but very little human interaction. They existed in a dimly lit, but clean and hygienic environment. They had adequate food, appropriate clothing with pastel colors, blankets, and regular medical care. They initially had no toys, although this changed with time. These babies had little visual stimuli, and, in fact, they had sheets hanging in between the cribs or cots—essentially creating a "solitary confinement." These babies had minimal human contact, limited primarily to feeding times. Spitz observed these children to deteriorate over time and to develop a group of symptoms, which he later termed *anaclitic depression*. This syndrome included the following symptoms: apprehension, sadness, weepiness, lack of contact, rejection of environment, withdrawal, retardation of development, retardation of reaction to stimuli, slowness of movement, dejection, stupor, loss of appetite, refusal to eat, loss of weight, and insomnia. He added that one additional symptom should be included, although it was difficult to describe. He portrayed it as a physiognomic expression, likening it to the expression of an adult who was depressed.

In 1945 Spitz compared children who were confined to institutions with same-age children living with their parents in either an urban or a rural area. The institutionalized children were the children of poor Latina women who did not have enough money to care for their infants. Their babies were generally healthy at first and were able to continue being breast-fed. Nonetheless, they remained in an institutional setting.

The other subgroup of babies were the children of what Spitz (1945, p. 60) termed "delinquent minors as a result of social maladjustment or feeblemindedness, or because they were psychically defective, psychopathic, or criminal." These mothers were prisoners in a penal institution. The babies of these women were weaned early and continued to receive care from their own mothers, with coaching from others.

The Latina foundling babies fared the worst. These babies experienced a drop in IQ from 124 to 72 over the first year (the other groups remained the same or improved) and fell to 45 by the end of the second year. In addition, Spitz found increased illness and infection rates in the foundling babies, high death rates, and developmental delays. Sadly, only 2 of 26 surviving 2½-year-old children could speak a couple of words, most were unable to do any self-care behaviors, and none had been toilet trained. Spitz argued that even though the Latina babies did have caregivers who were very sincere in their work with the babies, they did not have the time or the resources to adequately care for the babies. Essentially, he said, these babies were in "solitary confinement" as they rarely saw or interacted with a caregiver.

Freud and Burlingame (1944), Provence and Lipton (1962), and Dennis (1973), who also studied institutionalized children deprived of a mothering relationship, all came to the same general conclusions—that in spite of proper physical care, infants and children who lack an opportunity to emotionally bond with a "mother or mother-substitute" can lead to extreme forms of dysfunction in the child or death. These children often demonstrated decreased growth, decreased development, increased risk of psychiatric disturbances, increased levels of illness, and high death rates.

Hrdy (1999) states that what makes human primates different is the combination of our intelligence and the empathetic capacity. The empathetic component is the foundation of morality. Kochanska and Murray (2000) found that early mother–child relationships predicted preschool evaluations of the child's moral sense. The National Institute for Child Health and Development's daycare study found that the mother–child relationship explained more variance in child outcomes than the time in and quality of childcare environments (NICHD, 1999). Likewise, in a study of kibbutz infants, there was a difference in attachment security for infants sleeping with their mothers at night versus infants sleeping away from home, even though daytime contact with parents was similar (Sagi, van IJzendoorn, Aviezer, Konnell, and Mayseless, 1994). It thus seems that children need regular daily physical connections with their mothers in order to sustain secure attachments.

MATERNAL IMPACT

In 1951, the World Health Organization gave John Bowlby the task of exploring orphaned or homeless children. In understanding these children, Bowlby (1953, p. 11) determined that "what is believed to be essential for mental health is that the infant and young child should experience a warm, intimate, and continuous relationship with his mother (or permanent mother substitute—one person who steadily mothers him) in which both find satisfaction and enjoyment. It is this complex, rich, and rewarding relationship with the mother in early years . . . [that we] now believe to underlie the development of character and mental health." Not only was it determined that proper and adequate mothering was essential for proper growth, but it was determined that the mothering received during this period was also necessary for children's later ability to successfully mother their own children. Brody (1956, p. 377) writes "The genesis of motherliness is to be sought primarily in the quality of the child's attachment to her own mother in the first years of life. In that period the mother actively provides many passive satisfactions to the child, and is perceived as having the power to grant or withhold all of the pleasures that the child can imagine to be crucial. As the child grows capable of activity in her own right, she imitates the activity she is most familiar with, that of her mother."

The research generated by these two prophetic statements has supported the ideas that our mothering is important in who we become as individuals and parents. Through this research we have also learned about the nature and behaviors of mothering—what supports the developing child and what sets the child up for a negative life trajectory. Some of the specific behaviors of mothering found to have positive effects include sensitivity, affect attunement (Haft and Slade, 1989), empathy (Basch, 1983; Settlage, 1980), emotional availability (Emde, 1980; Settlage, 1980), touch or stimulation (Fields, 1994), reciprocation (Mahler, 1961; Mahler, Pine, and Bergman, 1975), ability to read and respond to child's cues (Sumner and Spietz, 1994), contingency (Sumner and Spietz, 1994), parental management and socialization processes (Greenberg, Speltz, and DeKlyen, 1993), and a history of secure relationships or attachments (Benoit and Parker, 1994; Slade and Cohen, 1996). The behaviors that lead to less desirable outcomes include things in direct opposition to those behaviors previously listed. A primary caregiver's insecure attachment history has also been shown to have a strong effect, as has the presence of trauma (Lyons-Ruth and Block, 1996).

BECOMING A MOTHER: A PATH TO WOMANHOOD

Conception marks the beginning of a transformation: that of a woman to a mother. The progression through pregnancy into motherhood leads to a second transformation: that of a woman with a newfound female identity (Pines, 1972), one developed out of the context of motherhood. Psychologically, pregnancy involves a series of transformations and becomes a period of introspection (Trad, 1990). The pregnancy changes women physically, altering the form and appearance of their bodies, as well as activating and changing certain functions of their bodies. These outward changes represent the inner work that needs to occur.

Women prepare to become the mothers of their children, while at the same time are still children of their mothers (Pines, 1972). These are among the first tasks of this developmental shift. Lester and Notman (1988) argued that pregnant women may experience a reactivation of feelings of dependency on their mothers as well as a wish for fusion with them. They need to understand who their mothers are, what they represent to them, what part of their mothers they want to incorporate into themselves, and how to incorporate the "ideal" mother images they have been developing and carrying within their own minds (Solchany, 2001). They come to understand their mothers from the perspective of another mother, creating a new level of relating. As this reworking of the relationship with their mothers continues, pregnant women also need to begin to develop and establish a relationship with their babies. This requires a psychological reckoning with both the long-imagined babies of their minds (Pines, 1972) and the perfect babies they had wished they would have been (Deutsch, 1945). Pines (1972, p. 336) summarized these processes by stating, "Motherhood is a three-generation experience."

Benedek (1959) clearly described the transformation to motherhood as a developmental stage at which motherhood acts as the catalyst for transformation of the identity of self (Demick, in Vol. 3 of this *Handbook*). As the mother begins to "mother" her child, she finds that she satisfies the infant's needs much of the time. She also finds that, at times, she fails to satisfy her baby's needs. Meeting baby's needs generates feelings of accomplishment, success, and competency within the mother. Failing to meet the perceived needs of the baby generates feelings of failure, inadequacy, and emotional pain within the mother. Benedek (1959, p. 392) called this "emotional symbiosis" and defined it as "the reciprocal interaction between mother and child which . . . creates structural change in each of the participants." In other words, the baby's experience with the mother affects the baby's psychological processes, just as the mother's experience with the baby affects the mother's psychological processes. Each time the mother feeds her hungry baby, the baby experiences the mother as a good mother who takes away the pain of hunger and replaces it with satiation, warmth, soothing, security, and safety—all is good in the world. When the baby does not get fed, the world becomes a bad, painful experience. For the mother, when she is able to feed and satisfy her hungry child, she feels satisfied herself; however, when she is unable to satisfy her infant, she feels less satisfied and frustrated in her own abilities. Benedek (1959) described this process for the baby as translating to *good mother = good self*; and a reciprocal process for the mother as *good-thriving-infant = good-mother-self*. Whatever the experience, one of satisfaction or one of frustration, it becomes integrated into the personalities of both the baby and the mother. With good mothering, the egos of each member of the dyad are fed and nurtured, building confidence. With disturbed mothering, the relationship within the dyad turns into a vicious circle, fed by aggression and a lack of mutual satisfaction (Benedek, 1959).

The transformation to motherhood requires women to accept and work through feelings of loss and grief. Barclay, Everitt, Rogan, Schmied, and Wyllie (1997) found women experienced a loss of a sense of self, of how they used their time, of freedom and independence, and of their life as it used to be. Women grieve over the changes in their bodies, their relationships, their professional lives, their activities, and the context in which they viewed and experienced life (Solchany, 2001). They need to reconcile with the facts that they will never again be women without children—even if the pregnancy they experience tragically ends through miscarriage or fetal death—and that their bodies and their lives are forever altered. Trad (1990, p. 359) described, "motherhood [as] a dynamic process in which change is virtually unceasing, [and] flexibility and the ability to deal with these transformations and concomitant losses are necessary traits of the adaptive mother." The processes of grief and loss often breed feelings of conflict, ambivalence, hostility, regression, aggression, and negativity.

Hartrick (1997, p. 271) described a period in which "the taken for granted infrastructure" the women had or had assumed they had in their lives "is questioned and begins to crumble." This idea is echoed by Barclay et al. (1997, p. 721), who found that women go through a period of realization of "the overwhelming process of becoming a mother and the consequences this has on one's life."

Hartrick (1997) described resolution of these issues through a reclaiming for women of certain parts of who they were and in the recognition that they had choices. Recognition of choice allowed them to lessen the ideas that motherhood had taken certain things from them. Loss took on a different meaning when it was understood within the context of personal choice.

PREPARING FOR MOTHERHOOD

Through their intimate involvement with women's childbearing experiences, nurses have historically been witnesses to women becoming mothers from physical, psychological, and social perspectives. Over the past four decades, nurses, especially Rubin (1967a, 1967b, 1977, 1984) and Mercer (1981, 1985), have captured the development of mothering through empirical studies. The primary process involved is attaining the maternal role, which includes the development of maternal identity and role competency. This process begins during pregnancy and continues into the postpartum period.

Attaining the Maternal Role: Processes in Pregnancy

Rubin (1984) reported on qualitative studies she conducted in the 1960s and 1970s of many women during the process of childbearing. Her work challenges the attribution that mothering is instinctual. She noted (1984, p. 2), "There is nothing particularly mysterious or exotically sex-linked in the activities of feeding, bathing, protecting or teaching the young. . . . Enduring love, altruistic self-denial, and empathy are not exclusive to the maternal woman or to the mother–child relationship. And yet, together these actions within the matrix of affiliate bonds comprise the characteristics of maternal behavior which are seen as the bottom line." Rubin went on to claim that there is nothing preprogrammed in maternal behavior; it is the product of an interaction between the mother's past and interaction with the developing child.

Rubin (1984) described the transition to motherhood as the development of the capacity for mothering. In her model there are four maternal tasks: (1) seeking safe passage for herself and her child through pregnancy, labor, and delivery; (2) ensuring the acceptance of her child by significant persons in the family of the child she bears; (3) "binding-in" to her unknown child and the idea of having a "real" child; and (4) learning to give of herself. These tasks occur throughout pregnancy and into the early phase of the postpartum period. Characteristics of each task are summarized from Rubin's work.

In *seeking safe passage*, Rubin (1984) found that a woman begins in the first trimester to concentrate on her personal well-being. She becomes concerned with what she eats and will often stop using alcohol or drugs. Fears of what this pregnancy and baby will mean to both her body and her life will take shape. By the second trimester, the pregnant woman's concern shifts to the welfare of her unborn child. She will become more sensitive to the impact of the outside environment on her unborn child. Her fears revolve around the baby's well-being, and she begins to closely monitor the activity of her unborn child. She also becomes susceptible to traditional fears, old wives' tales, and stories about behaviors potentially bringing harm to the baby. As she enters the third trimester, the pregnant woman has begun to view herself as "one" with her child. She experiences the baby and herself as inseparable; psychologically they become one entity. The pregnant woman will often develop fears about both her baby's and her own successful navigation of the delivery.

The third trimester is also a time during which the pregnant woman's increasing body size and decreased agility, as well as the pregnancy itself, become uncomfortable experiences. Psychologically she may begin to feel ugly, and normal events are perceived as dangerous to her. She avoids crowds, yet may dread being alone. By the eighth month of pregnancy she views delivery as a relief. She is hopeful that the physician or midwife will think she is about to deliver or will suggest she go to the hospital. False labor pains generally are felt in the last month of pregnancy, so she has continuous reminders about her transitional state. The pregnant woman finds herself constantly balancing the desire for the pregnancy to be over and her fears of labor and delivery.

Rubin (1984) saw the second task of *ensuring the acceptance of the child* by others as one of the most critical. Essentially, this involves the mother's developing a place both physically and psychologically for the child within the family, the more difficult of the two being the emotional fit. It is necessary for the mother and other family members to adjust their relationships; bonds among existing family members have to be loosened and redefined. This work begins as the mother becomes aware of the growing child within her. She begins sharing with family members and friends her thoughts, dreams, and aspirations about the child. Fantasies about the unborn child are ideally shared between family members as a way of envisioning the reality of accepting a new family member. The mother's objective is to gain unconditional acceptance, therefore any conditional acceptances based on gender of the child or normalcy pose a deep worry to the mother because of the fear of the child's being rejected if the condition is not met.

Binding-in, the third task, is a process that begins in pregnancy and generally results in a state at birth in which there already exists a bond between mother and infant. During the first trimester the binding-in begins with the acceptance and rejection process of the pregnancy. At first, even in planned pregnancies, there is the conscious processing of whether the mother really wants this child. We speculate that a woman does not seek confirmation of the pregnancy or prenatal care until she has come to an acceptance of the pregnancy. During the second trimester, the event of fetal movement evokes a special private experience. Use of technology may modify the expectant mother's psychological development. With the fetal image projected onto a video monitor by ultrasound and fetal heart tones made audible with Doppler radar, the pregnancy can be shared at a different level than previously allowed. Use of technology to enter the intimate and hidden environment of the womb can be a positive experience for some women yet have a dangerous impact on others (Solchany, 2001). For some women, seeing and sharing the images of their unborn child can be exciting and may intensify their feelings of love and bonding. For other women, seeing their unborn child in the early stages of development during which the fetus bears little resemblance to an already born healthy child can intensify fears and interfere with the development of love and bonding. The reality of the fetus does not match up with the fantasy image of a baby. Brazelton (1992, p. 5) suggested that the imagined baby parents tend to fantasize around reflects three different images: "the perfect four-month-old who rewards them with smiles and musical cooing, the impaired baby, who changes each day, and the mysterious real baby whose presence is beginning to be evident in the motions of the fetus." Not one of these matches fetal images.

Physical changes associated with pregnancy, the growing fetus' activity, and the sense of "life within her" make the mother more especially aware of the child. The child begins to be real for the mother long before the child becomes real for family members and friends; they must await the birth. Pressure often begins to build during the third trimester as those around the pregnant woman begin to ask "when is the baby coming?" and "how much longer?" The mother is just as eager for her child to arrive, but continues to experience anxiety around her own and the baby's safety.

Learning to give of oneself, the fourth task, begins in the first trimester as the woman begins to weigh the demands that pregnancy entails. The changes in body appearance, function, integrity, relationships, lifestyle, and life space represent both loss and change. The basic principle of what she needs to give up and what she will be gaining is evaluated during this time. During the second trimester her identification shifts to the child. Others bring special gifts to the mother for the baby. These gifts take on significant meaning for the mother as the importance lies not in the physical gift but in the meaning behind the giving—that the baby is being anticipated and will therefore be accepted into the mother's social circle. The third trimester brings to the surface the realization of the commitment required in giving birth. The danger of the delivery, the fears that the giving of self will be overwhelming, and that her capacity to give to the baby will not be enough are all commitments she is pondering. Mothers will often express the fear, "I can't do this!" during this period.

Rubin (1984) saw these tasks of pregnancy as preparing the woman for her continuing maternal role as she develops classical maternal concerns and worries on behalf of her child. This maternal role is characterized by the long-term giving of one's time and interest in the form of enduring love, altruistic self, self-denial, and empathy.

Attaining the Maternal Role: Processes in the Postpartum Period

Mercer (1981, 1985, 1986) later explored the relations of women's personal factors and contextual–situational influences with the ease of attaining the maternal role. She (1985, p. 178) asserted that, "A woman defines maternal role performance in interaction with her infant and responds according to the situational context, her perceptions of her past and present experience and her values." Personal factors include physical health, self-esteem, birth experience, level of commitment, and competence. Contextual–situational influences include anticipatory socialization, separation from the infant, social support, and societal value of the maternal role.

Mercer's (1981, 1985) work on maternal role attainment extended beyond Rubin's (1967a, 1967b) primary focus on pregnancy. Because Mercer's work was not as grounded in the physical experience of pregnancy, it may help to explain the process of maternal role attainment for women becoming mothers through other avenues, such as adoption. Mercer studied first-time mothers during the early postpartum period and at 1, 4, 8, and 12 months after birth. The endpoint of maternal role attainment was seen as maternal identity that encompassed confidence and competency in role performance.

Mercer (1981, 1985) applied rigorous, quantitatively oriented research methods. She compared the process of maternal role attainment in three age cohorts over time. Each of the age cohorts represented clusters of personal and contextual factors that could enhance or hinder maternal role attainment.

Mercer operationalized maternal role attainment as comprising *attachment*, *competency*, and *pleasure and gratification in the role*. Mercer (1985, 1986) found differences in these aspects of maternal role attainment across the age groups at different times of measurement. Feelings about the baby in all three maternal age groups peaked at the 4-month measure, coinciding with the height of infant social responsiveness. Gratification in the mothering role was initially highest for adolescent mothers and lowest for older mothers. Adolescent mothers reported a drop in gratification at 8 months, which continued to drop at 12 months. These drops coincided with challenging infant behavior such as separation anxiety at 8 months and increased mobility at 11 months. The older women (30 to 39 years of age) reported less gratification from the maternal role at each time point. Just the reverse was true for the mother's competency that was observed during the interviews. The teenage mothers demonstrated the least competency in role at all age periods and the older mothers the greatest competency. The least positive ways of disciplining the child occurred with greater frequency in the adolescent mothers. However, age alone does not account for differences in maternal role attainment among groups. Differences based on age are difficult to discern because of the presence of many age-related factors, such as level of education, stability in family life and other relationships, experience with competence in other roles, and socioeconomic status.

In defining their comfort with the maternal role, only 3% of the mothers claimed to have internalized the role by pregnancy, 49% by 2 months after birth, and 95% by 12 months. There was no significant difference in the age cohorts in reporting achievement of comfort in the maternal role. In other words, maternal role identity develops broadly throughout the first year after birth. A few women do not have maternal identity at the end of the first year.

Finally, a measure of role strain (Burr, 1972) reported items such as loss of personal time, gaining role skills, nighttime care and sleep, deprivation, total responsibility, and infant's changing behavior. The degree of role strain did not decrease over the first year; as some of the early challenges were mastered, the changes in the infant's behavior seemed to replace the necessary earlier adjustments.

CAPACITY FOR MOTHERING

Others have studied development of the capacity for mothering. Lederman (1984) studied the paradigm shift she claims a woman must make from her perception as woman without child to woman with child. Lederman's (Lederman, Lederman, Workk, and McCann, 1978) original study of women in labor prompted her to do further work on women's adaptation during pregnancy. Finding that there were women who demonstrated behavioral and physiological correlates of stress during labor that prolonged stage two of labor, Lederman was eager to study more fully what prenatal psychological factors predicted this difficulty of progressing in labor. She saw the woman as needing to make a paradigm shift from her former lifestyle and behaviors to attain this capacity to give to the child. Lederman proposed that the woman needs to be willing to give up her former self and learn to achieve satisfaction from giving in her relationship with the child.

If the woman has not resolved this paradigm shift during the pregnancy, as labor and delivery approach, she becomes more anxious. Lederman studied the relation between the outcome of labor and the pregnant woman's perceptions regarding this paradigm. The prenatal variables obtained through client interviews were acceptance of the pregnancy, identification of a motherhood role, relationship with own mother, and fears about pregnancy. The variables of acceptance of pregnancy and identification of the motherhood role had the most consistent correlations with progress during labor, including measures of uterine activity, plasma epinephrine, state anxiety, and duration of labor. These findings provide support for Rubin's (1967a, 1967b) assertion that acceptance of the pregnancy and child is an important maternal role attainment task.

Josten (1982) developed a method for prenatal assessment of mothering potential. The method involved review of individual women's prenatal clinic charts for the positive or negative evidence of the following aspects: (1) perception of the complexities of mothering, (2) attachment, (3) acceptance of child by significant others, (4) ensuring physical well-being, and (5) evidence of problem areas such as history of parenting difficulties, lack of knowledge about children, inadequate cognitive function, inadequate support, spousal abuse, mental illness, substance abuse, major stress, rejection of child, or inappropriate use of services.

Prenatal clinic charts were rated with the Parental Assessment Guide. A score of positive, negative, or neutral was assigned to each woman for each type of evidence defined. Josten (1982) studied 52 mothers, all part of a larger study at the University of Minnesota. In the larger study, the quality of care had been rated by independent observers. Excellent care was defined as meeting the physical and the psychological needs of the infant with sensitivity and cooperative handling by the mother, whereas inadequate care was defined as failure to take action to provide the basic physical or psychosocial care that, when absent, caused physical or psychological harm to the infant. Josten compared 27 mothers rated as providing excellent mothering with 25 mothers rated as providing inadequate care. From the prenatal chart reviews, the inadequate mothers had more negative scores on their perception of the complexities of the mothering role, acceptance of the child by significant others, and physical well-being during pregnancy. The majority of the inadequate mothers had therefore not prepared for pregnancy including dealing with the emotional tasks of pregnancy. It is apparent that high-risk women have little opportunity to do the psychological work to prepare for mothering.

In the late 1980s, through a research partnership with an Early Head Start program (Barnard, Spieker, and Huebner, 1996), we instituted a protocol, by utilizing the theories of Rubin and Mercer, to guide program mothers through their pregnancy. We found that the women were receptive to talking about their pregnancy and their role as mother (Solchany, Sligar, and Barnard, in press). It was the case that many mothers had not identified a maternal role model, rejecting their own mother as such a model. In fact, it was difficult for the home visitors who implemented the pregnancy protocol to help mothers find in their circle of friends a good maternal role model. In addition to difficulties and interference in taking on the maternal role, home visitors working with pregnant women were further challenged with issues such as maternal mental illness, difficulties or avoidance in making a connection with the unborn child, a lack of or a problematic social or familial network, and a lack of preparation for the baby. In reaction to these challenges, Solchany (2001) developed a book that addresses mental health theory, practice, and intervention during pregnancy, specifically as they pertain to maternal role attainment, mothering, and developing a healthy relationship with the child.

The capacity for forming relationships and confidence in visualizing self as mother are efficient predictors in anticipating parent–child and child outcomes (Heinicke, in Vol. 3 of this *Handbook*). A simple self-report measure of the transition to motherhood has been reported: Ruble et al. (1990) constructed a questionnaire and completed preliminary psychometric testing on the Childbearing Attitude Questionnaire. This scale contains 16 factors: maternal worries, maternal self-confidence, relationship with husband, relationship with mother, body image, identification with pregnancy, feelings about children, negative self-image, attitude toward breast-feeding, pain tolerance, interest in sex, denial, negative aspects of caregiving, feelings of dependency, social boredom, and information seeking. The questionnaire was given at three time points—prepregnancy, pregnancy, and postpartum—to 51 women. There was a consistency in perception of self and others across the time points, supporting the assumption that there is a lifelong developmental impact of one's self-confidence, social orientation, identification with motherhood, and attitude toward giving birth that remains stable during this transition.

There is no sure set of predictive variables; however, the strongest variables include a personal history of a poor childhood, history of psychopathology, current psychopathology, ambivalence about the pregnancy, lack of evidence of forming a positive relationship with the newborn, and lack of capacity for self-care (Gabinet, 1986). In one study of families of children with conduct disorders, mother's report of having been abused as a child and low family income were the most potent variables that differentiated abusive and nonabusive families (Webster-Stratton, 1985).

In our Early Head Start research we found that mothers with unresolved loss or trauma as identified from the baseline Adult Attachment Interview (Main and Goldwyn, 1994) were strongly associated with women who could not be emotionally available for their infants (Spieker, Solchany, McKenna, DeKlyen, and Barnard, 1999). A qualitative analysis of these most difficult mothers showed that they described having mothers present in their lives physically; however, these mothers were rarely emotionally or psychologically available to them. These women shared stories of their childhoods that were filled with incidents of rejection, abandonment, disregard for safety, inability to protect their child from sexually or physically abusive perpetrators, maternal mental illness and unpredictability, and an extreme lack of support for normal childhood experiences such as play and interaction with peers. These women not only experienced traumas such as abuse, they were further traumatized by unavailable mothers who showed little regard for them. Frequently, a case study integrates the circumstances better than the empirical evidence from groups or theories. The story of Amy, one of the traumatized mothers who was interviewed, is recounted to illustrate the obstacles and course of maternal role attainment:

> Amy was a 21-year-old, unmarried woman pregnant with her third pregnancy. Amy first became pregnant at the age of 16 years. She was, at the time, living with her mother, who refused to let Amy live with her if she chose to have the baby. Amy decided to abort that pregnancy. Amy soon became pregnant again when she was 17. This time she chose to leave her mother's home. Amy had the child and ended up homeless. When that child was 3 months old, she decided to relinquish him for adoption. At 21 years of age, Amy was now pregnant again, living with the baby's father who also happened to be her exhusband's brother.
>
> Amy had a long history of relationship trauma, as well as physical and sexual abuse. Sexual abuse began at the age of 4 years by her mother's drug dealers. By 5 years of age, she was removed from her mother's care and placed with her biological father, who began to molest her at the age of 6 years. She endured sexual as well as physical and emotional abuse for the following six years. Amy returned to her mother's care at the age of 14 years. By this time her mother had been diagnosed with bipolar disorder, was untreated, still abusing drugs, and prostituting.

Amy's past created many problems in her life. She experienced symptoms consistent with posttraumatic stress disorder, including vivid, violent nightmares, fear of others, paranoid thinking, isolation, fear of her own impulses (especially toward the baby), and a flat, unanimated affect. She had no support system and did not have the skills or the motivation to develop or even accept assistance in developing one.

Amy's past experiences created many obstacles for her in assuming the maternal role and in her ability to mother her child. She did not know what a mother should do; her mother models were inadequate or nonexistent. She was unable to discuss the changes in her body as her pregnancy progressed; these changes seemed to overwhelm her, and she responded to this by denying what was happening to her body. When the baby was born, she could not cuddle him or hold him close to her body. In fact, she could not hold her son when she fed him; instead she laid the baby in a babyseat and held the bottle to his mouth. Her inability to touch her baby seemed to come from her own discomfort with touch and intimate contact with her own body. These feelings generalized; she rarely touched the baby, she would not allow the baby to be completely naked during a bath, and she would stop others from touching and playing with her baby. Any intensity of emotion would be shut down; she did not have the capacity to tolerate extremes of emotion so she would shut them down. She did not play with her baby for she had never developed appropriate play skills herself as a child.

Her baby suffered from her stunted development and poor capacity to mother. He was essentially sensory deprived. He was not touched, he was not nurtured, he was not played with, he was not comforted, he was not cuddled, he was not held, and he was rarely talked to. At 14 months of age this baby did not speak, did not laugh, rarely smiled, had little range of affect, had a depressed response to pain, was clumsy, was disorganized in his interactions with his environment, had multiple environmentally induced developmental delays (fine motor, gross motor, speech, social ability), and had developed an insecure–avoidant attachment with his mother.

At the age of 19 months, this child was removed from his mother's care and placed with his father and his new wife. This woman assumed the mothering role for this child and nurtured and doted on him. Within a year of this placement, this child no longer qualified for disability services, was able to demonstrate a range of emotions, seemed happy, and played well by himself and with other children. His Baley Developmental score jumped 12 points in a 10-month period, and he demonstrated a newfound confidence in his interactions within his environment.

Amy seemed to have no ability to relate on an emotional level with this child. She was unable to become excited for or about him, and it was just as difficult for her to show frustration. Emotionally she responded by giving up, sighing loudly, walking away, retreating to her seat—in essence she was rejecting this baby repeatedly. The significance of maternal emotional availability is very apparent in this case. This child was left in a flat, empty, emotionless void when he was with her, which in turn stunted his own emotionality and ability to relate to others.

MOTHERING AS A "HOLDING ENVIRONMENT" FOR THE CHILD

To this point we have dealt with attainment of maternal role during pregnancy and the first year of life. Mercer's (1985, 1986) work embraces the first year of the child's life, yet it deals primarily with the mother's own perception of her role, how well she fulfills it, and how satisfying it is to her. The next step is to explore what it is that mothers actually do with children. We focus on mothers because in our experience, we have found that, in the vast majority of cultures around the world, the mother remains the primary caregiver of the young child. It is true in many cultures that the extended female family members such as mothers, mothers-in-law, sisters, and aunts are integrated into the caring role, either directly caring for the children or indirectly by caring for the mother and her household responsibilities. Stern and Bruschweiler-Stern (1998) described the psychological support women seek from other women after the birth of their baby. They described it in the same terms as those Winnicott (1990) used to describe the character of the environment needed by infants: a holding environment.

Winnicott (1990, p. 49) described the mothering role to be one of "holding." He defined holding for infants as involving (1) protection from physiological insult; (2) taking account of the infant's skin sensitivity, temperature, auditory sensitivity, visual sensitivity, sensitivity to failing, and lack of knowledge of existence of anything other than the self; (3) a routine of care through the entire day and following to the minute the day-to-day changes belonging to the infant's growth and development, both physical and psychological; and (4) physical holding of the infant, which is a form of love.

Taken in its totality, providing a holding environment for a child is a very demanding undertaking. Winnicott's (1990) formulation can be applied to any age; characteristics of the child form the changing nature of the child's needs for a holding environment. Providing a holding environment requires that the caregiver have the physical and psychological resources to be on alert to the child and respond in a manner that satisfies not only the child's need but also in a way that facilitates the child's ongoing development.

There are three aspects of the mothering role embedded in Winnicott's (1990) notation of the holding environment that are important to examine in relation to actual behavioral observation of maternal role performance. These aspects are (1) the monitoring–surveillance function, (2) expectant nurturing, and (3) responsive caregiving.

Monitoring–Surveillance Function

When talking with a mother of a young infant, one soon becomes aware that the mother's attention is riveted to the infant. Even though she may be engaged in a social exchange with other persons, she visually checks in on the infant's well-being approximately every 20 seconds. In our experience, mothers have reported that they develop a special sense for the infant's breathing and movement patterns that they monitor during the infant's sleep and that they arouse from their own sleep if they detect an unusual change in those patterns. Winnicott (1988) called this "maternal preoccupation" with the infant.

Infants are beginning to develop the ability to control their behavior, or self-regulate, through their sleeping, feeding, and responses to stress in their environments. This process begins shortly after birth. Part of the mothering role is to support and assist the infant in developing self-regulatory behavior. In observing parenting practices in relation to sleep, it has been established that in the first three months most infants are not put down to sleep until they are already fully asleep, reflecting the belief that infants need help in getting to sleep (Johnson, 1991). By 3 months of age, infants are put down for sleep by their parents while they are still awake, giving the infant a chance to regulate this basic process of self-soothing and putting one's self to sleep. Infants provided with the opportunity to self-soothe learn to get to sleep and stay asleep versus infants who are always put to sleep by their parents. Infants who are put to bed awake also are encouraged by parents to use transitional objects such as pacifiers and blanket ends to soothe or regulate their distress or arousal.

Infancy is a period of development when intensive monitoring is justified, relative to the infant's lack of physiological homeostasis and general helplessness (Bornstein, in Vol. 1 of this *Handbook*). Even after this period, however, the monitoring of the child's behavior and development is a vital role for the parent. There is evidence of this function in most homes. For example, parents often keep charts on which the infant's weight and length have been recorded, records of sleep and feeding patterns, marks on the kitchen doorframe indicating the height of each child, videotapes, and albums of pictures. As the child matures, the monitoring extends beyond the family when the child plays with peers. Mothers speculate how their child is doing in relation to others. As a child matures, the child can manage more and more behavior; knowing the child's capacity for self-regulation is the dynamic part of maternal surveillance. For the school-age child, the monitoring of the child's whereabouts is extremely important in controlling the situations appropriate for the child's decision-making competencies and supporting healthy social development (Collins, Madsen, and Susman-Stillman, in Vol. 1 of this *Handbook*). With adolescence there is the continuing need for structure and rules to help the teenager maintain a controllable environment (Steinberg and Silk, in Vol. 1 of this *Handbook*). In other words, teenagers need parameters within which they can make most of their own decisions.

Parental monitoring becomes less intense as children grow older. An ongoing challenge to mothers is how much freedom should they give their children to investigate their environment. Too close monitoring may stifle growing independence, whereas too little monitoring or supervision may lead to childhood behavior problems. One mother shared a clever example of how she negotiated the transition of her preteen son. She admitted she was not sure when she was being "too motherly," acknowledging his increasing need for freedom and independence. They agreed to come up with a code word that he could say to cue her to withdraw a little—he chose the words "Kelsey Grammer." This plan between mother and son helped to ease the tensions between them and to allow for a more supportive transition to increased independence for the child and decreased mothering for the mother.

Expectant Nurturing Functions

Expectant nurturing functions include caregiving behaviors such as providing nutrition for the grow-ing child, maintaining an environment that provides for the basic needs of health care, appropriate environmental temperature control, safe housing, maintainance of appropriate physical safety, and the meeting of general dependency needs. Expectant nurturing are those acts that are expected to be performed by the mother or a responsible caregiver to ensure the physical survival of the child. Only in the extreme circumstances are these basic human needs not met; when they are not provided this is labeled as neglect. Most cases of reported child abuse contain elements of chronic neglect. Neglect can have devastating effects on the developing child, especially when the neglect of basic needs is coupled with the neglect for psychological or social needs. Interestingly, there is less agreement on the expectant nurturing for psychological or social needs.

The primary focus of parenting in the early months of an infant's life is to establish routines, patterns of interaction, and patterns of communication (Bornstein, in Vol. 1 of this *Handbook*). Theories that attempt to explain the consolidation of the mother–infant relationship over time often reflect even larger endeavors to explain all of human relationships. A commonly held view, and basic tenet of "general systems theory," is that parents and children mutually influence and provide feedback to one another.

Especially for the infant there is a degree of dependency that makes survival questionable without the commitment of a caregiver. Infants cannot nourish themselves with food, nor can young infants manage to make the environment change or be predictable. Infants require adults for bringing objects into reach, to both provide and eliminate auditory stimulation, and to maintain the safety of the envi-ronment. Papoušek and Bornstein (1992) described two different forms of caregiving, responsive and didactic, which in turn have been related to different child outcomes. Responsive caregiving involves the social interaction between the partners, whereas didactic caregiving involves the transmission of information between mother and child. Mothers who engaged in more social interaction had infants doing more social orienting, whereas mothers who concentrated more on orienting the infant to the environment had infants who explored objects more and who later had higher verbal intelligence. As the infant develops, the adult is mediating the environment for the child. Only when the child begins to locomote and finally walks and talks does the child begin to have more control over how much stimulation she or he gets and what activities she or he engages in. Scarr and McCartney (1983) stated that it is before the child is 3 years old that the environment the child is provided has the most influences on the child's development. After the age of 3 years, the child has the ability to seek envi-ronments and activities independently. In studies of children coming from high-risk environments, we have discovered that the amount of caregiving and stimulation increases for children after the onset of walking and talking.

Because the infant has a limited capacity to accommodate, the quality of the socioemotional environment in the early infancy period is highly dependent on the social competence of the mother. Goldberg (1977) highlighted three areas of infant social competence that contribute optimally to infants' interactions with their caregivers: predictability of behavior (which includes regularity of biological rhythms), social responsiveness, and readability of cues. High-risk infants or infants with handicaps may be compromised in these areas of social competence. These infants may be frequently irritable, be difficult to soothe, be difficult to feed, reject holding or cuddling, and be unresponsive. The ability of the mother to interpret infant behavior and to respond contingently, as well as the infant's ability to give clear behavioral cues, influence the quality of mother–infant interactions.

Critical to the success of any interaction is the ability of the mother and the child to adapt to one another. Sander (1962, 1964) suggested that initial mother–infant adaptation involves the fitting together of the "active tendencies" of each partner. Parent–infant synchrony is facilitated by a sense of rhythmicity, which is proposed to be in underlying pattern in the flow of interactive behavior (Censullo, Bowler, Lester, and Brazelton, 1987; Censullo, Lester, and Hoffman, 1985; Lester, Hoffman, and Brazelton, 1985). When partners in an interaction are only passively involved, the interaction becomes less adaptive, less positive.

Responsive Caregiving–Social Partner Role

In any social interaction there is an exchange. In most partnerships this exchange is an equal one. Exchanged are feelings, emotions, and information. In the mother–child interaction, the roles are altered slightly in that the mother takes on more responsibility for the social exchange, depending on the child's capacity or developmental level. In parent–child exchanges, the parent or mother provides more feedback of an instructional nature during the exchange. Bornstein (1989) labeled this type of instructional feedback as *didactic* exchanges.

In a responsive caregiver–child interaction, there are certain behaviors that are cardinal to fulfilling the role. A fundamental aspect of responsiveness is contingency. The ability to monitor, interpret, and respond to the child's behavior in an immediate and appropriate manner is key to the child's developing a sense of the trustworthiness of his or her environment and that his or her behavior has an influence on others. The temporal nature of contingency is important. Often in situations in which the mother is preoccupied, the ability to be contingent is compromised. She may respond to the child but with a latency that does not allow the child to connect her behavior with the mother's response. It is in the response of others that the child develops meaning of her or his behavior. When the response is absent or inconsistent, it is more difficult for the child to assign meaning to her or his behavior. Often in families with high degrees of stress, it is observed that mothers are not responsive to the immediate behavior of the child. The lack of concordance between behavior and mother's response makes it difficult for the child to detect cause–effect relations. Successful child behavior management programs aim to help parents improve the concordance between the child's behavior and its consequences (Webster-Stratton, 1992).

Barnard, Hammond, Booth, Mitchell, and Spieker (1989) described the mother–infant interaction system as a dialogue or a mutually adaptive "waltz" between partners. For the waltz to flow smoothly, and for the infant to receive the quantity and quality of stimulation needed for optimum development, both the dance partners and the dialogue must have certain features:

(1) The partners in the dialogue must have a sufficient repertoire of behaviors so that interlocking sequences are possible and a smooth-flowing interactive system develops. Low-education mothers and preterm infants who are typically less responsive than term infants are both examples of partners with diminished interactive behaviors (Barnard, 1994; Morisset, 1994).
(2) The partners' responses must be contingent on one another; as the child matures, the mother must remain both consistent and contingent in responding to the child. Low-education mothers have been found to be less contingent (Barnard, 1994; Morrisett, 1994).
(3) Interactive content must be rich in terms of positive affect, verbal stimulation, and range of play materials provided.
(4) The adaptive patterns between mother and child must change over time relative to the emerging developmental capacities of the child.

Others have described the mutual mother–infant "dance" with terms such as contingency (Greenspan and Lieberman, 1980), attunement (Stern, 1985), emotional availability, reciprocity, or mutuality (Brazelton, Tronick, Adamson, Als, and Wise, 1975), and synchrony (Censullo et al., 1987).

MATERNAL RESPONSIBILITIES DURING INTERACTION

The mother–child relationship is initially embedded in acts of caregiving such as feeding, bathing, playing, and responding to the baby's signs of distress. A particularly challenging part of relating to the infant is learning how to monitor and read the nonverbal language of the infant. The baby has an organized set of nonverbal symbols that communicate the basic message of continue or stop this action. The engagement and disengagement cues of infants have been identified as present right at birth (Barnard, 1976; Sumner and Spietz, 1994). Examples of potent engagement cues are mutual gaze, reaching toward the caregiver, smiling, and turning to the caregiver. Subtle disengagement cues are more numerous and include back arching, crawling away, halt hand (putting hand up with palm facing out in a stoplike gesture), overhand beating movement of arms, pulling away, spitting up, tray pounding, and withdrawing from an active to a sleep state. There are also subtle engagement and disengagement cues. Each of these subtle cues in isolation has little meaning; however, when several subtle disengagement cues occur in rapid sequence, such as look away, tongue show, and hand behind ear, this signals distress in the baby; when the mother sees this activity and responds by slowing her pace, stopping, or changing the activity, she succeeds in responding to the child's communication about distress.

Empirical work suggests that the mother–child interaction aspect has the greatest impact on the child's subsequent development. Considerable research has demonstrated important links between qualities of mother–child interactions and child development outcomes (Barnard, 1994; Barnard and Kelly, 1989; Beckwith and Cohen, 1984; Bee et al., 1982; Bell and Ainsworth, 1972; Belsky, Rovine, and Taylor, 1984; Bornstein, 1989; Bornstein and Tamis-LeMonda, 1989; Clarke-Stewart, 1973; Coates and Lewis, 1984; Elardo, Bradley, and Caldwell, 1975; Hammond, Bee, Barnard, and Eyres, 1983; Morisset, 1994; Nelson, 1973; Olson, Bates, and Bayles, 1984; Papoušek and Bornstein, 1992; Ramey, Farran, and Campbell, 1979; Wachs, Užgiris, and Hunt, 1971; Yarrow, Rubenstein, and Pedersen, 1975). Researchers have established strong relations between specific elements of early mother–child interactions and later skills or qualities in the child. Overall, positive quality interactions during the first years of life tend to be positively linked to the child's subsequent intellectual and language capacities, to more secure attachments to major caregivers, and to more competent behavioral strategies (Kochanska and Aksan, 1995; Kochanska, Aksan, and Koenig, 1995; Kochanska and Murray, 2000; NICHD, in press).

The socioemotional environment relative to the mother–infant interactive system is established through reciprocal behaviors on the part of both infant and mother (Brazelton, Koslowski, and Main, 1974). During interaction both mother and infant reciprocally influence the behavior of the other in a way that is potentially rewarding for both of them. Through a process of social interaction and bidirectional influences, the mother and the infant learn to adapt, modify, and change their behaviors in response to the other. The achievement of heightened positive affect, increased alertness, and extended episodes of mutual attention provide the infant with a framework on which to build future social experience.

AFTER INFANCY: DEVELOPMENTALLY BASED MOTHERING

Mothering flexes and changes with the development of the child. Recall for a moment that early mothering behavior needs to provide a balance between offering security through nurturing, sensitivity, emotional availability, and reciprocal interaction and supporting exploration of the environment through being predictable, reliable, approachable, and responsive. When a baby is first born the balance needs to be more heavily centered on offering security. As the baby grows this balance begins to shift to support exploration. As the child grows and develops, this shift becomes heavier and heavier in the direction of supporting exploration. It is important to remember that this balance is fluid; if the attachment behavioral system is activated, then a shift back to security can occur as needed. Furthermore, the goal of mothering is to develop an underlying, internal strength that fuels a healthy ego, supports a working conscience, and constructs strong internal working models consistent with individuality; and that the ultimate mothering goal is a child, who can enter adulthood as an autonomous, individuated, responsible person secure in her or his relationships.

Children's needs change throughout development as their own abilities mature. Mothering needs to reflect these changes. Connolly (2000), in a qualitative study of mothering, found that during the beginning of childhood mothers engaged in more caregiving tasks, meeting the basic needs of the children. By adolescence, mothers took on a more supportive role and became more involved in the emotional aspects of their children's lives. McBride (1987) further described the adolescent years as not only requiring a shift in mothering and parenting, but also a period of self-reflection for the mother as she has to learn to let go of her child and allow the child to become a person in her or his own right.

It is difficult to discern the changes in mothering over time. Cultural factors, family patterns and traditions, personal beliefs, the presence or absence of risk factors, and the context of the environment all contribute to changes in the mothering role over the child's development. Additionally, the distinctions between mothering and parenting blur as the child ages. Does this mean that mothering ceases and parenting replaces it? Does it mean that actual mothering surfaces only as the child's needs demand it? What are the defining factors for mothering as opposed to parenting? Based on child development factors, mothering should see decreases in the amount of caregiving required and increases in the amount of strategies for enhancing the child's independence and autonomy. In addition, as the child ages, mothering needs to reflect the child's increasing capacity for self-reliance. Table 1.1 describes expectations of mothering in terms of acts of monitoring, expectant nurturing, and responsiveness, reflective of the developmental progression of the child.

CHALLENGES IN MOTHERING

Mothering can occur only within the context of a relationship between a mother and a child. Likewise, a child can survive to grow and develop only within the context of a caregiving relationship. It is clear that the most significant period of mothering appears to be during the early years while the child has the most dependency for care. The mother–child relationship is an asymmetrical relationship during this period, in which the child needs more and gives less than the mother.

At first it seems that it is the expectant nurturing aspect of mothering that is the most important, as it has a direct impact on the child's well-being. However, we believe it is the aspect of the mother's capacity to make an emotional connection with the infant that determines survival and the child's developmental trajectory. This emotional connection is the foundation on which the developmental trajectory will play out. Initially, the child needs mothering that reflects hands-on care and her physical presence. Over time, and as maturation progresses, these needs shift. The child no longer needs mothering to survive, the goal instead becomes one of preparation for individuation or becoming a functional, responsible, socially appropriate adult—and this goal is met through the emotional connections made between the mother and child.

The work we have done with mothers in Early Head Start programs has taught us strong lessons about emotional connections for children. For mothers whose past traumatic events were not resolved in their own psyche, we found they could not make space for their babies in their minds. We think Bergum's (1997) labeling the phenomenon of "a child on her mind" is the unique contribution that mothers make to children's well-being.

TABLE 1.1
Expectations of Mothering

Age (years)	Child's Needs and Actions	Maternal Responsibilities

Infancy: 0–3	Basic care-food, shelter, stimulation, interaction
	Temporal regularity of sleep and feeding patterns
	Opportunities for a few independent decisions
	  i.e., feeding self, on parent's lap or next to
	  parent, clothes preference
		Providing food, safety, stimulation
		  and security
		Providing consistency and
		  predictability
		Being emotionally available and present
		Responding to child's distress
		Developing routines, such as bedtime
		Responding in sensitive and empathetic

Preschool: 3–5	Spending longer periods of time independently
	  of primary caregivers
	Developing some autonomous actions
	Establishing a mental model of mother and
	  other primary caregivers
	Decision making about eating preferences, favorite
	  activities and toys, bedtime routines
		Setting well-defined and consistent
		  limits and routines
		Modeling and encouraging
		  expression of feelings
		Encouraging opportunities for age
		  appropriate independence from
		  caregiver
		Encouraging development of mental
		  models of mother through symbols,
		  transitional objects and imagery

Early School: 5–8	Opportunities and support for learning and
	  decision making
	Engaging in healthy competition
	Gaining competence and a positive sense of self
	Solidifying mental images of mother and other
	  significant caregivers and extended family
	Expanding emotional literacy and understanding
	  rights of others
		Providing discipline and limits
		Providing opportunities for
		  independence while still monitoring
		Supporting emotional development
		Setting limits on inappropriate
		  expression of feelings
		Promoting awareness of other's
		  values and beliefs

Middle School: 8–12	Establishing a sense of self, including mastery,
	  reliance, behavioral control, esteem, emotional
	  literacy, friendships, values and beliefs
	Participating in social activities with family
	  and peers
		Supporting self-reliance and
		  maturing abilities
		Honoring the developing sense of
		  self and emotional growth
		Providing discipline and limits

Preteen: 12–15	Understanding of sexual self
	Developing peer relationships
	Increasing autonomy
		Providing guidance in transition to
		  adulthood, peer network and
		  autonomy
		Listening to child's expression
		  of sexual and physical changes
		Monitoring peer network

Adolescence: 15–18	Discovering emerging adult self
	Evaluating values and beliefs
	Evaluating consequences of decisions
		Providing love and ongoing
		  support
		Supporting decision making
		Providing access to resources
		Empathizing with tensions in
		  transition to adulthood
		Advocating for child's rights

Infancy: 0–3	Basic care
	Temporal regularity
	Opportunities for a few independent
	  decisions, i.e., on parent's lap or next
	  to parent, holding parent's left hand
	  or right hand, and so forth
		Providing food, safety, stimulation, and
		  security
		Providing consistency and predicatability
		Developing routines for certain interactions,
		  such as going to bed
		Being emotionally available and present
		Responding in sensitive and empathetic ways

(Continued)

TABLE 1.2
(Continued)

Age (years)	Child's Needs and Actions	Maternal Responsibilities
Preschool: 3–5	Spending increasingly longer periods of time independently of primary caregivers to begin to develop autonomy	Encouraging and supporting self-control through the setting of well-defined and consistent limits and routines
	Developing a stronger mental model of mother or other primary caregiver for sustaining longer periods of separation	Modeling and encouraging expressions of feelings; setting limits on inappropriate expressions of feelings
	Structuring of decision-making opportunities, e.g., bath now or after dinner, dress or pants, careal or toast	Encouraging and providing opportunities for age-appropriate independence from caregiver
		Supporting and encouraging the development of mental models of mother through symbols, transitional objects, and mental imagery

One of the successful aspects of assuming the mothering role is to be able to think of one's self as a "mother" and to think of the child in your arms as "my daughter" or "my son." If the mother cannot take possession of the baby in her mind, she will never be able to fully take possession of the living and breathing baby in her life. When the mother has the baby "on her mind," it represents the emotional connection that the mother has made with the child. When a baby is never taken into a mother's mind, the child becomes an emotional orphan whether or not a mother is physically present. We saw this in some of our Early Head Start mothers who described their mothers as living with them and providing food and shelter, but who also described these same mothers as "not there for me." They described feelings of rejection, abandonment, and a sense that no one really ever cared for them. They talked about their childhood wishes and dreams of having mothers who could do things with them like homework or even simply talk with them.

We found that when the mothers' minds were full of their losses and traumatic experiences there was no room left for their babies. We videotaped the interactions of one mother with her 5-month-old baby, which demonstrated this vacancy quite dramatically. In feeding her infant she did so by giving him the bottle while he was in a plastic infant seat. She made no eye or body contact; rather she visually scanned the environment. She did not talk to her child and would dissuade him from exploring his environment by pushing his hands down anytime he reached up for the bottle or her hand. Witnessing the emptiness of this interaction left us feeling empty. When we understood the significance of her past experiences, her emotional trauma, and her lack of loving relationships (case of Amy), we could more readily understand her behavior and recognize the challenge of forging emotional connectedness for the baby. It is our speculation that approximately 25% of new mothers have unresolved trauma that interferes with the emotional connection and having the child on her mind.

Another factor we have recognized is the limited perspective new parents have had in observing maternal role models and how important this is to the formation of their own parenting. Again in our Early Head Start experience many of the women had been emotionally rejected by their own mothers and, in turn, became rejecting of their own mothers. They did not see their mothers as "models" of mothers whom they might look to, neither could they identify an alternative positive model from their network. If a woman does not have a model of mothering in her mind, where can it come from? Stern and Bruschweiler-Stern (1998) hypothesized about the need women experience after birth for contact with other women. Ongoing research with doulas (a birthing witness and support) seems to confirm that when low-income women have a doula that provides support, information, and coaching there is a much different outcome in the pregnant woman's ability to carry the fetus to term and in the incidence of continued breast-feeding (Chicago Health Connection, 2000). We need to evaluate in our current society a structure within which children learn mothering behaviors. Few new parents have had the luxury of watching younger siblings parenting or even watching care of children by other parents or in childcare. Yet it is our experience that women without good role models who realize this have a hunger for good role models once they are pregnant.

Another factor to consider is the aspect of the intergenerational patterns that have an impact on mother–child relationships. Again, the case of Amy is illustrative. She had no positive mothering figure. Amy's biological mother was emotionally and physically unavailable to her and used the "child Amy" in abusive ways to get her own needs met—she abandoned Amy to abuse and neglect. Her stepmother afforded Amy no sense of safety or protection—she abandoned Amy to abuse and condoned this abuse with her lack of action. Amy not only experienced the primary trauma of abuse and neglect, she also experienced relationship trauma through the inadequate and rejecting mothering she received. We could see this emotional unavailability passed on to her infant son whom she refused to touch or interact with as she fed him in a mechanical manner. Her son already mirrored her lack of affect and emotionless face by the time he was a year old. Observing them together was like peering into two deep holes, each an emotional abyss hungry to be filled but with no sense or expectation that filling these voids would ever occur.

Without intervention both this mother and her child would continue with the cycle of rejecting and empty relationships, always at risk for trauma. The mothers we have seen to be effective in breaking this intergenerational cycle are those who have been able to garner emotional support from persons outside their family systems. For some mothers this meant completely and physically separating from their families of origins; for others it meant learning to keep tight boundaries on their families and essentially separating from them emotionally. The actual breaking of this cycle is often a very painful experience for the mother doing the separating; one mother made the following comment:

"I look at my daughter, who is now 12, and I think about where I was at 12—my mother was boozing it up every night, no one was ever home, she didn't know where I was or what I was doing and I was living with different friends, smoking dope, drinking, and looking for guys to help me feel like I existed. Sarah is reading books and playing softball, we talk and have a good time, she likes to be with me and I like to be with her . . . sometimes I wonder why I was the chosen one, the one who had to stop it all."

When asked how she became the mother she is now she replied,

"I found it in everyone else I met, I watched people in church, I watched other kids at school, I asked for help and accepted the help offered, and I swore I would never be like my mom . . . I still work at it everyday, but I know I am the best mom I can possibly be."

In fact, this mother quit her drugs and alcohol, she joined Alcoholic's Anonymous by the age of 16 and has been clean and sober since that time, she sought counseling, joined a church supportive of her desire to change, and facilitated relationships with her "healthy" relatives and friends for emotional support—she refers to all of this as "I made my own family, a healthy one, where I knew I would be loved and supported." The change in this woman's life is quite striking; she calls it "working from the inside" and acknowledges it would not have occurred if she had remained emotionally enmeshed with her family of origin.

CONCLUSIONS

Information from the childcare study by the National Institute of Child Health and Development has demonstrated application of the concept Hrdy labels as *allomothers* (1999). Allomothering is "shared mothering," common in both human and animal species. It is a variation in mothering that includes all persons who mother or help to mother the child, including (but not limited to) the mother's mate, extended family, peers, and neighbors. Allomothering helps to spread out the cost and responsibility of the care and nurturance of the child. In childcare, those responsible for the caring for the children would be classified as allomothers. Allomothering of any child, of course, varies with each mother–child dyad.

In our culture, there was a great deal of involvement of the extended family in the early 1900s. By midcentury, in the 1950s, this involvement narrowed as young parents and families became more mobile and often moved out of the areas where they had the greatest amount of support. Nearing the end of the twentieth century, we saw a move to this increased involvement of others, or allomothering. This trend continues today, with increased support from extended family immediately after birth and a large shift of the care of infants to allomothers in the form of childcare. Recent estimates are that 74% of children under 1 year of age are in childcare (National Research Council and Institute of Medicine, 2000).

Although empirical data from the National Child Care Study supports the consistent impact of the mother–child relationship on the child's later cognitive, language, and social–emotional development, the fact that there were no differences in child outcomes based on exclusive nonmaternal care and exclusive maternal care (NICHD, in press) provides us with support for complementary care of young children by allomothers. At the same time, it is worthy to note the consistent role the mothering relationship has with developmental outcomes. When mothers were sensitive, responsive and nonintrusive and the children experienced a secure attachment their development course was optimized.

We should support a national policy of federal and state government involvement with childcare, adding a feature to create ways to support the mother–child relationship through parent education and support. Interestingly, a consistent factor predicting maternal behavior, parent–child relationships, and child outcomes is the educational level of the mother. We need to understand more fully what *educational level* involves. Is it a marker for more support during the woman's development? Does having had more teachers provide more role models of nurturing behaviors? Does education provide more knowledge and strategies for learning and coping? Childcare services that are available and of good quality are important in the care of young children, given the high rate of maternal employment; but we must realize that for the best child outcomes encouraging the involvement of the parents' relationship with the child must be on the agenda.

The challenges we suggest for future research on mothering are directed toward seeing how women can be assisted before and during pregnancy to assume the maternal role and have the "child on their mind"; this is particularly important for women with less education and with mental health issues. In addition we need to know more about how to encourage parental involvement when parents use nonparental childcare resources. Work with the parents is not a part of most contemporary childcare. It was a tradition in former cooperative preschools, and we need to restructure parental involvement through the childcare resource for parents with working schedules. The research shows the value of maternal involvement regardless of childcare. Mothering is one of the most important roles in society. More attention and support need to be directed to the preparedness of women to take on their mothering role.

REFERENCES

Badinter, E. (1981). *Mother love: Myth and reality.* New York: Macmillan.

Barclay, L., Everitt, L., Rogan, F., Schmied, V., and Wyllie, A. (1997). Becoming a mother—an analysis of women's experience of early motherhood. *Journal of Advanced Nursing, 25,* 719–728.

Barnard, K. E. (1976). *NCAST II learners' resource manual.* Seattle, WA: Nursing Child Assessment Satellite Training.

Barnard, K. E. (1994). What the feeding scale measures. In G. Sumner and A. Spietz (Eds.), *NCAST feeding manual* (pp. 98–121). Seattle, WA: Nursing Child Assessment Satellite Training. (Available only with training; telephone 206-543-8528.)

Barnard, K. E., Hammond, M. A., Booth, C. L., Mitchell, S. K., and Spieker, S. J. (1989). Measurement and meaning of parent–child interaction. In F. J. Morrison, C. E. Lord, and D. P. Keating (Eds.), *Applied development psychology* (Vol. 3, pp. 39–80). New York: Academic.

Barnard, K. E., and Kelly, J. F. (1989). Assessment of parent–child interaction. In S. J. Meisels and J. P. Shonkoff (Eds.), *Handbook of early childhood intervention* (pp. 278–302). New York: Cambridge University Press.

Barnard, K. E., Spieker, S. J., and Huebner, C. E. (1996). Attachment in Early Head Start: Process and outcomes. Unpublished manuscript.

Basch, M. F. (1983). Empathetic understanding: A review of the concept and some theoretical considerations. *Journal of the American Psychoanalytic Association, 31*, 101–126.

Beckwith, L., and Cohen, E. E. (1984). Home environment and cognitive competence in preterm children during the first 5 years. In A. W. Gottfried (Ed.), *Home environment and early cognitive development* (pp. 235–271). New York: Academic.

Bee, H. L., Barnard, K. E., Eyres, S. J., Hammond, M. A., Spietz, A. L., Snyder, C., and Clark, B. (1982). Prediction of IQ and language skill from perinatal status, child performance, family characteristics, and mother–infant interaction. *Child Development, 53*, 1134–1156.

Bell, S. M., and Ainsworth, M. D. S. (1972). Infant crying and maternal responsiveness. *Child Development, 43*, 1171–1190.

Belsky, J., Rovine, M., and Taylor, D. G. (1984). The Pennsylvania infant and family development project, III: The origins of individual differences in infant–mother attachment: Maternal and infant contributions. *Child Development, 55*, 718–728.

Benedek, T. (1959). Parenthood as a developmental phase: A contribution to the libido theory. *Journal of the American Psychoanalytic Association, 7*, 379–417.

Benoit, D., and Parker, K. C. H. (1994). Stability and transmission of attachment across three generations. *Child Development, 65*, 1444–1456.

Bergum, V. (1997). *A child on her mind*. Westport, CT: Bergin and Garvey.

Bornstein, M. H. (1989). Between caretakers and their young: Two modes of interaction and their consequences for cognitive growth. In M. H. Bornstein and J. S. Bruner (Eds.), *Interaction in human development* (pp. 197–214). Hillsdale, NJ: Lawrence Erlbaum Associates.

Bornstein, M. H., and Tamis-LeMonda, C. S. (1989). Maternal responsiveness and cognitive development in children. In M. H. Bornstein (Ed.), *Maternal responsiveness: Vol. 43. Characteristic and consequences. New directions for child development* (pp. 49–61). San Francisco: Jossey-Bass.

Bowlby, J. (1953). *Childcare and the growth of love*. Harmondsworth, England: Penguin.

Brazelton, T. B. (1992). *Touchpoints: Your child's emotional and behavioral development*. Reading, MA: Perseus.

Brazelton, T., Koslowski, B., and Main, M. (1974). The origins of reciprocity: The early mother–infant interaction. In N. Lewis and L. Rosenblum (Eds.), *The effect of the infant on its caregiver*. New York: Wiley.

Brazelton, T. B., Tronick, E., Adamson, L., Als, H., and Wise, S. (1975). Early mother–infant reciprocity. In *Parent–infant interaction* (Symposium of the CIBA Foundation) (137–153, New Serial., 33). Amsterdam: Elsevier.

Brody, S. (1956). *Patterns of mothering*. New York: International Universities Press.

Burr, W. R. (1972). Role transitions. A reformulation of theory. *Journal of Marriage and the Family, 34*, 407–416.

Censullo, M., Bowler, R., Lester, B., and Brazelton, T. B. (1987). An instrument for the measurement of infant–adult synchrony. *Nursing Research, 36*, 342–346.

Censullo, M., Lester, B., and Hoffman, J. (1985). Rhythmic patterning in mother–newborn interaction. *Nursing Research, 34*, 342–346.

Chicago Health Connection. (2000). *The Chicago Doula Project*. Chicago, IL: Author.

Clarke-Stewart, K. A. (1973). Interactions between mothers and their young children: Characteristics and consequences. *Monographs of the Society for Research in Child Development, 38* (153, Serial No. 38).

Coates, D. L., and Lewis, M. (1984). Early mother–infant interaction and infant cognitive status as predictors of school performance and cognitive behavior in six-year-olds. *Child Development, 55*, 1219–1230.

Connolly, E. F. (2000). Toward an understanding of mothering: A comparison of two motherhood stages. *American Journal of Occupational Therapy, 54*, 281–289.

Dennis, W. (1973). *Children of the creche*. New York: Appleton-Century-Crofts.

Deutsch, H. (1945). *The psychology of women* (Vol. 2). New York: Grune and Stratton.

Emde, R. N. (1980). Emotional availability: A reciprocal reward system for infants and parents with implications for prevention of psychosocial disorders. In P. M. Taylor (Ed.), *Parent–infant relationships* (pp. 87–115). Orlando, FL: Grune and Stratton.

Elardo, R., Bradley, R., and Caldwell, B. (1975). The relations of infants' home environments to mental test performance from six to thirty-six months: A longitudinal analysis. *Child Development, 46*, 71–76.

Fields, T. (1994). The effects of mother's physical and emotional unavailability on emotional regulation. In N. A. Fox (Ed.), *The development of emotion regulation: Biological and behavioral considerations*. Chicago: University of Chicago Press.

Freud, A., and Burlingame, D. (1944). *Infants without families*. New York: International Universities Press.

Freud, S. (1918). Totems and taboo: Resemblances between the psychic lives of savages and neurotics. Original paper published 1913. Translated by A. A. Brill, PhB, MD. New York: Vintage Books.

Gabinet, L. (1986). A protocol for assessing competence to parent a newborn. *General Hospital Psychiatry, 8*, 263–272.

Goldberg, S. (1977). Social competence in infancy: A model of parent–infant interaction. *Merrill-Palmer Quarterly, 23*, 163–177.

Greenberg, M. T., Speltz, M. L., and DeKlyen, M. (1993). The role of attachment in the early development of disruptive behavior problems. *Development and Psychopathology, 5*, 191–213.

Greenspan, S. I., and Lieberman, A. F. (1980). Infants, mothers, and their interaction: A qualitative clinical approach to developmental assessment. In S. Greenspan and G. H. Pollock (Eds.), *The course of life* (Vol. I, pp. 271–312). (DHHS Publication No. 80-786). Washington, DC: National Institute of Mental Health.

Haft, W. L., and Slade, A. (1989). Affect attunement and maternal attachment: A pilot study. *Infant Mental Health Journal, 10*, 157–171.

Hammond, M. A., Bee, H. L., Barnard, K. E., and Eyres, S. J. (1983). *Child health assessment: Part IV. Follow-up at second grade.* (Grant RO 1-NU-00816, Final Report of Division of Nursing, Bureau of Health Professions, Health Resources and Services Administration, U.S. Public Health Service). Seattle, WA: Nursing Child Assessment Satellite Training, University of Washington.

Hartrick, G. A. (1997). Women who are mothers: The experience of defining self. *Health Care for Women International, 18*, 263–277.

Hrdy, S. B. (1999). *Mother nature: A history of mothers and infants, and natural selection.* New York: Pantheon.

Johnson, M. C. (1991). Infant and toddler sleep: A telephone survey of parents in one community. *Journal of Developmental and Behavioral Pediatrics, 12*, 108–114.

Josten, L. (1982). Contrast in prenatal preparation for mothering. *Maternal–Child Journal, 11*, 65–73.

Jung, C. G. (1959). Psychological aspects of the mother archetype. In R. C. F. Hill (Trans.) *The collected works of C. G. Jung* (Vol. 9, pp. 75–84). Princeton, NJ: Princeton University Press. (Original work published 1938)

Kochanska, G., and Aksan, N. (1995). Mother–child mutually positive affect, the quality of child compliance to requests and prohibitions, and maternal control as correlates of early internalization. *Child Development, 66*, 236–254.

Kochanska, G., Aksan, N., and Koenig, A. L. (1995). A longitudinal study of the roots of preschoolers' conscience: Committed compliance and emerging internalization. *Child Development, 66*, 1752–1769.

Kochanska, G., and Murray, K. T. (2000). Mother–child mutually responsive orientation and conscience development: From toddler to early school age. *Child Development, 71*, 417–431.

Lederman, R. P. (1984). *Psychosocial adaptation in pregnancy.* Englewood Cliffs, NJ: Prentice-Hall.

Lederman, R., Lederman, E., Workk, B. A., and McCann, D. S. (1978). The relationship of maternal anxiety, plasma catecholamines and plasma control to progress in labor. *American Journal of Obstetrics and Gynecology, 132*, 495–500.

Lester, B. M., Hoffman, J., and Brazelton, T. B. (1985). The rhythmic structure of mother–infant interaction in term and preterm infants. *Child Development, 56*, 15–27.

Lester, E. P., and Notman, M. T. (1988). Pregnancy and object relations: Clinical considerations. *Psychoanalytic Inquiry, 8*, 196–221.

Lyons-Ruth, K., and Block, D. (1996). The disturbed caregiving system: Relations among childhood trauma, maternal caregiving, and infant affect and attachment. *Infant Mental Health Journal, 17*, 257–275.

Mahler, M. S. (1961). On sadness and grief in infancy and childhood. *The Psychoanalytic Study of the Child, 16*, 332–351.

Mahler, M. S., Pine, F., and Bergman, A. (1975). *The psychological birth of the human infant: Symbiosis and individuation.* New York: Basic Books.

Main, M., and Goldwyn, R. (1994). *Adult attachment rating and classification system.* Unpublished manuscript, University of California at Berkeley.

McBride, A. B. (1987). *How to enjoy a good life with your teenager.* Tucson, AZ: Fisher Books.

Mercer, R. T. (1981). A theoretical framework for studying factors that impact on the maternal role. *Nursing Research, 30*, 73–77.

Mercer, R. T. (1985). The process of maternal role attainment over the first year. *Nursing Research, 34*, 198–204.

Mercer, R. T. (1986). *First-time motherhood: Experiences from the teens to forties.* New York: Springer.

Morisset, C. E. (1994). What the teaching scale measures. In G. Sumner and A. Spietz (Eds.), *NCAST teaching manual* (pp. 100–127). Seattle, WA: Nursing Child Assessment Satellite Training. (Available only through training: telephone 206-543-8528.)

National Research Council and Institute of Medicine. (2000). *From neurons to neighborhoods: The science of early development.* Washington, DC: National Academy Press.

Nelson, K. (1973). Structure and strategy in learning to talk. *Monographs of the Society for Research in Child Development, 38* (1–2, Serial No. 149).

NICHD Early Child Care Research Network. (in press). Parenting and family influences when children are in childcare: Results from the NICHD study of early childcare. In J. G. Borkowski, S. Ramey, and Bristol-Power, M. (Eds.), *Parenting and the child's world: Influences on intellectual, academic and socioemotional development.* Mahwah, NJ: Lawrence Erlbaum Associates.

Olson, S. L., Bates, J. E., and Bayles, K. (1984). Mother–infant interaction and the development of individual differences in children's cognitive competence. *Developmental Psychology, 20*, 166–179.

Papoušek, H., and Bornstein, M. H. (1992). Didactic interaction: Intuitive parental support of vocal and verbal development in human infants. In H. Papoušek, U. Jurgens, and M. Papoušek (Eds.), *Nonverbal vocal communication: Comparative and developmental approaches* (pp. 209–229). Cambridge, England: Cambridge University Press.

Paxson, D. (1998). The matronae (the mothers), *Sage Woman, 43*, 35–41.

Pines, D. (1972). Pregnancy and motherhood: Interaction between fantasy and reality. *British Journal of Medical Psychology, 45*, 333–343.

Provence, S., and Lipton, R. C. (1962). *Infants in institutions*. New York: International Universities Press.

Ramey, C. T., Farran, D. C., and Campbell, F. A. (1979). Predicting IQ from mother–infant interactions. *Child Development, 50*, 804–814.

Rubin, R. (1967a). Attainment of the maternal role: Models and referents. *Nursing Research, 16*, 342–346.

Rubin, R. (1967b). Attainment of the maternal role: Processes. *Nursing Research, 16*, 237–245.

Rubin, R. (1977). Binding-in the postpartum period. *Maternal-Child Nursing Journal, 6*, 67–75.

Rubin, R. (1984). *Maternal identity and maternal experience*. New York: Springer.

Ruble, D. N., Fleming, A. S., Stangor, C., Brooks-Gunn, J., Fitzmaurice, G., and Deutsch, F. (1990). Transition to motherhood and the self: Measurement, stability, and change. *Journal of Personality and Social Psychology, 58*, 450–463.

Sagi, A., van IJzendoorn, M. H., Aviezer, O., Konnell, F., and Mayseless, O. (1994). Sleeping out of home in a kibbutz communal arrangement: It makes a difference for infant–mother attachment. *Child Development, 65*, 992–1004.

Sander, L. W. (1962). Issues in early mother–child interaction. *Journal of American Academy of Child Psychiatry, 1*, 141–166.

Sander, L. W. (1964). Adaptive relationships in early mother–child interaction. *Journal of American Academy of Child Psychiatry, 3*, 231–264.

Scarr, S., and McCartney, K. (1983). How people make their own environments: A theory of genotype to environment effects. *Child Development, 54*, 424–435.

Settlage, C. F. (1980). The psychoanalytic theory and the understanding of psychic development during the second and third years of life. In S. I. Greenspan and G. H. Pollack (Eds.), *The course of life: psychoanalytic contributions toward understanding personality development: Vol. 1. Infancy and early childhood* (pp. 523–539). (DHHS Publications No. ADM 80-786). Washington, DC: U.S. Government Printing Office.

Slade, A., and Cohen, L. J. (1996). The process of parenting and the remembrance of things past. *Infant Mental Health Journal, 17*, 217–238.

Solchany, J. E. (2001). *Rehearsal for mothering: A handbook for prenatal mental health, maternal role attainment, and the mother-child relationship*. Seattle, WA: Nursing Child Assessment Satellite Training, School of Nursing, University of Washington.

Solchany, J., Sligar, K., and Barnard, K. E. (in press). Attachment promoting interventions in pregnancy: The parent–child communication-coaching program. In J. M. M. Duran (Ed.), *Infant and early childhood mental health, models of clinical intervention*. Washington, DC: American Psychiatric Press.

Spieker, S., Solchany, J., McKenna, M., DeKlyen, M., and Barnard, K. (1999). The story of mothers who are difficult to engage in prevention programs. In J. Osofsky and H. E. Fitzgerald (Eds.), *WAIMH handbook of infant mental health* (Vol. 3, Chap. 6). New York: Wiley.

Spitz, R. A. (1945). Hospitalism: An inquiry into the genesis of psychiatric conditions in early childhood. *Psychoanalytic Study of the Child, 2*, 53–73.

Spitz, R. A. (1946). Anaclitic depression: An inquiry into the genesis of psychiatric conditions in early childhood, II. *Psychoanalytic Study of the Child, 2*, 313–342.

Stern, D. (1985). Selective attunement. In D. N. Stern (Ed.), *The interpersonal world of the infant* (pp. 297–311). New York: Basic Books.

Stern, D., and Bruschweiler-Stern, N. (1998). *The birth of a mother: How the motherhood experience changes you forever*. New York: Basic Books—Perseus Book Group.

Stone, J., and Church, J. (1957). *Childhood and adolescence*. New York: Random House.

Sumner, G., and Spietz, A. (Eds.). (1994). *NCAST: Feeding manual*. Seattle, WA: Nursing Child Assessment Satellite Training.

Trad, P. V. (1990). On becoming a mother: In the throes of developmental transformation. *Psychoanalytic Psychology, 7*, 341–361.

van der Heever, J. (1990). Maternal love. *Nursing RSA Verleding, 5*, 114–116.

Wachs, T. D., Užgiris, I. C., and Hunt, J. (1971). Cognitive development in infants of different age levels and from different environmental backgrounds: An explanatory investigation. *Merrill-Palmer Quarterly, 17*, 283–317.

Webster-Stratton, C. (1985). Comparison of abusive and nonabusive families with conduct-disordered children. *American Journal of Orthopsychiatry, 55*, 59–69.

Webster-Stratton, C. (1992). *The incredible years*. Toronto: Umbrella Press.

Winnicott, D. W. (1988). *Babies and their mothers*. Exeter, England: Short Run Press.

Winnicott, D. W. (1990). *The maturation process and the facilitating environment*. Exeter, England: BPCC Wheatons.

Yarrow, L. J., Rubenstein, J. L., and Pedersen, F. A. (1975). *Infant and environment: Early cognitive and motivational development*. Washington, DC: Hemisphere.

2

Fathers and Families

Ross D. Parke

University of California, Riverside

INTRODUCTION

Theoretical assumptions that guide research in this area both explain the choice of topics and provide an organizational structure for this chapter. First, to understand fully the nature of father–child relationships, it is necessary to recognize the interdependence among the roles and the functions of all family members. Families are best viewed as social systems. Consequently, to understand the behavior of one member of a family, the complementary behaviors of other members also need to be recognized and assessed. For example, as men's roles in families shift, changes in women's roles in families must also be monitored (Parke, 1996).

Second, family members—mothers, fathers, and children—influence one another both directly and indirectly (Parke, Power, and Gottman, 1979). Examples of fathers' indirect impact include various ways in which fathers modify and mediate mother–child relationships. In turn, women affect their children indirectly through their husbands by modifying both the quantity and the quality of father–child interaction. Children may indirectly influence the husband–wife relationship by altering the behavior of either parent that consequently changes the interaction between spouses.

Third, different levels of analysis are necessary in order to understand fathers. The individual level—child, mother, and father—remains a useful and necessary level of analysis, but recognition of relationships among family members as levels or units of analysis is also necessary. The marital, the mother–child, and the father–child relationships, require separate analyses. The family as a unit that is independent of the individual or dyads within the family requires recognition (Parke, 1996; Parke and McDowell, in press).

Fourth, families are embedded within a variety of other social systems, including both formal and informal support systems, as well as within the cultures in which they exist (Bronfenbrenner, 1989; Bronfenbrenner and Morris 1998; Parke and Buriel, 1998). These include a wide range of extrafamilial influences such as extended families, informal community ties such as friends and neighbors, work sites, and social, educational, and medical institutions (Parke and O'Neil, 2000; Tinsley and Parke, 1988).

A fifth assumption concerns the importance of considering father–child relationships from a variety of developmental perspectives. Developmental changes in child perceptual–cognitive and social–emotional capacities represent the most commonly investigated type of development. In addition, a lifespan perspective (Elder, 1998; Elder, Modell, and Parke, 1993; Parke, 1988, 1996) suggests the importance of examining developmental changes in the adult because parents continue to change and develop during adult years. For example, age at the time of the onset of parenthood can have important implications for how females and males manage their maternal and paternal roles. This involves an exploration of the tasks faced by adults, such as self-identity, education, and career and examination of relations between these tasks and the demands of parenting.

Another assumption involves recognition of the impact of secular shifts on families. In recent years, a variety of social changes in America has had a profound impact on families. These include the decline in fertility and family size, changes in the timing of the onset of parenthood, increased participation of women in the workforce, rise in rates of divorce, and subsequent increase in the number of single-parent families (Parke and Stearns, 1993; Parke and Tinsley, 1984). The ways in which these society wide changes impact on interaction patterns between parents and children merit examination.

Another closely related assumption involves the recognition of the importance of the historical time period in which the family interaction is taking place (Coltrane and Parke, 1998). Historical time periods provide the social conditions for individual and family transitions: Examples include the 1930s (the Great Depression), the 1960s (the Vietnam War era), or the 1980s (Farm Belt Depression). Across these historical time periods, family interactions may be quite different because of the peculiar conditions of the particular era (Elder et al., 1993).

These distinctions among different developmental trajectories, as well as social change and historical period effects, are important because these different forms of change do not always harmonize (Elder, 1998; Parke, 1988; Parke and Tinsley, 1984). For example, a family event such as the birth of a child—the transition to parenthood—may have very profound effects on a man who has just begun a career in contrast to the effects on one who has advanced to a stable occupational position. Moreover, individual and family developmental trajectories are embedded within both the social conditions and the values of the historical time in which they exist (Elder, 1998). The role of parents, as is the case with any social role, is responsive to such fluctuations.

A final assumption concerns the role of cognitive factors in understanding father–child relationships. Specifically, we assume that the ways in which parents perceive, organize, and understand both their children and their roles as parents will affect the nature of father–child interaction (Beitel and Parke, 1998; Goodnow and Collins, 1991).

To understand the nature of father–child relationships within families, a multilevel and dynamic approach is required. Multiple levels of analysis are necessary in order to capture the individual, dyadic, and family unit aspects of operation within the family itself as well as to reflect the embeddedness of families within a variety of extrafamilial social systems. The dynamic quality reflects the multiple developmental trajectories that warrant consideration in understanding the nature of families in children's development.

The substantive portion of this chapter begins with a discussion of the nature of the father–child relationships and how these shift across the development of the child. Next, the chapter moves to an examination of the determinants of father involvement to examine the impact of the marital relationship on the parent–child relationship. The effect of recent historical changes, namely shifts in work patterns of family members and changes in the timing of the onset of parenthood, on father–child relationships is reviewed. Finally, the implications of fathering for men themselves, their wives, and their children are examined.

This chapter is a review of recent work on fatherhood and devotes less attention to the historical aspects of the topic. However, several recent reviews caution against any simple and linear set of historical trends that lead clearly from the past to the present (LaRossa, 1997; La Rossa, Jaret, Gadgil, and Wynn, 2000; Parke and Stearns, 1993; Rotundo, 1993; Stearns, 1991). Perhaps most striking is the continued tension and variability in fathering behavior—a set of characteristics that have long marked definitions of fatherhood. There have always been counteracting forces that have both promoted and limited father involvement with their children and families. There have been "good dads and bad dads" (Furstenberg, 1988) throughout the course of the history of fatherhood. Even the venerable play orientation of fathers has its origins only recently in the past century (Stearns, 1991; Parke and Stearns 1993). Stearns (1991, p. 50) has recently characterized the shifts over the past century as follows:

> [M]ost pressing context for fatherhood over the past century has been the change in work—family relationship. . . . An 18th Century father would not recognize the distance contemporary men face between work and home or the importance of sports in father–child relations or the parental leadership granted to mothers or indeed the number of bad fathers. An 18th Century father would, however, recognize certain contemporary tensions such as a balance between seeking and giving love on the one hand and defining proper authority and he might feel kinship to present-day fathers who sense some tension between responses they regard as male and special restraints required for proper family life.

In sum, many of the themes that characterize contemporary thinking about fatherhood have clearer antecedents in the past century than we often assume (Coltrane and Parke, 1998). There has been a tendency to confuse the resurgence of interest in fathering as a research topic with the assumption that the changes in fathering activities have been only recent as well.

PATERNAL VERSUS MATERNAL INVOLVEMENT WITH CHILDREN

There are overall differences in the quantity of involvement for mothers and fathers, and there are important stylistic or qualitative differences as well. Not all forms of father involvement are conceptually equivalent (Barnett and Baruch, 1987; Lamb, Pleck, and Levine, 1985; Palkovitz, 1997; Parke, 2000; Radin, 1993). The most influential scheme was offered by Lamb and his colleagues (Lamb, 1987; Lamb et al., 1985), who suggested three components: interaction, availability, and responsibility (Lamb, Pleck, Charnov, and Levine, 1987, p. 125):

> Interaction refers to the father's direct contact with his child through caregiving and shared activities. Availability is a related concept concerning the child's potential availability for interaction, by virtue of being present or accessible to the child whether or not direct interaction is occurring. Responsibility refers to the role the father takes in ascertaining that the child is taken care of and arranging for resources to be available for the child.

As several authors (e.g., McBride, 1989; Palkovitz, 1997; Parke, 1995, 2000) note, the focus of research on fathers has been primarily on face-to-face parent–child *interaction*. To a large degree this emphasis reflects the common assumption that parental influence takes place directly through face-to-face contact or indirectly through the impact of the interaction on another family member. Similarly, the availability issue has been addressed, but largely through the research on father absence as a consequence of either divorce or unwed parenthood (Garfinkel, McLanahan, Meyer, and Seltzer, 1998; McLanahan and Sandefur, 1994; Mott, 1994). Less is known about the determinants or the consequences of availability of fathers among residential fathers. Only recently have researchers and theorists begun to recognize the "managerial" function of parents (the "responsibility" notion of Lamb et al., 1987) and to appreciate the impact of variations in how this managerial function influences the child development (Hartup, 1979; Parke, 1978; Parke and O'Neil, 2000). The term managerial refers to the ways in which parents organize and arrange the child's home environment and set limits on the range of the home setting to which the child has access and the opportunities for social contact with playmates and socializing agents outside the family (Parke, Killian, Dennis, Flyr, McDowell, Simpkins, Kim, and Wild, in press). The managerial role may be just as important as the parent's role as stimulator, because the amount of time that children spend interacting with the inanimate environment far exceeds their social interaction time (White, Kaban, Shapiro, and Attonucci, 1976).

Mothers and fathers differ in their degree of responsibility for management of family tasks. From their children's infancy through middle childhood, mothers are more likely to assume the managerial role than fathers. In the child's infancy, this means setting boundaries for play (Power and Parke, 1982), taking the child to the doctor, or arranging daycare. Russell and Russell (1987) found that, in the child's middle childhood, mothers continue to assume more managerial responsibility (e.g., directing the child to have a bath, to eat a meal, or to put away toys). Nor is the managerial role restricted to family activities, but rather includes initiating and arranging children's access to peers and playmates (Ladd, Profilet, and Hart, 1992; Mounts, 2000; Parke and Bhavnagri, 1989; Parke, Killian et al., in press). In addition, parents function as supervisors or overseers of children's interactions with agemates, especially with younger children. Both mothers and fathers are equally capable of this type of supervisory behavior, as shown in laboratory studies (Bhavnagri and Parke, 1991) and in home contexts, but fathers are less likely than mothers to perform this supervisory role (Bhavnagri and Parke, 1991; Ladd et al., 1992). Moreover, the effects are similar whether mother or father supervised the play of the two children; in home contexts fathers are less likely than mothers to engage in this type of supervisory behavior (Bhavnagri and Parke, 1991; Ladd et al., 1992). These activities may vary by ethnicity. Toth and Xu (1999) reported that African American and Hispanic fathers are more likely to report monitoring and supervising than European American fathers, but still do less than mothers. Coltrane (1996, p. 175) made the following observation:

> In most families, husbands notice less about what needs to be done, wait to be asked to do various chores and require explicit directions if they are to complete the tasks successfully . . . most couples continue to characterize husbands' contributions to housework or child care as "helping" their wives.

Radin (1993) also suggests that absolute and relative involvement needs to be distinguished because prior work (e.g., Pleck, 1985) argues that these two indices are independent and may affect both children's and adults' views of role distributions in different ways.

It is important to distinguish among domains of involvement, as fathers and mothers vary in their distribution of time across different child and household activities. Several distinctions have been made in the prior literature, including personal care activities, involvement in play, leisure and affiliative activities with children (Beitel and Parke, 1998; Radin, 1993). More recently, Yeung, Sandberg, Davis-Kean, and Hofferth (2001) have expanded the domain list to include not just personal care and play but achievement-related activities (e.g., homework, reading), household activities (e.g., housework, shopping), social activities (e.g., conversation, social events), and other activities (e.g., time in school, sleep). As noted in the next subsection, both the amount of time that fathers spend on these different activities and the determinants of involvement in these domains vary across fathers. Finally, recent estimates of father involvement have usefully distinguished between weekdays and weekends because both the types activities and levels of father involvement vary as a function of the time period being assessed (Yeung et al., 2001).

Quantitative Assessments of Father Involvement in Intact Families

The extent to which fathers in intact families participate in childcare needs to be distinguished from the level of involvement of fathers who are not coresident with their children for a variety of reasons, including divorce or out-of-wedlock births. In fact, this conceptual distinction reflects the contradictory trends in the fathering literature that Furstenberg (1988, p. 193) has characterized as the "two faces of fatherhood." On the one hand, fathers seem to be increasing their involvement and moving slowly toward more equal participation with their wives in the care and rearing of children. On the other hand, increases in father absence, nonpayment of child support, and denial of paternity suggest that a less desirable side of fatherhood is evident as well. As in prior decades, the movement is not linear and straightforward but is contradictory and inconsistent. Even among contemporary fathers in intact families, there is considerable variability in the level and type of involvement. For example, Jain, Belsky, and Crinic (1996) identified two major types of fathers, namely a set of progressive fathers who engaged in caregiving, play and teaching and a group of traditional fathers who were either disengaged or functioned as disciplinarians. In sum, both across time and in our own era, there are wide individual differences among fathers that are often obscured by our focus on overall trends and mother-father comparisons. In this subsection, the focus is on the former aspect of the issue, and in later subsections on adolescent fatherhood and father visitation the issue of nonresidential fatherhood is addressed.

In spite of current shifts in cultural attitudes concerning the appropriateness and the desirability of shared roles and equal levels of participation in routine caregiving and interaction for mothers and fathers, the shifts toward parity are small, but nonetheless real. In a recent review, Pleck (1997) cites a range of studies that document that father involvement has increased, albeit slowly. For example, Robinson (1988) compared levels of childcare by fathers in a small American city in 1966 and 1988 and found an increase. Employed fathers' time with children increased from 1.21 to 1.53 hr per week. This trend appears to be continuing. A national survey of men's childcare responsibilities found that the percentage of children whose fathers cared for them during their mothers' work hours rose from 15% in 1977 to 20% in 1991 (O'Connell, 1993). Pleck (1997, p. 74) noted that, "fathers are the primary care arrangement almost as often as are family day care homes (22%) and far more often than group care centers (14%) or grandparents (9%)." The fact that fathers are the primary caregivers during mothers' working hours in almost one out of five dual-career families with preschool children suggests that a much higher proportion of fathers have significant childcare responsibility than is usually thought. Some estimate that fathers' involvement in all aspects of childcare, not just during their wives' working hours, was nearly a third of the total childcare by U.S. dual-career couples in the 1990s. Although more mothers are entering the workforce, current occupational arrangements still mean that the vast majority of fathers have fewer opportunities for interaction with their children than mothers do (Coltrane, 1996; Lamb, 1987). As Pleck (1997, p. 71) noted, "Averaging across studies from the 1980s and 1990s, fathers proportional engagement is somewhat over two-fifths of mothers (43.5%) and their accessibility is two-thirds of mothers (65.6%)" (p. 71). These figures are higher than reports from the 1970s and early 1980s, which averaged one third for proportional engagement and one half for accessibility (Pleck, 1997).

In a recent critique of the prior work on father involvement, Yeung et al. (2001, p. 136) noted that "estimates of fathers' involvement vary widely for many reasons. Generalization and comparison over time or across age groups from results in previous research are difficult because studies on this topic differ in the samples used, the ages of the children covered, and the methodology employed in accounting for paternal involvement. Many of them are based on data collected from small local samples more than a decade ago, and most focus on fathers' involvement with infants and preschoolers."

To overcome these limitations and to provide a current estimate of the level of father involvement, Yeung et al. (2001) used a national representative sample of children in two-parent families in the United States in 1997. The sample included children aged 0 to 12 years and therefore allowed an assessment of the nature of paternal involvement across different developmental periods. Finally, because the data were collected in 1997, the study permitted a comparison of father involvement in the 1960s, 1980's, and the late 1990s to determine if there has been a historical shift in level of father involvement. These investigators confirmed Pleck's (1997) conclusion that there has been a gradual increase in the level of father involvement over the past four decades. Yeung et al. (2001) found that the relative time fathers in intact families were directly engaged with children was 67%

of the time that mothers were involved on weekdays and 87% of mothers engagement on weekends. Accessibility showed similar shifts across time that, in accord with earlier estimates (Pleck, 1997), were higher than levels of engagement. Finally, Yeung et al. found relatively few differences in level of father involvement (engagement or accessibility) as a function of ethnicity (African American, European American, and Latino). Others (Hossain and Roopnarine, 1994) reported similar findings. Involvement by African American fathers in middle-socioeconomic and lower-middle-socioeconomic, dual-earner families with infants and preschool children was similar to the levels of involvement of other ethnic groups.

Studies in other cultures confirm these findings. Evidence of mother–father differences in involvement comes from the longitudinal study of traditional and nontraditional families in Sweden conducted by Lamb and his colleagues (Lamb, Frodi, Hwang, and Frodi, 1982; Lamb, Frodi, Hwang, Frodi, and Steinberg, 1982). Families in which the father elected to stay home as primary caregiver for 1 month or more (nontraditional) were compared with families in which the father elected to be a secondary caregiver (traditional). In an analysis of home observations when infants were 8 and 16 months of age, mothers surpassed fathers in holding and affectional behavior regardless of family type. Further support for this pattern of gender-of-parent differences comes from a study of kibbutz families (Sagi, Lamb, Shoham, Dvir, and Lewkowicz, 1985). Although childcare was the primary responsibility of nonparental caregivers (metaplot) rather than that of either parent, gender differences in parental behavior similar to those observed in the United States and Sweden were found. Kibbutz mothers were more affectionate and engaged in more caregiving than were fathers. Finally, Ishii-Kuntz (1995, 2000) has reported similar findings for Japanese fathers; again, fathers engage in less direct caregiving than mothers.

These findings are consistent with the more general proposition that pregnancy and birth of a first child, in particular, are occasions for a shift toward a more traditional division of roles (Cowan and Cowan, 1992). Of particular interest is the fact that this pattern held regardless of whether the initial role division between husbands and wives was traditional or equalitarian (Cowan and Cowan, 1992). Cowan, Cowan, Coie, and Coie (1978, p. 20) observed that, "Despite the current rhetoric and ideology concerning equality of roles for men and women, it seems that couples tend to adopt traditionally defined roles during times of stressful transition such as around the birth of a first child."

The overall pattern of contact time between mothers and fathers with their children that is evident in infancy continues into middle childhood and adolescence (Collins and Russell, 1991). In a study of middle childhood (6- to 7-year-old children), Russell and Russell (1987) found that Australian mothers were available to children 54.7 hr/week compared with 34.6 hr/week for fathers. Mothers also spent more time alone with their children (22.6 hr/week) than did fathers (2.4 hr/week). However, when both parents and child were together, mothers and fathers initiated interactions with children with equal frequency and children's initiations toward each parent were similar. Adolescents spent less time with their parents than younger children did and less time alone with their father than with their mother (Larson and Richards, 1994). Montemayor (1982), in a study of 15- to 16-year-old teenagers, reported that more than twice as much time was spent with mother alone than with father alone each day. Similar findings were reported for 14- to 18-year-old teenagers by Montemayor and Brownlee (1987). In summary, mothers and fathers clearly differ in terms of their degree of involvement with their offspring from infancy through adolescence.

Although the relative difference in mother and father involvement is not markedly different across development, the absolute level of father involvement decreases as the child develops and the types of activities in which fathers and children interact also vary across development. In the survey by Yeung et al. (2001), for example, in the case of infants and toddlers (ages 0–2 years) fathers interact directly or are accessible to their children for approximately 3 hr/day. By the time the children are 9 to 12 years of age the level of involvement has decreased to $2\frac{1}{4}$ hr. Activities vary across age as well. Time in personal care with fathers (either interaction or accessibility) drops from 1 hr/day for infants to $\frac{1}{2}$ hr for 9- to 12-year-old children. Play or companionship activities with fathers are more common among infants and toddlers (44 min/day) than at later ages (23 min for 9- to 12-year-old children). While indoor games and toy play as well as outdoor activities and sports decrease, TV and video watching increase across age. Achievement-related activities, which include reading, educational play, and studying, increase from 7 to 27 min from toddlerhood to preadolescence. The pattern is similar on weekends, but the absolute amount of time in which fathers are either involved or accessible nearly doubles. Not unexpected is the rise in household activities (e.g., shopping) and social activities (e.g., religious services) on weekends for fathers and their children. As the study by Yeung et al. (2001) study clearly underscores, both age and type of activity need to be considered in descriptions of father involvement.

Competence Versus Performance

The lower level of father involvement in caregiving and other forms of interaction does not imply that fathers are less competent than mothers to care for infants and children. Competence can be measured in a variety of ways: One approach is to measure the parent's sensitivity to infant cues in the feeding context. Success in caregiving, to a large degree, depends on the parent's ability to correctly "read" or interpret the infant's behavior so that the parent's own behavior can be regulated to respond appropriately. Parke and Sawin (1975, 1976) found that fathers' sensitivities to a variety of cues—auditory distress signals during feeding (sneeze, spitup, cough), vocalizations, mouth movements—was just as marked as mothers' responsitivities to these cues. Both fathers and mothers adjusted their behavior (e.g., looked more closely, vocalized) in response to these infant cues. In a later study (Parke and Sawin, 1980), it was shown that parent vocalizations can modify infant vocalizations. Interaction between fathers and infants—even in the newborn period—is clearly bidirectional in quality; parents and infants mutually regulate each other's behavior in the course of interaction. In spite of the fact that they may spend less time overall in caregiving activities, fathers are as sensitive as mothers to infant cues and as responsive to them in the feeding context. Moreover, the amount of milk consumed by infants with their mothers and fathers in this study was very similar, which suggests that fathers and mothers are not only comparable in their sensitivity but equally successful in feeding the infant. If a competence–performance distinction is made, fathers may not necessarily be as frequent contributors to infant feeding, but when called on they have the competence to execute these tasks effectively.

Fathers' abilities to perform caregiving tasks do not appear to be different from those of mothers when their children are in middle childhood as well. As Russell and Russell (1987) found, both parents reported that they were involved on a regular basis in a variety of caregiving activities even though mothers were higher in their frequencies. For example, both mothers and fathers report "having a cuddle" very nearly every day and fathers as well as mothers "go over their child's day" and "sit and have a talk" almost every day. Moreover, the degree of warmth expressed by mothers and fathers to their children is similar, although the behavioral manifestations of how warmth is expressed varies as a function of both gender of parent and gender of child (Russell and Russell, 1989). Finally, as noted earlier, fathers can function effectively as managers and supervisors of their children's activities, but do so less than mothers on a routine basis (Bhavnagri and Parke, 1991; Coltrane, 1996; Ladd et al., 1992). Again it appears that fathers are capable of this type of caregiving function but execute this function less regularly than mothers. On balance, however, the evidence suggests that fathers are competent caregivers.

Qualitative Effects: Stylistic Differences in Mother and Father Interaction

Fathers participate less than mothers in caregiving but spend a greater percentage of the time available for interaction in play activities than mothers do. In the United States, Kotelchuck (1976) found that fathers spent a greater percentage of their time with their infants in play (37.5%) than mothers did (25.8%), although in absolute terms mothers spent more time than fathers in play with their children.

Similar findings have been reported from a longitudinal investigation of parent–infant interaction in England (Richards, Dunn, and Antonis, 1977). Playing with their infants at 30 and 60 weeks of age was the most common activity of fathers, and over 90% of the fathers played regularly with their infants. Lamb (1977) observed interactions among mothers, fathers, and infants in their homes when the infants 7 to 8 months of age and again when they were 12 to 13 months of age. Marked differences emerged in the reasons that fathers and mothers pick up infants: Fathers were more likely to hold the babies simply to play with them, whereas mothers were far more likely to hold them for caregiving purposes.

More recent studies of African American (Hossain and Roopnarine, 1994) and Latino (Hossain, Field, Malphurs, Valle, and Pickens, 1995) fathers yield a similar pattern: Fathers spend more of their time in play with their children. For example, African American fathers spent 54% of their time in play compared with only 38% for mothers. It is not only the quantity of time in play that discriminates between mother and father involvement in infancy; the quality of play activity does so as well. Power and Parke (1982) observed mothers and fathers interacting with their 8-month-old infants in a laboratory playroom. Fathers played more bouncing and lifting games, especially with boys, than mothers did. In contrast, mothers played more watching games in which a toy is presented and made salient by moving or shaking it. Observations of father– and mother–infant interactions in unstructured home contexts with older infants reveals similar mother–father differences in play style (Clarke-Stewart, 1978, 1980; Lamb, 1977).

Nor are these effects evident only during a child's infancy. MacDonald and Parke (1984), in an observational study of the play interaction patterns between mothers and fathers and 3- and 4-year-old toddlers, found that fathers engaged in more physical play with their children than mothers did, whereas mothers engaged in more object-mediated play than fathers did. According to MacDonald and Parke (1986), the fathers' distinctive role as a physical play partner changes with age, however. Physical play was highest between fathers and 2-year-old toddlers; when the children were between 2 and 10 years of age there was a decreased likelihood that fathers would engage their children physically.

In spite of the decline in physical play across age, fathers are still more often physical play partners than mothers. In an Australian study of parents and their 6- to 7-year-old children (Russell and Russell, 1987), fathers were more involved in physical or outdoor play interactions and fixing things around the house and garden than mothers were. In contrast, mothers were more actively involved in caregiving and household tasks and in school work. Mothers were also involved in more reading, playing with toys, and helping with arts and crafts.

In all studies reviewed, a reasonably consistent pattern emerges: Fathers are tactile and physical, and mothers tend to be verbal, didactic and toy mediated in their play. Clearly infants and young children experience not only more stimulation from their fathers, but a qualitatively different stimulatory pattern.

Is There a Universal Father Play Style?

Some cross-cultural studies support the generality of this pattern of mother–father differences in play style. Parents in England and Australia show similar gender differences (Russell and Russell, 1987; Smith and Daglish, 1977). However, other evidence suggests that this pattern of mother–father differences in play style may be, in part, culture bound. Specifically, neither in Sweden (Lamb, Frodi, Hwang, and Frodi, 1982) nor among Israeli kibbutz families (Sagi et al., 1985) were there clear gender-of-parent differences in the tendency to engage in play or in the types of play initiated. As Sagi et al. (1985, p. 283) observed: "Perhaps this reflects the more egalitarian arrangements effective (at least during observation period) in Sweden and Israel than in the United States. This would suggest that, at least in regard to Sweden and Israel, sex differences in maternal and paternal behavior, are influenced by the concrete competing demands on the parents' time, as well as by their socialization and biogenetic tendencies."

Similarly, Chinese Malaysian, Taiwanese, and Thai mothers and fathers reported that they rarely engaged in physical play with their children (Sun and Roopnarine, 1996; see Lamb, 1987, for review). Among middle-socioeconomic Indian families in New Delhi, fathers and mothers are more likely to display affection than to play with infants while holding them. Although mothers engaged in more object-mediated play than fathers, there were no other differences in the play styles of mothers and fathers. Most interesting was the finding that the frequency of rough physical play was very low—less than once per hour (Roopnarine, Hooper, Ahmeduzzaman, and Pollock, 1993). Observations of Aka pygmies of Central Africa by Hewlett (1991) are consistent with this pattern. In this culture, mothers and fathers rarely, if ever, engage in vigorous or physical type of play. Instead both display affection and engage in plenty of close physical contact. In other cultures, such as Italy, neither mothers nor fathers but other women in the extended family or within the community are more likely to play physically with infants (New and Benigni, 1987).

Whether these distinctively female and male play styles are due to cultural influences or to biological factors remains a puzzle for future researchers to solve. However, the fact that male monkeys show the same rough-and-tumble physical style of play as human fathers suggests that we cannot ignore a possible biological component in play styles of mothers and fathers (Lovejoy and Wallin, 1988; Parke and Suomi, 1981). Moreover, males monkeys tend to respond more positively to bids for rough-and-tumble play more than females do (Meany, Stewart, and Beatty, 1985). Perhaps, as Maccoby (1988, p. 271) states, "males may be more susceptible to being aroused into states of positive excitement and unpredictability than females"—a speculation that is consistent with gender differences in risk taking and sensation seeking. In addition, males, whether boys and young men, tend to behave more boisterously and show more positive affect than females (Maccoby, 1998). Together these threads of the puzzle suggest that predisposing biological differences between females and males may play a role in the play patterns of mothers and fathers. At the same time, the cross-cultural data clearly underscore the ways in which cultural and environmental contexts shape play patterns of mothers and fathers and remind us of the high degree of plasticity of human social behaviors.

DETERMINANTS OF FATHER INVOLVEMENT

The importance of examining the determinants of father involvement stems from the view that the paternal role is less culturally scripted and determined than the maternal role and few clear role models for defining fatherhood exist (Daly, 1993; Marsiglio, 1993). It is assumed that a multifactor approach to father involvement is necessary because a variety of factors determines the degree of father involvement with children. It is useful to distinguish individual, familial, and societal levels of analysis in assessing the determinants of father involvement with children (Doherty, Kouneski, and Erikson, 1998; Parke, 1996).

Biological Factors in Paternal Behavior

It has long been recognized that females undergo a variety of hormonal changes during pregnancy and childbirth that may facilitate maternal behavior. Rosenblatt (1969, 1995, in Vol. 2 of this *Handbook*), using the rat as an experimental model, showed that hormonal changes elicited maternal behavior, while other studies showed similar effects for human mothers (Fleming, Ruble, Krieger, and Wong, 1997). It was long assumed that hormones play an unimportant role in paternal behavior because a father's exposure to rat pups increases paternal activity without any changes in hormone levels (Fleming and Corter, 1995). More recent evidence has challenged the assumption that hormonal levels are unimportant determinants of paternal behavior when this issue was examined in species other than the rat, which is not a natural paternal species. In naturally paternal species, such as canid species who constitute less than 10% of mammalian species (Storey, Walsh, Quinton, and Wynne-Edwards, 2000), researchers have found that in a variety of animal species males experience hormonal changes, including increases in prolactin and decreases in testosterone before the onset of parental behavior and during infant contact (Fleming and Corter, 1995; Rosenblatt, 1995). Human fathers, too, undergo hormonal changes during their mates' pregnancy and childbirth. Storey et al. (2000) found that men experienced significant prenatal, perinatal, and postnatal changes in each of these hormones—prolactin, cortisol, and testosterone—a pattern of results which was similar to that of the women in their study. Specifically, prolactin levels were higher for both men and women in the late prenatal period than in the early prenatal period, and cortisol levels increased just before birth and decreased in the postnatal period for both men and women. Testosterone levels were lower in the early postnatal period, which corresponds to the first opportunity for interaction with their infants. Hormonal levels and changes were linked with a variety of social stimuli as well. Men with lower testosterone levels held test baby dolls longer and were more responsive to infant cues (crying) than were men with higher testosterone levels. Men who reported a greater drop in testosterone levels also reported more pregnancy or couvade symptoms. Together these findings suggest that lower testosterone levels in the postnatal period may increase paternal responsiveness, in part by reducing competitive nonnurturing behavior (Storey et al., 2000). Similarly prolactin levels were higher in men who showed greater responsiveness to infant cries and in men who reported more couvade symptoms during their mates' pregnancies. Finally, Storey et al. (2000, p. 91) argued that the "cortisol increases in late pregnancy and during labor may help new fathers focus on and become attached to their newborns." Men's changes in hormonal levels are linked not only with baby cries and the time in the pregnancy birth cycle but also to the hormonal levels of their partners. Women's hormonal levels were closely linked with the time remaining before delivery, and men's levels were linked with their partner's hormone levels, not with time to birth. This suggests that contact with the pregnant partner may play a role in paternal responsiveness, just as the quality of the marital relationship is linked with paternal involvement in later infancy. This suggests that social variables need to be considered in understanding the operation of biological effects. Perhaps intimate ties between partners during pregnancy stimulates hormonal changes, which in turn, are associated with more nurturance toward babies. This perspective recognizes the dynamic or transactional nature of the links between hormones and behavior in which behavior changes can lead to hormonal shifts and vice versa. In contrast to the myth of the biologically unfit father, this work suggests that men may be more prepared even biologically for parenting than previously thought. Finally, it is critical to underscore that these hormonal changes are not necessary for the elicitation of fathering behaviors in either animals or humans (Fleming and Corter, 1995; Corter and Fleming, in Vol. 2 of this *Handbook*). In humans, for example, studies of father–infant relationships in the cases of adoption clearly suggest that hormonal shifts are unnecessary for the development of positive father–infant relationships (Brodzinsky, Lang, and Smith, 1995). Next is a discussion of the social determinants of father involvement.

Individual Factors

Men's own psychological and family background, attitudes toward the fathering role, motivation to become involved, and childcare and childrearing knowledge and skills all play a role in determining men's level of involvement with their children. (See Pleck, 1997 for review of demographic correlates of father involvement.)

Men's relationships with their family of origin. The quality of relationship that fathers develop with their own mothers and fathers has been viewed as a possible determinant of fathers' involvement with their own children (Cabrera, Tamis-Le Monda, Bradley, Hofferth, and Lamb, 2000; Parke, 1996). However, evidence in support of this proposition is complex and by no means clear-cut. Two views have guided this inquiry (Russell, 1986; Snarey, 1993). First, from social learning theory (Bandura, 1989) comes a modeling hypothesis that suggests that men model themselves after their fathers, and this modeling process will be enhanced if their fathers were nurturant and accessible. Second, a compensatory or reworking hypothesis argues that fathers tend to compensate or make up for deficiencies in their childhood relationships with their own fathers by becoming better and more involved when they themselves assume this role. There is support for both views. In support of the modeling hypothesis, a number of studies suggest that positive relationships with fathers in childhood are related to higher levels of later father involvement (Cowan and Cowan, 1987, 1992; Sagi, 1982). Hofferth (1999) found that men whose fathers were active participants in rearing them are more involved with their own offspring, take more responsibility, are warmer, and monitor their children more closely than do men reared by less involved fathers. Moreover, fathers parent more like their own fathers than like their mothers (Losh-Hasselbart, 1987). Support for the second hypothesis is also evident in both early (Biller, 1971; Hetherington and Frankie, 1967) and more recent reports (Baruch and Barnett, 1986; Russell, 1986). Baruch and Barnett (1986) found that men who viewed their own relationships with their fathers as negative tended to be more involved with their 5- and 9-year-old children. As researchers have noted (Belsky, 1991; Snarey, 1993), the predictive power of earlier familial relationships is especially evident in single-earner families in which wives are not employed. In these instances, fathers have more discretion in determining their level of involvement with their children. Sagi (1982, p. 214) argues that these two hypotheses "are not mutually exclusive since either process is possible depending on the circumstances." In a qualitative study, Daly (1993) interviewed fathers of young children about the sources of their role models for their own fatherhood identity. Some fathers emulate their own fathers, others compensate, and still others report little influence of their own fathers as mentors or models (see also Hofferth, 1999). However, most of the fathers interviewed by Daly either did not view their fathers as a model or wanted to do better as fathers than their own fathers did. Many fathers in Daly's study opted for a piecemeal approach to defining fathering. Instead of emulating one person, many men tried to piece together an image of fathering from many different sources.

Men thus draw on models from their own generation of contemporary fathers as well as from fathers of earlier eras and past generations. As men become fathers, they struggle to reconcile past and present images and models of fathering behavior with the changed historical circumstances that face modern fathers. Even if they choose to emulate their own fathers, the rapid changes in our society make it difficult for current fathers to apply these lessons from the past in any simple way. A central aspect of learning to be a father is the construction of a set of images that makes sense in the contemporary era. It is clear that the process of intergenerational transmission of parenting is an active one in which the father himself plays a central role in sorting, retaining, and discarding images and guidelines from a variety of sources. There is no simple or single route to developing a father identity; there are many different paths just as there are many different kinds of fathers (Belsky and Pensky, 1988; Jain et al., 1996).

Socialization of boys into the fathering role.   It is not only the specific nature of the relationship a child develops with his parents but the ways in which girls and boys are differentially prepared for parenthood during childhood that determines the ways in which girls and boys enact their parenting roles in adulthood (Parke and Brott, 1999). It is well known that girls and boys are treated differently by parents during socialization (Bem, 1993; Maccoby, 1998), but most of this work focuses on occupational aspirations, activity and object preferences, and modes of relating to others. However, the differential treatment of girls and boys may help shape a boy's expectation about his future fathering role. A variety of strands of evidence supports this view. First, children's household chores are based on gender, with girls engaging in more household duties such as cleaning, ironing, cooking, and childcare, whereas boys take out the garbage and mow the lawn (Goodnow, 1988, 1999). Of particular importance is the differential opportunities afforded to girls and boys to learn childcare skills. Cross-cultural evidence (Whiting and Whiting, 1975; Whiting, Edwards, Ember, and Erchak, 1988) as well as evidence from our own culture suggests that boys are given dolls less than girls are and are discouraged from playing with dolls (Langlois and Downs, 1980; Pomerleau, Balduc, Malcuit, and Cossotte, 1990; Rheingold and Cook, 1975). In middle childhood, boys are less likely to be baby-sitters (Maccoby, 1998; Goodnow, 1999). This lack of opportunities for socialization into parenthood makes boys less prepared for fatherhood than girls are for motherhood.

Signs of girls' and boys' differing attitudes toward parenthood are evident very early. By the age of 4 or 5 years, girls interact more with babies than boys do. When asked to care for a baby, boys are more inclined to watch the baby passively, whereas girls actively engage in caregiving. In one study, Berman (1987, 1991) observed 3- to 6-year-old children when either a 1-year-old baby or a goldfish was present. Girls spent more time in the area than boys did when the baby was present, but children of both genders appreciated the goldfish equally often. Older boys spent significantly less time in the area than the younger boys did on baby days, which suggests that as boys get older they become gradually less attracted to babies.

This is all part of what Berman (1987) calls the "social scripts" that girls and boys develop long before they are 5 years old. "It is likely that parenting or caregiving scripts are assembled in a gradual but discontinuous manner throughout childhood, and it is reasonable to believe that these early scripts may be precursors of and contributors to scripts generated in adulthood" (Berman 1987, p. 49). Parenting scripts are in turn related to "self-efficacy," the feeling that we can successfully tackle a certain task. As our sense of self-efficacy in a particular activity increases, the more we are likely to continue investing time and effort in that activity (Bandura, 1997). According to Rose and Halverson (1996), differences in childhood opportunities provided to girls and boys contribute to later differences in parental self-efficiency for men and women.

Men's attitudes, motivation, and skills.   Paternal attitudes, motivation, skills and personality are important determinants of father involvement (Jain et al., 1996; Lamb, 1987; Lamb et al., 1987). There has been a considerable body of research concerning the relation between gender-role attitudes and paternal involvement. Gender-role attitudes are usually indexed by scales measuring masculinity, femininity, and androgyny. In spite of the early promise of laboratory studies, which showed a link between men's higher scores on the traditional femininity scale of the Bem Sex Role Inventory and their tendencies to engage in parenting behavior (e.g., interact with a baby), there has been less support for this position in studies of fathers' involvement with their own children. Russell (1983), in his work on shared-caregiving families in Australia, found that these fathers in comparison with fathers in traditional families were higher on femininity. Moreover, compared with those in traditional families, more fathers (and mothers) in the shared-caregiving families were androgynous, fewer mothers were feminine, and fewer fathers were masculine. However, in traditional families, Russell (1983) found no significant link between scores on the Bem Sex Role Inventory and level of father involvement. Kurdek (1998) provided evidence in support of the link between gender-linked attitudes and parental role satisfaction. Fathers' endorsement of instrumental characteristics (assertive, dominant) (a traditional notion of masculinity) in the first year of marriage predicted parenting satisfaction 8 years later, whereas mothers' year 8 parenting satisfaction was predicted by their own year 1 expressiveness (a traditional aspect of femininity). Of interest is the fact that these gender-role self-concepts were the only unique predictors (compared with marital relationships, social support, and child characteristics); even when marital satisfaction was controlled for, these gender-congruent self-concepts were predictive of parenting satisfaction, which suggests that these concepts are uniquely predictive of the child subsystems of the family. Finally, the effects of gender-role concepts on later parenting held across a variety of child variables (age, gender, and frequency of behavior problems). Any strong conclusions are tempered by the fact that others have failed to find links between gender-role attitudes and fathering behavior (De Frain, 1979; Lamb, Frodi, Hwang, Frodi, and Steinberg, 1982). Moreover, the direction of effect is not clear; prior experience may shape gender-role attitudes rather than vice versa.

When the focus is more specifically oriented toward beliefs about parental roles, clearer links between beliefs and behavior are evident. This work has been guided by identity theory, which recognizes that men play a variety of roles as spouse, parent, and worker and that the relative importance men assign to these roles in their formation of a self-identity is a useful predictor of father involvement (Marsiglio, 1995; Rane and McBride, 2000).

Paternal attitudes about parenting relate to measures of father involvement with their 3-month-old infants (Beitel and Parke, 1998). Specifically, fathers' beliefs in the biological basis of gender differences, their perceptions of their caregiving skills, and the extent to which they valued the fathers' role were predictors of fathers' involvement. These attitudinal factors predict when either mothers or fathers were reporters of the level of father involvement. When fathers' reports of their own involvement are used, assessment of their own motivation emerges as a significant predictor as well. Finally, a variety of types of involvement relates to paternal attitudes, including play, caregiving, and indirect care (e.g., packing diaper bag, changing crib linen).

Other studies have found that paternal attitudes are important beyond infancy. Russell (1983) found that Australian men who do not accept the notion of maternal instinct participate in childcare more with their 3- to 6-year-old children. However, Russell found that 51% of mothers and 71% of fathers believed in a "maternal instinct" with regard to childcare. Whereas 60% of the mothers felt that their husbands had the ability to care for children, only 34% of fathers considered themselves capable of taking care of their children. Moreover, most fathers perceived their role as beginning after the baby stage and believed that the father's role is more important later in the child's life, especially during adolescence.

McBride and Rane (1997) found that, consistent with the study by Russell (1983) fathers' attitudes about the importance of father for preschool-age children's development was linked to several indices of father involvement (responsibility, interaction, and accessibility). In addition, their perceived investment in the worker role was inversely related to their workday accessibility and responsibility. Rane and McBride (2000) found that fathers who considered the nurturing role highly central to their sense of self engaged in more interaction and assumed more responsibility behaviors with their children than did fathers who were low on nurturing role centrality. Bonney, Kelley, and Levant (1999) reported similar findings for fathers of preschool-age children; specifically they found that fathers with more liberal gender ideology and who view fathers as critical for child development and as capable of performing childcare as mothers have higher levels of involvement in childcare than do more traditional fathers.

Not only are attitudes important but personality is an important correlate of father involvement as well. Jain et al. (1996) found that in their study of fathers and their male toddlers, progressive fathers (caregivers, playmates and teachers) were less anxious, hostile and irritable than traditional fathers (disengaged or disciplinarian fathers).

In spite of the fact that men are competent caregivers (e.g., Parke and O'Leary, 1976; Parke and Sawin, 1976, 1980), there are wide individual differences among men in either their perceived or their actual level of skill in caregiving. In turn, these variations in skill may be related to the level of father involvement. Some of the most convincing evidence comes from intervention studies that show that skill-oriented training increases the level of father involvement. These studies show that fathers who receive training in caregiving and/or play that presumably increased their skill engage in higher levels of involvement with their infants (Dickie and Gerber, 1980; Palm, 1997; Parke and Beitel, 1986; Parke, Hymel, Power, and Tinsley, 1980; see Fagan and Hawkins, 2000).

Family Factors

Individual factors are not the only determinants of father involvement. Family-level variables including maternal attitudes concerning father involvement and the marital relationship are both family-level factors that require examination.

Maternal attitudes: Mother as gatekeeper.   Consistent with a family systems view, maternal attitudes need to be considered as a determinant of paternal participation in childcare. In spite of advances in women's participation in the workplace, many women still feel ambivalent about father involvement in domestic issues (Coltrane, 1996; Dienhart and Daly, 1997). Because in part of the "cult of maternalism" (Duffy, 1988), which stresses the notion that mothers are indispensable, natural, and necessary, many women are reluctant to actively and wholeheartedly involve fathers in the daily routines of caregiving. As Allen and Hawkins (1999, p. 202) suggest, their ambivalence "may be because increased paternal involvement intrudes on a previously held monopoly over the attentive and intuitive responsibilities of family work which if altered may compromise female power and privilege in the home." These maternal attitudes may lead to behavior that in turn limits father involvement and constitutes a form of gatekeeping. A major advance in conceptualization of gatekeeping was made by Allen and Hawkins (1999, p. 200), who defined the term as follows:

> Maternal gatekeeping is a collection of beliefs and behaviors that ultimately inhibit a collaboration effort between men and women in families by limiting men's opportunities for learning and growing through caring for home and children.

These investigators identified three conceptual dimensions: mothers reluctance to relinquish responsibility over family matters by setting rigid standards, external validation of a mothering identity, and differentiated conceptions of family roles. In a study of dual-earner families, Allen and Hawkins (1999) found that 21% of the mothers were classified as gatekeepers, who in turn did more hours of family work per week and had less equal divisions of labor than women classified as collaborators. Unfortunately, the scales used to measure gatekeeping included both housework and childcare, although Allen and Hawkins (1999, p. 210) noted that "separating housework and child care into unique measures produced similar results." Nor were the number and the ages of the children specified in these analyses. Other studies of gatekeeping have focused specifically on father involvement in child care.

Beitel and Parke (1998) examined the relation between maternal attitudes and father involvement with 3- to 5-month-old infants. A variety of maternal attitudes concerning father involvement with infants related to the level of father involvement in a sample of over 300 first-time parents. Mothers' judgments about their husbands' motivation and interest in participating in childcare activities, maternal perception of their husbands' childcare skills, and the value that the mother place on father involvement all predicted father involvement. Mothers' beliefs in innate gender differences in female and male abilities to nurture infants and the extent to which mothers viewed themselves as critical or judgmental of the quality of their husbands' caregiving were negatively related to father involvement. As these results suggest, maternal attitudes play a significant role in understanding father involvement, but the type of involvement needs to be considered, because different attitudes related to different types of involvement (e.g., play, role responsibility, indirect care). Moreover, maternal attitudes predicted the level of father involvement even after a variety of factors were controlled for, including amount of maternal outside employment, type of feeding (bottle versus breast), father involvement in birth preparation classes, and family history (parents' recollections of their relationships with their own parents). The general pattern was evident whether maternal or paternal reports of father involvement were used.

Nor are the effects restricted to infancy. Using a sample of parents with preschoolers, McBride and Rane (1997) found that maternal perceptions of their partners' investment in the parental as well as the spousal role were related to father involvement whereas their perceptions of their husbands' investment in the worker role was negatively related to fathers involvement. In fact, mothers' perceptions were the best predictors of total father involvement.

Other evidence suggests that fathers' participation may be more self-determined than these earlier studies suggest. Bonney et al. (1999) found that mothers' attitudes about the degree to which fathers should be involved in childcare were unrelated to fathers' participation in childcare. Instead, they found that fathers' participation appears to influence mothers' beliefs about the fathers' role. Longitudinal studies are needed to more definitively determine the direction of causality in this domain; or perhaps, as Bonney et al. (1999) argue, a transactional perspective best characterizes this relation between maternal attitudes and father involvement in which fathers who are more involved have female partners who develop more positive attitudes about their involvement, which, in turn, increases father level of participation.

Two qualifications to our discussion of gatekeeping are needed. First, the term is gender neutral and fathers as well as mothers engage in gatekeeping activities in other domains of family life (Allen and Hawkins, 1999). Second, gates can open as well as close, and the term needs to be broadened to recognize that parents—mother and fathers—can facilitate as well as inhibit the type and level of domestic involvement of each other. Work on "parental gatekeeping" needs to include gate opening as well as gate closing in order to underscore the dual nature of the inhibitory and facilitory processes that are part of the coparenting enterprise.

Marital relationships and father–child relationships. Models that limit examination of the effects of interaction patterns to only the father–child and the mother–child dyads and the direct effects of one individual on another are inadequate for understanding the impact of social interaction patterns in families (Belsky, 1984; Parke, 1988, 1996; Parke et al., 1979). From a family systems viewpoint, the martial relationship needs to be considered as well.

Several studies in both the United States (Dickie and Matheson, 1984; Pedersen, 1975) and other cultures (e.g., Japan; Durrett, Otaki, and Richards, 1984) support the conclusion that the degree of emotional–social support that fathers provide mothers is related to both indices of maternal caregiving competence as well as measures of the quality of infant–parent attachment. Other evidence suggests that the quality of the marital relationship is related to father–infant interaction patterns (Amato and Keith, 1991; Cummings and O'Reilly, 1997). Moreover, the evidence suggests that the father–child relationship is altered more than the mother–child relationship by the quality of the marriage. For example, Belsky, Gilstrap, and Rovine (1984) found that father's overall engagement of the infant was reliably and positively related to overall marital engagement when the infant was 1, 3, and 9 months of age, whereas maternal engagement was related to the marital relationship when the infant was only 1 month of age. In a second study, mother–infant, father–infant, and husband–wife interactions were observed during three separate naturalistic home observations when infants were 1, 3, and 9 months old (Belsky and Volling, 1986). As in the previous study by Belsky et al. (1984), in this second study there was a greater degree of relation between fathering and marital interaction than between mothering and marital interaction (see also Belsky, Youngblade, Rovine, and Volling, 1991).

Other evidence is consistent with the finding that spousal support is a stronger correlate of competence in fathers than in mothers (Dickie and Matheson, 1984). The level of emotional and cognitive support successfully discriminated high- and low-competent fathers but failed to do so in the case of mothers. This suggests that spousal support is more critical for adequate parenting on the part of fathers than on the part of mothers. In a short-term longitudinal study of the antecedents of father involvement, Feldman, Nash, and Aschenbrenner (1983) measured a variety of factors, including the marital relationship during the third trimester of the wives' pregnancies and again at 6 months postpartum. Marital relations predicted father involvement in caregiving, playfulness, and satisfaction with fatherhood. As Feldman et al. (1983, p. 1634) noted, "In our upper to middle class, highly educated sample, the quality of the marital dyad, whether reported by the husband or wife, is the most consistently powerful predictor of paternal involvement and satisfaction." Lamb and Elster (1985) addressed a similar question in a sample of adolescent mothers and their male partners. Using an observational scheme similar to that of Belsky et al. (1984), they observed mother, father, and infant at home in an unstructured context. Father–infant interaction positively related to the level of mother–father engagement. By contrast, mother–infant interaction was unrelated to measures of mother–father engagement.

Other studies (Coley and Chase-Lansdale, 1999; Levy-Shiff and Israelashvili, 1988; Volling and Belsky, 1991) report similar relations between marital satisfaction and father participation in childcare. However, both the identity of the reporter (mother versus father) and the quality versus quantity of father involvement need to be considered (NICHD Early Child Care Research Network, 2000). Fathers' perceptions of marital quality were related to paternal sensitivity (quality), whereas mothers' perceptions of marital quality were related to paternal engagement in caregiving activities (quantity) (NICHD Early Child Care Research Network, 2000).

Recently attention has focused on the impact of marital conflict on parenting, including father behavior and children's outcomes. Two perspectives concerning the link between marital conflict and children's adaptation can be distinguished. According to a direct-effects model, direct exposure to marital conflict influences children's behavior, whereas the indirect model suggests that the impact of marital conflict on children is indirectly mediated by changes in the parent–child relationship (Cummings and O'Reilly, 1997; Fincham, 1998; Grych and Fincham, 2001). Several decades of investigation have amassed considerable evidence that indicates that dimensions of marital functioning are related to aspects of children's long-term overall adjustment and immediate coping responses in the face of interparental conflict (Cummings and O'Reilly, 1997). A range of studies suggests that marital discord and conflict are linked to a variety of child outcomes, including antisocial behavior, internalizing and externalizing behavior problems, and changes in cognition, emotions, and physiology in response to exposure to marital conflict (Erel and Burman, 1995). Although less empirical work has been directed specifically toward examination of the "carryover" of exposure to marital conflict to the quality of children's relationships with significant others such as peers and siblings, a body of literature is beginning to emerge that indicates that exposure to marital discord is associated with poor social competence and problematic peer relationships (Katz and Gottman, 1994; Kerig, 1996).

Marital discord can have an indirect influence on children's adjustment through changes in the quality of parenting (Fauber and Long, 1991). Affective change in the quality of the parent–child relationship, lack of emotional availability, or adoption of less optimal parenting styles has each been implicated as a potential mechanism through which marital discord disrupts parenting processes. Several studies (Katz and Kahen, 1993; Cowan, Cowan, Schulz, and Heming, 1994) have found evidence that marital conflict is linked with poor parenting, which, in turn, is related to poor social adjustment of the children. Other work has focused on the specific processes by which the marital relationship itself directly influences children's immediate functioning and long-term adjustment. Several aspects of parental conflict appear to be relatively consistently associated with poor outcomes for children. More frequent interparental conflict and more intense or violent forms of conflict have been found to be particularly disturbing to children and likely to be associated with externalizing and internalizing difficulties (Cummings and O'Reilly, 1997), and poor peer relationships (Parke, Kim et al., 2001). Conflict that was child related in content was more likely than conflict involving other content to be associated with behavior problems in children (Grych and Fincham, 1993).

Other studies suggest that resolution of conflict reduces children's negative reactions to exposure to interadult anger and conflict. Exposure to unresolved conflict, for example, has been found to be associated with negative affect and poor coping responses in children (Cummings, Ballard, El-Sheikh, and Lake, 1991). In addition, the manner in which conflict is resolved may also influence children's adjustment. Katz and Gottman (1993), for example, found that couples who exhibited a hostile style of resolving conflict had children who tended to be described by teachers as exhibiting antisocial characteristics. When husbands were angry and emotionally distant while resolving marital conflict, their children were described by teachers as anxious and socially withdrawn.

Conflict is inevitable in most parental relationships and is not detrimental to family relationships and children's functioning under all circumstances. In particular, disagreements that are extremely intense and involve threat to the child are likely to be more disturbing to the child. In contrast, when conflict is expressed constructively, is moderate in degree, is expressed in the context of a warm and supportive family environment, and shows evidence of resolution, children may learn valuable lessons regarding how to negotiate conflict and resolve disagreements (Davies and Cummings, 1994).

Together these findings suggest that successful paternal parenting is more dependent on a supportive marital relationship than maternal parenting is. A number of factors may aid in explaining this relation. First, there is prior evidence that the father's level of participation is, in part, determined by the extent to which the mother permits participation (Beitel and Parke, 1998; Allen and Hawkins, 1999). Second, because the paternal role is less well articulated and defined than the maternal role, spousal support may serve to help crystallize the boundaries of appropriate role behavior. Third, men have fewer opportunities to acquire and practice skills that are central to caregiving activities during socialization and therefore may benefit more than mothers from informational (i.e., cognitive) support (Parke, 1996; Parke and Brott, 1999).

Changing Societal Conditions as Determinants of Father–Child Relationships

A number of society-wide changes in the United States have produced a variety of shifts in the nature of early family relationships. Fertility rates and family size have decreased, the percentage of women in the workforce has increased, the timing of onset of parenthood has shifted, divorce rates have risen, and the number of single-parent families has increased (for reviews see Furstenberg and Cherlin, 1991; Hernandez, 1993; Marsiglio, 1998). In this subsection, the effects of two of these changes— timing of parenthood and recent shifts in family employment patterns—are explored to illustrate the impact of social change on father–child and family relationships. Exploration of these shifts will serve to underscore an additional theme, namely the importance of considering the historical period or era in which social change occurs.

Timing of parenthood and the father's role. Patterns of the timing of the onset of parenting are changing, although those changes are not evident from an examination of the median age of parents at the time of the birth of their first child. In the first half of the 1950s the median age of woman at the birth of her first child was her early twenties, and in the 1990s it was approximately the same. This apparent pattern of stability, however, masks the impressive expansion of the range of the timing of first births during recent decades. During this period, women were having babies earlier *and* later than in previous decades. Two particular patterns can be identified. First, there was a dramatic increase in the number of adolescent pregnancies, and, second, there was an increase in the number of women who were postponing childbearing until their thirties. What are the consequences of this divergent pattern of childbearing?

A number of factors need to be considered in order to understand the impact on parenting of childbearing at different ages. First, the *life course context*, which is broadly defined as the point at which the individual has arrived in his or her social, educational, and occupational timetable, is an important determinant. Second, the *historical context*, namely the societal and economic conditions that prevail at the time of the onset of parenting, interacts with the first factor in determining the effects of variations in timing. Let us consider early and delayed childbirth in light of these issues.

The most significant aspect of *early entry into parenthood* is that it is a nonnormative event. Achieving parenthood during adolescence can be viewed as an accelerated role transition, as noted by McCluskey, Killarney, and Papini (1983, p. 49):

> School age parenting may produce heightened stress when it is out of synchrony with a normative life course. Adolescents may be entering parenting at an age when they are not financially, educationally, and emotionally ready to deal with it effectively.

In addition, adolescent childbearers are at higher medical risk because of poorer diets, malnutrition, and less intensive and consistent prenatal care (Hofferth, 1987; Moore and Brooks-Gunn, in Vol. 3 of this *Handbook*). Teenage childbearing is less likely to be planned and is strongly associated with higher levels of completed fertility, closer spacing of births (Brooks-Gunn and Chase-Lansdale, 1995; Furstenberg, Brooks-Gunn, and Chase-Lansdale, 1989) lower educational attainment—especially for females—and diminished income and assets as well as poverty, relative to individuals who delay childbearing (Card and Wise, 1978), and again the effect is particularly severe for women. In turn, this has long-term occupational consequences, with early childbearers overrepresented in blue-collar jobs and underrepresented in the professions. Finally, teenage marriages tend to be highly unstable;

separation or divorce is two to three times as likely among adolescents as among women who are 20 years of age or older (Furstenberg et al., 1989).

In part, this pattern is due to the fact that the fathers also are often adolescents and, as in the case of teenage mothers, are often unprepared financially and emotionally to undertake the responsibilities of parenthood (Lamb and Elster, 1985; Lerman and Ooms, 1993; Marsiglio and Cohan, 1997; Parke and Neville, 1987). As Lerman (1993, p. 47) noted, "young unwed fathers are generally less well educated, had lower academic abilities, started sex at earlier ages and engaged in more crime than did other young men." Low family income and having lived in a welfare household increase the likelihood of entry into young unwed fatherhood. This profile was especially evident for European American unwed fathers. In spite of the fact that African American males are four times as likely to be an unwed father as European American males, African American unwed fatherhood is less likely to be linked with adverse circumstances but is a more mainstream issue. Several factors reduce the likelihood of becoming a teenage father, including church attendance, military service, and higher reading scores. In view of the low rates of marriage and high rates of separation and divorce for adolescents, adolescent fathers, in contrast to "on-schedule" fathers, have less contact with their offspring. However, contact is not absent; in fact, studies of unmarried adolescent fathers indicate a surprising amount of paternal involvement for extended periods following the birth. Data (Lerman, 1993) based on a national representative sample of over 600 young unwed fathers indicated that three fourths of young fathers who lived away from their children at birth never lived in the same household with them. However, many unwed fathers remain in close contact with their children, with nearly half visiting their youngest child at least once a week and nearly one fourth almost daily. Only 13% never visited and 7% visited only yearly. These estimates were based on the fathers' own reports, but other work (Mott, 1994) that relies on maternal reports yield lower contact estimates. Mott found that approximately 40% visited once a week and a third never visited or visited only yearly. Several studies report declines in contact as the child develops (Lerman, 1993; Marsiglio and Cohan, 1997; Rangarajan and Gleason, 1998). According to Lerman's (1993) analysis of the national survey data, 57% visited once a week when the child was 2 years old or under, 40% for ages 2 to $4\frac{1}{2}$ years, 27% for ages $4\frac{1}{2}$ to $7\frac{1}{2}$, and 22% for $7\frac{1}{2}$ and older. Nearly one third of the fathers of the oldest group never visited their offspring.

Coley and Chase-Lansdale (1999) suggested that there is considerable instability in levels of father involvement with their children across time. In a sample of low-income, African American, unwed fathers, nearly 40% either increased or decreased their level of involvement between the child's birth and when the child was 3 years old. A variety of factors contributed to these variations: Paternal employment and education were both linked to higher levels of involvement, as was harmonious mother–father relations (romantic or not).

These declines in father participation appear to continue across childhood and adolescence. Furstenberg and Harris (1993) reported the pattern of contact between adolescent fathers and their offspring from birth through late adolescence. Under half of the children lived at least some time with their biological father at some time during their first 18 years, but only 9% lived with their father during the entire period. Instead, children spent approximately one third of their childhood with their fathers, and this was more likely to occur in early childhood. During the preschool period, nearly half of the children were either living with their father or saw him on a weekly basis. By late adolescence, 14% were living with him, and only 15% were seeing him as often as once a week; 46% had no contact, but 25% saw him occasionally in the preceding year.

Fathers who rarely or never visit are less likely to pay child support (Lerman, 1993), which, in turn, adds to the mothers' financial burden and may indirectly have negative effects on the children. The direction of effects is still being debated; perhaps fathers who can provide financial support are more likely to stay involved as a parent or, alternatively, those who stay involved are more likely to seek employment in order to fulfill their role as provider (Coley and Chase-Lansdale, 1999; Garfinkel et al., 1998). Finally, European American (30%) and Latino (37%) fathers are more likely to have no contact with their offspring than African American fathers (12%).

How have increases in the rate of adolescent childbirth altered the father's role? Or, to pose the question differently, how was being an adolescent father different in a historical period when adolescent childbearing was relatively rare compared with a period in which the rate is significantly higher? First, as rates of adolescent childbearing rise and the event becomes less nonnormative or deviant, the social stigma associated with the event may decrease. In combination with increased recognition that adolescent fathers have a legitimate and potentially beneficial role to play, adolescent fathers' opportunities for participation have probably expanded. Second, the increased availability of social support systems such as daycare may make it easier for adolescent fathers (and mothers) simultaneously to balance educational and occupational demands with parenting demands. Longitudinal studies of the long-term impact of achieving parenthood during adolescence are clearly necessary, as well as more investigation of the impact of adolescent parenthood during different historical periods (see Parke and Neville, 1987).

Finally, there is a variety of deleterious effects of early childbearing for the offspring. First, there is a greater risk of lower IQ (Brooks-Gunn and Furstenberg, 1986; Moore and Brooks-Gunn, in Vol. 3 of this *Handbook*). It also affects academic achievement and retention in grade (Furstenberg et al., 1989). Nor are the effects short lived; they tend to persist throughout the school years (Hoffreth, 1987). Social behavior is affected as well, with several studies showing that children of teenage parents are at greater risk of social impairment (e.g., under control of anger, feelings of inferiority, fearfulness) and mild behavior disorders (e.g., aggressiveness, rebelliousness, impulsivity; Brooks-Gunn and Furstenberg, 1986). In assessing the effects of early childbearing, it is important to remember that the deleterious impact on children is due to both teenage mothers and teenage fathers. Both contribute to these outcomes, and it is oversimplification to attribute the effects to fathers or mothers alone. Early fatherhood clearly has profound consequences for men, their partners, and their offspring. At the same time, we must keep in mind that there is variation among early fathers as well as late fathers. The image of all young fathers as uninvolved and uncaring is an outdated stereotype (Marsiglio and Cohan, 1997).

In contrast to adolescent childbearing, when *childbearing is delayed*, considerable progress in occupational and educational spheres has potentially already taken place. Education is generally completed, and career development is well underway for both males and females. Delayed-timing fathers have described themselves as being in more stable work situations than early-timing fathers, being more experienced workers, and having their jobs and careers more firmly established than early-timing peers (Daniels and Weingarten, 1982). Although they are expected to be more satisfied with their jobs, as job satisfaction has been found to be positively associated with age until midlife (Kalleberg and Loscocco, 1983), and less likely to experience the "life cycle squeeze," during which one's ability to generate income has not yet progressed as fast as the need for income with the introduction of children (Rodman and Safilios-Rothschild, 1983), support for this view is limited. Neville and Parke (1997), in a study of early-timing (under 25 years of age at first birth) and late-timing (over 30 years of age) fathers, found that delayed-timing fathers were more satisfied with their jobs, but the effect was due to socioeconomic status (SES) and salary differences between the groups rather than the timing of birth per se. The financial strains associated with early career status therefore may be more likely to create conflict between the work and family demands of early-timing or normal-timing fathers than those of delayed-timing fathers. Neville and Parke (1997) found some support for this proposition, but qualified it by the gender of the child. Specifically, younger fathers of girls and older fathers of boys reported more interference by work in family life than did older fathers of girls and younger fathers of boys.

What are the effects of late-timing parenthood for the father–child relationship? Are fathers who delay parenthood more or less involved with their offspring? Are their styles of interaction different from those of early-timing or on-time fathers? What are the consequences of late-timing parenthood for father involvement? Retrospective accounts by adults who were the firstborn children of older parents report that having older parents was an important influence in their lives. Many reported having felt especially appreciated by their parents (Yarrow, 1991) and described fathers who were between the ages 30 and 39 years when the respondent was born as more accepting than fathers who were younger or older (Finley, Janovetz, and Rogers, 1990). Parents' retrospective accounts of parenting have also been found to vary with timing. Daniels and Weingarten (1982) found that early-timing fathers are less involved in the daily care of a preschool-age child: Three times as many late-timing fathers, in contrast to their early-timing counterparts, had regular responsibility for some part of the daily care of a preschool-age child. Cooney, Pedersen, Indelicato, and Palkovitz (1993) found in a nationally representative sample that late-timing fathers were more likely to be classified as being highly involved and experiencing positive affect associated with the paternal role than were on-time fathers. Finally, men who delayed parenthood until their late twenties contributed more to indirect aspects of childcare, such as cooking, feeding, cleaning, and doing laundry than men who assumed parenthood earlier (Coltrane and Ishii-Kuntz, 1992).

The timing of the onset of parenthood is a powerful organizer of both maternal and paternal roles. In the future, investigators need to examine not only both maternal and paternal interaction patterns with each other and their children, but within the context of careers as well. More detailed attention to cohort issues is warranted, as indicated by the suggestive findings of Daniels and Weingarten (1982), who found that women who had children in the 1950s and the 1970s were more likely to follow different patterns of balancing work and family life. Late-timing mothers in the 1950s were more likely to follow a sequential pattern in which outside employment and parenthood follow one another. By the 1970s women were more likely to follow a simultaneous pattern in which outside work and parenting coexist in parents' lives. Presumably the decision to delay the onset of parenthood was easier in the 1970s than in earlier decades because of increased acceptance of maternal employment, less rigid role definitions for men and women, and the greater availability of support services such as daycare that permit simultaneous family and career options. It is likely that this shift toward a simultaneous pattern of work and childrearing helps to account for the increased levels of father involvement in late-timing families.

There are qualitative differences in styles of interaction for on-time versus late-timing fathers. In a self-report study, MacDonald and Parke (1986) found that the age of a parent is negatively related to the frequency of physical play. Even after the age of the child is controlled for, the size of the relation is reduced but generally reveals the same pattern. However, this relation appears stronger for some categories of play than for others. Some physical activities, such as bounce, tickle, chase, and piggyback, which tend to require more physical energy on the part of the play partner, show strong negative relations with the age of parent. The negative correlation between the age of a parent and physical play may be ascribable to either the unwillingness or the inability of older parents to engage in high-energy affectively arousing activities, such as physical play, or to the fact that children may elicit less physical activity from older parents. Moreover, Neville and Parke (1987, 1997) found that older parents were likely to engage in more cognitively advanced activities with children and to report holding their children more than younger fathers did. These and other studies (e.g., Zaslow, Pedersen, Suwalsky, Rabinovich, and Cain, 1985) suggest that older fathers may be less tied to stereotypical paternal behavior, adopting styles more similar to those that have been considered traditionally maternal.

Observational studies of father–child interaction confirm these early self-report investigations. Volling and Belsky (1991), who studied fathers interacting with their infants at 3 and 9 months of age, found that older fathers were more responsive, stimulating, and affectionate. In another observational study, Neville and Parke (1997) examined the play patterns of early- and late-timing fathers interacting with their preschool-age children. Early- and delayed-timing fathers' play styles differed; the early-timing fathers relied on physical arousal to engage their children, whereas the delayed-timing fathers relied on more cognitive mechanisms to remain engaged (see also Parke and Neville, 1995).

Timing effects are important not just for fathers but for grandfathers as well. Moreover, not only is age per se important, but the timing of entry into familial roles may be a determinant of interactional style as well. In their study of grandfathers interacting with their 7-month-old grandchildren, Tinsley and Parke (1988) found that grandfathers' ages related to the level of stimulating play. Grandfathers were divided into three categories: younger (36 to 49 years old), middle (50 to 56 old), and older (57 to 68 old). Grandfathers in the middle-aged group were rated significantly higher on competence (e.g., confident, smooth, accepting), affect (e.g., warm, interested, affectionate, attentive), and play style (e.g., playful, responsive, stimulatory). From a lifespan developmental perspective, the middle group of grandfathers could be viewed as being optimally ready for grandparenthood, both physically and psychologically (Parke, 1988; Tinsley and Parke, 1988). Unlike the oldest group of grandfathers, grandfathers in the middle group were less likely to be chronically tired or to have been ill with age-linked diseases; and, unlike the youngest grandfathers, they had completed the career-building portion of their lives and were prepared to devote more of their time to family-related endeavors. Moreover, the ages of the middle group of grandfathers fit the normative age at which grandparenthood is most often achieved; thus, for these men, the role of grandfather was more age appropriate than it was for the youngest and the oldest groups of grandfathers.

Women's and men's employment patterns and the parental roles in the family. The relations between employment patterns of both women and men and their family roles are increasingly being recognized (Deutsch, 1999; Gottfried, Gottfried, Bathurst, and Killian, 1999; Hoffman, 2000). In this subsection, a variety of issues concerning the links between the worlds of work and family is considered to illustrate the impact of recent shifts in work patterns on both men's and women's family roles. The impact of changes in the rate of maternal employment on both quantitative and qualitative aspects of father participation is examined, as well as the influence of variations in family work schedules.

Since the mid-1950s, there has been a dramatic shift in the participation rate of women in the labor force. The rise has been particularly dramatic for married women with children. Between 1950 and 1996, the employment rate for married mothers of children has increased dramatically to over 70%, and among mothers of adolescents it is even higher (80%) (Hoffman, 2000). How have these shifts affected the quantity and the quality of the father's contribution to family tasks such as housework and childcare?

Problems arise in interpreting the main data source—time-use studies—because these studies often fail to control for the family size and the age of children. As Hoffman (1984, p. 439) noted, "Since employed-mother families include fewer children, in general, and fewer preschoolers and infants, in particular, there are fewer childcare tasks to perform." Therefore the differences between families with employed and nonemployed mothers may, in fact, be underestimated. A second problem is that, as noted earlier, the differentiation of tasks performed by fathers is often very crude, and in some studies it is impossible to determine what specific aspects of the father's family work—such as primary childcare, non-care-related child contact, or housework—are affected (Coltrane, 1996, 2000). In spite of these limitations, some trends are clear.

One estimate by Coltrane (1996, pp. 173–174) suggests that "men's average contributions to inside housework have roughly doubled since about 1970, whereas women's contributions have decreased by a third . . . the late 1980's men were doing about 5 hours per week or about 20–25% of the inside chores." These trends are slightly higher in the case of dual-career families. For example, Bailey (1994) and Bonney et al. (1999) found that among European Americans, father participation in childcare was higher when mothers were employed outside the home. Similar findings are evident for African American and Mexican American fathers as well. Fagan (1998) found that as the number of hours that wives work increases, the amount of time African American fathers spend playing, reading, and directly interacting with their preschoolers increases. Evidence (NICHD Early Child Care Research Network, 2000) suggests that the relation between maternal employment and father involvement is, in part, dependent on fathers' childrearing beliefs. When mothers do not work or work only part time, fathers are more likely to participate in caregiving if they hold nontraditional views of parenting; when mothers are employed full time, father participation in caregiving is higher regardless of fathers' beliefs. However, there are exceptions to this overall pattern. Neither Kelley

(1997), in a study of low-income and blue-collar two-parent African American families, nor Hossain and Roopnarine (1994), in a study of middle-SES African American families, found a relation between maternal employment and paternal involvement in childcare. Similarly, Yeung et al. (1999), in their national sample, found no evidence of an increase in fathers' childcare responsibilities on weekdays as a function of the number of hours of maternal employment.

These trends do not negate the fact that the majority of household tasks are still performed by women, including childcare (Pleck, 1997). Moreover, this increase often emerges as a result of wives' reducing the amount of time they devote to housework and childcare rather than as a result of increases in the absolute amount of time men devote to these tasks. In a time-diary study of housework and childcare, Walker and Woods (1976) found that husbands' proportion of all family work (i.e., combining that performed by both husband and wife) rose from 16% (1.6 of 9.7 hr) to 25% (1.6 of 6.4 hr) when wives were employed. Other studies confirm the general finding that fathers' proportional shares increase, in part, because they are contributing more absolute time and because mothers are spending less time on home tasks (Pleck, 1983; 1997; Robinson, 1988; Robinson and Godbey, 1997; Shelton, 1992). These findings are not without significance for children's development because the impact of the mother and the father on children is likely to be different in families in which the father and the mother are more equal in their household participation.

However, there is less evidence for absolute increases in fathers' contributions to family work when wives are employed, especially in father–child contact. Although some investigators report a modest increase in absolute level (O'Connell, 1993; Pleck, 1997), other studies report no absolute increase (Blair et al. 1999; Gottfried et al. 1994) in father contact as a result of maternal employment.

One of the problems in this literature is the failure to recognize the importance of the temporal patterning of both mothers' and fathers' work hours and the degree to which there is overlap in the work schedules of mothers and fathers. As several investigators have found, as the overlap in spouses' work schedules decreases, husbands become more involved in family work (Presser, 1994) including childcare (Brayfield, 1994).

The observed proportional increase in father participation when mothers work outside the home fits well Rappaport's concept for a *psychosocial lag* (Rappaport, Rappaport, and Strelitz, 1977). According to this concept, men's roles in the family change at a slower rate than do shifts in women's roles in paid employment. Part of the explanation for the relatively modest size of the shift in men's family work when women enter the job market, according to Pleck (1983, p. 47) may be that there has been a "value shift in our culture toward greater family involvement by husbands . . . which has effects even on those husbands whose wives are not employed." A similar trend is found in the reduction in time devoted to household tasks by nonemployed women as well as by employed women (Coltrane, 2000; Hoffman, 1984; Robinson, 1988; Robinson and Godbey, 1997).

Unfortunately, a number of problems limit the value of these findings to our understanding of historical trends in fathering. Most of the available data come from cross-sectional comparisons of families in which wives are either employed outside the home or not. Although it is assumed that these concurrent data can be extrapolated backward to provide a picture of how men's participation in family activities has shifted across time as a result of the historically documented increases in women's presence in the work force, longitudinal studies of the same families as well as repeated cross-sectional comparisons across time are necessary to place this issue on a firmer empirical basis.

In current literature, cohort, time of testing, and age of children are often confounded. For example, in the studies that show that the fathers' participation is higher when infants and young children are involved, it is not clear whether this is due only to the age of the children or to the difference in the cohorts whose children are younger at the time of evaluation. Value shifts may elicit greater involvement in the current cohort of new parents that may not have affected more seasoned parents. Moreover, once a pattern of father participation has been established, possibly these families will continue to participate more equally in childrearing. If this analysis is correct, future surveys may indicate that father participation extends into later childhood age periods. Alternatively, fathers who are involved early may feel that they have contributed and do less at later ages. The importance of considering the timing of the mother's employment as a determinant of the degree of father involvement is clear. Age of the child is not the only variable, however; other factors such as employment onset in relation to the family's developmental cycle as well as the reason for employment need to be considered. Both the age of the parents and their point in the occupation cycle will affect paternal involvement and may interact with maternal employment.

Examination of the quantitative shifts in father behavior as a consequence of maternal employment is only one aspect of the problem; it is also necessary to examine the impact of this shift on the quality of the father–child relationship. Some evidence suggests that shifts in the quality of father–infant interaction may occur as a function of maternal employment. In one study, Pedersen, Anderson, and Cain (1980) assessed the impact of dual-wage-earner families on mother and father interaction patterns with their 5-month-old infants. Fathers in single-wage-earner families tended to play with their infants more than mothers did, but in the two-wage-earner families the mothers' rates of social play were higher than the fathers' rates of play. In fact, the fathers in these dual-wage-earner families played at lower rates than even the mothers in the single-wage-earner families. Because the observations took place in the evenings after both parents returned from their jobs, Pedersen at al. (1980, p. 10) suggested that the mother used increased play as a way of reestablishing contact with her infant after being away from home for the day: "It is possible that the working mother's special need to interact with the infant inhibited or crowded out the father in his specialty." However, as studies of reversed-role families suggest, the physical style of fathers play remains evident (Field, 1978). Together with the study by Pedersen et al. (1980), these data suggest that both mothers and fathers may exhibit distinctive play styles, even when family role arrangements modify the quantity of their interaction. However, the father–infant relationship appears to be altered as a result of maternal employment. Specifically, insecure infant–father attachment is higher in dual-career families, although only for sons and not for daughters (Belsky, Rovine, and Fish, 1989). Other evidence suggests that fathers in dual-earner families are less sensitive with their male infants at 4 and 12 months of age. These sons were more likely to have insecure attachments with their fathers (Braungart-Rieker, Courtney, and Garwood, 1999). Grych and Clark (1999) report similar findings, namely that in families in which mothers work full time (defined as 25 hr or more), fathers were more negative in interacting with their infants at 4 months of age, although the relation was not evident when their infants were 12 months of age. In contrast, in homes with a nonemployed mother, father caregiving participation was related to positive affect and behavior during play when their infants were 4 and 12 months of age and at 12 months for fathers whose wives worked part time (fewer than 25 hrs a week). Fathers whose wives do not work outside the home are likely to engage in these activities because they enjoy it, whereas fathers with full-time working wives are pressed into service and experience more tension in balancing work and home duties (Grych and Clark, 1999). Finally, McHale, Crouter, and Bartko (1991), in a sample of fourth- and fifth-grade children, found that both work status of spouses and role arrangements in families (traditional vs. egalitarian) may, in fact, be independent. To understand the effects of father participation on children, it is important to understand both the work status of parents and family type (traditional vs. egalitarian). McHale et al. (1991) found that an inequitable division of parents' work and family roles relate to poorer socioemotional adjustment of children. Children from traditional dual-earner families were more anxious and depressed and rated themselves lower in terms of both peer social acceptance and school competence than did children from families characterized by an equitable division in parents' work and family role (e.g., traditional single-earner and egalitarian dual-earner families).

Father's work quantity and quality and father involvement. Instead of examining whether or not one or both parents are employed, researchers have begun to address the issue of the impact of the quantity, quality, and nature of work on fathering behavior (Perry-Jenkins, Repetti, and Crouter, 2000). In terms of quantity, several studies found that fathers who are employed for more hours were less involved in caregiving than fathers who worked fewer hours (Coltrane, 1996; NICHD Early Child Care Network, 2000). Yeung et al. (2001, p. 148) made the following estimate: "for every hour a father is at work, there is an associated one-minute decrease in time a child spent with him on weekdays (mostly in play companionship activities)."

In terms of the quality issue, Crouter (1994) noted that there are two types of linkage between father work and fathering. One type of research focuses on work as an "emotional climate" (Kanter, 1977) that, in turn, may have carryover effects to the enactment of roles in home settings. The focus is generally on short-term or transitory effects. A second type of linkage focuses on the types of skill, attitude, and perspective that adults acquire in their work-based socialization as adults and on how these variations in job experience alter their behavior in family contexts. In contrast to the short-term perspective of the spillover of emotional climate research, this type of endeavor involves more enduring and long-lasting effects of work on family life.

Work in the first tradition has been conducted by Repetti (1989, 1994), who studied the impact of working in a high-stress job (air traffic controller) on subsequent family interaction patterns. She found that the male air traffic controllers were more withdrawn in marital interactions after high-stress shifts and tended to be behaviorally and emotionally withdrawn during interactions with their children as well. Although high workload is associated with withdrawal, negative social experiences in the workplace have a different effect. In addition, distressing social experiences at work were associated with higher expressions of anger and greater use of discipline during interaction with a child later in the day. Repetti views this as a "spillover effect" in which there is a transfer of negative feelings across settings. Similarly Crouter, Bumpus, Maguire, and McHale (1999) found that mothers and fathers who felt more pressure on the job reported greater role overload, which, in turn was linked to heightened parent–adolescent conflict (see Perry-Jenkins et al., 2000, for a review).

Other research suggests that positive work experiences can enhance the quality of fathering. Grossman, Pollack, and Golding (1988) found that high job satisfaction was associated with higher levels of support for fathers' 5-year-old children's autonomy and affiliation in spite of the fact that positive feelings about work were negatively related to the quantity of time spent interacting with their children. This finding underscores the importance of distinguishing quantity and quality of involvement. One caveat: In contrast to the Repetti studies, the study by Grossman et al. focused on general job satisfaction and demandingness rather than on daily fluctuations in the level of positivity or negativity experienced in the work setting. Future studies need to assess these two aspects of job-related affect and involvement separately.

Work patterns have long-term links with fathering as well. Fathers on air traffic controller teams with a poor social climate had less positive and more negative emotional tone in their interactions with their children (Repetti, 1994). This line of research underscores the importance of distinguishing among different types of work-related stress on subsequent father–child interactions and of considering the direct short-term carryover effects versus long-term effects of work on fathering. In fact, relatively little attention has been paid to the types of local events that account for daily fluctuations in fathering behavior.

Research in the second tradition of family–work linkage, namely the effects of the nature of men's occupational roles on their fathering behavior, dates back to Kohn and Schooler (1983) and Miller and Swanson (1958). Men who experience a high degree of occupational autonomy value independence in their children, consider children's intentions when considering discipline, and use reasoning and withdrawal of rewards instead of physical punishment. In contrast, men who are in highly supervised jobs with little autonomy value conformity and obedience, focus on consequences rather than on intentions, and use more physical forms of discipline. In short, they repeat their job-based experiences in their parenting roles (see Parcel and Menaghan, 1994, for a review of the impact of mother's work characteristics on parenting).

Greenberger and O'Neil (1991) extended the original work oh Kohn and Schooler (1983) by focusing on the implications of job characteristics not only for the parenting behavior of both mothers and fathers but, in turn, the effects of these variations in parenting for children's development. Fathers with more complex jobs (i.e., those characterized by mentoring others versus taking instruction or serving others) spend more time alone with sons and more time developing their sons' skills (e.g., academic, athletic, mechanical, interpersonal), but this is not the case for daughters. In fact, they spend more time in work and work-related activities if they have daughters. In addition, these fathers tend to behave more warmly and responsively to sons and use less harsh and less lax control of sons, but report more firm but flexible control with daughters. Fathers who have jobs characterized by a high level of challenge (e.g., expected to solve problems, high level of decision making) devote more time to developing sons' skills, give higher-quality explanations to their sons, and use less harsh and more firm but flexible control in their interactions with their boys. Finally, fathers with time-urgent jobs (work fast most of the day; have difficulty in taking a break) spend more time on work activities, less time interacting, and use less lax control if they have daughters. To summarize, when fathers have complex, stimulating, and challenging jobs, their boys seem to benefit much more than their girls do. According to these researchers, different processes may account for the work–home linkages because of stimulating or challenging jobs and complexity of occupation. Greenberger and O'Neil (1991, p. 13) argued that "spillover of positive mood" may account for the relationships between stimulating–challenging jobs and good fathering, whereas, "complexity of work with people may increase fathers' intellectual and emotional flexibility in dealing with their sons." Similarly Grimm-Thomas and Perry-Jenkins (1994) found that fathers with greater complexity and autonomy at work reported higher self esteem and less authoritarian parenting. Similarly, in a sample of European-American, rural, dual-earner couples, Whitbeck et al. (1997) found that fathers with more job autonomy had more flexible parenting styles that were linked to a sense of mastery and control in their adolescents. Interestingly, some evidence suggests that the effect of these job characteristics may be more evident for fathers than for mothers. Although some studies find that job characteristics are associated with maternal parenting (Parcel and Menaghan, 1994), others (Greenberger and O'Neil, 1991; Whitbeck et al., 1997) find that mothers' job qualities are less predictive of their parenting than are fathers' job attributes. Perhaps mothers show fewer links because of the more heavily culturally or evolutionarily scripted nature of maternal roles (Parke, 1996).

CONSEQUENCES OF FATHER–CHILD RELATIONSHIPS

Variations in father involvement have implications for men themselves and for their families, as well as for their children.

Consequences of Fatherhood for Men Themselves

Becoming a father has an impact on a man's own psychological development and well-being. As Parke (1981, p. 9) noted, "the father–child relationship is a two-way process and children influence their fathers just as fathers alter their children's development." Three aspects of this issue have been examined: (1) marital relationships, (2) work and occupational issues, and (3) "societal generativity" (to borrow Snarey's, 1993, phrase).

Impact on marital relationships.   Perhaps most attention has been devoted to the impact of the transition to parenthood on marriage. The general finding from a large number of studies is that there is a decline in marital satisfaction, especially on the part of men, as a consequence of the birth of a child (see Belsky and Pensky, 1988, for a review). The psychological adjustments associated with the transition to fatherhood are clearly evident in the longitudinal study by Cowan and Cowan (1985, 1992). Their project followed families from pregnancy until the children were 5 years of age. These investigators found that father's marital satisfaction showed a modest decrease from pregnancy to 6 months postpartum, but a sharp decline between 6 and 18 months postpartum. In contrast, mothers showed a much more linear decline, beginning in the postpartum period and continuing across the first 2 years. In this same period of 18 months, 12.5% of the couples separated or divorced; by the time the child was 5 years of age, this figure was up to 20%.

In spite of the dip in marital satisfaction, two caveats should be noted. First, even though marital satisfaction decreases for men (and women) after the onset of parenthood, marital stability (i.e., the likelihood of staying in the marriage) increases relative to childless couples, for whom the national average is 50% (Cowan and Cowan, 1992). As the Cowans (1992, p. 110) noted, "the marital stability of couples who have preschool children is protected. Although new parents may be experiencing increased tension or dissatisfaction as couples, their joint involvement with managing the baby's and the family's needs may lead them to put off, or possibly work harder on, the problems in their marriage—at least while the children are young."

Not all of the couples showed a decline in marital satisfaction: 18% of the couples showed increased satisfaction with their marital relationship. This figure rose to 38% for couples who participated in a supportive intervention program during the transition to parenthood (Cowan and Cowan, 1992; C. Cowan, 1988). Similar diversity in the pattern of change in father's marital satisfaction is evident in Belsky's longitudinal study (Belsky et al., 1984, 1989). During the transition to parenthood, marital quality declined in approximately 30% of the families, improved in another 30%, and in nearly 40% of the families showed no change.

A variety of reasons has been suggested for this decline in men's marital satisfaction, including (1) physical strain of childcare, (2) increased financial responsibilities, (3) emotional demands of new familial responsibilities, (4) the restrictions of parenthood, and (5) the redefinition of roles and role arrangements (Belsky and Isabella, 1985; Cowan and Cowan, 1992; Snarey, 1993). However, as Cowan and Cowan (1992) found, there is little support for the hypothesis that, as the number of negative changes increase, marital satisfaction declines. In their study, they found little relation between declining marital satisfaction and any single negative change. Perhaps a cumulative negative events model (Rutter, 1987) holds, in which an increase in the number—regardless of quality—of negative shifts is associated with shifts in marital satisfaction. However, several lines of evidence suggest that discrepancies in expectations on the part of mothers and fathers concerning the relative roles that each will play may be an important determinant of postpartum marital satisfaction. Cowan and Cowan (1987, 1992) found that when there was a larger discrepancy between the wives' expectations of their husbands' involvement in infantcare and his level of actual participation, there was a greater decline in wives' marital satisfaction between late pregnancy and 18 months postpartum. Belsky, Ward, and Levine (1986) found a similar decrease in marital satisfaction when mothers' expectations about father involvement were not met. Men showed a similar effect of a discrepancy between attitudes and behavior. McDermid, Huston, and McHale (1990) found greater negative impact of the onset of parenthood when there was a discrepancy between spouses' gender-role attitudes and the division of household and childcare labor, and McBride (1989) found that traditional fathers who held conservative gender-role attitudes, but were nonetheless involved in childcare, reported higher levels of dissatisfaction. Finally, Hock (1987) found similar results for mothers who wanted to work outside the home, but did not; they were more depressed than mothers whose attitudes and roles were congruent. On the positive side, when expectations and behaviors match, some evidence suggests that marital satisfaction is correspondingly high. Osofsky and Culp (1989) reported that in a 3-year longitudinal study of transitions to fatherhood, when fathers were satisfied with the division of family tasks and decisions, marital and sexual adjustments were satisfactory. In summary, research suggests that discrepancies in parental expectations about roles, rather than the level of change per se, may be a key correlate of men's marital satisfaction after the onset of fatherhood. It is important to underscore that marital relationships are both determinants as well as consequences of paternal involvement, as previously noted (Pleck, 1997).

One of the limitations of much of the literature is the focus on infancy. Less is known about the impact of being a father on marital satisfaction after the child's infancy. An exception is the longitudinal study by Heath (1976) and Heath and Heath (1991) that followed a cohort of college men born in the 1930s into their thirties and midforties. Competent fathers were in satisfying marriages. However, these two indices also related to psychological maturity, leaving open the possibility that fathering activities lead to marital satisfaction and maturity or that maturity is the common correlate of being both a competent father and husband. Because of limitations in sample size, reliance on qualitative indices, and the lack of adequate statistical analyses, these results remain suggestive rather than definitive. However, Snarey (1993) found support for the relation between paternal involvement in childhood or adolescence and marital satisfaction. In a follow-up longitudinal study of men originally studied in the 1940s and1950s by Glueck and Glueck (1950), Snarey (1993, p. 111) assessed the marital success of these men at midlife (age 47): "Fathers who provided high levels of social–emotional support for their offspring during the childhood decade (0–10 years) and high levels of intellectual, academic and social emotional support during the adolescent decade (11–21 years) were themselves as men at mid-life, more likely to be happily married."

In sum, it is clear that there are hints of long-term positive effects of father involvement on marriage, but these data must be interpreted cautiously for several reasons. First, it is clear that there are negative effects of increased father involvement, as noted earlier in the discussion of maternal gatekeeping. Some women may view increased father involvement as intrusive and unwelcome. Second, much of the literature is based on cohorts studied several decades ago. In light of the changing work and family lives of both men and women in the new millennium, conclusions based on earlier periods may not be readily applicable (Pleck, 1997).

Impact on occupational success.   There are two perspectives on this issue. First, a short-term perspective suggests that as fathers increase their involvement they perceive higher levels of work–family conflict (Baruch and Barnett, 1986). This work–family stress is more likely to be reported by fathers in dual-earner rather than in single-earner families (Volling and Belsky, 1991). Many fathers wish they had more time for family and more flexible job arrangements (Parke and Brott, 1999), and although there are clear trends toward more family-friendly policies, the workplace barriers remain formidable (Levine and Pittinsky, 1998; Parke and Brott, 1999). A long-term perspective, on the other hand, suggests that father involvement is positively linked with occupational mobility, but the evidence is rather meager and limited by reliance on studies from earlier (and perhaps inapplicable) historical eras. For example, occupational mobility is also affected by father involvement. In his longitudinal study, Snarey (1993) found that the father's childrearing involvement across the first two decades of the child's life moderately predicted the father's occupational mobility (at the age of 47 years) above and beyond other background variables (e.g., parent's occupation, his IQ, current maternal employment).

Fatherhood and men's self-identity.   Men's sense of themselves shifts as a function of the transition to fatherhood. A variety of dimensions has been explored in prior research, including fathers' role definitions, their self-esteem, and their sense of generativity. Roles change for both men and women after the onset of parenthood. Cowan and Cowan (1987, 1992) assessed role shifts during the transition to fatherhood and found that men who become fathers decreased the "partner/lover" aspect of their self and increased the "parent" percentage of their self-definition. In contrast, men who remained childless significantly increased the "partner/lover" aspect of their relationship over the 21-month assessment period. Self-esteem, however, was not affected by the transition to parenthood for either fathers (or mothers) in the Cowan's project. Grossman (1987), who studied men's transition to parenthood, found that first-time fathers who were both more affiliative (i.e., importantly connected to others, enjoyed empathetic relationships) and more autonomous, viewing themselves as separate and distinct from others, had significantly higher life adaptation scores. Fathers of firstborns who were more affiliative at 1 year of age also reported being higher in emotional well-being. As Grossman (1987, p. 10) indicates, these findings suggest that "separateness and individuation are not sufficient for men's well being; they need connections as well." Does fatherhood have a longer-term impact on men's psychological development? Heath (1977), in a longitudinal study of college men, found that fatherhood related to men's ability to understand themselves, to understand others sympathetically, and to integrate their own feelings.

Finally, does fatherhood affect *generativity*, a concept derived from Erikson's (1975) theoretical writings? Snarey (1993, pp. 18–19) provided a succinct summary:

> The psychosocial task of middle adulthood, Stage 7 [in Erikson's stage theory] is the attainment of a favorable balance of generativity over stagnation and self-absorption.... Most broadly, Erikson (1975) considers generativity to mean any caring activity that contributes to the spirit of future generations, such as the generation of new or more mature persons, products, ideas, or works of art.... Generativity's psychosocial challenge to adults is to create, care for, and promote the development of others from nurturing the growth of another person to shepherding the development of a broader community.

Other theorists have distinguished among different types of generativity (Hawkins and Dollahite, 1997; Kotre, 1984; Kotre and Hall, 1990). Snarey (1993) described three types that apply to fathers: (1) biological generativity (indicated by the birth of a child), (2) parental generativity (indicated by childrearing activities), and (3) societal generativity (indicated by caring for other younger adults: serving as a mentor, providing leadership, and contributing to generational continuity). Although serious questions have been raised about the utility of Erikson's stage notions, especially the inevitability of the ordering of the "stages" and their universal applicability (P. Cowan, 1988), the concept of generativity is nonetheless a useful marker for assessing the long-term relation between fathering behavior and other aspects of mature men's lives. Recently, Hawkins and Dollahite (1997) cast generative fathering as a theoretical corrective to earlier views of fathers as inadequate and deficient.

A series of studies has examined the relations between fatherhood, especially paternal competence, and involvement and social generativity. Heath and Heath (1991) noted a link between fatherhood satisfaction and community participation; fathers who were higher in reported parenting satisfaction were more likely to be active participants in community organizations or professions in the prior decade. Similarly, Valliant (1977) found a positive relation between societal generativity and social adjustment and paternal competence. Men who held positions of responsibility for other adults and who were well adjusted socially were rated higher in terms of their psychological closeness to their children. Is men's societal generativity at midlife related to the level of care and support they provide their children? Snarey (1993, p. 98) rated father's social generativity on a 3-point scale and tapped whether "he demonstrated a clear capacity for establishing, guiding and caring for the next generation through sustained responsibility for the growth, well-being or leadership of younger adults or the larger society . . . beyond the sphere of the nuclear family." Snarey found that men who nurtured their children's social–emotional development during childhood (0 to10 years) and who also contributed to both social–emotional and intellectual–academic development during the second decade (11 to 21 years) were at midlife more likely to become generative in areas outside their family. Again this contribution of fathering participation to societal generativity was evident after a variety of background variables was controlled for. Snarey offered several interpretations of these findings. First, a disequilibrium explanation suggests that parental childrearing responsibility results in demands that are difficult to meet and that, in turn, promote (Snarey, 1993, pp. 117–118) "increased complexity in the fathers' cognitive emotional and behavioral repertoire.... This commitment beyond the self, in turn, prepares the way for societal generativity which involves a commitment beyond the family." Second, perhaps a nurturing predisposition may underlie both parenting and societal generativity and account for the continuity across time. Third, the arrival of children often leads to increases in men's participation in neighborhood and community organizations on behalf of children, which, in turn, may continue into their midlife years. In summary, although the processes are not yet well understood, it is clear that involved fathering relates in positive ways to other aspects of men's lives. As Snarey (1993, p. 119) noted, "men who are parentally generative during early adulthood usually turn out to be good spouses, workers and citizens at mid life."

Other work (Palkovitz and Palm, 1998) inspired by this generative perspective suggests that engagement in fatherhood roles may present a sensitive period for men in the development of religious faith and in religious practice. Although further empirical work is necessary to adequately evaluate the utility of this emerging perspective, it represents a promising new direction for fatherhood research.

Implications of Father Involvement for Children's Development

Three types of approaches to the issue of the impact of father involvement on children's social, emotional, and cognitive development can be distinguished. First, in a modern variant of the earlier father-absence theme, sociologists, in particular, have recently examined the impact of nonresident fathers' frequency and quality of contact on children's development. In contrast to this paternal deprivation approach, a second strategy examines the impact of paternal enhancement. This approach asks about the lessons learned from focusing on unusually highly involved fathers, such as occurs in role-sharing and reversed-role families. The third or normative approach focuses on the consequences of the quality and the quantity of father–child interaction on children's development in intact families.

Contact between nonresident fathers and their children. Research in the sociological tradition has focused on large national samples of fathers and children, such as the National Longitudinal Study of Youth, the National Survey of Children, and the National Survey of Families and Households. These surveys reveal a high level of disengagement on the part of nonresident fathers but also, at the same time sufficient variability to permit an examination of the issue of the impact of contact on children's development. A meta-analysis of 63 studies of the associations between nonresident fathers and children's well-being was reported by Amato and Gilbreth (1999). Although they found weak associations between contact and academic success and internalizing problems, there was no link between contact and externalizing problems. In general, frequency of contact with nonresident fathers was not linked to child outcomes. This conclusion is consistent with earlier scholarly evaluations of the evidence (McLanahan and Sandefur, 1994; Seltzer, 1994).

However, quality, not contact or no contact alone, is important in assessing the impact of nonresident fathers. In a follow-up study of 18- to 21-year-old children of African American adolescent mothers, Furstenberg and Harris (1993) found little impact of contact alone on young adults' outcomes but clear beneficial effects if the *quality* of the relationship were taken into account. Those who reported a strong bond or attachment with their father during adolescence had higher educational attainment, were less likely to be imprisoned, and were less depressed. These effects were especially evident in the case of children living with the father and were only marginally evident for children of nonresident biological fathers. The data suggest that both presence and quality matters; but quality is especially important because fathers' presence is unrelated to outcomes when quality (degree of attachment to father) is controlled. The meta-analysis by Amato and Gilbreth (1999) confirms these earlier findings; a measure of the affective relationship between the father and child (feeling close) was positively associated with academic success and negatively with internalizing and externalizing problems. The effect sizes were modest in magnitude. Second, fathers' authoritative parenting was associated with higher academic success and fewer internalizing and externalizing problems for their children. Authoritative parenting was a better predictor than either frequency of contact or the "feeling close" measure. In addition to quality of involvement, one other variable, namely the amount of fathers' payments of child support, was a significant predictor of children's outcomes, including academic success and children's externalizing behavior although not internalizing behavior. This finding is not surprising, because, as Amato and Gilbreth (1999, p. 559) point out, "fathers financial contributions provide wholesome food, adequate shelter in safe neighborhoods, commodities (such as books, computers, and private lessons) that facilitate children's academic success and support for college attendance." Finally, this effect was evident for both boys and girls and African Americans and European American families. This work reflects earlier and recurring themes in the parent–child literature, namely that quality is the critical factor in determining children's development (Clarke-Stewart, 1988; Wachs, 2000).

Impact of normal variations in intact families on children's development. A voluminous literature has emerged over the past three decades that clearly demonstrates relations between quality of paternal involvement and children's social, emotional, and cognitive development (Biller, 1993;

Parke, 1979, 1996; Cabrera et al., 2000; Pleck, 1997). At the same time, considerable evidence shows a good deal of redundancy between fathers' and mothers' impacts on children. There is less evidence that fathers make a unique contribution to children's development.

In a review of the effects of fathers on children, Marsiglio, Amato, Day, and Lamb (2000) examined 72 studies published in the 1990s, with the majority involving young children or adolescents and the remaining concerning young adults. Their review revealed moderate negative associations between authoritative fathering and internalizing and externalizing problems (Baumrind, 1991). The relation held for children and adolescents regardless of age. Moreover, Amato and Rivera (1999) found that the positive influence on children's behavior was similar for European American, African American, and Latino fathers. Marsiglio et al. (2000, p. 1183) offer three important caveats to their conclusion that "positive father involvement is generally beneficial to children." First, most studies rely on a single data source, which raises the problem of shared method variance. Second, as others have noted as well (Parke, 1995, 1996; Amato and Rivera, 1999), many researchers do not control for the quality of the mother–child relationship when examining father effects. Because the behavior and the attitudes of parents are often highly related, this step is critical. Only 8 of the 72 studies reviewed by Marsiglio et al. (2000) did, in fact, control for the quality of the mother–child relationship; 5 of the 8 studies continued to show a father effect after taking into account mother–child effects. For example, Isley, O'Neil, and Parke (1996) found that fathers' levels of affect and control predicted children's social adaptation with peers both concurrently and 1 year later after maternal effects were controlled for (see also Hart, Nelson, Robinson, Olsen, and McNeilly-Choque, 1998; Mosley and Thompson, 1995). Although there is overlap between the effects of mothers and fathers on their children's academic, emotional, and social development, evidence is emerging that fathers make a unique contribution to their children's development (Parke, 1996; Rohner, 1998).

A third caveat concerns problems of inferring direction of causality because studies are correlational and involve concurrent rather than longitudinal assessments (Marsiglio et al., 2000). However, two strands of evidence suggest that the direction of effects can plausibly flow from paternal behavior to child outcomes. First, longitudinal studies support the view that fathers influence their children (for reviews, see Amato and Rivera, 1999; Parke, 1996; Pleck, 1997). For example, Gottman, Katz, and Hooven (1997) found that fathers' acceptance of and assistance with the emotions (sadness, anger) of their children at 5 years of age were related to higher levels of social acceptance with peers at the age of 8. Nor are the effects of fathering on developmental outcomes restricted to childhood. In a follow-up of the classic childrearing study of Sears, Maccoby, and Levin (1957), Koestner, Franz, and Weinberger (1990) reassessed a sample of the original children when they were 31 years old. The most powerful predictor of empathy in adulthood for both men and women was paternal child-rearing involvement when they were 5 years of age. This paternal factor was a better predictor than several maternal variables. In a further study (Franz, McClelland, and Weinberger, 1991), at the age of 41 years, men and women with better social relationships (marriage quality, extrafamilial ties) in midlife had experienced more paternal warmth as children. Although these studies support a father-effects perspective, it is likely that reciprocal relationships will become evident, in which children and fathers mutually influence each other across the life course (Cabrera et al., 2000; Marsiglio et al., 2000; Parke, 1996). (For a review of the father's role in the development of childhood psychopathology, see Phares, 1996.)

The other strand of evidence that supports the plausibility of a father to child direction-of-effects model comes from intervention, studies, and reports of reverse-role families. In recent years, a small minority of families have explicitly explored alternative family arrangements such as role sharing and reversing family roles. In spite of their rarity, these alternative family arrangements can inform us about the possible ways in which families can reorganize themselves to provide flexibility for mothers, fathers, and children (see Radin, 1993, for a recent review) and to assess the impact of increased father involvement on children's development. Russell (1983, 1986) examined Australian families in which fathers took major or equal responsibility for childcare. There are distinct consequences for mothers, fathers, and children from parents' role sharing. Most commonly, mothers experience difficulties associated with the physical and time demands of a dual role; in Russell's (1983) sample, 60% of the mothers reported this strain. On the positive side, mothers reported increased stimulation as a result of outside employment, greater independence, and increased self-esteem. Fathers have mixed reactions as well, with 48% reporting difficulties associated with the demands—the constancy and boredom—associated with their full-time caregiving role. On the positive side, 70% of fathers reported that their relationship with their children improved. Other advantages include greater understanding of children, greater awareness of mother–housewife roles, and freedom from career pressures. Although approximately one third of role-sharing parents felt that children improved their relationships with both parents, over one fourth of both parents viewed the mother–child relationship as less strong. In a 2-year follow-up (Russell, 1986), approximately a third of the original families were reinterviewed. Nearly two thirds of both parents continued to view improved father–child relationships as the major advantage of this sharing arrangement. There was an increase in tension and conflict in the father–child relationship as well—a not surprising finding in light of the father's increased caregiver role.

An Israeli study of primary caregiver fathers and their 3- to 6-year-old children (Sagi, 1982; Sagi, Koren, and Weinberg, 1987) found that this arrangement had clear benefits for the children. Over half of the fathers were either equally or more involved in childcare than the mothers were. In addition to the finding that children of fathers with intermediate and high involvement exhibited more internal locus of control than children of fathers with low involvement, it was also found that the intermediate- and high-involvement fathers had higher expectations for independence and achievement and offered more encouragement than low-involvement fathers. Empathy varied positively with involvement as well, with the children of the high-involvement fathers showing the highest empathy scores. Finally, there was evidence of more androgynous gender-role orientation on the part of girls— probably as a result of being reared by more nurturant, involved fathers who were not gender stereotyped themselves and who did not respond to girls in a gender stereotyped fashion (Radin and Sagi, 1982).

Confirmatory evidence of the impact of high levels of father participation on children's development comes from a US study. Radin (1982, 1988) studied 3- to 6-year-old children from families in which fathers were the primary caregivers. Children in these families showed higher levels of internality—a belief in their own ability to control events—than children in traditional families. In addition, children in the role-sharing families scored higher on verbal ability, and their fathers set higher educational standards and career expectations for their children than fathers in traditional families. However, gender-role orientations of the children were not different across the father and the mother primary caregiver families. An 11-year follow-up, when the children were adolescents, assessed the long-term consequences for children as a result of childrearing patterns assessed when the children were preschoolers and when they were 7 to 9 years old. Williams, Radin, and Allegro (1992) found that a greater amount of paternal involvement during the teen's preschool years was predictive of adolescent support for a nontraditional employment arrangement. This included greater approval of both spouses working full time and sharing childcare and less approval of the husbands working full time with his spouse not working and caring for the children on a full time basis. Second, children who experienced high paternal involvement at 7 to 9 years of age were supportive of more nontraditional childrearing arrangements (i.e., high father involvement or shared childcare). In summary, Radin (1993, p. 34) states that "norm-violating parental socialization practices do appear to have an impact on children's gender-related attitudes although it may take a decade to become evident." (Radia, 1993, p. 34). In a related report, Williams and Radin (1992) found no long-term impact of father involvement in childrearing on academic grades or expectations for higher education. Perhaps the models of involved fathers as nonachievement oriented may have diluted their impact on their children's achievement aspirations. In summary, gender roles especially seem to be altered by increased father caregiving participation, but the effects may depend on time of measurement in relation to the child's development.

However, caution is necessary because parents who reverse roles are still rare, and evidence suggesting that children from these families fare better is not conclusive. Such parents may be different in other ways from parents who maintain traditional roles and might have influenced their children differently than traditional parents, no matter which parent stayed home. Moreover, the effect of shared caregiving is usually confounded with the effects of related family characteristics such as maternal employment outside the home. However, it is likely that parents who reverse roles are significantly affected by their choice and that, therefore, the nontraditional environment is at least partially responsible for differences between children from traditional and nontraditional families. As new family role arrangements become more common and more intensively studied, the effects of role reversal and other innovations will be better understood. However, until there is some change in our traditional view about the roles that men and women can or should play in rearing children, few families will either try alternative patterns or persist in them for extended periods (Parke and Brott, 1999).

Finally, a variety of intervention studies aimed at increasing father involvement with their children provide some further evidence that the direction of effects flows in part from father to child (see Fagan and Hawkins, 2000, for a review). For example, studies of fathers and infants have found that fathers who receive parenting training not only increase their involvement (Parke and Beitel, 1986; Parke et al., 1980) but their infants show increased social responsiveness and more play initiations (Dickie and Gerber, 1980; Zelazo, Kotelchuck, Barber, and David, 1977). Studies of fathers with older children, too, show positive changes in father involvement, which in turn improves the father–child relationship (Levant, 1988). Unfortunately, relatively few of these studies systematically assess children's developmental outcomes as well. An exception is a recent study by Cowan and Cowan (2002) who used a randomized design and found that parents (mothers and fathers) who participated in a 16-week series of discussions groups on effective parenting just before to their children's entry into elementary school had children with better school adjustment and higher academic achievement than did parents in a nonparenting oriented discussion group condition. Moreover, the effects of the intervention were evident 6 years later. Although this study involved both mother and fathers as the unit of intervention, these data suggest that experimental modification of fathering behaviors can be an effective way of more clearly establishing the direction of causality in fathering research.

Beyond description: Processes that link fathering and child outcomes. Recent work that has focused on fathers' special style of interacting, namely play, has begun to reveal the processes through which fathers influence children's development (for reviews, see Parke, 1996; Parke and O'Neil, 2000). Parke and his colleagues, for example, examined the relation between father–toddler play and children's adaptation to peers. In one study (MacDonald and Parke, 1984), fathers and their 3- and 4-year-old girls and boys were observed in 20 minutes of structured play in their homes. Teachers ranked these sample children in terms of their popularity among their preschool classmates. For both girls and boys, fathers who were rated as exhibiting high levels of physical play with their children and elicited high levels of positive affect in their children during the play sessions had children who received the highest peer popularity ratings. For boys, however, this pattern was qualified by the fathers' level of directiveness. Boys whose fathers were both highly physical and low in directiveness received the highest popularity ratings, and the boys whose fathers were highly directive received lower popularity scores. Possibly children who interact with a physically playful father and at the same time have an opportunity to regulate the pace and the tempo of the interaction, a characteristic of low-directive fathers, learn how to recognize and send emotional signals during social interactions. Later studies confirmed these findings and showed a link between children's emotional encoding and decoding abilities that are presumably acquired, in part, in these playful interchanges and children's social adaptation to peers (Parke et al., 1988, 1994; Parke, McDowell et al., in press). In addition, fathers' affect displays, especially father anger, seem to be a potent correlate of children's social acceptance. In studies in both the laboratory (Carson and Parke, 1996) and the home (Boyum and Parke, 1995), fathers' negative affect is inversely related to preschool and kindergarten children's sociometric status. Mize and Pettit (1997) found that preschool children whose play with fathers is characterized by mutuality or balance in making play suggestions and following partners' suggestions were less aggressive, more competent, and better liked by peers. Similarly Hart and his colleagues (Hart et al., 1998, 2000) found that greater playfulness, patience, and understanding with children, especially on the part of the father, are associated with less aggressive behavior with peers. Although there is overlap between mothers and fathers, evidence is emerging that fathers make a unique and independent contribution to their children's social development.

Although father involvement in infancy and childhood is quantitatively less than mother involvement, the data suggest that fathers nevertheless do not have an important impact on their offspring's development. Just as earlier research indicated that quality rather than quantity of mother–child interaction was the important predictor of cognitive and social development, (e.g., Wachs, 2000), a similar assumption appears to hold for fathers as well.

REMAINING ISSUES AND FUTURE TRENDS

A number of issues remain to be examined in future research if we are to describe fully the complexities, specify the determinants and processes, and outline the consequences of father–child relationships. These include the choice of the unit of analysis, the effects of family variation, types of developmental change, the role of historical change, and methodological issues.

Unit of Analysis

Current work clearly recognizes the importance of considering fathers from a family systems perspective. However, our conceptual analysis of dyadic and triadic units of analysis is still limited (Barrett and Hinde, 1988; Parke, 1988; McHale et al., 2002). Considerable progress has been made in describing the behavior of individual interactants (e.g., mother, father, child) within dyadic and, to a lesser extent, triadic settings, but less progress has been achieved in developing a language for describing interaction in dyadic and triadic terms. Even if such terms as reciprocal or synchronous hold promise, there remains little real advance in this regard. In addition, greater attention needs to be paid to the family as a unit of analysis. A number of researchers have offered differing taxonomies of family types or typologies that move us to this level of analysis (Boss, 1980; Kreppner, 1989; Reiss, 1981; Sameroff, 1994), but only recently have there been efforts to apply these notions systematically to family relationships in childhood (see Dickstein et al., 1998, Hayden et al., 1998).

Another aspect of the unit of analysis issue concerns the focus on variables versus individuals. As Magnusson and Cairns (1996, p. 25) have noted "most analyses of behavior have been "variable-oriented" rather than "person-oriented." Instead of focusing on a variable approach in which the goal is to examine relations among variables, Magnusson and Bergmann (1990) advocate a person oriented approach in which questions are posed in terms of individuals and their profiles. Jain et al. (1996) recently applied this person-oriented approach to the description of types of fathers in intact families. Clusters of four types of fathers emerged: caretakers, playmates-teachers, disciplinarians and disengaged fathers. Moreover, the first two types of fathers were more educated, had more prestigious occupations, were less neurotic, had more confidence in the dependability of others and experienced fewer daily hassles than the disciplinarian and disengaged father types. This person-oriented approach to the classification of fathering types merits more attention by researchers in the future.

Fathers and Family Variation

One of the clear advances of the past decade is recognition of the importance of individual differences in children; one of the next advances will be the recognition of individual differences among families and fathers. Recognition of individual variability across families implies the necessity of expanding sampling procedures. In spite of demands for a greater awareness of family diversity, the range of family types that are studied is still relatively narrow. Although progress has been made in describing interaction patterns of fathers and children in different cultures (Bornstein, 1991; Demo et al., 2000; Ishii-Kuntz, 2000; Roopnarine and Carter, 1992) and in different ethnic groups and social classes in the United States (Deutsch, 1999; Gadsen, 1999; Leyendecker and Lamb, 1999; Parke Coltrane et al., in press), this work represents only a beginning, and much more detailed descriptive, as well as process-oriented work, is necessary if we are to achieve a balanced and nuanced understanding of how cultural beliefs and practices influence fathering behaviors. Another form of diversity that warrants more attention is structural variation. In view of the high rates of single mothers and divorced families, caution is necessary in generalizing from intact families to single-parent households (Amato and Booth, 1997; McLanahan and Sandefur, 1994). Moreover, although much of the work is based on survey methods and the amount of observationally based interactional work of fathers in families of different structures remains limited, recent work (e.g., Hetherington and Clingempeel, 1992; Hetherington and Stanley-Hagan, 1999, in Vol. 3 of this *Handbook*) is beginning to correct this situation. Finally, recent work on gay and lesbian families has raised provocative issues for the field of fatherhood research. As Patterson and her colleagues (Patterson, 1995, in Vol. 3 of this *Handbook*; Patterson and Chan, 1997) have suggested, children in families of same-gender parents develop adequately in terms of social–emotional adjustment. As Parke (2002, p. 78) has argued, "Our focus on the gender of the parent may too narrow; instead, it could be helpful to recast the issue and ask whether it is the extent to which exposure to males and/or females is critical or whether it is exposure to the interactive style typically associated with either mother or father that matters." Perhaps the style of parenting and the gender of the parent who enacts the style can be viewed as partially independent. More attention to the kinds of parenting styles evident in same-gender parental households will help us address the uniqueness of father and mother roles in the family and help provide needed clarity on the important issue of how essential opposite-gender parental dyads are for children's development (Parke, 2002; Silverstein and Auerbach, 1999).

Types of Developmental Change

Developmental issues need to be addressed more fully to include children at a wider range of ages. Moreover, we need to move beyond childhood and examine more closely father relationships with their adult children—if we are to achieve a lifespan view of fathering. Although development traditionally has marked change in the individual child, it is evident from this review that this perspective is too limited, and fathers, as well as children, continue to develop across time (Parke, 1988, 1990, 1996). Fathers' management of a variety of life course tasks, such as marriage, work, and personal identity, will clearly determine how they will execute parental tasks; in turn, these differences may find expression in measures of father–child interaction. Because developmental shifts in children's perceptual, cognitive, and social development in turn may alter parental attitudes and behaviors and the nature of the adults' own developmentally relevant choices, such as work or career commitment, this clearly argues for the recognition of two developmental trajectories—a child developmental course and an adult developmental sequence. The description of the interplay between these two types of developmental curves is necessary to capture adequately the nature of developmental changes in a father's role in the family (Parke, 1988, 1990).

Monitoring Secular Trends

There is a continuing need to monitor secular trends and to describe their impact on father–child interaction patterns (Coltrane and Parke, 1998; Parke and Stearns, 1993). Secular change is complex and clearly does not affect all individuals equally or all behavior patterns to the same extent. In fact, it is a serious oversimplification to assume that general societal trends can isomorphically be applied across all individual fathers and families. Moreover, better guidelines are necessary to illuminate which aspects of processes within families are most likely to be altered by historical events and which processes are less amenable to change. For example, the structural dynamics of early interaction (Stern, 1977) as well as some qualitative aspects of early parent–infant interactive style may be insulated from the influence of secular shifts. Are fathers biologically prepared to interact in a more physical way and mothers in a more verbal mode? If this assumption about differences in parental play style is, in fact, true, rates of interactions would be more likely to change than style as employment opportunities for women and men become more equal. Alternatively, the restraints may be more solely environmental, and as opportunities for adult female and male participation in childcare and childrearing equalize, some maternal–paternal stylistic differences may diminish.

Changes in technology represent another secular shift with potentially profound implications for fathers. Computer and communication technology can alter the relation between families and work. For example, researchers (Hill, Hawkins, and Miller, 1996) are beginning to explore the impact of telecommuting on fathers and families. As new work patterns that are due to advances in technology emerge, the effects on fathers merit examination. Even more profound is the potential impact of the new reproductive technologies on parenting in general and fathering in particular (Parke, 2002). New reproductive technologies are expanding the ways in which individuals become parents and opening up new possibilities for infertile as well as same-gender couples (Paulson and Sachs, 1999). The implications of these recent advances including in vitro fertilization, sperm donors, surrogate mothers, and indracyctoplasmic sperm injection for our definitions of parenthood, including fatherhood, are only beginning to be explored. Even less is known about the impact of these alternative pathways to fatherhood on children's development. Increasingly our definition of fatherhood is becoming divorced from biology and instead is recognized as a socially constructed category. New questions, both ethical and psychological, are likely to arise from these advances (see Parke, 2002).

To date, historical events, such as shifts in the timing of parenting or work participation, have been treated relatively independently, but, in fact, these events co-occur rather than operate in any singular fashion (Parke and Tinsley, 1984). Moreover, the impact of any historical change may be different as a result of its occurrence in the same period as another change or changes (Coltrane and Parke, 1998). For example, women's increased presence in the workplace and delay in the onset of parenthood vary, and probably each event has different meaning without the other change. This implies the research need for multivariate designs to capture the simultaneous impact of multiple events on fathering activities.

Methodological Issues

It is likely that no single methodological strategy will suffice for understanding of the development of the father's role in the family. Instead, a wide range of designs and data collection and data analysis strategies is necessary (Parke, 2000). To date, there is still a paucity of information concerning interrelations across molar and molecular levels of analysis. However, it is becoming increasingly clear that a microanalytic strategy is not always more profitable in terms of describing relationships among interactive partners; in fact, in some cases, ratings may be a more useful approach. A set of guidelines concerning the appropriate level of analysis for different questions would be helpful.

Men's own reports have been underutilized in most research. Self-reports are not a substitute for observational data but can provide important information that can aid in interpretation of observed patterns (Goodnow and Collins, 1991). Moreover, recent work on the cultural images of fatherhood that are shared by both fathers themselves and by the wider society have profited from reliance on men's own reports and narratives (Dollahite, Hawkins, and Brotherson, 1997; Marsiglio, 1993; Maurer, Pleck and Rane, 2001; Parke Coltrane et al., in press).

Reliance on nonexperimental strategies may be insufficient to address the important issue of direction of effects in work on the impact of fathers on children and families (Parke, 2000). Experimental strategies have been underutilized in studies of fathers. By experimental modification of either the type of paternal behavior or level of father involvement, firmer conclusions concerning the direct causative role that fathers play in modifying their children's and their wives development will be possible. Intervention studies (e.g., Fagan and Hawkins, 2000; Parke et al., 1980) aimed at modifying fathering behavior provide models for this type of work, and, if these studies are extended to include measures of child, mother, and father development, they could provide evidence of the impact of changes in fathering behavior on developmental outcomes. Moreover, these experimentally based interventions have clear policy implications by exploring the degree of plasticity of fathering behavior. Finally, these interventions can serve as a vehicle for evaluation of alternative theoretical views of fatherhood (Parke, 2000).

Contextual Issues

Greater attention needs to be paid to the role of context in determining father–child relationships. How do father–child interaction patterns shift between home and laboratory settings and across different types of interaction contexts such as play, teaching, and caregiving? Moreover, it is important to consider the social as well as the physical context. Recognition of the embeddedness of fathers in family contexts is critical, and, in turn, conceptualizing families as embedded in a variety of extrafamilial social settings is important for understanding variation in father functioning (Parke, 1996). In this regard, it is necessary to recognize that variations in family structure and in ethnicity and SES will modify significantly the ways in which social networks are organized and utilized. For example, the role of the extended family is much more prominent in some groups, such as African American and Mexican American than in other groups (Gadsen, 1999; Parke, Coltrane et al., in press; Wilson, 1986). Similarly, single-parent families may be more directly embedded in community-based social networks than two-parent families. Descriptions of these variations are necessary for an adequate understanding of the role of extrafamilial networks on fathers and family functioning.

CONCLUSIONS

In spite of a relatively brief recent history of serious research devoted to fatherhood, considerable progress has been achieved in our understanding of the paternal role and the impact of fathers on themselves and others. Several conclusions are warranted. First, some modest increases over the past several decades have occurred in the level of father involvement with children. However, not all types of involvement shown have been equally affected and managerial aspects of family life remain largely a maternal responsibility. Second, fathers are clearly competent caregivers and playmates in spite of their limited involvement. Third, stylistic differences in interaction with children between mothers and fathers continue to be evident in spite of recent shifts toward greater involvement, although some cross-cultural evidence suggests that the paternal physical play style may not be as universal as previously assumed. Fourth, the father role appears less scripted and less determined than the mother role, which may account for the variability that characterizes the enactment of fathering. Fathering is multidetermined with individual, family, institutional, and cultural factors all influencing this role. Fifth, the focus of the effects of fathers continues to be on children's development, and evidence continues to suggest that fathers do have an impact on children's social, emotional, and cognitive development. However, the quality of fathering remains an important determinant of paternal influence on children's development, and the independent contribution of fathers relative to mothers remains only weakly documented. Sixth, recent evidence suggests that fathering activities alter men's marital relationships as well as men's own sense of self and their societal generativity.

The study of father–child relationships has matured in the past two decades and is now a more fully contextualized issue. Fathers in the context of their social relationships both within and beyond the family are increasingly the appropriate point of entry for understanding the issue of both paternal roles and their impact on themselves and others. Our conceptual paradigms continue to outstrip our empirical understanding. To reduce this gap is the challenge of the next decades of research. Children, fathers, and families will benefit from this increased understanding.

ACKNOWLEDGMENTS

Preparation of this chapter was supported in part by National Institute of Mental Health grant RO1MH54154 and National Institute of Child Health and Human Development grant HT32391. Thanks to Heather Guzman and Faye Harmer for the preparation of this manuscript.

REFERENCES

Allen, J. M., and Hawkins, A. J. (1999). Maternal gatekeeping: Mothers' beliefs and behaviors that inhibit greater father involvement in family work. *Journal of Marriage and the Family, 61*, 199–212.

Amato, P. R., and Booth, A. (1997). *A generation a risk: Growing up in an era of family upheaval.* Cambridge, MA: Harvard University Press.

Amato, P. A., and Gilbreth, J. G. (1999). Nonresident fathers and children's well-being: A meta analysis. *Journal of Marriage and the Family, 61*, 15–73.

Amato, P. R., and Keith, B. (1991). Parental divorce and the well-being of children: A meta-analysis. *Psychological Bulletin, 110*, 26–46.

Amato, R. R., and Rivera, F. (1999). Paternal involvement and children's behavior. *Journal of Marriage and the Family, 61*, 375–384.

Bailey, W. T. (1994). Fathers' involvement and responding to infants: "More" may not be "better." *Psychological Reports, 74*, 92–94.

Bandura, A. (1989). Cognitive social learning theory. In R. Vasta (Ed.), *Six theories of child development.* Greenwich, CT: JAI.

Bandura, A. (1997). *Self-efficacy.* New York: Freeman.

Barnett, R. C., and Baruch, G. K. (1987). Determinants of fathers' participation in family work. *Journal of Marriage and the Family, 49*, 29–40.

Barrett, J., and Hinde, R. A. (1988). Triadic interactions: Mother–first born–second born. In R. A. Hinde and J. Stevenson-Hinde (Eds.), *Towards understanding families.* Oxford, England: Oxford University Press.

Baruch, G. K., and Barnett, R. C. (1986). Fathers' participation in family work and children's sex-role attitudes. *Child Development, 57*, 1210–1223.

Baumrind, D. (1991). The influence of parenting style on adolescent competence and substance use. *Journal of Early Adolescence, 11*, 56–95.

Beitel, A., and Parke, R. D. (1998). Maternal and paternal attitudes as determinants of father involvement. *Journal of Family Psychology, 12*, 268–288.

Belsky, J. (1984). Determinants of parenting: A process model. *Child Development, 55*, 83–96.

Belsky, J. (1991). Parental and nonparental child care and children's socioemotional development. In A. Booth (Ed.), *Contemporary families: Looking forward, looking back* (pp. 122–140). Minneapolis, MN: National Council on Family Relations.

Belsky, J., Gilstrap, B., and Rovine, M. (1984). The Pennsylvania infant and family development project, I: Stability and change in mother–infant and father–infant interaction in a family setting at one, three and nine months. *Child Development, 55*, 692–705.

Belsky, J., and Isabella, R. (1985). Marital and parent–child relationships in family of origin and marital change following the birth of a baby: A retrospective analysis. *Child Development, 56*, 342–349.

Belsky, J., and Pensky, E. (1988). Marital change across the transition to parenthood. In R. Palkowitz and M. B. Sussman (Eds.), *Transitions to parenthood* (pp. 133–156). New York: Haworth.

Belsky, J., Rovine, M., and Fish, M. (1989). The developing family system. In M. Gunnar and E. Thelen (Eds.), *Minnesota symposia on child psychology: Vol. 22. Systems and development* (pp. 119–166). Hillsdale, NJ: Lawrence Erlbaum Associates.

Belsky, J., and Volling, B. L. (1986). Mothering, fathering and marital interaction in the family triad: Exploring family systems processes. In P. Berman and F. Pedersen (Eds.), *Men's transition to parenthood: Longitudinal studies of early family experience* (pp. 37–64). Hillsdale, NJ: Lawrence Erlbaum Associates.

Belsky, J., Ward, H. J., and Levine, M. (1986). Prenatal expectations, postnatal experiences and the transition to parenthood. In R. Ashmore and D. Brodinsky (Eds.), *Perspectives on the family* (pp. 111–146). Hillsdale, NJ: Lawrence Erlbaum Associates.

Belsky, J., Youngblade, L., Rovine, M., and Volling, B. (1991). Patterns of marital change and parent–child interaction. *Journal of Marriage and the Family, 53*, 487–498.

Bem, S. L. (1993). *The lenses of gender.* New Haven, CT: Yale University Press.

Berman, P. (1987). Young children's responses to babies: Do they foreshadow differences between maternal and paternal styles. In A. Fogel and G. F. Melson (Eds.), *Origins of Nurturance* (pp. 25–26) Hillsdale, NJ: Lawrence Erlbaum Associates.

Berman, P. (1991). Children caring for babies: Age and sex differences in response to infant signals and to the social context. In M. Woodhead, R. Carr, and P. Light (Eds.), *Becoming a person: Child development in social context* (Vol. 1, pp. 300–327). London: Routledge.

Bhavnagri, N., and Parke, R. D. (1991). Parents as direct facilitators of children's peer relationships: Effects of age of child and sex of parent. *Journal of Social and Personal Relationships, 8*, 423–440.

Biller, H. B. (1971). The mother-child relationship and the father-absent boy's personality development. *Merrill-Palmer Quarterly, 17*, 227–241.

Biller, H. B. (1993). *Fathers and families.* Westport, CT: Auburn House.

Blair, S. L., Wenk, D., and Hardesty, C. (1994). Marital quality and paternal involvement: Interconnections of men's spousal and parental roles. *Journal of Men's Studies, 2*, 222–237.

Bonney, J. F., Kelley, M. L., and Levant, R. F. (1999). A model of father's involvement in child care in dual-earner families. *Journal of Family Psychology, 13*, 401–415.

Bornstein, M. H. (Ed.). (1991). *Cultural approaches to parenting.* Hillsdale, NJ: Lawrence Erlbaum Associates.

Boss, P. (1980). Normative family stress: Family boundary changes across the life span. *Family Relations, 29*, 445–450.

Boyum, L., and Parke, R. D. (1995). Family emotional expressiveness and children's social competence. *Journal of Marriage and Family, 57*, 593–608.

Braungart-Rieker, J., Courtney, S., and Garwood, M. M. (1999). Mother– and father–infant attachment: Families in context. *Journal of Family Psychology, 13*, 535–553.

Brayfield, A. (1994). Juggling jobs and kids: The impact of employment schedules on fathers caring for children. *Journal of Marriage and the Family, 57*, 321–332.

Brodzinsky, D. M., Lang, R., and Smith, D. W. (1995). Parenting adopted children. In M. Bornstein (Ed.), *Handbook of parenting: Vol. 3. Status and social conditions of parenting* (pp. 209–232). Mahwah, NJ: Lawrence Erlbaum Associates.

Bronfenbrenner, U. (1989). Ecological systems theory. In R. Vasta (Ed.), *Six theories of child development* (Vol. 6, pp. 187–250). Greenwich, CT: JAI.

Bronfenbrenner, U., and Morris, P. A. (1998). The ecology of developmental process. In R. Lerner (Vol. Ed.) and W. Damon (Series Ed.), *Handbook of child psychology* (4th ed., Vol. 1, pp. 993–1028). New York: Wiley.

Brooks-Gunn, J., and Chase-Lansdale, L. (1995). Adolescent parenthood. In M. Bornstein (Ed.), *Handbook of parenting: Vol. 3. Status and Social Conditions of Parenting* (pp. 113–150). Mahwah, NJ: Lawrence Erlbaum Associates.

Brooks-Gunn, J., and Furstenberg, F. F. (1986). The children of adolescent mothers: Physical, academic and psychological outcomes. *Developmental Review, 6*, 224–251.

Cabrera, N. J., Tamis-LeMonda, S., Bradley, R. H., Hofferth, S., and Lamb, M. E. (2000). Fatherhood in the twenty-first century. *Child Development, 71*, 127–136.

Card, J., and Wise, L. (1978). Teenage mothers and teenage fathers: The impact of early child-bearing on the parents' personal and professional lives. *Family Planning Perspectives, 10*, 199–205.

Carson, J., and Parke, R. D. (1996). Reciprocal negative affect in parent–child interactions and children's peer competency. *Child Development, 67*, 2217–2226.

Clarke-Stewart, K. A. (1980). The father's contribution to children's cognitive and social development in early childhood. In F. Pedersen (Ed.), *The father–infant relationship* (pp. 97–112). New York: Praeger.

Clarke-Stewart, K. A. (1978). And daddy makes three: The father's impact on mother and young child. *Child Development, 49*, 466–478.

Clarke-Stewart, K. A. (1988). Historical shifts and underlying themes in ideas about rearing young children in the United States. *Early Development and Parenting, 7*, 101–117.

Coley, R. L., and Chase-Lansdale, P. L. (1999). Stability and change in paternal involvement among urban African-American fathers. *Journal of Family Psychology, 13*, 416–435.

Collins, W. A., and Russell, G. (1991). Mother–child and father–child relationships in middle childhood and adolescence: A developmental analysis. *Developmental Review, 11*, 91–136.

Coltrane, S. (1996). *Family man.* New York: Oxford.

Coltrane, S. (2000). Research on household labor: Modeling and measuring the social embeddedness of routine family work. *Journal of Marriage and the Family, 62*, 1208–1233.

Coltrane, S., and Ishii-Kuntz, M. (1992). Men's housework: A life course perspective. *Journal of Marriage and the Family, 54*, 43–57.

Coltrane, S., and Parke, R. D. (1998). *Reinventing fatherhood: Towards an historical understanding of continuity and change in men's family life* (commissioned paper). Philadelphia, PA: National Center on Fathers and Families.

Cooney, T. M., Pedersen, F. A., Indelicato, S., and Palkovitz, R. (1993). Timing of fatherhood: Is "on-time" optimal? *Journal of Marriage and the Family, 55*, 205–215.

Cowan, C. P. (1988). Working with men becoming fathers: The impact of couples group intervention. In P. Bronstein and C. P. Cowan (Eds.), *Fatherhood today* (pp. 276–298). New York: Wiley.

Cowan, C. P., and Cowan, P. A. (1985, March). *Parents' work patterns, marital and parent-child relationships, and early child development.* Paper presented at the meetings of the Society for Research in Child Development, Toronto, Canada.

Cowan, C. P., and Cowan, P. A. (1987). Men's involvement in parenthood. In P. W. Berman and F. A. Pedersen (Eds.), *Men's transition to parenthood* (pp. 145–174). Hillsdale, NJ: Lawrence Erlbaum Associates.

Cowan, C. P., and Cowan, P. (1992). *When parents become partners.* New York: Basic Books.

Cowan, C. P., Cowan, P. A., Coie, L., and Coie, J. D. (1978). Becoming a family: The impact of a first child's birth on the couple's relationship. In W. B. Miller and L. F. Newman (Eds.), *The first child and family formation.* Chapel Hill, NC: Carolina Population Center.

Cowan, P. (1988). Becoming a father: A time of change, an opportunity for development. In P. Bronstein and C. P. Cowan (Eds.), *Fatherhood today* (pp. 13–35). New York: Wiley.

Cowan, P. A. and Cowan, C. P. (2002). What an intervention reveals about how parents affect their children's academic achievement and behavior problems. In J. Borkowski, S. Landesman Ramey, M. Bristol-Power (Eds.). *Parenting and the child's world: Influences on intellectual, academic and social-emotional development* (pp. 75–98). Mahwah, NJ: Lawrence Erlbaum Associates.

Cowan, P. A., Cowan, C. P., Schulz, M. S., and Heming, G. (1994). Prebirth to preschool family factors in children's adaptation to kindergarten. In R. D. Parke and S. G. Kellam (Eds.), *Exploring family relationships with other social contexts* (pp. 75–114). Hillsdale, NJ: Lawrence Erlbaum Associates.

Crockett, L. J., Eggebeen, D. J., and Hawkins, A. J. (1993). Fathers presence and young children's behavioral and cognitive adjustment. *Journal of Family Issues, 14*, 355–377.

Crouter, A. C. (1994). Processes linking families and work: Implications for behavior and development in both settings. In R. D. Parke and S. G. Kellam (Eds.). *Exploring family relationships with other social context* (pp. 9–28). Hillsdale, NJ: Lawrence Erlbaum Associates.

Crouter, A. C., Bumpus, M. R., Maguire, M. C., and McHale, S. M. (1999). Linking parents' work pressure and adolescents' well-being: Insights into dynamics in dual earner families. *Developmental Psychology, 35*, 1453–1461.

Cummings, E. M., Ballard, El-Sheikh. M., and Lake, M. (1991). Resolution and children's responses to interadult anger. *Developmental Psychology, 27*, 462–470.

Cummings, E. M., and O'Reilly, A. W. (1997). Fathers in family context: Effects of marital quality on child adjustment. In M. E. Lamb (Ed.), *The father's role in child development* (3rd ed.) New York: Wiley.

Daly, K. (1993). Reshaping fatherhood: Finding the models. *Journal of Family Issues, 14*, 510–530.

Daniels, P., and Weingarten, K. (1982). *Sooner or later: The timing of parenthood in adult lives.* New York: Norton.

Davies, P. T., and Cummings, E. M. (1994). Marital conflict and child adjustment: An emotional security hypothesis. *Psychological Bulletin, 116*, 387–411.

De Frain, J. (1979). Androgynous parents tell who they are and what they need. *The Family Coordinator, 28*, 237–243.

Demo, D. H., Allen, K. R., and Fine, M. A. (2000). (Eds.). Handbook *of family diversity.* New York: Oxford University Press.

Deutsch, C. (1999). *Having it all.* Cambridge, MA: Harvard University Press.

Dickie, J., and Gerber, S. C. (1980). Training in social competence: The effect on mothers, fathers and infants. *Child Development, 51*, 1248–1251.

Dickie, J. R., and Matheson, P. (1984, August). *Mother–father–infant: Who needs support?* Paper presented at meeting of the American Psychological Association, Toronto.

Dickstein, S., Seifer, R., Hayden, L. C., Schiller, M., Sameroff, A. J., Keitner, G., Miller, I., Rasmusen, S., Matzko, M., and Magee, K. D. (1998). Levels of family assessment: II. Impact of maternal psychopathology on family functioning. *Journal of Family Psychology, 21*, 23–40.

Dienhart, A., and Daly, K. (1997). Men and women cocreating father involvement in a nongenerative culture. In A. J. Hawkins and D. C. Dollahite (Eds.), *Generative fathering* (pp. 147–164). Thousand Oaks, CA: Sage.

Doherty, W. E. J., Kouneski, E. F., and Erikson, M. (1998). Responsible fathering: An overview and conceptual framework. *Journal of Marriage and the Family, 60*, 277–292.

Dollahite, D. C., Hawkins, A. J., and Brotherson, S. E. (1997). Father work: A conceptual ethic of fathering as generative work. In A. J. Hawkins and D. C. Doilahite (Eds.), *Generative father* (pp. 17–35). Thousand Oaks, CA: Sage.

Duffy, A. (1988). Struggling with power: Feminist critiques of family inequity. In N. Mandell and A. Duffy (Eds.), *Reconstructing the Canadian family: Feminist perspectives* (pp. 111–139). Toronto: Butterworths.

Durrett, M. E., Otaki, M., and Richards, P. (1984). Attachment and the mother's perception of support from the father. *International Journal of Behavioral Development, 7*, 167–176.

Elder, G. H. (1998). The life course and human development. In W. Damon (Series Ed.) and R. M. Lerner (Vol. ed.). *Handbook of child psychology* (4th ed., Vol. 1). New York: Wiley.

Elder, G. H., Modell, J., and Parke, R. D. (Eds.). (1993). *Children in time and place*. New York: Cambridge University Press.

Erel, O., and Burman, B. (1995). Interrelatedness of marital relations and parent–child relations: A meta-analytic review. *Psychological Bulletin, 118*, 108–132.

Erikson, E. (1975). *Life history and the historical moment*. New York: Norton.

Erikson, E. (1982). *The life cycle completed*. New York: Norton.

Fagan, J. (1998). Correlates of low-income African American and Puerto Rican fathers' involvement with their children. *Journal of Black Psychology, 24*, 351–367.

Fagan, J., and Hawkins, A. J. (2000). *Clinical and educational interventions with fathers*. Binghamton, NY: Haworth.

Fauber, R. L., and Long, N. (1991). Children in context: The role of the family in child psychotherapy. *Journal of Consulting and Clinical Psychology, 59*, 813–820.

Feldman, S. S., Nash, S. C., and Aschenbrenner, B. G. (1983). Antecedents of fathering. *Child Development, 54*, 1628–1636.

Field, T. M. (1978). Interaction behaviors of primary versus secondary caretaker fathers. *Developmental Psychology, 14*, 183–185.

Finley, G. E., Janovetz, V. A., and Rogers, B. (1990, March). *University students' perceptions of parental acceptance–rejection as a function of parental ages*. Poster presented at the Conference on Human Development, Richmond, VA.

Fincham, F. D. (1998). Child development and marital relations. *Child Development, 69*, 543–574.

Fleming, A. S., and Corter, C. M. (1995). Psychobiology of maternal behavior in nonhuman mammals. In M. Bornstein (Ed.), *Handbook of parenting: Vol 2. Biology and ecology of parenting* (pp. 59–85). Mahwah, NJ: Lawrence Erlbaum Associates.

Fleming, A. S., Ruble, D., Krieger, H., and Wong, P. Y. (1997). Hormonal and experimental correlates of maternal responsiveness during pregnancy and the puerperium in human mothers. *Hormones and Behavior, 31*, 145–158.

Franz, C. E., McClelland, D., and Weinberger, J. (1991). Childhood antecedents of conventional social accomplishment in midlife adults: A 26-year prospective study. *Journal of Personality and Social Psychology, 58*, 709–717.

Frodi, A. M., Lamb, M. E., Hwang, C. P., and Frodi, M. (1982, March). *The Swedish experiment: Paternal involvement in infant care*. Paper presented at the International Conference on Infant Studies, Austin, TX.

Furstenberg, F. F., Jr. (1988). Good dads—bad dads: Two faces of fatherhood. In A. J. Cherlin (Ed.), *The changing American family and public policy* (pp. 193–218). Washington, DC: Urban Institute.

Furstenberg, F. F., Jr., Brooks-Gunn, J., and Chase-Lansdale, L. (1989). Teenaged pregnancy and child bearing. *American Psychologist, 44*, 313–320.

Furstenberg, F. F., and Cherlin, A. J. (1991). *Divided families*. Cambridge, MA: Harvard University Press.

Furstenberg, F. F., and Harris, K. M. (1993). When and why fathers matter: Impacts of father involvement on children of adolescent mothers. In R. I. Lerman and T. J. Ooms (Eds.), *Young unwed fathers* (pp. 117–138). Philadelphia: Temple University Press.

Glueck, S., and Glueck, E. (1950). *Unraveling juvenile delinquency*. New York: Commonwealth Fund.

Gadsden, V. (1999). Black families in intergenerational and cultural perspective. In M. E. Lamb (Ed.), *Parenting and child development in "nontraditional" families* (pp. 221–246). Mahwah, NJ: Lawrence Erlbaum Associates.

Garfinkel, L., McLanahan, S., Meyer, D., and Seltzer, J. (1998). *Fathers under fire: The revolution of child support enforcement*. New York: Russell Sage Foundation Press.

Goodnow, J. J. (1988). Children's household work: Nature and functions. *Psychological Bulletin, 103*, 4–26.

Goodnow, J. J. (1999). From household practices to parents' ideas about work and interpersonal relationships. In S. Harkness, C. Super, and R. Niew (Eds.), *Parenting ethnotheories*. New York: Guilford.

Goodnow, J. J., and Collins, W. A. (1991). *Development according to parents: The nature, sources and consequences of parents ideas*. Hillsdale, NJ: Lawrence Erlbaum Associates.

Gottfried, A. E., Bathurst, K., and Gottfried, A. W. (1994). Role of maternal and dual-earner employment status in children's development. In A. E. Gottfried and A. W. Gottfried (Eds.), *Redifining families: Implications for children's development* (pp. 55–97). New York: Plenum.

Gottfried, A. E., Gottfried, A. W., Bathurst, K., and Killian, C. (1999), Maternal and dual-earner employment: Family enviroment, adaptations and the developmental impingement perspective. In M. E. Lamb (Ed.), *Parenting and child development in "nontraditional" families* (pp. 15–38). Mahwah NJ: Lawrence Erlbaum Associates.

Gottman, J. M., Katz, L., and Hooven, C. (1997). *Meta-emotion*. Mahwah, NJ: Lawrence Erlbaum Associates.

Greenberger, E., and O'Neil, R. (1991, April). *Characteristics of fathers' and mothers' jobs: Implications for parenting and children's social development*. Paper presented at the biennial meeting of the Society for Research in Child Development, Seattle, WA.

Grimm-Thomas, K., and Perry-Jenkins, M. (1994). All in a day's work: Job experiences self-esteem and fathering in working-class families. *Family Relations, 43*, 174–181.

Grossman, F. K. (1987). Separate and together: Men's autonomy and affiliation in the transition to parenthood. In P. W. Berman and F. A. Pedersen (Eds.), *Men's transition to parenthood* (pp. 89–112). Hillsdale, NJ: Lawrence Erlbaum Associates.

Grossman, F. K., Pollack, W. S., and Golding, E. (1988). Fathers and children: Predicting the quality and quantity of fathers. *Developmental Psychology, 24*, 82–91.

Grych, J. H., and Clark, R. (1999). Maternal employment and development of the father–infant relationship. *Developmental Psychology, 35*, 893–903.

Grych, J. H., and Fincham, F. D. (1993). Children's appraisals of marital conflict: Initial investigations of the cognitive-contextual framework. *Child Development, 64*, 215–230.

Grych. J. H., and Fincham, F. D. (Eds.). (2001). *Interparental conflict and child development.* New York: Cambridge University Press.

Hart, C. H., Nelson, D. A., Robinson, C. C., Olsen, S. F., and McNeilly-Choque, M. K. (1998). Overt and relational aggression in Russian nursery-school-age children: Parenting style and marital linkages. *Developmental Psychology, 34*, 687–697.

Hart, C. H., Nelson, D. A., Robinson, C. C., Olsen, S. F., McNeilly-Choque, M. K., Porter, C. L., and McKee, T. R. (2000). Russian parenting styles and family processes: Linkages with subtypes of victimization and aggression. In K. A. Kerns, J. M. Contreras, and A. M. Neal-Barnett (Eds.), *Family and peers: Linking two social worlds.* Westport, CT: Praeger.

Hartup, W. W. (1979). The social worlds of childhood. *American Psychologist, 34*, 944–950.

Hawkins, A. J., and Dollahite, D. C. (Eds.). (1997). *Generative fathering: Beyond deficit perspectives.* Thousand Oaks, CA: Sage.

Hayden, L. C., Schiller, M., Dickstein, S., Seifer, R., Sameroff, A. J., Miller, I., Keitner, G., and Rasmussen, S. (1998). Levels of family assessment: I. family, marital and parent-child interaction. *Journal of Family Psychology, 12*, 7–22.

Heath, D. H. (1977). Some possible effects of occupation on the maturing professional man. *Journal of Vocational Behavior, 11*, 263–281.

Heath, D. H. (1976). Competent fathers: Their personalities and marriages. *Human Development, 19*, 26–39.

Heath, D. H., and Heath, H. E. (1991). *Fulfilling lives: Paths to maturity and success.* San Francisco: Jossey-Bass.

Hernandez, D. J. (1993). *America's children.* New York: Russell Sage Foundation Press.

Hetherington, E. M. (1967). The effects of familial variables on sex typing, on parent–child similarity and on imitation in children. In J. P. Hill (Ed.), *Minnesota symposia on child psychology* (Vol. 1, pp. 82–107). Minneapolis: University of Minnesota Press.

Hetherington, E. M., and Clingempeel, W. G. (1992). Coping with marital transitions. *Monographs of the Society for Research in Child Development, 57* (Serial No. 227).

Hetherington, E. M., and Deur, J. (1972). The effects of father's absence. *Young Children, 26*, 233–248.

Hetherington, E. M., and Frankie, G. (1967). Effects of parental dominance, warmth, and conflict on imitation in children. *Journal of Personality and Social Psychology, 6*, 119–125.

Hetherington, E. M., and Stanley-Hagan, M. M. (1999). Step families. In M. E. Lamb (Ed.), *Parenting and child development in nontraditional families* (pp. 137–159). Mahwah, NJ: Lawrence Erlbaum Associates.

Hewlett, B. S. (1991). *Intimate fathers.* Ann Arbor: University of Michigan Press.

Hill, E. J., Hawkins, A. J., and Miller, B. C. (1996). Work and family in the virtual office. *Family Relations, 45*, 293–301.

Hock, E. (1987). Working and nonworking mothers and their infants: A comparative study of maternal caregiving characteristics and infant social behavior. *Merrill-Palmer Quarterly, 26*, 79–101.

Hoffman, L. W. (1984). Work, family and the socialization of the child. In R. D. Parke, R. Emde, H. McAdoo, and G. P. Sackett (Eds.), *Review of child development research: The family* (Vol. 7, pp. 223–282). Chicago: University of Chicago Press.

Hoffman, L. W. (2000). Maternal employment: Effects of social context. In R. D. Taylor and M. C. Wang (Eds.), *Resilience across contexts* (pp. 142–176). Mahwah, NJ: Lawrence Erlbaum Associates.

Hofferth, S. L. (1987). Social and economic consequences of teenage parenthood. In S. L. Hoffreth and C. D. Hayes (Eds.), *Risking the future* (Vol. 2, pp. 123–144). Washington, DC: National Academy Press.

Hofferth, S. (1999, April). *Race/ethnic differences in further involvement with young children: A conceptual framework and empirical test in two-parent families.* Paper presented at the Urban Seminar on Fatherhood, Harvard University, Cambridge, MA.

Hossain, Z., and Roopnarine, J. L. (1994). African-American fathers' involvement with infants: Relationship to their functioning style, support, education, and income. *Infant Behavior and Development, 17*, 175–184.

Hossain, T., Field, I., Malphurs, J. E., Valle, C., and Pickens, J. (1995). *Father caregiving in low income African-American and Hispanic-American families.* Unpublished manuscript, University of Miami Medical school, Miami, FL.

Ishii-Kuntz, M. (1995). Paternal involvement and perception toward fathers' roles: A comparison between Japan and the United States. In W. Marsiglio (Ed.), *Fatherhood contemporary theory, research and social policy* (pp.110–118). Thousand Oaks, CA: Sage.

Ishii-Kuntz, M. (2000). Diversity within Asian American Families. In D. H. Demo, K. R. Allen, and M. A. Fine (Eds.), *Handbook of family diversity* (pp. 274–292). New York: Oxford University Press.

Isley, S., O'Neil, R., and Parke, R. D. (1996). The relation of parental affect and control behavior to children's classroom acceptance: A concurrent and predictive analysis. *Early Education and Development, 7*, 7–23.

Jain, A., Belsky, J., and Crnic, K. (1996). Beyond fathering behaviour: Types of dads, *Journal of Family Psychology, 10*, 431–442.

Kalleberg, A. L., and Loscocco, K. A. (1983). Aging, values, and rewards: Explaining age differences in job satisfaction. *American Sociological Review, 48*, 78–90.

Kanter, R. M. (1977). *Work and family in the United States: A critical review of research and policy.* New York: Sage.

Katz, L. F., and Gottman, J. M. (1993). Patterns of martial conflict predict children's internalizing and externalizing behaviors. *Developmental Psychology, 29*, 940–950.

Katz, L. F., and Gottman, J. M. (1994). Patterns of marital interaction and children's emotional development. In R. D. Parke and S. Kellam (Eds.), *Exploring family relationships with other contexts* (pp. 49–74). Hillsdale, NJ: Lawrence Erlbaum Associates.

Katz, L. F., and Kahen, V. (1993, April). *Marital interaction patterns and children's externalizing and internalizing behaviors: The search for mechanisms.* Paper presented at the biennial meeting of the Society for Research in Child Development, New Orleans, LA.

Kelley, M. L. (1997). The division of family roles among low income African-American families. *Journal of African-American Men, 2,* 87–102.

Kerig, P. K. (1996). Assessing the links between interparental conflict and child adjustment: The conflicts and problem-solving scales. *Journal of Family Psychology, 10,* 454–473.

Koestner, R., Franz, C., and Weinberger, J. (1990). The family origins of empathic concern: A 26-year longitudinal study. *Journal of Personality and Social Psychology, 58,* 709–717.

Kohn, M. L., and Schooler, C. (1983). *Work and personality: An inquiry into the impact of social stratification.* Norwood, NJ: Ablex.

Kotelchuck, M. (1976). The infant's relationship to the father: Experimental evidence. In M. E. Lamb (Ed.), *The role of the father in child development* (pp. 123–157). New York: Wiley.

Kotre, J. (1984). *Outlining the self: Generativity and the interpretation of lives.* Baltimore: Johns Hopkins University Press.

Kotre, J., and Hall, E. (1990). *Seasons of life: Our dramatic journey from birth to death.* Boston: Little, Brown.

Kreppner, K. (1989). Linking infant development in context research to the investigation of life-span family development. In K. Kreppner and R. M. Lerner (Eds.), *Family systems and life-span development* (pp. 33–64). Hillsdale, NJ: Lawrence Erlbaum Associates.

Kurdek, L. A. (1998). Prospective predictors of parenting satisfaction for fathers and mothers with young children. *Journal of Family Psychology, 12,* 56–65.

Ladd, G. W., Profilet, S. M., and Hart, C. H. (1992). Parents management of children's peer relations: Facilitating and supervising children's activities in the peer culture. In R. D. Parke and G. W. Ladd (Eds.), *Family–peer relationships: Modes of linkage* (pp. 215–254). Hillsdale, NJ: Lawrence Erlbaum Associates.

Lamb, M. E. (1977). Father–infant and mother–infant interaction in the first year of life. *Child Development, 48,* 167–181.

Lamb, M. E. (Ed.). (1987). *The father's role: Cross-cultural perspectives.* Hillsdale, NJ: Lawrence Erlbaum Associates.

Lamb, M. E., and Elster, A. B. (1985). Adolescent mother–infant–father relationships. *Developmental Psychology, 21,* 768–773.

Lamb, M. E., Frodi, A. M., Hwang, C. P., and Frodi, M. (1982). Varying degrees of paternal involvement in infant care: Attitudinal and behavioral correlates. In M. E. Lamb (Ed.), *Nontraditional families.* Hillsdale, NJ: Lawrence Erlbaum Associates.

Lamb, M. E., Frodi, A. M., Hwang, C. P., Frodi, M., and Steinberg, J. (1982). Effects of gender and caretaking role on parent–infant interaction. In R. M. Emde and R. J. Harmon (Eds.), *Attachment and affiliative systems.* New York: Plenum.

Lamb, M. E., Pleck, J., Charnov, E. L., and Levine, J. A. (1987). A biosocial perspective on paternal behavior and involvement. In J. B. Lancaster, J. Altmann, A. Rossi, and L. R. Sherrod (Eds.), *Parenting across the life span: Biosocial perspectives.* Chicago: Aldine de Guyter.

Lamb, M. E., Pleck, J. H., and Levine, J. A. (1985). The role of the father in child development: The effects of increased paternal involvement. In B. Lahey and E. E. Kazdin (Eds.), *Advances in clinical child psychology* (pp. 229–266) (Vol. 8). New York: Plenum.

Langlois, J. H., and Downs, A. C. (1980). Mothers, father, and peers as socialization agents of sex-typed play behaviors in young children. *Child Development, 51,* 1217–1247.

LaRossa, R. (1997). *The modernization of fatherhood.* Chicago: University of Chicago Press.

LaRossa, Jaret, C., Gadgil, M., and Wynn, G. R. (2000). The changing culture of fatherhood in comic-strip families: A six-decade analysis. *Journal of Marriage and the Family, 62,* 375–387.

Larson R., and Richards, M. (1994). *Divergent realities.* New York: Basic Books.

Lerman, R. I. (1993). A national profile of young unwed fathers. In R. I. Lerman and T. J. Ooms (Eds.), *Young unwed fathers* (pp. 27–51). Philadelphia: Temple University Press.

Lerman, R. L., and Ooms, T. J. (Eds.). (1993). *Young unwed fathers.* Philadelphia: Temple University Press.

Levant, R. (1988). Education for fatherhood. In P. Bornstein and C. P. Cowan (Eds.), *Fatherhood today* (pp. 253–275). New York: Wiley.

Levine, J. A. (1976). *Who will raise the children: New options for fathers (and mothers).* New York: Lippincott.

Levine, J. A., and Pittinsky, T. L. (1998). *Working fathers.* Reading, MA: Addison-Wesley.

Levy-Shiff, R., and Israelashvili, R. (1988). Antecedents of fathering: Some further exploration. *Developmental Psychology, 24,* 434–440.

Leyendecker, B., and Lamb, M. E. (1999). In M. E. Lamb (Ed.), *Parenting and child development in "nontraditional" families* (pp. 247–262). Mahwah, NJ: Lawrence Erlbaum Associates.

Lovejoy, J., and Wallen, K. (1988). Sexually dimorphic behavior in group-house rhesus monkeys (*Macaca mulatta*) at 1 year of age. *Psychobiology, 16,* 348–356.

Losh-Hasselbart, S. (1987). The development of gender roles. In M. B. Sussman and S. Steinmetz (Eds.), *Handbook of marriage and family* (pp. 535–563). New York: Plenum.

Maccoby, E. E. (1988). Gender as a social category. *Developmental Psychology, 24*, 755–765.

Maccoby, E. E. (1998). *The two sexes: Growing up apart, coming together.* Cambridge, MA: Harvard University Press.

MacDonald, K., and Parke, R. D. (1984). Bridging the gap: Parent–child play interaction and peer interactive competence. *Child Development, 55*, 1265–1277.

MacDonald, K., and Parke, R. D. (1986). Parent-child physical play: The effects of sex and age of children and parents, *Sex Roles, 7–8*, 367–379.

Magnusson, D., and Bergman, L. R. (1990). A pattern approach to the study of pathways from childhood to adulthood in L. N. Robins and M. Rutter (Eds.), *Straight and devious pathways from childhood to adulthood* (pp. 101–115). Cambridge: Cambridge University Press.

Magnusson, D., and Cairns, R. B. (1996). Developmental Science: Toward a unified framework. In R. B. Cairns, G. H. Elder, and E. J. Costello (Eds.), *Developmental source* (pp. 7–30). New York: Cambridge University Press.

Marsiglio, W. (1993). Contemporary scholarship on fatherhood: Culture, identity and conduct. *Journal of Family Issues, 14*, 484–509.

Marsiglio, W. (Ed.). (1995). *Fatherhood: Contemporary theory, research, and social policy.* Thousand Oaks, CA: Sage.

Marsiglio, W. (1998). *Procreative man.* New York: New York University Press.

Marsiglio, W., Amato, P., Day, R. D., and Lamb, M. E. (2000). Scholarship on fatherhood in the 1990s and beyond. *Journal of Marriage and the Family, 62*, 1173–1191.

Marsiglio, W., and Cohan, M. (1997). Young fathers and child development. In M. E. Lamb (Ed.), *The role of the father in child development* 3rd ed. (pp. 227–244). New York: Wiley.

Maurer, T. W., Pleck, J. H., and Rane, T. R. (2001). Parental identity and reflected-appraisals: Measurement and gender dynamics, *Journal of Marriage and the Family, 63*, 309–321.

McBride, B. A. (1989). Stress and fathers' parental competence: Implications for family life and parent educators. *Family Relations, 38*, 385–389.

McBride, B. A., and Rane, T. R. (1997). Role identity, role investments, and paternal involvement: Implications for parenting programs for men. *Early childhood Research Quarterly, 12*, 173–197.

McCluskey, K. A., Killarney, J., and Papini, D. R. (1983). Adolescent pregnancy and parenthood: Implications for development. In E. C. Callahan and K. A. McCluskey (Eds.), *Life-span developmental psychology: Non-normative life events.* New York: Academic.

McDermid, S. M., Huston, T., and McHale, S. (1990). Changes in marriage associated with the transition to parenthood: Individual differences as a function of sex-role attitudes and changes in the division of household labor. *Journal of Marriage and the Family, 52*, 475–486.

McHale, J. P., Lauretti, A., Talbot, J., and Pouquette, C. (2002). Retrospect and Prospect in the Psychological study of coparenting and family group process. In J. P. McHale and W. Grolnick (Eds.), *Retrospect and prospect in the psychological study of families.* (pp. 127–166). Mahwah, NJ: Lawrence Erlbaum Association.

McHale, S. M., Crouter, A. C., and Bartko, W. T. (1991). Traditional and egalitarian patterns of parental involvement: Antecedents, consequences and temporal rhythms. In R. Lerner and D. Featherman (Eds.), *Advances in life-span development,* (pp. 117–131) (Vol. 9). Hillsdale, NJ: Lawrence Erlbaum Associates.

McLanahan, S., and Sandefur, G. (1994). *Growing up with a single parent.* Cambridge, MA: Harvard University Press.

Meany, M. J., Stewart, J., and Beatty, W. W. (1985). Sex differences in social play: The socialization of sex roles. In J. S. Rosenblatt, C. Bear, C. W. Bushnell, and P. Slater (Eds.), *Advances in the study of behavior* (Vol. 15, pp. 1–58). New York: Academic.

Miller, D. R., and Swanson, G. E. (1958). *The changing American parent.* New York: Wiley.

Mize, J., and Pettit, G. S. (1997). Mothers social coaching, mother–child relationship style and children's peer competence: Is the medium the message? *Child Development, 68*, 312–332.

Montemayor, R. (1982). The relationship between parent–adolescent conflict and the amount of time adolescents spend alone with parents and peers. *Child Development, 53*, 1512–1519.

Montemayor, R., and Brownlee, J. (1987). Fathers, mothers and adolescents: Gender-based differences in parental roles during adolescence. *Journal of Youth and Adolescence, 16*, 281–291.

Mosley, J., and Thompson, E. (1995). Fathering behavior and child outcomes: The role of race and poverty. In W. Marsiglio (Ed.), *Fatherhood: Contemporary theory, research, and social policy* (pp. 148–165). Thousand Oaks, CA: Sage.

Mott, F. L. (1994). Sons, daughters and fathers' absence: Differentials in father-leaving probabilities and in home environments. *Journal of Family Issues, 5*, 97–128.

Mounts, N. S. (2000). Parental management of adolescent peer relationships: What are its effects on friend selection? In K. A. Kerns, J. M. Contreras, and A. M. Neal-Barnett (Eds.), *Family and peers: Linking two social worlds* (pp. 169–193). Westport, CT: Praeger.

Neville, B., and Parke, R. D. (1997). Waiting for paternity: Interpersonal and contextual implications of the timing of fatherhood. *Sex Roles, 37*, 45–59.

New, R., and Benigni, L. (1987). Italian fathers and infants: Cultural constraints on paternal behavior. In M. E. Lamb (Ed.), *The father role: Cross-cultural perspectives*. New York: Wiley.

NICHD Early Childcare Research Network. (2000). Fathers caregiving activities and sensitivity with young children. *Journal of Family Psychology, 14*, 200–219.

O'Connell, M. (1993). *Where's Papa? Father's role in child care*. Washington DC: Population Reference Bureau.

O'Neil, R. (1991, April). *Fathers' work experiences and well being: Implications for parenting and children's achievement*. Paper presented at the biennial meeting of the Society for Research in Child Development, Seattle, WA.

Osofsky, H., and Culp, R. (1989). Risk factors in the transition to fatherhood. In S. Cath, A. R. Gurwitt, and L. Gunsberg (Eds.), *Fathers and their families* (pp. 145–165). Hillsdale, NJ: Analytic Press.

Palkovitz, R. (1997). Reconstructing "involvement," Expanding conceptualizations of men's caring in contemporary families. In A. J. Hawkins and D. C. Dollahite (Eds.), *Generative fathering: Beyond deficit perspectives* (pp. 200–216). Thousand Oaks, CA: Sage.

Palkovitz, R., and Palm, G. (1998). Fatherhood and faith in formation: The developmental effects of fathering on religiosity, morals and values. *Journal of Men's Studies, 7*, 33–51.

Palm, G. F. (1997). Promoting generative fathering through parent and family education. In A. J. Hawkins and D. C. Dollahite (Eds.), *Generative fathering* (pp. 167–182). Thousand Oaks, CA: Sage.

Parcel, T. L., and Menaghan, E. G. (1994). *Parents' jobs and children's lives*. New York: Aldine de Gruyter.

Parke, R. D. (1978). Parent–infant interaction: Progress, paradigms and problems. In G. P. Sackett (Ed.), *Observing behavior: Vol. 1. Theory and applications in mental retardation*. Baltimore: University Park Press.

Parke, R. D. (1979). Perspectives of father–infant interaction. In J. Osofsky (Ed.), *A handbook of infant development* (pp. 549–590). New York: Wiley.

Parke, R. D. (1981). *Fathers*. Cambridge, MA: Harvard University Press.

Parke, R. D. (1988). Families in life-span perspective: A multilevel developmental approach. In E. M. Hetherington, R. M. Lerner, and M. Perlmutter (Eds.), *Child development in life-span perspective* (pp. 159–190). Hillsdale, NJ: Lawrence Erlbaum Associates.

Parke, R. D. (1990). In search of fathers: A narrative of an empirical journey. In I. E. Sigel and G. H. Brody (Eds.), *Methods of family research* (Vol. 1, pp. 153–188). Hillsdale, NJ: Lawrence Erlbaum Associates.

Parke, R. D. (1995). Fathers and families. In M. H. Bornstein (Ed.), *Handbook of parenting: Status and social conditions of parenting, Vol. 3* (pp. 27–63). Hillsdale, NJ: Lawrence Erlbaum Associates.

Parke, R. D. (1996). *Fatherhood*. Cambridge, MA: Harvard University Press.

Parke, R. D. (2000). Father involvement: A developmental psychological perspective. *Marriage and Family Review, 29*, 43–58.

Parke, R. D. (2002). Parenting in the new millennium: Prospects, promises and pitfalls. In J. P. McHale and W. S. Grolnick (Eds.), *Retrospect and prospect in the psychological study of families* (pp. 65–93). Mahwah, NJ: Lawrence Erlbaum Associates.

Parke, R. D., and Beitel, A. (1986). Hospital based interventions for fathers. In M. E. Lamb (Ed.), *Fatherhood: Applied perspectives* (pp. 293–323). New York: Wiley.

Parke, R. D., and Bhavnagri, N. (1989). Parents as managers of children's peer relationships. In D. Belle (Ed.), *Children's social networks and social supports* (pp. 241–259). New York: Wiley.

Parke, R. D., and Brott, A. (1999). *Throwaway dads*. Boston: Houghton-Mifflin.

Parke, R. D., and Buriel, R. (1998). Socialization in the family: Ecological and ethnic perspectives. In W. Damon (Ed.), *Handbook of child psychology*. New York: Wiley.

Parke, R. D., Burks, V. M. Carson, J., Neville, B., and Boyum, L. A. (1994). Family-peer relationships: A tripartite model. In R. D. Parke and S. G. Kellam (Eds.), *Exploring family relationships with other social contexts* (pp. 115–145). Hillsdale, NJ: Lawrence Erlbaum Associates.

Parke, R. D., Coltrane, S., Borthwick-Duffy, S., Powers, J., Adams, M., Fabricius, W., Braver, S., and Saenz, D. (in press). Measurement of father involvement in Mexican American families. In R. Day and M. E. Lamb (Eds.), *Assessing father involvement*. Mahwah, NJ: Lawrence Erlbaum Associates.

Parke, R. D., Hymel, S., Power, T. G., and Tinsley, B. R. (1980). Fathers and risk: A hospital-based model intervention. In D. B. Sawin, R. C. Hawkins, L. O. Walker, and J. H. Penticuff (Eds.), *Psychosocial risks in infant-environment transactions* (pp. 174–189). New York: Brunner/Mazel.

Parke, R. D., Killian, C., Dennis, J., Flyr, M., McDowell, D., Simpkins, S., Kim, M., and Wild, M. (in press). Managing the external environment: The parent and child as active agents in the system. In L. Kuczynski (Ed.), *Handbook of dynamics of parent–child relations*. Thousand Oaks, CA: Sage.

Parke, R. D., Kim, M., Flyr, M., McDowell, D. J., Simpkins, S. D., Killian, C. M., and Wild, M. (2001). Managing marital conflict: Links with children's peer relationships. In J. Grych and F. Fincham (Eds.). *Child development and interparental conflict* (pp. 291–314). New York: Cambridge University Press.

Parke, R. D., MacDonald, K., Beitel, A., and Bhavnagri, N. (1988). The inter-relationships among families, fathers and peers. In R. D. Peters (Ed.), *New approaches to family research* (pp. 17–44). New York: Brunner/Mazel.

Parke, R. D., and McDowell, D. J. (in press). Fatherhood. *International Encyclopedia of Marriage and Family Relationships*. New York: Macmillan.

Parke, R. D., McDowell, D. J., Kim, M., Killian, C., Dennis, J. Flyr, M. L., and Wild, M. (in press). Father–child relationships and children relationships with peers. In C. S. Tamis-LeMonda and N. Cabrera (Eds.), *Handbook of father involvement: Multidisciplinary perspectives*. Mahwah. NJ: Lawrence Erlbaum Associates.

Parke, R. D., and Neville, B. (1987). The male adolescent's role in adolescent pregnancy and childbearing. In S. L. Hofferth and C. Hayes (Eds.), *Risking the future* (pp. 145–173). Washington, DC: National Academy Press.

Parke, R. D., and Neville, B. (1995). Late-timed fatherhood: Determinants and consequences for children and families. In J. Shapiro, M. Diamond, and M. Greenberg (Eds.), *Becoming a father: Social, emotional and psychological perspectives* (pp. 104–116). New York: Springer.

Parke, R. D., and O'Leary, S. (1976). Family interaction in the newborn period: Some findings, some observations, and some unresolved issues. In K. Riegel and J. Meacham (Eds.), *The developing individual in a changing world: Vol. 2. Social and environmental issues* (pp. 653–663). The Hague, The Netherlands: Mouton.

Parke, R. D., and O'Neil, R. (2000). The influence of significant others on learning about relationships: From family to friends. In R. Mills and S. Duck (Eds.), *The developmental psychology of personal relationships* (pp. 15–47). London: Wiley.

Parke, R. D., Power, T. G., and Gottman, J. M. (1979). Conceptualization and quantifying influence patterns in the family triad. In M. E. Lamb, S. J. Suomi, and G. R. Stephenson (Eds.), *Social interaction analysis: Methodological issues* (pp. 231–253). Madison: University of Wisconsin Press.

Parke, R. D., and Sawin, D. B. (1975, April). *Infant characteristics and behavior as elicitors of maternal and paternal responsibility in the newborn period*. Paper presented at the biennial meeting of the Society for Research in Child Development, Denver, CD.

Parke, R. D., and Sawin, D. B. (1976). The father's role in infancy: A reevaluation. *The Family Coordinator* [Invited article for special issue on fatherhood], *25*, 365–371.

Parke, R. D., and Sawin, D. B. (1980). The family in early infancy: Social interactional and attitudinal analyses. In F. A. Pedersen (Ed.), *The father–infant relationship: Observational studies in the family setting*. New York: Praeger.

Parke, R. D., and Stearns, P. N. (1993). Fathers and child rearing. In G. H. Elder, J. Modell, and R. D. Parke (Eds.), *Children in time and place* (pp. 147–170). New York: Cambridge University Press.

Parke, R. D., and Suomi, S. J. (1981). Adult male–infant relationships: Human and nonhuman primate evidence. In K. Immelmann, G. Barlow, M. Main, and L. Petrinovich (Eds.), *Behavioral development: The Bielefeld interdisciplinary project* (pp. 700–725). New York: Cambridge University Press.

Parke, R. D., and Tinsley, B. R. (1984). Fatherhood: Historical and contemporary perspectives. In K. McCluskey and H. Reese (Eds.), *Life span development: Historical and generational effects* (pp. 203–248). New York: Academic.

Patterson, C. J. (1995). Lesbian and gay parenthood. In M. Bornstein (Ed.), *Handbook of Parenting: Vol. 3. Status and social conditions of parenting* (pp. 255–274). Mahwah, NJ: Lawrence Erlbaum Associates.

Patterson, C. J., and Chan, R. W. (1997). Gay fathers. In M. E. Lamb (Ed.), *The role of the father in child development* (3rd ed., pp. 245–260). New York: Wiley.

Paulson, R. J., and Sachs, J. (1999). *Rewinding your biological clock: Motherhood late in life: Options, issues, and emotions*. San Francisco: Freeman.

Pedersen, F. A. (1975, September). *Mother, father and infant as an interactive system*. Paper presented at the Annual Convention of the American Psychological Association, Chicago.

Pedersen, F. A., Anderson, B. J., and Cain, R. L., Jr. (1980). Parent–infant and husband–wife interactions observed at age five months. In F. A. Pedersen (Ed.), *The father–infant relationship*. New York: Praeger.

Pedersen, F. A., Zaslow, M. J., Cain, R. L., and Anderson, B. J. (1981). Caesarean childbirth: Psychological implications for mothers *and* fathers. *Infant Mental Health Journal, 2*, 257–263.

Perry-Jenkins, M., Repetti, R. L., and Crouter, A.C. (2000). Work and family in the 1990's. *Journal of Marriage and the Family, 62*, 981–998.

Phares, V. (1996). *Fathers and developmental psychopathology*. New York: Wiley.

Pleck, J. H. (1983). Husbands' paid work and family roles: Current research issues. In H. Z. Lopata and J. H. Pleck (Eds.), *Research on the interview of social roles: Vol 3. Families and jobs*. Greenwich, CT: JAI.

Pleck, J. H. (1985). *Working wives, working husbands*. Beverly Hills, CA: Sage.

Pleck, J. H. (1997). Paternal involvement: Levels, sources and consequences. In M. E. Lamb (Ed.), *The role of the father in child development* (3rd ed., pp. 66–103). New York: Wiley.

Pomerleau, A., Balduc, D., Malcuit, G., and Cossotte, L. (1990). Pink or blue: Environmental gender stereotypes in the first two years of life. *Sex Roles, 22*, 359–367.

Power, T. G., and Parke, R. D. (1982). Play as a context for early learning: Lab and home analyses. In I. E. Sigel and L. M. Laosa (Eds.), *The family as a learning environment* (pp. 147–178). New York: Plenum.

Presser, H. B. (1994). Employment schedules among dual-earner spouses and the division of household labor by gender. *American Sociological Review, 59*, 321–332.

Radin, N. (1982). Primary caregiver and role sharing fathers. In M. E. Lamb (Ed.), *Nontraditional families* (pp. 173–204). Hillsdale, NJ: Lawrence Erlbaum Associates.

Radin, N. (1988). Primary caregiving fathers of long duration. In P. Bronstein and C. P. Cowan (Eds.), *Fatherhood-today* (pp.127–143). New York: Wiley.

Radin, N. (1993). Primary caregiving fathers in intact families. In A. Gottfried and A. Gottfried (Eds.), *Redefining families* (pp. 11–54). New York: Plenum.

Radin, N., and Sagi, A. (1982). Childrearing fathers in intact families in Israel and the U.S.A. *Merrill-Palmer Quarterly, 28*, 111–136.

Rane, T. R., and McBride, B. A. (2000). Identity theory as a guide to understanding fathers' involvement with their children. *Journal of Family Issues, 21*, 347–366.

Rappaport, R., Rappaport, R. N., and Strelitz, Z. (1977). *Fathers, mothers and society*. New York: Basic Books.

Rangarajan A., and Gleason, P. (1998). Young unwed fathers of AFDC children: Do they provide support? *Demography, 35*, 175–186.

Reiss, D. (1981). *The family's construction of reality*. Cambridge, MA: Harvard University Press.

Repetti, R. L. (1989). Effects of daily workload on subsequent behavior during marital interaction: The roles of social withdrawal and spouse support. *Journal of Personality and Social Psychology, 57*, 651–659.

Repetti, R. L. (1994). Short-term and long-term processes linking job stressors to father–child interaction. *Social Development, 3*, 1–15.

Rheingold, H. L., and Cook, K. V. (1975). The content of boys and girls rooms as an index of parent behavior. *Child Development, 46*, 459–463.

Richards, M. P. M., Dunn, J. F., and Antonis, B. (1977). Caretaking in the first year of life: The role of fathers' and mothers' social isolation. *Child: Care, Health and Development, 3*, 23–26.

Robinson, J. (1988). Who's doing the housework? *American Demographics, 10*, 24–28.

Robinson, J. P., and Godbey, G. (1997). *Time for life: The surprising ways Americans use their time*. University Park, PA: Pennsylvania State University Press.

Rodman, H., and Safilios-Rothschild, C. (1983). Weak links in men's worker–earner roles: A descriptive model. In H. Z. Lopata and J. H. Pleck (Eds.), *Research in the interweave of social roles: Vol. 3. Jobs and families* (pp. 239–250). Greenwich, CT: JAI.

Rohner, R. P. (1998). Father love and child development: History and current evidence. *Current Directions in Psychological Science, 1*, 157–161.

Roopnarine, J. L., and Carter, D. B. (Eds.). (1992). *Parent-child socialization in diverse cultures*. Norwood, NJ: Ablex.

Roopnarine, J. C., Hooper, F. H., Ahmeduzzaman, M., and Pollock, B. (1993). Gentle play partners: Mother–child, father–child play in New Delhi, India. In K. MacDonald (Ed.), *Parent–child play* (pp. 287–304). Albany: State University of New York Press.

Rose, H. A., and Halverson, C. F. (1996). A transactional model of differential self-socialization of parenting. Unpublished manuscript, University of Georgia, Athens, GA.

Rosenblatt, J. S. (1969). The development of maternal responsiveness in the rat. *American Journal of Orthopsychiatry, 39*, 39–56.

Rosenblatt, J. (1995). Hormonal basis of parenting in mammals. In M. Bornstein (Ed.), *Handbook of parenting: Vol. 2. Biology and ecology of parenting* (pp. 3–25). Mahwah, NJ: Lawrence Erlbaum Associates.

Rotundo, E. A. (1985). American fatherhood: A historical perspective. *American Behavioral Scientist, 29*, 7–25.

Rotundo, E. A. (1993). *American manhood*. New York: Basic Books.

Russell, A., and Russell, G. (1989). Warmth in mother–child and father–child relationships in middle childhood. *British Journal of Developmental Psychology, 7*, 219–235.

Russell, G. (1983). *The changing role of fathers*. St. Lucia, Australia: Queensland University Press.

Russell, G. (1986). Primary caretaking and role-sharing fathers. In M. E. Lamb (Ed.), *The father's role: Applied perspectives* (pp. 29–57). New York: Wiley.

Russell, G., and Russell, A. (1987). Mother–child and father–child relationships in middle childhood. *Child Development, 58*, 1573–1585.

Rutter, M. (1987). Psychosocial resilience and protective mechanisms. *American Journal of Orthopsychiatry, 51*, 316–331.

Sagi, A. (1982). Antecedents and consequences of various degrees of paternal involvement in childrearing: The Israeli project. In M. E. Lamb (Ed.), *Nontraditional families: Parenting and child development* (pp. 205–232). Hillsdale, NJ: Lawrence Erlbaum Associates.

Sagi, A., Koren, N., and Weinberg, M. (1987). Fathers in Israel. In M. E. Lamb (Ed.), *The father's role: Cross-cultural perspectives* (pp. 197–226). Hillsdale, NJ: Lawrence Erlbaum Associates.

Sagi, A., Lamb, M. E., Shoham, R., Dvir, R., and Lewkowicz, K. S. (1985). Parent–infant interaction in families on Israeli kibbutzim. *International Journal of Behavioral Development, 8*, 273–284.

Sameroff, A. J. (1994). Developmental systems and family functioning. In R. D. Parke and S. G. Kellam (Eds.), *Exploring family relationships with other social contexts* (pp. 199–214). Hillsdale, NJ: Lawrence Erlbaum Associates.

Schaffer, H. R. (1984). *The child's entry into a social world*. New York: Academic.

Sears, R. R., Maccoby, E. E., and Levin, H. (1957). *Patterns of childrearing*. Evanston, IL: Row, Peterson.

Seltzer, J. (1994). Consequences of marital dissolution for children. *Annual Review of Sociology, 20*, 235–266.

Shelton, B. A. (1992). *Women, men and time: Gender differences in paid work, housework and leisure*. New York: Greenwood.

Silverstein, L. B., and Auerbach, C. F. (1999). Deconstructing the essential father. *American Psychologist, 54*, 397–407.

Smith, P. K., and Daglish, L. (1977). Sex differences in parent and infant behavior in the home. *Child Development, 48*, 1250–1254.

Snarey, J. (1993). *How fathers care for the next generation.* Cambridge, MA: Harvard University Press.

Stearns, P. (1991). Fatherhood in historical perspective: The role of social change. In F. W. Bozett and S. M. H. Hanson (Eds.), *Fatherhood and families in cultural context* (pp. 28–52). New York: Springer.

Stern, D. N. (1977). *The first relationship.* Cambridge, MA: Harvard University Press.

Storey, A. E., Walsh, C. J., Quinton, R. L., and Wynne-Edwards, K. E. (2000). Hormonal correlates of paternal responsiveness in new and expectant fathers. *Evolution and Human Behavior, 21*, 79–95.

Sun, L. C., and Roopnarine, J. L. (1996). Mother-infant, father-infant interaction and involvement in childcare and household labor among Taiwanese familiar. *Infant Behaviour and Development, 19*, 121–129.

Tinsley, B. J., and Parke, R. D. (1984). The contemporary impact of the extended family on the nuclear family: Grandparents as support and socialization agents. In M. Lewis (Ed.), *Beyond the dyad* (pp. 161–194). New York: Plenum.

Tinsley, B. J., and Parke, R. D. (1988). The role of grandfathers in the context of the family. In P. Bronstein and C. P. Cowan (Eds.), *Fatherhood today* (pp. 236–250). New York: Wiley.

Toth, J. E., and Xu, X. (1999). Ethnic and cultural diversity in father's involvement: A racial/ethnic comparison of African American, Hispanic and White fathers. *Youth and Society, 31*, 76–79.

Valliant, G. (1977). *Adaptation to life.* Boston: Little, Brown.

Volling, B. L., and Belsky, J. (1991). Multiple determinants of father involvement during infancy in dual-earner and single-earner families. *Journal of Marriage and the Family, 53*, 461–474.

Wachs, T. (2000). *Necessary but not sufficient.* Washington DC: American Psychological Association.

Walker, K., and Woods, M. (1976). *Time use: A measure of household production of family goods and services.* Washington, DC: American Home Economics Association.

Whitbeck, L. B., Simons, R. L., Conger, R. D., Wickrama, K. A. S., Ackley, K. A., and Elder, G. H., Jr. (1997). The effects of parents' working conditions and family economic hardship on parenting behaviors and children's self-efficacy. *Social Psychology Quarterly, 60*, 291–303.

White, B. L., Kaban, B., Shapiro, B., and Attonucci, J. (1976). Competence and experience. In I. C. Užgiris and F. Weizmann (Eds.), *The structuring of experience* (pp. 115–152). New York: Plenum.

Whiting, B. B., Edwards, C. P., Ember, C. R., and Erchak, G. M. (1988). *Children of different worlds: The formation of social behavior.* Cambridge, MA: Harvard University Press.

Whiting, B., and Whiting, J. (1975). *Children of six cultures.* Cambridge, MA: Harvard University Press.

Williams, E., and Radin, N. (1992, May). *Predictors of adolescent achievement and expectations: An 11 year follow-up.* Paper presented at a meeting of the American Orthopsychiatric Association, New York.

Williams, E., Radin, N., and Allegro, T. (1992). Highly involved fathers' children: An 11 year follow-up focused on sex-role attitudes. *Merrill–Palmer Quarterly, 38*, 457–476.

Wilson, M. (1986) The Black extended family : An analytic consideration. *Developmental Psychology, 22*, 246–258.

Yarrow, A. L. (1991). *Latecomers: Children of parents over 35.* New York: Free Press.

Yeung, W. J., Sandberg, J. F., Davis-Kean, P. E., and Hofferth, S. L. (2001). Children's time with fathers in intact families *Journal of Marriage and the Family, 63*, 136–154

Zaslow, M., Pedersen, F., Suwalsky, J., Rabinovich, B., and Cain, R. (1985, April). *Fathering during the infancy period: The implications of the mother's employment role.* Paper presented at the meeting of the Society for Research in Child Development, Toronto.

Zelazo, P. R., Kotelchuck, M., Barber, L., and David, J. (1977, March). *Fathers and sons: An experimental facilitation of attachment behaviors.* Paper presented at the biennial meeting of the Society for Research in Child Development, New Orleans, LA.

3

Coparenting in Diverse
Family Systems

James McHale
Inna Khazan
Clark University
Pauline Erera
University of Washington
Tamir Rotman
Wendy DeCourcey
Melanie McConnell
Clark University

When a four-year-old is taller than her mother, maybe she is sitting on the shoulders of her father.

—Minuchin and Fishman (1981, p. 148)

INTRODUCTION

The majority of children throughout the world grow up in family systems in which there is more than one significant parenting figure guiding the child's socialization. Until recently, however, most empirical research investigating family socialization climates did not fully embrace this reality. Virtually all of psychology's guiding theories of child development depict such development as unfolding within the context of dyadic parent–child relationship systems. During the 1980s, important progress was made by developmental scientists in contextualizing such dyadic relationships within nuclear two-parent families; intensive focus was given to understanding how marital relationships affect children both directly (e.g., through direct exposure to marital violence or destructive marital conflict) and indirectly (by compromising or intensifying dyadic parent–child relationships). However, continuing on through the mid-1990s, still missing from this breaking wave of "family systems" research were studies that focused on the full family group as a unit. Over the past several years, that circumstance has begun to change. Yet to fully capture the diversity of today's families we need to acknowledge that the parenting figures in the full family group may include step-parents, grandparents, aunts or other extended family members, previous (ex-) spouses, and same-sex partners.

Anyone who has ever grown up with more than one parenting figure can describe ways in which the dynamics of their relationships with each of these people individually are transformed when their family is considered as a full interacting group. One defining feature of family units containing two or more adult parenting figures is the nature of the coparenting dynamic coconstructed by members of the unit's "executive subsystem" (Minuchin, 1974). Effectively functioning coparenting units are those in which the significant adult figures collaborate to provide a family context that communicates to children solidarity and support between parenting figures, a consistent and predictable set of rules and standards (regardless of whether the child lives in a single household or in multiple ones), and a safe and secure home base (McHale, Lauretti, Talbot, and Pouquette, 2002). Although intensive empirical research on coparenting in families is less than a decade old, empirical findings to date have substantiated the critical function that coordination between parenting figures can play.

Unfortunately, most of what we know about coparenting to date is based on research with heterosexual, married, European American or European, two-parent families. However, a good deal of family research, although not professing to study coparenting coordination per se, nonetheless provides helpful insights into the nature of interadult coparenting dynamics within families. Our modest goal in this chapter is to provide a broad overview of recent theory and research pertaining to the coordination between adult parenting figures from which future work might proceed. An adequate grounding already exists to help facilitate rapid expansion of this field of study by researchers concerned with establishing the generalizability and limits of the principles discussed in this chapter.

Our review of the coparenting field begins with a brief discussion of families in historical context, followed by a more recent history that traces the roots of contemporary coparenting research. We then outline central conceptual issues in current thinking about coparenting and summarize the essential tenets of structural family theory. This is followed by a review of coparenting research, emphasizing issues such as insider and outsider views of coparental and family dynamics and linkages between coparental functioning and child adjustment. We then provide a section on practical issues in coparenting that should be of interest to both scientists and professionals working with families, and close with a section summarizing future directions in coparenting theory and research. Among the topics we consider in this concluding section are limits of the coparenting construct, and applicability of current thinking about coparenting to diverse family systems and to the coparenting of multiple children in the same family.

In the next section, we provide a historical perspective on family group dynamics and trace the roots of present-day interest in coparenting dynamics within families.

HISTORICAL CONSIDERATIONS IN COPARENTING

Which Lens—The History of Coparenting Research or the History of Families?

Although the origins of current thinking about coparenting dynamics can be most clearly traced to shifts in the activities of fathers prompted by the Women's Movement in the United States some 30 years ago, many precursors to present-day notions about coparenting were evident in the writings of family clinicians as early as the 1950s. Some of the topics of concern to these early family clinicians, including contentiousness between wives and husbands in their marriage and disinterest in the family by one of the parenting figures—usually fathers—remain areas of intensive inquiry by researchers at the turn of the new millennium. This said, however, the more differentiated focus on roles that adults play as coparents—each person possessing her or his own unique ideas about how to rear children, unique methods for affecting those desired outcomes, and unique propensities for consulting and coordinating with the coparenting partner to afford children consistent rules and standards—is quite new. The first empirically based research reports on coparenting were published in the late 1970s, but these early studies focused almost exclusively on postdivorce coparenting relationships, including cooperation and antagonism between parents (Ahrons, 1981; Hetherington, Cox, and Cox, 1982). It was not until the mid-1990s that intensive empirical studies involving multisource data on coparenting coordination in families that had not undergone the divorce process began to appear (Belsky, Crnic, and Gable, 1995; McHale, 1995).

But what lens should we take in reviewing the history of coparenting relationships? There is the circumscribed history of active coparental engagement ushered in by the Women's Movement, and then there is the history of family dynamics across societies and time. In our view, one of the most important advances in socialization research in recent years has been a growing appreciation by psychologists for the importance of context—sociocultural, subcultural, and historical. Increasingly, we are recognizing that many of the most elemental, basic tenets in social science are in fact quite context specific.

At the same time, the temptation remains in science to ferret out basic underlying, guiding principles—if not laws—possessing universal (and even evolutionary) applicability. Apropos to this chapter on coparenting relationships, perhaps the most fundamental of all these "elemental" tenets in family research has been the often unspoken assumption that children's biological mothers are nature's natural and intended parents (see Corter and Fleming, 1995; Holmes, 1995). The predominant view has been that the roles and the responsibilities of other adult figures in the family (in psychology's central theories, these "other figures" have most often been defined as the child's biological father) are principally those of supporting player or assistant. The contributions of family assistants can come in myriad forms—providing for the mother's and children's sustenance but having little to do with children's essential upbringing; holding a circumscribed, albeit critical, family role such as that of child disciplinarian; assisting with basic childcare duties to spell mothers as they reach the ends of their ropes; or assuming a more proactive and egalitarian (although at least in the case of fathers, seldom fully "coequal") family role as caregiver and nurturer.

Given this elemental assumption about mothers, it may come as a surprise to learn that the "mother-at-hub/others auxiliary" family adaptation does not appear to have characterized many of the earliest human societies (McHale, Lauretti et al., 2001). According to the anthropologist Harrell (1997), in many early societies children were viewed as the responsibility of the entire group or "band," looked after by and maintaining emotional attachments to multiple others. Only when competition between growing numbers of different hunting, gathering, and foraging bands threatened the availability of subsistence resources did humans adapt by settling down in one area and cultivating land (the "sedentarization transformation"). It was at this point in human history that families underwent a fundamental reorganization in how they divided essential functions (procuring, processing, socializing children, and providing emotional support). One common adaptation pursuant to the establishment of family "homesteads" in some parts of the world was for one set of individuals to tend processing activities in the domestic sphere while others tended procurement activities and became more active in family expansion and political maneuverings. In most, although not all, societies, this breakdown occurred along gender lines, with women assuming the domestic and caregiving roles.

Even so, adaptations by families diverged markedly as a function of geographical locale and resource availability (Harrell, 1997). In resource-limited areas (such as certain oceanic nations), myriad adaptations, including adopting children out, were used to ensure ample resources for all members of the populace. Strategies and adaptations on the African continent, where land was wide open and subsistence resources were more plentiful, took a different turn, with large and extended family compounds emerging as a much more valuable commodity for attending ever-widening land claims. Thus the breakdown of family roles by gender (captured succinctly by Ehrensaft's, 1997, observation that "men do parenting, but women are parents") may not have been the state of affairs at the beginning of human history.

Moreover, the moment we move beyond the mother–father–child "primary triangle" (Fivaz-Depeursinge and Corboz-Warnery, 1999) to describe child socialization within extended family systems, we are faced with a very different set of circumstances concerning skills, resources, and roles. Family systems involving the child's biological parents and extended family members on one or both sides of the family have usually been the norm rather than the exception throughout human history (Bateson, 2000). One advantage of the extended family not shared by isolated single-parent (Weinraub, Horvath, and Gringlas, in Vol. 3 of this *Handbook*) or nuclear families is the vast repository of knowledge about childrearing afforded by others in the kin network. Indeed, in a long historical view, it might be argued that societal circumstances at one time favored grandparents (Smith and Drew, in Vol. 3 of this *Handbook*) rather than parents to serve as primary parenting figures for young children once the children had been weaned. Particularly in hunting and foraging societies, but in more recent family forms as well, group fitness may have been best served by an organization in which the grandparents drew on their greater accumulated wisdom to acculturate children while younger parents, possessing superior agility and stamina, focused on procurement. The proposition that grandparents may be better adapted to care for young children would undoubtedly be a very unpopular one in early twenty-first century North America, in which legislation has been advanced to protect "primary" rights of biological parents (especially mothers), and legal actions prohibiting grandparents from seeking claim to regular time with grandchildren in postdivorce family environments have increased in number (Azar, 2002; McHale, Lauretti et al., 2002).

Our point here is that researchers pondering the unique significance of coparenting coordination in families need first to appreciate that the very broad definition that has guided coparenting research to date—the coordination and support provided by adults rearing children together—is also likely to be the only one that could possibly have cross-historical and cross-cultural applicability. It is certainly true that, from the time of the Industrial Revolution, millions of Western children found themselves being reared in nuclear families by their biological mothers and fathers, apart from the regular presence of extended kin (Farrell, 1999). Even so, children across the globe continued to grow up in extended family systems. Moreover, at the turn of this new millenium, staggering numbers of the world's children are being reared in dual family systems by their biological parents and one or more stepparents (Erera, 2002; Hetherington and Stanley-Hagan, in Vol. 3 of this *Handbook*), by foster parents (Erera, 1997; Haugaard and Hazan, in Vol. 1 of this *Handbook*), by gay or straight adoptive parents (Brodzinsky and Pinderhughes, in Vol. 1 of this *Handbook*; Patterson, in Vol. 3 of this *Handbook*), by grandparents parenting alone or together with one or both biological parents—as well as by aunts, uncles, fictive kin, and in many, many other adaptive family systems (Erera, 2002; Minuchin, 2002).

From this vantage, the role of the child's biological mother (or father) as coparenting figure in such diverse family systems undoubtedly varies as a function of cultural mores and local adaptations. For example, although there has been a growing movement toward "Western" nuclear family systems (two-parent domiciles without extended family dwellers, greater father involvement in the day-to-day lives of children) in many urban areas of Pacific Rim countries, in rural areas of these same countries extended kin rather than fathers retain the greatest supportive role in both basic caregiving and acculturation activities (Belanger, 2000; Hirschman and Vu, 1996; Ho, 1986). Fathers' family roles are certainly not insignificant in many rural-dwelling families; men procure the family's subsistence resources, hold symbolic roles as family figurehead, and frequently take on responsibilities of family disciplinarian and teacher. Nonetheless, many Asian scholars advise that the relatively circumscribed nature of fathers' cultural socialization roles in the Asian family can be expected to result in far less variability in enacted family process than would be found in North American or European families (Chao and Tseng, in Vol. 4 of this *Handbook*; Ho, 1986). To the extent that this is so, fathers' active engagement in coparenting or disputes with mothers around childrearing themes would not be particularly salient concerns for most traditional Asian families. Dissonance between mothers and other family caregiving figures may be important, but only insofar as mothers insist on preferences and strategies that diverge markedly from those of cocaregiving adults.

As we close this brief consideration of coparenting in historical context, one other important consideration warrants mention. Most of what we currently know about coparenting alliances within families is owed to studies of nuclear families headed by a husband/father and a wife/mother. Perhaps the most predominant theme guiding family research efforts during the 1980s and 1990s was the notion that strain or distance in marital relationships compromises parenting efforts (Belsky, 1984;

Erel and Burman, 1995; Wilson and Gottman, in Vol. 4 of this *Handbook*). One variant on this theme, borrowing from Minuchin's observations (see next subsection), was that parents in distressed marital relationships often look to their children for the intimacy and closeness they cannot find in the marriage; such co-opting of children into adultlike relationships can create cross-generational coalitions that tip the family's power hierarchy and place children in confusing and potentially untenable circumstances (Christensen and Margolin, 1988; Kerig, 1995; Lindahl, Clements, and Markman, 1998; Sroufe, and others, 1985; Vuchinich, Emery, and Cassidy, 1988).

Clearly, this line of inquiry has pertinence for thinking about coparenting dynamics, as we outline later in this chapter. However, the view of marriage relationships as providing intimacy and emotional sustenance is a relatively new one. As outlined by Farrell (1999), throughout history and across different cultures, marriages have most frequently been unions of functional partnership, with most mothers indeed looking to their children for the closeness and intimacy not afforded by the marital partnership. Hence present-day notions of parent–child coalitions or alliances as problematic or as placing children at developmental risk—both widely accepted tenets in contemporary family theory and research—are actually historically specific ones. Without historical family analysis, we run the risk of overlooking how rooted in place and time many of our core assumptions about families actually turn out to be.

Tracing the Roots of Coparenting Research Within the Current Historical Context

Having reviewed some of the problems with taking time-limited views of the family and its interior dynamics, we acknowledge that ultimately the work of parents, educators, and professional helpers must indeed be carried out in a particular place and historical time. Therefore, in this subsection, we localize in historical time the particulars of how and why coparenting research emerged when it did. It is probably fair to say that empirical studies of coparenting were ushered onto the family map by two primary developments in the United States during the late twentieth century. As previously mentioned, the first was the Women's Movement, during which a society—perhaps it is most accurate to say, large factions of a society—questioned the prevailing ethos that the "intended" place of women was as the center of hearth and home and that men's primary importance to families was in providing resources. The qualification "large factions of a society" refers not only to the resistance that the Women's Movement received from the society's standing male-dominated power structure, but also to the split between women who embraced the Women's Movement and championed many of its advances and women who did not join with champions of the Women's Movement for philosophical reasons or who were left behind for other reasons. These critical subcultural issues (to which we return) notwithstanding, the Women's Movement not only called for women's finding success outside the home, but for men's finding success in the home as more involved partners in the rearing and caregiving of children.

The second historical development triggering a look at joint parenting was the staggering rise in the divorce rate in the United States at century's end. Of course, families have had to cope with separations for centuries—during historical epochs such as World War II and its aftermath, millions of fragmented families reconstituted in all types of functional configurations in Israel (Lavee and Katz, 2001). For many years, Jewish families and children found ways to adapt until coordinated reunion efforts could begin. During the years of slavery in the United States, African American families likewise had family members precipitously removed from their core but maintained a core of consanguineous kin relationships that continues through today. These are examples of family adaptation to forced separation. Widespread, elected family dissolution in the United States during the late twentieth century was a very different phenomenon. With more and more of the nation's children spending time being parented in two different households, and with preliminary investigations conducted during the 1970s and 1980s documenting significant adjustment difficulties for many children of divorce, postdivorce parenting coordination rapidly became an issue of central importance. Indeed, much of our current thinking about successful parenting coordination in nuclear families owes, ironically, to early studies of families in which the two parenting partners were not husband and wife at all. This distinction, between "marriages" and "coparenting relationships," is still a current area of controversy for at least some family researchers.

CENTRAL ISSUES IN COPARENTING

Psychology's central developmental theories—from Freud and his proteges at the twentieth century's and field's beginnings through Bowlby, Ainsworth, and attachment theory at century's end—have always viewed mother as the family's central figure and other family figures as auxiliary. This bias continues, despite the flurry of research documenting important and meaningful contributions for fathers in children's lives (Parke, in Vol. 3 of this *Handbook*). Perhaps this is because, in the overwhelming majority of mammalian species and in most cultures, children's biological mothers are indeed the ones ultimately charged by society with infant survival. We think this needs to be asserted at the outset to set the stage for our ensuing discussion, although clearly, family patterns can and do vary considerably both within and across cultures. Indeed, diversity in family socialization environments has been apparent from the earliest societies right on up through contemporary societies.

Be this as it may, the guiding conceptualization of family scholars in describing contemporary family situations has usually been that the alternative parenting figures were "standing in" for or augmenting the role of the child's biological mother. Perhaps the clearest illustration of the "biological mother is parent" principle is embedded in current research and thinking about maternal "gatekeeping." The term gatekeeping refers to a mother's monitoring and even titrating of her partner's involvement with her young child (DeLuccie, 1995; Jordan, 1995). Although cultures exist in which men assume principal responsibilities for socializing their sons from a very early age, we are aware of no cultural groups in which fathers are assigned the "power" to determine whether or not mothers will be afforded psychological access to their infants and young children. In lesbian-headed families following divorce, however, the biological father (the ex-husband) can deny the lesbian mother (his ex-wife) custody and visitation.

We belabor these points not to reify the notion of maternal primacy or to diminish the clear-cut evidence that there are and have always been myriad functional family forms. Rather, we think it important that readers be clear that the "co" in coparenting (which we have defined as the degree of collaboration and support between adults rearing children together) does not imply that these multiple coparenting figures—whoever they may be—share equally the roles of nurturer or principal attachment figure. Were this the metric, few families across the globe would approach a coequal nurturer standard. Although such coequal status may have beneficial outcomes (Baruch and Barnett, 1986; Radin and Russell, 1983; Schwartz, 1994), we do not believe it is a necessary component for well-functioning coparental units. Rather, we believe there to be many routes families can take to coconstruct an effective coparenting alliance that communicates to children solidarity between parenting figures, consistent and predictable rules and standards, and a safe and secure home base.

This said, to date, coparenting theory and research have focused in a more limited way on a small set of essential themes that organize intrafamily dynamics in nuclear family systems. Among these are the presence or absence of antagonism between the coparenting partners, the relative degree of balance (versus skew) in engagement and participation with children by the parenting partners, and the overall levels of cohesion and affective connection observed among family members (Belsky et al., 1995; Johnson, Cowan, and Cowan, 1999; Katz and Gottman, 1996; Lindahl and Malik, 1999; McHale, 1995). These coparenting and family dynamics, which can be reliably measured in two-parent families with small children, correlate with and predict young middle-socioeconomic North American children's adaptation in a diverse set of social and behavioral domains. However, their applicability in families beyond the two-parent nuclear structure is as yet unknown. Indeed, it is quite unlikely that a single set of guiding principles will operate across myriad diverse family forms.

As we discuss central conceptual issues, we address an issue that is turning out to be somewhat controversial in certain family research circles. When taking a narrow view of the coparental relationship as a relationship that crystallizes only in nuclear families in which there is a marriage and a pair of parent–child relationships, one reasonable question that surfaces is whether there is a need to hypothesize a distinctive role in families for coparental coordination at all. During the 1980s, beginning with the research studies of Cummings and colleagues (summarized in Cummings and Davies, 1994) and on through the 1990s, led by the theory and research efforts of Grych and Fincham (1990; Grych and Fincham, 2001; Grych, in Vol. 4 of this *Handbook*), the field established unequivocally that it was not just husband–wife marital violence but also high-intensity, destructive, and unresolved verbal conflict in the marriage (as distinguished from low intensity, constructive, and resolved conflict) that had particularly adverse effects on children's development. Destructive marital conflict frightened children and often led to clinically significant problems with depression or anxiety, modeled ineffective problem-solving approaches that were sometimes adopted in one form or another by the children themselves, and gave rise to biased information-processing styles that the children, in turn, visited on other social relationships outside the family. Given the overwhelming and pervasive impact that marital conflict appears to have on children's thinking, emotions, and behavior, it is probably not surprising that some scholars have been left wondering whether interadult coordination in parenting provides any meaningful additional insights into family functioning. Indeed, many marital researchers have not differentiated between marital conflict and coparenting relationships at all, implying either that the latter is but another area of dispute that the marital partners can be expected to dispense with in their prototypical problem-solving styles or ignoring coparenting dynamics altogether in their looks at two-parent families.

Several essential conceptual points lead into coparenting theory. First, viewing coparenting dynamics simply as a subset of marital relationships overlooks the fact that a great many coparenting partners are not married. The adults who coordinate in rearing children are often a mother and her own or her husband's extended family members; once married but now divorced, or never-married biological parents across different households; biological parents and nonblood fictive kin in any number of functional family relationships, and so forth. Second, even within two-parent nuclear families, there are not always direct correspondences between how marital and coparenting relationships are worked out in the family. Indeed, there is evidence that a common marital *quid pro quo*—in which parents commiserate that fathers' greater financial power and influence in non-child-related family matters will be balanced by greater maternal influence in child-related matters—may be further exaggerated in families in which one partner is particularly domineering in the working through of marital disputes. Among nonclinically referred middle-socioeconomic community families, when one parent (usually, although not always, the father) dominates in dispensing with marital disputes, closing off progress toward resolution through dismissing or blocking strategies, the other parent (typically, although not always, the mother) is more likely to hold a position of greater authorship in contacts with infant children (McHale, 1995). Cross-contextual coherence between marital and coparenting domains is apparent, but the power dynamics active in the marital relationship are not replicated, but rather counterbalanced, by the dynamics of the coparental relationship. Moreover, there is at least some limited evidence that unrest in the marriage may affect coparenting dynamics differently, depending on the child's gender. Coparenting dynamics in maritally distressed families are characterized more often by distance and disconnection if the child is a girl but hostile engagement and contentiousness when the child is a boy (Ablow, 1997; McHale, 1995).

Finally, allowing for the possibility that marital and coparenting relationships are related but at least partially distinct family domains in two-parent families permits clinicians and researchers to pose questions such as "What is going on in families in which parents are able to afford a warm, supportive, civil, and consistent family environment to their children even in the face of severe marital distress? and "Can we bottle this?" To be sure, couples who are able to manage engaged, cohesive coparental efforts in the context of a deteriorating marriage are probably the exception rather than the rule. However, to the extent that such families do exist, it may be possible to learn from them so as to promote coordinated parenting efforts in other families even when marriages cannot be salvaged.

We suspect that researchers will indeed uncover consistencies between problem-solving styles called on by intimate partners in handling major family conflicts, whether these conflicts be about coparenting children or about topics unrelated to the children. It may even turn out (e.g., El-Sheikh, Cummings, and Goetsch, 1989; Gerra et al., 1993; Gottman and Katz, 1989; Wilson and Gottman, in Vol. 4 of this *Handbook*) that interadult conflict on any level that is regularly argued out in front of young children fundamentally affects the children's physiological regulation and resulting defensive strategies (such as closing off or preemptively engaging in aggression). If conflict is conflict is conflict (Margolin, 1988), then the more subtle strains introduced by a disconnected coparenting partner, a pair or set of parenting figures who expect different things from the children, or an otherwise consistent set of parenting figures who derive no joy from the parenting enterprise will probably have a significant impact only in families in which pervasive destructive marital conflict is absent. This is an empirical question, of course, but one that will be laid to rest only once coparenting researchers and marital conflict researchers engage one another's work.

One last issue is worthy of comment here. As we outline in the next section, the conceptual underpinnings of coparenting theory owe largely to the work of Salvador Minuchin, founder of structural family theory and therapy. Perhaps because Minuchin's emphasis was on disturbances in children and families owing to coparental alliances that were not functioning adequately, most studies of coparenting in the child development literature have likewise focused on coparental relationships that are not working well. Although evidence is mounting that there are detrimental effects of coparental antagonism or nonsupport on child and parent adjustment in community families, often overlooked are the positive, health-promoting effects of well-functioning coparental alliances. Warm, supportive relations appear to be particularly important for children's social adjustment outside the family (Brody and Flor, 1996; Lindahl and Malik, 1999; McHale, Johnson and Sinclair, 1999), and support between mothers and fathers around childrearing challenges and dilemmas have the potential to strengthen and enhance the parenting practices of each individual parent (Ehrensaft, 1990; Floyd, Gilliom and Costigan, 1998; Jordan, 1995; Margolin, 2001; McBride and Rane, 1998). Additional conceptual and empirical contributions in the area of coparenting solidarity will strengthen considerably this burgeoning area of study.

THEORY IN COPARENTING

Consistent, predictable, contingent responsiveness is at the heart of most theories of effective parenting of infants and of small children. A logical corollary, then, is that parenting figures who are on the same page and who work in concert are in a better position to afford a stable, consistent, and predictable environment for children than are parents working at cross purposes. Consistency need not mean that the coparents embrace the same styles of playing and caregiving or that they spend like amounts of time administering to children. People are different, plain and simple, and when the family's key parenting adults include at least one male and one female figure, stylistic differences in ways of playing with and talking to children are often especially apparent (Lamb, 1995; Palm and Palkovitz, 1988; but see Silverstein, 2002, for a discussion of how such stylistic differences may not simply be gender tied). Rather, the operative element of consistency we refer to here as the centerpiece of effective coparenting efforts likely requires but a handful of basic accomplishments: agreement about basic elements of effective care and about preferred (culturally condoned) strategies for acculturating children; experiencing affirmation and support from the parenting partner for contributions made to child and family; trust that partners will carry through with agreed on acculturation strategies during their own dealings with children in a manner that children will find logically consistent; and of course, actual adherence to these agreed-on family "rules" during dealings with children both in, and especially outside of, the partner's presence. Such accomplishments are not easily achieved because parenting figures in many families possess at least somewhat dissonant ideas about how they would ideally wish to acculturate their children. But the essential notion is that children growing up in families that afford greater consistency will have an easier time divining and internalizing rules of comportment, achieving effective self-regulation, progressing apace through stages of moral development, and coming to perceive a stable and trustworthy interadult alliance in the family, than will children from families in which the coparents are less consistent.

The most well-articulated conceptual approach pertinent to current thinking about coparenting dynamics was offered by Minuchin (1974; Minuchin, Rosman, and Baker, 1978). Minuchin's structural family theory affords central roles to the importance of supportive relationships between adult caregiving figures in the "parental holon" (Minuchin and Fishman, 1981) or "executive subsystem" (Minuchin, 1974); to the maintenance of clear hierarchies between generations (including an absence of cross-generational coalitions and alliances); and to the importance of proximity, contact, and affiliation among family members (Jones and Lindblad-Goldberg, 2001). Although Minuchin never used the term coparenting in disseminating his work, the essence of the coparenting construct is clearly evident throughout his writings. Minuchin stressed the importance of hierarchy in the family, that is, an unequal distribution of power and authority across generations such that adult parenting figures possess more authority than do children. His clinical work with diverse family groupings emphasized that, regardless of whether the family's executive subsystem involves one or multiple adults, clear lines of parental authority and power in the family are essential (Minuchin, 1974; Minuchin, Rosman, and Baker, 1978).

Embedded in Minuchin's conceptualizations of families are the seeds of present-day thinking about how North American children and youth find themselves traveling down worrisome pathways. For example, in discussing multigenerational families in which a certain member emerges as a "symptom bearer" for the family (that is, as the person within the family unit who is identified as the "one" manifesting some form of maladjustment), Minuchin and Fishman (1981, p. 53) posited that "cross-generational coalitions may be scapegoating one family member or rendering certain holons dysfunctional." Minuchin's definition of coparental authority in such families is a properly flexible one; he described, for example, how a mother and grandmother living in the same household may cooperate in an organization with differentiated functions and expertise. It is only when the two parenting adults end up battling for a position of primacy in the family, and in so doing coopt the child into their struggle for ascendance, that the adaptive lines of adult authority crumble. Minuchin and colleagues (e.g., Minuchin and Fishman, 1981; Minuchin, Montalvo, Guerney, Rosman, and Schumer, 1967) also described "disorganized extended families," in which adults function in a disengaged or "centrifugal" fashion. A key organizing metaphor used by many family theorists contrasts centripetal emotionally "binding" and enmeshed families with "centrifugal," disconnected, or expelling ones (Walsh, 1993). According to Minuchin, it is in these latter families who often struggle under conditions of poverty and other burdens that many executive functions, including attentive childrearing, fall by the wayside or remain underdefined. Without an effectively monitoring executive parental subsystem, children often end up exiting the family before they are developmentally or emotionally prepared to do so. As a consequence, many fall prey to a variety of different societal risks such as drug and alcohol abuse, early pregnancy, gang membership and criminality, homelessness, various forms of victimization, and suicide.

Clearly the essential components of Minuchin's conceptualization stress cooperation, communication, and coordination between parenting adults, clear and agreed-on standards for children, and a clear demarcation of power in the family with the adults in charge and on the same page. Contemporary structural family theory (e.g., Jones and Lindblad-Goldberg, 2001) embellishes Minuchin's seminal work by integrating more extensively affective components of family commerce. Many of the metaphors in the writings of Minuchin and other structural family theorists have been those of "battles" with children—confrontation, winning and losing, shows of unity and force. To parents of willful toddlers or rebelling adolescents, such metaphors undoubtedly hit close to home. It is equally important, however, not to short schrift the importance of closeness, attachment, and emotion in the family. For example, the clinical concept of "scapegoating" (Vogel and Bell, 1960) derives from the premise that some parents react to an emotional rift between themselves by collaboratively diverting attention from their own growing emotional split onto a relatively safe scapegoat, chosen from among their children (Novak and van der Veen, 1970). Working on the same page and in tandem, the adults can collude to minimize their own emotional distress by localizing their concerns onto a vulnerable target. Whether or not this disturbing family dynamic, initially documented in clinically referred families, is also a commonplace "normal" family process (Walsh, 1993), it does serve to illustrate that, beyond hierarchy and coordination, affect and emotion must be more fully taken into account as essential features of the family's coparental dynamic (Gottman, Katz, and Hooven, 1997; Jones and Lindblad-Goldberg, 2002). Clear rules, limits, and sanctions without closeness and connection can be as damaging—if not more damaging—to children than inept organization, inadequate structure, and lax or inconsistent rule setting and enforcement (Kerig, 1995).

CLASSICAL AND MODERN RESEARCH IN COPARENTING

The first wave of coparenting research began to appear in the early 1980s, with the results of longitudinal investigations documenting how divorce affected the adjustment of cohorts of children in the 1970s. A major overarching theme of these reports was that children whose parents manifested an actively contentious postdivorce relationship fared very poorly (e.g., Emery, 1982; Hetherington et al., 1982; Wallerstein, 1984). Among the noxious dynamics documented were triangulation of the child into interadult conflicts, placing children in a position of having to choose sides by dividing their loyalties, and maintaining very different sets of standards for children across the two postdivorce parental households—all dynamics observed and reported by Minuchin and others working with families clinically (e.g., Satir, 1967). Another deleterious factor was the disparagement of children's parents, one by the other (Buchanan, Maccoby, and Dornbusch, 1991). In families marked by a confluence of these divisive relationship dynamics, children displayed difficulties managing their own conduct and, in some studies, manifested higher than would be expected symptoms of anxiety and depression (Buchanan et al., 1991; Camara and Resnick, 1989; Emery, 1982; Hetherington et al., 1982; Wallerstein, 1984; Whiteside and Becker, 2000).

Within a few years' time, a handful of researchers had begun looking for similar relationship dynamics within families in which parents had not moved toward divorce. One of the first studies of this population (Block, Block, and Morrison, 1981) used self-reported differences between parents on a parenting ideology index as a proxy for coparental disagreement. Findings from this study revealed that preschool-age children from families in which larger discrepancies existed between mother and father parenting beliefs exhibited more behavior problems than did children whose parents were in greater accord. These findings were replicated in 1989 by Deal, Halverson, and Wampler, who also used an index of childrearing disagreement, and in 1991 by Jouriles, Murphy, Farris, and Smith, who used a self-report estimate of the number of weekly child-related disputes as the index of coparental disagreement. Floyd and Zmich (1991), also using a self-report index, documented a similar relationship between the degree of support versus undermining of their partner in their parental role and the frequency of child behavior problems. Each of these studies was carried out in the broad shadow of Cummings' research on how children are affected by marital conflict (for a comprehensive review of this program of work see Cummings and Davies, 1994). Although there had been some speculations (e.g., Grych and Fincham, 1990) that children may be particularly adversely affected by child-related conflict (e.g., interparental disputes about discipline, peer relationships, dependence–independence, moral values, safety, self-defense, and so on), the paper by Jouriles et al. (1991) was important in providing clear empirical evidence that, beyond general marital conflict or distress, conflicts around the coparenting of children may be uniquely disruptive for the child and perhaps also more proximally linked to child adjustment difficulties than is general marital conflict or distress (see also Bearss and Eyberg, 1998; Snyder et al., 1988).

Also during the 1980s, a second thread pertaining to coparenting relationships in families was pursued in studies of the division of labor in two-parent middle-socioeconomic families. Several investigators, studying couples' adaptation across the transition to new parenthood (Belsky, Spanier, and Rovine, 1983; Belsky and Rovine, 1990; Cowan and Cowan, 1992; Levy-Shiff, 1994; Lewis, Owen, and Cox, 1988), documented declines in marital satisfaction following the birth of the baby. In fact, a report by Shapiro, Gottman, and Carrere (2000) puts the proportion of new mothers showing this decline at two thirds. One of the key correlates of these widespread declines in marital dissatisfaction during the transition to parenthood turned out to be maternal dissatisfaction with "who does what" childcare and housework (Crouter, Perry-Jenkins, Huston, and McHale, 1987; Deutsch, Lussier, and Servis, 1993). Following the baby's arrival, couples actually became more, rather than less, "traditional" in how they divided family work, with women shouldering the overwhelming majority of the domestic work duties (Aldous, Mulligan, and Bjarnason, 1998; Cowan and Cowan, 1988; Lamb, 1995) and men intensifying their work roles. Moreover, the greater the discrepancy between what women had expected would materialize during their pregnancies and what actually materialized once the baby was born, the greater was their dissatisfaction with the marriage (Cowan, Cowan, Heming, and Miller, 1991). Curiously, this linkage ran in different directions for "traditional" and feminist mothers. Whereas women who held more egalitarian views of the roles of men and women at work and in the home expressed the most dissatisfaction when men did less than they had expected, women with more traditional views of male–female roles were actually most dissatisfied when their partners did more than they had anticipated prenatally (Hackel and Ruble, 1992). This finding demands that we take into account men's and women's views of parental, coparenting, and family roles as determinants of the evolving coparental alliance (Lauretti and McHale, 2001).

Despite the simultaneous emergence of these two strands of research related to coparenting dynamics within families, it has never been fully clear whether linkages exist between parents' dissatisfaction with the division of family labor and the family's enacted coparenting process. In many traditional cultures, fathers do next to nothing in contributing to routine daily household or childcare work but are an important and active developmental force in their children's lives. In North America, many fathers in both single- and dual-earner families neglect to take on the work of routine care duties with their infants but at the same time remain strongly committed to child and family and spend regular and meaningful blocks of time engaging playfully with their infant children (Parke, 1996, in Vol. 3 of this *Handbook*). An empirical question for the field is whether the coparenting process is compromised in families in which mothers are dissatisfied with the division of labor in the family but in which fathers are nonetheless actively involved in their babies' lives as play partners. Does unhappiness with inequities in "who does what" eventually culminate in antagonism in the parenting of the child as she or he ages? Or are these two facets of coparenting relationships relatively independent? Preliminary work by Carleton, Rotman, and McHale (2000, 2001) suggests that, at 3 months postpartum, parents' dissatisfaction with the division of labor does not yet appear to show connections with negativity in the enacted coparenting process (see also Ehrenberg, Gearing-Small et al., 2001). More work in this area is clearly needed.

Up through the mid-1990s, most of what we knew about linkages between coparental disagreement and child behavior problems stemmed from studies in which self-report methodologies were used. Certainly, obtaining "insider" views of the family process is a critical enterprise in studies of coparenting. Still, as late as 1995, observationally based studies of the family group process remained quite rare, with most estimates of coparenting focusing either on discrepancies in self-reported parenting beliefs (Block et al., 1981) or on perceptions of the coparenting alliance including self-reported experiences of dissatisfaction (Cowan and Cowan, 1992) or support (Abidin and Brunner, 1995; Frank, Olmstead, Wagner, Laub et al. 1991), or self-reported estimates of coparenting contacts and conflicts (Ahrons, 1981; Jouriles et al., 1991). A few investigations of family group dynamics had appeared (e.g., Christensen and Margolin, 1988; Lewis et al., 1988; Russell and Russell, 1994; Sroufe, 1991), but the dearth of studies that used observations of the full family group to obtain data on coparental collaboration and coordination was perplexing to many clinically oriented researchers. Scientists knowledgeable about family theory and therapy recognized the unique power of whole family observation in revealing important underlying family themes (Byng-Hall, 1995), and the writings of Minuchin and others strongly suggested that one prominent theme for socialization researchers should be whether coparenting partners work collaboratively to maintain appropriate intergenerational boundaries and hierarchical authority in their families or, alternatively, whether they work at cross purposes in their parenting roles.

Observational Studies of Coparenting and Family Relationships

With this question in mind, two independent laboratories pursued observationally based studies of coparenting coordination within a family group process (Belsky et al., 1995; McHale, 1995). Both investigations established that problems with coparenting (including not only lack of support, but also active undermining of one parent by the other) were indeed more commonplace in families in which partners were struggling in their marriages. Belsky's study also indicated that coparenting solidarity was adversely affected when parents were deluged by high levels of daily hassles, and McHale's investigation suggested that child gender may be an important moderator of marital–coparenting linkages.[1] Findings substantiating the marital–coparenting link were soon reported by other investigators (Floyd et al., 1998; Frosch, Mangelsdorf, and McHale, 1998; Katz and Gottman, 1996; Kitzmann, 2000).

McHale (1997) also drew attention to the fact that coparenting solidarity involves far more than just the day-to-day rhythms of the enacted coparenting and family group process. Support parents offer to one another in disciplining a child, for example, is quickly undermined when one of the parents repairs the disciplinary act in private with the child. Indeed, what happens during alone, one-on-one time with the child may be as or more important in establishing a sense of coparental alliance and authority for the child as what happens when the partners are parenting together. Parents can use such time to either strengthen and support the child's sense of the integrity of the coparenting alliance, or deconstruct and undermine that sense of integrity. For example, during alone time with the child, a parent may disparage their partner to the child or convey that all disciplinary encounters are at the whim of the other parent, implicitly or explicitly suggesting to the child that the absent parent does not have the child's best interests at heart as clearly as the present parent. Ultimately, parents may have very different interactive styles, roles with the children, and intensities of respond-ing, but the most critical factor according to current thinking about coparenting is that the child receive consistent messages across parents and settings about the integrity of the family's executive subsystem. Without such a bedrock, the child may not only be at risk for problems with adjustment (see below) but may also fail to derive the necessary sense of "family-level" security (Cummings and Davies, 1996; Kerig, 2001; McHale, 1997).

Coparenting and Child Adjustment

The first studies tying observed coparenting antagonism and distress to child adjustment problems showed, as had earlier self-report studies, that the facet of child adjustment most reliably linked to coparenting conflict was externalizing-spectrum behavior problems. In a report by Belsky, Putnam, and Crnic (1996), children whose parents had exhibited more active undermining of one another's parenting during home-based observations child when the children were 2 years old showed higher levels of disinhibition at the age of 3 years than would have been predicted on the basis of their age 2

---

[1] At different points in this chapter, we refer to mediator and moderator effects. Our use of these terms mirrors that of Baron and Kenny (1986). When a variable, such as infant gender, moderates the relationship between two other variables, such as marital distress and coparenting conflict, this means that the relationship between the two variables differs as a function of the specific level or value of the moderator variable. By contrast, when a variable mediates the relationship between two other variables, it serves as the intermediary link through which the first variable has its effects on the third. That is, coparenting conflict may be the mediator through which marital distress has its effects on child adjustment.

temperament scores. McHale and Rasmussen (1998), following families for an even longer period of time, found that hostility and competitiveness in coparenting during the children's infancy (8 to 11 months) foreshadowed higher preschool teacher ratings of child aggression when children were 4 years of age. These findings were also mirrored in a rigorous small-N study by Fivaz-Depeursinge, Frascarolo, and Corboz-Warnery (1996). These researchers reported that all children in their sample whose family group dynamics during the infancy period (age 9 months) had been judged as reflecting "collusive alliances" (in which each parent intruded on and interfered with the other's interactions with the baby) manifested clinically significant symptomatology as rated by clinicians by the time the children were 4 years of age.

Furthermore, in a study that spanned a full preschool year, McHale, Johnson, and Sinclair (1999) found that $4^{1}/_{2}$-year-old children who came from families characterized by low levels of mutuality and support in coparenting were more likely than their classmates to show difficulties in social adjustment on the preschool playground. Following the naturally occurring peer interactions of a full preschool cohort for 4 months, McHale and colleagues discovered that children whose parents showed little warm contact with, support of, or validation of one another during joint teaching and play interactions with their child showed fewer positive and more negative (aggressive, withdrawn) activities over the 4-month observation period than did their classmates. The researchers also discovered that these links between coparenting and child difficulties were mediated by what they termed "children's representations of family." Boys who came from families showing coparenting distress (particularly absence of connection as unified parenting partners) and who projected aggression into a series of stories they narrated about families while using a set of doll figures as props showed the highest levels of playground aggression; boys from families showing these signs of coparenting distress but who revealed more benign family representations were not as aggressive. In a like manner, links between coparenting distress and isolated, withdrawn preschool behavior were themselves mediated by boys' discomfort during puppet stories querying the child about family anger. Boys from families showing coparenting distress who also exhibited discomfort with themes of family anger in the puppet task were among the most withdrawn in the cohort; boys from families exhibiting similar signs of coparenting distress but who were less upset by anger in the puppet family were not as withdrawn. McHale and colleagues argued that children are active processors of their family process, and that the interpretations they place on their family circumstances help to account for pathways between observed family dynamics and child outcomes. Moreover, data from this study highlighted the fact that young children are aware not only of active and overt coparenting conflict, but also of more subtle signs of disconnection and distance between adults in their coparenting roles. Similar linkages between low levels of family cohesiveness and behavior problems by young children from those families have also been reported by Lindahl and Malik (1999) and by Johnson, Cowan, and Cowan (1999).

Most studies of coparenting–child linkages have been conducted with families of children aged 0 to 5 years. However, studies linking coparenting conduct to maladjustment in school-age children have been reported by McConnell and Kerig (in press) and by Brody and colleagues (e.g. Brody and Flor, 1996; Brody, Flor, and Neubaum, 1998; Brody, Stoneman, Smith, and Gibson, 1999), who have studied both coparental and cocaregiving conflict and support in rural African American families with preadolescent youth. Brody's program of work has substantiated the importance of both fathers and extended family members in contributing to children's self-regulatory capacities. He and his colleagues also found that parents' perceptions of caregiving support received from extended family members may not be as relevant as perceived caregiving conflict in predicting measures of child adjustment (Brody et al., 1999). The work of McConnell and Kerig (in press) reveals clear linkages between observed coparental conflict in the families of latency-age children and concurrent externalizing symptomatology demonstrated by the youth. In one of the few studies to look specifically at interparental consistency during adolescence, Fletcher, Steinberg and Selters (1999) suggest that a unified front is important only insofar as the stance presented is an authoritative one. If parents agree but are permissive, neglectful, as authoritarian, adolescent outcomes are not as positive as when at least one adult maintains an authoritative posture.

The organizing theme being pursued in most ongoing research is that poor coordination, active undermining and disparagement, lack of cooperation and warmth, and disconnection by one parenting partner—either alone or in combination with overinvolvement by the other—are all conditions that place children at developmental risk in their families. By contrast, coparental solidarity, cooperation and warmth show clear ties to children's prosocial behavior and peer competence. An auxilliary point of special interest is that studies that have examined the incremental contribution of coparenting process in predicting child developmental outcomes have typically found the relationship between coparenting and child adjustment to remain significant even after taking into account parent–child relationship quality and general marital distress. In other words, after the deleterious effects of insecure attachments, insensitive parenting, low parental well-being, or marital distress are accounted for, it is helpful to have information about the quality of the family's coparenting process to determine which children will struggle with adjustment difficulties and which will not (McHale, Kuersten, and Lauretti, 1996).

Undoubtedly, in many families in which parent–child or marital relationships are strained, the coparental alliance can come to serve either an ameliorating or exacerbating function. Likewise, in many families in which there are no particularly damaging parent–child or marital difficulties, antagonism in the coparenting realm can breed trouble for the child and family. Research is making good headway on identifying predictors of the quality of coparental alliances themselves (McHale and Fivaz-Depeursinge, 1999), but lacks a comprehensive, multifaceted family model to guide predictions about when coparenting dynamics might be expected to make a major difference in affecting children's development and when they would probably be of relatively little import compared with other family factors. We also lack well-defined theories predicting why it is that some children from families showing coparental contentiousness develop externalizing-spectrum symptoms, whereas others develop internalizing behavior problems. Some earlier mechanisms proposed, such as the disruption of emotional security (Davies and Cummings, 1994), modeling of antagonistic problem-solving approaches (Emery, 1982), and blockage of the child's ability to rely on the family as a coping resource (Tolan and Gorman-Smith, 1997) are not themselves particularly helpful in explaining how and why children migrate toward one form of adjustment difficulties rather than another. Furthermore, studies examining the impact of interadult conflict on child adjustment have repeatedly drawn attention to the potential moderating role of child gender (e.g., Kerig, Fedorowicz, Brown, Patenaude, and Warren, 1998).

Other factors operating within the child, such as a temperamental predisposition toward approach or avoidance of stimulation, and factors operating within the child's parents, such as personal capacities for restraint (low impulsivity, high self-control or ego resilience) or depressive symptomatology, have also been suggested as key moderating variables that alter pathways between coparental distress and child behavior problems (McHale, Talbot, Lauretti, Pouquette, and Zaslavsky, 2000). For example, McHale, Talbot et al. (2000) hypothesized that boys who are exposed to pervasive coparenting conflict between their mothers and fathers may be at greater risk for problems with disinhibition if the father figure is impulsive and surgent, but for problems with action and initiative if the father figure is depressed or ineffective. However, because few empirical data are available to substantiate these notions, much work remains for researchers in empirically testing these intriguing possibilities. As McHale and Fivaz-Depeursinge (1999) have outlined, coparenting dynamics are initially shaped by personal qualities and attributes of key parenting figures and their personal relationship predating the arrival of the children, but they are also altered by qualities of the individual child or children themselves (see also Van Egeren, 2000).

We emphasize also that comprehensive family models will need to account more adequately for the complex multivariate nature of relationship influences (such as coparental and parenting or attachment relationships affecting one another in circular fashion through time; see Minuchin, 2001). For example, coparental difficulties (such as one parent' s disparagement of the other parenting figure to the child) have the potential to disrupt the quality of children's specific attachment relationships (e.g., Frosch, Mangelsdorf and McHale, 2000; Greenberg, Speltz, and DeKlyen, 1993).

However, preliminary data show few linear, one-to-one associations between toddler attachment security and coparental and family group process (McHale, Lauretti, and Kuersten-Hogan, 1999; McHale, Lauretti, and Talbot, 1998), suggesting the possibility that secure attachments with one or both parents could potentially buffer children from disruptive coparenting influences and that adequate and supportive coparental relationships could buffer children from the potentially deleterious effects of an insecure attachment.

Another critical factor not adequately accounted for in most coparenting studies to date is the likelihood that coparenting dynamics can be expected to change over time with normative and non-normative child and family change. To date, our models of coparenting trajectories have been more linear than developmental, although we know from Kreppner's (1988) study of family changes following the birth of a second child that family reorganizations are the rule rather than the exception. Furthermore, the evidence is good that there are bidirectional and reciprocal effects between marital and coparental relationships. Prebirth marital distress may set the stage for difficulties in establishing a respectful and well-coordinated coparental alliance (Lewis et al., 1988; Lindahl et al., 1998; McHale and Fivaz-Depeursinge, 1999), but there is also emerging evidence that the quality of the coparental alliance may likewise affect the quality of the marital relationship over time (Belsky and Hsieh, 1998; Hetherington et al., 1999). And at base, central to most conceptualizations guiding studies of coparenting is the notion that coparental dynamics must be taken into account in studies of socialization because such dynamics both mediate the effects of marital distress on child adjustment (Cohen and Weissman, 1984; Gable, Belsky, and Crnic, 1992; McHale and Rasmussen, 1998) and mediate the impact of marital distress on, and perhaps even alter the trajectory of, individual parenting practices over time (Floyd, Gilliom and Costigan, 1998; Margolin, 2001; McBride and Rane, 1998). We emphasize once more that none of the important conceptual advances needed in coparenting research will proceed with the necessary pace in the years ahead unless family researchers take pains to distinguish coparental dynamics within the family from marital conflict and adjustment, or from the well-known dyadic parenting influences of children's caregivers typically studied when the caregivers are engaged with the child alone. Research also needs to be conducted with a diversity of family configurations (step-families, grandparent–headed families, adoptive families), ethnicities, and social status groups in order to be relevant to families in the 21st century.

PRACTICAL INFORMATION ABOUT COPARENTING

Despite the newness of coparenting research, it is already becoming clear that the most important story likely to come from this field of inquiry will concern its practical implications for children and families. However, controlled clinical studies substantiating the potential value of focused coparenting interventions have yet to be completed. Hence the tenor of this section is necessarily more one of promise than of proof. Still, we see many implications of work to date (see McHale, Fivaz-Depeursinge, and Corboz-Warnery, 2000), and several of these are summarized below.

First, early signs of miscoordination in the coparenting alliance observed as early as 3 or 4 months postpartum can be anticipated by information specifically relevant to family "triads" gathered during the third trimester of the mother's first pregnancy (Lauretti and McHale, 2001). For example, in one prospective study of parents expecting their first baby, Fivaz-Depeursinge, Frascarolo, Corboz-Warnery, Carneiro, and Montfort (2000) asked the imminent coparenting partners to play-enact their first encounter with the infant by using a life-sized doll and negotiating the first three stages of Fivaz-Depeursinge and Corboz-Warnery's, Lausanne triadic play paradigm (LTP), in which (1) one partner engages en face with the infant while the second attends, (2) the partners switch roles, and then (3) the two partners and infant engage in a "three-together" en face interaction. The researchers documented not only striking diversity in parents' emotional responsiveness to this prebirth enactment, but also statistically significant relationships between the degree of connectedness between the adults during the prebirth family scenario and subsequent coordination among the partners in the actual triad at 4 months postpartum.

In related work, von Klitzing, Simoni, and Burgin (1999) studied interview-based indicators of expectant parents' "triadic capacities," which they defined as the interviewees' spontaneous (unsolicited) propensities to portray the postbirth family unit as a threesome rather than dwelling principally on the self–infant unit. They found that their triadic capacity index showed prospective linkages with the actual quality of triadic interaction in the LTP at 4 months postpartum. These findings are given additional poignance in light of Fivaz-Depeursinge and Corboz-Warnery's (1999) finding that the quality of triadic coordination, or, in the researchers' parlance, the family alliance type, shows striking stability from these early postpartum months through the end of the child's first year. Although the definitive longitudinal studies have yet to be completed, the systematic ties between coparental and family-related cognitions and behaviors during the latter stages of pregnancy and subsequent coparental and family process during the early postpartum months suggest that there may be value in studying professionals' prebaby contacts with families centered around fostering coordination and cooperation in future coparental partnerships (Talbot, Pouquette, and McHale, 1999).

Second, as studies replicate and refine prior findings on the possibilities of forecasting coparental alliances from earlier information about the parenting partners as individuals and as a couple, it is going to be important for researchers and practitioners to be aware of prototypical trajectories of coparental alliances through time. Normatively, it appears that there is more disorganization in family alliances during the early postpartum months than there is either in pregnancy or at 1 year postpartum. The prospective study by Fivaz-Depeursinge et al. (2000) charting coparental relationships from the prebirth LTP variant previously described through the end of the family's first year together documented a U-shaped curve wherein coordination declined from pregnancy through 3 months postpartum, but rebounded again by 12 months postpartum. Elsewhere, we have speculated that another major period of disequilibrium for the family may be provoked by the separation–individuation issues arising during the child's move into toddlerhood (McHale and Fivaz-Depeursinge, 1999). Here, when many fathers begin to parent children more actively than they did during infancy and when the key parenting issues shift from dependency to limit setting, a new coparenting organization comes to be required of the family, and hence there may be temporary disruptions in the functioning of the coparental alliance. Knowing typical periods of developmental stability and reorganization in the coparental and family system will be critical for tailoring interventions to meet families where they are. Subsequent research could contribute to this enterprise by charting individual family growth trajectories; for even if the quadratic function we have proposed does accurately portray coparenting change from pregnancy through the "terrible twos" at a group level, different families will show different coparenting trajectories over time (some steadily deteriorating, others strengthening rather than showing temporary disorganization during the toddler years, and so on). An important pursuit for subsequent research studies will be not just in defining such individual growth curves, but also in determining whether different courses can be forecast from information available about the family's interpersonal relationships and belief structure before the child's arrival on the scene (Lauretti and McHale, 2001; Van Egeren, 2000).

Third, families can be expected to struggle in forging a workable coparental alliance during the early stages of family formation, but as Fivaz-Depeursinge and Corboz-Warnery (1999) documented, there is also striking stability in triadic family patterns from 3 months postpartum forward. These researchers focused on the quality of the enacted family process in the standardized LTP assessment. Of interest were qualities of the family process akin to those outlined earlier—interference and miscoordination, withdrawal and disengagement by one partner, low levels of affective matching and connection. Although there were a few families studied by Fivaz-Depeursinge and Corboz-Warnery at 3 months postpartum who shifted their core interpersonal dynamics over subsequent assessment periods in a meaningful fashion, the overwhelming majority of families in their sample remained through the child's first year true to the core underlying relational themes seen first at 3 months postpartum. These data suggest that, for professionals concerned with strengthening coparental alliances or curbing interparental antagonism, it may never be too early to intervene. Indeed, in the absence of change efforts, coparenting and family distress as early as the first year places children at risk for later adjustment difficulties during the toddler and the preschool years (Belsky et al., 1996; Fivaz-Depeursinge and Corboz-Warnery, 1999; Frosch, Mangelsdorf, and McHale, 2000; McHale and Rasmussen, 1998).

Fourth, from an interventionist's standpoint, the strong and reciprocal linkage that has been demonstrated between the quality of marital and coparental relationships in many investigations suggests that there may be positive benefits for enhancing the coparental alliance by intervening directly with the marital subsystem. At the same time, the fact that indicators of the coparental and family alliance may be more closely connected to child behavior problems than marital adaptation (Bearss and Eyberg, 1998; Jouriles et al., 1991; McHale and Rasmussen, 1998) and the fact that coparenting interactions, rather than marital relationships, are the more proximal context for child development suggest that the coparental and family alliance may be a more useful place to begin when intervening with families of young children. Longstanding marital dynamics may be more intractible than the coparenting process, and distressed couples otherwise reticent to enter into marital counseling may be more willing to engage clinically around issues that concern the health and well-being of their children. In the ideal, enduring systemic change would be expected to be greatest in circumstances in which interventions successfully targeted positive change in both marital and coparental subsystems. This is an empirical question calling out for focused research efforts.

Fifth, although strengthening marital relationships may have beneficial carryover effects in the coparental domain, intervening with dyadic parent–child subsystems may not have the same effect. Research to date has revealed a fair degree of conceptual independence between parenting and co-parenting systems. Parents who bicker as coparenting partners, who witness a family group dynamic in which one partner draws away while the other intensifies involvement with the child, or who show low levels of positive affective connection in the family group are not necessarily more rigid, harsh, negativistic, or insensitive with children when parenting alone; indeed, trying to estimate the family group dynamic solely on the basis of information about each parent–child dyad individually is some-times an impossible task, as empirical data reported by McHale, Kuersten, Lauretti, and Rasmussen (2000) illustrate. At the same time, conceptual independence is not absolute. For example, McHale, Lauretti et al. (2002) showed that cohesive family group dynamics (whether child or parent centered) are more commonplace in families in which fathers show high levels of warmth and whimsy during dyadic (one-on-one) play with their toddler-age children. Nonetheless, because several studies have shown that coparental dynamics continue to explain unique variance in child outcome measures even after the effects of parenting behavior have been taken into consideration (Belsky et al., 1996; McHale, Johnson, and Sinclair, 1999), interventionists should be aware that working separately with one or both parent–child dyads without bringing the family in together may not meaningfully alter the coparental or family group process.

A sixth related point is that triadic and family group assessments should not be reified as a "holy grail" in work with families or be expected to substitute for well-founded, dyadic parent–child assess-ments. Indeed, the investigation by McHale, Kuersten et al. (2000), showing that assessing dyadic relationships separately provides a completely different picture of the family than does assessing the family as a group, indicates that it would be just as shortsighted to neglect parent–child dyads in clinical assessments as it would be to neglect coparenting and family group dynamics. There are no shortcuts, and responsible clinical evaluations need to involve both parent–child and whole family assessments. For example, the study by Lauretti and McHale (1997) of parenting behavior in dyadic and family group contexts showed that in families in which the couple is experiencing marital problems, both mothers' and fathers' parenting behavior showed a more pronounced shift as the parent moved from the dyadic to the triadic context than did the behavior of parents in families in which the couple is not martially distressed. More specifically, mothers in the study by Lauretti and McHale who were in distressed couple relationships were judged to be less sensitive when parenting their toddler-age children in their husband's presence (relative to when they were parenting the children alone), whereas mothers in nondistressed marriages were much more consistent in the levels of sensitivity they showed between dyadic and whole family settings. Maritally distressed fathers showed a much more precipitous decline in involvement with their toddlers when they moved from parenting in the dyad to parenting in the family setting than did fathers in nondistressed marriages. Hence the very consistency and predictability of parental behavior is more likely to be compromised across parenting settings when the marital relationship is in trouble. This critical finding would have been missed had parenting behavior been examined only in dyadic or only in whole family contexts.

The seventh and final point is that marital conflict researchers (e.g., Cummings, Davies, and Simpson, 1994; Grych, 1998; Grych and Fincham, 1993; Kerig et al., 1998; Grych, Seid and Fincham, 1992) have used children's reports of marital conflict with substantial success, and data linking parent- and child-generated perceptions of coparenting and family relationships to observed family process indicate that both parents and children appear to be good observers of such family dynamics (McHale Johnson, and Sinclair, 1999; McHale, Neugebauer, Asch, and Schwartz, 1999). Such knowledge is not usually utilized in clinical contacts with families, but it could and should be. Parents' capability of reporting on their own coparenting-related behavior suggests some cognizance of what they are doing and can be capitalized on not only for screening purposes but also as a tool in working with the family to affect coparenting change. Furthermore, the ability of young children, as early as at the ages of $2^1/_2$ to 3 years, to communicate through play their perceptions of family group process is quite striking (McHale, Neugebauer, Asch, and Schwartz, 1999). In many cases, such child reports can be used effectively as a tool in providing feedback to parents about how children have come to view the family process (McHale, McConnell, Lauretti, and Neugebauer, 2002).

FUTURE DIRECTIONS IN COPARENTING THEORY AND RESEARCH

What Are the Limits of the Coparenting Construct?

The work described thus far has sensitized socialization researchers to look beyond parent–child and marital relationships to ask what happens in families in which adults undermine one another's parenting, in which one parent disengages from the executive parenting subsystem, or in which there is little joy or life within an otherwise adequately functioning coparental and family system. We have suggested that in many families in which there is little volatile marital conflict or no major disruptions in attachment, the presence or absence of divisive or disconnected coparenting dynamics may be an important prognosticator of which children will experience strain and struggle. Still, we are left with the following question: Does miscoordination between parenting adults explain a clinically significant proportion of the variance in child outcomes in families other than the middle-socioeconomic nuclear families about which we know the most? Is coordination between parenting figures a less important factor in families in which one or more of these key parenting persons is not the child's biological parent—or a more important one? Answers to these questions lie on the frontier of coparenting research; below, we summarize some of what we know to date.

Applicability to extended or multigenerational families.   Minuchin himself was among the first to alert us to the deleterious role that conflict about childrearing issues between parents and actively involved grandparents can have in children's lives. This theme also appears in the work of several other researchers, including those of Apfel and Seitz (1996, 1999), Chase-Lansdale and Brooks-Gunn (1994), Brody et al. (1998, 1999), and Brody and Flor (1996). Moreover, Brody's work suggests that African American youths who come from families in which there is significant disagreement about the children between mothers and grandmothers experience the same types of problems with behavioral regulation as do youths in families in which the antagonism is between the child's biological parents (Brody et al., 1998). Clearly, when children are being actively parented by two involved adults and the adults are at odds about house rules and what is best for the children, this has the potential to cause confusion for the children and to heighten the risk for children's acting out when the standards for comportment are not clear or reliably enforced. We have had a tendency in the socialization literature to look at consistency as a within-parent variable but it now seems clear that consistency may be as or more important between parenting figures.

Before prematurely concluding that coparental coordination is just as relevant in extended or multigenerational families as it is in nuclear families, it is important to examine key differences in such family systems. One major difference between multigenerational and nuclear family systems lies in the degree of knowledge about childrearing possessed by the cocaregiving partners from the outset. In outlining the "building blocks" of the emerging coparenting and triadic family process in two-parent nuclear families following the transition to parenthood, McHale and Fivaz-Depeursinge (1999) highlighted how mothers do not necessarily start out as more adept parents than fathers. Generally, neither parent feels adequately prepared for their new parenting role, and there are many fits and starts along the way as both individuals learn by trial and error. However, given the societal dictate that it is the mothers who are ultimately responsible for babies' lives, women have traditionally become "expert" more quickly than men, connecting with a largely female network to gain information and advice during the early stages (Silverstein and Auerbach, 1989; Stern, 1995). Fathers then look to mothers as the experts, and the skill and knowledge difference gradually begins to expand to favor mothers. It is this greater mastery that permits a subset of mothers to wield "gatekeeping" prerogatives.

But what happens in a family in which the coparenting partner is not the father, but rather a more experienced grandmother? Does a similar gatekeeping phenomenon occur, and with what regularity? And, perhaps more to the point, which person is the gatekeeper and with what implications for the coparental and family group process? In nuclear families, when fathers who might potentially otherwise assume more active roles with their children face blocked or only partial access to their children as a function of maternal gatekeeping efforts, many accept this circumstance. When this happens, the family unit may develop a dynamic wherein the mother assumes a primary parenting role, with the father assuming a secondary, more limited but complimentary role. However, in other families the mother's dominance in the parenting sphere may render father only a shadow-parenting figure. In still other families, the fathers may indeed remain involved despite their partners' gatekeeping efforts; one outcome of such uninvited involvement can be high levels of oppositionality between fathers and mothers in the coparental system with attendant negative implications for the children. What we do not know at present is whether the processes that eventuate in multigenerational families following gatekeeping maneuvers by one or the other coparenting figure are akin to these nuclear family processes or whether other types of adjustments are made.

Clearly extended family members have the potential to serve a stabilizing or disrupting effect as coparenting figures (Kellam, Adams, Brown, and Ensminger, 1982). Indeed, whereas mothers may become relatively impervious to critiques of their caregiving by the children's fathers, who are usually in a one-down position with respect to parenting knowledge after the first few months of parenthood, mothers appear to be quite sensitive to critiques from other family members (Cohen, 1999). Moreover, it is not just the presence of additional caregivers but rather the quality of coparental support provided by these individuals that is clearly critical in determining both parenting success and child outcome. For example, the work of Apfel and Seitz (1996, 1999) with young adolescent African American mothers indicated that the most negative long-term consequences were found in families in which maternal grandmothers provided either too much aid (comandeering primary control as the grandchild's main parenting figure) or too little aid (abandoning the daughter and leaving her with no caregiving support). In these two groups, adolescent mothers were more likely to subsequently have another child in rapid succession, and were less likely to be the primary parent for the first child at the age of 12 years.

Hence evidence to date hints that there does seem to be value in examining qualities of coparental or "cocaregiving" support provided by members of the extended family. Just as in two-parent nuclear families, children fare less well when they are receiving dissonant messages from different parenting figures or being drawn into age-inappropriate alliances with adult family members, one against another. This said, researchers must always be clearly attuned to the family's parenting map before attempting to measure family process (Demo and Cox, 2000). Undoubtedly there exist but a finite number of basic functions that absolutely must be carried out in all families of infants and young children (Bornstein, in Vol. 1 of this *Handbook*); in many families, these essential functions are then augmented by an auxiliary set of important enrichment activities. This full set of basic and enrichment activities can all be carried out by a single person or can be shared in an infinite number of permutations among two or more parenting figures. The division of roles and responsibilities is organized in large part by cultural mores, but even so there are nuances to be negotiated and worked out by individual families. The basic principle that we would expect to obtain is that, regardless of who does what, socialization and acculturation of young children would proceed most efficiently when there is functional agreement and coordination among parenting figures, whoever these figures may be. Research on functional coparenting arrangements in multigenerational and extended families, on individual differences in both the process and outcomes of such arrangements (i.e., what is happening when coparenting arrangements are working well, and what is happening when they are not?), and, most importantly, on unique family dynamics attendant to extended families (i.e., negotiation between mothers and more experienced family members) will all be welcome additions to the landscape of coparenting research.

Applicability to single-parent families. Not all single parents have functional coparenting partners (Weinraub, Horvath, and Gringlas, in Vol. 3 of this *Handbook*). Many parents rear their children by themselves, with no siblings, grandparents, friends, or other relatives to share the load. The utility of the coparenting construct for such families is not clear. At base, coparenting alliances are alliances of a family's executive subsystem. That subsystem can be composed of a single person or of multiple others, but in either case the lines of parental authority must be clear. When a single parent recruits a neighbor, a baby-sitter, or (more commonly) her or his older children to assist with caring for younger children (Zukow-Goldring, in Vol. 3 of this *Handbook*), is it appropriate to view these people as coparenting partners? Although they are vested with responsibility and some authority, ultimately they are not privy to executive decision-making functions, and as such the single parent remains the one ultimately responsible for ensuring that all basic care and enrichment activities take place. The roles of positive male role models outside the family (e.g., Florsheim, Tolan, and Gorman-Smith, 1998), of daycaregivers, and of other institutions in the lives of these individuals—as well as in the lives of all families (Florsheim et al., 1998)—are certainly worthy of study, but it may be stretching the essential notion of coparenting (collaboration and support between adults rearing children together) to concoct a coparental alliance and dynamic in families in which none exist. Nonetheless, the guiding notion of a coparental alliance has been used clinically by Minuchin to describe the nature of the working alliance between single parents and therapists dealing with multiproblem children, and a similar metaphor—establishing functional connections with others to guide the parenting enterprise—has potential utility for those single parents in search of such supports.

Applicability to stepfamilies. Coparenting relationships in step-families are very complex (Hetherington and Stanley-Hagan, in Vol. 3 of this *Handbook*), and competent studies of the coparental dynamics in such families are quite important. One major distinction between nuclear and stepfamilies is the ambiguity of appropriate parenting roles for the nonbiological parent in stepfamilies. According to Boss and Greenberg (1984), the concept of "family boundaries" is a useful one for defining who belongs in a family and what functions each person will perform in that system; stress and dysfunction are commonplace when a lack of boundary clarity exists in families. However, as Erera (1997) noted, although it is certainly true that nuclear families uncertain about whether a member does or does not belong are experiencing family boundary ambiguity, in stepfamilies in which residential birth and nonbiological parents share parenting of half-siblings and stepchildren with nonresidential birth parents and nonresidential, nonbiological parents, families need to maintain ambiguous boundaries for different members to function in adaptive fashion. Indeed, some studies have found that when stepparents attempt to assume the same position of parental authority with stepchildren as they would with their own children, this often engenders conflict not only with the stepchild but also with their partner, the child's biological parent (Ganong and Coleman, 1992; Visher and Visher, 1979). It is usually stepfathers who attempt to take on this "birth parent" role (Erera-Weatherly, 1996), although some studies also find that approximately one fourth of stepmothers likewise view themselves as having the same role as birth parents (Ahrons and Wallisch, 1987).

Stepparents themselves are often unclear as to their spouse's expectations of them as coparents (Giles-Simes, 1984; Whitsett and Land, 1992), and often with good reason. Several studies have indicated that birth parents may view their new parenting partner as a threat to the exclusive bond they share with their birth children (Erera-Weatherly, 1996). If birth parents forge and maintain strong coalitions with birth children and exclude the stepparent from executive decisions in the reconstituted family, the stepparent never becomes fully integrated either as parent or coparenting partner (Giles-Simes, 1984). Even in families in which stepparents are granted authority to participate as coparents, however, gatekeeping by the birth parent (especially when this parent is the child's mother) is the rule and not the exception, and so gate keeping is best considered as a "normal family process" in stepfamilies. Under such circumstances, the family processes that follow are necessarily different in certain important respects from those of nuclear families (Bronstein, Clauson, Stoll, and Abrams, 1993). Indeed, of various possible parenting roles assumed by stepparents (birth parent style, "supergood" stepmother; detached; uncertain; friendship style), all create different levels of strain, animosity, and disciplinary challenges (Erera-Weatherly, 1996). On the basis of her research, Erera proposed that the most effective style for stepparents, particularly those with adolescent children, may be the friendship style—certainly a different role than that recommended for parents in nuclear families.

The legitimacy of the stepparent as coparental partner may also be affected by the relationship the child and the family maintain with the nonresidential biological parent. Here, findings are somewhat inconsistent (Clingempeel and Segal, 1986; Furstenberg, 1987; Pink and Wampler, 1985; Santrock and Sitterle, 1987), with some studies showing that good relationships with the noncustodial parent enhance the stepparent's legitimacy with the stepchild, and others indicating no relation between these variables. Clingempeel and Segal (1986) proposed that some of the variability lies in whether the contact with the noncustodial parent allays the child's fear of abandonment and eases acceptance of the new parenting figure or confuses the child as to appropriate authority figures and forces the stepparent to adopt a friendship rather than a parental role with the stepchild. Also, in all of the preceding work, child age clearly matters; younger children are far more likely than older children to eventually accept the stepparent as legitimate coparenting figure—although perhaps also more likely to be "protected" from the stepparent's active parenting efforts by the birth parent, especially early on in the remarriage (Visher and Visher, 1990).

Clearly models of coparenting need to be rethought when applied to the functioning of stepfamilies, and thoughtful research in this area will be a boon to the coparenting literature.

Applicability to families headed by gay and lesbian parents.   Most coparenting research to date with gay and lesbian families with children has focused on lesbian parenting partners, with a few important exceptions (e.g., Patterson, in Vol. 3 of this *Handbook*; Silverstein, 2002). Because such families are very diverse, there is no one set of guiding principles that can be readily applied to help understand coparenting by gay or lesbian partners—except that virtually all families headed by gay and lesbian parents must rear their children in social climates dominated by homophobia, stigma, prejudice, and discrimination both in societies at large and in their legal systems (Duran-Aydintug and Causey, 1996; Erera and Fredricksen, 1999; Rothblum, 1985). To understand coparenting dynamics within families headed by gay and lesbian partners, it is important to know how such families formed. Children can come into the lives of gay and lesbian partners through many different means, each with different implications for the emergence of the family's coparenting alliance. At present, most lesbian families come into being with one of the partners bringing children from a former, heterosexual union (Lewin, 1993), although the past decade has seen an increase in the number of families in which the partners actively seek either a known or unknown sperm donor and begin parenthood together (Erera and Fredricksen, 1999; Gartrell et al., 1999). Both lesbian and gay partners rearing children together can also begin their family by adoption of a nonbiological child (Brodzinsky and Pinderhughes, in Vol. 1 of this *Handbook*; Pies, 1989; Rohrbaugh, 1992). It should be noted, however, that this is possible only in some states. Many states prohibit adoption by the second parent in a same-sex couple (in 2001, only three states—New Mexico, New York, and Rhode Island—had legislation or regulations permitting gay and lesbian adoption). Moreover, some states (such as Florida and New Hampshire) prohibit gays and lesbians from qualifying as adoptive or foster parents. And, while Nevada's regulations permit placement of children with lesbian and gay individuals, state laws do not allow adoption by unmarried couples (Erera, 2002).

Formation of families through these different means can prompt different kinds of coparenting dynamics and challenges. In families in which the partners have adopted a child together, the co-parents are often on more equal footing both as the child's legal parents and as authority figures. In such families, roles and responsibilities must be worked out as in heterosexual two-parent adoptive families, but the family form itself does not inherently constrain or shape the types of adaptations ultimately made by the parenting partners. Indeed, although conventional provider–nurturer roles are sometimes adopted by the parents, perhaps in response to internalized heterosexual cultural norms (Pies, 1989), it is also the case that such partnerships are typically characterized by a more egalitarian division of labor than in most heterosexual couples (Sullivan, 1996). Moreover, many partners break set and invent "new" family roles, as did the "mommy–daddies" in Silverstein's research with gay male adoptive partners.

When the lesbian couple's child is born within the partnership by natural childbirth with an outside donor, there is also more egalitarianism in the division of labor than in heterosexual couples, but the birth mother is usually the one more involved in childcare (Hare and Richards, 1993; Patterson, 1995; Rohrbaugh, 1992; Sullivan, 1996). Reasons for this division are many (Erera and Fredrikson, 1999), but most accounts highlight the biological ties between mother and child as leading to the tendency of these women to assume more parental responsibility. Because of discrimination in the legal system and the lack of protection of legal marriage in most places, nonbirth mothers in lesbian partnerships also face the specter of being denied parental rights, custody, and visitation rights in the event of partnership dissolution. Whether or not this circumstance plays a role in couples' decisions about who will be the birth mother or in the extent to which the nonbirth mother consciously or unconsciously enters fully into the psychological and emotional coparenting role has not been definitively demonstrated. Also unclear is the extent to which "gatekeeping" processes occur in lesbian partnerships in which the child was born within the couple union. It is clear, however, that birth mothers who bring a child to a new lesbian partnership from a prior heterosexual union are more likely to play a gatekeeping role with "their" children, much as are birth parents in other stepfamilies (Erera and Fredricksen, 1999a). Indeed, lesbian families that form as a stepfamily confront many of the challenges of heterosexual stepfamilies previously described, including role ambiguity (Erera and Fredricksen, 1999). Fortunately, there is now a critical mass of high-quality research underway examining common challenges faced by gay and lesbian families (Kenney and Tash, 1993; Muzio, 1993; Patterson, in Vol. 3 of this *Handbook*), both as parents and as coparents, and important advances can be expected from this field of study over the next decade.

What do we know about cross-national applicability?   Virtually all coparenting studies published in the peer-reviewed literature to date have involved families from North America or Europe, and hence there is little to say about cross-national applicability outside of these limited regions of the world. There are, however, some very basic considerations to ponder. First, given that over 40% of the world's children are malnourished, have no access to clean water, and struggle just to survive (DeLoache, 2001), coparenting factors such as dissonance in parenting practices, divestment from active parenting by a significant family adult, or low levels of positive family affect should not be expected to have any kind of incremental formative impact in the lives of such children. Second, even in regions where day-to-day survival is not at issue, most of the world's children live in poverty. Cross nationally, most families must rely on preadolescent children, rather than on adults, for daily care of infants and small children. Indeed, it is not uncommon for children as young as 4 or 5 years old to be solely responsible for large blocks of time in the caregiving of their infant siblings or cousins (Zukow-Goldring, in Vol. 3 of this *Handbook*). When families' lives are focused on ensuring more basic survival needs, coparental coordination again fades as an important family force in child socialization and development.

However, what about regions of the world where poverty and concerns about sustenance are not as all encompassing, but where patterns of family life are very different from those of Western societies? Family compounds remain very commonplace in areas of Africa and Asia (Belanger, 2000; Dasgupta and Mukhopadhyay, 1993; Sigwana-Ndulo, 1998), and in such compounds virtually all child-related responsibilities continue to be handled by children's mothers and female members of either the mothers' or their partners' extended families (DeSai and Jain, 1994; Mullatini, 1995; Suppal and Roopnarine, 1999). Studies of coparenting coordination in such societies would seem a very important next frontier in testing the generalizability of basic notions about the importance of coparental coordination and solidarity in helping to explain individual developmental trajectories of young children. It is becoming clear from studies of mothers and grandmothers rearing children together in the United States that undermining of one woman by the other can be as confusing and disruptive to children as undermining of a father by a mother, or mother by a father, in a two-parent nuclear family (Brody et al., 1998). These findings linking coparenting dissonance and children's adjustment describe what happens in families rearing children in a particular cultural context, in which the goals of childrearing are in inculcating independence rather than filial piety and in which there may or may not be neighborhood, school, and other cultural supports for families. Coparenting events such as openly aired interadult disputes about the child's comportment or activities or more protracted sequences such as one adult's permitting certain forms of "misbehavior" prohibited by the other may never occur in other cultural contexts—or if they do, they are integrated into the family's reality in a very different fashion that then comes to guide the child's experience. Most Asian scholars believe there to be much more within-culture consistency in family and childrearing beliefs in collectivist Asian countries than in "every family for itself" Western nations, and hence much less likelihood that Asian coparents—whether father and mother or mother and extended family—would be working at cross purposes or disengaging from important coparental roles if such roles were culturally prescribed and expected.

It is also important for scholars studying family processes cross-nationally to be sensitive to within-culture variability (Ho, 1986). For example, one study with mothers of preschool children in urban Beijing, China, replicated findings from North American samples by establishing linkages between maternal reports of coparental conflict and child behavior problems (McHale, Rao, and Krasnow, 2000). However, a number of recent shifts in Beijing toward life circumstances that shadow "Western" cultures (i.e., women in the workplace, single-family dwellings without living space for extended kin, paternal involvement in day-to-day contacts with children, childcare by nonfamily members) may make this region of China an unusual and perhaps atypical site for testing the generalizability of coparenting constructs in traditional cultures. Family structure and process in rural areas of Asian countries may prove to be much more meaningful sites for providing "true" tests of cross-national generalizability of coparental conflict and coordination. At the same time, such work makes the most sense when carried out by indigenous scholars who take an "emic" approach, refining and adding a culturally meaningful lens to research on coparental and family group processes.

Is Coparenting Competition Most Relevant in Middle-Socioeconomic
Two-Parent Families?

When we began studying whole family group dynamics in the late 1980s, we were so captivated by the phenomenon of mother–father competitiveness that we never stopped to wonder whether this coparenting process was an epiphenomenon of a cultural curiosity—highly involved, motivated fathers who felt entitled to parent their young children shoulder-to-shoulder with their wives. We wonder about this now. At the same time as we believe that contentiousness between the child's key parenting figures about childrearing matters interferes with the establishment of order and predictability for children at home, we also wonder whether the propensities of educated, white-collar American fathers to question their wives' manner of dealing with child-related issues—and even, as some writers have proposed, to "appropriate" their sons' socialization as boys enter adolescence (Gullette, 2001)—have parallels in families from other walks of life, whether in the United States or in other places around the globe. Contemporary middle- and upper-middle-socioeconomic men who grew up in the United States during the 1970s and 1980s, in the wake of profound changes in family life inspired by the Women's Movement, may have been exposed to very different family events than men who grew up in blue-collar families during this same time period with fathers who were at home less or in which the breakdown of family-related functions may have been along more traditional gender lines. Indeed, there is evidence that contemporary fathers from blue-collar families may be more likely to carefully watch and model the child-related ministrations of their wives than are middle-socioeconomic fathers, who parent based on their own convictions and preferences (Entwisle and Doering, 1981). As such, it is conceivable that there may exist more coparental consistency in blue-collar than in white-collar families.

Do fathers from cultural groups and socioeconomic backgrounds besides those of the European American middle-socioeconomic men who have populated most coparenting studies also try to remedy matters when they perceive their wives as providing too much or too little guidance in teaching new skills, not permitting their children enough freedom and independence, encouraging timidity in the children rather than boldness, or reprimanding the child too often for too trivial matters? Certainly, at least in the socialization of male children, fathers often complain when they perceive their wives to be "babying" the boys or fostering dependency behavior, and coparenting conflicts often arise during the latency years when mothers and fathers have different notions about whether their sons need to be taught to "defend themselves" by fighting with other boys once challenged. In understanding the significance of such events, however, it is important to ask whether they are unusual occurrences in the life of the family or recurring patterns that place children "in the middle" day in and day out. Why do such antagonistic coparenting dynamics become part of the fabric of life in some middle-socioeconomic families but not in others? Are social status and education key contextual variables? If so, why are more educated fathers in other cultural groups not equally likely to take a contentious and assertive role in parenting? And is such contentiousness most prominent in rearing male children? When and under what circumstances are female children exposed to similar family dynamics, and what unique coparenting patterns emerge in the parenting of girls? All of these questions demand further inquiry, and they lead us to our final recommendation regarding future research.

How Do We Understand the Coparenting of Multiple Children
in the Same Family?

Research to date has most often examined interadult coordination in parenting a single child within the family, and hence the body of knowledge generated on coparenting dynamics may misrepresent the complexities of the majority of families with multiple children. Clearly not all children within the same family receive similar treatment from their parents (Brody, Stoneman, and Burke, 1987; Bryant and Crockenberg, 1980; Conger and Conger, 1994), and hence differential patterns of coparenting might also be expected, depending on such factors as the children's ages and genders (McHale, Crouter, McGuire, and Updegraff, 1995; Volling and Elins, 1998). Moreover, coparenting dynamics can be conceptualized either with respect to each of the children in the family individually or as a collective effort wherein the family's parenting figures simultaneously parent all children as a group. Undoubtedly, children themselves are aware of both sets of realities (how they, individually, fit into the parent-parent–self system and how they are situated relative to their siblings in receiving parenting from the coparental partners). The evidence is clear that when children receive differential treatment this triggers sibling conflict and other forms of child distress (Brody et al., 1987; Dunn, Stocker, and Plomin, 1990; Stocker, Dunn, and Plomin, 1989). Thus far, most studies have examined differential treatment from the perspective of the conduct of each parent individually (Brody et al., 1987; Brody, Stoneman, and McCoy, 1992; Bryant and Crockenberg, 1980; Volling and Belsky, 1992), although a few studies have attempted to study family-level patterns by comparing the favoritism, affection, and discipline demonstrated by mothers and fathers toward their different children (McHale et al., 1995; Volling, 1997; Volling and Elins, 1998).

These latter studies provide very important information about coparenting dynamics in families with multiple children. Conventional wisdom has held that the most negative outcomes for children are likely to occur in families in which the same child is targeted by both parents for harsher discipline, and there is now some limited empirical evidence indicating that this is so (Kerig, 1995; Volling and Elins, 1998). At the same time, differential treatment of a particular child by one parent combined with equal treatment of the children by the other parent can also be a sign of underlying marital and family distress (Minuchin, 1974). The investigations of Volling (1997) and Volling and Elins (1998) indicate that it is important to ask (1) what type of differential treatment is being considered? and (2) what are the ages of the children in the family being considered? When Volling and Elins scrutinized the coparenting patterns of families with children aged $1^1/_2$ and 4 years, they found that differential *favoritism* directed toward a particular child by one parent, when combined with equal treatment of the children by the other (a pattern they termed "incongruent"), could be tied to low levels of love in the marriage, as both Minuchin's (1974) theory and scattered empirical studies (Brody et al., 1992; Deal, 1996; McHale et al., 1995; Volling, 1997) had suggested. At the same time, they found that differential *discipline* directed toward the older child by the father in combination with equal disciplinary treatment of the children by the mother (also an incongruent pattern) did not carry the same meaning. According to Volling and Elins (1998), not only was this latter pattern correlated with less marital conflict, but it also predicted the best outcomes for the families' preschoolers.

Hence congruence does not always translate into favorable outcome or incongruence into negative outcome. As previously noted, when families in the study by Volling and Elins (1998) showed congruence in discipline (with both of the parents disciplining the older child more) preschoolers showed the most problematic adjustment. In families characterized by differential discipline in which fathers took the disciplinarian role with the older child while mothers disciplined equally, preschoolers and marriages were faring very well. However, when it was the *mothers* rather than the fathers who disciplined the preschooler more while fathers disciplined the children equally, marital conflict was usually high. In this last case, the importance of considering family and child development becomes most apparent. Kreppner's work (1988; Kreppner, Paulsen, and Schuetze, 1982) showed that, after a second child is born, fathers typically take on more responsibilities with the older child while mothers attend to the infant. If fathers do not assume this responsibility, mothers must pull double duty, and hence the family's patterns of coparenting the two children can be a sign of underlying marital distress. It is important to note also that functional coparenting patterns are likely to change as children age (Volling, 1997), and hence research will profit most from longitudinal inquiry guided by a developmental lens.

CONCLUSIONS

The emergence of this new area of inquiry has led to a number of important insights about multicaregiver families and parenting. In most families in which multiple caregivers rear children together, there is usually at least some dissonance in the different parenting adults' beliefs about optimal parenting practices. Be that as it may, families then go on to chart distinctively different pathways in resolving such differences. Some adaptations that the coparenting adults strike upon are functional, in the sense that they are acceptable to all parties involved. Others cause strain, resentment, conflict, or disengagement between the parenting partners. Moreover, strategies that work in one family may be ill suited for others because of the personal characteristics and preferences of the parenting figures involved, needs of the child, extant life circumstances that have an impact on the family, and so on. Attempting to divine common, universal principles governing adaptive coparental relations and dynamics across social status, cultures, and family structures may be an impossible task—but we do believe that collaboration and solidarity between parenting partners, in whatever form, will leave children in better stead than will divisiveness and inconsistency of standards.

How do parents learn about the origins and significance of coparenting conflict and coordination for both the family and the child? We know of few institutional practices that specifically aim to validate the inevitability of and strains caused by caregiver differences, but are hopeful that the recent boon in coparenting research will sensitize parents and professionals to the importance of strengthening coparental support and solidarity, given mounting evidence that such collaboration fosters children's social and emotional development. We have suggested that it may never be too early to encourage and promote coparental support and coordination. Coparenting dynamics emerge and crystallize early, with early emerging dynamics foreshadowing later patterns of child and family adjustment. It will be important for professionals working with families to keep in mind that they should always assess whole families in action together, rather than simply relying on assessments of each parent engaged individually with the child. Available data indicate that these two assessment contexts can provide very different impressions of families, with family group assessments particularly well suited for revealing core coparenting dynamics.

In conclusion, despite the formidable progress that has been made in describing the context, determinants, and sequelea of various coparenting dynamics over the past several years, much work remains in clarifying the meaning, developmental significance, and nuances of such dynamics in a wide variety of family groups. We see this area of study as a vibrant, exciting, and significant new domain for research in the field of parenting and expect investigations over the next decade to teach us a great deal about when, why, and how coparenting dynamics are important in the lives of children and families.

ACKNOWLEDGMENTS

Work on this chapter and several of the findings reported herein was supported in part by National Institutes of Health grant HD 37172, "Coparenting and Family Processes during Infancy and Toddlerhood."

REFERENCES

Abidin, R. R., and Brunner, J. F. (1995). Development of a parenting alliance inventory. *Journal of Clinical Child Psychology, 24,* 31–40.

Ablow, J. (1997, April). *Marital conflict across family contexts: Does the presence of children make a difference?* Poster presented at the Biennial Meeting of the Society for Research in Child Development, Washington, DC.

Ahrons, C. R. (1981). The continuing coparental relationship between divorced spouses. *American Journal of Orthopsychiatry, 51,* 415–428.

Ahrons, C. R., and Wallisch, L. S. (1987). The relationship between former spouses. In D. Perlman and S. Duck (Eds.), *Intimate relationships: Development, dynamics, and deterioration* (pp. 269–296). Newbury Park, CA: Sage.

Aldous, J., Mulligan, G. M., and Bjarnason, T. (1998). Fathering over time: What makes the difference? *Journal of Marriage and the Family, 60,* 809–820.

Apfel, N., and Seitz, V. (1996). African American adolescent mothers, their families, and their daughters: A longitudinal perspective over twelve years. In: B. Leadbeater and N. Way (Eds.); *Urban girls: Resisting stereotypes, creating identities.* New York: New York University Press, (p. 149–170).

Apfel, N., and Seitz, V. (1999, April). Style of family support predicts teen mothers' subsequent childbearing and parenting success. Paper presented at the Society for Research in Child Development, Albuquerque, NM.

Azar, S. T. (2001). Family research and the law. In J. McHale and W. Grolnick (Eds.), *Retrospect and prospect in the psychological study of families* (pp. 283–320). Mahwah, NJ: Lawrence Erlbaum Associates.

Baron, R., and Kenny, D. (1986). The moderator-mediator variable distinction in social psychological research: Conceptual, strategic, and statistical considerations. *Journal of Personality and Social Psychology, 51,* 1173–1182.

Baruch, G., and Barnett, R. (1986). Consequences of fathers' participation in family work: Parents' role strain and well-being. *Journal of Personality and Social Psychology, 51,* 983–992.

Bateson, M. (2000). *Full circles, overlapping lives: Culture and generation in transition.* New York: Random House.

Bearss, K. E., and Eyberg, S. (1998). A test of the parenting alliance theory. *Early Education and Development, 9,* 179–185.

Belanger, D. (2000). Rural differences in household composition and family formation patterns in Viet Nam. *Journal of Comparative Family Studies, 31,* 171–189.

Belsky, J. (1984). The determinants of parenting: A process model. *Child Development, 55,* 83–96.

Belsky, J., Crnic, K., and Gable, S. (1995). The determinants of coparenting in families with toddler boys: Spousal differences and daily hassles. *Child Development, 66,* 629–642.

Belsky, J., Spanier, G., and Rovine, M. (1983). Stability and change in marriage across the transition to parenthood. *Journal of Marriage and the Family, 45,* 567–577.

Belsky, J., and Hsieh, K. H. (1998). Patterns of marital change during the early childhood yeas: Parent personality, coparenting, and division-of-labor correlates. *Journal of Family Psychology, 12,* 511–528.

Belsky, J., Putnam, S., and Crnic, K. (1996). Coparenting, parenting, and early emotional development. In J. P. McHale and P. A. Cowan (Eds.), *Understanding how family-level dynamics affect children's development: Studies of two-parent families* (pp. 45–55). San Francisco: Jossey-Bass.

Belsky, J., and Rovine, M. (1990). Q-sort security and first-year nonmaternal care. *New Directions for Child Development, 49,* 7–22.

Block, J. H., Block, J., and Morrison, A. (1981). Parental agreement–disagreement on child-rearing orientations and gender related personality correlates in children. *Child Development, 52,* 965–974.

Boss, P., and Greenberg, J. (1984). Family boundary ambiguity: A new variable in family stress theory. *Family Process, 23,* 535–546.

Brody, G. H., and Flor, D. L. (1996). Coparenting, family interactions, and competence among African-American youths. In J. P. McHale and P. A. Cowan (Eds.), *Understanding how family-level dynamics affect children's development: Studies of two-parent families* (pp. 77–91). San Francisco: Jossey-Bass.

Brody, G. H., Flor, D. L., and Neubaum, E. (1998). Coparenting processes and child competence among rural African-American families. In M. Lewis and C. Feiring (Eds.), *Families, risk, and competence* (pp. 227–243). Mahwah, NJ: Lawrence Erlbaum Associates.

Brody, G. H., Stoneman, Z., and Burke, M. (1987). Child temperaments, maternal differential behavior, and sibling relationships. *Developmental Psychology, 23,* 354–362.

Brody, G. H., Stoneman, Z., and McCoy, J. K. (1992). Associations of maternal and paternal direct and differential behavior with sibling relationships: Contemporaneous and longitudinal analyses. *Child Development, 63,* 82–92.

Brody, G. H., Stoneman, Z., Smith, T., and Gibson, N. M. (1999). Sibling relationships in rural African American families. *Journal of Marriage and the Family, 61,* 1046–1057.

Bronstein, P., Clauson, J., Stoll, M., and Abrams, C. (1993). Parenting behavior and children's social, psychological, and academic adjustment in diverse family structures. *Family Relationships, 42,* 268–276.

Bryant, B., and Crockenberg, S. (1980). Correlates and dimensions of pro-social behavior: A study of female siblings with their mothers. *Child Development, 51,* 354–362.

Buchanan, C. M., Maccoby, E., and Dornbusch, S. M. (1991). Caught between parents: Adolescents' experience in divorced homes. *Child Development, 62,* 1008–1029.

Byng-Hall, J. (1995). *Rewriting family scripts: Improvisation and systems change.* New York: Guilford.

Camara, K. A., and Resnick, G. (1989). Styles of conflict resolution and cooperation between divorced parents: Effects on child behavior and adjustment. *American Journal of Orthopsychiatry, 59,* 560–575.

Carleton, M., Rotman, T., and McHale, J. (2000, July). *Assessing the familys coparenting dynamic at infant age 3 months.* Paper presented at the International Conference on Infant Studies, Brighton, England.

Carleton, M., Rotman, T., and McHale, J. (2001, April). *Linking observational and narrative indices of coparental coordination and collaboration at 3 months postpartum.* Paper presented at the Biennial Meeting of the Society for Research in Child Development, Minneapolis, MN.

Chase-Lansdale, P. L., and Brooks-Gunn, J. (1994). Young African-American multigenerational families in poverty: Quality of mothering and grandmothering. *Child Development, 65. (Special Issue: Children and Poverty),* 373–393.

Christensen, A., and Margolin, G. (1988). Conflict and alliance in distressed and non-distressed families. In R. A. Hinde and J. Stevenson-Hinde (Eds.), *Relationships within families* (pp. 263–282). Oxford, England: Clarendon.

Clingempeel, W. G., and Segal, S. (1986). Stepparent–stepchild relationships and the psychological adjustment of children in stepmother and stepfather families. *Child Development, 57,* 474–484.

Cohen, N. E. (1999, April). *Mother/co-caregiver relationships, social support, parenting, and child adjustment in single-parent African-American families.* Paper presented at the Biennial Meeting of the Society for Research in Child Development, Albuquerque, NM.

Cohen, N. E., and Weissman, S. (1984). The parenting alliance. In R. Cohen, B. Cohler, and S. Weissman (Eds.), *Parenthood: A psychodynamic perspective* (pp. 33–49). New York: Guilford.

Conger, K. J., and Conger, R. D. (1994). Differential parenting and change in sibling differences in delinquency. *Journal of Family Psychology, 8,* 287–302.

Corter, C., and Fleming, A. (1995). Psychobiology and maternal behavior in human beings. In M. Bornstein (Ed.), *Handbook of Parenting: Vol. 2. Biology and ecology of parenting* (pp. 87–116). Mahwah, NJ: Lawrence Erlbaum Associates.

Cowan, C. P., and Cowan, P. A. (1988). Who does what when partners become parents: Implications for men, women, and marriage. *Marriage and Family Review, 12,* 105–131.

Cowan, C. P., and Cowan, P. A. (1992). *When partners become parents: The big life change for couples.* New York: Basic Books.

Cowan, C. P., Cowan, P. A., Heming, G., and Miller, N. B. (1991). Becoming a family: Marriage, parenting, and child development. In P. A. Cowan and E. M. Hetherington (Eds.), *Family transition: Advances in family research series* (pp. 79–109). Hillsdale NJ: Lawrence Erlbaum Associates.

Crouter, A. C., Perry J. M., Huston, T. L., and McHale, S. M. (1987). Processes underlying father involvement in dual earner and single earner families. *Developmental Psychology, 23,* 431–440.

Cummings, E. M., and Davies, P. (1994). *Children and marital conflict: The impact of family dispute and resolution.* New York: Guilford.

Cummings, E. M., and Davies, P. (1996). Emotional security as a regulatory process in normal development and the development of psychopathology. *Development and Psychopathology, 8,* 123–139.

Cummings, E. M., Davies, P., and Simpson, K. (1994). Marital conflict, gender, and childrens appraisals and coping efficacy as mediators of child adjustment. *Journal of Family Psychology, 8,* 141–149.

Dasgupta, S., and Mukhopadhyay, R. (1993). Nuclear and joint family households in West Bengal villages. *Ethnology, 32,* 339–358.

Davies, P., and Cummings, E. M. (1994). Marital conflict and child adjustment: An emotional security hypothesis. *Psychological Bulletin, 116,* 387–411.

Deal, J. E. (1996). Marital conflict and differential treatment of siblings. *Family Process, 35,* 333–346.

Deal, J., Halverson, C., and Wampler, K. (1989). Parental agreement on child-rearing orientations: Relations to parental, marital, family, and child characteristics. *Child Development, 60,* 1025–1034.

DeLoache, J. (2001). *A world of babies: Imagined childcare guides for seven societies.* Cambridge, England: Cambridge University Press.

DeLuccie, M. F. (1995). Mothers as gatekeepers: A model of maternal mediators of father involvement. *The Journal of Genetic Psychology, 156,* 115–131

Demo, D., and Cox, M. (2000). Families with young children: A review of research in the 1990s. *Journal of Marriage and the Family, 62,* 876–895.

DeSai, S., and Jain, D. (1994). Marital and change in family: The social context of women's work in rural Southern India. *Population and Development Review, 20,* 115–136.

Deutsch, F. M., Lussier, J. B., and Servis, L. J. (1993). Husbands at home: Predictors of parental participation in childcare and housework. *Journal of Personality and Social Psychology, 65,* 1154–1166.

Dunn, J. F., Stocker, C., and Plomin, R. (1990). Non-shared experiences within the family: Correlates of behavior problems in middle childhood. *Development and Psychopathology, 2,* 113–126.

Duran-Aydintug, C., and Causey, K. A. (1996). Child custody determination: Implications for lesbian mothers. *Journal of Divorce and Remarriage, 25,* 55–74.

Ehrensaft, D. (1990). Parenting together: Men and women sharing the care of their children. Urbana, IL: University of Illinois Press.

Ehrensaft, D. (1997). *Spoiling childhood: How well-meaning parents are giving children too much—but not what they need.* New York: Guilford.

Ehrenberg, M., Gearing-Small, M., Hunter, M., and Small, B. (2001). Childcare task division and shared parenting attitudes in dual-earner families with young children. *Family Relations, 50,* 143–153.

El-Sheikh, M., Cummings, E. M., and Goetsch, V. L. (1989). Coping with adults' angry behavior: Behavioral, physiological, and verbal responses in preschoolers. *Developmental Psychology, 25,* 490–498.

Emery, R. E. (1982). Interparental conflict and the children of discord and divorce. *Psychological Bulletin, 92,* 310–498.

Entwisle, D., and Doering, S. (1981). *The first birth: A turning point.* Baltimore: Johns Hopkins University Press.

Erel, O., and Burman, B. (1995). Interrelatedness of marital relationships and parent–child relationships: a meta-analytic review. *Psychological Bulletin, 118,* 108–132.

Erera, P. I. (1997). Foster parents' attitudes toward birth parents and caseworkers: Implications for visitations. *Families in Society, 78,* 511–519.

Erera, P. (2002). Family diversity: *Continuity and change in the contemporary family.* Thousand Oaks, CA: Sage Publications.

Erera, P. I., and Fredricksen, K. (1999). Lesbian stepfamilies: A unique family structure. *Families in Society, 80*, 263–270.

Erera-Weatherley, P. I. (1996). On becoming a stepparent: Factors associated with the adoption of alternative stepparenting styles. *Journal of Divorce and Remarriage, 25*, 155–174.

Farrell, B. G. (1999). *Family: The making of an idea, an institution, and a controversy in American culture.* Boulder, CO: Westview.

Fivaz-Depeursinge, E., and Corboz-Warnery, A. (1999). *The primary triangle: A developmental systems view of mothers, fathers, and infants.* New York: Basic Books.

Fivaz-Depeursinge, E., Frascarolo, F., and Corboz-Warnery, A. (1996). Assessing the triadic alliance between fathers, mothers, and infants at play. In J. P. McHale and P. A. Cowan (Eds.), *Understanding how family-level dynamics affect children's development: Studies of two-parent families* (pp. 27–44). San Francisco: Jossey-Bass.

Fivaz-Depeursinge, E., Frascarolo, F., Corboz-Warnery, A., Carneiro, C., and Montfort, V. (2000, July). *Constituting a family alliance: Relations with prenatal coparenting and the infants handling of triangular interactions.* Paper presented at the International Conference on Infant Studies, Brighton, England.

Fletcher, A., Steinberg, L., and Sellers, E. (1999). Adolescents' well-being as a function of perceived inter-parental consistency. *Journal of Marriage and the Family, 61*, 599–610.

Florsheim, P., Tolan, P., and Gorman-Smith, D. (1998). Family relationships, parenting practices, the availability of male family members, and the behavior of inner-city boys in single-mother and two-parent families. *Child Development, 69*, 1437–1447.

Floyd, F. J., Gilliom, L. A., and Costigan, C. L. (1998). Marriage and parenting alliance: Longitudinal prediction of change on parenting perceptions and behaviors. *Child Development, 62*, 1434–1479.

Floyd, F. J., and Zmich, D. E. (1991). Marriage and parenting partnership: Perceptions and interactions of parents with mentally retarded and typically developing children. *Child Development, 62*, 1434–1448.

Frank, S., Olmstead, C., Wagner, A., Laub, C. et al. (1991). Child illness, the parenting alliance, and parenting stress. *Journal of Pediatric Psychology, 16*, 361–371.

Frosch, C. A., Mangelsdorf, S. C., and McHale, J. L. (1998). Correlates of marital behavior at 6 months postpartum. *Developmental Psychology, 34*, 1438–1449.

Frosch, C. A., Mangelsdorf, S. C., and McHale, J. L. (2000). Marital behavior and the security of preschooler–parent attachment relationships. *Journal of Family Psychology, 14*, 144–161.

Furstenberg, F. F. (1987). The new extended family: The experience of parents and children after remarriage. In K. Pasley and M. Ihinger-Tallman (Eds.), *Remarriage and stepparenting: Current research and theory* (pp. 42–61). New York: Guilford.

Gable, S., Belsky, J., and Crnic, K. (1992). Marriage, parenting, and child development: Progress and prospects. *Journal of Family Psychology, 5. (Special Issue: Diversity in Contemporary Family Psychology)*, 276–294.

Ganong, L. H., and Coleman, M. (1992). Gender differences in expectations of self and future partner. *Journal of Family Issues, 13*, 55–64.

Gartrell, N., Banks, A., Hamilton, J., Reed, N., Bishop, H., and Rodas, C. (1999). The national lesbian family study: II. Interviews with mothers of toddlers. *American Journal of Orthopsychiatry, 69*, 362–369.

Gerra, G., Caccavari, R., Delsignore, R., Passeri, M., Fertonani, G. A., Maestri, D., Monica, C., and Brambilla, F. (1993). Parental divorce and neuroendocrine changes in adolescents. *Acta Psychiatrica Scandinavica, 87*, 350–354.

Giles-Simes, J. (1984). The step-parent role. *Journal of Family Issues, 5*, 116–130.

Gottman, J. M., and Katz, L. F. (1989). Effects of marital discord on young children's peer interaction and health. *Developmental Psychology, 25*, 373–381.

Gottman, J. M., Katz, L. F., and Hooven, C. (1997). *Meta-emotion: How families communicate emotionally.* Mahwah, NJ: Lawrence Erlbaum Associates.

Greenberg, M. T., Speltz, M. L., and DeKlyen, M. (1993). The role of attachment in the early development of disruptive behavioral problems. *Development and Psychopathology, 5*, 191–213.

Grych, J. H. (1998). Childrens appraisals of interparental conflict: Situational and contextual inflences. *Journal of Family Psychology, 12*, 1–17.

Grych, J. H., and Fincham, F. D. (1990). Marital conflict and children's adjustment: A cognitive–contextual framework. *Psychological Bulletin, 108*, 267–290.

Grych, J. H., and Fincham, F. D. (1993). Childrens appraisals of marital conflict: Initial investigations of the cognitive–contextual framework. *Child Development, 64*, 251–230.

Grych, J. H., and Fincham, F. D. (2001). *Child development and interparental conflict.* New York: Cambridge University Press.

Grych, J., Seid, M., and Fincham, F. (1992). Assessing marital conflict from the child's perspective: The Children's Perception of Interparental Conflict Scale. *Child Development, 63*, 558–572.

Gullette, M. (2001). *The broken shovel.* Unpublished manuscript.

Hackel, L. S., and Ruble, D. N. (1992). Changes in the marital relationship after the first baby is born: Predicting the impact of expectancy disconfirmation. *Journal of Personality and Social Psychology, 62*, 944–957.

Hare, J., and Richards, L. (1993). Children raised by lesbian couples: Does context of birth affect father and partner involvement? *Family Relations, 42*, 249–255.

Harrell, S. (1997). *Human families.* Boulder, CO: Westview.

Hetherington, E. M., Cox, M., and Cox, R. (1982). Effects of divorce on parents and children. In Lamb, M. E. (Ed.), *Nontraditional families.* Hillsdale, NJ: Lawrence Erlbaum Associates.

Hetherington, E. M., Henderson, S. H., Reiss, D., Anderson, E. R., Bridges, M., Chan, R. W., Insabella, G. M., Jodl, K. M., Kim, J. E., Mitchell, A. S., O'Connor, T. G., Skaggs, M. J., and Taylor, L. C. (1999). Adolescent siblings in stepfamilies: Family functioning and adolescent adjustment. *Monographs of the Society for Research in Child Development, 64,* (Serial No. 222).

Hirschman, C., and Vu, M. (1996). Family and household structure in Viet Nam: Some from a recent survey. *Pacific Affairs, 69,* 229–249.

Ho, D. (1986). Chinese patterns of socialization: A critical review. In M. H. Bond (Ed.), *The psychology of the Chinese people* (pp. 1–37). New York: Oxford University Press.

Holmes, J. (1995). "Something there is that doesn't love a wall": John Bowlby, Attachment theory, and psychoanalysis. In S. Goldberg, R. Muir, and J. Kerr (Eds.), *Attachment theory: Social, developmental, and clinical perspectives* (pp. 19–44). Hillsdale, NJ: U.S. Analytic.

Johnson, V., Cowan, P., and Cowan, C. (1999). Children's classroom behavior: The unique contribution of family organization. *Journal of Family Psychology, 13,* 355–371.

Jones, W., and Lindblad-Goldberg, M. (in press). Structural family therapy: Elaborations of theory and practice. In F. Kaslow (Series Ed.) and R. Massey and S. Massey (Vol. Eds.), *Comprehensive handbook of psychotherapy: Vol III. Interpersonal, humanistic, and existential models.* New York: Wiley.

Jordan, P. L. (1995). The mother's role in promoting fathering behavior. In J. L. Shapiro and M. J. Diamond (Eds.), *Focus on men: Vol. 8. Becoming a father: Contemporary, social, developmental, and clinical perspectives* (pp. 61–71). New York: Springer.

Jouriles, E., Murphy, C., Farris, A., and Smith, D. (1991). Marital adjustment, parental disagreements about child-rearing, and behavior problems in boys: Increasing the specificity of the marital assessment. *Child Development, 62,* 1424–1433.

Katz, L. F., and Gottman, J. M. (1996). Spillover effects of marital conflict: In search of parenting and coparenting mechanisms. In J. P. McHale and P. A. Cowan (Eds.), *Understanding how family-level dynamics affect children's development: Studies of two-parent families* (pp. 57–76). San Francisco: Jossey-Bass.

Kellam, S. G., Adams, R. G., Brown, C. H., and Ensminger, M. E. (1982). The long-term evolution of the family structure of teenage and older mothers. *Journal of Marriage and the Family, 44,* 539–554.

Kenney, J. W., and Tash, D. T. (1993). Lesbian childbearing couples' dilemmas and decisions. In P. N. Stern (Ed.), *Lesbian health: What are the issues?* (pp. 119–129). Washington, DC: Taylor and Francis.

Kerig, P. K. (1995). Triangles in the family circle: Effects of family structure on marriage, parenting and child adjustment. *Journal of Family Psychology, 9,* 28–43.

Kerig, P. K. (2001). Introduction and overview: Conceptual issues in family observational research. In P. K. Kerig and K. M. Lindahl (Eds.), *Family observational coding systems: Resources for systemic research* (pp. 1–22). Mahwah, NJ: Lawrence Erlbaum Associates.

Kerig, P. K., Fedorowicz, A., Brown, C., Patenaude, R., and Warren, M. (1998). When warriors are worriers: Gender, appraisals, and childrens strategies for coping with interparental violence. *Journal of Emotional Abuse, 1,* 89–114.

Kitzmann, K. M. (2000). Effects of marital conflict on subsequent triadic family interactions and parenting. *Developmental Psychology, 36,* 3–13.

Kreppner, K. (1988). Changes in parent–child relationships with the birth of the second child. *Marriage and Family Review, 12,* 157–181.

Kreppner, K., Paulsen, S., and Schuetze, Y. (1982). Infant and family development: From triads to tetrads. *Human Development, 25,* 373–391.

Lamb, M. E. (1995). The changing roles of fathers. In J. L. Shapiro and M. J. Diamond (Eds.), *Focus on men: Vol. 8. Becoming a father: Contemporary, social, developmental, and clinical perspectives: Springer series, focus on men* (pp. 18–35). New York: Springer.

Lauretti, A., and McHale, J. (1997, April). Shifting patterns of coparenting styles between dyadic and family settings: The role of marital distress. Paper presented at the Society for Research in Child Development, Atlanta, GA.

Lauretti, A., and McHale, J. (2001, April). Charting the early evolution of the coparental alliance. Symposium presented at the Society for Research in Child Development, Minneapolis, MN.

Lavee, Y. and Katz, R. (in press). The family in Israel: Between tradition and modernity. In C. Hennon and T. Brubaker (Eds.), *Diversity in families: A global perspective.* Belmont, CA: Wadsworth.

Levy-Shiff, R. (1994). Individual and contextual correlated of marital change cross the transition to parenthood. *Developmental Psychology, 30,* 591–604.

Lewin, E. (1993). *Lesbian mothers: Accounts of gender in American culture.* Ithaca, NY: Cornell University Press.

Lewis, J. M., Owen, M. T., and Cox, M. J. (1988). The transition to parenthood: III. Incorporation of the child into the family. *Family Process, 27,* 411–421.

Lindahl, K., Clements, M., and Markman, H. (1998). The development of marriage: A 9 year perspective. In T. N. Bradbury (Ed.), *The developmental course of marital dysfunction* (pp. 205–236). New York: Cambridge University Press.

Lindahl, K., and Malik, N. (1999). Marital conflict, family process, and boys' externalizing behavior in Hispanic and European-American families. *Journal of Clinical Child Psychology, 28*, 12–24.

Margolin, G. (1988). Marital conflict is not marital conflict is not marital conflict. In R. DeV. Peters and R. McMahon (Eds.), *Social learning and systems approaches to marriage and the family* (pp. 193–216). New York: Brunner/Mazel.

Margolin, G. (2001). Coparenting: A link between marital conflict and parenting in two-parent families. *Journal of Family Psychology, 15*, 3–21.

McBride, B. A., and Rane, T. R. (1998). Parenting alliance as a predictor of father involvement: An exploratory study. *Family Relationships: Interdisciplinary Journal of Applied Family Studies, 47*, 229–236.

McConnell, M. C., and Kerig, P. K. (in press). Assessing coparenting in families of school age children: Validation of the Coparenting and Family Rating System. *Canadian Journal of Behavioural Science.*

McHale, J. (1995). Co-parenting and triadic interactions during infancy: The roles of marital distress and child gender. *Developmental Psychology, 31*, 985–996.

McHale, J. (1997). Overt and covert coparenting process in the family. *Family Process, 36*, 183–210.

McHale, J., and Fivaz-Depeursinge, E. (1999). Understanding triadic and family group process during infancy and early childhood. *Clinical Child and Family Psychology Review, 2*, 107–127.

McHale, J., Fivaz-Depeursinge, E., and Corboz-Warnery, A. (2000, July). *What do studies of the formation of the family triad contribute to clinical practice?* Paper presented at the World Association for Infant Mental Health, Montreal, Canada.

McHale, J., Johnson, D., and Sinclair, R. (1999). Family dynamics, preschoolers' family representations, and preschool peer relationships. *Early Education and Development, 10*, 373–401.

McHale, J., Kuersten, R., and Lauretti, A. (1996). New directions in the study of family-level dynamics during infancy and early childhood. In J. P. McHale and P. A. Cowan (Eds.), *Understanding how family-level dynamics affect children's development: Studies of two-parent families* (pp. 5–26). San Francisco: Jossey-Bass.

McHale, J., Kuersten, R., Lauretti, A., and Rasmussen, J. (2000). Parental reports of coparenting and observed coparenting behavior during the toddler period. *Journal of Family Psychology, 14*, 220–237.

McHale, J., Lauretti, A., and Kuersten-Hogan (1999, April). *Linking family-level patterns to father–child, mother–child, and marital relationship qualities.* Paper presented at Society for Research and Child Development, Albuquerque, NM.

McHale, J., Lauretti, A., and Talbot, J. (1998, April). *Security of attachment, family-level dynamics, and toddler adaptation.* Paper presented at the International Conference on Infant Studies, Atlanta, GA.

McHale, J., Lauretti, A., Talbot, J., and Pouquette, C. (2002). Retrospect and prospect in the psychological study of coparenting and family group process. In J. McHale and W. Grolnick (Eds.). *Retrospect and prospect in the psychological study of families* (p. 127–166). Mahwah, NJ: Lawrence Erlbaum Associates.

McHale, J., McConnell, M., Lauretti, A., and Neugebauer, A. (in preparation). Using semi-structured family doll play tasks to understand 2 to 4-year olds' views of the family. In D. Gordon (Ed.), *What play tells us.* No publisher yet secured.

McHale, J., Neugebauer, A., Asch, A., and Schwartz, A. (1999). Preschooters characterizations of multiple family relationships during family doll play. *Journal of Clinical Child Psychology, 28*, 256–268.

McHale, J., Rao, N., and Krasnow, A. (2000). Constructing family climates: Chinese mothers' reports of their coparenting behavior and preschoolers' adaptation. *International Journal of Behavioral Development, 24*, 111–118.

McHale, J., and Rasmussen, J. (1998). Coparental and family group-level dynamics during infancy: Early family precursors of child and family functioning during preschool. *Development and Psychopathology, 10*, 39–58.

McHale, J., Talbot, J., Lauretti, A., Pouquette, C. and Zaslavsky, I. (2000, July). Does knowledge of parents' or infants' traits facilitate predictions about the family's group dynamics? Paper presented at the World Association for Infant Mental Health, Montreal, Canada.

McHale, S. M., Crouter, A. C., McGuire, S. A., and Updegraff, K. A. (1995). Congruence between mothers' and fathers' differential treatment of siblings: Links with family relationships and children's well-being. *Child Development, 66*, 116–128.

Minuchin, P. (2002). Looking toward the horizon: Present and future in the study of family systems. In J. McHale and W. Grolnick (Eds.), *Retrospect and prospect in the psychological study of families* (p. 259–278). Mahwah, NJ: Lawrence Erlbaum Associates.

Minuchin, S. (1974). *Families and family therapy.* Cambridge, MA: Harvard University Press.

Minuchin, S., and Fishman, H. C. (1981). *Techniques of family therapy.* Cambridge, MA: Harvard University Press.

Minuchin, S., Montalvo, B., Guerney, B., Rosman, B., and Schumer, F. (1967). *Families of the slums.* New York: Basic Books.

Minuchin, S., Rosman, B. L., and Baker, L. (1978). *Psychosomatic families: Anorexia nervosa in context.* Cambridge, MA: Harvard University Press.

Mullatini, L. (1995). Families in India: Beliefs and realities. *Journal of Comparative Family Studies, 26*, 11–25.

Muzio, C. (1993). Lesbian co-parenting: On being/being with the invisible (m)other. *Smith College Studies in Social Work, 63 (Special Issue: Lesbians and lesbian families: Multiple reflections)*, 215–229.

Novak, A., and van der Veen, F. (1970). Family concepts and emotional disturbance in the families of disturbed adolescents with normal siblings. *Family Process, 9*, 157–172.

Palm, G. F., and Palkovitz, R. (1988). *The challenge of working with new father: implications for support providers.* Newark, NJ: Haworth.

Parke, R. D. (1996). *Fatherhood*. Cambridge, MA: Harvard University Press.

Patterson, C. J. (1995). Families of the lesbian baby boom: Parents' division of labor and chidren's adjustment. *Developmental Psychology, 31*, 115–124.

Pies, C. A. (1989). Lesbians and the choice to parent. *Marriage and Family Review, 14*, 137–154.

Pink, J. E., and Wampler, K. S. (1985). Problem areas in stepfamilies: Cohesion, adaptability, and the stepfather–adolescent relationship. *Family Relationships: Journal of Applied Family and Child Studies, 34*, 327–335.

Radin, N., and Russell, G. (1983). Increased father participation and child development outcomes. In M. Lamb and A. Sagi (Eds.), *Fatherhood and family policy* (pp. 191–218). Hillsdale, NJ: Lawrence Erlbaum Associates.

Rohrbaugh, J. (1992). Lesbian families: Clinical issues and professional implications. *Professional Psychology: Research and Practice. 23*, 467–473.

Rothblum, E. D. (1985). *Lesbianism: Affirming nontraditional roles*. Paper presented at the Annual Meeting of the Association for Advancement of Behavior Therapy, Houston, TX.

Russell, A., and Russell, G. (1994). Coparenting early school-age children: An examination of mother–father interdependence within families. *Developmental Psychology, 30*, 757–770.

Santrock, J. W., and Sitterle, K. A. (1987). Parent–child relationships in stepmother families. In K. Pasley and M. Ihinger-Tallman (Eds.), *Remarriage and stepparenting: Current research and theory* (pp. 273–299). New York: Guilford.

Satir, V. M. (1967). Family systems and approaches to family therapy. *Journal of the Fort Logan Mental Health Center, 4*, 81–93.

Schwartz, P. (1994). *Peer Marriage: How Love between Equals Really Works*. New York: the Free Press.

Shapiro, A. F., Gottman, J. M., and Carrere, S. (2000). The baby and the marriage: identifying factors that buffer against decline in marital satisfaction after the first baby arrives. *Journal of Family Psychology, 14*, 59–70.

Sigwana-Ndulo, N. (1998). Rural African family structure in the Eastern Cape Province, South Africa, *Journal of Comparative Family Studies, 29*, 407–417.

Silverstein, L. (2002). Fathers and families. In J. McHale and W. Grolnick (Eds.), *Retrospect and prospect in the psychological study of families* (p. 35–64). Mahwah, NJ: Lawrence Erlbaum Associates.

Silverstein, L.B., and Auerbach, C. F. (1999). Deconstructing the essential father. *American Psychologist, 54*, 397–407.

Snyder, D. K., Klein, M. A., Gdowski, C. L., Faulstich, C., et al. (1988). Generalized dysfunction in clinic and nonclinic families: A comparative analysis. *Journal of Abnormal Child Psychology, 16*, 97–109.

Sroufe, J. (1991). Assessment of parent-adolescent relationships: Implications for adolescent development. *Journal of Family Psychology, 5*, 21–45.

Sroufe, L. A., Jacobvitz, D., Mangelsdorf, S., DeAngelo, E., and Ward, M. (1985). Generational boundary dissolution between mothers and their preschool children: A relationship systems approach. *Child Development, 56*, 317–325.

Stern, D. (1995). *The motherhood constellation: A unified view of parent–infant psychotherapy*. New York: Basic Books.

Stocker, C., Dunn, J., and Plomin, R. (1989). Sibling relationships: Links with child temperament, maternal behavior, and family structure. *Child Development, 60*, 715–727.

Sullivan, M. (1996). Rozzie and Harriet? Gender and family patterns of lesbian coparents. *Gender and Society, 10*, 747–767.

Suppal, P., and Roopnarine, J. (1999). Paternal involvement in child care as a factor of maternal employment and extended families in India. *Sex Roles, 40*, 731–744.

Talbot, J., Pouquette, C., and McHale, J. (1999, April). *The second wave of transition to parenthood research in context*. Paper presented at Society for Research in Child Development, Albuquerque, NM.

Tolan, P. H., and Gorman-Smith, D. (1997). Families and the development of urban children. In H. J. Walberg and O. Reyes (Eds.), *Children and youth: Interdisciplinary perspectives: Issues in children's and families' lives* (Vol. 7, pp. 67–91). Thousand Oaks, CA: Sage.

Van Egeren, L. A. (2000, July). *Prebirth predictors of parenting alliance trajectories in early infancy*. Paper presented at the World Association for Infant Mental Health, Montreal, Canada.

Visher, E. B., and Visher, J. S. (1979). Impressions of psychiatric problems and their management: China, 1977. *American Journal of Psychiatry, 136*, 28–32.

Visher, E. B., and Visher, J. S. (1990). Dynamics of successful stepfamilies. *Journal of Divorce and Remarriage, 14*, 3–12.

Vogel, E., and Bell, N. (1960). The emotionally disturbed child as a family scapegoat. In N. Bell and E. Vogel (Eds.), *A modern introduction to the family*, New York: Free Press. 21–42.

Volling, B. (1997). The family correlates of maternal and paternal perceptions of differential treatment in early childhood. *Family Relations, 46*, 227–236.

Volling, B. L., and Belsky, J. (1992). The contribution of mother–child and father–child relationships to the quality of sibling interaction: A longitudinal study. *Child Development, 63*, 1209–1222.

Volling, B. L., and Elins, J. L. (1998). Family relationships and children's emotional adjustment as correlated of maternal and paternal differential treatment: A replication with toddler and preschool siblings. *Child Development, 69*, 1640–1656.

Von Klitzing, K., Simoni, H., and Burgin, D. (1999, July). Child development and early triadic relationships. *International Journal of Psychoanalysis, 80*, 71–89.

Vuchinich, S., Emery, R. E., and Cassidy, J. (1988). Family members and third parties in dyadic family conflict: Strategies, alliances, and outcomes. *Child Development, 59,* 1293–1302.

Walsh, F. (1993). *Normal family processes.* New York: Guilford.

Wallerstein, J. (1984). Children of divorce: Preliminary report of a ten-year follow-up of young children. *American Journal of Orthopsychiatry, 54,* 444–458.

Whiteside, M. F., and Becker, B. J. (2000). Parental factors and the young child's postdivorce adjustment: A meta analysis with implications for parenting arrangements. *Journal of Family Psychology, 14,* 5–26.

Whitsett, D., and Land, H. (1992). Role strain, coping, and marital satisfaction of stepparents. *Families in Society, 73,* 79–92.

4

Single Parenthood

Marsha Weinraub
Danielle L. Horvath
Temple University
Marcy B. Gringlas
Thomas Jefferson University

INTRODUCTION

The proportion of children living in single-parent families has increased markedly around the world since 1960, and this increase has been especially significant in the United States (Burns, 1992; Hobbs and Lippman, 1990). The United States has a higher proportion of single-parent households than that of any other developed country. The proportion of children in the United States living with only one parent increased from 9.1% in 1960 to 28% in 1997 (U.S. Bureau of the Census, 1998). Although there are differences in the prevalence of single-parent families across ethnic groups, with nearly 47% of African American children living in single-parent families, this increase has affected all groups of Americans (U.S. Bureau of the Census, 2000). Given current divorce and remarriage trends, demographers predict that more than half of all America's children will spend some part of their formative years in a single-parent family (Ahlburg and DeVita, 1992; Bianchi, 1995).

For observers on the national scene in the early 1990s, this changing family pattern was viewed as particularly alarming. Considered a prime symptom of the erosion of American culture, single-parent families were reputed by many to be responsible for society's declining values and the breakdown of the social fabric. In an *Atlantic* magazine article entitled "Dan Quayle was right," Whitehead (1993, p. 77) characterized the family disruption associated with the rise in single-parent families as "a central cause of many of our most vexing social problems." Indeed, the term single-parent family became almost a euphemism for family breakdown, a kind of social pathology, and a major contributor to all that is wrong with our society (Kamerman and Kahn, 1988).

To some extent, this alarmist view of the early 1990s contains a grain of truth. A wide range of research from sociologists and psychologists has shown that children of single-parent families are more likely to have difficulties with emotional and psychological adjustment and with school performance and educational attainment, and they are also more likely to have behavioral adjustment problems, later marriage, and earlier childbearing compared with children of two-parent families. Because single-parent children appear more vulnerable to a wide variety of societal problems, these children have been routinely referred to as at risk for developmental difficulties. However, new studies that have appeared within the past decade are raising questions about these families and whether or not children growing up in single-parent families are necessarily at risk, particularly in the child's early years (e.g., Ricciuti, 1999).

To say that a child is at risk is a statistical statement, indicating that, probabilistically speaking, children in single-parent families are generally more likely to have developmental difficulties than other children are. One of the reasons children from single-parent families may be at risk is that single-parent families are also disproportionately poor compared with other families. According to Garfinkel and McLanahan (1986), no other major demographic group is so poor and no other group stays poor for so long. International studies show that poverty rates are higher among children in single-parent families than those in all other family types in every country studied (Hobbs and Lippman, 1990). Data from the 2000 census indicate that 34% of single-parent homes headed by a woman and 16% of single-parent families headed by a man live in poverty (June 2001 US Census Bureau). As a consequence of poverty alone, many children of single parents grow up in deteriorated and dangerous neighborhoods, often with inferior housing and educational systems. How much of the single-parent risk status is related to poverty and how much of the single-parent risk status is due to other factors also associated with single-parent families are questions with important psychological and social policy implications.

Increasingly, signs have emerged that perceptions and acceptance of single-parent families are changing. More and more single-parent families are emerging very visibly on the national scene, and the public has become more accustomed to seeing them. When Ingrid Bergman conceived a child out of wedlock in 1950, writers of the movie star columns were aghast, and Ingrid Bergman was effectively blackballed for nearly a decade from the American screen. In the 1990s, derision and concern greeted the television character Murphy Brown's birth of her out-of-wedlock child. However, in the year 2000, Madonna, a real-life rock star, birthed a baby son Rocco, and the event was greeted with as much joy and interest as the birth of any baby to a prominent rock star. Shortly after Rocco's birth, Madonna married the child's father; there may have been more interest in Madonna's subsequent marriage than in the birth of her child. Could this be indicative of a changing view of nonmarital births? Could public perceptions of social clocks and developmental sequences of "first marriage, then baby carriage" be changing at the beginning of the twenty-first century? Could changes in public perceptions of births to single parents also be related to changes in our understanding of the risks related to growing up in a single-parent home?

To unravel the multiple factors that may be related to our understanding of whether or not children of single-parent families are at at risk, it is necessary to identify the many similar and divergent characteristics of single-parent families. One of the most important characteristics of single-parent families and their children is their heterogeneity. Although about half of all children growing up in single-parent families live in poverty, many do not. Similarly, contrary to stereotypical views and journalistic ravings, not all single-mother families are on welfare. Although many single mothers draw funds from public assistance, more than half do not (Kamerman and Kahn, 1988).

The phenomenological experience of growing up in a single-parent family varies depending on the nature of the family, the experiences of the parent, and the family context. Single parents may be divorced, widowed, or unmarried; they may be teenaged or older; they may have been previously married or not. Although most single parents are women, the number of male single parents is increasing. Although legally single, some parents classified by Census statisticians and researchers as single may be living in a committed, partnered relationship not legally acknowledged (see Patterson, in Vol. 3 of this *Handbook*, for information about lesbian and gay parenting). These statistically single parents are often rearing their children in the context of a committed, partnered relationship. For some single parents, becoming a single parent may have been a planned and conscious decision; for others it was not. Some single parents may have chosen to have and to rear their children with another adult parent; they became single parents when this partnership did not work out, resulting in divorce, separation, or widowhood. Other single parents may have decided to become parents knowing that they would be without partners. The commonality across these varied types of single parents is that the parent does not have a legally married partner in the home. How these individuals came to be parents, the choices they made, and the experiences that were thrust on them, all have differential implications for their family's life circumstances.

Differences in how the parents came to be single parents affect individuals' employment, their financial circumstances, their relationships with other adults, their involvement with their child, and their competence as parents. The etiology of the parent's single parenthood also may have implications for the child's perceptions and experiences growing up. For example, imagine that 10 children from different types of single-parent families are brought together to discuss their experiences. They would describe many common experiences, such as not having enough money, missing their mothers or fathers, and problems getting along with their single parent. These concerns, however, do not differ from those of children living in *all* families. Those issues that are *unique* to single-parent families are issues for which there are large individual differences across single-parent families. Depending on their age, children from recently divorced single-parent families might talk of anger at their parents' separation, of fights between mom and dad over custody and child support, and about what happens on dad's day for visitation (see Hetherington and Stanley-Hagan, in Vol. 3 of this *Handbook*, for more information about parenting in divorced and remarried families). Some children of divorce may wonder why dad and mom are not living together anymore; others may be relieved to be free finally from the marital discord. Children of widowed single parents may be mourning their parent's loss, whereas children of adolescent single mothers may have difficulty with mom's inexperienced and immature ways and wonder when mom will ever finish going to school. Children of never-married mothers may wonder about their father, who he is, and what he is like. Some children may be confused about who their fathers are, and why they are not around, whereas other children, albeit a minority, may be learning to live without a mother. Some children may feel isolated and alone, whereas others are living in cramped households, with not too much in the way of material goods but plenty of people to be with and love. Researchers need to unravel these various psychological experiences to understand what it is about the single-parent family that might contribute to the at-risk status of these children.

These issues are our foci in this chapter: to describe the changing demographics of single-parent families, to describe similarities and differences across parenting situations in single-parent families, and to explore some of the parenting factors that might be responsible for the at-risk status of children growing up in single families. In the first section, we consider the changing demographics of single-parent families over the past several decades. We show that not only is the number of single-parent families increasing, but also the circumstances that are responsible for the formation of single-parent families—divorce and separation, widowhood, and out-of-marriage births—are changing too. In the next section, we summarize the literature on parenting in common types of single-parent families—divorced parents, adolescent parents, and "not-married" mothers—with the intent of identifying parenting features both unique to these specific single-parent family types and common to single parents as a group. We examine in this section the differences between mother-headed and father-headed single-parent families. We suggest that single-parent families that arise from different circumstances differ in a number of important ways, and these differences need to be considered before any understanding of the more general effects of rearing children in a single-parent family is attained. In the third section, we consider research directions that appear especially promising.

Because so much critical attention has been focused on the effects on child development of growing up in a single-parent family (examples of excellent reviews include those of Herzog and Sudia, 1973; as well as Amato, 1988; Amato and Keith, 1991a, 1991b; Cashion, 1982; McLanahan and Bumpass, 1988; and Ricciuti, 1999), we direct our attention in this chapter to describing and understanding the situations single parents face during the time of their single parenthood and how these situations may influence their behavior toward their children.

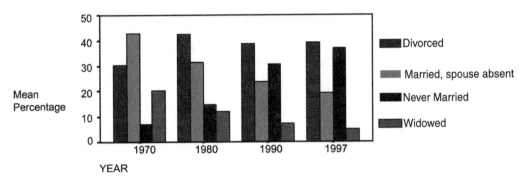

FIGURE 4.1. Percentage of children under 18 years of age living with one parent, by marital status of parent: 1970, 1980, 1990, and 1997. (Source: U.S. Bureau of the Census, *Current Population Reports,* 2000.)

DEMOGRAPHIC CHANGES IN SINGLE-PARENT FAMILY FORMATION

Not only has the prevalence of single-parent families changed over the past four decades, but so have the conditions that have lead to the formation of single-parent families (Amato, 2000; U.S. Bureau of the Census, 1992). As Figure 4.1 shows, in 1997 most children were in single-parent families, either mother or father headed, created by divorce or separation, and nearly 40% of children who were living in single-parent homes had parents who had never been married. However, what cannot be as easily discerned from Figure 4.1 is that the proportion of single-parent children living in a family created by divorce or separation (columns one and two combined) declined from 86% in 1970, to 73% in 1990, to 58% in 1997. Also declining, from 20% in 1970 to 5% in 1997, is the proportion of children living in single-parent families created by the death of a parent. Of all single-parent families, the most significant is the increase in children in single-parent families headed by a never-married parent. This group increased from approximately 6% in 1970, to 26% in 1990, to 37% in 1997. This increase reflects both increases in births to unmarried individuals and single-parent adoptions. In addition, the increase in the proportion of children living in a home with a never-married parent is partly a function of the decrease in the proportion of single-parent families created by divorce, separation, or the death of a parent. This increase may also reflect, not necessarily changes in attitudes toward marriage, but changes in women's willingness to enter into marital unions that place them at serious economic and social disadvantage (Edin, 2000).[1]

Many women have children outside of marriage; the past few decades have seen fluctuations in the rates of nonmarital births. In the 1960s, nonmarital birthrates increased steadily, averaging 285,600 per year. This number quadrupled over the next two decades to approximately 1.1 million by 1990 and peaked in 1994 at nearly 1.3 million. However, since 1994, the rates of births to nonmarried women have been decreasing. Before a U.S. House of Representatives Subcommittee hearing on Reducing Nonmarital Births, Stephanie Ventura (June, 1999), researcher and demographer for the Centers for Disease Control and Prevention, stressed the following four points regarding recent trends in nonmarital births:

> "Nonmarital births skyrocketed from 1940–1990 but trends have stabilized in the 1990's, with a decline since 1994. Teens are not the only women having nonmarital births; two-thirds of nonmarital births are to women 20 and older. Teen birth rates have declined considerably since 1991, with declines in all states and racial and ethnic groups. Nonmarital birth rates have fallen for all population groups, but most sharply for African American women."

---

[1] At the same time, there is some suggestion that from 1996 to 2000, there have been increases in the incidence of single parents cohabiting with their unmarried spouses in response to new welfare regulations.

Although premarital births have been more common among African American women since at least the early 1960s, responsibility for the increase over the past 40 years in premarital births has been shared across racial groups. According to Ventura (1999), two trends have contributed to the rising numbers of premarital births. First, there has been a large increase in the number of unmarried women in the childbearing years, and, second, there has been a 40% decrease in birthrates for married women since 1940.

More interesting is the changing character of the women having out-of-marriage births. The largest percentage of increases in births outside of marriages has been for European American, employed, college-educated women (Bachu, 1998). For a number of reasons—increased employment, delayed marriage, reduced likelihood of marriage, and delayed childbearing—single motherhood has increased dramatically among affluent and well-educated women. This trend for births outside of marriage has been particularly dramatic among mothers in managerial and professional occupations, for whom the percentages more than doubled from 3.1% in 1980 to 8.2% in 1990. According to Bachu (1998), the "propensity to marry," that is, the tendency to avoid an out-of-wedlock birth with a forced marriage, decreased most dramatically for European American women by over 30% from the 1930s to the 1990s. The desire to marry to avoid an out-of-wedlock birth has historically been lower for African American women than for European American women, but the propensity to marry has also decreased for African American women (Bachu, 1998; Cherlin, 1998). The statistics of the declining propensity to marry partially symbolize the abating stigma associated with an out-of-wedlock birth and the concurrent financial gains women have made. Furthermore, for low-income women in general, they report that there are fewer eligible or appealing men to marry (Cherlin, 1998; Edin, 2000).

As Figure 4.2 shows, the percentage of increase in women having children out of marriage is particularly large for older women, especially for women in their thirties. In fact, even though teen birthrates have fallen for all population groups, the drop in teen birthrates has been sharpest for African American women (Ventura, 1999). In 1975 one half of all nonmarital births were to teenagers. This number decreased to one third in 1997, largely because many women over 20 years old are having nonmarital births.

Across racial groups, the number of never-married single mothers increased by 9% between 1990 and 1997, the number of married but separated mothers decreased by 23%, and the number of mothers who were single because of divorce increased over this same time by 4%. However,

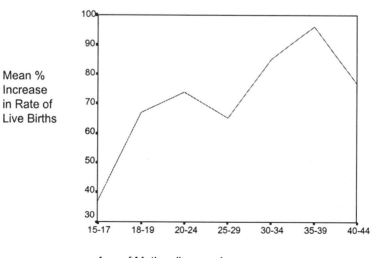

Age of Mother (in years)

FIGURE 4.2. Percentage of increase in rates of live births to unmarried women by age of mother: 1980 to 1997.

overall the proportion of children living in single-parent homes *headed by a mother* has decreased since 1990. This is largely because the number of father-headed single-parent homes increased from 12% of all single-parent homes in 1990 to 18% in 1997. The large increase in the number of never-married single fathers has contributed to this growth. The number of never-married single-father families increased by 50%; the number of families of divorced single fathers with custody increased by one third. These general trends are mirrored within each of the ethnic groups.

At the same time, the number of single parents, both male and female, who adopted children increased dramatically in the 1980s (Groze, 1991). The majority of adoptions are by women. Estimating the exact increase in single-parent adoptions is not possible because of differences in sampling strategies across studies, and the number of families of single parents who adopt children is still low compared with the number of single-parent households in the general population (Groze, 1991). Shireman (1995, 1996) and others (e.g., Feigelman and Silverman, 1977; Shireman and Johnson, 1976) have suggested that most single-parent adoptions are to women, and when single parents adopt they tend to adopt children of the same gender as themselves. Adoptions by single fathers are still uncommon, but adoptions by single mothers are not. In fact, in some places in the United States approximately 30% of all adoptions are to single women (V. Groza, personal communication, August 24, 2000). Perhaps as a consequence of the fact that most single adoptive parents are women, single-parent adoptive families tend to have lower incomes than dual-parent adoptive families (Groze, 1991; Shireman, 1996; Shireman and Johnson, 1976).

Finally, single parenthood is a transitional, not a permanent, status for many parents. Garfinkel and McLanahan (1986) estimate that the median length of time children spend in a mother-only family is approximately 6 years, approximately one third of the time most children remain in a household. Whether this single-parent experience begins early in the child's life or late may lead to very different experiences, with different consequences for parents and their children.

African American Families

Although the dramatic increase in single-parent families pervades all social strata and ethnic groups (Garcia-Coll, Meyer, and Brilliz in this handbook), the preponderance of single-parent families in African American families deserves special note (see also McAdoo, in Vol. 4 of this *Handbook*). According to Cherlin (1998), the fact that a far higher proportion of African American children are born to young unmarried mothers than is the case for other American families reflects historical trends concerning marriage and childbearing rather than a result of increased sexual activity among young African American unmarried women. To put it another way, over the past four decades African American women have postponed marriage but not childbearing. African American unmarried teens and unmarried young women between 20 and 24 years of age were no more likely to give birth in the late 1980s than they were in the 1960s. What has happened is that births to married African American women dropped precipitously, along with declines in childbearing across all groups from 1960 to 1970, and then births to married women leveled off. Meanwhile, fewer and fewer African American women married during the decades from 1960 to 1980, resulting in the fact that a greater proportion of births to African Americans were to unmarried women (69% in 1997; Ventura, 1999).

Overall, although there are more European American children reared in single-parent homes, an African American child is more likely to grow up in a single-parent home than a European American child is because there is a disproportionately large number of single African American parents. There are two reasons for this: One, the marriage rate for African Americans is lower than that of European Americans, and, two, African Americans are more likely to get divorced or separated than European Americans. The declining marriage rate among African Americans, according to Cherlin (1998, p. 56), can be accounted for by the "inseparable web of society-wide cultural change, the African American cultural heritage, and worsening economic constraints." Chronic male unemployment, recent increases in male unemployment, and the increasingly low ratio of male to female wages have made African American women less likely to marry and less tolerant of unsatisfactory relationships.

In addition, long-standing cultural traditions stemming from African styles of family life, specifically the greater emphasis on ties to a network of kin that extend across households (Garcia-Coll et al., 1995), have contributed to a reduced emphasis on marriage as the foundation of family life. Contrary to popular stereotypes, the dramatic increase in the number of African American single-parent families appears to be largely a response to the health of the American economy rather than a contribution to our nation's social or economic problems. Although economic problems contribute to higher rates of single-parent families in the African American community, the processes by which these economic factors influence parenting behavior within single-parent African American (McLoyd, Jayaratne, Ceballo, and Borquez, 1994) and two-parent European American (Conger, Ge, Elder, Lorenz, and Simons, 1994) families appear to be similar.

African American women have made significant educational gains in the past 20 years. The number of bachelor degrees awarded to African American women increased by 77% from 1977 to 1997. African American women are more educated than ever, but the number of bachelor degrees awarded to African American men over this same period increased by only 30% (Shepard, July 26, 2000). The educational discrepancy can manifest as a future earnings discrepancy, with African American women making significantly more than their potential mate. Indeed, for every three African American women in their twenties, there is only one African American male with earnings above the poverty level (Cherlin, 1998). This discrepancy may contribute to the incidence of single parenthood among African American families.

Single-Father Families

One group of single-parent families that has shown tremendous and well-documented increases, especially in the past decade, is that of single-father families. Approximately 18% of all single-parent families in 1997 were headed by fathers, up one third since 1990, and three times the number of single-father families in 1970 (U.S. Bureau of the Census, 1998). Single-parent fathers comprise almost 20% of single-parent families today. Compared with single-parent families headed by mothers, single-parent families headed by fathers are more often created by circumstances of divorce, and the fathers are more likely to be employed and less likely to be economically disadvantaged. Evidence also suggests that single-parent fathers are more likely to have custody of older children and males and are proportionally more likely to be of European American background than single-parent mothers are (U.S. Bureau of the Census, 1991). Telephone interviews with a subsample of single-parent families pulled from the Survey of Children and Parents, a nationally representative sample of 1,738 parents and 929 children aged 10 to 17 years, led Smith (1993) to report that single fathers were more likely to have been created by circumstances of divorce. They also had higher annual incomes, were more likely to be employed full time and less likely to be nonemployed, and less likely to be living in poverty than were single-parent mothers.

Over the past few decades, the reasons for fathers becoming single parents have changed. Instead of becoming single parents from widowhood, as was common around the turn of the twentieth century, most fathers, and single parents in general, are becoming single parents because of divorce or separation or are assuming responsibility for the child from an out-of-wedlock birth (Amato, 2000). It is important to note that nearly one in five children living in a single-parent home is living with the father. It is a misconception therefore to assume that nearly all children living with a single parent are living with their mother. Furthermore, it would be an oversight for researchers to continue to overlook this large population of families (Greif, 1995; Greif and DeMaris, 1995).

With the increase in single-parent father homes, the gap between single fathers who are divorced and single-parent fathers who have never been married is narrowing. Indeed, the fastest growing group of single-parent fathers living with their children includes single-parent fathers who have never been married. The number of single fathers who have never been married doubled from 3% in 1990 to 6% in 1998. Very little is known about this segment of fathers and their families. What is known is that across all ethnic groups, the proportions of never-married, separated, and divorced single fathers are remarkably similar. However, across ethnic groups, the average age of single fathers differs. European American single fathers are the oldest (the majority 40 to 44 years old), followed by African American single fathers (the majority 30 to 34 years olds); Latino single fathers are the youngest, with the majority 20 to 24 years of age. The age of the single father matters in that age is related to educational attainment and financial status, with older fathers likely to be more affluent than younger fathers (Amato, 2000).

Summary

There is great heterogeneity across single-parent families with regard to the conditions that lead to their formation, and these conditions have been growing more variable over the past decade. Whereas 10 years ago, the preponderance of single-parent families had been created from situations of divorce and widowhood, today there are nearly as many single parents who were not married when they become parents. Nonmarried mothers are more likely to be older and better educated than previous single-parent mothers were. Increasingly, single fathers are becoming primary custodial parents.

In the next section, unique features of each of these single-parent family types are examined for better understanding of the heterogeneity of single-parent families and for understanding why it may be highly misleading to generalize across single-parent families when describing parent circumstances and parenting behaviors.

SIMILARITIES AND DIFFERENCES ACROSS DIFFERENT TYPES OF SINGLE-PARENT FAMILIES

In this section we descibe the similarities and the differences in family situations in the many different types of single-parent families. We begin by addressing the following question: Are there differences between mother-only and father-only households? This is followed with a more specific discussion of the special circumstances of divorced parents with custody, adolescent parents, and various other forms of single-parent families.

Comparisons Between Single Fathers and Single Mothers

Are single-parent fathers as a group of single parents unique from single-parent mothers? Most of what is known about single-parent fathers comes from small, select samples of volunteers; generally, they are compared with single mothers or married fathers (e.g., DeFrain and Eirick, 1981; Dornbusch and Gray, 1988; Greif, 1985; regarding lesbian and gay single-parents, see Turner, Scadden, and Harris, 1990; Patterson, in Vol. 3 of this *Handbook*). This literature suggests that, demographically, single-parent fathers are different from single-parent mothers. However, as the number of single-parent father families grows and the homogeneity among single-parent fathers as a group decreases, differences between single fathers and single mothers are coming under renewed scrutiny. In the past, samples were fairly homogeneous, made up of European American, middle-socioeconomic, divorced, college-educated men. However, with more never-married, younger, lower-income men heading up single-parent homes and fathers gaining custody after divorce, this profile is likely to change and look more like that of fathers in general. Furthermore, comparisons of parental character-istics between single mothers and fathers may look different (Eggebeen, Snyder, and Manning, 1996; Greif, 1995). In comparison with married fathers, single-parent fathers have substantially less in-comes, and since 1984 this gap has been widening (Brown, 2000). It is estimated that single fathers' incomes are somewhere between those of single-parent mothers and married fathers (Meyer and Garasky, 1993).

Although there are more single-parent father homes now than ever before, the differences in how they came about may have significant ramifications in terms of the economic status of the single-parent family. Most single-parent fathers are divorced, whereas there is nearly an equal percentage of never-married and divorced single-parent mother homes. Overall, divorced single parents are better off financially than never-married or separated single parents. Thus, with fewer single mothers from divorce compared with single fathers, financially, single fathers are better off (Amato, 2000).

A more pressing and more complicated issue than demographic differences between single mothers and single fathers concerns the relationship between demographic variables and parenting practices. To the extent that a single parent's parenting style is influenced by demographic variables such as educational attainment and socioeconomic status, the parenting styles of single-parent mothers and fathers may be different (Avenevoli, Sessa, and Steinberg, 1999; Hill and Hilton, 2000; Hilton and Devall, 1998; Kleist, 1999). Research suggests that a single parent's parenting behavior is negatively affected by both satisfaction at work and economic status, both of which are higher for single fathers than for single mothers (Christoffersen, 1998). Likewise, compared with single mothers, single fathers seem to have better overall psychological well-being, but this difference is at least partially accounted for by their increased economic status and educational attainment (Amato, 2000; Christoffersen, 1998). It is even possible that these demographic variables operate differently in how they influence parenting styles of mothers and fathers. Nevertheless, as discussed in the next subsection, within divorced families, custodial parents, whether fathers or mothers, often face similar challenges.

The Special Circumstances of Divorced Parents with Custody

The majority of divorced parents with custody are mothers (85%; U.S. Bureau of the Census, 2000). However, the increasing divorce rates, along with changing views of gender roles since the 1970s, have meant that fathers' opportunities for winning custody in the courts have increased, and fathers have been more interested and willing to take custody of their children. Studies suggest that, prior to their divorce, single fathers were not different from other married fathers. Predivorce, these fathers were often not unusually involved in childrearing or household chores, at least, not until their marriage began to deteriorate (Gersick, 1979; Greif, 1985). They became custodial parents either because the mother did not want custody when the marriage ended or because the father did not want to leave the family home. According to what single fathers told Greif (1985), fathers received custody generally because they were open to the possibility of being a single parent and because either the mother did not want to continue in her custodial role or because the mother was perceived to be incompetent. In some cases, the father received custody because the children wanted to remain in the home with their father. It is rare for fathers to gain custody as a result of contested custodial court trials (Greif, 1985). However, fathers who do obtain custody in this manner report more troubled relationships with their children later, possibly because they face more adjustment difficulties than other divorced fathers with custody (Greif and DeMaris, 1995).

When marriages end in divorce, newly single parents have to come to terms with the loss of their marriage and often with the failure of their marital hopes and expectations. The single parent's partner may have served as an attachment figure, or even a best friend, and these emotional losses can be devastating (Weiss, 1979). Resolving these emotional experiences can take months or, in many cases, years. During this time, these emotional experiences may affect the parent's adjustment, well-being, relationships with other adults, and interactions with the children.

During the time of separation and divorce, household routines are being reorganized, and children are often more angry, aggressive, and resentful (Bolton and MacEachron, 1986). These conditions pose significant challenges for competent parenting. Also during this time, many families experience dramatic changes in financial status (Cherlin, 1992). Although mothers seem to suffer more financial setbacks postdivorce, fathers too are affected. According to a March 2000 Census report, even though 58% of all custodial parents had child support awards (61% for mothers and 40% for fathers) and

70% of mothers and 57% of fathers awarded these awards actually received a portion of the award, 33% of custodial mothers and 14% of custodial fathers still are considered poor.

As a further stress on financial resources following an emotionally upsetting divorce, some families experience employment and housing changes and disturbances, creating adjustment difficulties for parents as well as for children (Jones, 1984; Richard, 1982). Common parental responses to divorce and the subsequent life-altering events are anger, anxiety, and depression, with possible impulsive and antisocial behavior and excessive swings of mood and self-confidence (Hetherington, 1993). Reoccurring health problems and difficulties with the immune system are not uncommon (Hetherington and Stanley-Hagan, in Vol. 3 of this *Handbook*; Richard, 1982).

Given what is known about how economic and psychosocial stress may affect parents (McLoyd, 1990; McLoyd et al., 1994), it is not surprising that during the first months and years after divorce, divorced parents are more irritable and unresponsive in their interactions with their children (Thiriot and Buckner, 1991). They show poor supervision and erratic and sometimes punitive discipline (Camara and Resnick, 1988; Hetherington, Cox, and Cox, 1982; Wallerstein, Corbin, and Lewis, 1988). As Hetherington and Stanley-Hagan note (1995), many of these symptoms subside as families attain a new homeostasis, usually within 2 years. "Divorced adults may continue to feel more depressed and more anxious than their nondivorced counterparts, and some custodial parents may continue to find single parenting stressful. In spite of this, most restabilized single-parent families function reasonably well, provided they are not faced with sustained or new adversities." (Hetherington and Stanley-Hagan, in Vol. 3 of this *Handbook*).

Financial security, employment stability and satisfaction, "neutral if not positive relationships" with their exspouses, confidence in their parenting skills, and the formation of a new intimate support relationship are factors that affect well-being and parenting skills of the custodial parent (Richard, 1982; Thiriot and Buckner, 1991). As Hetherington and Stanley-Hagan (in Vol. 3 of this *Handbook*) report, loneliness, task overload, and increased child rearing stress are common experiences of divorced custodial parents. Nevertheless, within two years,

> three fourths of divorced women report that they are happier in their new situation than in the last year of their marriage, and most, in spite of the stresses, find rearing children alone easier than with a disengaged, undermining, or acrimonious spouse.... Furthermore, in addition to perceiving themselves as more able parents than mothers in conflictual, unsatisfying marriages, divorced women on the average are less depressed, show less state anxiety, drink less, and have fewer health problems than those in unhappy, acrimonious, or emotionally disengaged marriages.

Thus the diminished parenting associated with divorce results from the disorganization and change after the dissolution of the marriage. As these stresses subside and as relationships with the noncustodial spouse reach equilibrium, the stresses these families experience become increasingly related to the difficulties of having only one adult parent. This parent frequently must combine parenting and financial responsibilities. As a single wage earner, the divorced parent may be limited in earning power and opportunity for workplace advancement. In terms of role transition following divorce, generally, mothers have to adjust to a new role as a financial supporter, and fathers have to adjust to a new role as a homemaker (Hill and Hilton, 2000). Each role transition has unique and shared responsibilities and stresses for men and women. In an investigation of 626 divorced single mothers and 100 divorced single fathers with custody, satisfaction with the new role was the strongest predictor of depression in both groups (Hill and Hilton, 2000).

There are differences in the situations between custodial fathers and mothers. Divorced custodial mothers and fathers both face new challenges in trying to balance family and career goals. New challenges for custodial fathers in the primary caregiver role include cutting back on hours at the office or work and conflicts in scheduling business trips. For mothers, adding the primary provider role may be especially frustrating. Although women have made considerable gains in the American workplace in the past few decades, women still earn only 73% of what their male counterparts earn (U.S. Bureau of the Census, 2000). According to Hill and Hilton (2000), it may be easier for fathers to incorporate the primary parenting role than it is for mothers to add the primary provider role. To the extent that custodial mothers improve their standard of living, by educational and economic attainment, to levels comparable with those of custodial fathers, differences in psychological adjustment and parenting behaviors between custodial mothers and fathers may diminish.

Notwithstanding, custodial fathers have somewhat different circumstances from those of custodial mothers. Custodial divorced fathers are often older, better educated, and earn better incomes (DeFrain and Eirick, 1981; Dornbusch and Gray, 1988; Greif, 1985). Custodial divorced fathers are less likely to move to either an apartment or a relative's home after the divorce, and they are more likely to be living in their predivorce homes than divorced mothers. Compared with mothers who must return to work (Jones, 1984), newly divorced fathers rarely need to find new employment, most continue in their same jobs, and income levels rarely plummet as they do for newly divorced mothers. Many fathers cut back on employment so that they can devote more time to household and childrearing duties. Fathers report that because employers are unsympathetic to their situation of having to combine childrearing and employment, full-time employment is sometimes difficult to maintain.

Divorced fathers receive more offers of support from their relatives and community, but they are less likely to take them. Sometimes, their lack of experience with housekeeping, household chores, childrearing, and arranging childcare and activity schedules make the transition more difficult for fathers than for mothers, but most fathers adjust quite quickly, soliciting help from their children, particularly older children, and most particularly daughters (Greif, 1985; Kissman and Allen, 1993). Although it is generally assumed that fathers are more likely to hire housekeepers, except for widowers, Greif did not find this to be the case in his 1982 survey of 1,136 custodial fathers.

At the time of divorce, fathers, like mothers, undergo considerable interpersonal stress, with increases in anger, loss, loneliness, lack of self-esteem, and lowered self-confidence (Pichitino, 1983). In contrast, men are less likely than women to have friendships and close emotional relationships outside their marriage, and they may be more likely than women to turn feelings of Greif into anger (Kissman and Allen, 1993; Nieto, 1990; Pasick, 1990). Often they are less likely to seek therapy, and they often feel less comfortable with it (Kissman and Allen, 1993).

However, as time goes on, both divorced fathers and mothers develop a household and social routine adequate to their family needs. DeFrain and Eirick (1981) questioned 33 divorced single-parent fathers and 38 comparable single-parent mothers on a wide variety of topics and found substantial similarities between fathers and mothers. Both reported that their marriages before the divorce were "more bad than good," with lack of communication, extramarital affairs, sexual problems, and loss of interest given as reasons for the breakup. Both mothers and fathers rated divorce as a medium-high to highly stressful event. Both men and women reported that their moods had improved since the divorce and many of their initial fears had subsided, with the majority of both groups feeling that they were doing "reasonably well." The minority of parents who reported yelling and/or hitting their children after the divorce said that those behaviors had decreased over time, and they found it much easier to control their children since the divorce. Both men and women reported they did not get to spend as much time with their children as they would prefer. Nevertheless, fathers reported feeling quite satisfied with themselves for coping as well as they did in their new role as a single parent.

Other investigators have reported similarities and differences in fathers' and mothers' childrearing behaviors. Hilton and Devall (1998) reported that single mothers and fathers provide their children with different types of care. The mothers in their study talked to their children more, and fathers provided their children with more economic and material resources. Also, as in previous investigations, the fathers reported being more confident in their role, and they commanded more respect and authority with their children than mothers did. Dornbusch and Gray (1988) reported that, like single mothers, single fathers tend to be more permissive than their married counterparts.

Contrary to expectations, both fathers and mothers report having an easier time with younger than with older children (Greif, 1985). Both mothers and fathers report more difficulties with sons than daughters, but single-parent fathers experience more childrearing problems with daughters than single-parent mothers do (Greif, 1985; Santrock, Warshak, and Elliott, 1982). Compared with their agemates, boys in single-parent father homes appear equally sociable and mature; daughters in single-parent father families are less sociable, less independent, and more demanding (Santrock et al., 1982). Many fathers in Greif's study reported difficulties understanding and meeting their daughters' emotional needs, and they sometimes called on their daughters to shoulder childcare and household chores disproportionately. Puberty seems especially difficult for fathers and their daughters, with fathers uncomfortable talking about maturation and sexual matters (Greif, 1985).

Socially, divorced men and women are both equally interested in dating, with nearly four out of five of the parents in Greif's (1985) study reporting that they were currently dating. In a follow-up investigation Greif (1995) found that the most well-adjusted fathers were satisfied with their social life. However, the single father's greater financial resources often made finding substitute childcare easier (Kissman and Allen, 1993). Although no overall differences in dating patterns have been documented, the remarriage rate is higher for divorced men than for divorced women. This may be because some men feel that they can best fulfill their childrearing responsibilities by remarrying (Kissman and Allen, 1993).

One of the greatest stresses reported by divorced custodial fathers is combining work and child-rearing (Greif, 1985; Kissman and Allen, 1993), with nearly four out of five fathers in Greif's sample reporting that this was difficult. Men reported that, compared with their experiences before divorce, after divorce they had more interruptions in their daily work schedules and fewer opportunities to take on additional hours and projects, inhibiting their hope for career progress and higher incomes. Of the 1,136 fathers Greif interviewed, 66 men had to quit their job because of conflicts with childrearing responsibilities, and 43 men reported being fired. They also experienced problems with having to arrive at work late or leave early, missing workdays, or not being able to engage in work-related travel. Only 27% of the men interviewed reported that no work-related changes were necessary.

As stressful as these childrearing–employment conflicts are for single-parent fathers, they are often even more stressful for single-parent mothers. In Greif's (1985) comparison of single divorced mothers who were asked the same questions as men, women reported greater employment–childrearing conflicts than men. Only 10% of the women said that work had *not* been difficult; and more mothers than fathers were fired from or had to quit their jobs. Although the difficulties that fathers and mothers have juggling employment and family conflicts may be similar in some respects, these experiences may be different for men and women because of early socialization differences. Men may not be as prepared for coping with these conflicts as women, and they may not understand these conflicts as well. They may continue to evaluate themselves against standards that they had used previously when they had a wife who performed childcare and household tasks for the entire family. As Greif (1985, p. 70) describes it, a man "has to change the way he feels about himself as a *MAN*". In contrast, women's difficulties with employment–childrearing conflicts may stem from problems associated with less education, less employment experience, lower occupational prestige, and a lower-paying job along with reduced flexibility for juggling childcare and employment demands.

Finally, the dynamics of single-parent mother and single-parent father families, relative to relationships predivorce, may be different. Anecdotal reports indicate that noncustodial mothers may be more active parents in their children's lives after the divorce than are noncustodial fathers (Greif, 1985; Kissman and Allen, 1993). Although divorce in the custodial mother family may cause both mothers and fathers to move away from close supervision of their children and involvement in their children's lives, single fathers are often drawn into *closer* contact with their children and have more involvement in their children's lives after than *before* the divorce. In contrast, after the divorce custodial mothers often may have a somewhat reduced involvement in their parenting role because of increased financial responsibilities than before divorce. In a comparison of 30 single-parent mother and 30 single-parent father homes, Hilton and Devall (1998) reported that single mothers became less positive in their parenting following divorce and single fathers became more positive. This may be the case because following a divorce as the mother is adding her primary provider role, she has less time to spend with her children, and she may not be as psychologically available to her children in the time that she does have. Fathers, in contrast, in adding the primary caregiver role probably find themselves spending more time with their children than they did before the divorce. The custodial father's higher involvement with his children and his more frequent performance of traditionally female tasks, compared with those of other nondivorced fathers, may lead children of single-father families to develop more flexible notions of childrearing and gender roles than children in custodial mother or married, two-parent settings (Lamb, Pleck, and Levine, 1986).

In sum, divorced parents are still the largest group of single parents. Economically, divorced single parents are the most prosperous of all single parents. Divorced fathers are more financially stable than mothers are. Earlier research often examined gender differences in parenting styles isolated from the differential experiences divorced mothers and fathers have following a divorce. Current research suggests that divorced mothers and fathers are more similar in their parenting style to the extent that their economic and educational backgrounds are similar. Divorced fathers and mothers must adjust to a new role as primary caretaker or provider respectively. Men and women's adjustment to their new roles is affected by institutional barriers in the workforce, barriers that reflect society's acceptance, or lack, of the notion of a father as a primary care provider or mother as primary provider. As time goes on, mothers and fathers alike seem able to adjust and accept the marital dissolution and the challenges of single parenthood.

Single Parents Who are Not Married When They Become Parents

In this subsection we examine the different types of single-parent homes created by a nonmarital birth. Many women have what in the past have been called out-of-wedlock births. Different circumstances lead different women to have sometimes planned and sometimes unplanned premarital births. Individuals at different life stages vary in their capacity to meet the challenges of single parenthood. In this subsection we examine these different types of situations and how different types of single parents cope with and adjust to single parenthood.

Adolescent single parents. Many adolescent parents are also single parents. Although the adolescent birthrate is at an all-time low (U.S. Bureau of the Census, 2000), approximately one third of all births to single mothers are to teen mothers (Ventura, Martin, Curtain, Mathews, and Park, 2000; see also Figure 2). The relation between adolescent parenting and single parenting can also be presented in another way: Of all adolescent mothers, 79% are not married (Ventura et al., 2000). Two changes have occurred that have affected the statistics regarding the incidence of adolescent parenting, single parenting, and their relation. First, teen births have declined over the past four decades. Second, teens who do give birth are less likely to be married now than in previous decades.

Considerable ethnic differences exist in the proportion of adolescent mothers who are single. Although the African American teen birthrate has fallen the most dramatically, African American teen mothers are less likely to be married than either Latina, or non-Hispanic European American adolescent mothers (Child Trends, 1992; Kamerman and Kahn, 1988).

To what extent is the adolescent experience of being a single parent unique from the experiences of other single parents? According to Astone (1993), adolescent parenting contributes additional information needed to predict parental income five years after childbirth than that which can be predicted by single parenthood alone. To understand the uniqueness of the adolescent single-parenting situation, researchers are using approaches that tease out preexisting differences in young women who become adolescent mothers from those who delay childbearing and exploring developmental and contextual pathways in the lives of young mothers as they affect the childrearing process (e.g., Moore and Brooks-Gunn, in Vol. 3 of this *Handbook*).

Adolescent parents are perhaps the most disadvantaged of single parents. They usually come from poor families of low educational backgrounds. They are likely to be from impoverished neighborhoods, they have attended poor-quality schools, and they have suffered school failure and low educational aspirations (Furstenberg, Brooks-Gunn, and Chase-Lansdale, 1989; Hayes, 1987; Miller and Moore, 1990; Scott-Jones, 1991). These conditions do not disappear with the birth of the child, but continue to limit the young mothers' movements toward self-sufficiency (Furstenberg et al., 1989). Compared with other teens, teenage mothers are more likely to drop out of high school, but many circumstances affect the teen mothers' likelihood of dropping out (Scott-Jones, 1991). In 1997, National Longitudinal Youth Survey researchers reported that only 35% of teen mothers finished high school, compared with 85% of nonchildbearers (Hotz, Mullin, and Sanders, 1997). However, it is important to note that it is less common now than in past decades for teen mothers to terminate their educational career (Coley and Chase-Lansdale, 1998). Teen mothers who drop out of school come from poorer backgrounds than teen mothers who do not drop out of school do, and they are less likely to be receiving sufficient support both economically and emotionally from their families. However, even when teen mothers graduate from high school, they are less likely than other women to go on for postsecondary schooling.

Many adolescent single mothers and their children live with their family of origin, and African American mothers are more likely to coreside than European American single mothers (Moore and Brooks-Gunn, in Vol. 3 of this *Handbook*). There are benefits and drawbacks to coresidential living, and the effects of these family of origin arrangements may depend on the age of the single mothers, with more positive effects on the young teen mother and her child than on older teen mothers. In general, some studies have found coresidence with family members to be beneficial for the young mother in terms of further educational attainment (Furstenberg, 1981) and more fertility control (Black and Nitz, 1996). For the most part, families are willing to help the adolescent mother, especially in the first few years after her pregnancy (Furstenberg, 1981; Wakschlag, Chase-Lansdale, and Brooks-Gunn, 1996). The level of support seems to vary depending on whether the mother decides to remain at home, whether the parent stays in school, and on the family's ability to provide support. Teen mothers who remain with their families of origin are more likely to have returned to school, graduated, to be employed, and not receiving welfare (Cooley and Unger, 1991).

As Prater (1995) pointed out, the decision to establish an independent household and not remain in the family of origin is not necessarily an affirmative decision as much as a reflection of a lack of alternatives. Sometimes teen mothers are asked to move out, and sometimes they leave voluntarily. Regardless of the circumstances surrounding the separation from the family of origin, teen mothers who move out face the challenge of meeting the demands of adulthood and parenthood more so than other teen mothers. Teen mothers who do not live with their families of origin are more likely to be older, welfare dependent, and depressed (Prater, 1995).

Compared with other single mothers, teen mothers have more difficulty finding and maintaining stable employment, are more likely to collect welfare, and are less likely to marry than teens who are not mothers (Moore and Brooks-Gunn, in Vol. 3 of this *Handbook*; Prater, 1995). When they do marry, their divorce rates are higher than those of the general population; although no more likely to have more children than women who delay childbearing, adolescent mothers are more likely to have children closely spaced. Mott (1986) found that, to further strain a most likely already dire economic situation, a female giving birth before the age of 16 years has a 26% likelihood of having another child within 2 years.

Like other mothers, teen mothers have the predictable difficulties of balancing childcare, education, work, and leisure. However, in light of their lower education, poorer earning power, and reliance on family members and neighbors for support, these balancing difficulties are often more severe for the adolescent parent. Childcare is more likely to be provided by other family members and more often comprises makeshift arrangements (Cherlin, 1995). Compared with other women their age, women who give birth as teenagers continue to have low levels of employment and educational attainment. However, the Baltimore study (Furstenberg, Brooks-Gunn, and Morgan, 1987) and the New Haven study (Horwitz, Klerman, Kuo, and Jekel, 1991) showed surprising diversity on outcomes among these parents' situations, with striking individual differences in educational attainment, employment success, and subsequent births. For example, in the Baltimore study, by

17 years after the initial contact many teen mothers had continued their schooling, three fourths of the mothers were employed, and only one fourth were on welfare.

Higher educational attainment and fertility control have consistently been identified as effective means of bettering the life course of a teenage mother. Furstenberg et al. (1989) reported that 17 years after a teen pregnancy young mothers who finished high school, did not have a repeat pregnancy (within 5 years), and were married were no different from older childbearers from similar backgrounds. In sharp comparison was the young mother who managed none of these things, whom Furstenberg et al. (1989, p. 316) described as a "chronic welfare mom, with a number of children and few prospects of future betterment." In addition, the adolescent children of the teen mothers in the study of Furstenberg et al. improved or deteriorated in school (cognitively and socially) as their mother made her life better or worse (Furstenberg, Hughes, and Brooks-Gunn, 1992). In a study that examined the life courses of teenage mothers and teenagers who were pregnant but miscarried from similar, poor backgrounds, Hotz et al. (1997) found that the girls who miscarried were not more likely to have higher educational attainment than the mothers who gave birth. Furthermore, at the age of 34 years the mothers who miscarried were in fact less successful in the labor market than women who had become teen mothers. Finally, there were no differences in fertility control between the two groups of mothers (Hotz et al., 1997).

Less is known about the psychological adjustment and coping skills of single teenage mothers over time. There is some evidence that adolescent parents are more depressed than older mothers (Amato, 2000; Carter, Osofsky, and Hann, 1991; Osofsky, Eberhart-Wright, Ware, and Hann, 1992; Wasserman, Rauh, Brunelli, Garcia-Castro, and Necos, 1990), especially if they establish a household independently of their family of origin (Prater, 1995). Because many adolescent mothers live with their mothers, separation and autonomy become important issues to negotiate. Many adolescent mothers depend on their own mothers, not only for financial support and living arrangements, but also for childcare, guidance, parental supports, and information about parenting (Moore and Brooks-Gunn, in Vol. 3 of this *Handbook*). The results of studies that have looked at cohabiting teenage mothers have been mixed, with results indicating that for some teenage mothers it is better, in terms of child outcomes and the mothers' well-being, to live at home, but for others it is not. These mixed results may be partially due to the finding that the adolescent mother's mother is not typically a better parent than the adolescent mother herself (Oyerserman, Radin, and Benn, 1993). Also, adolescent mothers who live at home frequently experience and expose themselves and their child to conflict in the home that occurs at this time as the family renegotiates roles (Unger and Cooley, 1992).

Both adolescence as a life stage and the birth of a child contribute to shifts in family relationships and dynamics. When these shifts occur simultaneously, as they do in adolescent families, the families in which adolescent mothers live may experience tremendous stress. As Moore and Brooks-Gunn (in Vol. 3 of this *Handbook*) suggest, the task of developing an identity as a young woman at the same time as developing an identity as a mother may pose a more challenging task than negotiating the identity issues facing other teenagers who are not parents. Difficulties in developing an identity as a competent parent may be further challenged by the increased likelihood of having a premature, low-birthweight or sick child, circumstances that often co-occur with adolescent pregnancy. Finally, combining these changes with the many changes that may accompany the young woman's changing status from teenager to mother—changes in school, employment, family, and social status—may pose cumulative risks that further inhibit the adolescent mother's adjustment and coping.

Researchers have reported that adolescent parents have more unrealistic expectations for their children, are more restrictive, and provide a less stimulating, responsive, and well-regulated affective and intellectual environment for their children than do comparison groups of adult mothers (Brooks-Gunn and Furstenberg, 1986; Osofsky, Hann, and Peebles, 1994). However, the comparison groups that researchers include are often not appropriate, and often age and marital status are confounded (Moore and Brooks-Gunn, in Vol. 3 of this *Handbook*). More serious confounding variables include differences in education, employment, verbal ability, and poverty status. When these variables are controlled, as in a study by Chase-Lansdale, Brooks-Gunn, and Zamsky (1994), parental age does not seem to relate to parental affect, disciplinary style, or problem-solving style. As Hotz et al. (1997) found in their study of teen mothers and comparable teens who had miscarried, the actual age of first birth seems to matter less than more contextual factors, such as education and poverty status, that may affect a young mother and her child's chances at success.

Interventions aimed at improving the parenting skills of teen parents have not been successful (Brooks-Gunn, 1990), perhaps because these programs are generally of limited intensity (Roosa, 1986). Interventions that are comprehensive, offering childcare and development education, in addition to emotional, financial, and employment support, seem to be beneficial (Prater, 1995). Programs created with the young mother's needs and concerns in mind appear most beneficial. For instance, visiting the young mothers in the home may be more time consuming and expensive for clinicians, but it may be more effective because it eliminates travel and babysitting costs for the young mother. Furthermore, comprehensive programs that include financial and educational support will be most beneficial to young mothers in that they may assist the families' financial status and the mothers decision-making ability, self-efficacy, and psychological well-being (Kissman and Allen, 1993; Moore and Brooks-Gunn, in Vol. 3 of this *Handbook*).

Other single mothers.   The fastest growing group of single parents is that of the non adolescent, nonmarried woman. Some of these mothers may be living in partnered relationships, some may not. Observers have noted several cultural changes that have contributed to this international trend for women to have and rear children outside of traditional marital relationships. These include later age of marriage for men and women, increased infertility and childlessness of later marrying women, increasing divorce rates, and changing social attitudes (Burns and Scott, 1994; Edin, 2000; Kamerman and Kahn, 1988). The social stigma attached to having a child out of marriage has been declining since the 1960s, as witnessed by the increasing acceptance of unmarried mothers as public figures and as characters in popular films and television programs. Even the politicized labels that have been used to describe unmarried mothers and their children—"out-of-wedlock mothers" with "illegitimate children" —have been replaced in the popular literature with more morally neutral terms. There is also evidence that the liklihood of a "shotgun" wedding, getting married after learning of a pregnancy, is declining (Bachu, 1998). Some observers have even attributed the increasing number of women having children outside the traditional two-parent family structure to the decreasing "complementarity" of men's and women's gender roles in today's culture (Burns and Scott, 1994).

Within the group of nonmarried single-parent families, there is great diversity, and this diversity has important implications for understanding the parents, the parents' circumstances, and the possible effects of these differences on parenting and subsequent child outcomes. In this subsection, three groups of single parents are considered: unmarried single parents who are living with partners outside of a formal legal contract, "single mothers by choice," and a more inclusive group, whom we call solo mothers. Each is described in turn.

Unmarried couples by choice.   Women included in the statistical reports of women unmarried at childbirth include those who are unmarried but living with a partner in an extralegal relationship. Although many of these couples are composed of a man and woman, some may also be same-gender pairs (see Patterson, in Vol. 3 of this *Handbook*, for a description of parenting by lesbian and gay couples). Estimating the true proportion of these families is difficult, as statistics on these families are not registered anywhere. It is possible that, when the numbers of unmarried mothers living in committed relationships and rearing children with a partner is taken into consideration, the number of single parents is lower than generally thought.

Eiduson and Weisner (1978) and Weisner and Garnier (1992) included "social contract" or "unmarried couples by choice" in their early study of nonconventional family lifestyles. Generally, these were women and men who were experimenting with living together, they may or may not have married later. In many ways, the circumstances of unmarried mothers living with male partners were similar to those of married women (Eiduson, 1983), except that their partnerships tended to be more unstable and the values and beliefs about childrearing authority relationships and morality were less traditional. Compared with married couples and their children, these mothers and their children experienced relatively more frequent changes in their household composition, lived on lower and more unpredictable incomes, and often faced various social stigmas, such as lower teacher expectations (Weisner and Garnier, 1992). Regardless of these potential risks, Weisner and Garnier noted that when parents from nonconventional lifestyles had a strong commitment to their chosen family style, their children did not differ from children living in more traditional families on measures of adjustment and school performance.

Less is known about unmarried couples rearing children together. Edin (2000) interviewed 292 European American and African American low-income mothers in three U.S. cities. She found that almost all of the low-income single mothers she interviewed reported that they preferred to live separately or to cohabit with the fathers of their children rather than marry. Cohabitation allowed these mothers to enforce a "pay and stay" rule. If the father contributed to the household and followed the agreed-on rules, he could stay. If not, the mother had the power to evict him, because his name was generally not on the rental lease or mortgage. How frequently single-parent mothers are cohabiting with their partners or the fathers of their children is not known, and so it is hard to know whether there are changes in the rates of cohabitation or demographic differences in the frequency. More information about these families could help researchers understand the frequency and consequences of actual single parenting as opposed to the instances of cohabitation partnered parenting.

Single mothers by choice.   Another group of women who have nonmarital births are described as single mothers by choice (SMCs) by a national support and informational group founded in New York City in 1981. This organization SMC, defines a single mother by choice as a woman who starts out rearing her child without a partner. She may have decided to have or adopt a child, knowing she will be her child's sole parent, at least at the outset (Mattes, 1994). Bock (2000) pointed out that the label *single mother by choice* serves to differentiate these mothers from other single mothers. The words "by choice" imply that other single mothers did not choose to be single parents, or at least did not come to choose this way of life as conscientiously and responsibly as these single mother's by choice did. Single mothers choice, as defined above, are unique from other single mothers, and some feel faced with a struggle to assert their legitimacy as competent parents because they are different from both married parents and other single parents. However, just how different they are from other single mothers who choose to remain single may be open to some question.

Information concerning the incidence of single mothers by choice, their living circumstances, their parenting experiences, and effects on children growing up in these homes is limited. Existing information generally comes from the SMC organization in the form of surveys or anecdotal reports of members. Most research in this area is in the form of in-depth interviews with women identified as members of SMC. Generally there are no comparison groups, and the sample sizes are not large.

The profile of a single mother by choice is rather homogeneous. Single mothers by choice appear to be in their middle to upper thirties, European American, and of upper-middle-socioeconomic status. They are financially secure, well educated, and employed in well-paying professional jobs (Bock, 2000; Kamerman and Kahn, 1988; Mannis, 1999; Mattes, 1994). The SMC organization stresses that most of their members decided a priori to be single parents. The majority of these mothers gave very serious attention to either becoming pregnant or adopting a child. Nevertheless, there are also some single mothers by choice who became pregnant accidentally and found themselves delighted at the possibility of having children even though they were not married. Although the single mothers studied by Eiduson and Weisner in 1978 chose their lifestyle as a result of feminist concerns and the desire to live independently of traditional family styles, the single mothers by choice of the 1980s and the 1990s appear to be motivated by the "ticking of their biological clock," often heard ticking most loudly around a hallmark birthday such as the thirty-fifth or fortieth, at this time women reported feeling that they had fallen behind developmentally (Bock, 2000; Kamerman and Kahn, 1988; Mattes, 1999).

For many women, the decision to become a single parent is a long and difficult one (Kamerman and Kahn, 1988). As a participant–observer in a Single Mothers by Choice support group for two years, Bock (2000) concluded that all 26 of the single mothers by choice she interviewed decided to have or adopt a child only after serious thought and consideration of the child's ultimate well-being. They often sought guidance from various sources including their SMC support group, members of their religious or spiritual community, parents, and friends. Single Mothers by Choice reported that for a woman to embark on this endeavor, there are several criteria. These include being older and having lived in the world and being responsible, emotionally mature, and financially capable. Indeed, Bock noted that women were often discouraged from having or adopting children if they failed to meet these criteria. Many of the single mothers by choice Bock interviewed made serious lifestyle changes before having or adopting a child. Some of these changes included buying a new home in a more child-friendly community, saving money for the child, and changing jobs or careers to be better prepared to be both a mother and a solo provider.

Observers of single parents by choice who adopt children report that these parents have a high level of emotional maturity, have a high capacity for frustration tolerance, and are not overly influenced by others' opinions (Branham, 1970; Groze, 1991). Shireman (1995, 1996) reported that most single-parent adoptions are to women, and most parents adopt children of the same gender. Often a high level of maturity is necessary because, as Shireman (1995) reported, many of these children have special needs. Adoptive single parents are often oriented toward children and derive great personal fulfillment from their interactions with them (Jordan and Little, 1966; Shireman and Johnson, 1976). The single adoptive parents that Groze (1991, p. 326) observed "had an ability to give of themselves, were not possessive of their children, and were capable of developing a healthy relationship with their children." In recent decades, international adoptions have become more common for both singles and married couples. Upper-middle-socioeconomic single parents are more likely than other parents to pursue international adoptions (V. Groza, personal communication, August 24, 2000). Different countries have different rules about who is allowed to adopt, but overall, single women are permitted to adopt in more countries than are single men.

Single women by choice, whether they have or adopt a child, face similar difficulties as other single parents face in meeting the demands of single parenthood. Like other single parents they have difficulty procuring quality childcare, balancing motherhood and career plans, and obtaining emotional support for themselves (Kamerman and Kahn, 1988). However, as Kamerman and Kahn (1988) pointed out, these are concerns that affect any working woman, single or married, wealthy or not. The extent to which single mothers by choice have recognized and prepared for these difficulties may help them better adapt to these circumstances than other single parents.

Some observers have questioned whether this classification of mothers as single by choice is useful from a scientific, descriptive point of view. Clearly these mothers do not have to contend with the effects of divorce and separation or contested custody or child support payments, and they are older than adolescent mothers. To what extent is this SMC category a socioeconomic, sociopolitical distinction, based solely on a mother's access to resources? To what extent is the SMC category an attempt on the part of some women to distance themselves from stereotypes of poor and adolescent single mothers? As Bock (2000) reported, the single mothers she interviewed see themselves as at the top of the single-parenthood hierarchy. However, many women—poor as well as rich—find themselves pregnant and choose to remain single and rear their child without the presence of a male partner. Could they too not be considered single mothers by choice?

There is some reason to believe that many more women are single mothers by choice than commonly believed. Census data indicate that women are not only less likely than ever before to marry, but also today's women are less likely to marry to avoid an out-of-wedlock birth. Contemporary women—rich and poor alike—think hard before entering the institution of marriage. In her interviews with less privileged single mothers in Chicago, Charleston, South Corolina, and Camden, New Jersy, Edin (2000) learned that poor mothers held strong reasons for avoiding marriage. Economic factors emerged as most important. Poor mothers were reluctant to take in a husband who does not contribute to the family's economic welfare. Not only how much money is earned, but how the money is earned is important. Men with illegal earnings and unstable employment contribute to the economic instability and are viewed by poor women as poor economic risks. The women Edin interviewed held marriage in high esteem, and they wanted to be sure to find worthy partners who would treat them fairly. They worried that a man who was frequently out of work or engaged in criminal activity would not only be a poor economic risk, but also he would neither enhance their status nor be a worthy parental role model. Noting the possibly stalled gender-role revolution among the lower-socioeconomic groups, Edin reported that women were also unwilling to enter relationships in which they perceived they would have a subservient role in bargaining and decision making. They were also fearful of being joined legally to a man whom they might not fully trust emotionally to support them or their children. Finally, approximately half of the European American women and approximately a fifth of the African American women Edin interviewed reported concerns about domestic violence. The women Edin interviewed chose to have their children outside of marriage, not because they did not value marriage as an institution, but because they preferred to forego marriage until a worthy partner could be found. Edin's findings suggest that low-income women have high ideals for marriage and resist unions that promise trouble.

Thus many rich and poor single mothers can be said to be "single mothers by choice," remaining single for a number of clear and easily understood reasons. Like the single women in Bock's study, the women in Edin's study were not opposed to the idea of marriage; they simply wanted to wait until the right man came along. A major difference between the women whom Bock and Edin interviewed has to do with legal regulations concerning child support. Because they are dependent on federal or state subsidies to rear their children, the poor women in Edin's study are required to identify the children's fathers for child support. Another difference may be related to the amount of preparation that went into deciding to become a single parent before pregnancy or adoption that was reported by the women in Bock's study. Certainly the women in Bock's study were better educated and had better access to the media. They may have been more career oriented. No doubt, because they have more money, they are perceived to be better able to provide for their children. But the similarities between these two sets of women raise questions about the unique denomination of "single mothers by choice" selected by some women over others.

Solo mothers.   In this subsection, we discuss the findings from three studies with a focus on the results as they pertain to mothers who appear to be rearing their children outside a partnered union. These are studies that looked at the class of single mothers without regard to the reasons for their single-parent status. One is a small study that relied primarily on interviews with parents and observations of them with their children. The other two studies used large-scale national data sets and utilized mainly questionnaire-type measures.

In a series of reports, Weinraub and Wolf (1983, 1987), Gringlas and Weinraub (1995), Weinraub (1986), and Wolf (1987) focused on a group of women they call solo mothers: adult women rearing their children from birth without a male partner. This group of single mothers includes single mothers by choice as well as other mothers who may not have deliberately chosen to be single as they reared their children. As a result of circumstances not always under their control, these solo mothers had been rearing their children from birth or shortly thereafter without a male father figure in the home. Children of solo mothers are those who have had, at least in their memory, no experience living with a father figure in the home, and more importantly, no experience of family dissolution, marital discord, or family realignment. Since early in life, or at least before the onset of language, these children were reared by their mothers, within either a single-parent household or an extended household. Some mothers made a conscious and deliberate choice to become single mothers; others did not.

Weinraub and her colleagues studied this group of nonrepresentative single-parent families in order to understand the effects on the young child of growing up in a family without the full-time presence of father, when these effects are not confounded by poverty, immature parenting, or the trauma of separation or divorce. Because this group of single parents is another group of single parents with unique circumstances that help us to understand the heterogeneity of single-parent families and because this is the only longitudinal, observational study focusing on these single-parent families that has taken into consideration the parent's characteristics, circumstances, parenting behavior, and child outcome, this research is described in some detail.

Weinraub and Wolf (1983, 1987) identified single-parent and two-parent families matched on a variety of characteristics, including maternal age, education, race, per capita income, neighborhood, child age, and child gender. The solo mothers were a varied group. Some mothers were not married or had already been divorced when they unintentionally conceived; some were married and then separated from their husbands soon after conception or pregnancy; and some mothers deliberately became pregnant with full understanding that there would be no father in their young child's life. Some of these mothers could be classified as single mothers by choice, some could be seen as divorced mothers. In their small sample, no differences between these two groups could be discerned. Most of the mothers were college educated and had professional employment.

Observational measures of maternal and child behavior were taken in the laboratory when the children were between 27 and 55 months of age, and parents completed questionnaires and in-depth interviews in their homes. Of the families, 70% returned for observation and interviews when the children were between 8 and 13 years of age (Gringlas and Weinraub, 1995). For the older children, child measures included a self-perception profile and maternal and teacher reports of behavior problems, social competence, and academic performance. Maternal measures included maternal and child reports of parenting practices, social supports, and stress.

Comparisons between solo-parent mothers and comparable married mothers highlight some of the important ways in which even the most stable of single-parent families differ from married parent families. First, despite careful attempts to match single- and two-parent mothers on employment status, single parents worked longer hours both when their children were in preschool and at preadolescence. When their children were in preschool, single parents reported more difficulties coping with finances, more daily hassles, and slightly more stresses relating to employment. Single mothers of sons reported more stressful life events relating to interpersonal areas of their lives. The largest difference between the mothers concerned social supports. During the preschool period, single parents received fewer emotional and parenting supports (Weinraub and Wolf, 1983, 1987). During the preadolescent period, only single-parent mothers of sons reported lower satisfaction with their emotional supports (Gringlas and Weinraub, 1995). Their friends and relatives either did not understand or did not address their emotional and parenting needs as well as those of solo mothers of daughters or two-parent mothers.

When the children were in their preschool years, observational measures of parents administering a teaching task to the children revealed few overall differences in mothers' or children's behavior, but differences emerged in single mother's parenting as a function of the child's gender. Although no differences in maternal communications and degrees of maternal nurturance were observed, single mothers had difficulties exercising control over and setting appropriate maternal demands on their sons. Not surprisingly, preschool boys in single-parent homes were less compliant with their mothers' requests than boys from two-parent homes (Weinraub and Wolf, 1987). By preadolescence, teachers reported that children of solo mothers had more behavior problems, lower social competence, and poorer school performance than children of married mothers (Gringlas and Weinraub, 1995).

Within each group, maternal social support predicted parenting and child outcomes. During the preschool period, maternal social supports contributed to more optimal parent–child interaction for both single- and two-parent families. The more mothers received support in their role as parents, the more optimal was their behavior in interaction with their preschool child (Weinraub and Wolf, 1983, 1987). During preadolescence, only for solo parents was social support predictive of children's academic performance (Gringlas and Weinraub, 1995).

Maternal stress also had different effects in the solo- and the two-parent families. At both assessment periods, more stressful life events predicted less optimal outcomes, but only for solo-parent families. During the preschool period, solo mothers with frequent stressful life events had less optimal interactions with their children in a teaching task, had children who were perceived as more moody and who had lower intelligence and readiness-to-learn scores. More frequent stressful life events were associated with reduced parental effectiveness, poorer communication, and less nurturance in solo-parent families. The effects of stress in the preschool period not only indirectly affected child outcome by means of maternal parenting behavior, but also had direct effects on child outcome independently of the solo mother's parenting behavior (Weinraub and Wolf, 1987). During preadolescence, children from solo parent families with high levels of maternal stress were described by teachers and mothers as having the most behavior problems. However, children from low-stress solo-parent families were indistinguishable from children from two-parent families (Gringlas and Weinraub, 1995).

These results are similar to other findings documenting the psychological vulnerability of women rearing their children alone (Burden, 1986; Compas and Williams, 1990; Elder, Eccles, Ardelt, and Lord, 1993; Hastings-Storer, 1991; McLanahan, 1983). This vulnerability seems to affect children of single-parent families not only indirectly through parenting behavior, but possibly directly as well. These findings suggest that reduced social supports and increased stresses may be more common for solo parents, even when there are no separation, divorce, and custody difficulties and even when the mothers are mature, well educated, and from secure financial circumstances. Differences in social support and stress can affect parent behavior and child outcome, especially in solo-parent families. Most importantly, stress may be the main factor placing solo-parent children at risk, and children from solo-parent families with low stress do not appear to be at any increased risk.

Because Weinraub's and her colleagues' sample of solo mothers is small and unrepresentative, more systematic research with broader samples of single mothers from varied circumstances is needed to identify the conditions of maternal stress and sources of social support that may help explain differences in parental behavior and subsequent child outcome. At the expense of rich qualitative data, large national data sets can provide a wealth of information regarding how different types of single parents and solo mothers in particular differ from each other in their standard of living and parenting practices. Numerous researchers have published research by using data from Great Britain's public data set and other national surveys much like the U.S. census reports, comparing single mothers who have never married with married mothers.

Lone mothers.   In Great Britain, single mothers are referred to as lone mothers. In a number of studies, lone mothers have been identified as having poorer physical as well as mental health (e.g., Benzeval, 1998; Hope, Power, and Rodgers, 1999; Macran, Clarke, and Joshi, 1996; Whitehead, Burstroem, and Diderrichsen, 2000). Various researchers have examined why lone mothers and particularly never-married lone mothers have significantly poorer health compared with that of their married counterparts. According to these studies, the poorer health of the lone mothers appears to stem from the higher levels of psychological distress they experience. These higher levels of psychological distress that characterize lone mothers are related to financial hardship and lack of support both from the community and from friends and family (Benzeval, 1998; Hope et al., 1999). Surprisingly, employment status has not been found to be related to either improved psychological or physical health (Baker and North, 1999).

Using a large American data set, Amato (2000) examined data from the 1987–1988 National Survey of Households and Families (NSHF). Focusing on 1,515 single parents who were not cohabitating, Amato examined how different groups of single-parents varied along such measures such as income, psychological well-being, and relationships with children. With regards to income, Amato (2000, pp. 161–162) found that the poorest single parents "were mothers, high school dropouts, separated or never married, aged 24 or younger and living with kin." With regards to psychological well-being, Amato found no significant differences between men and women or never-married and other women on indices of happiness, depression, and health. Single parents who reported being separated from their spouse reported being the least happy and most depressed of the single parents who were widowed, divorced, or never married. In terms of parent–child relationships, gender and education were the best predictors of authoritative parenting: Mothers were more authoritative than fathers, and more educated single parents were more authoritative than other single parents.

In the NSHF survey, Amato found no one single, social address variable that most effectively predicted parenting, but he did identify a complex, intertwined combination of factors that affected the parents' situation and ability to effectively parent. Having a child outside of marriage did not necessarily put a mother at risk for being stressed, depressed, unemployed, or a bad parent. However, having an early out-of-marriage birth in combination with little education put a mother and her child at risk for living in poverty. Poverty placed families and children at developmental risk, in that parents and children in poverty had to contend with a myriad of stresses and strains, including hunger, lack of material necessities, poor educational resources, and unsafe, crime ridden neighborhoods (Amato, 2000; Magnuson and Duncan, in Vol. 4 of this *Handbook*).

Summary. The group of mothers commonly identified as unmarried mothers is actually quite varied and diverse. Some of these parents may not be truly "single" parents; while unmarried, they may be living in homes with a committed partner. As the research of Eiduson and Weisner (1978) and Patterson (1995) has shown, when nonmarried parents are committed to their chosen lifestyle, their children do not differ from children of more traditional household unions on measures of psychological adjustment and school performance. Other mothers rearing their children alone may be single or divorced, and their children are being reared in homes that are truly single-parent homes. Family circumstances vary widely among single-parent homes, with important variations in maternal stress and social supports. As the research of Weinraub and her colleagues shows, variations in these stressful life events and social supports may influence the quality of the mother's interactions with her child. These social context differences and the differential effects they may have on single parents may ultimately be the most important differences separating single-parent from two-parent families.

Summary

Several types of single-parent families exist, and differing circumstances characterize each family type. Although single-parent fathers and single-parent mothers may differ from each other in a variety of ways, divorced custodial fathers and divorced custodial mothers both face similar problems after the breakup of their marriage. For divorced families, disruption of the family members' lives and their household is a major challenge. How the divorced parent negotiates these challenges has important implications for the child's temporary coping and long-term adjustment. Among adolescent mothers, negotiating the multiple challenges of personal identity, preparation for adulthood, and parenthood itself poses significant risks for the adolescent and her child, especially because the adolescent is often coming from a situation of economic and educational disadvantage. Finally, unmarried couples by choice, single mothers by choice, solo mothers, and lone mothers may also face different life circumstances. The degree of social support and the frequency of daily life stresses in these parents' lives may hold the keys for predicting whether or not single parenthood will affect children's development.

PROMISING RESEARCH DIRECTIONS IN SINGLE PARENTHOOD

We must progress beyond both nostalgia about the way we wish families were and moral panic about the loss of family values to deal with families as they really were and are.

—Fine, Demo, and Allen (2000, p. 445)

For too long, researchers have focused on the differences in child outcomes between single- and two-parent families. Researchers are now beginning to examine more thoroughly the differences in family processes between single- and two-parent families and within different types of single-parent families that may be responsible for some of the observed differences in child outcomes.

Focus on Process

Dynamic family processes in single-parent families, as in other families, contribute to the overall emotional climate of the household and affect the experience of developing in a particular family. An example of research on how family processes work in single-parent families is the research by Larson and Gillman (1999). Larson and Gillman examined the transmission of negative emotions in an ethnically and economically diverse sample of single-mother homes with adolescent children. Researchers "beeped" the single mothers and adolescent children randomly throughout the day. At each beep, parents were asked to record their moods, including, for example, anxiety, stress, sadness, and happiness. In addition, researchers assessed maternal parenting style, maternal life events, social support, and time spent alone. The results indicated that maternal anxiety and anger predicted the adolescents' anger and anxiety in both lower- and middle-income homes. However, adolescent anger and anxiety did not relate to mothers' subsequent negative emotions. Rather, it was maternal time spent alone and parenting style that more strongly predicted the mothers' flow of negative emotions. Larson and Gillman speculated that competent parents, single or wed, may actively circumvent their negative emotions so as not to affect their children. By including a representative cross section of single mothers, Larson and Gillman showed that it was family process variables, and not family status or income levels, that regulated child and maternal adjustment in these families.

Studies of the contribution of family structure may need to yield to studies that focus on understanding family processes. Minturn and Lambert (1964) studied families in six different cultures. They concluded that more relevant for predicting child outcome than specific childrearing technologies were household composition, family size, and parental work load. They argued that these variables were more important than other variables because these variables influence the time and energy that mothers have available to care for their children. Family structure may serve only as a "social address" for locating these more important, process-oriented variables.

The longitudinal study by Eiduson (1983) and Eiduson and Weisner (1978) of nontraditional families of the 1960s suggested that the goals and values of parents may also transcend the importance of family structure. For Eiduson and Weisner, nonmarried parents whose goals were literacy, pronaturalism, or nonconventional achievement had children who were as successful on adjustment and school performance measures as did children of other, more conventional families. Parents' involvement in their children's schooling and parents' commitment to coherent activities and values were more important than family structure on predicting successful child outcome. As Weisner and Garnier (1992, p. 628) argued, "the categories used to group families, such as single-parents, unwed mothers, divorced unmarried couples or married couples, are not capturing important differences in values, commitment and stability, which influence children living in these types of families." As important as differences across different types of single-parent family structure may be, ultimately we need to focus on more proximal characteristics within families that directly affect parenting behavior. Researchers may need to look beyond demographics and family structural variables in order to understand the true role of family structure in affecting child development.

Do we know more about family demographics than family processes in single-parent families? Probably, and this needs redress. Fine et al. (2000) advised researchers to study dynamic family process variables as they relate to static social address variables. Single-parent family processes need to be studied in context, with careful attention to both similarities and differences between and within different single-parent family forms.

Appreciating the diversity between and within different types of single-parent families requires that researchers be specific in describing the dynamic processes characteristic of particular types of single-parent families. A prime example of this approach to research is a study in which Acock and Demo (1994) examined adjustment and academic performance among adolescents living in five prevalent family structures. Two-parent family units, divorced families, single-parent families, step-families, and never-married noncohabiting families were found to vary dramatically on measures of family functioning and adolescent behavior. Compared with the other family types, divorced and stepparent families reported the most mother–child conflict and the lowest levels of parental control and parent–child interaction. As a result, it was not surprising that children in these families experienced more personal and emotional adjustment problems and had more difficulties with school performance. Although striking socioeconomic differences were observed, with never-married mothers singularly disadvantaged, it was not economic differences across families but differences in mother–child interaction that were most predictive of child outcome.

The role of fathers.   Studies comparing different types of single-parent families have yielded some useful information about the role of fathers in child development (Parke, in Vol. 3 of this *Handbook*). Research on children of remarried single-parent families (e.g., Acock and Demo, 1994; Amato and Keith, 1991b; Steinberg, 1987; Vuchinich, Hetherington, Vuchinich, and Clingempeel, 1991; Zimiles and Lee, 1991), showing that children whose mothers have remarried do not necessarily show better psychological adjustment than children whose mothers have not remarried, suggests that the presence of a male figure in the home may not be the critical variable responsible for the at-risk status of single-parent families. Similarly, studies of two-adult households in which one parent is not a father figure (e.g., Kellam, Ensminger, and Turner, 1977; Patterson, 1992) indicate that children reared in these households may not differ substantially from those in households in which there is a father, suggesting further that it may not be the father's "genderness" that is responsible for his important contribution to the family so much as it is his role as a "second," although not second-class, parent. The importance of father's contributions may derive more from his serving as one of two involved, accepting, warm, nurturing caregivers who support each other emotionally and financially more than it derives from the uniqueness of his male gender (Weinraub, 1978).

More information on unmarried single fathers.   Researchers are beginning to unravel the differences and the similarities between divorced single mothers and fathers with custody. However, we are unaware of research that examines differences and similarities between never-married fathers who assume responsibility for a child following an out-of-wedlock birth and other fathers. Obtaining samples of single parents, especially single fathers now, compared with even a decade ago, can be much easier thanks to the Internet. Although individuals who can be reached by the Internet are likely to be of higher socioeconomic status than those who cannot be reached through electronic media, the Internet can be a valuable recruitment tool. Currently there are numerous Web sites devoted to all types of single parents receiving many "hits" per day, with proper recruitment a somewhat diverse sample might be attained.

Teasing Out the Effects of Differing Variables on Different Child Outcome Variables

Studies that include large samples of single parents can help tease out specific contextual and psychological features that contribute to the at-risk status of children growing up in single-parent families. Father absence, economic deprivation, increased stressful life events, decreased social and instrumental supports, diminished parental role models, parental involvement, and lax child supervision may all contribute to placing children at risk, and these factors often co-occur. Statistical manipulations in which data from large archival data sets, such as the NSFH and the National Survey of Family Growth are used (see Brooks-Gunn, Philips, and Elder 1991, for a wider discussion of archival data sets) make it possible to separate the influence of co-occurring factors, identifying critical factors that require social policy and intervention efforts. The study by McLanahan and Bumpass (1988) of the inter-generational consequences of family disruptions applied proportional hazard models to the National Survey of Family Growth to test several competing experiences for intergenerational consequences of growing up in a single-parent families on young women. With this data set, the researchers tested three hypotheses regarding growing up in a single-parent home and later family planning behavior: the economical deprivation hypothesis—that growing up in poverty affects development; the social hypothesis—that the amount and the quality of social support in the community affect the child and family; and the stress hypothesis—that frequency, type, and impact of stresses affect development. They found results consistent with the argument that parental role models and parental supervision are the primary factors in determining offspring's future family formation behavior. Likewise, Duncan, Brooks-Gunn, and Klebanov (1994) found that income and poverty status account almost entirely for differential intelligence scores found in single- and two-parent families. In contrast, family structure effects, despite controls for income and poverty, predicted child adjustment scores. Studies such as these applied to a wide variety of child outcomes would illuminate the possible different processes that simultaneously influence various aspects of child and later adult development.

The main thrust of this chapter has been the argument that different types of single-parent families exist, and differing circumstances characterize each family type. At the same time as we examine processes, we also need to continue to assess the contributions of ethnicity and social status within family types. Are differences between single-parent families equally valid for families of all economic and education levels, all ethnic backgrounds, and for rural as well as urban families? Or are some of these differentiations more meaningful for some groups than for others? A report by Hanson, McLanahan, and Thomson (1997) showed just how complicated these effects can be. In their analysis of the NSFH study, Hanson et al. (1997) found that authoritative parenting practices had more beneficial effects on poor children than on nonpoor children. In two-parent families, praising and hugging children were more likely to positively influence child outcome in poor children's homes than in nonpoor children's homes. However, in single-parent families, parent practices were more influential for nonpoor children than for poor children. Hanson et al. (1997, p. 220) wondered whether the effects of being in a single-parent family and in poverty combined "to reduce the children's capacity to respond positively to good parenting practices." One may also speculate that having two parents acting positively is a more powerful influence on children than having only one parent acting positively, and this is especially true when there are no additional countervailing pressures.

Making Sense of Multiple Methods and Multiple Measures

To better understand numerous equally plausible rival hypotheses, family systems researchers utilize various complementary qualitative and quantitative measures. For instance, Bock (2000) and Edin (2000) used in-depth, probing interviews to better understand their samples of single mothers. The data obtained were detailed individual life histories, essential for helping to understand why and how different women become single mothers. In contrast, using a large public data set (Panel Study of Income Dynamics), Foster, Jones, and Hoffman (1998) painted a very different picture of what it means to be single mother. Foster et al. (1998, p. 165) reported that "only a minority of unmarried women having children after age twenty are European American women giving birth for the first time. Even fewer of these women are faring well economically." Obviously, different types of data sets can yield dissimilar results; dissimilar, but not incompatible. With further research with both large quantitative data sets and smaller qualitative measures, rich meaningful theories concerning how family processes relate specifically to single-parent families can be further developed.

Gender differences and intergenerational effects. An area of research often overlooked concerns gender differences in intergenerational continuity from one family to the next. McLanahan and Bumpass (1988) focused on predictors of family formation in young adult women, and Furstenberg et al. (1987) examined the influences of growing up in adolescent mothers' families on young women's negotiation of identity. Equally important is understanding those variables that influence adult family-related behavior in young men. Simmons, Lin, Grordan, Conger, and Lorenz (1999) described research that suggests that the absence of biological fathers can profoundly affect their sons' adjustment and well-being. Even after custodial mothers' depression, parenting style, and financial status after the divorce were controlled for, sons were still significantly depressed. From this study, it is impossible to know whether the boys' depression is related to father absence or the discord in the predivorce marital relationship, but future research will need to tease out these effects. How might this depression continue into adolescence and beyond?

In a television documentary, Williams (1992) described his search for his father and his attempt to derive a sense of personal identity and destiny from knowledge of his father. His mother's brief liaison more than 21 years earlier had resulted in his birth. Although reared sensitively and lovingly by his mother and other female relatives, Williams sought his father to answer questions of what kind of a father he himself would be. Would he ever get married? What would be his own role in nurturing his own children? Research on fatherhood has begun to tell us much about the further life consequences of early fathering experiences (Snarey, 1993). Similar longitudinal studies of young men from less economically advantaged and more ethnically diverse situations may yield useful information on the impact of growing up without a father's presence on life course choices and developmental pathways for men as well as for women.

Overlapping status. Not only is single parenthood a transitory status, but none of these particular single-parent types is mutually exclusive; overlapping single-parent categorizations are possible. At the time that we study her, an adolescent mother may be divorced, and she may also be living in a committed, partnered relationship. The possibility that the effects of single-parent status may differ for parents of different backgrounds and that parents may have multiple single-parent status classifications suggests that describing families in terms of their family structure may be less meaningful than looking at specific process-oriented features of their experiences.

CONCLUSIONS

Understanding the diverse etiology and nature of single-parent families requires that we consider the specific contextual issues and factors confronting these families. These issues and factors may pose both significant risks as well as important benefits to the successful socialization and parenting of children. Single-parent families are a heterogeneous group, and knowing that a parent is single may not be as helpful as knowing how she or he became a single parent and the parent's specific life circumstances.

Single parenting is a difficult process. Single parents who face the challenges of parenting without the supportive assistance of or collaboration with other concerned and involved adults may find their parenting abilities strained beyond limit. Economic disadvantage, employment, minimal social supports, and exhaustion can exact a toll on a single parent's parenting abilities and resources. Poor parental psychological well-being hinders parents' ability to develop and maintain child-directed energy, optimism, and commitment (Gringlas, 1994). Primary risks to the development of children living in single-parent homes can derive from an ongoing pattern of stress, exhaustion, depression, and isolation experienced by the family (Sargent, 1992). Economic difficulties, chronic illness, and intellectual, academic, or emotional child difficulties place increased stress and demands on single-parent families. If a single parent is frequently unavailable because she or he is overly stressed exhausted or depressed, the disciplining of older children may be erratic and inconsistently enforced, and younger children may be at risk for social withdrawal and depression.

Given this myriad of potential difficulties, it is critical to remember that single parents can and often do rear their children successfully. In a chapter on family variations, Sargent (1992) described what he believes to be central features that lead to effective childrearing in single-parent families. He cited emotional support from a social network, secure financial status, quality of alternative sources of childcare, capacity to maintain appropriate discipline, capacity to parent when exhausted or overwhelmed, ability to develop, one's own rewarding social life and relationships, and capacity to collaborate effectively in childrearing with other involved adults. These parenting variables, and not family structure alone, may be critical in understanding and predicting successful child outcomes.

Single parents are a strikingly diverse group, yet single parents have the same hopes and dreams for their children as their married counterparts do. Despite concerns that the increasing incidence of single-parent families reflects growing disaffection with marriage and two-parent childrearing, there is reason to believe that the rising incidence of single-parent families may reflect the high esteem that many parents still hold for the institution of marriage. It may be precisely because of this high regard for the institution of marriage that parents are reluctant to commit to a relationship that does not promise continuity, trust, intimacy, safety, and love. Similarly, the poverty associated with single-parent families may be as much a contributor to the increased incidence of single-parent families as it is a result of being in a single-parent family. Poor women report that they do not want to weigh themselves down with a husband who does not contribute to the family's overall welfare. As women see themselves growing more competent and powerful in the workplace, they may be less inclined to commit themselves to a marriage in which they are challenged economically and subjugated personally.

Given the biological clocks that govern our lives and the difficulties many women perceive in finding a trusting familial relationship, the United States may be on the cusp of enormous cultural change in how families are created and maintained. One possibility is that the predictable developmental sequence of marriage and childrearing is being reversed. First may come the baby carriage and only afterward marriage—and only if the relationship benefits the child's mother and continues to grow stronger. It is also possible that something even more dramatic is occurring, reflecting a changing cultural *Zeitgeist* in which men and women are increasingly coming to believe that the social, emotional, and economic supports so necessary to facilitate childrearing can be obtained from sources other than the marital relationship. Only time, careful data collection, and sensitive, thoughtful data analyses and interpretation will tell whether it is only the predictable sequences that are changing or the nature of the social–emotional demands adults place on each other as partners and team players in the complicated process of childrearing.

ACKNOWLEDGMENTS

This chapter was written while the first author was supported by the National Institute of Child Health and Human Development Study of Early Child Care and Youth Development (U10-HD25455). We are indebted to Ronald Taylor, Elizabeth Jaeger, and Laurence Steinberg for suggestions and comments on early drafts of this manuscript and for their continuing support and inspiration. Also, we extend our appreciation to Jennifer Tweed for her enthusiastic editorial and bibliographic help in the first edition of this chapter. Finally, we express our caring and appreciation to Anne and Emma all the other single-parent families who have taught us so much about parenting and child development.

REFERENCES

Acock, A. C., and Demo, D. H. (1994). *Family diversity and well being*. Thousand Oaks, CA: Sage.

Ahlburg, D. A., and DeVita, C. J. (1992). New realities of the American family. In *Population Bulletin* (Vol. 47, No. 2). Washington, DC: Population Reference Bureau.

Amato, P. R. (1988). Long-term implications of parental divorce for adult self-concept. *Journal of Family Issues, 9*, 201–213.

Amato, P. R. (2000). Diversity within single-parent families. In D. H. Demo, K. R. Allen, and M. A. Fine (Eds.), *Handbook of family diversity* (pp.149–172). New York: Oxford University Press.

Amato, P. R., and Keith, B. (1991a). Parental divorce and adult well-being: A meta-analysis. *Journal of Marriage and the Family, 53*, 43–58.

Amato, P. R., and Keith, B. (1991b). Parental divorce and the well-being of children: A meta-analysis. *Psychological Bulletin, 110*, 26–46.

Astone, N. M. (1993). Are adolescent mothers just single mothers? *Journal of Research on Adolescence*, *3*, 353–373.

Avenevoli, S., Sessa, F. M., and Steinberg, L. (1999). Family structure, parenting practices, and adolescent adjustment: An ecological examination. In E. M. Heatherington (Ed.), *Coping with divorce, single-parenting, and remarriage: A risk and resiliency perspective* (pp. 65–92). Mahwah, NJ: Lawrence Erlbaum Associates.

Bachu, A. (1998). *Trends in marital status of U.S. women at first birth.* (Population Division Working Paper No. 20). Washington, DC: U.S. Government Printing Office.

Baker, D., and North, K. (1999). Does employment improve the health of lone mothers? *Social Science and Medicine*, *49*, 121–131.

Benzeval, M. (1998). The self-reported health status of lone parents. *Social Science and Medicine*, *46*, 1337–1353.

Bianchi, S. M. (1995). The changing demographic and socioeconomic characteristics of single-parent families. In S. M. Hanson, M. L. Heims, D. Julian, and M. B. Sussman (Eds.), *Single-parent families: Diversity, myths and realities.* New York: Hawthorne.

Black, M. M., and Nitz, K. (1996). Grandmother co-residence, parenting and child development among low income, urban teen mothers. *Journal of Adolescent Health*, *18*, 218–226.

Bock, J. D. (2000). Doing the right thing? Single mothers by choice and the struggle for legitimacy. *Gender and Society*, *14*, 62–86.

Bolton, F. G., and MacEachron, A. (1986). Assessing child maltreatment risk in the recently divorced parent-child relationship. *Journal of Family Violence*, *1*, 259–275.

Branham, E. (1970). One parent adoptions. *Children*, *17*, 103–107.

Brooks-Gunn, J. (1990). Promoting healthy development in young children: What educational interventions work? In D. E. Rogers and E. Ginzberg (Eds.), *Improving the life chances of children at risk* (pp. 125–145). Boulder, CO: Westview.

Brooks-Gunn, J. (1992). Growing up female: Stressful events and the transition to adolescence. In T. M. Field and P. M. McLabe (Eds.), *Stress and coping in infancy or childhood*, pp. 119–145.

Brooks-Gunn, J., and Furstenberg, F. F., Jr. (1986). Antecedents and consequences of parenting: The case of adolescent motherhood. In A. Fogel and G. Melson (Eds.), *Origins of nurturance: Developmental, biological and cultural perspectives on caregiving* (pp. 233–258). Hillsdale, NJ: Lawrence Erlbaum Associates.

Brooks-Gunn, J., Philips, E., and Elder, G. H. (1991). Studying lives through time: Secondary data analysis in *Developmental Psychology*, *27*(6) 899–910.

Brown, B. V. (2000). The single father family: Demographic, economic, and public transfer characteristics. *Marriage and Family Review*, *29*, 203–220.

Burden, D. S. (1986). Single-parents and the work setting: The impact of multiple job and home life responsibilities. *Family Relations Journal of Applied Family and Child Studies*, *35*, 37–43.

Burns, A. (1992). Mother-headed families: An international perspective and the case of Australia. *Social Policy Report*, *6*, 8–17.

Burns, A., and Scott, C. (1994). *Mother-headed families and why they have increased.* Hillsdale, NJ: Lawrence Erlbaum Associates.

Camara, K. A., and Resnick, G. (1988). Interparental conflict and cooperation: Factor moderating children's post-divorce adjustment. In E. M. Hetherington and J. D. Arasteh (Eds.), *Impact of divorce, single-parenting, and stepparenting on children* (pp. 169–195). Hillsdale, NJ: Lawrence Erlbaum Associates.

Carter, S. L., Osofsky, J. D., and Hann, D. M. (1991). Speaking for the baby: A therapeutic intervention with adolescent mothers and their infants. *Infant Mental Health Journal*, *12*, 291–301.

Cashion, B. G. (1982). Female-headed families: Effects on children and clinical implications. *Journal of Marital and Family Therapy*, *8*, 77–86.

Chase-Lansdale, P. L., Brooks-Gunn, J., and Zamsky, E. S. (1994). Young African American multigenerational families: Quality of mothering and grandmothering. *Child Development*, *65*, 373–393.

Cherlin, A. J. (1992). *Marriage, divorce, remarriage* (2nd ed.). Cambridge, MA: Harvard University Press.

Cherlin, A. J. (1998). Marriage and marital dissolution among Black Americans. *Journal of Comparative Family Studies*, *29*, 147–158.

Cherlin, A. J. (1995). Child care for poor children: Policy issues. In P. L. Chase-Lansdale and J. Brooks-Gunn (Eds.), *Escape from poverty: What makes a difference for poor children?* New York: Cambridge University Press.

Child Trends. (1990, November). *Facts at a Glance.*

Child Trends. (1992, November). *Assessing the Condition of Children.*

Christoffersen, M. N. (1998). Growing up with dad: A comparison of children aged 3–5 years old living with their mothers or fathers. *Childhood: A Global Journal of Child Research*, *5*, 41–54.

Coley, R. L., and Chase-Lansdale, P. L. (1998). Adolescent pregnancy and parenting. *American Psychologist*, *53*, 152–166.

Cohen, R. (1993, May). Values are important, but the radical transformation of the family may be the key. *The Philadelphia Inquirer*, p. A08.

Compas, B. E., and Williams, R. A. (1990). Stress, coping, and adjustment in mothers and young adolescents in single- and two-parent families. *American Journal of Community Psychology*, *18*, 525–545.

Conger, R. D., Ge, X., Elder, G. H., Jr., Lorenz, F. O., and Simons, R. L. (1994). Economic stress, coercive family process, and developmental problems of adolescents. *Child Development, 65*, 541–561.

Cooley, M. L., and Unger, D. G. (1990). The role of family support in determining developmental outcomes of teen mothers. *Child Psychiatry and Human Development, 21*(3), 217–234.

DeFrain, J., and Eirick, R. (1981). Coping as divorced single-parents: A comparative study of fathers and mothers. *Family Relations, 30*, 265–273.

Dornbusch, S. M., and Gray, K. D. (1988). Single-parent families. In S. M. Dornbusch and M. H. Strober (Eds.), *Feminism, children, and the new families*. New York: Guilford.

Duncan, G. J., Brooks-Gunn, J., and Klebanov, P. K. (1994). Economic deprivation and early childhood development. *Child Development, 65*, 296–318.

Edin, K. (2000). What do low-income single mothers say about marriage? *Social Forces, 47*, 112–133.

Eggebeen, D. J., Snyder, A. R., and Manning, W. D. (1996). Children in single father families in demographic perspective. *Journal of Family Issues, 17*, 441–465.

Eiduson, B. T. (1983). Conflict and stress in nontraditional families: Impact on children. *American Journal of Orthopsychiatry, 53*, 426–435.

Eiduson, B. T., and Weisner, T. S. (1978). Alternative family styles: Effects on young children. In J. H. Stevens, Jr. and M. Matthews (Eds.), *Mother/child father/child relationships* (pp. 197–221). Washington, DC: National Association for the Education of Young Children.

Elder, G. H., Jr., Eccles, J. S., Ardelt, M., and Lord, S. (1993, March). *Inner city parents under economic pressure: Perspectives on the strategies of parenting*. Paper presented at the Society for Research on Child Development, New Orleans, LA.

Feigelman, W., and Silverman, A. R. (1977). Single-parent adoptions. *Social Casework, 58*, 418–425.

Fine, M. H., Demo, D. H., and Allen, K. R. (2000). Family diversity in the 21st century: Implications for research, theory and practice. In D. H. Demo, K. R. Allen, and M. A. Fine (Eds.), *Handbook of family diversity* (pp. 149–172). New York: Oxford University Press.

Foster, E. M., Jones, D., and Hoffman, S. (1998). The economic impact of nonmarital childbearing: How are older single mothers faring? *Journal of Marriage and the Family, 60*, 163–174.

Furstenberg, F. F., Jr. (1981). Implicating the family: Teenage parenthood and kinship involvement. In T. Ooms (Ed.), *Teenage pregnancy in a family context* (pp. 131–164). Philadelphia: Temple University Press.

Furstenberg, F. F., Jr., Brooks-Gunn, J., and Chase-Lansdale, L. (1989). Adolescent fertility and public policy. *American Psychologist, 44*, 313–320.

Furstenberg, F. F., Jr., Brooks-Gunn, J., and Morgan, P. (1987). *Adolescent mothers in later life*. New York: Cambridge University Press.

Furstenberg, F. F., Jr., Hughes, M. E., and Brooks-Gunn, J. (1992). The next generation: Children of teenage mothers grow up. In M. K. Rosenheim and M. F. Testa (Eds.), *Early parenthood and coming of age in the 1990's* (pp. 113–135). New Brunswick, NJ: Rutgers University Press.

Garcia-Coll, C. T., Meyer, E. L., and Brilliz, L. Handbook Vol. 3. Bio. and Eco. of printing. Parenting(?)

Garfinkel, I., and McLanahan, S. S. (1986). *Single mothers and their children: New American dilemma*. Washington, DC: Urban Institute Press.

Garfinkel, I., Miller, C., McLanahan, S., and Hanson, T. L. (1998). Dead beat dads of inept states: A comparison of child support enforcement systems. *Evaluation Review, 22*(6) 717–750.

Gersick, K. (1979). Fathers by choice: Divorced men who receive custody of their children. In G. Levinger and D. C. Moles (Eds.), *Divorce and separation*. New York: Basic Books.

Goldsmith, J. (1976). A child of one's own: Unmarried women who choose motherhood (Doctoral dissertation, California School of Professional Psychology, 1975). *Dissertation Abstracts International, 36*, 3602–3603B.

Greif, G. L. (1985). *Single fathers*. Lexington, MA: Heath.

Greif, G. L. (1995). Single fathers with custody following separation and divorce. In S. M. Hanson, M. L. Heims, D. Julian, and M. B. Sussman (Eds.), *Single-parent families: Diversity, myths and realities*. New York: Hawthorne.

Greif, G. L., and DeMaris, A. (1995). Single fathers with custody: Do they change over time? In W. Marsiglio (Ed.), *Fatherhood: Contemporary theory, research, and social policy* (pp. 193–210). New York: Sage.

Gringlas, M. (1994). *Maternal psychological well-being: Determinants of a mother's parenting behavior*. Unpublished doctoral dissertation, Temple University, Philadelphia, PA.

Gringlas, M., and Weinraub, M. (1995). The more things change: Single parenting revisited. *Journal of Family Issues, 16*, 29–52.

Groze, V. (1991). Adoption and single-parents: A review. *Child Welfare, 70*, 321–332.

Hanson, T. L., McLanahan, S. S., and Thomson, E. (1997). Double Jeopardy: Printal conflict and stepfamily outcomes for children. *Journal of Marriage and the Family, 58*, 141–154.

Hastings-Storer, J. (1991). Parenting stress in rural, low-income African American mothers of young children (Doctoral dissertation, University of Missouri-Columbia, 1991). *Dissertation Abstracts International, 52*, 3318B.

Hayes, C. D. (Ed.). (1987). *Risking the future: Adolescent sexuality, pregnancy, and childbearing* (Vol. 1). Washington, DC: National Academy of Science Press.

Heath, T. D., and Orthner, D. K. (1999). Stress and adaptation among male and female single-parents. *Journal of Family Issues, 20,* 557–587.

Herzog, E., and Sudia, C. (1973). Children in fatherless families. In B. M. Caldwell and H. N. Ricciuti (Eds.), *Review of child development research* (Vol. 3, pp. 141–232). Chicago: University of Chicago Press.

Hetherington, E. M. (1993). An overview of the Virginia longitudinal study of divorce and remarriage: A focus on early adolescence. *Journal of Family Psychology, 7,* 39–56.

Hetherington, E. M., Cox, M., and Cox, R. (1982). Effects of divorce on parents and children. In M. E. Lamb (Ed.), *Nontraditional families* (pp. 233–288). Hillsdale, NJ: Lawrence Erlbaum Associates.

Hetherington, E. M., and Stanley-Hagan, M. M., Parenting in divorced and remarried families. In M. Bornstein (Ed.), *Handbook of parenting: Vol. 3. Status and social conditions of parenting* (pp. 233–254). Mahwah, NJ: Lawrence Erlbaum Associates.

Hill, L. C., and Hilton, J. M. (2000). Changes in roles following divorce: Comparison of factors contributing to depression in custodial single mothers and custodial single fathers. *Journal of Divorce and Remarriage, 31,* 91–114.

Hilton, J. M., and Devall, E. L. (1998). Comparison of parenting and children's behavior in single-mother, single-father, and intact families. *Journal of Divorce and Remarriage, 29,* 23–53.

Hobbs, F., and Lippman, L. (1990). Children's well-being: An international comparison. *International Population Reports Series* (Series P95, No. 80). Washington, DC: U.S. Government Printing Office.

Hope, S., Power, C., and Rodgers, B. (1999). Does financial hardship account for elevated psychological distress in lone mothers? *Social Science and Medicine, 49,* 1637–1649.

Horwitz, S. M., Klerman, L. V., Kuo, H. S., and Jekel, J. F. (1991). School-age mothers: Predictors of long-term educational and economic outcomes. *Pediatrics, 87,* 862–867.

Hotz, V. J., Mullin, C. H., and Sanders, S. G. (1997). The costs and consequences of teenage childbearing for mothers. In R. A. Maynard (Ed.), *Kids having kids: Economic costs and consequences of teenage pregnancy* (pp. 54–94). Washington, DC: Urban Institute Press.

Jones, S. C. (1984). Going to work: A challenging time for single mothers. *Journal of Employment Counseling, 21,* 7–12.

Jordan, V., and Little, W. (1966). Early comments on single-parent adoptive homes. *Child Welfare, 45,* 536–538.

Kamerman, S. B., and Kahn, A. J. (1988). *Mothers alone: Strategies for a time of change.* Dover, MA: Auburn House.

Kellam, S. G., Ensminger, M. E., and Turner, R. J. (1977). Family structure and the mental health of children. *Archives of General Psychiatry, 34,* 1012–1022.

Kissman, K., and Allen, J. A. (1993). *Single-parent families.* Newbury Park, CA: Sage.

Kleist, D. M. (1999). Single-parent families: A difference that makes a difference? *Family Journal of Counseling and Therapy for Couples and Families, 7,* 373–378.

Lamb, M. E., Pleck, J. H., and Levine, J. (1986). The role of the father in child development. In A. Kazdin (Ed.), *Advances in clinical child psychology* (Vol. 8, pp. 229–266). New York: Plenum.

Larson, R., and Gillman, S. (1999). Transmission of emotions in the daily interactions of single mother families. *Journal of Marriage and the Family, 61,* 21–37.

Macran, S., Clarke, L., and Joshi, H. (1996). Women's health: Dimensions and differentials. *Social Science and Medicine, 42,* 1203–1216.

Mannis, V. S. (1999). Single mothers by choice. *Family Relations: Interdisciplinary Journal of Applied Family Studies, 48,* 121–128.

Mattes, J. (1994). *Single mothers by choice: A guidebook for single women who are considering or have chosen motherhood.* New York: Times Books.

McLanahan, S. S. (1983). Family structure and stress: A longitudinal comparison of two-parent and female-headed families. *Journal of Marriage and the Family, 45,* 347–357.

McLanahan, S. S., and Bumpass, L. L. (1988). Intergenerational consequences of family disruption. *American Journal of Sociology, 94,* 130–152.

McLoyd, V. C. (1990). The impact of economic hardship on Black families and children: Psychological distress, parenting, socioemotional development. *Child Development, 61,* 311–346.

McLoyd, V. C., Jayaratne, T. E., Ceballo, R., and Borquez, J. (1994). Unemployment and work interruption among African American single mothers: Effects on parenting and adolescent socioemotional functioning. *Child Development, 65,* 562–589.

Meyer, D. R., and Garasky, S. (1993). Custodial fathers: Myths, realities and child support policies. *Journal of Marriage and the Family, 45,* 73–87.

Miller, B. C., and Moore, K. A. (1990). Adolescent sexual behavior, pregnancy, and parenting: Research through the 1980s. *Journal of Marriage and the Family, 52,* 1025–1044.

Minturn, L., and Lambert, W. W. (1964). *Mothers of six cultures.* New York: Wiley.

Mott, F. L. (1986). The pace of repeated childbearing among young African American mothers. *Family Planning Perspectives, 18,* 5–12.

Mullis, R. L., and Mullis, A. K. (1985). Parenting education for single-parent families: Focusing community resources. *Journal of Child Care*, *2*, 29–36.

Nieto, D. S. (1990). The custodial single father: Who does he think he is? *Journal of Divorce and Remarriage*, *13*, 27–43.

Osofsky, J. D., Eberhart-Wright, A., Ware, L. M., and Hann, D. M. (1992). Children of adolescent mothers: A group at risk for psychopathology. *Infant Mental Health Journal*, *13*, 119–131.

Osofsky, J. D., Hann, D. M., and Peebles, C. (1994). Adolescent parenthood: Risks and opportunities for parents and infants. In C. Zeanah (Ed.), *Handbook of infant mental health*. New York: Guilford, Press.

Oyerserman, D., Radin, N., and Benn, R. (1993). Dynamics in a three-generational family: Teens, grandparents and babies. *Developmental Psychology*, *29*, 564–572.

Pasick, R. (1990). Friendship between men. In R. C. Meth and R. S. Pasick (Eds.), *Men in therapy: The challenge of change*. New York: Guilford.

Patterson, C. J. (1992). Children of lesbian and gay parents. *Child Development*, *63*, 1025–1042.

Patterson, C. J. (1995). Lesbian and gay parenthood. In M. Bornstein (Ed.), *Handbook of parenting: Vol. 3, Status and social conditions of parenting* (pp. 255–274). Mahwah, NJ: Lawrence Erlbaum Associates.

Pichitino, J. P. (1983). Profile of the single father: A thematic integration of the literature. *Personnel and Guidance Journal*, *9*, 295–299.

Potter, A. E., and Knaub, P. K. (1988). Single motherhood by choice: A parenting alternative. *Family and Economic Issues*, *9*, 240–249.

Prater, L. P. (1995). Never-married/ biological teen mother headed households. In Hanson, S. M., Heims, M. L., Julian, D., and Sussman, M. B. (Eds.), *Single-parent families: diversity, myths and realities*. New York: Hawthorne.

Ricciuti, H. N. (1999). Single parenthood and school readiness in white, black and hispanic 6 and 7 year olds. *Journal of Family Psychology*, *13*(3) 450–465.

Richard, J. V. (1982). Addressing stress factors in single-parent women-headed households. *Women and Therapy*, *1*, 15–27.

Roosa, M. W. (1986). Adolescent mothers, school drop-outs, and school-based intervention programs. *Family Relations*, *35*, 313–317.

Santrock, J. W., Warshak, R. A., and Elliot, G. L. (1982). Social development and parent–child interaction in father custody and stepmother families. In M. E. Lamb (Ed.), *Nontraditional families* (pp. 289–314). Hillsdale, NJ: Lawrence Erlbaum Associates.

Sargent, J. (1992). Family variations. In M. D. Levine, W. B. Carey, and A. C. Crocker (Eds.), *Developmental-behavioral pediatrics*. Philadelphia: Saunders.

Scott-Jones, D. (1991). Adolescent childbearing: Risks and resilience. *Education and Urban Society*, *24*, 53–64.

Shepard, P. (July 26, 2000). A portrait of progress and setbacks an Urban League report noted Blacks' economic gains, but a gender gap in education. *The Philadelphia Inquirer*.

Shireman, J. F. (1995). Adoptions by single-parents. *Marriage and Family Review*, *20*, 367–388.

Shireman, J. F. (1996). Single-parent adoptive homes. *Children and Youth Services Review*, *18*, 23–36.

Shireman, J., and Johnson, P. (1976). Single-parents as adoptive parents. *Social Service Review*, *50*, 103–116.

Simmons, R. L., Lin, K. H., Grordan, L., Conger, R., and Lorenz, F. (1999). Explaining the higher incidence of adjustment problems among children of divorce compared with those in two parent homes. *Journal of Marriage and the Family*, *61*, 1020–1033.

Smith, E. W. (1993, March). *Life circumstances and experiences in single-parent households: Data from a national survey*. Paper presented at the Society for Research in Child Development, New Orleans, LA.

Snarey, J. (1993). *How fathers care for the next generation: A four decade study*. Cambridge, MA: Harvard University Press.

Steinberg, L. D. (1987). Single-parents, stepparents, and the susceptibility of adolescents to antisocial peer pressure. *Child Development*, *58*, 269–275.

State of America's Children Yearbook (1994). Washington, DC: Children's Defense Fund.

Thiriot, T. L., and Buckner, E. T. (1991). Multiple predictors of satisfactory post-divorce adjustment of single custodial parents. *Journal of Divorce and Remarriage*, *17*, 27–48.

Turner, P. H., Scadden, L., and Harris, M. B. (1990). Parenting in gay and lesbian families. *Journal of Gay and Lesbian Psychotherapy*, *1*, 55–66.

Unger, D. G., and Cooley, M. L. (1992). Partner and grandmother contact in black and white teen parent families. *Journal of Adolescent Health*, *13*, 546–552.

U.S. Bureau of the Census. (1991). Child Support and Alimony: 1989. *Current Population Reports* (Series P60, No. 173). Washington, DC: U.S. Government Printing Office.

U.S. Bureau of the Census. (1992). Households, families, and children: A 30 year perspective. *Current Population Reports* (Series P23, No. 181). Washington, DC: U.S. Government Printing Office.

U.S. Bureau of the Census. (1998). Washington, DC: U.S. Government Printing Office.

U.S. Bureau of the Census. (March 2000). Census Brief: Women in the United States: A profile. *Current Population Reports*. Washington, DC: U.S. Government Printing Office.

U.S. Bureau of the Census. (2001). America's families and living arrangements: Population characteristics. *Current Population Report* (Series P20, No. 537). Washington, DC: U.S. Government Printing Office.

Ventura, S. (June 29, 1999). Testimony before subcommittee on human resources of the house committee on ways and means: Hearing on reducing nonmarital births. http://www.house.gov/ways_means/humres/106cong/6-29-99. Committee on ways and means, subcommittee or human resources, 6-29-99 testimony.

Ventura, S., Martin, J., Curtain, S., Matthers, T. J., and Park, M. M. (2000). Births: Final data for 1998. *National Vital Statistics Report, 48* (3).

Vuchinich, S., Hetherington, E., Vuchinich, R., and Clingempeel, W. (1991). Parent-child interaction and gender differences in early adolescents' adaption to stepfamilies. *Developmental Psychology, 27,* 618–626.

Wakschlag, L. S., Chase-Lansdale, P. L., and Brooks-Gunn, J. (1996). Not just "ghosts in the nursery": Contemporary intergenerational relationships and parenting in young African American families. *Child Development, 67,* 2131–2147.

Wallerstein, J. S., Corbin, S. B., and Lewis, J. M. (1988). Children of divorce: A ten-year study. In E. M. Hetherington and J. D. Arasteh (Eds.), *Impact of divorce, single-parenting, and stepparenting on children* (pp. 198–214). Hillsdale, NJ: Lawrence Erlbaum Associates.

Wasserman, G. A., Rauh, V. A., Brunelli, S. A., Garcia-Castro, M., and Necos, B. (1990). Psychosocial attributes and life experiences of minority mothers: Age and ethnic variations. *Child Development, 61,* 566–580.

Weinraub, M. (1978). Fatherhood: The myth of the second-class parent. In J. H. Stevens, Jr., and M. Matthews (Eds.), *Mother/child father/child relationships* (pp. 109–133). Washington, DC: National Association for the Education of Young Children.

Weinraub, M. (1986, August). Growing up in single-parent families: Effects on child development. *Invited Fellows Symposium: Psychology of Women—Current Issues and Research.* Paper presented at meetings of the American Psychological Association, Washington, DC.

Weinraub, M., and Wolf, B. (1983). Effects of stress and social supports on mother–child interactions in single and two-parent families. *Child Development, 54,* 1297–1311.

Weinraub, M., and Wolf, B. (1987). Stressful life events, social supports, and parent-child interactions: Similarities and differences in single-parent and two-parent families. In Z. Boukydis (Ed.), *Research on support for parents and infants in the postnatal period* (pp. 114–135). Norwood, NJ: Ablex.

Weisner, T. S., and Garnier, H. (1992). Non-conventional family life-styles and school achievement: A 12-year longitudinal study. *American Education Research Journal, 29,* 605–632.

Weiss, R. S. (1979). *Going it alone: The family life and social situation of the single-parent.* New York: Basic Books.

Whitehead, B. D. (1993). Dan Quayle was right. *The Atlantic, 271,* 47–84.

Whitehead, M., Burstroem, B., and Diderichsen, F. (2000). Social policies and the pathways to inequalities in health: A comparative analysis of lone mothers in Britain and Sweden. *Social Science and Medicine, 50,* 255–270.

Williams, M. (1992). The single-parent family: In search of my father [Television film]. Conjure Films.

Wolf, B. M. (1987). Stress and social supports: Impact on parenting and child development in single-parent and two-parent families (Doctoral dissertation, Temple University, Philadelphia, 1987). *Dissertation Abstracts International, 48,* 1171B–1172B.

Zimiles, H., and Lee, V. (1991). Adolescent family structure and educational progress. *Developmental Psychology, 27,* 314–320.

5

Grandparenthood

Peter K. Smith
University of London
Linda M. Drew
University of Southern California

INTRODUCTION

Grandparenting it is an important part of the life cycle. In the United States, some three fourths of adults will become grandparents (Giarrusso, Silverstein, and Bengtson, 1996); the average age of becoming a grandparent is approximately 50 years for women and a couple of years older for men. Many people will remain grandparents for some 25 years, or approximately a third of their lifespan. A more exact calculation in the United States comes from a study by Rossi and Rossi (1990) of some 2,000 respondents in the Boston area; the mean generational gap was 28 years. With high death rates in the late 70s (especially men) and 80s (especially women), this means that children will typically grow up with both sets of grandparents, but lose perhaps grandfathers when they are in adolescence and grandmothers as young adults. The findings of Rossi and Rossi suggest that not so many adults have living grandparents—the proportion falls from 62% in the 20s to 27% by the 30s. Great-grandparenthood is correspondingly rare; typically, as adults go through their 50s, their parents die and their grandchildren are born.

The findings of Rossi and Rossi do "demythologize" the idea of common or extensive four-generation families; in their sample, only 1.3% of Bostonians have any living great-grandparents (whereas one in four have at least one living grandparent, and one in four have a grandchild). Equally, the figures confirm that grandparenting is a common experience. Rossi and Rossi describe the three-generation family as modal; it can be considered normative today for children up to early adulthood to have grandparents and for people in their late 50s onwards to have grandchildren.

Terms such as grandparent, parent, child, and grandchild are relative; someone may be both a parent and a child, for example. Many researchers use generational labels such as G1, G2, and G3 to avoid this ambiguity. However, this device has its own difficulties, as, if G1 refers to a grandparental generation, then there is no appropriate label for any great-grandparents. In this chapter, we take grandchildren as the reference point and refer to their parents, grandparents, and great-grandparents.

The majority of the research literature on grandparenting is relatively recent, and this chapter starts with an examination of historical considerations and then the classical research in this area. Following a review of theories bearing on the study of grandparenthood, the central issues covered by research are outlined in some detail. Two particularly interesting issues—grandparents as surrogate parents, and the intergenerational transmission of attitudes and behaviors—each has its own major section. Some practical issues of grandparenting are then considered, and finally future directions for research are indicated.

HISTORICAL ISSUES IN THE STUDY OF GRANDPARENTING

Development takes place in an historical context, and cross-sectional studies of development thus confound age effects with cohort effects (Baltes, Reese, and Lipsitt, 1980). The cohort of contemporary grandparents in their 70s, for example, as well as being older than parents and grandchildren, will also have experienced less formal schooling. Bengtson (1987) similarly distinguishes period effects (historical period), cohort effects (when you were born while living in an historical period), and lineage effects (different generations within a family structure). Bengtson's emphasis on *lineage* rather than on *age* is appropriate for this chapter, in which we are primarily looking at the generational relationship of grandparenthood. Grandparents can of course vary in age a great deal, whereas lineage remains constant. Age then becomes one mediating factor (among many others) to be considered as affecting grandparental relations.

Most of our evidence on grandparenthood comes from modern urban, industrial societies, particularly the United States and, to a lesser extent, Western Europe. As LeVine and White (1987) point out, generational relations would have been (and still are) very different in agrarian societies. They were embedded in a system with strong kinship ties and strong expectations of reciprocity. Parents tended to have many children, mortality was relatively high, and parents expected children to support them in their later years. The urban-industrial revolution reduced the salience of kinship and parentage; and the concept of childrearing changed from one of lifelong reciprocity to one of launching children into an autonomous maturity in which their future relationship with parents was optional.

The last few centuries in urban-industrial societies have seen numerous changes, partially linked but proceeding at different rates in different countries such as England, France, Germany, Scandinavia, and the United States (LeVine and White, 1987). These include the demographic transition to lower birthrates and deathrates and longer lifespan expectancy; rise of technology; mass public schooling; greater public interest and concern in children (LeVine and White, 1987); and greater parental involvement in children, although with some reduction in parental (especially paternal) control over matters such as marriage and career (Vinovskis, 1987). In the past few decades, there has been an increase in divorce rates and in numbers of reconstituted families and stepkin (Hetherington and Stanley-Hagan, in Vol. 3 of this *Handbook*); greater health and financial security in older generations; and with this some greater ambiguity in the role of the grandparental lineage (Rossi and Rossi, 1990).

These factors need to be borne in mind when the nature and the role of grandparenthood are considered, but some recent changes may have also influenced the extent to which grandparenting has been an object of social scientific and psychological research. Most of the research has been in the past 20 years. Tinsley and Parke (1984) suggested four reasons for this. The first is the demographic change resulting in substantial increases in life expectancy, with more people becoming grandparents. The second is the tendency to view the family as nuclear, comprising only parents and children; although psychologists started looking beyond the mother to the father and siblings in the 1970s, it is only more recently that this "wider social network" has extended to grandparents. Third, consideration of grandparent–grandchild relationships forces investigators to think in a lifespan framework and to consider processes of intergenerational influence. However, the lifespan perspective in developmental and child psychology became influential only in the 1980s; before that, developmental psychology and child development were often seen as virtually synonymous, in practice if not in theory; and this narrowed vision of developmental processes as more or less ceasing at adulthood or "maturity" would not encourage thinking about grandparents. Fourth, some methodological difficulties are associated with working with grandparents. Older persons may be ill or in some ways less suitable research participants, and theoretical and statistical models need to be more complex to cope with the triadic or polyadic relations and patterns of direct and indirect influence likely to be encountered in analyzing grandparent–grandchild influence and interaction.

CLASSICAL RESEARCH IN GRANDPARENTING

The first few articles about grandparents appeared in the 1930s and 1940s (Smith, 1991). Usually written by psychiatrists or clinicians, these gave a rather negative view of grandparental influence. Articles by Vollmer (1937) titled "The Grandmother: A Problem in Child Rearing" and by Strauss (1943) titled "Grandma made Johnny Delinquent" each berated the adverse influence of grandmothers who interfere with the mother's childrearing in old-fashioned and didactic ways. Vollmer ended (1937, p. 382) by stating that "The practical conclusion is that the grandmother is not a suitable custodian of the care and rearing of her grandchild: She is a disturbing factor against which we are obliged to protect the child according to the best of our ability."

Staples (1952) presented a more balanced view, at the same time emphasizing problems of grandparents being coresident with children and grandchildren. She concluded (1952, p. 340) that "the well-liked grandmother . . . keeps up with the times . . . can easily make the transition from a position of responsibility in the family to one of rendering interested, helpful services. The disliked grandmother is unable to adjust to change and is unpleasantly aggressive in her contacts with her family." Staples and Smith (1954) interviewed 87 grandmother–mother pairs and found the grandmothers to have stricter and more authoritarian views than the mothers, on every subscale. Views of grandmothers (and of mothers) were particularly strict when both lived in the same three-generation household (48% of her sample) and when they had fewer years of formal education.

From the 1960s, grandparents started to be presented much more favorably. Smith (1991) suggests that this development reflects some actual changes in grandparental attitudes and roles; although the early studies are probably unrepresentative in terms of sampling, there is some evidence that more grandparents were coresident, and had a more authoritative attitude, earlier in the century. However, by the 1960s certainly, many grandparents accepted a "formal" or "fun-seeking" role, clearly demarcating grandparental and parental roles. In the study by Neugarten and Weinstein (1964), only a very small proportion of grandparents saw themselves as "reservoirs of family wisdom." This decrease in formality and authority probably allowed more indulgent and warm relationships between grandparents and other family members (Apple, 1956).

Studies by Kahana and Kahana (1970) and Robertson (1977) of the perception of grandparenthood continued this more positive picture and set a trend for much subsequent research. Kornhaber and Woodward (1981) described the "vital connection" of grandparents and grandchildren, although worried by now that some grandparents were becoming remote and detached. Tinsley and Parke (1984) reviewed the importance of grandparents as support and socialization agents. Bengtson and Robertson (1985) provided a clear compilation of the more positive research and views of grandparenthood that had accumulated over the previous decade. Cherlin and Furstenberg (1986) gave a thorough account of "the new American grandparent." Mangen, Bengtson, and Landry (1988) provided a comprehensive review of methodological issues in studying intergenerational relationships. Smith (1991) gave a selection of studies of grandparenthood from different industrialised countries, helping to balance the great bulk of research from the United States. In overview, the past two decades have seen a great increase in research on grandparenting, with generally a more positive view of the role than was given in the earlier studies.

THEORETICAL PERSPECTIVES APPLICABLE
TO GRANDPARENTHOOD

Several theoretical perspectives can be used to structure research and interpret data on grandparenting. These include evolutionary theory, psychoanalysis and attachment theory, family sociology and family systems theory, and lifespan development and gerontology.

Evolutionary Theory

Evolutionary theory has had application in several areas of understanding grandparenthood. First, it is relevant to the evolution of features of the human lifespan such as the menopause and senescence. In nonhuman primates there does not seem to be a clear menopause—reproductive senescence does not proceed more rapidly or earlier than senescence in other systems (Altmann, 1987). Evolutionary theories of senescence generally predict the maximum lifespan being set at the point at which the probability of further reproduction is zero (Leek and Smith, 1991; Turke, 1988; Williams, 1957). In humans, however, the menopause at 45–55 years of age clearly precedes likely mortality by some 20, 30, or even 40 years. Turke (1988) argued that this atypical primate pattern suggests that older humans (especially older women, who have a menopause) were able to help children and grandchildren effectively and enhance their own reproductive success more by this than by having yet further children themselves. On this line of reasoning, it is perhaps no accident that the age of menopause is not greatly different from the likely age of becoming a grandparent.

Besides perhaps explaining the advent of the menopause, this approach leads to the prediction that grandparents could and often would provide support for children and grandchildren. Several studies in nonurban societies (the Micronesian atoll community of Ifaluk; Hadza hunter–gatherers in Tanzania; the Gambia) confirm this (Hawkes, O'Connell, and Blurton Jones, 1997; Mace, 2000; Turke, 1988). Hawkes et al. (1997) found that grandmothers were an important source of extra food for grandchildren, especially when the mother had a new baby. Mace (2000) found evidence for mothers having a child earlier and for children having higher survival rates when the mother's mother was alive.

Degree of relatedness should be a predictor of helping; again this is confirmed by many studies. As Rossi and Rossi (1990, p. 491) put it for relationships generally, "what mattered most for obligation level was not a specific *type* of kinperson, but the degree of relatedness of ego to the various kintypes." The greater risk of step-grandchildren for abuse (Margolin, 1992) would also be predicted.

Smith (1991) in Canada and Euler and Weitzel (1996) in Germany found differences in grand-parental involvement and investment (maternal grandmother > maternal grandfather = paternal grandmother > paternal grandfather) and explained these in terms of certainty of (genetic) relatedness; whereas mothers are certain of relatedness to their children, fathers are not so certain. The relatedness to maternal grandmother is definitely one fourth (of genes shared by common descent), whereas for paternal grandfather it is on average somewhere between one fourth and zero, with both links (grandfather–son and son–grandson) potentially uncertain. (For maternal grandfather and paternal grandmother there is one potentially uncertain link.) Pashos (2000) reported similar findings in urban Greece, but, contrary to this and the Canadian and the German findings, greater involvement of paternal than maternal grandparents in rural Greece, suggesting the importance of cultural factors.

Following genetic similarity theory (Rushton, Russell, and Wells, 1984), Leek and Smith (1991) suggested that grandparents might use indicators of phenotypic similarity as cues for relatedness, such that perceived similarity between grandparent and grandchild would also predict involvement or investment. They looked at both perceived similarity in physical appearance and perceived similarity in personality. Similarity in physical appearance did not yield any significant correlations, but perceived personality similarity did correlate with perceived value of help given to children and grandchildren.

There is scope for predictions of when conflict should arise among grandparents, their children, and grandchildren. Parent–offspring conflict theory (Trivers, 1974) has been extended to three generations (Fagen, 1976; Partridge and Nunney, 1977). Thus grandparents might be expected to encourage more cooperation among their grandchildren (who are cousins to each other) than the grandchildren themselves might wish.

Evolutionary theories have a role to play in our understanding of grandparenthood and can and should be integrated with more proximal, and cultural, explanations of relevant data, rather than seen as antithetical to them. For example, Archer (1999) suggests that explanations of greater grief in maternal grandmothers at death of a grandchild, while having evolutionary theory as a distal factor, require strength of attachment as a proximate causative variable.

Psychoanalysis and Attachment Theory

Psychoanalytic views of grandparent–grandchild relationships were prominent in earlier reports, especially by clinicians. These used psychoanalytic ideas such as the "Oedipus complex" (in which an infant boy represses sexual desire for his mother and murderous wishes to his father) and "transference" (in which someone may, for a period, transfer powerful but repressed emotional feelings for someone onto a substitute, as is regularly thought to happen in therapy). Strauss (1943) explained the delinquency of a child called Johnny in terms of the Oedipal complex between the grandmother and Johnny's father, and the hostility to Johnny's mother that was then transferred to Johnny when his mother died. More recently, Battistelli and Farneti (1991) used ideas concerning the Oedipus complex and the transference of a child's feeling from parent to grandparent to throw light on the kinds of associations and dreams that children had about grandparents, as well as developmental trends in these. They argued that grandparents may have a "transitional object role" toward the adolescent grandchild (being a substitute figure for the parent, helping the adolescent during the process of separation).

Although the influence of psychoanalytic ideas in developmental psychology waned after the 1960s, some have had a revival by means of the subsequent developments in attachment theory and the rapprochement among developmental psychologists, systems theorists, and psychoanalysts in this area (Fonagy, 1999; Cummings and Cummings, in Vol. 5 of this *Handbook*). It is possible that psychoanalytic ways of describing and explaining complex emotional dynamics (such as rivalry, jealousy, and projection)—seen clearly in case studies such as those of Cohler and Grunebaum (1981), who draw on psychoanalytic concepts in this way—may be reworked in the future in productive ways more compatible with mainstream developmental ideas (Cohler and Paul, in Vol. 3 of this *Handbook*).

Family Sociology and Family Systems Theory

Concepts from family sociology have been used extensively in describing aspects of grandparental relationships. Key concepts have been cohesion or solidarity, refined into associational, affectual, consensual, functional, normative and goal components, and measures of intergenerational family structure (McChesney and Bengtson, 1988).

Sociological studies such as those by Cunningham-Burley (1984, 1985) and Cotterill (1992) drew attention to how grandparents perceive their role and possible contradictions between such roles and wider familial or societal expectations. The in-depth, qualitative nature of these studies yields findings that are not appropriate for statistical generalization, but that do give a rounded picture of behavior in real-life situations.

Family systems theory (Minuchin, 1988) has potential in elaborating the nature of three-generation family structure further, and it could be used in complementary fashion to some of the psychoanalytic concepts to explore more complex issues such as scapegoating, marginalizing, coalitions, and exclusions in larger family groups. Family systems theory has begun to be recognized as an effective theory for grandparenting research, especially with the increased perception within society that grandparents are an integral part of the family unit.

LifeSpan Development and Gerontology

Lifespan development provides an important way of viewing intergenerational phenomena, and the lifespan concepts of Baltes et al. (1980) can be used as a framework for the impact of nonnormative life events—for example, how grandparents play a buffering role for children in divorcing families or for how historical changes have affected grandparental roles. Bengtson (1987) has emphasized the importance of cohort and period effects. The lifespan perspective can also be seen as lying behind the distinction between direct and indirect influences of grandparents to grandchildren (Tinsley and Parke, 1984), as well as the understanding of bidirectional effects in development (Bengtson, 1987).

Aging and gerontology provide another perspective for studying grandparenthood. Even though many grandparents are not "aged" in the conventional sense, they may experience negative stereotypes of aging. A significant proportion of grandparents will indeed be in their later years or suffer from particular infirmities of age such as senile dementia (Creasey, Myers, Epperson, and Taylor, 1989). More positively, aging can be seen as leading to more mature concepts of morality and greater wisdom (Clayton and Birren, 1980; Sternberg, 1990). In some traditional agricultural societies, grandparenthood can be a precondition for achieving the status of respected elder in the community (Sangree, 1992). In general, theories from gerontology could be integrated with a lifespan perspective to give insights into grandparenting insofar as it inevitably involves aging.

CENTRAL ISSUES IN STUDYING GRANDPARENTHOOD

The main issues central to the study of grandparenthood in contemporary society discussed here are the frequency and the nature of contacts between grandparents and grandchildren; the mediating role of proximity; varying characteristics of grandparents and grandchildren; great-grandparents; styles of grandparenting; perceptions of grandparents; grandparents affected by divorce or death of a grandchild; step-grandparents; grandparents and lesbian mothers; grandparents of grandchildren with disabilities; and the nature of grandparenting in different cultures. In later sections we consider indirect and direct patterns of grandparent–grandchild influence, including intergenerational transmission and acting as a surrogate parent.

Contacts Between Grandparents and Grandchildren: How Frequent and How Satisfying?

The consensus of a considerable number of studies on contemporary grandparents and grandchildren is that they see each other moderately frequently, and the relationship is usually (although not invariably) quite close and satisfying, rather than conflictual. However "frequent" and "satisfying" are somewhat relative terms, and how one sees the typical grandparent–grandchild relationship may depend on one's expectations. Kivett (1985) reported the grandfather role to be of little relative importance as seen through low levels of interaction and low priority as a role. However, Kivett's actual data on grandfathers showed that 82% of them were visited by grandchildren and 37% had visits once a week or more; 26% also attended church several times a month with grandchildren, and 88% of grandfathers said they felt very close to the grandchild with whom they had most contact. These data are not out of line with many other studies in the United States. The grandfathers in Kivett's study tended to rank grandfatherhood as the third most important role in their life, after being a spouse or parent. This seems realistic. Being a grandparent does not rank as high as being a husband (or wife) or being a parent, and it is true that some grandparents see some grandchildren seldom, if ever. However, the modal tendency is for grandparents to see grandchildren often enough to share a quite close and satisfying relationship.

Several studies in the United States have reported on the perceptions that college students or young adults have of their grandparents. For example, Eisenberg (1988) gave questionnaires to

120 undergraduates, aged 18 to 23 years. On average, grandchildren had contact with grandparents approximately once or twice a month and rated the relationship as "close" (3 on a 5-point scale). Creasey and Koblewski (1991) surveyed 142 college students, mean age 19 years. Again, most managed to visit grandparents once a month or so and telephoned more often. Relationships were generally good; on 5-point scales, grandparents rated high on continuity (4.1) and affection (4.0), mutual respect (3.9) and satisfaction (3.5), and low on power (1.7) and conflict (1.6). Creasey and Koblewski (1991, p. 384) concluded that "it is clear that most grandparents continue to play a relatively active role within their adolescent grandchildren's social networks."

Hodgson (1992) reported results from a national telephone survey, which obtained data from 208 grandchildren, mostly aged 18 to 40 years, about the relationship with their closest grandparent. The majority were in some contact with the grandparent several times a month, 40% weekly (although 13% interacted only once a year or less). On a 4-point scale of closeness, the mean response was 3 ("quite close"). Hodgson (1992, p. 222) concludes that, despite variability, "the grandchild/grandparent bond continues with surprising strength into adulthood."

In a national study in the United States, Cherlin and Furstenberg (1986) reported that 60% of grandparents saw their grandchildren at least once or twice a month. In Great Britain, direct contact between grandparents and grandchildren was weekly to monthly for 75% of a national sample, and grandparents saw the relationship as rewarding (National Centre for Social Research, 1999). In Finland, Ruoppila (1991) found that 70% of grandparents, even when quite elderly, saw their grandchildren at least once a week; and most saw the relationship in positive terms. Sticker (1991) reported on several studies in Germany; generally, grandparents saw grandchildren weekly or, in the case of grandchildren who were of preschool age, more often. Approximately three fourths of grandparent–grandchild dyads were characterized by "high" or "very high" emotional closeness. In Poland, Tyszkowa (1991) found that a majority of students (aged 15 to 23 years) visited grandparents at least once a month, and the emotional tone of the relationship was generally positive. Not all grandchildren get on with their grandparents, of course. In Tyskowa's (1991, p. 56) study, one student reported "I don't like my grandmother; she's sloppy and disagreable . . . I don't like visiting her"; and another "she's always running about, grumbling, nagging and shouting."

The wider nature of family relationships involving grandparents can be very complex, as is well brought out in case studies. Cohler and Grunebaum (1981) reported four detailed studies of three-generation Italian American families. In one, Ms. Scardoni, aged 53 years, is the mother of Ms. Russo, aged 27 years, and grandmother of Charlotte. Ms. Scardoni experienced violence from her own father and later her husband (with whom she had 11 children). Her ambivalence comes out in jealously and continual criticism of her son-in-law, Mr. Russo, and overworrying about her grandchildren. Ms. Russo is strongly influenced by her mother and talks to her on the telephone at least once a day, but is torn between loyalty to her and to her husband. By the age of 6 years, Charlotte appeared well behaved, but, according to Cohler and Grunebaum (1981, p. 350), subdued and compliant, "suggesting that Charlotte may have joined her mother and grandmother in the continuation of family conflicts into the third generation."

In summary, most grandparents see many grandchildren at least once a month, sometimes much more often; and generally the relationship is seen as positive, and important, by both generations. However, this general picture should not be allowed to hide the very great variation in contact and satisfaction in grandparent–grandchild relationships.

The Nature of Contacts Between Grandparents and Grandchildren

The range of activities that grandparents and grandchildren engage in is wide and obviously varies greatly with age; the particular role of surrogate parenting will be discussed later. Eisenberg (1988) found that a majority of her grandchildren reported having done the following activities with grandparents: having treats, giving a sense of family, imparting family history, taking part in family events, playing games, going on trips, baby-sitting, making you feel good, giving emergency help, giving personal advice, being someone to talk to, joining in religious activity, and giving advice on school. Tyszkowa (1991, p. 20) reported "conversations" as being prominent in activities reported by Polish grandchildren. "When we go fishing with Grandpa, we talk. We tell each other about ourselves"; "with Grandma I can talk about my problems." This is echoed by some of the German grandchildren in Sticker's (1991, p. 37) study: "... we talk about everything, also about confidences which concern our family as a whole"; "if I don't like anything, I can say it, whatever it is ... I'm not afraid ... sometimes I also tell Grandma a secret." Because they are close but do not have a parental authority role, grandparents can sometimes act as confidants in situations in which an older child might not wish to confide in a parent.

Also, grandparents will often know more about family history than anyone else and can provide a sense of continuity in family traditions that may be of considerable interest to grandchildren as they get older. They can pass on national history; Tyszkowa (1991) found that 20% of grandchildren reported that grandparents had told them about episodes such as the Second World War in Poland.

The Mediating Role of Proximity

Proximity has been found to be the most important factor in frequency of contact and level of emotional closeness between grandparents and grandchildren. In Hodgson's (1992) sample, nearly one half of grandparents lived within 25 miles of grandchildren; but a fourth lived more than 500 miles away. This variation in proximity was the strongest factor in predicting frequency of contact. Kivett (1985) found that in 93% of cases the grandchild with whom a grandfather had the most contact was also the closest geographically. In a study of 171 undergraduates in Western Canada, Boon and Brussoni (1996) reported that emotional closeness of the grandparent–grandchild relationship was related to frequency of contact. In a sample of 4,629 grandparent–grandchild dyads, Uhlenberg and Hammill (1998) found six factors that predicted contact between grandparents and grandchild, geographic proximity being the strongest, followed by the quality of the parent–grandparent relationship.

In a study of intergenerational interaction in Finnish families with 12-year-old grandchildren, Hurme (1988) found that most had some grandparents within 60 kilometers, and a third had a maternal grandmother in the same town (only 1.5% in the same house). In Great Britain 30%–40% of grandparents' live within 15 minutes travel of a grandchild (National Centre for Social Research, 1999) although 25% have a grandchild living more than 100 miles away (Age Concern, 1998). Hurme found a sharp decline in frequency for contact when distance exceeded 20 kilometers, but little change in the perceived importance of the relationship when distance was up to 60 kilometers.

Changes in transportation and communication provide other avenues to maintain contact and possibly remove proximity as the barrier to contact that it once was (Thompson, Scalora, Limber, and Castrianno, 1991). In Great Britain, 86% of grandparents and grandchildren keep in regular phone contact and 4% are in contact by the Internet or e-mail (Age Concern, 1998). Ponzetti (1992) found that the frequency of phone calls was more effective than letters as a predictor of grandparent–grandchild closeness. Creasey (1993) found phone contact to play an important role in sustaining the relationship between adolescent grandchildren and paternal grandparents.

Varying Characteristics of Grandparents and Grandchildren

External factors such as proximity of residence affect grandparent–grandchild contacts and activities, and so too do factors such as gender, lineage, age, and health of the grandparent, and the particular grandchild and age of grandchild.

Gender. The grandparenting role is related to overall life satisfaction and morale in both genders (Kivnick, 1982). However, just as mothers are more often the closer parent to children, many studies find that grandmothers are more involved with grandchildren than are grandfathers.

Grandmothers and grandfathers have been argued to approach their roles from different perspectives; Kornhaber and Woodward (1981) called grandmothers the "heart" and grandfathers the "head." Grandmothers anticipate and become involved in the role sooner than grandfathers (Creasey and Koblewski, 1991) and have greater satisfaction with their current and expected grandparenting role than do grandfathers (Somary and Stricker, 1998; Thomas, 1989). Expectant grandmothers are more likely to emphasize the joy of indulging the grandchild, being a valued older person, and being central to the grandchild's life than expectant grandfathers are, whereas expectant grandfathers had warmer attitudes toward caregiving of the grandchild before birth than grandmothers did.

Tinsley and Parke (1988) found that grandfathers, when involved, are able to nurture and respond to children's needs as effectively as grandmothers; some grandfathers are more nurturing than they were as fathers (Kornhaber, 1996). However, grandmothers are more likely to care for grandchildren and find a personal sense of biological renewal in the role. Grandfathers most often view their role as an opportunity for emotional fulfilment and place greater stress on the continuation of the family through the grandchildren and indulging them (Kivnick, 1982; Neugarten and Weinstein, 1964; Thomas, 1989) and influencing young adult grandchildren in instrumental ways, such as jobs and finances (Hagestad, 1985).

Kornhaber and Woodward (1981) found that children view their grandparents in stereotypical roles: a grandfather is to "do things with" and "get advice from"; a grandmother is to "take care of you" and "teach you a lot, and you can talk to her about everyday things." These views held by the grandchildren might influence their behavior and how grandparents respond to their grandchildren. More research needs to be conducted into gender-role differences in grandparenting and the impact these roles have on the grandchildren and vice versa.

Lineage.   Grandparents through the mother's side—maternal grandmother and maternal grandfather—are more involved than those through the father's side—paternal grandmother and paternal grandfather. Gender and lineage of grandparent may interact as influences, with the maternal grandmother often appearing as having the most contact and closest relationship with grandchildren. Kahana and Kahana (1970), Eisenberg (1988), and Hodgson (1992) found the maternal grandmother to be perceived as closest and seen most often by grandchildren in the United States, followed by the maternal grandfather, and then the paternal grandparents. Battistelli and Farneti (1991) in Italy, Smith (1991) in Canada, and Tyszkowa (1991) in Poland reported a similar pattern; although Pashos (2000) found a different pattern in rural Greece (see the subsection on evolutionary theory). The age of a grandparent can be an interacting factor here; because on average women marry slightly older men, maternal grandmothers are often the youngest of all four grandparents. However, the main explanation probably lies in the strength of mother–daughter bonds, often reinforced by societal expectations and perhaps in a more distal causal sense by certainty of relatedness.

Age and health of grandparent.   As noted earlier, the age of a grandparent will interact with other factors, notably health, age of grandchildren, cohort effects, and the image of grandparents as older persons. For example, Johnson (1983) found that grandparents over the age of 65 years had less favorable attitudes to cohabitation (probably a cohort effect), were less family oriented and more friend oriented (probably reflecting older age and greater independence of grandchildren), and had less contact with grandchildren.

Thomas (1986) compared grandparents aged 45 to 60, 61 to 69, and 70 to 90 years; the ages of grandchildren averaged from 7 to 17 years; in this entirely European American sample, no grandparents shared a household with grandchildren, but 63% lived within 30-minutes travel of at least one grandchild. Thomas found no age differences in satisfaction with the role of grandparent or in the amount of helping grandchildren. However, the two younger groups expressed greater responsibility for grandchildren's discipline and for giving childrearing advice. This latter finding probably reflects an age-of-grandchild effect (the oldest group mostly had adolescent grandchildren, the younger groups mostly preadolescents), although it could reflect either age-of-grandparent or cohort effects.

Kennedy (1991) looked at reasons given by college students for closeness to their most close grandparent. Younger grandparents (50 to 60 years of age) received more reasons to do with love and appreciation, intimacy, and shared activities; older grandparents, especially those over 75 years of age, received more reasons to do with caring for the grandparent. Older grandparents are of course less likely to be in good health, and this can affect the relationship. Mild health problems may not decrease relationship satisfaction and may indeed elicit caring from grandparents (Cherlin and Furstenberg, 1985; Troll, 1985).

Creasey et al. (1989) compared grandparent–grandchild relationships when grandparents in their 60s and 70s did or did not have senile dementia of the Alzheimer's type. In both groups, grandchildren saw the grandparents about once a week; but, not surprisingly, grandchildren had poorer relationships with grandparents with Alzheimer's disease, perceiving lower companionship, intimacy, and affection (although not differing in nurturance).

Particular grandchild.   The relationship of the grandparent has usually been generalized to all of their grandchildren; but different grandchildren may have different needs and personalities that result in different forms of contact. Fingerman (1998) interviewed 91 grandparents who provided information about each of their 346 grandchildren. Grandparents identified a special grandchild, and a few described a tumultuous relationship with a grandchild. Grandchildren who were identified as special were defined in terms of the grandchild's personal attributes, accomplishments, or love, and grandparents not surprisingly spent more time with these grandchildren than with those who were described as "irritating" to the grandparent.

Age of grandchild.   Some studies have reported on age of grandchild as a factor in relationships with grandparents. Given the rapid developmental changes of childhood, attribution of findings to age (rather than historical period or age of grandparent) may be more plausible than in the corresponding analyses of grandparent age. Kahana and Kahana (1970) gave interviews and questionnaires to children aged 4 to 5, 8 to 9, and 11 to 12 years about their grandparents. The two older groups had more contact with grandparents, especially paternal grandparents. The youngest group saw paternal grandparents least, perhaps because they were most dependent on family (and mother's) arrangements; the older grandchildren had greater independent mobility, and also were more likely to verbalize a desire to treat all grandparents equally (Kahana and Kahana, 1970, p. 102): "you have to love all your grandparents the same," "I love them all the same." In terms of describing the relationship, the youngest children often referred to indulgent grandparents who gave them gifts or treats—"egocentric" responses; the 8- to 9-year-old children gave reasons based more on mutuality and fun-sharing activities, and the 11- to 12-year-old children were generally more diverse in their reasons.

Battistelli and Farneti (1991) gave a questionnaire on grandparents to children aged 8 to 9, 12 to 13, and 16 to 17 years. The youngest group more often described playing with grandparents. Older grandchildren, however, even if they saw grandparents as somewhat less important, also saw them as more patient and understanding than parents, with adolescents being much less likely to argue with grandparents than with parents. Consistent with the findings of Kahana and Kahana, perhaps, these Italian children grew toward a more homogenized evaluation of different grandparents, the maternal grandparents (who received more positive evaluation in younger children) being evaluated equally with the paternal grandparents by adolescence.

Creasey and Kaliher (1994) used the Network of Relationships Inventory with 169 children aged 9 to 13 years; older grandchildren perceived less supportive relationships with grandparents than did younger ones; paternal grandfathers were perceived as least supportive, but there were few other gender differences.

Mills (1999) utilized data from the University of Southern California Longitudinal Study of Generations, spanning 23 years between 1971 and 1994, and explored the role transition of the grandchild from adolescent to adult for the impact on the solidarity of the grandparent–grandchild relationship.

Obtained roles were defined for the grandchild as employment, marriage, parenthood, or remarriage after divorce; lost roles were unemployment or divorce. Overall, greater familial solidarity between grandparent and grandchild was not dependent on acquisition or loss of a role; however, role transitions were greater predictors of grandchildren's solidarity with grandfathers than with grandmothers.

Great-Grandparents

The relatively small number of studies on great-grandparenthood finds contact to be less frequent and the role to be less intense or clear than that of grandparent. Wentowski (1985) interviewed 19 great-grandmothers, aged 66 to 92 years. As 92-year-old Ms. Smith commented; "when you're a grandparent, you love 'em, you're glad to have them come, you fix 'em food, do things for 'em because they're precious to you. When you're a great-grandparent, you're older and you can't do as much. It's different." However, even the youngest and healthiest great-grandmothers (aged 66 and 71 years) were not so involved with great-grandchildren as with grandchildren (Wentowski, 1985, p. 594): "Other people take care of this now." Ms. Smith saw some local great-grandchildren weekly with her daughter and granddaughter, but had never seen some nonlocal great-grandchildren. Ruoppila (1991) found that elderly Finnish people saw great-grandchildren much less frequently than they did grandchildren; this was especially true for men. Nevertheless, most saw great-grandchildren at least monthly.

Doka and Mertz (1988) described the role of great-grandparent as fulfilling but remote, as contact was limited more to holidays and birthdays. They identified three roles for the great-grandparent: personal and family renewal, diversion in their lives, and a mark of their longevity. Reese and Murray (1996) interviewed eight European American and eight African American great-grandmothers, aged 75 to 89 years, who saw their role as intrinsic to the family system; they either initiated family gatherings or were the cause of them. However, from the perspective of 297 adult great-grandchildren, Roberto and Skoglund (1996) reported the role of the great-grandparent as not clear. Although 33% of great-grandchildren reported having respect for them and 24% saw them as a teacher, 56% reported having little to no contact with their great-grandparent while growing up and currently.

Burton and Bengtson (1985), in a study of young grandmothers, interviewed a number of great-grandmothers aged 46 to 73 years and regarded those aged up to 57 years as "early" in the role; they also interviewed seven great-great-grandmothers and one great-great-great-grandmother! Generally, as will be discussed later, these "early" grandmothers and great-grandmothers do not like being seen in this role because of their own conflicting life concerns and also what they perceive as an association of (great-)grandparenthood with aging and its associated negative stereotypes.

Styles of Grandparenting

In describing variations in grandparent–grandchild relationships, researchers have devised typologies of grandparenting or different styles of grandparenting. The earliest, and one that has remained influential, is that of Neugarten and Weinstein (1964). From interviews with 70 sets of grandparents, they delineated five major styles: *formal* (following prescribed roles with a clear demarcation between parenting and grandparenting responsibilities); *fun seeker* (seeing grandchildren as fun and a source of self-indulgence or mutuality of satisfaction); *surrogate parent* (taking actual caregiving responsibility); *reservoir of family wisdom* (dispensing special skills or resources, with authority); and *distant* (only infrequent contacts with grandchildren on ritual occasions). They found the formal role to be more frequent in grandparents over 65 years of age, whereas the fun seeker and distant styles were more frequent in younger grandparents. This typology has been used in several other studies. McCready (1985) compared different U.S. ethnic groups in this way; Sticker (1991) summarized results from several studies, including a number of studies in Germany, which point to the fun-seeking style's predominating with younger grandchildren, and the formal style's increasing with older grandchildren.

The roles described by Neugarten and Weinstein are in fact a mixture of intrinsically age-related roles (especially "surrogate parent") with styles that may be overlapping rather than discrete (thus McCready combined the "formal" and the "distant" types). Inclusive, discrete typologies were produced by Robertson (1977) and Cherlin and Furstenberg (1985). Robertson assessed the personal meanings (meeting individual needs) and the social role meanings (meeting social norms) grandparents used to describe relationships with grandchildren; this yielded four styles, *apportioned* (high on both), *remote* (low on both), *individualized* (high on personal only), and *symbolic* (high on social only). Cherlin and Furstenberg (1985) distinguished two main aspects of grandparent–grandchild relationships, measured by scales of several items: those relating to exchange of services (giving and receiving help) and those relating to exerting parental-type influence (disciplining, advising on problems). Also, they took account of infrequent (less than once a month) or more frequent contact. This gave them a fivefold typology. *Detached* grandparents were low on both scales and had infrequent contact; *passive* grandparents were low on both scales and had more frequent contact; *supportive* grandparents were high on exchange of services; *authoritative* grandparents were high on parentlike influence; and those high on both scales were *influential*. More African American grandparents (especially grandmothers) were authoritative or influential.

Mangen and McChesney (1988) described 14 types of grandparent role based on a heirarchical cluster analysis of a large number of different measures of cohesion in a sample of over 2,000 respondents. The types vary in terms of amounts of contact and exchange, degree of reciprocity, emotional closeness, and geographical distance.

Perceptions of Grandparents

However social scientists describe grandparent roles, it is another matter whether grandparents themselves have a clear idea of their own role and how this is viewed by society generally. We discuss here societal views of grandparenthood and stereotypes of aging; on-time and off-time grandparenthood as perceived by grandparents; and perceptions of different generations.

Societal views of grandparenthood.   There have been changes through the past century in the extent to which grandparents have been expected to have "authoritarian" or "authoritative" parental-type duties or just be "supportive" (Kornhaber and Woodward, 1981). One view of grandparents is of someone who spoils grandchildren, being overlenient or indulgent. As one U.K. song puts it (Miller, 1989),

> Granny spoils us, oh what fun, Have some sweets and a sticky bun, Don't tell mum you were up till ten, I want to come and babysit again.

This image of spoiling has some basis in reality. In interviews of 155 older people with grandchildren in Great Britain, Townsend (1957, p. 106) reported that "the grandparents were notably lenient towards grandchildren." This leniency and spoiling may have been a reaction, both real and perceived, against the strict and authoritarian role of grandparents that was, by the 1950s, being rejected. As one of Townsend's (1957, pp. 106–107) informants put it, "I used to slosh my children. But I don't like to see my grandchildren walloped," and another said "the grandmother can be free and easy. She [her daughter] has to be fairly strict with them."

Johnson (1983) found that U.S. grandmothers had not often consciously conceptualized the role and thus could mold it to their own lifestyle and that of their families. However, individual grandmothers were quite able to give a list of rules that they used to regulate their behavior with their grandchildren. The "shoulds" typically included being an advocate, mediator, support, and source of enjoyment; the "should nots" involved not being too intrusive, overprotective, or parental—too "old fashioned," in fact. Many of these 1980s grandmothers seem to have taken a "supportive" role and rejected an "authoritative" role more common a generation or so before. Tunaley (2000) reported contemporary U.K. grandparents as being able to find a balance in their role of supporting the family through emotional and practical help, but of noninterference in the parenting style of their adult child and son-in-law or daughter-in-law.

Stereotypes of grandparents and aging.   The media and children's books often portray grandparents as aged, fussy, domesticated, and sedentary, probably with infirmities. Janelli (1988) surveyed 42 North American children's books, published between 1961 and 1983; she found that 55% of grandmothers had white or gray hair, 31% wore glasses, and 31% had aprons; 39% of grandfathers had bald heads, and 36% had both white hair and glasses. Many U.K. children's books show grandparents in a similar way (Smith, 1991).

This stereotype is out of step with demographic realities. Most grandchildren who read children's books will have grandparents in their 40s, 50s, and 60s. As Hagestad (1985, pp. 35–36) similarly pointed out for TV commercials, "Often, the grandmother presented on the screen should be a great-grandmother. The woman who has small, golden-haired grandchildren is not likely to have silver hair in a bun, serve lemonade on the porch, or worry about slipping dentures and "irregularity." She would more realistically be portrayed dressed in a jogging suit on her way to aerobic dancing or in a suit coming home from work."

This association of grandparenthood with old age and negative stereotypes associated with aging can have a negative effect on how grandparents and grandchildren view the role; in a study of drawings of young and old people by 10- to 11-year-old children in Scotland, Falchikov (1990) reported that the content of the drawings of older people showed glasses, rocking chairs, walking frames, and smaller figures—generally, aging as a degenerative biological process. Nevertheless, Marcoen (1979) found that children's drawings of their own grandparents were more realistic and less influenced by these negative stereotypes.

On-time and off-time grandparents.   For most people, becoming a grandparent is described as a positive experience; but this can depend on the age at which it happens. Nearly one third of grandparents experience grandparenthood "off time," that is, either before the age of 40 years or after the age of 60 years (Szinovacz, 1998). Burton and Bengtson (1985) interviewed African American grandmothers and described those who experienced the transition between 42 and 57 years of age as being "on time," within the normal range of variation. However, those women who became grandmothers "early," between 25 and 37 years of age, were discontented, feeling obligations placed on them for which they were not ready: "I don't have time to do what I would like to do as a grandmother. I work everyday. I have young children. Right now I'm just too busy." They were also affected by the stereotypes associated with grandparenting and age (Burton and Bengtson, 1985, p. 68): "I am just too young to be a grandmother. That's something for old folks, not for me."

Timberlake and Chipungu (1992) compared the perceived value of grandchildren to African American grandmothers who became grandmothers either between the ages of 30 and 41 or between the ages of 45 and 60 years. The former had a significantly lower evaluation of what their grandchildren meant to them. Watson (1997) found younger European American and African American grandmothers to have a less good understanding of their grandchildren and to experience more frustration in the role.

By contrast, Burton and Bengtson (1985) found that those grandparents who experienced the transition "late," for example in their 70s, were likely to be disappointed that they would have relatively little time left to enjoy their grandchildren and would be less likely to be sufficiently well and physically active to make the most of the grandparental role. Off-time grandparents, whether early or late, were likely to experience more difficulties in the role than were on-time grandparents.

Perceptions of different generations.   Although three generations are involved in grandparent–grandchild relationships, most studies have focused on the viewpoint of only one generation.

Sometimes the views of grandparents have been elicited; more often, the perspective of the grandchild. However, the differing perceptions of differing generations may be important information. The few studies that have obtained multiple perspectives regularly report some incongruence. Hurme (1988) found that 38% of her Finnish grandmothers rated their relationship with the grandchild as "very important," whereas only 27% of mothers so rated it. Mangen and Miller (1988) reported that correlations across generations for amount of contact, seemingly an objective fact, varied between .41 and .75. Disagreements here often signified relationship difficulties; one father claimed to visit the children's grandmother once a month, but the grandmother complained that he hardly ever came and (Mangen and Miller, 1998, p. 121) that "I do not see my son's children enough to know their middle names." Landry and Martin (1988) found reasonable levels of agreement across generations about attitudes, but with the grandparent's generation underestimating the grandparent–parent difference and the grandchild's generation overestimating differences with their parents. These differing perceptions deserve more attention in future, both for their theoretical interest and for possible practical benefits that might ensue if misunderstandings can be avoided.

Grandparents, Grandchildren, and Parental Divorce

The incidence of separation and divorce has risen over the past few decades in many countries, including the United States and Great Britain (Rodgers and Pryor, 1998). When parents separate and divorce, this can have a tremendous impact on grandparent–parent–grandchild relationships. Although much research has looked at the effect of parental separation or divorce on the Parent–child relationship (Hetherington and Stanley-Hagan, 1999, in Vol. 3 of this *Handbook*), few studies have looked at its impact on the grandparents. The relationship of grandparents to parents, particularly to a custodial parent (or one who has care and control of the grandchildren) becomes a crucial issue.

If the grandparent–parent relationships are harmonious, this opens opportunities for a supportive role; grandparents can provide stability, support, and nurturance to the grandchild(ren) and family, often providing financial assistance or childcare (Aldous, 1985; Clingempeel, Colyar, Brand, and Hetherington, 1992; Gladstone, 1987; Johnson, 1988; Kennedy and Kennedy, 1993; Kivett, 1991; Myers and Perrin, 1993). They can negotiate relationship difficulties between the parent and grandchild (Barranti, 1985) and be a "stress buffer" during times of family distress, which can benefit grandchildren even when their relationship with the grandparent is not intense (Derdeyn, 1985; Kennedy, 1990, 1992; Kornhaber and Woodward, 1981; McCrimmon and Howell, 1989; Wallerstein, 1986).

Gladstone (1987) found a significant increase in the frequency of face-to-face contact between grandmothers and their grandchildren following an adult child's separation or divorce. The increase was dependent on the geographical proximity and mobility of the grandparents and on the custodial status of the child of the separated or divorced parent. In a study of 77 grandchild–grandparent pairs after divorce, Schutter, Scherman, and Carroll (1997) identified healthier grandparents and those who lived closer as having greater contact with their grandchildren.

A difficult or disrupted grandparent–parent relationship can threaten proximity of grandparents to grandchildren, contact, involvement, and fulfillment of a satisfying grandparental role (Lavers and Sonuga-Barke, 1997). Contact can be significantly reduced when the relationship with the custodial parent is poor to nonexistent (Kruk, 1995). Marital discord was found by Rossi and Rossi (1990) to affect all grandparent–grandchild relationships negatively except that of maternal grandmother and granddaughter. Although parental custody has been suggested as the greater variable in grandchild–grandparent contact after divorce and not the maternal or paternal family relationship per se (Hilton and Macari, 1997), if (as is usually the case) the children reside with their mother, then paternal grandparents may have to "tread carefully" in obtaining access to their grandchildren. With some 50% of noncustodial fathers in Great Britain, the United States, and Canada gradually losing all contact with their children (Kruk and Hall, 1995), paternal grandparents are at a higher risk of losing contact with their grandchildren than are maternal grandparents.

The consequences of unwanted loss of contact with grandchildren can be devastating. Kruk (1995) in Canada and Drew and Smith (1999) in England sampled grandparents who were members of support groups; both studies found that, after loss of contact with their grandchildren that was due to parental divorce, grandparents reported symptoms of bereavement and negative effects on their physical and emotional health. In a further study with 192 grandparents who were not members of a grandparent support group, following loss of contact with a grandchild (which was due to divorce and also to family feud), Drew (2000) found a range of negative consequences, including intense chronic grief, symptoms of posttraumatic stress disorder, cognitive intrusion and avoidance, mental health problems, and lowered life satisfaction, with some being clinically depressed). One grandparent stated (Drew, 2000, p. 152), "My feelings most days are as if my heart is being torn from my body." Many of these grandparents were experiencing a threefold grief: grieving for their adult child, grieving for their grandchild, and their own loss of the grandchild relationship and role. Additionally, the pining or yearning of the grandparents was related to the "hope" of reunion with their grandchildren; although not totally unrealistic, these hopes make it difficult to work through the grief process.

Grandparents can sometimes learn to negotiate their relationship with the custodial parent in order to have contact with their grandchild (Schutter et al., 1997). The personality, resources, and coping strategies of grandparents can be important in maintaining contact after divorce. King and Elder (1998) found that grandparents who have greater self-efficacy in the grandparenting role find ways to be involved in their grandchild's life even when obstacles stand in the way. With time, also, grandchildren become more independent; Thompson and Walker (1987) found that, if young adult granddaughters had a close intimate relationship with their grandmother, then after parental divorce they would bypass the parent generation and maintain contact.

Death of a Grandchild

The few studies that have investigated how the death of a grandchild has an impact on grandparents have all reported similar findings, despite the varying grandchild ages or causes of the death—such as accident or sudden infant death syndrome (Defrain, Ernest, Jakub, and Taylor, 1992; Defrain, Jakub, and Mendoza, 1991–1992; Fry, 1997; Ponzetti, 1992; Ponzetti and Johnson, 1991; Roskin, 1984). Tremendous anguish, grief, sadness, and emotional and physical pain were reported. Grandparents focused more on the needs of their adult child than their own grief (Ponzetti, 1992). Grandmothers were more likely than grandfathers to discuss the death of their grandchild.

Step-Grandparenthood

Johnson and Barer (1987) pointed out the complexity of three-generation family relationships that can ensue after divorce. A grandchild could have three types of step-grandparent, resulting from a parent remarrying (the most usual), a grandparent remarrying, or from the parent of a stepparent remarrying! Sanders and Trygstad (1989) compared U.S. college student grandchildren's perceptions of grandparents and step-grandparents. They found that grandparent–grandchild relationships were closer in terms of more frequent contact, greater emotional involvement, and role expectations than were step-grandparent–grandchild relationships. Nevertheless, approximately half their grandchild sample saw the step-grandparent relationship as important. The differences appeared to be partly, but not completely, a product of the length of time for which they had known the (step-)grandparent. Henry, Ceglian, and Matthews (1992) obtained the views of 62 mothers on grandparent relations with grandchildren and step-grandchildren; the relationships were perceived as different, with more steprelationships described as "remote" in Robertson's (1977) typology.

Henry, Ceglian, and Ostrander (1993) identified four developmental stages and corresponding tasks that a step-grandparent transcends in accepting the new blended family: *accepting the losses* (the grieving of the lost family and the loss of traditional grandparenthood); *accepting the adult child's single status* (accepting the change of family boundaries and acknowledging ambiguity in family roles, and finding ways to maintain contact with grandchildren); *accepting the adult child's entrance into a new relationship* (building a relationship with the new daughter-in-law or son-in-law and accepting new family members); and *establishing new relationships within the stepfamily context* (finding opportunities to build the new relationships and share the family history with the new family members).

Grandparents and Lesbian Mothers

Little is known about the grandparent role in lesbian families (Patterson, in Vol. 3 of this *Handbook*). Patterson, Hurt, and Mason (1998) interviewed 37 lesbian mother families with children aged 4 to 9 years, who lived with either their biological or adopted lesbian mother. The majority of grandchildren were in monthly contact with their grandparents and had fewer behavior problems than did those with less frequent contact. Contact with biological grandparents was higher than that for nonbiological grandparents; Patterson et al. suggested that this is either a symptom of a history of more supportive family interaction or the nonbiological grandparents' lack of acceptance of their lesbian daughter's identity.

Grandparents of Grandchildren with Disabilities

A growing research area is the role of grandparents within the family when their grandchild has a disability (Hodap, in Vol. 1 of this *Handbook*; Melamed, in Vol. 5 of this *Handbook*). Some studies do not identify a specific disability (Hornby and Ashforth, 1994; Scherman et al., 1995; Seligman et al., 1997), whereas others are more focused: cerebral palsy (Schilmoeller and Baranowski, 1999), Down syndrome (Byrne, Cunningham, and Sloper, 1988), autism (Glasberg and Harris, 1997; Harris, Handleman, and Palmer, 1985), developmental delays (George, 1988), deafness (Nybo, Scherman, and Freeman, 1998), and sickle cell disease (Dillworth, 1994). A great deal of this research has been conducted from a clinical perspective. Researchers have identified the need for a theoretical focus, and many have suggested family systems theory (Mirfin-Veitch, Bray, and Watson, 1997; Nybo et al., 1998; Scherman et al., 1995; Schilmoeller and Baranowski, 1999; Seligman et al., 1997).

Several studies have identified grandparents as vital sources of emotional and practical support when a grandchild has a disability (Kazak and Marvin, 1984; Mirfin-Veitch, Bray, and Watson, 1996). However, sometimes the grandparent's immediate inability to accept a grandchild's disability can be a source of stress to the family system. Myer and Vadasy (1986) reported that the birth of a grandchild with a disability evokes emotions that are different from those experienced when the grandchild is healthy. The grandparents often experience a threefold anxiety: for their newborn grandchild's health, their adult child's ability to cope, and their role as a grandparent. Nybo et al. (1998) and Scherman et al. (1995) suggested that grandparents are frequently trapped in disappointment and grieve for their grandchild as well as for their adult child.

The majority of research on grandchildren with disabilities finds that maternal grandparents provided more emotional support to families (Byrne et al., 1988; Hornby and Ashforth, 1994; Seligman et al., 1997). Maternal grandparents were more likely to learn sign language to communicate with their deaf grandchild than paternal grandparents were because of their closer relationship with their grandchild's mother (Nybo et al., 1998). Maternal grandmothers were more accurately able to assess the development of their grandchild with autism than the paternal grandmothers were (Glasberg and Harris, 1997).

Grandparents who attended support or educational groups related to their grandchild's disability had more positive feelings (George, 1988; Vadasy, Fewell, and Meyer, 1986). Schilmoeller and Baranowski (1999) found grandparent education about their grandchild's disability was associated with greater acceptance and more involvement with their grandchild. Educational workshops for grandparents about their grandchild's deafness were helpful in not only educating the grandparent but letting go of their denial about their grandchild's disability.

In Panama, the parents of disabled children provided very little information to grandparents about their grandchild's condition, which is different than in Western society, but is indicative of the Panamanian culture (Scherman et al., 1998). Scherman et al. (1995) found that, in general, once grandparents of children with disabilities were over the immediate shock they were prepared to provide support and engage in the family system.

Cultural Differences and Grandparents

The literature on grandparenting outside the Western industrialized countries is scattered. In the Pacific Rim countries of China, Japan, and Korea, family ties including grandparental bonds tend to be especially close. In China, many grandparents still live in three-generation households, and family ties are perceived as very close (Shu, 1999). A survey of Chinese children by Falbo (1991) found that grandparental preschool care was associated with somewhat better school performance than was parental care; there are possible confounds in this finding (such as socioeconomic status), but frequency of grandparental contact, plus grandparental educational attainment, did predict language and mathematics scores in first- and fifth-grade children. Similarly, Korean grandmothers from a sample of 1,326 extended families were accredited with increasing their grandchildren's resiliency by providing sources of attachment, affection, and knowledge, as well as having indirect effects through their support of parents (Hwang and St. James-Roberts, 1998).

In many non-Western societies, grandparents have a respected role as elders in the community. Sangree (1992) investigated Kenyan and Nigerian families in the districts of Tiriki and Irigwe. Every-where, grandparenthood was a prerequisite for elderhood; but the grandparent status as the valued elder varies among townships. Grandparents in Tiriki were more involved in their grand-children's lives and felt more appreciated by their adult children than in Irigwe, where the status of grandparents had decreased from the mid-1960s to 1980. Sangree suggested that changes within these societies' age norms or roles of parent and grandparent were responsible for the resulting difference.

African American grandparents. Several studies have documented the particular impor-tance of grandparents, especially the maternal grandmother, in many African American families (McAdoo, in Vol. 4 of this *Handbook*). Approximately one-half of African American children live in single-parent female-headed households, approximately three times the figure for European Amer-ican families; also, the generation gap tends to be shorter (Burton and Dilworth-Anderson, 1991; Tolson and Wilson, 1990). There is thus more opportunity in African American families for younger grandparents to be involved with and to support their grandchildren.

Historically, African American grandmothers were important figures of support and continuity (Hill-Lubin, 1991) and often acted as supplementary or surrogate parents (Burton and Dilworth-Anderson, 1991). Pearson, Hunter, Ensminger, and Kellam (1990) studied a predominantly African American community in Chicago and found that 10% of households with target 6- to 8-year-old children had coresident grandmothers. The grandmothers had substantial childrearing roles in these families, in control, support, and punishment. They were approximately half as active as the mothers in these areas and considerably more active than fathers (if present) and grandfathers. Timberlake and Chipungu (1992) found that active help with grandchildren was associated with more positive evaluation of the grandparental role in a sample of 100 African American grandmothers. Stevens (1984) found that African American grandmothers were supportive of teenage daughters with young grandchildren (13–30 months of age); they passed on useful information about norms of development and modeled a more responsive and less punitive interaction style with the infants.

Acculturation and the grandparent role.   Acculturation refers to changes in the cultural behavior and thinking of an individual or group through contact with another culture. Typically through the influence of the peer group (Harris, 1998), children of immigrant parents and grandparents adopt the language, styles, and customs of a new, larger culture they are in. These processes can lead to intergenerational difficulties and disagreements, with changes in perceptions of the parent or the grandparent role families (Garcia Coll and Pachter, in Vol. 4 of this *Handbook*).

In a sample of 54 Muslim mothers in extended families in Britain, acculturation was found to contribute to discrepancies in childrearing practices with grandmothers, often resulting in the mothers having unusually high levels of depression and anxiety (Sonuga-Barke, Mistry, and Qureshi, 1998). The more acculturated the intergenerational family, the greater the amount of discrepancy found in childrearing practices; grandmothers were more authority orientated and mothers more child centred.

In the United States, Pettys and Balgopal (1998) found that Indo-American grandparents were more accepting of their grandchildren's moving away from the culture, than they were of their adult children's. They believed it was necessary for their grandchildren to change in order to get ahead in the American culture, which they perceived as positive, whereas they expected their adult children to stay close to their ethnic origins. Silverstein and Chen (1999) found that the extent of acculturation of 375 adult Mexican American grandchildren affected the amount of contact they reported with their grandparents; however, grandparents did not feel a sense of loss of closeness. Grandparents may have been minimizing the cultural gap to lessen their feelings of aloneness resulting from their immigration to a foreign country.

Issues of acculturation also affect grandchildren of mixed cultural background. Anderson (1999) interviewed several families in Athens, Greece, with a Greek father and a British mother. He found that the differing views of grandparents and parents were difficult to accommodate for grandchildren from two cultural backgrounds when they were developing their own cultural identity, for example of Greekness and Britishness.

DIRECT AND INDIRECT INFLUENCES OF GRANDPARENTS ON GRANDCHILDREN

What influence do grandparents have on the development of grandchildren? Tinsley and Parke (1984) distinguished between *direct influences*, resulting from contact and face-to-face interaction, and *indirect influences*, mediated by other means such as parental behavior.

One source of indirect influence of grandparents is through financial support. For example, Dickemann (1979) argued that, in traditional societies, dowry can be seen as maternal grandparents' investing resources to place a daughter in an advantageous position on the marriage market, thus enhancing the reproductive success of their grandchildren. Rather more studies have focused on how grandparents, by acting as parents themselves, will have influenced the way in which their children act as parents to the grandparents' grandchildren; essentially, intergenerational transmission of parenting, a topic we review in detail.

Examples of direct influence are giving gifts, being a companion and confidant, acting as an emotional support or "buffer" at times of family stress, passing on family history or national traditions, and acting as a role model for aging. The most direct form of grandparent–grandchild influence is through acting as a surrogate parent. Jendrek (1994) distinguished three levels of this: temporary childcare or daycare, in which the grandchild goes to the grandparent's house; coresident grandparenting, in which grandparents live in a three-generation household with the grandchild; and the grandparent-maintained household or "skipped-generation" family, in which the grandchild is cared for directly by the grandparent(s). We review these three areas after the subsection on intergenerational transmission.

Indirect Influence: Intergenerational Transmission

A vigorous research area is looking at the transmission of attitudes and behaviors across generations—the intergenerational transmission of parenting. Some of this work has been within the domain of attachment theory; other work has used more general assessments of parenting styles.

The attachment theory perspective utilizes the concept of internal working models of relationships. Main, Kaplan, and Cassidy (1985) described internal working models as being internalized representations acquired in infancy and childhood, which reflect aspects such as trust or ambivalence learned in primary relationships. These are assessed in infancy in the Strange Situation (SS), yielding classifications of secure, avoidant, ambivalent, and disorganized attachment with mother or caregiver. In adult life the Adult Attachment Interview (AAI) provides a means of assessing an adult's model of their relationships with their parents; it yields four categories: autonomous (recalling earlier attachment-related experiences objectively and openly, even if these were not favorable); dismissive (earlier attachment-related experiences seen as of little concern, value or influence); preoccupied (still dependent on parents and actively struggling to please them); and unresolved (a trauma involving, or early death of, an attachment figure, which has not been worked through).

There is a quite strong predictive link between the child's SS category with (usually) mother and the mother's AAI classification reflecting her model of the relationship with her own parents (her child's grandparents). In a meta-analysis, van IJzendoorn (1995) examined 18 AAI studies totaling 854 parent–child dyads and found 75% concordance between secure/insecure on the SS and autonomous/nonautonomous on the AAI. Part of this intergenerational transmission appears to be due to maternal sensitivity to infant signals. Benoit and Parker (1994) demonstrated these links across three generations; mothers' AAI scores during pregnancy and when infants were 11 months old were compared with infant's SS classification at 12 months of age, and the maternal grandmother's AAI status measured at any time during the study. They found that 65% of grandmother–mother–infant triads had concordant attachment classifications.

Attachment theory emphasizes consistency over generations, but it also predicts that adults can work through or resolve unsatisfactory relations with their parents and modify their internal working models, either through self-reflection or with the aid of therapy or counseling. An ongoing study of survivors of the Holocaust in World War II (Bar-On et al., 1998) finds that, although many survivors (now grandparents) score unresolved on the AAI, because of the traumatic way in which they lost their parents at an early age, few of their children score unresolved, and their grandchildren appear to be indistinguishable from the remaining population in terms of attachment characteristics.

Other studies have been less tied to attachment theory, but have looked at transmission of more general qualities such as warmth, autonomy, depression, and aggression. Wakschlag, Chase-Lansdale, and Brooks-Gunn (1996) found modest relations between mother–grandmother and mother–child interactions; in particular, mothers who were autonomous with grandmothers were more flexible, warm, and supportive with their children. Warner, Weissman, Mufson, and Wickramaratne (1999) found that when both the parent and the grandparent were depressed the grandchild was at a high risk for anxiety, and 49% of these grandchildren had some form of psychopathology.

Ruoppila (1991) found significant correlations between grandparental and parental childrearing attitudes and practices in his Finnish sample. These were most marked for grandmothers and their daughters, but there also appeared to be important influences from grandfathers to their sons, in terms of attitudes to childcare. Rossi and Rossi (1990) linked indices of marital relationship, cohesion, and attitudes across generations. They found (p. 358) that "the quality of G1 parents' marriage was echoed in the marital happiness of G2 adult children" and "a significant tendency for parents to transmit the same skills their own parents had taught them to their own children." Family cohesion tended to be stable across generations and especially for women; attitudes, too, showed more influence from mothers than from fathers.

Vermulst, de Brock, and van Zutphen (1991) utilized Belsky's (1984) model of parental functioning across the generations in a sample of Dutch grandmother–mother dyads. They noted overall differences between generations, with mothers scoring higher than grandmothers on educational level, affection, and perceived support, but lower on conformity and restriction. However, they were more interested in the variations within each generation and how they connected. They found strong grandmother–mother links for educational level, and also for affection, and conformity; and also from grandmother affection to mother's psychological well-being. Approximately one third of the variation found in mother's parental functioning could be explained in terms of earlier parental functioning of the grandmother.

Research on children's antisocial behavior has also pointed to intergenerational influences. The use of physically aggressive and punitive techniques in the grandparent–parent generation predicts similar behavior in the parent–grandchild generation and to antisocial behavior in the grandchildren (Farrington, 1993; Lefkowitz, Eron, Walder, and Huesmann, 1977; Murphy-Cowan and Stringer, 1999). Caspi and Elder (1988) found a reinforcing dynamic between problem behavior and unstable ties in the family across four generations of women in their Berkeley Guidance Study. Stein, Newcomb, and Bentler (1993) documented relations between both grandparent and maternal drug abuse and behavioral or developmental problems in (grand)children aged 2 to 8 years, especially for boys.

Kornhaber (1996) suggested "clinical grandparenting" as a new field investigating the pathology of grandparenting, its etiology and treatment. His findings are based on a 3-year longitudinal study in which 300 grandparents and grandchildren (as well as some parents) were interviewed. The primary interest was in the roles and styles of grandparenting, but this led to an examination of functional and dysfunctional styles of grandparenting. He suggested categories of grandparent identity disorder (intentional lack of involvement with grandchildren), grandparent activity disorder (conflicts and alienation), and grandparent communication disorder (inability to communicate openly about actions or feelings); these categories of dysfunctional grandparenting were contrasted with functional grandparenting, characterized by altruism and open and effective communication with children and grandchildren. Kornhaber does not use an attachment theory perspective, but insecure attachment can be predicted to relate to difficulties in relationships and to the kinds of clinical grandparenting difficulties described; Drew, Richard, and Smith (1998) hypothesized that insecure–avoidant relationships would predict to grandparent identity disorder and grandparent communication disorder, whereas insecure–ambivalent attachment would predict to grandparent activity disorder.

Direct Influence: Surrogate Parenting

Childcare and grandparents. Daycare or regular childcare from grandparents can provide regular help for the middle generation. The decision to care has often been found to be initiated by the grandparent and related to the "impulse to care"; most are not paid for the daycare provided, and the majority are maternal grandparents who care for their daughter's children and not their son's (Jendrek, 1994). Grandchild care can later lead to very close grandparent–grandchild relationships, as reported by Hodgson (1992, p. 219): "My grandmother took me in for five years. You can get pretty close in five years of living together." Observational studies have shown that grandparents can act as a source of secure attachment for young children.

Cotterill (1992, p. 614) noted that some grandmothers, especially paternal grandmothers, may be reluctant to provide long-term support of childcare for working mothers: "One thing I've always said, even with my own daughter, I would never look after grandchildren on the same basis during the day whilst they go to work. I don't agree with that. I've brought up my own children and I don't want to be tied down every day looking after grandchildren."

Parent-maintained households with coresident grandparents. Although more the norm in some traditional societies, the prevalence of three-generation households can be substantial in Western societies. The 1997 U.S. Census Bureau reported an increase of children living with one parent (father or mother) and either one or two of their grandparents, in comparison with previous census reports, in which coresident grandmothers (70%) were more prevalent than coresident grandfathers (17%) or both grandparents (13%) (Bryson and Casper, 1998). A large proportion (45%) of these grandchildren (aged from 6 to 17 years) were in foreign-born or immigrant families in which the parent is supporting both the older and the younger generations.

High rates of coresident grandparents in three-generational households are found in African American families (Apfel and Seitz, 1991; Burton and DeVries, 1993; Martin and Martin, 1978). Pearson et al. (1990) studied a predominantly African American community in Chicago and found that 10% of households with 6- to 8-year-old children had coresident grandmothers. The grand-mothers had substantial childrearing roles in these families, in control, support, and punishment. Tolson and Wilson (1990) compared African American families with one or two parents and with or without a coresident grandmother; their results (limited by small sample size) mainly suggest the influence of number of caregivers rather than who the extra caregiver is (usually, father or grandmother).

Radin, Oyserman, and Benn (1991) and Oyserman, Radin, and Benn (1993) examined 64 families in which teen mothers of children under the age 2 years were assisted by grandparents. They found that the grandmother had little effect on the child's development, but that involved grandfathers did have a positive influence, probably by modeling a male role of nurturance and cooperation. These were father-absent families, so perhaps the grandparents had a well-marked role to play. The relationship of grandmothers with adolescent mothers or mothers-to-be can be emotionally charged and rivalrous or conflictual as well as supportive (Musick, 1994).

Grandparent-maintained households.   The 1997 U.S. Census Bureau indicated a dramatic increase of 1.3 million grandparents rearing grandchildren between 1980 and 1992. The primary reasons have been identified as an increase in drug use, teenage pregnancy, divorce, mental and physical illness, AIDS, child abuse, and parental incarceration. A secondary reason is the landmark Supreme Court case of *Youakim v. Miller* (1979), which upheld a lower court's decision that federal foster care benefits could not be withheld from relatives who were eligible. Following this decision, states began placing children with relatives in support of the policy of "kinship care" (George, Wulczyn, and Harden, 1995). In 1997, a plateau seemed to have been reached, with nearly 4 million children living with their grandparents or with other relatives (Bryson and Casper, 1998).

Grandparent-headed households are more common in African American (9.2%) than in European American (2.3%) families (Bryson and Casper, 1998). The 1990 U.S. Census Bureau reported that 5.8% of Latino or Hispanic children lived with their grandparents. Women, recently bereaved parents, and African American families have double the odds of becoming caregiving grandparents (Fuller-Thomson, Minkler, and Driver, 1997). Typically the grandchildren are under 6 years of age, the grandparents are young, and the families poor and without health care, with those headed by grandmothers being the most poverty stricken (Bryson and Casper, 1998). Grandchildren reared in grandparent-headed households have poorer academic performance than do similar children in parent-headed households (Solomon and Marx, 1995).

Hayslip, Shore, Henderson, and Lambert (1998) reported that custodial grandfathers had higher levels of satisfaction in rearing their grandchild than did custodial grandmothers. Several researchers have found grandparents in grandparent-headed households to have a higher incidence of depres-sion, anxiety, and risk for physical and emotional health problems than noncaregivers (Burnette, 1999; Emick and Hayslip, 1999; Minkler, Fuller-Thomson, Miller, and Driver, 1997; Roe, Minkler, Saunders, and Thomson, 1996; Strawbridge, Wallhagen, Shema, and Kaplan, 1997; Szinovacz, DeViney, and Atkinson, 1999). However, data from the 1997 U.S. Census Bureau suggest that 36% of these grandparents have excellent or very good health and work outside the home. Sands and Goldberg-Glen (1998) found in a sample of 123 grandparent caregivers that 65% were experiencing good to excellent health; for those who were experiencing physical and emotional health problems a relationship was found with being European American and unemployed.

In a telephone questionnaire survey, Pruchno (1999) found similarities and differences in a comparison of 398 European American and 319 African American grandmothers rearing their grandchildren. The similarities included grandparent age, education, relationship to the child, age of the grandchild, reasons for rearing the grandchild, behavior characteristics of the grandchild, and impacts on the grandmother's employment. Both African American and European American grandmothers had high levels of satisfaction with themselves as a function of their grandparent role. However, more European American grandmothers reported feeling trapped in their role, not having enough time for themselves, lack of privacy, and unwanted change in the their home environment. African American grandmothers were more likely to have friends or other family members rearing grandchildren, which may account for their feeling less tired or isolated.

In a questionnaire study with 74 custodial Latino grandparents from New York, Burnette (1999a,b) found that poverty in these grandparent-headed families was three times the national average of other custodial grandparents and that they were experiencing double the amount of physical and emotional health problems. Grandparent-headed families within the Latino or the Hispanic culture bring to the surface specific issues of acculturation, language barriers, and legal aspects of immigration laws. Further exploration of this particular population as well as of other cultural groups that may have specific needs is necessary.

Custodial grandparents are conducting a service to their communities as well as their families and need support at a national and community level to continue effectively. In the United States the American Association of Retired Persons provides support, advice, and education to grandparent caregivers. The Brookdale Grandparent Caregiver Information Project in the United States has been tracking some of the smaller community organizations that provide support to custodial grandparents (Minkler, Driver, Roe, and Bedeian, 1993); these services help grandparents feel less isolated and help them cope with the demands and challenges of their new role, but suffer from lack of financial support and proper evaluation.

Sexual abuse by grandparents.   As with some parents, close contact with grandchildren through supplementary or surrogate parenting also gives grandparents opportunities for abuse. Although rare, some 10% of all reported cases of intrafamilial childhood sexual abuse involve grandfathers and granddaughters (Goodwin, Cormier, and Owen, 1983). Margolin (1992) also reported this to be the most common form of grandparent–grandchild sexual abuse, and both reports concur that such abuse is neither gentle nor benign. Margolin found the risk of abuse to be significantly higher for step-grandchildren (as predicted by evolutionary theory).

TWO PRACTICAL ASPECTS OF GRANDPARENTING

The increased recognition of the practical importance of grandparenthood is shown by two developments in modern industrial societies. One is the advent of courses for effective grandparenting and of foster grandparent programs. The other is the growing pressure for grandparents to have visitation rights in cases of family separation and divorce.

Grandparents in Society

In the United States there are now courses for grandparents. Strom and Strom (1989) offer "an educational program for grandparents to help strengthen families" including components on: sharing feelings and ideas with peers, listening to the views of younger people, learning about lifespan development, improving family communication skills, and focusing self-evaluation. Educational programs have been used to evaluate the needs of Mexican American grandparents in America (Strom, Buki, and Strom, 1997), Japanese grandparents (Strom et al., 1995), and Taiwanese grandparents

(Strom, Strom, Shen, Li, and Sun, 1996). Interventions following these programs were self-evaluated and found to be effective within these communities.

Kennedy and Keeney (1988) described the running of a psychotherapy group for grandparents who were the primary caregivers for children receiving mental health treatment. There are intergenerational programs, such as the Three Generation Project (Hansen and Jacob, 1992), which aim to help both new parents and grandparents cope with shifts in family relationships that the transition to (grand)parenthood brings. Ingersoll-Dayton and Neal (1991) described an evaluation of bringing grandparents into family therapy sessions.

There are also foster grandparent programs. Werner (1991, p. 78) described how these give "elders with low income the opportunity to provide companionship and caring for a variety of high-risk children and youths in return for a tax-exempt stipend." These take place in hospitals, residential institutions, daycare programs, and family shelters. The evaluation of these programs appears to be positive.

Obtaining Contact: The Courts or Mediation?

An important issue for grandparents is what access and visitation rights they have with grandchildren of noncustodial parent families. Mediation has been found to be effective in some cases; however, sometimes legal contact orders are the only way of preserving the child's continued contact with their grandparent. Grandparent visitation rights first appeared in the courts in the United States over 100 years ago; in 1894 the appellate court ruled that grandparent visitation was a moral, not a legal, obligation, and parents could not be forced legally to allow grandparent visitations (Wacker, 1995). Thompson, Tinsley, Scalora, and Parke (1989) reviewed the then-legal situation in the United States; statutes granting grandparents legal standing to petition for legally enforceable visitation with their grandchildren, even over parental objections, had been passed in all 50 states. However, in many states these laws have since been rescinded because of parents challenging the laws on the basis that the statute is an infringement of their fundamental constitutional right to raise their children as they see fit (Kornhaber, 1996). Contact orders were transferable from state to state as of December, 1998, when the Visitation Rights Enforcement Act became law (Kornhaber, 1999). In a recent landmark decision (June, 2000), the U.S. Supreme Court struck down the law in Washington State that gave grandparents rights to contact with their grandchildren. The decision leans toward the rights of parents versus the rights of children. This decision is likely to have ramifications for other states and possibly other countries such as Great Britain and Australia, who have similar laws.

In Great Britain, the 1989 Children Act, which highlights the interests of children, also allows any person (not just grandparents or relatives) to request a leave to seek an order for contact with a child (Douglas and Lowe, 1990; Crook, 1994). When deciding whether to grant a leave, the court will consider the applicant's connection with the child. However, even if the grandparent has obtained a contact order there is little that holds the parent to abide by the court ruling. Parents who do not do so can be held in contempt of court and serve 28 days in prison. However, few grandparents would wish to take such action and risk their grandchildren being placed in care; additionally, this sort of action by the grandparent would only increase the anger of the parents, leaving the grandparent with less long-term opportunity of seeing their grandchildren. All of these court proceedings are very expensive and often beyond the means of grandparents who have retired and are on fixed incomes.

There are considerable problems in using legal measures, which are probably best seen as a last-resort option that, even when granted, may not always be properly enforceable (Drew, 2000; Drew and Smith, 1999; Kruk, 1994). Any negativity that exists between the family members is likely to become only more enhanced in the courtroom (Kornhaber, 1996). Grandparents often stress the importance of attempting nonlegal forms of resolution first, such as mediation, while opting for legal action as a final resort (Drew, 2000; Drew and Smith, 1999).

FUTURE DIRECTIONS FOR THEORY AND RESEARCH
IN GRANDPARENTING

Despite a productive two decades of research, there are limitations to research on grandparenting to date. These include a somewhat limited use of methods of obtaining data, a narrow cultural range, and a lack of strong theoretical guidance.

Methods of Obtaining Data

A wider range of methodologies might be usefully utilized. Most studies of grandparenthood have used interviews or else structured or semistructured questionnaires. These are straightforward ways of getting someone's perceptions of a role or relationship, but may not always be reliable indices of behavior. A few studies of grandparental relationships have used direct observation of behavior in standard situations (Myers, Jarvis, and Creasey, 1987; Tomlin and Passman, 1989). Radin et al. (1991) and Tinsley and Parke (1987) recorded grandparent behavior with infants in the home, finding them often to be involved in play and nurturing activities, although perhaps less competently than with their parents. More naturalistic home observations of grandparent–grandchild interaction might well be worthwhile in checking results based on attitude and perception against behavioral reality.

Other kinds of methodologies could be used more to elicit more complex, emotional, or unconscious feelings toward grandparents. These could be more projective or open-ended methods, for example, writing essays about grandparents (Ponzetti and Folkrod, 1989; Tyszkowa, 1991) or analyzing drawings that grandchildren draw of grandfathers and grandmothers (Marcoen, 1979). Case studies (Cohler and Grunebaum, 1981) and more qualitative approaches (Cunningham-Burley, 1984, 1985; Musick, 1994; Tunaley, 2000) can add important insights and complement more quantitative results.

Wider Cultural Comparisons

With some exceptions (e.g., Smith, 1991), most research on grandparenthood has been carried out in the United States. This has included descriptions of subcultural variations, not only African American families but other ethnic groups (e.g., McCready, 1985; Schmidt and Padilla, 1983; Werner, 1991). A greater number of comparable studies of grandparenthood in different cultures, including Eastern as well as Western, nonindustrial as well as urban, will give a greater picture of variety (Sangree, 1992). This, in turn, will provide a better testing ground for integrated biocultural theories, which could attempt to account for both the differences between cultures and the commonalties across cultures.

The Need for Theory

A major requirement is for greater theoretical underpinning to research in grandparenthood. Mancini and Blieszner (1989, p. 283) wrote of intergenerational relationships that "relatively little research appears to be guided a priori by theories or conceptual frameworks. Most of the work is concerned with addressing a defined problem. Although research driven by problem solving is not without merit, when it is devoid of a theoretical context the understanding of the larger picture is stunted." This is rather true of research on grandparenthood, in which many articles simply describe the amounts and kind of contact between grandparents and grandchildren, the influence of such factors as type of grandparent, age of grandchild, proximity, and so forth. It is important to get this descriptive information, but now there is sufficient data to look for a wider theoretical framework in which to interpret them.

There are several relevant theoretical traditions. The use of family systems theory in the area of grandchildren with disabilities provides one promising area of focus. Other areas are attachment theory in understanding intergenerational transmission and conflict, and evolutionary theory in understanding kinship asymmetries. Rather than seeing these perspectives as opposed, it will be help-ful to work toward some expansion and integration. Hagestad (1987) saw a need to move beyond the dyad and to reconcile the developmental studies of infancy and childhood with the sociological and gerontological studies of older persons. To this, we would add the need to integrate evolutionary theories with developmental and sociocultural ones (Rossi and Rossi, 1990). Research on grandpar-enthood has spanned a number of different disciplines; this has been part of its interest, but it also presents us with a challenge for future integration.

CONCLUSIONS

Grandparenthood is a fascinating area of research that has been relatively neglected until the past two decades. Yet demographic tendencies in modern industrialized societies mean that it is an important part of the lifespan for most people. In understanding grandparenthood, theoretical perspectives can be brought to bear from evolutionary theory, psychoanalysis and attachment theory, family systems theory, family sociology, lifespan development, and gerontology.

Being a grandparent does not usually have as much significance as being a parent; but relationships with grandchildren are usually seen as being positive and satisfying. Typically, grandparents may see grandchildren once or a few times a month. Grandparents engage in a variety of activities with grandchildren, including acting as family historian, as a confidant, and as a support in times of family discord. Living close to grandchildren, being a grandmother (especially maternal grandmother), being relatively younger and healthy, all predict greater contact. In addition there are individual and cultural differences in style and role perceptions: Among African Americans, for example, the maternal grandmother tends to have a particularly influential role.

Grandparents can be on time or off time, depending on when they first become a grandparent; generally, on-time grandparents experience the most satisfaction in the role. Great-grandparents and step-grandparents tend to have less contact and lower satisfaction.

Grandparents can influence their grandchildren's development in many ways. Some are direct, by contact. Some grandparents become particularly close to young grandchildren by acting as a surrogate parent or running a grandparent-maintained household. Some are indirect, by support of parents and intergenerational transmission of parenting skills. Generally, the influence of grandparents can be very positive. On occasions it can be less so, if grandparents conflict with parents on childrearing values or even abuse grandchildren.

Some issues connected to grandparenthood have direct societal implications. For example, there are courses for grandparents and foster grandparent programs. In the United States grandparents are at risk of losing their rights of access to grandchildren separated from them by their children's divorce.

Research on grandparenthood is growing in strength and relevance; future directions may usefully see a broadening in methodology, studies in a greater variety of different cultures, and a more thorough application of theory to data collection and interpretation.

REFERENCES

Age Concern (1998). *Across the generations.* London: Author.

Aldous, J. (1985). Parent–adult child relations as affected by the grandparent status. In V. L. Bengtson and J. F. Robertson (Eds.), *Grandparenthood* (pp. 117–132). Beverley Hills, CA: Sage.

Altmann, J. (1987). Life span aspect of reproduction and parental care in anthropoid primates. In J. B. Lancaster, J. Altmann, A. S. Rossi, and L. R. Sherrod (Eds.), *Parenting across the life span: Biosocial dimensions* (pp. 15–29). New York: Aldine de Gruyter.

Anderson, M. (1999). Children in-between: Constructing identities in the bicultural family. *Royal Anthropological Institute, 5,* 13–26.

Apfel, N. H., and Seitz, V. (1991). Four models of adolescent mother–grandmother relationships in Black inner-city families. *Family Relations, 40*, 421–429.

Apple, D. (1956). The social structure of grandparenthood. *American Anthropologist, 58*, 56–63.

Archer, J. (1999). *The nature of grief.* London: Routledge.

Baltes, P. B., Reese, H. W., and Lipsitt, L. P. (1980). Life-span developmental psychology. *Annual Review of Psychology, 31*, 65–110.

Bar-On, D., Eland, J., Kleber, R. J., Krell, R., Moore, Y., Sagi, A., Soriano, E., Suedfeld, P., van der Velden, P. G., and van IJzendoorn, M. H. (1998). Multigenerational perspectives on coping with the holocaust experience: An attachment perspective for understanding the developmental sequelae of trauma across generations. *International Journal of Behavioural Development, 22*, 315–338.

Barranti, C. C. R. (1985). The grandparent/grandchild relationship: Family resource in an era of voluntary bonds. *Family Relations, 34*, 343–352.

Battistelli, P., and Farneti, A. (1991). Grandchildren's images of their grandparents: A psychodynamic perspective. In P. K. Smith (Ed.), *The psychology of grandparenthood: An international perspective* (pp. 143–156). London: Routledge.

Belsky, J. (1984). The determinants of parenting: A process model. *Child Development, 55*, 83–96.

Bengtson, V. L. (1987). Parenting, grandparenting, and intergenerational continuity. In J. B. Lancaster, J. Altmann, A. S. Rossi, and L. R. Sherrod (Eds.), *Parenting across the life span: Biosocial dimensions* (pp. 435–456). New York: Aldine de Gruyter.

Bengtson, V. L., and Robertson, J. F. (Eds.). (1985). *Grandparenthood.* Beverley Hills, CA: Sage.

Benoit, D., and Parker, K. (1994). Stability and transmission of attachment across three generations. *Child Development, 65*, 1444–1456.

Boon, S. D., and Brussoni, M. J. (1996). Young adults' relationships with their "closest" grandparents: Examining emotional closeness. *Journal of Social Behavior and Personality, 11*, 439–458.

Bryson, K., and Casper, L. M. (1998). *Coresident grandparents and grandchildren.* In *Current population reports: Special studies for the U.S. Census Bureau.* Washington, DC: U.S. Census Bureau.

Burnette, D. (1999a). Custodial grandparents in Latino families: Patterns of service use and predictors of unmet needs. *Social Work, 44*, 22–34.

Burnette, D. (1999b). Physical and emotional well-being of custodial grandparents in Latino families. *American Journal of Orthopsychiatry, 69*, 305–318.

Burnette, D. (1999). Social relationships of Latino grandparent caregivers: A role theory perspective. *The Gerontologist, 39*, 49–58.

Burton, L. M., and Bengtson, V. L. (1985). Black grandmothers: Issues of timing and continuity of roles. In V. L. Bengtson and J. F. Robertson (Eds.), *Grandparenthood* (pp. 61–77). Beverley Hills, CA: Sage.

Burton, L. M., and DeVries, C. (1993). Challenges and rewards: African American grandparents as surrogate parents. In L. M. Burton (Ed.), *Families and aging.* Amityville, NY: Baywood.

Burton, L. M., and Dilworth-Anderson, P. (1991). The intergenerational family roles of aged Black Americans. In S. K. Pfelfer and M. B. Sussman (Eds.), *Families: Intergenerational and generational connections* (pp. 311–330). Binghampton, NY: Haworth.

Byrne, E. A., Cunningham, C. C., and Sloper, P. (1988). *Families and their children with Down's syndrome.* London: Routledge.

Caspi, A., and Elder, G. H. (1988). Emergent family patterns: The intergenerational construction of problem behaviour and relationships. In R. A. Hinde and J. Stevenson-Hinde (Eds.), *Relationships within families: Mutual influences* (pp. 218–260). Oxford, England: Oxford University Press.

Cherlin, A., and Furstenberg, F. F. (1985). Styles and strategies of grandparenting. In V. L. Bengtson and J. F. Robertson (Eds.), *Grandparenthood* (pp. 97–116). Beverley Hills, CA: Sage.

Cherlin, A., and Furstenberg, F. F. (1986). *The new American grandparent.* New York: Basic Books.

Clayton, V., and Birren, J. E. (1980). Age and wisdom across the life span: Theoretical perspectives. In P. B. Baltes and O. G. Brim, Jr. (Eds.), *Life-span development and behavior* (Vol. 3, pp. 103–135). New York: Academic.

Clingempeel, W. G., Colyar, J. J., Brand, E., and Hetherington, E. M. (1992). Children's relationships with maternal grandparents: A longitudinal study of family structure and pubertal status effects. *Child Development, 63*, 1404–1422.

Cohler, B. J., and Grunebaum, H. U. (1981). *Mothers, grandmothers, and daughters: Personality and childcare in three-generation families.* New York: Wiley.

Cotterill, P. (1992). 'But for freedom, you see, not to be a babyminder': Women's attitudes towards grandmother care. *Sociology, 26*, 603–618.

Creasey, G. L. (1993). The association between divorce and late adolescent grandchildren's relations with grandparents. *Journal of Youth and Adolescence, 22*, 515–529.

Creasey, G. L., and Kaliher, G. (1994). Age-differences in grandchildrens perceptions of relations with grandparents. *Journal of Adolescence, 17*, 411–426.

Creasey, G. L., and Koblewski, P. J. (1991). Adolescent grandchildren's relationships with maternal and paternal grandmothers and grandfathers. *Journal of Adolescence, 14*, 373–387.

Creasey, G. L., Myers, B. J., Epperson, M. J., and Taylor, J. (1989). Grandchildren of grandparents with Alzheimer's disease: Perceptions of grandparent, family environment, and the elderly. *Merrill-Palmer Quarterly, 35*, 227–237.

Crook, H. (1994). Grandparents and the Children Act 1989. *Family Law, 24*, 135–138.

Cunningham-Burley, S. (1984). 'We don't talk about it . . .': Issues of gender and method in the portrayal of grandfatherhood. *Sociology, 18*, 325–338.

Cunningham-Burley, S. (1985). Constructing grandparenthood: Anticipating appropriate action. *Sociology, 19*, 421–436.

Defrain, J., Ernest, L., Jakub, D., and Taylor, J. (1992). *Sudden infant death: Enduring the loss.* Lexington, MA: Lexington Books.

Defrain, J. D., Jakub, D. K., and Mendoza, B. L. (1991–1992). The psychological effects of sudden infant death on grandmothers and grandfathers. *Omega, 24*, 165–182.

Derdeyn, A. P. (1985). Grandparent visitation rights: Rendering family dissention more pronounced? *American Journal of Orthopsychiatry, 55*, 277–287.

Dickemann, M. (1979). The ecology of mating systems in hypergynous dowry societies. *Social Science Information, 18*, 163–195.

Dillworth, P. (1994). The importance of grandparents in extended kin caregiving to black children with sickle cell disease. *Journal of Health and Social Policy, 5*, 185–202.

Doka, K. J., and Mertz, M. E. (1988). The meaning and significance of great-grandparenthood. *The Gerontologist, 28*, 192–197.

Douglas, G., and Lowe, N. (1990). Grandparents and the legal process. *Journal of Social Welfare Law, 2*, 89–106.

Drew, L. M. (2000). *What are the implications for grandparents when they lose contact with their grandchildren?* Ph.D. thesis, Goldsmiths College, University of London.

Drew, L. M., Richard, M., and Smith, P. K. (1998). Grandparenting and its relation to parenting. *Clinical Child Psychology and Psychiatry, 3*, 465–480.

Drew, L. M., and Smith, P. K. (1999). The impact of parental separation/divorce on grandparent–grandchild relationships. *International Journal of Aging and Human Development, 48*, 191–215.

Eisenberg, A. R. (1988). Grandchildrens' perspectives on relationships with grandparents: The influence of gender across generations. *Sex Roles, 19*, 205–217.

Emick, M. A., and Hayslip, B. (1999). Custodial randparenting: stresses, coping skills, and relationships with grandchildren. *International Journal of Aging and Human Development, 48*, 35–61.

Euler, H. A., and Weitzel, B. (1996). Discriminative grandparental solicitude as reproductive strategy. *Human Nature, 7*, 39–59.

Fagen, R. M. (1976). Three-generation family conflict. *Animal Behaviour, 24*, 874–879.

Falbo, T. (1991). The impact of grandparents on childen's outcomes in China. *Marriage and Family Review, 16*, 369–376.

Falchikov, N. (1990). Youthful ideas about old age: An analysis of children's drawings. *International Journal of Aging and Human Development, 31*, 79–99.

Farrington, D. P. (1993). Understanding and preventing bullying. In M. Tonry (Ed.), *Crime and Justice: An Annual Review of Research* (Vol. 17, pp. 381–458). Chicago: University of Chicago Press.

Fingerman, K. L. (1998). The good, the bad, and the worrisome: Emotional complexities in grandparents' experiences with individual grandchildren. *Family Relations, 47*, 403–414.

Fonagy, P. (1999). Psychoanalytic theory from the viewpoint of attachment theory and research. In J. Cassidy and P. R. Shaver (Eds.), *Handbook of Attachment* (pp. 595–624). New York: Guilford.

Fry, P. S. (1997). Grandparents' reactions to the death of a grandchild: An exploratory factor analytic study. *Omega, 35*, 119–140.

Fuller-Thomson, E., Minkler, M., and Driver, D. (1997). A profile of grandparents raising grandchildren in the United States. *The Gerontologist, 37*, 406–411.

George, J. D. (1988). Therapeutic interventions for grandparents and extended family of children with developmental delays. *Mental Retardation, 26*, 369–375.

George, R. M., Wulczyn, F. H., and Harden, A. (1995). *Foster care dynamics, 1988–1993: An update from the Multistate Foster Care Data Archive.* Chicago: University of Chicago, Chapin Hall Center for Children.

Giarrusso, R., Silverstein, M., and Bengtson, V. L. (1996). Family complexity and the grandparenting role. *Generations Quarterly Journal of the American Society on Aging, 20*, 17–23.

Gladstone, J. W. (1987). Factors associated with changes in visiting between grandmothers and grandfathers following an adults child's marriage breakdown. *Canadian Journal on Aging, 6*, 117–127.

Glasberg, B. A., and Harris, S. L. (1997). Grandparents and parents assess the development of their child with autism. *Child & Family Behavior Therapy, 19*, 17–27.

Goodwin, J., Cormier, L., and Owen, J. (1983). Grandfather–granddaughter incest: A trigenerational view. *Child Abuse & Neglect, 7*, 163–170.

Hagestad, G. O. (1985). Continuity and connectedness. In V. L. Bengtson and J. F. Robertson (Eds.), *Grandparenthood* (pp. 31–48). Beverly Hills, CA: Sage.

Hagestad, G. O. (1987). Parent–child relations in later life: Trends and gaps in past research. In J. B. Lancaster, J. Altmann, A. S. Rossi, and L. R. Sherrod (Eds.), *Parenting across the life span: Biosocial dimensions* (pp. 405–433). New York: Aldine de Gruyter.

Hansen, L. B., and Jacob, E. (1992, October). Intergenerational support during the teansition to parenthood: Issues for new parents and grandparents. *Families in Society: The Journal of Contemporary Human Services*, pp. 471–479.

Harris, J. R. (1998). *The nurture assumption.* New York: Touchstone.

Harris, S. L., Handleman, J. S., and Palmer, C. (1985). How parents and grandparents view the autistic child. *Journal of Autism and Developmental Disorders, 15*, 127–137.

Hawkes, K., O'Connell, J. F., and Blurton Jones, N. G. (1997). Hadza women's time allocations, offspring provisioning, and the evolution of long postmenopausal life spans. *Current Anthropology, 38*, 551–577.

Hayslip, B., Shore, R., Henderson, C. E., and Lambert, P. L. (1998). Custodial grandparenting and the impact of grandchildren with problems on role satisfaction and role meaning. *Journal of Gerontology: Social Sciences, 53B*, S154–S173.

Henry, C. S., Ceglian, C. P., and Matthews, D. W. (1992). The role behaviors, role manings, and grandmothering styles of grandmothers and stepgrandmothers: Perceptions of the middle generation. *Journal of Divorce and Remarriage, 17*, 1–22.

Henry, C. S., Ceglian, C. P., and Ostrander, D. L. (1993). The transition to stepgrandparenthood. *Journal of Divorce and Remarriage, 19*, 25–44.

Hetherington, E. M., and Stanley-Hagan, M. (1999). The adjustment of children with divorced parents: A risk and resiliency perspective. *Journal of Child Psychology and Psychiatry, 40*, 129–140.

Hill-Lubin, M. A. (1991). The African-American grandmother in autobiographical works by Frederick Douglass, Langston Hughes, and Maya Angelou. *International Journal of Aging and Human Development, 33*, 173–185.

Hilton, J. M., and Macari, D. P. (1997). Grandparent involvement following divorce: A comparison in single-mother and single-father families. *Journal of Divorce and Remarriage, 28*, 203–224.

Hodgson, L. G. (1992). Adult grandchildren and their grandparents: The enduring bond. *International Journal of Aging and Human Development, 34*, 209–225.

Hornby, G., and Ashforth, T. (1994). Grandparents' support for families who have children with disabilities: A survey for parents. *Journal of Child and Family Studies, 3*, 403–412.

Hurme, H. (1988). *Child, mother and grandmother: Intergenerational interaction in Finnish families.* Jyvaskyla, Finland: University of Jyvaskyla Press.

Hwang, H. J., and St. James-Roberts, I. (1998). Emotional and behavioural problems in primary school children from nuclear and extended families in Korea. *Journal of Child Psychology and Psychiatry, 39*, 973–979.

Ingersoll-Dayton, B., and Neal, M. B. (1991). Grandparents in family therapy: A clinical research study. *Famly Relations, 40*, 264–271.

Janelli, L. M. (1988). Depictions of grandparents in children's literature. *Educational Gerontology, 14*, 193–202.

Jendrek, M. P. (1994). Grandparents who parent their grandchildren: Circumstances and decisions. *The Gerontologist, 34*, 206–216.

Johnson, C. L. (1983). A cultural analysis of the grandmother. *Research on Aging, 5*, 547–567.

Johnson, C. L. (1988). Active and latent functions of grandparenting during the divorce process. *The Gerontologist, 28*, 185–191.

Johnson, C. L., and Barer, B. M. (1987). Marital instability and the changing kinship networks of grandparents. *The Gerontologist, 27*, 330–335.

Kahana, B., and Kahana, E. (1970). Grandparenthood from the perspective of the developing grandchild. *Developmental Psychology, 3*, 98–105.

Kazak, A. E., and Marvin, R. S. (1984). Differences, difficulties and adaptation: Stress and social networks in families with a handicapped child. *Family Relations, 33*, 67–77.

Kennedy, G. E. (1990). Quality in grandparent/grandchild relationships. *International Journal of Aging and Human Development, 35*, 83–98.

Kennedy, G. E. (1991). Grandchildren's reasons for closeness with grandparents. *Journal of Social Behavior and Personality, 6*, 697–712.

Kennedy, G. E. (1992). Shared activities of grandparents and grandchildren. *Psychological Reports, 70*, 211–227.

Kennedy, G. E., and Keeney, V. T. (1988). The extended family revisited: Grandparents rearing grandchildren. *Child Psychiatry and Human Development, 19*, 26–35.

Kennedy, G. E., and Kennedy, C. E. (1993). Grandparents—A special resource for children in stepfamilies. *Journal of Divorce and Remarriage, 19*, 45–68.

King, V., and Elder, G. E. (1998). Perceived self-efficacy and grandparenting. *Journal of Gerontology, 53B*, S249–S257.

Kivett, V. R. (1985). Grandfathers and grandchildren: Patterns of association, helping, and psychological closeness. *Family Relations, 34*, 565–571.

Kivett, V. R. (1991). The grandparent–grandchild connection. *Marriage and Family Review, 16*, 267–290.

Kivnick, H. Q. (1982). Grandparenthood: An overview of meaning and mental health. *The Gerontologist, 22*, 59–66.

Kornhaber, A. (1996). *Contemporary grandparenting*. Newbury Park, CA: Sage.

Kornhaber, A. (1999). Foundation for Grandparenting Web site [on-line]. Available: www.grandparenting.org/kornhaber/htm.

Kornhaber, A., and Woodward, K. (1981). *Grandparents/grandchildren: The vital connection*. Garden City, NY: Doubleday.

Kruk, E. (1994). Grandparent visitation disputes: Multigenerational approaches to family mediation. *Mediation Quarterly*, *12*, 37–53.

Kruk, E. (1995). Grandparent–grandchild contact loss: Findings from a study of "Grandparents Rights" members. *Canadian Journal on Aging*, *14*, 737–754.

Kruk, E., and Hall, B. L. (1995). The disengagement of paternal grandparents subsequent to divorce. *Journal of Divorce and Remarriage*, *23*, 131–147.

Landry, P. H., Jr., and Martin, M. E. (1988). Measuring intergenerational consensus. In D. J. Mangen, V. L. Bengtson, and P. H. Landry, Jr. (Eds.), *Measurement of intergenerational relations* (pp. 126–155). Newbury Park: Sage.

Lavers, C. A., and Sonuga-Barke, E. J. S. (1997). Annotation: On the grandmothers' role in the adjustment and maladjustment of grandchildren. *Journal of Child Psychology and Psychiatry*, *38*, 747–753.

Leek, M., and Smith, P. K. (1991). Cooperation and conflict in three-generation families. In P. K. Smith (Ed.), *The psychology of grandparenthood: An international perspective* (pp. 177–194). London: Routledge.

Lefkowitz, M. M., Eron, L. D., Walder, L. O., and Huesmann, L. R. (1977). *Growing up to be violent*. New York: Pergamon.

LeVine, R. A., and White, M. (1987). Parenthood in social transformation. In J. B. Lancaster, J. Altmann, A. S. Rossi, and L. R. Sherrod (Eds.), *Parenting across the life span: Biosocial dimensions* (pp. 271–293). New York: Aldine de Gruyter.

Mace, R. (2000). Evolutionary ecology of human life history. *Animal Behaviour*, *59*, 1–10.

Main, M., Kaplan, N., and Cassidy, J. (1985). Security in infancy, childhood, and adulthood: A move to the level of representation. In I. Bretherton and E. Waters (Eds.), *Growing points of attachment and research* (pp. 66–104). Chicago: University of Chicago Press.

Mancini, J. A., and Blieszner, R. (1989). Aging parents and adult children: Research themes in intergenerational relations. *Journal of Marriage and the Family*, *51*, 275–290.

Mangen, D. J., Bengtson, V. L., and Landry, P. H., Jr. (Eds.). (1988). *Measurement of intergenerational relations*. Newbury Park: Sage.

Mangen, D. J., and McChesney, K. Y. (1988). Intergenerational cohesion: A comparison of linear and nonlinear analytical approaches. In D. J. Mangen, V. L. Bengtson, and P. H. Landry, Jr. (Eds.), *Measurement of intergenerational relations* (pp. 208–221). Newbury Park, CA: Sage.

Mangen, D. J., and Miller, R. B. (1988). Measuring intergenerational contact in the family. In D. J. Mangen, V. L. Bengtson, and P. H. Landry, Jr. (Eds.), *Measurement of intergenerational relations* (pp. 98–125). Newbury Park, CA: Sage.

Marcoen, A. (1979). Children's perception of aged persons and grandparents. *International Journal of Behavioral Development*, *2*, 87–105.

Margolin, L. (1992). Sexual abuse by grandparents. *Child Abuse & Neglect*, *16*, 735–741.

Martin, E., and Martin, J. (1978). *The black extended family*. Chicago: University of Chicago Press.

McChesney, K. Y., and Bengtson, V. L. (1988). Solidarity, integration and cohesion in families: Concepts and theories. In D. J. Mangen, V. L. Bengtson, and P. H. Landry, Jr. (Eds.), *Measurement of intergenerational relations* (pp. 15–30). Newbury Park: Sage.

McCready, W. C. (1985). Styles of grandparenting among white ethnics. In V. L. Bengtson and J. F. Robertson (Eds.), *Grandparenthood* (pp. 49–60). Beverly Hills, CA: Sage.

McCrimmon, C. A., and Howell, R. J. (1989). Grandparents' legal rights to visitation in the fifty states and the District of Columbia. *Bulletin of American Academic Psychiatry Law*, *17*, 355–366.

Miller, J. (1989). *Myself*. Christchurch, Dorset, England: Golden Apple Productions.

Mills, T. L. (1999). When grandchildren grow-up: Role transition and family solidarity among baby boomer grandchildren and their grandparents. *Journal of Aging Studies*, *13*, 219–239.

Minkler, M., Driver, D., Roe, K. M., and Bedeian, K. (1993). Community interventions to support grandparent caregivers. *The Gerontologist*, *33*, 807–811.

Minkler, M., Fuller-Thomson, E., Miller, D., and Driver, D. (1997). Depression in grandparents raising grandchildren: Results of a national longitudinal study. *Archive of Family Medicine*, *5*, 445–452.

Minuchin, P. (1988). Relationships within the family: a systems perspective on development. In R. A. Hinde and J. Stevenson-Hinde (Eds.), *Relationships within families: Mutual influences* (pp. 7–26). Oxford, England: Oxford University Press.

Mirfin-Veitch, B., Bray, A., and Watson, M. (1996). "They really do care": Grandparents as informal support sources for parents of children with disabilities. *New Zealand Journal of Disability Studies*, *2*, 136–148.

Mirfin-Veitch, B., Bray, A., and Watson, M. (1997). "We're just that sort of family": Intergenerational relationships in families including children with disabilities. *Family Relations*, *46*, 305–311.

Murphy-Cowan, T., and Stringer, M. (1999). Physical punishment and the parenting cycle: A survey of Northern Irish parents. *Journal of Community & Applied Social Psychology*, *9*, 61–71.

Musick, J. S. (1994). Grandmothers, and grandmothers-to-be: Effects on adolescent mothers and adolescent mothering. *Infants and Young Children, 6*, 1–9.

Myer, D. J., and Vadasy, P. F. (1986). *Grandparent workshops: How to organize workshops for grandparents of children with handicaps.* Seattle: University of Washington Press.

Myers, B. J., Jarvis, P. A., and Creasey, G. L. (1987). Infants' behavior with their mothers and grandmothers. *Infant Behavior and Development, 10*, 245–259.

Myers, J. E., and Perrin, N. (1993). Grandparents affected by parental divorce: A population at risk? *Journal of Counseling and Development, 72*, 62–66.

National Centre for Social Research (1999). *British social attitudes, the 16th Report.* NCSR: London.

Neugarten, B. L., and Weinstein, K. K. (1964). The changing American grandparent. *Journal of Marriage and the Family, 26*, 199–204.

Nybo, W. L., Scherman, A., and Freeman, P. L. (1998). Grandparents' role in family systems with a deaf child: An exploratory study. *American Annals of the Deaf, 143*, 260–267.

Oyserman, D., Radin, N., and Benn, R. (1993). Dynamics in a three-generation family: Teens, grandparents, and babies. *Developmental Psychology, 29*, 564–572.

Partridge, L., and Nunney, L. (1977). Three-generation family conflict. *Animal Behaviour, 25*, 785–786.

Pashos, A. (2000). Dores paternal uncertainty explain discriminative grandparental solicitude? A cross-cultural study in Greece and Germany. *Evolution and Human Behavior, 21*, 97–109.

Patterson, C. J., Hurt, S., and Mason, C. D. (1998). Families of the lesbian baby boom: Children's contact with grandparents and other adults. *American Journal of Orthopsychiatry, 68*, 390–399.

Pearson, J. L., Hunter, A. G., Ensminger, M. E., and Kellam, S. G. (1990). Black grandmothers in multigenerational households: Diversity in family structure and parenting involvement in the Woodlawn community. *Child Development, 61*, 434–442.

Pettys, G. L., and Balgopal, P. R. (1998). Multigenerational conflicts and new immigrants: An Indo-American experience. *Families in Society: The Journal of Contemporary Human Services, 74*, 410–423.

Ponzetti, J. J. (1992). Bereaved families: A comparison of parents' and grandparents' reactions to the death of a child. *Omega, 25*, 63–71.

Ponzetti, J. J., and Johnson, M. A. (1991). The forgotten grievers: Grandparents' reactions to the death of grandchildren. *Death Studies, 15*, 157–167.

Ponzetti, J. J., Jr., and Folkrod, A. W. (1989). Grandchildren's perceptions of their relationships with their grandparents. *Child Study Journal, 19*, 41–50.

Pruchno, R. (1999). Raising grandchildren: The experiences of Black and White grandmothers. *The Gerontologist, 39*, 209–221.

Radin, N., Oyserman, D., and Benn, R. (1991). Grandfathers, teen mothers and children under two. In P. K. Smith (Ed.), *The psychology of grandparenthood: An international perspective* (pp. 85–99). London: Routledge.

Reese, C. G., and Murray, R. B. (1996). Transcendence: the meaning of great-grandmothering. *Archives of Psychiatric Nursing, 4*, 245–251.

Roberto, K. A., and Skoglund, R. R. (1996). Interactions with grandparents and great-grandparents: A comparison of activities, influences, and relationships. *International Journal of Aging and Human Development, 43*, 107–117.

Robertson, J. F. (1977). Grandmotherhood: A study of role conceptions. *Journal of Marriage and the Family, 39*, 165–174.

Rodgers, B., and Pryor, J. (1998). *Divorce and separation: The outcomes for children.* York, England: Joseph Rowntree Foundation.

Roe, K. M., Minkler, M., Saunders, F., and Thomson, G. E. (1996). Health of grandmothers raising children of the crack cocaine epidemic. *Medical Care, 34*, 1072–1084.

Roskin, M. (1984). Emotional reactions among bereaving Israeli parents. *Israel Journal of Psychiatry and Related Sciences, 21*, 73–84.

Rossi, A. S., and Rossi, P. H. (1990). *Of human bonding: Parent–child relations across the life course.* New York: Aldine de Gruyter.

Ruoppila, I. (1991). The significance of grandparents for the formation of family relations. In P. K. Smith (Ed.), *The psychology of grandparenthood: An international perspective* (pp. 123–139). London: Routledge.

Rushton, J. P., Russell, R. J. H., and Wells, P. A. (1984). Genetic similarity theory: beyond kin selection. *Behaviour Genetics, 14*, 179–193.

Sanders, G. F., and Trygstad, D. W. (1989). Stepgrandparents and grandparents: The view from young adults. *Family Relations, 38*, 71–75.

Sands, R. G., and Goldberg-Glen, R. S. (1998). The impact of employment and serious illness on grandmothers who are raising their grandchildren. *Journal of Women & Aging, 10*, 41–58.

Sangree, W. H. (1992). Grandparenthood and modernization: The changing status of male and female elders in Tiriki, Kenya, and Irigwe, Nigeria. *Journal of Cross-Cultural Gerontology, 7*, 331–361.

Scherman, A., Efthimiadis, M. S., Gardner, J. E., and McLean, H. M. (1998). The role of Panamanian grandmothers in family systems that include grandchildren with disabilities. *Educational Gerontology, 24*, 233–246.

Scherman, A., Gardner, J. E., Brown, P., and Schutter, M. (1995). Grandparents' adjustment to grandchildren with disabilities. *Educational Gerontology, 21*, 261–273.

Schilmoeller, G. L., and Baranowski, M. D. (1999). Intergenerational support in families with disabilities: grandparents' perspectives. *Families in Society: The Journal of Contemporary Human Services, 79*, 465–476.

Schmidt, A., and Padilla, A. M. (1983). Grandparent-grandchild interaction in a Mexican American group. *Hispanic Journal of Behavioral Sciences, 5*, 181–198.

Schutter, M. E., Scherman, A., and Carroll, R. S. (1997). Grandparents and children of divorce: Their contrasting perceptions and desires for the postdivorce relationship. *Educational Gerontology, 23*, 213–231.

Seligman, M., Goodrich, C., Paschal, K., Applegate, A., and Lehman, L. (1997). Grandparents of children with disabilities: Perceived levels of support. *Education and Training in Mental Retardation and Developmental Disabilities, 32*, 293–303.

Shu, S. (1999). *Grandparents, parents and children: A study of three-generation family structure and intergenerational relationships in contemporary China.* M.Phil. Thesis, Goldsmiths College, University of London.

Silverstein, M., and Chen, X. (1999). The impact of acculturation in Mexican American families on the quality of adult grandchild-grandparent relationships. *Journal of Marriage and the Family, 61*, 188–198.

Smith, M. S. (1991). An evolutionary perspective on grandparent-grandchild relationships. In P. K. Smith (Ed.), *The psychology of grandparenthood: An international perspective* (pp. 157–176). London: Routledge.

Smith, P. K. (1991). Introduction: The study of grandparenthood. In P. K. Smith (Ed.), *The psychology of grandparenthood: An international perspective* (pp. 1–16). London: Routledge.

Solomon, J. C., and Marx, J. (1995). "To grandmother's house we go": Health and school adjustment of children raised solely by grandparents. *The Gerontologist, 35*, 386–394.

Somary, K., and Stricker, G. (1998). Becoming a grandparent: A longitudinal study of expectations and early experiences as a function of sex and lineage. *The Gerontologist, 38*, 53–61.

Sonuga-Barke, E. J. S. Mistry, M., and Qureshi, S. (1998). The mental health of Muslim mothers in extended families living in Britain: The impact of intergenerational disagreement on anxiety and depression. *British Journal of Clinical Psychology, 37*, 399–408.

Staples, R. (1952). Appreciations and dislikes regarding grandmothers as expressed by granddaughters. *Journal of Home Economics, 44*, 340–343.

Staples, R., and Smith, J. W. (1954). Attitudes of grandmothers and mothers toward child rearing practices. *Child Development, 25*, 91–97.

Stein, J. A., Newcomb, M. D., and Bentler, P. M. (1993). Differential effects of parent and grandparent drug use on behavior problems of male and female children. *Developmental Psychology, 29*, 31–43.

Sternberg, R. J. (1990). *Wisdom*. Cambridge, England: Cambridge University Press.

Stevens, J. H., Jr. (1984). Black grandmothers' and black adolescent mothers' knowledge about parenting. *Developmental Psychology, 20*, 1017–1025.

Sticker, E. J. (1991). The importance of grandparenthood during the life cycle in Germany. In P. K. Smith (Ed.), *The psychology of grandparenthood: An international perspective* (pp. 32–49). London: Routledge.

Strauss, C. A. (1943). Grandma made Johnny delinquent. *American Journal of Orthopsychiatry, 13*, 343–347.

Strawbridge, W. J., Wallhagen, M. I., Shema, S. J., and Kaplan, G. A. (1997). New burdens or more of the same? Comparing grandparent, spouse, and adult-child caregivers. *The Gerontologist, 37*, 505–510.

Strom, R. D., Buki, L. P., and Strom, S. K. (1997). Intergenerational perceptions of English speaking and Spanish speaking Mexican-American grandparents. *International Journal of Aging and Human Development, 45*, 1–21.

Strom, R., and Strom, S. (1989). Grandparents and learning. *International Journal of Aging and Human Development, 29*, 163–169.

Strom, R., Strom, S., Collinsworth, P., Sato, S., Makino, K., Sasaki, Y., Sasaki, H., and Nishio, N. (1995). Grandparents in Japan: A three-generational study. *International Journal of Aging and Human Development, 40*, 209–226.

Strom, R., Strom, S., Shen, Y.-L., Li, S.-J., and Sun, H.-L. (1996). Grandparents in Taiwan: A three-generational study. *International Journal of Aging and Human Development, 42*, 1–19.

Szinovacz, M. (1998). Grandparents today: A demographic profile. *The Gerontologist, 38*, 37–52.

Szinovacz, M. E., DeViney, S., and Atkinson, M. P. (1999). Effects of surrogate parenting on grandparents' well-being. *Journal of Gerontology: Social Sciences, 54B*, S376–S388.

Thomas, J. L. (1986). Age and sex differences in perceptions of grandparenting. *Journal of Gerontology, 41*, 417–423.

Thomas, J. L. (1989). Gender and perceptions of grandparenthood. *International Journal of Aging and Human Development, 29*, 269–282.

Thompson, L., and Walker, A. J. (1987). Mothers as mediators of intimacy between grandmothers and their young adult granddaughters. *Family Relations, 36*, 72–77.

Thompson, R. A., Scalora, M. J., Limber, S. P., and Castrianno, L. (1991). Grandparent visitation rights: A psycholegal analysis. *Family and Conciliation Courts Review, 29*, 9–25.

Thompson, R. A., Tinsley, B. R., Scalora, M. J., and Parke, R. D. (1989). Grandparents visitation rights: Legalizing the ties that bind. *American Psychologist, 44*, 1217–1222.

Timberlake, E. M., and Chipungu, S. S. (1992). Grandmotherhood: Contemporary meaning among African American middle-class grandmothers. *Social Work, 37,* 216–221.

Tinsley, B. J., and Parke, R. D. (1984). Grandparents as support and socialization agents. In M. Lewis (Ed.), *Beyond the dyad* (pp. 161–194). New York: Plenum.

Tinsley, B. J., and Parke, R. D. (1987). Grandparents as interactive and social support agents for families with young infants. *International Journal of Aging and Human Development, 25,* 259–277.

Tolson, T. J. F., and Wilson, M. N. (1990). The impact of two- and three-generational black family structure on perceived family climate. *Child Development, 61,* 416–428.

Tomlin, A. M., and Passman, R. H. (1989). Grandmothers' responsibility in raising two-year-olds facilitates their grand-children's adaptive behavior: A preliminary intrafamilial investigation of mothers' and maternal grandmothers' effects. *Psychology and Aging, 4,* 119–121.

Townsend, P. (1957). *The family life of old people.* London: Routledge & Kegan Paul.

Trivers, R. L. (1974). Parent-offspring conflict. *American Zoologist, 14,* 249–264.

Troll, L. E. (1985). The contingencies of grandparenting. In V. L. Bengtson and J. F. Robertson (Eds.), *Grandparenthood* (pp. 135–149). Beverly Hills: Sage.

Tunaley, J. (2000). *The grandparenting role: Negotiation within the family.* A paper presented at the 'Grandparents in the 21st Century' Conference, Royal Institute of British Architects, London, 14 March 2000.

Turke, P. W. (1988). Helpers at the nest: childcare networks on Ifaluk. In L. Betzig, M. Borgerhoff Mulder, and P. Turke (Eds.), *Human reproductive behavior: A Darwinian perspective* (pp. 173–188). Cambridge: Cambridge University Press.

Tyszkowa, M. (1991). The role of grandparents in the development of grandchildren as perceived by adolescents and young adults in Poland. In P. K. Smith (Ed.), *The psychology of grandparenthood: An international perspective* (pp. 50–67). London: Routledge.

Uhlenberg, P., and Hammill, B. (1998). Frequency of grandparent contact with grandchild sets: Six factors that make a difference. *The Gerontologist, 38,* 276–285.

Vadasy, P., Fewell, R., and Meyer, D. (1986). Grandparents of children with special needs: Insights into their experiences and concerns. *Journal of the Division for Early Childhood, 10,* 36–44.

van IJzendoorn, M. H. (1995). Adult attachment representations. *Psychological Bulletin, 117,* 387–403.

Vermulst, A. A., de Brock, A. J. L. L., and van Zutphen, R. A. H. (1991). Transmission of parenting across generations. In P. K. Smith (Ed.), *The psychology of grandparenthood: An international perspective* (pp. 100–122). London: Routledge.

Vinovskis, M. A. (1987). Historical perspectives on the development of the family and parent–child interactions. In J. B. Lancaster, J. Altmann, A. S. Rossi, and L. R. Sherrod (Eds.), *Parenting across the life span: Biosocial dimensions* (pp. 295–312). New York: Aldine de Gruyter.

Vollmer, H. (1937). The grandmother: A problem in child rearing. *American Journal of Orthopsychiatry, 7,* 378–382.

Wacker, J. A. (1995). Legal issues and family involvement. In R. Blieszher and V. H. Bedfore (Eds.), *Handbook of aging and the family* (pp. 284–306). Wesport, CT: Greenwood.

Wakschlag, L., Chase-Lansdale, P. L., and Brooks-Gunn, J. (1996). Not just "Ghosts in the nursery": Contemporaneous intergenerational relationships and parenting in young African-American families. *Child Development, 67,* 2131–2147.

Wallerstein, J. S. (1986). Child of divorce: An overview. *Behavioral Science and the Law, 4,* 105–118.

Warner, V., Weissman, M., Mufson, L., and Wickramaratne, P. J. (1999). Grandparents, parents, and grandchildren at high risk for depression: A three-generation study. *Journal of American Academy of Child Adolescent Psychiatry, 38,* 289–296.

Watson, J. A. (1997). Grandmothering across the lifespan. *Journal of Gerontological Social Work, 28,* 45–62.

Wentowski, G. J. (1985). Older women's perceptions of great-grandmotherhood: a research note. *The Gerontologist, 25,* 593–596.

Werner, E. E. (1991). Grandparent–grandchild relationships amongst US ethnic groups. In P. K. Smith (Ed.), *The psychology of grandparenthood: An international perspective* (pp. 68–82). London: Routledge.

Wilks, C., and Melville, C. (1990). Grandparents in custody and access disputes. *Journal of Divorce, 13,* 1–4.

Williams, G.C. (1957). Pleiotropy, natural selection, and the evolution of senescence. *Evolution, 11,* 32–39.

Wood, V. (1982). Grandparenthood: An ambiguous role. *Generations: Journal of the Western Gerontological Society,* (Winter), 18–24.

6

Adolescent Parenthood

Mignon R. Moore
Jeanne Brooks-Gunn
Columbia University

INTRODUCTION

Teenage pregnancy and parenthood have always existed. However, before 1975 they received little attention or comment in the United States. In brief, the rapid rise in the number of younger adolescents having intercourse, in their birthrate, and in babies born to single teenage mothers all contributed to concern about early parenthood (Brooks-Gunn and Furstenberg, 1989; Coley and Chase-Lansdale, 1998; Furstenberg, Brooks-Gunn, and Chase-Lansdale, 1989; Maynard, 1997; Moore et al., 1993). The upward trend witnessed in the 1980s regarding the proportion of European American and African American adolescent girls who had never had sexual intercourse was followed by stabilization in 1990s rates of sexual debut, although the percentage of Latina adolescents initiating intercourse continued to increase. By the mid-1990s, 60% of African American, 56% of Latin American, and 51% of non-Hispanic European American teenagers between 15 and 19 years old reported having initiated intercourse (Besharov and Gardiner, 1997; Singh and Darroch, 1999). Approximately 77% of females and 85% of males report having initiated intercourse by the age of 20 years (Brown, 2000). Moreover, sexual intercourse is also becoming increasingly common for young women earlier in adolescence (Brooks-Gunn and Paikoff, 1993).

Although there has been a steady increase in the percentage of sexually experienced teenagers reporting current use of a contraceptive method during intercourse, the frequency of contraceptive use among youth continues to be inconsistent (Piccinino and Mosher, 1998). Although adolescent males reported using condoms more frequently in the 1990s than earlier (36% in the 1980s and 54% in the 1990s [Ku, Sonenstein, and Pleck, 1992], a response in part to concerns about HIV and AIDS, Brooks-Gunn and Furstenberg, 1990; Sonenstein, Pleck, and Ku, 1989), most boys and girls do not use contraceptives every time they have intercourse (Besharov and Gardner, 1997; Glei, 1999; Piccinino and Mosher, 1998); unprotected sexual intercourse, then, is common.

It comes as no surprise that approximately one fourth of all girls become pregnant by the end of their nineteenth year (Moore et al., 1993). The trend is most pronounced for African American women and Latinas. In 1995, approximately one out of three sexually active African American and Latin American teenagers became pregnant compared with approximately one out of six sexually active European American teenagers (U.S. Department of Health and Human Services, 2000). 30% of teenage pregnancies are terminated voluntarily, a proportion that has declined among adolescents since the mid-1980s (Ventura and Freedman, 2000; U.S. Department of Health and Human Services, 2000). Even so, in 1997, 23% of all African American first births, 17% of all Latin American first births, and 11% of all European American first births were to teenage mothers (U.S. Census Bureau, 1999a). Nevertheless, the numbers of pregnancies and births to adolescents of all ages have declined steadily since 1991, continuing a trend that began in 1960, with the exception of a sharp upturn between 1985 and 1991. In 1999, there were 49.6 births per 1000 women aged 15 to 19 years, down from 62.1 births in 1991 (Curtin and Martin, 2000). The trend is most pronounced among African American teenagers, who experienced the steepest declines in birthrates in every age category since 1960, when data for African American women first became available. Between 1991 and 1999, African American women aged 15 to 19 years saw a 30% decline in total number of births, compared with a 13% decline for Latin American women and a 21% decline for non-Hispanic European American women (Curtin and Martin, 2000). In 1998, Asian American or Pacific Islander teenagers and Native Americans experienced declines in teenage births of roughly 16% (Ventura, Mathews, and Curtin, 1999).

The decline in rates of teenage pregnancy and childbearing is widespread and is occurring across the industrialized world (with the exception of a few Eastern European countries, which saw their rates increase between 1970 and 1990); nevertheless, the United States continues to have the highest teenage pregnancy and childbearing rates of most Western countries (Singh and Darroch, 2000). At the same time the rates of sexual activity are quite similar across nations (Alan Guttmacher Institute, 1994; Jones et al., 1988; Reiss, 1997; Warren, 1992). The disparity in teenage birthrates between the United States and other Western nations has not been attributed to levels of immigration or U.S. racial and ethnic composition, as rates for European American teenagers were among the highest when compared with those of other developed countries, suggesting that the U.S. differential was only partially associated with the higher rates found among African American and Latin American youth (Jones et al., 1988). Rather, the gap in birthrates reflects divergent patterns of contraceptive use. Despite evidence suggesting increases in the availability of information about contraceptives and use among sexually experienced teens in America (Ventura and Freedman, 2000), adolescents in Western Europe continue to receive more information about sexuality and the practice of safe sex, have greater access to contraceptives, and see more public health campaigns that promote use of contraceptives. More generally, urging teenagers to practice safe sex receives greater acceptance from the public, and facetious debates about the role of families and societal institutions (school, media) in controlling adolescent sexuality or in aiding adolescents manage sexuality are not part of the political landscape as they are in the United States (Brooks-Gunn and Paikoff, 1993; Jones et al., 1988; Warren, 1992).

The majority of girls who do carry their babies to term are not married (79% in 1998). Despite the decline in teenage birthrates, nonmarital births as a proportion of all births to women aged 15 to 17 years increased between 1997 and 1998 because of the decline in marital births for women in this age group (Ventura et al., 1999). In 1998, 96% of births to African American teenagers, 72% of births to non-Hispanic European American teenagers, and 73% of births to Latin American teenagers were nonmarital (Ventura, Curtin, and Mathews, 2000). Childbearing outside the context of marriage has become normative for the teenage mother, just as has sexual intercourse. Never-married single parenthood also has become more common across the reproductive years. In 1998, 33% of all births were to unmarried women (Ventura and Bachrach, 2000).

The increased concern about early parenthood is due to the changed context in which it occurs. Today, teenage parenthood is almost synonymous with single parenthood. Teenage mothers are disproportionately represented on welfare rolls and as high school dropouts. Policies and programs have been developed to prevent the number of teenage births as well as to provide services to young mothers and their children. The declining age of intercourse, the increasing rate of nonmarital births, and the disappearance of teenage marriage mean that the young parent finds herself in a different situation today than previously (Finkel, 1995; Maynard, 1997). Additionally, she is able to stay in school today (pregnancy meant almost certain dismissal from high school thirty years ago).

The vast majority of teenage pregnancies are unplanned (Alan Guttmacher Institute 1994; Henshaw, 1998). The decision to continue a pregnancy is associated with school plans and aspirations, academic standing, perceptions of family support, number of friends who are already parents, religiosity, marital status at time of pregnancy, and attitudes towards abortion (Cervera, 1993; Frost and Oslak, 1999; Furstenberg et al., 1989; Scaramella, Conger, Simons, and Whitbeck, 1998). Little is known about the male partner's role in the girl's decision to continue a pregnancy (Harris, 1993).

Typically, teenage girls do not have educational or job skills, making it difficult for them to be financially independent. In addition, because so few marry and their male partners, even though typically a few years older, also are not in positions to be self-supporting, teenage mothers turn to family for help, shelter, and childcare. This is true whether or not a girl receives welfare supplements (East and Felice, 1996; Harris, 1997; Hogan, Hao, and Parish, 1990). Coresidence with parents enables many teenagers to finish high school and obtain childcare. Indeed, African American females are more likely to complete high school after becoming mothers than are European Americans and Latin Americans, perhaps because of help from families and lower marriage rates (Forste and Tienda, 1992; Jones, Astone, Keyl, Kim, and Alexander, 1999; Klepinger, Lundberg, and Plotnick, 1995; Testa, 1992). However, a large proportion of teenage mothers do not complete high school. Mothers who live with their families for several years after the birth are more likely to complete high school than mothers who do not. These outcomes affect ultimate economic self-sufficiency throughout the life course (Brooks-Gunn, and Furstenberg, 1986a; Furstenberg, Brooks-Gunn, and Morgan, 1987; Hoffman, Foster, and Furstenberg, 1993; Unger, Molina, and Teran, 2000).

We emphasize the importance of such contextual features of teenage parenthood throughout this chapter, as we stress the importance of developmental issues. Not only does the teenage parent face a number of developmental challenges, but her family members face new challenges as well (Chase-Lansdale, Brooks-Gunn, and Paikoff, 1991; Prater, 1995). Our focus is on the offspring of the teenage mother as well as on the teenage mother's family, specifically the kin involved in childcare. Literature on the father of the child is not reviewed extensively because the family system in which the teenage mother of today lives is typically her family of origin. More attention would have been paid to the father 25 years ago because so many teenage mothers got married; the lack of attention to the father, or, more accurately, the low attachment of teenage fathers to their children in many families with single teenage parents, is addressed elsewhere (see Chase-Lansdale and Vinovskis, 1995; Coley and Chase-Lansdale, 1999; Furstenberg et al., 1989; Furstenberg and Harris, 1993; Gohel, Diamond, and Chambers, 1997; Joshi and Battle, 1990).

This chapter is organized around themes central to understanding adolescent parenthood. The concept of timing of transitions (in this case the timing of adolescent parenthood) is the organizing feature of much of the work on this topic. As it is so relevant to a developmental perspective, we first present a brief discussion of this concept. Next, we turn to the more specific conceptual frameworks that have been invoked when the effects of teenage parenthood on various family members are described. Then the life course of the teenage mother is reviewed from two perspectives—the consequences of adolescent parenthood for the young mother vis-à-vis work, education, and family and the psychological response to becoming a mother. The life course of the children of teenage mothers is discussed next. The impact of the birth of a child on the adolescent's family is reviewed, with a focus on the female kin who live in the household, often participate in childcare, or coparent. The chapter concludes with a brief discussion of policy implications of these findings.

ADOLESCENT PARENTHOOD AS A DEVELOPMENTAL TRANSITION

Timing is a feature of all role transitions; one that has been studied extensively is parenthood. Sociologists have distinguished individual, family, and historical time: (1) individual time refers to each family member's life course; (2) family time connotes the interweaving of individual members' life courses; and (3) historical time suggests the timing patterns within a societal and historical context (Elder, 1977; Hagestad, 1986). Adolescent parenthood is defined as off time or early today. However, teenage motherhood has been, in previous eras, normative, as girls married and became mothers as teenagers (Furstenberg et al., 1989). In part, the rise in age of childbearing is due to lower fertility and infant mortality rates as well as higher rates of employment and high school graduation by women. First-time parenthood has been extended in timing to the middle 30s and 40s, so that variability is quite great.

However, it is important to remember that, even within a society, subgroups may perceive timing norms quite differently: Some work on perceived and desired normative role timing among young adolescent women has found an association between birth expectations and racial or ethnic background, with African American and Latin American adolescents reporting earlier optimal ages for first birth compared with those of European American and Asian American girls (East, 1998). Moreover, teenage parenthood is much more common in neighborhoods characterized by poverty, high rates of unemployment, and low rates of college attendance (Brooks-Gunn, Duncan, Klebanov, and Sealand, 1993; Crane, 1991; Sucoff and Upchurch, 1998). Consequently, characterizations of teenage parenthood as being early or off time may be less true in contexts in which a relatively large proportion of individuals are becoming mothers at a young age. Without making any casual attributions among these factors, it is true that girls in such neighborhoods not only know more peers who are mothers but give a lower age at which they could themselves become mothers (Furstenberg, Levine, and Brooks-Gunn, 1990).

The three timing dimensions are not always in synchrony. Individual timing of transitions must be considered in light of the life course decisions of other family members as well as the family as a whole. To complicate matters further, each individual has multiple roles within the family, making the timing of transitions in each relevant. Therefore becoming a teenage mother may influence the timing of high school graduation and entrance into the workforce. Moreover, the life course trajectories of other family members may influence the timing of these events as well. If the teenager's mother is in the workforce and not near retirement, her ability to help the teenager with childcare in order to encourage high school completion may be hampered. If the teenager's mother is elderly and not well, childcare may be more difficult (anecdotal evidence from multigenerational studies of young mothers, grandmothers, and toddlers shows that grandmothers with arthritis or sore backs find it quite uncomfortable to move the toddler around or feel that they could no longer care for the child given her or his weight; Chase-Lansdale, Brooks-Gunn, and Zamsky, 1994). Empirical data confirm the relation between a grandmother's health and her ability or willingness to care for young children (Baydar and Brooks-Gunn, 1998). If a grandmother in a multigenerational or married household has young children (her own or other grandchildren) in the home, childcare may be shared among adult relatives; however, if the grandmother is the sole caregiver, an additional grandchild may be a burden. Clearly the timing of transitions around the family members needs to be considered.

In the late 1980s and early 1990s, a line of research emerged that conceptualized timing somewhat differently from what has been discussed here. Geronimus (1987; Geronimus and Bound, 1990) suggested that early childbearing might not be disadvantageous for health outcomes for young poor African American women. Her thesis was based on the fact that, because of poverty and discrimination, African Americans are likely to have increased rates of morbidity and mortality at earlier ages than European Americans Geronimus provided evidence, termed the *weathering hypothesis*, for a number of illnesses. She then went on to argue that early childbearing may be advantageous. Her arguments were based on health outcomes of babies born to teenage mothers being no different or even better than those born to older mothers. The corresponding literature supported this hypothesis, suggesting few adverse effects and possible positive effects of early motherhood on neonatal health with proper prenatal care (McCarthy and Hardy, 1993). In an extension of this work, Geronimus and Korenman (1992) went on to argue that early childbearing also has fewer economic and social consequences for African American mothers than the current literature would indicate. They conducted further analyses, comparing sisters who do and do not become adolescent mothers and arguing that within-family designs control much better for selection factors than do across-family, cross-sectional studies. However, their work and subsequent work in this area found that analyses based on such a design reduced but did not eliminate the differences in outcomes between teenage mothers and their relatives who delayed childbearing (analyses of the Panel Study of Income Dynamics [PSID] and the National Longitudinal Study of Youth [NLSY]; Hoffman et al., 1993; Moore et al., 1993).

FRAMEWORKS USED IN THE STUDY OF ADOLESCENT PARENTHOOD

Research focusing on adolescent parenthood appears in several separate lines of inquiry. The major thematic thrusts include the following. One line defines the transition into parenthood as a normative life challenge. The role changes that accompany parenthood, including the psychological preparation for parenthood, the realignment of relationships with one's own parent and spouse (or boyfriend), the negotiation of childcare responsibilities within the family, and the possible redefinition of one's identity (including motherhood into one's identity) are all aspects of the transition to parenthood (Belsky, 1984; Cowan and Cowan, 1992; Deutsch, Ruble, Fleming, Brooks-Gunn, and Stangor, 1988; Parke, 1988; Ruble, Fleming, Hackel, and Stangor, 1988). Interestingly, research focusing on teenage parents does not use often use transition frameworks. We review work on psychological adaptation to motherhood and attempt to link this tradition with what is known about teenage parenthood.

The second and perhaps the most well-known approach to understanding teenage parenthood does not focus on parenting explicitly, but on the consequences of early parenthood on the mother herself. This approach is not psychologically driven, nor does it consider the meaning of parenthood or relational realignments of parenthood. Instead, the life course of teenage mothers is explored from a sociological and demographic viewpoint. Life course transitions are of interest, of course, but not from a psychological perspective or from a developmental viewpoint (i.e., the competing developmental demands of adolescence and parenthood are not studied, nor is parenthood in the context of the particular life stage in which it occurs).

A third body of work takes the life course perspective as a starting point and incorporates a more family-oriented approach to the study of young parents. The effects of early parenthood on the offspring as well as on the parents of young mothers are studied. Interest in the intersections of lives has led to a consideration of how young mothers' life decisions and situations unfold in the lives of their own children. The linking of lives within families is a major contribution of the teenage parenthood literature to developmental theory more generally (Chase-Lansdale and Brooks-Gunn, 1994).

Direct observation of the parenting behavior of young mothers has been a response to the belief that the offspring of adolescent mothers on the average fare more poorly than the offspring of older mothers (Brooks-Gunn and Furstenberg, 1986b). This research tradition borrows directly from the research on parenting behavior and mother-child interaction during the infancy and preschool years and focuses on the socialization practices of young mothers in the traditions described by Maccoby and Martin (1983). However, it is rather static in that longitudinal work is rare, comparisons with samples of older mothers who are from the same social and economic background are not always made, within-group analyses are not conducted to unveil the mechanisms underlying adequate or poor parenting practices, contextually detailed observations are not included, and the complexity of family life for young mothers and their children is not acknowledged (Chase-Lansdale, Brooks-Gunn, and Paikoff, 1991).

An even more finely detailed family-oriented approach has emerged in the study of young mothers. So-called family systems approaches focus on effects of young parenthood not only on individual family members but also on the family as a whole (Chase-Lansdale, Gordon, Coley, Wakschlag, and Brooks-Gunn, 1999; Chase-Lansdale, Wakschlag, and Brooks-Gunn, 1995). The formation of multigenerational households for the care of the young mother and her offspring is one impetus for this line of research. Another area involves the effect of adolescent childbearing on the behavior and attitudes of other household members, including the sexual activity of younger siblings, the extent and nature of mother–adolescent communication, as well as the quality of mother's parenting.

Research that uses these five frameworks is reviewed in this chapter. All five not only have heuristic value, but describe somewhat different aspects of the experiences of teenage mothers and their families.

THE LIFE COURSE OF ADOLESCENT MOTHERS

Effects of Adolescent Parenthood on Work and Family Trajectories

The literature has made significant advances in its consideration of the life trajectory of adolescent mothers and their various adaptations to early childbearing. Indeed, the life course of adolescent mothers has been described in great detail, with much of this work coming from sociological and demographical approaches (Bachrach and Carver, 1992; Baldwin, 1993). We know about adolescent mothers' eventual marital, fertility, work, education, and living situations (Bennett, Bloom and Miller, 1995; Furstenberg et al., 1987; Hotz, McElroy, and Sanders, 1997; Maynard, 1997; Moore et al., 1993). Studies have either included appropriate comparison groups or have charted developmental courses within samples of teenage mothers. A few studies now look at the life courses of teenage mothers and their sisters who did not become teenage mothers in an effort to control for a variety of familial factors correlated with young motherhood (Geronimus and Korenman, 1992; Hoffman et al., 1993). Other work examines within-group differences in long-term outcomes for disadvantaged women who gave birth during adolescence and those whose first birth occurred in adulthood (Grogger and Bronars, 1993; Hotz et al., 1997). A less well-developed literature exists on the educational and work lives of young fathers, although researchers are making strides in this area (Brien and Willis, 1997; Coley and Chase-Lansdale, 1999; Lerman, 1993; Wilson and Brooks-Gunn, 2001).

To give a face to teenage mothers, three examples of the educational, work, and family lives over a 17-year period are presented. These are taken from the Baltimore Study of Teenage Motherhood. Over 300 primarily low-income African American families have been followed for over 20 years. The three case histories are taken from the book *Adolescent Mothers in Later Life* (Furstenberg et al., 1987, pp. 23–25).

The first woman, whom we shall call Doris, was 34 at the time of the interview. In many respects she resembles the popular stereotype of a teenage mother. Doris was unmarried and a school dropout when she became pregnant in 1966 at the age of 16. She went on welfare immediately and continued to receive public assistance for the next 17 years, even during the period of her brief marriage, which lasted for only 3 years. Doris had three children by three different men, none of whom was her husband. She had been employed periodically but never for more than a few years at a time and never yielding enough income to lift her off the welfare rolls. During her late twenties, she had a lengthy relationship with Harris, who fathered her third child. But in 1980, Harris left the household, and Doris has been living alone with her three children, and her grandchild, the 2-year-old son of Dalia, Doris's second oldest child. By the end of this chapter, we will know how many women in our sample resemble Doris.

Other Baltimore mothers may be more like Iris. Iris became pregnant at 16 and waited to marry the baby's father until finishing high school, the year after her child was born. Her marriage lasted about 10 years, during which time she had a second child. Except for the period right after her children were born, Iris has always worked. After her marriage broke up, she received public assistance for 2 years; she began a new relationship with a man named Lester, which was brief. When it dissolved, Iris moved in with her mother for a year as an alternative to going back on welfare. As soon as she could afford it, she moved out and is now living with her two children as a single parent. For the past 5 years, Iris has been steadily employed as a business administrator for the Baltimore School District.

Iris has managed reasonably well with the occasional assistance of her family and supportive services from the government. Her best financial years were when she was married and working at the same time. But most of her adult life, she has been economically hard pressed, relying primarily on her own income to support her children.

Helena's life history is different still. At her parents' insistence, Helena delayed her marriage to Nelson, the father of her child, until she had completed her schooling and had a secure job. She and Nelson were married in 1971 around her 20th birthday. They have been married continuously for nearly 14 years. During most of this period, both Helena and Nelson have been steadily employed. They now live in a comfortable garden apartment on the outskirts of Baltimore with their two children.

These three case histories, although unique in some sense, were selected to represent prototypes of varying adaptations to early childbearing. Despite efforts to find employment and settle into a stable relationship, Doris has not managed to achieve domestic or economic security. Iris has done somewhat better, although she, too, has struggled to maintain economic independence and has barely scraped by as a single mother for the past 5 years. Both would envy Helena's marital and economic career, which since her early twenties has been progressively secure and stable.

Comparisons with Older Mothers

In general, the life course of teenage mothers looks different from agemates who do not become mothers early. The former are less likely to complete high school and go on to postsecondary education, marry, avoid welfare, be employed, be stably employed, earn other than minimum-wage incomes, and, if married, avoid divorce. Of utmost concern from a policy perspective is that, if girls leave school before or just after becoming mothers, their chances of completing high school are reduced (Jones et al., 1999; Upchurch and McCarthy, 1990). In contrast, young mothers who stay in school are more likely to finish high school (these trends are most pronounced for those youngsters who have not failed a grade). Special school programs throughout the United States for pregnant teenagers may in part explain the relatively high rates of high school completion for girls who are "on track" academically at the time of the pregnancy. Of interest from a two-generational perspective are those programs that offer childcare and parenting classes, given that childcare is one of the unmet needs for many young mothers (Cherlin, 1995; Clewell, Brooks-Gunn, and Benasich, 1989; Seitz, Apfel, and Rosenbaum, 1991; Wilson, Ellwood, and Brooks-Gunn, 1995).

Context and Selection

These negative consequences of early parenthood are due to multiple factors. Teenage mothers are unable to afford childcare and have difficulty locating childcare given their low earning power (similar to that of other poor mothers). Additionally, the Personal Responsibility and Work Opportunity Reconciliation Act of 1996, designed specifically to address adolescent and nonmarital births, requires that young mothers live with a legal parent or guardian and stay in school, so that income cannot be earned (even if low-paying jobs were available; Chase-Lansdale and Vinouskis, 1992; Chase-Lansdale and Brooks-Gunn, 1995; Coley and Chase-Lansdale, 1998). Relatives typically provide childcare, so that the young mother is dependent on her family for support; other family members also work, so that childcare often comprises makeshift arrangements (Cherlin, 1995). Juggling childcare, education, work, and leisure is difficult for all mothers, but teenage mothers may have special problems given their low education, poor earning ability, and reliance on others for support. Problems are compounded if young mothers have more children (Harris, 1997). Not all studies find teenage mothers to have more children than older childbearers from the same educational, economic, and racial strata. However, teenage mothers may be more likely to have their children more closely spaced. Having more than one child while still a teenager is a major risk factor for eventual economic dependency (Furstenberg et al., 1987; Harris, 1997).

An additional point needs to be made vis-à-vis the factors that place teenagers at risk for becoming a mother. Living in poor neighborhoods, attending low-quality schools, residing in a family in which the parents have low education and are poor, school failure, low aspirations—all are associated with teenage parenthood (Brewster, Billy, and Grady, 1993; Cherlin, Kiernan, and Chase-Lansdale, 1995; Coley and Chase-Lansdale, 1998; Furstenberg et al., 1989; Hardy et al., 1997; Luker, 1996). These so-called contextual precursors do not disappear after the birth of a child, but continue, further exacerbating the trends away from self-sufficiency. Research suggests that these factors explain much of the deleterious effects of teenage motherhood on subsequent life course, but being a young mother in and of itself seems to influence later experiences as well (although research often cannot totally separate selection effects based on background variables from effects of young parenthood; Bachrach, Clogg, and Carver, 1993; Chase-Lansdale, Brooks-Gunn, and Paikoff, 1991; Hardy, Astone, Brooks-Gunn, Shapiro, and Miller, 1998; Miller, 1992, 1993).

Another selection factor has to do with being a single mother. There is a nearly universal link between teenage motherhood and single motherhood for African Americans and a strong link for European Americans. Astone (1993) looked at the amount of variance in household income in the 5 years following the birth of a child that can be accounted for by single motherhood, as opposed to teenage motherhood (by using the PSID national data set; Hill, 1992). Single motherhood was highly predictive of low subsequent family incomes, but did not totally explain differences between women who give birth in their teenage years and those who give birth in their twenties (see also Hardy et al., 1998). At the same time, both groups look more disadvantaged than those mothers who delay childbearing until their midtwenties. Astone questioned the usefulness of distinguishing between childbearing in the teenage years and in the early adult years vis-à-vis income (even though she acknowledged the possibility of parenting or psychological differences between these two groups).

In an attempt to account for the selective differences in the background and the personal characteristics of teen mothers, Hotz et al. (1997) used data from the NLSY to compare women whose first teen pregnancy resulted in a live birth with those who miscarried at first teen pregnancy. The women shared similar socioeconomic characteristics, yet women who experienced a teenage birth had more births by the age of 30 years and spent more time as single mothers. Nevertheless, early childbearing has few adverse effects on subsequent labor market activity. Whereas at early ages, teen mothers worked less than did their nonchildbearing counterparts, by their midtwenties and early thirties these mothers worked more hours and reported higher earnings at every age through 34 years. Moreover, Hotz et al. found that delaying childbirth reduced welfare benefit receipts during the mothers' teen years but made no difference during their early twenties and increased the amount of benefits received at older ages. Other studies attempting to correct for selection bias present a similar conclusion to the work of Hotz et al.: Failure to account for this bias has overestimated the negative consequences of teenage childbearing for later socioeconomic attainment of young mothers (Geronimus and Korenman, 1992, 1993; Bronars and Grogger, 1994; Grogger and Bronars, 1993).

There is also research suggesting racial and ethnic differences in the effects of early childbearing. Delaying childbirth until the age of 25 years or later is associated with higher family incomes for European Americans, but not for African Americans. These findings suggest that delayed childbirth may not confer as many benefits to African American women, a thesis put forth by Geronimus and colleagues (Geronimus and Korenman, 1992), and debated by Hoffman et al. (1993) and Moore et al. (1993).

Moore et al. (1993) also presented analyses relevant to the issue of selection (see Bachrach et al., 1993; Baldwin, 1993). Using the NLSY (see Brooks-Gunn, Berlin, Leventhal, and Fuligni, 2000; Brooks-Gunn, Phelps, and Elder, 1991; Chase-Lansdale, Mott, Brooks-Gunn, and Phillips, 1991, for a brief discussion of the national data sets), Moore et al. considered the effect of age at first birth on income at the age of 27 years, finding effects for three ethnic–racial groups—European Americans, African Americans, and Latin Americans. The authors were interested in seeing how early childbearing might influence subsequent income, specifically poverty. Factors differed by ethnic group. For African Americans (for whom the age of birth effect was the weakest), the only mediator was number of children born before the mother was 27 years old. For European Americans, timing of marriage, family size and employment–earnings mediated the link between the mother's age at first birth and her income at the age of 27 years. Astone (1993) also reported that marriage (specifically current marital status) is an important predictor of family income for European Americans but not for African Americans.

Both of these analyses present a welcome trend in the literature on early childbearing, in that they go beyond documenting ill effects on subsequent well-being (in this case defined by income) and document the pathways through which teenage parenthood may exert effects on employment and school completion. A complementary approach involves separating the effects of high school dropout and teenage parenthood. Teenage childbearing is clearly and strongly associated with reduced schooling (Klepinger et al., 1995; Upchurch and McCarthy, 1989), but how the two interrelate is open to question (Upchurch and McCarthy, 1990). Using a transitions framework that focuses on the timing and sequencing of events occurring in early adulthood, with NLSY data, Upchurch (1993) compared groups of teenage girls in respect to the timing of high school dropout and teenage parenthood. Not surprisingly, the young women who drop out of school, become mothers, or both, come from more impoverished backgrounds than adolescents who do neither. Teenage mothers who do not drop out of school come from less disadvantaged families than those young mothers who drop out of school or childless young women who drop out of school. The teenage mother high school graduates are disadvantaged vis-à-vis their family background relative to high school graduates who are not mothers. They also are less likely to go on for postsecondary schooling (generally, models need to look at the predictors of high school graduation and postsecondary schooling separately; Brooks-Gunn, Guo, and Furstenberg, 1993; Haveman, Wolfe, and Spaulding, 1991). This line of research uses a more detailed framework for looking at teenage mothers (timing and sequencing framework), considers possible selection factors (in this case, an examination of the backgrounds from which the different groups come), highlights the variability of outcomes, and argues for more contextually based research (see Brooks-Gunn, Duncan et al., 1993, for a discussion of the effects of neighborhood residence on teenage motherhood and high school dropout rates).

Research in this area shows that early childbearing lowers the educational attainment of young women, but several analyses estimating high school completion for teen mothers separately by race and ethnicity have reported that African American teen mothers are more likely to complete high school compared with European American and Latin American adolescent mothers (Forste and Tienda, 1992; Jones et al., 1999; Upchurch and McCarthy, 1990). However, there is no overarching theoretical framework from which to interpret these findings. In the Upchurch and McCarthy analysis, women of all racial and ethnic groups who had a child while in school were more likely to graduate than drop out, and African American women were more likely to have a child while enrolled in school. Forste and Tienda (1992) suggest that African American teen mothers are more likely to remain at home and receive parental support, which facilitates school completion.

Predictors of Long-Term Outcomes

A final line of work focuses on long-term outcomes, taking a within-group perspective rather than the across-group comparisons just reviewed. Long-term follow-ups suggest that teenage mothers continue to do less well in the employment and the educational realms as they enter middle age. However, one of the surprising results of follow-up studies is the diversity in outcomes. The findings from the Baltimore Study of Teenage Motherhood and the New Haven Teenage Mother Study are illustrative (Brooks-Gunn and Furstenberg, 1986a; Horwitz, Klerman, Kuo, and Jekel, 1991).

The Baltimore and the New Haven studies address only the long-term trajectories of African American families (European American girls were included in the Baltimore Study, but the sample was too small to analyze). Additionally, both studies focus on urban families in the Northeast. Rates of teenage parenthood are also high in other regions of the country. A lack of information about teenage parenthood in the context of rural poverty is notable (but see Scaramella et al., 1998, for a discussion of pregnancy risk among European American, rural, adolescent women). Both the Baltimore and the New Haven studies would have benefited from more psychologically oriented measures. For example, information on self-efficacy, depressive affect, cognitive test scores, and coping strategies all would further our understanding of the life courses of teenage mothers.

Many of the young women continued to make efforts to improve their life options in both studies. In Baltimore, for example, many continued with schooling through the 17 years following the birth of the child. Approximately one third had completed high school (of those who had not completed it earlier), and almost one third had received some postsecondary schooling. Many more were in the workforce than might have been anticipated, given the results from shorter-term studies. Approximately three fourths were working in 1983–1984, when the 17-year follow-up was conducted. Only one fourth were receiving welfare. In terms of fertility, the Baltimore Study mothers had, on average, a little over two children, which is similar to the average number of children found in samples of older childbearers. However, this sample differs from other samples in that many of the young women were married at the time of the birth or within the first year after their child was born. However, the majority of these marriages did not last (only 16% of the firstborn children were living with their father in 1983–1984; Furstenberg et al., 1987).

What factors predict positive outcomes for teenage mothers? Positive outcomes were defined as a family annual income of $25,000 of more, no receipt of welfare in the past year, and having fewer than three children. The most potent influences involved educational experience—being on grade level at the time of the pregnancy, having parents with more education (more than tenth grade), attending a special school for pregnant youngsters in Baltimore, and having high aspirations for further schooling at the time of the birth. Other significant predictors included finishing high school within 4 to 5 years of the birth of the first child, limiting subsequent childbearing, and growing up in a family that did not receive welfare. Another factor promoting economic well-being was continuing in an early marriage. However, marriage might be considered a risky strategy for ensuring later success, in that so many of these marriages did not last. Mothers who got married early were less likely to complete their schooling, leaving those divorced mothers in a particularly bad situation in the job market (Brooks-Gunn and Chase-Lansdale, 1991; Brooks-Gunn and Furstenberg, 1987).

DEVELOPMENTAL ISSUES AND THE TRANSITION TO MOTHERHOOD

The birth of a first child, a major period of transition in the life of a woman, is marked by dramatic changes in self-related information seeking, self-definitions, and roles (Cowan and Cowan, 1992; Deutsch et al., 1988; Heinicke, in Vol. 3 of this *Handbook*). It may also herald alterations in adjustment, as inferred through postpartum increases in depressive affect, psychiatric illness, and marriage difficulties (Belsky, 1984; Ruble et al., 1988). Antecedents of postpartum adjustment, such as the mental health of the mother, satisfaction with the motherhood role, and actual parenting behavior have been studied, as have the consequences of women's attitudes, self-definitions, and adjustment vis-à-vis parenting behaviors and relationships (Belsky, 1984; Cowan and Cowan, 1988; Parke, 1988).

This literature does not focus on mothers who are young (i.e., teenagers), living without a partner, or who come from socioeconomically disadvantaged socioeconomic backgrounds. However, the approaches used to explain the transition to motherhood in the so-called "traditional" family may provide insights into how this transition is experienced in other family structures and by other ethnic groups. Here we consider the applicability of four research traditions on the transition to motherhood for teenage mothers: (1) intrapsychic, (2) self-definitional, (3) coping and stressful life events, and (4) adaptation to life changes framework.

Intrapsychic Perspectives on Becoming a Mother

Intrapsychically oriented models focus on adjustment to becoming a mother. They often stress that role definitions occur through identification with significant others—in the case of motherhood, typically identification with the pregnant woman's own mother. Indeed, positive relationships with one's mother are associated with self-confidence and perceived positive mothering characteristics in pregnant women. These associations are *not* due to self-esteem, information seeking, relationship with husband, and other factors (Deutsch et al., 1988). Frequency of maternal contact (both emotional support and physical sharing of childcare) may also predict a sense of maternal competence (Abernathy, 1973).

In the case of the adolescent parent, her relationship with her mother may assume an even greater importance than for older mothers. There are several reasons for this conjecture. First, adolescent girls are more likely than older women to be redefining their relationships with their mothers (Blos, 1967; Brooks-Gunn and Zahaykevich, 1989; Graber and Brooks-Gunn, 1999; Hauser, Borman, Powers, Jacobson, and Noam, 1990; Osofsky, Hann, and Peebles, 1993). This process not only takes several years but also may be truncated by an early pregnancy in that the adolescent may have to reinterpret what separation from her mother means. She is, on the one hand, dependent on her mother for financial resources (teenage mothers typically do not have the resources to move out of their family's home). On the other hand, she is individuated from the mother in that her actions have created a new and separate human being. Her struggles with autonomy may render the maternal relationship more salient, although not necessarily more conflict free (Chase-Lansdale et al., 1999).

Second, the adolescent girl may become reliant on the mother for information about parenthood, especially if few of her friends have become pregnant, if school dropout narrows her circle of friends, and if, like many women (young and old alike), she does not receive much information about pregnancy from doctors and other health professionals. In older European American middle-socioeconomic women, reading material is the primary source of pregnancy and parenthood information (Deutsch et al., 1988). The teenage mother is very likely to have been a poorer student than the older mother (Furstenberg et al., 1989; Hofferth 1987; Moore et al., 1993), making it likely that she will not turn to books readily.

Third, the adolescent girl may be less likely to have a male figure available for emotional support than might older women (Furstenberg et al., 1987). For some adolescent mothers, boyfriends are perceived to provide emotional support, which is related to positive adaptation (it is unclear whether this association is due to actual male support or only to perceptions). Additionally, in larger families, childcare by older siblings, especially sisters, may still be commonplace (Burton and Bengston, 1985). Finally, even in the United States earlier in this century and in the last century, when childbearing spanned a longer period of time, families often included young children and older adolescents, and experience with caregiving by teenagers was probably frequent (Modell and Goodman, 1990).

Finally, the adolescent's mother may be more emotionally involved in her young daughter's pregnancy. Because mothers often find the separation process difficult (as do their teenage daughters; Paikoff and Brooks-Gunn, 1991), the pregnant adolescent's mother may be preparing to become a mother of a young child again, in that she expects to take care of the new child, or at least to take a major role in caregiving (Burton, 1990). Given that a majority of teenage mothers live with their mothers in the first years after the birth, these expectations may be quite realistic (Hernandez and Myers, 1993).

Other intrapsychically oriented approaches have focused on constructs such as ego strength and maturity, both of which are associated with responsivity and reciprocity directed toward infants of middle-socioeconomic mothers (Cowan and Cowan, 1992). Teenage mothers are believed to have lower levels of ego strength and to be less mature socially and emotionally because of the necessity of negotiating the developmental tasks of adolescence (Hamburg, 1986). However, few studies have directly tested this hypothesis. Early case studies tended to report difficulties in psychoanalytic terms (teenage pregnancies represent "hysterical disassociation states," Kasanin and Handschin, 1941, "passive dependencies." Barglow, Bornstein, Exum, Wright, and Vitosky, 1968), although little verification exists in the developmental literature (Brooks-Gunn and Furstenberg, 1986a).

Lack of maturity may be inferred from indicators of self-orientation during pregnancy. In samples of middle-income married women, women who are preoccupied with themselves, as measured by physical and sexual concerns, seem to show less effective parenting patterns in the postpartum years (Grossman et al., 1980). Directed inward, these mothers may not be especially sensitive to their children's needs (Cowan and Cowan, 1992). Whether this would be more true of teenage mothers than of older mothers is not known, although it is plausible, given the former's lower scores on many measures of maturity (see study by Osofsky, Hann, and Peebles, 1993, reporting more identity diffusion for teenage than for older childbearers).

Another possible intrapsychic construct has been identified by Boyce, Schaefer, and Uitti (1985, p. 1281), who suggested that adjustment generally, and specifically as linked to social support, may be influenced by a sense of stability and permanence, the "belief or perception that certain central, valued elements of life experience are stable and enduring." Included in the construct (Boyce et al., 1985, p. 1282) is "an awareness of the self as consistent, of relationships as stable, of places as special referent points, of routines as predictable, and of universal order." Perceived social support in a small sample of teenage girls who were pregnant was associated with high levels of permanence. Interestingly, both social support and a sense of permanency were related to birth outcomes (as determined by medical records) as well as maternal positive affect (as determined by self-report). The authors speculate that a sense of permanence may influence the effects of social support and stress on adaptation to early parenthood. Whether a sense of permanence is more likely in older than younger childbearers is not known.

Social and intrapsychic constructs may interact with cognitive competence. Cognitive complexity increases during the adolescent years (Keating, 1990). By middle adolescence, however, cognitive skills are similar to those of young adults. At the same time, specific aspects of reasoning and social cognition might distinguish adolescents and young adults (Case, 1985; Keating, 1990). A relevant construct that might properly be considered social cognition is the Concepts of Development Questionnaire (CODQ), developed by Sameroff and colleagues (Gutierrez and Sameroff, 1990; Sameroff, Seifer, Barocas, Zax, and Greenspan, 1987). It conceptualizes beliefs about parenting in a four-stage sequence, ranging from fairly concrete and single-cause notions about parenting to more multicausal, reciprocal, and complex beliefs. More complex stages of reasoning are associated with better child outcomes, both higher intelligence test scores and lower behavior problems (Benasich and Brooks-Gunn, 1996; Liaw and Brooks-Gunn, 1994; Sameroff et al., 1987; Sameroff, Seifer, Baldwin, and Baldwin, 1993). Teenage mothers may have less complex and multilevel beliefs about parenting, as an analysis of a multisite study of over 800 mothers suggests (Benasich and Brooks-Gunn, 1996). Another study that used the CODQ did not focus on teenage mothers, but on children, adolescents, and young adults (Pratt et al., 1993). In this small, nonrepresentative sample, adolescents had lower scores than young adults (i.e., less multicausal beliefs). The scores on the CODQ were associated with an integrative complexity score as well as a Piagetian task. Compared with adults, teenagers may have difficulty in conceptualizing parenthood as a complex, multifaceted task that involves reciprocal interactions with the child. Such a stance toward parenting might explain, in part, the differences between younger and older mothers in actual parenting behavior.

Self-Definitional Approaches to Becoming a Mother

Cognitive developmentalists argue that when important life changes occur individuals become motivated to examine and modify self-conceptions to fit the changing circumstances (e.g., Kohlberg, 1966; Ruble, 1983). For example, pregnancy has been described as "anticipatory parenthood"

(Jessner, Weigert, and Fay, 1970), because at this time a sense of self as a mother seems to emerge (Ballou, 1978; Leifer, 1980). Pregnant women begin to visualize themselves as mothers, which is associated with postpartum adjustment and greater satisfaction with the mothering role (Oakley, 1980; Shereshefsky and Yarrow, 1973). Late-pregnancy self-definitions as a mother are also associated with self-confidence as a mother and the perception of oneself as possessing mothering characteristics, both concurrently and several months postpartum (Deutsch et al., 1988).

Women also (1) actively seek information in anticipation of a first birth, (2) use this information to construct identities incorporating motherhood, and (3) seek more information as the event becomes closer (i.e., information seeking about labor is greatest in the second and the third trimesters, information about childcare in the third trimester). Such information is a primary determinant of self-definitions of motherhood in primarily middle-income European American women living with a male partner (Deutsch et al., 1988; Ruble et al., 1990). It is unclear whether young mothers would as actively construct a self-definition of motherhood as do older mothers, given that the former are still constructing their self-definitions as independent and sexually mature women. Additionally, if information seeking about the pregnancy is more passive for young mothers (given the possible reliance on mothers' and friends' advice, rather than actively seeking out reading material or seeing health personnel), then their self-definitions may be less developed than those of older women. Because self-definitions in pregnancy are associated with subsequent satisfaction with mothering and possibly with responsivity to the infant (Ruble et al., 1988), a teenage mother's difficulty in forming a maternal self-definition may be detrimental to her early childrearing experience. In turn, this difficulty in maternal self-definition may set the stage for future interactional difficulties, as has been found in some samples of teenage mothers who have been observed interacting with their young children (Berlin, Brady-Smith, and Brooks-Gunn, in press; Field, 1982; Osofsky, Hann, and Peebles, 1993).

Maternal self-definitions are influenced by direct experience with children. These associations are more pronounced after the birth of the child; indeed, the basis of self-definition seems to shift from primarily indirect (outside the self) prenatally to primarily direct (experience with childcare) postnatally, as one might expect (Deutsch et al., 1988). Teenage mothers, being children themselves, may not have had as much caregiving experience as older women, at least in the role of caregiver rather than as an occasional baby-sitter. In other cultures, caregiving by teenagers and prepubertal girls is common and may act as a preparatory experience for the motherhood role (Whiting, 1981; Whiting and Edwards, 1988). In societies that require girls to go to school, this anticipatory training may be less likely to occur. Ethnographic studies of multigenerational households, particularly African American families, report extensive sibling care as well (Burton, 1995; Jarrett, 1990; Zukow-Goldring, in Vol. 3 of this *Handbook*). Other studies of the younger siblings of parenting teens have found high levels of coparticipation in childcare through their performance of secondary, instrumental tasks such as giving the child a bottle or watching the child for short periods of time (East and Felice, 1996). We do not know how frequently sibling care occurs in teenage mother-headed families.

Characteristics of the child also influence parenting patterns and self-definitions (Bell, 1968; Belsky, 1984). For example, mothers who reported having temperamentally "easy" babies considered themselves better mothers than did mothers who reported having "difficult" babies (Deutsch et al., 1988; Putnam, Sanson, and Rothbart, in Vol. 1 of this *Handbook*). Having an easy baby, one perceived as being relatively happy, predictable, soothable, and sociable, may enhance a mother's feelings that she is an efficacious, good, and competent mother. It may also influence actual interactions with the child (see studies of mother–infant interaction and temperament with at-risk children for related findings; Brooks-Gunn and Lewis, 1984; Field, 1980). If teenage mothers have had little previous experience with infants (and thus little information with which to compare their baby's behavior), they may perceive them to be more difficult or be less aware of developmental milestones (Benasich and Brooks-Gunn, 1996; Frodi, 1983; Osofsky, Eberhart-Wright, and Ware, 1992; Osofsky, Hann, and Peebles, 1993). At the same time, teenage mothers may be less skilled at handling a difficult baby (see studies on the problems that mothers have in modulating their interactions with low-birthweight babies; Field, 1982; Goldberg and DiVitto, in Vol. 1 of this *Handbook*; as well as work with teenage mothers; Hann, Castino, Jarosinski, and Britton, 1991; Hann, Robinson, Osofsky, and Little, 1991; Osofsky, Hann, and Peebles, 1993; Pope, Casey, Bradley, and Brooks-Gunn, 1993). Reasons for the lack of skill include teenage mothers' lack of experience, concern with other developmental issues, possible lack of a well-formed maternal self-definition, and sharing of childcare with their own mothers (leading to less "experience" with their own child).

Finally, possible interactional difficulties or low maternal self-definitions may be exacerbated by any of several events that can co-occur with becoming a young mother; these would include having a low-birthweight or preterm infant, having a sick infant, becoming depressed during the pregnancy or after the birth, changing residence or school attendance patterns, or constricting one's social network. In a study of the transition to parenthood, Cowan and Cowan (1992) documented the difficulties that middle-income women (and men) in relatively stable relationships and with fairly good social networks have in managing the multiple events that co-occur with the birth of a child. Teenage mothers may not have a realistic idea of infant developmental progressions, in part because of their lack of caregiving experience and lowered information seeking. Some studies have found that younger mothers, compared with older mothers overestimate or underestimate their children's attainment of developmental milestones (Benasich and Brooks-Gunn, 1996; Field, 1981; Frodi, 1983). Teenage mothers may expect too little too late in the areas of cognition and language, which is possibly related to the lower rates of contingent vocalizations seen in teenage mothers (Berlin et al., in press; Field, 1981; Osofsky and Osofsky, 1970).

Adjustment to parenting and the specific challenges of teenage parenthood may be mediated by social support other than that provided by the mother. Perceived social support provided by the father of the child is quite important to teenage mothers (Colletta, Hadler, and Gregg, 1981; Crnic, Greenberg, Ragozin, Robinson, and Basham, 1983; Crockenberg, 1987; Unger and Wandersman, 1985). Whether these effects are long term remains to be determined, especially because so many of the boyfriends of teenage mothers do not remain very involved in the rearing of their children, as measured by frequency of contact and support provided several years after the birth of the baby (Furstenberg et al., 1987; Furstenberg and Harris, 1993). However, analyses on the partners of women in the Baltimore study report two distinctive types of involvement: men who are highly active and supportive, and those who are disengaged and uninvolved in the lives of their partners and children (Coley and Chase-Lansdale, 1999). Moreover, there is significant complexity and fluidity of fathers' behavior over time, with significant increases and decreases in levels of involvement. Unger and Wandersman (1985) made the point that social support from the father of the baby or the girl's own mother may influence the teenage mother's behavior. We need more research that explores the relation between increased paternal support and adolescent mothers' behavior.

Coping Frameworks

How women manage crises and stressful life events and whether transitional events constitute a crisis are questions addressed by coping frameworks. Crises may be defined as "acute, short term, and intense"; the period in which the young girl learns that she is pregnant and tells her family may be characterized in terms of a crisis model.

Teenage motherhood as a crisis.   Those who see pregnancy and childbirth as a crisis might hypothesize that pregnancy is more of a crisis for the younger than for the older woman, as the former in all likelihood did not plan her pregnancy and was indeed quite surprised when it occurred (Brooks-Gunn and Furstenberg, 1989; Hofferth, 1987). However, there is little evidence that teenage pregnancy is perceived as a crisis because the period of active upset is quite short. Having a child as a single mother does not seem to be met with universal community disapproval today as it was earlier (Furstenberg, 1976; see Sung, 1992, for a description of the community sanctions on out-of-wedlock childbearing in Korea; the description is similar to what was reported in the United States 25 years ago). Indeed, most family members, although acknowledging the difficulties inherent in having to rear a young infant, particularly in terms of juggling school, childcare, work, and leisure activities, respond positively to the birth (Burton, 1996. This research is focused on African American families; it is presumed that family members greet the new baby positively in other ethnic groups as well.) In addition, responses at the time of the birth are not associated with later maternal or child outcomes (Furstenberg et al., 1987). However, very little information exists on possible factors that might increase the likelihood that a teenage pregnancy may be seen as a crisis (i.e., emotional state). Most studies to date have been more sociologically oriented, so that psychological evidence for early acceptance or emotional upset is sparse.

Teenage mothers have been found to be more depressed than older mothers in two studies conducted by Osofsky—the Topeka, Kansas, and the New Orleans, Louisiana, studies (Carter, Osofsky, and Hann, 1991; Hann, Robinson et al., 1991; Osofsky and Eberhart-Wright, 1988). Levels of depression and self-esteem were also found to be associated with more behavior problems in the toddler period in the Topeka study (Osofsky, Culp, Eberhart-Wright, Ware, and Hann, 1988).

Anecdotal evidence from a study of disadvantaged teenage mothers in Newark, New Jersey, suggests that many teenage mothers have very subdued affect and seem to have difficulty managing everyday tasks (Aber, Brooks-Gunn, and Maynard, 1995; see also Berlin et al., in press). It is not known whether these behaviors are indicative of depressive tendencies or the cumulative stress of being a mother, a teenager, and a poor person simultaneously. Depressed mood states and anxiety during pregnancy are associated with less effective parenting behavior in the year following the birth of a child in middle-income married women (Ruble et al., 1988). Whether such associations would be found in samples of teenage mothers has not been tested, although we suspect that such links would be.

That most young mothers seem to accept an unplanned pregnancy (after a brief period of upset) may be explained if we distinguish between life crises and life changes (Stewart, Sokol, Healy, and Chester, 1986). Crises, as defined above, are intense and of short duration and may characterize the period immediately following the teenager's first awareness of her pregnancy. It may also be a time of increased risk for emotional problems (Pearlin, 1975). After a crisis, individuals tend to return to their precrisis level of emotional functioning. Becoming a mother, then, might be conceptualized as a role transition, necessitating the changes in self-definitions and behaviors described earlier (Cowan and Cowan, 1992) or as an event that heralds multiple stressors, given the requirement for changes in many aspects of life (Cohen and Lazarus, 1977). Much literature considers the possible negative effects of multiple stressors, including decrements in mental and physical health. These have been documented for the maternal transition in samples of middle-income married women (Oakley, 1980; Shereshefsy and Yarrow, 1973).

Stressors that the teenage mother often confronts include poverty and family mandates for early childbearing. First, stability and change in socioeconomic conditions are proposed mechanisms that set the stage for the type of socialization that occurs within the family and neighborhood. Exemplars exist in the research on the very disadvantaged (Wilson, 1987, 1996). In neighborhoods with persistent concentrated poverty, such as in many large inner cities, rates of unemployment for African American teenage and young adult males have reached alarming proportions. This has co-occurred with early childbearing (although it is difficult to determine a causal link). However, if a community is characterized as (1) having few job opportunities, (2) providing little demonstrable evidence within a particular neighborhood that completing school will alter substantially one's life chances, and (3) perceiving out-of-wedlock childbearing as normative, then a form of implicit socialization for early parenthood may exist (Brooks-Gunn, et al., 1993; Klebanov, Brooks-Gunn, and Duncan, 1994). In such a context, the transition to motherhood may not be as stressful, particularly if other changes do not co-occur with the child's birth. The fact that the vast majority of teenage mothers today do not marry, and most stay with their own mothers, might lessen the possibility of stress.

Second, family mandates also may exist for early childbearing, as Burton and Dilworth-Anderson (1991) suggest on the basis of a 3-year ethnographic investigation of families in a rural community and in a small city. Such mandates seem to "require" that teenage girls have babies in order to allow their mothers to parent. In these families, direct responsibility for parenting (at least in the previous two generations) typically occurred when a woman became a grandmother. The teenager gave childcare responsibility to her mother with the expectation that her daughter would eventually do the same for her (see Ward, 1986, for similar findings). At the same time, the teenage mother was expected to care for her grandmother, as her own mother was busy with her child. As the authors suggested, teenage mothers in this community experienced stress because they were responsible for an elderly grandmother or for multiple generations rather than for their own young child.

In brief, teenage motherhood may be perceived as a crisis given that it is often unplanned and often requires family realignments. Teenage motherhood often signals changes in requests for help within the family. It often occurs in the context of persistent family poverty, neighborhood poverty, or both; poverty in and of itself renders coping with everyday tasks difficult. Becoming a young mother in the context of poverty is likely to be stressful.

Teenage motherhood as a challenge.   More positive aspects of coping are emphasized in some approaches, such as that of Lazarus and Folkman (1984), who considered the ways in which life events may be seen as challenges. These challenges may be growth enhancing as well as restricting, given the situations in which they occur and the characteristics of the individual. Indeed, the great diversity seen in the outcomes of the teenage mothers the Baltimore study suggests that many young mothers manage to overcome the inherent difficulties of having a child while school, job, and male relationships are being sorted out. Clearly, some women manage to cope well with this challenge, whereas others do not. Individual and environmental factors predict successful or unsuccessful adaptation, or, in the terminology of Lazarus and Folkman, how and in what circumstances the developmental challenge of early motherhood becomes growth enhancing (Furstenberg et al., 1987; Osofsky, Peebles, Fick, and Hann, 1992). However, little research addresses the positive aspects of teenage parenthood.

Adaptation to Life Changes

Adaptation to life changes has been conceptualized as a sequence of emotional responses, with the work of Freud and Erikson providing the wellspring (Stewart, 1982; Stewart et al., 1986). Any change is hypothesized to induce a heightened state of awareness of the environment, which is both exciting and confusing. Four phases are hypothesized in an individual's response to life changes. In an effort to create meaning and understanding of a new set of circumstances, Stewart postulated that the sense of self is diminished, autonomy is reduced, and dependency feelings are enhanced in the first phase. This receptive, dependent phase is gradually replaced with more autonomous functioning as the individual masters new aspects of the environment. The third phase is characterized by greater assertion as the individual begins to take more initiative. The final phase is a more integrated one than the second or third, in that autonomous functioning is coupled with an understanding of roles and feelings of others. Life changes such as pregnancy may result in a temporary, possibly adaptive, dependency phase; an individual may need to be less active and efficacious while learning and observing what is expected and needed to interact successfully in a new situation. Stewart and her colleagues showed that new mothers go through a more dependent phase following the birth of a child. This is replaced with more autonomous functioning after several years, at least for those mothers who do not experience multiple life events (such as illness or death of a relative, marital changes, work or residence changes) following the birth of the child. That is, the mothers who had other changes with which to cope were less able to progress to a more independent emotional stance (Stewart et al., 1986).

These findings have clear implications for understanding teenage mothers. Younger mothers may be less likely than older mothers to progress from a more dependent to a more autonomous emotional stance. First, the teenage girl, before becoming pregnant, is experiencing a number of role and life changes (separation from the mother, formation of other intimate relationships, entrance into sexual relationships, and so forth), making it likely that she is less mature than older mothers. Second, the advent of the birth of a child is likely to precipitate other changes in school, job, living arrangements, and male relationships. In all probability, a young mother will have experienced multiple life changes simultaneously. Research on adolescents who are not mothers suggests that the experience of multiple life events has deleterious effects on school achievement, peer relationships, and mental health (Brooks-Gunn, 1991; Brooks-Gunn and Peterson, 1991; Simmons and Blyth, 1987). The teenage mother is also likely to have experienced other events such as marital and school disruptions that are considered risky, and may contribute to poor outcomes in work and metal health through the pathways suggested by those who study cumulative risks in families (Brooks-Gunn, Klebanov, and Liaw, 1994; Sameroff et al., 1993). Future research needs to address how many teenage mothers reach more autonomous and integrated emotional phases, when this occurs, and the individual and environmental conditions that facilitate this process (Chase-Lansdale, Wakschlag, and Brooks-Gunn, 1995; Paikoff and Brooks-Gunn, 1991).

THE LIFE COURSE OF THE OFFSPRING OF ADOLESCENT MOTHERS

It is commonly presumed that early childbearing affects children adversely, but until the 1990s, only a limited amount of evidence had been marshaled to demonstrate this proposition, and almost all of this literature was confined to the period of infancy and early childhood (e.g., Brooks-Gunn and Furstenberg, 1986a; Osofsky, Hann, and Peebles, 1993). However, since the mid-1990s, several studies have been able to examine long-term effects of teen childbearing on children's outcomes into adolescence and adulthood (Hardy et al., 1997, 1998; Menaghan, Kowaleski-Jones, and Mott, 1997).

In the first year or two of life, few differences are seen between infants born to teenage mothers and those born to older mothers. This is true for measures of cognitive development (Coll, Vohr, Hoffman, and Oh, 1986) as well as for measures of social development (with secure attachment being studied most intensively; Benn and Saltz, 1989; Hann, Osofsky, Stringer, and Carter, 1988; Ward, Carlson, Plunkett, and Kessler, 1988). By the preschool years, small but consistent differences in cognitive functioning and psychosocial problems between offspring of early and later childbearers appear in preschool and continue into elementary school (Broman, 1981; Marecek, 1979, 1987; Moore, Morrison, and Greene, 1997). Such cognitive and psychosocial differences may set the stage for later school and social difficulties. By adolescence, school achievement among the offspring of teenage mothers is markedly lower and misbehavior, juvenile conduct disorders, and other school problems are markedly higher (Brooks-Gunn and Furstenberg, 1986a; Moore et al., 1997). For example, in the Baltimore Study of Teenage Motherhood, approximately one-half of the adolescents of the teenage mothers had failed a grade, compared with approximately one in five from an appropriate comparison group from the National Study of Children (Furstenberg et al., 1987; Furstenberg, Hughes, and Brooks-Gunn, 1992; see also Horwitz et al., 1991, for similar results in the New Haven study). However, in an analysis of data from the children born to young women (teenage and young adult childbearers) in the NLSY, mother's age at first birth was less important as a predictor of children's cognitive scores than were mothers' cognitive scores (Moore and Snyder, 1991).

Adolescent offspring of teenage mothers are also more likely to become teenage parents, as seen in the NLSY and Pathways to Adulthood data sets (Furstenberg et al., 1990; Hardy et al., 1997, 1998). Moreover, the disadvantage of being born to an early childbearer appears to persist into adulthood. In our analysis of data from the Pathways to Adulthood and Johns Hopkins Collaborative Perinatal Studies, the children of teenage mothers fared less well in adulthood than did the children of older mothers with respect to education, mental health, financial independence, and deviant behavior, including heavy alcohol and marijuana use (Hardy et al., 1997, 1998).

The question still remains as to what factors account for these differences. Precise causal links between early childbearing and the well-being of children have not been well delineated, especially if parenting goes well (Chase-Lansdale and Brooks-Gunn, 1994). Several factors may be operating, including the adverse social and economic effects associated with early parenthood, emotional immaturity associated with teenage motherhood, and/or less experienced and/or less adequate mothering by the young parent. The risks associated with becoming a teenage mother also operate later to affect the mother and her offspring. Living in poor families, as most of the offspring of teenage mothers do, affects children (Brooks-Gunn, 1995a; Brooks-Gunn and Duncan, 1997; Duncan and Brooks-Gunn, 1997; Duncan, Yeung, Brooks-Gunn, and Smith, 1998; McLoyd, 1990). Residing in poor neighborhoods also exacts a toll on children and youth (Brooks-Gunn, Duncan, and Aber, 1997; Duncan, Brooks-Gunn, and Klebanov, 1994; Leventhal and Brooks-Gunn, 2000).

EFFECTS OF THE LIVES OF TEENAGE MOTHERS ON THEIR CHILDREN

Children's lives are influenced by the choices made by and the situations of their mothers. The Baltimore Study of Teenage Motherhood follows the tradition of Elder (1974) in *Children of the Great Depression* and Werner and Smith's (1982) study of the children of Kauai by looking at the intersection between the lives of mothers and their children. We found that characteristics of the teenage mothers' lives had large effects on their children's outcomes, as measured by low preschool readiness scores and behavior problems during the preschool years and grade retention, high school dropout, low literacy, early sexual intercourse, teenage parenthood, and behavior problems in the adolescent years. At each time period, maternal characteristics such as welfare receipt, low education and cognitive achievement, large family size, and single parenthood were associated with poorer child and adolescent outcomes (Baydar, Brooks-Gunn, and Furstenberg, 1993; Brooks-Gunn, Guo, and Furstenberg, 1993; Furstenberg et al., 1987; Guo, Brooks-Gunn, and Harris, 1996).

Of more interest is the fact that the maternal characteristics were linked with the various indices of child success and failure somewhat differently as a function of age and outcome. Marital status was not predictive of preschool outcomes to any great extent, but was more important for adolescent outcomes, especially those concerned with sexuality and behavior problems. The presence of a father figure might be important in terms of supervision of girls or support of the mother in the supervision of girls during the transition to sexual maturity. The birth of additional children was more important for preschool than for adolescent outcomes, perhaps indicating the importance of adult time available to spend with preschoolers (Baydar, Brooks-Gunn, and Senior, 1995). Furthermore, maternal circumstances influenced child outcomes when those circumstances changed. For example, if a mother went off welfare between her child's preschool and adolescent years, the likelihood of grade failure was reduced during the elementary and the middle school years. This was true even though the preschool readiness scores predicted school-related problems in adolescence, and welfare receipt in the preschool years was highly associated with low school readiness scores. When these relations are taken into account, going off welfare decreases the child's chances of repeating a grade.

These findings are relevant for current policy debates about the benefits of helping mothers move off of welfare and into the workforce. Additionally, such analyses are the heart of development research, speaking to continuity and change, both in outcomes and in process or mediators (Bornstein and Krasnegor, 1989).

DEVELOPMENTAL ISSUES IN ADOLESCENT MOTHERS' PARENTING

Much research has focused specifically on the actual parenting behavior of adolescent parents. Most of this work considers the teenage mother and her infant. The first wave of research, as reviewed by Baldwin and Cain (1980) and Brooks-Gunn and Furstenberg (1986a), suggested that mothers differed primarily in terms of verbal responsivity to children's cues (see also Osofsky, Hann, and Peebles, 1993). Young mothers also perceived their infants to be more difficult and had unrealistic expectations for their developmental courses (Field, 1980; Osofsky, Peebles et al., 1992). Generally, teenage mothers seem to be as warm as older mothers toward their children. More recent work has replicated the early findings, as teenage mothers seem to provide a less stimulating and verbal environment for their young children and may also be more restrictive and disengaged (Berlin et al., in press; Crockenberg, 1987; Culp, Appelbaum, Osofsky, and Levy, 1988; Culp, Culp, Osofsky, and Osofsky, 1991; Parks and Arndt, 1990). The environment of teenage mothers' homes may be less geared toward learning as well (Wasserman, Brunelli, Rauh, and Alvarado, 1994). Using national data sets such as the children of the NLSY (Chase-Lansdale, Mott et al., 1991) confirms the findings on home environment from the smaller-scale studies (Luster and Dubow, 1990; Moore and Snyder, 1991).

Another line of research on teenage mothers' parenting was conducted by Osofsky and colleagues (1988, 1993). Using a risk and vulnerability model adapted from the field of developmental psychopathology, Osofsky looked at the links between parenting and child outcomes, with a particular focus on maternal affect regulation and parent–child interaction as they feed into the child's own affect regulation and emotional development. Arguing that many young mothers have difficulty regulating their own emotional states, as evidenced by high rates of depression and possible emotional liability, she studied how such regulatory disturbances might influence parent–child interactions. Depressed mothers sometimes have difficulty responding to their children's cues, with resulting impacts on their children (Downey and Coyne, 1990; Field, Healy, Goldstein, and Guthertz, 1990; Zahn-Waxler, Kochanska, Krupnick, and McKnew, 1990). Adolescent mothers often have problems in affect regulation, not just difficulties in responsivity (Berlin et al., in press; Carter et al., 1991; Hann, Castino, et al., 1991; Leadbeater and Linares, 1992).

Osofsky also raised the critical issue of emotional availability of the teenage mother to the child (Osofsky, Eberhart-Wright, 1998; Sameroff and Emde, 1992). Young mothers are less available to their children, both in the infancy and the toddler periods (Berlin et al., in press; Osofsky, Hann, and Peebles, 1993). These patterns of parenting may play a role in the more frequent observation of insecure attachment and disorganized attachment in infants of teenage mothers compared with those of older mothers (Hann, Castino, et al., 1991; Hann, Robinson et al., 1991; Lamb, Hopps, and Elster, 1987). However, research has not directly addressed the link between maternal availability and attachment in teenage mothers.

Of particular concern in this line of work is the use of comparison groups. Even if ethnicity and neighborhood are comparable across groups (a requirement that not all studies meet), some studies use as their comparison older married mothers, thus confounding age and marital status. A more profitable approach is to compare teenage mothers with older mothers who are also single as well as with those who are married in order to investigate the effects of being a single parent versus being a young mother (research has shown moderate effects of single parenthood in the context of divorce and childbearing outside of marriage on children's outcomes; Brooks-Gunn, 1995b; Cherlin et al., 1991; Hetherington, 1993; McLanahan, 1997; McLanahan and Sandefur, 1994; Smith, Brooks-Gunn, and Klebanov, 1997; Thomson, Hanson, and McLanahan, 1994; Thomson, McLanahan, and Curtin, 1992; Weinraub, Horvath, and Gringlas, in Vol. 3 of this *Handbook*).

Research in the middle to late 1990s included some of the controls missing in earlier works. For example, the Baltimore Multigenerational Family Study compared young women who became mothers in their teenage years with those who become mothers in their early twenties. The study's design allowed for observation of mothers and grandmothers separately with preschoolers. Mothers' ages at first birth ranged from 13 to 25 years, with a mean of approximately 18 years. Parenting behaviors were coded from a problem-solving task (a semistructured puzzle task adapted by Goldberg and Easterbrooks, 1984, from a tool task developed by Matas, Arend, and Sroufe, 1978). Both mothers and grandmothers were observed interacting with the toddlers. Parental affect, parenting disciplinary style (disengaged, authoritative, authoritarian), and problem-solving style (quality of assistance, supportive presence) were coded (see Baumrind, 1989; Chase-Lansdale et al., 1994). Other examples are analyses of the Early Head Start and the Infant Health and Development Program evaluations (Berlin et al., in press; Brooks-Gunn, Klebanov, Liaw, and Duncan, 1995). It is important to note that education, Aid to Families with Dependent Children (AFDC) participation, marital status, and verbal ability are controlled in order to see the effects of age (some women who become mothers at an early age are quite different in demographic characteristics from those who postpone motherhood).

Also, research has not looked at parenting practices vis-à-vis harshness and disciplinary styles. Nor has much work considered links between teenage parenting behaviors and child outcomes after the infancy period. Consistency and change in parenting behaviors over time have not been topics of investigation. A particularly provocative issue is whether teenage mothers become more adequate parents or alter their behavior to become more responsive and less harsh as they become older and possibly less centered on themselves (Chase-Lansdale and Brooks-Gunn, 1994).

The interpretation of findings from this work merits a cautionary note. This research relies on measures of parent–child interaction derived from work with primarily middle-income, married, older mothers. For example, most studies of teenage mothers have focused on the following constructs: maternal warmth, maternal responsivity or sensitivity, verbal interchanges, harsh parenting, and combinations of warmth and control (as in the dimensions originally identified by Baumrind, 1989; Maccoby and Martin, 1983; Matas et al., 1978). Many of the differences seem to be focused on verbal interchanges. Given that teenage mothers are on average likely to have lower verbal ability scores as well as less education, even when other demographic characteristics are controlled for (Miller and Moore, 1990), it may not be surprising that differences might exist in the verbal arena.

Other aspects of parenting remain somewhat untapped. For example, the Baltimore Multigenerational Family Study shows teenage mothers playing more with toys on their own in free-play situations than do grandmothers. Sometimes young mothers engage in what looks like parallel play—they play with some toys while their preschool children play with others. This is a type of behavior that we have not seen in work on older mothers. The same observation has been made in the Teenage Parent Demonstration, a sample of teenage mothers from Newark (Brooks-Gunn, Duncan, et al., 1993). Measures of parallel play might be developed and added to protocols involving teenage mothers.

Another problem with the current literature on parenting behavior of teenage mothers involves the transference coding systems from nonminority to minority households (Doucette-Gates, Brooks-Gunn, and Chase-Lansdale, 1998). This issue transcends the teenage mother literature, being relevant for all studies of minority children and their parents (McLoyd, 1990; McLoyd and Steinberg, 1998). It arises in the teenage parenthood literature because so many of the studies have focused on African American multigenerational families. Multigenerational households are a common response to young single parenthood across ethnic groups, but are typically studied in only African American families.

Exceptions include work by Wasserman, Field, Berlin, Garcia-Coll, and their colleagues. Wasserman and her colleagues (Wasserman, Brunelli, and Rauh, 1990; Wasserman et al., 1994; Wasserman, Rauh, Brunelli, Garcia-Castro, and Necos, 1990) conducted a study focusing on parenting behavior and attitudes as well as social support as they are associated with toddlers' outcome in Latin American adolescent and adult mothers. Two groups of Latin American immigrants residing in New York City were included—mothers from the Dominican Republic and from Puerto Rico as well as a sample of African American mothers. Teenage mothers from all groups were less likely to be married than older mothers, and marriage was least likely in the African American teenage mother sample. Teenage mothers were more likely to be depressed than adult mothers, although differences among ethnic groups were not found. Teenage mothers also had lower Home Observation for Measurement of the Environment (HOME) scores than the adults, lived in more crowded households, and performed less childcare than older mothers. However, teenage and adult mothers had similar child-rearing attitudes, although ethnic differences appeared. African American mothers reported greater social support than Latin American mothers, and Puerto Rican mothers perceived greater support than mothers from the Dominican Republic. Latin American mothers had more strict childbearing attitudes than African American mothers across age; mothers from the Dominican Republic had stricter attitudes than mothers from Puerto Rico.

Garcia Coll has focused on Latin American young mothers; her work has included samples of island Puerto Ricans, mainland African Americans, and mainland European Americans (Garcia Coll, 1989; Lester, Garcia Coll, and Sepkoski, 1983). Garcia Coll looked at culture-specific patterns of pregnancy timing, marriage, and social support from the family as possible explanations for these differences (see also Leadbeater and Linares, 1992).

Field and her colleagues (Field and Widmayer, 1981) looked at young mothers (not all of whom were teenage mothers) in interaction with their 4-month-old infants. Groups included mainland Puerto Rican and Cuban families residing in Miami, Florida. Interactions were more positive in the mainland Puerto Rican mothers than in the Cuban mothers. Both groups exhibited more positive behavior than the sample of African American mothers from Miami. Little is known about the cultural context of childbearing in the Puerto Rican and Cuban communities in Miami, information necessary to understand the origin and meaning of such differences.

Using data from the Early Head Start Research and Evaluation Project, Berlin et al. (in press) compared teenage mothers with older mothers vis-à-vis parenting interactions in the home when the children were 14 months of age. Ratings were based on the codes developed for the National Institute of Child Health and Human Development Study of Early Childcare. A unique feature of this sample is that, by definition, all mothers were poor (an eligibility requirement for Early Head Start). Moreover, 17 sites are included in the Early Head Start evaluation. Controlling for a host of demographic characteristics, Berlin et al. found that teenage mothers were less supportive, more detached, and more intrusive than older mothers. The effects were most pronounced for African American mothers, in part because they were relatively more disadvantaged (i.e., less likely to be married, less likely to have completed high school, and more likely to be in concentrated poverty) than European American and Latin American mothers in the sample.

Little work has focused on possible constructs of relevance for subgroups (e.g., defined by culture, ethnicity, language, or maternal age). As an illustration, in the study by Kohen and Brooks-Gunn (2001) of the Infant Health and Development Program, mothers and toddlers (2½ years old) were observed in a free-play setting within a larger clinic setting. Videotaped interactions were coded for authoritarian and authoritative parenting behavior (Baumrind, 1973; Maccoby and Martin, 1983). Cluster analyses were used to identify four groups of mothers based on their parenting behavior: (1) high authoritative–low authoritarian, (2) high authoritarian–low authoritative, (3) low on both, and (4) moderate authoritative and authoritarian. Although the first two groups mirror the two original behavioral "styles" outlined by Baumrind and the third mirrors the original disengaged "style," the forth represents what might be termed a "tough-love" approach to parenting, one in which mothers are very warm but also very directive. From the demographic characteristics of these four groups of mothers, it was evident that the teenagers in the sample (regardless of race) were almost all in the very authoritarian group. The fourth group consisted primarily of older African American mothers, and the first group was almost all older European American mothers. Child outcomes in the authoritative and the tough-love groups were similarly high, whereas the worst child outcomes were found in the group of highly authoritarian teenage mothers. These results suggest the importance of an additional parenting "style" not considered in Baumrind's original conceptualization, one that might be associated with better outcomes for children in certain contexts. The results also suggest that teenage mothers across racial or ethnic groups might be more similar to one another than are older mothers from different ethnic groups.

In summary, the research on parenting behavior would benefit from an expansion to other ethnic groups, a consideration of the applicability of current coding systems for young and minority mothers, and more analyses focusing on subgroups of teenage mothers (such as those who have not finished high school, who are or are not residing with their mothers).

FAMILY SYSTEMS APPROACHES: PATERNAL INVOLVEMENT, MULTIGENERATIONAL, AND SIBLING EFFECTS

The advent of teenage motherhood has effects on other family members, not just on the teenage mother. Research in this area has begun to focus on multiple family members as well as on family climate or emotional quality, which is important because a family systems approach includes individual family members as well as the family as a whole (Hinde and Stevenson-Hinde, 1988; Reiss, 1981). Because young mothers are highly likely to spend the first years after the birth of a child in a multigenerational household, the study of family systems is critical (Chase-Lansdale, Brooks-Gunn, and Paikoff, 1991; Chase-Lansdale et al., 1999). In addition, new work has begun to estimate the influence of sibling childbearing patterns on the risk of teen parenthood for younger adolescents. Finally, after a lengthy period of neglect, scholars have begun to examine the influence of teenage and unmarried fathers as sources of social and economic support for their children and for early childbearers.

The parents of a teenager are often unhappy about the impending birth, but typically provide support to their daughter during the pregnancy and to the daughter and baby during the first few years after delivery (as studied in African American families; Chase-Lansdale and Brooks-Gunn, 1995; Furstenberg, 1976). This support often includes coresidence, which is particularly common among African American families (Boyd-Franklin, 1989; Bryson and Casper, 1999; Hogan et al., 1990; McAdoo, 1988). Coresidence is approximately twice as likely among African American than among European American single mothers (Bryson and Casper, 1999; Hernandez and Myers, 1993; McAdoo, in Vol. 4 of this *Handbook*; Paikoff, Brooks-Gunn, and Baydar, 1993; Smith and Drew, in Vol. 3 of this *Handbook*). Research has begun to describe the prevalence of grandmother involvement in teenage mothers' lives. It is clear that multigenerational residence is more likely when the mother is young, as assessed in the Children of the National Longitudinal Survey of Youth (NLSY) (Baydar and Brooks-Gunn, 1991; Hogan et al., 1990; Paikoff et al., 1993). In one paper using those data, it was found that 11% of grandparents were primary caregivers of their grandchildren (Fuller-Thomson, Minkler, and Driver, 1997). Another line of research using the National Study of Families and Households was used, examined grandmothers' involvement with grandchildren. Baydar and Brooks-Gunn (1998) derived a profile of grandmothers in the United States and assessed the extent of regular care to children of their adult child. Approximately 12% of grandmothers resided with a grandchild (the numbers of those who have ever lived with a grandchild will presumably be much higher), and approximately 43% provided childcare to their grandchildren on a regular basis—a figure four times as high as the 11% reported by Fuller-Thomson et al. (1997). Cluster analyses identified four groups of grandmothers. Of interest to us here are the two groups providing significant amounts of childcare. The first group, whom we termed homemaker grandmas, made up 19% of the sample and was composed of older, married women who provided care. One fifth in this grouping had a grandchild living with them in their home. The second cluster, termed young and connected grandmas, constituted 23% of the sample. This group consisted primarily of younger women who worked and provided care. Three fourths of them participated in social or community organizations, and the group was split between married and unmarried, with one fifth having a grandchild living with them. This second group, given their age, is likely to have teenage daughters who are mothers. It is the group on which almost all of the research on multigenerational households focuses (Burton, 1990; Burton and Bengston, 1985; Chase-Lansdale, Mott, et al., 1991). In the Baltimore Multigenerational Family Study, for example, approximately one third of the adolescent mothers identified in the late 1960s lived with their mothers when their children were young. In the next generation of teenage mothers (based on data from the firstborn children of the original mothers) approximately three fifths were living with their mothers (Furstenberg et al., 1990; Hardy et al., 1998). Historical changes in living arrangements, if they have occurred as the Baltimore study data suggest, may have implications for interactions among generations. We address this topic here.

How does extended and often intensive support influence the family with regard to parenting behaviors exhibited across generations? Several lines of evidence point to both benefits and disadvantages of such support. We review research in four areas—grandmothers as parental role models, formation of multigenerational households, shared caregiving of grandmothers and mothers, and the relationship between teenage mothers and their mothers.

Grandmothers as Parental Role Models

One potential benefit of coresidence with the grandmother is the provision of a role model for young mothers to emulate with respect to their own parenting behavior. Consequently, continuity across generations in parenting behavior might be predicted. Most research exploring continuity has considered parents' experiences when they were children to ascertain whether early parenting experiences influence subsequent parenting behavior (Rutter, 1989). Usually the early parenting experience is assessed retrospectively. Such studies suggest some continuity, especially in terms of harsh and negative parenting (Caspi and Elder, 1988; Egeland, Jacobvitz, and Sroufe, 1988; Quinton and Rutter, 1988).

In the case of teenage mothers and their own mothers, continuity may be examined concurrently because both generations interact and care for the teenager's young child. We explored issues centering on continuity by examining low-income African American families in the Baltimore Multigenerational Family Study (Chase-Lansdale et al., 1994, 1999). Generally, concordance between mother and grandmother parenting was seen only for negative dimensions of parenting and only for younger mothers and grandmothers. Other research suggests that punitive, negative ways of interacting with children are more likely to be modeled than positive interactive styles (Patterson, 1986). More positive aspects of parenting were only associated across generations when the mother and the grandmother were not living together and when the mother was older.

Formation of Multigenerational Households

Research conducted in the late 1960s and early 1970s indicated that coresidence had greater benefits for the offspring of teenage mothers when compared with those residing in single-parent families (Furstenberg, 1976; Horwitz et al., 1991; Kellam, Ensminger, and Turner, 1977). These studies typically focused on relatively young mothers who resided in multigenerational households. The authors of these early studies noted that these benefits might be time limited: Coresidence might be a good solution when the offspring and mothers are young, but less beneficial as family members age. In the Baltimore Study of Teenage Mothers, for example, long-term residence in the mother's household predicted long-term welfare dependency in the daughters (Furstenberg et al., 1987).

Studies in the 1980s and 1990s do not all document positive effects of coresidence on children. Using the Children of the NLSY, Paikoff and colleagues (1993) find that multigenerational coresidence in the first years of life is associated with lower reading achievement scores at ages 5 and 6 in European American children of teenage and young adult mothers, controlling for a host of social and demographic characteristics. Other studies report no negative effect of multigenerational households on children's outcomes. For example, among African American young mothers residing in Newark, New Jersey, half of whom participated in a jobs-, skills-, and education-training program predicated on the federal Job Opportunities and Basic Skills (JOBS) program, coresidence was associated with lower verbal ability scores when the children (third generation) were between 3 and 5 years of age (Aber et al., 1995). Coresidence was also beneficial in a sample of low-birthweight children residing in eight sites. Pope et al. (1993) report that coresidence of teenage mothers is associated with higher children's intelligence test scores at the age of 3 years.

These possible differential effects of multigenerational households on children may be played out in family interactions. Of particular interest are the parenting styles and quality exhibited by young mothers and their mothers. We have outlined four hypotheses. Hypothesis 1, called modeling and support, draws on work initiated a generation ago that suggests that grandmothers' presence provides economic and emotional support and examples of good parenting to young mothers. The prediction in coresident households would be positive effects on mothers' parenting with no effect on grandmothers' parenting. Hypothesis 2, called conflict, poses that living together and sharing child-rearing are difficult and that conflict between mothers and grandmothers would negatively affect both mothers' and grandmothers' parenting, as can occur in mother–father families (e.g., Emery, 1982). Hypothesis 3, called mutual support, suggests that coresidence is an adaptive response to scarce resources and that mothers' and grandmothers' mutual support would have positive effects on both individuals' parenting quality (e.g., Stack, 1974). Finally, Hypothesis 4, burden on grandmother, poses that coresidence is difficult for grandmothers and drains their resources. Grandmothers' parenting would be negatively affected, whereas mothers' parenting would be positive or neutrally affected (e.g., Burton, 1990).

Findings from the Baltimore Multigenerational Family Study suggest that coresidence with grandmothers has negative consequences for the parenting of both mother and grandmother (Chase-Lansdale et al., 1994, 1999). It appears that multigenerational living arrangements are often stressful for young mothers and young grandmothers—the conflict hypothesis seems to fit these data. Living together may be difficult for—the young mother who is balancing needs for autonomy and need for childcare simultaneously, as well as the grandmother who is balancing the demands of adult midlife (work, relationships, parenting) with unanticipated childcare demands. Add to the equation the fact that these households are struggling with the demands of poverty, and intergenerational strain is not surprising.

Multigenerational residence may not be as beneficial today as in the past in part because of the deteriorating economic environment, the rise in single-parent childbearing, and the increase in neighborhoods with large numbers of poor people (Hogan et al., 1990; Wilson, 1987, 1996). These conditions make it more difficult to provide a supportive household environment. They may also render multigenerational residences more common, although little evidence exists on this topic. One exception is the work of Hernandez and Myers (1993), who estimate that the percentage of children in mother-only families with a grandparent living in the home decreased to between 11% and 14% in the 1970s, after a steady increase from 20% to 27% between 1940 and 1960. However, since the late 1970s, the proportion of children in single-mother, multigenerational families has risen continuously. In 1980, 22% of mothers who had ever been married were in multigenerational households, and when 1990 Census reports began to distinguish between single mothers who live in a parent's home and single mothers who have a parent living with them in their own household, it was shown that in 1998, 27% of children in mother-only families had a grandparent living with them in their mother's home, and an additional 12% of children in mother-only families were living in a grandparent's home. Combined, these figures suggest that 39% of children in mother-only families are actually multigenerational households (U.S. Census Bureau, 1998, Tables 4 and 6).

In part as a response to the conflicting findings from the studies of the 1960s and the 1970s compared with studies in the 1990s, we hypothesized that the effect of coresidence might vary depending on the age of the young mother. Coresidence might be a more positive experience when the second-generation mother is younger. Sharing parenting might be accepted by the teenage mother who is uncertain of her own parenting skills and who, still negotiating many of the normative challenges of adolescence, invests less in parenthood. The young mother may welcome the help of her own mother who, by taking on parental responsibility, allows the teenager to engage in adolescent activities (going out with friends, dating, and so forth), without alternative childcare arrangements. In contrast, as young women make the transition toward early adulthood, they may be less tolerant of sharing parenting decisions and of maternal monitoring (Crouter and Head, in Vol. 3 of this *Handbook*).

Indeed, coresidence influenced both mothers' and grandmothers' parenting, depending on the age of the young mother. For families in which the mother was very young (16 years of age and under at first birth), coresiding mothers and grandmothers exhibited more positive and less harsh parenting than those who did not live together. In contrast, for families in which the mother was older at the birth of the first child, coresidence had negative ramifications (Chase-Lansdale et al., 1994).

Shared Caregiving

A feature of multigenerational households is that parenting is often shared by members of two generations. Burton (1990, 1995) described various configurations of support and shared caregiving seen in three-generation families. She made the point that support does not always flow from the older to the younger generations and often involves one generation supporting and caring for other generations.

Other investigations have focused more specifically on how multiple generations share in the care of young children. Four modes of caregiving were identified by Apfel and Seitz (1991) in a study of low-income African American adolescent mothers, their mothers, and their 18-month-old children. Intensive interviews of the women allowed for a characterization of daily household activities and responsibilities, as well as time spent in caregiving and play, by all members of the household. The first mode of joint caregiving involves the replacement of the young mother with the grandmother as the primary caregiver. Contrary to popular opinion, this caregiving mode was relatively rare (10% of the sample). The next mode, labeled *parental supplement* by the authors, was the most common (50% of the sample). Young mothers shared childrearing tasks with their own mothers and other kin. Sharing was sometimes seen by task or by time of day. The third mode involved the grandmother acting as a role model to her daughter. It appeared that the grandmothers were engaged in training their daughter for eventual self-sufficiency. Although low frequency (10% of the sample), this mode of shared caregiving might be expected to result in shorter lengths of coresidence and, ultimately, greater maturity and more adequate parenting on the part of the young mother. Indeed, findings from the Baltimore Multigenerational Family Study tend to support this view in that the young women who did not coreside with their own mothers during their twenties (i.e., those who had been able to move out) exhibited the most positive parenting styles, as did their own mothers. The last mode in the study by Apfel and Seitz was labeled the *supported primary parent*. In these families, the grandmothers provided some caregiving help but were definitely not coparents. Grandmother support existed but was not high. In the Baltimore Multigenerational Family Study, the teenage mothers who coresided with their mothers might best represent these families. This group of teenagers left home very early; even though these young women had contact with their mothers, primary support and caregiving were not typically provided.

Apfel and Seitz (1996) also interviewed their multigenerational families when the child was approximately 6 years old. They reported that family placement among the four groups had changed. The mode in which the young mother (now in her twenties) is the primary support with some but fairly low caregiving was now characteristic of 50% of the families. Role modeling had withered away. Parental replacement was seen in 16% of the families, similar to what was seen earlier. Approximately 30% of families practiced parental supplement (down from 50%). Movement among caregiving arrangements was seen as well. The two arrangements most likely to result in self-sufficiency, or sufficiency in the context of limited but appropriate support from other family members, were the role model and the parental supplement styles. In both cases grandmothers offered help, but did not either "take over" the child (the replacement mode) or ignore the child (the supported primary parent mode).

The authors suggested that either extreme on the shared caregiving and support continuum might be detrimental for the eventual well-being of young mothers vis-à-vis their ability to move toward a primary parenting role. In essence, the two groups in which grandmothers played an important but secondary role in the rearing of the grandchild may have helped balance the young mother's need to emerge as an independent young woman with her need for reliance on others for childcare and support.

Relationship of the Young Mother and Grandmother

The complexity of caregiving roles and responsibilities in multigenerational families may play out in the ways in which young mothers parent and move toward independence. The quality of mother–daughter relationships in the context of multigenerational childrearing might be affected by the ways in which caregiving and living arrangements are managed. Indeed, the quality of these relationships may be the mechanism underlying the effects of coresidence and age on parenting behaviors and child outcomes. However, little is known about the interactions between young mothers and their own mothers because the relatively few investigations to date have focused on interactions with the children of young mothers and the phenomenon of shared caregiving itself.

In the Baltimore Multigenerational Family Study, we assessed the quality of the mother–grandmother relationship based on discussions of current disagreements (as defined by the mother and grandmother). We asked the mother and grandmother each to identify an area in which they disagreed. They were given 5 to 8 minutes to discuss each disagreement. The Scale of Intergenerational Relationship Quality (Wakschlag, Chase-Lansdale, and Brooks-Gunn, 1996; Wakschlag, Pittman, Chase-Lansdale, and Brooks-Gunn, in press) was developed for this sample. It integrates concepts from developmental and family research with those derived from more culturally specific studies of the African American family. Four factors were identified from the items on this scale—emotional closeness (emotional context of the relationship), dyadic positive affect (engaged, animated), grandmother affirmative parenting style (grandmother expresses herself in a firm, positive, and self-confident manner), and mother autonomy (young mother's ability to communicate clearly and to maintain her separateness while maintaining an atmosphere of mutuality). Mother autonomy within the context of the relationship with the grandmother was a strong predictor of mothers' parenting (and neither mother autonomy nor parenting was associated with maternal age). Mothers who had mature, flexible, and autonomous interactions with their own mothers were likely to be emotionally supportive, positive affectively, facilitative of children's puzzle-solving attempts, and authoritative. Surprisingly, emotional closeness and dyadic positive affect were not associated with young mothers' parenting. These findings highlight the role of autonomy for young women who are combining the transition to young adulthood with parenthood. Women who had high scores on autonomy were able to disagree with their mothers while, at the same time, listening to their mothers' point of view. The women with low scores seemed sullen, withdrawn, or uncommunicative with their mothers (Wakschlag et al., 1996, in press).

Autonomy was more tightly linked with parenting behavior in the two living situations that we previously identified as disadvantageous—not living with one's mother while being a teenage mother and coresidence with one's mother while being an older mother. That is, autonomy played more of a protective function in these families vis-à-vis parenting behavior.

These qualities of the mother–daughter relationship played less of a role in the expression of the grandmothers' parenting. However, emotional closeness was higher in families in which the grandmother and mother did not coreside. Perhaps grandmothers' parenting styles are influenced more by previous events and contextual factors (e.g., coresidence; East and Felice 1996; Wakschlag et al., 1996). Alternatively, their parenting may be more linked to other current life stage concerns, such as other caregiving responsibilities, work commitments, male relationships, and other factors (Burton, 1990).

Another research tradition focuses on the possible indirect effects of grandmothers' parenting on children through effects on adolescent mothers' behavior (Crockenberg, 1981; McNair, 1991). Nurturance and responsivity of the grandparent to the young mother have been identified as critical in these two studies. One study reported a more positive effect of grandfather nurturance on teenage parenting behavior than grandmother nurturance (in one of the few studies of primarily European American teenage mothers coresiding with their parents; Oyserman, Radin, and Benn, 1993). In brief, the emotional stances taken by the teenage mother and grandmother may influence the child, especially in terms of emotional relationships and the process of separation and individuation that occurs during the toddler and the early childhood years (Bowlby, 1960; Mahler, Pine, and Bergman, 1975; Sroufe, 1979). A mother who is not emotionally integrated may find it difficult to promote autonomy in her young child. Having a grandmother who may perform the functions of an autonomous and integrated mother may buffer the young child from the less developed emotional functioning of the mother.

These studies are welcome additions to the field. They show the family-oriented approach, sensitivity to reciprocal and indirect effects within the family, and consideration of the links between parenting and other salient aspects of family life. Of particular importance is the focus on individual differences in how family members share childcare and interact with one another. More information is needed on the ways in which families negotiate disagreements and the effects of family conflict on the children.

Impact of Older Sibling Early Childbearing

Family systems approaches to the study of adolescent sexual activity and parenthood have begun to emphasize other influences of family context in addition to the mother–daughter relationship. One line of research extends this approach to include effects of adolescent childbearing on younger siblings in the home. These studies have advanced our understanding in three ways. First, they have documented an association between adolescent childbearing in older siblings and early sexual activity among younger female siblings. Studies conducted in the early 1990s used sibling comparison data to examine this relation in the context of trying to tease apart the effects of family background and socioeconomic disadvantage on adult outcomes of teenage childbearers (Furstenberg, 1991; Geronimus and Korenman, 1992, 1993; Hoffman et al., 1993). Other work has estimated the risk of teenage childbearing for the siblings of adolescent mothers, finding that the sisters of teenage mothers transition to first intercourse and pregnancy at younger ages and experience higher rates of teenage pregnancy compared with the sisters of women who do not bear children in adolescence (Cox, Emans, and Bithoney, 1993; East, 1996, East, Felice, and Morgan, 1993; East and Jacobson, 2001).

The study of sibling effects on early childbearing has also examined differences in attitudes and incidence of problem behavior between the siblings of teen and nonteen childbearers. In a series of studies, East and colleagues (1993, 1996, 2001) found that girls with older, parenting adolescent sisters perceived younger optimal ages for sexual initiation, parenthood, and marriage, reported a greater acceptance of teen and nonmarital childbearing, placed less emphasis on achieving school and career goals, and were more likely to engage in delinquent activities including school truancy, cigarette smoking, and drug and alcohol use (East, 1996; East et al., 1993).

In seeking to identify the processes and mechanisms by which older siblings' sexual activity affects younger sisters, East found that their childbearing primarily affects the behavior of their younger siblings through changes the elders' new status brings to the family system, particularly with regard to changes in parent–child relationships, parenting style, and quality of parenting toward the childbearers and their siblings (East, 1998, 1999). Hao, Hotz, and Jin (2000) showed evidence of parental attempts to regulate younger siblings' childbearing decisions by limiting the amount of financial and social support given to older daughters who have early births. This change in parenting behavior reduces the likelihood of teen births for younger siblings.

Involvement and Impact of Young Fathers

It was once assumed that the male partners of unmarried teenage mothers were weak sources of support and played a limited fathering role, but 1990s work in this area has found significant variability in contact and involvement among this group, particularly in the first few years after a child's birth (Black, Dubowitz, and Starr, 1999; Coley and Chase-Lansdale, 1998, 1999). For example, in a nationally representative survey, Lerman (1993) reported that approximately half of young fathers visited their children weekly, and almost 25% had daily contact. However, the consistency and the quality of long-term relationships between young unmarried partners and between noncustodial fathers and their children tend to decline over time, their link to the household made even more tenuous by limited financial support (Lerman, 1993; Sullivan, 1990, 1993). Contact is less likely to be sustained in unmarried couples who are not cohabitating if the father is a teenager than if he is older (Wilson and Brooks-Gunn, 2001). In the Baltimore Multigenerational Study, we relied on mothers' reports to measure five different constructs of father involvement: financial contributions, frequency of visitation with child, father's provision of childcare, level of parental responsibility undertaken, and closeness of father–child relationship. Strong and close relationships between mother and father, male employment, and paternal grandmother involvement are related to high father financial and emotional involvement (Coley and Chase-Lansdale, 1999; Chase-Lansdale et al., 1999). These findings only begin to address the complexity and fluidity of behavior and relationships between father and child and between father and mother in disadvantaged and young childbearing families.

CONCLUSIONS

The study of adolescent parents has direct relevance to public policy. Indeed, much of the debate about how to structure welfare programs centers on young parents. The reason is that single young mothers are the group of parents most likely to be poor, and to remain poor, for many years. Over one half of all adolescent mothers, and approximately three fourths of all single adolescent mothers, join the welfare rolls in the 4 years after the birth of the child (Bane and Ellwood, 1986; Moore et al., 1993). Teenage mothers also account for a disproportionate amount of the funds spent on welfare, in part because they spend more time on welfare than older mothers do.

This state of affairs and concerns about the difficulty that young mothers have in completing high school and in entering the workforce have resulted in specific policy recommendations being written for them in the Family Support Act of 1988 (Chase-Lansdale and Brooks-Gunn, 1995; Chase-Lansdale and Vinovskis, 1995). Young women who become mothers as teenagers are required to stay in high school in order to receive welfare benefits. The policy may have unintended effects on the family system. For all practical purposes, young women cannot stay in school unless they have child-care and unless someone is supporting them (welfare benefits in most states would not enable young women to set up their own households, given rental prices, and to purchase childcare, given the cost of care; Brooks-Gunn et al., 1995; Cherlin, 1995). This requirement was preserved in the welfare reform act of 1996. Consequently, the Family Support Act implicitly sets up a situation in which the young mother's family in most cases will have to help with childcare as well as household arrangements. Child support by noncustodial fathers of never-married mothers is very low (Furstenberg, 1995; Garfinkel and McLanahan, 1995). The research that we have reviewed suggests that coresidence is not always a positive experience for the young mother, the grandmother, or the child.

Many programs for teenage mothers recognize the need for childcare. School-based services often provide childcare for young mothers. A few of the school-based endeavors have been evaluated (Benasich, Brooks-Gunn, and Clewell, 1992; Clewell et al., 1989). However, not enough school-based childcare services exist for all teenage mothers who have not completed high school. Fewer programs have focused on grandmothers explicitly. Marx, Bailey, and Francis (1988) suggested that many programs focusing on teenagers do provide services to others in the household, or at least recognize the need for such services. No evaluations have been conducted, nor has much attention been placed on the type of services that multigenerational families might need.

Another major thrust of the welfare act of 1988 for women on welfare has to do with the movement of women from welfare toward self-sufficiency or toward less dependency on federal support. These programs, under the JOBS title, offer employment, training, and educational services to mothers of all ages (Wilson et al., 1995). However, several demonstration programs have targeted young mothers, given that they have the most difficulty in making the transition toward work. The Teenage Parent

Demonstration program, the Young Single Women Demonstration Program, Project Redirection, and Project MATCH are exemplars (Aber et al., 1995; Halpern, 1993; Polit, 1989). Most report that intensive job-training programs reduce teenage mothers' dependency on welfare, but only modestly. At the same time, great variability exists vis-à-vis mothers' responses to these programs. For example, many mothers are more likely to enter the workplace if they are first given job training rather than remedial education. Perhaps school-oriented programs are too similar to the arena in which so many young mothers have already failed. Mothers often do not see the payoff in such programs. In contrast, bringing home a paycheck or working in a very low-paying job highlights the importance of further education as a way to increase earning power (Halpern, 1993).

Teenage mother programs also offer childcare referral as well as parenting classes, speaking to the recognition of the need for the former and the lack of experience and skill in the latter. Most have not conducted the developmentally oriented studies needed to demonstrate efficacy. Additionally, most programs offer parenting modules of low intensity; research from early childhood education would suggest that such approaches might not alter parenting behavior directly (Benasich et al., 1992; Bronfenbrenner, 1979; Brooks-Gunn, 1990; Brooks-Gunn, Burchinal, and Lopez, 2001; Gomby, 1999; Ramey et al., 1992; Reichman and McLanahan, 2001). However, they might influence parenting indirectly. Young mothers who enter the workforce may have increased levels of self-efficacy and psychological well-being more generally, which might influence their parenting behavior (Wilson et al., 1995; Zill, Moore, Smith, Stief, and Coiro, 1995). For example, in a follow-up of young mothers who participated in Project Redirection, home environment scores were higher as were children's verbal ability scores, even though few differences in maternal outcomes were found between families who participated in the project and those who did not (Polit, 1989), although these effects were not sustained (Reichman and McLanahan, 2001). Several work–welfare demonstration projects collect information on parenting behavior and actual observations of parent–child interactions to understand what aspects of parenting might be influenced (Duncan and Brooks-Gunn, 2001; Morris et al., 2001; Smith, 1995a, 1995b; Zaslow et al., 1998). These projects are a much–needed blend of developmental approaches to studying teenage mothers and their families and programs developed to help teenage mothers overcome the disadvantages inherent in early single parenthood.

The study of adolescent parenthood has come a long way since Campbell's now-famous quote about life scripts of early childbearers. Not only are researchers stressing variability in outcomes, but they are now also focusing on subgroups of teenage mothers and prospective mothers in order to understand the life courses within specific groups of teenage mothers (Baldwin, 1993; Berlin et al., in press; Hardy et al., 1998).

Some work is considering how outcomes for teenage mothers are linked rather than considering them separately. An example is the work considering school leaving and teenage births simultaneously (Upchurch, 1993). Measures of competency, mental health, and life satisfaction need to be considered over and above the well-studied (and important) outcomes involving school, fertility, marriage, and occupation. However, the range of outcomes studied needs to be broadened.

Work is commencing on intrafamilial differences, as well as the effects of timing of events within families (Geronimus, 1991). The within-family level analyses have, to date, focused on mean comparisons rather than or explanations for different analyses within families. The field is posed to take the intrafamilial methodology to a more process-oriented analysis. A developmental perspective demands that we look at how experiences in different life epochs contribute to an individual's life choices and emotional states. As Elder (1974) demonstrated, experience of events such as parental job loss influences children and adolescents quite differently, which has implications for long-term adaptation.

Timing of events must be studied more explicitly. Spacing of children made a difference in the life course trajectories of the teenage mothers in the Baltimore Study of Teenage Motherhood. It also made a difference in how the firstborn children fared: Births while the firstborn was still a preschooler had negative effects, whereas births later on did not. The divorce literature suggests differential effects on children and adolescents, depending on the timing of the divorce and the type of subsequent transition experienced by the family (Booth and Dunn, 1995; Chase-Lansdale, Cherlin, and Kiernan, 1995; Chase-Lansdale and Hetherington, 1990; Hetherington and Stanley-Hagan in Vol. 3 of this *Handbook*; Moore and Chase-Lansdale, 2001).

Intergenerational approaches are emerging as reviewed in this chapter (Hardy et al., 1997, 1998). Looking at mothers, grandmothers, and other adult kin allows for a better understanding as to how families provide a context in which teenage childbearing is encouraged or discouraged.

A few scholars have considered cohort effects. Given changes in the demographics of teenage parenthood (in particular the rise in nonmarital childbearing and, to a lesser extent, the rise in number of teenage mothers completing high school/general equivalency diploma), it is important to place each study in its historical context. For example, the comparison of teenage mothers in the Baltimore Study with their firstborn girls who also became teenage mothers illustrates a few differences that are cohort driven. These differences have vast implications for the life courses of these two cohorts (with mostly negative implications for the current generation of teenage mothers; Furstenberg et al., 1992).

A limitation of current research is that race and ethnicity are treated quite differently across studies, making it difficult to make cross-study comparisons for race and ethnicity. A few studies look at the different patterns of associations for ethnic groups separately. Clearly, given different housing, immigration, job patterns, as well as other pervasive effects of discrimination, the ways in which family support or schooling influence the outcomes of teenage mothers on their children might differ for European Americans, African Americans, and Latin Americans.

The adolescent experience is missing from much of the work. We need to look at the role of arousal and the difficulty youth have in managing those feelings. We need to understand how youth negotiate sexual decisions between boys and girls. Little is known about whether, and in what ways, teenage mothers manage autonomy and identity development differently from teenagers who are not mothers.

Research designs often do not focus on change. More attention must be paid to looking at change in different circumstances that each influence family members (teenage mother, teenage father, child, grandmother). In the Baltimore study, moving off welfare after the preschool years reduced the likelihood of school failure and early sexuality. To conduct longitudinal, process-oriented studies, attention must be paid to neighborhood, school, peer, family, and individual processes (Bronfenbrenner and Weiss, 1983).

ACKNOWLEDGMENTS

The writing of this chapter was supported by the National Institute of Child Health and Human Development Research Network on Children and Family Well-Being as well as the March of Dimes Foundation, the W. T. Grant Foundation, and the National Institute of Mental Health (NIMH) Administration for Children and Families (ACF) Consortium on Mental Health in Young Children. We are grateful for the insights of the National Institute of Mental Health Family Research Consortium. We thank Lindsay Chase-Lansdale for her insight and support. Work by Magdalena Hernandez, Christina Borberly, and Uchenna Evans on manuscript preparation is greatly appreciated.

REFERENCES

Aber, J. L., Brooks-Gunn, J., and Maynard, R. (1995). Effects of welfare reform on teenage parents and their children. *The future of children: Critical issues for children and youth, 5*, 53–71.

Abernathy, V. (1973). Social network and response to the maternal role. *International Journal of Sociology of the Family, 3*, 86–96.

Alan Guttmacher Institute (1994). *Sex and America's teenagers*. New York: Alan Guttmacher Institute.

Apfel, N. H., and Seitz, V. (1991). Four models of adolescent mother–grandmother relationships in Black inner-city families. *Family Relations, 40*, 421–429.

Apfel, N. H., and Seitz, V. (1996). African-American mothers, their families, and their daughters: A longitudinal perspective over 12 years. In B. J. Leadbeater and N. Way (Eds.), *Urban adolescent girls: Resisting stereotypes* (pp. 149–172). New York: New York University Press.

Astone, N. M. (1993). Are adolescent mothers just single mothers? *Journal of Research on Adolescence, 3*, 353–373.

Bachrach, C. A., and Carver, K. (1992, May). *Outcomes of early childbearing: An appraisal of recent evidence*. Summary of a conference convened by the National Institute of Child Health and Development, Bethesda, MD.

Bachrach, C. A., Clogg, C. C., and Carver, K. (1993). Outcomes of early childbearing: Summary of a conference. *Journal of Research on Adolescence, 3*, 337–349.

Baldwin, W. (1993). The consequences of early childbearing: A perspective. *Journal of Research on Adolescence, 3*, 349–353.

Baldwin, W., and Cain, V. S. (1980). The children of teenage parents. *Family Planning Perspectives, 12*, 34–43.

Ballou, J. W. (1978). *The psychology of pregnancy: Reconciliation and resolution*. Lexington, MA: Heath.

Bane, M. J., and Ellwood, D. T. (1986). Slipping into and out of poverty: The dynamics of spells. *Journal of Human Resources, 21*, 1–23.

Barglow, P., Bornstein, M., Exum, D. B., Wright, M. K., and Visotsky, H. M. (1968). Some psychiatric aspects of illegitimate pregnancy in early adolescence. *American Journal of Orthopsychiatry, 38*, 672–678.

Baumrind, D. (1989). Rearing competent children. In W. Damon (Ed.), *Child development today and tomorrow* (pp. 349–378). San Francisco: Jossey-Bass.

Baumrind, D. (1973). The development of instrumental competence through socialization. In A. Pick (Ed.), *Minnesota symposium on child psychology* (Vol. 7). Minneapolis: University of Minnesota Press.

Baydar, N., and Brooks-Gunn, J. (1991). Effects of maternal employment and childcare arrangements on preschoolers' cognitive and behavioral outcomes: Evidence from the children of the National Longitudinal Survey of Youth. *Developmental Psychology, 27*, 932–945.

Baydar, N., and Brooks-Gunn, J. (1998). Profiles of grandmothers who help care for their grandchildren in the United States. *Family Relations, 47*, 385–393.

Baydar, N., and Brooks-Gunn, J., and Furstenberg, F. F., Jr. (1993). Early warning signs of functional illiteracy: Predictors in childhood and adolescence. *Child Development, 64*, 815–829.

Baydar, N., Brooks-Gunn, J., and Senior, A. M. (1995). *How do living arrangements affect the development of Black infants?* Unpublished manuscript.

Bell, R. Q. (1968). A reinterpretation of the direction of effects in studies of socialization. *Psychological Review, 75*, 81–95.

Belsky, J. (1984). The determinants of parenting: A process model. *Child Development, 55*, 83–96.

Benasich, A. A., and Brooks-Gunn, J. (1996). Maternal attitudes and knowledge of childrearing: Associations with family and child outcomes. *Child Development, 67*, 1186–1205.

Benasich, A. A., Brooks-Gunn, J., and Clewell, B. C. (1992). How do mothers benefit from early intervention programs? *Journal of Applied Developmental Psychology, 13*, 311–362.

Benn, R., and Saltz, E. (1989, April). *The effects of grandmother support on teen parenting and infant attachment patterns within the family*. Paper presented at the meeting of the Society for Research in Child Development, Kansas City, MO.

Bennett, N. G., Bloom, D. E., and Miller, C. K. (1995). The influence of nonmarital childbearing on the formation of first marriages. *Demography, 32*, 47–62.

Berlin, L. J., Brady-Smith, C., and Brooks-Gunn, J. (in press). Links between childbearing age and observed maternal behaviors with 14-month-olds in the Early Head Start Research and Evaluation Project. *Infant Mental Health Journal*.

Besharov, D., and Gardiner, K. (1997). Trends in teen sexual behavior. *Children and Youth Services Review, 19*, 341–367.

Black, M. M., Dubowitz, H., and Starr, R. H., Jr. (1999). African American fathers in low income, urban families: Development, behavior, and home environment of their three-year-old children. *Child Development, 70*, 967–879.

Blos, P. (1967). The second individuation process. In P. Blos (Ed.), *The adolescent passage: Developmental issues at adolescence* (pp. 141–170). New York: International Universities Press.

Booth, A., and Dunn, J. (Eds.). (1994). *Stepfamilies: Who benefits? Who does not?* Hillsdale, NJ: Lawrence Erlbaum Associates.

Bornstein, M. H., and Krasnegor, N. E. (Eds.). (1989). *Stability and continuity in mental development: Behavioral and biological perspectives*. Hillsdale, NJ: Lawrence Erlbaum Associates.

Bowlby, J. (1960). Separation anxiety: A critical review of the literature. *Child Psychology and Psychiatry, 1*, 251–269.

Boyce, T., Schaefer, C., and Uitti, C. (1985). Permanence and change: Psychosocial factors in the outcome of adolescent pregnancy. *Social Science Medicine, 21*, 1279–1287.

Boyd-Franklin, N. (1989). *Black families in therapy: A multisystems approach*. New York: Guilford.

Brewster, K. L., Billy, J. O. G., and Grady, W. R. (1993). Social context and adolescent behavior: The impact of community on the transition to sexual activity. *Social Forces, 71*, 713–740.

Brien, M. J., and Willis, R. J. (1997). Costs and consequences for the fathers. In R. Maynard (Ed.), *Kids having kids: Economic costs and social consequences of teen pregnancy* (pp. 95–144). Washington, DC: Urban Institute Press.

Broman, S. H. (1981). Longterm development of children born to teenagers. In K. Scott, T. Field, and E. Robertson (Eds.), *Teenage parents and their offspring* (pp. 195–224). New York: Grune and Stratton.

Bronars, S. G., and Grogger, J. (1994). The economic consequences of unwed motherhood: Using twin births as a natural experiment. *The American Economic Review, 84,* 1141–1156.

Bronfenbrenner, U. (1979). *The ecology of human development: Experiments by nature and design.* Cambridge, MA: Harvard University Press.

Bronfenbrenner, U., and Weiss, H. (1983). Beyond policies without people: An ecological perspective on child and family policy. In E. F. Zigler, S. L. Kagan, and E. Klugman (Eds.), *Children, families, and government: Perspectives on American social policy* (pp. 393–414). Cambridge, England: Cambridge University Press.

Brooks-Gunn, J. (1990). Promoting healthy development in young children: What educational interventions work? In D. E. Rogers and E. Ginzberg (Eds.), *Improving the life chances of children at risk* (pp. 125–145). Boulder, CO: Westview.

Brooks-Gunn, J. (1991). How stressful is the transition to adolescence in girls? In M. E. Colten and S. Gore (Eds.), *Adolescent stress: Causes and consequences* (pp. 131–149). Hawthorne, NY: Aldine de Gruyter.

Brooks-Gunn, J. (1994). Research on step-parenting families: Integrating discipline approaches and informing policy. In A. Booth and J. Dunn (Eds.), *Stepfamilies: Who benefits? Who does not?* Hillsdale, NJ: Lawrence Erlbaum Associates.

Brooks-Gunn, J. (1995a). Children and families in communities: Risk and intervention in the Bronfenbrenner tradition. In P. Moen, G. H. Elder, and K. Lusher (Eds.), *Examining lives in context: Perspective on the ecology of human development* (pp. 467–519). Washington DC: American Psychological Association.

Brooks-Gunn, J. (1995b). Opportunities for change: Effects of intervention programs on mothers and children. In P. L. Chase-Lansdale and J. Brooks-Gunn (Eds.), *Escape from poverty: What makes a difference for children?* New York: Cambridge University Press.

Brooks-Gunn, J., Burchinal, M., and Lopez, M. (2001). *Enhancing the cognitive and social development of young children via parent education in the Comprehensive Child Development Program.* Manuscript submitted for publication.

Brooks-Gunn, J., Berlin, L. J., Leventhal, T., and Fuligni, A. (2000). Depending on the kindness of strangers: Current national data initiatives and developmental research. [Special Issue on "New Directions for Child Development in the Twenty-First Century"]. *Child Development, 71,* 257–267.

Brooks-Gunn, J., and Chase-Lansdale, P. L. (1991). Children having children: Effects on the family system. *Pediatric Annals, 20,* 467–481.

Brooks-Gunn, J., and Duncan, G. J. (1997). The effects of poverty on children. *Future of Children, 7*(2), 55–71.

Brooks-Gunn, J., Duncan, G. J., and Aber, J. L. (Eds.). (1997). *Neighborhood poverty: Context and consequences for children.* (Volume 1). *Policy implications in studying neighborhoods* (Volume 2). New York: Russell Sage Foundation Press.

Brooks-Gunn, J., and Duncan, G. J., Klebanov, P. K., and Sealand, N. (1993). Do neighborhoods influence child and adolescent development? *American Journal of Sociology, 99,* 353–395.

Brooks-Gunn, J., and Furstenberg, F. F., Jr. (1986a). Antecedents and consequences of parenting: The case of adolescent motherhood. In A. Fogel and G. Melson (Eds.), *Origins of nurturance: Developmental, biological and cultural perspectives on caregiving* (pp. 233–258). Hillsdale, NJ: Lawrence Erlbaum Associates.

Brooks-Gunn, J., and Furstenberg, F. F., Jr. (1986b). The children of adolescent mothers: physical, academic and psychological outcomes. *Developmental Review, 6,* 224–251.

Brooks-Gunn, J., and Furstenberg, F. F., Jr. (1987). Continuity and change in the context of poverty: Adolescent mothers and their children. In J. J. Gallagher and C. T. Ramey (Eds.), *The malleability of children* (pp. 171–188). Baltimore: Brookes.

Brooks-Gunn, J., and Furstenberg, F. F., Jr. (1989). Adolescent sexual behavior. *American Psychologist, 44,* 249–257.

Brooks-Gunn, J., and Furstenberg, F. F., Jr. (1990). Coming of age in the era of AIDS: Sexual and contraceptive decisions. *Milbank Quarterly, 68,* 59–84.

Brooks-Gunn, J., Guo, G., and Furstenberg, F. F., Jr. (1993). Who drops out of and who continues beyond high school? A 20-year follow-up of Black urban youth. *Journal of Research on Adolescence, 3,* 271–294.

Brooks-Gunn, J., Klebanov, P. K., and Duncan, G. (1996). Ethnic differences in children's intelligence test scores: Role of economic deprivation, home environment, and maternal characteristics. *Child Development, 67,* 396–408.

Brooks-Gunn, J., Klebanov, P. K., and Liaw, F. (1994). The learning, physical and emotional enviornment of the home in the context of poverty: The infant health and development program. *Children and Youth Services Review, 17,* 251–276.

Brooks-Gunn, J., Klebanov, P. K., Liaw, F., and Duncan, G. (1995). Toward an understanding of the effects of poverty upon children. In H. E. Fitzgerald, B. M. Leister, and B. Zuckerman (Eds.), *Children of poverty: Research, health care, and policy issues.* New York: Garland.

Brooks-Gunn, J., and Lewis, M. (1984). Maternal responsivity in interactions with handicapped infants. *Child Development, 55,* 782–793.

Brooks-Gunn, J., and Paikoff, R. L. (1993). "Sex is a gamble, kissing is a game": Adolescent sexuality, contraception, and pregnancy. In S. Millstein, A. C. Peterson, and E. O. Nightingale (Eds.), *Promoting the health of adolescents: New directions for the twenty-first century* (pp.180–208). New York: Oxford University Press.

Brooks-Gunn, J., and Peterson, A. C. (1991). Studying the emergence of depression and depressive symptoms during adolescence. *Journal of Youth and Adolescence, 20,* 115–119.

Brooks-Gunn, J., Phelps, E., and Elder, G. H., Jr. (1991). Studying lives through time: Secondary data analysis in developmental psychology. *Developmental Psychology, 27*, 899–910.

Brooks-Gunn, J., and Zahaykevich, M. (1989). Parent–daughter relationships in early adolescence: A developmental perspective. In K. Kreppner and R. M. Lerner (Eds.), *Family systems and life-span development* (pp. 223–246). Hillsdale, NJ: Lawrence Erlbaum Associates.

Brown, B. (2000). *Trends in the well-being of America's children and youth* (4th ed.). Washington, DC: U.S. Department of Health and Human Services, Office of the Assistant Secretary for Planning and Evaluation.

Brunnquell, D., Crichton, L., and Egeland, B. (1981). Maternal personality and attitude in disturbances of childrearing. *American Journal of Orthopsychiatry, 51*, 680–691.

Bryson, K., and Casper, L. M. (1998). Household and family characteristics, Current Population Reports, Series P-20: Population Characteristics, No. 509, Apr. 1998. U.S. Bureau of the Census: Washington, D.C.

Burton, L. M. (1990). Teenage childbearing as an alternative life-course strategy in multigeneration Black families. *Human Nature, 1*, 123–143.

Burton, L. M. (1995). Intergenerational patterns of providing care in African-American families with teenage childbearers: Emergent patterns in an ethnographic study. In K.W. Schaie, V. L. Bengtson, and L. M. Burton (Eds.), *Intergenerational issues in aging.* New York: Springer.

Burton, L. M. (1996). Age norms, the timing of family role transitions, and intergenerational caregiving among aging African-American women. *The Gerontologist, 36*, 199–208.

Burton, L. M., and Bengston, V. L. (1985). Black grandmothers: Issues of time and continuity of roles. In V. L. Bengston and J. Robertson (Eds.), *Grandparenthood* (pp. 61–77). Beverly Hills, CA: Sage.

Burton, L. M., and Dilworth-Anderson, P. (1991). The intergenerational family roles of aged Black Americans. *Marriage and Family Review, 16*, 311–330.

Caldwell, B. M., and Bradley, R. H. (1984). *Home observation for measurement of the environment.* Little Rock, AR: Authors.

Carter, S. L., Osofsky, J. D., and Hann, D. M. (1991). Speaking for the baby: A therapeutic intervention with adolescent mothers and their infants. *Infant Mental Health Journal, 12*, 291–301.

Case, R. (1985). *Intellectual development: Birth to adulthood.* New York: Academic.

Caspi, A., and Elder, G. (1988). Emergent family patterns: The intergenerational construction of problem behavior and relationships. In R. Hinde and J. Stevenson-Hinde (Eds.), *Relationships within the family: Mutual influences* (pp. 218–240). Oxford, England: Clarendon.

Cervera, N. (1993). Decision making for pregnant adolescents: Applying reasoned action theory to research and treatment. *Families in Society, 74*, 355–365.

Chase-Lansdale, P. L., and Brooks-Gunn, J. (1994). Correlates of adolescent pregnancy. In C. B. Fisher and R. M. Lerner (Eds.), *Applied developmental psychology*, New York: McGraw-Hill.

Chase-Lansdale, P. L., and Brooks-Gunn, J. (Eds.). (1995). *Escape from poverty: What makes a difference for children?* New York: Cambridge University Press.

Chase-Lansdale, P. L., Brooks-Gunn, J., and Paikoff, R. L. (1991). Research and programs for adolescent mothers: Missing links and future promises. *Family Relations, 40*, 396–404.

Chase-Lansdale, P. L., Brooks-Gunn, J., and Zamsky, E. S. (1994). Young African-American multigenerational families in poverty: Quality of mothering and grandmothering. *Child Development, 65*, 373–393.

Chase-Lansdale, P. L., Cherlin, A. J., and Kiernan, K. E. (1995). The long-term effects of parental divorce on the mental health of young adults: A developmental perspective. *Child Development, 66*, 1614–1634.

Chase-Lansdale, P. L., Gordon, R. A., Coley, R. L., Wakschlag, L., and Brooks-Gunn, J. (1999). Young African American multigenerational families in poverty: The contexts, exchanges and processes of their lives. In E. M. Hetherington (Ed.), *Coping with divorce, single parenting and remarriage: A risk and resiliency perspective.* Mahwah, NJ: Lawrence Erlbaum Associates.

Chase-Lansdale, P. L., and Hetherington, E. M. (1990). The impact of divorce on life-span development: Short- and long-term effects. In P. B. Baltes, D. L. Featherman, and R. M. Lerner (Eds.), *Life span development and behavior* (Vol. 10, pp. 107–151). Hillsdale, NJ: Lawrence Erlbaum Associates.

Chase-Lansdale, P. L., Mott, F. L., Brooks-Gunn, J., and Phillips, D. (1991). Children of the NLSY: A unique research opportunity. *Developmental Psychology, 27*, 918–931.

Chase-Lansdale, P. L., and Vinovskis, M. A. (1992). Adolescent pregnancy and child support. In R. Wollons (Ed.), *Children at risk in America: History, concept, and public policy* (pp. 202–229). Albany: State University of New York Press.

Chase-Lansdale, P. L., and Vinovskis, M. A. (1995). Whose responsibility? An historical analysis of the changing roles of mothers, fathers, and society. In P. L. Chase-Lansdale and J. Brooks-Gunn (Eds.), *Escape from poverty: What makes a difference for children?* New York: Cambridge University Press.

Chase-Lansdale, P. L., Wakschlag, L. S., and Brooks-Gunn, J. (1995). A psychological perspective on the development of caring in children and youth: The role of the family. *Journal of Adolescence, 18*, 515–556.

Cherlin, A. J. (1995). Childcare for poor children: Policy issues. In P. L. Chase-Lansdale and J. Brooks-Gunn (Eds.), *Escape from poverty: What makes a difference for children?* New York: Cambridge University Press.

Cherlin, A. J., Furstenberg, F. F., Chase-Lansdale, P. L., Kiernan, K. E., Robins, P. K., Morrison, D. R., and Teitler, J. O. (1991). Longitudinal studies of effects of divorce on children in Great Britain and the United States. *Science, 252*, 1386–1389.

Cherlin, A. C., Kiernan, K. E., and Chase-Lansdale, P. L. (1995). Parental divorce in childhood and demographic outcomes in young adulthood. *Demography, 32*, 299–318.

Clewell, B. C., Brooks-Gunn, J., and Benasich, A. A. (1989). Evaluating child-relating outcomes of teenage parenting programs. *Family Relations, 38*, 201–209.

Cohen, J. B., and Lazarus, R. S. (1977). *Social Support Questionnaire*. Berkeley: University of California.

Coley, R. L. and Chase-Lansdale, P. L. (1998). Adolescent pregnancy and parenthood: Recent evidence and future directions. *American Psychologist, 53*, 152–166.

Coley, R. L., and Chase-Lansdale, P. L. (1999). Stability and change in paternal involvement among urban African American fathers. *Journal of Family Psychology, 13*, 416–435.

Coll, C. G., Vohr, B. R., Hoffman, J., and Oh, W. (1986). Maternal and environmental factors affecting developmental outcomes of infants of adolescent mothers. *Developmental and Behavioral Pediatrics, 7*, 230–236.

Colletta, N. D., Hadler, S., and Gregg, C. H. (1981). How adolescents cope with the problems of early motherhood. *Adolescence, 63*, 499–512.

Cowan, C. P., and Cowan, P. A. (1988). Who does what when partners become parents: Implications for men, women, and marriage. *Marriage and Family Review, 12*, 105–131.

Cowan, C. P., and Cowan, P. A. (1992). *When partners become parents: The big life change for couples*. New York: Basic Books.

Cox, J., Emans, S. J., and Bithoney, W. (1993). Sisters of teen mothers: Increased risk for adolescent parenthood. *Adolescent and Pediatric Gynecology, 6*, 138–142.

Crane, J. (1991). The epidemic theory of ghettos and neighborhood effects on dropping out and teenage childbearing. *American Journal of Sociology, 96*, 1226–1259.

Crnic, K. A., Greenberg, M. T., Ragozin, A. S., Robinson, N. M., and Basham, R. B. (1983). Effects of stress and social support on mothers and premature and full term infants. *Child Development, 54*, 209–217.

Crockenberg, S. (1981). Infant irritability responsiveness, and social support influences on the security of infant–mother attachment. *Child Development, 52*, 857–865.

Crockenberg, S. (1987). Predictors and correlates of anger toward and punitive control of toddlers by adolescent mothers. *Child Development, 58*, 964–975.

Culp, R. E., Appelbaum, M. I., Osofsky, J. D., and Levy, J. A. (1988). Adolescent and older mothers: Comparison between prenatal maternal variables and newborn interaction measures. *Infant Behavior and Development, 11*, 353–362.

Culp, R. E., Culp, A. M., Osofsky, J. D., and Osofsky, H. J. (1991). Adolescent and toddler mothers' interaction patterns with their six-month-old infants. *Journal of Adolescence, 14*, 195–200.

Curtin, S. C., and Martin, J. A. (2000). Births: Preliminary data for 1999. In *National vital statistics reports* (Vol. 48, No. 14). Hyattsville, MD: National Center for Health Statistics.

Deutsch, F. M., Ruble, D. N., Fleming, A., Brooks-Gunn, J., and Stangor, C. (1988). Information-seeking and self-definition during the transition to motherhood. *Journal of Personality and Social Psychology, 55*, 420–431.

Doucette-Gates, A., Brooks-Gunn, J., and Chase-Lansdale, P. L. (1998). The role of bias and equivalence in the study of race, class, and ethnicity. In V. McLoyd and L. Steinberg (Eds.), *Studying Minority Adolescence* (pp. 211–236). Hillsdale, NJ: Lawrence Erlbaum Associates.

Downey, G., and Coyne, J. C. (1990). Children of depressed parents: An integrative review. *Psychological Bulletin, 108*, 50–76.

Duncan, G. J., and Brooks-Gunn, J. (1997). Income effects across the life span: Integration and interpretation. In G. J. Duncan and J. Brooks-Gunn (Eds.) *Consequences of growing up poor*. (pp. 596–610). New York: Russell Sage Foundation Press.

Duncan, G. J., and Brooks-Gunn, J. (2001). Family poverty, welfare reform, and child development. *Child Development, 71*, 188–196.

Duncan, G. J., Brooks-Gunn, J., and Klebanov, P. K. (1994). Economic deprivation and early-childhood development. *Child Development, 65*, 296–318.

Duncan, G. J., Yeung, W. J., Brooks-Gunn, J., and Smith, J. R. (1998). How much does childhood poverty affect the life chances of children? *American Sociological Review, 63*, 406–423.

Dyer, E. D. (1963). Parenthood as crisis: A restudy. *Marriage and Family Living, 25*, 196–201.

East, P. L. (1996). The younger sisters of childbearing adolescents: Their attitudes, expectations, and behaviors. *Child Development, 67*, 267–282.

East, P. L. (1998). Racial and ethnic differences in girls' sexual, marital, and birth expectations. *Journal of Marriage and the Family, 60*, 150–162.

East, P. L. (1999). The first teenage pregnancy in the family: Does it affect mothers' parenting, attitudes, or mother–adolescent communication? *Journal of Marriage and the Family, 61*, 306–319.

East, P. L., and Felice, M. E. (1996). *Adolescent pregnancy and parenting: Findings from a racially diverse sample*. Mahwah, NJ: Lawrence Erlbaum Associates.

East, P. L., Felice, M. E., and Morgan, M. C. (1993). Sisters' and girlfriends' sexual and childbearing behavior: Effects on early adolescent girls' sexual outcomes. *Journal of Marriage and the Family, 55*, 953–963.

East, P. L., and Jacobson, L. J. (2001). The younger siblings of teenage mothers: A follow-up of their pregnancy risk. *Developmental Psychology, 37*, 254–264.

Egeland, B., Jacobvitz, D., and Sroufe, L. A. (1988). Breaking the cycle of abuse. *Child Development, 59*, 1080–1088.

Elder, G. H. (1974). *Children of the great depression: Social change in life experience.* Chicago: University of Chicago Press.

Elder, G. H. (1977). *Children of the great depression.* Chicago: University of Chicago Press.

Emery, R. E. (1982). Interparental conflict and the children of discord and divorce. *Psychological Bulletin, 92*, 310–330.

Featherman, D. L., and Spencer, K. I. (1988). Class and the socialization of children: Constancy, change or irrelevance? In E. M. Hetherington, R. M. Lerner, and M. Perlmutter (Eds.), *Child development in life-span perspective* (pp. 67–90). Hillsdale, NJ: Lawrence Erlbaum Associates.

Feldman, S. S., and Nash, S. C. (1985). Antecedents of early parenting. In A. Fogel and G. F. Melson (Eds.), *Origins of nurturance: Developmental, biological and cultural perspectives on caregiving* (pp. 209–232). Hillsdale, NJ: Lawrence Erlbaum Associates.

Field, T. (1980). Interactions of high risk infants: Quantitative and qualitative differences. In D. B. Sawin, R. C. Hawkins, L. D. Walker, and J. H. Penticull (Eds.), *The exceptional infant* (Vol. 4, pp. 120–143). New York: Brunner/Mazel.

Field, T. (1981). Infant arousal, attention, and affect during early interactions. In L. Lipsitt and C. K. Rovee-Collier (Eds.), *Advances in infancy research* (Vol. 1, pp. 58–100). Norwood, NJ: Ablex.

Field, T. (1982). Affective displays of high-risk infants during early interactions. In T. M. Field and A. Fogel (Eds.), *Emotion and early interactions* (pp. 101–125). Hillsdale, NJ: Lawrence Erlbaum Associates.

Field, T. M., Healy, B., Goldstein, S., and Guthertz, M. (1990). Behavior–state matching and synchrony in mother–infant interactions of non-depressed versus depressed dyads. *Developmental Psychology, 26*, 7–14.

Field, T. M., and Widmayer, S. M. (1981). Mother–infant interaction among lower SES Black, Cuban, Puerto Rican, and South American immigrants. In T. M. Field, A. M. Sostek, P. Vietze, and P. H. Liederman (Eds.), *Culture and early interactions* (pp. 41–62). Hillsdale, NJ: Lawrence Erlbaum Associates.

Finkel, M. L. (1995). Focus on adolescent pregnancy and childbearing: A bit of history and implications for the 21st century. *Bulletin of the New York Academy of Medicine, 72*, 500–511.

Forste, R., and Tienda, M. (1992). Race and ethnic variation in the schooling consequences of female adolescent sexual activity. *Social Science Quarterly, 73*, 12–30.

Frodi, A. (1983). Attachment behavior and sociability with strangers in premature and full-term infants. *Infants Mental Health Journal, 4*, 13–22.

Frost, J. J., and Oslak, S. (1999). Teenagers' pregnancy intentions and decisions: A study of young women in California choosing to give birth (Occasional Report No. 2). New York: The Alan Guttmacher Institute.

Fuller-Thomson, E., Minkler, M., and Driver, D. (1997). A profile of grandparents raising grandchildren in the United States. *The Gerontologist, 37*, 406–411.

Furstenberg, F. F., Jr. (1976). *Unplanned parenthood: The social consequences of teenage childbearing.* New York: Free Press.

Furstenberg, F. F., Jr. (1991). As the pendulum swings: Teenage childbearing and social concern. *Family Relations, 40*, 127–138.

Furstenberg, F. F., Jr. (1995). Dealing with dads: The changing roles of fathers. In P. L. Chase-Lansdale and J. Brooks-Gunn (Eds.), *Escape from Poverty: What makes a difference for children?* New York: Cambridge University Press.

Furstenberg, F. F., Jr., Brooks-Gunn, J., and Chase-Lansdale, P. L. (1989). Adolescent fertility and public policy. *American Psychologist, 44*, 313–320.

Furstenberg, F. F., Jr., Brooks-Gunn, J., and Morgan, P. (1987). *Adolescent mothers in later life.* New York: Cambridge University Press.

Furstenberg, F. F., and Harris, K. M. (1993). When and why fathers matter: Impacts of father involvement on the children of adolescent mothers. In R. I. Lerman and T. J. Ooms (Eds.), *Young unwed fathers: Changing roles and emerging policies* (pp. 117–183). Philadelphia: Temple University Press.

Furstenberg, F. F., Hughes, M. E., and Brooks-Gunn, J. (1992). The next generation: Children of teenage mothers grow up. In M. K. Rosenheim and M. F. Testa (Eds.), *Early parenthood* (pp. 113–135). New Brunswick, NJ: Rutgers University Press.

Furstenberg, F. F., Levine, J. A., and Brooks-Gunn, J. (1990). The daughters of teenage mothers: Patterns of early childbearing in two generations. *Family Planning Perspectives, 22*, 54–61.

Garcia Coll, C. T. (1989). The consequences of teenage childbearing in traditional Puerto Rican culture. In J. K. Nuent, B. Lester, and T. B. Brazelton (Eds.), *The cultural context of infancy: Vol. 1. Biology, culture, and infant development* (pp. 111–132). Norwood, NJ: Ablex.

Garfinkel, I., and McLanahan, S. S. (1995). The effects of child support reform on child well-being. In P. L. Chase-Lansdale and J. Brooks-Gunn (Eds.), *Escape from poverty: What makes a difference for poor children?* New York: Cambridge University Press.

Geronimus, A. (1987). On teenage childbearing and neonatal morality in the United States. *Population and Development Review, 13,* 245–280.

Geronimus, A. (1991). Teenage childbearing and social and reproductive disadvantage: The evolution of complex questions and the demise of simple answers. *Family Relations, 40,* 463–471.

Geronimus, A. T., and Bound, J. (1990). Black/White differences in women's reproductive-related health status: Evidence from vital statistics. *Demography, 27,* 457–466.

Geronimus, A., and Korenman, S. (1992). The socioeconomic consequences of teen childbearing reconsidered. *Quarterly Journal of Economics, 107,* 1187–1214.

Geronimus, A., and Korenman, S. (1993). The costs of teenage childbearing: Evidence and interpretation. *Demography, 30,* 281–290.

Glei, D. (1999). Measuring contraceptive use patterns among teenage and adult women. *Family Planning Perspectives, 31,* 73–80.

Gohel, M, Diamond, J. J., and Chambers, C. V. (1997). Attitudes toward sexual responsibility and parenting: An exploratory study of young urban males. *Family Planning Perspectives, 29,* 280–283.

Goldberg, W. A., and Easterbrooks, M. A. (1984). Toddler development in the family. Impact of father involvement and parenting characteristics. *Child Development, 55,* 740–752.

Gomby, D. S. (1999). Understanding evaluations of home visitation programs. *The future of children, 9*(1), 27–43.

Graber, J. A., and Brooks-Gunn, J. (1999). "Sometimes I think that you don't like me": How mothers and daughters negotiate the transition into adolescence. In M. Cox and J. Brooks-Gunn (Eds.), *Conflict and cohesion in families: Causes and consequences* (pp. 207–242). Mahwah, NJ: Lawrence Erlbaum Associates.

Grogger, J., and Bronars, S. (1993). The socioeconomic consequences of teenage childbearing: Findings from a natural experiment. *Family Planning Perspectives, 25,* 156–161, 174.

Grossman, F. K., Eichler, L. S., Winickoff, S. A., Anzalone, M. K., Gofseyeff, M. H., and Sargent, S. P. (1980). *Pregnancy, birth, and parenthood.* San Francisco: Jossey-Bass.

Guo, G., Brooks-Gunn, J. and Harris, K. M. (1996). Parent's labor-force attachment and grade retention among urban black children. *Sociology of Education, 69,* 217–236.

Gutierrez, J., and Sameroff, A. (1990). Determinants of complexity in Mexican-American and Anglo-American mother's conceptions of child-development. *Child Development, 61,* 384–394.

Hagestad, G. O. (1986). Dimensions of time and the family. *American Behavioral Scientist, 29,* 679–694.

Halpern, R. (1993). Poverty and infant development. In C. Zeanah (Ed.), *Handbook of infant mental health* (pp. 73–86). New York: Guilford.

Hamburg, B. A. (1980). Developmental issues in school-age pregnancy. In E. Purcell (Ed.), *Aspects of psychiatric problems of childhood and adolescence* (pp. 299–325). New York: Macy Foundation.

Hamburg, B. A. (1986). Subsets of adolescent mothers: Developmental, biomedical, and psychosocial issues. In J. B. Lancaster and B. A. Hamburg (Eds.), *School-age pregnancy and parenthood: Biosocial dimensions* (pp. 115–145). New York: Aldine de Gruyter.

Hann, D. M., Castino, R. J., Jarosinski, J., and Britton, H. (1991, April). Relating mother–toddler negotiation patterns to infant attachment and maternal depression with an adolescent mother sample. In J. D. Osofsky and L. Hubbs-Tait (Chairs), *Consequences of adolescent parenting: Predicting behavior problems in toddlers and preschoolers.* Symposium conducted at the biennial meeting of the Society for Research in Child Development, Seattle, WA.

Hann, D. M., Osofsky, J. D., Stringer, S. S., and Carter, S. S. (1988, April). *Affective contributions of adolescent mothers and infants to the quality of attachment.* Paper presented at the International Conference on Infant Studies, Washington, DC.

Hann, D. M., Robinson, J. L., Osofsky, J. D., and Little, C. (1991, April). *Emotional availability in two caregiving environments: Low-risk adult mothers and socially at-risk adolescent mothers.* Paper presented at the biennial meeting of the Society for Research in Child Development, Seattle, WA.

Hao, L., Hotx, V. J., and Jin, G. Z. (2000). *Games daughters and parents play: Teenage childbearing, parental reputation, and strategic transfers.* Unpublished manuscript.

Hardy, J. B., Astone, N. M., Brooks-Gunn, J., Shapiro, S., and Miller, T. L. (1998). Like mother, like child: Intergenerational patterns of age at first birth and associations with childhood and adolescent characteristics and adult outcomes in the second generation. *Developmental Psychology, 34,* 1220–1232.

Hardy, J. B., Shapiro, S., Astone, N. M., Brooks-Gunn, J., Miller, T. L., and Hilton, S. C. (1997). Adolescent childbearing revisited: The age of inner-city mothers at delivery is a determinant of their children's self-sufficiency at age 27–33. *Pediatrics, 100,* 802–809.

Harris, G. W. (1993). Ethical dimensions of young unwed fatherhood. In R. I. Lerman and T. J. Ooms (Eds.), *Young unwed fathers: Changing roles and emerging policies* (pp. 170–192). Philadelphia: Temple University Press.

Harris, K. M. (1997). *Teen mothers and the revolving welfare door.* Philadelphia: Temple University Press.

Hauser, S. T., Borman, E. H., Powers, S. I., Jacobson, A. M., and Noam, G. G. (1990). Paths of adolescent ego development: Links with family life and individual adjustment. *Psychiatric Clinics of North America, 13,* 489–510.

Haveman, R., Wolfe, B., and Spaulding, J. (1991). Childhood events and circumstances influencing high school competition. *Demography*, *28*, 133–157.

Henshaw, S. K. (1998). Unintended pregnancy in the United States. *Family Planning Perspectives*, *30*, 24–29, 46.

Hernandez, D. J., and Myers, D. E. (1993). *America's children: Resources from family, government, and the economy.* New York: Sage.

Hetherington, E. M. (1993). An overview of the Virginia longitudinal study of divorce and remarriage: A focus on early adolescence. *Journal of Family Psychology*, *7*, 39–56.

Hill, M. S. (1992). *The Panel Study of Income Dynamics: A user's guide.* Beverly Hills, CA: Sage.

Hinde, R., and Stevenson-Hinde, J. (1988). *Relationships within families: Mutual influences.* Oxford, England: Clarendon.

Hofferth, S. L. (1987). The effects of programs and policies on adolescent pregnancy and childbearing. In S. L. Hofferth and C. D. Hayes (Eds.), *Risking the future: Vol. 2. Adolescent sexuality, pregnancy, and childbearing* (pp. 207–263). Washington, DC. National Academy of Sciences.

Hoffman, S. D., Foster, E. M., and Furstenberg, F. F., Jr. (1993). Reevaluating the costs of teenage childbearing. *Demography*, *30*, 1–14.

Hogan, D. P., and Astone, N. M. (1986). The transition to adulthood. *Annual Review of Sociology*, *12*, 109–130.

Hogan, D. P., Hao, L. X., and Parish, W. L. (1990). Race, kin networks and assistance to mother-headed families. *Social Forces*, *68*, 797–812.

Horwitz, S. M., Klerman, L. V., Kuo, H. S., and Jekel, J. F. (1991). School-age mothers: Predictors of long-term educational and economic outcomes. *Pediatrics*, *87*, 862–867.

Hotz, V. J., McElroy, S. W., and Sanders, S. G. (1997). The impacts of teenage childbearing on the mothers and the consequences of those impacts for government. In R. Maynard (Ed.), *Kids having kids: Economic costs and social consequences of teen pregnancy.* Washington, DC: Urban Institute.

Huston, A. C. (Ed.). (1991). *Children in poverty: Child development and public policy.* New York: Cambridge University Press.

Jarrett, R. L. (1990). *A comparative examination of socialization patterns among low-income African-Americans, Chicanos, Puerto-Ricans, and Whites: A review of the ethnographic literature.* New York: Social Science Research Council.

Jessner, L., Weigert, E., and Fay, J. L. (1970). The development of parental attitudes during pregnancy. In E. J. Anthony and T. Benedeck (Eds.), *Parenthood: Its psychology and psychopathology* (pp. 209–244). Boston: Little, Brown.

Jones, A. S., Astone, N. M., Keyl, P. M., Kim, Y. J., and Alexander, C. S. (1999). Teen childbearing and educational attainment: A comparison of methods. *Journal of Family and Economic Issues*, *20*, 387–418.

Jones, E. F., Forrest, J. D., Goldman, N., Henshaw, S. K., Silverman, J., and Torres, A. (1988). Unintended pregnancy, contraceptive practice and family planning services in developed countries. *Family Planning Perspectives*, *20*, 53–67.

Joshi, N., and Battle, S. (1990). Adolescent fathers: An approach for intervention. *Journal of Health and Social Policy*, *1*, 17–33.

Kasanin, J., and Handschin, S. (1941). Psychodynamic factors in illegitimacy. *American Journal of Orthopsychiatry*, *11*, 66–84.

Keating, D. P. (1990). Adolescent thinking. In S. S. Feldman and G. R. Elliot (Eds.), *At the threshold: The developing adolescent* (pp. 54–91). Cambridge, MA: Harvard University Press.

Kellam, S. G., Ensminger, M. E., and Turner, R. J. (1977). Family structure and the mental health of children: Concurrent and longitudinal community-wide studies. *Archives of General Psychiatry*, *34*, 1012–1022.

Klebanov, P. K., Brooks-Gunn, J., and Duncan, G. J. (1994). Does neighborhood and family affect mothers' parenting, mental health, and social support? *Journal of Marriage and the Family*, *56*, 441–455.

Klepinger, D., Lundberg, S., and Plotnick, R. (1995). Adolescent fertility and the educational attainment of young women. *Family Planning Perspectives*, *27*, 23–28.

Klerman, G. L. (1974). Depression and adaptation. In R. C. Friedman and M. M. Katz (Eds.), *The psychology of depression* (pp. 127–146). Washington, DC: Winston.

Kohen, D., and Brooks-Gunn, J. (2001). *Mothers who are not authoritative or authoritarian: "Tough love" as a parenting style.* Unpublished manuscript, Center for Children and Families, Teacher's College, Columbia University, New York.

Kohlberg, L. (1966). A cognitive-development analysis of children's sex-role concepts and attitudes. In E. E. Maccoby (Ed.), *The development of sex differences* (pp. 82–173). Stanford, CA: Stanford University Press.

Ku, L., Sonenstein, F., and Pleck, J. (1992). The association of AIDS education and sex education with sexual behavior and condom use among teenage men. *Family Planning Perspectives*, *24*, 100–106.

Lamb, M. E., Hopps, K., and Elster, A. B. (1987). Strange situation behavior of infants with adolescent mothers. *Infant Behavior and Development*, *10*, 39–48.

Lazarus, R. S., and Folkman, S. (1984). *Stress appraisal and coping.* New York: Springer-Verlag.

Leadbeater, B. J., and Linares, O. (1992). Depressive symptoms in Black and Puerto Rican adolescent mothers in the first three year postpartum. *Development and Pyschopathology*, *4*, 451–468.

Leifer, M. (1980). *Psychological aspects of motherhood: A study of first pregnancy.* New York: Springer-Verlag.

LeMasters, E. E. (1957). Parenthood as crisis. *Marriage and Family Living*, *19*, 352–353.

Lerman, R. I. (1993). A national profile of young unwed fathers. In R. I. Lerman and T. Ooms (Eds.), *Young unwed fathers: Changing roles and emerging policies*. Philadelphia: Temple University Press.

Lester, B., Garcia Coll, C. T., and Sepkoski, C. (1983). A cross-cultural study of teenage pregnancy and neonatal behavior. In T. M. Field and A. Sostek (Eds.), *Infants born at risk: Physiological, perceptual, and cognitive processes* (pp. 147–169). New York: Grune and Stratton.

Leventhal, T., and Brooks-Gunn, J. (2000). The neighborhoods they live in: The effects of neighborhood residence upon child and adolescent outcomes. *Psychological Bulletin, 126*(2), 309–337.

Liaw, F., and Brooks-Gunn, J. (1994). Cumulative familial risks and low-birthweight children's cognitive and behavioral development. *Journal of Clinical Psychology, 23*, 360–372.

Luker, K. (1996). *Dubious conceptions: The politics of teenage pregnancy*. Cambridge, MA: Harvard University Press.

Luster, T., and Dubow, E. (1990). Predictors of the quality of the home environment that adolescent mothers provide for their school-aged children. *Journal of Youth and Adolescence, 19*, 475–495.

Maccoby, E. E., and Martin, J. A. (1983). Socialization in the context of the family: Parent–child interaction. In P. H. Mussen (Series Ed.) and E. M. Hetherington (Vol. Ed.), *Handbook of child psychology: Vol. 4. Socialization, personality, and social development* (4th ed., pp. 755–911). New York: Wiley.

Mahler, M. S., Pine, F., and Bergman, A. (1975). *Psychological birth of the human infant: Symbiosis and individuation*. New York: Basic Books.

Marecek, J. (1979). *Economic, social, and psychological consequences of adolescent childbearing: An analysis of data from the Philadelphia Collaborative Perinatal Project* (Final report to the National Institute of Child Health and Human Development). Swathmore, PA: Swathmore College.

Marecek, J. (1987). Counseling adolescents with problem pregnancies. *American Psychologist, 42*, 89–93.

Marx, F., Bailey, S., and Francis, J. (1988). *Childcare for the children of adolescent parents: Findings from a national survey and case studies* (Working paper No. 184). Wellesley, MA: Wellesley College, Center for Research on Women.

Matas, L., Arend, R., and Sroufe, A. L. (1978). Continuity of adaptation in the second year: The relationship between quality of attachment and competence. *Child Development, 49*, 547–556.

Maynard, R. A. (Ed.). (1997). *Kids having kids: Economic costs and social consequences of teen pregnancy*. Washington, DC: Urban Institute.

McAdoo, H. P. (Ed.). (1988). *Black families* (2nd ed.). Newbury Park, CA: Sage.

McCarthy, J., and Hardy, J. (1993). Age at first birth and birth outcomes. *Journal of Research on Adolescence, 3*, 373–392.

McLanahan, S. S., (1997). Parent absence or poverty: Which matters more? In G. J. Duncan and J. Brooks-Gunn (eds.), *Consequences of growing up poor* (pp. 35–48). New York: Russell Sage.

McLanahan, S. S., and Sandefur, G. (1994). *Growing up with a single parent: What hurts, what helps*. Cambridge, MA: Harvard University Press.

McLoyd, V. C. (1990). The impact of economic hardship on Black families and children: Psychological distress, parenting, socioeconomic development. *Child Development, 61*, 311–346.

McLoyd, V. C., and Steinberg, L. (Eds.). (1998). *Studying minority adolescents: Conceptual, methodological, and theoretical issues*. Hillsdale, NJ: Lawrence Erlbaum Associates.

McNair, S. (1991, April). *Gender difference in nurturance and restrictiveness in grandparents of young children of teen mothers*. Paper presented at the biennial meeting of the Society for Research in Child Development, Seattle, WA.

Menaghan, E. G., Kowaleski-Jones, L., and Mott, F. L. (1997). The intergenerational costs of parental social stressors: Academic and social difficulties in early adolescence for children of young mothers. *Journal of Health and Social Behavior, 38*, 72–86.

Miller, B. C. (1992). Adolescent parenthood, economic issues, and social policies. *Journal of Family and Economic Issues, 13*, 467–475.

Miller, B. C. (1993). Families, science, and values: Alternative views of parenting effects and adolescent pregnancy. *Journal of Marriage and the Family, 55*, 7–21.

Miller, B. C., and Moore, K. A. (1990). Historical perspectives. In S. S. Feldman and G. R. Elliot (Eds.), *At the threshold: The developing adolescent* (pp. 93–123). Cambridge, MA: Harvard University Press.

Modell, J., Furstenberg, F., and Hershberg, T. (1976). Social change and transitions to adulthood in historical perspective. *Journal of Family History, 1*, 7–32.

Modell, J., and Goodman, M. (1990). Historical perspectives. In S. S. Feldman and G. R. Elliot (Eds.), *At the threshold: The developing adolescent* (pp. 93–123). Cambridge, MA: Harvard University Press.

Moore, K. A., Morrison, D. R., and Greene, A. D. (1997). Effects on the children born to adolescent mothers. In R. A. Maynard (Ed.), *Kids having kids: Economic costs and social consequences of teen pregnancy*. Washington, DC: Urban Institute.

Moore, K. A., Myers, D. E., Morrison, D. R., Nord, C. W., Brown, B., and Edmonston, B. (1993). Age at first childbirth and later poverty. *Journal of Research on Adolescence, 3*, 393–422.

Moore, K. A., and Synder, N. O. (1991). Cognitive attainment among firstborn children of adolescent mothers. *American Sociological Review, 56*, 612–624.

Moore, M. R., and Chase-Lansdale, P. L. (2001). Sexual intercourse and pregnancy among African-American adolescent girls in high-poverty neighborhoods: The role of family and perceived community environment. *Journal of Marriage and the Family, 63*, 1146–1157

Morris, P. A., Huston, A. C., Duncan, G. J., Crosby, D. A., and Bos, J. M. (2001). How welfare and work policies affect children: A synthesis of research. New York: The Next Generation, Manpower Demonstration Research Corporation.

Oakley, A. (1980). *Women confined: Towards a sociology of childbirth.* New York: Schochen Books.

Osofsky, J. D., Culp, A. W., Eberhart-Wright, A., Ware, L. M., and Hann, D. M. (1988). *Intervention program for adolescent mothers and their infants* (Final report to Kenworthy Foundation, Meninger Clinic, Topeka, Kansas, and Louisiana State University, New Orleans, LA). New Orleans: Louisiana State University.

Osofsky, J. D., and Eberhart-Wright, A. (1988). Affective exchanges between high risk mothers and infants. *International Journal of Psycho analysis, 69*, 221–231.

Osofsky, J. D., Eberhart-Wright, A., and Ware, L. M. (1992). Children of adolescent mothers: A group at risk for psychopathology. *Infant Mental Health Journal, 13*, 119–131.

Osofsky, J. D., Hann, D. M., and Peebles, C. (1993). Adolescent parenthood: Risks and opportunities for parents and infants. In C. H. Zeanah, Jr. (Ed.), *Handbook of infant health.* New York: Guilford.

Osofsky, H. J., and Osofsky, J. D. (1970). The adolescent mother: Factors related to their children's development. *American Journal of Orthopsychiatry, 40*, 825–834.

Osofsky, J. D., Peebles, C., Fick, A., and Hann, D. M. (1992). *Personality development in African-American adolescent mothers and high-risk adolescent females.* Unpublished manuscript.

Oyserman, D., Radin, N., and Benn, R. (1993). Dynamics in a three-generational family: Teens, grandparents, and babies. *Developmental Psychology, 29*, 564–572.

Paikoff, R., and Brooks-Gunn, J. (1991). Do parent-child relationships change during puberty? *Psychological Bulletin, 110*, 47–66.

Paikoff, R., Brooks-Gunn, J., and Baydar, N. (1993, March). Multigenerational co-residence in a sample of 6–7 year-olds. NLSY. Paper presented at the biennial meeting of Society for Research in Child Development, New Orleans, LA.

Parke, R. D. (1988). Families in life-span perspective: A multilevel developmental approach. In E. M. Hetherington, R. M. Lerner, and M. Perlmutter (Eds.), *Child development in life-span perspective* (pp. 159–190). Hillsdale, NJ: Lawrence Erlbaum Associates.

Parks, P. L., and Arndt, E. K. (1990). Difference between adolescents and adult mothers of infants. *Journal of Adolescent Health Care, 11*, 248–253.

Patterson, G. (1986). Performance models for antisocial boys. *American Psychologist, 41*, 432–444.

Pearlin, L. (1975). Sex roles and depression. In N. Datan and L. Ginsberg (Eds.), *Life-span development psychology: Normative life crises* (pp. 198–208). New York: Academic.

Piccinino, L., and Mosher, W. (1998). Trends in contraceptive use in the United States 1982–1995. *Family Planning Perspectives, 30*, 4–10.

Polit, D. F. (1989). Effects of a comprehensive program for teenage parents: Five years after project redirection. *Family Planning Perspectives, 21*, 164–169.

Pope, S., Casey, P., Bradley, R., and Brooks-Gunn, J. (1993). The effect of intergenerational factors on the development of low birth weight infants born to adolescent mothers. *Journal of the American Medical Association, 269*, 1396–1400.

Prater, L. P. (1995). Never married/biological teen mother headed households. *Marriage and Family Review, 20*, 305–324.

Pratt, M. W., Hunsberger, B., Pancer, S. M., Roth, D., and Santolupo, S. (1993). Thinking about parenting: Reasoning about development issues across the lifespan. *Developmental Psychology, 29*, 585–595.

Quinton, D., and Rutter, M. (1988). *Parenting breakdown: The making and breaking of intergenerational links.* Aldershot, England: Avebury.

Ramey, C. T., Bryant, D. M., Wasik, B. H., Sparling, J. J. Fendt, K. H., and LaVenge, L. M. (1992). The Infant Health and Development Program elements, family participation, and child intelligence. *Pediatrics, 89*, 454–465.

Reichman, N. E., and McLahanahan, S. (2001). Self-sufficiency programs and parenting interventions: Lessons from New Chance and the Teenage Parent Demonstration. *Social Policy Report, 15*(2).

Reiss, D. (1981). *The family's construction of reality.* Cambridge, MA: Harvard University Press.

Reiss, I. (1997). *Solving America's sexual crisis.* Amherst, NY: Prometheus Books.

Ruble, D. N. (1983). The development of social-comparison processes and their role in achievement-related self-socialization. In E. T. Higgins, D. N. Ruble, and W. W. Hartup (Eds.), *Social cognition and social development: A sociocultural perspective* (pp. 134–157). New York: Cambridge University Press.

Ruble, D. N., Brooks-Gunn, J., Fleming, A. S., Fitzmaurice, G., Stangor, C., and Deutsch, F. (1990). Transition to motherhood and the self: Measurement, stability, and change. *Journal of Personality and Social Psychology, 58*, 450–463.

Ruble, D. N., Fleming, A. S., Heckel, L. S., and Stangor, C. (1988). Changes in the marital relationship during the transition to first-time motherhood: Effects of violated expectations concerning division of household labor. *Journal of Personality and Social Psychology, 55*, 78–87.

Rutter, M. (1989). Pathways from childhood to adult life. *Journal of Child Psychiatry and Psychology and Applied Disciplines*, *30*, 23–51.

Sameroff, A. J., and Emde, R. N. (Eds.). (1992). *Relationship disturbances in early childhood: A developmental approach.* New York: Basic Books.

Sameroff, A. J., and Feil, L. (1985). Parental conceptions of developmental. In I. E. Sigel (Ed.), *Parental belief systems: The psychological consequences for children* (pp. 83–105). Hillsdale, NJ: Lawrence Erlbaum Associates.

Sameroff, A. J., Seifer, R., Baldwin, A., and Baldwin, C. (1993). Stability of intelligence from preschool to adolescence: The influence of social and family risk factors. *Child Development*, *64*, 80–97.

Sameroff, A. J., Seifer, R., Barocas, R., Zax, M., and Greenspan, S. (1987). IQ scores of 4-year-old children: Social–environmental teenagers. In K. G. Scott, T. Field, and E. G. Robertson (Eds.), *Teenage parents and their offspring* (pp. 249–263). New York: Grune and Stratton.

Scaramella, L. V., Conger, R. D., Simons, R. L., and Whitbeck, L. B. (1998). Predicting risk for pregnancy by late adolescence: A social contextual perspective. *Developmental Psychology*, *34*, 1233–1245.

Seitz, V., Apfel, N. H., and Rosenbaum, L. K. (1991). Effects of an intervention program for pregnant adolescents: Educational outcomes at two years postpartum. *American Journal of Community Psychology*, *19*, 911–930.

Shereshefsky, P. M., and Yarrow, L. J. (1973). *Psychological aspects of a first pregnancy and early postnatal adaptation.* New York: Raven.

Simmons, R. G., and Blyth, D. A. (1987). *Moving into adolescence: The impact of pubertal change and school context.* New York: Aldine de Gruyter.

Simmons, R. L., Whitbeck, L. B., Conger, R. D., and Chyi-in, W. (1991). Intergenerational transmission of harsh parenting. *Developmental Psychology*, *27*, 159–171.

Singh, S., and Darroch, J. (1999). Trends in sexual activity among adolescent American women: 1982–1995. *Family Planning Perspectives*, *31*, 212–9.

Singh, S., and Darroch, J. E. (2000). Adolescent pregnancy and childbearing: Levels and trends in developed countries. *Family Planning Perspectives*, *32*, 14–23.

Smith, S. (1995a). *Two-generational programs for families in poverty.* Norwood, NJ: Ablex.

Smith, S. (1995b). Two-generational program models: A new strategy and direction for future research. In P. L. Chase-Lansdale and J. Brooks-Gunn (Eds.), *Escape from poverty: What makes a difference for children?* New York: Cambridge University Press.

Smith, J. R., Brooks-Gunn, J., and Klebanov, P. K. (1997). The consequences of living in poverty for young children's congnitive and verbal ability and early school achievement. In G. Duncan and J. Brooks-Gunn (Eds.), *Consequences of growing up poor* (pp. 132–189). New York: Russell Sage Foundation.

Sonenstein, F. L., Pleck, J. H., and Ku, L. C. (1989). Sexual activity, condom use, and AIDS awareness among adolescent males. *Family Planning Perspectives*, *21*, 152–158.

Speiker, S. J. (1991, April). *Mothers in adolescence: Factors related to infant attachment and disorganization.* Paper presented at the biennial meeting of the Society for Research in Child Development, Seattle, WA.

Sroufe, A. L. (1979). The coherence of individual development. *American Psychologist*, *34*, 834–841.

Stack, C. B. (1974). *All our kin: Strategies for survival in a Black community.* New York: Harper & Row.

Stewart, A. J. (1982). The course of individual adaptation to life changes. *Journal of Personality and Social Psychology*, *42*, 1100–1113.

Stewart, A. J., Sokol, M., Healy, J. M., and Chester, N. L. (1986). Longitudinal studies of psychology consequences of life changes in children and adults. *Journal of Personality and Social Psychology*, *50*, 143–151.

Sucoff, C. A., and Upchurch, D. M. (1998). Neighborhood context and the risk of childbearing among metropolitan-area black adolescents. *American Sociological Review*, *63*, 571–585.

Sullivan, M. L. (1990). *The male role in teenage pregnancy and parenting: New directions for public policy.* New York: Vera Institute of Justice.

Sullivan, M. L. (1993). Culture and class as determinants of out-of wedlock childbearing and poverty during late adolescence. *Journal of Research on Adolescence*, *3*, 295–317.

Sung, K. (1992). Teenage pregnancy and premarital childbirth in Korea: Issues and concerns. In M. K. Rosenheim and M. F. Testa (Eds.), *Early parenthood and coming of age in the 1900s* (pp. 173–183). New Brunswick, NJ: Rutgers University Press.

Testa, M. F. (1992). Racial and ethnic variation in the early life course of adolescent welfare mothers. In M. K. Rosenheim and M. F. Testa (Eds.), *Early parenthood and coming of age in the 1990s* (pp. 89–112). New Brunswick, NJ: Rutgers University Press.

Thomson, E., Hanson, T. L., and McLanahan, S. S. (1994). Family structure and child well-being: Economic resources vs. parental behaviors. *Social Forces*, *73*, 221–242.

Thomson, E., McLanahan, S. S., Curtin, R. B. (1992). Family structure, gender, and parental socialization. *Journal of Marriage and the Family*, *54*, 368–378.

Unger, J., Molina, G., and Teran, L. (2000). Perceived consequences of teenage childbearing among adolescent girls in an urban sample. *Journal of Adolescent Health, 26,* 205–212.

Unger, D. G., and Wandersman, L. P. (1985). Social support and adolescent mothers: Action research contributions to theory and application. *Journal of Social Issues, 41,* 29–45.

Upchurch, D. M. (1993). Early schooling and childbearing experiences: Implications for postsecondary school attendance. *Journal of Research on Adolescence, 3,* 423–445.

Upchurch, D. M., and McCarthy, J. (1989). Adolescent childbearing and high school completion in the 1980s: Have things changed? *Family Planning Perspectives, 21,* 199–202.

Upchurch, D. M., and McCarthy, J. (1990). The timing of first birth and high school completion. *American Sociological Review, 55,* 224–234.

U.S. Census Bureau (1999). *Statistical abstract of the United States,* Vital Statistics Table 99. Washington, DC: U.S. Government Printing Office.

U.S. Census Bureau (1998). Marital status and living arrangements: March 1998. In *Current population reports* (Series P-20, No. 514). Washington, DC: U.S. Government Printing Office.

U.S. Department of Health and Human Services. (2000). Trends in pregnancies and pregnancy rates by outcome: Estimates for the United States. In *Vital and health statistics* (Series 21, No. 56). Washington, DC: DHHS in Silver Spring, MD.

Ventura, S. J., and Bachrach, C. A. (2000). Nonmarital childbearing in the United States, 1940–99. In *National vital statistics reports,* (Vol. 48, No. 16). Hyattsville, MD: National Center for Health Services.

Ventura, S. J. and Freedman, M. (2000). Teenage childbearing in the United States, 1960–97. *American Journal of Preventive Medicine, 19,* (Supplement), 18–25.

Ventura, S. J., Mathews, T. J., and Curtin, S. C. (1999). Declines in teenage birth rates, 1991–1998: Update of national and state trends. In *National vital statistics reports* (Vol. 47, No. 26). Hyattsville, MD: National Center for Health Services.

Ventura, S. J., Curtin, S. C., and Mathews, T. J. (2000). Variations in teenage birth rates, 1991–1998: National and state trends. In *National vital statistics reports* (Vol. 48, No. 6). Hyattsville, MD: National Center for Health Services.

Wakschlag, L. S., Chase-Lansdale, P. L., and Brooks-Gunn, J. (1996). Not just ghosts in the nursery: The influence of current intergenerational processes on parenting and young African-American families. *Child Development, 67,* 2131–2141.

Wakschlag, L. S., Pittman, L. D., Chase-Lansdale, P. L., and Brooks-Gunn, J. (in press). "Mama, I'm a person, too!": Individuation and young African-American mothers' parenting competence. In A. M. Cause and S. Hauser (Eds.), *Adolescence and beyond: Family processes and development.* Mahwah, NJ: Lawrence Erlbaum Associates.

Ward, M. K. (1986). *Them children: A study in language learning.* New York: Waveland.

Ward, M. J., Carlson, E., Plunkett, S. W., and Kessler, D. B. (1988, March). Adolescent mother–infant attachment: Interactions, relationships, and adolescent development. In *Adolescents as mothers: Family processes and child outcomes.* Presented at the symposium conducted at the biennial meeting of the Society for Research on Adolescence, Alexandria, VA.

Warren, C. (1992). Perspectives on international sex practices and American family sex communication relevant to teenage sexual behavior in the United States. *Health Communication, 4.2,* 121–136.

Wasserman, G. A., Brunelli, S. A., and Rauh, V. A. (1990). Social support and living arrangements of adolescent and adult mothers. *Journal of Adolescent Research, 5,* 54–66.

Wasserman, G. A., Brunelli, S. A., Rauh, V. A., and Alvarado, L. E. (1994). The cultural context of adolescent childrearing in three groups of urban minority mothers. In G. Lamberty and C. Garcia Coll (Eds.), *Puerto Rican woman and children: Issues in health, growth, and development.* New York: Plenum.

Wasserman, G. A., Rauh, V. A., Brunelli, S. A., Garcia-Castro, M., and Necos, B. (1990). Psychological attributes and life experiences of disadvantaged minority mothers: Age and ethnic variations. *Child Development, 61,* 566–580.

Werner, E. E., and Smith, R. S. (1982). *Vulnerable but inconvincible: A longitudinal study of resilient children and youth.* New York: McGraw-Hill.

Whiting, B. (1981). Environmental constraints constraints on infant care practices. In R. H. Munroe, R. L. Munroe, and B. B. Whiting (Eds.), *Handbook of cross-cultural human development* (pp. 155–179). New York: Garland.

Whiting, B. B., and Edwards, C. P. (1988). *Children of different worlds: The formation of social behavior.* Cambridge, MA: Harvard University Press.

Wilson, J. B., and Brooks-Gunn, J. (2001). Health status and behaviors of unwed fathers. *Children and Youth Services Review, 23,* 377–401.

Wilson, J. B., Ellwood, D. T., and Brooks-Gunn, J. (1995). Welfare to work through the eyes of children: The impact on parenting of movement from AFDC to employment. In P. L. Chase-Lansdale and J. Brooks-Gunn (Eds.), *Escape from poverty: What makes a difference for children?* New York: Cambridge University Press.

Wilson, W. J. (1987). *The truly disadvantaged.* Chicago: University of Chicago Press.

Wilson, W. J. (1996). *When work disappears: The world of the new urban poor.* New York: Knopf.

Zahn-Waxler, C., Kochanska, G., Krupnick, J., and McKrew, D. (1990). Patterns of guilt in children of depressed and well mothers. *Developmental Psychology, 26,* 51–59.

Zaslow, M. J., Oldham, E., Moore, K. A., and Magenheim, E. (1998). Welfare families' use of early childhood care and education programs, and implications for their children's development. *Early Childhood Research Quarterly, 13*(4), 535–563.

Zill, N., Moore, K. A., Smith, E. W., Stief, T., and Coiro, M. J. (1995) The life circumstances and development of children in welfare families: A profile based on national survey data. In P. L. Chase-Lansdale and J. Brooks-Gunn (Eds.), *Escape from poverty: What makes a difference for children?* New York; Cambridge University Press.

7

Nonparental Caregiving

K. Alison Clarke-Stewart
Virginia D. Allhusen
University of California

INTRODUCTION

The past quarter century has seen dramatic changes in family life in the United States. One of the most notable of these changes is the trend toward greater labor force participation by mothers, coupled with greater involvement of caregivers other than parents in the care of young children. In 1975, just over one third of married women with children under the age of 6 years were employed; by 1998, the rate of employment had risen to approximately two thirds (U.S. Bureau of the Census, 1999). In 1975, approximately 4 million American children under the age of 6 years were cared for by someone other than their mothers for a significant portion of each week; today, more than 10 million young children are in childcare of some type (U.S. Bureau of the Census, 1997). Some families have relatives (grandparents, aunts, older siblings) available to care for young children while the mother works. The trend observed in all Western societies toward smaller, more geographically spread out families, however, has clearly increased parents' need to find childcare outside the family.

The issue of the effects of nonparental care, often even *nonfamilial* care, on young children's social and cognitive development has raised many questions among child development researchers. What is the significance of children's daily separations from their mothers? What is the nature of the attention children receive from their daycare providers? What are the effects of having multiple caregivers? What does it mean if these caregivers are unrelated to the family and if their styles of interacting with the child are different from the parents' and from each other's? Are children who spend several hours each day with other children more dependent on their peers? Are they more aggressive with other children? Can children in daycare facilities with large groups of children and few caregivers be given enough stimulation to ensure their intellectual growth? Are daycare providers as committed as parents to fostering children's social and intellectual development? Questions such as these have engendered research and controversy among developmental scientists and others.

In this chapter, we review the theories and studies bearing on these questions. We summarize the history of daycare as it has developed in the United States and describe its current forms. We offer a brief review of the types of childcare that exist in a few other countries. We describe the roles of nonparental caregivers and the factors that influence caregivers' behavior. We review the research that compares children with and without nonparental childcare experience and those enrolled in care of varying quality. Finally, we look at the joint influences of family and childcare and the direction of future research aimed at further understanding the effects of nonparental care in the context of the child's complete world.

THEORIES OF NONPARENTAL CARE

Several theories in developmental science have been applied to the topic of nonparental care, particularly in the first few years of a child's life. We discuss the three most significant of these theories in this section. Later in the chapter we evaluate the empirical data bearing on issues raised by each of the three theories.

Attachment Theory

Attachment theory has been considered by many to be the most germane of existing child development theories to the issue of childcare and its potential effect on children's development. John Bowlby, whose name has become synonymous with attachment theory, emphasized the primacy of the infant's relationship with a primary caregiver for the child's subsequent psychological development (Bowlby, 1969). From the quality of the interactions between caregiver and child during the earliest years of the child's life, he suggested, the infant constructs an "internal working model" of the self and of the attachment figure—a set of expectations concerning that person's availability and a complementary view of the self as worthy or unworthy of such care. The child who enjoys a secure relationship with a primary attachment figure is thus fueled with the confidence to venture out and explore the world.

Bowlby's focus was almost exclusively on the mother as the primary attachment figure, primarily because, in most cultures, historically it has been the mother who serves as the infant's primary caregiver. A large body of empirical work, inspired by Bowlby's theory, focused primarily on the mother as the primary attachment figure and examined the relation between the quality of that attachment relationship and subsequent child development (see review by Lamb, Thompson, Gardner, and Charnov, 1985). However, many of these studies were conducted at a time when the vast majority of infants in the countries in which the studies took place were being cared for primarily by their mothers. As a result, attachment theorists developed their notions about the unique importance of the mother–infant relationship within the social and cultural context of the traditional maternal role—at home rearing children.

As more mothers of very young children began to participate in the workforce, attachment theory adapted to the changing social context. A number of attachment theorists (e.g., Sroufe, 1983) acknowledged that children form attachments to several people during early childhood, including fathers and other caregivers. However, the mother–infant relationship was assumed to be at the base of a hierarchy of relationships; the mother was still viewed as the adult with whom the child forms the first and most influential attachment relationship, thereby setting the stage for the formation of subsequent relationships with a wider circle of partners (Ainsworth, 1982). Any internal working models formed from other adult–child attachments would be influenced by the working models formed originally within the mother–child bond. Others, however, have argued that in the modern era, when many young infants spend a significant proportion of time in the care of someone other than the mother, it is reasonable to expect that the child would develop distinct working models of her or his relationship with each of these caregiving adults, and that each of them would contribute to the later relationships that the child develops.

The view that the mother retains a special, unique place in each child's emotional life, regardless of how many significant attachment relationships she or he may form with other caregivers, has been at the heart of the controversy as to whether early, extensive daily separations from the mother place the child at risk for later emotional maladjustment.

Sociobiological Theories

The view that the mother is uniquely important in the infant's emotional life, regardless of the experiences the individual child may have with other caregiving adults, also has roots in sociobiological theory, that is, the theory that adults are more likely to care for and protect those who will carry their genes into the next generation (i.e., their biological offspring; Hamilton, 1964; Rushton, Russell, and Wells, 1984).

Favoritism toward one's close relatives has been demonstrated in a variety of studies. Segal (1984) observed more cooperation and altruism on joint tasks in monozygotic than dizygotic twins in middle childhood. Freedman (1979) found that biological relatives expressed stronger feelings of family ties than did nonbiological relatives. Barash (1979) demonstrated that parents prefer to rear their own children rather than adoptive children. In fact, resistance to adoption is not an uncommon experience among childless couples who hope to have children (Brodzinsky and Pinderhughes, in Vol. 1 of this *Handbook*). Moreover, several researchers have found an elevated risk of child abuse associated with stepparenting (Lightcap, Kurland, and Burgess, 1982; Wilson, Daly, and Weghorst, 1980; see Hetherington and Stanley-Hagan, in Vol. 3 of this *Handbook*). These studies and others suggest that degree of genetic relatedness influences one's level of positive feelings, expectations, and behaviors toward a child.

From a sociobiological perspective, we might expect that the closer the genetic relation of a caregiver to a child, the greater will be the caregiver's investment in providing the best quality care for that child. An implication of this theory is that biological relatives, particularly parents and to a lesser extent grandparents, aunts, and uncles, are most invested in providing the best quality care for their children. On the other hand, it does not automatically follow that parents or other relatives are equipped to offer the best care. "Professional" caregivers often have more training and experience in child development than parents. In addition, parents, being more invested in their child's future, are not always objective about the child's behavior. These tendencies may balance or outweigh the advantages of parental or familial childcare.

Cognitive and Social Stimulation Theories

The third set of theories of relevance to the issue of nonparental caregiving consists of those focused on the stimulation of children's cognitive and social development. It has long been believed that providing young children with toys and lessons and verbal interactions with a responsive adult will promote their cognitive development, whereas the absence of such stimulating opportunities will delay or depress development (Dennis, 1973; Hunt, 1961). The preschool intervention movement of the 1960s and 1970s, including Project Head Start, was premised on this cognitive stimulation theory (e.g., Schweinhart, Weikart, and Larner, 1986); that is, on the belief that children from "deprived" environments could be offered stimulation in preschool programs that would "compensate" for their lack of educational experience at home. Proponents of daycare suggested that a high-quality daycare setting offers the young child the same kinds of stimulation as a cognitively oriented preschool program (e.g., Caldwell, 1970; Scarr and Weinberg, 1986). The daycare setting provided by a professional daycare home provider or a center, like that of a preschool or Head Start program, is designed to be a stimulating environment for young children. The room setup and materials are geared to the size and the developmental level of the child; the primary goal of the caregiver is to provide appropriate interaction for the well-being of the children in care. In contrast, the mother at home with her child must divide her time among multiple tasks, only one of which is childcare.

Of course there are limits to the stimulation that can be provided in a daycare setting. In a group setting, in which the adult's attention is spread thin because of the large number of children in care, even a professional caregiver will not be able to provide a steady diet of stimulating experiences for each child. The fear has been expressed that children in daycare will suffer the same deprivation that has been observed for children growing up in residential institutions. On the basis of cognitive stimulation theory (e.g., Wachs and Gruen, 1982), however, it would be expected that children who receive stimulating nonparental care in a materially varied daycare environment with a moderate number of children would have advanced cognitive development, whereas the development of children in an unstimulating or overcrowded childcare environment would be impaired.

Childcare arrangements outside the family, in addition to exposing children to cognitive enrichment or deprivation, typically provide young children with their first regular experience with peers. This social stimulation, too, can contribute—positively or negatively—to children's development. On the negative side, fears have been expressed that early rearing in a peer-oriented environment will deter the development of children's individuality and individualism, fantasy, and creativity, that in a peer culture children become dependent on peers rather than on adult authority and will be less likely to conform to standards for socially acceptable behavior, such as courtesy and cooperation (Suransky, 1982).

On the positive side, it has been suggested that experience playing with peers at an early age fosters the development of children's social competence. Howes (1988) presents one model for the development of social competence with peers for children who are in daycare. Although children who are not in daycare may "catch up" or go through the developmental stages quickly to reach their age-appropriate form of social competence when placed in group care, at the age of 4 years, children who entered care as infants are advanced in the frequency and they quality of their play with both familiar and unfamiliar peers because they have had more time to practice and perfect their social skills (Howes, 1991). There may even be something about the absence of the mother that encourages a positive orientation toward peers. Infants and young children in parent-cooperative arrangements have been found to be more sociable and socially skilled and less aggressive with peers when their own mother is out of the room than when she is present (Field, 1979; Smith and Howes, 1994). When the mother is present, children focus their attention on her rather than participate in the peer group. According to Howes' model, children who never spend time away from the mother may have difficulty with the initial step toward social competence with peers, that is, with developing enough interest to attempt interaction.

Theoretical Predictions Summarized

From the perspectives of these different theories, predictions about the effects of nonparental care on children's development are mixed. Traditional attachment theorists would predict that early separation from the mother creates a "risk" of later emotional difficulties for the child. This risk would be heightened if the alternative care were of poor quality. Sociobiologists would argue for the merits of childcare provided by a biological relative and for the special advantage of parents because they are the child's closest relatives. Cognitive and social stimulation theorists, in contrast, would predict positive outcomes for the child from the enrichment provided by an alternative care arrangement that is of high quality, with a responsive caregiver and a balance of stimulating experiences with adults, peers, and materials. In fact, such an enriched environment should produce greater cognitive and social development than an unstimulating home environment. There is not one single theoretical position that predicts the effects of nonparental care, but several, with quite different outcomes.

HISTORY OF DAYCARE IN THE UNITED STATES

The use of nonparental caregivers for young children is not a new phenomenon, even in the United States. Only its prevalence has changed. What was once a service for a minority of families—the affluent, with their nannies, and the urban poor, whose children were in day nurseries—has become the norm for the majority of American families today.

As a formal service, the history of daycare in the United States goes back well into the nineteenth century, when day nurseries were established in response to the flood of immigration that brought more than 5 million foreign families to the United States between 1815 and 1860 and to the industrialization and urbanization that took women from their homes to factories during this period. Young children were left to fend for themselves—locked up at home, allowed to roam the streets, or put under the casual supervision of a neighbor or relative. The situation was ripe for philanthropic intervention, and wealthy women and well-meaning service organizations, appalled by this neglect, organized day nurseries to provide care for these children. The first American day nursery was opened in Boston in 1838 to provide care for the children of seamen's working wives and widows. By 1898 approximately 175 day nurseries were operating in various parts of the country, enough to warrant the creation of a National Federation of Day Nurseries.

Over the next decade, expansion of daycare continued. Day nurseries were most often set up in converted homes. They were open 6 days a week, 12 hours a day. Most were simply custodial, run by overworked matrons with one or two assistants, who had to do the laundry, cooking, and cleaning as well as look after the children. They did not have the benefit of public support, monetary or ideological; the day nursery was considered a last resort for children who could not be cared for at home.

A few day nurseries with more energetic directors offered not only clean, safe places to keep children but something of interest to occupy their time. Beginning in the 1890s, some of the better day nurseries also began to offer a modest educational program, by hiring kindergarten teachers to come in and teach the children for several hours a day. They also offered services to working mothers beyond a place to leave their children: classes in sewing, cooking, English, and childcare, access to job training and opportunities, and help with practical family problems. In the 1920s these mothers were also given help with family-centered psychological problems.

In 1933, to alleviate effects of the Great Depression, President Roosevelt initiated the Federal Economic Recovery Act and the Works Project Administration. Public funds for the expansion of daycare became available for the first time to supply jobs for unemployed teachers, nurses, cooks, and janitors. By 1937 these programs had set up 1,900 day nurseries, caring for 40,000 children. Then, with World War II and the massive mobilization of women into war-related industries, a further surge in daycare occurred. By 1945, more than a million and a half children were in daycare. With the end of the war and the withdrawal of federal funds in 1946, this daycare boom ended as precipitously as it had begun. Nearly 3,000 centers closed, and by 1950 only 18,000 children were in daycare centers. From 1950 to 1965, daycare again became a marginal service for the poor, with an emphasis on social work and problem families. Unexpectedly, however, although the centers closed, women continued to work, and those who were not poor enough to qualify for publicly supported daycare used the few available private daycare centers or made other arrangements for childcare with relatives, neighbors, or housekeepers. Only in the mid-1960s did attitudes toward daycare begin to become more positive as it was recognized that mothers were already working and as it seemed that provision of daycare would allow more women to get off welfare. Federal support for daycare became available once more, although still only for poor families.

This change in attitude and legislation was influenced also by what was happening in early childhood education. People were focusing their attention on the preschool years as a critical period for stimulating intellectual development, hoping for later benefits in scientific program and national achievement. For 1967 to 1970, enrollment in nursery schools and kindergartens increased markedly (from one-fourth to one-half of all eligible 3- to 5-year-old children), and enrollment in licensed daycare centers doubled.

By the beginning of the 1970s, then, daycare was on many people's minds, and efforts to support more and better services were becoming stronger. However, with President Nixon's veto of the Comprehensive Child Development Act in 1972, hopes of further federal support for childcare were dashed. In the ensuing years, daycare enrollment in the United States has grown dramatically, increasing almost threefold through the end of the century. Unfortunately, this remarkable growth has taken place in the absence of any type of comprehensive national system for increasing the availability of childcare, providing financial assistance to families or facilities, or monitoring childcare quality. At present, daycare is a hodgepodge of arrangements, varying from state to state and family to family. The three most common types of care used today in the United States are described in the next section.

FORMS OF DAYCARE IN THE UNITED STATES

Table 7.1 shows the distribution of the major types of childcare arrangements currently being used by working mothers of preschool children (U.S. Bureau of the Census, 1999). Approximately one fourth of the families in which mothers work manage to cover childcare by juggling the parents' schedules or by taking the child along to work. Another fourth rely on other adult relatives (e.g., grandparents, aunts) to provide childcare. Approximately half of all children under 5 years of age whose mothers are employed, however, are cared for by a nonfamilial adult, either in the child's home or, more typically, in the adult's home or a daycare center. A small number of the families who use a nonrelated caregiver are able to afford a caregiver who comes to or lives in their home; most enroll their children in daycare homes or, more commonly, in daycare centers, with the latter, more formal type of care arrangement being used more frequently for older children.

In Child's Home

Care in the child's own home while mother works is most commonly provided by a relative, either the father or another relative. The caregiver is usually untrained, unlicensed, and unmonitored. Except when the caregiver is the father, in-home caregivers tend to be older women (over 40 years of age). If the in-home caregiver is related to the child, this is the most economical and stable of all daycare arrangements; if the caregiver is not a relative, this form of care is the least stable. If the caregiver is trained in child development—a professional nanny—in-home care is the most expensive kind of care. Educational or group activities with peers are uncommon in in-home care.

Daycare Home

A family daycare home is a care arrangement in which an adult (almost always a woman) cares for a small group of children in her own home. Two national surveys conducted in the 1990s (Kisker, Hofferth, Phillips, and Farquhar, 1991; U.S. Department of Education, National Center for Education Statistics, 1998) provide some descriptive facts about family daycare. Most daycare homes have no

TABLE 7.1
Primary Childcare Arrangements Used by Working Parents for Children Under
5 Years of Age

Type of Care	Infants and Toddlers (%)	Preschool Children (%)
Familial		
Parents themselves	24	23
Another relative	29	21
Nonfamilial		
In child's home	6	4
Daycare home	18	14
Daycare center	23	38

Note. Statistics are based on the most recent data available (U.S. Bureau of the Census, 1999).

more than three or four children (aged 18 to 36 months) and one care provider present at one time. The typical daycare home provider is a young married woman with young children of her own. She is a high-school graduate with 6 years of childcare experience, but she is likely to be untrained and unlicensed. She provides childcare because she is fond of children and she wants to provide playmates for her own child while at the same time supplementing the family income. Most daycare home providers see their role as caring for children's physical needs and to be "like a mother" to the children. They spend approximately half of their time interacting with the children and the rest of the time on housework or personal activities (Stallings, 1980). They are unlikely to offer organized educational games or structured activities; rather, children in daycare homes spend most of their day in free play (Eheart and Leavitt, 1989; Pence and Goelman, 1987). In short, the main goal of most family daycare providers is to provide a warm "homelike" atmosphere for the children.

Daycare Center

A daycare center is the most visible and easily identified childcare arrangement. The average daycare center provides care for 60 children. Children are usually divided into classes according to their age. The average group size is 7 infants, 10 toddlers, or 14 preschoolers (Kisker et al., 1991), but these sizes can vary enormously. Most children in daycare centers are 3 or 4 years old, although center care for infants and toddlers has steadily risen in popularity over the past decade, now accounting for approximately one quarter of all care utilized by families for children in this age group. Teachers in the centers tend to be women (97%[1]) under 40 years of age. Most have attended college (Whitebook, Howes, and Phillips, 1990) and have received training in child development (U.S. Department of Education, National Center for Education Statistics, 1998). They are likely to offer children educational opportunities and the chance to play with other children in a child-oriented, safe environment that is rich in materials and equipment. These qualities of staff training and a child-development-oriented program are especially likely in nonprofit, government-supported centers (Kagan, 1991; Whitebook et al., 1990).

Many researchers have attempted to detail differences in the "ecology" of center-based and family daycare. On the average, physical conditions (space, ventilation, light, toilets, cleanliness, toys, safety, nutrition, and immunization) are better in daycare centers, whereas daycare homes rank higher in social–personal conditions (fewer children per adult, more interaction with the caregiver, more conversation, more socialization attempts, more emotional input, and more sensitive approaches to the child by the caregiver; see Clarke-Stewart, Gruber, and Fitzgerald, 1994). Kisker et al. (1991) found that children in daycare centers spent most of their time in free-choice activities, adult-directed creative activities, physical exercise, and instruction, whereas children in home daycare spent somewhat more than half the day in free-choice activities and physical exercise and less than one third of their time in adult-directed creative activities and instruction. Less is known about the differences between center or home daycare and nonparental care in the child's own home. In contrast to center and home daycare, nonparental care in the child's own home has not been studied very extensively, perhaps because of the "private" nature of this form of care.

DAYCARE IN OTHER COUNTRIES

Thus far we have limited our focus in this chapter to the situation in the United States, where daycare takes many different forms as working parents search to make arrangements for their children's care in the absence of a national daycare system. In many other countries, by contrast, childcare services are widely available and well organized. Indeed, researchers have often surveyed the characteristics of

---

[1]Given the preponderance of female caregivers in homes and centers, we use the feminine pronouns ("she," "her") in our discussion.

daycare in other countries with an eye toward informing U.S. policy (for excellent reviews of childcare forms and features in other countries see Cochran, 1993; Kamerman, 1991; Lamb, Sternberg, Hwang, and Broberg, 1992; Melhuish and Moss, 1991; and Petrogiannis and Melhuish, 2001). In this section we describe the forms of daycare in three different countries, each of which has approached the issue of daycare in a different way.

Italy

The Italian national daycare system includes *asili nido* (nurseries) for infants and toddlers to the age of 3 years and *scuole materne* (preschools) for children ages 3 to 6 years. *Scuole materne* in Italy today are seen as an extension of primary school education, and although attendance is not mandatory, virtually every Italian child (94%) is enrolled. Class sizes and teacher–child ratios vary, but average somewhere around 24 and 1:12, respectively. Parents see the primary benefits of their children's attendance in these schools as providing opportunities for social contacts with peers and for learning more about the world (Pistillo, 1989).

Slower to gain public acceptance have been *asili nido*. A concern existed, as it has in many other countries, that early and extensive separations from the parent could be detrimental to the very young child's development. Today, Italy boasts a generous national parental leave policy that allows mothers to stay home with their infants at full salary for the first 5 months of the child's life and at half salary for six additional months (Ghedini, 2001); thus infants are rarely placed in center care before the age of 6 months (Lally, 2001). Owing in part to progressive and innovative approaches to early childcare that have evolved in Italy over the past 20 years, however, infant centers are now seen as the preferred childcare arrangement for older infants and toddlers. Centers are viewed as providing rich social and cognitively stimulating environments for children, as well as bases for parent networking and social support (Mantovani, 2001). The typical *asilo nido* class contains one caregiver for every 5 to 7 children. The center is typically broken down into three age groups: 10 to 18 months, 18 to 24 months, and 24 to 36 months. Caregivers' preservice educational training is limited; thus centers generally provide extensive in-service training for care providers. Unique to the Italian childcare system is a recognition that, to best care for the child, a relationship must be established with the parent. Caregivers view themselves as partners with parents in fostering the growth and development of the child as well as supporting the parents. Parents, in turn, view the caregivers as professionals to whom they can turn for "expert" advice on parenting issues. Within the group, each child is assigned a primary caregiver who serves as the child's primary attachment figure within the center and as a "mediator of socialization" for the child (Mantovani, 2001). This same caregiver cares for the child for the entire 3 years of the *nido* program, facilitating the development of a strong bond not just between caregiver and child, but also between caregiver and parent as well.

Sweden

Sweden has long been regarded as the model for providing social services for all individuals, from birth to the later years of life. Parental leave and childcare figure prominently in the government's provision of such services. At the core of such Swedish policies is a general belief that children belong at home with their mothers and fathers in the earliest months of their lives and, further, that the government should be involved in making that feasible for young families (Hwang and Broberg, 1992). To that end, Sweden offers generous paid parental leaves. The country is also often cited as having perhaps the most progressive views on the important role of fathers in the family's adaptation to its newest member; men, too, are entitled to paid leave following the birth of a child. Parents are entitled to a total of 450 days of leave, to be divided between mother and father, with at least 30 days reserved for each parent. As a result, most children (84%) do not enter nonparental child care before the age of approximately 17 months (Hwang and Broberg, 1992). Family-friendly work policies do not end there, however; parents are entitled to 120 days of paid leave (at 75% of their income) to care for a sick child and a reduced work week for both parents (6 hours per day until the child is 8 years old).

The government is involved not just in ensuring that children stay at home in the earliest months of their lives, but also in ensuring that, once they are placed in nonparental child care, children receive the highest-quality care possible. Approximately half of all Swedish children, beginning at approximately $1\frac{1}{2}$ years of age are placed in childcare. The government sponsors two types of public childcare (center and home based), and subsidizes even private childcare (e.g., parent cooperatives, church-run daycare centers). Currently, approximately 38% of all Swedish children under the age of 6 years are cared for in centers, and 23% are cared for in daycare homes (Directorate General for Research, 1997). Parents pay a small fee for childcare on a sliding scale basis that takes into account family size and income.

Daycare centers (*daghems*) are of uniformly high quality, spacious, well equipped, educational, and located in buildings specifically designed for that purpose. Teachers are well trained in early childhood education, and, in addition, the center staff includes adults trained as children's nurses. Classes generally consist of one adult for every three toddlers or preschoolers under the age of 3 years, with a total group size of approximately 10 to 12 children. Older children (age 3 to 6 years) are generally cared for in groups of 15 to 18 children with 3 adults.

Supplementing daycare centers are licensed family daycare homes (*familjedaghem*). Unlike centers, in which quality is closely regulated, Swedish family daycare homes are not carefully monitored. Perhaps for that reason, greater variability is seen in the features of family daycare homes than in centers. The typical *familjedaghem* consists of one adult, usually a mother herself, caring for six children including her own. As in the United States, the main reason Swedish daymothers give for providing care is that they can stay at home with their own young children. Care providers receive a small equipment grant from the government to stock their homes with toys and materials for the children. In some communities, groups of four to six daymothers and their children get together at a community center or other public area on a regular basis and conduct larger group activities with the children.

Israel

Daycare in Israel takes one of three forms, with the quality of care ranging from abysmal to outstanding. Perhaps the most internationally well known is the kibbutz system, in which children are cared for by a metapelet (caregiver) in an "Infant House" or "Children's House" beginning when the children are as young as 6 weeks of age. Today, most kibbutzim provide daytime care, in which children spend approximately 50 hours per week in the care of metaplot; in some, however, the children actually live with metaplot rather than with their own families. Parents visit with their children at certain times of the day, but the primary responsibility of raising the children (including instruction, discipline, and physical caregiving) rests with the metaplot. In general, the quality of care found on both types of kibbutzim is high; metaplot are carefully trained, the physical setting is spacious, well organized, and well equipped, the group is small (six children with two adults), and, perhaps owing at least in part to these favorable structural features, the caregivers provide high-quality care (Rosenthal, 1991).

The socioeconomic situation in Israel in the early 1900s, in which it was often necessary for both parents to work long hours outside the home, together with a social ideology that stressed communal living, gave rise to this unique form of childrearing. Today, kibbutzim account for only a tiny proportion of childcare arrangements used by Israeli families. Most childcare is subsumed under the Israeli national daycare system, which consists of daycare centers and family daycare homes. Both of these types of care facilities are subsidized by the federal government but are typically run by local authorities or women's organizations. In contrast to the kibbutz childcare system, national daycare centers are characterized by very large groups of children with few caregivers. The ratio of adults to children can reach 1:14 in infant classrooms, and 1:19 in toddler classrooms. Very few teachers have received any training at all; most have completed 12 years or fewer of education of any type (Rosenthal, 2001). As might be expected, the quality of care in such settings is custodial at best; routine caregiving tasks such as feeding or diapering are carried out in seconds, with virtually no positive engagement observed between adult and child, and children are frequently neither greeted on arrival at the center nor bid goodbye at departure (Koren-Karie, et al., 1998). The situation is much better in the national Family Day Care Home system, however, with structural features of the care settings approximating those found on kibbutzim. In a typical childcare home, one adult cares for five children. The care provider typically has not completed specialized training or earned an advanced degree of any type, but she is supervised by a local social worker or early childhood education professional. In research comparing the quality of care received in family daycare homes, centers, and kibbutzim, the quality of care received in the daycare homes was comparable with that received in the kibbutzim (Rosenthal, 1991). Care in the day-care centers, by contrast, was characterized by frequent negative exchanges between caregivers and children.

THE ROLES OF NONPARENTAL CAREGIVERS

Despite the fact that childcare takes many different forms in countries around the world, and even within countries, one common denominator is evident: the nonfamilial care provider is an important figure in the social networks of children who spend a significant portion of every day in nonparental care. The caregiver serves as a teacher and disciplinarian, a nurturer, and playmate, and she may occupy a place in the child's hierarchy of attachment figures.

Teachers

Whether they do so formally and deliberately or not, nonfamilial caregivers teach children many things. Caregivers in daycare centers are more likely than caregivers in family daycare settings to think of themselves as teachers (Pence and Goelman, 1987) and to use more academic teaching methods. They spend a major proportion of their time in curriculum planning and implementation (Phillips and Whitebook, 1990); they plan educational activities and pepper the children with questions. Teaching in family daycare is more informal. Children learn through free exploration and in the context of "real-life" tasks and situations.

Caregivers in homes and in centers may also teach children social rules. In groups of children, in which there is a higher probability that children will at least occasionally find themselves in conflict with peers, teaching social rules becomes quite important (Finkelstein, 1982). Children benefit from positive caregiver interventions in mediating peer conflicts; if left alone, children will most likely resort to aggression to resolve conflicts. Caregivers are more likely to intervene in negative toddler peer interactions (either spontaneously or after a child requests it) than in positive interactions. Interventions are most commonly verbal, and they often include explanations for the intervention; that is, caregivers use the negative peer interaction to teach a social rule to the children involved. Unfortunately, by ignoring positive peer encounters, caregivers miss opportunities to reinforce such behavior (Russon, Waite, and Rochester, 1990).

Disciplinarians

Caregivers also serve as disciplinarians. This may be especially important in a setting populated by a large group of children who are close in age. Praise is one way caregivers try to discipline or manage children. Praise can be used effectively to manipulate children's behavior in the daycare setting. If children are consistently praised for it, researchers have demonstrated, they will stay close to the caregiver and interact with her. They will play with a child they would ordinarily ignore if the teacher praises them for it. They will be more cooperative or more competitive, depending on which the caregiver praises. They will play with dolls rather than trucks if the caregiver rewards them for doing so (Serbin, Connor, and Denier, 1978). They will persist longer at tasks if they have been praised for working (Fagot, 1973). When caregivers do not expect children to behave in particular ways (e.g., cooperative, assertive, persistent, quiet, polite) and do not consistently encourage them to act in these ways and praise them for doing so, children are unlikely to learn these behaviors. Researchers have found that, when childcare teachers' discipline is lax, children misbehave more (Arnold, McWilliams, and Arnold, 1998).

Nurturers and Attachment Figures

Daycare providers in both center-based and family daycare settings often describe their main goal as providing children with love and affection in a warm, loving environment (Eheart and Leavitt, 1989; Kisker et al., 1991; Nelson, 1990). In several studies, daycare providers in high-quality childcare settings have been shown to be sensitive and responsive to children and to engage them in positive social and physical interactions (Allhusen, 1992; Anderson, Nagle, Roberts, and Smith, 1981; Howes, 1983). These types of interactions are generally thought of as being associated with optimal development in general, and, more specifically, the formation of a secure attachment bond (Belsky, 1984).

Because daycare providers spend significant portions of each day involved in caregiving and nurturant interactions with children, they are natural candidates for attachment figures in the hierarchy of children's attachment networks. A growing body of research suggests that not only do children in daycare form attachment relationships with their caregivers (Goossens and van IJzendoorn, 1990; Howes and Hamilton, 1992; van IJzendoorn, Sagi, and Lambermon, 1992), but this has positive implications for the children's development. Children who are rated as securely attached with their caregivers are more competent in cognitive play (Cassibba, van IJzendoorn, and D'Odorico, 2000), in their interactions with peers (Howes, 2000; Howes and Hamilton, 1993; Howes, Matheson, and Hamilton, 1994; Howes, Phillips, and Whitebook, 1992; van IJzendoorn et al., 1992), and with adults (Howes, Rodning, Galluzzo, and Myers, 1988). In the last study, children who were insecure with both their mothers and their caregivers were rated lower in social competence than children who had at least one secure relationship, suggesting that a secure attachment with a daycare provider can play a compensatory role for an insecure relationship with the mother. In fact, in a study conducted in Israel and The Netherlands, children's development and well-being were more highly related to having a number of secure attachments to caregivers than to being securely attached to both parents (van IJzendoorn et al., 1992). Children are more likely to be securely attached to the caregiver if they spend at least 20 hours a week with her (Howes and Matheson, 1992) and if they have a good relationship with their own mother (Pierrehumbert, Ramstein, Karmaniola, and Halfon, 1996). Studies have consistently shown, however, that, although children form attachments to their childcare providers, they prefer their mothers over these other caregivers (e.g., Farran and Ramey, 1977; Kagan, Kearsley, and Zelazo, 1978; Sagi et al., 1985; see reviews by Clarke-Stewart and Fein, 1983; Rutter, 1982).

Caregivers Versus Mothers

Daycare settings are different from most children's homes because of the number of other children who are present. Caregivers must make certain adjustments to adapt to the unique dynamics of caring for these children, who are often very close in age. There are likely to be more competing demands made on the caregiver and more conflicts between children that the caregiver must help to resolve. Although caregivers fill many of the same roles as mothers, differences between these settings require that they behave differently from one another in some ways. Interactions with the adult are less frequent in group care settings than they are in the child's home; in daycare, the peer group becomes more important (Rubenstein and Howes, 1983). The larger the peer group and the more their competing demands, the less stimulating and responsive are caregivers (Stith and Davis, 1984).

From a sociobiological standpoint, one would assume that most mothers are often more emotionally invested in the child than are nonfamilial caregivers, just by virtue of their relationship to the child. In fact, researchers have found that mother–child interactions are more emotionally charged and affectionate than caregiver–child interactions (Clarke-Stewart et al., 1994; Stith and Davis, 1984). In one study it was found that both caregivers and parents view physical contact between children and their daycare providers as less appropriate than contact between children and their parents (Hyson, Whitehead, and Prudhoe, 1988); thus it appears that caregivers may deliberately keep a certain degree of emotional distance from the children in their care.

As to whether mothers or caregivers are more sensitive, or appropriately responsive, toward the child, the data are not completely consistent. In two studies, mothers were found to be more stimulating and sensitive with their infants than were the infants' caregivers (Caruso, 1989; Stith and Davis, 1984), and in a third study, infants were found to be more likely to be securely attached to their mothers than to their nonparental caregivers (Galinsky, Howes, Kontos, and Shinn, 1994). However, Goossens and van IJzendoorn (1990) found that caregivers were more sensitive than either mothers or fathers in their interactions with the same child.

In terms of disciplinary styles, caregivers in daycare centers and nursery schools have been observed to be less directive and authoritarian, less critical and restrictive, and more likely to help, suggest activities, make tasks into games, respond to children's initiation of play, and mediate interactions with other children than are mothers (Hess, Price, Dickson, and Conroy, 1981; Howes, and Rubenstein, 1981; Rubenstein and Howes, 1983; Tizard, Carmichael, Hughes, and Pinkerton, 1980). Children also see their mother's role as being distinct from their caregiver's role: Mothers are perceived to be more involved in the children's physical care, whereas preschool teachers are seen more as providing play and stimulation (Smith, Ballard, and Barham, 1989).

Even when the daycare setting is a home, differences between mothers and caregivers are found. Family daycare providers differ from both daycare center teachers and mothers in their interactions with children. Compared with teachers, home care providers interact more with each child individually, especially when there are only one or two children in the care arrangement, and they may be more positive and sensitive in their approach to children. They also do more supervisory disciplining. Compared with mothers, family daycare providers are more emotionally distant; they engage in less positive physical contact with the child (kissing, caressing), and they are less playful and stimulating (Stallings, 1980). However, the more similar the childcare setting is to a homelike setting, the higher the concordance of attachment relationships between the child and each of the caregiving adults (family daycare provider and mother; Howes and Matheson, 1992).

Nonparental Caregivers in Brief

Taken together, these last two subsections suggest that not only do nonparental childcare arrangements fall into two general categories of physical settings (homes and centers), but in fact the adults in these different types of settings define their roles somewhat differently. That is, although there is some overlap in the roles that home and center caregivers fill, caregivers in home settings think and act more like "substitute mothers" toward the children, whereas caregivers in center-based settings behave more like teachers.

However, a description of the general types of daycare available in the U.S. today and the roles that caregivers play in those settings provides only part of the picture of children's experiences with nonparental caregivers. The crucial piece to fill in, of course, is the issue of the effects of nonparental care experiences on children's development. This issue is addressed in the next section.

DEVELOPMENTAL OUTCOMES FOR CHILDREN WITH AND WITHOUT NONPARENTAL CHILDCARE EXPERIENCES

Effects of Infant Daycare

The extent to which nonfamilial care affects infants has been a hotly debated issue. In particular, researchers have grappled with the question of whether or not early, extensive nonparental care leads to emotional insecurity and social maladjustment (Belsky, 1988, 1992; Clarke-Stewart, 1989, 1992). Research consistently shows that infants of working mothers form attachment relationships with them and prefer their mothers to their daycare providers. Some have argued, however, that infants are affected detrimentally by nonmaternal care, because the quality of their attachment to their mothers was found across a number of studies to be less secure and their later behavior with peers, more aggressive (Belsky, 1988, 1992).

This association with attachment to mother was not always observed. Studies based on rating children's behavior with their mothers at home after observing a substantial period of unstructured, natural interaction (Waters and Deane, 1985) did not reveal significant differences between children with extensive early daycare experience and those without (Howes et al., 1988; Strayer, Moss, and Blicharski, 1989; Weinraub, Jaeger, and Hoffman, 1988). However, the consistency of the differences observed across a substantial number of studies assessing children's attachment security in Ainsworth's Strange Situation led to a barrage of research to investigate whether infant care leads to attachment insecurity.

The results of this research generally indicates that infant care, per se, is not a risk factor for the development of emotional insecurity (although, as we discuss later in the chapter, childcare may compound the negative effects of inadequate care from mother). Consistently across studies, no link has been found between attending daycare in the first year and attachment behavior assessed in infancy or toddlerhood (Burchinal, Bryant, Lee, and Ramey, 1992; McKim, Cramer, Stuart, and O'Connor, 1999; Rauh, Ziegenhain, Mueller, and Wijnroks, 2000; Roggman, Langlois, Hubbs-Tait, and Rieser-Danner, 1994; Symons, 1998; see meta-analysis by Erel, Oberman, and Yirmiya, 2000) or later (Field, 1994; Pierrehumbert et al., 1996). In the National Institute of Child Health and Human Development (NICHD) Study of Early Child Care, more than 1,100 infants, living in 10 different regions of the country, were assessed in the Strange Situation at 15 months of age and a modified Strange Situation at 36 months. No significant main effects of infant childcare experience (amount, age at which care began, type or quality of care) on attachment security were found in either assessment (NICHD Early Child Care Research Network, 1997b, 2001a). Childcare was a small but significant predictor of maternal sensitivity and child engagement observed in a brief semistructured interaction with toys (NICHD Early Child Care Research Network, 1999a)—more hours of care predicted less sensitivity and engagement—but this was not an effect of infantcare, per se; the pattern of association was observed at older ages as well. Lamb (1998, 1999) concluded in his review of the research that the available evidence now indicates quite clearly that nonparental care, in and of itself, does not harm infant–mother attachment.

The pattern of recent research results regarding the possible contribution of infantcare to children's later behavior problems is also relatively benign. Two researchers uncovered links with aggressive behavior in preschool (Honig and Park, 1993) and kindergarten (Egeland and Hiester, 1995), but this was not so in school years (Egeland and Hiester, 1995). Other researchers found that aggression and other behavior problems in preschool were not more likely for children who attended infantcare (Balleyguier and Melhuish, 1996; Creps and Vernon-Feagans, 1999; Hausfather, Toharia, LaRoche, and Engelsmann, 1997; NICHD Early Child Care Research Network, 1998a) or for children whose mothers were employed in the first two years and who therefore were likely to be in infantcare (Greenstein, 1995; Harvey, 1999; Parcel and Menaghan, 1994; Vandell and Ramanan, 1992). In fact, children who attended infantcare were observed to have more positive social competence with peers in preschool (Creps and Vernon-Feagans, 1999; Howes, 1991) and more friends in school (Field,

1994). If there is a risk inherent in early nonparental care, it may be how much time is spent in the care arrangement. Children who spent more hours in care (full time rather than part time) were more likely to act aggressively in their interactions with other children in care—but they also engaged in more cooperative play (Field, 1994).

A third area of concern is whether children who were in infantcare are disadvantaged intellectually. Most of this concern comes from one data set, the National Longitudinal Study of Youth (NLSY). This national sample, which includes a relatively high proportion of young, low-income mothers, has been probed repeatedly by different researchers using different analyses and including sample sizes varying from 189 to 2,040. Several analyses revealed negative effects of early maternal employment on children's verbal intelligence scores—at least for some groups, such as boys from high-income families (Bayder and Brooks-Gunn, 1991; Desai, Chase-Lansdale, and Michael, 1989); other analyses did not (Greenstein, 1995; Parcel and Menaghan, 1994; Vandell and Ramanan, 1992). In analyses of the NLSY with larger, updated samples from this data set, Harvey (1999) found no main effect for mother's employment status in first year on children's scores, although when mothers worked more hours (in the first 3 years) children's cognitive scores were slightly lower through the age of 9 years and their academic achievement scores were slightly lower through the age of 6 years. Also, using up-to-date samples from the NLSY, Ruhm (2000) found that mothers' employment in the first year was associated with reductions in the verbal ability of 3- and 4-year-old children, but these reductions were partially offset by increases in scores related to employment during the second and the third years. Han, Waldfogel, and Brooks-Gunn (2000) found that the effects of maternal employment persisted to the ages of 7 or 8 years for children whose mothers started work early in the first year, but only when mothers worked in first year and then left the labor force was there a significant long-term negative effect of that first year. Taking into account the limitations of the NLSY data set and the complexity of its results, it seems safe to conclude that this study does not prove that children are damaged intellectually by being in nonparental care in infancy. Of particular importance, the NLSY is a study of maternal employment, not of nonparental care, per se. Han et al. (2000) also reported that children in their sample of the NLSY who were in nonparental care in the first year—relative care, nonrelative care, and center care—while their mothers worked had higher scores at ages 3 to 4 years than children of working mothers cared for by their parents.

Effects of Preschool Daycare

Cognitive development.   Children who attend daycare during the preschool years have quite consistently been found to have advanced cognitive and language development relative to children who are at home (Andersson, 1989; Burchinal, Lee, and Ramey, 1989; Clarke-Stewart et al., 1994; Garber and Hodge, 1989; Osborn and Millbank, 1987; Robinson and Corley, 1989; see reviews by Belsky, 1984; Clarke-Stewart and Fein, 1983; Hayes, Palmer, and Zaslow, 1990). This difference is not always found (e.g., Ackerman-Ross and Khanna, 1989; Vandell and Corasaniti, 1990, see meta-analysis by Erel et al., 2000), but there is a substantial body of research suggesting that the intellectual development of children who attend relatively high-quality daycare centers, nursery schools, or early childhood programs in the preschool years is advanced over the development of children from comparable family backgrounds who do not. Lamb concluded from his review that experimental research shows that nonparental childcare can have positive and enduring effects on cognitive performance, especially for children from less stimulating homes, although nonexperimental studies paint a less impressive picture (Lamb, 1998, 1999).

This acceleration in cognitive development has not usually been observed for children in daycare homes or with in-home caregivers. Although in some studies no significant differences between children in home daycare and daycare centers have been found, when there is a difference in intellectual development, it favors children in center-based care. On various measures of intellectual development, children in family daycare or in-home care perform at levels similar to those of children at home with their mothers, whereas children in daycare centers may do better (Andersson, 1989;

Bos and Granger, 1999; Clarke-Stewart, 1987; Clarke-Stewart et al., 1994; NICHD Early Child Care Research Network, 2000b).

In the study by Clarke-Stewart et al. (1994), a clear difference was found between children in home care (with parents, in-home caregiver, or daycare home provider) and center care (in nursery school, daycare center, or combined center and sitter arrangement), favoring the children attending centers, on a variety of measures of intellectual competence. The children in centers were, on the average, 6 to 9 months advanced over children cared for at home by their mothers or babysitters or in daycare homes. The differences appeared for children of all family backgrounds, for both boys and girls, after as little as 6 months in daycare. Two other studies support this finding of an advantage accruing from attendance at a daycare center. Broberg, Wessels, Lamb, and Hwang (1997) found that children's scores at the age of 8 years were related to the number of months they had spent in high-quality, Swedish daycare centers in the first $3\frac{1}{2}$ years, and in the NICHD study (NICHD Early Child Care Research Network, 2000b) cumulative experience in center care was associated with higher scores on cognitive tests when childern were 36 months of age.

Differences between children in daycare centers and daycare homes are less when the daycare homes are of high quality. For example, in one study, although the language competence of children in unlicensed daycare homes was inferior to that of children in centers, the language competence of children in regulated homes was equivalent (Goelman and Pence, 1987a). More telling, in another study, when care in daycare homes was enriched by the experimental addition of an educational curriculum, the intellectual performance of the children was observed to improve to the level of children in daycare centers (Goodman and Andrews, 1981). The effects of variations in daycare quality on children's development are described more fully in a later section.

Social development.   Children who attend daycare programs have also been shown to differ from children without nonfamilial care experience in their ability to interact with other children and adults. Compared with children without nonfamilial care experience, daycare children are more self-confident, outgoing, assertive, verbally expressive, self-sufficient, and comfortable, and less distressed, timid, and fearful in new situations (Fowler, 1978; Kagan et al., 1978; Moskowitz, Schwarz, and Corsini, 1977). They are more independent of their mothers in such situations; they go farther away and spend more time away and out of the mother's sight (Wynn, 1979). They exhibit more social skills and initiate more interaction in play with unfamiliar peers (Herwig, 1989; Wille and Jacobson, 1984). They play with peers at a more advanced level (Aureli and Colecchia, 1996). They know more about social rules (Siegal and Storey, 1985). They exhibit higher levels of social competence in the preschool years (Balleyguier and Melhuish, 1996; NICHD Early Child Care Research Network, in 2001b). In elementary school, they have more friends and extracurricular activities and are more popular (Field, 1991). In one recent 14-year longitudinal study in Sweden (Campbell, Lamb, and Hwang, 2000), the amount of time children spent in care before 3 years of age shaped their social skills with peers, and these individual differences in social competence remained stable through childhood and early adolescence. Like the differences in intellectual competence, differences in social competence appear frequently, although not invariably (e.g., Lamb, Hwang, Broberg, and Bookstein, 1988; Schenk and Grusec, 1987; see meta-analysis by Erel et al., 2000). Also, paralleling the results for cognitive development, children in centers have been found to be more socially competent than children in daycare homes (Clarke-Stewart et al., 1994; Wessels, Lamb, Hwang, and Broberg, 1997).

Researchers have also found, however, that, in addition to being more independent and outgoing, children attending daycare programs in the preschool years are sometimes less polite, agreeable, and compliant with their mother's or caregiver's request, louder and more boisterous, more irritable and rebellious, more likely to swear and have temper tantrums, and more likely to have behavior problems than children who are not or who have not been in daycare (Rabinovich, Zaslow, Berman, and Heyman, 1987; Robinson and Corley, 1989; Rubenstein and Howes, 1983; Sternberg et al., 1991; Thornburg, Pearl, Crompton, and Ispa, 1990). With peers, children in preschool daycare have been observed to be more aggressive and to engage in more negative interactions (Bates et al., 1991; Belsky, 1999; Haskins, 1985; Thornburg, Pearl, Crompton, and Ispa, 1990; Wille and Jacobson, 1984)—although this finding, too, is not inevitable (e.g., Hegland and Rix, 1990).

An argument has been made that the reason for this mixed bag of results is that participation in a stimulating daycare program fosters children's social development—social competence and independence—as it promotes their intellectual performance, but that because few programs focus on teaching children social rules—that is, teaching them effective ways of solving social problems—the consequence is that children express their competence and independence in less than polite ways with parents, peers, and other people (Clarke-Stewart, 1992). This explanation has not, as yet, been empirically investigated. An alternative argument is that these aggressive children are acting out the emotional maladjustment they have suffered as a consequence of having formed an insecure attachment to their mothers earlier on (Belsky, 1988, 1992). This second explanation seems unlikely, given the lack of connection between daycare attendance and the formation of insecure attachment to mother. Yet another explanation is that enrollment in daycare during the preschool years does not reliably facilitate or impede the development of positive relationships with peers. Instead, the quality of care is important: Children receiving high-quality care have better skills; children in poor care have deficient social skills and may be more aggressive (Lamb, 1998, 1999). We consider this possibility in the next section.

VARIATIONS IN THE QUALITY OF NONPARENTAL CAREGIVING AND THEIR OUTCOMES FOR CHILDREN'S DEVELOPMENT

Studies comparing developmental outcomes for children who have or have not experienced daycare are limited in their ability to explain within-group differences. Not all children who attend daycare programs show advances in cognitive development or exhibit aggression on the playground. This is because, just as not all families are created equal, not all daycare environments are created equal. Nonparental care, whether in daycare centers, family daycare homes, or with a caregiver in the child's own home, ranges from custodial to excellent in quality (Zigler and Freedman, 1990). It is illogical to try to evaluate whether daycare is universally harmful or helpful to children's development; rather, this question must be answered by taking into account the quality of the specific caregiving arrangements experienced by the individual child as well as other influential environmental factors in the child's ecology. In the next subsection, we review research that examines variations in caregiving quality and their effects on children's social and cognitive development. In this section, we take a closer look at how children's development is related to the quality of nonparental care.

A substantial number of investigators have documented significant associations between global measures of daycare quality—in centers and daycare homes—and children's cognitive development as assessed by observations of cognitive play and tests of intelligence and language ability (e.g., Broberg et al., 1997; Burchinal, Roberts et al., 2000; Burchinal, Roberts, Nabors, and Bryant, 1996; Cost, Quality and Child Outcomes Study Team, 1995; Howes, 1988; Kontos, 1994; Kontos, Hsu, and Dunn, 1994; Kwan, Sylva, and Reeves, 1998; NICHD Early Child Care Research Network, 2000b; Peisner-Feinberg and Burchinal, 1997; Phillips, McCartney, and Scarr, 1987; Phillips, Scarr, and McCartney, 1987; Pierrehumbert et al., 1996; Schliecker, White, and Jacobs, 1991; Whitebook et al., 1990), social development assessed by ratings of sociability, considerateness, compliance, self-regulation, positive peer interactions, and prosocial skills (e.g., Cost, Quality and Child Outcomes Study Team, 1995; Howes, 1990; Howes and Olenick, 1986; Howes and Stewart, 1987; Kontos, 1994; NICHD Early Child Care Research Network, 1998a, in press-b; Peisner-Feinberg and Burchinal, 1997; Phillips, McCartney, and Scarr, 1987; Phillips, Scarr, and McCartney, 1987; Vandell, Henderson, and Wilson, 1988), emotional well-being, indexed by interest, participation, self-esteem, social adjustment, and lack of anger, defiance, and other behavior problems (Cost, Quality and Child Outcomes Study Team, 1995; Hausfather et al., 1997; Kontos, 1991; NICHD

Early Child Care Research Network, 1998a), and positive relations with the caregiver (Cost, Quality and Child Outcomes Study Team, 1995; Galinsky, Howes, Kontos, and Shinn, 1994; Howes et al., 1992; Volling and Feagans, 1995). These associations are statistically significant, but modest in size, and do not usually last beyond the preschool years. In a follow-up of their study in Bermuda (Phillips, McCartney, and Scarr, 1987; Phillips, Scarr, and McCartney, 1987), for example, Chin-Quee and Scarr (1994) found a lack of longitudinal effects of the quality of infant and preschool childcare on school-age children's social and intellectual development. In a follow-up of the three-state study by Scarr, Phillips, McCartney, and Abbott-Shim (1993), Deater-Deckard, Pinkerton, and Scarr (1996) found no long-term effects of daycare center quality on school-age children's behavioral adjustment. Scarr (1998) concluded in her review of these and other studies that research to date on quality differences does not show major, long-term impacts on the development of children from ordinary homes. The results may be different for children from disadvantaged homes, for whom quality may supply missing elements in their lives.

Included in the measures of overall quality used in these studies were the amount or appropriateness of attention the child receives, the safety and stimulation in the physical setting, the educational curriculum that is followed, the size of the class and the classroom—factors that daycare professionals agree indicate high-quality care. However, global indexes of quality are not helpful for uncovering connections between children's development and specific kinds of daycare experience. More useful are those studies in which researchers have examined the associations between separate components of the daycare environment and particular developmental outcomes. In the next subsection, therefore, we focus on the results of these studies, and more specifically on studies of those aspects of daycare that relate to the caregiver herself—her behavior and the factors that influence her behavior.

Caregivers' Behaviors

Not surprisingly, studies of daycare show quite consistently that caregivers' behaviors predict the performance and development of the children in their care. Although associations between teacher–child interactions and children's social outcomes (attachment, social skills, behavior problems) have not been documented in every study (McCartney et al., 1997), there is a body of research suggesting that involved, stimulating, and responsive caregivers can foster children's development. Children whose teachers talk to them more are advanced in communication and language skills and score higher on intelligence tests (NICHD Early Child Care Research Network, 2000b; Phillips, McCartney, and Scarr, 1987; Phillips, Scarr, and McCartney, 1987; Rubenstein and Howes, 1983; Ruopp, Travers, Glantz, and Coelen, 1979; Whitebook et al., 1990). Even more closely related to children's performance and development is the quality of the attention the caregiver offers. Children whose caregivers are stimulating, educational, and respectful, who offer the children "intellectually valuable" experiences, especially language mastery experiences, have more advanced social and intellectual skills (Carew, 1980; Clarke-Stewart et al., 1994; Golden et al., 1978; McCartney, 1984; NICHD Early Child Care Research Network, 2000b; Phillips, Scarr and McCartney, 1987). Children spend more time working on a task, play at more complex levels, and perform better on tests of intelligence and achievement when their teachers are more positive and responsive to their questions, less physically affectionate, critical, and directive, and use positive rather than negative reinforcement (Clarke-Stewart et al., 1994; Miller, Bugbee, and Hybertson, 1985). Stimulation of children's development can begin in infancy: Infants who received enriched language intervention in infant daycare centers were well above norms for verbal and cognitive skills (Fowler, Ogston, Roberts-Fiati, and Swenson, 1997); they developed to gifted levels, excelled academically, and became strongly motivated to acquire multiple interests and competencies. They also enjoyed excellent relations with peers and adults and often became intellectual and social leaders. Other studies also demonstrate that children are more socially competent if teachers encourage their self-direction and independence, cooperation and knowledge, self-expression and social interaction (Miller and Dyer, 1975; Schweinhart et al., 1986). When the caregiver is sensitive and children's bids are answered consistently and appropriately

(Allhusen, 1992; Galinsky et al., 1994; Howes et al., 1992; van IJzendoorn et al., 1992), and when the caregiver is more involved and interactive (Elicker, Fortner-Wood, and Noppe, 1999; Seltenheim, Ahnert, Rickert, and Lamb, 1997), children are more likely to develop secure attachments with their nonfamilial caregivers. Children with teachers who are more highly engaged also display more intense positive affect and less intense negative affect in their activities with the caregiver (Hestenes, Kontos, and Bryan, 1993).

Studies such as these clearly indicate that the caregiver's behavior toward the child is a central mediator of the child's experience in nonfamilial care and therefore of the effects of nonfamilial care on the child's development. Certain characteristics of the caregiver (e.g., education and training, experience, stability and consistency, commitment to the child, and gender) may each play a role in the way the caregiver interacts with the child. We discuss the research on these characteristics next.

Caregivers' Characteristics

Education and training. Many researchers have demonstrated a link between the level of education and/or training that a caregiver has received and her behavior with the children in her care. Home care providers are more likely to be rated as sensitive, observed as responsive, and assessed as providing higher-quality care when they have higher levels of education (Galinsky et al., 1994). Center caregivers with higher levels of education work in centers that provide a higher overall quality of care (Cost, Quality and Child Outcomes Study Team, 1995). Those with higher levels of early childhood training implement more developmentally appropriate practices in their classrooms (Love, Ryer, and Faddis, 1992). More specifically, teachers who have completed a bachelor degree in early childhood education provide more appropriate caregiving and are more sensitive and less detached than teachers with vocational-level or high-school-level training (Whitebook et al., 1990); those with an associate degree or a and certificate in child development are more effective than teachers with some college or just high school plus workshops (Howes, 1997). With more training in child development, daycare providers are more knowledgeable, interactive, helpful, talkative, playful, positive, affectionate, involved, and didactic, and less authoritarian toward the children in their care (Berk, 1985; Fosburg et al., 1980; Kinney, 1988; Tyler and Dittman, 1980). When teachers have higher levels of education, the quality of center care is rated higher.

In turn, the children whose caregivers have higher levels of education and/or training in child development are more involved, cooperative, persistent, competent in play, and learn more (Arnett, 1989; Clarke-Stewart, 1987; Howes, 1983; Kontos et al., 1994; Lazar, Darlington, Murray, Royce, and Snipper, 1982; Ruopp et al., 1979; Whitebook et al., 1990). They have more secure attachments to their caregiver (Galinsky, Howes, and Kontos, 1995) and more advanced cognitive and language development (Burchinal et al., 2000; Dunn, 1993).

Despite the consistency and the reasonableness of these links with caregivers' education and training, significant associations have not always been documented. In the NICHD Study of Early Child Care (NICHD Early Child Care Research Network, 2000a), positive caregiving was more likely when home or center caregivers were more educated and held more child-centered beliefs about childrearing, but caregivers' behavior was not related to the amount of training they had in child development. In a study by Kontos (1994), quality of care was not related to home care providers' education or training. The reason that these studies failed to find the expected associations may have been that their measures of training were not specific enough or the range of caregivers' training was not extreme enough to detect variation. In a detailed analysis of data from the Cost, Quality, and Outcomes Study, Blau (2000) concluded that there is little question that training in early childhood education is related to childcare quality. However, the significance of the specific level of training—high school, college, college graduation, workshops—depends on what other variables are controlled. Education and training matter, but the precise form of education and training that is most productive depends on which unobserved differences are accounted for.

Center caregivers who have more education and training report higher levels of personal accomplishment (Manlove, 1993). They are more likely to rely on professional resources for information and to belong to professional childcare organizations; thus it may be that one way in which training can lead to provision of high quality care is by means of the increased reliance of more highly trained caregivers on professional sources to gauge and improve their own performance (Powell and Stremmel, 1989). Use of professional resources by family daycare providers has also been linked to provision of better quality care: Daycare home providers who consider themselves childcare professionals, read books on childcare or child development, attend meetings, and take classes in child development are more likely to talk, help, teach, and play with the children and to provide a physical environment with more music, dancing, books, and nutritious meals (Stallings, 1980). Caregivers who provide family daycare only because no better job is available, or as an informal agreement with friends, neighbors, or relatives, are less interactive and stimulating and spend more time on housework.

However, teachers with very high levels of training in child development may develop an academic orientation, emphasizing school activities (reading, counting, lessons, learning) to the exclusion of activities that promote children's social or emotional development. In Clarke-Stewart's (1987) study, children whose caregivers had more formal training in child development were advanced intellectually but were significantly less competent in interactions with an unfamiliar peer; children whose caregivers had a moderate level of training were more competent in both social and cognitive realms.

Experience. Another factor that predicts caregivers' behavior is their previous experience. With fewer than 2 or 3 years of experience in childcare, there is a tendency for daycare providers simply to go along with children and not initiate educational activities. With more professional childcare experience, caregivers report higher levels of personal accomplishment (Manlove, 1993) and are likely to be more stimulating, responsive, accepting, and positive (Clarke-Stewart et al., 1994; Howes, 1983; Kontos and Fiene, 1987; NICHD Early Child Care Research Network, 2000a). This relation is not always found, however. For example, in the National Day Care Study (Ruopp et al., 1979), teachers with more extensive experience were observed to provide less stimulating and educational interaction than caregivers with less experience. In the National Day Care Home Study (Fosburg et al., 1980; Stallings, 1980), caregivers with more experience were not markedly different from caregivers with less experience. With more than 10 years of experience, there is a tendency for teachers and caregivers to be less stimulating, stricter, and more controlling (Kontos and Fiene, 1987; Phillips, Scarr, and McCartney, 1987; Ruopp et al., 1979). Thus a moderate amount of experience may be most clearly related to higher-quality caregiving and more positive outcomes for children's development.

Stability and consistency. Another factor that influences the quality of care that providers offer is the length of time they have been in the particular daycare setting with a particular child. In stable childcare settings, the caregiver has more opportunity to get to know the child, read her or his signals more accurately, and respond appropriately. The more time children spend in a daycare setting, the more likely they are to form close relationships with their caregivers (Cummings, 1980; Elicker et al., 1999; Howes et al., 1988; Howes and Matheson, 1992; Smith, 1980). In one study, for example, 91% of infants who had been with their teacher for more than 1 year were securely attached to her, compared with 67% who had spent 9 to 12 months with her and 50% who had spent 5 to 8 months (Raikes, 1993). Toddlers prefer long-term stable care providers (Barnas and Cummings, 1994). Children who experience many changes in their childcare arrangements (either because of caregiver turnover or because the parents change the care arrangement) have been shown to perform poorly on intelligence tests (Whitebook et al., 1990), to be more insecure in their attachments with their mothers (Vaughn, Gove, and Egeland, 1980), to be less competent in their play with adults and peers (Howes and Stewart, 1987), and to exhibit more behavior problems (Bos and Granger, 1999). This association appears to be mediated by the nature of the caregiver's behavior; it is not just spending time together that matters, but that the caregiver and the infant are interactively involved (Elicker et al., 1999). However, there may be a ceiling on the positive effects of caregiver stability: beyond 3 or 4 years, there is no evidence that staying longer improves the quality of care (Clarke-Stewart et al., 1994). Caregiver stability is important not only because it is facilitates the formation of close relationships between children and their daycare providers, but also because stability is an indicator of good working conditions, adequate wages, and high staff morale. Stable home care providers are more likely to report high levels of job satisfaction, to work longer hours, to have previously held child-related jobs, and to have their own young children at home (Bollin, 1993). Caregivers provide higher-quality care when they are satisfied with their jobs (Whitebook et al., 1990).

Commitment to the child and the job. Another characteristic that may affect the caregiver's behavior with the child is the degree of her commitment to or emotional investment in the child. Caregivers who are less committed or emotionally invested are likely to keep an emotional distance from the children they care for; this in turn decreases the likelihood that the child will form a secure attachment relationship with the caregiver (Smith, 1980). Although it is intuitively reasonable to suspect that nonfamilial caregivers may be less emotionally committed to the children they care for and that children would be more likely to develop secure attachments with relatives than with nonfamilial caregivers, there are no data to bolster this view. In fact, in one study, children whose security scores with their daycare providers were very low were more likely to be cared for by a relative than in center-based or family daycare (Howes, Hamilton, and Allhusen, in preparation). Providers are more sensitive and responsive when they are committed to taking care of children and are doing so from a sense that this work is important and it is what they want to be doing; they seek out opportunities to learn about children's development and childcare; participate in family childcare training; think ahead about what the children are going to do and plan experiences for them; seek out the company of others who are providing care and are more involved with other providers; and charge higher rates and follow standard business practices (Galinsky et al., 1994). Center caregivers provide higher-quality care when they receive higher wages (Scarr, Eisenberg, and Deater-Deckard, 1994).

Gender. Does the gender of the caregiver make a difference in children's experiences in child-care? Very little research is available to help answer this question, primarily because, as mentioned earlier, the overwhelming majority of childcare providers are women. The few studies that have been done of teachers in daycare centers suggest that men and women differ in their teaching styles and behaviors. For instance, although both male and female teachers are likely to encourage what might be considered more feminine behavior (sitting quietly, reading, painting, working on puzzles) in both boys and girls in daycare, male teachers are less likely to do so. For boys, this may have a positive effect on academic achievement.

Some have argued that adults treat boys and girls differently because the children behave differently; others, that differences in adults' treatment of male and female infants has less to do with actual differences in the infants' characteristics or behaviors than in the adults' gender-stereotyped beliefs about boys and girls (see Leaper, in Vol. 1 of this *Handbook*). Adults may be more likely to resort to gender-stereotyped treatment of an infant when the infant is unfamiliar to them, but even mothers and fathers tend to interact more with same-gender than with opposite-gender infants (Parke and Sawin, 1980). If this is true for nonparental caregivers as well, then we might expect that girls in daycare settings would receive more attention than boys, given that most caregivers are female. Several studies appear to support this conjecture: Female caregivers were more affectionate (Botkin and Twardosz, 1988), sensitive, responsive, and stimulating (Allhusen and Cochran, 1991; NICHD Early Child Care Research Network, 1997a) with girls than with boys, and girls are more likely than boys to spend time in close proximity to teachers (Carpenter and Huston-Stein, 1980). Studies that compare male and female caregivers are needed to answer the question of whether the caregiver's gender, the child's gender, or both influence the quality of care that nonparental caregivers provide.

Researchers can also investigate whether the effects of nonparental care are related to the child's gender. Concern has been raised that boys are more affected than girls by early care. In one study, earlier entry into *low*-quality care was particularly associated with problem behavior and anger for boys (Hausfather et al., 1997). In two other studies in Sweden, boys benefited more than girls from their early experience in *good*-quality care in terms of school performance (Andersson, 1996) and decreased fear and unhappiness and increased social skills (Hagekull and Bohlin, 1995). However, most researchers, using large samples, have failed to find significant interactions with gender (e.g., Burchinal, Peisner-Feinberg, Bryant, and Clifford, 2000; Cost, Quality and Child Outcomes Study Team, 1995; Han, Waldfogel, and Brooks-Gunn, 2000; NICHD Early Child Care Research Network, 1998a, 2000b). In the NICHD Study (NICHD Early Child Care Research Network, 1997b), although a significant interaction with gender was reported for attachment at 15 months—boys with many hours of care and girls with few hours were more likely to be insecurely attached to their mothers—no interaction was observed at 36 months (NICHD Early Child Care Research Network, in 2001a), and the interaction at 15 months was not replicated by Canadian researchers (McKim et al., 1999), who suggested that the NICHD finding was probably spurious. It remains an open question whether gender—of child or caregiver—is reliably related to childcare and its effects.

Caregivers: The Key to Quality

Clearly, as the results of research discussed in this section have shown, the caregiver plays a crucial role in determining the quality of the child's experience in nonparental care. As we discussed, the caregiver's behavior and personal characteristics (e.g., education and training, experience, stability and consistency, commitment to the child, and gender) have been consistently related to various social and cognitive outcomes for the children in her care. However, caregiving does not take place in a vacuum; characteristics of the daycare setting itself also impinge on the quality of care that the nonparental caregiver provides. These setting characteristics are reviewed in the next section.

FACTORS THAT INFLUENCE CAREGIVER BEHAVIOR AND THAT ARE MEDIATED BY THE CAREGIVER

Structural aspects of the caregiving environment, such as the number of children in the care arrangement, the number of adults available to care for them, aspects of the physical environment, and the inclusion of an educational curriculum in the program, have been repeatedly shown to be important indicators of daycare quality (Clarke-Stewart, 1992; Howes et al., 1992; Phillips and Howes, 1987). In this section, we consider the ways in which each of these factors affects the caregiver's behavior or is mediated by her. As in the last section, these factors indirectly affect children's development by influencing the quality of nonfamilial care that the child receives.

Adult–Child Ratio and Group Size

The ratio of adults to children and the total number of children in the group are the two indicators of daycare quality most likely to have a direct effect on caregiver–child interaction (Howes, 1990; NICHD Early Child Care Research Network, 2000a). These factors have a substantial range from one setting to another. Government-mandated staff–child ratios for infants, for instance, have ranged from 1:3 to 1:12; for 4-year-old children, ratios in different states have ranged from 1:5 to 1:20. Significant associations showing the detrimental effect of low adult–child ratios and high class sizes for children's behavior and development have been found in a substantial number of studies (Burchinal, Roberts et al., 2000; Holloway and Reichhart-Erickson, 1988; Howes, 1983, 1987; Howes et al., 1988; Howes and Rubenstein, 1985; Lamb, Sternberg, Knuth, Hwang, and Broberg, 1991; NICHD

Early Child Care Research Network, 1999b, Phillips, McCartney, and Scarr, 1987; Phillips, Scarr, and McCartney, 1987; Ruopp et al., 1979; Sylva, Roy, and Painter, 1980; Whitebook et al., 1990). Children who are cared for in large groups or with many children per adult are less competent and more hostile with their peers; they are less cooperative and have more conflicts; they are less likely to be securely attached with their nonfamilial caregivers; and they spend more time in aimless activity (Howes et al., 1992; Ruopp et al., 1979; Smith and Connolly, 1980; Sylva et al., 1980).

Presumably the reason for these associations with child outcomes is that, when ratios are worse, the quality of nonparental care is worse. Correlational studies have shown that, with less favorable ratios and larger groups, the quality of care is lower: Caregivers interact less with the children, are less responsive and less positive in affect, spend less time stimulating children cognitively or socially, provide fewer activities, are less appropriate in their caregiving, and are more likely to be restrictive and negative (Blau, 2000; Cost, Quality and Child Outcomes Study Team, 1995; Howes, 1983; Howes et al., 1992; NICHD Early Child Care Research Network, 1996; Whitebook et al., 1990). In the NICHD Study, for example, when the ratio was 1:1, 38% of caregivers of infants were rated as highly sensitive; when the ratio was 1:2, only 17% of the caregivers received a rating of highly sensitive, and with a ratio of 1:4, only 8% of caregivers were rated as highly sensitive. This link with child–caregiver ratio was moderately strong, significant when other dimensions were controlled, and consistent across different types of care. In preschool care, differences related to ratio are still significant, but more modest in size (Blau, 2000; NICHD Early Child Care Network, 2000a). In childcare homes, differences related to the number of children in care are especially marked when children are in care full time rather than part time (Kontos, 1994).

Group size also may exert an effect on caregiving quality independent of the adult–child ratio. That is, even when the ratio of caregivers to children is kept small by adding caregivers to the class, the higher noise level and confusion of a larger class make it more difficult for caregivers to notice and attend to individual children's needs (Allhusen, 1992). Children from crowded classrooms have most behavioral disturbance and do worst on embedded-figures tests (Maxwell, 1996).

When researchers have experimentally reduced the adult–child ratio from 1:4 to 1:10 or 1:12 (Asher and Erickson, 1979; Smith and Connolly, 1980), children have been observed to have less contact with the caregiver, to have fewer of their questions answered, to engage in shorter conversations, and to be subject to more prohibitions. Increasing the ratio from 1:7 to 1:9, however, did not result in a measurable decline in the quality of care—although the caregivers themselves thought that quality had deteriorated (Love et al., 1992). Decreasing the ratio from 1:6 to 1:4 increased child-oriented activities and close interaction with the children only if the staff agreed on goals and methods in their work (Palmerus and Haegglund, 1991). Thus it appears that the quality of nonparental care is related to the number and ratio of children in the group, but this is not the only important factor.

Physical Environment

Another factor that matters is the physical environment. In the NICHD Study (NICHD Early Child Care Research Network, 1996, 2000a), across ages and different types of care, positive caregiving was consistently and significantly higher when the physical environment was safer and more stimulating. This link between care and context is also reflected in the children's behavior. Children do better when the daycare setting is divided into interest areas (Holloway and Reichhart-Erickson, 1988) and varied, age-appropriate, and educational toys, materials, and equipment are available (Goelman and Pence, 1987a; Holloway and Reichhart-Erickson, 1988; Howes and Rubenstein, 1985; Zajdeman and Minnes, 1991), much as these aspects of the home environment are related to children's development (see Bradley, in Vol. 2 of this *Handbook*). Simply adding novel materials to preschool classrooms or having more varied materials accessible, however, does not necessarily lead to cognitive gains; toys alone were not a direct promoter of development in two studies (Golden et al., 1978; Rubenstein and Howes, 1979). It was in combination with teachers' more stimulating behavior that aspects of the physical environment had an impact on children's development (Holloway and

Reichhart-Erickson, 1988; Ruopp et al., 1979). Adding books to the environment may be beneficial because these materials elicit increased interaction around literacy. In one recent study, researchers observed that adding five high-quality children's books per child to the daycare classroom led to more teacher–child reading, and children received higher scores on tests of literacy 6 months later in kindergarten (Neuman, 1999).

Educational Program

Studies of daycare have also shown that children in more educationally oriented daycare programs (those including prescribed educational activities such as lessons, guided play sessions, story reading, teaching of specific content, and more direct teacher instruction) differ from those in less educationally oriented programs. In these educational programs, children have been observed to spend more time in constructive and complex play with materials and with peers and to score higher on intelligence and achievement tests (e.g., Goelman and Pence, 1987a; Goodman and Andrews, 1981; Lazar, Hubbell, Murray, Rosche, and Royce, 1977; McCartney, 1984; Miller and Dyer, 1975; Sylva et al., 1980; Warash and Markstrom-Adams, 1995). When children spend their time in the daycare center just playing around with other children, they experience less "rich" play and are less competent in social and cognitive ways (McCartney, 1984; Phillips, McCartney, and Scarr, 1987; Phillips, Scarr, and McCartney, 1987; Sylva et al., 1980). This is one reason for the differences in children's development associated with being in a home care setting versus a center (described earlier in this chapter). Centers typically have more structured educational programs than childcare homes and children's play there is more complex (Clarke-Stewart et al., 1994; Kontos et al., 1994). On the other hand, there is no simple correlation between the level of educational curriculum and child outcomes (Kontos et al., 1994), and having too much structured activity, too much academic pressure, may predict less advanced social and cognitive development (Hirsh-Pasek, Hyson, and Rescorla, 1990; Miller and Dyer, 1975; Sylva et al., 1980).

Mediating Factors

The body of research reviewed in this section clearly shows that factors such as adult–child ratios, group size, physical setting, and an educational program all play important mediating roles in determining children's development in nonparental care. As suggested in the last section, however, the caregiver remains perhaps the most influential factor in the equation; the daycare setting factors discussed in this section merely influence her behavior or are mediated by her. However, the story of nonparental care is still not complete. The effects of childcare on children's development are determined not only by their experiences within nonparental care settings, but also by their experiences at home. Familial factors are considered in the next section.

FAMILY AND CHILDCARE INFLUENCES JOINTLY CONSIDERED

In our discussion of the relevance of attachment theory to research on nonparental caregiving and again in the section on the effects of daycare on infants, we discussed the widely held belief about the primacy of the mother in the young child's life and the concern expressed by some researchers that children's development may be at risk if they enter nonparental care in the first year of life. It is interesting to note, however, that until quite recently, family factors had not been taken into consideration in studying the effects of nonparental care on children's development. Yet if the child's family, and particularly the mother, plays such a central influential role in the child's development, then it seems clear that family factors must also be entered into the equation in determining what effects nonparental care experiences have on children's development. To explore the issue of how family and daycare experiences *together* contribute to children's development, researchers have begun to include assessments of family variables in studies of daycare children, that is, to consider both daycare and family predictors in a more integrated way. From these studies we are beginning to form a picture of how family and daycare variables interrelate and how both daycare and family variables together predict children's development.

Family Selection Factors

First, researchers have demonstrated the obvious—that children are not "randomly assigned" to nonparental care. Parents select childcare providers deliberately or are limited in their selection by their means and the availability of care, by their goals and characteristics—although the links are not simple or inevitable. Parents tend to select caregivers of the same ethnic group as their own (Kontos, Howes, Shinn, and Galinsky, 1997). They select a center care arrangement rather than a home care arrangement or no care at all if they value education more (Fuller, Holloway, and Liang, 1996). They may select caregivers with whom they share childrearing values and attitudes: For example, in one study, more authoritarian and punitive parents chose lower-quality care, in which, presumably, caregivers were more authoritarian and punitive (Bolger and Scarr, 1995). They select childcare of higher quality if their own parenting is of high quality (Burchinal et al., 1996; NICHD Early Child Care Research Network, 1999a). Nevertheless, these associations have not been observed in all studies: Parents did not choose home care providers who resembled them in childrearing preferences or quality of care in one study of home care (Kontos, 1994), and the quality of center care was not related to mothers' education or family functioning in another study (Hausfather et al., 1997) or to mother's education, ethnicity, or attitudes in a third (NICHD Early Child Care Research Network, 1997a). Relations with family income are more consistent—but not linear: When they are looking for home care, parents with higher incomes can find and select more sensitive caregivers and higher-quality care environments (Kisker, Hofferth, Phillips, and Farquhar, 1991; Kontos, 1994; Kontos et al., 1997; Phillips, 1995). However, when they select center care, the picture is more complicated. Parents with high incomes can afford and find the highest-quality care; parents with very low incomes are eligible for subsidized care, which is typically of high quality. It is middle-income families that can find or afford only the poorest-quality care (Cost, Quality and Child Outcomes, 1995; NICHD Early Child Care Research Network, 1997a; Phillips, Voran, Kisker, Howes, and Whitebook, 1994). It is important to take these complex selection factors into account in investigating the effects of nonparental care.

Controlling for Family Selection

Some researchers have dealt with the issue of these selection differences simply by statistically controlling for them in their analyses of daycare effects. Of course, when family and daycare quality are truly confounded, it is impossible to covary out all family effects, but researchers have at least tried to contain the overlap by imposing statistical controls. Doing so typically reduces the size of the associations between nonparental care and child outcomes. For example, in one study, although nonmaternal daycare appeared to be associated with higher levels of child behavior problems, the difference disappeared when family socioeconomic status was controlled (Poteat, Snow, Ironsmith, and Bjorkman, 1992). In another study, the quality of nonparental care was related to the level of child behavior problems, but the association was reduced to nonsignificance when family variables were controlled (NICHD Early Child Care Research Network, 1998a). However, associations between nonparental care quality and some aspects of children's behavior and development have still been significant in most major studies. The quality of center care was related to preschool children's cognitive and socioemotional development even with family selection factors controlled in the Cost, Quality and Outcomes Study (Peisner-Feinberg and Burchinal, 1997), and in the NICHD Study (NICHD Early Child Care Research Network, 2000b) analyses controlling for maternal intelligence, family income, the quality of parental care at home, and observed maternal cognitive stimulation, indicated that quality of care was still consistently—although modestly—related to children's cognitive and language outcomes through the age of 3 years. Today, and in future research, it is essential to include family variables when analyzing the effects of nonparental care.

Who Has More Influence—Parents or Nonparental Caregivers?

Rather than simply controlling for family factors, some researchers have included both family and daycare variables in their analyses in order to compare the relative influence of the two sets of variables. A number of these investigators have found that family variables are more strongly predictive of children's development than are daycare variables. Family variables were more predictive of children's cognitive, language, and social development than whether or not the child attended daycare, the type of daycare attended, or the quality of the daycare program in studies by Bates et al. (1991), Broberg, Hwang, Lamb, and Bookstein (1990), Goelman and Pence (1987b), Howes (1988), Kontos (1994), Melhuish, Lloyd, Martin, and Mooney (1990), Wadsworth (1986), and in the NICHD Study of Early Child Care (NICHD Early Child Care Research Network, 1998a). In several other studies, however, daycare attendance or quality was as highly predictive of children's development as family variables (Lamb et al., 1991; Phillips, Scarr, and McCartney, 1987; Vandell and Corasaniti, 1990; Wasik, Ramey, Bryant, and Sparling, 1990).

More important, perhaps, than which set of variables is more strongly predictive of child outcomes is whether the "influence" of the parents is reduced when the child is in nonparental care. One fear about early childcare is that children in nonparental care could lose out on the input from their parents that would ordinarily contribute to their cognitive and language development. This question was explored in analyses of the NICHD Study data (NICHD Early Child Care Research Network, 1998b). Results indicated that being in daycare does not, overall, reduce or eliminate the influence of the family. Children were selected from two groups: in full-time care (30+ hours of routine nonparental care from the age of 4 months to 3 years) or in maternal care (never more than 10 hours per week of routine care by anyone other than the mother). Correlations were calculated between family predictors and child outcomes for the two groups. Overall, there was not a significant difference between the two sets of correlations, suggesting that family influence is not "lost" when children are in care. Consistent with other research on family predictors of child development, children with higher levels of cognitive and language development came from more affluent families and their mothers were observed to be more sensitive and warm and less intrusive in play and to exhibit more positive involvement with them at home—irrespective of whether or not the children were in nonparental care.

Combined Effects of Parents and Nonparental Caregivers

Additive effects of family and childcare.   Other researchers have taken the strategy of investigating the combined effects of home and daycare environments on children's development. Using regression analyses, path analyses, or structural equations, they have found that the level of predictability of children's development is greater when both sets of variables are included in the analyses. Optimal development is supported when children receive high-quality care, stimulation, and encouragement in *both* home and daycare settings (Clarke-Stewart et al., 1994; Goelman and Pence, 1987b; Hausfather et al., 1997; Holloway and Reichhart-Erickson, 1989; Kontos, 1994; Laosa, 1982; Sternberg et al., 1991). One example demonstrating how children are affected by their experiences both at home *and* in nonparental care is provided by the NICHD Study. Recall that infantcare did not have a direct effect on the security of children's attachment to mother in that study. However, when the infant was in poor-quality, extensive, or unstable nonparental care—*combined with* having an insensitive mother at home—this led to elevated rates of insecure attachment at 15 months of age (NICHD Early Child Care Research Network, 1997b) and disorganized attachment at 36 months of age (NICHD Early Child Care Research Network, 2001a). This finding of attachment differences at 15 months of age was replicated by McKim et al. (1999): Age of entry into care, type, stability, and quality of care were not related to children's attachment security, but children with less sensitive mothers using extensive out of home care were least secure 6 months after care started. Thus research demonstrates that the effects of parental and nonparental care can be additive.

Family moderation of childcare effects.   Researchers have also found that another way family and nonparental care characteristics act together is that family characteristics may moderate the effects of childcare. In a number of studies, the positive effects of full-time high-quality daycare– like the effects of early maternal employment (Caughy, DiPietro, and Strobino, 1994; Harvey, 1999) were greatest for children whose home environments were least advantageous (Jarvis, 1987; Peisner-Feinberg and Burchinal, 1997; Scarr, Lande, and McCartney, 1988; Schlieker et al., 1991), and the negative effects of poor quality care (or maternal employment; Caughy et al., 1994; Han et al., 2000; Ruhm, 2000) were just as great or greater for children from more advantaged families (Peisner-Feinberg and Burchinal, 1997). Moderation is not always observed. In other studies, family factors did not significantly moderate the effects of childcare quality; quality of care was related to children's cognitive and social development across all levels of maternal education, ethnicity, income, and home quality (Burchinal et al., 1996; Burchinal, Peisner-Feinberg et al., 2000; Cost, Quality and Child Outcomes Study Team, 1995; NICHD Early Child Care Research Network, 1998a; 2000b). Nevertheless, even among these studies, associations were especially strong for minority children with less educated mothers (Burchinal, Peisner-Feinberg et al., 2000; Cost, Quality and Child Outcomes Study Team, 1995).

Parental mediation of childcare effects.   Yet another way that researchers have probed the joint contributions of parental and nonparental care is by analyzing statistical interactions between childcare and family effects, searching for ways in which parents might mediate the effects of nonparental care. Evidence of mediation was found by Belsky (1999), who observed that the quality of parenting mediated the negative effect of nonmaternal care on externalizing problems in 5-year-old boys; when children were in care for more hours, mothers were more negative and fathers were less positive in their interactions with the child. This is a promising approach, which can be followed up in future research. It suggests that it is important to look for the effects of nonparental care on parents' behavior as well as on their children.

   Another way in which researchers have explored the possibility of parental mediation of nonparental care effects is by asking how effects of nonparental care are affected by parents' attitudes toward nonparental care. Several researchers have found that childcare effects apparently depend on the mother's attitude toward using nonparental care. In the NICHD Study (NICHD Early Child Care Research Network, 1998b), when the mother believed—at the time the child was born—that maternal employment was beneficial for children's development, this predicted higher school readiness for children in full-time care (i.e., whose mothers were employed) and lower school readiness for children in maternal care (i.e., whose mothers were not employed) when the children were 3 years old. This finding suggests that when maternal attitudes toward care coincide with mothers' actual employment, then children benefit, whereas when attitudes and employment are at odds, children suffer. McKim et al. (1999), similarly, reported that employed mothers who preferred to stay home were more depressed and their children were more likely to experience unstable care than those who were working and wanted to work.

Nonparental care as a buffer for family effects.   One final way in which families and nonparental caregivers both contribute to children's development and well-being is when childcare serves as a buffer against deficiencies or problems in the family. We know that, when parents are stressed and family resources are limited, it is more difficult to provide good parental care and children may suffer. This can happen over the long run, as a result of chronic conditions in the family such as poverty or single parenthood; it can be the result of more acute conditions, such as having a bad day at work or feeling socially isolated. In one study, for example, it was documented that mothers respond to job stress by withdrawing from their children—they talk less and express less affection—on days when they experience greater workloads or interpersonal stress at work (Repetti and Wood, 1997). On days like these, it may benefit the child to be in a stable, high-quality nonparental care arrangement. Zajdeman and Minnes (1991) observed that children who made the most positive adjustment to being in daycare were those whose mothers were most socially isolated.

Several researchers have found evidence supporting the proposition that good daycare can buffer children against negative family circumstances. Hausfather et al. (1997) found that, when children were in high-quality centers, stress in their families was not related to angry behavior in the children—as it was for children in less adequate childcare, or, presumably would have been if they were not in care. Pierrehumbert et al. (1996) found that children who were insecurely attached to their mothers in infancy exhibited more externalizing behavior problems at the age of 5 years if they were in parental care but not if they had an extended experience of nonparental care. In the NICHD Study (NICHD Early Child Care Research Network, 1998b), too, childcare appeared to serve as a buffer: The cognitive and language development of children who were at home with their mothers was more strongly affected by the mother's depression than that of children who were in full-time nonparental care. Moreover, children from single-parent families and children with authoritarian mothers had poorer cognitive and socioemotional functioning if they were home with their mother but not if they were in full-time nonparental care.

Families and Childcare Together

Nonparental care should not be considered as an alternative to parental care or a competitor for the child's development. Nonparental care can support both children and families. Researchers have not done as much to document the positive effects of good nonparental care on family functioning as they have to demonstrate the effects of good care on child development; but these efforts are beginning. Research now confirms that, when children are in good-quality care, their parents are happier. Mothers are more satisfied with care when staff turnover is low and providers are sensitive and responsive; when caregivers are detached in their interactions with the children or the setting is chaotic, mothers miss their children and are less likely to believe that they are benefiting from care (Shinn, Phillips, Howes, Galinsky, and Whitebook, 1990).

Just as we were finishing this chapter, a colleague received a message from a young mother in Portland, Oregon, who had consulted her about childcare (M. Weinraub, personal communication, August 25, 2000). After staying at home with their child, now 6 months old, she and her husband wanted to know, should she return to employment? Money was getting tight, and she was offered a good position. If she did return to work, what should she do about childcare? She was wary of group childcare. Ultimately, she and her husband interviewed a number of care providers and went with group care. In her message was a paragraph describing her experiences visiting Henry, in his childcare center, unannounced:

> today i paid a surprise visit to the infants room at st. james. i had a no-show appointment not too far away and popped over to visit henry. i walked in and spied him in the lap of another woman! shannon was holding him on her lap and talking with him while chrissy, another "teacher" was bending over kissing him and they were all laughing and giggling together. henry was beaming from ear to ear and cooing like a little dove while his little dimples lit up the room. it did my heart good. sometimes, paranoid mom that i am, i think that they must, when they know I'm coming, stage little scenes like this to keep me coming back as a paying customer. but today, i know for sure this is a place i feel good about leaving my baby. there's a lot of love at st. james and it begins to feel like an extension of family. I've learned so much about mom-stuff by watching the staff interact with the kids. and I've been given the opportunity to appreciate my child through the eyes of a group of women who care about him very much. i feel so lucky. this kind of place is priceless. i think i would choose to work just so that my kids could go here! and THAT gives me a feeling of great joy.

This mother's testimonial provides a nice balance to the recent survey that revealed that most working parents with preschool children in this country believe they would do a better job looking after their youngsters than any nonparental caregiver (Public Agenda, August 23, 2000). More than 60% of the parents surveyed by Public Agenda disagreed that a "top-notch" center could provide a child with care as good as a stay-at-home parent. They expressed strong concern that children could suffer abuse there and said that daycare should be the option of last resort. In another recent nationwide survey published by *Parents Magazine* and the I Am Your Child Foundation (Hickey, 2000), similarly, 77% of mothers wished they could stay home full time to rear their children, and a poll conducted by the *Los Angeles Times* (Decker, 1999) showed that 81% of mothers would rather stay home with their children than work, if circumstances allowed. The tensions expressed by these parents, who are using nonparental care and worrying about it, suggest that researchers have a role to play in continuing to monitor positive and negative effects of nonparental care on children's development and family well-being and communicating our findings to parents.

FUTURE DIRECTIONS OF CHILDCARE RESEARCH

Nonparental caregivers play an important role in the lives of a majority of young children in the United States today. There is wide variation in the quality of care that nonparental caregivers provide, and children's development is affected by the quality of that care. However, as the research reviewed in the previous section illustrates, daycare is only part of the picture: Children not only attend daycare programs of different kinds and qualities, they also live in families of different kinds and qualities. To understand the complex picture of the effects of nonfamilial caregiving experiences on children's development, it is necessary to study not just variations in the quality of care that children experience in those settings, but also the additive, complementary, or compensatory effects of their experiences at home.

As we have described, the recent wave of childcare research, with its much more sophisticated designs and comprehensive focus on child and family development, has allowed us to begin to understand the proximal and distal effects of childcare on children's development in a more complete way than ever before. As this line of research continues into the next century, we will be in a position to gain an even clearer understanding of the potential effects of childcare experience on young children and their families. At least three issues will be important to consider as this research continues to develop. First, what are the longer-range impacts of early childcare on children's development? Longitudinal studies such as the NICHD Study of Early Child Care, which is following children into preadolescence (age 12 years) and perhaps beyond, will allow us to address this question. Second, what roles do societal and cultural values play in the effects of childcare on children's and families' development and well-being? The argument has been made that the preponderance of childcare research that has been conducted up to this point has adopted European American, middle-socioeconomic values and ideologies regarding childhood, child development, and the role of the family (Rosenthal, 1999). Future research needs to take culture and societal values into account when considering the effects of childcare on child and family development. Third, how large are the "effects" of nonparental care on children's development, that is, *how much* does childcare actually affect children? The issue of effect sizes is an important one in developmental science (McCartney and Rosenthal, 2000), particularly in this area, in which the size of statistical associations has practical implications for childcare policy. Decisions about whether the government should invest resources in improving adult–child ratios or training caregivers in childcare centers, for example, may be based, in part, on the magnitude of associations between these factors and childcare quality or child outcomes. It is essential to consider whether the correlations revealed by research have social and practical importance as well as statistical significance. A related issue is how to determine effect sizes. A controversy is brewing about how much statistical control should be imposed in weighing the effects of childcare above and beyond the contribution of the family. In one camp are those who argue that the latest research on the effects of childcare has been "overcontrolled" statistically; that is, too many family factors—demographic variables, parenting attitudes and behavior, child characteristics, and so forth—have been included in the analyses, washing out childcare effects that would otherwise be apparent. Others argue that the same research has not been sufficiently controlled for various important family and selection factors (Blau, 2000). In either case, the argument has been made that the "true" effects of childcare on child outcomes have not been adequately measured (Lamb, 2000). Only large-scale, comprehensive studies of childcare will make it possible for researchers to examine this issue by comparing the results obtained with statistical models with greater versus fewer numbers of selection factors. In the future, researchers will look to these large studies and data sets for answers to these difficult questions.

CONCLUSIONS

The organization of this discussion of nonparental care and its effects on children's development has roughly paralleled the historical development of this body of research. One is reminded of Bronfenbrenner's (1979) concentric circles of the child's world from microsystem to macrosystem. The first attempts at characterizing the effects of daycare on development consisted primarily of comparisons between daycare and home-reared children. Next, researchers began to look more closely at variations within daycare and to link those variations to differences in child outcomes. As a third step, researchers began to construct their findings as flow charts, with some characteristics of the daycare setting having a direct influence on the child and others having indirect effects by means of other daycare characteristics. In the most recent (and most complex) set of studies, researchers inserted familial influences into the diagram, recognizing that daycare factors alone cannot paint the complete picture of the effects of nonparental caregiving experiences on children's development.

   The data we have reviewed suggest that theory, too, must take this broad perspective on the multiple determinants of developmental outcomes for children in nonparental care. Traditional attachment theory and sociobiological theory place mothers and other biologically related individuals at the center of influence on children's development. Although noone would disagree that mothers fill a very important role in young children's lives, the controversy begins when we assume that children who spend less than full time at home with their mothers are at risk. In contrast to these theories, cognitive and social stimulation theories suggest that nonparental care that is of high quality is associated with developmental gains. The problem here is that the developmental gains that have been observed have been disappointingly modest. What is left for the future is the development of theory and research that will integrate these diverse views of development and that will go beyond a focus on either parental care or nonparental care to illuminate the larger and more complex ecology of contemporary children's lives.

ACKNOWLEDGMENT

We thank Darlene Clements for contributions to the first edition of this chapter. We also acknowledge the support of the National Institute of Child Health and Human Development (430-HD 25456).

REFERENCES

Ackerman-Ross, S., and Khanna, P. (1989). The relationship of high quality day care to middle-class 3-year-olds' language performance. *Early Childhood Research Quarterly, 4,* 97–116.
Ainsworth, M. D. S. (1982). Attachment: Retrospect and prospect. In C. M. Parkes and J. Stevenson-Hinde (Eds.), *The place of attachment in human behavior* (pp. 3–30). New York: Basic Books.

Allhusen, V. D. (1992, May). *Caregiving quality and infant attachment in day care contexts of varying quality.* Poster presented at the Eighth International Conference on Infant Studies, Miami, FL.

Allhusen, V. D., and Cochran, M. M. (1991, April). *Infants' attachment behaviors with their day care providers.* Poster presented at the biennial meetings of the Society for Research in Child Development, Seattle, WA.

Anderson, C. W., Nagle, R. J., Roberts, W. A., and Smith, J. W. (1981). Attachment to substitute caregivers as a function of center quality and caregiver involvement. *Child Development, 52*, 53–61.

Andersson, B.-E. (1989). Effects of public day care: A longitudinal study. *Child Development, 60*, 857–866.

Andersson, B.-E. (1996). Children's development related to day-care, type of family and other home factors. *European Child and Adolescent Psychiatry, 5*(Suppl. 1), 73–75.

Arnett, J. (1989). Caregivers in day-care centers: Does training matter? *Journal of Applied Developmental Psychology, 10*, 541–552.

Arnold, D. H., McWilliams, L., and Arnold, E. H. (1998). Teacher discipline and child misbehavior in daycare: Untangling causality with correlational data. *Developmental Psychology, 34*, 276–287.

Asher, K. N., and Erickson, M. T. (1979). Effects of varying child–teacher ratio and group size on day care children's and teachers' behavior. *American Journal of Orthopsychiatry, 49*, 518–521.

Aureli, T., and Colecchia, N. (1996). Day care experience and free play behavior in preschool children. *Journal of Applied Developmental Psychology, 17*, 1–17.

Balleyguier, G., and Melhuish, E. C. (1996). The relationship between infant day care and socio-emotional development with French children aged 3–4 years. *European Journal of Psychology of Education, 11*, 193–199.

Barash, D. (1979). *The whisperings within.* New York: Harper & Row.

Barnas, M. C., and Cummings, E. M. (1994). Caregiver stability and toddlers' attachment-related behavior towards caregivers in day care. *Infant Behavior and Development, 17*, 141–147.

Bates, J. E., Marvinney, D., Bennett, D. S., Dodge, K. A., Kelly, T., and Pettit, G. S. (1991, April). *Children's daycare history and kindergarten adjustment.* Paper presented at the biennial meetings of the Society for Research in Child Development, Seattle, WA.

Bayder, N., and Brooks-Gunn, J. (1991). Effects of maternal employment and child-care arrangements on preschoolers' cognitive and behavioral outcomes: Evidence from the children on the National Longitudinal Survey of Youth. *Developmental Psychology, 27*, 932–945.

Belsky, J. (1984). Two waves of day care research: Developmental effects and conditions of quality. In R. C. Ainslie (Ed.), *The child and the day care setting* (pp. 1–34). New York: Praeger.

Belsky, J. (1988). The "effects" of infant day care reconsidered. *Early Childhood Research Quarterly, 3*, 235–272.

Belsky, J. (1992). Consequences of child care for children's development: A deconstructionist view. In A. Booth (Ed.), *Child care in the 1990s: Trends and consequences* (pp. 83–94). Hillsdale, NJ: Lawrence Erlbaum Associates.

Belsky, J. (1999). Quantity of nonmaternal care and boys' problem behavior/adjustment at ages 3 and 5: Exploring the mediating role of parenting. *Psychiatry: Interpersonal and Biological Processes, 62*, 1–20.

Berk, L. (1985). Relationship of educational attainment, child oriented attitude, job satisfaction, and career commitment to caregiver behavior toward children. *Child Care Quarterly, 14*, 103–129.

Blau, D. M. (2000). The production of quality in child-care centers: Another look. *Applied Developmental Science, 4*, 136–148.

Bolger, K. E., and Scarr, S. (1995). Not so far from home: How family characteristics predict child care quality. *Early Development and Parenting, 4*, 103–112.

Bollin, G. G. (1993). An investigation of job stability and job satisfaction among family day care providers. *Early Childhood Research Quarterly, 8*, 207–220.

Bos, J. M., and Granger, R. C. (1999, April). *Estimating effects of day care use on child outcomes: Evidence from the New Chance Demonstration.* Paper presented at the biennial meetings of the Society for Research in Child Development, Albuquerque, NM.

Botkin, D., and Twardosz, S. (1988). Early childhood teachers' affectionate behavior: Differential expression to female children, male children, and groups of children. *Early Childhood Research Quarterly, 3*, 167–177.

Bowlby, J. (1969). *Attachment and loss: Vol 1. Attachment.* New York: Basic Books.

Broberg, A. G., Hwang, C.-P., Lamb M. E., and Bookstein, F. L. (1990). Factors related to verbal abilities in Swedish preschoolers. *British Journal of Developmental Psychology, 8*, 335–349.

Broberg, A. G., Wessels, H., Lamb, M E., and Hwang, C. P. (1997). Effects of day care on the development of cognitive abilities in 8-year-olds: A longitudinal study. *Developmental Psychology, 33*, 62–69.

Bronfenbrenner, U. (1979). *The ecology of human development: Experiments by nature and design.* Cambridge, MA: Harvard University Press.

Burchinal, M. R., Bryant, D. M., Lee, M. W., and Ramey, C. T. (1992). Early day care, infant/mother attachment, and maternal responsiveness in the infant's first year. *Early Childhood Research Quarterly, 7*, 383–396.

Burchinal, M. R., Lee, M., and Ramey, C. (1989). Type of day care and preschool intellectual development in disadvantaged children. *Child Development, 60*, 128–137.

Burchinal, M. R., Peisner-Feinberg, E., Bryant, D. M., and Clifford, R. (2000). Children's social and cognitive development and child-care quality: Testing for differential associations related to poverty, gender, or ethnicity. *Applied Developmental Science, 4*, 149–165.

Burchinal, M. R., Roberts, J. E., Nabors, L. A., and Bryant, D. M. (1996). Quality of center child care and infant cognitive and language development. *Child Development, 67*, 606–620.

Burchinal, M. R., Roberts, J. E., Riggins, R., Jr, Zeisel, S. A., Neebe, E., and Bryant, D. (2000). Relating quality of center-based child care to early cognitive and language development longitudinally. *Child Development, 71*, 338–357.

Caldwell, B. (1970). The rationale for early intervention. *Exceptional Children, 36*, 717–726.

Campbell, J. J., Lamb, M. E., and Hwang, C. P. (2000). Early child-care experiences and children's social competence between 1.5 and 15 years of age. *Applied Developmental Science, 4*, 166–175.

Carew, J. (1980). Experience and the development of intelligence in young children. *Monographs of the Society for Research in Child Development, 45*(6–7, Serial No. 187).

Carpenter, C. J., and Huston-Stein, A. (1980). Activity structure and sex-typed behavior in preschool children. *Child Development, 51*, 862–872.

Caruso, D. (1989). Quality of day care and home-reared infants' interaction patterns with mothers and day care providers. *Child and Youth Care Quarterly, 18*, 177–191.

Cassibba, R., Van IJzendoorn, M. H., and D'Odorico, L. (2000). Attachment and play in child care centres: Reliability and validity of the Attachment Q-sort for mothers and professional caregivers in Italy. *International Journal of Behavioral Development, 24*, 241–255.

Caughy, M. O., DiPietro, J A., and Strobino, D. M. (1994). Day-care participation as a protective factor in the cognitive development of low-income children. *Child Development, 65*, 457–471.

Chin-Quee, D., and Scarr, S. (1994). Lack of longitudinal effects of infant and preschool child care on school-age children's social and intellectual development. *Early Development and Parenting, 2*, 103–112.

Clarke-Stewart, K. A. (1987). Predicting child development from daycare forms and features: The Chicago study. In D. A. Phillips (Ed.), *Quality in child care: What does research tell us? Research Monographs of the National Association for the Education of Young Children* (Vol. 1, pp. 21–42). Washington, DC: National Association for the Education of Young Children.

Clarke-Stewart, K. A. (1989). Infant day care: Maligned or malignant? *American Psychologist, 44*, 266–273.

Clarke-Stewart, K. A. (1992). Consequences of child care for children's development. In A. Booth (Ed.), *Child care in the 1990s: Trends and consequences* (pp. 63–82). Hillsdale, NJ: Lawrence Erlbaum Associates.

Clarke-Stewart, K. A., and Fein, G. G. (1983). Early childhood programs. In P. H. Mussen, M. Haith, and J. Campos (Eds.), *Handbook of child psychology* (Vol. 2, pp. 917–1000). New York: Wiley.

Clarke-Stewart, K. A., Gruber, C. P., and Fitzgerald, L. M. (1994). *Children at home and in day care*. Hillsdale, NJ: Lawrence Erlbaum Associates.

Cochran, M. M. (1993). *International handbook of child care policies and programs*. Westport, CT: Greenwood.

Cost, Quality and Child Outcomes Study Team. (1995). *Cost, quality, and child outcomes in child care centers* (Public Report, 2nd ed.). Denver: Economics Department, University of Colorado at Denver.

Creps, C. L., and Vernon-Feagans, L. (1999). Preschoolers' social behavior in day care: Links with entering day care in the first year. *Journal of Applied Developmental Psychology, 20*, 461–479.

Cummings, E. M. (1980). Caregiver stability and day care. *Developmental Psychology, 16*, 31–37.

Deater-Deckard, K., Pinkerton, R., and Scarr, S. (1996). Child care quality and children's behavioral adjustment: A four-year longitudinal study. *Journal of Child Psychology and Psychiatry and Allied Disciplines, 37*, 937–948.

Decker, C. (1999, June 13). Parents tell of decisions, struggles in child-rearing. *The Los Angeles Times* [On-line]. Available: www.latimes.com/news/timespoll/state/lat_poll990613.htm

Dennis, W. (1973). *Children of the creche*. New York: Appleton-Century-Crofts.

Desai, S., Chase-Lansdale, P. L., and Michael, R. T. (1989). Mother or market? Effects of maternal employment on the intellectual ability of four-year-old children. *Demography, 26*, 545–561.

Directorate General for Research. (1997). *Social and labour market policy in Sweden*. Social Affairs Series, W13 [On-line]. Available: http://www.europarl.eu.int/dg4/wkdocs/soci/w13/en/text2.htm

Dunn, L. (1993). Proximal and distal features of day care quality and children's development. *Early Childhood Research Quarterly, 8*, 167–192.

Egeland, B., and Hiester, M. (1995). The long-term consequences of infant day-care and mother–infant attachment. *Child Development, 66*, 474–485.

Eheart, B. K., and Leavitt, R. L. (1989). Family day care: Discrepancies between intended and observed caregiving practices. *Early Childhood Research Quarterly, 4*, 145–162.

Elicker, J., Fortner-Wood, C., and Noppe, I. C. (1999). The context of infant attachment in family child care. *Journal of Applied Developmental Psychology, 20*, 319–336.

Erel, O., Oberman, Y., and Yirmiya, N. (2000). Maternal versus nonmaternal care and seven domains of children's development. *Psychological Bulletin, 126*, 727–747.

Fagot, B. E. (1973). Influence of teacher behavior in the preschool. *Developmental Psychology, 9*, 198–206.

Farran, D. C., and Ramey, C. T. (1977). Infant day care and attachment behaviors toward mothers and teachers. *Child Development, 48*, 1112–1116.

Field, T. M. (1979). Infant behaviors directed toward peers and adults in the presence and absence of mother. *Infant Behavior and Development, 2*, 47–54.

Field, T. M. (1991). Quality infant day-care and grade school behavior and performance. *Child Development, 62*, 863–870.

Field, T. M. (1994). Infant day care facilitates later social behavior and school performance. In H. Goelman and E. V. Jacobs (Eds.), *Children's play in child care settings* (pp. 69–84). Albany, NY: State University of New York Press.

Finkelstein, N. W. (1982). Aggression: Is it stimulated by day care? *Young Children, 37*, 3–12.

Fosburg, S., Hawkins, P. D., Singer, J. D., Goodson, B. D., Smith, J. M., and Brush, L. R. (1980). *National Day Care Home Study.* Cambridge, MA: Abt Associates.

Fowler, W. (1978). *Day care and its effects on early development: A study of group and home care in multi-ethnic, working-class families.* Toronto: Ontario Institute for Studies in Education.

Fowler, W., Ogston, K., Roberts-Fiati, G., and Swenson, A. (1997). The effects of enriching language in infancy on the early and later development of competence. *Early Child Development and Care, 135*, 41–77.

Freedman, D. G. (1979). *Human sociobiology.* New York: Free Press.

Fuller, B., Holloway, S. D., and Liang, X. (1996). Family selection of child-care centers: The influence of household support, ethnicity, and parental practices. *Child Development, 67*, 3320–3337.

Galinsky, E., Howes, C., and Kontos, S. (1995). *The family child care training study.* New York: Families and Work Institute.

Galinsky, E., Howes, C., Kontos, S., and Shinn, M. (1994). *The Study of Children in Family Child Care and Relative Care.* New York: Families and Work Institute.

Garber, H. L., and Hodge, J. D. (1989). Risk for deceleration in the rate of mental development. *Developmental Review, 9*, 259–300.

Ghedini, P. (2001). Change in Italian national policy for children 0–3 years old and their families: Advocacy and responsibility. In L. Gandini and C. P. Edwards (Eds.), *Bambini: The Italian approach to infant/toddler care* (pp. 38–48). New York: Teachers College Press.

Goelman, H., and Pence, A. R. (1987a). Effects of child care, family, and individual characteristics on children's language development: The Victoria Day Care Research Project. In D. A. Phillips (Ed.), *Quality in child care: What does research tell us?* (pp. 89–104). Washington, DC: National Association for the Education of Young Children.

Goelman, H., and Pence, A. R. (1987b). Some aspects of the relationship between family structure and child language in three types of day care. In I. E. Sigel, D. L. Peters, and S. Kontos (Eds.), *Annual advances in applied developmental psychology* (Vol. 2, pp. 129–149). Norwood, NJ: Ablex.

Golden, M., Rosenbluth, L., Grossi, M. T., Policare, H. J., Freeman, H., and Brownlee, E. M. (1978). *The New York City Infant Day Care Study.* New York: Medical and Health Research Association of New York City.

Goodman, N., and Andrews, J. (1981). Cognitive development of children in family and group day care. *American Journal of Orthopsychiatry, 51*, 271–284.

Goossens, F. A., and van IJzendoorn, M. H. (1990). Quality of infants' attachments to professional caregivers: Relation to infant–parent attachment and day-care characteristics. *Child Development, 61*, 832–837.

Greenstein, T. N. (1995). Are the "most advantaged" children truly disadvantaged by early maternal employment? *Journal of Family Issues, 16*, 149–169.

Hagekull, B., and Bohlin, G. (1995). Day care quality, family and child characteristics and socioemotional development. *Early Childhood Research Quarterly, 10*, 505–526.

Hamilton, W. D. (1964). The genetical evolution of social behavior I. *Journal of Theoretical Biology, 7*, 1–16.

Han, W.-J., Waldfogel, J., and Brooks-Gunn, J. (2000). The effects of early maternal employment on later cognitive and behavioral outcomes. Unpublished manuscript, Columbia University, New York.

Harvey, E. (1999). Short-term and long-term effects of early parental employment on children of the National Longitudinal Survey of Youth. *Developmental Psychology, 35*, 445–459.

Haskins, R. (1985). Public school aggression among children with varying day-care experience. *Child Development, 56*, 689–703.

Hausfather, A., Toharia, A., LaRoche, C., and Engelsmann, F. (1997). Effects of age of entry, day-care quality, and family characteristics on preschool behavior. *Journal of Child Psychology and Psychiatry and Allied Disciplines, 38*, 441–448.

Hayes, C. D., Palmer, J. L., and Zaslow, M. J. (1990). *Who cares for America's children?* Washington, DC: National Academy Press.

Hegland, S. M., and Rix, M. K. (1990). Aggression and assertiveness in kindergarten children differing in day care experiences. *Early Childhood Research Quarterly, 5*, 105–116.

Herwig, J. E. (1989, April). *Longitudinal effects of preschool experience on social and cognitive play behaviors of preschoolers.* Paper presented at the biennial meetings of the Society for Research in Child Development, Kansas City, MO.

Hess, R. D., Price, G. G., Dickson, W. P., and Conroy, M. (1981). Different roles for mothers and teachers: Contrasting styles of child care. In S. Kilmer (Ed.), *Advances in early education and day care* (Vol. 2, pp. 1–28). Greenwich, CT: JAI.

Hestenes, L. L., Kontos, S., and Bryan, Y. (1993). Children's emotional expression in child care centers varying in quality. *Early Childhood Research Quarterly, 8,* 295–307.

Hickey, M. C. (2000, March). The parent trap. *Parents Magazine* (pp. 124–129).

Hirsh-Pasek, K., Hyson, M. C., and Rescorla, L. (1990). Academic environments in preschool: Do they pressure or challenge young children? *Early Education and Development, 1,* 401–423.

Holloway, S. D., and Reichhart-Erickson, M. (1988). The relationship of day care quality to children's free-play behavior and social problem-solving skills. *Early Childhood Research Quarterly, 3,* 39–53.

Holloway, S. D., and Reichhart-Erickson, M. (1989). Child care quality, family structure, and maternal expectations: Relationship to preschool children's peer relations. *Journal of Applied Developmental Psychology, 10,* 281–298.

Honig, A.S., and Park, K. J. (1993). Effects of day care on preschool sex-role development. *American Journal of Orthopsychiatry, 63,* 481–486.

Howes, C. (1983). Caregiver behavior in centers and family day care. *Journal of Applied Developmental Psychology, 4,* 99–107.

Howes, C. (1987). Social competency with peers: Contributions from child care. *Early Childhood Research Quarterly, 2,* 155–167.

Howes, C. (1988). Peer interaction of young children. *Monographs of the Society for Research in Child Development, 53* (Serial No. 217).

Howes, C. (1990). Current research on early day care. In S. S. Chehrazi (Ed.), *Psychosocial issues in day care* (pp. 21–35). Washington, DC: American Psychiatric Press.

Howes, C. (1991). A comparison of preschool behaviors with peers when children enroll in child care as infants or older children. *Journal of Reproductive and Infant Psychology, 9,* 105–115.

Howes, C. (1997). Children's experiences in center-based child care as a function of teacher background and adult: child ratio. *Merrill-Palmer Quarterly, 43,* 404–425.

Howes, C. (2000). Social–emotional classroom climate in child care, child–teacher relationships and children's second grade peer relations. *Social Development, 9,* 191–204.

Howes, C., and Hamilton, C. E. (1992). Children's relationships with caregivers: Mothers and child care teachers. *Child Development, 63,* 859–866.

Howes, C., and Hamilton, C. E. (1993). The changing experience of child care: Changes in teachers and in teacher–child relationships and children's social competence with peers. *Early Childhood Research Quarterly, 8,* 15–32.

Howes, C., Hamilton, C., and Allhusen, V. D. (2001). Using the Attachment Q-set to describe non-familial attachments. Manuscript in preparation.

Howes, C., and Matheson, C. C. (1992). Contextual constraints on the concordance of mother–child and teacher–child relationship. In R. C. Pianta (Ed.), *Beyond the parent: The role of other adults in children's lives* (pp. 25–39). San Francisco: Jossey-Bass.

Howes, C., Matheson, C. C., and Hamilton, C. E. (1994). Maternal, teacher and child care history correlates of children's relationships with peers. *Child Development, 65,* 264–272.

Howes, C., and Olenick, M. (1986). Family and child care influences on toddler's compliance. *Child Development, 57,* 202–216.

Howes, C., Phillips, D. A., and Whitebook, M. (1992). Thresholds of quality: Implications for the social development of children in center-based child care. *Child Development, 63,* 449–460.

Howes, C., Rodning, C., Galluzzo, D. C., and Myers, L. (1988). Attachment and child care: Relationships with mother and caregiver. *Early Childhood Research Quarterly, 3,* 403–416.

Howes, C., and Rubenstein, J. L. (1981). Toddler peer behavior in two types of day care. *Infant Behavior and Development, 4,* 387–394.

Howes, C., and Rubenstein, J. L. (1985). Determinants of toddlers' experience in day care: Age of entry and quality of setting. *Child Care Quarterly, 14,* 140–151.

Howes, C., and Stewart, P. (1987). Child's play with adults, toys, and peers: An examination of family and child-care influences. *Developmental Psychology, 23,* 423–430.

Hunt, J. McV. (1961). Intelligence and experience. New York: Ronald.

Hwang, C. P., and Broberg, A. G. (1992). The historical and social context of child care in Sweden. In M. E. Lamb, K. J. Sternberg, C. P. Hwang, and A. G. Broberg (Eds.), *Child care in context: Cross-cultural perspectives.* Hillsdale, NJ: Lawrence Erlbaum Associates.

Hyson, M. C., Whitehead, L. C., and Prudhoe, C. M. (1988). Influences on attitudes toward physical affection between adults and children. *Early Childhood Research Quarterly, 3,* 55–75.

Jarvis, C. H. (1987, August). *Kindergarten days: Too much, too soon?* Paper presented at the meeting of the American Psychological Association, New York.

Kagan, J., Kearsley, R. B., and Zelazo, P. R. (1978). *Infancy: Its place in human development.* Cambridge, MA: Harvard University Press.

Kagan, S. L. (1991). Examining profit and nonprofit child care: An odyssey of quality and auspices. *Journal of Social Issues, 47,* 87–104.

Kamerman, S. B. (1991). Child care policies and programs: An international overview. *Journal of Social Issues*, *47*, 179–196.

Kinney, P. F. (1988). *Antecedents of caregiver involvement with infants and toddlers in group care.* Unpublished doctoral dissertation, University of Maryland, College Park.

Kisker, E. E., Hofferth, S. L., Phillips, D. A., and Farquhar, E. (1991). *A profile of child care settings: Early education and care in 1990* (Report prepared for the U.S. Department of Education, Contract No. LC88090001). Princeton, NJ: Mathematica.

Kontos, S. J. (1991). Child care quality, family background, and children's development. *Early Childhood Research Quarterly*, *6*, 249–262.

Kontos, S. (1994). The ecology of family day care. *Early Childhood Research Quarterly*, *9*, 87–110.

Kontos, S., and Fiene, R. (1987). Child care quality, compliance with regulations, and children's development: The Pennsylvania Study. In D. A. Phillips (Ed.), *Quality in child care: What does research tell us?* (pp. 57–80). Washington, DC: National Association for the Education of Young Children.

Kontos, S., Howes, C., Shinn, M., and Galinsky, E. (1997). Children's experiences in family child care and relative care as a function of family income and ethnicity. *Merrill-Palmer Quarterly*, *43*, 386–403.

Kontos, S., Hsu, H.-C., and Dunn, L. (1994). Children's cognitive and social competence in child care centers and family day-care homes. *Journal of Applied Developmental Psychology*, *15*, 387–411.

Koren-Karie, N., Egoz, N., Sagi, A., Joels, T., Gini, M., and Ziv, Y. (1998, July). *The emotional climate of center care in Israel.* Paper presented at the XVth Biennial Meetings of the International Society for the Study of Behavioural Development, Bern, Switzerland.

Kwan, C., Sylva, K., and Reeves, B. (1998). Day care quality and child development in Singapore. *Early Child Development and Care*, *144*, 69–77.

Lally, J. R. (2001). Infant care in the United States and how the Italian experience can help. In L. Gandini and C. P. Edwards (Eds.), *Bambini: The Italian approach to infant/toddler care* (pp. 15–22). New York: Teachers College Press.

Lamb, M. E. (1998). Nonparental child care: Context, quality, correlates, and consequences. In W. Damon (Gen. Ed.) and I. E. Sigel and A. Renninger (Vol. Eds.), *Handbook of child psychology: Vol. 4. Child psychology in practice* (5th ed., pp. 73–133). New York: Wiley.

Lamb, M. E. (1999). Nonparental child care. In M. E. Lamb (Ed)., *Parenting and child development in "nontraditional" families* (pp. 39–55). Mahwah, NJ: Lawrence Erlbaum Associates.

Lamb, M. E. (2000). The effects of quality of care on child development. *Applied Developmental Science*, *4*, 112–115.

Lamb, M. E., Hwang, C.-P., Broberg, A., and Bookstein, F. L. (1988). The effects of out-of-home care on the development of social competence in Sweden: A longitudinal study. *Early Childhood Research Quarterly*, *3*, 379–402.

Lamb, M. E., Sternberg, K. J., Hwang, C. P., and Broberg, A. G. (1992). *Child care in context.* Hillsdale, NJ: Lawrence Erlbaum Associates.

Lamb, M. E., Sternberg, K. J., Knuth, N., Hwang, C. P., and Broberg, A. G. (1991). Peer play and nonparental care experiences. In H. Goelman (Ed.), *Play and child care* (pp. 37–52). Albany, NY: State University of New York Press.

Lamb, M. E., Thompson, R. A., Gardner, W., and Charnov, E. L.(1985). *Infant–mother attachment: The origins and developmental significance of individual differences in Strange Situation behavior.* Hillsdale, NJ: Lawrence Erlbaum Associates.

Laosa, L. M. (1982). Families as facilitators of children's intellectual development at 3 years of age: A causal analysis. In L. M. Laosa and I. E. Sigel (Eds.), *Families as learning environments for children* (pp. 1–46). New York: Plenum.

Lazar, I., Darlington, R. B., Murray, H., Royce, J., and Snipper, A. (1982). Lasting effects of early education. *Monographs of the Society for Research in Child Development*, *47* (2–3, Serial No. 195).

Lazar, I., Hubbell, R., Murray, H., Rosche, M., and Royce, J. (1977). *The persistence of preschool effects: A long-term follow-up of fourteen infant and preschool experiments* (Final Report to Office of Human Development Services, Grant No. 18-76-07843). Ithaca, NY: Cornell University.

Lightcap, J. L., Kurland, J. A., and Burgess, R. L. (1982). Child abuse: A test of some predictions from evolutionary theory. *Ethology and Sociobiology*, *3*, 61–67.

Love, J. M., Ryer, P., and Faddis, B. (1992). *Caring environments: Program quality in California's publicly funded child development program* (Report on the Legislatively mandated 1990–91 Staff/Child Ratio Study). Unpublished manuscript, RMC Research Corporation, Portsmouth, NH.

Manlove, E. E. (1993). Multiple correlates of burnout in child care workers. *Early Childhood Research Quarterly*, *8*, 499–518.

Mantovani, S. (2001). Infant-toddler centers in Italy today: Tradition and innovation. In L. Gandini and C. P. Edwards (Eds.), *Bambini: The Italian approach to infant/toddler care* (pp. 23–37). New York: Teachers College Press.

Maxwell, L. E. (1996). Multiple effects of home and day care crowding. *Environment and Behavior*, *28*, 494–511.

McCartney, K. (1984). Effect of quality of day care environment on children's language development. *Developmental Psychology*, *20*, 244–260.

McCartney, K., and Rosenthal, R. (2000). Effect size, practical importance, and social policy for children. Child Development, *71*, 173–180.

McCartney, K., Scarr, S., Rocheleau, A., Phillips, D., Abbott-Shim, M., Eisenberg, M., Keefe, N., Rosenthal, S., and Ruh, J. (1997). Teacher–child interaction and child-care auspices as predictors of social outcomes in infants, toddlers, and preschoolers. *Merrill-Palmer Quarterly, 43*, 426–450.

McKim, M. K., Cramer, K. M., Stuart, B., and O'Connor, D. L. (1999). Infant care decisions and attachment security: The Canadian Transition to Child Care Study. *Canadian Journal of Behavioural Science, 31*, 92–106.

Melhuish, E. C., Lloyd, E., Martin, S., and Mooney, A. (1990). Type of child care at 18 months—II. Relations with cognitive and language development. *Journal of Child Psychology and Psychiatry, 31*, 861–870.

Melhuish, E. C., and Moss, P. (1991). *Day care for young children: International perspectives.* New York: Routledge.

Miller, L. B., Bugbee, M. R., and Hybertson, D. W. (1985). Dimensions of preschool: The effects of individual experience. In I. E. Sigel (Ed.), *Advances in applied developmental psychology* (Vol. 1, pp. 25–90). Norwood, NJ: Ablex.

Miller, L. B., and Dyer, J. L. (1975). Four preschool programs: Their dimensions and effects. *Monographs of the Society for Research in Child Development, 40* (5–6, Serial No. 162).

Moskowitz, D. W., Schwarz, J. C., and Corsini, D. A. (1977). Initiating day care at three years of age: Effects on attachment. *Child Development, 48*, 1271–1276.

Nelson, M. K. (1990). *Negotiated care: The experience of family day care providers.* Philadelphia: Temple University Press.

Neuman, S. B. (1999). Books make a difference: A study of access to literacy. *Reading Research Quarterly, 34*, 286–311.

NICHD Early Child Care Research Network. (1996). Characteristics of infant child care: Factors contributing to positive caregiving. *Early Childhood Research Quarterly, 11*, 269–306.

NICHD Early Child Care Research Network. (1997a). Familial factors associated with the characteristics of nonmaternal care for infants. *Journal of Marriage and the Family, 59*, 389–408.

NICHD Early Child Care Research Network. (1997b). The effects of infant child care on infant–mother attachment security: Results of the NICHD study of early child care. *Child Development, 68*, 860–879.

NICHD Early Child Care Research Network. (1998a). Early child care and self-control, compliance, and problem behavior at 24 and 36 months. *Child Development, 69*, 1145–1170.

NICHD Early Child Care Research Network. (1998b). Relations between family predictors and child outcomes: Are they weaker for children in child care? *Developmental Psychology, 34*, 1119–1128.

NICHD Early Child Care Research Network. (1999a). Child care and mother-child interaction in the first three years of life. *Developmental Psychology, 35*, 1399–1413.

NICHD Early Child Care Research Network. (1999b). Child outcomes when child care center classes meet recommended standards for quality. *American Journal of Public Health, 89*, 1072–1077.

NICHD Early Child Care Research Network. (2000a). Characteristics and quality of child care for toddlers and preschoolers. *Journal of Applied Developmental Science, 4*, 116–135.

NICHD Early Child Care Research Network. (2000b). The relation of child care to cognitive and language development. *Child Development, 71*, 960–980.

NICHD Early Child Care Research Network. (2001a). Child care and family predictors of MacArthur preschool attachment and stability from infancy. *Development Psychology, 37*, 847–862.

NICHD Early Child Care Research Network. (2001b). Child care and children's peer intractions at 24 and 36 months: The NICHD Study of Early Child Care. *Child Development, 72*, 1478–1500.

Osborn, A. F., and Milbank, J. E. (1987). *The effects of early education.* Oxford, England: Clarendon.

Palmerus, K., and Haegglund, S. (1991). The impact of children/caregiver ratio on activities and social interaction in six day care centre groups. *Early Child Development and Care, 67*, 29–38.

Parcel, T. L., and Menaghan, E. G. (1994). Early parental work, family social capital, and early childhood outcomes. *American Journal of Sociology, 99*, 972–1009.

Parke, R. D., and Sawin, D. B. (1980). The family in early infancy: Social interactional and attitudinal analysis. In F. A. Pedersen (Ed.), *The father–infant relationship: Observational studies in the family setting* (pp. 44–70). New York: Praeger.

Peisner-Feinberg, E. S., and Burchinal, M. R. (1997). Relations between preschool children's child-care experiences and concurrent development: The Cost, Quality, and Outcomes Study. *Merrill-Palmer Quarterly, 43*, 451–477.

Pence, A. R., and Goelman, H. (1987). Who cares for the child in day care? An examination of caregivers from three types of care. *Early Childhood Research Quarterly, 2*, 315–334.

Petrogiannis, K., and Melhuish, E. C. (2001). *The preschool period: Care, education, development.* Athens, Greece: Kastaniotis.

Phillips, D. (1995). *Child care for low-income families: Summary of two workshops.* Washington, DC: National Academy Press.

Phillips, D. A., and Howes, C. (1987). Indicators of quality in child care: Review of research. In D. A. Phillips (Ed.). *Quality in child care: What does the research tell us?* (pp. 1–19) Washington, DC: National Association for the Education of Young Children.

Phillips, D. A., McCartney, K., and Scarr, S. (1987). Child-care quality and children's social development. *Developmental Psychology, 23*, 537–543.

Phillips, D. A., Scarr, S., and McCartney, K. (1987). Dimensions and effects of child care quality: The Bermuda study. In D. A. Phillips (Ed.), *Quality in child care: What does research tell us?* (pp. 43–56). Washington, DC: National Association for the Education of Young Children.

Phillips, D. A., Voran, M., Kisker, E., Howes, C., and Whitebook, M. (1994). Child care for children in poverty: Opportunity or inequity? *Child Development, 65,* 472–492.

Phillips, D. A., and Whitebook, M. (1990). The child care provider: Pivotal player in the child's world. In S. S. Chehrazi (Ed.), *Psychosocial issues in day care* (pp. 129–146). Washington, DC: American Psychiatric Press.

Pierrehumbert, B., Ramstein, T., Karmaniola, A., and Halfon, O. (1996). Child care in the preschool years: Attachment, behaviour problems and cognitive development. *European Journal of Psychology of Education, 11,* 201–214.

Pistillo, F. (1989). Preprimary education and care in Italy. In P. Olmsted and D. Weikart (Eds.), *How nations serve young children: Profiles of child care and education in 14 countries* (pp. 151–202). Ypsilanti, MI: The High/Scope Press.

Poteat, G. M., Snow, C. W., Ironsmith, M., and Bjorkman, S. (1992). Influence of day care experiences and demographic variables on social behavior in kindergarten. *American Journal of Orthopsychiatry, 62,* 137–141.

Powell, D. R., and Stremmel, A. J. (1989). The relation of early childhood training and experience to the professional development of child care workers. *Early Childhood Research Quarterly, 4,* 339–355.

Public Agenda. (August 23, 2000). "Survey Finds Parents Don't Trust Day Care." Reuters/Washington Post, on the Internet.

Rabinovich, B. A., Zaslow, M. J., Berman, P. W., and Heyman, R. (1987, April). *Employed and homemaker mothers' perceptions of their toddlers' compliance behavior in the home.* Paper presented at the biennial meetings of the Society for Research in Child Development, Baltimore, MD.

Raikes, H. (1993). Relationship duration in infant care: Time with high-ability teacher and infant/teacher attachment. *Early Childhood Research Quarterly, 8,* 309–325.

Rauh, H., Ziegenhain, U., Mueller, B., and Wijnroks, L. (2000). Stability and change in infant–mother attachment in the second year of life: Relations to parenting quality and varying degrees of day-care experience. In P. M. Crittenden and A. H. Claussen (Eds.), *The organization of attachment relationships: Maturation, culture, and context* (pp. 251–276). New York: Cambridge University Press.

Repetti, R. L., and Wood, J. (1997). Effects of daily stress at work on mothers' interactions with preschoolers. *Journal of Family Psychology, 11,* 90–108.

Robinson, J., and Corley, R. (1989, April). *The effects of day care participation: Sex differences in early and middle childhood.* Paper presented at the biennial meetings of the Society for Research in Child Development, Kansas City, MO.

Roggman, L., Langlois, J., Hubbs-Tait, L., and Rieser-Danner, L. (1994). Infant day care, attachment, and the "file drawer problem." *Child Development, 65,* 1429–1443.

Rosenthal, M. K. (1991). Daily experiences of toddlers in three child care settings in Israel. *Child & Youth Care Forum, 20,* 37–58.

Rosenthal, M. K. (1999). Out-of-home child care research: A cultural perspective. *International Journal of Behavioral Development, 23,* 477–518.

Rosenthal, M. K. (2001). Early child care and education in Israel. In K. Petrogiannis and E. Melhuish (Eds.), The preschool period: Care, education, development (pp. 313–348). Athens, Greece: Kastaniotis.

Rubenstein, J. L., and Howes, C. (1979). Caregiving and infant behavior in day care and in homes. *Developmental Psychology, 15,* 1–24.

Rubenstein, J. L., and Howes, C. (1983). Social–emotional development of toddlers in day care: The role of peers and of individual differences. In S. Kilmer (Ed.), *Advances in early education and day care* (Vol. 3, pp. 13–45). Greenwich, CT: JAI.

Ruhm, C. J. (2000). Parental employment and child cognitive development. Unpublished manuscript, University of North Carolina at Greensboro.

Ruopp, R., Travers, J., Glantz, F., and Coelen, C. (1979). *Children at the center.* Cambridge, MA: Abt Associates.

Rushton, J. P., Russell, R. J. H., and Wells, P. A. (1984). Genetic similarity theory: Beyond kin selection. *Behavior Genetics, 14,* 179–193.

Russon, A. E., Waite, B. E., and Rochester, M. J. (1990). Direct caregiver intervention in infant peer social encounters. *American Journal of Orthopsychiatry, 60,* 428–439.

Rutter, M. (1982). Social–emotional effects of day care for preschool children. In E. Zigler and E. W. Gordon (Eds.), *Day care: Scientific and social policy issues* (pp. 3–32). Boston: Auburn House.

Sagi, A., Lamb, M. E., Lewkowicz, K. S., Shoham, R., Dvir, R., Estes, D. (1985). Security of infant–mother, –father, and –metapelet attachments among kibbutz-reared Israeli children. In I. Bretherton and E. Waters (Eds.), *Growing points of attachment theory and research* (pp. 257–275). *Monographs of the Society for Research in Child Development, 50* (1–2, Serial No. 209).

Scarr, S. (1998). American child care today. *American Psychologist, 53,* 95–108.

Scarr, S., Eisenberg, M., and Deater-Deckard, K. (1994). Measurement of quality in child care centers. *Early Childhood Research Quarterly, 9,* 131–151.

Scarr, S., Lande, J., and McCartney, K. (1988). Child care and the family: Complements and interactions. In J. Lande, S. Scarr, and N. Gunzenhauser (Eds.), *Caring for children: Challenge to America* (pp. 1–21). Hillsdale, NJ: Lawrence Erlbaum Associates.

Scarr, S., Phillips, D., McCartney, K., and Abbott-Shim, M. (1993). Quality of child care as an aspect of family and child care policy in the United States. *Pediatrics, 91*, 182–188.

Scarr, S., and Weinberg, R. A. (1986). The early childhood enterprise. *American Psychologist, 41*, 1140–1146.

Schenk, V. M., and Grusec, J. E. (1987). A comparison of prosocial behavior of children with and without day care experience. *Merrill-Palmer Quarterly, 33*, 231–240.

Schliecker, E., White, D. R., and Jacobs, E. (1991). The role of day care quality in the prediction of children's vocabulary. *Canadian Journal of Behavioural Science, 23*, 12–24.

Schweinhart, L. J., Weikart, D. P., and Larner, M. D. (1986). Consequences of three preschool curriculum models through age 15. *Early Childhood Research Quarterly, 1*, 15–45.

Segal, N. L. (1984). Cooperation, competition, and altruism within twin sets: A reappraisal. *Ethology and Sociobiology, 5*, 163–177.

Seltenheim, K., Ahnert, L., Rickert, H., and Lamb, M. E. (1997, May). *The formation of attachments between infants and care providers in German day care centers.* Paper presented at the meeting of the American Psychological Society, Washington, DC.

Serbin, L. A., Connor, J. M., and Denier, C. (1978). *Modification of sex typed activity and interactive play patterns in the preschool classroom: A replication and extension.* Paper presented at the Annual Meeting of the Association for the Advancement of Behavior Therapy, Chicago, IL.

Shinn, M., Phillips, D., Howes, C., Galinsky, E., and Whitebook, M. (1990). *Correspondence between mothers' perceptions and observer ratings of quality in child care centers.* New York: Family and Work Institute.

Siegal, M., and Storey, R. M. (1985). Day care and children's conceptions of moral and social rules. *Child Development, 56*, 1001–1008.

Smith, A. B., Ballard, K. D., and Barham, L. J. (1989). Preschool children's perceptions of parent and teacher roles. *Early Childhood Research Quarterly, 4*, 523–532.

Smith, E. W., and Howes, C. (1994). The effect of parents' presence on children's social interactions in preschool. *Early Childhood Research Quarterly, 9*, 45–59.

Smith, P. K. (1980). Shared care of young children: Alternative models to monotropism. *Merrill-Palmer Quarterly, 26*, 371–389.

Smith, P. K., and Connolly, K. J. (1980). *The ecology of preschool behaviour.* Cambridge, England: Cambridge University Press.

Sroufe, L. A. (1983). Infant–caregiver attachment and patterns of adaptation in preschool: The roots of maladaptation and competence. In M. Perlmutter (Ed.), *Minnesota symposium in child psychology* (Vol. 16, pp. 41–83). Hillsdale, NJ: Lawrence Erlbaum Associates.

Stallings, J. A. (1980). An observation study of family day care. In J. C. Colberg (Ed.), *Home day care: A perspective.* Chicago: Roosevelt University.

Sternberg, K. J., Lamb, M. E., Hwang, C.-P., Broberg, A., Ketterlinus, R. D., and Bookstein, F. L. (1991). Does out-of-home care affect compliance in preschoolers? *International Journal of Behavioral Development, 14*, 45–65.

Stith, S. M., and Davis, A. J. (1984). Employed mothers and family day-care substitute caregivers: A comparative analysis of infant care. *Child Development, 55*, 1340–1348.

Strayer, F. F., Moss, E., and Blicharski, T. (1989). Biosocial bases of representational activity during early childhood. In L. T. Winegar (Ed.), *Social interaction and the development of children's understanding* (pp. 21–44). Norwood, NJ: Ablex.

Suransky, V. P. (1982). *The erosion of childhood.* Chicago: University of Chicago Press.

Sylva, K., Roy, C., and Painter, M. (1980). *Child watching at playgroup and nursery school.* London: Grant McIntyre.

Symons, D. K. (1998). Post-partum employment patterns, family-based care arrangements, and the mother–infant relationship at age two. *Canadian Journal of Behavioural Science, 30*, 121–131.

Thornburg, K. R., Pearl, P., Crompton, D., and Ispa, J. M. (1990). Development of kindergarten children based on child care arrangements. *Early Childhood Research Quarterly, 5*, 27–42.

Tizard, B., Carmichael, H., Hughes, M., and Pinkerton, B. (1980). Four-year-olds talking to mothers and teachers. In L. A. Hersov and M. Berger (Eds.), *Language and language disorders in childhood* (pp. 49–77). London: Pergamon.

Tyler, B., and Dittman, L. (1980). Meeting the toddler more than halfway: The behavior of toddlers and their caregivers. *Young Child, 35*, 39–46.

U.S. Bureau of the Census (1997). *Who's minding our preschoolers?* (Current Population Reports, P70-62). Washington, DC: U.S. Government Printing Office.

U.S. Bureau of the Census (1999). *Statistical abstract of the United States* (119th ed.). Washington, DC: U.S. Government Printing Office.

U.S. Department of Education, National Center for Education Statistics. (1998). *Characteristics of children's early care and education programs* (Data from the 1995 National Household Education Survey, NCES 98-128, by S. L. Hofferth, K. A. Shauman, R. R. Henke, and J. West). Washington, DC: U.S. Department of Education.

van IJzendoorn, M. H., Sagi, A, and Lambermon, M. W. E. (1992). The multiple caretaker paradox: Data from Holland and Israel. In R. C. Pianta (Ed.), *Beyond the parent: The role of other adults in children's lives* (pp. 5–24). San Francisco: Jossey-Bass Inc.

Vandell, D. L., and Corasaniti, M. A. (1990). Variations in early child care: Do they predict subsequent social, emotional, and cognitive differences? *Early Childhood Research Quarterly, 5*, 555–572.

Vandell, D. L., Henderson, V. K., and Wilson, K. S. (1988). A longitudinal study of children with day-care experiences of varying quality. *Child Development, 59*, 1286–1292.

Vandell, D. L., and Ramanan, J. (1992). Effects of early and recent maternal employment on children from low-income families. *Child Development, 63*, 938–949.

Vaughn, B. E., Gove, F. L., and Egeland, B. (1980). The relationship between out-of-home care and the quality of infant-mother attachment in an economically disadvantaged population. *Child Development, 51*, 1203–1214.

Volling, B. L., and Feagans, L. V. (1995). Infant day care and children's social competence. *Infant Behavior and Development, 18*, 177–188.

Wachs, T. D., and Gruen, G. E. (1982). *Early experience and human development*. New York: Plenum.

Wadsworth, M. E. J. (1986). Effects of parenting style and preschool experience on children's verbal attainment: Results of a British longitudinal study. *Early Childhood Research Quarterly, 1*, 237–248.

Warash, B. G., and Markstrom-Adams, C. (1995). Preschool experiences of advantaged children. *Psychological Reports, 77*, 89–90.

Wasik, B. H., Ramey, C. T., Bryant, D. M., and Sparling, J. J. (1990). A longitudinal study of two early intervention strategies: Project CARE. *Child Development, 61*, 1682–1696.

Waters, E., and Deane, K. E. (1985). Defining and assessing individual differences in attachment relationships: Q-methodology and the organization of behavior in infancy and early childhood. In I. Bretherton and E. Waters (Eds.), *Growing points of attachment theory and research, Monographs of the Society for Research in Child Development, 50* (1–2, Serial No. 209, pp. 42–65).

Weinraub, M., Jaeger, E., and Hoffman, L. W. (1988). Predicting infant outcomes in families of employed and non-employed mothers. *Early Childhood Research Quarterly, 3*, 361–378.

Wessels, H., Lamb, M. E., Hwang, C. P., and Broberg, A. G. (1997). Personality development between 1 and 8 years of age in Swedish children with varying child care experiences. *International Journal of Behavioral Development, 21*, 771–794.

Whitebook, M., Howes, C., and Phillips, D. (1990). *Who cares? Child care teachers and the quality of care in America* (Final Report. National Child Care Staffing Study). Oakland CA: Child Care Employee Project.

Wille, D. E., and Jacobson, J. L. (1984, April). *The influence of maternal employment, attachment pattern, extrafamilial child care, and previous experience with peers on early peer interaction.* Paper presented at the International Conference on Infancy Studies, Beverly Hills, CA.

Wilson, M. I., Daly, M., and Weghorst, S. J. (1980). Household composition and the risk of child abuse and neglect. *Journal of Biosocial Science, 12*, 333–340.

Wynn, R. L. (1979, March). *The effect of a playmate on day-care and home-reared toddlers in a strange situation.* Paper presented at the biennial meetings of the Society for Research in Child Development, San Francisco, CA.

Zajdeman, H. S., and Minnes, P. M. (1991). Predictors of children's adjustment to day-care. *Early Child Development and Care, 74*, 11–28.

Zigler, E. F., and Freedman, J. (1990). Psychological–developmental implications of current patterns of early child care. In S. S. Chehrazi (Ed.), *Psychosocial issues in day care* (pp. 3–20). Washington, DC: American Psychiatric Press.

8

Sibling Caregiving

Patricia Zukow-Goldring
University of California

In the small farming community of Santa Ana y Lobos at the southeastern edge of Guanajuato in Central Mexico, six children of ages 2 to 10 engage in very elaborate imaginative play. Next to the courtyard fence in a shady spot, Sara aged 10 and Cristina aged 7 managed to organize an enactment of tortilla making amidst countless interruptions. The sisters, with the elder firmly guiding the others, call out directions and revisions to each other as they all simultaneously and continuously constitute and negotiate the emerging event. Sara and Cristina must chide Lalo aged 3 for his incessant requests for more water and temporarily banish Juana aged 2 for carelessly smashing a prized jarrita, a miniature clay jar. These sisters demonstrate in play their mastery of a complex skill central to attaining competence in the most basic, yet the most difficult, achievement of Mexico's culinary arts. To make tortillas, they gather implements, grind corn (dirt), mix the result with water to make masa *(dough), shape balls of* masa, *pat them out to form rounds, and cook them on a* comal *(round cookstone).*

Twenty to 30 feet away, adults and adolescent siblings at work or at rest after long hours in the fields share checking out details of care only when something may be amiss. They call out only when a child elsewhere needs tending or when Juana, shamed by being sent away, goes to her father who with an older brother teases her gently. Using a younger male cousin as a lure, first Sara, then Cristina ask Juana to rejoin them. Juana refuses Sara's invitation. A few moments later Juana walks to the infant now held by Cristina. She sweetly chucks him under the chin, murmuring niño = niño = niño/little boy = little boy = little boy *as she accepts the second face-saving bid to go back to the group activity. Soon Sara seats her among the others and encourages her several times saying,* ¡echa una tortillita!/pat out a little tortilla!. *With little urging, Juana awkwardly and enthusiastically takes a ball of* masa *prepared by her sisters and pats it into the proper flattened shape.*

—Zukow (AMR, March 3, 1982[1])

---

[1] Here and in other vignettes of interaction, the initials refer to the child recorded and the date to the day data were collected.

INTRODUCTION

This segment of interaction, embedded in the most mundane daily activities of a Mexican family living in a rural, agrarian community of 700 people, illustrates the multifaceted role of sibling caregiving. Functional and adaptable, sibling care helps the family in its maintenance and survival. Siblings assist in socializing cultural ways of knowing and perceiving. Sibling caregivers select and promote detection of cultural practices within levels of shared care. Age and gender affect who plays or works together. These activities, whether involving groups or an individual, co-occur in the courtyard. Family members consider conflict and cooperation to be unavoidable and beneficial, both contributing to socializing members of the culture. Within this milieu, the social setting meets, shapes, and is shaped by the child. The primary question is not whether the social setting has or has not met the needs of the individual child, but whether the child assists the family in meeting its needs.

What roles do sibling caregivers play in the development of their younger sisters and brothers? How does giving care affect the development of older siblings? Answers to these questions reflect a dichotomy between findings arising from research conducted in urban–technological societies and those in rural–agrarian societies. In small, non-Western agrarian societies the mother's workload correlates significantly with children's assistance in household work (Harkness and Super, in Vol. 2 of this *Handbook*; Whiting and Edwards, 1988; Whiting and Whiting, 1975). Older siblings are highly valued caregivers of younger family members in agrarian societies whose assistance frees the mother to engage in economically more productive work (Rogoff, Sellers, Piorrata, Fox, and White, 1975; Weisner and Gallimore, 1977; Werner, 1979; Whiting and Edwards, 1988; Whiting and Whiting, 1975). A family's survival depends on successfully socializing sibling caregivers. In turn, manifesting these caregiving practices marks older siblings as taking important steps toward becoming competent and appreciated members of society (Weisner, 1987). Not surprisingly, sibling caregiving is taken for granted in cultures that depend on the involvement of older brothers and sisters on a daily basis.

Conversely, most adults in Western technological cultures do not acknowledge the important function of sibling caregiving (Bank and Kahn, 1982; Lamb and Sutton-Smith, 1982; Zukow, 1989b). Despite circumstances of great hardship, members of technological societies have often ignored siblings as a resource for families, even among those with children who are handicapped (Weisner, 1993a). Individuals may judge such care as neglect, bad parenting, or worse, even when economics force all adult members of a family to work outside the home. Only recently have investigators in painstaking naturalistic observation grounded in ethological studies and ethnographies of daily life concluded that young siblings display sophisticated knowledge of the social world (Dunn, 1988; Dunn and Kendrick, 1982a). Older siblings function as competent socializing agents of younger children in the family, not merely as monitors of the young child's most basic biological needs (Martini, 1994; Maynard, 1999, 2000; Watson-Gegeo and Gegeo, 1989; Zukow, 1989b).

Disciplinary, theoretical, cultural, economic, historical, and generational forces all contribute to the assumptions held by members of technological societies regarding sibling caregivers. Unexamined presuppositions held by researchers in technological societies may bias "facts" that emerge from empirical studies. Interpretation, influenced by disciplinary bias, can cloud further the questions scholars need to ask about sibling caregiving around the world.

In this chapter I first examine existing biases that may prevent members of technological societies from appreciating the value of sibling caregiving. Subsequently, I define parenting goals, discuss their realization within agrarian and technological societies, and consider the functions and contributions of sibling caregiving within this framework. I next address the empirical research that documents the range of activities in which sibling caregivers engage, including who gives and gets care, how siblings achieve the prerequisites for competent sibling caregiving, who socializes sibling caregivers, and how they do so. Then I consider the significance of authority versus conflict, novice–expert roles, and the effective socializing of cultural practices manifested in the domains of cognition, play, and language. Finally, I look at future directions for research on sibling caregiving and what sibling research offers theories of child development and social policy.

THE STUDY OF SIBLING CAREGIVING: BIASES AND OPPORTUNITIES

Sibling caregiving is very widespread, yet it is understudied, even unseen. Why have theorists and researchers overlooked siblings as an important resource in the process of socializing younger children? Examining certain biases provides answers to this question. Theoretical approaches informing the study of siblings cluster at two ends of a continuum. Some theoretical perspectives and research flowing from psychology focus nearly exclusively on the individual child's development or individual differences among or between groups in culturally limited settings, whereas other views informed by anthropology, psychology, and sociology look at the child "coming of age" within her or his particular culture. Before discussing the benefits that both offer, I address unexamined assumptions characteristic of each. These assumptions as well as historical and generational influences have impeded research on sibling caregiving and its implications for theory.

Biases

Western researchers perceive how children become competent members of their cultures and view children as individuals who can recognize, participate in, and communicate about ongoing events in a variety of ways. Investigation of these processes has been pursued within a near "crazy quilt" of theoretical approaches, including attachment, behavioral genetics, ecocultural, ecological, exchange, family systems, general systems, hermeneutics, language socialization, organismic, personality (birth order, individual differences), Piagetian, psychodynamic, sociobiological, Vygotskian, and more. Theories, however, are ways of knowing that focus as well as limit what adherents notice and interpret. Much like the elephant described by the three blind men, the lens of a powerful *zeitgeist* can make some relations prominent and others nearly invisible, ultimately distorting what is understood about the whole.

Fewer than 25 years ago, a cluster of empirical studies documented the notion that older siblings play an important role in their younger sisters' and brothers' development (Dunn and Kendrick, 1982a; Hartup, 1979; Lamb, 1982; Sutton-Smith, 1982; Weisner and Gallimore, 1977). Within psychology three biases in particular have contributed to overlooking and underestimating the significant contribution of siblings to each others' development. First, members of Western technological societies often assume that the nuclear family is the norm (Weisner and Gallimore, 1977), oblivious to influences from extended family members, such as relatives near in age (cousins, aunts, and uncles). Second, psychological theories reflect cultural values and beliefs that hold individual achievement in particularly high esteem and may ignore achievements arising from interdependence (LeVine, 1980). Third, psychodynamic theories of personality or psychological development did not identify siblings as important socializing agents (Lamb, 1982). They focused instead on sibling rivalry, the conflict and competitiveness presumed to arise inevitably as brothers and sisters vied for maternal love and affection (Dunn, 1988; Dunn and Kendrick, 1982a, 1982b; Nuckolls, 1993a). In harmony with this view, researchers concentrated almost exclusively on the mother's role in her child's development rather than on that of any other family member (Dunn and Kendrick, 1982b; Lamb, 1976). Recently, historical overviews of childrearing practices among nonhuman primates and our human ancestors draw a picture dramatically different from the Freudian perspective.

Shared caregiving among nonhuman primates.   In the wild, exclusive maternal care of offspring is rarely the rule in primate development (Bard, in Vol. 2 of this *Handbook*). Older siblings who experience positive interactions with their own mothers, peers, and infants are more likely to become good mothers themselves (Nicolson, 1991). Speculating from data documenting surrogate care among some Old World monkeys, McKenna (1987) suggested that allomothering has adaptive significance. Younger females assisting in infantcare would release the mother to forage more efficiently. Under those circumstances, surrogate caregivers and infants would establish and strengthen bonds. If a mother should die, a female who had previously handled the infant might adopt that infant.

Shared caregiving among humans.   Paralleling McKenna (1987), Lamb and Sternberg (1992) argued on the basis of the interplay between biological and economic necessity that exclusive maternal care of infants and children has rarely occurred throughout human history. Documentation of childcare in eighteenth- and nineteenth-century England and the United States describes women's work as requiring a system of shared caregiving, including sibling caregiving. Even within the past few hundred years, death during childbirth, maternal employment outside the home, and the overseeing of large families and heavy workloads within the home were common experiences (Getis and Vinovskis, 1992; Hareven, 1989; Melhuish and Moss, 1992). In these situations, elder sisters often took on caregiving responsibilities and became surrogate parents if one or both parents died (Hareven, 1989). From this and other evidence, Lamb and Sternberg (1992) asserted that it is a myth to assume that maternal care is somehow normal, natural, or traditional. Problems may arise if an elite, dominant group holds this view. These individuals may judge deviations from this standard as alarming and disadvantageous. Such ethnocentrism affects members of every cultural group, including scholars who may unwittingly blind themselves to the functions, advantages, disadvantages, and routine practice of sibling care.

Generational exclusion.   Membership in a particular generation can exclude an individual from participating in the activities of another cohort. Siblings commonly "educate" each other by sharing cultural practices. Most adults cannot observe these activities because adults have no access to many day-to-day interactions among siblings (Zukow, 1989a). What is hidden from easy view is unlikely to be investigated, although researchers should not so readily accept such a limited perspective. Conducting ethnographies of daily life before conducting investigations would reveal what people actually do on a daily basis and thus contribute to more rigorous research designs (Jessor, Colby, and Shweder, 1996; Weisner, 1996b).

Studies of lineage.   In contrast to psychologists who concentrate on child development and socialization within the nuclear family, anthropologists have studied the whole range of family forms as well as how individuals in agrarian societies govern each other within kin-based societies. For example, anthropologists have examined descent, the tracing of an individual's lineage or ancestry, and its relation to social solidarity in patrilineal societies without governments. Within this area of study, being a sibling merely marked group membership and was not considered functionally relevant to considerations of rank and position within the larger group. Because siblings are located at the same genealogical level, the analysis of antecedents may have concealed from investigators the importance of siblinghood (Nuckolls, 1993a). As interest has shifted away from investigating patriarchal lines of power and authority exclusively, the personnel and the settings in which socializing new members takes place have gained more prominence.

Summary.   Powerful theories of social organization and human development arising in the past century and a quarter combined with the limiting lenses of adult status may have influenced scholars to overlook the importance of sibling caregiving. These theories directed researchers away from siblings altogether or toward sibling discord and investigations of the nuclear family, individual achievement, the mother's role in child development, and the lineage of power and authority. These same theories turned researchers away from the positive potential of sibling caregiving.

Opportunities

A number of researchers who have straddled more than one intellectual and cultural world have achieved some success in combining "rigorous" quantitative and "authentic" ethnographic (qualitative) methods (Cole, Hood, and McDermott 1978, Price-Williams, 1975; Rogoff, Mistry, Göncü, and Mosier, 1993; Scribner and Cole, 1981). Furthermore, integrating these perspectives has born fruit in the form of theories or thought-provoking essays that acknowledge that the ecocultural context is the matrix in which the novice–child member develops (Laboratory of Comparitive Human Cognition, 1986; Rogoff, 1990; Super and Harkness, 1986, 1997; Watson-Gegeo and Gegeo, 1989, 1992; Weisner, 1989a, 1996b; Whiting and Edwards, 1988; Whiting and Whiting, 1975).

Research grounded in Western psychological theory also contributes to understanding sibling caregiving, especially those informed by Piaget and Vygotsky. Studies grounded in Piagetian theorems as well as those inspired by information-processing models usually investigate the cognitive development of the individual child, actively and independently exploring the child's rather passive environment. In contrast, research derived from Vygotsky or from the notion of "scaffolding" (Wood, Bruner, and Ross, 1976; Wood and Middleton, 1975) characterizes both the child and the environment as active. These investigations often focus on the crucial role of the more adept or expert person who assists the novice's participation in common, ordinary activities during social interaction.

Most of the research reviewed in this chapter was inspired by ecocultural, cognitive, or social interactive theories along with a sprinkling from the other theories mentioned earlier. All contribute to understanding sibling caregiving, but so far no theory of child development encompasses what is known about sibling caregiving. In everyday life, however, there is little debate over the usefulness of sibling caregiving. The majority of the world's parents assume their children will become competent caregivers and depend on their assistance in socializing younger sisters and brothers.

THE BASES OF SIBLINGS' CAREGIVING PRACTICES

Ethnographers work from the hypothesis that members' daily practices embody the beliefs and values of a culture (Jessor et al., 1996). The most mundane activities of daily life can reveal coherent cultural themes as members interpret each other within these frames of meaning. To understand sibling caregiving, socializing practices must be considered so that the function and accomplishments of children in different societies can be appreciated (e.g., Demuth, 1984; Gaskins, 2000; Martini, 1994; Ochs, 1988; Schieffelin, 1990; Watson-Gegeo and Gegeo, 1989).

Universal Parenting Goals

LeVine (1977) proposed that parents first seek to ensure the survival (health and safety) of their offspring, then they provide the means for the child to learn economic self-sufficiency, and finally they inculcate cultural values. Achievement at each level is a prerequisite for and interdependent with that which follows. How these achievements relate to each other depends on both the demands of daily life and the developmental level of the individuals. For instance, a neonate must survive the perils of infancy and develop motorically, perceptually, and intellectually during the intervening years in order to engage in chores that contribute to the welfare of the family. After basic subsistence needs are met, time and energy can be devoted to the fulfillment of an individual child's culturally defined aesthetic, spiritual, and self-actualizing activities. These "native" practices then presumably instantiate parental guidance regarding prestige, wealth, intellectual achievement, ethical conduct, and so forth (also Weisner, 1987; Whiting and Edwards, 1988).

Parents' investment of time, attention, and economic resources, of course, depends on local conditions (LeVine, 1977, 1980, 1988; Weisner, 1987, 1989b; Whiting and Edwards, 1988). What is optimal in a rural–agrarian society will not be optimal in one that is urban–technological. In an agrarian setting, parents value highly children's relatively unskilled assistance in food and artifact production and especially their assistance in tending younger siblings. Shared caregiving frees more mature individuals in these societies to engage in higher-yield economic work that requires more complex abilities, helping to ensure the family's survival. Children have such value in some Pacific Island societies that they belong to the community, not to the biological parents (Martini and Kirkpatrick, 1992).

Sources of Variation

The methods for achieving parental goals as well as the characteristics parents encourage their children to display vary between agrarian and technological cultures. In agrarian societies, a more sociocentric self embodies a more interdependent system of status and role (Nuckolls, 1993a; Shweder, 1991). A "we-ness" is fostered across the lifespan through practices that encourage solidarity along with emotional and economic exchanges. It is not surprising then that interdependence is a central goal of socialization in agrarian societies (Greenfield, 1994; LeVine, 1980; Mundy-Castle, 1974; Weisner, 1989b). According to Harrison, Wilson, Pine, Chan, and Buriel (1990), the socialization of ethnic minority children in the United States occurs within an extended family rooted in a similar collectivist world view that emphasizes interdependence as well. In contrast, members of the dominant group in technological societies typically encourage innovation and change (LeVine, 1980; Weisner, 1989b). In technological cultures the definition of self is more egocentric and autonomous. This view leads both to less intense family bonds as family members change and grow and to an emphasis on the individual's future, tangible achievements (Borstelmann, 1977). Independence and individual difference highlight the socializing aims of members of the dominant group within urban–technological societies (LeVine, 1980; Weisner, 1989b).

LeVine (1980) discussed concepts and topics in psychological research that reflect the implications of these cultural assumptions. The Western ideal of self-reliance and self-confidence is set within a frame of egalitarian ideology. Parents greet behavior embodying these characteristics with elaborate displays of praise and reinforcement. Consequently, at the slightest accomplishment a child may draw excessive attention to herself or himself. In contrast, praising children for their achievements is rare indeed in agrarian societies (Gaskins, 1999; Maynard, 1999) as being overproud (of individual accomplishments) works against interdependence (Martini and Kirkpatrick, 1992; Weisner, 1987; Whiting and Edwards, 1988). Children are often scolded or teased for "showing off or putting on airs" (Martini and Kirkpatrick, 1992; Schieffelin, 1990). In South India a new baby is not viewed as someone exceptional to cherish but another person who requires a particular kind of care (Seymour, 1993). If family members were to shower the baby with attention, then the other children might vie for attention as well. Family members encourage children to experience their acts as contributions to work, providing intrinsic satisfaction according to the degree it helps the group as a whole (LeVine, 1988).

Summary

The core of parenting goals is universal but the particulars are realized quite differently, depending on the specific setting. Preparing a child to become a competent member of an agrarian culture requires a different set of priorities than those needed for full membership in a technological one. Interdependence is crucial to the survival of the entire family in agrarian societies, whereas independence is prized in technological ones. The degree to which children participate in parenting younger sisters and brothers directly reflects the importance of shared caregiving to the economic welfare of the family. However, wherever cultures lie on the continuum between small-scale, rural–agrarian societies and very complex, urban–technological ones, siblings must pay attention to these goals before they can assist in socializing younger family members.

SIBLING CAREGIVING: WHO CARES FOR WHOM, WHERE, AND WHY

The process of socializing sibling caregivers entails who gives care and who gets it. A child's own level of development affects her or his becoming a caregiver, because adults require and value particular prerequisites before entrusting the child with caring for a younger sibling. A range of family members using a variety of practices socializes child caregivers. They convey where, when, and how to engage in activities during the course of the day. The preponderance of studies that explicitly document the work of sibling caregivers comes from cross-cultural investigations of agrarian and foraging groups who highly value this contribution to daily life.

In this chapter I describe central tendencies as well as variations in sibling care. Differences in the form and the function of sibling caregiving occur throughout the world as do intracultural variations in practice. This diversity relates to work load, cultural models and norms, availability of other adult caregivers, local demography, gender balance, child temperament and more (Harkness and Super, 1992; Weisner, 1982; Weisner and Gallimore, 1977).

Pervasiveness of sibling caregiving in agrarian societies. The Whitings and those who collaborated with them have produced a body of work that provides the most comprehensive picture of sibling caregiving (Whiting, 1963; Whiting and Edwards, 1988; Whiting and Whiting, 1975). Their Six Cultures studies sampled behavior in small villages or towns in Mexico, India, the Philippines, Kenya, Okinawa (Japan), and the United States. A "new" sample added Peru, Guatemala, Liberia, several more groups in Kenya and India, and an upper-middle-socioeconomic suburban community in the United States. These investigations documented the quality, quantity, and omnipresence of sibling care in agrarian cultures. Numerous investigations have supplemented and expanded these studies, including the review by Weisner and Gallimore (1977) and more recent investigations of agrarian communities located in Africa, the Pacific Islands, Central America, South Asia/India, and Turkey.

Who Becomes a Sibling Caregiver?

Most siblings engage in caregiving from the age of 5 to 10 years. Where mothers have very high work loads, children of 2 years of age may infrequently assist minding a younger infant. Girls fill this role far more often than boys and begin a year or two earlier than boys. Most frequently, the mother assigns caregiving responsibilities to the eldest daughter. However, Ochs (1988) did not observe more girls than boys acting as sibling caregivers in Samoa. All school-age children attended class regularly, and each was kept home to assist in caregiving in an apparent rotating system. In agrarian societies, boys commonly serve as caregivers in the absence of an available elder sister, but rarely engage in caregiving after 7 years of age.

Sources of variation in technological settings. Weisner (1987) stressed that common stages in the life course differ across cultures. In middle-socioeconomic North America the sequence relating to childcare usually consists of getting married, setting up a household, and then childcare. Non-Western societies have a different pattern. Childcare occurs first, and much later in life comes marriage and a new household. Perhaps because of this difference, only a small number of studies have directly documented sibling care in technological societies. The Whitings and their colleagues investigated families of normally developing children in a small New England town (Fischer and Fischer, 1963; Whiting and Edwards, 1988; Whiting and Whiting, 1975). The few intraethnic investigations available are ethnographies by Ward (1971) among African American blue-collar children in Louisiana and by Heath (1983) in South Carolina. In these families, the ubiquity of older girls (referred to by Stack in Weisner, 1987, as boss girls) organizing and maintaining the sibling play group may reflect the pressures arising from caring for numerous children in the extended family, when mothers often work outside the home. Mirroring the basis for sibling caregiving in agrarian societies, the mother's work load, agrarian roots, a collectivist attitude, and a clear hierarchy among household work assignments in the family also influence the frequency of sibling caregiving in African American families. Similar dynamics hold for Latino families living in blue-collar neighborhoods in Los Angeles (Zukow-Goldring, fieldnotes, 1987 to 1994). In families with siblings who are delayed, physically disabled, chronically ill, or mentally ill, older *and* younger nonhandicapped brothers and sisters often provide essential caregiving assistance. These studies attest to the importance, benefits, and appreciation of sibling care in families with special needs (Bluebond-Langer, 1996; *Journal of the California Alliance for the Mentally Ill*, 1992; Lobato, 1990; McHale and Crouter, 1996; McHale and Pawletko, 1992; Stoneman and Berman, 1993).

Sibling caregiving: Resource rather than neglect. In the main, school occupies much of school-age children's day, segregating them in age-graded groups tended by adults (Gottfried, Gottfried, and Bathurst, in Vol. 2 of this *Handbook*; Rogoff et al., 1993). With the increase of dual-wage-earner families, parents who can afford afterschool care further decrease siblings' time together. For those who cannot, the number of "latchkey" siblings whose afterschool activities at home and in the neighborhood are unsupervised until parents return from work grows in number. However, siblings do spend many hours together in early morning, late afternoon, evenings, weekends, holidays, and vacation. In Los Angeles, for instance, children attend school only 180 days a year.

What occurs during the time these siblings spend together? Ethnographic studies designed to describe what siblings do after school might provide the basis for a large social policy benefit. The functional and adaptive value of deploying sibling caregivers to assist while parents work has an unexplored potential in technological settings. Organizing programs to encourage and take advantage of supervised sibling caregiving by grandparents and/or young single mothers would provide employment for the unemployed and turn what has been termed neglect or bad parenting from risk into benefit.

Who Gives and Who Gets Care?

In this subsection I examine the age range of siblings who receive care, the age of siblings who give care, and the variety of ages found in sibling groups. Most sibling groupings in high-fertility, low-mortality, child-sharing communities are composed of a mixture of sisters and brothers.

The sibling group. The structure of living arrangements and the distribution of work organize the population of children receiving care. The sibling group includes siblings, half-siblings in polygynous societies, cousins or "classificatory siblings," and young aunts and uncles (Nuckolls, 1993a; Seymour, 1993; Watson-Gegeo and Gegeo, 1989; Whiting and Edwards, 1988; Zukow, 1989b). In the Solomon Islands, the children of one's mother's sisters and father's brothers are classified as siblings and have the same obligations throughout the lifespan (Watson-Gegeo and Gegeo, 1989), whereas in Southern India, only the children of a father's brothers are included in this category (Nuckolls, 1993a; Seymour, 1993). Nuckolls noted that Westerners assigned the term classificatory to designate this basic kinship category as if such siblings were somehow less real or significant than "true" biological siblings.

Whiting and Edwards (1988) classified children in sibling groups by age based on Margaret Mead's (1935) system. Children from approximately birth to 1 year of age are called lap children, those from 2 to 3 years old are knee children, from 4 to 5 years old yard children, and from 6 to 10 community children/schoolchildren. Yard and community children/schoolchildren usually care for lap and knee children. However, children appreciate from very early in development that they are embedded within nested levels of care (Ochs, 1988; Weisner, 1982). As members of the household move through daily work schedules, a particular child may be in charge of a smaller infant and simultaneously be deferring to and receiving guidance from a still older sibling.

Siblings who give care. Girls usually have the responsibility of lap children and are observed more often in their company. Knee children receive more varied care. In one community in Kenya, Nyansango, the 2- to 3-year-old toddlers preferred to be with the boys herding cattle, whereas in one small Indian village children of this age were not left with older siblings. Young children customarily play alone in this community. Girls far more frequently tend children of 5 to 7 years old than do boys. Seymour's (1993) Indian sample demonstrates differences across castes. Among lower-caste families, most mothers had employment that took them outside the home. Girls tended siblings six times as often as girls in middle- and upper-class families. Lower-status boys cared for siblings twice as frequently as middle-class boys did. Upper-class boys never engaged in such behavior. Whiting and Edwards (1988, p. 125) summarized these observations succinctly: "girls work while boys play."

Implications of shared care.   Many people share in the care of a younger child. Shared caregiving affords multiple sources of affection as well as possible strife (Martini and Kirkpatrick, 1992). The resulting lack of competition for care appears to reduce rivalry (Seymour, 1993). Furthermore, if the children giving and getting care encounter some incompatibility, finding an alternative among several available caregivers resolves the conflict (Draper and Harpending, 1987). The fostering of children illustrates this common practice in Africa (Goody, 1982; Haugaard and Hazan, in Vol. 1 of this *Handbook*; Nsamenang, 1992). Parents loan or foster children out of their natal homes for many reasons, including learning a trade, strengthening social bonds, and disciplining recalcitrant children by those less emotionally attached than the immediate family. In Central Mexico, a difficult child might be sent to live in the compound of another family member nearby (Zukow, field notes, 1981 to 1982).

Technological settings.   Studies conducted in technological societies support cross-cultural findings that girls engage in more infantcare. The research by Kreppner, Paulsen, and Schuetze (1982), documenting that more girls fulfill the "parenting" role, may be directly related to the findings by Kramer and Noorman (1993) that plans to involve the elder child in infantcare affected daughters most frequently. However, "going it alone" or "making it on your own" starts early in the United States. Whiting and Edwards (1988) noted that parents leave children alone far more of the time in the United States than parents do in other cultures and assign them by far the fewest chores. Mothers and fathers in the United States do not perceive children of 5 to 9 years of age as competent to care for others, preferring those of 12 years old or more. Even so, baby-sitting by preadolescent and adolescents may not be explicitly acknowledged as sibling care. Indeed, rather than contributing to the family's economic welfare, children in the same family receive payment to tend one another in middle-socioeconomic families.

Turning from who gives and receives care, I address in the next section the bases for selecting sibling caregivers.

PREREQUISITES FOR SIBLING CAREGIVING

Although very young children of even 2 years of age may assist with tending a baby, given the mother has a burdensome work load, sibling caregivers typically range in age from 7 to 13 or 14 years (Whiting and Edwards, 1988). Mothers prefer ages 7 or 8 to 10 years (Rogoff et al., 1975, Whiting and Edwards, 1988). Why does this preference exist? On the one hand, adults do not consider the younger siblings fully competent; on the other, some adolescent siblings are unavailable. These older siblings may have married, been fostered, have other economic tasks to perform, or may be serving an apprenticeship in another locale (Weisner, 1987, 1989b). Under these circumstances, cultural beliefs regarding children's emerging abilities support an increase in the assignment of caregiving responsibilities at ages 5 to 7 years (Rogoff, 1996; Rogoff et al., 1975). Adults regard a child of this age teachable and as having "reason," common sense, and a stable personality.

Cognitive Achievements

Weisner (1987, 1996a) reviewed cultural pressures underlying this preference and developmental milestones related to the shift that occurs at ages 5 to 7 years. Rogoff et al. (1975) provided findings that permit piecing this relation together. They argued that household chores provide the foundation for learning more general practices. Within the domestic setting two naturally occurring abilities that develop during middle childhood relate to the cognitive skills necessary for competently caring for others (Nerlove, Roberts, Klein, Yarbrough, and Habicht, 1974). The first, *self-managed sequencing of activities*, refers to the child's ability to carry out a sequence of acts in an exact order without supervision, such as preparing corn for *masa*. This activity involves removing the dried kernels from the cobs, preparing the lime-laced water, soaking the kernels in that water, removing the husks from the kernels, judging the proper texture of the kernels for grinding, and so forth. If anything goes wrong during the sequence, the child must have enough flexibility to find alternative solutions. The second, *voluntary social activities*, entails knowing the goals and rules of everyday life, such as the appropriate ways of acting toward each member of the family in accord with their place in the kinship hierarchy. At least a minimal attainment of these two cultural practices appears to underlie assignment of caregiving responsibilities to siblings during middle childhood.

Social and Emotional Achievements

Although these cognitive achievements are clearly important to caregiving, some qualitative descriptions by Whiting and Edwards (1988) make it dramatically evident that dynamic social and emotional abilities play a part as well. Sibling caregivers of 3 to 5 years old and those older caregivers who are overburdened tend to overstimulate an infant and to become quite upset themselves when they cannot soothe a fussy baby. The inability to assess the internal state of another (treating a crying baby as if she is cranky when instead she is sleepy), to foresee the implications of one's acts in relation to another person's response (more bouncing will not satisfy a hungry baby), to find alternative solutions (continuing to bounce a baby who persists in crying, rather than stopping, and then walking with or singing to the baby), and to control one's own impulses (slapping a fussy baby in frustration) illustrate missing competence. The following segments of interaction contrasting sibling caregivers of 5 and 8 years old in Central Mexico illustrate some aspects of the discrepancy. Note that the boys are from different levels within the lowest socioeconomic group known as *marginados* who live on the outskirts of Mexico City (Lomnitz, 1975). Mario who is 5 years old, belongs to the very poorest level composed mainly of recent immigrants living without the basic utilities, whereas Jaime, who is 8 years old, lives with his extended family in a home with running water, gas, and electricity. Mario's mother came from a very "rustic" region in the mountains in the state of Puebla and her work load was very high. Because Mario was not old enough to attend school and his mother expected him to assist her on a daily basis, his responsibilities for caregiving his younger sisters were much closer to that of the traditional rural culture than Jaime's. Jaime's mother, who was born in Mexico City, expected him to attend school regularly and look after his brother in the afternoons if none of the older girls in the family were available. There were six children under 10 years of age in both households (Zukow, field notes, 1981 to 1982).

Mario, 5, lives with his family in a semi-rural section of Mexico City a short walk from the pit in which his parents make bricks by hand. Mario has carried Irene, 21 months, to see their father working in the 20-foot-deep pit. He points at his father who is at least 35 feet away saying *¡Mira, allí está papi!/Look, there's Daddy!* His younger sister does not respond but glances about vaguely. Mario repeats the same gesture and variations of the same verbal message a dozen or more times as he attempts quite unsuccessfully to refocus her attention. He does not walk closer taking the pathway down into the pit or pick up a rock or shard of pottery to toss toward the place his father is standing. His mother in a similar situation had revised her message by eventually throwing a rock at the place she wanted Irene to notice (Zukow, 1990). Mario's responses were inflexible and displayed an insensitivity regarding the perceptual information that might have redirected his sister's attention to her father (Zukow, IGS, April 29, 1982).

In contrast, Jaime, nearly 8 years old, who lives in a nearby *colonia popular*, working-class neighborhood, resolves ambiguity for Juan, 21 months old. Jaime guides Juan's gaze to the target of attention, when his younger brother does not understand his message. Their aunt beats egg whites for a very special treat, *chiles rellenos*. The children of the family crowd into the small kitchen to watch in delight as some of the egg white spatters on their sister Beti's dress. Jaime points across the room to her as everyone laughs. He notices that Juan does not understand what is funny. Jaime uses his index finger to trace a trajectory for Juan to follow with his gaze. He begins at the corner of his brother's eye, walks across the room pointing, and ends the trajectory's path all the way across the room as he touches the egg white on Beti's dress. Juan then walks to his sister, reaches up to touch the egg white, and explores this unfamiliar experience by feeling its texture between his fingers. Clearly, Jaime revised his message on the basis of what his brother needed to perceive, quickly providing a re-viewing of the event that effectively guided Juan's knowing (Zukow, JLA, July 9, 1982).

Nascent social understanding.   Although this older sibling of nearly 8 years of age was more skilled than his 5-year-old counterpart in assisting his younger brother to perceive the target of his point, "younger" older siblings exhibit considerable understanding of infants. According to Dunn and Kendrick (1982a) and Wolf, Rygh, and Altshuler (1984), young children in their second and third years in England and the United States may not have an understanding of others as mental agents, but what they do know can be seen in their actions and speech. In action they display that they appreciate the consequences of their own acts and what another might feel. These abilities emerge very early in development. Young children express the same sensitivity to others in rural settings in Central Mexico as well (Zukow, LMF, May 5, 1982):

> Lilia, 17 months, lived in a small farming *ejido*, cooperative, about 175 miles northwest of Mexico City in the state of Guanajuato. She behaved quite possessively about a small green rush-bottomed chair. While playing together, Ana, a courtyard cousin closer to 3 years of age, took the chair quite deliberately. Ana, very sturdily built, set the chair down carefully a short distance away. She bent forward elaborately and slowly lifted her bottom up and back in order to sit squarely on the tiny chair. As she began to lower herself, Lilia moved smoothly into the gap between "up and back" and "down." She efficiently walked behind her cousin and without hesitation lifted the seat away at the exact instant that seat and bottom were meant to meet. A look of quiet satisfaction met Ana's loud protestations.

Was this outcome mere happenstance, or is there more supportive evidence that very young children understand the feelings and needs of others? In the literature, researchers and theorists first focused on the age between 3 and 5 years at which preschoolers achieve an initial understanding of others as agents who know (Tomasello, 1999; Wellman and Hinkling, 1994). Looking for precursors, many researchers have begun to explore how children under the age of 3 years come to understand the perceptions, emotions, actions, and communications of others. Candidate possibilities include attuning to emotional expression (Hobson, 1993), identifying and simulating the actions of others (Harris, 1991, 1996), detecting amodal invariant relations during social interaction (Zukow-Goldring, 1997, 2001; Zukow-Goldring and Rader, 2001), active intermodal mapping during reciprocal imitation (Meltzoff and Moore, 1999), understanding others as intentional agents (Tomasello, 1999), and the maturing of innate modules (Baron-Cohen, 1995). Except for Zukow-Goldring's naturalistic investigations, their explanations primarily rest on laboratory data documenting what children know at a particular point in time under controlled circumstances in unfamiliar settings with strangers.

Naturalistic evidence suggests that the development of social understanding comes not from the child alone but from the interplay between the changing cognitive, perceptual, and social abilities displayed by the child and the continual adjustment of the social environment to the developing child. In their longitudinal studies, Dunn and her colleagues (Dunn, 1988, 1991, 1996; Dunn and Kendrick, 1982a, 1982b) have demonstrated that during interaction siblings reveal a remarkable understanding of each other. They reasoned that children would display far more advanced behavior at home in a familiar setting, going about the most mundane routines of daily life. To become a "person," Dunn and her colleagues emphasized that the child must be able to recognize and share emotional states, anticipate and interpret how others will respond, understand relationships between important other people, know which behaviors are appropriate and which are sanctioned, and comprehend that punishments follow violations. Dunn and her co-workers viewed the infant as rather wise, using social understanding achieved through careful observation of people and events to gain her or his own special interests, often by playing on their fears and preferences.

Dunn (1989, p. 107) described what happened after an 18-month-old toddler overheard his mother telling the observer that his older sister detested a particularly fearsome toy spider: "Mother to observer: 'Anny [sibling] is really frightened of spiders. In fact there's a particular toy spider we've got that she just hates.' Child runs to next room, searches in toy box, finds toy spider, runs back to front room, pushes it at sibling—sibling cries." This 18-month-old toddler knew exactly how to upset her older sister. She exhibited consummate skill as she forced her older sister to notice a loathsome object that predictably made her cry. To date, children who participate in laboratory experiments do not display an understanding of the relations between perception and emotion until 12 months later at the age of 30 months (Wellman, Phillips, and Rodriguez, 2000). These findings add some weight to Dunn's proposal that behaviors manifest in the home setting earlier than in the laboratory.

Interactional bases for social understanding.   Younger siblings pay a great deal of attention to older siblings (Dunn and Kendrick, 1982a; Martini and Kirkpatrick, 1992; Zukow, 1989b), often imitating their actions. Dunn and her co-workers (Dunn, 1988; Dunn and Kendrick, 1982a) proposed that early play routines among siblings, such as tag, give-and-take, and mimicking that entail variation, elaborations, accelerating affect, and role reversals, provide an arena for understanding another person is "like me." Some support for these speculations comes from research documenting that imitation of other children occurs quite early and reliably in development. Novice peers of 14 to 18 months of age imitate object manipulation modeled by expert peers despite delays of up to 48 hours and changes in the context of the original action and personnel (Hanna and Meltzoff, 1993). Bouts of imitation among peers in which both the initiator of the action and the introduction of variations in action switch back and forth occur robustly between 16 and 28 months of age (Eckerman, 1993). Meltzoff and Moore (1999) have argued that reciprocal imitation games provide infants with the means to know that others are "like me" at the level of action. They speculated that there may be a developmental progression from knowing that someone acts like me to sharing goals, desires, and intentions. Although imitation may be a building block for treating others as "like the self," how the content and organization of countless sequences of imitation among siblings evolve over time and affect development remain unexamined.

Several researchers note that older siblings also imitate "regressive" activities, such as the way infants of 8 months of age or less act with bottles and blankets (Dunn and Kendrick, 1982a; Stewart, Mobley, van Tuyl, and Salvador, 1987). Dunn and Kendrick (1982a) cautioned about making premature negative interpretations of these actions, because their findings documented that these same behaviors correlated with warm and affectionate future relationships between the siblings. Whereas Stewart and his co-workers interpreted this mimicry of the new baby as bids for attention from the parents, there may be a more positive interpretation of enacting "babyish" behavior. The child may detect invariant relations or regularities common to the feelings displayed by the infant and to the co-occurring feeling qualities within the self (Zukow-Goldring, 1997, pp. 217–220). That is, through these actions the older sibling might renew knowing what a baby experiences. If so, those regressive imitations may serve the very important function of providing access to the infant sibling's state and, as such, another opportunity to perceive that a younger sister or brother is "like me".

Having a sibling apparently contributes to knowing what others do not know as well. Siblings from larger families, independent of birth order, could predict actions of a falsely informed story character more accurately than could siblings from smaller families (Perner, Ruffman, and Leekam, 1994). Clarifying these findings, Ruffman, Perner, Naito, Parkin, and Clements (1998) demonstrated that having older, not younger, siblings enhances a child's understanding of false belief. They speculated that the counterfactual states of affairs embodied in pretend play with older siblings might account for this superior performance.

Early expressions of comfort.   Not unexpectedly, siblings know how to soothe as well as torment their siblings. Siblings observed in the home comfort each other as early as the second year of life. Whereas Whiting and Edwards (1988) speculated that 3- to 5-year-old children may be unable to assess the internal states of others, Dunn and her colleagues (Dunn, 1988; Dunn and Kendrick, 1982a, 1982b) provided evidence that children of even 3 years of age had a nascent or "practical" understanding of the feelings of others. For example, the responses of siblings of 2 and 3 years old to the distress of a younger sibling changed as the children developed. The distress of an infant sibling clearly upset the youngest 2-year-old toddlers. By the second half of the second year they made rather awkward, formulaic attempts to comfort the other with kissing, patting, and going to the mother for help. Finally, during the third year siblings tailored comfort more exactly to the infant's needs. Children of 2 and 3 years of age also displayed an understanding of the connection between their own actions and other family members' fury, pleasure, or joy.

The relation of age to expressions of care continues according to related work conducted in the home by Gottlieb and Mendelson (1990). These researchers reported that older sisters of 38 to 57 months of age behaved with greater affection toward a newborn sister or brother and comforted with more sensitivity than those of 28 to 37 months old. Studies by Stewart and his colleagues (Stewart, 1983a, 1983b; Stewart and Marvin, 1984) demonstrated that children under 5 years old sometimes comfort younger siblings. These researchers linked perspective-taking skills among older siblings of 3 to 5 years old with their expression of empathy toward a distressed younger sibling during observations in a modified "Strange Situation" in the laboratory. The greater degree of comfort expressed in the familiar home setting observed by Dunn and her colleagues (Dunn, 1988; Dunn and Kendrick, 1982a, 1982b) suggests that the strangeness of the laboratory setting and the procedure itself may have inhibited how often siblings comforted one another. In a shortened, less aversive, modified Strange Situation, Howe and Ross (1990) found that comfort expressed by elder siblings of 36 to 58 months of age to their 14-month-old siblings was directly related to the intensity of the younger sibling's distress, not to perspective taking. These authors suggested that comforting another may arise simply from recognizing affective cues or from gratifying self-interest by eliminating aversive crying. Work by Garner, Jones, and Palmer (1994) confirmed among similarly aged, low-income and minority preschoolers that the ability to comfort a distressed younger sibling related to affective knowledge and skills rather than to perspective taking.

Self-interest as the core of conflict.   Although sibling caregivers must be able to comfort a younger sibling, competent caregiving requires more than this newfound sensitivity. Clearly the elder siblings in Dunn's studies did not manifest one of the other prerequisites for caregiving suggested by Whiting and Edwards. Putting the needs of another before those of the self is not found at 3 years of age. To the contrary, the self-interest of one sibling is often at odds with that of the other. At this age, threats to the child's self-interest are the core of conflict (Dunn, 1988). In related work (Dunn and Shatz, 1989; Slomkowski and Dunn, 1992), younger siblings of 33 months of age successfully turned the topic of talk during arguments from others to the self. In a similar vein, in the Strange Situation, less securely attached elder siblings of 2 to 7 years old "threatened" by the mother's leaving were less likely to comfort younger siblings of 1 to 2 years old than those siblings who were securely attached (Teti and Ablard, 1989). In more extreme situations, when younger siblings expressed very high levels of distress, even less securely attached elder siblings overcame their reticence and did comfort their younger siblings. Because the securely attached child did not need comfort in this setting, this child could attend more easily to the needs of the sibling. Investigating parental behaviors that might contribute to secure attachment, Murphy (1992) found a relation between contingent responding by adults to the elder child's needs and that child's empathic responses to the younger brother or sister. If elder siblings feel frightened, upset, or want nurturing, they may find it quite difficult to comfort someone else. Although expressions of care involve increasing levels of social understanding and secure attachment, the role of elder sibling itself also plays a part in the quality of sibling interaction.

Pelletier-Stiefel et al. (1986) observed more prosocial behavior in elder children of the ages of 3 to $4\frac{1}{2}$, $4\frac{1}{2}$ to 6, and 6 to $7\frac{1}{2}$ years than in their siblings who were $1\frac{1}{2}$ years younger. However, the relative proportion of prosocial behaviors did not change with age. Apparently the key to prosocial acts is having someone to nurture rather than being cognitively more advanced. Little wonder that children in agrarian societies display comfort and nurturance earlier. Their apprenticeship begins at 2 years of age and is more pervasive because of the sheer number of young children continuously available in the sibling group (Whiting and Edwards, 1988). Among the Maya of Guatemala, 5-year-old children provide routine care to younger siblings for several hours at a time (Gaskins, 1999). Although there is considerable evidence that young children can and do comfort each other when their own needs have been met, how do they come to put their own concerns aside in the face of another's distress?

Overcoming self-interest. Murphy's (1992) investigation of sibling–infant relationships among school-age children of 5 to 11 years old provides a means to understand how siblings overcome self-interest as well as achieve the other prerequisites for competent sibling caregiving suggested by Whiting and Edwards (1988). A competent sibling caregiver can modulate the intensity of interaction depending on the response of the younger sibling and display flexibility in finding alternative solutions for comforting an unhappy baby. Some of Murphy's findings relate to the emergence of these abilities. Future research can extend her findings by determining how characteristics of sibling mutuality relate to competent sibling caregiving. Areas with potential for study include the relation between parents who respond contingently to the elder child's needs and who, in turn, responds contingently to her or his younger brother or sister; parents who do not encourage the elder child to interact when she or he is cranky; and those parents who educate the elder to pick up perceptual information relating to the feelings and needs expressed by the infant. Interestingly, Kramer and Radey (1997) demonstrated that training elder siblings to notice and communicate with peers about possibly conflicting preferences resulted in improved sibling interactions.

Summary

Competent sibling caregivers understand the emotional states of younger sisters and brothers, know how to comfort a child in distress, can see more than one way to resolve a problem, and can put another's needs before their own. Children of 2 and 3 years of age display the rudiments of social understanding. Before the ages 5 to 7 years, children rarely can tailor care to the particular needs of a younger sibling and put self-interest aside. The experiences that precipitate the transition to more sophisticated levels of social understanding require further investigation. Imitation may provide the interactional basis through perception and action for knowing that the other is like the self and for coming to know what the other knows. The effectiveness and the function of this relation require clarification beyond detecting that your sibling experiences a similar range of emotional states. However, even if siblings display these social and cognitive skills, sibling caregiving does not occur unless the organization and the structure of the culture and the family foster this role (Weisner, 1987, 1996a).

SOCIALIZING SIBLING CAREGIVERS

Rather than assuming that developmental changes prompt different socialization pressures from caregivers, Whiting and Edwards (1988) argued that economic and cultural forces manifested in the organization and structure of daily life informed socialization. A child becoming a caregiver receives "on-the-job training" during "apprenticeship experiences" in which the child learns by doing and by observing (Weisner, 1987). What sibling caregivers learn depends on "activity settings" within a particular "cultural place" (Weisner, 1989a, 1993a): where they are, whom they are with, and what others are doing (Whiting and Edwards, 1988). Children are not separated or excluded from the ebb and flow of daily life in agrarian societies. As a matter of course, they are immersed in nearly the full range of social and economic activities that continuously unfold in family courtyards, neighborhoods, and nearby fields (Mundy-Castle, 1974). In technological societies, the reverse holds: The separation of home, workplace, and social activities of adults prevents children from observing many aspects of economic and social life.

Maternal Socializing Practices

The 5- to 8-year-old children who serve as child nurses receive clear training messages. Most of the instructions direct children of these ages to attend to chores and other socially useful activities. Whiting and Edwards (1988) asserted that children learn through imitating a model, by trial-and-error followed by successful repetition, and by direct tuition. The mother often remains in the vicinity when she assigns caregiving to a novice caregiver. She models and teaches appropriate behavior. Mothers most frequently use demonstration as their method of instruction. Weisner (1989b) noted that the Abaluyia of Kenya express most of these messages nonverbally. Research investigating mothers' messages to daughters learning cultural practices in a different domain confirm the widespread use of nonverbal messages in agraraian societies. Greenfield and her colleague (Childs and Greenfield, 1980; Greenfield, 1984) contrasted informal and formal teaching methods.[2] The informal style is characterized by nonverbal guidance that rarely permitted any failure among the Zinacatecan Mayans in Southern Mexico who were teaching their daughters to weave. According to Gaskins (2000), Yucatec Mayans rarely push a child to perform at the limits of their competence, as the increased errors and need to more closely monitor the child's participation would be counterproductive economically in this subsistence society.

In Senegal, Rabain-Jamin (1998) argued that the preparation for transferring caregiving responsibilities to older siblings appeared in maternal speech during triadic dialogue. Wolof mothers modeled the caregiving role for the older sibling by using the verbal routine of reported speech, a very common and important form in traditional oral societies. By saying that the elder had said "don't do X" to the younger, these mothers modeled what to say, gave the older authority, and directed the younger's attention to the elder child as a legitimate caregiver.

Interaction as a Training Ground for Nurturance

In agrarian societies, interacting with lap and very young knee children from birth to 18 months of age affords a training ground for nurturance. Whiting and Edwards (1988) argued that infants come into the world with natural abilities to elicit and maintain involvement. Papoušek and Papoušek (in Vol. 2 of this *Handbook*) elaborated the related notion of "intuitive parenting." However, what is learned and what is "natural" is unclear (Dent, 1990; Zukow, 1990). Caregivers adjust an infant's posture, facing them toward others for interacting and communicating as early as at 4 months of age (Ochs, 1988; Schieffelin, 1990). From a Vygotskian and various ecological perspectives, interaction may be the teacher precipitating cycles of contingent responding that benefit the infant receiving care and the child who is giving it (Whiting and Edwards, 1988; Zukow, 1989b, 1990). Soothing the infant gives immediate feedback to the older sibling, clearly attesting to the elder's competence. Furthermore, while teaching the sibling caregiver how to calm the infant, more competent caregivers may embed the practices within a cultural framework. For example, because Marquesans discourage any preoccupation with internal states, they guide preschool caregivers to jostle the infant primarily to return her or him to social life, not just to relieve immediate distress (Martini and Kirkpatrick, 1992). These Marquesan novice caregivers also learn a baby's likes, dislikes, and habits.

---

[2]The formal, verbal style, however, is common among highly educated caregivers in technological societies.

Harder lessons require that young elder siblings of 2 to 6 years of age learn to put aside their own wants and needs and, instead, to attend to those of others. Sibling "nurses" begin by offering food and soothing fussy infants. However, natural generosity is not the source of such actions, but gentle prodding. "Personal trainers" reside in all cultures (Zukow, MGMF, March 26, 1982):

> Cousins, Joana (15 months) and Beto (9 months), lived in a small farming community of 700 inhabitants in Guanajuato, Mexico. One day for 25 minutes, Joana energetically and persistently attempted to take Beto's sucker. In seamless counterpoint, her mother patiently guided her to first enjoy some of the sweet herself, then to share it with the serendipitously disinterested infant, and finally to smile and coo at the baby when he tasted the sucker. After 5 more months of encouragement and immersion in daily opportunities to share, Joana often shared food on request.

In Senegal, children share both food and the initial source of comfort as soon as possible. Wolof caregivers encourage a recently weaned child to share his food with other siblings and the younger sibling who had taken his place at their mother's breast (Zempleni-Rabain, 1973).

Among the Kahluli in New Guinea, mothers use a "feeling-sorry voice" to teach caring for younger siblings (Schieffelin, 1990). Requests for food in this plaintive voice tell the older sibling what to do from the content as well as how to feel from the form of the message. As a lesson in interdependence, the younger sibling learns to appeal for help and/or compassion, whereas the older one learns to assist others and feel compassion for someone dependent or helpless. Summarizing the developmental course of sharing and caring for others' needs, Watson-Gegeo and Gegeo (1989) noted that Solomon Islanders begin instructing an infant to share at 6 months of age. By 18 months of age the child shares without hesitation on request, by 3 years of age shares without prompting, and by 6 years of age may give her or his entire portion to a younger sibling if there is insufficient food for everyone.

Confirming that children of 3 years of age or more share without guidance, Martini and Kirkpatrick (1992) documented parallel exchanges among siblings of 3 to 5 years old in the Marquesas. Similarly, half a world away in Senegal, siblings of 3 to 8 years old, enacted the Wolof's "law of brothers and equals" as they worked out sharing food without adult assistance (Zempleni-Rabain, 1973). These siblings also shared objects and protected younger siblings from being hurt by others. This attention to sharing resources reflects its critical significance for group survival. For instance, the Wolof consider nonsharing to be the most antisocial act (Rabain-Jamin, 1994).

"Practice makes perfect".   According to Whiting and Edwards (1988), girls are assigned caregiving more often than boys. In addition, girls interact more with young children, and in the company of their mothers continuously see them engaging in caregiving behavior with younger siblings. In a reflexive cycle, girls receive more practice and become more adept at empathetic and nurturant actions. Whiting and Edwards argued that practice relates to greater nurturing. Supporting their position, boys who act as caregivers nurture others outside of the caregiving role itself more than boys who do not (Ember, 1973). Given this broad foundation, girls have more confidence in these abilities and find the experience pleasurable.

Niche picks or niche picking.   Another twist on the arguments over who is socializing whom relates to the degree to which children pick learning environments compatible with their own individual characteristics. Although behavioral geneticists and others argue forcefully that genetic endowments in the form of behavioral predispositions guide much of development (Dunn, 1983; Dunn and Plomin, 1990; Scarr, 1992; Scarr and McCartney, 1983), a particular social milieu and exposure to members of the culture are necessary before someone "can learn what s/he was born to be" (Draper and Harpending, 1987, p. 212). The following description of socialization among the Kwara'ae of the Solomon Islands suggests that the "niche" picks the child rather than the reverse (Watson-Gegeo and Gegeo, 1989; personal communication, March and June, 1994):

> From the earliest observations of Susuli at 9 months she was sensitive, easily upset, and sometimes selfish. At the same time, she was quick to learn and perceptive towards the social relations around her. At 3 and 6 years old she was usually very responsible and skilled in performing work tasks in the home and garden, including caregiving of younger siblings. On the other hand, at times she threw temper tantrums and was moody and stubborn. These bouts of ill-temper interfered with her being a good model for her younger siblings, from her parents' point of view. By age 9 Susuli had become more stubborn, was taking advantage of her younger sister, and was not doing well in school. She carried out her work at home less and less willingly. Because the Kwara'ae believe that it is unhealthy for a person to be emotionally labile, Susuli's mood swings were disruptive to the family. Further, an important cultural value held by the Kwara'ae is that the needs of the group come before those of the individual. Susuli's parents felt that she was too focused instead on herself.
>
> Two years later Susuli seemed transformed: relaxed, calm, happy, gentle, nurturing toward her siblings, and showing a high level of responsibility. In the 2 intervening years, Susuli had received intensive *Fa'amanata'anga* (counseling sessions), from her parents, her father's sister, and her grandfather. Despite initial resistance from Susuli, these adults had gently, patiently, and unremittingly insisted that she change. The transformed Susuli was poised, self-confident, and had willingly taken the role in the family that they had envisioned for her. She was highly valued within her family and by others in the village.

As this summary of field notes from the Solomon Islands illustrates, ultimately, culture strongly affects how individual behaviors are played out (Weisner, 1993b). Further, culture and parental discipline constrains the range of conduct that different siblings can express.

Effects of a New Baby on Family Practices

In technological cultures, researchers overwhelmingly consider the theme of individual development, not interdependence, when investigating adjustment to a new baby. Most studies focus nearly exclusively on what negative effects the baby's arrival will have on the firstborn and/or on how to avoid disruptions to her or him (Dunn and Kendrick, 1982a; Kreppner, 1988; Kreppner et al., 1982; Stewart, 1990; Sutton-Smith and Rosenberg, 1970). Apparently no one assumes that older siblings will welcome the new infant and gradually take on caregiving responsibilities that will contribute to the overall well-being of the family group. As noted, the notion of sibling rivalry from psychodynamic theory continues to strongly influence the direction of this research (Cohler and Paul, in Vol. 3 of this *Handbook*; Furman and Lanthier, in Vol. 1 of this *Handbook*). Rather than presupposing a limitation of resources, another approach might be the allocation of bountiful resources. In settings in which shared caregiving is common, the mother is not the exclusive source of nurturance. When the mother is not available, others fill in for her. Thus, receiving less from the mother may not be so traumatic in situations in which surrogate care is the norm rather than in situations in which it is not, that is, in the nuclear family. Supporting this notion is evidence that the involvement of the father ameliorates the level of stress within the Western family during the infant's first 2 years of life (Kreppner, 1988; Kreppner et al., 1982).

Dunn and her colleagues (Dunn, 1988; Dunn and Kendrick, 1982a) speculated that having a younger sibling precipitates noticing the characteristics of self and other. The mother's comments regarding the baby as a person with desires, preferences, and intentions affect the pattern of interaction between the siblings. In a case study of his own children, Mendelson (1990) described in detail the methods he and his wife used to prepare their 4-year-old son for the arrival of his new sibling and to guide him in becoming a sibling himself. Mendelson summarized the highlights as including ceaseless changes in infant and sibling that continuously elicited and shaped the behavior to come.

In addition, the parents informally "taught" the eldest about his infant brother as they chatted about his care, emotions, and growing abilities. They also took care to sustain their relationship with their firstborn son. These parents also recognized that their elder son's negative behavior was often simply clumsiness or intrusiveness in the service of curiosity. They kept stern correction to a minimum. Mendelson confirmed much of Dunn's theorizing: During both pleasurable and aversive interactions, the eldest child and the infant learned about the self as well as about each other as they grew and changed.

How might the experience of having a sibling precipitate expressions of comfort? Perhaps the raw emotions perceived and felt provide a ground for detecting an intersubjectivity or invariance of experience across persons (Zukow-Goldring, 1997). The other cries and, although the elder child may not be crying now, she or he has cried on other occasions. The experience of crying provides a means to understand that the other is both like the self who has cried in the past and unlike the self who is not crying now. Parents often tell an older child that the younger sibling's state "is just like" what you used to do, still do, or is more or less intense. In the future, researchers may find that caregivers who guide children to notice the similarities or differences in experience have provided the basis for accurate detection of the state of another. (For the related topic of active intermodal mapping during reciprocal imitation, see Meltzoff and Moore, 1999.)

Extending and confirming many of Dunn and Mendelson's findings, researchers have investigated the experiences of siblings of 3 to 11 years of age who express and enact warmth and care to their younger siblings (Howe and Ross, 1990; Kramer and Noorman, 1993; Murphy, 1992, 1993). Because prior research primarily investigated firstborn elder siblings and their secondborn brothers and sisters, Murphy (1993) extended this work by including some elder siblings who were laterborn children themselves. Conditions that contribute to sibling mutuality include an initial interest in the infant as proposed by Whiting and Edwards (1988; see also section titled Prerequisites to Sibling Caregiving), many uninterrupted opportunities to interact that are accompanied by very little correction, contingent responses to the needs of the elder sibling by the parents, parents who include and share responsibility of the infant with the elder child, parents who focus the elder child's attention on the cues used to read the infant's needs and feeling, and parents who do not press the elder child to interact when she or he is tired or fussy. Of these, Murphy (1993) speculated that the accessibility of and responsibility for the infant are most critical to the elder child's becoming a caregiver during the first 18 months of the new baby's life. Presumably practice nurturing encourages nurture in technological settings just as it does in agrarian ones.

Summary

In many agrarian societies, elder siblings constantly have opportunities to observe and imitate other more competent caregivers as they interact with younger children in the family. Siblings can and do imitate and observe each other's emotional state. However, caregivers constantly refine young children's interpretations of the "here and now" and also embed what siblings perceive and know about others in a web of interrelated cultural practices. With seemingly infinite patience seasoned with cajoling, correcting, threatening, and teasing, caregivers guide older siblings as they learn to tend fussy, hungry, angry, sleepy younger siblings. This guidance provides siblings with a flexible repertoire of responses to their younger siblings. Framed by vivid and predictable affect, the children themselves apparently detect what produces annoyance and all too often use that information to provoke each other. Finally, by distracting, pushing, and prodding, more mature caregivers help older siblings to overcome self-interest so that they automatically tend to the needs of others before their own. Although this pattern has not been documented to the same degree among parents in technological societies (Gottfried et al., in Vol. 2 of this Handbook), clearly learning the potential benefits of sibling caregiving from traditional societies might assist overburdened dual wage earners of today.

SIBLING CONFLICT: AUTHORITY OR RIVALRY?

Permitting children to socialize each other may be necessary and intrinsic to the development and smooth functioning of hierarchical sibling relationships (Seymour, 1993). The conflict associated with sibling care need not be construed negatively. Traditional societies, instead, interpret conflict in terms of how it might serve continuity and cohesion as related to the group's survival. In contrast, since Cain and Abel, Western culture has highlighted the injurious effects to individual sisters and brothers of sibling rivalry arising from limited resources. More recently, studies in technological cultures have considered the positive effects of sibling discord, especially how conflict relates to practices that promote the needs or achievements of the individual.

The Interplay of Cooperation and Conflict

In many societies, such as those in the Pacific Islands, Africa, South Asia, and Central America, group survival depends on shared resources and cooperation. Because siblings directly play the most important role in each other's lives both economically and socially across the lifespan, these relationships are more elaborated than those of parents and children or of spouses (Nuckolls, 1993a, 1993b; Weisner, 1993b; also B. B. Schieffelin, personal communication, Fall, 1979). In these cultures, siblings have power over many decisions affecting economic (exchange/sharing, inheritance, and marriage payments), protection/defense, and ceremonial (age, initiation) obligations (Maynard, 1999; Nuckolls, 1993a, 1993b; Watson-Gegeo and Gegeo, 1989; Weisner, 1987; Zempleni-Rabain, 1973; also B. B. Schieffelin, personal communication, Fall, 1979).

In fact, in South Asia the great epics and legends extol the relationships among mythic siblings. The literary, mythological, and scriptural texts of South Asia that depict sibling relationships include the *Ramayana*, the *Mahabharata*, and the *Mitakshara* (Beals and Eason, 1993; Nuckolls, 1993a, 1993b; Seymour, 1993). People frequently refer to these models of ideal conduct to resolve immediate problems and to socialize children (Beals and Eason, 1993; Nuckolls, 1993a). To ground these findings, Nuckolls (1993a) contrasted the perspectives of anthropologists informed by theories of symbolic interaction with those of developmental psychologists and psychological anthropologists. Anthropologists view systems of meaning (ideologies, conceptual systems, unconscious processes, symbolic frameworks) as the phenomena that form behavior. Psychologists study the processes that promote the development of abilities that permit survival within any particular culture. Nuckolls noted the low probability of psychologists' considering the influence of ancient texts on contemporary socialization practices. To overcome such omissions, he called for an integration of behavioral and symbolic approaches, arguing that they both direct attention to important aspects of sibling relations that neither alone acknowledge (see also Zukow, 1989a).

Beals and Eason (1993) challenged implicit, common assumptions regarding what is normal by arguing that a competitive society forces Western children to "repress" humanity's natural preference for harmony. Thomas (as cited in Martini, 1994, p. 99) referred to a "cooperation deficit." However, although siblings continually monitor and adjust to each other's needs (Nuckolls, 1993a), scholars do not paint a picture of life in agrarian societies as a Rousseau-like utopian paradise without dissension (Beals and Eason, 1993; Nuckolls, 1993a; Ochs, 1988; Schieffelin, 1990; Seymour, 1993; Weisner, 1987, 1989b; Whiting and Edwards, 1988; Whittemore and Beverly, 1989). Members of agrarian cultures continuously attempt to gain benefits from or maintain advantages over one another as adults, often struggling over all manner of assets including power, emotional well-being, spiritual practices, and material goods. Even with these exigencies of everyday life, within hierarchical societies cooperation keeps the system running smoothly, whereas too much conflict endangers the delicate balance. Enhancing cooperation and muting conflict need not suggest that these qualities are two ends of a continuum, but may be manifestations of separate dimensions that interact. Researchers regard conflict as a natural outgrowth and support of the organization and structure of these societies.

Authority Embodying Interdependence

Whiting and Edwards (1988) and others (Ochs, 1988; Schieffelin, 1990) contended that in stratified[3] societies prosocial dominance follows from variations in status. Older siblings have legitimate power when caring for younger children that embodies their lifetime relationship. Elder siblings learn to exercise this authority as they socialize one another, whereas younger siblings get used to another's will (Whittemore and Beverly, 1989). In this unequal relationship the elder has and wields power, whereas the younger negotiates for possessions and status (Nuckolls, 1993a; Zempleni-Rabain, 1973). The giver gains respect and self-esteem "by renouncing the doubtful advantage of possessing something" (Zempleni-Rabain, 1973, p. 229). Within this framework, no one gains and much can be lost if younger siblings express rivalry (Beals and Eason, 1993).

In everyday expressions of their authority, elder siblings use simple commands and coercive techniques to persuade their charges to behave appropriately and not hurt themselves (Whiting and Edwards, 1988). Sibling caregivers find caring for toddlers of 2 and 3 years of age more difficult and may chide them a great deal. Because adults consider the tantrums, rages, and expressions of hostility of younger children as normal, squabbling among children close in age receives little attention. Adults and older children greet these behaviors with teasing at most and usually simply ignore them. On occasion an older sibling's self-centered behavior negatively affects that of a younger child or results in actually hurting someone. The elder child who has overextended the authority granted to her or him will eventually be punished, especially if the conflict interferes with adult work. A younger sibling risks collective shaming that might involve everyone nearby, if she or he does not heed the guidance of elder siblings (Ochs, 1988). Siblings soon learn not to let problems get to older persons (Ochs, 1988) but, instead, monitor and criticize each other constantly (Martini, 1994; Watson-Gegeo and Gegeo, 1986).

Conflict Promoting Individual Development

Most researchers in technological societies study conflict in terms of the individual's course of development in contrast to conflict as it relates to the group. Research conducted under the sway of psychodynamic theory focused on the negative effects of siblings' rivalrous feelings and actions arising from a continuous tug-of-war over the affectional resources of the mother (Cohler and Paul, in Vol. 2 of this *Handbook*; Furman and Lanthier, in Vol. 1 of this *Handbook*; Lamb, 1976; Sutton-Smith and Rosenberg, 1970). Offering a different interpretation, Dunn (1988) argued that conflict within the family has beneficial effects. Sibling conflict is the emotional crucible that drives the emergence of a "practical" understanding of other people's feelings and intentions. Day in and day out, teasing and provoking are directly experienced as annoying and upsetting to the self and to one's sibling (Dunn and Munn, 1985). However, these conflicts are resolved and discussed. Dunn and her colleagues (Dunn, 1988, 1991, 1996; Dunn and Kendrick, 1982a) emphasized the many positive effects of conflict, especially the importance of mothers' elaborating general moral tenets underlying the particulars of family rules and regulations. Eventually children invoke social rules to justify their behavior. Ross and her colleagues concur, based on their findings showing that middle-socioeconomic parents actively intervene in more than half of the conflicts arising between siblings of 2 to 4 years of age (Ross, Filyer, Lollis, Perlman, and Martin, 1994). They caution, however, that current models of parent intervention do not predict which rules siblings adopt and which they do not. In addition, Shantz and Hobart (1989) emphasized that paradoxically conflict demonstrates connectedness through providing practice in negotiating mutual consensus. In the same vein, Kramer and Baron (1995) noted that nonaggressive sibling conflict may promote social development. In

---

[3]Ochs (1988) defines a stratified society as one in which power and prestige derive from distinctions based on such characteristics as age, sex, personal qualities, and, perhaps more crucially, from the rank of particular 'titles' that individuals may hold during their lifetime.

research supporting this view, Kramer and Radey (1997) found that increasing warmth or closeness enhanced sibling relationships more than misguided attempts to eliminate conflict. Across cultures sibling discord provides children with a means to explore the nuances and limits of their social world and to evaluate and calibrate emotional reactions.

SIBLING NOVICES AND EXPERTS

Technological Cultures

By imitating and responding to sibling guidance and seeking information from them, younger siblings display that they notice and gather information while interacting with their older brothers and sisters. First, numerous investigations have reported that preschoolers and school-age siblings imitate their elder siblings far more frequently than they are imitated (Abramovitch, Corter, and Lando, 1979; Abramovitch, Corter, Pepler, and Stanhope, 1986; Berndt and Bulleit, 1985; Dunn and Kendrick, 1982a; Stoneman, Brody, and MacKinnon, 1984). Summers, Summers, and Ascione (1993) found far greater imitation of older siblings in single-parent families, pointing to their importance as role models. Second, studies document that younger siblings comply with the instructions of older siblings (Abramovitch et al., 1986) and play the part of the learner during games (Brody, Stoneman, and MacKinnon, 1982; Stoneman et al., 1984). Third, younger siblings ask older siblings for suggestions, demonstrating that they view them as having important cultural practices to impart (Azmitia and Hesser, 1993; Handel, 1986). In broad terms, younger siblings pay attention to what their older siblings do, repeat it, and in structured activities follow their directions.

Imitation's role in theory. Piaget's theory (1962) and approaches informed by child language studies (Bloom, Hood, and Lightbown, 1974; Greenfield and Smith, 1976; Nelson, Carskaddon, and Bonvillian, 1973; Snow, 1981) propose that children imitate actions just coming into their repertoires. These findings imply, at the very least, that older siblings indirectly affect the younger child's development. Normally younger children can imitate immediately or slightly after observing the activities of older siblings that are within their range of actions. A Vygotskian interpretation (Vygotsky, 1978; Wertsch, 1985) focuses on guidance provided during social interaction as the matrix within which more competent persons serve as the source of cultural knowledge to others less fully informed. Although robust evidence demonstrates that younger siblings witness new activities while interacting with older siblings and enact them autonomously only after some delay (Azmitia and Hesser, 1993), these findings from studies of imitation do not differentiate between the theoretical views. In the analysis of play and language that follows, this puzzle is taken up again.

Giving and taking directions. Besides serving as witting or unwitting models, in the manager role older siblings produce many more directives across a range of activities than the younger sibling (Tomasello and Mannle, 1985) and more than the mother when forbidding actions or guiding the younger child's play (Dunn and Kendrick, 1982a). These specific studies and those of Brody and Stoneman (Brody et al., 1982; Stoneman et al., 1984) did not assess the effectiveness of these directives, simply that older siblings tried to direct the interactions. However, investigations of teaching and tutoring at home have shown that older sibling did guide the activities of the younger sibling (Cicirelli, 1972; Ellis and Rogoff, 1982; Koester and Johnson, 1984; Stewart, 1983b; Vandell, Minnett, and Santrock, 1988), sometimes with cascading effects (Azmitia, Cooper, Garcia, and Dunbar, 1996). That is, older siblings taught chores to younger ones who, in turn, taught them to even smaller sisters and brothers in lower-income, Mexican American families. For skills required outside the home, siblings can play an important teaching/tutoring role. If parents were not familiar with schoolwork, siblings helped with homework, conveying the "tricks of the trade" in African American, European American, Mexican American, and Vietnamese American families (Azmitia et al., 1996; Blankston, 1998; Pérez et al., 1994; Smith, 1993; Snow, Barnes, Chandler, Goodman, and Hemphill, 1991). The degree of success depended on the task, the ages of the siblings, and the presence of adults.

Coregulation of sibling interactions.   Azmitia and Hesser (1993) examined the roles of 9-year-old sibling and peer teachers and 7-year-old sibling learners. Confirming others, the authors found that younger children looked at siblings' models more than at peers', imitated siblings more often, and directed more questions and requests for help to siblings. The siblings provided more spontaneous teaching than did peers, but girls taught more than boys overall. Their most important finding highlights the role of the younger child. The younger siblings elicited many more explanations from their older siblings than from the peer, signaling that brothers and sisters enjoyed a "privileged" teaching status. Furthermore, the younger siblings took more responsibility themselves when with a sibling as they more often blocked the older sibling from taking over a task. This study draws attention to the need to consider how "novice" and "expert" coregulate interactions.

Summary.   In technological societies, older siblings often act and are treated as experts, whereas younger siblings embody the novice role most often. Studies of play and language provide evidence that interaction with siblings creates an environment in which more adept children supply unique information to those less competent, using methods rather different from those of adults.

Play

Vygotsky (1978) asserted that play is the setting within which cultural knowing emerges. In this view, children engage in cultural activities earlier and more frequently during interaction with more competent members of their culture and only manifest this knowing on their own at a later time.[4] From a Piagetian perspective, the younger sibling actively seeks information. Without guidance, the child purportedly can absorb what she or he requires at any particular level of development through observation alone. This view interprets guidance as interfering at best (Piaget, 1962; Zukow, 1984a, 1989b). Does Vygotsky's or Piaget's view best account for the data? Is life a catered affair, or is it a cafeteria from which the child selects whatever she or he considers a nutritious developmental diet?

Unique and effective role of older siblings in agrarian settings.   In agrarian societies and among blue-collar African Americans, the play of young children occurs almost exclusively among siblings (Farver, 1999; Farver and Wimbarti, 1995; Gaskins, 2000; Göncü, Mistry, and Mosier, 2000; Martini, 1994; Ward, 1971; Watson-Gegeo and Gegeo, 1989; Zukow, 1989b). Zukow (1984b, 1986) documented that play with adult and sibling caregivers is more advanced than unguided play. Furthermore, she demonstrated that play with siblings was significantly more advanced than play with adult caregivers. Older siblings of 4 to 11 years of age often succeeded in enticing younger siblings of 12 to 27 months of age to leave less challenging and self-involved play with objects for more elaborate enactments of scenes from everyday life. In the segment that opened this chapter, Juana was repeatedly invited to refrain from taking apart and putting together a plastic egg in favor of joining in the tortilla making by sisters of 7 and 10 years old, guiding her from the *level of actual development* to the *level of potential development*. Farver's research in Mexico and Indonesia (Farver, 1999; Farver and Wimbarti, 1995) also documented that younger siblings engaged in more frequent and complex play with older siblings than with mothers. Nevertheless, how effective or

---

[4]A large body of research informed by Vygotsky's theory (1978) has investigated his assertion that the input of more competent persons affects that of a novice in a broad range of activities at home and at school (Moll, 1990; Wertsch, 1985). However, Bornstein and Tamis-LeMonda (1995) argue that attachment theory and the ethological approach also support this view in their more comprehensive overview of theoretical perspectives that may enlarge our understanding of the play literature.

"finely tuned" sibling guidance might be to the younger sibling's level of development cannot be determined from these few studies.

Zukow-Goldring and co-workers (Zukow, 1989b, 1990; Zukow-Goldring, 1996, 2001; Zukow-Goldring, Romo, and Duncan, 1994) argued that caregivers who disambiguate their messages and actions by making perceptual information prominent and available assist children in achieving consensus about ongoing events. More studies examining whether younger siblings benefit from such guidance can fill in the gaps and eventually contribute to more comprehensive theories of the emergence of cultural practices. In an ethnographic investigation of teaching in the context of play, elder Zinacantec Maya siblings apparently adapt or finely tune what they say and do while caring for and teaching younger sisters and brothers (Maynard, 1999, 2000). They provided verbal messages and perceptual information to enhance the understanding of everyday tasks. Siblings of 8 to 11 years of age supplied the structure and organization of tasks, served as models, broke activities into doable parts, put the younger child through the motions of a new action, and encouraged them to persevere. At 6 to 7 years old, siblings gave many orders, set up materials, rarely simplified a task, and gave a modicum of explanation and feedback. From 3 to 5 years of age, brothers and sisters did the task themselves, mainly serving as models.

In similar situations when the younger sibling responded inadequately (Zukow, 1989b), older siblings of 3 to 5 years old with eagerness and impatience displayed their own competence by enacting requested actions. For instance, Marta, the mother of 21-month-old Irene, asked her to wash a doll in a basin of water by saying *báñala* (*bathe her*). Irene did not immediately douse the doll with water. After a brief pause, 3½-year-old Maximina chimed in with *¡YO lo hago!* (*I'LL do it!*). She washed the doll, providing a clear perceptual model of "appropriate" conduct that Irene promptly imitated. Sometimes the older child is blunt and critical. For instance, 4-year-old Victoria told 26-month-old Lucha with great disdain *¡Mira, tu no sabes!* (*Look, you don't know how!*) as she showed apprehensive Lucha how to hold a wriggling rabbit by its ears. Children of 3 to 5 years of age need not take another's perspective, guess what the other needs to know, and/or scaffold carefully to promote a younger sibling's development as adult caregivers in Central Mexico often do. By displaying their own competence, slightly older siblings make their own definition of adequate behavior quite available. Younger older siblings do not mince words, in stark contrast to adults' usual gentle adjustments. Being told and shown you are doing it wrong "may be quite as informative as gradually getting it right" (Zukow, 1989b, p. 98). Pérez-Granados and Callanan (1997) in the United States provide some confirmation from an unexpected source. In a sorting task, these researchers found that older siblings of 5 to 8 years of age corrected far more than did mothers, pointed to correct choices more often, or did the task for the younger siblings of 3 to 5 years old. The younger siblings categorized more accurately during the "explicit teaching" session with their siblings than in those with their mothers who were more easygoing about placing puzzling items.

Returning to an agrarian site and to the study of play, Martini's (1994) ethnography of play in a sibling group numbering 13 in the Marquesas describes how children learn stratified roles, such as peripheral toddler, initiate, noisy leader, and quiet leader. These roles parallel the hierarchical interrelationships of the larger society. Children of 2 to 5 years of age learn self-reliance and emotional control as they negotiate dominance, consensus, and adherence to social rules with little or no adult assistance. Marquesans value the "sacredness of the individual and of personal plans" as long as they do not intrude on the interests of others. However, in the play group leaders quickly make evident the limits of "doing your own thing." One day all the children pretended to load water on an imaginary outrigger canoe except one initiate named Rora. As Rora instead washed the deck, Justin, a "noisy" leader, knocked the water out of his hands. The initiate swung at the older child who responded by hitting him roughly and causing Rora to cry. Soon afterwards Justin patted Rora on the head and handed him a container of water to load, quietly letting him know what he ought to do. In this stratified environment, the older siblings teach their younger brothers and sisters to pay attention to the group purpose, deal with frustration appropriately, and make light of an attack.

From pretend play partners to methodological inconsistencies in technological settings.
In contrast to parents in agrarian societies, parents in technological societies do play with their children. Parents play at a more advanced level with a daughter or son of 12 to18 months of age than to
older siblings who are from 1 to 6 years older (Stevenson, Leavitt, Thompson, and Roach, 1988; Teti,
Bond, and Gibbs, 1988). Although Hartup and Laursen (1991) described the role of the play group
as vague, pretend play occurs almost exclusively with siblings and peers (Dunn, 1988; Dunn and
Kendrick, 1982a; Stevenson et al., 1988; White and Woollett, 1992; Youngblade and Dunn, 1995a,
1995b). Research from several investigations supports the notion that the internal state language expressed in fantasy play with siblings contributes to the development of social understanding of other's
feeling and actions (Brown, Donelan-McCall and Dunn, 1996; Howe, Petrakos, and Rinaldi, 1998;
Youngblade and Dunn, 1995a, 1995b. These abilities, in turn, may underlie knowing what others
know as tested in false-belief tasks (Ruffman et al., 1998; Youngblade and Dunn, 1995a, 1995b).

Dunn (1983) suggested that play with parents provides the impetus for developmental change,
whereas play with siblings serves to consolidate those modifications, especially in pretend play. In
technological societies this observation may hold, but clearly "cultural place" plays a part. In many
agrarian societies siblings introduce each other to the layout of the rural setting, daily practices, and
preferred behavior. Methodological inconsistencies, especially the effect of violating ecological validity, may account for some of these contradictory results (Cole et al., 1978; Malpass, 1977; Mischel,
1977). The unfamiliar laboratory setting, parents remaining in the room while their siblings play,
and novel toys contribute to mistaking "stimulus" equivalence for "functional" equivalence. Further,
interpreting the "directiveness" of older siblings as negative, rather than recognizing the unique and
powerful advantage that explicit correction can make, may obscure the benefits of sibling interaction.

Summary. During play children learn about the organization and structure of everyday events,
the affordances of objects, social roles and practices, and the preferred degree of interdependence or
independence in particular cultures. Findings from current studies of play, both in agrarian and technological settings, favor a Vygotskian interpretation in highlighting and confirming the importance
of social interaction with more expert partners as the source of knowing.

Language

Effective and unique role of older siblings in agrarian settings. Although comprehension
of speech pervasively precedes speech production, most child language research focuses on the
child's speech production. For the most part, investigations of sibling speech do not depart from this
pattern. Nonetheless, how caregivers treat the unintelligible utterances of language learning children
and prompt them to talk does not explicate how children learn the relation between words and
world in the first place. In Central Mexico and in the United States among European American and
Latino caregivers, those who interact with children do revise their own miscomprehended utterances,
so that infants can perceive the correspondence between words and ongoing events. Siblings do
too. Caregivers carefully coordinate the temporal synchrony of action/gesture and word providing
perceptual information that marks the relation between what they are saying and what is happening
(Zukow, 1989b; Zukow-Goldring, 1990, 1996, 2001; Zukow-Goldring and Ferko, 1994). Some can
articulate what should be done when a child miscomprehends speech (Zukow, 1991). These practices
disambiguate speech and correlate significantly with the child's later production (Zukow-Goldring,
2001), as described in the following vignette (Zukow, 1989b, p. 95):

> For instance, Jaime, almost 8, and Juan, his younger brother of 22 months, play in the bedroom with a
> toy monkey. At the time Juan could neither comprehend nor express location. Jaime asks him to place
> the monkey halfway across the room, pointing and saying ¡*Páralo allí!/Stand it up there!*. When Juan
> repeats ¿*Eh?/Hm?* several times, Jaime catches his gaze, walks to the place, and bends over. He carefully
> coordinates saying ¡*Aquí, páralo!/Here, stand it up!* and point-touching the place on the floor.

In this segment, Jaime provided a tangible, perceptual translation of his verbal message to assist his younger brother in comprehending what he had just said. Just as siblings carefully adjust problematic aspects of their messages to assist in their younger siblings' lexical growth, they also play a role in the emergence of other aspects of language.

In the Pacific Islands and in Africa, triadic conversations with infant, older sibling, and mother provide settings in which much language socialization takes place (Ochs, 1988; Rabain-Jamin, 1998; Schieffelin, 1990; Watson-Gegeo and Gegeo, 1989). Although these authors described the role of siblings as important for the learning of lexical items and the rules and uses of language, they provided little specific detail. In contrast, Demuth (1984, 1996) argued that among the Basotho of Lesotho in southern Africa siblings learn to use advanced linguistic forms, in particular relative clauses, during interaction with the sibling group. Utterances such as *bring that thing that you found* occur far more frequently when younger siblings of 25 to 55 months of age play with older siblings of 5 to 10 years of age than when interacting with adults. Mothers concur that children who interact frequently with other children speak earlier and better than those who stay with their mothers. Even though Zeisler and Demuth (1995) provided evidence that even siblings of 5 years of age appropriately use a special simplified speech register when talking to younger siblings, K. A. Demuth (personal communication, January, 1995) speculated that older siblings sometimes do not attend as carefully as adults might to what a younger sibling is saying and doing. This proposed variability in attentiveness may force the younger child to work harder at making herself or himself understood (Demuth, 1984). Aware of the valuable role of sibling caregiving, researchers conducting studies in agrarian societies have looked for and found that siblings perform an important function in the language development of their younger sisters and brothers.

Illuminating the positive role of older siblings in technological settings.   Much research in the 1970s and 1980s emphasized that certain characteristics of caregiver speech observed in European American middle-socioeconomic mothers, such as finely tuning utterances to the child's level of development and disentangling the meaning of the child's unintelligible speech, facilitate language learning (Barnes, Gutfreund, Satterly, and Wells, 1983; Cross, 1977; Ryan, 1974; Snow, 1977; Snow, Perlmann, and Nathan, 1987). The ways that mothers talk to an individual child differ markedly from 3- to 5-year-old siblings' speech to infants of 12 to 23 months of age or speech during triadic infant–sibling–mother conversations (Dunn and Kendrick, 1982a; Jones and Adamson, 1987; Tomasello and Mannle, 1985; Woollett, 1986). The benefits attributed to the speech of mothers especially adapted to language-learning children naturally led to speculations regarding the probable deleterious language environment of later siblings who would receive input from siblings as well. Pervasive, unexamined assumptions regarding the superior achievement of firstborn children[5] may have added weight to this conjecture.

Nonetheless, these researchers and those that followed focused mostly on the potential benefits of learning language in a richer social environment that includes mothers and siblings (Barton and Tomasello, 1991, 1992; Dunn and Shatz, 1989; Hoff-Ginsberg, 1998; Hoff-Ginsberg and Krueger, 1991; Jones and Adamson, 1987; Mannle, Barton, and Tomasello, 1992). Why? Despite variations in language environment, children learn how to talk. Findings from the Pacific Islands document that adult caregivers in these settings do not finely tune speech to children, scaffold, and usually

---

[5]Before the midtwentieth century and in more traditional societies even today, allocation of family resources to the eldest male's education may have primed the person receiving such benefits for higher achievement (Ernst and Angst, 1983). Recent comprehensive surveys of the relation of birth order to occupational status, IQ, school achievement, and personality demonstrate that social status and other variables better account for observed differences in sibling accomplishments than does birth order (Ernst and Angst, 1983; Zajonc and Bargh, 1980; cf. Zajonc and Marcos, 1975. More to the point, empirical research suggests that socioeconomic status plays a more important role in early language development than does birth order (Hoff-Ginsberg, 1993). And, reversing the original received idea of firstborn superiority, Sulloway (1996) has argued from a family dynamics perspective that many more laterborns than firstborns produce unorthodox, innovative adancements in human understanding.

ignore children's poorly formed early speech (Ochs, 1988; Schieffelin, 1990). This research may have influenced researchers in technological settings to revise received opinions regarding the sibling speech environment.

In harmony with this larger perspective, later children gain many pragmatic abilities that assist them in participating as conversational partners. Triadic conversations consist of far less scaffolded speech to the infant and far more complex speech than that usually directed to younger children in dyadic interactions (Dunn and Shatz, 1989; Hoff-Ginsberg and Krueger, 1991; Mannle et al., 1992). Even so, younger siblings consistently display that they can comprehend much of ongoing speech in these settings by participating actively and appropriately (Barton and Tomasello, 1991; Dunn and Shatz, 1989). Because preschool siblings do not adjust speech as much for younger siblings, this situation may precipitate the younger to work harder at expressing herself or himself (Demuth, 1984; Dunn and Shatz, 1989; Jones and Adamson, 1987; Mannle et al., 1992; Woollett, 1986). Furthermore, as several researchers speculated (Dunn and Kendrick, 1982; Dunn and Shatz, 1989; Oshima-Takane, 1988; Woollett, 1986), being exposed to references to the self and others in "overheard" rather than "child-directed" speech untangles the usage of personal pronouns. Oshima-Takane, Goodz, and Derevensky (1996) confirmed that later children at 21 and 24 months of age display a more advanced understanding and use of personal pronouns than do firstborn siblings.

Recent studies do not support the earlier opinions that firstborns learn language earlier and better, nor that all sibling utterances are dramatically different from those of mothers. Laterborns do not lag far behind firstborns in lexical growth (Hoff-Ginsberg and Krueger, 1991; Pine, 1993), especially if socioeconomic status is taken into consideration (Hoff-Ginsberg, 1998). Furthermore, although for "starters" children must have the lexical "building" blocks in the language game, the rules for combining lexical "pieces" and strategies for communicating make a player competent. Firstborns of 18 to 26 months of age may have the lead for some aspects of syntax, whereas laterborn siblings have the edge in the area of pragmatics (Hoff-Ginsberg, 1998). Hoff-Ginsberg and Krueger (1991) demonstrated that 7- to 8-year-old siblings' speech to younger siblings of 18 to 36 months of age, provided far more of the characteristics of mother's speech than did that of 4- to 5-year-old siblings. These authors noted that much of the "dismal" early evaluation of sibling speech may be due to choosing to study preschoolers, rather than 7- to 8-year-old children whose age is similar to that of sibling caregivers in agrarian societies. Finally, in a provocative twist regarding the assumed benefits of adult caregiver speech to infants, Trehub, Unyk, and Henderson (1994) speculated that older caregivers appropriated the childlike characteristics of "motherese" from the vocal and singing patterns of siblings. Perhaps older caregivers notice how the higher pitch, exaggerated speech contours, slower tempo, and shorter utterances of young siblings enhance gathering attention during interaction (Zukow-Goldring, 1997). Clearly the study of siblings' contribution to each other's language development in all cultures is only in its infancy.

CONCLUSIONS

Sibling caregiving has many guises across cultures. Whether explicit or implicit, whether labeled caregiving or not, the impact of siblings is ubiquitous and universal as they teach each other about life during the most mundane daily activities of their cultures. In agrarian societies, sibling caregivers do more than attend to immediate biological needs and keep younger children amused. Siblings are "culture brokers," introducing their sisters and brothers to ways of acting and knowing through unique styles of interaction. Only in the past decade and a half have researchers in technological settings discovered the positive effect of sibling caregiving, better known as interaction, in studies of play, cognitive, and language development of the individual child.

Although not perceived as "prerequisites" to sibling caregiving in technological societies, a very similar pattern of social, emotional, perceptual, and cognitive milestones underlies being a competent elder sibling anywhere on this planet. The older sibling's shifts from overwhelming self-interest related to the most basic necessities to the display of competence in cultural tasks to putting the needs of others before the self mirror LeVine's (1980) description of parental goals. Parents and other caregivers apparently do successfully socialize their children for self-survival, inculcate cultural practices that will lead to economic self-sufficiency, and, finally, provide a frame through which to see the self in terms of cultural practices embodied through the care of others.

Two ends may be coming toward the middle. As agrarian people move to urban settings and as schooling becomes available in rural areas, sibling caregiving may be quietly "falling apart" in some societies (Broberg and Hwang, 1992; Harkness and Super, 1982; Lamb and Sternberg, 1992; Nsamenang, 1992), while adjusting to new circumstances and continuing to thrive in others (Gaskins, in press; Weisner, 1997, 2000). In technological settings, dual-wage-earner families who cannot provide afterschool care for their children leave the sibling caregiving potential to go begging. Urgent social policy questions for the future entail how each group can learn from the other. Ethnographies of patterns of care and need in all settings can inform resolution of these global problems.

Paraphrasing John Kennedy's famous words, Mace (1977, p. 43) called for his colleagues to "ask not what's in your head, but what your head's inside of." Although Mace was addressing a different set of problems, that play on words points to one way to examine the cornucopia or cacophony of theoretical voices within sibling caregiving research. From the bewildering array of theories influencing ongoing empirical research, a more coherent pattern can emerge. Findings from cross-cultural studies based on ecocultural models highlight sibling caregiving and its variations, challenging more insular theories to be more inclusive. Exposure to the empirical content of cross-cultural studies can benefit theories arising from Western psychological approaches by prompting them to ask new questions and be less ethnocentric and egocentric. In the same vein, theories and research explaining and investigating social, emotional, perceptual, and language development broaden and contribute to understanding sibling caregiving. A coherent theory of child development will weave the many into one.

ACKNOWLEDGMENTS

The author's research conducted in Mexico was supported by National Institute of Mental Health Postdoctoral Fellowship No. 5 F32 MH 07996-02 and by a Spencer Foundation Grant awarded to Patricia Greenfield. The studies conducted in the United States with Latino and European American families were funded by a grant to the author by the Spencer Foundation and by the Michelle F. Elkind Foundation. I express my gratitude to Tom Weisner for perceptive comments and, especially, for his generosity during his reading of several versions of this manuscript. Special thanks go to Karen Watson-Gegeo, Cathy Dent-Read, and Marc Bornstein for their extremely careful readings.

REFERENCES

Abramovitch, R., Corter, C., and Lando, B. (1979). Sibling interaction in the home. *Child Development, 50*, 997–1003.

Abramovitch, R., Corter, C., Pepler, D. J., and Stanhope, L. (1986). Sibling and peer interaction: A final follow-up and a comparison. *Child Development, 57*, 217–229.

Azmitia, M. Cooper, C. R., Garcia, E. E., and Dunbar, N. D. (1996). The ecology of family guidance in low-income Mexican-American and European-American families. *Social Development, 5*, 1–23.

Azmitia, M., and Hesser, J. (1993). Why siblings are important agents of cognitive development: A comparison of siblings and peers. *Child Development, 64*, 430–444.

Bank, P. B., and Kahn, M. D. (Eds.). (1982). *The sibling bond.* New York: Basic Books.

Baron-Cohen, S. (1995). *Mindblindness: An essay on autism and theory of mind.* Cambridge, MA: MIT Press.

Barnes, S., Gutfreund, H., Satterly, D., and Wells, G. (1983). Characteristics of adult speech which predict children's language development. *Journal of Child Language, 10*, 65–84.

Barton, M. E., and Tomasello, M. (1991). Joint attention and conversation in mother–infant–sibling triads. *Child Development, 62*, 517–529.

Barton, M. E., and Tomasello, M. (1992). The rest of the family: The role of fathers and siblings in early language development. In B. Richards and C. Gallway (Eds.), *Language addressed to children* (pp. 109–134). London: Cambridge University Press.

Beals, A. R., and Eason, M. A. (1993). Siblings in North America and South Asia. In C. W. Nuckolls (Ed.), *Siblings in South Asia: Brothers and sisters in cultural context* (pp. 71–101). New York: Guilford.

Berndt, T. J., and Bulleit, T. N. (1985). Effects of sibling relationships on preschoolers' behavior at home and at school. *Developmental Psychology, 56*, 761–767.

Blankston, III, C. L. (1998). Sibling cooperation and scholastic performance among Vietnamese-American secondary school students: An ethnic social relations theory. *Sociological Perspectives, 41*, 167–184.

Bloom, L., Hood, L., and Lightbown, P. (1974). Imitation in language development: If, when, and why. *Cognitive Psychology, 6*, 380–420.

Bluebond-Langer, M. (1996). *In the shadow of illness: Parents and siblings of the chronically ill child.* Princeton, NJ: Princeton University Press.

Bornstein, M. H., and Tamis-LeMonda, C. S. (1995). Parent–child symbolic play: Three theories in search of an effect. *Developmental Review, 15*, 382–400.

Borstelmann, L. J. (1977). Child rearing in the United States (1620–1970). In B. B. Wolmen (Ed.), *International encyclopedia of psychiatry, psychology, psychoanalysis, and neurology* (pp. 143–146). New York: Produced for Aesculapius Publishers by Van Nostrand Reinhold Co.

Broberg, A. G., and Hwang, C. P. (1992). The shaping of child-care policies. In M. E. Lamb, K. J. Sternberg, C. P. Hwang, and A. G. Broberg (Eds.), *Child care in context: Cross-cultural perspectives* (pp. 509–521). Hillsdale, NJ: Lawrence Erlbaum Associates.

Brody, G. H., Stoneman, Z., and MacKinnon, C. (1982). Role asymmetries among school-age children, their younger siblings, and their friends. *Child Development, 53*, 1364–1370.

Brown, J. R., Donelan-McCall, N., and Dunn, J. (1996). Why talk about mental states? The significance of children's conversations with friends, siblings, and mothers. *Child Development, 67*, 836–849.

Childs, C. P., and Greenfield, P. M. (1980). Informal modes of learning and teaching: The case of Zincanteco weaving. In N. Warren (Ed.), *Studies in cross-cultural psychology* (Vol. 2, pp. 269–316). London: Academic.

Cicirelli, V. G. (1972). The effect of sibling relationships on concept learning of young children taught by child teachers. *Child Development, 43*, 282–287.

Cole, M., Hood, L., and McDermott, R. P. (1978). Concepts of ecological validity: Their differing implications for comparative cognitive research. *The Quarterly Newsletter of the Laboratory of Comparative Human Cognition, 2*, 34–37.

Cross, T. (1977). Mother's speech adjustments: The contribution of selected child listener variables. In C. Snow and C. Ferguson (Eds.), *Talking to children*. London: Wiley.

Demuth, K. A. (1984). *Aspects of Sesotho language acquisition*. Bloomington, IN: Indiana University Linguistics Club.

Demuth, K. A. (1996). Collecting spontaneous production data. In D. McDaniel, C. McKee, and H. S. Cairns (Eds.), *Methods for assessing children's syntax* (pp. 3–22). Cambridge, MA: MIT Press.

Dent, C. (1990). An ecological approach to language development: An alternative functionalism. In C. Dent and P. G. Zukow (Eds.), The idea of innateness: Effects on language and communication research [Special issue]. *Developmental Psychobiology, 23*, 679–704.

Draper, P., and Harpending, H. (1987). Parent investment and the child's environment. In J. B. Lancaster, J. Altmann, A. S. Rossi, and L. R. Sherrod (Eds.), *Parenting across the life span: Biosocial dimensions* (pp. 207–235). New York: Aldine de Gruyter.

Dunn, J. (1983). Sibling relationships in early childhood. *Child Development, 54*, 787–811.

Dunn, J. (1988). *The beginnings of social understanding. Cambridge*, MA: Harvard University Press.

Dunn, J. (1989). Siblings and the development of social understanding in early childhood. In P. G. Zukow (Ed.), *Sibling interaction across cultures: Theoretical and methodological issues* (pp. 106–116). New York: Springer-Verlag.

Dunn, J. F. (1991). Sibling influences. In M. Lewis and S. Feinman (Eds.), *Social influences and socialization in infancy* (pp. 97–109). New York: Plenum.

Dunn, J. (1996). Arguing with siblings, friends, and mothers: Developments in relationships and understanding. In D. I. Slobin, J. Gerhardt, A. Kyratzis, and J. Guo (Eds.), *Social interaction, social context, and language: Essays in honor of Susan Ervin-Tripp* (pp. 191–204). Mahwah, NJ: Lawrence Erlbaum Associates.

Dunn, J., and Kendrick, C. (1982a). *Siblings: Love, envy, and understanding*. Cambridge, MA: Harvard University Press.

Dunn, J., and Kendrick, C. (1982b). The speech of two- and three-year olds to infant siblings: "Baby Talk" and the context of communication. *Journal of Child Language, 9*, 579–597.

Dunn, J., and Munn, P. (1985). Becoming a family member: Family conflict and the development of social understanding. *Child Development, 56*, 480–492.

Dunn, J., and Plomin, R. (1990). *Separate lives: Why siblings are so different*. New York: Basic Books.

Dunn, J., and Shatz, M. (1989). Becoming a conversationalist despite (or because of) having an older sibling. *Child Development, 60*, 399–410.

Eckerman, C. O. (1993). Toddlers' achievement of coordinated action with conspecifics: A dynamic systems perspective. In L. B. Smith and E. Thelen (Eds.), *A dynamic systems approach to development* (pp. 333–357). Cambridge, MA: MIT Press.

Ellis, S., and Rogoff, B. (1982). The strategies and efficacy of child versus adult teachers. *Child Development, 43*, 730–735.

Ember, C. (1973). Feminine task assignment and the social behavior of boys. *Ethos, 1*, 424–439.

Ernst, C., and Angst, J. (1983). *Birth order: Its influence on personality*. Berlin: Springer-Verlag.

Farver, J. (1999). Activity setting analysis; A model for examining the role of culture in development. In A. Göncü (Ed.), *Children's engagement in the world: Sociocultural perspectives* (pp. 99–127). New York: Cambridge University Press.

Farver, J., and Howes, C. (1993). Cultural differences in American and Mexican mother–child pretend play. *Merrill-Palmer Quarterly, 39*, 344–358.

Farver, J., and Wimbarti, S. (1995). Indonesian children's play with their mothers and older siblings. *Child Development, 66*, 1493–1503.

Fischer, J. L., and Fischer, A. (1963). The New Englanders of Orchard Town, U.S.A. In B. B. Whiting (Ed.), *Six cultures: Studies of child rearing*. New York: Wiley. (Reprinted as a separate volume, 1966.)

Garner, P. W., Jones, D. C., and Palmer, D. J. (1994). Social cognitive correlates of preschool children's sibling caregiving behavior. *Developmental Psychology, 30*, 905–911.

Gaskins, S. (1999). Children's daily lives in a Mayan village: A case study of culturally constructed roles and activities. In A. Göncü (Ed.), *Children's engagement in the world: Sociocultural perspectives* (pp. 25–61). New York: Cambridge University Press.

Gaskins, S. (2000). Children's daily activities in a Mayan village: A culturally grounded description. *Cross-Cultural Research, 34*, 375–389.

Gaskins, S. (in press). From corn to cash: The impact on children of continuities and change in work patterns within the Mayan farming household. In G. Clark (Ed.), *Gender and economic life*. Lanham, MD: Altamira press.

Getis, V. L., and Vinovskis, M. A. (1992). History of child care in the United States before 1950. In M. E. Lamb, K. J. Sternberg, C.-P. Hwang, and A. G. Broberg (Eds.), *Child care in context: Cross-cultural perspectives*. Hillsdale, NJ: Lawrence Erlbaum Associates.

Göncü, A. Mistry, J., and Mosier, C. (2000). Cultural variations in the play of toddlers. *International Journal of Behavioral Development, 24*, 321–329.

Goody, E. N. (1982). *Parenthood and social reproduction: Fostering and occupational roles in West Africa*. Cambridge, England: Cambridge University Press.

Gottlieb, L. N., and Mendelson, M. J. (1990). Parental support and firstborn girls' adaptation to the birth of a sibling. *Journal of Applied Developmental Psychology, 11*, 29–48.

Greenfield, P. M. (1984). A theory of the teacher in the learning activities of everyday life. In B. Rogoff and J. Lave (Eds.), *Everyday cognition: Its development in social context* (pp. 117–138). Cambridge, MA: Harvard University Press.

Greenfield, P. M. (1994). Independence and interdependence as developmental scripts: Implications for theory, research, and practice. In P. M. Greenfield and R. R. Cocking (Eds.), *Cross-cultural roots of minority child development* (pp. 1–39). Hillsdale, NJ: Lawrence Erlbaum Associates.

Greenfield, P. M., and Smith, J. H. (1976). *The structure of communication in early language development*. New York: Academic.

Handel, G. (1986). Beyond sibling rivalry: An empirically grounded theory of sibling relationships. In P. A. Adler and P. Adler (Eds.), *Sociological studies of child development* (pp. 105–122). Greenwich, CT: JAI.

Hanna, E., and Meltzoff, A. N. (1993). Peer imitation by toddlers in laboratory, home, and daycare contexts: Implications for social learning and memory. *Developmental Psychology, 29*, 701–710.

Hareven, T. K. (1989). Historical changes in children's networks in the family and community. In D. Belle (Ed.), *Children's social networks and social supports* (pp. 15–36). New York: Wiley.

Harkness, S., and Super, C. M. (1992). Shared child care in East Africa: Sociocultural origins and developmental consequences. In M. E. Lamb, K. J. Sternberg, C. P. Hwang, and A. G. Broberg (Eds.), *Child care in context: Cross-cultural perspectives*. Hillsdale, NJ: Lawrence Erlbaum Associates.

Harris, P. (1991). The work of the imagination. In A. Whiten (Ed.), *Natural theories of mind* (pp. 283–304). Oxford, England: Blackwell.

Harris, P. (1996). Desires, beliefs, and language. In P. Carruthers and P. Smith (Eds.), *Theories of theories of mind* (pp. 200–222). Cambridge, England: Cambridge University Press.

Harrison, A. O., Wilson, M. N., Pine, C. J., Chan, S. Q., and Buriel, R. (1990). Family ecologies of ethnic minority children. *Child Development, 61*, 363–383.

Hartup, W. W. (1979). The social world of children. *American Psychologist, 34*, 944–950.

Hartup, W. W., and Laursen, B. (1991). Relationships as developmental contexts. In R. Cohen and A. W. Siegel (Eds.), *Context and development* (pp. 253–279). Hillsdale, NJ: Lawrence Erlbaum Associates.

Heath, S. B. (1983). *Ways with words: Language, life, and work in communities and classrooms*. New York: Cambridge University Press.

Hobson, P. (1993). *Autism and the development of mind*. Hillsdale, NJ: Lawrence Erlbaum Associates.

Hoff-Ginsberg, Erika. (1998). The relation of birth order and socioeconomic status to children's language experience and language development. *Applied Psycholinguistics*, 19, 603–629.

Hoff-Ginsberg, E., and Krueger, W. M. (1991). Older siblings as conversational partners. *Merrill-Palmer Quarterly*, 37, 465–482.

Howe, N., Petrakos, H., and Rinaldi, C. M. (1998). "All the sheeps are dead. He murdered them": Sibling pretense, negotiation, internal state language, and relationship quality. *Child Development*, 69, 182–191.

Howe, N., and Ross, H. S. (1990). Socialization, perspective-taking, and the sibling relationship. *Developmental Psychology*, 26, 160–165.

Howrigan, G. A. (1988). Fertility, infant feeding, and change in Yucatan. In R. A. LeVine, P. M. Miller, and M. M. West (Eds.), *Parental behavior in diverse societies* (pp. 3–12). New Directions in Child Development, No. 40. San Francisco: Jossey-Bass.

Jessor, R., Colby, A., and Shweder, R. A. (Eds.). (1996). *Ethnography and human development: Context and meaning in social inquiry*. Chicago: University of Chicago Press.

Jones, C. P., and Adamson, L. B. (1987). Language use in mother–child and mother–child–sibling interactions. *Child Development, 58*, 356–366. *Journal of the California Alliance for the Mentally Ill.* (1990). *3*(1), 1–2.

Koester, L. S., and Johnson, L. S. (1984). Children's instructional strategies: A comparison of sibling and peer tutoring. *Acta Paedologica, 1*, 23–32.

Kramer, L., and Baron, L. A. (1995). Parental perceptions of children's sibling relationships. *Family Relations, 44*, 95–103.

Kramer, L., and Noorman, S. (1993, March). *Maternal expectations and children's adaptation to becoming a sibling.* Poster presented at the meeting of the Society for Research in Child Development, New Orleans, LA.

Kramer, L., and Radey, C. (1997). Improving sibling relationships among young children: A social skills training model. *Family Relations, 46*, 237–246.

Kreppner, K. (1988). Changes in dyadic relationships within a family after the arrival of a second child. In R. A. Hinde and J. Stevenson-Hinde (Eds.), *Relationships within families: Mutual influences* (pp. 143–167). Oxford, England: Clarendon.

Kreppner, K., Paulsen, S., and Schuetze, Y. (1982). Infant and family development: From triads to tetrads. *Human Development, 25*, 373–391.

Laboratory of Comparative Human Cognition. (1986). Contribution of cross-cultural research to educational practices. *American Psychologist, 41*, 1049–1058.

Lamb, M. E. (1976). *The role of the father in child development.* New York: Wiley.

Lamb, M. E. (1982). Sibling relationships across the lifespan: An overview and introduction. In M. E. Lamb and B. Sutton-Smith (Eds.), Sibling relationships (pp. 1–11). Hillsdale, NJ: Lawrence Erlbaum Associates.

Lamb, M. E., and Sternberg, K. (1992). Sociocultural perspectives on nonparental child care. In M. E. Lamb, K. J. Sternberg, C.-P. Hwang, and A. G. Broberg (Eds.), *Child care in context: Cross-cultural perspectives* (pp. 1–23). Hillsdale NJ: Lawrence Erlbaum Associates.

Lamb, M. E., and Sutton-Smith, B. (1982). *Sibling relationships.* Hillsdale, NJ: Lawrence Erlbaum Associates.

LeVine, R. A. (1977). Child rearing as cultural adaptation. In P. H. Leiderman, S. R. Tulkin, and A. Rosenfeld, (Eds.), *Culture and infancy: Variations in the human experience* (pp. 15–27). New York: Academic. Press.

LeVine, R. A. (1980). Anthropology and child development. In C. M. Super and S. Harkness (Eds.), *Anthropological perspectives on child development* (pp. 71–86). San Francisco: Jossey-Bass.

LeVine, R. A. (1988). Human parental care: Universal goals, cultural strategies, individual behavior. In R. A. LeVine, P. M. Miller, and M. M. West (Eds.), *Parental behavior in diverse societies* (pp. 3–12). New Directions in Child Development, No. 40. San Francisco: Jossey-Bass.

Lobato, D. J. (1990). *Brothers, sisters, and special needs.* Baltimore: Brookes.

Lomnitz, L. (1975). *Como sobreviven los marginados.* Mexico, DF: Siglo Veinti-uno Editores.

Mace, W. (1977). Ask not what's in your head, but what your head's inside of. R. E. Shaw and J. Bransford (Eds.), *Perceiving, acting, and knowing* (pp. 43–65). Hillsdale, NJ: Lawrence Erlbaum Associates.

Mannle, S., Barton, M., and Tomasello, M. (1992). Two-year-old's converstions with their mothers and preschool-aged siblings. *First Language, 12*, 57–71.

Malpass, R. S. (1977). Theory and method in cross-cultural research. *American Psychologist, 32*, 1069–1079.

Martini, M. (1994). Peer interactions in Polynesia: A view from the Marquesas. In J. L. Roopnarine, J. E. Johnson, and F. H. Hooper (Eds.), *Children's play in diverse cultures* (pp. 73–103). Albany: State University of New York Press.

Martini, M, and Kirkpatrick, J. (1992). Parenting in Polynesia: A view from the Marquesas. In J. L. Roopnarine and D. B. Carter (Eds.), *Parent–child socialization in diverse cultures* (pp. 199–223). Norwood, NJ: Ablex.

Maynard, A. E. (1999, November). The social organization and development of teaching in Zinacantec Maya sibling play. In P. Greenfield (Chair), *Cultural context and developmental theory: Evidence from the Maya of Mexico.* Symposium conducted at the meeting of American Anthropological Association, Chicago.

Maynard, A. E. (in press). *Cultural teaching: The development of teaching skills in Maya sibling interactions. Child Development.*

McHale, S. M., and Crouter, A. C. (1996). The family contexts of children's sibling relationships. In G. H. Brody (Ed.), *Sibling relationships: Their causes and consequences* (pp. 173–195). Norwood, NJ: Ablex.

McHale, S. M., and Pawletko, T. M. (1992). Differential treatment of siblings in two family contexts. *Child Development*, *63*, 68–81.

McKenna, J. J. (1987). Parental supplements and surrogates among primates: Cross-species and cross-cultural comparisons. In J. B. Lancaster, J. Altmann, A. S. Rossi, and L. R. Sherrod (Eds.), *Parenting across the life span: Biosocial dimensions* (pp. 143–184). New York: Aldine de Gruyter.

Mead, M. (1935). *Sex and temperament in three primitive societies*. New York: Morrow.

Melhuish, E., and Moss, P. (1992). Day care in the United Kingdom in historical perspective. In M. E. Lamb, K. J. Sternberg, C.-P. Hwang, and A. G. Broberg (Eds.), *Child care in context: Cross-cultural perspectives*. Hillsdale, NJ: Lawrence Erlbaum Associates.

Meltzoff, A. N., and Moore, M. K. (1999). Persons and representation: Why infant imitation is important for theories of human development. In J. Nadel and G. Butterworth (Eds.), *Imitation in infancy* (pp. 9–35). Cambridge, England: Cambridge University Press.

Mendelson, M. J. (1990). *Becoming a brother: A child learns about life, family, and self*. Cambridge, MA: MIT Press.

Mischel, W. (1977). On the future of personality measurement. *American Psychologist*, *32*, 246–254.

Moll, L. C. (Ed.). (1990). *Vygotsky and education: Instructional implications and applications of sociohistorical psychology*. New York: Cambridge University Press.

Mundy-Castle, A. C. (1974). Social and technological intelligence in Western and non-Western cultures. *Universitas*, *4*, 46–52.

Murphy, S. O. (1992). Using multiple forms of family data: Identifying pattern and meaning in sibling-infant relationships. In J. F. Gilgum, K. Daly, and G. Handel (Eds.), *Qualitative methods in family research* (pp. 146–171). Newbury Park, CA: Sage.

Murphy, S. (1993, March). Parent strategies and the transition to siblinghood. In D. Teti (Chair), *Becoming a sibling: Family-contextual factors and the transition to siblinghood*. Symposium conducted at the meeting of the Society for Research in Child Development, New Orleans, LA.

Nelson, K. E., Carskaddon, G., and Bonvillian, J. (1973). Syntax acquisition: Impact of experimental variation in adult verbal interaction with the child. *Child Development*, *44*, 497–504.

Nerlove, S. B., Roberts, J. M., Klein, R. E., Yarbrough, C., and Habicht, J. P. (1974). Natural indicators of cognitive development: An observational study of rural Guatemalan children. *Ethos*, *2*, 265–295.

Nicolson, N. A. (1991). Maternal behavior in human and nonhuman primates. In J. D. Loy and C. B. Peters (Eds.), *Understanding behavior: What primate studies tell us about human behavior* (pp. 17–50). New York: Oxford University Press.

Nsamenang, B. A. (1992). Early childhood care and education in Cameroon. In M. E. Lamb, K. J. Sternberg, C.-P. Hwang, and A. G. Broberg (Eds.), *Child care in context: Cross-cultural perspectives*. Hillsdale, NJ: Lawrence Erlbaum Associates.

Nuckolls, C. W. (1993a). An introduction to the cross-cultural study of sibling relations. In C. W. Nuckolls (Ed.), *Siblings in South Asia: Brothers and sisters in cultural context* (pp. 19–41). New York: Guilford.

Nuckolls, C. W. (1993b). Sibling myths in a South Indian fishing village: A case study in sociological ambivalence. In C. W. Nuckolls (Ed.), *Siblings in South Asia: Brothers and sisters in cultural context* (pp. 191–217). New York: Guilford.

Ochs, E. (1988). *Culture and language development: Language acquisition and socialization in a Samoan village*. Cambridge, England: Cambridge University Press.

Oshima-Takane, Y. (1988). Children learn from speech not addressed to them: The case of personal pronouns. *Child Language*, *15*, 95–108.

Oshima-Takane, Y., Goodz, E., and Derevensky, J. L. (1996). Birth order effects on early language development: Do secondborn children learn from overheard speech? *Child Development*, *67*, 621–634.

Pelletier-Stiefel, J., Pepler, D., Crozier, K., Stanhope, L., Corter, C., and Abramovitch, R. (1986). Nurturance in the home: A longitudinal study of sibling interaction. In A. Fogel and G. F. Melson (Eds.), *Origins of nurturance: Developmental, biological and cultural perspectives on caregiving* (pp. 1–24). Hillsdale NJ: Lawrence Erlbaum Associates.

Pérez, D., Barajas, N., Domínguez, M., Goldberg, J., Juarez, X., Saab, M., Vergara, F., and Callanan, M. (1994). Siblings providing one another with opportunities to learn. *Focus on Diversity*, *5*, 1–5.

Pérez-Granados, D. R., and Callanan, M. A. (1997). Conversations with mothers and siblings: Young children's semantic and conceptual development. *Developmental Psychology*, *33*, 120–134.

Perner, J., Ruffman, T., and Leekam, S. R. (1994). Theory of mind is contagious: You catch it from your sibs. *Child Development*, *65*, 1228–1238.

Piaget, J. (1962). *Play, dreams, and imitation in childhood*. New York: Norton Library.

Pine, J. (1995). Variation in vocabulary development as a function of birth order. *Child Development*, *66*, 272–281.

Price-Williams, D. R. (1975). *Explorations in cross-cultural psychology*. San Francisco: Chandler and Sharp.

Rabain-Jamin, J. (1994). Language and socialization of the child in African families living in France. In. P. M. Greenfield and R. Cocking (Eds.), *Cross-cultural roots of minority child development* (pp. 147–166). Edison, NJ: Lawrence Erlbaum Associates.

Rabain-Jamin, J. (1998). Polyadic language socialization strategy: The case of toddlers in Senegal. *Discourse Processes*, *26*, 43–65.

Rogoff, B. (1990). *Apprenticeship in thinking: Cognitive development in social context*. New York: Oxford University Press.

Rogoff, B. (1996). Developmental transitions in children's participation in sociocultural activities. In A. J. Sameroff and M. H. Haith (Eds.), *The five to seven year shift: The age of reason and responsibility* (pp. 273–294). Chicago: University of Chicago Press.

Rogoff, B., Mistry, J., Göncü, A., and Mosier, C. (1993). Guided participation in cultural activity by toddlers and caregivers. *Monographs of the Society for Research in Child Development, 58* (8, Serial No. 236).

Rogoff, B., Sellers, M. J., Piorrata, S., Fox, N., and White, S. (1975). Age of assignment of roles and responsibilities to children: A cross-cultural survey. *Human Development, 18*, 353–369.

Ross, H. S., Filyer, R. E., Lollis, S. P., Perlman, M., and Martin, J. L. (1994). Administering justice in the family. *Journal of Family Psychology, 8*, 254–273.

Ruffman, T., Perner, J., Naito, M., Parkin, L., and Clements, W. A. (1998). Older (but not younger) siblings facilitate false belief understanding. *Developmental Psychology, 34*, 161–174.

Ryan, J. (1974). Early language development: Towards a communicative analysis. In M. P. M. Richards (Ed.), *The integration of the child into the social world* (pp. 185–213). Cambridge England: Cambridge University Press.

Scarr, S. (1992). Developmental theories for the 1990's: Development and individual differences. *Child Development, 63*, 1–19.

Scarr, S., and McCartney, S. K. (1983). How people make their own environment: A theory of genotype environment effects. *Child Development, 54*, 424–435.

Schieffelin, B. B. (1990). *The give and take of everyday life: Language socialization of Kaluli children.* Cambridge, England: Cambridge University Press.

Scribner, S., and Cole, M. (1981). *The psychology of literacy.* Cambridge, MA: Harvard University Press.

Seymour, S. (1993). Sociocultural contests: Examining sibling roles in South Asia. In C. W. Nuckolls (Ed.), *Siblings in South Asia: Brothers and sisters in cultural context* (pp. 45–69). New York: Guilford.

Shantz, C. U., and Hobart, C. J. (1989). Social conflict and development: Peers and siblings. In T. H. Berndt and G. W. Ladd (Eds.), *Peer relationships in child development* (pp. 71–94). New York: Wiley.

Shweder, R. A. (1991). *Thinking through culture.* Cambridge, MA: Harvard University Press.

Slomkowski, C. L., and Dunn, J. (1992). Arguments and relationships within the family: Differences in young children's disputes with mother and sibling. *Developmental Psychology, 28*, 919–924.

Smith, T. E. (1993). Growth in academic achievement and teaching younger siblings. *Social Psychology Quarterly, 56*, 77–85.

Snow, C. E. (1977). The development of conversation between mothers and babies. *Journal of Child Language, 4*, 1–11.

Snow, C. E. (1981). The uses of imitation. *Journal of Child Language, 8*, 205–212.

Snow, C. E., Barnes, W. S., Chandler, J., Goodman, I. F., and Hemphill, L. (1991). *Unfulfilled expectations: Home and school influences on literacy.* Cambridge, MA: Harvard University Press.

Snow, C. E., Perlmann, R., and Nathan, D. (1987). Why routines are different: Toward a multiple-factor model of the relation between input and language acquisition. In K. E. Nelson and A. van Kleeck (Eds.), *Children's language* (Vol. 6, pp. 65–97). Hillsdale, NJ: Lawrence Erlbaum Associates.

Stevenson, M. B., Leavitt, L. A., Thompson, R. H., and Roach, M. A. (1988). A social relations model analysis of parent and child play. *Developmental Psychology, 24*, 101–108.

Stewart, R. B. (1983a). Sibling attachment relationships: Child–infant interactions in the strange situation. *Developmental Psychology, 19*, 192–199.

Stewart, R. B. (1983b). Sibling interaction: The role of the older child as teacher for the younger. *Merrill-Palmer Quarterly, 29*, 47–68.

Stewart, Jr., R. B. (1990). *The second child: Family transition and adjustment.* Newbury Park, CA: Sage.

Stewart, R. B., and Marvin, R. S. (1984). Sibling relations: The role of conceptual perspective-taking in the ontogeny of sibling caregiving. *Child Development, 55*, 1322–1332.

Stewart, R. B., Mobley, L. A., Van Tuyl, S. S., and Salvador, M. A. (1987). The firstborn's adjustment to the birth of a sibling: A longitudinal assessment. *Child Development, 58*, 341–355.

Stoneman, Z., and Berman, P. (Eds.). (1993). *The effects of mental retardation, disability, and illness on sibling relationships: Research issues and challenges.* Baltimore: Brookes.

Stoneman, Z., Brody, G. H., and MacKinnon, C. (1984). Naturalistic observations of children's activities and roles while playing with their siblings and friends. *Child Development, 55*, 617–627.

Sulloway, F. J. (1996). *Born to rebel: Birth order, family dynamics, and creative lives.* New York: Pantheon Books.

Summers, M., Summers, C. R., and Ascione, F. R. (1993). A comparison of sibling interaction in intact and single-parent families. Unpublished manuscript.

Super, C. M., and Harkness, S. (1982). The infant's niche: A conceptualization at the interface of child and culture. *International Journal of Behavioral Development, 9*, 545–569.

Super, C. M., and Harkness, S. (1986). The developmental niche: A conceptualization at the interface of child and culture. *International Journal of Behavioral Development, 9*, 1–25.

Super, C. M., and Harkness, S. (1997). The cultural structuring of child development. In J. W. Berry, P. R. Dasen, and T. S. Saraswathi (Eds.), *Handbook of cross-cultural psychology: Vol. 2. Basic processes and human development* (pp. 1–38). Toronto: Allyn and Bacon.

Sutton-Smith, B. (1982). Epilogue: Framing the problem. In M. E. Lamb and B. Sutton-Smith (Eds.), *Sibling relationships* (pp. 383–386). Hillsdale, NJ: Lawrence Erlbaum Associates.

Sutton-Smith, B., and Rosenberg, B. G. (1970). *The sibling*. New York: Holt, Rinehart and Winston.

Teti, D., and Ablard, K. E. (1989). Security of attachment and infant-sibling relationships: A laboratory study. *Child Development, 60*, 1519–1528.

Teti, D. M., Bond, L. A., and Gibbs, E. D. (1988). Mothers, fathers, and siblings: A comparison of play styles and their influence upon infant cognitive level. *International Journal of Behavioral Development, 11*, 415–432.

Tomasello, M. (1999). *The cultural origins of human cognition*. Cambridge, MA: Harvard University Press.

Tomasello, M., and Mannle, S. (1985). Pragmatics of sibling speech to one-year-olds. *Child Development, 56*, 911–917.

Trehub, S. E, Unyk, A. M. M., and Henderson, J. L. (1994). Children's songs to infant siblings: Parallels with speech. *Journal of Child Language, 21*, 735–744.

Vandell, D. L., Minnett, A. M., and Santrock, J. W. (1988). Age differences in sibling relationships during middle childhood. *Journal of Applied Developmental Psychology, 8*, 247–257.

Vygotsky, L. S. (1978). Play and its role in the mental development of the child. In M. Cole, V. John-Steiner, S. Scribner, and E. Souberman (Eds.), *Mind in society*. Cambridge, MA: Harvard University Press.

Ward, M. C. (1971). *Them children: A study in language learning*. New York: Holt, Rinehart and Winston.

Watson-Gegeo, K. A., and Gegeo, D. (1986). The social world of Kwara'ae: Acquistion of language and values. In J. Cook-Gumpertz, W. Corsaro, and J. Streek (Eds.), *Children's language and children's world* (pp. 109–127). The Hague: Mouton.

Watson-Gegeo, K. A., and Gegeo, D. W. (1989). The role of sibling interaction in child socialization. In P. G. Zukow (Ed.), *Sibling interactions across cultures: Theoretical and methodological issues* (pp. 54–76). New York: Springer-Verlag.

Watson-Gegeo, K. A., and Gegeo, D. W. (1992). Schooling, knowledge, and power: Social transformation in the Solomon Islands. *Anthropology and Education Quarterly, 23*, 10–29.

Weisner, T. S. (1982). Sibling interdependence and child caretaking: A cross-cultural view. In M. Lamb and B. Sutton-Smith (Eds.), *Sibling relationships: Their nature and significance across there lifespan* (pp. 305–327). Hillsdale, NJ: Lawrence Erlbaum Associates.

Weisner, T. S. (1987). Socialization for parenthood in sibling caretaking societies. In J. B. Lancaster, J. Altmann, A. S. Rossi, and L. R. Sherrod (Eds.), *Parenting across the life span: Biosocial dimensions* (pp. 237–270). New York: Aldine de Gruyter.

Weisner, T. S. (1989a). Comparing sibling relationships across cultures. In P. G. Zukow (Ed.), *Sibling interactions across cultures: Theoretical and methodological issues* (pp. 11–25). New York: Springer-Verlag.

Weisner, T. S. (1989b). Cultural and universal aspects of social support for children: Evidence from Abaluyia of Kenya. In D. Belle (Ed.), *Children's social networks and social supports* (pp. 70–90). New York: Wiley.

Weisner, T. S. (1993a). Ethnographic and ecocultural perspectives on sibling relationships. In Z. Stoneman and P. W. Berman (Eds.), *The effects of mental retardation, disability and illness on sibling relationships: Research issues and challenges* (pp. 51–83). Baltimore: Brookes.

Weisner, T. S. (1993b). Overview: Sibling similarity and difference in different cultures. In C. W. Nuckolls (Ed.), *Siblings in south Asia: Brothers and sisters in cultural context* (pp. 1–17). New York: Guilford.

Weisner, T. S. (1996a). The 5 to 7 transition as an ecocultural project. In A. J. Sameroff and M. M. Haith (Eds.), *The five to seven shift: The age of reason and responsibility* (pp. 295–326). Chicago: University of Chicago Press.

Weisner, T. (1996b). Why ethnography should be the most important method in the study of human development. In R. Jessor, A. Colby, and R. A. Shweder (Eds.), *Ethnography and human development: Context and meaning in social inquiry* (pp. 305–324). Chicago: University of Chicago Press.

Weisner, T. S. (1997). Support for children and the African family crisis. In T. S. Weisner, C. Bradley, and P. L. Kilbride (Eds.), *African families and the crisis of social change* (pp. 20–44). Westport, CT: Bergin and Garvey.

Weisner, T. S. (2000). Culture, childhood, and progress in sub-Saharan Africa. In L. E. Harrison and S. P. Huntington (Eds.), *Culture matters: How values shape human progress* (pp. 141–157). Cambridge, MA: Basic Books.

Weisner, T. S., and Gallimore, R. (1977). My brother's keeper: Child and sibling caretaking. *Current Anthropology, 18*, 169–190.

Wellman, H. M., and Hickling, A. K. (1994). The mind's "I": Children's conception of the mind as an active agent. *Child Development, 65*, 1564–1580.

Wellman, H. M., Phillips, A. T., and Rodriguez, T. (2000). Young children's understanding of perception, desire, and emotion. *Child Development, 71*, 895–912.

Werner, E. E. (1979). *Cross-cultural child development: A view from planet Earth*. Monterey, CA: Brooks/Cole.

Wertsch, J. (1985). *Vygotsky and the social formation of mind*. Cambridge, MA: Harvard University Press.

White, D., and Woollett, A. (1992). *Families: A context for development*. London: Falmer.

Whiting, B. B. (Ed.). (1963). *Six cultures: Studies of child rearing*. New York: Wiley.

Whiting, B. B., and Edwards, C. P. (1988). *Children of different worlds: The formation of social behavior*. Cambridge, MA: Harvard.

Whiting, B. B., and Whiting, J. W. (1975). *Children of six cultures*. Cambridge, MA: Harvard.

Whittemore, R. D., and Beverly, E. (1989). Trust in the Mandinka way: The cultural context of sibling care. In P. G. Zukow (Ed.), *Sibling interactions across cultures: Theoretical and methodological issues* (pp. 26–53). New York: Springer-Verlag.

Wolf, D. P., Rygh, J., and Altshuler, J. (1984). Agency and experience: Actions and states in play narratives. In I. Bretherton (Ed.), *Symbolic play: The development of social understanding* (pp. 195–218). Orlando, FL: Academic.

Wood, D., Bruner, J. S., and Ross, G. (1976). The role of tutoring in problem solving. *Journal of Child Psychology and Psychiatry, 17,* 89–100.

Wood, D., and Middleton, D. A. (1975). A study of assisted problem-solving. *British Journal of Psychology, 66,* 181–191.

Woollett, A. (1986). The influence of older siblings on the language environment of young children. In M. Barrett and M. Harris (Eds.), Language and cognition in early social interaction [Special issue]. *British Journal of Developmental Psychology, 4,* 235–246.

Youngblade, L. M., and Dunn, J. (1995a). Individual differences in young children's pretend play with mother and sibling: Links to relationships and understanding of other people's feelings and beliefs. *Child Development, 66,* 1472–1492.

Youngblade, L. M., and Dunn, J. (1995b). Social pretend with mother and sibling: Individual differences and social understanding. In A. D. Pellegrini (Ed.), *The future of play theory: A multidisciplinary inquiry into the contributions of Brian Sutton-Smith* (pp. 221–240). Albany: State University of New York Press.

Zajonc, R. B., and Bargh, J. (1980). Birth order, family size, and decline of SAT scores. *American Psychologist, 35,* 662–668.

Zajonc, R. B., and Marcos, G. B. (1975). Birth order and intellectual deveopment. *Psychological Review, 82,* 74–88.

Zeisler, Y. L., and Demuth, K. A. (1995). Noun class prefixes in Sesotho child-directed speech. In E. Clark (Ed.), *Proceedings of the 26th Annual Child Langue Research Forum* (pp. 1–10). Stanford, CA: Center for the Study of Language and Information.

Zempleni-Rabain, J. (1973). Food and the strategy involved in learning fraternal exchange among Wolof children. In P. Alexandre (Ed.) *French perspectives in African studies* (pp. 221–233). London: Oxford University Press.

Zukow, P. G. (1981–1982). [Field notes.]. Unpublished raw data.

Zukow, P. G. (1984a). Criteria for the emergence of symbolic conduct: When words refer and play is symbolic. In L. Feagans, C. Garvey, and R. Golinkoff (Eds.), *The origins and growth of communication.* Norwood, NJ: Ablex.

Zukow, P. G. (1984b, November). *The relative contribution of sibling and adult caregivers to the emergence of play in Central Mexico.* Paper presented at the American Anthropological Association Meetings, Denver, CO.

Zukow, P. G. (1986). The relationship between interaction with the caregiver and the emergence of play activities during the one-word period. *British Journal of Developmental Psychology, 4,* 223–234.

Zukow, P. G. (1987–1994). [Field notes.]. Unpublished raw data.

Zukow, P. G. (1989a). Communicating across disciplines: On integrating psychological and ethnographic approaches. In P. G. Zukow (Ed.), *Sibling interactions across cultures: Theoretical and methodological issues* (pp. 1–8). New York: Springer-Verlag.

Zukow, P. G. (1989b). Siblings as effective socializing agents: Evidence from Central Mexico. In P. G. Zukow (Ed.), *Sibling interactions across cultures: Theoretical and methodological issues* (pp. 79–105). New York: Springer-Verlag.

Zukow, P. G. (1990). Socio-perceptual bases for the emergence of language: An alternative to innatist approaches. In C. Dent and P. G. Zukow (Eds.), The idea of innateness: Effects on language and communication research. [Special issue]. *Developmental Psychobiology, 23,* 679–704.

Zukow, P. G. (1991). A socio-perceptual/ecological approach to lexical development: Affordances of the communicative context. *Anales de Psicologia, 7,* 151–163.

Zukow-Goldring, P. (1996). Sensitive caregivers foster the comprehension of speech: When gestures speak louder than words. *Early Development and Parenting, 5*(4), 195–211.

Zukow-Goldring, P. (1997). A social ecological realist approach to the emergence of the lexicon: Educating attention to amodal invariants in gesture and speech. In C. Dent-Read and P. Zukow-Goldring (Eds.), *Evolving explanations of development: Ecological approaches to organism-environment systems* (pp. 199–250). Washington, DC: American Psychological Association.

Zukow-Goldring, P. (2000, July). *Saying and doing: Caregiver gestures cultivate the lexical development of Latino and Euro-American infants.* Poster presented at the International Conference of Infant Studies, Brighton, England.

Zukow-Goldring, P. (2001). Perceiving referring actions: Latino and Euro-American caregivers and infants comprehending speech. In K. L. Nelson, A. Aksu-Koc, and C. Johnson (Eds.), *Children's language* (Vol. 11, pp. 139–165). Hillsdale, NJ: Lawrence Erlbaum Associates.

Zukow-Goldring, P. and Ferko, K. (1994). Socializing attention: A socio-perceptual/ecological approach to the mergence of the lexicon. In V. John-Steiner, C. Panofsky, and L. Smith (Eds.), *Interactionist approaches to language and literacy* (pp. 170–190). New York: Cambridge University Press.

Zukow-Goldring, P., and Rader, N. (2001). Commentary: Perceiving referring actions. *Developmental Science, 4,* 28–30.

Zukow-Goldring, P., Romo, L., and Duncan, K. (1994). The relation of cultural heritage to the repair of communicative breakdowns in early educational settings. In A. Alvarez and P. del Rio (Eds.), *Education as cultural construction* (pp. 227–238). Madrid: Fundacion Infancia y Aprendizaje.

9

Parenting in Divorced and Remarried Families

E. Mavis Hetherington
University of Virginia
Margaret Stanley-Hagan
University of North Carolina at Charlotte

INTRODUCTION

The definition of family has become increasingly complex over the past 30 to 40 years. Marriage rates, particularly among adolescents, have declined significantly, and adults are older when they first marry, an average of 24 years of age for women and 26 years for men. The current 43.5% divorce rate represents a continued modest decline from the peak in the early 1980s (U.S. Bureau of the Census, 1998). It may be tempting to suggest that delayed first marriages and declining divorce rates represent a return to traditional views of families. However, these changes are accompanied by dramatically escalating rates of cohabitation and births outside of marriage. More than half of adults cohabit before their first marriage, and almost two thirds of divorced adults cohabit before entering a second marriage (Seltzer, 2000). By the late 1990s, 25% of children born in the United States were born outside of marriage (Teachman, Tedrow, and Crowder, 2000), in part a product of changed attitudes about cohabitation and single-parent lifestyles. Families headed by single parents have always been part of the demographic landscape, but before the 1960s the most some common cause of single parenthood was death (Weinraub, Horvath, and Gringlas, in Vol. 3 of this *Handbook*). In contrast to the uncontrollable and unintentional nature of death, the voluntary nature of divorce and having a child out of wedlock have led some politicians, social critics, and scholars to view single parenthood as an ethical problem. This problem is seen as a moral issue in which the self-indulgent behavior of parents places their own well-being above that of their children (Amato, 2000).

As parents move in and out of intimate relationships, their children are exposed to the stresses associated with multiple family transitions. Only 68% of children under the age of 18 years live with their married biological parents, a decrease of 4.4% between 1990 and 1998 (U.S. Bureau of the Census, 1998). It is estimated that 40% of children born to married parents will experience their parents' divorce. However, approximately 65% of divorced women and 75% of divorced men eventually remarry (Bumpass and Raley, 1995; Cherlin and Furstenberg, 1994). In 1998 the number of remarriages equaled the number of first marriages. Approximately 27% of all married couples in the United States include at least one previously married spouse (Wineberg and McCarthy, 1998). Half of these families include children from one spouse's or both spouses' previous relationships. Unfortunately, the divorce rate for second marriages is higher than that for first marriages, particularly for couples with children (Martin and Bumpass, 1989; Tzeng and Mare, 1995). For children whose parents cohabit, the risk is even higher. The instability experienced by many cohabiting partners carries over to their marriages. Compared with couples who never cohabit before marriage, couples who do have a 50% higher divorce rate (Seltzer, 2000). Those who cohabit with multiple partners before marriage have an 84% higher divorce rate. Thus, for many adults and children, the definition of family evolves over time, changing as cohabiting and marital partners and their children enter and leave the household, and the family grows in complexity as children are born and kinship networks expand.

As the numbers of divorced and remarried families increased dramatically through the 1960s and 1970s, understandably so did interest in the adjustment of members, especially children, within these families. The early researchers approached the study of divorced and remarried families with the expectation that most divorced parents and their children were doomed to troubled lives marked by deviant behavior and psychopathology. In the 1980s social scientists and feminists began to point out that it was family process, not family structure, that was most important in child adjustment and that competent children could develop in mother-headed families. Some researchers agreed, but noted that divorced and remarried families encounter stresses that put them at risk for disruptions both in family process and in child adjustment (Brand, Clingempeel, and Bowen-Woodward, 1988; Bray, 1988; Hetherington, 1989). Others (Amato and Keith, 1991; Amato, 2001), based on meta-analyses of children's adjustment, argued that the effect size in differences in adjustment between children in nondivorced and divorced families was small, although often statistically significant. Now many researchers (Amato and Booth, 1997; McLanahan and Sandefur, 1994; Popenoe, Elshtain, and Blankenhorn, 1996; Waite and Gallagher, 2000) and clinicians (Wallerstein, Lewis, and Blakeslee, 2000) appear to have come full circle and are again arguing that a stable family headed by two married biological parents is the most salutary for the development of children and that in most cases the hazards of divorce for the well-being of children are too great to risk.

Studies based on a pathogenic or deficit model have been sustained by evidence that individual adjustment and family relationships in divorced and remarried families often differ from those observed in nondivorced families and with evidence that children from "broken homes" are over-represented in antisocial and delinquent populations. Many of the early studies, however, were methodologically limited. Cross-sectional studies on small nonrepresentative and clinical samples were common. Early studies and many contemporary survey studies frequently used a social address model (Bronfenbrenner, 1986) in which mean differences among individuals in different family structures on some characteristic or outcome are the only comparisons made, in which findings are based on the reports of a single family member, and in which measures of family process are absent or inadequate. Often, critical factors such as the age of parents and children, time since transition, the availability of extended family and extrafamilial supports, and preexisting pathology are not examined. More recent work by psychologists has used multiple methods, measures, and informants to get a more comprehensive assessment of family functioning and child adjustment in divorced and remarried families (Bray, 1999; DeGarmo and Forgatch, 1999; Hetherington, 1993; Hetherington and Clingempeel, 1992; Hetherington et al., 1999). This work has revealed not only great diversity in the adjustment of both parents and children from divorced and remarried families, but great diversity in the complex interacting factors that facilitate or impede adjustment and growth.

Many contemporary researchers use multidimensional risk and resiliency models to focus on the interactions among diverse experiences and family processes that contribute to individual differences in adjustment (Amato, 1999a; Hetherington, 1989, 1991, 1993, 1999a,b; Hetherington and Clingempeel, 1992; Hetherington and Jodl, 1994; Wolin and Wolin, 1993). Multidimensional risk and resiliency models often combine aspects of lifespan, family systems, or ecological perspectives to identify and explain the profile of dynamic interactions among risk and supportive factors unique to each family.

From a developmental lifespan perspective, divorce and remarriage are viewed as steps in a long series of family transitions. Each transition requires changes in family relationships and experiences that can have an impact on parent and child adjustment, and there will be notable individual differences in response to these altered life situations. Family members may be more sensitive to the stresses associated with a family transition when a transition occurs concurrently with a normative developmental transition, such as entry into adolescence. Moreover, certain developmental changes such as those associated with adolescence may trigger latent delayed effects of divorce and remarriage. The family systems perspective offers a view of the family as an interdependent system wherein changes in family structure or in any family member or family subsystem prompt changes throughout the system. Thus this perspective has led to an examination of relationships and adjustments within and between marital, parent–child, and sibling subsystems as well as less frequently to an appraisal of family functioning in divorced and remarried families at the level of the whole family system (Bray and Berger, 1993). The ecological perspective extends this framework by examining the roles of contextual and extrafamilial factors (e.g., the peer group, educational institutions, employment, extended family and extrafamilial supports, legal and social norms) in explaining individual adjustment and family process differences.

The most marked disruptions in personal adjustment and family process and reported distress are found in the first few years following a marital transition, with the gradual establishment of new roles and relationships and a new family homeostasis emerging over time (Bray, 1992; Cherlin and Furstenberg, 1994; Hetherington, 1991, 1993; Hetherington and Clingempeel, 1992; Kitson and Holmes, 1992). Achieving a new homeostasis following divorce typically takes two to three years (Hetherington, 1989), and it has been estimated that restabilization in stepfamilies may take as long as five to seven years (Cherlin and Furstenberg, 1994; Hetherington et al., 1999; Hetherington and Kelly, in press). Multidimensional risk and resiliency models can provide a framework appropriate for identifying complex, interacting individual, relationship, and contextual circumstances that influence and predict diverse parent, child, and family outcomes. Although divorce and remarriage may confront parents and children with new stresses and challenges, in many families it also offers an escape from lonely, unsatisfying, or conflictual family relationships and an opportunity for more fulfilling family relationships and personal growth. As families negotiate divorce and remarriage, the dynamic balance of risk and protective factors unique to each family and each family member influences adjustment. These shift as the individuals and their life circumstances change and as new life challenges are faced. Parents and children with many protective factors are better able to be resilient in coping with the stresses associated with divorce, life in a single-parent household, and remarriage than those with few resources and many vulnerabilities.

Much of the research on divorce and remarriage has focused on child adjustment. Parenting is typically studied as it directly affects child adjustment or mediates the impact of contextual changes and risks on child well-being. It has been common to focus on the divorced-single-mother families and stepfather families, the family structures in which the majority of the children reside. Only in recent years have researchers begun to examine family processes and adjustment in less common structures, including single-father families, stepmother families, and complex stepfamilies. The discussion presented in this chapter reflects this research balance. Following a brief overview of children's adjustment, the empirical results of studies of parenting in divorced families are presented, with separate emphases given to parenting of custodial mothers and fathers, parenting of noncustodial mothers and fathers, and the qualities and impact of different types of coparenting relationships. Parenting in remarried families is presented next, including discussions of parenting of custodial and noncustodial parents and stepparents and the interdependence between marital and parent–child relationships. The final section includes a discussion of individual, family, and contextual factors that contribute to the diversity found in parenting skills and parent–child relationships.

CHILD ADJUSTMENT IN DIVORCED AND REMARRIED FAMILIES

The adjustment of children in divorced-single-parent families and in stepfamilies is similar (Amato, 1994; Bray, 1999; Cherlin and Furstenberg, 1994; Hetherington, 1993; Hetherington and Clingempeel, 1992; Hetherington and Jodl, 1994). Most children experience emotional and behavioral problems in the months immediately following parental divorce or remarriage (for reviews see Amato and Keith, 1991a, 1991b; Cherlin and Furstenberg, 1994; Hetherington, Bridges, and Insabella, 1998; Hetherington and Stanley-Hagan, 1999). Although these problems diminish with time, children from divorced and remarried families on the average exhibit more behavior problems and are less academically, socially, and psychologically well adjusted than those in nondivorced families (Amato, 1999a, in press; Amato and Keith, 1991a, 1991b; Avenevoli, Sessa, and Steinberg, 1999; Bray, 1999; Capaldi and Patterson, 1991; Chase-Lansdale, Cherlin, and Kiernan, 1995; Hetherington, 1999a; Hetherington and Clingempeel, 1992; McLanahan, 1999; Zill, 1994; Zill, Morrison, and Coiro, 1993). Furthermore, in adolescence and young adulthood, problems in adjustment, family relations, and the formation of stable intimate relationships can emerge or intensify (Amato, 1999a; Amato and Booth, 1997; Amato and Keith, 1991a; Bray, 1999; Bray and Berger, 1993; Buchanan, Maccoby, and Dornbusch, 1996; Cherlin, Chase-Lansdale, and McRae, 1998; Hetherington, 1993; Hetherington and Clingempeel, 1992; Hetherington et al., 1999; McLanahan and Sandefur, 1994; Powell and Parcel, 1997; Simons and Associates, 1996; Wolfinger, 2000; Zill et al., 1993).

In nondivorced families and in divorced-single-parent and remarried households, children's adjustment is associated with the quality of the parenting environment regardless of the number of family reorganizations or the time since each transition (Baumrind, 1991; Fine and Kurdek, 1994; Forgatch, Patterson, and Ray, 1996; Hetherington, 1991, 1993, 1999b; Hetherington and Clingempeel, 1992; O'Connor, Thorpe, Dunn, and Golding, 1999; Simons, 1996). Parenting quality not only affects children directly, but also modifies the impact of many ecological stressors associated with family transitions (DeGarmo and Forgatch, 1999; Hetherington, 1993, 1999b; Hetherington and Clingempeel, 1992; Simons and Associates, 1996). Children adjust best when the custodial parent is authoritative. An authoritative parent is warm, supportive, responsive to the child's needs, open in communication, monitors the children's activities, and exerts firm, consistent control (Hetherington and Clingempeel, 1992; Steinberg, Mounts, Lamborn, and Dornbusch, 1991). Uniquely important to the adjustment of children in divorced and remarried homes is the degree to which divorced mothers and fathers are able to establish and maintain cooperative, shared parenting relationships and the quality of children's relationships with parents and stepparents. Although there are few systematic studies comparing the effects of divorce and remarriage on children in different ethnic groups, McLanahan (1999) in her reanalysis of 10 large survey data sets reports that European American children in single-parent families are more disadvantaged compared with those of two-parent families than are African American and Latin American families. Being in a single-parent family led to a greater increase in the risk of school dropout, low academic attainment, not completing college, and teen births for European American than for African American and Latin American offspring. In contrast, African American youths in single-parent families were more disadvantaged than European American youths in labor market detachment, that is, in being out of school and out of work. Furthermore, living with a stepfather was more likely to increase the chance of an African American than a European American stepson's finishing high school. These ethnic differences in child adjustment in different family types did not seem to be associated with the effectiveness of authoritative parenting as a protective factor in different ethnic groups. Differences in authoritative parenting between divorced and married parents vary little across ethnic groups. Authoritative parenting is generally beneficial to children in all ethnic groups for most areas of adjustment; however, in the areas of distress and grade point average, middle-class African American adolescents benefit less from authoritative parenting than do adolescents in other ethnic groups (Avenoli et al., 1999). In antisocial behavior, the area in which the largest differences between the adjustment of children in divorced and remarried families and those in nondivorced families usually are obtained, authoritative parenting serves as an equally effective buffer.

PARENTING IN DIVORCED FAMILIES

For all families, separation and divorce set in motion a series of changes that are potentially stressful for family members and that make effective parenting difficult. In the months immediately following divorce, families are frequently faced with radically changing financial circumstances that can result in shifts in residence and new or second jobs or increased work hours. Family environments are often chaotic as household routines break down and parents struggle to adapt to single-parent roles that combine house care and childcare tasks previously performed by two adults (Cohen, 1995).

The stresses associated with these changes place both parents at risk for psychological and physical disorders that may interfere with their ability to be competent parents (Chase-Lansdale and Hetherington, 1990; Forgatch et al., 1996; Hetherington, 1993; Hetherington and Kelley, in press; Kitson and Holmes, 1992). During and after marital dissolution, adults often suffer anger, anxiety, irritability, and depression and exhibit impulsive and antisocial behavior. It is not unusual for custodial parents to report feeling optimistic about their abilities to manage single-parent demands one moment, only to doubt their competence the next. Moreover, psychological stress can be exacerbated by reoccurring health problems. There is evidence that the stresses associated with marital disruption can lead to an altered immune system that in turn makes the divorced parent more susceptible to chronic and acute medical problems (Kiecolt-Glaser et al., 1987).

Custodial Mothers

A sense of positive well-being is a strong predictor of the postdivorce adjustment of single, custodial mothers (Thiriot and Buckner, 1991). However, this sense of well-being depends on their sense of financial security and employment satisfaction, neutral if not positive relationships with their ex-spouses, a perception that their parenting skills are positive and effective, and, most notably, on the formation of a new, intimate support relationship (DeGarmo and Forgatch, 1999; Hetherington, Cox, and Cox, 1982; Kitson and Holmes, 1992; Thiriot and Buckner, 1991). Unfortunately, for most newly single mothers, stressful disruptions in their financial and employment statuses as well as in their relationships with their ex-spouses and children are common, and loneliness and depression are frequent complaints of both divorced custodial mothers and fathers (Shapiro and Lambert, 1999; Simons and Associates, 1996).

Compared with noncustodial fathers, whose financial resources usually remain stable or improve after divorce, the typical divorced mother experiences a significant decline in her financial resources (Amato, 2000; Arendell, 1995; Bursik, 1999; Meyer and Garasky, 1993) estimated to be 13 to 30%. The decline can be attributed in part to the failure of noncustodial fathers to pay child support. Only 56% of custodial mothers with children have active child support orders, and only one fourth receive the full amount owed them (U.S. Bureau of the Census, 1995). Moreover, child support collection has changed little during recent years, despite stricter enforcement efforts (Amato, 2000; Hanson, Garfinkel, McLanahan, and Miller, 1996). Adding to the standard of living decline is job instability. Although income decline for custodial mothers has decreased as women become better educated (Forgatch et al., 1996; Furstenberg, 1990; McLanahan, 1999), compared with parents in two-parent households, single custodial mothers are three times more likely to be unemployed during the first critical years following divorce, and those who are employed are more likely to experience changes in employment (Forgatch et al., 1996). As a result of income declines and job instability, between 30% and 40% of new custodial, single mothers temporally receive some form of government assistance (U.S. Bureau of the Census, 1995).

Regardless of family structure, parent well-being and parent–child relationships are negatively affected by financial distress (Amato, 2000; Cohen, 1995; Meyer and Garasky, 1993; Simons and Associates, 1995). In divorced-mother-headed families, financial decline has been linked to the use of less effective discipline and monitoring by mothers (Amato, 2000; Bank, Forgatch, Patterson, and Fetrow, 1993; Simons and Associates, 1996), to behavioral problems in children (Morrison and

Cherlin, 1995; Simons and Associates, 1996), and to mother (Amato, 2000) and child depression (Morrison and Cherlin, 1995). Moreover, concerns about financial settlements and child support can fuel ongoing conflict between ex-spouses. Disagreements about finances and childrearing practices are common, and many divorcing adults report that the conflict evident before and during the divorce is maintained or escalates after the divorce (Hetherington et al., 1982; Tshann, Johnston, Kline, and Wallerstein, 1991; Maccoby, Depner, and Mnookin, 1990). Thus a positive or even neutral relationship between former spouses is attained by few. When conflict between mothers and fathers is high, fathers are more likely to disengage from parenting and stop paying child support, leaving mothers with total parenting and financial responsibilities (Seltzer, 1991).

Parenting is a challenge when there are two involved parents, but parenting problems may be exacerbated when custodial mothers suddenly find themselves alone as they juggle financial, housework, and childcare responsibilities (Hetherington et al., 1982). When emotionally and physically stressed mothers face children who are angry, depressed, noncompliant, and demanding, parenting is particularly difficult. Thus it is common for the mothers to experience an initial period of diminished parenting characterized by irritability, unresponsiveness, poor monitoring and control, and erratic and sometimes punitive discipline (Hetherington, 1993, 1999a; Hetherington and Clingempeel, 1992; Hetherington et al., 1982; Hetherington and Jodl, 1994; Simons, 1996). Moreover, mother–child relationships are often conflicted, and escalating, mutually coercive interchanges are common, particularly with sons (Hetherington, 1993, 1999a; Hetherington and Clingempeel, 1992; Hetherington and Jodl, 1994).

Even when divorced households have restabilized they may still confront more negative life events and be more chaotic than nondivorced households, and many mothers report that the term task overload continues to be an accurate description of their lives (Hetherington et al., 1982; Stolberg, Camplair, Currier, and Wells, 1987). However, by two years following divorce three fourths of divorced women report that they are happier in their new situation than in the last year of their marriage, and most, in spite of the stresses, find rearing children alone easier than with a disengaged, undermining, or acrimonious spouse (Hetherington, 1993). Furthermore, in addition to perceiving themselves as more able parents than mothers in conflictual, unsatisfying marriages, divorced women on the average are less depressed, show less state anxiety, drink less, and have fewer health problems than those in unhappy, acrimonious, or emotionally disengaged marriages. Many divorced women comment on the independence, self-fulfillment, and new competencies they developed in response to the challenges of divorce and being a single parent (Hetherington, 1993; Hetherington and Kelly, in press). These changes are reflected in improvements in mother–daughter relationships, with divorced mothers and their preadolescent daughters often developing close, harmonious, companionate relationships (Hetherington and Clingempeel, 1992). As daughters enter adolescence, however, conflict between divorced mothers and daughters may reemerge, especially if the daughter becomes sexually active or becomes involved in antisocial activities. Divorced mothers who have earlier granted their children considerable autonomy may attempt ineffectively to increase monitoring and control of their adolescent daughters' behaviors (Hetherington, 1993, 1999a; Hetherington and Clingempeel, 1992). Approximately one third of adolescents in divorced and remarried families disengage and maintain physical and emotional distance from their families. Sometimes these adolescents form a close relationship with a friend's family, teacher, coach, or other relative such as an aunt or grandparent, and this may be a successful solution to a difficult conflictual family environment. However, adolescents, especially adolescent boys, who do disengage from their families and have no close relationship with a caring adult, are more susceptible to the influences of delinquent peers (Hetherington, 1991, 1992; Hetherington and Kelly, in press; Steinberg, 1987).

Even after the family has attained a new equilibrium, custodial mothers, especially mothers of sons, on the average report more childrearing stress than do those in nondivorced families (Colletta, 1981; Hetherington, 1993). The most sustained problems for them appear to be in the areas of monitoring and control, and these problems are to some extent associated with the precocious autonomy and greater power of children in divorced families (Bank et al., 1991; Hetherington and Clingempeel, 1992; Hetherington, Cox, and Cox, 1985; Hetherington and Kelly, in press).

Weiss (1979) has commented on the fact that children in divorced families grow up faster. More recent researchers confirm that this precocious development is associated with less supervision of activities, more power in decision making, and children's assumption of parent roles, a process referred to as parentification (Hetherington, 1991, 1999a; Johnston, 1990). Both custodial mothers and fathers often expect children, especially daughters, to assume instrumental roles such as house care and sibling care. However, mothers are more likely than fathers to expect daughters to provide emotional support and to serve as advisors and confidants. The assignment of responsibilities is sometimes associated with unusual social competence, greater cognitive agency, and fewer antisocial behaviors in daughters. However, they are also more likely to have lower self-worth and to be more depressed. Low self-esteem, anxiety, depression, and compulsive caregiving are more likely to occur when the roles assumed are age inappropriate or beyond the capabilities of the child (Hetherington, 1999a). In addition, children in divorced families have more power in family decision making and are less competent and responsive to their mothers' commands (Hetherington, 1989, 1999a). This accelerated independence often makes the challenges associated with normative family realignments and autonomy seeking in early adolescence or the move into a stepfamily difficult.

Custodial Fathers

Since the mid-1970s, many states have changed custody laws to eliminate gender biases in custody decisions and to encourage if not mandate joint custody. Despite these changes and despite evidence that fathers are no less competent parents than mothers (Amato and Gilbreth, 1999) and that they can play a positive role in the postdivorce adjustment of their children, fewer than 12% of fathers are awarded physical custody of their children at the time of divorce (U.S. Bureau of the Census, 1998). A distinction must be made between joint legal custody, wherein both parents are held responsible for the welfare of their children regardless of residency arrangements, and joint physical custody, wherein the children alternately reside with both parents. Although both joint legal and physical custody have become more common over the past decade, even when joint physical custody is awarded, most children reside almost full time with their mothers (Hetherington and Stanley-Hagan, 1997; Maccoby and Mnookin, 1992; Teachman et al., 2000). The implication is that many physical custody decisions are made by the divorcing parents, not the courts, and there is evidence that these decisions may reflect concerns fathers themselves have about assuming full-time parenting (Maccoby and Mnookin, 1992). Many fathers report that they would like sole or joint physical custody of their children but choose not to pursue it because (1) they believe their children would benefit more from the closer relationship children are perceived to have with their mothers, (2) fathers' job responsibilities are not flexible enough to accommodate the time demands of single parenthood, and (3) fathers want to avoid exposing their children to prolonged negative custody battles (Hetherington and Stanley-Hagan, 1997; Maccoby, Buchanan, Mnookin, and Dornbusch, 1993).

Although researchers have begun to focus attention on the quality of relationships custodial fathers have with their children, it is still the case that less is known about relationships in father-custody homes than in mother-custody homes. Available research indicates that newly divorced custodial fathers and mothers appear to share many of the same stresses and concerns. Both report feeling overloaded and socially isolated and worried about their parenting competence (Hetherington, 1993; Simons, 1996). On the other hand, custodial fathers have greater job stability and more economic resources that may enable the fathers to hire others to help with house care and childcare (Amato, 2000; Braver et al., 1993; Furstenberg, 1990). Custodial fathers also tend to have more extensive support systems than custodial mothers, and, once their families have restabilized, custodial fathers report better relationships and fewer problems with their children (Furstenberg, 1988).

Researchers have found differences between the parenting of custodial fathers and that of custodial mothers. For example, fathers are more likely to assign household responsibilities to children than are mothers (Chase-Lansdale and Hetherington, 1990). In addition, in contrast to custodial mothers, custodial fathers do not have similar problems in control and discipline, although they have been found to be less competent monitors of their children's activities, a problem associated with more delinquent activities by adolescents (Buchanan, Maccoby, and Dornbusch, 1991; Maccoby and Mnookin, 1992). Moreover, fathers are less likely to communicate and self-disclose openly with their children or to praise, hug, and spend time with their children (Amato, 2000). Custodial fathers' interactions with their children tend to focus on skills training and education attainment. Custodial mothers are more likely to focus on a wider range of issues, including emotional well-being and social relationships. More custodial mothers know the names of their children's friends (Downey, 1994). Despite these differences, once their families restabilize, custodial fathers report less childrearing stress, better parent–child relationships, and fewer behavior problems in their children than do custodial mothers (Amato and Keith, 1991a; Clarke-Stewart and Hayward, 1996).

Although both mothers and fathers can be competent parents, there is some inconsistent evidence that children, especially preadolescent boys, may develop fewer problems in father-custody homes (Amato and Keith, 1991a). For example, the coercive cycles characteristic of mother–son interactions are rare between custodial fathers and sons. School-age boys in father custody appear to have higher self-esteems, to be more socially competent, and to have fewer behavior problems. It has been suggested that children may fare better in father-custody situations in part because the children are less likely to be exposed to risks associated with economic difficulties (McLanahan, 1999; McLanahan and Sandefur, 1994). Support for this position is found in research that indicates that children who live with affluent custodial mothers have fewer behavior problems than do children living with financially distressed single mothers (Amato and Keith, 1991a). However, other researchers have found that, even when economic circumstances are controlled, children in father-custody families have fewer problems than those in mother-custody families (Clarke-Stewart and Hayward, 1996). The suggestion that children may fare better in the custody of fathers and the degree to which risks associated with temporary and long-term financial adversities place children and parent–child relationships at risk warrant further study. However, regardless of custody arrangements, children benefit from living with an authoritative parent in a family environment devoid of interparental conflict.

Noncustodial Parents

Although custodial parents are more salient than noncustodial parents in the adjustment of children, noncustodial parents who remain involved can contribute to their children's development (see Amato and Gilbreth, 1999, for a meta-analysis). However, methodologically sound studies of relationships between noncustodial parents and their children have appeared only recently. Available research suggests that noncustodial mothers and noncustodial fathers differ in both their levels of involvement in childrearing and the types of relationships they have with their children.

Noncustodial fathers.   Most noncustodial fathers become increasingly uninvolved over time (Amato and Gilbreth, 1999; Furstenberg, 1988; Hetherington and Jodl, 1994; Hetherington and Kelly, in press; Minton and Pasley, 1996; Seltzer, 1991). Only 25% of children see their fathers once a week or more, and over 33% do not see their fathers at all or see them only a few times a year (Seltzer, 1991). Recognizing the important roles fathers can play, particularly if they can establish an authoritative relationship with their child and a cooperative coparenting relationship with their ex-spouse, researchers have tried to identify the factors associated with continued involvement. Fathers are more likely to remain involved with sons than daughters and with older children and adolescents than with younger children (Hetherington, 1989; Hetherington and Kelly, in press). Fathers are likely to reduce contact if they remarry or if they or their former wives relocate geographically (Gunnoe, 1993). However, regardless of child age or gender and geographic proximity, the best predictors of continued paternal involvement appear to be the degree to which the father identifies with parenting roles (Ihinger-Tallman, Pasley, and Buehler, 1995; Minton and Pasley, 1996; Stone and McKenry, 1998), the father's relationship with his former spouse, and his perceived control in decisions about the child's activities and well-being (Amato and Gilbreth, 1999; Arditti and Allen, 1993; Arditti and Madden-Derdich, 1995; Braver et al., 1993). Fathers who strongly identify with their parenting roles and who rank parenting roles and responsibilities high on their list of life priorities are more likely to remain involved with their children after they and their wives separate and divorce (Ihinger-Tallman et al., 1995; Minton and Pasley, 1996; Stone and McKenry, 1998). Fathers with a strong parent identity typically view themselves as competent parents, an important perspective given that fathers who withdraw after divorce are more likely to believe they are less competent than other parents (Arendell, 1995; Dudley, 1996; Seltzer, 1991, 1998). Regardless of parent identity, fathers are more likely to report being dissatisfied with parenting and to disengage when the legal wranglings with their former wives at the time of divorce were stressful, when interparental conflict remains high, when these conflicts center around disagreements over childrearing practices, and when joint custody is not granted and the fathers believe they have little say in their children's upbringing.

There is some evidence that suggests that noncustodial fathers, may not be dropping out as much as they have in the past (Emery, 1999; Seltzer, 1998). Maccoby et al. (1993) proposed that changes in custody laws and changing gender norms are not only encouraging continued paternal contact and involvement but are beginning to make such involvement easier. However, frequency of contact between noncustodial fathers and their children is generally unrelated to child adjustment. What matters is the quality of the relationship. Children are more successful in school and show fewer externalizing and internalizing problems when nonresident fathers are authoritative and fathers and children feel close to one another (Amato, 1999b; Amato and Gilbreth, 1999). However, for those noncustodial fathers who remain involved, a pattern of intermittent and infrequent visitations appears to affect the type of relationships they have with their children. They are more likely to be permissive than authoritative parents and to assume more of a recreational, companionate role than the role of teacher or disciplinarian (Furstenberg, 1990; Furstenberg and Cherlin, 1991; Gunnoe, 1993; Hetherington, 1993).

Continued involvement of the noncustodial father also has an indirect effect on children's adjustment. Involved fathers are more likely to pay child support, and child support is associated with better parenting by the custodial mother and with fewer behavior problems and greater education attainment in children (Amato and Gilbreth, 1999).

Finally, a provocative finding was reported in a meta-analysis of the effects of nonresident fathers on children's well-being (Amato and Gilbreth, 1999): The association between paternal contact and children's well-being has become stronger over time. Amato and Gilbreth speculated that this may be because recent cohorts of fathers are becoming more involved and committed to their parental role or because fathers are displaying better parenting skills. It also may be because of the increase in divorce mediation and in joint custody, which increases paternal contact.

Noncustodial mothers. Even less is known about the behavior of noncustodial mothers than that of noncustodial fathers. What information there is indicates that noncustodial mothers have about twice as much contact with their children as do noncustodial fathers (Gunnoe, 1993; Hetherington, 1993; Hetherington and Jodl, 1994) and that this contact seems to decline less over time or following the remarriage of the custodial father (Gunnoe, 1993; Santrock, Sitterle, and Warshak, 1988; Santrock and Warshak, 1979). Although the research is not entirely consistent in this regard, increasing evidence indicates that mothers, like fathers, are more apt to maintain contact with sons than with daughters (Hetherington et al., 1982; Gunnoe, 1993).

In contrast to noncustodial fathers, noncustodial mothers are more likely to adopt a traditional parenting role and are more likely to arrange their living situations to facilitate visits from their children (Furstenberg, 1990; Gunnoe, 1993; Hetherington and Kelly, in press). Although notably poorer at monitoring and controlling their children's behaviors than nondivorced mothers, noncustodial mothers show greater monitoring and control than do noncustodial fathers (Gunnoe, 1993; Hetherington and Jodl, 1994). They also are more sensitive to their children's emotional needs, communicate better, are more supportive in times of stress, and are more knowledgeable and interested in their children's activities (Furstenberg and Nord, 1987; Gunnoe, 1993). It is therefore not surprising that children report feeling closer to noncustodial mothers than to noncustodial fathers (Gunnoe, 1993).

Furthermore, compared with contact with noncustodial fathers, contact with noncustodial mothers has been more strongly and consistently found to be positively associated with the adjustment of children, especially that of daughters (Arditti, 1992; Gunnoe, 1993; Johnston, Kline, and Tschann, 1989).

Shared Parenting

The move toward joint physical custody and joint legal custody and facilitating visitation is based on the assumptions that continued contact with both parents is desirable and that parents can attain some modicum of cooperative, constructive parenting that puts the well-being of the child before their own feelings of acrimony or resentment (Furstenberg, 1990; Maccoby et al., 1990). The superiority of joint over sole physical custody measured in terms of positive child adjustment and parental satisfaction has not been clearly demonstrated (Furstenberg, 1990; Maccoby et al., 1990). In fact, there is some evidence that in high-conflict divorces children exhibit more problems under joint custody (Johnston, 1994; Johnston et al., 1989). However, parents who report being satisfied with shared physical custody also report that (1) they had positive relationships with their former spouses, particularly over parenting issues, before divorce; (2) there is congruence between their childrearing practices; (3) neither residence is considered to be the children's primary residence, and the schedule for the children's shifts in residence is formalized; and (4) there was little conflict before the divorce and has been low to moderate conflict since (Benjamin and Irving, 1990). Dissatisfied parents share few if any of these characteristics and are likely to believe that they were coerced into the arrangement by the courts or the other parent. Mothers may have acquiesced out of guilt at denying their children access to their fathers or out of fear of loss of their children in a custody battle, and some parents are likely to have believed that a shared-parenting relationships that necessitates continued contact might lead to a reconciliation.

Contemporary researchers have extended the definition of shared parenting or coparenting to include the degree to which parents remain involved and work together to provide mutual parenting support and a more stable parenting environment for their children regardless of physical custody arrangements. Maccoby et al. (1990, 1993) identified three parenting patterns that can be used to describe shared parenting in sole or joint custody families. *Cooperative* parents talk with each other about the children, avoid arguments, and support rather than undermine each other's parenting efforts. *Conflicted* parents talk with each other about the children but with criticism, acrimony, defensiveness, and attempts to undermine each other's parenting. *Disengaged* parents are both involved with their children but adopt what Furstenberg (1990) has termed a parallel parenting model. Each parent adopts her or his own style and does not interfere with the other's parenting. Communication with each other is avoided except perhaps through their children. This reduces the likelihood of direct conflict but also reduces cooperation.

Cooperative coparenting is most satisfying to parents and children. When the biological parents are cooperative coparents, their children adjust better to the divorce and adjust more easily to one or both parents' remarriages, and the children's relationships with their stepparents are more positive (Bray and Berger, 1993). Parents are more likely to be cooperative when they are able to establish relationship boundaries that clearly define the former partner as a coparent but not as a spouse (Emery, 1994), when there are a small number of children who are of school age, when there was little conflict at the time of divorce or since, and when both parents express an ongoing concern about the children's well-being (Maccoby et al., 1993).

Unfortunately, feelings of anger and resentment are difficult if not impossible for many divorced parents to control, and even two years after divorce approximately one quarter of divorced parents are involved in conflicted parenting (Maccoby and Mnookin, 1992). The adverse effects on children of exposure to ongoing parental conflict have been well documented (Emery, 1994; Hetherington et al., 1982; Simons and Associates, 1996). However, mere exposure may not be as detrimental as experiencing loyalty conflicts by being caught in the middle of parental conflict (Buchanan et al., 1991, 1996; Hetherington, 1993). Children forced to serve as go-betweens may learn to exploit their parents and to play one off against the other, and, when older, escape careful monitoring of their activities (Hetherington and Kelly, in press).

Although cooperative coparenting is associated with positive adjustment, in cases in which both parents remain involved, the disengaged or parallel style of shared parenting is most common (Furstenberg, 1990; Maccoby et al., 1990; Maccoby and Mnookin, 1992). Parents of young children are more likely to be conflicted initially. Over time, however, conflict in coparenting decreases and disengaged parenting increases as the children move into adolescence (Maccoby and Mnookin, 1992). Moreover, even initially cooperative parents are likely to become conflicted or disengaged when one or both parents become involved in new relationships. Although a disengaged style is not the ideal, children have been found to adjust well, provided that their parents do not interfere with each other's parenting, conflict is low, and the children are not asked to act as go-betweens (Buchanan et al., 1996).

Summary

Concerns about the difficulties divorced, single parents face and about the adjustment of their children have led to the emergence of an old question: Should parents stay together for the sake of their children? The healthiest environment for children is a harmonious, low-conflict two-parent household (Simons, 1996). However, the answer to the question relies less on family structure than on income, parental conflict, and the quality of parenting. Prospective studies that separated nondivorced families into those with high or low conflict or those who would later divorce found that the child adjustment problems in those who later divorced were intermediate to the other two groups (Hetherington, 1999a). When divorce is associated with a move to a more harmonious, less stressful family situation, children in divorced families are similar to children in low-conflict nondivorced families in adjustment (Amato, Loomis, and Booth, 1995; Hetherington, 1999a). However, when divorce is associated with increased stress, conflict, and adversity, children in divorced families tend to be less well adjusted than children in either low conflict or high-conflict nondivorced families. In other words, if children are going to be exposed to parental conflict, they may fare better in a nondivorced household characterized by marital conflict than in a divorced household characterized by ongoing conflict between resident and nonresident parents (Amato et al., 1995; Hetherington, 1999a). However, after an initial period of stress and conflict, most divorced parents are able to establish a disengaged if not cooperative coparenting relationship.

The family disequilibrium that accompanies the divorce transition is stressful for all family members, and many divorced women and children encounter the risks associated with poverty. However, many divorced mothers also report that they eventually gain greater self-confidence and self-fulfillment as a result of escape from an unsatisfying marriage and coping with the challenges faced as they work toward a new family equilibrium. Critical to the adjustment of children is the presence of an authoritative custodial parent, but whether or not parents are able to establish or maintain an authoritative approach to parenting depends on the degree to which they must cope with concurrent adversities. When custodial parents are faced with ongoing financial strain or with the full house care and childcare responsibilities in the absence of a close personal relationship and support from kin or extrafamilial sources, the psychological and physical well-being of parents and parenting quality often suffer.

Recent research indicates that neither mothers nor fathers are superior custodial parents. Although there is some inconsistent evidence that children may adapt better in the custody of fathers, children function well in the custody of either parent provided that the parent can maintain a relatively authoritative approach and provided that the family is not faced with new or continuing adversities. There is a growing emphasis on shared parenting. However, even if the courts may mandate a shared legal responsibility or even shared physical custody, courts cannot mandate a cooperative, consensual shared parenting relationship. Again, being caught in the middle of acrimonious parental relationships can have deleterious effects on children's development.

PARENTING IN STEPFAMILIES

Stepfamilies occur in diverse sizes and organizations. The custodial and the noncustodial parents and stepparent all may have been married and divorced, often more than once. The parents may have residential or nonresidential children from a previous marriage or cohabitation, and a large network of grandparents and other relatives may remain involved in the children's lives. Regardless of form and size, however, all newly reconstituted families face tasks unique to their status. The couple must define and strengthen their marriage while simultaneously renegotiating the biological parent–child relationships and establishing stepparent–stepchild and stepsibling relationships. The family must establish roles and relationships with the stepparent who has not participated in the shared family history and whose entry upsets the relationships established in the single-parent household. Extrafamilial relationships, especially those with the noncustodial parents, will influence and will be changed by the remarriage. This complex network of new and old extended family relationships must be altered and integrated in the absence of clear guiding or agreed-on norms (Bray, 1999; Fine, Coleman, and Ganong, 1999; Hetherington and Jodl, 1994).

How successful families are in accomplishing these tasks depends in part on their beliefs and expectations at the outset. Clinicians have suggested that when remarried families believe that the traditional nuclear model is the ideal against which they should measure themselves, problems are virtually inevitable (Bray and Berger, 1993; Burchardt, 1990; Visher and Visher, 1994). In contrast to what many families expect or hope, adjustment is likely to be slow (Hetherington and Clingempeel, 1992). Affection between the stepparent and the stepchildren may develop slowly, if at all, and the role of a disciplinarian may never be adopted. Newly remarried families are families in transition, and the remarriage is but one in a series of transitions. There is some evidence that multiple transitions are more difficult to negotiate (DeGarmo and Forgatch, 1999), especially if the transitions are widely spaced and a new homeostasis has been established in the previous family form (Anderson, Greene, Hetherington, and Clingempeel, 1999). Thus the reorganization is likely to take longer than did the reorganization following the initial divorce, and, once a new equilibrium has been achieved, family relationships and processes in a stepfamily are likely to look different from those found in nondivorced families (Bray, 1999; Hetherington and Clingempeel, 1992; Hetherington and Kelly, in press; Hetherington et al., 1999).

Remarried Mothers

Despite the various possible forms a stepfamily may take, 84% of remarried households are stepfather families, formed when a custodial mother with children from a previous relationship marries, and children of the stepfather's first marriage are usually nonresidential (U.S. Bureau of the Census, 1998). For these mothers and their children, remarriage can signal a significant improvement in the family situation. The remarriage typically results in a positive change in their financial status and provides the custodial parent with emotional support and help with household and childcare responsibilities.

However, these positive changes are not reflected in improvement in the adjustment of stepchildren, which remains similar to the adjustment of children in single-parent households. Why should this be? Some investigators have suggested that the greater prevalence of behavior problems in children in stepfamilies is attributable to conflict and other adverse experiences they encounter during divorce and life in a single-parent family (Anderson et al., 1999). They propose that children already have more problems in adjustment and family relations when they enter a new stepfamily and that many of the problems in parent–child relationships in stepfamilies may be child driven (Anderson et al., 1999; Hetherington and Clingempeel, 1992; Hetherington and Kelly, in press). Other researchers point out that, even if more positive life changes are found in stepfamilies than in single-parent families, more negative life changes than are found in nondivorced families also occur as the challenges of integrating a new member into the existing family system are confronted (Bray, 1999; Hetherington, 1993). Moreover, when families are faced with sharing financial resources with the stepfather's family from his first marriage and stepfather–stepchild relationships are troubled, initially high expectations are likely to fall.

As a result of the stresses associated with integrating a stepfather into the family and their concern about the marital relationship, many newly remarried mothers experience a temporary decline in their monitoring and control. Moreover, when remarriage occurs when children are preadolescents, monitoring and control problems are accompanied by an increase in conflictual mother–child exchanges. Remarried mothers are more likely to be poorer monitors of sons' behaviors, but conflict is likely to be higher with daughters. The early monitoring problems may represent a continuation of the poor monitoring found in divorced single mothers, but mother–daughter conflict appears in response to the remarriage. In contrast to the mutually coercive relationships of divorced mothers and sons, daughters often have close, confiding, compassionate relationships with their divorced mothers during their time in a single-parent household. Once remarried, the mother's attention, time, and affection are shared with her new husband. Thus the entry of the stepfather marks a significant change in the daughter's status in the family, which can lead to resentment and conflict with both the mother and the stepfather (Bray, 1999; Bray and Berger, 1993; Hetherington and Clingempeel, 1992; Hetherington and Jodl, 1994; Hetherington and Kelly, in press).

The age of the child at the time of the mother's remarriage has been found to be a factor in the long-term adjustment of the mother–child relationship. When children are preadolescents at the time of the remarriage, maternal monitoring and control problems improve by approximately two years after the remarriage but often reemerge when the children reach adolescence (Hetherington, 1993). On the other hand, if the remarriage takes place when children are negotiating with stresses associated with the developmental transition into adolescence, the risks of long-term problems in the mother–child relationship increase. Decreases in warmth, monitoring, and control and increases in conflict are not uncommon as parents and children in all families realign their relationships (Hetherington, 1993). When the remarriage occurs as the child is moving into adolescence, problems may be magnified. Maternal monitoring and control can stabilize in these families but often at levels lower than those in first-marriage families. Despite this evidence, most remarried mothers' relationships with their children are renegotiated and tend to restabilize in a pattern fairly similar to that of nondivorced mothers (Bray, 1999; Hetherington and Clingempeel, 1992; Hetherington and Kelly, in press; Gunnoe, 1993; Pink and Wampler, 1985).

Stepfathers

For new stepfathers, a primary source of stress is the lack of clear stepparent roles (Marsiglio, 1992). Although a few states have recently passed laws that require stepparents to contribute to the financial support of their stepchildren, stepparents have virtually no legal parenting rights or responsibilities. The lack of legal guidelines reflects a comparable lack of social norms. Stepfathers often report feeling poorly prepared for the task of integrating themselves into a preexisting family (Fine et al., 1999; Marsiglio, 1992). However, over half of remarried mothers and stepfathers believe that the stepparent should assume an active parenting role and share equally childcare responsibilities (Marsiglio, 1992). In families in which mothers welcome such involvement and stepfathers are able to establish authoritative relationships with their stepchildren, children, particularly preadolescent boys, manifest fewer adjustment problems.

Unfortunately, many stepchildren believe, in contrast to parent and stepparent expectations, that the stepparents should not be parents (Fine et al., 1999; Visher and Visher, 1988), and stepfathers' efforts to adopt a positive parental role too soon are often met with resentment and resistance from children, particularly early adolescents (Hetherington, 1988, 1989; Hetherington and Clingempeel, 1992; Hetherington and Jodl, 1994). Younger children are more likely than adolescents eventually to accept a stepfather as a parent. However, even with preadolescents, their precocious independence and power in the family make a stepfather's assertion of authority and control problematic (Hetherington and Anderson, 1987; Hetherington and Clingempeel, 1992; Hetherington and Kelly, in press). There is accumulating evidence that early in a remarriage, young adolescents may have a more salient role in shaping stepfathers than the reverse. Over time, stepfathers may respond to the resistant, aversive, and troubled behavior of early young adolescents with increasing negativity, low positivity, and disengagement (Anderson et al., 1999; Hetherington, 1993; Hetherington and Clingempeel, 1992). Moreover, children's repeated rejections of the stepfather may lead to the development of strong maladaptive mother–child alliances that can put the marriage in jeopardy (Bray, 1999). Although stepfathers with early adolescent stepchildren appear to have the most difficulty assuming a positive parental role, comparisons of well-functioning and dysfunctional stepfamilies reveal that, regardless of children's ages, stepchildren in dysfunctional stepfamilies tend to respond with resistant, negative behavior to stepfathers' attempts at warmth and authority (Anderson et al., 1999; Bray, 1999; Brown, Green, and Druckman, 1990; Hetherington and Clingempeel, 1992). The most successful strategy for stepfathers may be to build a warm, involved relationship with the children initially and to support the discipline of the mother (Bray and Berger, 1993; Fine, Voydanoff, and Donnelly, 1993; Hetherington and Clingempeel, 1992; Hetherington and Jodl, 1994). The move toward authoritative parenting should be gradual and in some families should not occur at all. However, in stepfamilies, as in divorced and nondivorced families, authoritative parenting is associated with more positive adjustment of children (Anderson et al., 1999; DeGarmo and Forgatch, 1999; Hetherington and Jodl, 1994; Hetherington and Kelly, in press).

As a result of ambiguous role definitions and family expectations as well as family experiences (e.g., age of the children, time since divorce), great diversity has been found in the parenting of stepfathers, particularly when compared with that of biological fathers in nondivorced homes (Hetherington and Clingempeel, 1992). Most stepfathers are less involved and communicative with stepchildren (Fine et al., 1999; Hetherington and Clingempeel, 1992; Hetherington and Kelly, in press), are less nurturing and warm (Amato, 1987; Hetherington and Clingempeel, 1992), exert less control (Amato, 1987), and have less positive perceptions of their relationships with stepchildren (Fine et al., 1993; Hetherington and Clingempeel, 1992). Evolutionary psychologists have proposed that parents are more likely to be attached, involved, and protective with their biological children than with stepchildren. They suggest that human beings use reproductive strategies that increase the chances of survival of their genes into the next generation (Daly and Wilson, 1989). However, equally plausible explanations involve the high levels of resistance and noxious behavior in stepchildren encountered by many stepparents and the involuntary nature of the parenting role. A frequent mantra of stepfathers is "I married her, not her kids."

Over time, aproximately one third of stepfathers, particularly those with young children, in contrast to over one half of nondivorced fathers, become active and involved authoritative parents (Hetherington and Clingempeel, 1992), and stepchildren, particularly boys, benefit from this relationship (Bray, 1999; Gunnoe, 1993; Hetherington et al., 1999; Hetherington and Jodl, 1994). However, most stepfathers remain or become disengaged, but to varying degrees. Some who disengage do so completely. They are inattentive to their stepchildren and unsupportive of the mothers' parenting (Santrock et al., 1988). Others disengage only from an active disciplinarian role but develop close affective relationships with their stepchildren and are supportive of the mothers' discipline and control efforts. Research to date suggests that when full authoritative involvement is not possible, an indirect engagement style may be best for children. Children have been found to adjust well when their custodial mother is authoritative and retains full responsibility for discipline while their stepfather is warm and supportive toward them and involves himself indirectly in discipline through his support of the mother (Bray, 1999; Bray and Berger, 1993; Fine et al., 1993; Hetherington, 1989; Hetherington and Clingempeel, 1992; Hetherington and Jodl, 1994).

Stepmothers

An estimated 13 million women in the United States are stepmothers, but only 8%, slightly more than 1 million, actually live with their stepchildren full time (Cherlin and Furstenberg, 1994). Stepmothers have many of the same initial concerns expressed by stepfathers. They worry that they will not be able to be as nurturant with stepchildren as the children's biological mothers or to control and discipline the children as well as their biological fathers (Salwen, 1990). When stepmothers suppress their concerns and become active in disciplining their stepchildren, the result is likely to be similar to that found in stepfather families, conflict with their stepchildren, particularly stepdaughters (Brand et al., 1988; MacDonald and DeMaris, 1996).

However, as is found with stepfathers, whether or not stepmothers successfully negotiate their place in the stepfamily depends largely on their expectations and on those held by their new spouse and his children. Women enter stepfamilies with diverse ideas about what their roles should be and the emphasis they should place on their relationships with stepchildren relative to that placed on the marital relationship. In an investigation of stepmothers' expectations about stepfamilies, Church (1999) identified five different kinship models. However, more than 80% of the stepmothers adopted one of three models, the nuclear, extended, or couple model. The models differ on the primacy of the marital relationship, the parental role adopted by the stepmothers, and the inclusion or exclusion of stepchildren, new in-laws, and former in-laws and spouses in the stepfamily system. Approximately 22% of the stepmothers studied adopted a *nuclear model* because they believed the nondivorced, two-parent model to be ideal. To foster this ideal, the stepmothers give primacy to the family system, sometimes at the expense of the marital relationship, trying to assume a full parenting role, including disciplining their stepchildren and trying to restrict the children's involvement with their mothers and both biological relatives and steprelatives. These stepmothers become stressed when family members fail to recognize their efforts and when the stepchildren's biological mother remains an involved parent. Approximately 27% of stepmothers adopted an *extended model* that parallels the nuclear model only in the stepmother's perception that their stepchildren are related to them. These women identify an extended kinship network as the ideal, a network that includes the women's family of origin and all children and in-laws from former marriages and the current marriage. They propose that all benefit from the enlarged, complex network and are stressed when others in the network do not share their views. The stepmothers argue that they are coparents with the stepchildren's biological parents and, as such, their role is not to replace a biological parent but to be a source of support and diverse experiences for their stepchildren. Another 31% adopted a *couple model*, wherein the relationship with the husband is placed first and relationships with stepchildren are placed second. These stepmothers devote themselves to establishing a strong marriage because they believe that they and their partners, children, and stepchildren benefit from a strong marital relationship. Although the stepmothers resist personal contact with their husband's former spouse, they believe that both biological parents should be involved with their children. The stepmothers expect to provide warmth and support to their stepchildren as they become the children's friend, but they also expect to leave discipline to the children's biological parents.

Recent research indicates that the couple model may be the most adaptive. Stepmothers are less stressed, stepchildren have fewer chronic adjustment problems, and marriages are stronger when both newly married spouses primarily focus on establishing a strong marriage (Bray, 1999; Cherlin and Furstenberg, 1994; Minuchin and Nichols, 1994; Neilson, 1999; Visher and Visher, 1996), when the stepmother does not feel that she is competing with her husband's ex-wife for his love and attention (Quick, McKenry, and Newman, 1994), and when the stepmother leaves child discipline to her husband (Fine and Kurdek, 1994; Papernow, 1993). Unfortunately, regardless of the parenting model stepmothers try to adopt, they are usually more involved in parenting, including discipline, than are stepfathers (Fine et al., 1993; Thomson, McLanahan, and Curtin, 1992; Whitsett and Land, 1992). Gender norms make it difficult if not impossible for stepmothers to assume a parental role gradually or to disengage when faced with resistant, noncompliant stepchildren. Therefore, compared with stepfathers, residential stepmothers appear to have a more difficult and stressful time fitting themselves into the family system (Cherlin and Furstenberg, 1994; Papernow, 1993; Whitsett and Land, 1992).

Although both stepmothers and stepchildren find their relationships more stressful than comparable relationships in stepfather families, most stepmothers and their stepchildren do eventually get along reasonably well (Fustenberg and Cherlin, 1991; Ganong and Coleman, 1994; Hetherington and Jodl, 1994: Quick et al., 1994). Moreover, few child adjustment differences have been found between stepfather and stepmother families (Ganong and Coleman, 1994).

Noncustodial Parents

Early investigations of remarried families paid little attention to the complex relationships between residential and nonresidential family members. However, as interest in postdivorce shared-parenting relationships has grown, researchers have begun to assess the impact that continued involvement of the noncustodial parent has on the remarried family. For example, investigators have proposed that the problems residential stepmothers have in establishing positive, effective relationships with their stepchildren may be exacerbated by the fact that the children's noncustodial mother is likely to visit frequently and to be actively involved with the children (Brand et al., 1988). It is interesting to note, however, that continued involvement of noncustodial fathers has not been found to have a similar impact on stepfather–child relationships (Brand et al., 1988; Furstenberg, 1988; Hetherington and Kelly, in press). This seeming discrepancy may result because of the greater disengagement of step-fathers or the more companionable role of noncustodial fathers. In one report from a study based on a national sample, Gunnoe (1993) indicated that noncustodial mothers' monitoring, aggression, and positivity, and daughters' feelings of being caught between noncustodial mothers and stepmothers, are associated with girls' conduct problems, depression, and social responsibility. Noncustodial fathers' monitoring serves as a deterrent to sons' conduct problems and depression. Biological mothers who were involved and competent before divorce stay involved even after the remarriage of the custodial father (Hetherington, 1993). Children in stepfamilies often report feeling caught between their mothers and stepmothers, and these perceived loyalty conflicts can lead to difficulties in the stepmother–stepchild relationship (Gunnoe, 1993; Hetherington and Kelly, in press; Salwen, 1990). Thus residential stepmothers who adopt an active parenting role are in competition with involved non-custodial mothers, a situation exacerbated by the fact that children typically feel much closer to their noncustodial mothers (Gunnoe, 1993). If residential stepfathers establish an affectionate bond with the children and do not adopt a disciplinarian role, they are not in competition with the noncustodial fathers who remain actively involved in parenting (Bray, Berger, and Boethal, 1994; Brooks-Gunn, 1994; Cherlin and Furstenberg, 1994; Hetherington and Henderson, 1997; Visher and Visher, 1996). On the other hand, the noncustodial father who is permissive and who plays a less instrumental role is less likely to be competing with an authoritative stepfather (Gunnoe, 1993; Hetherington, 1993; Hetherington and Jodl, 1994; White, 1994). Thus it is not contact with the noncustodial parent per se but the quality of the parent–child relationship that is important in children's adjustment, and these relationships vary with the gender of the noncustodial parent and child.

Associations Between Marital and Parent–Child Relationships in Remarried Families

A close marital relationship is often viewed as a firm foundation for positive family functioning, a foundation that promotes both responsive, competent parenting and the psychological well-being of children (Kerig, Cowan, and Cowan, 1993). The associations between the marital and the parent–child subsystems and their impact on child adjustment in nondivorced families have been well documented and a comparable pattern of positive associations has been found in remarried families (Bray, 1999; Bray and Berger, 1993; Fine and Kurdek, 1994; Hetherington and Clingempeel, 1992). However, exceptions to this pattern, especially in stepfamilies with preadolescent children, have been found, and the interactions among subsystems in remarried families may differ from those typical in nondivorced families (Bray and Berger, 1993; Hetherington and Clingempeel, 1992).

In stepmother families, higher marital quality has been found to be associated with more positive stepmother–stepson relationships and better stepson adjustment, but with less positive stepmother–stepdaughter relationships and poorer stepdaughter adjustment (Brand and Clingempeel, 1987). In stepfather families, stepfathers with close satisfying conjugal relationships are more positive toward stepchildren of both sexes (Brand et al., 1988; Bray, 1988; Bray and Berger, 1993; Hetherington and Clingempeel, 1992). However, the quality and the extent of the association between the marital relationship and stepfathers' and stepchildren's behavior toward each other may differ and may be related to the age of the child at the time of remarriage, the time since the remarriage, and the stepfathers' involvement in parenting.

In the months immediately following remarriage, stepfathers report higher marital satisfaction if they are not expected to either bond with or discipline their stepchildren immediately (Bray, 1988, 1999). Extending this line of investigation in long-term follow-ups of adjustment in a sample of stepfather families, Bray and Berger (1993) found that, as remarried families begin to adjust, the marital satisfaction of both partners remains higher if stepfathers establish close emotional bonds with their stepchildren but support the mothers' discipline efforts rather than getting directly involved themselves. Interestingly, once the families had restabilized after five years, little evidence of a relation between the marital relationship and parenting was found, a result that supports the findings of other researchers who have observed marital satisfaction and parenting to be less closely related in remarried than in nondivorced families (Hetherington, 1991, 1993).

The association of the quality of the marital relationship with children's behavior toward the stepfather varies with the age of the child. In newly remarried families with preadolescent children, especially with daughters, a close marital relationship is associated with high levels of negative, resistant behavior from children toward both the mother and the stepfather. This relation is not significant for preadolescent boys after two years of remarriage but is sustained for girls (Hetherington, 1993; Hetherington and Jodl, 1994). Furthermore, with preadolescent children, even in the longer remarried families, a close satisfying marital relationship is associated with both internalizing and acting out behavior in stepdaughters but with lower externalizing with stepsons (Hetherington, 1993). A satisfying marital relationship may be seen as more of a threat to continuation of close relationships between preadolescent daughters and their divorced mothers than it was to the frequently conflictual relations found between divorced mothers and sons.

In contrast to the findings with younger children when remarriages occur when children are early adolescents, both stepsons and stepdaughters are better adjusted and exhibit more positive, less conflictual parent–child relationships if parents have a close satisfying marital relationship (Hetherington, 1993; Hetherington and Clingempeel, 1992). Why should there be these differences in the correlates of marital satisfaction and the behavior of stepdaughters in preadolescent and early adolescent children? At this time, marked physical changes are occurring in children, and they are becoming sensitive to issues of intimate relationships and sexuality. Many nondivorced fathers are disconcerted by their adolescent daughters' burgeoning sexuality (Hill, Holmbeck, Marlow, Green, and Lynch, 1985a, 1985b) and are concerned about the proper expression of physical affection at this time. Concerns about affection and sexuality may be more severe in the case of stepfathers and stepdaughters. A close marital relationship may be seen by adolescent daughters and their parents as a buffer against the threat of inappropriate intimacy between stepfathers and stepdaughters (Hetherington, 1993; Hetherington and Kelly, in press).

Compared with first-marriage families, second-marriage families that include children appear to be have more permeable boundaries (Bray, 1999; Bray and Berger, 1993; Hetherington and Clingempeel, 1992). This greater permeability is reflected in greater complaints about childrearing conflict and stress in stepfamilies (Hetherington and Jodl, 1994) and the significantly higher rates of divorce in stepfamilies in which children are present (Tzeng and Mare, 1995). However, how adaptive or detrimental stepfamily subsystem permeability may be has yet to be determined. On the one hand, the permeability may provide adaptive flexibility in stepfamilies. On the other hand, greater permeability may mean that the new marriage is more vulnerable to child adjustment problems and difficulties in parent–child and stepparent–stepchild subsystems and relationships outside of the household.

Further investigations on the linkages among family subsystems, how they change over time, and how they affect child adjustment are needed. Moreover, studies of different kinds of stepfamilies also are needed. Some recent research suggests that complex stepfamilies such as blended families in which children share different patterns of biological relationships with parents in the household show more problems in family relationships, parenting, and child adjustment than do simple stepfamilies in which the only children present are from a mother's previous marriage (Dunn, Davies, O'Connor, and Sturgess, in press; Hetherington et al., 1999). Most critically required, however, are longitudinal studies that will permit some disentangling of direction of effects influences among systems such as between the parent–child and the marital systems and between parents' and children's behavior. Although it has been customary to think of parents as influencing children's behavior, it is apparent that, in adapting to divorce and remarriage, children play an important role in modifying the behavior of parents and stepparents (Anderson et al., 1999).

Summary

The challenges of establishing constructive, functional relationships within the family and with extended family members contribute to the risk of problems following remarriage. However, most family members, including children, perceive the remarriage as a positive life event (Anderson et al., 1999) and over time many remarried families appear able to achieve a workable integration of marital, parent–child, stepparent–child, and sibling subsystems. However, the higher divorce rate in remarried families and the frequent finding that multiple marital transitions are associated with inept parenting and poor adjustment in parents and children indicate that stepfamilies are high-risk situations. But, as Rutter (1998) has asked, "Does the risk lie in the person or the experience?" There is considerable evidence that antisocial individuals who indulge in risk behaviors and get involved in stressful life experiences tend to marry those with problems (DeGarmo and Forgatch, 1999; Dunn et al., in press). They also lack the self-regulation and interpersonal sensitivity and skills that are related to sustaining a satisfying marriage or to being a competent parent. To some extent these attributes are genetically based (McGue and Lykken, 1992; Reiss, Neiderhiser, Hetherington, and Plomin, 2000) and may contribute to multiple marital transitions, poor parenting, and problems in adjustment in children in divorced and remarried families. Genetic research studies of assortative mating and of the direction of effects between children's and parents' behavior are leading to innovative considerations about parenting and the development of children in divorced and remarried families.

DIVERSITY IN DIVORCED AND REMARRIED FAMILIES

The diversity evident in the responses of both parents and children to divorce and remarriage can be attributed to complex interactions among many factors including (1) parent and child gender, (2) the child's developmental status, (3) parent and child temperaments and personalities, and (4) the availability of both informal and formal supports. What follows is a brief summary of what is known about how these factors affect the immediate and the long-term adjustment of parents and children.

Parent and Child Gender

Although gender effects were commonly found in early studies of divorce, they are less frequently found in more recent studies (Amato and Keith, 1991a). Furthermore, whether or not gender is a factor in children's adjustment following marital transitions depends on the age of the child at the time of the family transition and at the time of assessment. Gender differences have been found in the adjustment of younger children to divorce and remarriage but are rarely found with adolescents in divorced families. Regardless of the custody arrangement following divorce, younger boys act out more than do girls in divorced families or children in nondivorced families (Allison and Furstenberg, 1989; Amato, 2001; Buchanan et al., 1996; Emery, 1994; Hetherington et al., 1985; Parke, 1996; Pasley and Ihinger-Tallman, 1994). Children in divorced families are more likely to exhibit more behavioral, emotional, social, and learning problems than are children in intact families, and these problems are more marked and enduring for young boys than for girls (Guidubaldi, Perry, and Nastasi, 1987; Hetherington et al., 1985; Zaslow, 1988).

In adolescence (Hetherington, 1993; Hetherington and Clingempeel, 1992; McLanahan and Sandefur, 1994) and in young adulthood (Zill et al., 1993) as girls are becoming more involved in heterosexual relationships, delayed effects may occur in previously well-adjusted daughters of divorced mothers in the form of early sexuality, teenage pregnancy, and unstable intimate relationships. Problems in precocious sexuality and substance abuse are especially likely to occur in early physically maturing girls who associate with older peers and have a nonauthoritative mother who is overtly sexually active with multiple partners (Hetherington, 1993; Hetherington and Kelly, in press). Furthermore, high stress, the absence of the biological father because of divorce, and the presence of a stepfather stimulate earlier menarche (Ellis and Garber, 2000; Hetherington, 1993). Thus more girls in divorced-mother-custody and stepfather families are likely to mature early, and their early maturity interacts with other factors to put them at risk for precocious sexual behavior (Hetherington, 1993; Hetherington and Kelly, in press).

The pattern of gender differences following remarriage of the custodial parent differs from that of the divorced parent. Young girls in both stepfather and stepmother families have more trouble adjusting to the entry of the stepparent than do boys (Brand et al., 1988; Hetherington and Clingempeel, 1992). Although both boys and girls may be initially upset and resistant to the new stepparent, preadolescent boys appear to adapt more quickly and benefit from the presence of an authoritative stepfather, and even in adolescence the presence of a stepfather protects boys against school dropout (Gunnoe, 1993; Hetherington, 1991, 1993; Hetherington and Clingempeel, 1992; Zill et al., 1993).

The gender differences found in the adjustment of younger children and in the qualities of interactions of the divorced parent and child may result from complex reciprocal interactions between adults and children. On the one hand, the gender differences found in young children in divorced families may be attributed to differences in how parents treat girls versus boys. For example, in divorcing families, sons are more likely than daughters to be exposed to parental conflict and to be exposed for longer periods of time (Hetherington, 1989; Hetherington et al., 1982). They may even have been exposed to more conflict before the divorce because parents with sons are more likely to stay together than are parents with daughters (Hetherington et al., 1982). Given that boys are more responsive to conflict (Anderson et al., 1999) and interpret family disagreements less positively than do girls (Epstein, Finnegan, and Gythall, 1979) and are less able to express their feelings in constructive ways or to solicit support from others when stressed, coping with such family conflict may be more difficult for boys than girls (Hetherington, 1989). Congruently, because preadolescent boys tend to be more noncompliant and aggressive than girls, their behavior may exacerbate the problems of the already stressed divorced mother.

In remarried families, differences in how nondivorced parents and stepparents act toward boys versus girls may be a reaction to the different behaviors exhibited by the children. For example, in one longitudinal study of adjustment in nondivorced, divorced-single-mother, and stepfather families, it was found that parenting of early adolescents in stepfather families may be more reactive than proactive (Anderson et al., 1999; Hetherington and Clingempeel, 1992). Earlier child externalizing was associated with increased subsequent negativity on the part of stepfathers. In addition, warm, supportive parenting by the remarried mother and stepfather was more likely to be evident in response to the children's earlier social competence. In remarried families, it is not surprising that stepparent–stepdaughter relationships are usually characterized as conflictual, given that stepdaughters tend to be more resistant and combative than stepsons when a new stepfather or stepmother enters the family (Bray and Berger, 1993; Hetherington and Clingempeel, 1992).

Children's Developmental Status

Researchers and practitioners alike have expressed concerns about how the timing of a divorce or remarriage relative to a child's developmental status affects the parent–child relationship and child adjustment. Unfortunately, studies of the effects of children's age at divorce or remarriage on children's adjustment to family transitions have produced inconsistent results. Some researchers have found that preschoolers who are unable to understand the reasons for the family disruption or to seek out extrafamilial supports are more adversely affected by their parents' divorce than are older children or adolescents (Allison and Furstenberg, 1989; Zill et al., 1993) and that these effects of timing of divorce extend into young adulthood (Amato and Keith, 1991a; Chase-Lansdale et al., 1995; Zill et al., 1993). Others have found evidence that adolescents are as adversely affected as young children (Frost and Pakiz, 1990; Needle, Su, and Doherty, 1990).

Although less work has been done on the timing of remarriage, there are indications that early adolescence may be an especially difficult time in which to have a remarriage occur. Younger children, especially boys, may eventually adapt to and directly benefit from the presence of a warm, involved stepfather and may benefit indirectly from improvements in the custodial mother's parenting associated with the support of a new spouse (Hetherington et al., 1985; Thomson et al., 1992). Furthermore, older adolescents and young adults feel some relief from the responsibility of economic, emotional, and social support of their divorced mother when a remarriage occurs. However, similar benefits have not been found when the remarriage occurs in early adolescence. At this time, dealing with the stresses associated with family formation may exacerbate problems in trying to cope with the pubertal transition, particularly those associated with autonomy and sexuality (Hetherington, 1991, 1993). Moreover, even in restabilized divorced-mother-headed and remarried families, in early adolescence family relationships may be disrupted, family cohesion may decline, and behavior problems may emerge in previously well-adjusted children (Bray, 1990; Hetherington, 1989, 1991; Hetherington and Clingempeel, 1992). For late adolescents, ongoing family conflict can lead to early disengagement from both divorced single-parent families and stepfamilies. Approximately one third of adolescent boys and one fourth of adolescent girls disengage and spend little time in family activities or at home. Home leaving, which is higher in girls in stepfamilies than in any other group, places adolescents at risk if they associate with antisocial peers without adult supervision (Cherlin and Furstenberg, 1994; Hetherington, 1999a).

Preexisting Problems, Temperament, and Personality

It has long been assumed that postdivorce and postremarriage problems observed in parent–child relationships and individual adjustment are caused by the stresses associated with family reorganization. However, this assumption can be attributed in part to the fact that most research has measured adjustment only after the marital transition occurred. Thus the degree to which preexisting conditions contribute to an initial divorce or to problems in subsequent marriages has rarely been examined. There is evidence, however, that for some children and their parents, greater emotional, behavioral, and academic problems and poorer parenting skills may be present before the divorce (Block, Block, and Gjerde, 1989; Bray and Berger, 1993; Capaldi and Patterson, 1991; Cherlin et al., 1991; Elder, Caspi, and Van Nguyen, 1992; Hetherington, 1991, 1999b).

Parents who are depressed or have antisocial personalities are more likely to divorce, to go through multiple marital transitions, and to be unskilled parents and less adaptable in the face of stresses associated with marital transitions (Block et al., 1989; Capaldi and Patterson, 1991; Emery, 1999b). Antisocial or depressed parents may find it particularly difficult to deal with the emotional acting-out behavior in children associated with divorce or remarriage. These difficulties are likely to be exacerbated if the parent relies on distancing or escape–avoidance coping strategies (Holloway and Machida, 1991). On the other hand, parents who normally rely on more active behavioral and cognitive coping strategies in stressful life circumstances are more likely to feel they are in control in childrearing situations and are more capable of maintaining an authoritative parenting style.

Children whose parents will later divorce exhibit more behavior problems before their parents' divorce than do children in nondivorced families (Block et al., 1989; Capaldi and Patterson, 1991; Cherlin et al., 1991; Hetherington, 1999b). Some researchers have suggested that children who are troubled before the divorce are simply responding to family problems, conflict, and inept parenting already evident. However, in a study of adjustment problem among late adolescents and young adults of divorced parents, Chase-Lansdale et al. (1995) found that adjustment problems remain high even when problems evident before the divorce are controlled.

It may be that a coping pattern similar to that observed in parents appears in children. Temperamentally difficult children are more likely than temperamentally easy children to elicit and receive their parents' criticism and displaced anger and anxiety, especially when parents are stressed, and they are less able to cope with erratic parenting and adverse life circumstances when they occur (Rutter, 1987; Werner, 1988). Furthermore, children with difficult temperaments are more likely to have preexisting emotional and behavioral problems that are exacerbated by the stresses of family disruption and reorganization (Block et al., 1989; Hetherington, 1989, 1991; Patterson and Dishion, 1988). Moreover, it may be that having to deal with difficult children strains troubled marriages to the breaking point (Hetherington and Mekos, 1992). In contrast, children who are socially competent, intelligent, high in self-esteem, have an internal locus of control, and a good sense of humor are more likely than temperamentally difficult children to evoke positive responses from potential support figures and to adapt to the challenges associated with family transitions (Hetherington, 1989, 1991).

Support Systems

Perceived availability and use of both informal supports (e.g., friends, extended family members) and formal supports (e.g., divorce mediation, shared-parenting classes) can do much to ameliorate the negative impact of adverse life events including the stresses associated with marital transitions (Aseltine and Kessler, 1993; DeGarmo and Forgatch, 1999; Hughes, Good, and Candell, 1993; Simons, Beaman, Conger, and Chao, 1993). To date, however, most of the research on the associations between supports and family transition adjustment has been limited to studies of divorced families, particularly divorced-single-mother families. The impact on remarried family adjustment has been largely unexplored.

Informal support systems. Social support promotes the psychological well-being of divorced women and enhances their problem solving, and protective function occurs through the support of both kin and friends. Approximately one third of the children of single mothers live in a household with adult kin in addition to their mothers, with this rate being higher in African American than in European American families. Coresidence often is a temporary arrangement because most parents when they become economically self-sufficient prefer living on their own. Still, those single mothers who opt to live with kin report less depression, greater happiness, and better physical health than mothers who live alone. They also report fewer behavior problems among their adolescent children, perhaps because there are more adults available to supervise and monitor the adolescents' activities (Amato, 2000).

For children whose home environments are changing and whose parents are temporarily unresponsive, support can come from outside the home. For example, daycare centers and schools that offer warm, structured, and stable environments can provide the stability children lack at home

(Hetherington and Kelly, in press; Hetherington and Jodl, 1994). Responsive adults such as teachers, coaches, or parents of friends can help children maintain feelings of self-worth, competence, and self-control (Guidubaldi et al., 1987; Hetherington et al., 1982, 1985; Rutter, 1987). As children get older and move into adolescence, siblings and peers can be important sources of support, and children in divorced and remarried families are especially susceptible to peer pressure (Hetherington, 1991).

Divorce Mediation

Some states now require divorcing parents to submit parenting plans detailing how they will rear their children and deal with conflict, visitation, residence, custody, and relocation. Although there is little rigorous research evaluating the effects of parenting plans on parental behavior, participating in parenting plans has seemed to encourage and increase the rate of joint legal custody (Ellis, 1990). Sometimes parenting plans are incorporated as part of the process of divorce mediation, which has been instituted in many states in an effort to reduce the conflict that often erupts and escalates when divorcing couples disagree about child support, custody, or visitation arrangements. Participation is recommended in some states, required in others, and the content and the quality of divorce mediation programs are as diverse as the families they are designed to assist. The primary goal of most mediation programs, however, is to provide the opportunity for couples to reach decisions about child custody and visitation in an environment less acrimonious and adversarial than a court setting. Decisions about disputed assets and financial support typically are resolved through court litigation.

Generally, couples who resolve custody and visitation disputes through mediation rather than through more adversarial court litigation are less likely to need or pursue further court hearings, more likely to reach resolutions more quickly, and more likely to comply with agreements (Emery, 1999a, Emery, Matthews, and Wyer, 1991). Early studies of the impact of divorce mediation on parents' satisfaction with the resolution process also suggested that parents are more satisfied with the resolution process when disputes are mediated rather than litigated (Emery et al., 1991). However, the results of additional work indicate that beliefs about the fairness of the resolution process and satisfaction with agreements differ for fathers and mothers (Emery, 1994). Despite the legal emphasis on gender-neutral custody decisions, many courts still interpret the "best interests of the child" as mother custody. Thus when custody disputes are litigated in the court rather than mediated in a less adversarial setting, fathers are still more likely to lose the custody battle. When arrangements are worked out through mediation, however, joint legal custody is the more likely outcome (Emery and Wyer, 1987; Emery et al., 1991). Not surprisingly, compared with fathers who go through litigation, fathers who go through mediation are more likely to report that their interests and rights have been protected and that they are satisfied with the agreements. For mothers, the picture is less clear. Although both mothers who go through mediation and mothers who go through litigation report that their rights have been protected, litigating mothers who are more likely to receive sole custody are more satisfied with the resultant agreements (Emery et al., 1991; Emery and Wyer, 1987).

Shared-Parenting Programs

Although divorce mediation can help parents reach custody and financial settlements with less conflict than found when decisions are litigated, divorce mediation does not appear to promote better psychological well-being for either parents or children (Emery et al., 1999) and rarely addresses coparenting after the legal divorce. However, evidence that a cooperative, consensual coparenting arrangement is in the best interests of the child has fostered a rapid growth in shared-parenting programs. Many use cognitive therapy and family systems principles to help divorced couples learn shared-parenting skills (see Kramer and Washo, 1993; Leek, 1992) with the goals of improving communication between the parents and helping them develop a pattern of functioning that is adaptive for each family member. In order to work, the programs frequently must help couples come to terms with their own preexisting problems and recognize that their problems are between them and involving their children is likely to prove detrimental to their children's adjustment. Shared-parenting programs are promising, but it might be expected that, unless court mandated, only exceptionally concerned child-oriented parents would become involved in such programs.

Stepfamily therapy. Compared with therapies and programs designed to help divorced-single-parent families restabilize, therapies and programs that address the special needs of stepfamilies in transition are relatively new, and there is little research to measure their success. However, what little is known indicates that stepfamilies benefit from programs that help them to validate their lives, strengthen the marital relationship, and develop a parenting coalition (Visher and Visher, 1994).

The 1990s witnessed a rapid rise in interventions and support programs such as divorce mediation, shared-parenting classes, changes in custody laws, and targeted therapies and coping-skills training programs for children and their parents. Such programs indicate an increasing awareness of the need to address those factors that are most likely to ameliorate or exacerbate problems in divorced homes, but more longitudinal evaluative research needs to be conducted before firm conclusions are reached about their effectiveness (Emery, 1999a; Grych and Fincham, 1992; Patterson, 1992). With growing recognition of the number of children living in remarried families, more policies and more programs designed to meet the special needs of these families are to be expected. At present, however, there is little empirical evidence to guide these efforts (Emery, 1999a; Maccoby et al., 1993; Visher and Visher, 1994).

CONCLUSIONS

Each marital transition is characterized by an initial period of disequilibrium followed by reorganization and eventual restabilization. The patterns of equilibrium attained, however, are likely to differ from either the patterns that existed before the transition or the patterns observed in many nondivorced families. These differences may be due to the stresses during and following transition, and they may reflect adaptive changes in interaction processes rather than the presence of problems within the families (Bray and Berger, 1993).

In the past two decades, a substantial body of research knowledge has been gathered on the functioning of divorced families and the adjustment of children in mother-headed households. Less is known about the family system, family processes, and the development of children in father-custody or remarried families. What is notable is the great diversity in children's responses to their parents' marital transitions and the central role that involved, responsive parenting plays in the resiliency and adaptability of children in all families.

Research findings indicate that children are more resilient than was once thought. Studies of children's adjustment to divorce and remarriage have shown that relatively few children and adolescents experience enduring problems (Amato and Keith, 1991a; Hetherington and Clingempeel, 1992; Hetherington and Kelly, in press; Hetherington et al., 1998). Rather than concluding that parental divorce and remarriage are preludes to serious or pervasive adjustment problems in most children, it would be more accurate to conclude that family transitions place children at risk. Whether or not they experience severe problems is likely to be determined by complex interactions among many factors. Some of the important factors appear to be those associated with adjustment problems in any family, the presence of concurrent stressors such as continued financial distress in the household, household disorganization, children's involvement in parental conflict, disrupted parenting practices, and lack of effective support systems. Although all of these variables are important, the presence of an involved, caring, responsive authoritative adult plays a critical role in protecting children from the possible adverse effects of divorce and remarriage and in promoting children's psychological well-being when they are coping with the changes and challenges associated with marital transitions.

REFERENCES

Allison, P. D., and Furstenberg, F. F. (1989). How marital dissolution affects children: Variations by age and sex. *Developmental Psychology, 25*, 540–549.

Amato, P. R. (1987). Parental divorce and attitudes toward family life. *Journal of Marriage and the Family, 50*, 453–461.

Amato, P. R. (1994). The implications of research findings on children in stepfamilies. In A. Booth and J. Dunn (Eds.), *Stepfamilies: Who benefits? Who does not?* (pp. 81–87). Hillsdale, NJ: Lawrence Erlbaum Associates.

Amato, P. R. (1999a). Children of divorced parents as young adults. In E. Hetherington (Ed.), *Coping with divorce, single parenting, and remarriage* (pp. 147–163). Mahwah, NJ: Lawrence Erlbaum Associates.

Amato, P. R. (1999b). Nonresident fathers and children's well-being: A meta-analysis. *Journal of Marriage and the Family, 61*, 557–573.

Amato, P. R. (2000). Diversity within single parent families. In D. H. Demo, K. R. Allen, and M. A. Fine (Eds.), *Handbook of family diversity* (pp. 149–172). New York: Oxford University Press.

Amato, P. (2001). Children of divorce in the 1990's: An update of the Amato and Keith (1991) meta-analysis. *Journal of Family Psychology, 15*, 355–370.

Amato, P. R., and Booth, A. (1997). *A generation at risk: Growing up in an era of family upheaval.* Cambridge, MA: Harvard University Press.

Amato, P. R., and Gilbreth, J. G. (1999). Nonresident fathers and children's well being: A meta-analysis. *Journal of Marriage and the Family, 61*, 557–573.

Amato, P. R., and Keith, B. (1991a). Parental divorce and the well-being of children: A meta-analysis. *Psychological Bulletin, 110*, 26–46.

Amato, P. R., and Keith, B. (1991b). Parental divorce and adult well-being: A meta-analysis. *Journal of Marriage and the Family, 53*, 43–58.

Amato, P. R., Loomis, L. S., and Booth, A. (1995). Parental divorce, marital conflict, and offspring well-bring during early adulthood. *Social Forces, 73*, 895–915.

Anderson, E. R., Greene, S. M., Hetherington, E. M., and Clingempeel, W. G. (1999). The dynamics of parental remarriage: Adolescent, parent, and sibling influences. In E. M. Hetherington (Ed.), *Coping with divorce, single parenting and remarriage: A risk and resiliency perspective* (pp. 295–319). Mahwah, NJ: Lawrence Erlbaum Associates.

Arditti, J. A. (1992). Differences between fathers with joint custody and noncustodial fathers. *American Journal of Orthopsychiatry, 62*, 186–194.

Arditti, J. A., and Allen, K. R. (1993). Understanding distressed fathers' perceptions of legal and relational inequalities postdivorce. *Family and Conciliation Courts Review, 31*, 699–712.

Arditti, J. A., and Madden-Derdich, D. A. (1995). No regrets: Custodial mothers' accounts of the difficulties and benefits of divorce. *Contemporary Family Therapy, 17*, 229–248.

Arendell, T. (1995). *Fathers and divorce.* Thousand Oaks, CA: Sage.

Aseltine, R. H., and Kessler, R. C. (1993). Marital disruption and depression in a community sample. *Journal of Health and Social Behavior, 34*, 237–251.

Avenoli, S., Sessa, F. M., and Steinberg, L. (1999). Family structure, parenting practices, and adolescent adjustment: An ecological examination. In E. M. Hetherington (Ed.), *Coping with divorce, single parenting and remarriage: A risk and resiliency perspective* (pp. 65–90). Mahwah, NJ: Lawrence Erlbaum Associates.

Bank, L., Forgatch, M. S., Patterson, G. R., and Fetrow, R. A. (1991). *Parenting practices: Mediators of negative contextual factors in divorce.* Unpublished manuscript.

Baumrind, D. (1991). Effective parenting during the early adolescent transition. In P. A. Cowan and E. M. Hetherington (Eds.), *Family transitions* (pp. 111–163). Hillsdale, NJ: Lawrence Erlbaum Associates.

Benjamin, M., and Irving, H. H. (1990). Comparison of the experience of satisfied and dissatisfied shared parents. *Journal of Divorce and Remarriage, 14*, 43–61.

Block, J., Block, J. H., and Gjerde, P. F. (1989). Parental functioning and the home environment in families of divorce: Prospective and concurrent analyses. *Annual Progress in Child Psychiatry and Child Development, 12*, 192–207.

Brand, E., and Clingempeel, W. G. (1987). Interdependence of marital and stepparent–stepchild relationships and children's psychological adjustment: Research findings and clinical implications. *Family Relations Journal of Applied Family and Child Studies, 36*, 140–145.

Brand, E., Clingempeel, W. G., and Bowen-Woodward, K. (1988). Family relationships and children's psychosocial adjustment in stepmother and stepfather families. In E. M. Hetherington and J. D. Arasteh (Eds.), *The impact of divorce, single-parenting, and stepparenting on children* (pp. 299–324). Hillsdale, NJ: Lawrence Erlbaum Associates.

Braver, S. L., Wolchik, S. A., Sandler, I. N., Sheets, V. L., Fogas, B., and Bay, R. C. (1993). A longitudinal study of non-custodial parents: Parents without children. *Journal of Family Psychology, 7*, 1–16.

Bray, J. H. (1988). Children's development in early remarriage. In E. M. Hetherington and J. D. Arasteh (Eds.), *The impact of divorce, single-parenting, and step-parenting on children* (pp. 279–298). Hillsdale, NJ: Lawrence Erlbaum Associates.

Bray, J. H. (1990). Impact of divorce on the family. In R. E. Rakel (Ed.), *Textbook of family practice* (4th ed., pp. 111–122). Philadelphia: Saunders.

Bray, J. H. (1992). Family relationships and children's adjustment in clinical and nonclinical stepfather families. *Journal of Family Psychology*, *6*, 60–68.

Bray, J. H. (1999). From marriage to remarriage and beyond: Findings from the Developmental Issues in Stepfamilies Research Project. In E. M. Hetherington (Ed.), *Coping with divorce, single parenting, and remarriage: A risk and resiliency perspective* (pp. 253–271). Mahwah, NJ: Lawrence Erlbaum Associates.

Bray, J. H., and Berger, S. H. (1993). Developmental issues in stepfamilies research project: Family relationships and parent–child interactions. *Journal of Family Psychology*, *7*, 1–17.

Bray, J. H., Berger, S. H., and Boethal, C. (1994). Role integration and marital adjustment in stepfather families. In K. Pasley and M. Ihinger-Tallman (Eds.), *Stepparenting* (pp. 69–87). Westport, CT: Greenwood.

Bronfenbrenner, U. (1986). Ecology of the family as a context for human development. *Developmental Psychology*, *22*, 723–742.

Brooks-Gunn, J. (1994). Research on stepparenting families. In A. Booth and J. Dunn (Eds.), *Stepfamilies* (pp. 157–189). Hillsdale, NJ: Lawrence Erlbaum Associates.

Brown, A. C., Green, R. J., and Druckman, J. (1990). A comparison of stepfamilies with and without child-focused problems. *American Journal of Orthopsychiatry*, *60*, 556–566.

Buchanan, C. M., Maccoby, E. E., and Dornbusch, S. M. (1991). Caught between parents: Adolescents' experience in divorced homes. *Child Development*, *62*, 1008–1029.

Buchanan, C. M., Maccoby, E. E., and Dornbusch, S. M. (1996). *Adolescents after divorce*. Cambridge, MA: Harvard University Press.

Bumpass, L. L., and Raley, R. K. (1995). Redefining single-parent families: Cohabitation and changing family therapy. *Demography*, *32*, 97–109.

Burchardt, N. (1990). Stepchildren's memories: Myth, understanding, and forgiveness. In R. Samual and P. Thompson (Eds.), *The myths we live by* (pp. 239–251). London: Routledge.

Bursik, K. (1999). Correlates of women's adjustment during the separation and divorce process. *Journal of Divorce and Remarriage*, *14*, 137–162.

Capaldi, D. M., and Patterson, G. R. (1991). Relation of parental transitions to boys' adjustment problems: I. A linear hypothesis. II. Mothers at risk for transitions and unskilled parenting. *Developmental Psychology*, *27*, 489–504.

Chase-Lansdale, P. L., Cherlin, A. J., and Kiernan, K. K. (1995). The long-term effects of parental divorce on the mental health of young adults: A developmental perspective. *Child Development*, *66*, 1614–1634.

Chase-Lansdale, P. L., and Hetherington, E. M. (1990). The impact of divorce on life-span development: Short and long term effects. In P. B. Baltes, D. L. Featherman, and R. M. Lerner (Eds.), *Life-span development and behavior* (Vol. 10, pp. 105–150). Hillsdale, NJ: Lawrence Erlbaum Associates.

Cherlin, A. J., Chase-Lansdale, P. L., and McRae, B. (1998). Effects of parental divorce on mental health throughout the life course. *American Sociological Review*, *63*, 239–249.

Cherlin, A. J., and Furstenberg, F. F. (1994). Stepfamilies in the United States. *Review of Sociology*, *20*, 359–381.

Cherlin, A. J., Furstenberg, F. F., Chase-Lansdale, P. L., Kiernan, K. E., Robins, P. K., Morrison, D. R., and Teitler, J. O. (1991). Longitudinal studies of the effects of divorce on children in Great Britain and the United States. *Science*, *252*, 1386–1389.

Church, E. (1999). Who are the people in your family: Stepmothers' divorce notions of kinship. *Journal of Divorce and Remarriage*, *31*, 83–104.

Clarke-Stewart, K. A., and Hayward, C. (1996). Advantages of father custody and contract for the psychological well-being of school-age children. *Journal of Applied Developmental Psychology*, *17*, 239–270.

Cohen, O. (1995). Divorced fathers raise their children by themselves. *Journal of Divorce and Remarriage*, *23*, 55–73.

Colletta, N. D. (1981). Social support and risk of maternal rejection by adolescent mothers. *Journal of Psychology*, *109*, 191–197.

Daly, M., and Wilson, M. (1989). The Darwinian psychology of discriminative parental solicitude. In J. Berman (Ed.). *Nebraska symposium on motivation* (pp. 211–234). Lincoln, NE: University of Nebraska Press.

DeGarmo, D. S., and Forgatch, M. S. (1999). Contexts as predictors of changing maternal parenting practices in diverse family structures: A social interactional perspective of risk and resiliency. In E. M. Hetherington (Ed.), *Coping with divorce, single parenting, and remarriage: A risk and resiliency perspective* (pp. 227–252). Mahwah, NJ: Lawrence Erlbaum Associates.

Downey, D. B. (1994). The school performance of single mother and single father families: Economic or interpersonal deprivation? *Journal of Family Issues*, *15*, 129–147.

Dunn, J., Davies, L., O'Connor, R., and Sturgess, M. (in press). Parents' and partners' life course and family experiences: Links with parent-child relationships in different family settings. *Journal of Family Psychology*.

Ellis, J. W. (1990). Plans, protections, and professional intervention: Innovations in divorce custody reform and the role of legal professionals. *University of Michigan Journal of Law Reform*, *24*, 65–188.

Ellis, B. J., and Garber, J. (2000). Psychosocial antecedents of variation in girls' pubertal timing: Maternal depression, stepfather presence, and marital and family stress. *Child Development*, *71*, 485–501.

Emery, R. E. (1994). *Renegotiating family relationships: Divorce, child custody, and mediation*. New York: Guilford.

Emery, R. E. (1999a). Psychological interventions for separated and divorced families. In E. M. Hetherington (Ed.), *Coping with divorce, single parenting, and remarriage: A risk and resiliency perspective* (pp. 253–271). Mahwah, NJ: Lawrence Erlbaum Associates.

Emery, R. E. (1999b). *Marriage, divorce and childrens' adjustment*. Thousand Oaks, CA: Sage.

Emery, R. E., Matthews, S. G., and Wyer, M. M. (1991). Child custody mediation and litigation: Further evidence on the differing views of mothers and fathers. *Journal of Consulting and Clinical Psychology*, *59*, 410–418.

Emery, R. E., and Wyer, M. M. (1987). Child custody mediation and litigation: An experimental evaluation of the experience of parents. *Journal of Consulting and Clinical Psychology*, *55*, 179–186.

Epstein, N., Finnegan, D., and Gythall, D. (1979). Irrational beliefs and perceptions of marital conflict. *Journal of Consulting and Clinical Psychology*, *67*, 608–609.

Fine, M. A., Coleman, M., and Ganong, L. H. (1999). A social constructionist multi-method approach to understanding the stepparent role. In E. M. Hetherington (Ed.), *Coping with divorce, single parenting, and remarriage: A risk and resiliency perspective* (pp. 273–294). Mahwah, NJ: Lawrence Erlbaum Associates.

Fine, M. A., and Kurdek, L. A. (1994). A model of family adjustment. In K. Pasley and M. Ihinger-Tallman (Eds.), *Stepparenting* (pp. 33–51). Westport, CT: Greenwood.

Fine, M., Voydanoff, P., and Donelly, N. W. (1993). The relations between parental control and warmth and child well being in stepfamilies. *Journal of Family Psychology*, *7*, 222–232.

Forgatch, M. S., Patterson, G. R., and Ray, J. A. (1996). Divorce and boys' adjustment problems: Two paths with a single model. In E. M. Hetherington and E. Blechman (Eds.), *Stress, coping, and resiliency in children and the family* (pp. 67–105). Mahwah, NJ: Lawrence Erlbaum Associates.

Frost, A. K., and Pakiz, B. (1990). The effects of marital disruption on adolescents: Time as a dynamic. *American Journal of Orthopsychiatry*, *60*, 544–555.

Furstenberg, F. F. (1988). Child care after divorce and remarriage. In E. M. Hetherington and J. Arasteh (Eds.), *Impact of divorce, single-parenting, and stepparenting on children* (pp. 245–261). Hillsdale, NJ: Lawrence Erlbaum Associates.

Furstenberg, F. F. (1990). Divorce and the American family. *Annual Review of Sociology*, *16*, 379–403.

Furstenberg, F. F., and Cherlin, A. (1991). *Divided families: What happens to children when parents part*. Cambridge, MA: Harvard University Press.

Furstenberg, F. F., and Nord, C. W. (1987). Parenting apart: Patterns of childrearing after marital disruption. *Journal of Marriage and the Family*, *47*, 893–904.

Ganong, L. H., and Coleman, M. (1994). *Remarried Family Relationships*. Thousand Oaks, CA: Sage.

Grych, J. H., and Fincham, F. D. (1992). Marital conflict and children's adjustment: A cognitive–contextual framework. *Psychological Bulletin*, *108*, 267–290.

Guidubaldi, J., Perry, J. D., and Nastasi, B. K. (1987). Growing up in a divorced family: Initial and long-term perspectives on children's adjustment. *Applied Social Psychology Annual*, *7*, 202–237.

Gunnoe, M. L. (1993, June). *Noncustodial mothers' and fathers' contributions to the adjustment of adolescent stepchildren*. Unpublished doctoral dissertation, University of Virginia Charlottesville.

Hanson, T. L., Garfinkel, I., McLanahan, S. S., and Miller, C. K. (1996). Trends in child support outcomes. *Demography*, *33*, 483–496.

Hetherington, E. M. (1988). Parents, children, and siblings six years after divorce. In R. Hinde and J. Stevenson-Hinde (Eds.), *Relationships within families* (pp. 311–331). Cambridge, England: Cambridge University Press.

Hetherington, E. M. (1989). Coping with family transitions: Winners, losers, and survivors. *Child Development*, *60*, 1–14.

Hetherington, E. M. (1991). Families, lies, and videotapes. *Journal of Research on Adolescence*, *1*, 323–348.

Hetherington, E. M. (1993). An overview of the Virginia longitudinal study of divorce and remarriage with a focus on early adolescence. *Journal of Family Psychology*, *7*, 1–18.

Hetherington, E. M. (1999a). Should we stay together for the sake of the children? In E. M. Hetherington (Ed.), *Coping with divorce, single parenting, and remarriage: A risk and resiliency perspective* (pp. 93–116). Mahwah, NJ: Erlbaum Associates.

Hetherington, E. M. (1999b). Social capital and the development of youth from Nondivorced, divorced, and remarried families. In J. A. Collins and B. Laursen (Eds.), *Relationships as developmental contexts: The 29th Minnesota symposium on child psychology* (Vol. 30, pp. 177–210). Mahwah, NJ: Lawrence Erlbaum and Associates.

Hetherington, E. M., and Anderson, E. R. (1987). The effects of divorce and remarriage on early adolescents and their families. In M. D. Levine and E. R. McAnarney (Eds.), *Early adolescent transitions* (pp. 49–67). Lexington, MA: Heath.

Hetherington, E. M., Bridges, M., and Insabella, G. M. (1998). What matters? What does not?: Five perspectives on the association between marital transitions and children's adjustment. *American Psychologist*, *53*, 167–184.

Hetherington, E. M., and Clingempeel, W. G. (1992). Coping with marital transitions: A family systems perspective. *Monographs of the Society for Child Development* (Serial No. 227, *57*, Nos. 2–3).

Hetherington, E. M., Cox, M., and Cox, R. (1982). Effects of divorce on parents and children. In M. E. Lamb (Ed.), *Nontraditional families* (pp. 233–288). Hillsdale, NJ: Lawrence Erlbaum Associates.

Hetherington, E. M., Cox, M., and Cox, R. (1985). Long-term effects of divorce and remarriage on the adjustment of children. *Journal of the American Academy of Child Psychiatry, 24*, 518–530.

Hetherington, E. M., and Henderson, S. H. (1997). Fathers in stepfamilies. In M. Lamb (Ed.), *The father's role in child development* (pp. 212–226). New York: Wiley.

Hetherington, E. M., Henderson, S. H., Reiss, D., Anderson, E. R., Bridges, M., Chan, R., Insabella, G. M., Jodl, K. M., Jungmeen, E., Mitchell, A. S., O'Connor, T. G., Skaggs, M. J., and Taylor, L. C. (1999). Adolescent siblings in step-families: Family functioning and adolescent adjustment. *Monographs of the Society for Research in Child Development, 64* (4).

Hetherington, E. M., and Jodl, K. (1994). Stepfamilies as settings for development. In A. Booth and J. Dunn (Eds.), *Stepfamilies* (pp. 55–80). Cambridge, MA: Harvard University Press.

Hetherington, E. M., and Kelly, J. (in press). For better or for worse: Divorce reconsidered. New York: Norton.

Hetherington, E. M., and Stanley-Hagan, M. (1997). The effects of divorce on fathers and their children. In M. Lamb (Ed.), *The role of the father in child development* (pp. 191–211). New York: Wiley.

Hetherington, E. M., and Stanley-Hagan, M. (1999). Diversity in stepfamilies. In D. Demo, K. Allen, and M. Fine (Eds.), *Handbook of family diversity* (pp. 173–196). New York: Wiley.

Hill, J., Holmbeck, G., Marlow, L., Green, T., and Lynch, M. (1985a). Menarcheal status and parent–child relations in families with seventh grade girls. *Journal of Youth and Adolescence, 14*, 301–316.

Hill, J., Holmbeck, G., Marlow, L., Green, T., and Lynch, M. (1985b). Pubertal status and parent–child relations in families of seventh grade boys. *Journal of Early Adolescence, 5*, 31–44.

Holloway, S. D., and Machida, S. (1991). Child-rearing effectiveness of divorced mothers: Relationship to coping strategies and social support [Special issue: Women and divorce/men and divorce]. *Journal of Divorce and Remarriage, 14*, 179–201.

Hughes, R., Good, E. S., and Candell, K. (1993). A longitudinal study of the effects of social support on the psychological adjustment of divorced mothers. *Journal of Divorce and Remarriage, 19*, 37–57.

Ihinger-Tallman, M., Pasley, K., and Buehler, C. (1995). Developing a middle-range theory of father involvement postdivorce. In W. Marsiglio (Ed.), *Fatherhood: Contemporary theory, research, and social policy: Research on men and masculinit* (Series 7, pp. 57–77). Thousand Oaks, CA: Sage.

Johnston, J. R. (1990). Role diffusion and role reversal: Structural variations in divorced families and children's functioning. *Family Relations, 39*, 405–413.

Johnston, J. R. (1994). High conflict divorces. *The Future of Children, 4*, 165–182.

Johnston, J. R., Kline, M., and Tschann, J. (1989). Ongoing post-divorce conflict in families contesting custody: Effects on children of joint custody and frequent access. *American Journal of Orthopsychiatry, 59*, 576–592.

Kerig, P. K., Cowan, P. A., and Cowan, C. P. (1993). Marital quality and gender differences in parent–child interaction. *Developmental Psychology, 29*, 931–939.

Kiecolt-Glaser, J. K., Fisher, L. D., Ogrocki, P., Stout, J. C., Speicher, C. E., and Glaser, R. (1987). Marital quality, marital disruption, and immune function. *Psychosomatic Medicine, 49*, 13–34.

Kitson, G. C., and Holmes, W. M. (1992). *Portrait of divorce: Adjustment to marital breakdown*. New York: Guilford.

Kramer, L., and Washo, C. A. (1993). Evaluation of a court mandated prevention program for divorcing parents: The Children First Program. *Family Relations, 42*, 179–186.

Leek, D. F. (1992). Shared parenting support program. *American Journal of Forensic Psychology, 10*, 49–64.

Maccoby, E. E., Buchanan, C. M., Mnookin, R. H., and Dornbusch, S. M. (1993). Post-divorce roles of mothers and fathers in the lives of their children. *Journal of Family Psychology, 7*, 1–15.

Maccoby, E. E., Depner, C. E., and Mnookin, R. H. (1990). Co-parenting in the second year after divorce. *Journal of Marriage and the Family, 52*, 141–155.

Maccoby, E. E., and Mnookin, R. H. (1992). *Dividing the child: Social and legal dilemmas of custody*. Cambridge, MA: Harvard University Press.

MacDonald, W. L., and DeMaris, A. (1996). Parenting stepchildren and biological children: The effects of stepparents' gender and new biological children. *Journal of Family Issues, 17*, 5–25.

Marsiglio, W. (1992). Stepfathers with minor children living at home: Parenting perceptions and relationship quality. *Journal of Family Issues, 13*, 195–214.

Martin, T., and Bumpass, L. (1989). Recent trends in marital disruption. *Demography, 26*, 37–51.

McGue, M., and Lykken, D. T. (1992). Genetic influence on the risk of divorce. *Psychological Science, 3*, 368–373.

McLanahan, S. (1999). Father absence and the welfare of children. In E. M. Hetherington (Ed.), *Coping with divorce, single parenting, and remarriage: A risk and resiliency perspective* (pp. 117–145). Mahwah, NJ: Lawrence Erlbaum Associates.

McLanahan, S., and Sandefur, G. (1994). *Growing up with a single parent*. Cambridge, MA: Harvard University Press.

Meyer, D. R., and Garasky, S. (1993). Custodial fathers: Myths, realities, and child support policy. *Journal of Marriage and the Family, 55*, 73–89.

Minton, C., and Pasley, K. (1996). Fathers' parenting role identity and father involvement: A comparison of nondivorced and divorced, nonresident fathers. *Journal of Family Issues, 17*, 26–45.

Minuchin, S., and Nichols, M. (1994). *Family healing*. New York: Simon and Schuster.

Morrison, D. R., and Cherlin, A. J. (1995). The divorce process and young children's well being: A prospective study. *Journal of Marriage and the Family, 57*, 800–812.

Needle, R. H., Su, S. S., and Doherty, W. J. (1990). Divorce, remarriage and adolescent substance abuse: A prospective longitudinal study. *Journal of Marriage and the Family, 52*, 157–169.

Neilson, L. (1999). Stepmothers: Why so much stress? A review of the research. *Journal of Divorce and Remarriage, 30*, 115–148.

O'Connor, T. G., Thorpe, K., Dunn, J., and Golding, J. (1999). Parental divorce and adjustment in adulthood: Findings from a community sample. *Journal of Child Psychology and Psychiatry and Allied Disciplines, 40*, 777–789.

Papernow, P. (1993). *Becoming a stepfamily*. San Francisco: Jossey-Bass.

Parke, R. D. (1996). *Fatherhood*. Cambridge, MA: Harvard University Press.

Pasley, K., and Ihinger-Tallman, M. (1994). *Stepparenting issues in theory, research, and practice*. Westport, CT: Greenwood.

Patterson, G. R. (1992). Developmental changes in antisocial behavior. In R. D. Peters, R. J. McMahon, V. L. Quinsey (Eds.), *Aggression and violence throughout the life span* (pp. 52–82). Newbury Park, CA: Sage.

Patterson, G. R., and Dishion, T. J. (1988). Multilevel family process models: Traits, interactions and relationships. In R. A. Hinde and J. Stevenson-Hinde (Eds.), *Relationships within families* (pp. 283–310). London: Clarendon.

Pink, J., and Wampler, K. (1985). Problem areas in stepfamilies: Cohesion, adaptability and the stepparent-adolescent relationship. *Family Relations, 34*, 327–335.

Popenoe, D., Elshtain, J. B., and Blankenhorn, D. (Eds.). (1996). *Promises to keep: Decline and renewal of marriage in America*. Lanham, MD: Rowman and Littlefield.

Powell, M. A., and Parcel, T. L. (1997). Effects of family structure on the earnings process: Differences by gender. *Journal of Marriage and the Family, 59*, 419–433.

Quick, D., McKenry, P., and Newman, B. (1994). Stepmothers and their adolescent children. In K. Pasley and M. Ihinger-Tallman (Eds.), *Stepparenting* (pp. 105–127). Westport, CT: Greenwood.

Reiss, D., Neiderhiser, J. M., Hetherington, E. M., and Plomin, R. (2000). *The relationship code: Deciphering genetic and social influences on adolescent development*. Cambridge, MA: Harvard University Press.

Rutter, M. (1987). Psychosocial resilience and protective mechanisms. *American Journal of Orthopsychiatry, 57*, 316–331.

Rutter, M. (1998). Some research considerations on intergenerational continuities and discontinuities. *Developmental Psychology, 34*, 1269–1273.

Salwen, L. V. (1990). The myth of the wicked stepmother [Special issue: Motherhood: A feminist perspective]. *Women and Therapy, 10*, 117–125.

Santrock, J. W., Sitterle, K. A., and Warshak, R. A. (1988). Parent–child relationships in stepfather families. In P. Bronstein and C. P. Cowan (Eds.), *Fatherhood today: Men's changing roles in the family*. New York: Wiley.

Santrock, J. W., and Warshak, R. A. (1979). Father custody and social development in boys and girls. *Journal of Social Issues, 35*, 112–125.

Seltzer, J. A. (1991). Relationships between father and children who live apart: The father's role after separation. *Journal of Marriage and the Family, 53*, 79–101.

Seltzer, T. A. (1998). Father by law: Effects of joint legal custody on nonresident fathers' involvement with children. *Demography, 35*, 135–146.

Seltzer, J. A. (2000). Families formed outside of marriage. *Journal of Marriage and the Family, 62*, 1247–1268.

Shapiro, A., and Lambert, J. D. (1999). Longitudinal effects of divorce on the quality of the father–child relationship and on fathers' psychological well-being. *Journal of Marriage and the Family, 61*, 397–408.

Simons, R. L. (1996). The effect of divorce on adult and child adjustment. In R. L. Simons (Ed.), *Understanding differences between divorced and intact families: Stress, interaction, and child outcomes* (pp. 3–20). Thousand Oaks, CA: Sage.

Simons, R. L. (1994). The impact of mothers' parenting, involvement by nonresidential fathers, and parental conflict on the adjustment of adolescent children. *Journal of Marriage and the Family, 56*, 356–374.

Simons, R. L., and Associates. (1996). Understanding differences between divorced and intact families. Thousand Oaks, CA: Sage.

Simons, R. L., Beaman, J., Conger, R. D., and Chao, W. (1993). Stress, support, and antisocial behavior trait as determinants of emotional well being and parenting practices among single mothers. *Journal of Marriage and the Family, 55*, 385–398.

Steinberg, L. (1987). Single parents, stepparents, and the susceptibility of adolescents to antisocial peer pressure. *Child Development, 58*, 269–275.

Steinberg, L., Mounts, N. S., Lamborn, S. D., and Dornbusch, S. M. (1991). Authoritative parenting and adolescent adjustment across varied ecological niches. *Journal of Research on Adolescence, 1*, 19–36.

Stolberg, A. L., Camplair, C. W., Currier, K., and Wells, M. J. (1987). Individual, familial, and environmental determinants of children's post-divorce adjustment and maladjustment. *Journal of Divorce, 11*, 51–70.

Stone, G., and McKenry, P. (1998). Nonresidential father involvement: A test of a mid-range theory. *Journal of Genetic Psychology, 159*, 313–336.

Teachman, J. D., Tedrow, L. M., and Crowder, K. D. (2000). The changing demography of America's families. *Journal of Marriage and the Family, 62*, 1234–1246.

Thiriot, T. L., and Buckner, E. T. (1991). Multiple predictors of satisfactory post-divorce adjustment of single custodial parents. *Journal of Divorce and Remarriage, 17*, 27–48.

Thomson, E., McLanahan, S. S., and Curtin, R. B. (1992). Family structure, gender, and parental socialization. *Journal of Marriage and the Family, 54*, 368–378.

Tshann, J. M., Johnston, J. R., Kline, M., and Wallerstein, J. S. (1991). Conflict, loss, change, and parent–child relationships: Predicting children's adjustment during divorce. *Journal of Divorce, 13*, 1–22.

Tzeng, J. M., and Mare, R. D. (1995). Labor market and socioeconomic effects on marital stability. *Social Science Research, 24*, 329–351.

U.S. Bureau of the Census. (1995). *Statistical abstract of the United States: 1995* (115th ed.). Washington, DC: U.S. Government Printing Office.

U.S. Bureau of the Census. (1998). *Current population reports, Marital Status and Living Arrangements: March 1998 (Update)*. (P20-514). Washington, DC: U.S. Department of Commerce, Economics and Statistics Administration.

Visher, E. B., and Visher, J. S. (1988). *Old loyalties, new ties: Therapeutics strategies with stepfamilies*. New York: Brunner/Mazel.

Visher, E. B., and Visher, J. S. (1994). The core ingredients in the treatments of stepfamilies. *Family Journal, 2*, 208–214.

Visher, E. B., and Visher, J. S. (1996). *Therapy with stepfamilies*. New York: Brunner/Mazel.

Waite, L. J., and Gallagher, M. (2000). *The case for marriage: Why married people are happier, healthier and better off financially*. New York: Doubleday.

Wallerstein, J. S., Lewis, J. M., and Blakeslee, S. (2000). *The unexpected legacy of divorce: A 25 year landmark study*. New York: Hyperion.

Weiss, R. S. (1979). Growing up a little faster: The experience of growing up in a single-parent household. *Journal of Social Issues, 35*, 97–111.

Werner, E. E. (1988). Individual differences, universal needs Zero to Three: Bulletin of National Center for Clinical Infant Programs, 8, 1–15.

White, L. (1994). Stepfamilies over the life course: Social support. In A. Booth and J. Dunn (Eds.), *Stepfamilies: Who benefits? Who does not?* (pp. 109–138). Hillsdale, NJ: Lawrence Erlbaum Associates.

Whitsett, D. P., and Land, H. M. (1992). Role strain, coping, and marital satisfaction of stepparents. *Families in Society, 73*, 79–92.

Wineberg, H., and McCarthy, J. (1998). Living arrangements after divorce: Cohabitation versus remarriage. *Journal of Divorce and Remarriage, 29*, 131–146.

Wolfinger, N. H. (2000). Beyond the intergenerational transmission of divorce. *Journal of Family Issues, 21*, 1061–1086.

Wolin, S., and Wolin, S. (1993). *The resilient self: How survivors of troubled families rise above adversity*. New York: Villard.

Zill, N. (1994). Understanding why children in stepfamilies have more learning and behavior problems than children in nuclear families. In A. Booth and J. Dunn (Eds.), *Stepfamilies: Who benefits? Who does not?* (pp. 97–106). Hillsdale, NJ: Erlbaum Associates.

Zill, N., Morrison, D. R., and Coiro, M. J. (1993). Long-term effects of parental divorce on parent–child relationships, adjustment, and achievement in young adulthood. *Journal of Family Psychology, 7*, 1–13.

10

Lesbian and Gay Parenthood

Charlotte J. Patterson
University of Virginia

INTRODUCTION

The central heterosexist assumption that everyone is or ought to be heterosexual is nowhere more prevalent than in the area of parent–child relations. Not only are children usually assumed to be heterosexual in their orientation, but mothers and fathers are also generally expected to exemplify heterosexuality in their attitudes, values, and behavior. From such a perspective, children with lesbian and gay parents seem not to exist; for some people, the idea of lesbian or gay parenthood may be difficult even to imagine. In contrast to such expectations, however, many lesbian women and gay men are parents.

In this chapter, I first review the historical context in which lesbian and gay parenting has emerged. I then provide an overview of lesbian and gay parenthood today, including information about the prevalence and diversity of lesbian and gay parenting and about the legal contexts in which lesbian and gay families currently live. I then describe the results of research on lesbian and gay parents and their children and discuss some implications of the research findings for theories of psychological development and for the politics of family life. Next, I describe services that have been developed specifically for lesbian and gay families. The chapter concludes with a discussion of future directions for research, service, and advocacy relevant to the needs of lesbian mothers, gay fathers, and their children.

HISTORICAL CONTEXT OF LESBIAN AND GAY PARENTHOOD

The emergence of large numbers of openly self-identified lesbian women and gay men is a historical phenomenon of relatively recent vintage (Boswell, 1980; D'Emilio, 1983; Faderman, 1981, 1991). Although the origins of homophile organizations date to the 1950s and even earlier (D'Emilio, 1983; Faderman, 1991), the origins of contemporary gay liberation movements are generally traced to police raids on the Stonewall bar in the Greenwich Village neighborhood of New York City in 1969 and to the resistance shown by gay men and lesbian women to these attacks (Adam, 1987; D'Emilio, 1983). In the years since that time, more and more gay men and lesbian women have abandoned secrecy, declared their identities, and begun to work actively for lesbian and gay rights (Blumenfeld and Raymond, 1988).

With greater openness among lesbian and gay adults, a number of family forms are becoming more and more visible in which one or more of a child's parents identify as lesbian or gay. Many such families involve children from a previous marriage. Others involve children born or adopted after the parents have identified themselves as gay or lesbian. In the past 10 to 20 years, such families have been the subject of increasing attention in the media and in the popular press (Goleman, 1992; Gross, 1991; Martin, 1993; Rafkin, 1990; Schulenberg, 1985).

Although it is widely believed that family environments exert important influences on children who grow up in them, authoritative scholarly reviews of such matters are only now beginning to consider children growing up in families with gay and/or lesbian parents (e.g., Lamb, 1999). Given the multiplicity of new lesbian and gay families and in view of their apparent vitality, scientists today are faced with remarkable opportunities to study the formation, growth, and impact of new family forms.

To the extent that parental influences are seen as critical in psychosocial development and to the extent that lesbians and/or gay men may provide different kinds of influences than heterosexual parents, then the children of gay men and lesbians can been expected to develop in ways that are different from those of children of heterosexual parents. Whether any such differences are expected to be beneficial, detrimental, or nonexistent depends, of course, on the viewpoint from which the phenomena are observed. Lesbian and gay families with children thus present an unusual opportunity to test basic assumptions that many scientists have long taken for granted.

LESBIAN AND GAY PARENTHOOD TODAY

How many lesbian and gay families with children are there in the United States today? What are the important sources of diversity among them? And what is the nature of the legal context within which lesbian and gay families are living? In this section, I discuss each of these questions in turn.

Prevalence of Lesbian and Gay Parenthood

For many reasons, no accurate count of the numbers of lesbian and gay families with children is available. First, the numbers of lesbian and gay male adults in the United States today cannot be estimated with confidence. Because of fear of discrimination, many take pains to conceal their sexual orientation (Blumenfeld and Raymond, 1988; Herek, 1995). It is especially difficult to locate lesbian and gay parents. Concerned that they might lose child custody and/or visitation rights if their sexual orientation were to be known, some lesbian and gay parents attempt to conceal their gay or lesbian identities (Pagelow, 1980), sometimes even from their own children (Dunne, 1987).

Despite acknowledged difficulties, estimates of the numbers of lesbian and gay families with children in the United States have been offered (see Patterson and Friel, 2000, for a review and critique). One approach to making estimates of this kind is to extrapolate from what is known or believed about base rates in the population. For example, there are approximately 106 million women and approximately 98 million men over 18 years of age in the United States today (U. S. Bureau of the Census, 2000). If one assumes that approximately 4% of the population is gay or lesbian, that would place the numbers of lesbian and gay adults in the United States today at approximately 4.2 million and 3.9 million, respectively. According to some large-scale survey studies (e.g., Bell and Weinberg, 1978; Blumstein and Schwartz, 1983), approximately 20% of lesbians and approximately 10% of gay men are parents, most of whom have children from a heterosexual marriage that ended in divorce. Calculations with these figures suggest that there may be well over a million gay or lesbian parents in the United States today. If, on average, each parent has two children, that would mean that there could be more than two million children with lesbian and gay parents in the United States today.

The accuracy of such estimates is, of course, no better than that of the figures on which they are based (Michaels, 1996). The data of Bell and Weinberg (1978) were drawn from a large and diverse sample of lesbian and gay adults, but the sample was not intended to be representative of the population of the United States; indeed, all the respondents lived in a single geographical area. Moreover, the average age of the respondents was 35 years of age, so ultimate levels of fertility could not be assessed. For these and related reasons (see Patterson and Friel, 2000), the data of Bell and Weinberg (1978), although valuable, cannot be seen as definitive.

Efforts have been made by Badgett (1998) and by Patterson and Friel (2000) to estimate the numbers of lesbian and gay parents in the United States by drawing on data from nationally representative (or near-representative) samples of American adults of childbearing age. Badgett (1998) used data from voter exit polls, and Patterson and Friel used data from the National Health and Social Life Survey (NHSLS; Laumann, Gagnon, Michael, and Michaels, 1994). These authors estimated that there are between one and five million lesbian and gay parents in the United States today, with the lower numbers taken from the very most conservative assessments on the NHSLS (Patterson and Friel, 2000) and the higher numbers drawn from the more liberal assessments used in the NHSLS and in the voter exit polls (Badgett, 1998; Patterson and Friel, 2000). Projecting from these estimates of the numbers of parents, and assuming that each parent has on average only one child, one finds then that there would be between one and five million children with lesbian and gay parents in the United States today. If one makes the estimates assuming that each parent has more than one child, then estimated numbers of children with lesbian and gay parents would of course be larger.

Although the exact numbers will probably never be known with certainty, it does seem clear that a substantial number of people are involved. In addition to those who had children in the context of a heterosexual marriage, many lesbian and gay adults are also having children after assuming nonheterosexual identities, so the characteristics of the population may also be changing (Gartrell et al., 1996; Martin, 1993; Patterson, 1994b; Ricketts, 1991). Whatever estimates one adopts, it seems clear that many children are growing up with lesbian or gay parents.

Diversity Among Lesbian Mothers, Gay Fathers, and Their Children

The numbers of lesbian and gay families with children would thus appear to be sizable. When the numbers are considered, however, it is important not to overlook the many sources of diversity among these families. In an effort to begin to characterize the diversity that characterizes lesbian and gay families with children, some of the differences among such families are examined next.

As previously suggested, one important distinction among lesbian and gay families with children involves the sexual identity of parents at the time of a child's birth or adoption. Probably the largest group of children with lesbian and gay parents today are those who were born within the context of heterosexual relationships between biological parents and whose parent or parents subsequently identified as gay or lesbian. These include families in which the parents divorced when the husband came out as gay, families in which the parents divorced when the wife came out as lesbian, families in which the parents divorced when both parents came out, and families in which one or both of the parents came out and the parents decided not to divorce. Gay or lesbian parents may be single or they may have same-gender partners. A gay or lesbian parent's same-gender partner may or may not assume stepparenting relationships with the children. If the partner has also had children, the youngsters may or may not also assume stepsibling relationships with one another. In other words, lesbian and gay families with children born in the context of heterosexual relationships are themselves a relatively diverse group.

In addition to children born within the context of heterosexual relationships between parents, lesbians and gay men are believed increasingly to be choosing parenthood (Patterson, 1994a, 1994b; Pies, 1985, 1990). Many such children are conceived by means of donor insemination (DI). Lesbians who wish to bear children may choose a friend, relative, or acquaintance to be the sperm donor, or may choose instead to use sperm from an unknown donor. When sperm donors are known, they may take parental or avuncular roles relative to children conceived by means of DI or they may not (Patterson, 1994a, 1994b; Pies, 1985, 1990). Gay men may also become biological parents of children whom they intend to parent, whether with a single woman (who may be lesbian or heterosexual), with a lesbian couple, or with a gay male partner. Many adoption agencies are open to working with lesbian and gay prospective adoptive parents (Brodzinsky, Patterson, and Vaziri, 2001), and options pursued by gay men and lesbians include both adoption and foster care (Ricketts, 1991). Thus children are today being brought up in a diverse array of lesbian and gay families.

In addition to differences in parents' sexual identities at the time of a child's birth, another set of distinctions concerns the extent to which family members are related biologically to one another (Pollack and Vaughn, 1987; Riley, 1988; Weston, 1991). Although biological relatedness of family members to one another is taken for granted less and less as heterosexual stepfamilies proliferate, it is often even more prominent as an issue in lesbian and gay than in heterosexual families (Wright, 1998). When children are born by means of DI into lesbian families, they are generally related biologically only to the birth mother, not to her partner. Similarly, when children are born by means of surrogacy to a gay couple, only the father who served as a sperm donor is likely to be biologically related to the child. In adoption and foster care, of course, the child will probably have no biological relation to any adoptive or foster parent.

Another issue of particular importance for lesbian and gay families concerns custodial arrangements for minor children. As in heterosexual families, children may live with one or both biological parents, or they may spend part of their time in one parent's household and part of their time in another's. Many lesbian mothers and gay fathers have, however, lost custody of their children to heterosexual spouses following divorce, and the threat of custody litigation almost certainly looms larger in the lives of most divorced lesbian mothers than it does in the lives of divorced heterosexual ones (Lyons, 1983; Pagelow, 1980). Although no authoritative figures are available, it seems very likely that a greater proportion of lesbian and gay than of heterosexual parents have lost custody of children against their will. Probably for this reason, more lesbians and gay men seem to be noncustodial parents (i.e., do not have legal custody of their children) and nonresidential parents (i.e., do not live in the same household with their children) than might otherwise be expected.

Beyond these basic distinctions, many others can also be considered. Other important ways in which lesbian and gay families with children may differ from one another include income, education, race/ethnicity, gender, and culture. Difficulties and ambiguities in the definition of sexual orientation should also be acknowledged (Brown, 1995; Fox, 1995). Although such variability undoubtedly contributes to differences in the qualities of life, little research has yet been directed to understanding such differences among lesbian and gay families.

Legal and Public Policy Issues

When considering the environment within which lesbian and gay parenting takes place, one must acknowledge that the legal system in the United States has long been hostile to lesbians and to gay men who are or who wish to become parents (Editors of the Harvard Law Review, 1990; Falk, 1989; Patterson and Redding, 1996; Polikoff, 1990; Rivera, 1991). Lesbian mothers and gay fathers have often been denied custody and/or visitation with their children following divorce (Falk, 1989). Although some states now have laws stipulating that parental sexual orientation as such cannot be a factor in determining child custody following divorce, in other states gay or lesbian parents are presumed to be unfit as parents (Patterson and Redding, 1996). Regulations governing foster care and adoption in many states have also made it difficult for lesbians and gay men to adopt or to serve as foster parents (Ricketts, 1991; Ricketts and Achtenberg, 1990). It is clear that college students expect children of lesbian mothers to have more behavior problems than other children (King and Black, 1999), and this bias may be shared by judges and policymakers.

One of the central issues underlying judicial decision making in custody litigation and in public policies governing foster care and adoption has been questions about the fitness of lesbians and gay men to be parents. Specifically, policies have sometimes been constructed and judicial decisions have often been made on the assumptions that gay men and lesbians are mentally ill and hence not fit to be parents, that lesbians are less maternal than heterosexual women and hence do not make good mothers, and that lesbians' and gay men's relationships with sexual partners leave little time for ongoing parent–child interactions (Editors of the Harvard Law Review, 1990; Falk, 1989). Because these assumptions have been important ones in denying or limiting lesbian and gay parental rights and because they are open to empirical evaluation, they have guided much of the research on lesbian and gay parents, which is discussed below.

In addition to judicial concerns about parents themselves, three principal kinds of fears about effects of lesbian and gay parents on children have also been reflected in judicial decision making about child custody and in public policies such as regulations governing foster care and adoption (Patterson, 1997; Patterson and Redding, 1996). One of these concerns is that development of sexual identity among children of lesbian and gay parents will be impaired. For instance, judges may fear that children will themselves grow up to be gay or lesbian, an outcome that they generally view as negative. Another concern is that lesbian and gay parents will have adverse effects on other aspects of their children's personality development. For example, judges may fear that children in the custody of gay or lesbian parents will be more vulnerable to behavior problems or to mental breakdown. A third general concern is that these children will have difficulties in social relationships. For instance, judges may believe that children will be teased or stigmatized by peers because of their parent's sexual orientation. Because such concerns have often been explicit in judicial determinations when lesbian or gay parents' custody or visitation rights have been denied or curtailed (Editors of the Harvard Law Review, 1990; Falk, 1989; Patterson and Redding, 1996) and because these assumptions are open to empirical test, they have provided an important impetus to research.

RESEARCH ON LESBIAN MOTHERS AND GAY FATHERS

Case reports about lesbian mothers, gay fathers, and their children began to appear in the psychiatric literature in the early and the mid-1970s (e.g., Osman, 1972; Weeks, Derdeyn, and Langman, 1975), but systematic research on these families is more recent. Despite the diversity of lesbian and gay parenting communities, research to date has, with few exceptions, been conducted with relatively homogeneous groups of participants. Parents have been mainly European American, well educated, affluent, and living in major urban centers. Any studies that provide exceptions to this rule are specifically noted as such. In this section, research on those who became parents in the context of heterosexual relationships, before coming out as lesbian or gay, is presented first. Studies of lesbians who became parents after coming out are described next. For other reviews of research on lesbian and gay parents, see Brewaeys and Van Hall (1997), Kirkpatrick (1996), Patterson (1995a, 1995b, 1997, 1998, 2000), Patterson and Chan (1996), Perrin (1998), and Tasker and Golombok (1991, 1997).

Lesbians and Gay Men Who Became Parents in the Context of Heterosexual Relationships

One important impetus for research in this area has come from extrinsic sources, such as judicial concerns about the psychological health and well-being of lesbian mothers compared with those of heterosexual mothers. Other work has arisen from concerns that are more intrinsic to the families themselves, such as what and when children should be told about their parents' sexual orientation. In this subsection, I review first the research arising from extrinsic concerns and then the work stemming from intrinsic concerns. Because studies tend to focus either on mothers or on fathers, I present first the research on mothers, then that on fathers. Although some of these parents may not have been married to the heterosexual partner with whom they had children, it is likely that most of the research participants were married. To avoid the use of more cumbersome labels, then, I refer to divorced lesbian mothers and to divorced gay fathers.

Divorced lesbian mothers. Because the overall mental health of lesbian mothers compared with that of heterosexual mothers has often been raised as an issue by judges presiding over custody disputes (Falk, 1989), a number of studies have focused on this issue. Consistent with data on the mental health of lesbian women in general (Gonsiorek, 1991), research in this area has revealed that divorced lesbian mothers score at least as high as divorced heterosexual mothers on assessments of psychological health. For instance, studies have found no differences between lesbian and heterosexual mothers on self-concept, happiness, overall adjustment, or psychiatric status (Falk, 1989; Patterson, 1995a, 1997).

Another area of judicial concern has focused on maternal gender-role behavior and its potential impact on children (Falk, 1989). Stereotypes cited by the courts suggest that lesbians might be overly masculine and/or that they might interact inappropriately with their children. In contrast to expectations based on the stereotypes, however, neither lesbian mothers' reports about their own gender-role behavior nor their self-described interest in childrearing have been found to differ from those of heterosexual mothers. Reports about responses to child behavior and ratings of warmth toward children have been found not to differ significantly between lesbian and heterosexual mothers (Kweskin and Cook, 1982; Mucklow and Phelan, 1979; Thompson, McCandless, and Strickland, 1971).

Some differences between lesbian and heterosexual mothers have also been found. Lyons (1983) and Pagelow (1980) reported that divorced lesbian mothers had more fears about loss of child custody than did divorced heterosexual mothers. Similarly, Green, Mandel, Hotvedt, Gray, and Smith (1986) reported that lesbian mothers were more likely than heterosexual mothers to be active in feminist organizations. Given the environments in which these lesbian mothers were living, findings like these are not surprising. How such differences may affect parenting behavior, if at all, is at present unknown.

A few other scattered differences seem more difficult to interpret. For instance, Miller, Jacobsen, and Bigner (1981) reported that lesbian mothers in their sample were more child centered than heterosexual mothers were in their discipline techniques. In a sample of African American lesbian mothers and African American heterosexual mothers, Hill (1987) found that lesbian mothers reported being more flexible about rules, more relaxed about sex play and modesty, and more likely to have nontraditional expectations for their daughters.

Several studies have also examined the social circumstances and relationships of lesbian mothers. Divorced lesbian mothers have consistently been reported to be more likely than divorced heterosexual mothers to be living with a romantic partner (Harris and Turner, 1985/1986; Kirkpatrick, Smith, and Roy, 1981; Pagelow, 1980). Whether this represents a difference between lesbian and heterosexual mother-headed families, on the one hand, or reflects sampling biases of the research, on the other, cannot be determined on the basis of information in the published reports. Information is sparse about the impact of such relationships in lesbian mother families, but what has been published suggests that, like heterosexual stepparents, coresident lesbian partners of divorced lesbian mothers can be important sources of conflict as well as support in the family (Kirkpatrick, 1987).

Relationships with the fathers of children in lesbian mother homes have also been a topic of study. Few differences in the likelihood of paternal financial support have been found for lesbian and heterosexual families with children; Kirkpatrick et al. (1981) reported, for example, that only approximately half of heterosexual and approximately half of lesbian mothers in their sample received any financial support from the fathers of their children. Findings about frequency of contact with fathers are mixed, with some (e.g., Kirkpatrick et al., 1981) reporting no differences in frequency of contact as a function of maternal sexual orientation and others (e.g., Golombok, Spencer, and Rutter, 1983) reporting more contact with fathers among lesbian than among heterosexual mothers.

Although most research has involved assessment of possible differences in personality and social behavior between lesbian and heterosexual mothers, a few studies have reported other types of comparisons. For instance, in a study of divorced lesbian mothers and divorced gay fathers, Harris and Turner (1985/1986) found that gay fathers were likely to report greater financial resources and to say that they encouraged more gender-typed toy play among their children, whereas lesbian mothers were more likely to describe benefits such as increased empathy and tolerance for differences among their children as a result of having lesbian or gay parents. In comparisons of relationship satisfaction among lesbian couples who did or did not have children, Koepke, Hare, and Moran (1992) reported that couples with children scored higher on overall measures of relationship satisfaction and of the quality of their sexual relationship. These findings are intriguing, but much more research will be needed before their interpretation will be clear.

Another important set of questions, as yet little studied, concerns the conditions under which lesbian mothers experience enhanced feelings of well-being and support. Rand, Graham, and Rawlings (1982) reported that psychological health of lesbian mothers was associated with mothers' openness about their sexual orientation with employers, exhusbands, children, and friends, and with their degree of feminist activism. Kirkpatrick (1987) reported that lesbian mothers living with partners and children had greater economic and emotional resources than did those living alone with their children. Much is still to be learned about determinants of individual differences in psychological well-being among lesbian mothers.

Many other issues that have arisen in the context of divorced lesbian mother families are also in need of study. For instance, when a mother is in the process of coming out as a lesbian to herself and to others, at what point in that process should she address the topic with her child and in what ways should she do so—if at all? Also, what influence ought the child's age and circumstances to have in such a decision? Reports from research and clinical practice suggest that early adolescence may be a particularly difficult time for parents to initiate such conversations, and that disclosure may be less stressful at earlier points in a child's development (Patterson, 1992, 1997), but systematic research on these issues is just beginning. Similarly, many issues remain to be addressed regarding stepfamily and blended family relationships that may emerge as a lesbian mother's household seeks new equilibrium following her separation or divorce from the child's father (Wright, 1998).

Divorced gay fathers. Although considerable research has focused on the overall psychological adjustment of lesbian mothers compared with that of heterosexual mothers, no published studies make such comparisons of gay fathers with heterosexual fathers. This fact may be attributable to the greater role of judicial decision making as an impetus for research on lesbian mothers. In jurisdictions in which the law provides for biases in custody proceedings, these are likely to favor female and heterosexual parents. Perhaps because, other things being equal, gay fathers are extremely unlikely to win custody battles over their children after divorce, fewer such cases seem to have reached the courts. Consistent with expectations based on this view, only a small minority of divorced gay fathers have been reported to live in the same households with their children (Bigner and Bozett, 1990; Bozett, 1980, 1989).

Research on the parenting attitudes of gay versus heterosexual divorced fathers has, however, been reported (Barret and Robinson, 1990). Bigner and Jacobsen (1989a, 1989b) compared gay and heterosexual fathers, each of whom had at least two children. Results showed that, with one exception, there were no significant differences between gay and heterosexual fathers in their motives for parenthood. The single exception concerned the greater likelihood of gay than heterosexual fathers to cite the higher status accorded to parents compared with that of nonparents in the dominant culture as a motivation for parenthood (Bigner and Jacobsen, 1989a).

Bigner and Jacobsen (1989b) also asked gay and heterosexual fathers in their sample to report on their own behavior with their children. Although no differences emerged in the fathers' reports of involvement or intimacy, gay fathers reported that their behavior was characterized by greater responsiveness, more reasoning, and more limit setting than that of heterosexual fathers. These reports by gay fathers of greater warmth and responsiveness, on the one hand, and greater control and limit setting, on the other, are strongly reminiscent of findings from research with heterosexual families and would seem to raise the possibility that gay fathers are more likely than their heterosexual counterparts to exhibit authoritative patterns of parenting behavior such as those described by Baumrind (1967; Baumrind and Black, 1967). Caution must be exercised, however, in the interpretation of results such as these, which stem entirely from paternal reports about their own behavior.

In addition to research comparing gay and heterosexual fathers, a few studies have made other comparisons. For instance, Robinson and Skeen (1982) compared gender-role orientations of gay fathers with those of gay men who were not fathers and found no differences. Similarly, Skeen and Robinson (1985) found no evidence to suggest that gay men's retrospective reports about relationships with their own parents varied as a function of whether or not they were parents themselves. As noted in the subsection on divorced lesbian mothers, Harris and Turner (1985/1986) compared gay fathers and lesbian mothers, reporting that, although gay fathers had higher incomes and were more likely to report encouraging their children to play with gender-typed toys, lesbian mothers were more likely to believe that their children received positive benefits such as increased tolerance for diversity from growing up with lesbian or gay parents. Studies like these begin to suggest a number of issues for research on gender, sexual orientation, and parenting behavior, and it is clear that there are many valuable directions in which future work in this area could go.

A great deal of research in this area has arisen from concerns about the gay father identity and its transformations over time. Thus the work by Miller (1978, 1979) and Bozett (1980, 1981a, 1981b, 1987) has sought to provide a conceptualization of the processes through which a man who considers himself to be a heterosexual father may come to identify himself, both in public and in private, as a gay father. From extensive interviews with gay fathers both in the United States and Canada, these authors have emphasized the centrality of identity disclosure and of the reactions to disclosure by significant people in a man's life. Miller (1978) suggested that, although a number of factors such as the extent of occupational autonomy and the amount of access to gay communities may affect how rapidly a gay man discloses his identity to others, the most important of these is likely to be the experience of falling in love with another man. It is this experience, more than any other, Miller argued, that leads a man to integrate the otherwise compartmentalized parts of his identity as a gay father. This hypothesis is very much open to empirical evaluation, but such research has not yet been reported.

In summary, results of research with gay fathers suggest that their parenting attitudes and practices are very similar to those of heterosexual fathers. Other studies have examined the emergence of gay father identities, suggesting that for men who became fathers in the context of a heterosexual relationship, gay father identities emerge slowly and over considerable periods of time, often in response to the experience of falling in love with another man. Existing data suggest a number of directions for future studies, and additional research is needed.

Lesbians and Gay Men Who Choose to Become Parents

Although for many years lesbian mothers and gay fathers were generally assumed to have become parents in the context of previous heterosexual relationships, both men and women are believed increasingly to be undertaking parenthood in the context of preexisting lesbian and gay identities (Beers, 1996; Crawford, 1987; Gartrell et al., 1996, 1999; Patterson, 1994a, 1994b). A substantial body of research addresses the transition to parenthood among heterosexuals (e.g., Cowan and Cowan, 1992; Heinicke, in Vol. 3 of this *Handbook*), but very little research has explored the transition to parenthood for gay men or lesbian women. Many issues that arise for heterosexuals also face lesbian women and gay men (e.g., concerns about how children will affect couple relationships, economic concerns about supporting children), but gay men and lesbian women must also cope with many additional issues because of their situation as members of stigmatized minorities. These issues are best understood when viewed against the backdrop of heterosexism and antigay prejudice.

Antigay prejudice is evident in institutions involved with health care, education, and employment that often fail to support and, in some cases, are openly hostile to lesbian and gay families (Casper and Schultz, 1999; Casper, Schultz, and Wickens, 1992; Martin, 1993; Perrin, 1998). Lesbian and gay parents may encounter antigay prejudice and bigotry even from members of their families of origin (Pollack and Vaughn, 1987). Many, if not most, of the special concerns of lesbian and gay parents and prospective parents stem from problems created by such hostility.

A number of interrelated issues are often faced in particular by lesbians and gay men who wish to become parents (Beers, 1996; Crawford, 1987; Martin, 1989, 1993; Patterson, 1994b). One of the first needs among prospective lesbian and gay parents is for accurate, up-to-date information on how lesbians and gay men can become parents, how their children are likely to develop, and what supports are available to assist them. In addition to such educational needs, lesbians and gay men who are seeking biological parenthood are also likely to encounter various health concerns, ranging from medical screening of prospective birth parents to assistance with DI techniques, prenatal care, and preparation for birth. As matters progress, a number of legal concerns about the rights and responsibilities of all parties are likely to emerge. Associated with all of these will generally be financial issues; in addition to the support of a child, auxiliary costs of medical and legal assistance may be considerable. Finally, social and emotional concerns of many different kinds are also likely to emerge (Pies, 1985, 1990; Patterson, 1994b; Pollack and Vaughn, 1987; Rohrbaugh, 1988).

As this brief outline of issues suggests, numerous questions are posed by the emergence of prospective lesbian and gay parents. What are the factors that influence lesbians' and gay men's inclinations to make parenthood a part of their lives? What effects does parenting have on lesbians or gay men who undertake it, and how do these effects compare with those experienced by heterosexuals? How effectively do special services such as support groups serve the needs of lesbian and gay parents and prospective parents for whom they were designed? What are the elements of a social climate that is supportive for lesbian and gay parents and their children? As yet, little research has addressed such questions.

In one study of gay men who were not parents, Beers (1996) found that approximately half of the participants reported that they would like to become parents. Interestingly, those who expressed a desire to become parents were also described as being at higher levels of psychosocial development (assessed within an Eriksonian framework) and at higher levels of identity formation with regard to their gay identities. There were no differences, however, in retrospective reports of experiences with their own parents (Beers, 1996). These results suggest the possibility that internalized negative attitudes about homosexuality may be associated with reluctance on the part of gay men to become parents, but further evidence on this point is lacking.

The earliest studies of childbearing among lesbian couples were reported by McCandlish (1987) and by Steckel (1985, 1987). Both investigators reported research based on small samples of lesbian couples who had given birth to children by means of DI. Their focus was primarily on the children in such families, and neither investigator conducted systematic assessments of mothers. McCandlish (1987) did, however, highlight some events and issues that were significant among families in her sample. For instance, she noted that, regardless of their interest in parenting before birth of the first child, the nonbiological mothers in each couple unanimously reported an "unexpected and immediate attachment" to the child (McCandlish, 1987, p. 28). Although both mothers took part in parenting, they reported shifting patterns of caregiving responsibilities over time, with the biological mother taking primary responsibility during the earliest months, and the nonbiological mother's role increasing in importance after the child was 12 or more months of age. Couples also reported changes in their own relationships following the birth of the child, notably a reduction or cessation in sexual intimacy. That lesbian couples reported less sexual activity after the birth of a child in the McCandlish (1987) study would seem to be at odds with the finding reported by Koepke et al. (1992) that lesbian couples with children were more satisfied with their sexual relationship than were those without children. Further research will be needed to provide a definitive interpretation of these apparently contradictory results and to clarify the associations of such variables with the qualities of actual behavior in parenting roles.

An early study by Hand (1991) examined the ways in which 17 lesbian and 17 heterosexual couples with children under 2 years of age shared childcare, household duties, and occupational roles. Her principal finding was that lesbian couples reported sharing parental duties more equally than did heterosexual couples. Lesbian nonbiological mothers were significantly more involved in childcare than were heterosexual fathers. The lesbian nonbiological mothers also regarded their parental role as significantly more salient than did heterosexual fathers. Lesbian biological mothers viewed their maternal role as more salient than did any of the other mothers, whether lesbian or heterosexual. Fathers viewed their occupational roles as more salient than did any of the mothers, whether lesbian or heterosexual.

Another study conducted at approximately the same time (Osterweil, 1991) involved 30 lesbian couples with at least one child between 18 and 36 months of age. Consistent with Hand's results for parents of younger children, Osterweil's results showed that biological mothers viewed their maternal role as more salient than did nonbiological mothers. In addition, although household maintenance activities were shared fairly equally, biological mothers reported having more influence in family decisions and more involvement in childcare. Osterweil (1991) also reported that the couples in her study scored at approximately the mean for normative samples of heterosexual couples in overall relationship satisfaction. Taken together, results of the Hand and the Osterweil studies thus suggest that lesbian couples who have chosen to bear children are likely to share household and childcare duties more equally than do heterosexual couples and that lesbians are relatively satisfied with their couple relationships.

Patterson (1995b) studied 26 families headed by lesbian couples who had children between 4 and 9 years of age. Consistent with other investigators (Koepke et al., 1992; Osterweil, 1991), Patterson (1995a, 1995b, in press) found that lesbian parents' mental health and their relationship satisfaction were generally high, relative to norms for heterosexual couples. Although they reported sharing household tasks and decision making equally, couples in this study reported that biological mothers were more involved in childcare and that nonbiological mothers spent longer hours in paid employment. The differences reported by Patterson (1995b) between lesbian parents' involvement in childcare were smaller by far, however, than those reported by Hand (1991) between heterosexual parents. Within this context, Patterson (1995b) also found that children were better adjusted and parents were more satisfied in lesbian mother families when childcare was shared more equally between parents.

Chan, Brooks, Raboy, and Patterson (1998) studied a group of 80 families formed by lesbian and by heterosexual parents by means of DI, and reported similar findings, as did Tasker and Golombok (1998) with a group of 99 lesbian and heterosexual British families. In the study by Tasker and Golombok's (1998), lesbian couples with children who had been conceived by means of DI were more likely to share childcare duties evenly than were heterosexual couples who had conceived children by means of DI or heterosexual couples who had conceived children in the conventional way.

A study of gay couples who chose parenthood was conducted by McPherson (1993), who assessed division of labor, satisfaction with division of labor, and satisfaction with couple relationships among 28 gay and 27 heterosexual parenting couples. Consistent with evidence from lesbian parenting couples (Chan et al., 1998; Hand, 1993; Osterweil, 1991; Patterson, 1995b; Tasker and Golombok, 1998), the findings of McPherson (1993) showed that gay couples reported a more even division of responsibilities for household maintenance and childcare than did heterosexual couples. Gay parenting couples also reported greater satisfaction with their division of childcare tasks than did heterosexual couples. Finally, gay couples also reported greater satisfaction with their couple relationships, especially in the areas of cohesion and expression of affection.

Sbordone (1993) studied 78 gay men who had become parents through adoption or through surrogacy arrangements and compared them with 83 gay men who were not fathers. Consistent with the findings of Skeen and Robinson (1985) with divorced gay fathers, there were no differences between fathers and nonfathers on reports about relationships with the men's own parents. Gay fathers did, however, report higher self-esteem and fewer negative attitudes about homosexuality than did gay men who were not fathers.

An interesting result of Sbordone's (1993) study was that 54% of the gay men who were not fathers indicated that they would like to rear a child. Those who said they wanted children were younger than those who said they did not, but the two groups did not otherwise differ (e.g., on income, education, race, self-esteem, or attitudes about homosexuality). Given that fathers had higher self-esteem and fewer negative attitudes about homosexuality than did either group of nonfathers, Sbordone speculated that gay fathers' higher self-esteem might be a result rather than a cause of parenthood.

As this brief discussion has revealed, research on lesbians and gay men who have chosen to become parents is quite sparse. Most research has been conducted on a relatively small scale, and many important issues have yet to be addressed. Existing research suggests, however, that lesbian and gay parenting couples are more likely than heterosexual couples to share tasks involved in childcare relatively evenly and perhaps also to be more satisfied than heterosexual couples with their arrangements. Much remains to be learned about the determinants of lesbian and gay parenting, about its impact on lesbian and gay parents themselves, and about its place in contemporary communities. In the next section, I summarize what is known about the impact of parental sexual orientation on children.

RESEARCH ON CHILDREN OF LESBIAN AND GAY PARENTS

As with research on parents, an important impetus for studies of children with lesbian and gay parents has been the issues raised by the courts in the context of child custody hearings. Reflecting concerns that have been seen as relevant in the largest number of custody disputes, most of the research on children of lesbian and gay parents compares the development of children with custodial lesbian mothers with that of children with custodial heterosexual mothers. Because many children living in lesbian mother-headed families have undergone the experience of parental separation and divorce, it has been widely believed that children of divorced but heterosexual mothers provide the best comparison group. Research has also focused mainly on age groups and topics relevant to the largest numbers of custody disputes. Thus most research compares children of divorced custodial lesbian mothers with children of divorced custodial heterosexual mothers, and most studies focus on school-age children. Other reviews of this literature can be found in the works of Brewaeys and Van Hall (1997), Parks (1998), Patterson (1995b, 1997), Perrin (1998), Tasker and Golombok (1991, 1997), and Victor and Fish (1995).

One main area of concern discussed by judges in custody proceedings involves the development of sexual identity among children of lesbian and gay parents (Patterson, 1992, 1997). Studies of gender identity and of gender-role behavior have, however, revealed few, if any, significant differences between children of lesbian or gay parents, on the one hand, and those of heterosexual parents, on the other. For instance, in one study (Gottman, 1990), 35 adult daughters of divorced lesbian mothers did not differ on indexes of gender-role preferences either from 35 adult daughters of divorced heterosexual mothers who had remarried or from 35 adult daughters of divorced heterosexual mothers who had not remarried (see also Green, 1978; Hoeffer, 1981).

An area of perennial concern in the area of sexual identity is that of the development of sexual orientation. Are the offspring of lesbian and gay parents themselves more likely to become lesbian or gay? Research to date gives precious little evidence to support the view that having nonheterosexual parents predisposes a child to become gay or lesbian (Patterson, 1992; Tasker and Golombok, 1997). In Gottman's (1990) study, for example, the percentage of adult daughters who self-identified as lesbian did not differ as a function of mothers' sexual orientations. Similar results have been reported by other investigators (Bailey and Dawood, 1998; Golombok and Tasker, 1996). Adolescent and young adult offspring of lesbian and gay parents in these studies, contrary to some expectations, were not significantly more likely to report lesbian or gay identities than were the offspring of heterosexual parents.

Other concerns voiced by judges about lesbian mother homes include worries about other aspects of personal development and about social relationships among the children (Patterson, 1992). Research relevant to these issues has, however, found no evidence to sustain any of these concerns. Children of lesbian mothers have proven to have no particular behavioral or emotional problems, no special difficulties with self-concept (Huggins, 1989), and no evidence of disruption in their social relationships with children or adults. For example, Golombok et al. (1983) compared school-age children of divorced lesbian mothers with same-age children of divorced heterosexual mothers on a wide array of assessments of behavioral problems, issues in peer relations, and relationships with adults. They found no differences, except that lesbian mothers reported that their children had more contact with their fathers than did those of heterosexual mothers. Children's contacts with fathers were also studied by Kirkpatrick et al. (1981), who reported no differences between children of divorced lesbian and divorced heterosexual mothers. Overall, then, the picture drawn by the existing research is one of great similarity between children of lesbian and heterosexual divorced mothers.

Some research has also been conducted to describe development among children born to or adopted by lesbian parents. The earliest studies in this area were those by McCandlish (1987) and Steckel (1985, 1987), both of whom reported similarities in overall patterns of development among young children born to lesbian couples and children born to heterosexual couples. This general pattern of findings has also been reported in studies of behavioral adjustment by Patterson (1994a, in press; Chan, Raboy, and Patterson, 1998), by Flaks, Ficher, Masterpasqua, and Joseph (1995), by Gartrell and her colleagues (Gartrell et al., 1996, 1999), and by Golombok and her colleagues (Golombok, Cook, Bish, and Murray, 1995; Golombok, Tasker, and Murray, 1997). Results of research on lesbian childrearing converge on the conclusion that children of lesbian mothers are developing in a normal fashion.

Despite the diversity evident within lesbian and gay communities, research on variations among lesbian and gay families with children is as yet quite sparse. Existing data suggest that children may fare better when mothers are in good psychological health (e.g., Patterson, in press). Children have also been described as more well adjusted when their lesbian mothers reported sharing childcare duties more evenly (e.g., Chan, Brooks, et al., 1998). Existing data also suggest the value of a supportive milieu, in which parental sexual orientation is accepted by other significant adults and in which children have contact with peers in similar circumstances. Research findings are still few in number, however, and much remains to be learned in this area.

SERVICES FOR LESBIAN AND GAY FAMILIES

In response to the varied special concerns of lesbian and gay families with children, many services and programs have been created. In this section, examples of programs and services that have arisen in three different contexts are described: parent groups, health care centers, and legal advocacy groups. For more detailed discussion of these issues, see Patterson (1994b).

Parent Groups

Lesbian and gay parents have formed many different kinds of support groups in localities in the United States and around the world. These include informal children's play groups arranged by friends, regional associations that hold picnics, carnivals, and other community events, and international organizations that publish newsletters and sponsor conferences. Many groups, in addition to addressing the needs of existing families, also provide services and programs for lesbians and gay men who are considering parenthood.

The largest such group in North America is the Family Pride Coalition (formerly Lesbian and Gay Parents' Coalition International). Family Pride Coalition lists more than 100 chapters across the United States, and its newsletter is also sent to readers in many other countries. It contains news of national and chapter activities, interviews with lesbian and gay parents, reports of current legal issues, and notices about other matters of interest for lesbian and gay parents and prospective parents. Beginning in 1990, the group also sponsored Children of Lesbians and Gays Everywhere, an organization for children of lesbian and gay parents, which in 1999 became an indepedently chartered group.

Through its central office and local chapters, Family Pride Coalition sponsors numerous activities for parents and prospective parents, including annual conferences; collects information regarding the policies of adoption agencies, sperm banks, and fertility programs; researches state laws as they pertain to adoption by openly lesbian families; creates lists of supportive gynecologists and fertility specialists in every state; and disseminates this information.

Much of the support that the Family Pride Coalition provides to prospective parents is made available through the efforts of local chapters that sponsor workshops and support groups for gay men and lesbians who are interested in parenthood. Many chapters sponsor support groups for individuals and couples who are in various stages of considering parenthood through DI, adoption, and/or surrogacy arrangements. Through such activities, prospective lesbian and gay parents can learn more about local parenting opportunities, legal issues, and medical resources, as well as meet others in the lesbian and gay community who are interested in becoming parents (Patterson, 1994b).

Health Care Centers

Some medical clinics that focus on the health care needs of lesbian and gay communities also provide services for parents and prospective parents. Such clinics have generally not been formally affiliated with hospitals or medical schools but have been established as free-standing primary-care centers for urban lesbian and/or gay communities. Two well-known examples are the Lyon-Martin Women's Health Services in San Francisco and the Whitman-Walker Clinic in Washington, D.C.

Lyon-Martin Women's Health Services, founded in 1978, is a primary-care community clinic specifically for women, with a primary focus on health care for lesbians and bisexual women. The clinic provides an array of medical and health-related services, including preventive and primary health care, HIV services, support services for mothers, and programs for sexual minority youth. It also sponsors the Lyon-Martin Lesbian/Gay Parenting Services (LGPS), which provides services for current and prospective lesbian and gay male parents.

Over the past 20 years, the LGPS has offered a broad array of programs for lesbian and gay families with children. These include an information and referral service, support groups for prospective parents, and workshops, forums, and special events for lesbian and gay families. Support groups are led by professional health educators and range from 8-week groups for lesbians considering parenthood to 6-week childbirth education classes. Many informational meetings and workshops on Considering Parenthood, Legal Issues, Adoption, Choices in Pregnancy and Birth and Lesbians and Gay Men Parenting Together are also offered by the Lyon-Martin LGPS. Panel participants include professionals in health care, social services, and the law, all speaking from a lesbian- and gay-affirmative perspective.

LGPS also sponsors, in addition to educational programming, a number of special events that are primarily social and recreational in character. Examples include a lesbian and gay family picnic and a parenting fair that provides access to information on a range of local parenting resources in a festive atmosphere. These kinds of community events offer valuable information, support, and recreational opportunities for lesbian and gay families.

Under the auspices of its Lesbian Choosing Children Project (LCCP), the Whitman-Walker Clinic also makes available services for lesbian and gay male parents and prospective parents. The LCCP has also sponsored workshops on creating alternative families. In addition, the LCCP has sponsored Maybe Baby groups for lesbians considering parenthood, and workshops on special topics such as

Options and Issues for Non-Biological Mothers. Similar programs are available in many other urban areas.

Legal Advocacy Groups

Legal advocacy groups within lesbian and gay communities also provide services to current and prospective lesbian parents. Especially prominent among such groups are the Lambda Legal Defense and Education Fund (LLDEF) and the National Center for Lesbian Rights (NCLR).

The LLDEF, founded in 1973 and based in New York City, works to advance the rights of sexual minorities through litigation and to provide education to the public, the legal profession, and the government about discrimination based on sexual orientation. The work of LLDEF covers a broad spectrum of issues including, "... discrimination in employment, in housing, in immigration, and in the military; AIDS and HIV-related issues; parenting and relationship issues; domestic partner benefits; and constitutional rights" (Perkins, 1992, p. 2). For many years, LLDEF has filed *amicus* briefs in cases involving the rights of lesbian nonbiological parents (Perkins, 1992; Perkins and Romo-Carmona, 1991). For instance, an attorney for LLDEF represented the plaintiff in Alison D. v. Virginia M., a well-known New York case in which a nonbiological mother sought visitation rights following the breakup of her relationship with her child's biological mother (Rubenstein, 1991). LLDEF attorneys also worked on important cases involving same-gender marriage, such as Baehr v. Miike (which sought unsuccessfully to establish the legality of same-gender marriage in Hawaii) and Baker v. Vermont (which established the rights of lesbian and gay adults to have their relationships treated in equal fashion, resulting in civil unions for same-gender couples in Vermont). Work by LLDEF in these and related cases has been influential in legal advocacy for causes that are critical to lesbian and gay families with children.

The NCLR, founded in 1977 and based in San Francisco, promotes awareness, respect, and recognition of lesbians and their rights (Chasnoff, 1992). The NCLR offers legal representation, *amicus* work, and technical assistance to cooperating counsel and other attorneys around the country. For example, NCLR has filed *amicus* briefs in cases involving the rights of nonbiological lesbian parents following the death of a biological parent and the breakup of a relationship between biological and nonbiological parents.

The NCLR has also been a pioneer in second-parent adoptions (Chasnoff, 1992; Ricketts and Achtenberg, 1990). Second-parent adoptions enable an unmarried parent to adopt a child without another parent of the same sex giving up his or her legal rights or responsibilities as a parent. Because they secure legal recognition of the relationship between nonbiological parents and their children, the availability of second-parent adoptions is of particular importance to lesbian and gay couples who wish to parent. Because in part of the efforts of NCLR attorneys, second-parent adoptions have been granted to date in at least 15 states and in the District of Columbia (Patterson and Redding, 1996).

An additional aspect of NCLR activities in support of lesbian and gay families with children is the NCLR publications program. They include a variety of materials relevant to lesbian and gay parenting, including "AIDS and Child Custody: A Guide to Advocacy," "Lesbians Choosing Motherhood: Legal Implications of Donor Insemination and Co-Parenting," and "Model Documents for Second Parent Adoption." These publications can assist parents and prospective parents in their efforts to secure legal protection for their families.

DIRECTIONS FOR RESEARCH, SERVICE, AND ADVOCACY

Although some innovative programs and services are available for lesbian mothers, gay fathers, and their children, their availability is still extremely limited. In this section, directions for research, service, and advocacy relevant to lesbian and gay families with children are described.

Directions for Research

One of the important directions for research is to identify and to explore factors that influence lesbian and gay couples' and individuals' inclinations to make parenthood a part of their lives (Crawford, 1987). Having lived so long in the shadow of antigay prejudice, many lesbians and gay men do not consider parenthood as an option. What kinds of influences are important in this regard? Does the degree of an individual's or a couple's integration with different parts of gay or lesbian and/or heterosexual communities make a difference? What roles do personal, social, and economic variables play in such decisions? We need to know more about the factors that influence decisions about parenthood among lesbians and gay men.

A related direction for research is assessment of the climate for lesbian and gay parenting in various areas. What are the important criteria that should be used in such an assessment, and how do different locales measure up against them? One approach might be to use state-level indicators as rough indices. For example, a statewide gay and lesbian rights law would be a positive indicator with regard to the climate for lesbian and gay parenting, as would the accomplishment of second-parent adoptions in that state. On the other side, negative indicators would include the existence of sodomy laws and/or other adverse legal precedents. One might also review regulations pertaining to adoption and foster care placements. Ratings of this sort could be useful for couples and individuals seeking parenthood, parents considering relocation, and for activists and advocacy groups deciding how best to direct their activities.

The climates of local communities might also be assessed with the needs of lesbian and gay parents and their children in mind. For instance, one might ask whether there are lesbian and gay parent groups already in existence, whether any second-parent adoptions have been completed within this community, and whether relevant health care and medical resources are available to lesbian and gay families. Such assessments should be geared to specific locales, because communities that are located in geographical proximity to one another may vary tremendously in the climates they provide for lesbian and gay families with children.

Such efforts to examine and to describe the atmosphere for lesbian and gay family life also raise questions about what aspects of a community make it an attractive place for lesbian and gay parents and their children to live. Such characteristics might in some cases be similar to those for heterosexual families (e.g., safe streets, good schools), whereas in other cases they might vary even among lesbian and gay families as a function of the family's other identities, interests, or needs. For instance, multiracial families might value especially the opportunity to live in multiracial neighborhoods.

It would also be valuable to learn more about the effectiveness of existing services for lesbian and gay families. Although many new services and programs have emerged for prospective parents as well as for parents and their children, there have been few attempts to evaluate their effectiveness. How effectively do available services fill the needs that they are intended to address? What populations are targeted by existing programs, and with what success do programs and services reach the communities for which they are intended? What are the essential elements of effective programs? How can existing programs be improved? All of these are critical questions for community-oriented research on lesbian and gay parenting services (see D'Augelli and Garnets, 1995).

Finally, the knowledge base relevant to lesbian and gay parenting is still somewhat limited. Courts need accurate information about the impact, if any, of parental sexual orientation on the development of children. Lesbians and gay men interested in parenting often want descriptive information about child and adolescent development among the offspring of lesbian and gay parents. Many lesbians and gay men considering parenthood also have questions about the ways in which parenthood can be expected to affect existing couple relationships in lesbian and gay families. Others are concerned about relationships with members of their families of origin as well as with friends, neighbors, and colleagues. Still others focus on family members' interactions with institutional contexts such as educational, legal, and medical settings. Scientists want to develop better understanding of the important variables in parenting and parent–child interactions, and this requires greater knowledge about parenting and about child development in lesbian and gay families. Such topics are open to empirical study, and the work has begun, but much remains to be accomplished.

Directions for Service

There are a number of ways in which efforts to provide improved services for lesbian and gay parents might be directed. In part because services for lesbian and gay parents are so new, and in part because of widespread discrimination, expanded services are needed at all levels. At the national level, an organization like the Family Pride Coalition has the potential to develop lists of health care, legal, and other resources on a state-by-state basis, as well as to provide technical assistance to local groups. At regional and local levels, individual parent groups are mounting educational events and other programs in support of lesbian and gay parenting in local communities. Even in major urban areas, however, most such programs are in a nascent state, depend heavily on the efforts of volunteers, and reach mainly affluent well-educated segments of lesbian and gay communities. In many smaller towns and rural areas, there are as yet no services at all.

One of the major needs, then, is for expansion of services. Programs and services should be developed by and for low-income and ethnic minority lesbian and gay individuals and couples who are parents or who wish to become parents. Of necessity, such work would involve identification of medical, legal, and other resources that are open to members of sexual minorities as well as to ethnic minorities and low-income communities. Services could also be developed for the children of lesbian and gay parents.

In seeking to expand services for sexual minority parenting communities, it will be important not to overlook important resources outside lesbian and gay communities themselves. For instance, building public library collections in areas relevant to lesbian and gay parenting can provide an important resource that is available to a large number of people, regardless of sexual orientation. Educational institutions such as high schools, colleges, and universities can also provide important resources for prospective lesbian and gay parents by including accurate information in the curriculum, by providing speakers and other relevant programming, and by making available to students articles, books, and video materials that relate to parenting by individuals with sexual minority identities (Casper and Schultz, 1999; Casper et al., 1992). Similarly, religious groups can offer meaningful support by providing special activities for lesbian and gay families with children and by educating all members of congregations about lesbian and gay parenting (Kahn, 1991).

Another major aim of service to prospective lesbian and gay parents is to eliminate discrimination against lesbian and gay parents and their children. To the degree that this effort meets with success, many of the special needs of gay or lesbian parents and their children will decrease in significance. Although it is unlikely that antigay prejudice will be eliminated in the foreseeable future, work in this direction is nevertheless an item of great importance. Prevention efforts relevant to lesbian and gay parenting should be designed to counter unfavorable stereotypes of lesbians and gay men with accurate information about the realities of life in lesbian and gay families and to provide an understanding of psychosocial processes underlying prejudice and discrimination.

Directions for Advocacy

Among the greatest current needs of lesbian and gay families with children is for activism to promote social and political change. Lesbian and gay parents and their children have issues in common with those of many other families, but they also have unique concerns that arise from prejudice against lesbian and gay families.

The basic issues of children and families in the United States are, in many cases, also the issues of lesbian and gay families with children. For instance, many families with children would benefit from enhanced neighborhood safety, better public schools, flexible working hours for parents, and better access to health care. A more equal distribution of economic resources would benefit children in economically stressed lesbian and gay families, just as it would benefit children in other economically disadvantaged homes. In other words, a common stake is held by gay, lesbian, and heterosexual families in many issues of public policy relevant to families with children.

Even allowing for overlap with the needs of other families, though, lesbian and gay families with children also have unique needs. Lesbian and gay families with children are less likely than heterosexual families to enjoy legal recognition for their family relationships, equal access to medical care, or freedom from harassment, bigotry, and hate crimes. The quality of life for lesbian and gay parents would be greatly enhanced if they could be confident that their sexual orientation would not be held against them as they pursue parenthood, bring up their children, or seek custody of their children after a partner's death or the breakup of an intimate relationship between parents. Like the offspring of heterosexual parents, children of lesbian and gay parents would feel more secure if their relationships with parents were protected by law. Accomplishment of such aims is an important goal for advocacy efforts on behalf of lesbian and gay families with children (Patterson and Redding, 1996; Polikoff, 1990; Rubinstein, 1991).

CONCLUSIONS

Research on lesbian mothers, gay fathers, and their children is coming of age. Systematic study of lesbian and gay families with children began in the context of judicial challenges to the fitness of lesbian and gay parents. For this reason, much research has been designed to evaluate negative judicial presumptions about the psychological health and well-being of parents and children in lesbian and gay families. Although much remains to be done to understand conditions that foster positive mental health among lesbian mothers, gay fathers, and their children, results of the early research were unusually clear. Findings of studies to date suggest that children of lesbian and gay parents develop in much the same ways that other children do and do not support the idea that children of lesbian or gay parents suffer debilitating disadvantages resulting from parental sexual orientation. In short, the results of research provide no justification for denying or curtailing parental rights because of variations in parental sexual orientation (Patterson and Redding, 1996).

With these conclusions in mind, researchers are now beginning also to turn their attention to areas of diversity among lesbian and gay families and are starting to explore conditions that help lesbian and gay families to flourish. This transition, now well underway, appears to be gathering momentum, and it suggests that research on lesbian and gay families has reached a significant turning point (Patterson, 1992, 1997). Having addressed negative assumptions represented in psychological theory, judicial opinion, and popular prejudice, researchers are now in a position to explore a broader range of issues.

From a methodological viewpoint, a number of directions seem especially promising. Longitudinal research is needed to follow families over time and to illuminate how changing life circumstances affect both parents and children. There is also a clear need for observational studies and for work conducted with large samples. A greater focus on family interactions and processes as well as on structural variables is also likely to be valuable (Patterson, 1992, 1997).

From a substantive point of view, many issues relevant to lesbian and gay families are in need of study. First, and most obvious, is that studies representing the demographic diversity of lesbian and gay families are needed. With few exceptions (e.g., Hill, 1987), existing research has involved European American, well-educated, middle-socioeconomic level families who live in urban areas of the United States. More work is needed to understand differences that are based on race and ethnicity, family economic circumstances, and cultural environments. Research of this kind should elucidate differences as well as commonalities among lesbian and gay families with children.

Future research should also, insofar as possible, encompass a larger number of levels of analysis. Existing research has most often focused on children or on their parents, considered as individuals. As valuable as this emphasis has been, it will also be important to consider couples and families as such. Assessments of dyadic adjustment or family climate could enhance understanding of individual-level variables such as self-esteem. When families are considered at different levels of analysis, nested within the neighborhood, regional, and cultural contexts in which they live (Lerner, Rothbaum, Boulos, and Castellino, in Vol. 2 of this *Handbook*), a more comprehensive understanding of lesbian and gay families is likely to emerge.

In this effort, it will be valuable to devote attention to family process as well as to family structure. How do lesbian and gay families negotiate their interactions with institutional settings such as the school and the workplace (e.g., Casper and Schultz, 1999)? How are family processes and interactions affected by economic, cultural, religious, and legal aspects of the contexts in which these families live (e.g., Badgett, 1998)? How do climates of opinion that prevail in their communities affect lesbian and gay families, and how do families cope with prejudice and discrimination when they are encountered?

Gender is a matter deserving of special attention in this regard. Inasmuch as lesbian and gay relationships encourage the uncoupling of gender and behavioral roles, one might expect to find considerable variability among families in the ways in which they carry out essential family, household and childcare tasks (Chan, Brooks, et al., 1998; Hand, 1991; McPherson, 1993; Osterweil, 1991; Patterson, 1995a, 1995b; Tasker and Golombok, 1998). In what ways do nontraditional divisions of labor affect children who grow up in lesbian and gay homes? And in what ways does the performance of nontraditional tasks affect parents themselves? In general terms, it will be valuable to learn more about the relative importance of gender and behavioral roles in lesbian and gay families with children.

One additional issue that should be given special emphasis involves the conceptualization of parents' sexual identities. In research on lesbian and gay parenting, scant attention has been devoted to possible changes in sexual identities over time or to the implications of any such fluidity for children (Brown, 1995). For instance, many parents are probably bisexual to some degree, rather than exclusively heterosexual, gay, or lesbian, yet this has rarely been noted or studied directly in the existing research literature. Increasing numbers of adults seem to be identifying themselves as bisexual (Fox, 1995). Future research might benefit from closer attention to issues in assessment of parental sexual orientation.

Although research to date on lesbian mothers, gay fathers, and their children has been fruitful, there is yet much important work to be done. Having addressed many of the heterosexist concerns of jurists, theorists, and others, researchers are now poised to examine a broader range of issues raised by the emergence of different kinds of lesbian and gay families with children. Results of future work in this area have the potential to increase our knowledge about lesbian and gay parenthood, stimulate innovations in our theoretical understanding of human development, and inform legal rulings and public policies relevant to lesbian mothers, gay fathers, and their children.

ACKNOWLEDGMENTS

I gratefully acknowledge support from the Society for Psychological Study of Social Issues, from the Lesbian Health Fund of the Lesbian and Gay Medical Association, and from the Roy Scrivner Fund of the American Psychological Foundation for my own research on lesbian families with children.

REFERENCES

Adam, B. D. (1987). *The rise of a gay and lesbian movement.* Boston: Twayne.

Badgett, M. V. L. (1998). The economic well-being of lesbian, gay and bisexual adults' families. In C. J. Patterson and A. R. D'Augelli (Eds.), *Lesbian, gay and bisexual identities in families: Psychological perspectives.* New York: Oxford University Press.

Bailey, J. M., and Dawood, K. (1998). Behavior genetics, sexual orientation, and the family. In C. J. Patterson and A. R. D'Augelli (Eds.), *Lesbian, gay and bisexual identities in families: Psychological perspectives.* New York: Oxford University Press.

Barret, R. L., and Robinson, B. E. (1990). *Gay fathers*. Lexington, MA: Lexington Books.

Baumrind, D. (1967). Childcare practices anteceding three patterns of preschool behavior. *Genetic Psychology Monographs*, *75*, 43–88.

Baumrind, D., and Black, A. E. (1967). Socialization practices associated with dimensions of competence in preschool boys and girls. *Child Development*, *38*, 291–327.

Beers, J. R. (1996). *The desire to parent in gay men*. Unpublished doctoral dissertation, Columbia University, New York, New York.

Bell, A. P., and Weinberg, M. S. (1978). *Homosexualities: A study of diversity among men and women*. New York: Simon & Schuster.

Bigner, J. J., and Bozett, F. W. (1990). Parenting by gay fathers. In F. W. Bozett and M. B. Sussman (Eds.), *Homosexuality and family relations* (pp. 155–176). New York: Harrington Park.

Bigner, J. J., and Jacobsen, R. B. (1989a). The value of children to gay and heterosexual fathers. In F. W. Bozett (Ed.), *Homosexuality and the family* (pp. 163–172). New York: Harrington Park.

Bigner, J. J., and Jacobsen, R. B. (1989b). Parenting behaviors of homosexual and heterosexual fathers. In F. W. Bozett (Ed.), *Homosexuality and the family* (pp. 173–186). New York: Harrington Park.

Blumenfeld, W. J., and Raymond, D. (1988). *Looking at gay and lesbian life*. Boston: Beacon.

Blumstein, P., and Schwartz, P. (1983). *American couples*. New York: Morrow.

Boswell, J. (1980). *Christianity, social tolerance, and homosexuality: Gay people in Western Europe from the beginning of the Christian era to the fourteenth century*. Chicago: University of Chicago Press.

Bozett, F. W. (1980). Gay fathers: How and why they disclose their homosexuality to their children. *Family Relations*, *29*, 173–179.

Bozett, F. W. (1981a). Gay fathers: Evolution of the gay-father identity. *American Journal of Orthopsychiatry*, *51*, 552–559.

Bozett, F. W. (1981b). Gay fathers: Identity conflict resolution through integrative sanctioning. *Alternative Lifestyles*, *4*, 90–107.

Bozett, F. W. (1987). Children of gay fathers. In F. W. Bozett (Ed.), *Gay and lesbian parents* (pp. 39–57). New York: Praeger.

Bozett, F. W. (1989). Gay fathers: A review of the literature. In F. W. Bozett (Ed.), *Homosexuality and the family* (pp. 137–162). New York: Harrington Park.

Brewaeys, A., and Van Hall, E. V. (1997). Lesbian motherhood: The impact on child development and family functioning. *Journal of psychosomatic obstetrics and gynecology*, *18*, 1–16.

Brodzinsky, D. M., Patterson, C. J., and Vaziri, M. (2001). Adoption agency perspectives on lesbian and gay adoptive parents: A national study. Unpublished manuscript, Rutgers University, Piscataway, NJ.

Brown, L. (1995). Lesbian identities: Conceptual issues. In A. R. D'Augelli and C. J. Patterson (Eds.), *Lesbian, gay and bisexual identities across the lifespan*. New York: Oxford University Press.

Casper, V., and Schultz, S. (1999). *Gay parents, straight schools: Building communication and trust*. New York: Teachers College Press.

Casper, V., Schultz, S., and Wickens, E. (1992). Breaking the silences: Lesbian and gay parents and the schools. *Teachers College Record*, *94*, 109–137.

Chan, R. W., Brooks, R. C., Raboy, B., and Patterson, C. J. (1998). Division of labor among lesbian and heterosexual parents: Associations with children's adjustment. *Journal of Family Psychology*, *12*, 402–419.

Chan, R. W., Raboy, B., and Patterson, C. J. (1998). Psychosocial adjustment among children conceived via donor insemination by lesbian and heterosexual mothers. *Child Development*, *69*, 443–457.

Chasnoff, D. (1992, Spring). *Newsletter of the National Center for Lesbian Rights*. San Francisco: National Center for Lesbian Rights.

Cowan, C. P., and Cowan, P. A. (1992). *When partners become parents: The big life change for couples*. New York: Basic Books.

Crawford, S. (1987). Lesbian families: Psychosocial stress and the family-building process. In Boston Lesbian Psychologies Collective (Ed.), *Lesbian psychologies: Explorations and challenges* (pp. 195–214). Urbana, IL: University of Illinois Press.

D'Augelli, A. R., and Garnets, L. (1995). Lesbian, gay and bisexual communities. In A. R. D'Augelli and C. J. Patterson (Eds.), *Lesbian, gay and bisexual identities across the lifespan*. New York: Oxford University Press.

D'Emilio, J. (1983). *Sexual politics, sexual communities: The makings of a homosexual minority in the United States, 1940–1970*. Chicago: University of Chicago Press.

Dunne, E. J. (1987). Helping gay fathers come out to their children. *Journal of Homosexuality*, *13*, 213–222.

Editors of the Harvard Law Review (1990). *Sexual orientation and the law*. Cambridge, MA: Harvard University Press.

Faderman, L. (1981). *Surpassing the love of men*. New York: Morrow.

Faderman, l. (1991). *Odd girls and twilight lovers: A history of lesbian life in twentieth century America*. New York: Columbia University Press.

Falk, P. J. (1989). Lesbian mothers: Psychosocial assumptions in family law. *American Psychologist*, *44*, 941–947.

Flaks, D. K., Ficher, I., Masterpasqua, F., and Joseph, G. (1995). Lesbians choosing motherhood: A comparative study of lesbian and heterosexual parents and their children. *Developmental Psychology*, *31*, 105–114.

Fox, R. C. (1995). Bisexual identities. In A. R. D'Augelli and C. J. Patterson (Eds.), *Lesbian, gay and bisexual identities across the lifespan*. New York: Oxford University Press.

Gartrell, N., Banks, A., Hamilton, J., Reed, N., Bishop, H., and Rodas, C. (1999). The national lesbian family study: II. Interviews with mothers of toddlers. *American Journal of Orthopsychiatry, 69*, 362–369.

Gartrell, N., Hamilton, J., Banks, A., Mosbacher, D., Reed, N., Sparks, C. H., and Bishop, H. (1996). The national lesbian family study: I. Interviews with prospective mothers. *American Journal of Orthopsychiatry, 66*, 272–281.

Goleman, D. (1992, December 2). Studies find no disadvantage to growing up in a gay home. *New York Times*, p. C14.

Golombok, S., Cook, R., Bish, A., and Murray, C. (1995). Families created by the new reproductive technologies: Quality of parenting and social and emotional development of the children. *Child Development, 66*, 285–298.

Golombok, S., Spencer, A., and Rutter, M. (1983). Children in lesbian and single-parent households: Psychosexual and psychiatric appraisal. *Journal of Child Psychology and Psychiatry, 24*, 551–572.

Golombok, S., and Tasker, F. (1996). Do parents influence the sexual orientation of their children? Findings from a longitudinal study of lesbian families. *Developmental Psychology, 32*, 3–11.

Golombok, S., Tasker, F. L., and Murray, C. (1997). Children raised in fatherless families from infancy: Family relationships and the socioemotional development of children of lesbian and single heterosexual mothers. *Journal of Child Psychology and Psychiatry, 38*, 783–791.

Gonsiorek, J. C. (1991). The empirical basis for the demise of the illness model of homosexuality. In J. C. Gonsiorek and J. D. Weinrich (Eds.), *Homosexuality: Research implications for public policy*. Beverly Hills, CA: Sage.

Gottman, J. S. (1990). Children of gay and lesbian parents. In F. W. Bozett and M. B. Sussman (Eds.), *Homosexuality and family relations* (pp. 177–196). New York: Harrington Park.

Green, R. (1978). Sexual identity of 37 children raised by homosexual or transsexual parents. *American Journal of Psychiatry, 135*, 692–697.

Green, R., Mandel, J. B., Hotvedt, M. E., Gray, J., and Smith, L. (1986). Lesbian mothers and their children: A comparison with solo parent heterosexual mothers and their children. *Archives of Sexual Behavior, 7*, 175–181.

Gross, J. (1991, February 11). New challenge of youth: Growing up in a gay home. *New York Times*, pp. A1, B7.

Harris, M. B., and Turner, P. H. (1985/1986). Gay and lesbian parents. *Journal of Homosexuality, 12*, 101–113.

Hand, S. I. (1991). *The Lesbian Parenting Couple*. Unpublished doctoral dissertation, The Professional School of Psychology, San Francisco.

Hand, S. I. (1993). *The Lesbian Parenting Couple*. Unpublished Doctoral Dissertation, The Professional School of Psychology, San Francisco, CA.

Herek, G. (1995). Psychological heterosexism in the United States. In A. R. D'Augelli and C. J. Patterson (Eds.), *Lesbian, gay and bisexual identities over the lifespan: Psychological perspectives*. New York: Oxford University Press.

Hill, M. (1987). Child-rearing attitudes of black lesbian mothers. In the Boston Lesbian Psychologies Collective (Ed.), *Lesbian Psychologies: Explorations and challenges* (pp. 215–226). Urbana: University of Illinois Press.

Hoeffer, B. (1981). Children's acquisition of sex-role behavior in lesbian-mother families. *American Journal of Orthopsychiatry, 5*, 536–544.

Huggins, S. L. (1989). A comparative study of self-esteem of adolescent children of divorced lesbian mothers and divorced heterosexual mothers. In F. W. Bozett (Ed.), *Homosexuality and the family* (pp. 123–135). New York: Harrington Park.

Kahn, Y. H. (1991, Spring). Hannah, must you have a child? *Out/Look* (12), 39–43.

King, B. R., and Black, K. N. (1999). College students' perceptual stigmatization of the children of lesbian mothers. *American Journal of Orthopsychiatry, 69*, 220–227.

Kinsey, A. C., Pomeroy, W. B., and Martin, C. E. (1948). *Sexual behavior in the human male*. Philadelphia: Saunders.

Kirkpatrick, M. (1987). Clinical implications of lesbian mother studies. *Journal of Homosexuality, 13*, 201–211.

Kirkpatrick, M. (1996). Lesbians as parents. In R. P. Cabaj and T. S. Stein (Eds.), *Textbook of homosexuality and mental health*. Washington, DC: American Psychiatric Press.

Kirkpatrick, M., Smith, C., and Roy, R. (1981). Lesbian mothers and their children: A comparative survey. *American Journal of Orthopsychiatry, 51*, 545–551.

Kleber, D. J., Howell, R. J., and Tibbits-Kleber, A. L. (1986). The impact of parental homosexuality in child custody cases: A review of the literature. *Bulletin of the American Academy of Psychiatry and Law, 14*, 81–87.

Koepke, L., Hare, J., and Moran, P. B. (1992). Relationship quality in a sample of lesbian couples with children and child-free lesbian couples. *Family Relations, 41*, 224–229.

Kweskin, S. L., and Cook, A. S. (1982). Heterosexual and homosexual mothers' self-described sex-role behavior and ideal sex-role behavior in children. *Sex Roles, 8*, 967–975.

Lamb, M. E. (Ed.). (1999). *Parenting and child development in nontraditional families*. Mahwah, NJ: Lawrence Erlbaum Associates.

Laumann, E. O., Gagnon, J. H., Michael, R. T., and Michaels, S. (1994). *The social organization of sexuality: Sexual practices in the United States*. Chicago: University of Chicago Press.

Lyons, T. A. (1983). Lesbian mothers' custody fears. *Women and Therapy, 2*, 231–240.

Martin, A. (1989). The planned lesbian and gay family: Parenthood and children. *Newsletter of the Society for the Psychological Study of Lesbian and Gay Issues, 5,* 6, 16–17.

Martin, A. (1993). *The lesbian and gay parenting handbook: Creating and raising our families.* New York: HarperCollins.

McCandlish, B. (1987). Against all odds: Lesbian mother family dynamics. In F. Bozett (Ed.), *Gay and lesbian parents* (pp. 23–38). New York: Praeger.

McPherson, D. (1993). *Gay parenting couples: Parenting arrangements, arrangement satisfaction, and relationship satisfaction.* Unpublished doctoral dissertation, Pacific Graduate School of Psychology.

Michaels, S. (1996). The prevalence of homosexuality in the United States. In R. P. Cabaj and T. S. Stein (Eds.), *Textbook of homosexuality and mental health.* Washington, DC: American Psychiatric Press.

Miller, B. (1978). Adult sexual resocialization: Adjustments toward a stigmatized identity. *Alternative Lifestyles, 1,* 207–234.

Miller, B. (1979). Gay fathers and their children. *Family Coordinator, 28,* 544–552.

Miller, J. A., Jacobsen, R. B., and Bigner, J. J. (1981). The child's home environment for lesbian versus heterosexual mothers: A neglected area of research. *Journal of Homosexuality, 7,* 49–56.

Mucklow, B. M., and Phelan, G. K. (1979). Lesbian and traditional mothers' responses to adult responses to child behavior and self concept. *Psychological Reports, 44,* 880–882.

Osman, S. (1972). My stepfather is a she. *Family Process, 11,* 209–218.

Osterweil, D. A. (1991). *Correlates of relationship satisfaction in lesbian couples who are parenting their first child together.* Unpublished doctoral dissertation, California School of Professional Psychology, Berkeley/Alameda.

Pagelow, M. D. (1980). Heterosexual and lesbian single mothers: A comparison of problems, coping and solutions. *Journal of Homosexuality, 5,* 198–204.

Parks, C. A. (1998). Lesbian parenthood: A review of the literature. *American Journal of Orthopsychiatry, 68,* 376–389.

Patterson, C. J. (1992). Children of lesbian and gay parents. *Child Development, 63,* 1025–1042.

Patterson, C. J. (1994a). Children of the lesbian baby boom: Behavioral adjustment, self-concepts, and sex-role identity. In B. Greene and G. Herek (Eds.), *Contemporary perspectives on lesbian and gay psychology: Theory, research, and applications* (pp. 156–175). Beverly Hills, CA: Sage.

Patterson, C. J. (1994b). Lesbian and gay couples considering parenthood: An agenda for research, service, and advocacy. *Journal of Gay and Lesbian Social Services, 1,* 33–55.

Patterson, C. J. (1995a). Lesbian mothers, gay fathers, and their children. In A. R. D'Augelli and C. J. Patterson (Eds.), *Lesbian, gay and bisexual identities across the lifespan.* New York: Oxford University Press.

Patterson, C. J. (1995b). Families of the lesbian baby boom: Parents' division of labor and children's adjustment. *Developmental Psychology, 31,* 115–123.

Patterson, C. J. (1997). Children of lesbian and gay parents. In T. Ollendick and R. Prinz (Eds.), *Advances in clinical child psychology* (Vol. 19, pp. 235–282). New York: Plenum.

Patterson, C. J. (1998). Family lives of children with lesbian mothers. In C. J. Patterson and A. R. D'Augelli (Eds.), *Lesbian, gay and bisexual identities in families: Psychological perspectives* (pp. 154–176). New York: Oxford University Press.

Patterson, C. J. (2000). Family relationships of lesbians and gay men. *Journal of Marriage and the Family, 62,* 1052–1069.

Patterson, C. J. (in press). Families of the lesbian baby boom: Maternal mental health and child adjustment. *Journal of Gay and Lesbian Psychotherapy.*

Patterson, C. J., and Chan, R. W. (1996). Gay fathers and their children. In R. P. Cabaj and T. S. Stein (Eds.), *Textbook of homosexuality and mental health* (pp. 371–393). Washington, DC: American Psychiatric Press.

Patterson, C. J., and Friel, L. V. (2000). Sexual orientation and fertility. In G. R. Bentley and N. Mascie-Taylor (Eds.), *Infertility in the modern world: Biosocial perspectives.* Cambridge, England: Cambridge University Press.

Patterson, C. J., Hurt, S., and Mason, C. D. (1998). Families of the lesbian baby boom: Children's contacts with grandparents and other adults. *American Journal of Orthopsychiatry, 68,* 390–399.

Patterson, C. J., and Redding, R. (1996). Lesbian and gay families with children: Public policy implications of social science research. *Journal of Social Issues, 52,* 29–50.

Perkins, P. (Ed.). (1992). *The Lambda Update* (Vol. 9, No. 1). New York: Lambda Legal Defense and Education Fund.

Perkins, P., and Romo-Carmona, M. (1991). *The Lambda Update* (Vol. 8, No. 1). New York: Lambda Legal Defense and Education Fund.

Perrin, E. C. (1998). Children whose parents are lesbian or gay. *Contemporary Pediatrics, 15,* 113–130.

Pies, C. (1985). *Considering parenthood.* San Francisco: Spinsters & Aunt Lute.

Pies, C. (1990). Lesbians and the choice to parent. In F. W. Bozett and M. B. Sussman (Eds.), *Homosexuality and family relations* (pp. 137–154). New York: Harrington Park.

Polikoff, N. (1990). This child does have two mothers: Redefining parenthood to meet the needs of children in lesbian mother and other nontraditional families. *Georgetown Law Review, 78,* 459–575.

Pollack, S., and Vaughn, J. (Eds.). (1987). *Politics of the heart: A lesbian parenting anthology.* Ithaca, NY: Firebrand.

Rafkin, L. (Ed.). (1990). *Different mothers: Sons and daughters of lesbians talk about their lives.* Pittsburgh, PA: Cleis.

Rand, C., Graham, D. L. R., and Rawlings, E. I. (1982). Psychological health and factors the court seeks to control in lesbian mother custody trials. *Journal of Homosexuality, 8,* 27–39.

Ricketts, W. (1991). *Lesbians and gay men as foster parents*. Portland, ME: National Child Welfare Resource Center for Management and Administration.

Ricketts, W., and Achtenberg, R. (1990). Adoption and foster parenting for lesbians and gay men: Creating new traditions in family. In F. W. Bozett and M. B. Sussman (Eds.), *Homosexuality and family relations* (pp. 83–118). New York: Harrington Park.

Riley, C. (1988). American kinship: A lesbian account. *Feminist Issues, 8*, 75–94.

Rivera, R. (1991). Sexual orientation and the law. In J. C. Gonsiorek and J. D. Weinrich (Eds.), *Homosexuality: Research implications for public policy* (pp. 81–100). Newbury Park, CA: Sage.

Robinson, B. E., and Skeen, P. (1982). Sex-role orientation of gay fathers versus gay nonfathers. *Perceptual and Motor Skills, 55*, 1055–1059.

Rohrbaugh, J. B. (1988). Choosing children: Psychological issues in lesbian parenting. *Women and Therapy, 8*, 51–63.

Rubenstein, W. B. (1991). We are family: A reflection on the search for legal recognition of lesbian and gay relationships. *The Journal of Law and Politics, 8*, 89–105.

Sbordone, A. J. (1993). *Gay men choosing fatherhood*. Unpublished doctoral dissertation, Department of Psychology, City University of New York.

Schulenberg, J. (1985). *Gay parenting: A complete guide for gay men and lesbians with children*. New York: Anchor.

Skeen, P., and Robinson, B. (1985). Gay fathers' and gay nonfathers' relationships with their parents. *Journal of Sex Research, 21*, 86–91.

Steckel, A. (1985). *Separation–individuation in children of lesbian and heterosexual couples*. Unpublished doctoral dissertation, The Wright Institute Graduate School, Berkeley, CA.

Steckel, A. (1987). Psychosocial development of children of lesbian mothers. In F. W. Bozett (Ed.), *Gay and lesbian parents* (pp. 75–85). New York: Praeger.

Tasker, F. L., and Golombok, S. (1991). Children raised by lesbian mothers: The empirical evidence. *Family Law, 21*, 184–187.

Tasker, F. L., and Golombok, S. (1997). *Growing up in a lesbian family: Effects on child development*. New York: Guilford.

Tasker, F. L., and Golombok, S. (1998). The role of co-mothers in planned lesbian-led families. In G. A. Dunne (Ed.), *Living Difference: Lesbian Perspectives on Work and Family Life*. New York: Harrington Park Press.

Thompson, N., McCandless, B., and Strickland, B. (1971). Personal adjustment of male and female homosexuals and heterosexuals. *Journal of Abnormal Psychology, 78*, 237–240.

United States Bureau of the Census (2000). [On-line]. Available: http://www.census.gov/population/estimates/nation2/html.

Victor, S. B., and Fish, M. C. (1995). Lesbian mothers and their children: A review for school psychologists. *School Psychology Review, 24*, 456–479.

Weeks, R. B., Derdeyn, A. P., and Langman, M. (1975). Two cases of children of homosexuals. *Child Psychiatry and Human Development, 6*, 26–32.

Weston, K. (1991). *Families we choose: Lesbians, gays, kinship*. New York: Columbia University Press.

Wright, J. M. (1998). *Lesbian stepfamilies: An ethnography of love*. New York: Harrington Park Press.

11

Parenting and Contemporary Reproductive Technologies

Susan Golombok

City University, London

INTRODUCTION

The reproductive technology that resulted in the birth in 1978 of Louise Brown, the first "test-tube" baby (Steptoe and Edwards, 1978), has led to the creation of families that would not otherwise have existed. This procedure, more appropriately described as *in vitro* fertilization (IVF), has not only allowed many people who would have remained childless to become mothers and fathers but has also had a fundamental impact on the way in which parents may be related to their children. With IVF, when the mother's egg and the father's sperm are used, both parents are genetically related to the child. When a donated egg is used, the father is genetically related to the child but not the mother; and when donated sperm are used, the mother is genetically related to the child but not the father. When both egg and sperm are donated, both parents are genetically unrelated to the child, a situation that is like adoption except that the parents experience the pregnancy and the child's birth. In the case of surrogacy, neither, one, or both parents may lack a genetic link with the child, depending on the use of a donated egg, sperm, or both. As Einwohner (1989) has pointed out, it is now possible for a child to have five parents: an egg donor, a sperm donor, a birth mother who hosts the pregnancy, and the two social parents whom the child knows as mom and dad. In addition, an increasing number of lesbian and single heterosexual women are opting for assisted reproduction (Patterson, in Vol. 3 of this *Handbook*), particularly donor insemination, to allow them to conceive a child without the involvement of a male partner. In these families, there is no father present right from the start, and many lesbian families are headed by two mothers.

In this chapter families created by the different types of contemporary reproductive technology are examined, with particular attention given to the issues and concerns that have been raised by these procedures and to the findings of research on parenting in these new family forms. Although there is a growing body of empirical research on families created by assisted reproduction, many investigations have focused on children and not on parents. Only those studies that have addressed parenting are discussed in this chapter.

This chapter is organized according to the three major types of contemporary reproductive technology: IVF, donor insemination, and egg donation. Within each section the concerns that have been raised regarding parenting are discussed, followed by an examination of the empirical evidence. This chapter ends with a consideration of future directions in the development of contemporary reproductive technologies and general conclusions about parenting in these new family forms.

PARENTING CHILDREN CONCEIVED BY IVF

Although IVF may be carried out with donated eggs, sperm, or both, in the large majority of cases the gametes of the prospective parents are used. The following discussion of IVF families focuses on parents who are genetically related to their child.

Concerns About Parenting in IVF Families

IVF involves the fertilization of an egg with sperm in the laboratory and the transfer of the resulting embryo to the mother's womb. It may seem that having a genetically related child by IVF is just the same as having a child by natural conception; all that is different is the process of conception. However, there are a number reasons why having a child by IVF may result in a rather different experience for parents than having a child in the usual way. One very apparent difference is the higher incidence of multiple births, preterm births, and low-birthweight infants following IVF (Australian In Vitro Fertilization Collaborative Group, 1985; Beral, Doyle, Tan, Mason, and Campbell, 1990; Lancaster, 1987; Society for Assisted Reproductive Technology [SART] Registry, 1999; Tanbo, Dale, Lunde, Moe, and Abyholm, 1995; Wang et al., 1994; Westergard, Johansen, Erb, and Andersen, 1999). Whereas only 1% of natural births involve twins, triplets, or more, this is true of more than one fourth of births resulting from IVF (Medical Research Council, 1990; SART Registry, 1999). Parents who have multiple births (Lytton with Gallagher, in Vol. 1 of this *Handbook*) have to cope with not only two or more infants born at once but also with infants who may have greater needs as a result of prematurity and low birthweight (Botting, MacFarlane, and Price, 1990).

It has also been suggested that the stress associated with the experience of infertility and its treatment, often lasting for many years, may result in parenting difficulties when a baby eventually arrives (Burns, 1990). Certainly it is the case that infertility can be deeply upsetting. In an investigation by van Balen, Trimbos-Kemper, Van Hall, and Weeda (1989), infertility was viewed by more than 40% of women as the worst experience of their life. The negative impact of infertility on psychological functioning is also evident from studies that show raised levels of anxiety among couples, particularly women, undergoing infertility treatment, and of clinical depression among women whose treatment was unsuccessful (Eugster and Vingerhoets, 1999; Golombok, 1992; Leiblum, 1997; Leiblum, Kemmann, and Lane, 1987). Kopitzke and Wilson (2000) concluded that the physical discomfort caused by infertility treatment faded into insignificance compared with the emotional agonies involved. Women at their clinic reported that their lives were diminished and that it was hard to visualize the future. Social relationships were dramatically affected because of feelings of alienation from friends and relatives with children, and family get-togethers and even trips to shopping centers full of mothers with baby strollers could be a source of pain.

Infertility may also constitute a threat to a woman's sense of identity (Miall, 1986, 1989). Evidence from Miall's research showed that the large majority of infertile women saw infertility as a personal failure. Among the 71 infertile women studied, 89% reported that motherhood was either important or very important to their notion of themselves as persons, and 78% had always wanted to have children. Although studies that have included men have shown them to be less emotionally distressed than women about their failure to have a child, many men are also upset about their inability to become fathers (Eugster and Vingerhoets, 1999; Golombok, 1992; Leiblum, 1997; Leiblum et al., 1987).

According to Burns (1990), the stresses produced by infertility are likely to result in dysfunctional patterns of parenting. She argued that parents who had difficulty in conceiving may be overprotective of, and emotionally overinvested in, their much longed-for child. Other authors have also suggested that those who become parents after a period of infertility may be overprotective of their children, or may have unrealistic expectations of them, or of themselves as parents, because of the difficulties they experienced in their attempt to give birth (McMahon, Ungerer, Beaurepaire, Tennant, and Saunders, 1995; Mushin, Spensley, and Barreda-Hanson, 1985; van Balen 1998). Psychological disorder and marital difficulties have also been predicted for those who become parents following IVF (McMahon et al., 1995).

Research on Parenting in IVF Families

Contemporary reproductive technologies have advanced at such a pace that studies of the families that are created as a result of these procedures have lagged far behind. The psychological literature that exists has largely addressed concerns that conception by IVF may have a detrimental effect on children's cognitive and emotional development. Less attention has been paid to the impact of IVF on parenting. The investigations subsequently described have tended to look at families with a single child born as a result of assisted reproduction to avoid the confounding effect of a multiple birth. However, many of the children studied had older or younger siblings.

In a prospective study of IVF families in Australia, psychological adjustment to first-time motherhood was assessed when the baby was 4 months old (McMahon, Ungerer, Tennant, and Saunders, 1997). Sixty-five IVF families were compared with 62 families with no history of infertility. The aim of the study was to determine whether mothers who conceived by IVF differed from the matched comparison group of natural conception mothers with respect to adjustment to early parenthood, specific adjustment to the maternal role, and quality of the parent–child relationship. Anxiety was assessed with the State Anxiety Inventory (Spielberger, Gorusch, and Lushene, 1970); the Edinburgh Postnatal Depression Scale (Cox, Holden, and Sagovsky, 1987) was used to screen for postnatal depression; marital adjustment was assessed with the Dyadic Adjustment Scale (Spanier, 1976); and self-esteem as a woman was measured with a modification of a scale developed by Rosenberg (1965).

Measures of adjustment to motherhood included the Being a Parent Questionnaire, which was developed specifically for the study to assess the mother's sense of competence and satisfaction, the Maternal Self-Efficacy Scale (Teti and Gelfand, 1991), the Maternal Postnatal Attachment Questionnaire (Condon, 1993) to assess the mother's feelings about her infant, and the Maternal Separation Anxiety Scale (Hock, DeMeis, and McBride, 1988). In addition, an observational assessment of mother–infant interaction was carried out with the still-face procedure (Gianino and Tronick, 1985; Tronick, Als, Adamson, Wise, and Brazelton, 1978). Maternal behavior was coded according to both positive (e.g., baby-talk, frequency and variety of games) and negative (e.g., intrusiveness, overriding behaviors, and teasing) interactive styles to assess the mother's sensitivity to her infant.

There were no differences between the two groups of mothers for anxiety, postnatal depression, marital adjustment, or feelings of attachment toward the infant, and the observational assessment showed no difference in maternal behavior during the still-face procedure between the two groups of mothers. However, the IVF mothers reported lower self-esteem and lower maternal self-efficacy. McMahon et al. (1997) concluded that the overall findings were reassuring for parents who conceive by IVF and that the specific differences identified between the IVF and the natural conception mothers may be explained by the IVF mothers judging themselves too harshly.

The 65 IVF families and 61 of the natural conception families were followed up when the babies were 1 year old by use of many of the same measures as in the original investigation (Gibson, Ungerer, Leslie, Saunders, and Tennant, 1999; Gibson, Ungerer, Tennant, and Saunders, 2000). Additional assessment instruments included the Intimate Bond Measure (McMahon et al., 1997) and the Partner Involved Scale (B. Heubeck, personal communication) to assess marital quality; the Center for Epidemiological Studies of Depression Scale (Radloff and Locke, 1986); the Family Support Scale and the Inventory of Socially Supportive Behaviors (Barrera, 1981; Dunst, Jenkins, and Trivette, 1984) to measure social support; and the Parenting Attitudes to Child Rearing Scale (Goldberg and Easterbrooks, 1984). Mothers were also administered the Parenting Stress Index (Abidin, 1990) and were interviewed about their feelings in relation to protectiveness toward the child, frequency of thoughts about the child's vulnerability (e.g., the risk of illness or injury), and perceptions of the child's "specialness." The mother–child relationship was assessed through videotaped observational procedures scored blind to IVF status. Maternal sensitivity, structuring, and hostility during a period of play were measured with the Emotional Availability Scales.

The findings showed that IVF mothers and fathers reported similar general psychological adjustment and parenthood-specific adjustment relative to the natural conception parents. The two groups of parents did not differ on the measures of anxiety, depression, and social support, or on measures more specific to parenthood such as attachment to the child, attitudes to childrearing, separation anxiety, and parenting stress. There was, however, a nonsignificant trend toward the IVF mothers who reported lower self-esteem and less parenting competence than did the natural conception mothers. In addition, although there were no group differences in protectiveness, the IVF mothers saw their children as significantly more vulnerable and "special." The IVF fathers reported significantly lower self-esteem and marital satisfaction but no less competence in parenting. There were no differences between the IVF and the natural conception mothers for any of the measures of interaction during play as assessed by the Emotional Availability Scales.

Gibson et al. (1999, 2000) concluded that the IVF parents' adjustment to parenthood when their child was 1 year old was similar to that of the natural conception families. Nevertheless, there were minor differences among the IVF parents that reflected heightened child-focused concern and less confidence in parenting for mothers, less satisfaction with the marriage for fathers, and vulnerable self-esteem for both parents. Gibson et al. (1999, 2000) emphasized that, although the IVF mothers continued to have higher levels of concern over child well-being and notions of child "specialness," their concerns did not appear to be associated with more protective parenting compared with mothers who had conceived naturally. In addition, these parenting attitudes did not seem to translate into differences or impairments in the quality of mother–child interaction. They did suggest, however, that the IVF mothers' concerns may cause them to be preoccupied with their children and to exclude their husbands, thereby contributing to the fathers' lower marital satisfaction and self-esteem.

In France, Raoul-Duval, Bertrand-Servais, Letur-Konirsch, and Frydman (1994) studied 33 families with an IVF child compared with matched groups of 33 families with a history of infertility (who conceived their child through ovarian stimulation) and 33 families with a naturally conceived child. The families were first seen in the hospital after delivery, and then followed up at home after 9 months, 18 months, and 3 years. Each assessment involved a semistructured interview regarding the well-being of the mother and her relationship with her child. The mother–child relationship was assessed on the basis of the mother's body language (the way in which the mother held her child), vocal dialogue (the way in which the mother addressed her child), visual dialogue (the way in which the mother looked at her child), and attitude toward breast-feeding. There were no significant differences among the three family types in the incidence of either maternal depression or problems in the relationship between the mother and the child at any of the assessment periods. It should be noted, however, that by the time of the 3-year-old assessment, only 39% of the natural conception mothers and 33% of the mothers with a history of infertility remained in the study, although a higher proportion of IVF families (76%) was retained. As Raoul-Duval et al. (1994) pointed out, if the other types of family were lost because of difficulties in family functioning, this would give greater weight to the conclusion that the IVF families were not at risk.

In the United Kingdom, 20 couples who had conceived by IVF were compared with a matched group of 20 couples who had conceived without medical assistance when their babies were between 15 and 27 months old (Weaver, Clifford, Gordon, Hay, and Robinson, 1993). The parents' emotional health and marital adjustment were assessed by the Crown-Crisp Experiential Index (Crown and Crisp, 1979) and the Dyadic Adjustment Scale (Spanier, 1976) respectively. Questionnaires measuring quality of life (Campbell, Converse, and Rodgers, 1976) and parents' feelings about their babies (Reading, Cox, Sledmere and Campbell, 1984) were also administered together with the Mother–Child Relationship Evaluation Manual (Roth, 1980), a measure of parenting attitudes that produces scores on subscales of acceptance, overprotection, overindulgence, and rejection.

There were no differences between the two groups of parents for emotional health or marital adjustment, and their scores were closely comparable with general population norms. The IVF parents reported significantly more positive feelings toward their babies than did the natural conception parents and rated themselves as feeling significantly less tied down on the quality of life measure. With respect to the measure of parenting attitudes, the IVF parents reported being more protective toward their child than did the natural conception parents. It may be relevant that these parents were the first to give birth to an IVF child in this area of the country. It should also be noted that these findings were based on questionnaire data only.

IVF families with children between the ages of 24 and 30 months in Belgium were studied by Colpin, Demyttenaere, and Vandemeulebroecke (1995), who used both self-report questionnaires and observational measures of mother–child interaction. Thirty-one families with an IVF child were compared with 62 natural-conception families with no history of infertility, representing response rates of 87% and 93%, respectively. The parents' anxiety, depression, and marital relationship were assessed with the State-Trait Anxiety Inventory (Speilberger, 1966), the Zung Depression Scale (Zung, 1965), and the Maudsely Marital Questionnaire (Crowe, 1978). The Parental Bonding Instrument (Parker, Tupling, and Brown, 1979) was also completed by parents to assess mothers' and fathers' experiences with their own parents on four dimensions: mother's affection, mother's overprotection, father's affection, and father's overprotection. Mother–child interaction was assessed with the Rating Scales for Interactive Tasks (Erickson, Sroufe, and Egeland, 1985). During a home visit, the child was videotaped interacting with the mother in a series of problem-solving tasks. The child's behavior was rated on four task-oriented scales (enthusiasm for the tasks, persistence in attempting to solve them, reliance on the mother for help, and compliance for task directions suggested by the mother) and three mother-oriented scales (avoidance of the mother, hostility, and the expression of positive feelings toward her). The mother's behavior was assessed on four dimensions (supportive presence, respect for the child's autonomy, structure and limit setting, and hostility expressed toward the child). Fathers' and mothers' representations of their relationship with their child were assessed with a Dutch translation (Lambermon, 1991) of the Questionnaire of Parental Attitudes and Emotions (Engfer and Schneewind, 1976), which produces subscale scores of empathy, rigidity, strain, frustration, depression, tendency to punish, role reversal between parents and children, and anxious overconcern.

No differences were identified between the IVF families and the natural conception families for any of the measures of the parents' psychological functioning or the mother's relationship with her child. The only difference to emerge related to the subgroup of IVF mothers who were employed; those who were employed showed less respect for their child's autonomy during problem solving than both the nonemployed IVF mothers and the employed natural conception mothers. A possible explanation for this finding put forward by Colpin et al. (1995) was that it may be more difficult for IVF mothers to resume work outside the home than it is for natural conception mothers and that they may compensate by inhibiting their child from being autonomous. Certainly, the IVF mothers who resumed work were more likely to have done so for financial reasons than the mothers of a naturally conceived child. Nevertheless, an alternative explanation is that this finding represented a chance effect resulting from the large number of group comparisons carried out.

In a study of IVF families with 2- to 4-year-old children in The Netherlands, van Balen (1996) included a comparison group of formerly infertile parents with a naturally conceived child to control for the experience of infertility, in addition to a comparison group of natural conception families with no history of infertility. Forty-five IVF parents, 35 formerly infertile parents, and 35 fertile parents completed questionnaires on parenting behavior and on their child. A modified version of the Child-Rearing Practices Report (Block, 1965; Dekovic, Jansen, and Gerris, 1991) was used to

measure parental concern, emotional involvement, and expectations. Parental stress was assessed with the Nijmegen Questionnaire of Child Rearing Circumstances (Robbroeckx and Wels, 1989) to give scores on two dimensions; parental competence (ability to handle the child) and parental burden (feeling burdened by the child).

The IVF mothers and the previously infertile mothers differed from the natural conception mothers with respect to emotional involvement with their child. They reported experiencing more pleasure in their child and stronger feelings toward their child than did mothers with no history of infertility. The IVF and the previously infertile mothers also reported greater parental competence than did the fertile mothers. There were no differences regarding the mothers' reports of parental concern, parental expectations, or parental burden. Fathers did not differ on any of the measures. It seems therefore that where differences existed the findings of this study pointed to positive outcomes for mothers of 2- to 4-year-old children with a history of infertility whether or not the child was conceived by IVF. It is important to point out that these results are based on self-report questionnaires and that the response rate was low (ranging from 69% for the IVF mothers through 52% for the previously infertile mothers to 35% for the fertile mothers). An advantage of the study, however, was the inclusion of a comparison group of previously infertile couples who did not conceive by IVF.

The European Study of Assisted Reproduction Families has examined the quality of parenting in families created as a result of both IVF and donor insemination compared with families with a naturally conceived child and a group of adoptive families. In the first phase of the study, conducted when the children were between the ages of 4 and 8 years, representative samples of 41 families with a child conceived by IVF and 45 families with a child conceived by donor insemination were recruited through infertility clinics throughout the United Kingdom (Golombok, Cook, Bish, and Murray, 1995). The comparison groups of 43 families with a naturally conceived child and 55 families with a child adopted in the first 6 months of life were recruited through the records of maternity wards and adoption agencies, respectively, and matched to the assisted reproduction families as closely as possible with respect to demographic characteristics such as the age of the mother, social status, and family size.

Quality of parenting was assessed by standardized interview with the mother, by use of an adaptation of a technique developed by Quinton and Rutter (1988). Four overall ratings were made: (1) Mother's warmth toward the child was based on the mother's tone of voice and facial expression when talking about the child, spontaneous expressions of warmth, sympathy, and concern about any difficulties experienced by the child, and enthusiasm and interest in the child as a person. (2) Emotional involvement, which represented anxious overinvolvement at the extreme end, took account of the extent to which the family day was organized around the child, the extent to which the needs or interests of the child were placed before those of other family members, the extent to which the mother was overconcerned, overprotective, or inhibited the child from age-appropriate independent activities, the extent to which the mother was willing to leave the child with other caregivers, and the extent to which the mother had other interests or engaged in activities apart from those relating to the child. (3) Mother–child interaction and (4) father–child interaction were ratings of the quality of interaction between the parent and the child based on mothers' reports of the extent to which the parent and the child enjoyed each other's company, wanted to be with each other, spent time together, enjoyed joint play activities, and showed physical affection to one another. In addition, the short form of the Parenting Stress Index (Abidin, 1990) was administered to all mothers and fathers. The psychological functioning of the parents was assessed with the State-Trait Anxiety Inventory (Spielberger, 1983), the Beck Depression Scale (Beck and Steer, 1987), and the Golombok Rust Inventory of Marital Satisfaction (Rust, Bennun, and Golombok, 1990). The findings relating to the IVF families are presented here, and the donor insemination families are discussed in the next section.

It was found that parents with a child conceived by IVF obtained significantly higher ratings for mother's warmth to the child, mother's emotional involvement with the child, and mother–child interaction and father–child interaction than did the natural conception parents. The adoptive parents' ratings on these variables were closely comparable with those of the IVF parents. In line with these findings, mothers and fathers of naturally conceived children reported significantly higher levels of stress associated with parenting. Thus the findings of this study indicated that the quality of parenting in families with a child conceived by IVF was superior to that shown by families with a naturally conceived child. Where parents in the different family types differed with respect to anxiety, depression, or marital satisfaction, this reflected greater difficulties among the natural-conception parents.

In the second phase of the research, the study was expanded to include an additional country from northern Europe (The Netherlands) and two countries from southern Europe (Spain and Italy) in order to increase the sample size and to allow the examination of the influence of culturally determined attitudes toward assisted reproduction on the functioning of families that have resulted from these techniques. The procedures used in The Netherlands, Spain, and Italy were identical to those used in the United Kingdom. The inclusion of these three countries brought the total number of IVF, donor insemination, adoptive, and naturally conceived families to 116, 111, 115, and 120, respectively. The findings regarding the donor insemination families are presented in the next section.

The results of the extended study confirmed the findings of the original investigation (Golombok et al., 1996). Mothers of children conceived by IVF were found to express greater warmth to their child, to be more emotionally involved with their child, to interact more with their child, and to report less stress associated with parenting than did the mothers in the comparison group who conceived their child naturally. In addition, IVF fathers were reported by mothers to interact with their child more than fathers with a naturally conceived child.

In the United Kingdom, the families were followed up as the children approached adolescence (Golombok, MacCallum and Goodman, 2001). Thirty-four of the IVF families, 49 of the adoptive families, and 38 of the natural conception families were assessed as close as possible to the child's twelfth birthday (see the next section for a follow-up of donor insemination families). This represented response rates of 87%, 89%, and 97%, respectively, excluding those who could not be traced. The focus of the study was on parent–child relationships with a emphasis on warmth and control, two aspects of parenting that are considered important for the psychological adjustment of the adolescent child (Baumrind, 1989, 1991; Maccoby and Martin, 1983; Patterson, 1982; Patterson, Reid, and Dishion, 1992).

The mothers and fathers were interviewed separately with a modification of the standardized interview technique, designed to assess the quality of parenting, that was used in the earlier investigation (Quinton and Rutter, 1988). The data obtained from these interviews were coded to give ratings of sensitive responding, emotional involvement, mother-to-child warmth, father-to-child warmth, severity of disputes with child, frequency of disputes with child and disciplinary indulgence. In addition, the Expression of Affection Inventory (Hetherington and Clingempeel, 1992) was completed by mothers (regarding the child), fathers (regarding the child), and children (once for each parent) to provide a standardized assessment of the total occurrence of affectionate behaviors between them. The Conflict Tactics Scale (Straus, 1979) was administered in the same way to assess how parents and children act during conflict. Data on parenting were also obtained from an interview with the child by the Child and Adolescent Functioning and Environment Schedule (John and Quinton, 1991) to produce ratings of warmth, dependability, and quality of discipline from mothers and fathers.

IVF parents continued to have a good relationship with their child, characterized by a combination of affection and appropriate control. Some differences were found between families in which parents experienced a period of infertility before the birth of their child and the natural conception families, but these were not specific to IVF families. Instead, they were characteristic of both IVF and adoptive families, suggesting that the experience of infertility, rather than the lack of a genetic relationship between the mother and the child, was associated with differences in parent–child relationships. These differences were found to be both negative and positive. In particular, mothers who had experienced infertility were found to show less sensitive responding toward their child, and their children found them to engage in less reasoning during disputes, suggesting greater detachment, but they were also viewed by their children as more dependable. The only difference to emerge between IVF and adoptive families was for maternal and paternal affection, indicating that a genetic link between parents and children may be related to greater affection toward the child (Bjorklund, Yunger, and Pelligrini, in Vol. 2 of this *Handbook*). However, this finding was not reflected in IVF children's perceptions of parental affection toward them, indicating that this effect, to the extent that it did not simply result from a social desirability bias, was not large.

The finding of the initial study of 4- to 8-year-old children (Golombok et al., 1995) that IVF mothers and fathers were more involved parents than mothers and fathers of naturally conceived children was no longer apparent when the children were 12 years old. Examination of the variables for which data were collected on both occasions showed that the natural conception mothers had relatively higher scores at follow-up than in the initial study and not that the IVF mothers obtained lower ratings. For those measures of parenting for which less positive outcomes were found for the IVF and the adoptive mothers, the scores did not reflect dysfunctional relationships but were instead indicative of average rather than high levels of functioning.

Conclusion

Contrary to the concerns that have been raised regarding the potentially negative consequences of IVF for parenting, studies of these families have generally found IVF parents to be well adjusted and to have good relationships with their children. To the extent that differences have been found between IVF and natural conception parents, in the early years these have tended to reflect higher levels of anxiety about parenting by IVF mothers. For example, McMahon et al. (1997) found IVF mothers of 4-month-old infants to report lower self-esteem and lower maternal self-efficacy than natural conception mothers, although these differences had lessened by the child's first birthday (Gibson et al., 2000). In addition, several studies indicated that IVF mothers were more protective of their child (Weaver et al., 1993), allowed their child less autonomy (Colpin et al., 1995), and saw their child as more vulnerable and "special" (Gibson et al., 2000).

These findings must be viewed in the context of a lack of difference between IVF and natural conception families with respect to other measures of maternal feelings, attitudes, and behavior such as separation anxiety and observational measures of maternal behavior (McMahon et al., 1997; Gibson et al., 2000); maternal interaction with the child (Raoul-Duval et al., 1994); acceptance, overindulgence, and rejection of the baby (Weaver et al., 1993); maternal attitudes and emotions and observational measures of maternal interaction (Colpin et al., 1995); and maternal concerns, expectations, and burden (van Balen, 1996). There were also more positive results for IVF mothers with respect to feelings toward their baby (Weaver et al., 1993) and emotional involvement with their child (van Balen, 1996). No differences were identified between IVF and natural conception fathers, with the exception of lower self-esteem and marital satisfaction among IVF fathers of 1-year-old children in the Australian study (Gibson et al., 2000).

Findings from the European Study of Assisted Reproduction Families (Golombok et al., 1995, 1996) indicated that in the early school years positive effects for IVF families prevailed. IVF mothers and fathers were found to be more involved with their children than natural conception parents. By the time their children were 12 years old this advantage had disappeared. The quality of parenting in IVF families continued to be good, characterized by affection and appropriate control, but few differences in parenting were found between IVF and natural conception mothers and fathers, and those differences identified were both positive and negative.

A number of methodological problems have been associated with studies of IVF families. In particular, mothers of IVF children are generally older than mothers who have given birth without medical intervention, and attempts to match natural conception mothers for maternal age has presented difficulties as has matching for birth order of the target child and number of children in the family. These confounding factors may well explain the differences identified between IVF and natural conception parents, although some researchers have attempted to control for these variables statistically. Furthermore, some of the samples studied have been small and the cooperation rates have been less than ideal, and few studies have included an additional comparison group of natural conception parents with a history of infertility. Nevertheless, the available data on parenting in families created by IVF are generally reassuring. Even if the more positive findings for IVF parents can be explained by factors such as fewer children in the family, there is no evidence to suggest that IVF mothers and fathers experience marked difficulties in parenting compared with their natural conception counterparts. Neither is there evidence for a higher incidence of marital or psychological problems among IVF parents. To the contrary, where differences have emerged, these reflect greater psychological adjustment and marital satisfaction among parents of an IVF child.

PARENTING CHILDREN CONCEIVED BY DONOR INSEMINATION

There are concerns additional to those expressed in relation to IVF regarding potentially negative consequences for parenting in families in which donated sperm have been used in the child's conception.

Concerns About Parenting in Donor Insemination Families

If a woman is able to have children but her husband is infertile, the couple may opt to have a child by donor insemination. With this procedure, the woman is inseminated with the sperm of a man who is not her husband or partner. Although donor insemination is generally classified as a contemporary reproductive technology, the first reported case took place in 1884 (Achilles, 1992), and the procedure itself is not "high tech" at all, involving the transfer of semen to the vagina by syringe. Although this can be carried out without medical intervention, insemination usually takes place at a clinic so that an anonymous donor can be used and characteristics of the donor can be matched to those of the couple who will become the parents of the child. Clinics can also screen donors for disorders that could be passed on to the child to ensure that only healthy men are allowed to donate.

Because donor insemination is like adoption in that one parent, the father, has no genetic link with the child, it is often assumed that the experience of parenting a child conceived by donor insemination is similar to parenting an adoptive child. Father–child relationships in adoptive families are generally positive when the child has been adopted at birth (Brodzinsky and Pinderhughes, in Vol. 1 of this *Handbook*; Brodzinsky, Smith, and Brodzinsky, 1998), the situation that is most closely comparable with that of donor insemination families, suggesting that difficulties in father–child relationships would not be a feature of donor insemination families. Moreover, donor insemination differs from adoption in that the child has a genetic relationship with the mother, the child is born to the mother, the child has not been given up by existing parents, and the father is present during the pregnancy and birth. In all of these ways, donor insemination families are more like natural conception families than adoptive families.

Parallels have also been drawn between donor insemination families and stepfather families in that both family types lack a genetic tie between the father and the child (Hetherington and Stanley-Hagan, in Vol. 3 of this *Handbook*). Studies of stepfather families point to difficult relationships between stepfathers and stepchildren (Hetherington and Clingempeel, 1992; Dunn et al., 1998). However, the formation of a stepfamily brings with it a number of stresses that may affect the quality of fathering that are not present in donor insemination families, including the disruption of the relationship with an existing father and the need to negotiate relationships with new family members. Interestingly, Dunn, Davies, O'Connor, and Sturgess (2000) found parents in stepfamilies to be less affectionate toward, and less supportive of, their stepchildren than toward their own biological children. Nevertheless, donor insemination families differ from stepfamilies in important ways; the father has chosen to rear the child, has done so from birth, and presents the child to others as his own. It cannot be assumed therefore that donor insemination fathers will be like stepfathers with respect to the quality of their relationship with their nongenetic child.

Although donor insemination has been practiced for more than a century to enable couples with an infertile male partner to have children, the majority of adults and children conceived in this way remain unaware that the person they know of as their father is not their genetic parent. In the first reported case of donor insemination, not even the mother of the child was told by her doctor that she had been inseminated with the sperm of another man (Achilles, 1992). It was not until the introduction of the new reproductive technologies in the late 1970s that public awareness of donor insemination increased, and even today it remains cloaked in secrecy (Haimes and Daniels, 1998). In sharp contrast to the openness of adoptive parents, most donor insemination parents keep the circumstances of conception secret from their child.

In recent years there has been growing unease about the secrecy that surrounds families created by donor insemination. It has been argued that secrecy will have an insidious and damaging effect on family relationships and consequently on the child (Baran and Pannor, 1993; Daniels and Taylor, 1993; Landau, 1998; Snowden, 1990; Snowden, Mitchell, and Snowden, 1983). Findings suggestive of an association between secrecy and negative outcomes for children have come from two major sources: research on adoption (Hoopes, 1990; Schechter and Bertocci, 1990) and the family therapy literature (Bok, 1982; Karpel, 1980; Papp, 1993). It is now generally accepted that adopted children benefit from knowledge about their biological parents, and there is a commonly held view that children who are not given such information may become confused about their identity and at risk for emotional problems (Hoopes, 1990; Sants, 1964; Schechter and Bertocci, 1990; Triseliotis, 1973). In the field of assisted reproduction, parallels have been drawn with the adoptive situation, and it has been suggested (Clamar, 1989; Daniels and Taylor, 1993) that lack of knowledge of, or information about, the donor may be harmful for the child.

Family therapists have argued that secrecy can jeopardize communication among family members, cause tension, and result in a distancing of some members of the family from others (Bok, 1982; Karpel, 1980; Papp, 1993). In relation to donor insemination, Clamar (1989) has argued that keeping the circumstances of conception secret will separate those who know the secret (the parents) from those who do not (the child). Studies have shown that children can often sense when they are not being told something because a taboo surrounds the discussion of certain topics (De Paulo, 1992). Parents often give themselves away by their tone of voice, facial expression, or body posture, or by abruptly changing the subject. It is not known whether children conceived by donor insemination become aware that a secret about their parentage is being kept from them, but it is likely that they will become suspicious if their parents always change the topic of conversation whenever the subject of whom they look like comes up.

Research on Parenting in Donor Insemination Families

Rather fewer studies have been carried out of parenting in families created by donor insemination than of IVF families in which the child is genetically related to both parents. This is perhaps not surprising, given parents' desire to maintain secrecy about the nature of their child's conception. In a review of the 12 studies of parents' disclosure of donor insemination published between 1980 and 1995, Brewaeys (1996) found that few parents (between 1% and 20%) intended to tell their child about her or his genetic origins, and in 8 of the 12 studies fewer than 10% of parents intended to tell. Although it might be expected that a higher proportion of parents in the more recent studies would be open with their children, this was not the case, a finding duplicated by van Berkel, van der Veen, Kimmel, and te Velde (1999) in a comparison between recipients of donor insemination in 1980 and 1996. The move toward greater encouragement of disclosure does not appear to have resulted in more parents telling their child.

It is noteworthy that, in spite of their decision to opt for secrecy, almost half of the parents included in Brewaeys's (1996) review had told at least one other person that they had conceived as a result of donor insemination, thus creating a risk that the child would find out through someone else. However, many parents regretted their earlier openness once the child had been born (Amuzu, Laxova, and Shapiro, 1990; Back and Snowden, 1988; Klock and Maier, 1991).

Brewaeys (1996) also examined studies of the characteristics of donor insemination parents. She found that, in the large majority of cases, donor insemination was felt to be a positive choice and, with few exceptions, fathers reported that donor insemination did not influence their relationship with their child and that they felt themselves to be "real" fathers. However, these investigations were based on questionnaire data of variable quality, and no control groups were used. With respect to psychological adjustment, there was little indication of disturbance in couples who opted for donor insemination (Klock, Jacob, and Maier, 1994; Klock and Maier, 1991; Owens, Edelman, and Humphrey, 1993; Reading, Sledmere, and Cox, 1982; Schover, Collins, and Richards, 1992). In addition, these couples had a low divorce rate and high marital satisfaction (Humphrey and Humphrey, 1987; Klok et al., 1994; Klok and Maier, 1991; Schover et al., 1992).

In the first controlled study of families with a child conceived by donor insemination, Kovacs, Mushin, Kane, and Baker (1993) examined Australian children's psychological development, but did not assess parenting. However, the authors commented on the fact that in most of these families both parents took part in the study, which was interpreted as reflecting an active involvement in parenting by both mothers and fathers.

Parenting in donor insemination families was a major focus of the European Study of Assisted Reproduction Families (Golombok et al., 1995). Details of the samples investigated and the measures used are described in the previous section on IVF families. In addition to these measures, mothers of children conceived by donor insemination were interviewed about their openness regarding their child's genetic origins. The findings relating to the quality of parenting were the same as for the IVF families, suggesting that genetic ties are less important for family functioning than a strong desire for parenthood. Whether the child was genetically related to two parents (in the case of IVF), genetically related to one parent (in the case of donor insemination), or genetically unrelated to both parents (in the case of adoption), the quality of parenting in families in which the mother and father had gone to great lengths to have children was superior to that shown by mothers and fathers who had achieved parenthood in the usual way.

It was striking, however, that not one set of donor insemination parents had told their child that she or he had been conceived with the sperm of an anonymous donor. Thus not one of the donor insemination children was aware that his or her father was not the genetic parent. Most mothers (80%) reported that they definitely had decided not to tell, 16% were undecided, and 4% planned to tell their child. Nevertheless, half of the donor insemination mothers had told a member of their family, and almost one third had told one or more friends, so the risk of disclosure to the child would always be there. The main reasons for the parents' decision not to tell the child were concern that the child would love the father less, protection of the father from the stigma associated with infertility, and uncertainty about what and when to tell the child (Cook, Golombok, Bish, and Murray, 1995).

Similar results were obtained with the inclusion of the additional samples from Italy, Spain, and The Netherlands (Golombok et al., 1996). Once again, whether or not donor sperm had been used to conceive the child seemed to make little difference to the quality of parenting in assisted reproduction families. Donor insemination parents did not differ from IVF parents for any of the parenting measures, and the adoptive families were similar to the assisted reproduction families. Significant group × country interactions were not identified for any of the variables, showing that the findings were alike in each of the four countries studied.

Perhaps surprisingly, there was no evidence that attitudes toward assisted reproduction differed between predominantly Protestant Northern Europe and predominantly Catholic Southern Europe. Not one of the parents with a child conceived by donor insemination in any of the four countries studied had told the child about her or his method of conception. When mothers were asked whether they planned to tell their child in the future, most (75%) reported that they had definitely decided not to tell, 13% were undecided, and only 12% planned to tell their child. A significant difference among countries was found with respect to attitude toward telling the child. The Italian parents were most against telling, with 100% having decided never to tell, followed by the United Kingdom and Dutch parents, of whom 80% and 76%, respectively, had decided never to tell. In Spain, the parents seemed more open to considering the idea of telling, with only 48% having definitely decided never to tell.

Although the majority of donor insemination parents had decided against telling their child, once again it was found that more than half had told a friend or family member. A significant difference between countries was not identified for this variable. The mothers of donor insemination children were also asked about which members of the family had been told. Although the majority of parents had not told the child's grandparents, more than one third of the maternal grandparents had been told, compared with less than one fourth of paternal grandparents. There was no significant difference among countries with respect to telling either maternal or paternal grandparents. In addition, there was no significant difference among countries in telling friends. Overall, 71% of the sample had not told any friends, 28% had told very few friends, and only 1% had told many friends.

In the United Kingdom, the families were followed up as the children approached adolescence (Golombok, MacCallum, Goodman, and Rutter, in press). It is at adolescence that issues of identity become salient. Thus it is at adolescence that difficulties for donor insemination children may be expected to arise. To the extent that the experiences of adopted children are relevant to children conceived by donor insemination, early adolescence is the time when adopted children begin to show a greater incidence of behavioral problems compared with their nonadopted counterparts (Maughan and Pickles, 1990; Miller, Fan, Christensen, Grotevant, and van Dulmen, 2000), alongside a greater interest in their biological parents (Hoopes, 1990).

Of the donor insemination families, 37 were examined when the child was 12 years old compared with (1) a new group of 91 natural conception families who had experienced infertility before conceiving their child spontaneously or with minimal medical intervention and (2) 49 of the adopted families recruited to the original investigation. The response rate for donor insemination and adoptive families was 82% and 89%, respectively. The former comparison group controlled for the desire to have children, and the latter controlled for the absence of a genetic link between the father and the child. The measures are described in the previous section in relation to the 12-year-old follow-up of IVF children.

The findings suggest that the nature of the differences in parent–child relationships among donor insemination families and the other family types are distinct for mothers and fathers; mother–child relationships differ with respect to warmth, whereas father–child relationships differ with respect to control. The pattern of results relating to warmth from the mothers' data indicated that donor insemination mothers showed higher levels of expressive warmth toward their children. However, this was not reflected in the findings from the children. From the perspective of donor insemination children, their mothers were just as affectionate, but not more so, than mothers in the other family types. A possible explanation for the greater expressive warmth of donor insemination mothers is related to the imbalance in genetic relatedness between the parents and the child. In the donor insemination families, the mother, but not the father, has a genetic link with the child, whereas adoptive parents both lack a genetic relationship and natural conception parents are both genetically linked. It is conceivable that donor insemination mothers feel that they have a special relationship with their child because they are the only parent with a genetic bond. Alternatively, donor insemination mothers may feel a greater need to overtly demonstrate their affection toward their child because of the stigma associated with the nature of their child's conception.

Fathers of donor insemination children were less likely to become involved in serious disputes with their children and, when conflict did occur, they considered themselves to be less likely to reason with them, suggesting greater detachment from their children than the other fathers felt. It may be the case that donor insemination fathers feel less entitlement, or less interest in, disciplining their children because they lack a genetic bond. Interestingly, these findings are in line with clinical data on donor insemination families in which fathers have reported less involvement in disciplining their child (Baran and Pannor, 1993). Although the findings of the present study support the hypothesis that donor insemination fathers are more distant from their children, it is important to point out that this finding was not duplicated by the children's data, and mothers in families with a nongenetic parent reported more help from fathers with issues of control than did natural conception mothers. In addition, there was no difference in expressive or instrumental warmth between donor insemination fathers and their children compared with that of the other family types, as assessed independently by both fathers and children, which suggests that donor insemination fathers were just as close to their children.

It is important to emphasize that the differences identified among donor insemination families and the other family types generally reflect either more positive or different, but not necessarily negative, relationships between donor insemination parents and their children. These results are thus broadly similar to the findings of the first phase of the study conducted 6 years earlier (Golombok et al., 1995). At that time, the more positive parent–child relationships found in donor insemination families compared with those of natural conception families were thought to result from the donor insemination parents' greater desire to have a child. However, these differences remained at the 12-year-old follow-up despite the recruitment of a new comparison group of natural conception families with a history of infertility to control for this potentially confounding effect. It seems therefore that the differences in parenting between donor insemination and natural conception families cannot be explained by a difference in the desire for a child between parents in the two family types. More likely, the explanation lies in a difference in attitude between couples who have a child who is genetically unrelated to the father and couples who simply seek medical intervention to have their own genetic child.

Of particular interest is the finding that only 2 of the 37 12-year-old donor insemination children had been told about their genetic origins Golombok, MacCallum, Goodman, and Rutter (in press). In spite of the parents' decision not to tell, it appears that the children at the age of 12 years were functioning well and did not seem to be experiencing negative consequences arising from the absence of a genetic link with their fathers or from the secrecy surrounding the circumstances of their birth. Nevertheless, this does not necessarily mean that it is better for children not to be told about donor insemination. Research on adoption has demonstrated that adopted children welcome information about their genetic parents (Brodzinsky et al., 1998; Grotevant and McRoy, 1998), and many adoptees do not begin to seek out their genetic parents until they reach adulthood (Howe and Feast, 2000). As their children grow older, it becomes more difficult for parents to tell them that they were conceived by use of donor sperm. Some parents in the present study regretted not having told their child from the start but felt that it would now present too much of a shock for them and that it was too late (MacCallum et al., 2001).

More is known about lesbian mothers with a child born through donor insemination (Patterson and Fisher, in Vol. 5 of this *Handbook*) than about single heterosexual women who have a child in this way. In recent years, several controlled studies of parenting by lesbian couples who conceived their child by donor insemination, albeit with small samples, have been reported. These mothers planned their family together after coming out as lesbian. In the United States, Flaks, Ficher, Masterpasqua, and Joseph (1995) compared 15 lesbian donor insemination families with 15 heterosexual donor insemination families with respect to the quality of the parents' relationship and their awareness of parenting skills. Although there were no group differences in relationship quality, the lesbian parents were more aware of the skills necessary for effective parenting than were their heterosexual counterparts. However, further analyses revealed that this was related to the parents' gender rather than to their sexual orientation, as both lesbian and heterosexual mothers demonstrated a greater awareness of parenting skills than did heterosexual fathers. Also in the United States, Chan, Raboy, and Patterson (1998) studied 55 donor insemination families headed by lesbian parents compared with 25 donor insemination families headed by heterosexual parents and found no group differences in relationship quality, parenting stress, depression, or self-concept as assessed by standardized questionnaires.

In the United Kingdom, 30 lesbian donor insemination families were compared with 41 heterosexual two-parent donor insemination families and 42 families headed by a single heterosexual mother by use of a standardized interview assessment of parenting quality and questionnaire assessments of anxiety, depression, and relationship satisfaction (Golombok, Tasker, and Murray, 1997). The results showed that mothers in the fatherless families expressed greater warmth toward, and interacted more, with their child. There were no group differences in parental adjustment. Similarly, Brewaeys, Ponjaert, Van Hall, and Golombok (1997) studied 30 lesbian mother families with a 4- to 8-year-old child compared with 38 heterosexual families with a donor insemination child and 30 heterosexual families with a naturally conceived child in Belgium. The quality of the couples' relationship and the quality of mother–child interaction did not differ between lesbian mother families and either of the heterosexual family groups. The most striking finding to emerge was that comothers in the lesbian families were more involved with their children than were fathers in the heterosexual families. Moreover, comothers in lesbian families were regarded by children to be as much a "parent" as fathers in both types of heterosexual family. All of the lesbian mothers intended to tell their children that they had been conceived by donor insemination, and 56% would have opted for an identifiable donor had that been possible (Brewaeys, Ponjaert, Van Hall, Helmerhorst, and Devroey, 1995). The attitude of lesbian mothers toward this issue is in striking contrast to that of heterosexual parents who prefer not to tell.

No studies have been carried out on parenting by single women who opt for donor insemination as a means of having a child. A small, uncontrolled study of 10 single women requesting donor insemination (cited by Fidell and Marik, 1989) found that an important reason for opting for this procedure was to avoid using a man to produce a child without his knowledge or consent. Donor insemination also meant that they did not have to share the rights and responsibilities for the child with a man to whom they were not emotionally committed. Although rare, women who have never experienced a sexual relationship with either sex have also had donor insemination to produce so-called virgin births (Jennings, 1991).

Research on single-mother families in general has shown that difficulties in parenting are associated with both economic hardship and lack of social support (Ferri, 1976; McLanahan and Sandefur, 1994; Weinraub, Horvath, and Gringlas, in Vol. 3 of this *Handbook*). In addition, emotional distress and an associated reduction in parental functioning is common among single mothers following divorce (Amato, 1993; Chase-Lansdale and Hetherington, 1990; Hetherington and Stanley-Hagan, in Vol. 3 of this *Handbook*). In single-mother families with a child conceived by donor insemination, it is important to take social context into account. Single-mother families are not all the same, and anecdotal reports suggest that single women requesting donor insemination tend to be financially secure and to have access to social support from family and friends. Moreover, they have not experienced conflict with, or separation from, the father of their child. Such circumstances may reduce the potentially negative consequences for parenting of rearing a child alone.

Conclusion

From the information that is currently available, there is no evidence to suggest that the quality of parenting in donor insemination families is compromised by the absence of a genetic link between the father and the child. Nevertheless, in spite of the recent move toward encouraging openness with children conceived by donor insemination, it seems that parents continue to withhold information from children about their origins. Although it has been argued on the basis of research on adoption that such information is important for children's emotional well-being, it seems that the areas presenting most difficulty for disclosure are precisely those in which donor insemination differs from adoption: the stigma associated with donor insemination, acknowledgement of the father's fertility problem, uncertainty about the best time and method of telling the child, and lack of information to give the child about the genetic father (Cook et al., 1995; Nachtigall, Pitcher, Tschann, Becker, and Szkupinsku Quiroga, 1997; Snowden et al., 1983). Unlike adoption, there are no generally accepted stories of what to tell the child about donor insemination, and parents have to explain the facts of life and discuss the father's infertility in order for the child to understand. Moreover, if an anonymous donor has been used, they have little information to give the child about her or his genetic father. Because of these factors, the situation for donor insemination parents is different from that of adoptive parents and, as a result, most heterosexual donor insemination parents seem to have concluded that nondisclosure is desirable for the protection of both the father and the child. Interestingly, however, in a study of parents who had told their children, the majority (57%) reported feeling good about having done so (Rumball and Adair, 1999). In lesbian donor insemination families in which the child grows up without a father, mothers are more open with their children about the method of their conception. Whether single heterosexual mothers with a child conceived by donor insemination opt for secrecy or disclosure remains to be seen. A study of single women requesting donor insemination suggested that they were more likely than married women to intend to tell (Klock, Jacob, and Maier, 1996).

Although the absence of psychological problems in children and of problems in parent–child interaction in donor insemination families suggests that secrecy does not have an adverse effect on family functioning, it must be remembered that the children studied so far are young and have not yet developed a sophisticated understanding of their relationship with their parents. In addition, a potential difficulty facing these families is that the children may find out about their genetic origins by accident, or at a time of family trauma such as divorce, as many parents have told someone other than the child. Little is known about children who are aware of their conception by donor insemination, or about the impact of this knowledge on their relationship with their parents, as the only study of such families did not distinguish between parents who had actually told their child about donor insemination and those who simply intended to tell (Nachtigall et al., 1997). Nevertheless, no association was found in this study between attitude toward disclosure and parenting quality. Instead, fathers who were most concerned about the stigma associated with donor insemination reported less warmth and less fostering of independence in their child, suggesting that perceptions of stigma may have an adverse effect on the relationship between donor insemination fathers and their children. A major problem with investigations of donor insemination families is the low cooperation rate associated with the parents' desire to maintain secrecy about their child's conception. Parents who are most concerned about secrecy are least likely to take part in research. Until families who have told their child have been compared with those who have not, it is not possible to come to a clear understanding of the consequences of secrecy versus disclosure on parenting in donor insemination families.

Anecdotal reports from adults who are aware of their conception by donor insemination shed some light on the longer-term effects. Whereas some adults report good relationships with their parents (Snowden et al., 1983), others report more negative feelings, including hostility, distance, and mistrust (Cordray, 1999; Donor Conception Support Group of Australia, 1997; Turner and Coyle, 2000). As these adults are not representative of people conceived by donor insemination in general, it is not possible to generalize from their experiences. Most likely, children's reaction to discovering that they were conceived by donor insemination will depend on a number of factors, including the quality of their relationship with their parents before the disclosure and the manner in which they find out. It is only through systematic, controlled studies of representative samples that the long-term consequences of donor insemination can be fully understood.

PARENTING CHILDREN CONCEIVED BY EGG DONATION

Concerns About Parenting in Egg Donation Families

Although the use of donor sperm to enable couples with an infertile male partner to have children has been practiced for many years, it is only since 1983, following advances in IVF, that infertile women have been able to conceive a child by using a donated egg (Lutjen et al., 1984; Trounson, Leeton, Besanka, Wood, and Conti, 1983). Egg donation is a much more complex procedure than donor insemination, involving fertilization of the donated egg with the father's sperm in the laboratory, followed by the transfer of the resulting embryo to the mother's uterus. Women who donate eggs must take hormonal medication, undergo a series of ultrasound scans, and have the eggs surgically removed from their ovary—a much more intrusive and unpleasant experience than that of men who donate semen.

Egg donation is like donor insemination in that the child is genetically related to only one parent, but in this case it is the mother and not the father who is genetically unrelated to the child. Thus egg donation has made it possible for children to be born to, and reared by, mothers with whom they have no genetic link. The concerns that have been expressed about egg donation are similar to those raised by donor insemination. It is the absence of a genetic bond between the mother and the child and the effect of secrecy about the child's conception that have been the topics of greatest debate. However, unlike donor insemination, for which the donor is usually anonymous, egg donors are more often relatives or friends of the parents and may remain in contact with the family as the child grows up. Contact with the genetic mother has been viewed by some as a positive experience for children in that they have the opportunity to develop a clearer understanding of their origins. However, it is not known what the impact of two mothers will be on a child's social, emotional, and identity development through childhood and into adult life or how contact between the genetic mother and the child will affect the social mother's security in her parenting role.

Research on Parenting in Egg Donation Families

The first study of parenting in families with a child conceived by egg donation was conducted in France (Raoul-Duval et al., 1994). All of the donors were anonymous. Raoul-Duval et al. reported on 12 families assessed when their children were 9 and 18 months old and 9 of these families when their children were 36 months old. The quality of the relationship between the mother and her infant was assessed by the procedure previously described by Raoul-Duval et al. (1994) for IVF families based on the mother's body language, vocal dialogue, visual dialogue, and attitude toward breast-feeding. It was reported that all of the mother–infant relationships were excellent. However, no details were given on the way in which an "excellent" mother–infant relationship was defined.

A group of 21 families with a 3- to 8-year-old child conceived by egg donation was recruited in the United Kingdom, allowing a contrast to be made between families in which the child is genetically related to the father but not to the mother (egg donation families) and families in which the child is genetically related to the mother but not to the father (donor insemination families) (Golombok, Murray, Brinsden, and Abdalla, 1999). The only difference to emerge between egg donation and donor insemination families was that mothers and fathers of children conceived by egg donation reported lower levels of stress associated with parenting than did parents of a donor insemination child. It seems, from the limited information available, that egg donation families, like donor insemination families, are functioning well. However, most of the children in these families had been conceived with the egg of an anonymous donor. What is not known is the effect on parenting of the child being conceived with the egg of a known donor—a relative or family friend—who continues to play a part in family life. Only one set of parents with a child conceived by egg donation had told their child about his genetic origins.

In Finland, a cohort of 49 families with an egg donation child between the ages of 6 months and 4 years was compared with 92 families with a child born through IVF, representing a response rate of 100% and 95%, respectively (Soderstrom-Anttila, Sajaniemi, Tiitinen, and Hovatta, 1998). The large majority of egg donors (84%) were anonymous. However, the eight known donors (sisters or friends) saw the child regularly with no reported difficulties in the relationship between the donor and the mother. Thirty-eight percent of all parents intended to tell their child that she or he had been conceived by egg donation, a proportion that is higher than that generally reported for donor insemination parents. Of the eight parents who used a known donor, only two intended to tell the child. As with the donor insemination parents, a high proportion (73%) had told someone other than the child. With respect to parenting, significantly fewer egg donation parents than IVF parents expressed concern about their child's behavior.

Conclusion

It appears from the few investigations carried out so far that having a child by egg donation does not have a detrimental effect on parenting. However, most of the parents studied to date conceived their child by using the egg of an anonymous donor. Little is known about the consequences of egg donation when the donor is a relative or friend, a situation that may have more far-reaching effects on family relationships.

FUTURE DIRECTIONS IN CONTEMPORARY REPRODUCTIVE TECHNOLOGIES

The introduction of IVF has paved the way for increasingly "high tech" reproductive procedures such as intercytoplasmic sperm injection (ICSI), in which a sperm is injected directly into an egg, and embryo donation (sometimes described as prenatal adoption) in which a donated egg is fertilized by donated sperm in the laboratory and the resulting embryo is placed in the womb of the mother-to-be. Of all the different ways in which families can be built today, it is the practice of surrogacy, in which a woman bears a child for another woman, that is the most controversial. There are two types of surrogacy: partial surrogacy, in which conception occurs through the use of the commissioning father's sperm and the surrogate mother's egg, and full surrogacy, in which both the egg and the sperm come from the commissioning parents. As yet, no controlled studies have been carried out on the consequences for parenting of conceiving a child in these different ways. Whereas it is not necessarily expected that ICSI would have a major impact on parenting, embryo donation and surrogacy raise more questions. With surrogacy, for example, it is not known how the involvement of the surrogate mother with the family as the child grows up will affect the feelings and behavior of the commissioning mother, particularly when the surrogate mother and the commissioning father are the genetic parents of the child. Although existing knowledge about the impact of the contemporary reproductive technologies does not give undue cause for concern, there remain many unanswered questions about the consequences for parenting of creating families in this way.

CONCLUSIONS

Creating families by means of contemporary reproductive technologies has raised a number of concerns about potentially adverse consequences for parenting and child development. It has been argued, for example, that dysfunctional patterns of parenting may be a feature of these families because of the difficulties experienced by these mothers and fathers in their quest for a child. It seems, however, from the evidence available so far that such concerns are unfounded. Parents of children conceived by assisted reproduction appear to have good relationships with their children, even in families in which one parent lacks a genetic link with the child.

Although the focus of this chapter is on parenting, it is important to point out that the children born by IVF, donor insemination, and egg donation also appear to be functioning well. They are well adjusted in terms of social, emotional, and identity development and show positive relationships with their parents and peers. There is no evidence to suggest that they are at risk for emotional or behavioral difficulties arising from the nature of their conception. Little is known, however, about children born through a surrogacy arrangement or to single heterosexual women by donor insemination. With respect to cognitive development, any impairments reported seem to be associated with the higher incidence of preterm and multiple births found among children born as a result of IVF techniques. Although there is some concern that children conceived by ICSI may show a higher incidence of sex chromosome abnormalities (Bonduelle et al., 1999), this has yet to be confirmed. Detailed information on the outcomes of assisted reproduction for child development can be found in reviews by Brewaeys (1996) and van Balen (1998).

The issue that continues to be the subject of greatest controversy is whether parents should be open with children conceived by gamete donation about their genetic origins and whether identifying information about the donor should be available to the child. In some parts of the world, including Sweden and New Zealand, children have a legal right to the identity of their donor, and in other places, including some parts of the United States, prospective parents can opt for a donor who is willing to be identified. At present, the large majority of parents of donor offspring decide not to tell their child. Thus the consequences of disclosure for parenting remain, as yet, to be seen.

REFERENCES

Abidin, R. (1990). *Parenting Stress Index Test manual*. Charlottesville, VA: Pediatric Psychology Press.

Achilles, R. (1992). *Donor insemination: an overview*. Ontario, Canada: Royal Commission on New Reproductive Technologies.

Amato, P. R. (1993). Children's adjustment to divorce: Theories, hypotheses and empirical support. *Journal of Marriage and the Family, 55*, 23–38.

Amuzu, B., Laxova, R., and Shapiro, S. (1990). Pregnancy outcome, health of children and family adjustment of children after DI. *Obstetrics and Gynecology, 75*, 899–905.

Australian In Vitro Fertilisation Collaborative Group. (1985). High incidence of preterm births and early losses in pregnancy after in vitro fertilisation. *British Medical Journal, 291*, 1160–1163.

Back, K., and Snowden, R. (1988). The anonymity of the gamete donor. *Journal of Psychosomatic Obstetrics and Gynecology, 9*, 191–198.

Baran, A., and Pannor, R. (1993). Perspectives on open adoption. *Future of Children, 3*, 119–124.

Barrera, M. J. (1981). Social support in the adjustment of pregnant adolescents: assessment issues. In R. H. Price (Ed.), *Social networks and social support* (pp. 69–96). Thousand Oaks, CA: Sage.

Baumrind, D. (1989). Rearing competent children. In W. Damon (Ed.), *Child development today and tomorrow* (pp. 349–378). San Fransisco: Jossey-Bass.

Baumrind, D. (1991). Effective parenting during the early adolescent transition. In P. A. Cowen and M. Hetherington (Eds.), *Family transitions* (pp. 111–163). Hillsdale, NJ: Lawrence Erlbaum Associates.

Beck, A., and Steer, R. (1987). *The Beck Depression Inventory manual*. San Antonio, TX: Psychological Corporation.

Beral, V., Doyle, P., Tan, S. L., Mason, B. A., and Campbell, S. (1990). Outcome of pregnancies resulting from assisted conception. *British Medical Bulletin, 46*, 753–768.

Block, J. H. (1965). *The child-rearing practices report*. Berkeley: University of California, Berkeley Institute of Human Development.

Bok, S. (1982). *Secrets*. New York: Pantheon.

Bonduelle, M., Camus, M., De Vos, A., Staessen, C., Tournaye, H., Van Assche, E., Verheyen, G., Devroey, P., Liebaers, I., and Van Steirteghem, A. (1999). Seven years of intracytoplasmic sperm injection and follow-up of 1987 subsequent children. *Human Reproduction, 14*, (Suppl. 1), 243–264.

Botting, B. J., MacFarlane, A. J., and Price, F. V. (1990). *Three, four and more. A study of triplet and higher order births*. London: HMSO.

Brewaeys, A. (1996). Donor insemination, the impact on family and child development. *Journal of Psychosomatic Obstetrics and Gynecology, 17*, 1–13.

Brewaeys, A., Ponjaert, I., Van Hall, E., and Golombok, S. (1997). Donor insemination: Child development and family functioning in lesbian mother families. *Human Reproduction, 12*, 1349–1359.

Brewaeys, A., Ponjaert, I., Van Hall, E., Helmerhorst, F. M., and Devroey, P. (1995). Lesbian mothers who conceived after donor insemination: A follow-up study. *Human Reproduction, 10*, 2731–2735.

Brodzinsky, D. M., Smith, D. W., and Brodzinsky, A. B. (1998). *Children's adjustment to adoption. Developmental and clinical issues*. London: Sage.

Burns, L. H. (1990). An exploratory study of perceptions of parenting after infertility. *Family Systems Medicine, 8*, 177–189.

Campbell, A., Converse, P., and Rodgers, W. (1976). *The quality of American life*. New York: Sage.

Chan, R. W., Raboy, B., and Patterson, C. J. (1998). Psychosocial adjustment among children conceived via donor insemination by lesbian and heterosexual mothers. *Child Development, 69*, 443–457.

Chase-Lansdale, P. L., and Hetherington, E. M. (1990). The impact of divorce on life-span development: Short and long-term effects. In P. B. Baltes., D. L. Featherman, and R. M. Lerner (Eds.), *Life-span development and behavior* (Vol. 10, pp. 105–150). Hillsdale, NJ: Lawrence Erlbaum Associates.

Clamar, A. (1989). Psychological implications of the anonymous pregnancy. In J. Offerman-Zuckerberg (Ed.), *Gender in transition: A new frontier* (pp. 111–121). New York: Plenum.

Colpin, H., Demyttenaere, K., and Vandemeulebroecke, L. (1995). New reproductive technology and the family: The parent–child relationship following *in vitro* fertilization. *Journal of Child Psychology and Psychiatry, 36,* 1429–1441.

Condon, J. T. (1993). The assessment of antenatal emotional attachment: Development of a questronnarie instrument. *British Journal of Medical Psychology, 66,* 167–183.

Cook, R., Golombok, S., Bish, A., and Murray, C. (1995). Disclosure of donor insemination: Parental attitudes. *American Journal of Orthopsychiatry, 65,* 549–559.

Cordray, B. (1999, May). *Speaking for ourselves: Quotes from men and women created by DI/remote father conception.* Paper presented at the 11th World Congress of In Vitro Fertilization and Human Reproductive Genetics, Sydney, Australia.

Cox, J. L., Holden, J. M., and Sagovsky, R. (1987). Detection of postnatal depression: Development of the 10-item Edinburgh Postnatal Depression Scale. *British Journal of Psychiatry, 150,* 782–786.

Crowe, M. J. (1978). Conjoint marital therapy: A controlled outcome study. *Psychological Medicine, 8,* 623–636.

Crown, S., and Crisp, A. H. (1979). *Manual of the Crown-Crisp experiential index.* London: Hodder and Stoughton.

Daniels, K., and Taylor, K. (1993). Secrecy and openness in donor insemination. *Politics and Life Sciences, 12,* 155–170.

Dekovic, M., Jansen, J., and Gerris, J. (1991). Factor structure and construct validity of the Block child-rearing practices report. *Psychological Assessment, 3,* 182–187.

De Paulo, B. M. (1992). Nonverbal behavior and self-presentation. *Psychological Bulletin, 111,* 203–243.

Donor Conception Support Group of Australia. (1997). *Let the offspring speak: Discussions on donor conception.* New South Wales: Sydney, Georges Hall.

Dunn, J., Davies, L. C., O'Connor, T. G., and Sturgess, W. (2000). Parents' and partners' life course and family experiences: Links with parent–child relationships in different family settings. *Journal of Child Psychology and Psychiatry, 41,* 955–968.

Dunn, J., Deater-Deckard, K., Pickering, K., O'Conner, T. G., Golding, J., and the ALSPAC Study Team. (1998). Children's adjustment and prosocial behaviour in step-, single-parent, and non-stepfamily settings: Findings from a community study. *Journal of Child Psychology and Psychiatry, 39,* 1083–1095.

Dunst, C. J., Jenkins, V. and Trivette, C. M. (1984). Family support scale: reliability and validity. *Journal of Individual Family Community Wellbeing, 1,* 45–52.

Einwohner, J. (1989). Who becomes a surrogate: Personality characteristics. In J. Offerman-Zuckerberg (Ed.), *Gender in transition: A new frontier* (pp. 123–132). New York: Plenum.

Engfer, A., and Schneewind, K. (1976). *Ein Fragebogen selbstperzipiertes elterlichen Erziehungseinstellungen.* Unpublished manuscript, Trier, Germany: Trier University.

Erickson, M, Sroufe, L. A., and Egeland, B. (1985). The relationship between quality of attachment and behavior in preschool in a high risk sample. In I. Bretherton and E. Waters (Eds.), *Growing points in attachment theory and research, Monographs of the Society for Research in Child Development, 50* (1-2, Serial No. 209, pp. 147–166).

Eugster, A., and Vingerhoets, A. J. J. M. (1999). Psychological aspects of in vitro fertilization: A review. *Social Science and Medicine, 48,* 575–589.

Ferri, E. (1976). *Growing up in a one parent family.* Slough, England: NFER Nelson.

Fidell, L., and Marik, J. (1989). Paternity by proxy: Artificial insemination by donor sperm. In J. Offerman-Zuckerberg (Ed.), *Gender in transition: A new frontier* (pp. 93–110). New York: Plenum.

Flaks, D. K., Ficher, I., Masterpasqua, F., and Joseph, G. (1995). Lesbians choosing motherhood: A comparative study of lesbian and heterosexual parents and their children. *Developmental Psychology, 31,* 105–114.

Gianino, A., and Tronick, E. (1985). The mutual regulation model: The infant's self and the interactive regulation and coping and defence capacities. In R. Field., P. McCabe, and N. Schneiderman (Eds.), *Stress and coping* (pp. 47–68). Hillsdale, NJ: Lawrence Erlbaum Associates.

Gibson, F. L., Ungerer, J. A., Leslie, G. I., Saunders, D. M., and Tennant, C. (1999). Maternal attitudes to parenting and mother-child relationship and interaction in IVF families: A prospective study. *Human Reproduction, 14* (Suppl. 1), 131–132.

Gibson, F. L., Ungerer, J. A., Tennant, C. C., and Saunders, D. M. (2000). Parental adjustment and attitudes to parenting after in vitro fertilization. *Fertility and Sterility, 73,* 565–574.

Goldberg, W. A., and Easterbrooks, M. A. (1984). Role of marital quality in toddler development. *Developmental Psychology, 20,* 504–514.

Golombok, S. (1992). Psychological functioning in infertility patients. *Human Reproduction, 7,* 208–212.

Golombok, S., Brewaeys, A., Cook, R., Giavazzi, M. T., Guerra, G., Mantovanni, A., Van Hall, E., Crosignani, P. G., and Dexeus, S. (1996). The European study of assisted reproduction families. *Human Reproduction, 11,* 2324–2331.

Golombok, S., Cook, R., Bish, A., and Murray, C. (1995). Families created by the new reproductive technologies: Quality of parenting and social and emotional development of the children. *Child Development, 66,* 285–298.

Golombok, S., MacCallum, F., and Goodman, E. (2001). The 'test-tube' generation: Parent–child relationships and the psychological well-being of IVF children at adolescence. *Child Development, 72,* 599–608.

Golombok, S., MacCallum, F., and Goodman, E., and Rutter, M. (in press). *Families with children conceived by donor insemination: A follow-up at age 12. Child Development.*

Golombok, S., Murray, C., Brinsden, P., and Abdalla, H. (1999). Social versus biological parenting: Family functioning and the socioemotional development of children conceived by egg or sperm donation. *Journal of Child Psychology and Psychiatry, 40,* 519–527.

Golombok, S., Tasker, F., and Murray, C. (1997). Children raised in fatherless families from infancy: Family relationships and the socioemotional development of children of lesbian and single heterosexual mothers. *Journal of Child Psychology and Psychiatry, 38,* 783–792.

Grotevant, M. D., and McRoy, R. G. (1998). *Openness in adoption: Exploring family connections.* New York: Sage.

Haimes, E., and Daniels, K. (1998). International social science perspectives on donor insemination: An introduction. In K. Daniels and E. Haimes (Eds.), *Donor insemination: International social science perspectives* (pp. 1–6). Cambridge, England: Cambridge University Press.

Hetherington, E. M., and Clingempeel, W. G. (1992). Coping with marital transitions. *Monographs of the Society for Research in Child Development, 57* (2-3, Serial No. 227).

Hock, E., DeMeis, D. K., and McBride, S. L. (1988). Maternal separation anxiety: Its role in the balance of employment and motherhood in mothers of infants. In A. E. Gottfried. and A. W. Gottfried (Eds.), *Maternal employment and children's development: longitudinal research* (pp. 191–229). New York: Plenum.

Hoopes, J. L. (1990). Adoption and identity formation. In D. M. Brodzinsky and M. D. Schechter (Eds.), *The psychology of adoption* (pp. 144–166). Oxford, England: Oxford University Press.

Howe, D., and Feast, J. (2000). *Adoption, search and reunion: The long term experiences of adopted adults.* London: The Childrens Society.

Humphrey, M., and Humphrey, H. (1987). Marital relationships in couples seeking donor insemination. *Journal of Biosocial Sciences, 19,* 209–219.

Jennings, S. (1991). Virgin birth syndrome. *The Lancet, 337,* 559–560.

John, K., and Quinton, D. (1991). *Child and adolescent functioning and environment schedule (revised).* London: MRC Child Psychiatry Unit.

Karpel, M. A. (1980). Family secrets: I. Conceptual and ethical issues in the relational context. II. Ethical and practical considerations in therapeutic management. *Family Process, 19,* 295–306.

Klock, S., and Maier, D. (1991). Psychological factors related to donor insemination. *Fertility and Sterility, 56,* 549–559.

Klock, S., Jacob, M., and Maier, D. (1994). A prospective study of donor insemination recipients: Secrecy, privacy and disclosure. *Fertility and Sterility, 62,* 477–484.

Klock, S. C., Jacob, M. C., and Maier, D. (1996). A comparison of single and married recipients of donor insemination. *Human Reproduction, 11,* 2554–2557.

Kopitzke, E., and Wilson, J. F. (2000, June). *ART and quality of life: Physical and emotional distress.* Paper presented at the 16th Annual Meeting of the European Society for Human Reproduction and Embryology, Bologna, Italy.

Kovacs, G. T., Mushin, D., Kane, H., and Baker, H. (1993). A controlled study of the psycho-social development of children conceived following insemination with donor semen. *Human Reproduction, 8,* 788–790.

Lambermon, M. W. E. (1991). *Video of folder? Karte- en lange termijneffecten van voorlichting over vroegkinderlijke opvoeding.* Unpublished doctoral dissertation, State University, Leyden, The Netherlands.

Lancaster, P. A. L. (1987). Congenital malformations after in-vitro fertilization. *Lancet, 2,* 1392–1393.

Landau, R. (1998). Secrecy, anonymity, and deception in donor insemination: A genetic, psycho-social and ethical critique. *Social Work and Health Care, 28,* 75–89.

Leiblum, S. R. (1997). *Infertility: Psychological issues and counselling strategies.* New York: Wiley.

Leiblum, S. R., Kemmann, E., and Lane, M. K. (1987). The psychological concomitants of in vitro fertilization. *Journal of Psychosomatic Obstetrics and Gynaecology, 6,* 165–178.

Lutjen, P., Trounson, A., Leeton, J., Findlay, J., Wood, C., and Renou, P. (1984). The establishment and maintenance of pregnancy using in vitro fertilization and embryo donation in a patient with primary ovarian failure. *Nature (London), 307,* 174.

MacCallum, F., Goodman, E., Kerai, V., and Golombok, S. (2001). *Parents' attitudes towards disclosure in donor insemination families.* Manuscript in preparation.

Maccoby, E. E., and Martin, J. A. (1983). Socialization in the context of the family: Parent–child interaction. In P. H. Mussen (Series Ed.) and E. M. Hetherington (Vol. Ed.), *Handbook of child psychology: Vol. 4. Socialization, personality, and social development* (4th ed., pp. 1–101). New York: Wiley.

Maughan, B., and Pickles, A. (1990). Adopted and illegitimate children growing up. In L. N. Robins and M. Rutter (Eds.), *Straight and devious pathways from childhood to adulthood* (pp. 36–61). New York: Cambridge University Press.

McLanahan, S., and Sandefur, G. (1994). *Growing up with a single parent: What hurts, what helps.* Cambridge, MA: Harvard University Press.

McMahon, C., Ungerer, J., Beaurepaire, J., Tennant, C., and Saunders, D. (1995). Psychosocial outcomes for parents and children after in vitro fertilization: A review. *Journal of Reproductive and Infant Psychology, 13,* 1–16.

McMahon, C. A., Ungerer, J., Tennant, C., and Saunders, D. (1997). Psychosocial adjustment and the quality of the mother–child relationship at four months postpartum after conception by in vitro fertilization. *Fertility and Sterility, 68,* 492–500.

Medical Research Council Working Party on Children Conceived by In Vitro Fertilization. (1990). Births in Great Britain resulting from assisted conception, 1978–87. *British Medical Journal, 300*, 1229–1233.

Miall, C. E. (1986). The stigma of involuntary childlessness. *Social Problems, 33*, 268–282.

Miall, C. E. (1989). Reproductive technology vs. the stigma of involuntary childlessness. *Social casework: The journal of contemporary social work*, January, 43–50.

Miller, B. C., Fan, X., Christensen, M., Grotevant, H. D., and van Dulmen, M. (2000). Comparisons of adopted and nonadopted adolescents in a large, nationally representative sample. *Child Development, 71*, 1458–1473.

Mushin, D., Spensley, J., and Barreda-Hanson, M. (1985). Children of IVF. *Clinics in Obstetrics and Gynecology, 12*, 865–875.

Nachtigall, R., Pitcher, L., Tschann, J., Becker, G., and Szkupinski Quiroga, S. (1997). Stigma, disclosure and family functioning among parents of children conceived through donor insemination. *Fertility and Sterility, 68*, 83–89.

Owens, D., Edelman, R., and Humphrey, M. (1993). Male infertility and donor insemination: Couples decisions, reactions, and counselling needs. *Human Reproduction, 8*, 880–885.

Papp, P. (1993). The worm in the bud: Secrets between parents and children. In E. Imber-Black (Ed.), *Secrets in families and family therapy* (pp. 66–85). New York: Norton.

Parker, G., Tupling, H., and Brown, L. B. (1979). A parental bonding instrument. *British Journal of Psychology, 51*, 1–10.

Patterson, G. R. (1982). *Coercive family process*. Eugene, OR: Castalia.

Patterson, G., Reid, J., and Dishion, T. (1992). *Antisocial boys*. Eugene, OR: Castalia.

Quinton, D., and M. Rutter (1988). *Parenting breakdown: The making and breaking of intergenerational links*. Aldershot, England: Avebury Gower.

Radloff, L. S., and Locke, B. Z. (1986). The community mental health survey and the CES-D Scale. In M. M. Weissman, J. K. Myers, and C. E. Ross (Eds.), *Community surveys of psychiatric disorders*. New Brunswick, NJ: Rutgers University Press.

Raoul-Duval, A., Bertrand-Servais, M., Letur-Konirsch, H., and Frydman, R. (1994). Psychological follow-up of children born after in-vitro fertilization. *Human Reproduction, 9*, 1097–1101.

Reading, A., Sledmere, C., and Cox, D. (1982). A survey of patient attitudes towards artificial insemination by donor. *Journal of Psychosomatic Research, 26*, 429–433.

Reading, A. E., Cox, D. N., Sledmere, C. M., and Campbell, S. (1984). Psychological changes over the course of pregnancy: A study of attitudes toward the fetus/neonate. *Health Psychology, 3*, 211–221.

Robbroeckx, L. M. H., and Wels, P. M. A. (1989). *Nijmeegse vragenlijst voor de opvoedingssituatie (NVOS)* [Nijmegen questionnaire regarding child-rearing circumstances]. Nijmegen, The Netherlands: Institute voor Orthopedagogiek, Katholieke Universiteit Nijmegen.

Rosenberg, M. (1965). *Society and the adolescent self-image*. Princeton, NJ: Princeton University Press.

Roth, R. M. (1980). *The mother–child relationship evaluation manual*. Los Angeles: Western Psychological Services.

Rumball, A., and Adair, V. (1999). Telling the story: parents' scripts for donor offspring. *Human Reproduction, 14*, 1392–1399.

Rust, J., Bennun, I., and Golombok, S. (1990). The GRIMS: A psychometric instrument for the assessment of marital discord. *Journal of Family Therapy, 12*, 45–57.

Sants, H. J. (1964). Genealogical bewilderment in children with substitute parents. *British Journal of Medical Psychology, 37*, 133–141.

Schechter, M. D., and Bertocci, D. (1990). The meaning of the search. In D. M. Brodzinsky and M. D. Schechter (Eds.), *The psychology of adoption* (pp. 62–92). New York: Oxford University Press.

Schover, L. R., Collins, R. L., and Richards, S. (1992). Psychological aspects of donor insemination: evaluation and follow up of recipient couples. *Fertility and Sterility, 57*, 583–590.

Snowden, R. (1990). The family and artificial reproduction. In D. R. Bromham, M. E. Dalton, and J. C. Jackson (Eds.), *Philosophical ethics in reproductive medicine* (pp. 70–185). Manchester, England: Manchester University Press.

Snowden, R., Mitchell, G. D., and Snowden, E. M. (1983). *Artificial reproduction: A social investigation*. London: Allen and Unwin.

Society for Assisted Reproductive Technology Registry. (1999). Assisted reproductive technology in the United States: 1996 results generated from the American Society for Reproductive Medicine/Society for Assisted Reproductive Technology Registry. *Fertility and Sterility, 71*, 798–807.

Soderstrom-Anttila, V., Sajaneimi, N., Tiitinen, A., and Hovatta, O. (1998). Health and development of children born after oocyte donation compared with that of those born after in-vitro fertilization, and parents' attitudes regarding secrecy. *Human Reproduction, 13*, 2009–2015.

Spanier, G. B. (1976). Measuring dyadic adjustment: New scales for assessing the quality of marriage and similar dyads. *Journal of Marriage and the Family, 38*, 15–38.

Spielberger, C. D. (1966). Theory and research on anxiety. In C. D. Spielberger (Ed.), *Anxiety and behavior* (pp. 3–20). New York: Academic.

Spielberger, C. (1983). *The handbook of the State-Trait Anxiety Inventory*. Palo Alto, CA: Consulting Psychologists Press.

Spielberger, C. D., Gorusch, R. L., and Lushene, R. (1970). *The State-Trait Anxiety Inventory test manual*. Palo Alto, CA: Consulting Psychological Press.

Steptoe, P. C., and Edwards, R. G. (1978). Birth after reimplantation of a human embryo. *Lancet, 2,* 366.

Straus, M. (1979). Measuring intrafamily conflict and violence: The Conflict Tactics (CT) Scales. *Journal of Marriage and the Family, 41,* 75–88.

Tanbo, T., Dale, P. O., Lunde, O., Moe, N., and Abyholm, T. (1995). Obstetric outcome in singleton pregnancies after assisted reproduction. *Obstetrics and Gynecology, 86,* 188–192.

Teti, D. M., and Gelfand, D. (1991). Behavioral competence among mothers of infants in the first year: The mediational role of maternal self efficacy. *Child Development, 62,* 918–929.

Triseliotis, J. (1973). *In search of origins: The experiences of adopted people.* London: Routledge & Kegan Paul.

Tronick, E., Als, H., Adamson, J., Wise, S., and Brazelton, T. B. (1978). The infant's response to entrapment between contradictory messages in face-to-face interaction. *Journal of the American Academy of Child and Adolescent Psychiatry, 17,* 1–13.

Trounson, A., Leeton, J., Besanka, M., Wood, C., and Conti, A. (1983). Pregnancy established in an infertile patient after transfer of a donated embryo fertilized in vitro. *British Medical Journal, 286,* 835–838.

Turner, A. J., and Coyle, A. (2000). What does it mean to be a donor offspring? The identity experiences of adults conceived by donor insemination and the implications for counselling and therapy. *Human Reproduction, 15,* 2041–2051.

van Balen, F. (1996). Child-rearing following in vitro fertilization. *Journal of Child Psychology and Psychiatry, 37,* 687–693.

van Balen, F. (1998). Development of IVF children. *Developmental Review, 18,* 30–46.

van Balen, F., Trimbos-Kemper, G., Van Hall, E., and Weeda, W. C. (1989, May). *Involuntary childlessness, long term coping strategies and psychosomatic symptoms.* Paper presented at the 9th International Congress of Psychosomatic Obstetrics and Gynaecology, Amsterdam.

van Berkel, D., van der Veen, L., Kimmel, I. and te Velde, E. (1999). Differences in the attitudes of couples whose children were conceived through artificial insemination by donor in 1980 and in 1996. *Fertility and Sterility, 71,* 226–231.

Wang, J. X., Clark, A. M., Kirby, A., Philipson, G., Petrucco, O., Anderson, G., and Matthews, C. D. (1994). The obstetric outcome of singleton pregnancies following in-vitro fertilization/gamete intra-fallopian transfer. *Human Reproduction, 9,* 141–146.

Weaver, S. M., Clifford, E., Gordon, A. G., Hay, D. M., and Robinson, J. (1993). A follow-up study of 'successful' IVF/GIFT couples: Social–emotional well-being and adjustment to parenthood. *Journal of Psychosomatic Obstetrics and Gynecology, 14,* 5–16.

Westergard, H. B., Johansen, A. M. T., Erb, K., and Andersen, A. N. (1999). Danish national in vitro fertilization registry 1994 & 1995: A controlled study of births, malformations and cytogenic findings. *Human Reproduction, 14,* 186–902.

Zung, W. (1965). A self-rating depression scale. *Archives of General Psychiatry, 12,* 63–70.

PART II

BECOMING AND BEING
A PARENT

12

The Transition to Parenting

Christoph M. Heinicke

University of California at Los Angeles

INTRODUCTION

The transition to becoming a parent represents a major life change. Interest in this developmental change is universal. Professionals writing in the 1940s through the 1960s stressed the adjustments necessary to deal with the arrival and care of the infant. Global descriptions of the essence of these adjustments differed. Some authors concluded that the birth of the infant represented a crucial positive fulfillment of the developmental and psychic needs of the woman (Deutsch, 1945). Other writers characterized pregnancy and the transition to parenthood as a period of crisis (Bibring, Dwyer, Huntington, and Valenstein, 1961; Hill, 1949). Shereshefsky and Yarrow (1973) saw this developmental disequilibrium as an opportunity to facilitate positive change through intervention. They systematically assessed the impact of counseling on the adjustment to pregnancy and early infancy. One of their most important findings was that clarity and confidence in visualizing themselves as future parents anticipated a more adequate postnatal adjustment.

Other pioneering longitudinal studies (Grossman, Eichler, and Winikoff, 1980) stimulated detailed description of the transition to parenting and to delineation of those aspects of the family system likely to influence family development. Both for its own sake and as a guide to more effective intervention, investigators recognized the need for more specific information about the determinants of parenting.

Interest in the transition to and determinants of parenting grows out of efforts in the late 1970s to define those prebirth and ongoing parent personality and support characteristics that were likely to be associated with the positive development of the child's security of attachment, autonomy, and task orientation. Once one had defined such potential "paths" of influence, the task of intervention would be to change not only the child's behavior and the parent–child transactions, but the functioning of the parents as well. We carried out such an intervention with the preschool child (Heinicke, 1977) and achieved some significant changes in all of the above domains, but the extent of the impact on the child's task orientation was not that extensive. Reviews of the literature (Belsky, 1984;

Heinicke, 1984) outlined the significant determinants of responsive parenting, such as the mother's adaptive functioning and quality of her partner support. These reviews also stressed that these personality and support characteristics could be the subject of intervention before the child is born, thereby altering the quality of parenting and child development. This reasoning led to the decision to initiate family intervention in the third trimester of pregnancy.

The next task became to summarize the research findings delineating the developmental track from parent prebirth and ongoing functioning to postbirth parenting and their child's development. What longitudinal associations can be established and justify initiating intervention in pregnancy? The primary task of this chapter is to answer that question.

In organizing this review and preparing for the definition of an eventual intervention, we also addressed the question of what areas of functioning were likely to respond to an environmental intervention. Hypotheses about the relative influence of genetic and environmental determinants, and particularly their interaction in influencing a particular area of functioning, governed my conceptualization. This emphasis on the interaction of "nature and nurture" in the determination of parenting and family development has been clearly stated and supported with much research evidence by Collins, Maccoby, Steinberg, Hetherington, and Bornstein (2000).

Even if one works within an interactionist framework, it could be argued that the initial characteristics of the child, and his or her impact on the family, are the major determinants of the nature of the family development. As a first response to this assumption, care has been taken to include those studies that indeed test the potential influence of the child's characteristics on the family's development. A second response to the assumption that the child's characteristics are the predominant determinant is to assess parent personality, relationship functioning, and support system *before* the birth of the child, that is, before the child can influence that functioning. If variations in these prebirth characteristics predict variations in the postnatal parent–child and child functioning, such associations cannot be accounted for solely by the impact of the child; those parent characteristics that are relatively stable in the pre- to postbirth period make an independent contribution to these associations.

However, even if it is granted that the associations between parent functioning and parent–child and child functioning are not exclusively determined by endogenous child influences, it is conceivable that latent endogenous factors influence *both* parent and child functioning and thus determine their association. For example, the significant association between prebirth assessments of the mother's secure-autonomous functioning and the secure attachment of her 1–year–old child could be determined by an as yet not discovered endogenous factor.

Following one of the arguments of Collins et al. (2000), if an environmental intervention can alter both the parent and child functioning as well as their interrelationship, then the argument for an exclusive underlying endogenous influence is less convincing. I return to these considerations at the end of the chapter.

With this background in mind, this chapter examines the research that is now available on delineating the impact of prebirth parent personality and relationship functioning on key areas of parent and child development. A number of propositions guide this review. The first proposition states that parent personality and marital functioning are relatively stable in the transition to parenthood. Parents who function more adequately than other parents before the birth of their child also tend to function more adequately after the birth. Within this relatively consistent impact, it is also proposed that differences in the quality of the prebirth parent personality and experienced support anticipate differences in parent–child and child functioning. The above propositions imply a focus on (1) the expectable stabilities and changes in the couples' transition to parenthood and (2) how variations in prebirth parent personality and support characteristics influence variations in future parenting. Accordingly, the two major goals of this chapter are to summarize the available evidence on (1) the stability of parent personality and support characteristics in the transition to parenting and (2) the evidence linking variations in prebirth parent personality and support characteristics to variations in family development.

Two conceptual frameworks are outlined to organize the summary of research. The first is a summary of a family systems framework that provides a larger context for the research summarized here. The second focuses more specifically on the definition of the parent personality and marital and support characteristics that anticipate parenting and child's development.

A FAMILY SYSTEMS MODEL OF PARENTING

Cowan, Powell, and Cowan (1998) have proposed that, in order to understand variations in developing parent–child relationships and their effects on children's development, information about six domains of family functioning are needed. These are:

(1) The biological and psychological characteristics of each individual in the family;
(2) The quality of relationships in parents' families of origin and in current relationships among grandparents, parents, and grandchildren;
(3) The quality of the relationship between the parents, with special emphasis on their division of roles, communication patterns, and roles as coparents to their children;
(4) The quality of relationship between the siblings;
(5) The relationships between nuclear family members and key individuals or institutions outside the family (friends, peers, work, childcare, school, ethnic group, government, etc.) as sources of stress, support, models, values, and beliefs;
(6) The quality of the relationship between each parent and child.

In documenting the significance of one domain influencing another, including the influence over time, Cowan et al. (1998) cited associations that are particularly relevant to the findings presented in this chapter. They emphasized the central role of marital quality in family adaptation (see Grych, in Vol. 4 of this *Handbook*). They document that both the quality of the intimate partner relationship and whether they can successfully coparent have a significant impact on the parent–child relationship and that both are likely to be influenced negatively as the number of stresses in other domains increase.

Cowan et al. (1998) also stressed the importance of one domain influencing another over time in citing evidence for the three–generational transmission of parenting patterns. To give an example, and as will be documented further below, if the mother is characterized by an insecure working model of her early attachments as assessed *before* the birth of her child, then her child will tend to have a less secure attachment to her. Illustrating their emphasis on considering many interacting influences, the above is not true if women classified as insecure had spouses who were secure.

Although it is essential to keep the concept of interacting domains of a family-system model in mind, to summarize the findings on the association between prebirth parent characteristics and early family development, the concepts being used to describe each of the domains needs to be defined more specifically. They will be used in relation to both of my goals: (1) to document stability and change in the parent personality and support characteristics and (2) to cite the evidence linking variations in prebirth personality and support characteristics to variations in family development.

PREBIRTH DETERMINANTS, PARENTING, AND THE CHILD'S DEVELOPMENT: A CONCEPTUAL FRAMEWORK

Characterization of the mother's and father's personalities has scrutinized their *adaptation-competence*, *capacity for positive sustained relationships*, and *self-development*. Consideration of their supportive relationships focuses on their *partners* (including marital) and their *extended family*.

Characterization of parenting was defined by three parent–infant transactions (social interaction variables) and the associated components of the child's emerging self (personality variables). It is recognized that even if one limits oneself to tracing interconnections between personality and social interaction variables across the transition to family formation, the number of potential mutual influences and levels of abstraction is great. In organizing this chapter, I address those interconnections that have actually been studied and specified.

Turning to the definition of parent personality concepts, *adaptation-competence* refers to the efficient, nonanxious, persistent, and flexible approach to problem solving. It has been operationally specified as ego strength (Barron, 1953), adaptation-competence (Heinicke, Diskin, Ramsey-Klee, and Given, 1983)—and, more recently, as maternal competence (Teti, Gelfand, and Pompa, 1990)—and the absence of task-related anger (Heinicke, 1993).

The *capacity for positive sustained relationships* refers to empathy and positive mutuality expressed by the parent in an ongoing relationship. It has been operationally specified in relation to parenting by the mother's and father's coherent, objective, and balanced account of their childhood relationship experiences (Fonagy, Steele, and Steele, 1991; Main and Goldwyn, in press) and by the parent's recall of their own parenting as loving (Main and Goldwyn, 1994), low in conflict (Cowan, Cowan, Schulz, and Heming, 1994), and generally positive (Heinicke and Guthrie, 1992). It is also defined by sensitivity to other's needs (Brunnquell, Crichton, and Egeland, 1981) and being trusting as opposed to skeptical of interpersonal relationships (Pianta, Egeland, and Erickson, 1989).

Definition of the *parent's self-development* has involved their experienced autonomy and confidence as opposed to insecurity. It has been operationally specified in relation to parenting as clarity and confidence in visualizing oneself as a parent (Heinicke et al., 1983; Shereshefsky and Yarrow, 1973). Cowan and colleagues (1985) assessed both the parent's self-esteem and which life roles were most important to them: partner, lover, worker, and so on. Diamond, Heinicke, and Mintz (1996) operationally defined the autonomy of each parent using concepts of individuation-separation. The link of self-development to past and current relationships is stressed by examining relations to the family of origin, self–directed autonomous activities, and mutuality with and differentiation from the current partner.

The *parent's positive experience of their partnerships* (including marriage) is also central to this organization of literature. Specific definitions have focused on different aspects of this experience. Cowan and Cowan (1988) stressed the importance of the partner's consensus on their mutual role arrangements (who does what) and the openness of their communication. Both inventories (Belsky, Rovine, and Fish, 1989; Cowan and Cowan, 1988) and interviews (Heinicke et al., 1983) have been used to define the expressed satisfaction with the partner. Direct observations of the quality of the marital interaction of parents underline the importance of both expressing negative affects and remaining on the task of resolving conflicts (Balaguer and Markman, 1991; Heinicke and Guthrie, 1996; Pratt, Kerig, Cowan, and Cowan, 1988).

Whereas it has generally been assumed that the quality of support experienced in the partnership (married or not) plays a central role in family adaptation (Belsky, 1984; Cowan et al., 1998), the *support received from family and friends* also exerts a beneficial impact on parent–child relationships (Belsky, 1984). Such support may be emotional or involve instrumental assistance. It is very likely related to the mother's adaptation–competence and capacity for relationships, but has been considered as an independent influence in the research being considered here.

In defining the likely link of prebirth parent characteristics to postnatal family development, it is most meaningful to focus on those qualities of parenting that are not only likely to link to prebirth parent characteristics, but are in turn a part of significant transactions defined by both parenting and child qualities. Thus, I highlight certain qualities of parenting by relating them to the development of the child's self. The key forms of parenting are teaching and exposing the child to new cognitive experiences, responding to the needs of the infant, and promoting the autonomy of the child. (For operational definition of these parent–infant transactions, see Ainsworth, Blehar, Waters, and Wall, 1978; Bornstein, in Vol. 1 of this *Handbook*; Heinicke and Guthrie, 1992.)

Consistent with Sroufe's (1989) discussion of relationships, self, and individual adaptation, components of the self are defined as emerging from the interaction of early infant characteristics and the constellation of parent characteristics and parenting relationship potentials. Self as an organization integrates the infant's adaptation and accompanying feelings and thoughts. The development of the components of the self can be related to the quality and goals of these relationships (Sroufe, 1989).

The "competent self" is associated with a sense of being an agent (Stern, 1985), task orientation, attention (Heinicke, 1980), and self–regulation. It emerges out of and continues in the context of the type of parental responsiveness that teaches and exposes the child to new cognitive experiences (Bornstein and Tamis–LeMonda, 1989). The emphasis on adaptive capacities includes early modes of self–regulation or defense such as suppression, turning the passive into active, avoidance, and control. The "secure self" (Ainsworth et al., 1978) and the closely associated "expectation of being cared for" (Heinicke and Guthrie, 1992), "sense of self as worthy" (Sroufe, 1989), and "modulation of aggression" (Heinicke, Diskin, Ramsey–Klee, and Oates, 1986) emerge out of and continue in a relationship characterized by parents' responsiveness to the needs of the infant (Bornstein and Tamis–LeMonda, 1989). The "separate self," or subjective awareness of the self and other (Stern, 1985), begins in the second half of the first year of life and is seen as emerging out of and continuing in a relationship that prepares for and promotes autonomy as well as providing control (limits) for that expansion (Heinicke and Guthrie, 1992).

The above profile of variables has guided my integration of the research findings, but it is important to note that the definition and measurement of the variables are clarified in each study reviewed. Before examining whether the relative standing of couples on various prebirth parent qualities within a sample remain *stable* from the pre- to postbirth period, and then formulating specific statements linking these parent qualities to parent and parent–child *variations* in development, I provide a narrative description of one family. The concepts used are illustrated and the findings to be presented are anticipated.

THE DEVELOPMENT OF LAURIE'S FAMILY FROM PREGNANCY TO 4 YEARS OF AGE

The father, Mark, and the mother, Nancy, had been married for 11 years. They were 39 and 32 years old respectively, as they expected their first child. Their prebirth adaptation, capacity for relationship, mutuality, as well as sense of autonomy were, by comparison with other couples in the research sample, at the highest level (Heinicke and Guthrie, 1992). Moreover, their level of role differentiation and capacity to resolve conflictual issues was sustained throughout their daughter's first four years. Three important events impacted this positive stability and represented a challenge: the mother's return to full-time work, a recurrence of the father's chronic illness when the daughter, Laurie, was 1 year old, and the mother becoming pregnant with her second child when Laurie was 17 months old.

Prebirth Assessments

Review of the prebirth interview, psychological testing, home visits, and marital interaction data by three different clinicians before the birth of Laurie led to the following summary and predictions:

This is a very attractive couple in the sense of being competent and giving. Their relationship is mutually satisfying and supportive. They communicate clearly and, especially, what they expect of each other. They have dealt with changes in a flexible manner, and the expectation is that they will make the adjustments to include their infant in a "very close" dyad. They recognize that a sense of control that they now have over their lives and being together will be seriously changed. They are able to resolve this by talking about a sanctuary both in terms of being alone and having time to themselves. This issue is raised in the following recorded marital interaction, and different perspectives are given in the context of positive regard:

Mother:	...We should probably really keep in mind to make time for us to just be by ourselves, not necessarily get a babysitter when we're going out with somebody else but to have time for ourselves to do things, 'cause we really need that.
Father:	I just guess I don't quite believe that it takes as much time as people say it does. 'Cause I just feel like we'll have time for each other but—
Mother:	Well, it will probably take more time than we think, but I feel like we shouldn't assume that one hundred percent of our time from the time the baby is born has to be directed toward the baby. I think that it'd be good if there are times when we could sort of let the baby play by itself. You know, some people never do that. They're always involved with the baby. They never give the baby any time to itself. Maybe that's something we should remember and it'll help us have a little more time. There are times when the baby can play quietly.
Father:	But you never know. I mean, we might be really pulled toward the baby too, you know, and away from each other ...
Mother:	Yeah, which I think we should be careful of ... 'cause otherwise we'll be faced with getting to know each other again. When the baby starts to be old enough so that it needs to be independent it can; I think babies need to be independent at a very early age. I mean, maybe have some time by themselves.

Their enthusiasm for the birth, their confidence as future parents, as well as their warmth, individuality, and competence lead to the expectation that they would be responsive to the needs of their infant and promote learning and autonomy in their child.

The clinicians reviewing their prebirth material also articulated that there would be two particular challenges to this positive adjustment: The possible deterioration in the father's health and the mother's return to work at a very early date. It was anticipated that, because of financial pressures and the mother's wish to pursue her work, she would be less flexible in this question. It was also anticipated that this might be partially resolved by the father sharing in the caregiving.

After a lengthy labor, Laurie was delivered by Caesarian section. Both parents were thrilled with their baby girl. The hospital observer described her as a very beautiful, nicely formed, large baby with pink skin and light brown hair. There were no obstetrical complications (Littman and Parmalee, 1974). Summary comments from the Brazelton Behavior Assessment Scale (Brazelton, 1973) were: "Laurie is a very pretty baby. She aroused to the alert state quickly. She was very responsive to stimulation (animate), and was mature in several of her responses."

After several efforts, the mother successfully nursed her new infant on the fourth day. She continued the nursing more than the prescribed time: "It made no sense to pull her off the breast just because the clock said a certain time." The mother stroked her back and neck and spoke softly to her in soothing tones when she was awake. She mentioned that she thought the baby liked her and liked being held closely. This pleased her immensely because, as she said, "I love to hold her." Thus, a responsive mother and responsive infant formed a positive relationship in the first few days: "I just can't believe it, here she is and she's so perfect. I can't believe she's really mine." She talked in the same positive tone about her husband and then became concerned that she might have to go back to work for financial reasons.

Observations in the home revealed that in 1 month the bodily closeness to the infant included the father. He enjoyed Laurie deeply, was beaming with pride, and was often tempted to pick her up even when he knew he shouldn't. The baby was responsive to voices and made good eye contact. The mother was pleased with her increasing ability to read Laurie's signals. She often stroked her hair and would lean forward to kiss her. Laurie responded to this loving care by lengthening her nighttime sleep periods and continuing to be easy to nurse. As the mother's attachment grew she became increasingly conflicted about returning to work, yet the financial pressures to do so were considerable. It was also clear that the cries of a dependent infant taxed her need to control her life. In her first contact with the mother–infant group when Laurie was 5 weeks old, Nancy recounted how terrible the first few weeks had been, and that now during Laurie's fussy times between 10 p.m. and 1 a.m. she often finds herself crying along with the baby.

In the next two mother–infant group sessions, the group leader noted that Nancy "enjoys her baby and within their tight closeness has a very nice, gentle way with her." When the mother removed her wet diaper, Laurie responded to her freedom with gurgling, movement, and visual contact. Nancy told the other mothers that she was surprised at how reluctant she had become to leave her infant and go to work again. Having to replace her initial sitter again activated her doubts.

As the return to work actually occurred, Laurie adjusted well. Observations in the home at 3 months emphasized that the mutual responsiveness of mother, father, and infant was continuing. Being with the baby-sitter had encouraged Laurie to experiment more and move into the environment more. By contrast, the mother was less able in the evening to put her down and have her be apart: "I haven't been with her all day."

Family Development at 6 Months

At 6, 12, 24, and 48 months, the parents and infant were assessed through interviews, testing, and observations in the home.

From both the interview and observation in the home at 6 months, it became clear that Laurie had been successfully integrated into her parent's positive mutuality. Mother's intense affection continued to be expressed through holding, kissing, and nursing her in the morning and evening. But by this age, the mother was also encouraging exploration, helped her to stand up, and let her roam on the floor. The father–daughter relationship was by now one of obvious infatuation. As the father played various games with her on the floor, he would often spontaneously hug and kiss her. Laurie would make everyone laugh with her happy vocalizations and noises.

During the Bayley Scale Assessment, Laurie showed above-average goal directedness, attention, and endurance. Both her mental and motor development were above average; the Mental Development Index was 129 and the Motor Development Index was 112. The examiner made the following observations: "Mother and infant share a calm and deliberate physical space reflecting a relaxed, secure relationship. Laurie's primary orientation is toward the social, but she also examined each stimulus with interest. The mother encouraged this with a moderate amount of exposing and teaching."

As part of the Bayley assessment, the infant's reaction to a brief separation was tested (Heinicke, Recchia, Berlin, and James, 1993). Initially vigilant, Laurie soon cried and pushed away from the examiner. Upon reunion, Laurie immediately visually engaged and cuddled her mother and then reengaged the examiner visually and vocally. This reaction to separation was scored as demonstrating low anxiety with positive reunion.

Global ratings have been used to summarize the home observations (Heinicke et al., 1993). Table 12.1 presents the ratings for each month:

As shown in the table, the 6–month global ratings indicate a positive family development. In terms of the major transactions that are the focus of this chapter, all ratings are high (i.e., 4 or 5):

(1) The child's expectation of being cared for (an index of the secure self) interacting with mother responsiveness to need;
(2) the child's sense of separate self interacting with the mother encourages autonomy;
(3) the child's adaptation–competence interacting with the mother stimulates cognitive experiences.

The global parent–child ratings for the father were very similar to those on the mother. Changes in these indices of family development did occur. The reasons for these changes are discussed later.

Family Development at 12 Months

Whereas the various assessments of development had been uniformly positive up to 6 months, at 12 months some indications confirmed the continuing positive development, whereas others showed signs of stress. Nancy and Mark had further pursued their careers and continued to be close not only

TABLE 12.1
Global Child and Mother–Child Ratings at Four Assessment Points with 5-Point Scales
(Five Is High)

Ratings	Months			
	6	12	24	48
Global Child				
Expectation of being cared for	5	5	4	3
Sense of separate self	4	5	5	4
Sense of positive self	5	5	4	3
Adaptation competence	5	5	4	3
Global Mother–Child				
Mother affection	5	5	4	3
Mother responsive to need	4	5	5	4
Mother encourages autonomy	4	4	5	4
Mother stimulates cognitive experience	4	5	4	3

with each other, but with Laurie. In her more intimate interview with her social worker, Nancy's depression concerning her husband's illness was evident. This was not evident in her interaction with Laurie at home or in the laboratory test situation. In the test situation the mother offered appropriate demonstrations and affectionate approval. Anticipating Laurie's frustration on a particular task, she gave her a hug, and this allowed Laurie to reengage. The observation in the home pictured a very alert, energetic, interested child who made numerous forays into every corner of the room, bringing out all her favorite toys. When tired, Laurie would allow herself to be picked up, caressed, and then would again "read a book" or experiment with a toy. The mother could mostly sit back, name or point to things when invited, and was no longer as driven to pick her up. She was clearly comfortable in her mothering, and especially so since a very affectionate daily in–house caregiver had been with them in the last 6 months. Ratings done by the home observer at 12 months reflected a very positive parent–child and child development (see Table 12.1).

The test examiner also concluded that "Laurie shows a secure attachment to a responsive mother." However, Laurie was noticeably less social than at 6 months, and while making eye contact with and reaching for her mother during the reunion after a brief separation, there was an absence of any obvious feeling. A muted and even defensive response was suggested. Taken together with the decline in her general social responsiveness, this momentary defensiveness did raise the question of whether some insecurity in the child was enhanced by the mother's daily absence and/or the concern about the father's illness.

Family Development at 24 Months

At this point in Laurie's life, her mother was 7 months pregnant. Although tired, the mother still had a soft, gentle way with her daughter. Laurie's extensive vocabulary allowed her to communicate her needs, which the mother responded to with sensitivity. The mother avoided control battles with Laurie and instead facilitated her daughter's involvement with activities of Laurie's own choosing.

The excellent communication, role differentiation, and positive mutuality between the parents came into play, as Nancy had concluded that she was missing too much of her daughter's development. She and Mark agreed that she would take care of Laurie in the mornings and he would be home in the afternoon.

In the Bayley testing situation, both mother and daughter displayed a mutually accepting, quiet, and reflective manner. Laurie was cooperative, attentive, and goal directed. This task persistence was clearly associated with a Mental Development Index of 121 (above average) and a Motor

Development Index of 131 (superior). Within the above positive context of family development, the Bayley assessment situation also suggested signs of distress in the mother–daughter relationship. The examiner noted a lack of exuberance, both in the daughter and the mother. There were next to no playful interactions. When separated from her mother, she reassured herself with "Mommy right back," pointed to the door, turned to the examiner for comfort. But, despite an affectionate invitation from the mother at reunion, she was unresponsive, did not return her mother's hug, and turned instead to her own play. The examiner inferred that her daughter's actual and anticipated lack of attention from her pregnant mother could be accentuating both anger and unresponsiveness.

The observations of the family made shortly after the birth of the baby brother, Tim, were best summarized by the phrase "a lovely family," and this was reflected in the ratings shown in Table 12.1. A quiet enthusiasm was associated with various family activities. The parents reported that Laurie "socializes easily" with other children, likes to read books, but, as she says, "likes to talk too." During the visit she played on her own but also became involved in family tasks. There were no problems regarding control or aggression. The parents were responsive to their children and to each other. They expressed some concern about Laurie's nail biting and that she doesn't like to be left alone. As if this last quality were somehow negative, they quickly added that she does not get that upset or have a fit. This report of her reaction to being left was consistent with what had been observed during the separation from the mother in the test situation. Yet the predominant picture emerging from the total assessment was that both individually and in their interactions, this family was continuing to develop in a very positive direction.

Family Development at 48 Months

As at previous assessment points, observations were made in the home, the mother was interviewed, and Laurie was tested (the Weschler Pre–School Test of Intelligence). The observer, the parents, and the preschool teacher also filled out the California Child Q-Sort (Block and Block, 1980). One hundred descriptions of child functioning were judged as most versus least characteristic of Laurie.

Both the positive communication between the parents and the acceptance by both of them of their respective roles had further insured an overall positive family development. The mother had decided to quit her job and be at home full-time; it was clear from her behavior and answers to the interview questions that she had never been so happy. The father's increasing business success had brought greater financial security, and thus in part made this possible.

The parents were also clearly enchanted with their 2-year-old son. As the observer described it: "He has that cherubic kind of glow about him that you just want to pick him up and play with him." Not surprisingly, Laurie had difficulty with a rival that would so easily receive positive attention. At times she would get impatient and interrupt. Though not openly aggressive, her interaction was often controlling. On one occasion she grabbed his shirt and said, "Wait a minute, big boy."

Another adaptation to the newcomer was to be boyish and very active. She greeted the observer in a Superman outfit. "Oh," said the observer, "you are Superwoman." "No, no," she said, "I am Superman," and proceeded to jump all over the couch. The mother added that when her daughter is in doubt she becomes a Superhero.

But clearly, most difficult for the parents was Laurie's reaction to separation; she just didn't like her mother to drop her off at the play group: "Don't go Mommy." Yet, the mother added, she reacts fairly quietly and does not throw a fit. The difficulty in being away from her mother interfered with her IQ test performance. She had to check on her mother in the adjoining room and had difficulty completing the subtest. Thus, her verbal IQ of 115 was probably an underestimate. On the performance IQ she scored 123. She had an excellent fund of information, a good vocabulary, and a good concept of numbers.

Moreover, her overall capacity for engagement in the IQ test was reflected in the Q-sort items that the teacher, parents, and observer agreed were most characteristic: is attentive and able to concentrate; is curious and exploring, eager to learn, and open to new experiences; and is persistent in activities. Several items reflected her autonomy and independence: is self-assertive and seeks to be independent and autonomous. There was also agreement on her pride: tends to be pleased with her products and accomplishments. Her energy level was seen as very characteristic: is vital, energetic, lively; is agile and well coordinated; and has a rapid personal tempo. Other items agreed on were: responds to humor; is creative in perception, thought, work, or play; and does not tease children or her sibling.

In regard to social interaction, after a period of great difficulty following the birth of her brother, she did at this time play with him and had some playmates. In preschool, she tended to avoid the rough boys and was often by herself. In the home, the observer noted that she was not easy to engage and at times seemed like an unhappy child. The father commented that he loves to talk to her but that the "sweetness" isn't always there; sometimes she is difficult to reach and seeks attention in a boisterous way.

The global ratings for the 48–month points when compared with the 6-month points reveal a decline in the expectation of being cared for, the sense of a positive self, and her adaptation–competence. By contrast, the sense of a separate self remained the same. Declines were also seen in the mother stimulating Laurie's cognitive experiences, and especially in affection. Although there was therefore less affectionate involvement, the mother's response to her daughter's needs and the encouragement of autonomy did not decline.

Summary of Family Development

Longitudinal observation of Nancy, Mark, Tim, and Laurie illustrates the major findings of this chapter. Prebirth characteristics of the couple and of each individual partner anticipate qualities of their parenting, and especially their responsiveness to need and encouragement of autonomy. Their capacity for efficient adaptation, positive mutuality, and evolving security in their role could be linked to the development of security, autonomy, and competent cognitive functioning in their child. This was especially evident in the first 2 years of life. Crucial to the family functioning was the parent's ability to confront difficult problems, express their feelings, and come to some resolution. This was seen in relation to protecting their need for alone time as a couple in the prebirth marital interaction, and was evidenced postnatally in the way in which the parents resolved the issue of how much, if at all, the mother should work.

Within this picture of positive adjustment, the increasing charm and security of 2–year–old Tim had threatened the security of his 4–year–old sister. Her boisterous, attention-seeking and anxious/defensive reaction to separation from her mother irritated the other members of the family. However, her task motivation, independence, and learning were not impaired. Given the resources of the parents and the continuing response to Laurie's needs and encouragement of autonomy, it was anticipated that this issue would be resolved in a positive direction.

I now turn to a summary of the research findings documenting both the stability of parental characteristics and how differences in those characteristics influence differences in family development.

THE STABILITY OF PARENT PERSONALITY AND MARITAL CHARACTERISTICS

Review of the research literature suggests a striking consensus that a considerable number of parent personality and marital characteristics are stable across the transition to parenthood, and thus are likely to exert a continuing and generally consistent influence on postnatal family development. Grossman et al. (1980) showed that the mother's emotional well-being, marital adjustment, and level of anxiety and depression during pregnancy and at 2 months postpartum correlated significantly with measures of those same qualities as assessed at 12 months postpartum. Similarly, these authors demonstrated that measures of the father's marital adjustment and level of anxiety assessed during pregnancy and at 2 months postpartum anticipated assessment of that same quality at 12 months postpartum.

Although they delineated change in certain domains of couple functioning, Cowan and Cowan (1988) documented the relative stability of the following characteristics by citing the correlation between the prebirth and 18-month assessments as follows: Marital satisfaction ranges from 0.50 to 0.70; role satisfaction is 0.56 for men and 0.62 for women; self–esteem is 0.75 for men and 0.76 for women. Similarly, Wolkind and Zajicek (1981) found that assessments of the mother's self–esteem at 4 and 14 months after the birth of her child tended to be highly consistent. Huston and McHale (1983) compared the marital relationship of samples of families who had a child during approximately the first year after their marriage with those who did not. Couples who had children shared more joint activities (almost exclusively in childcare) and also moved toward more traditional sex roles in terms of instrumental activities. Having a child did not, however, differentially affect involvement with kin and friends or the overall evaluation of and the expression of affection within the marriage. Although these last two indexes of the marriage declined, the magnitude of the change in evaluation of the marriage was not great. Consistent with these findings, Cox and Owen (1993) found that prenatal and 3–month assessments of marital discord were significantly correlated.

Findings from two longitudinal studies (Heinicke and Guthrie, 1992) also support the hypothesis that measures of both personality functioning and marital quality significantly correlate even when the time interval extends from prebirth to the child's fourth birthday. Factor scores describing the mother's positive experience of the marriage based on ratings of recorded interviews with her during pregnancy and at 1, 6, 12, 24, 36, and 48 months of age were significantly correlated. With the exception of the correlation between the prebirth and 6–month assessments, all intercorrelations were statistically significant.

As cited earlier, Cowan and Cowan (1988) also reported the consistency in marital functioning, but noted that there is a lower correlation between pregnancy and 6 months than pregnancy and 18 months. This exception suggests the possible impact of the transition to parenthood. Indeed, there is variation in the patterns of change in marital patterns (Heinicke and Guthrie, 1992). However, the relative position of each couple within a group of families remains stable from prebirth to 48 months. Indices of the mother's adaptation–competence and warmth are also significantly intercorrelated in the period from prebirth to 48 months (Heinicke and Lampl, 1988). Schaeffer, Edgerton, and Hunter (1983) found similar levels of association between pregnancy and postpartum measures of a quality closely linked to adaptation–competence, namely, maternal locus of control.

The Adult Attachment Interview (AAI) categorizations (George, Kaplan, and Main, 1996), which assess an adult's state of mind with respect to attachment, have also been found to be stable across a period of time. Most relevant to an interest in the span from pregnancy to postbirth status is the study by Benoit and Parker (1994). Using three categories to compare the AAI done in pregnancy with that administered when the mother's child was 12 months showed a 90% agreement. Van IJzendoorn and Bakermans–Kranenburg (1996) have summarized additional evidence showing the considerable stability of the AAI.

In summary, previous findings suggest considerable stability in global indexes of marital quality and personality functioning when prebirth and postnatal assessments are compared. This stable and consistent impact on postnatal family development of both personality and marital characteristics begs the question of which of these characteristics link to emerging parent transactions with the infant, and thus influence infant development. Ideally, answers to this question would involve a particular study that includes assessments of all six domains of family functioning stipulated by the Cowan et al. (1998) family system model and, following the focus of this chapter, repeats such measures from the prebirth to postbirth period. Such studies are not currently available. At this point, the existing research is best organized by linking prebirth *maternal*, prebirth *paternal*, and prebirth *couple* characteristics to selected social–emotional parent–child and child functioning. At the risk of oversimplification, but to make the findings more accessible, I summarize the findings by initial statements that I feel are supported by those findings. Although the primary focus of the studies cited tends to fall on the association of the domains being documented, in many instances a particular study includes consideration of other domains in the design, for example, the mother's level of prenatal family support and the child's 1-month social responsiveness (Isabella and Gable, 1993).

THE IMPACT OF PREBIRTH PARENT CHARACTERISTICS ON POSTNATAL FAMILY DEVELOPMENT

Maternal Prebirth Functioning, Mother's Responsiveness, and the Security of Her Child

The mother's prebirth adaptive competence and capacity to sustain positive relationships (especially those with her partner) anticipate her responsiveness to the needs of her infant in the period from 1 month to 4 years of age. Moreover, these same prebirth characteristics anticipate the development of security in her child. The previous two statements can be rephrased as follows: If, before the birth of her child, the mother copes well with various life issues, has the capacity to form positive, trusting relationships, and has a mutually positive relationship with her partner, then she is more likely to be responsive to her child's needs, and her child will develop greater security in the first 4 years of life. This reflects the fact that the transaction of parent responsiveness to need and the child's security are intercorrelated. Moreover, this transactional association is reflected in the first set of findings. Based on the review of research available at the time (Belsky, 1984; Heinicke, 1984), a hypothesized path analysis was formulated and reported in Heinicke et al. (1986; see Figure 12.1).

Focusing on statistically significant associations relevant to the development of security, it was found that husband–wife adaptation, maternal adaptation–competence, and maternal warmth all have a direct and independent impact on variations in parent responsiveness to need at 1 month, and that 1-month parent responsiveness impacts infant fretting at 3 months. Three–month infant fretting, in turn, anticipates child modulation of aggression and parent responsiveness at 2 years. Modulation of aggression is here being used as an index of the child's security (Heinicke et al., 1986; Heinicke and Guthrie, 1992). That is, these two research reports document the potential chain of effects from prebirth to 1 month, 3 months, and then to 2 years. Suggesting the continuing influence of stable parent characteristics is the direct association (path) from prebirth husband–wife adaptation, maternal adaptation–competence, and maternal warmth to 2-year modulation of aggression (see Figure 12.1).

A number of other prospective longitudinal studies starting with assessments of the parents before the birth of their first child have reported findings consistent with the aforementioned model. Belsky and Isabella (1986) found that mothers who scored poorly before the birth of their first child on both ego strength and interpersonal affection were likely to experience the most negative change in their marriage. In addition, these two personality characteristics, the quality of the postnatal marital experience, as well as the perceptions of their child as becoming less adaptable all contributed to the development of an insecure infant–mother relationship at 12 months as measured by the child's reaction to separation from and reunion with the mother. Findings by Grossman et al. (1980) are also consistent with the hypotheses outlined in that parent responsiveness and infant soothability at 2 months are anticipated by prenatal indexes of maternal adaptation, anxiety, and marital style in the case of the firstborn child. Moreover, with respect to maternal personality, Moss (1967) demonstrated that accepting the prebirth nurturant role and viewing the care of a baby as gratifying rather than burdensome are associated with each other: Both these factors in turn anticipate the mother's actual responsiveness to her baby as observed at 3 weeks and 3 months.

Results from the Minnesota Mother–Child Interaction project reported by Egeland and his colleagues (Brunnquell et al., 1981; Egeland and Farber, 1984; Pianta et al., 1989) also support the power of prebirth measures of the mother's emotional stability as predictors of maternal responsive caregiving and a secure infant attachment. In their poverty at-risk sample, mothers who scored significantly higher on a prebirth factor entitled Level of Personality Integration (Brunnquell et al., 1981) met the physical and emotional needs of their children at 3 months, and their children at 12 months

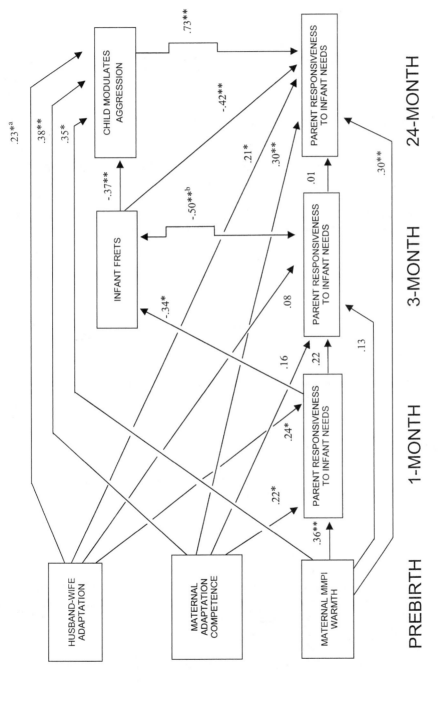

FIGURE 12.1. Path analysis diagram for two indexes of 24-month positive parent–child mutuality: child aggression modulation and parent responsiveness to need ($N = 44$).

*$p < 0.05$.   **$p < 0.01$.

[a] Beta weights placed by across time paths.

[b]Vertical lines indicate cross-sectional correlations. Copyright © 1986 by the American Psychological Association. Reprinted with permission.

were more frequently classified as secure (Egeland and Farber, 1984). Level of Personality Integration is "composed of an amalgam of affective and intellectual elements, each of which contributes to the overall conception of the mother's recognition of her own psychological needs and process, her ability to perceive those needs and processes in others, and her ability to integrate the two sets of needs and processes" (Brunnquell et al., 1981). Among the measures related to this construct are IQ, locus of control, the feeling of being able to control what happens to oneself, and the Cohler Scales—such as encouragement versus discouragement of reciprocity, appropriate versus inappropriate control of the child's aggression, and acceptance versus denial of emotional complexity in childcare. Further analyses of these data revealed that prebirth maternal characteristics were also associated with whether or not the mother anticipated and in fact found her child "difficult" as opposed to "easy" at 3 and 6 months (Vaughn, Deinard, and Egeland, 1980; Vaughn, Taraldson, Chrichten, and Egeland, 1981). The importance of the contribution of the mother's adaptation–competence and capacity for relationships to her future caregiving is supported by the fact that the best discriminator of the maltreating and inadequate caring mothers, as followed up in this sample at child 64 months, of age was the emotional stability scale of the 16PF Personality test, also administered at this time. Pianta et al. (1989) discussed two concepts in relation to this scale: emotional instability (impulsiveness) and being skeptical of interpersonal relationships.

In another longitudinal study, Isabella and Gable (1993) found that mother's prenatal reports of personal sympathy were predictive of both sensitive responsivity and rejection at three postnatal measurement periods. Mothers who had described themselves as compassionate, empathic, and sensitive to the needs of others were likely to exhibit sensitively responsive and nonrejecting behaviors at 1, 4, and 9 months, whereas insensitivity and rejection were most likely observed in mothers who had described themselves as inconsiderate and slow to recognize the needs of others. Measures of the type of social support and marital quality were also associated with maternal interactive behavior. Women who reported higher levels of prenatal family support were likely to exhibit more sensitively responsive behaviors at 4 months and less rejecting behaviors at both 4 and 9 months. Linking marital quality to mothering revealed that mothers who were more satisfied with their marriages prenatally were likely to exhibit higher levels of sensitivity at 9 months. In additional analyses, Isabella and Gable (1993) found that the association between prenatal maternal sympathy and 1–month sensitivity was no longer significant when the impact of the child's social responsiveness was considered. However, prenatal sympathy did anticipate the change in the mother's sensitivity from 1 to 4 months. Again by contrast, the change in maternal sensitivity from 4 to 9 months was not predicted by any variable. The authors suggest that this may be due to the high correlation between the 4– and 9–month maternal behavior—that is, there is little change. In summary, these authors suggested that in the first month the focus is on immediate mutual mother–infant adjustment, that in the next 3 months (1 to 4 months) changes in maternal responsiveness are to a great extent governed by aspects of the mother's personality, but because of the considerable stability in her sensitivity during the 4– to 9–month period, this sensitivity is no longer subject to prenatally assessed personality influences.

The complexity of intercorrelations among prebirth parent characteristics, parenting, and infant characteristics is underlined by the fact that, contrary to the above findings, Heinicke and Lampl (1988) found that 1–month parent responsiveness to the infant's needs was anticipated by the mother's prebirth adaptation–competence and positive marital adjustment even when 1–month infant social responsiveness was taken into account. Indeed, the influence of prebirth marital adaptation on parent responsiveness and child security was seen throughout the first 4 years of life.

One study has specifically addressed the issue of the relative contribution of three of the family system domains, namely parent, parent–infant, and infant characteristics to the development of a secure attachment at 1 year of age. Del Carmen, Pedersen, Huffman, and Bryan (1993) studied the relative power of prebirth maternal anxiety, postbirth 3-month maternal response to distress, and the infant characteristic of negative affect as predictors of security of attachment at 1 year of age. The results indicated that 3–month distress management and prenatal maternal anxiety were the strongest predictors in classifying security of attachment. The authors' interpretation of these findings was consistent with the emphasis of this chapter on the importance of regulating affect. Mothers who could not manage their own affect (distress) have experienced difficulty managing the distress (affect) of their 3–month-old infant.

What other evidence is there that parental adaptation–competence as well as parental relationship capacity are likely to influence variation in the child's development of security? Main and Goldwyn (1994) showed that the classification from the Adult Attachment Interview stressing the mother's coherent, objective, and balanced account of her childhood is significantly associated with the development of security in her infant's attachment. Very relevant to predicting the transaction of parental responsiveness to the needs of the infant and the security of the child are findings of Ward and Carlson (1995) linking the classification derived from the prebirth Adult Attachment Interview to maternal sensitivity and security of attachment in children at 15 months. Mothers classified as autonomous as opposed to dismissing, preoccupied, or unresolved showed higher levels of sensitivity at 3 and 9 months, and their infants were more frequently classified as secure at 15 months. However, maternal sensitivity at 3 and 9 months was not significantly associated with security of attachment at 15 months. The authors suggest that the meaning of sensitivity may have been affected by whether the adolescent mothers were or were not the primary caregiver; many of them were not. In a similar study, Benoit and Parker (1994) found an 81% match between AAIs administered in pregnancy and the three-category Ainsworth Strange Situation assessment at 12 months.

As part of a meta-analysis on the predictive validity of the Adult Attachment Interview, van IJzendoorn (1995) summarized the findings from all available studies linking three forms of maternal representations as assessed by the AAI before birth to the postbirth threefold infant security of attachment classification; he found a 69% correspondence for the three-way classifications. That is, his meta-analysis not only showed the significant relation between parent's attachment representations and the security of the child's attachment relationship with the parents in a large sample (N = 854), but analysis of the more limited sample specifically showed the relation of the prebirth AAI and postbirth infant security of attachment. Although not confined to the prebirth AAIs, in this same meta-analysis van IJzendoorn (1995) also showed the power of the Adult Attachment Interview to predict the mother's responsiveness to the needs of her infant.

As the experience of classifying the responses to the attachment interview suggests, the categories being used seem to speak as much to issues of adaptation–competence or current ego functioning as they do to the capacity to form an empathic trusting relationship (Main and Goldwyn, 1994). A prospective study by Fonagy et al. (1991) linking the prebirth Adult Attachment Interview classifications to the developing security of the 1-year-old child permits further discussion of this question. The Adult Attachment Interview was administered to 100 mothers expecting their first child and, at 1–year follow-ups, 96 mothers were again seen with their infants in the Strange Situation to assess the quality of their child's attachment. Maternal representations of attachment (autonomous versus dismissing or preoccupied) predicted subsequent infant–mother attachment patterns (secure versus insecure) 75% of the time. In addition to deriving these major classifications, each interview was also rated on eight 9-point scales describing the adult's probable childhood experience of having been parented, the current state of mind with respect to attachment, and the overall coherence of the interview. Both anxious resistant and secure, as opposed to avoidant, children had mothers who recalled their relationship with their mothers as significantly more loving and less rejecting, whereas coherence was highest among mothers of securely attached infants. So, both the parent's specific positive remembrance of their own parenting and an index of ego integration (i.e., coherence) anticipate the development of a secure child attachment. The question then arises of whether alternate measures of the mother's organizational functioning not necessarily tied to questions about her relationship history would predict her child's secure attachment. Fonagy, Steele, Steele, Moran, and Higgitt (1991) studied this issue in terms of the capacity of the mother to reflect on her mental functioning. All recorded Adult Attachment Interviews were rated on the absence or presence of reflective functions. Strong evidence of self–reflection was seen in statements indicating the mother's ability to understand psychological states, including conscious and unconscious motivations under-lying their own reactions and those of others. Relating this measure of the mother's functioning to the ratings of the Adult Attachment Interview and the security of the child, it was found that the mother's self-reflection was highly correlated (0.73) with the previous ratings of quality of recall and coherence; that, as already noted, the coherence of the mother's interview predicted a secure child attachment; and when reflective self–function was controlled for, coherence no longer related significantly to infant security. This suggests that self-reflection is an essential component of the mother's ability to organize her relationship experiences.

Related to further search for those maternal adaptive functions that predict secure attachment and parent sensitivity to the child's need (Ainsworth et al., 1978), Teti et al. (1990) found that this sensitivity correlated with the availability and adequacy of attachment figures, marital harmony, major negative life events, daily hassles, infant difficulty, and maternal depression, but all these significant relations became nonsignificant when controlled for by maternal self-efficacy in dealing with the child. So in this study, even when other family system domains were included in the design, the mother's self–efficacy was the most powerful predictor of her sensitivity.

An initial summary statement and the supporting research findings have focused on the association of the mother's prebirth characteristics and her responsiveness to the needs of her infant. Several other studies either focus on the father or include both mother and father.

Paternal Prebirth Functioning and Father's Positive Relationship to His Child

The father's prebirth adaptive competence and capacity to sustain positive relationships (especially those with his partner) anticipate a positive relationship with his child during the first year of life as well as the security of his child. Research evidence supporting this statement is limited but consistent. Steele, Steele, and Fonagy (1996) showed not only that mothers classified as secure on the prebirth Adult Attachment Interview (AAI) have children who are secure in the infant–mother Strange Situation at 12 months, but fathers who are classified as secure on the AAI have children who are secure in the 18-month infant–father Strange Situation. Although these associations were independent of each other, secondary analyses showed that the mother's security as derived from the AAI may also be significantly associated with infant–father security. The authors discuss the potentially greater influence of the mother's status on the child's development of security and also consider the potential influence of the child's temperament in accounting for variations in infant security.

Other studies that support the generalization being discussed not only trace the influence of the father's competence and capacity for relationship, but increasingly include measures of marital adjustment as significant predictors. Thus, Grossman et al. (1980) found that an interview measure of the father's positive relationship to his child at 2 months postpartum is anticipated by the following first-trimester measures: the father's tendency to identify positively with his own mother and good marital adjustment. Similarly, Feldman, Nash, and Aschenbrenner (1983) showed that the father's caregiving and playfulness with his 6–month–old infant and his satisfaction with fatherhood are anticipated by prebirth indices of general adjustment and marital happiness as reported by the husband and/or wife. For example, satisfaction with fatherhood was predicted by the father's empathy with his wife, few if any problems in the marriage, a match between the desired and actual sex of the baby, and a self–description low in characteristics like gullible and childlike.

In a series of reports, Cox and her colleagues showed how prebirth measures of father *and* mother functioning anticipate postnatal parent responsiveness and child security. The first report (Cox, Owen, Lewis, and Henderson, 1989) used both an interview-based 3–month parent attitude as well as observations of sensitive parental behavior as outcome measures. Mothers had a more positive attitude toward their 3–month–old infant if that infant was a son and if their own prebirth psychological assessment (adaptation–competence) was adequate. Both this adequate adjustment and the positive quality of their marriage anticipated sensitive behavioral responding to their infant. Similarly, but also slightly different, both an adequate prebirth adjustment and positive marriage anticipated the father's positive attitude toward his 3–month–old child. The father was likely to respond warmly if his own adjustment was adequate and his infant was a son. A second report (Cox, Owen, Henderson, and Margaund, 1992) showed that an expanded version of the previous 3-month parent attitudinal and observational variables predicted a 12-month secure attachment continuum. Twelve-month infant–mother security was anticipated by the mother's positive and sensitive interaction with her infant, her physical affection, and the total amount of time spent with her infant, but not by her attitude toward her infant. Infant–father security at 12 months was anticipated by all of the aforementioned 3–month variables. However, the association between time spent and infant–father security was negative. Although not easy to interpret, this last finding points to the importance of considering these variables in a total family context. Cox and Owen (1993) reported that prebirth measures of marital discord and psychological adjustment anticipated both 3–month parent positive interaction/attitude and 12–month infant security. Infant–father attachment security at 12 months was anticipated directly (negatively) by the father's positive interaction/attitude toward his 3–month–old child and by prebirth marital discord. The father's prebirth psychological adjustment also had a significant impact on his child's security, but indirectly so, via marital discord and father positive interaction/attitude. The comprehensive analysis of the same variables predicting to infant–mother security was not significant. However, significant correlations emerged when the association of variables was evaluated separately by gender. For boys, security of 12–month attachment was significantly associated with the mother's 3–month parenting, but was not related to marital discord or mother's adjustment. For girls, prebirth marital relations predicted 12–month security.

In overview, if the mother copes well with various life issues, has the capacity to form positive and trusting relationships, and has a mutually positive relationship with her partner before the birth of her child, she is more likely to be responsive to her child's needs and her child will develop greater security in the first 2 years of life. There is some evidence to suggest that similar statements also apply to the father. Most important, the studies of the impact of the individual maternal and paternal characteristics frequently included assessments of the quality of their relationship to their partner. Indeed, many studies of the association between prebirth determinants and postbirth family development are best summarized by focusing on the quality of the couple's functioning, and that will be the form for the presentation below.

PREBIRTH COUPLE FUNCTIONING AND FAMILY DEVELOPMENT UNTIL KINDERGARTEN

Couples characterized by prebirth and continuing positive mutuality, partner autonomy, and the ability to confront problems and regulate negative affect are responsive to the needs of their infants, promote their autonomy, and have more secure and autonomous children as seen throughout the first 4 years of life. The children from these families are also more task oriented in preschool, are less aggressive and shy in early kindergarten, and score higher on achievement tests at the end of kindergarten.

In tracing the link from prebirth measures of partner personality and marital functioning to the security and autonomy of the child and to the subsequent academic achievement and social competence in kindergarten, Cowan et al. (1994) proceed in two longitudinal steps. The first related prebirth, 6–month, and 18–month measures of relationship functioning to observations of marital interaction and the parent's interaction with their child when the child is in preschool (or 3½ years). A second step linked this marital interaction and parent–child interaction with measures of the child's academic achievement and social competence in late kindergarten. The first set of findings involved a self-report measure of marital satisfaction (Locke and Wallace, 1959) in pregnancy and at 18 months. The decline in marital satisfaction during this period was associated with the observed angry, cold, and competitive as opposed to warm, responsive, and cooperative marital interaction when the child is 3½ years. This conflictual marital interaction was in turn associated with both the father and mother being less warm with their child and the father communicating less well and not being able to present the assigned tasks in a manner that helped the preschool child to manage them. Pratt et al. (1988) showed that parents who are warm and structuring also tend to provide scaffolding for their children—to move in at the appropriate level when their children are having difficulty and back off when their children are succeeding on their own. Another prebirth measure, the Family Environment Scale (Moos, 1974), was linked to marital stress at 6 months, to the decline in marital quality (prebirth to 18 months) and to marital and parent–child interaction at 3½ years. Parents who, during pregnancy, remember the atmosphere in the families in which they grew up as high in conflict and experienced more stress at 6 months were more conflicted in their marital interaction when their child was 3½ years old. Further analyses showed that high levels of stress at 6 months linked directly to less adequate parenting styles and indirectly via the decline in marital satisfaction from prebirth to 18 months. As already discussed, this decline anticipated conflicted marital interaction and less responsive parenting styles when the child was 3½ years old.

Cowan et al. (1994) also documented the association between these preschool variables and children's kindergarten assessments. The kindergarten children who scored lower on the Peabody Individual Achievement Test (reading recognition, reading comprehension, spelling, mathematics, and general information) had parents who were more conflicted in their interaction with each other and less warm and encouraging of the autonomy of their preschool child. For this outcome variable (i.e., academic achievement) the prebirth-to-18-months quality of relationship variables had an indirect effect via the preschool status; there were no direct links from prebirth to kindergarten.

Variation in the preschool parent and parent–child interaction measures also anticipated variation in the kindergarten child's shyness and aggression. Parents who were competitive and hostile in their marital interaction and did not work cooperatively in front of their preschooler tended to have children who showed more aggressive interactions or who were shy and withdrawn with their classmates 2 years later. Further findings were that low levels of father and mother warmth and responsiveness at 3½ years linked to high levels of classroom aggressiveness. However, different levels of parent structuring did not predict levels of aggression.

In contrast to the prediction of academic achievement, there were direct as well as indirect links from the prebirth family relationship to the kindergarten child's level of shyness and aggressiveness. Thus, parents who during pregnancy remembered the atmosphere in the families they grew up in as high in conflict tended to have children who were rated as shy and/or aggressive.

Evidence from the Pennsylvania State Family Development Project linked a declining postnatal marital pattern to the development of an insecure attachment at 1 year of age. Belsky, Youngblade, Rovine, and Volling (1991) showed the association between these declining marital patterns and observations of fathers and mothers interacting with their 3-year-old children in a free-play and teaching-task situation. Relevant to the parent facilitating the autonomy of the child was the finding that in declining marital relationships, fathers were more intrusive and aversive as opposed to positive and facilitative.

Path analysis diagrams (Figures 12.2 and 12.3) best summarize our findings on the antecedents of 4-year-old children's task orientation and modulation of aggression (Heinicke and Lampl, 1988). Consistent with the emphasis of Cowan et al. (1994), that the prebirth and continuing positive quality of husband–wife adaptation is central to family adaptation, Figures 12.2 and 12.3 show that this prebirth quality is the only direct link to both aggression modulation and task orientation. Also consistent with the results reported by Cowan et al. (1994) is the finding that, even when all previous influences are allowed for, both child indices are still correlated with their respective preschool transactional counterparts: Parent responsiveness to infant needs correlates with "child modulates aggression" (0.75) and child task orientation correlates with "parent stimulates child's cognitive and verbal experiences" (0.34).

These same diagrams also show the indirect influence on aggression modulation of variations in early child and prebirth maternal characteristics. Thus, prebirth husband–wife adaptation and

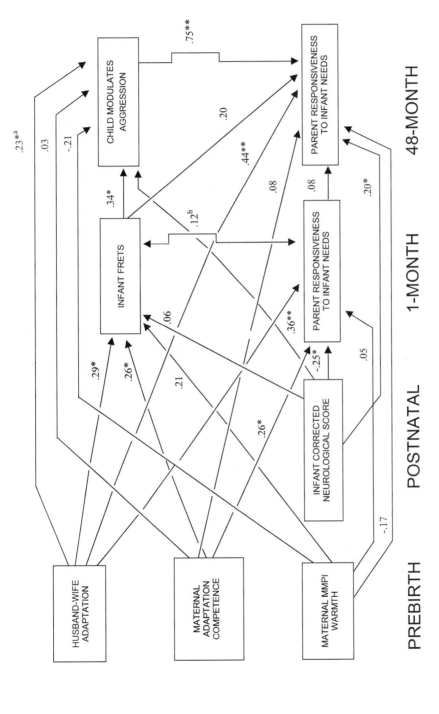

FIGURE 12.2. Path analysis diagram for two indexes of 48-month positive parent–child mutuality: child aggression modulation and parent responsiveness to need ($N = 44$).

$*p < 0.05.$ $**p < 0.01.$

[a]Beta weights placed by across time paths.

[b]Vertical lines indicate cross-sectional correlations. Reprinted from *Infant Behavior and Development, Vol. 11.* Heinicke, C. M. and Lampl, E. Pre- and post-birth antecedents of 3- and 4-year-old attention, IQ, verbal expressiveness, task orientation, and capacity for relationships. Copyright © 1988, pp. 381–410, with permission from Elsevier Science.

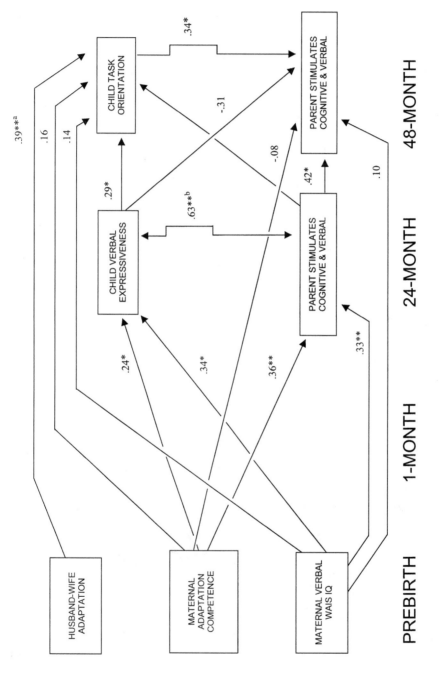

FIGURE 12.3. Path analysis diagram for 48-month task orientation and parental stimulation of cognitive and verbal cognitive antecedents ($N = 44$). Reprinted from *Infant Behavior and Development, Vol. 11.* Heinicke, C. M. and Lampl, E. Pre- and post-birth antecedents of 3- and 4-year-old attention, task orientation, and capacity for relationships. Copyright © 1988, pp. 381—410 with permission from Elsevier Science.

*$p < 0.05$. **$p < 0.01$.

[a] Beta weights placed by across time paths.

[b] Vertical lines indicate cross-sectional correlations.

maternal adaptation–competence influence the 1–month infant's fretting, and variation in this quality anticipates variation in aggression modulation (see Figure 12.2).

Another early infant characteristic, postnatal neurological adaptation, affects the parent responsive to need aspect of the transaction being discussed. At 1 and 48 months, the parent's response to the needs of their infant is influenced not only by their prebirth marital adaptation, but by the adaptive (neurological) characteristics of their infant. At 1 month there is a negative association. The more difficult the infant, the more responsive the parent. A form of compensation is suggested. By 48 months there is a positive link between infants who show an optimal response right after birth and optimal parent responsiveness. I assume that the compensatory behavior is not maintained and the infant's initial status has some prevailing impact on parent–infant mutuality.

In a similar way, 48–month task orientation is directly anticipated by husband–wife adaptation and prior 24–month child verbal expressiveness and parental stimulation of cognitive and verbal experiences (see Figure 12.3). Each of these parts of a correlated transaction (child verbal expressiveness and parent stimulation) is anticipated by prebirth maternal adaptation–competence and maternal verbal IQ. Given all of the previous significant influences, we concluded (as did Cowan et al., 1994) that task orientation is influenced both by a social–emotional network (here represented by the parent's marital quality) and by intellectual and adaptive antecedents (such as maternal adaptation and verbal IQ).

Just as Cowan et al. (1994) analyzed steps in the influence of couple functioning and Belsky et al. (1991) focused on declining marital patterns, further analyses on a sample of 96 families included a time dimension by defining six different patterns of postnatal marital development. Three positive patterns were shown to be associated with the development of those parent–child interactions (responsiveness to need and promotion of autonomy) that enhance a secure and separate self in the first 2 years of life (Heinicke and Guthrie, 1992). Moreover, the more positive marital patterns were anticipated by ratings of the parent's open discussion and remembrance in the prebirth period of their own positive parenting experience, and by indices of maternal adaptation–competence derived from prebirth videotaped interviews with the mother and by her Minnesota Multiphasic Personality Inventory (MMPI) responses. Equally striking, the overall incidence of divorce among the 96 families in the first 4 years of life was 17%, but only three divorces occurred in the 48 families with positive marital patterns, whereas 14 of the 25 families characterized by negative marital patterns experienced divorce (Heinicke, Guthrie, and Ruth, 1997).

Because the aforementioned results were based on prebirth parent responses to self inventories and interviews, the question arises as to whether indices of the quality of the husband–wife relationship derived from direct observation of their prebirth marital interaction also anticipate variation in postnatal family development. We assumed that the individual adaptation of each partner, as well as their adaptation to each other when asked to resolve a conflict between them, would be a valid assessment of their ability to deal with future challenges of parenting. Studies by Howes and Markman (1991) and Heinicke and Guthrie (1996) are relevant to this question. The couples of the second cohort (N = 46) were, in the prebirth period, asked to discuss and resolve differences on three important issues (Heinicke and Guthrie, 1996). Systematic coding resulted in classifications contrasting those who could realistically confront the tasks and express negative feelings while maintaining a context of positive mutuality from those who could not. Those who could not resolve issues were either consistently low or decreased in their postnatal marital adjustment. As already documented, the positive patterns of postnatal marital changes were associated with the development of a secure attachment in the first child and their capacity to promote autonomy when that child was 2 years old. Similarly, Markman and his colleagues (Balaguer and Markman, 1991; Howes and Markman, 1991) documented an association between premarital and prebirth marital interaction measures and the development of attachment and self-concepts in the child. Thus, premarital relationship-problem discussions were coded and related to measures of attachment (the Waters Q–sort) when the first child was between 1 and 3 years of age. Correlational results indicated that avoidance of conflict and emotional invalidation in the parent's premarital relationship predicted less secure attachment relationships between mothers and their firstborns. Codes describing women as facilitating the resolution of conflict during premarital discussions predicted more secure attachment relationships between fathers and their firstborns. Howes and Markman (1991, p. 10) summarized these as well as other findings by concluding that "abilities in regulating negative affect by acknowledging and addressing differences appears to be critical to both spousal and parent–child relationships". Similarly, Balaguer and Markman (1991) found an association between the quality of marital interaction both before marriage and before the birth of the first child and measures of the child's self concept at ages 4 to 7. A mother's support of her future husband, and both partners' support of each other in problem–solving marital interactions before the birth of their first child anticipate the child's experience of the self as part of positive family interaction. They stressed the importance to the child of not being exposed to destructive conflict. The additional finding that negative escalation as seen in both father and mother during prebirth interactions anticipates lower levels of the child's experience of positive self affect is consistent with this emphasis.

In a subsequent study of the same sample (Renick and Odell, 1993), it was shown that codes of family interaction videotaped when the child was 4 to 7 years old were associated with both the child's concurrent positive self-ratings and the couple's premarital negative escalation. That is, those families that could cooperate in a game and showed positive self–esteem avoided negative escalation during a premarital interaction session.

In overview, the parent's ability to confront conflictual issues, regulate negative affect, and resolve differences is associated with a setting in which children develop greater security and autonomy. These results, based on observed interaction, are consistent with those based on inventory and interview data.

THE UCLA FAMILY DEVELOPMENT PROJECT

Given the above findings on the *interrelationship* of parent adaptation, partner and family support, and key areas of parent–child interaction and child development, it was reasoned that the intervention needed to address all these domains to bring about a sustained change.

These longitudinal findings also suggested that the specific areas of functioning that would likely change. Because security of attachment, autonomy, and task orientation were shown to be related to parent behavior which influences those developments, efforts to change such behavior as well as the child's development should have considerable potential. Indeed, the early family intervention did bring about changes in most of the areas that were expected to change. This would contrast with child IQ as an outcome measure, because variations in child IQ are found to be influenced primarily by the genetic IQ profile of the parents and relatively less by parenting behavior (Heinicke and Lampl, 1988; Reznick, Corley, and Robinson, 1997; Scarr, 1985).

We compared two samples of mothers who were identified as at–risk for inadequate parenting in the third trimester of pregnancy with their first child. The primary risk characteristics were poverty and lack of support. Thirty–one of these mothers experienced the intervention, and 33 did not. Mothers given the opportunity of a positive trusting and working relationship with a weekly home visitor as well as a mother–infant group scored significantly higher on measures of their experienced partner and family support. The intervention also made a significant impact on three critical social–emotional mother–infant transactions in the first 2 years of life. Thus, on a variety of indices, including the responses to the Ainsworth Strange Situation, the children in the intervention group were more secure and their mothers were responsive to their needs. Children experiencing the intervention were also more autonomous and task oriented, and were encouraged in this regard by their mothers. When their children were 2 years old, the mothers experiencing the intervention, in comparison with those who did not, also used verbally persuasive as opposed to coercive intrusive methods of control, and their children responded more positively to these controls. Thus, the relation–based intervention clearly made an impact on certain aspects of the family's development from pregnancy to the child's age of 2 years (Heinicke, Fineman, Ponce, and Guthrie, 2001).

Even if one can demonstrate an effect, the question arises as to what are the paths of influence. Hierarchical regression and tests of mediation were used to arrive at some preliminary answers. One sequence of influences is consistent with the longitudinal findings summarized in this chapter. The mother's prebirth capacity to form positive relationships anticipates the quality of her partner support when the child is 6 months old, and this quality of partner support anticipates her ability to form an effective working relationship with the home visitor in the 6– to 12–month interval (Heinicke et al., 2000). The effectiveness of that working relationship in turn anticipates variations in the mother's responsiveness to the needs of her infant at 12 months, and the latter is correlated with her child's security of attachment. However, the level of partner support at 6 months also directly anticipates the child's 12–month security of attachment.

This finding raised the question of whether the level of partner support was mediating the effects of the intervention. Following a model of analysis proposed by James and Brett (1984), the hypothesis that the intervention impacted partner support and that this in turn impacted such functioning as 12–month mother responsiveness to need and 12–month child security of attachment was not supported. Rather, just as the longitudinal research summarized in this chapter suggested that several domains of family functioning would have to be addressed to bring about sustained change, and the intervention was indeed designed and implemented to achieve that, so the initial findings indicate that the mother's adaptive functioning, her partner support, her responsiveness to her child, and the secure attachment of her child were all very likely affected directly, and no one change was the mediator leading to other changes (Heinicke et al., 1998).

CONCLUSIONS

The research on the prebirth determinants of family development permits several general conclusions. Parents who are capable of efficient, nonanxious, flexible problem solving, able to sustain a positive mutuality, especially with their partner, and also able to maintain their autonomy and self-esteem are more likely to provide an optimal parenting environment. In the context of the studies reviewed, this optimal parenting includes responsiveness to need, encouragement of autonomy, and exposure to cognitive experiences. It is shown that variations in these qualities of parenting are of central significance in family interactions enhancing security, autonomy, and task motivation in the child. These developments in turn are associated with higher academic achievement and less disruptive aggression in kindergarten. That is, the motivation to learn and modulation of aggression, which are crucial to later academic and social development, are influenced by parent and marital characteristics that are present before birth and tend to have a consistent influence in the emerging family interactions.

Although several studies included the relative contribution of early child characteristics, these were not found to be a major source of influence on the aspects of family development considered here. Heinicke and Lampl (1988) did show that the child's postnatal neurological adaptation and fretting were part of an emerging interacting family development. An interactional model of that development is most useful to guide further research in this area.

Emphasizing again the interaction of endogenous and exogenous factors, if an environmental intervention can change parent personality and support characteristics as well as associated parent–child and child development, then it is less likely that these family developments are exclusively a function of endogenous determinants. Guided by this assumption and the specific research findings summarized in this chapter, the UCLA Family Development Project, an early family intervention, was designed, and its efficacy was tested in a randomized trial.

The longitudinal research findings on the impact of prebirth and continuing parent characteristics on family development and the interventions to affect that development stress the interacting influences of the various family domains. Moreover, these findings do not support the assumption of general or dominating main effects. They do support the assumption that the family domains considered are subject to change, especially if the intervention addresses all aspects of the interrelated family system (Cowan and Cowan, 1992). It follows that if such environmentally induced changes can be brought about in certain areas of development, such as the parent's responsiveness to the needs of her infant and the associated security of attachment, then the anticipation of these developments by characteristics of the parents before the child is even born is not likely to be accounted for exclusively by unfolding endogenous factors related to both. The search for such endogenous factors that interact with these environmentally influenced family domains will of course continue.

Although the above conclusions are likely to be confirmed by further research, generalizations must be viewed with some caution. The conclusion that prebirth parent characteristics have a significant impact on parenting and child development is based on the prebirth measurement and proven stability of these characteristics. These prebirth assessments reflect family system characteristics that continue, and are influenced by, but not exclusively determined by, the characteristics of the child. However, it may be possible that other influences, such as a profile of genetic determinants, could affect both pre– and postbirth developments. Much more research is needed to clarify these issues. Some clarification will come from "interventions with human parents" (Collins et al., 2000).

ACKNOWLEDGMENTS

This research was supported by the Atlas Family Foundation and the National Institute of Mental Health, grant no. MH45722. Victoria A. Ponce provided invaluable assistance in the preparation of this document.

REFERENCES

Ainsworth, M. D. S., Blehar, M. D., Waters, E., and Wall, S. (1978). *Patterns of attachment: A psychological study of the Strange Situation.* Hillsdale, NJ: Lawrence Erlbaum Associates.

Balaguer, A., and Markman, H. J. (1991). *The effects of marital communication and conflict management on child self-concept: A longitudinal perspective.* Unpublished manuscript.

Barron, F. (1953). An ego-strength scale which predicts response to psychotherapy. *Journal of Consulting Psychology, 17,* 327–333.

Belsky, J. (1984). The determinants of parenting: A process model. *Child Development, 55,* 83–96.

Belsky, J., and Isabella, R. (1986). Maternal, infant, and social–contextual determinants of attachment security. In J. Belsky and R. Isabella (Eds.), *Clinical implications of attachment* (pp. 41–94). Hillsdale, NJ: Lawrence Erlbaum Associates.

Belsky, J., Rovine, M., and Fish, M. (1989). The developing family system. In M. Ganner and E. Thelen (Eds.), *Systems and development: Minnesota Symposium on Child Psychology* (Vol. 22, pp. 119–166). Hillsdale, NJ: Lawrence Erlbaum Associates.

Belsky, J., Youngblade, L., Rovine, M., and Volling, B. (1991). Patterns of marital change and parent–child interaction. *Journal of Marriage and the Family, 53,* 487–498.

Benoit, D., and Parker, K. (1994). Stability and transmission of attachment across three generations. *Child Development, 65,* 1444–1456.

Bibring, C. S., Dwyer, T. F., Huntington, D. S., and Valenstein, A. F. (1961). A study of the psychological processes in pregnancy and the earliest mother–child relationship. In *The psychoanalytic study of the child* (Vol. 16, pp. 9–72). New York: International Universities Press.

Block, J., and Block, J. H. (1980). *The California Child Q-set.* Palo Alto, CA: Consulting Psychologists.

Bornstein, M. H., and Tamis-LeMonda, C. S. (1989). Maternal responsiveness and cognitive development in children. In M. H. Bornstein (Ed.), *Maternal responsiveness: Characteristics and consequences* (pp. 49–71). San Francisco: Jossey-Bass.

Brazelton, T. B. (1973). *Neonatal Behavior Assessment Scale* (Clinics in Development Medicine No. 50). Philadelphia: Lippincott.

Brunnquell, D., Crichton, L., and Egeland, B. (1981). Maternal personality and attitude in disturbances of child-rearing. *Journal of Orthopsychiatry, 51,* 680–691.

Collins, W. A., Maccoby, E. E., Steinberg, L., Hetherington, E. M., and Bornstein, M. H. (2000). Contemporary research on parenting: The case for nature and nurture. *American Psychologist, 55,* 218–232.

Cowan, C. P., and Cowan, P. A. (1992). *When partners become parents.* New York: Basic.

Cowan, C. P., Cowan, P. A., Heming, G., Garrett, E., Coysh, W. S., Curtis-Boles, H., and Boles, A. J. (1985). Transitions to parenthood: His, hers, and theirs. *Journal of Family Issues, 6,* 451–481.

Cowan, P. A., and Cowan, C. P. (1988). Changes in marriage during the transition to parenthood: Must we blame the baby? In G. Michaels and W. A. Goldberg (Eds.), *The transition to parenthood: Current theory and research* (pp. 114–154). Cambridge, England: Cambridge University Press.

Cowan, P. A., Cowan, C. P., Schulz, M., and Heming, G. (1994). Pre-birth to preschool family factors in children's adaptation to kindergarten. In R. Parke and S. Kellam (Eds.), *Exploring family relationships with other social contexts: Advances in family research* (Vol. 4, pp. 1–65). Hillsdale, NJ: Lawrence Erlbaum Associates.

Cowan, P. A., Powell, D., and Cowan, C. P. (1998). Parenting interventions: A family systems perspective. In I. E. Sigel and K. A. Renninger (Eds.), *Handbook of child psychology: Volume 4. Child psychology in practice* (5th ed.). New York: Wiley.

Cox, M. J., and Owen, M. T. (1993). Marital conflict and conflict negotiation. *Abstracts of the Biannual Meeting of the Society for Research in Child Development, 9.*

Cox, M. J., Owen, M. T., Henderson, V. K., and Margaud, N. A. (1992). Prediction of infant–father and infant–mother attachment. *Developmental Psychology, 28,* 474–483.

Cox, M. J., Owen, M. T., Lewis, J. M., and Henderson, V. K. (1989). Marriage, adult adjustment, and early parenting. *Child Development, 60,* 1015–1024.

Del Carmen, R., Pedersen, F. A., Huffman, L. C., and Bryan, Y. E. (1993). Dyadic distress management predicts subsequent security of attachment. *Infant Behavior and Development, 16,* 131–147.

Deutsch, H. (1945). *The psychology of women: Motherhood* (Vol. 2). New York: Grune and Stratton.

Diamond, D., Heinicke, C. M., and Mintz, J. (1996). *Separation–individuation as a family transactional process in the transition to parenthood. Infant Mental Health Journal, 17,* 24–42.

Egeland, B., and Farber, E. A. (1984). Infant–mother attachment: Factors related to its development and changes over time. *Child Development, 55,* 753–771.

Feldman, S. S., Nash, S. C., and Aschenbrenner, R. B. (1983). Antecedents of fathering. *Child Development, 54,* 1628–1636.

Fonagy, P., Steele, H., and Steele, M. (1991). Maternal representations of attachment during pregnancy predict the organization of infant–mother attachment at one year of age. *Child Development, 62,* 891–905.

Fonagy, P., Steele, M., Steele, H., Moran, G. S., and Higgitt, A. C. (1991). The capacity for understanding mental states: The reflective self in parent and child and its significance for security of attachment. *Infant Mental Health Journal, 13,* 200–216.

George, C., Kaplan, N., and Main, M. (1996). *Adult attachment interview* (3rd ed.). Unpublished manuscript, University of California, Berkeley.

Grossman, F. K., Eichler, L. W., and Winikoff, S. A. (1980). *Pregnancy, birth and parenthood.* San Francisco, CA: Jossey-Bass.

Heinicke, C. M. (1977). *Relationship opportunities in day care and the child's task orientation.* (Final report to Office of Child Development, Department of Health, Education and Welfare, Vols. 1 and 2).

Heinicke, C. M. (1980). Continuity and discontinuity of task orientation. *Journal of the American Academy of Child Psychiatry, 19,* 637–653.

Heinicke, C. M. (1984). Impact of pre-birth parent personality and marital functioning on family development: A framework and suggestions for further study. *Developmental Psychology, 20,* 1044–1053.

Heinicke, C. M. (1993). Maternal personality, involvement in interaction, and family development. *Abstracts of the Biannual Meeting for the Society for Research in Child Development, 9,* 116.

Heinicke, C. M., Diskin, S., Ramsey-Klee, D., and Given, K. (1983). Pre-birth parent characteristics and family development in the first year of life. *Child Development, 54,* 194–208.

Heinicke, C. M., Diskin, S. D., Ramsey-Klee, D. M., and Oates, D. S. (1986). Pre- and postbirth antecedents of two-year-old attention, capacity for relationships, and verbal expressiveness. *Developmental Psychology, 22,* 777–787.

Heinicke, C. M., Fineman, N. R., Ponce, V. A., and Guthrie, D. (2001). Relation based intervention with at-risk mothers: Outcome in the second year of life. *Infant Mental Health Journal, 22*(4), 431–462.

Heinicke, C. M., Goorsky, M., Moscov, S., Dudley, K., Gordon, J., and Guthrie, D. (1998). Partner support as a mediator of intervention outcome. *American Journal of Orthopsychiatry, 68,* 534–541.

Heinicke, C. M., Goorsky, M., Moscov, S., Dudley, K., Gordon, J., Schneider, C., and Guthrie, D. (2000). Relationship based intervention with at-risk mothers: Factors affecting variations in outcome. *Infant Mental Health Journal, 21,* 133–155.

Heinicke, C. M., and Guthrie, D. (1992). Stability and change in husband–wife adaptation and the development of the positive parent–child relationship. *Infant Behavior and Development, 15,* 109–127.

Heinicke, C. M., and Guthrie, D. (1996). Pre-birth marital interactions and post-birth marital development. *Infant Mental Health Journal, 17,* 140–151.

Heinicke, C. M., Guthrie, D., and Ruth, G. (1997). Marital adaptation, divorce, and parent–infant development: A prospective study. *Infant Mental Health Journal, 18,* 282–299.

Heinicke, C. M., and Lampl, E. (1988). Pre- and post-birth antecedents of 3- and 4-year-old attention, IQ, verbal expressiveness, task orientation, and capacity for relationships. *Infant Behavior and Development, 2,* 381–410.

Heinicke, C. M., Recchia, S., Berlin, P., and James, C. (1993). *Manual for coding global child and parent–child ratings.* Unpublished manuscript.

Hill, R. (1949). *Families under stress.* New York: Harper.

Howes, P. W., and Markman, H. J. (1991). Longitudinal relations between premarital and prebirth adult interaction and subsequent parent–child attachment. *Abstracts of the Biannual Meeting of the Society for Research in Child Development, 8.*

Huston, J. L., and McHale, S. M. (1983). Changes in the topography of marriage following the birth of the first child. *Abstracts of the Biannual Meeting of the Society for Research in Child Development, 4.*

Isabella, R. A., and Gable, S. (1993). *The determinants of maternal behavior across the first year: An ecological consideration.* Unpublished manuscript.

James, L. R., and Brett, J. M. (1984). Mediators, moderators, and tests for mediation. *Journal of Applied Psychology, 69,* 307–321.

Littman, B., and Parmalee A. H., Jr. (1974). *Manual for obstetrical complications.* Los Angeles: University of California, Marion Davie's Children's Center.

Locke, H., and Wallace, K. (1959). Short marital adjustment and prediction tests: Their reliability and validity. *Marriage and Family Living, 21,* 251–255.

Main, M., and Goldwyn, R. (in press). Interview-based adult attachment classifications: Related to infant–mother and infant–father attachment. *Developmental Psychology.*

Moos, R. H. (1974). *Family environment scale.* Palo Alto, CA: Consulting Psychologists.

Moss, H. (1967). Sex, age, and state as determinants of mother–infant interaction. *Merrill-Palmer Quarterly, 13,* 19–36.

Pianta, R., Egeland, B., and Erickson, M. F. (1989). The antecedents of maltreatment: Results of the Mother–Child Interaction Research Project. In D. Cichetti and V. Carlson (Eds.), *Child maltreatment: Theory and research on the causes and consequences of child abuse and neglect* (pp. 203–253). New York: Cambridge University Press.

Pratt, M. W., Kerig, P. K., Cowan, P. A., and Cowan, C. P. (1988). Mothers and fathers teaching 3-year-olds: Authoritative parenting and adult's use of the zone of proximal development. *Developmental Psychology, 24,* 832–839.

Renick, M. J., and Odell, S. (1993). Premarital communication, family interaction, and children's self-esteem. *Abstracts of the Biannual Meeting of the Society for Research in Child Development, 9,* 564.

Reznick, J. S., Corley, R., and Robinson, J. (1997). A longitudinal twin study of intelligence in the second year. *Monographs of the Society for Research in Child Development, 62,* 1–154.

Scarr, S. (1985). Constructing psychology: Making facts and fables for our times. *American Psychologist, 40,* 499–512.

Schaefer, F. S., Edgerton, M., and Hunter, M. (1983). *Childbearing and child development correlates of maternal locus of control.* Paper presented at the August meeting of the American Psychological Association, Los Angeles, CA.

Shereshefsky, P. M., and Yarrow, L. J. (1973). *Psychological aspects of a first pregnancy and early postnatal adaptation.* New York: Raven.

Sroufe, L. A. (1989). Relationships and relationship disturbances. In A. J. Sameroff and R. N. Emde (Eds.), *Relationship disturbances in early childhood* (pp. 97–124). New York: Basic.

Steele, M., Steele, H., and Fonagy, P. (1996). Associations among attachment classifications of mothers, fathers, and their infants: Evidence for a relationship-specific perspective. *Child Development, 67,* 541–555.

Stern, O. N. (1985). *The interpersonal world of the infant.* New York: Basic.

Teti, D. M., Gelfand, D. M., and Pompa, J. (1990). Depressed mothers behavioral competence with their infants: Demographic and psychosocial correlates. *Development and Psychopathology, 2,* 259–270.

Van IJzendoorn, M. H. (1995). Adult attachment representations, parental responsiveness, and infant attachment: A meta-analysis on the predictive validity of the adult attachment interview. *Psychological Bulletin, 177,* 387–403.

Van IJzendoorn, M. H., and Bakermans-Kranenburg, M. J. (1996). Attachment representations in mothers, fathers, adolescents, and clinical groups: A meta-analytic search for normative data. *Journal of Consulting and Clinical Psychology, 64,* 8–21.

Vaughn, B., Deinard, A., and Egeland, B. (1980). Measuring temperament in pediatric practice. *Journal of Pediatrics, 96,* 510–514.

Vaughn, B., Taraldson, B., Crichton, L., and Egeland, B. (1981). The assessment of infant temperament: A critique of the Carey infant temperament questionnaire. *Infant Behavior and Development, 4,* 1–17.

Ward, M. J., and Carlson, E. A. (1995). Associations among adult attachment representations, maternal sensitivity, and infant–mother attachment in a sample of adolescent mothers. *Child Development, 66,* 69–79.

Wolkind, S., and Zajicek, E. (1981). *Pregnancy: A psychological and social study.* London: Academic Press.

13

Stages of Parental Development

Jack Demick
University of Massachusetts Medical School

INTRODUCTION

A recent chapter (Demick, 1999, p. 177) on parental development began with the following paragraphs:

> I have a seven year-old daughter and a four year-old son. After recently being instructed to wear a coat in below freezing temperatures, my daughter informed me that she did not have to comply with my directive because she was accountable to only two people in the world: God and Bill Clinton. During a recent dinner conversation in which my daughter was asking about foreign languages, my son's eyes piqued as he asked, "Dad, how do you say 'vagina' in Spanish?" Not usually at a loss for words, I needed several moments to regain cognitive equilibrium before attempting to respond to these novel and unexpected stimuli.
>
> While numerous life events have the potential to lead to higher stages of development and, specifically, to foster cognitive development, the experience of parenthood as one such life event is a relatively unequivocal example. As Berger (1994, p. 478) has noted, "From the birth of a first child, which tends to make both parents feel more 'adult'—thinking about themselves and their responsibilities differently—through the unexpected issues raised by adolescent children, parenthood is undoubtedly an impetus for cognitive growth" (Feldman, Biringen, and Nash, 1981; Flavell, 1970; Galinsky, 1981). That not only cognitive but also psychosocial development is affected by parenthood has been supported by several sources of work reported in our (Demick, Bursik, and DiBiase, 1993) recently edited volume on *Parental Development*.

Since that time, my daughter and son, now aged 15 and 12 years, respectively, have continued to supply unexpected stimuli, though differing in content and form. These stimuli, which have necessitated the continued reestablishment of dynamic equilibrium in my self-world relationships, or in what I have alternatively termed my person-in-environment system (e.g., Wapner and Demick, 1998), have clearly been occasions for my own cognitive and psychosocial development. As Gutmann

(1975, p. 1) has stated, "Parenthood is a powerful generator of development. It gives us an opportunity to refine and express who we are, to learn what we can be, to become different." However, assuming that parenthood is a powerful generator of growth and change, the questions become, What is the genesis of parental growth and/or change? Are there stages of parental development and, if so, what are their determinants? If there are stages, what motivates a parent to move from one stage to another?

Thus my purpose in this chapter is threefold: (1) to present theory and research on the concept of stages of parental development and related constructs (e.g., stages of the family life cycle); (2) to evaluate the theory on stages of parental development in light of recent empirical data, contemporary psychological criticism, changing family demographics, and the like; and (3) to propose an alternative conceptualization of the stages of parental development construct based on an holistic, developmental, systems-oriented approach to person-in-environment functioning across the lifespan (e.g., Wapner and Demick, 1998, 1999, 2000, in press-a, in press-b, in press-c). Toward this end, theory and research on stages of parental development are now reviewed.

THEORY AND RESEARCH ON STAGES OF PARENTAL DEVELOPMENT

Theory and research on stages of parental development have drawn on several related strands of research, namely, work on (1) parenthood as a developmental stage (primarily from a psychoanalytic viewpoint); (2) transition to parenthood (with respect to individual, marital, and family functioning); and (3) stage theories of parenthood–family life cycle (drawing on a variety of developmental theories, namely, those influenced by Piaget and Kohlberg and those informed by psychoanalytically oriented adult developmentalists such as Levinson and Gould). Brief reviews of the first two lines of inquiry with a focus on their implications for conceptualizing stages of parental development (see Heinicke, 1984, 1990, in Vol. 3 of this *Handbook*, for more complete discussions of the transition to parenthood) are presented first. Then, two lines of specific work on stages of parental development are addressed. In each instance, theoretical and methodological critiques as well as directions for future research are interwoven throughout.

Parenthood as a Developmental Stage

Parenthood as a developmental phase[1] was first conceptualized in the psychoanalytic literature by Benedek (1959). Specifically, parenthood was first seen as a powerful stage in the development of women (e.g., Benedek, 1959; Chodorow, 1978; Deutsch, 1945) and then of both women and men more generally (Anthony and Benedek, 1970; cf. Group for the Advancement of Psychiatry, 1975).

---

[1]The distinction between "phase" and "stage" is relevant here. Although both terms have often been used interchangeably by psychoanalytically oriented writers (e.g., Benedek, 1959; Freud, 1935, 1938), there is a technical difference between the two. According to Reber (1995), the term phase has been used to designate a temporary stage in a person's life in which characteristic behaviors are observed; nontechnical writings have typically used the word phase to connote a period during which children exhibit behaviors that their parents hope will soon cease. However, such usage is not proper because the notion of recurrence is missing. That is, a phase has more specifically been defined (Reber, 1995, p. 562) as "an aspect or appearance or state of some thing or event which recurs as the thing or event passes cyclically through various modes or conditions"; in this definition, the key word is "recur." Psychoanalytically oriented writers therefore are correct to use "phase" as a synonym for "stage" if they are implying that issues associated with particular phases (e.g., phallic phase) recur at later points in development. This appears to be the case generally (e.g., psychoanalytically oriented investigators assumed that individuals become fixated, that is, continue to derive gratification from particular erogenous zones, throughout life) and specifically (e.g., parenthood as a developmental phase). In this latter context, such authors (e.g., Benedek, 1959, 1970) postulated a cyclic nature to parenthood when they highlighted that (1) the stressful aspects of the transition to parenthood may recur with the addition of each new child and (2) parents relive their own developmental issues through their children (cf. Buchholz, 2000). From this point forward, the more precise and technically correct term stage is used.

For example, with respect to the former, Deutsch (1945) proposed that parenthood (specifically, giving birth) represents the crucial, positive fulfillment of a woman's needs. In line with the latter, Benedek (1970, p. 124) held that "... the study of the family as a field of transactional processes ... is based on the proposition that the parents' drive-motivated, emotional investment in the child brings about reciprocal intrapsychic processes in the parents, which normally account for changes in their personalities." Arguing that successful (unsuccessful) relationships with children make for advances (regressions) in the parent's personality (e.g., superego, self-esteem), Benedek (1970, p. 131) explained that "in terms of dynamic psychology it means that while the parent consciously tries to help the child achieve his developmental goal, he cannot help but deal with his own conflicts unconsciously and by this, normally, achieve a new level of maturation."

Thus adults' conscious and unconscious ways of navigating the world were thought to change when they became parents, often leading them to relive some of their own psychological vulnerabilities with their children. For example, Buchholz (2000, p. 441) stated that "... when a child enters school, a parent's own fear and resistance against the authority of the school may erupt and cause the parent, child or both specific difficulties. When children reach adolescence, parents have to confront their own sexuality once again." It must be noted, however, that the bulk of this psychoanalytic work on parenthood has been based on parents in psychiatric treatment and may thus not generalize to parents at large (e.g., it was not until the 1970s that psychoanalytically oriented investigators turned to the examination of normal, as distinguished from pathological, adult development; see Levinson, 1978). Nonetheless, Benedek (1959) also made inroads into the general problem of stages of parental development. Specifically, laying the groundwork for future theory and research, she suggested three broad stages: (1) stage one, from conception to the child's entry into school, this is a period of "total parenthood" during which parents perceive children as completely their own; (2) stage two, the point in time at which the youngest child reaches adolescence and parents must deal with the "empty nest" phenomenon; and (3) stage three, beginning when parents become grandparents and indulge their grandchildren instinctively.

Further support for the notion of parenthood as a developmental stage has come from the work of Erikson (1950, 1968, 1982). Modifying Freudian theory in two major ways, Erikson proposed that (1) in addition to their psychosexual aspects, stages have psychosocial aspects, which involve major social conflicts that the individual must resolve at each stage (e.g., basic trust versus mistrust, autonomy versus shame and doubt, and initiative versus guilt in the oral, anal, and phallic stages, respectively); and (2) social development continues postadolescence (even if intellectual development does not) and leads to consideration of three additional developmental stages (and social conflicts), namely, young adulthood (intimacy versus isolation), adulthood (generativity versus stagnation), and maturity (integrity versus despair). The seventh stage, generativity versus stagnation, corresponds to middle adulthood. Generativity refers to the ability to give of oneself to another person or persons. Although generativity may be achieved in numerous ways (e.g., transmission of knowledge through teaching and writing, provision of empathy and/or protection to individuals, groups, social institutions, or societal activities; see McAdams, de St. Aubin, and Logan, 1993, for an elaborated concept of generativity), it is ideally expressed in the context of parenthood in which parents derive fulfillment by investing in their children's lives, sharing their life experiences, and guiding and teaching them. According to Erikson, few life experiences provide as much opportunity to care for others, to realize our "need to be needed," and to exercise our innate wish to teach as parenthood.

Thus early psychoanalytically driven theory and research made several important contributions to the study of stages of parental development. These contributions included conceptualization of parenthood as (1) a major life stage with powerful potential for parents' reorganization of self (e.g., mastery of intrapsychic conflicts, increased self-esteem) and of environment (e.g., heightened focus on family relationships, decreased focus on other relationships); (2) a life stage of some duration with at least a clear beginning, middle, and end (paralleling the child's development); (3) a stage with significant current and future developmental implications (e.g., setting the stage for the subsequent evaluation of one's life in the context of dealing with integrity versus despair); and (4) a general framework within which parents might occupy several stages concurrently (e.g., in the middle phase with some children and in the early phase with others).

Transition to Parenthood

Not surprisingly, once parenthood was conceptualized as a developmental stage, interest primarily in the beginning and secondarily in the end of this period grew; to date, significantly less research has focused on the middle phase of parenthood (see Demick, 2000d). For example, early sociological work (e.g., Bibring, Dwyer, and Valenstein, 1961; Emmerich, 1969; Hill and Mattesich, 1979; LeMasters, 1965; cf. Leifer, 1980; Rossi, 1971) led to the initial conceptualization of the transition to parenthood as a relatively time-limited period of "crisis" for new parents (e.g., see Fedele, Golding, Grossman, and Pollack, 1988, on the regressive impact of first-time parenthood as often manifest in the appearance of psychopathology and postpartum depression in parents). However, subsequent psychological research has qualified this notion. That is, some psychologists (e.g., Antonucci and Mikus, 1988; Sirigano and Lachman, 1985)—also focusing on individual functioning, viz., personality and attitude change over the transition to parenthood—have provided extensive information on, for example, personality characteristics associated with the parental role (e.g., see Belsky and Barends, in Vol. 3 of this *Handbook*), factors (e.g., infant temperament) mediating the impact of parenthood on personality, and areas of change within parents (e.g., affective states, personal maturity, self-efficacy, self-perception, and values). Others (e.g., Cowan and Cowan, 1988, 1992; Heinicke, 1984, in Vol. 3 of this *Handbook*) have treated the impact of the transition to parenthood on the marital relationship and on developmental change in the family system (cf. Cowan and Hetherington, 1991; McKenry and Price, 2000; Michaels and Goldberg, 1988). For example, Cowan and Cowan (1992) provided a structural model of marital and familial adaptation that focused on the developmentally advanced state of balancing individuality and mutuality; empirical findings documented that couples characterized by positive mutuality over the transition to parenthood exhibit optimal parenting, which leads to positive child outcomes at least through the kindergarten years (see Heinicke, in Vol. 3 of this *Handbook*). Consistent with such work has been the research of Belsky (1978, 1984) and Belsky and Pensky (1988), who have attempted to document the determinants of parenting. These researchers have identified as primary factors including child characteristics (e.g., temperament), the personal–psychological well-being of parents, and contextual sources of support and stress (cf. Azar, 1986, 1991, and Demick and Azar, 2001, on determinants of maladaptive parenting in the context of child abuse and/or neglect).

Summarily, theory and research on the transition to parenthood have suggested the following as key to the conceptualization of stages of parental development. First, the transition to parenthood—beginning at conception and continuing through birth and into the child's first years—represents a significant stage that must be incorporated into any stage theory of parental development. Second, empirical findings on the adaptation of marital couples to parenthood has generally reinforced the usefulness of comprehensive conceptualization (cf. Belsky, 1984) as well as the role of individual differences in adaptation (cf. Heinicke, in Vol. 3 of this *Handbook*). Third, comparative research on the determinants of parenting in both adaptive (normal) and maladaptive (e.g., child abuse) contexts has the potential to advance our understanding of family processes and their development more generally (cf. Demick and Wapner, 1988a, 1988b, 1992).

Stage Theories of Parental Development

On the most general level, stage theory has been one of the strongest traditions in developmental psychology (e.g., as exemplified in the work of Gesell, Freud, Havighurst, Piaget, Erikson, Levinson, and others). From the notion that there are universal sequences of change, stage theories tend to have an underlying organismic root metaphor, which leads them to attribute change primarily to an innate blueprint that governs development similarly in all members of a species (although the role of the environment is acknowledged but to varying degrees). The stages are viewed as sequential so that successful completion of one stage is necessary for successful progression to the next (and, as a corollary, failure to acquire skills or resolve issues at an earlier stage undercuts success at later stages). Although stage theories gained enormous popularity in the 1950s and 1960s (and received a much-needed boost from Levinson's, 1978, theory of adult life), they are not without their longstanding critics. Such critics (e.g., Kaplan, 1966, 1983) object to their use on the basis of such issues as the following: an overemphasis on chronological age hides variation in individual lives; there are often no clear markers for beginning and ends of stages; stage models downplay the role of the sociohistorical context; and stages offer a blueprint of idealized normality (so that deviation from the ideal is often perceived as abnormality). These and other criticisms, particularly as they relate to work on stages of parental development, are subsequently discussed.

More specific theory and research on stages of parental development have been generated from within two developmental frameworks, namely, one influenced by Piaget (1952a, 1952b, 1970a, 1970b), Kohlberg (1969, 1981), Loevinger (1976), and Selman (1980) and a second informed by the theory and research of psychoanalytically oriented adult developmentalists such as Levinson (1978, 1986) and Gould (1972). Each is discussed in turn. Lesser known theories that have focused primarily on cognitive stages of parental development are presented first followed by a discussion of what has come to be known as the classic research on stages of parental development. This classic work, which has utilized a more holistic concept of development, then serves as the focus for the remainder of the discussion.

Cognitive stages of parental development.   Relevant here is the work of Sameroff (1975a, 1975b, 1975c), Sameroff and Feil (1985), Newberger (1977, 1980, 1987), Newberger and Cook (1983), and Newberger and White (1989) on parental conceptions of the child and/or of the parental role. Taken together, these theories have outlined a descriptive, developmental continuum of parental social–cognitive awareness, which has been conceptualized in an analogous manner to Piaget's (1952a, 1952b, 1970a, 1970b) stages of intellectual development of the child. According to these theories, the parent's conceptions of the child and/or of the parental role have been seen as representing a cognitive structure of parenthood. Cognitive structures refer to stable patterns of thought that define how an individual (here, parent) makes sense out of her or his experience and organizes her or his responses to it. Related to increased interaction with the environment, the structure of a person's (parent's) thinking broadens (allowing her or him to consider a wider array of information and perspectives) as well as reflects increased flexibility in thinking. Thus the development of the cognitive structure of parenthood has been seen as aiding parents in interpreting their children's responses and behavior and in formulating policies to guide their parental actions.

Stated simply, Sameroff (1975a, 1975b, 1975c) and Sameroff and Feil (1985) ordered parents' conceptions of their children's development into four stages, corresponding to Piaget's four stages of the child's intellectual development, namely, *symbiotic* (sensorimotor), *categorical* (preoperational), *compensating* (concrete operational), and *perspectivistic* (formal operational). For example, Sameroff and Feil (1985, pp. 86–87) characterized the parent's earliest conceptions of her or his child as symbiotic whereby she or he ". . . is concerned primarily with the immediate relationship to the child [and] . . . responds in a here and now fashion to the child's behavior. . . . The skin to skin contact in breast feeding. . . are interpreted as consequences of the mother's efforts and serve to produce a positive affectional bond between mother and child. . . . This lack of differentiation between oneself and one's child makes the ability to reflect on the developmental process impossible."

Subsequent stages were seen as reflecting increasing differentiation between parent and child. For example, once the parent is able to differentiate between self and child as independent entities, she or he has advanced to the categorical stage in which (Sameroff and Feil, 1985, p. 87) "the child's actions can be viewed as being intrinsic characteristics of the child" independent of whether the parent characterizes the child positively or negatively. The highest level of reasoning has been termed perspectivistic insofar as parents at this stage are capable of thinking hypothetically and interpreting their child's behavior in light of the complexity of experience, context, and endowment; furthermore, parents at this stage are able to think constructively about remediation to overcome either general or selected deficiencies in the child.

Although framed somewhat similarly, the work of Newberger (1977, 1980, 1987) and Newberger and her colleagues (1983, 1989) has been developed more extensively. First, Newberger (1987) distinguished between what she termed "parental awareness" (as embodied in her stages) and parental attitudes. Specifically, she assumed that parental awareness represents an underlying cognitive structure of concepts of people and of roles, whereas parental attitudes reflect more superficial points of view about caregiving behaviors and styles. Thus parental awareness, which reflects the complexity and flexibility of the underlying cognitive resources available to the parent, is (unlike some attitudes) not a correct or an incorrect but rather a deeper mode of thinking and thus might be more amenable to intervention. Second, Newberger's theory has received some empirical validation; moreover, there have been some attempts to incorporate her ideas into parent education programs aimed at fostering parental development (see following discussion).

Specifically, Newberger's orientations, levels, and stages have been described as follows:

(1) *Egoistic orientation.* Here, a parent is self-focused (considering only her or his own interests and needs) and perceives the child merely as a projection of her or his own experience (e.g., in terms of the effect of the child on the parent). An example of a mother who is functioning at this level may be seen in the following quotation (Thomas, 1996, p. 189): "I enjoy that she is getting more independent. I can sit down and read a magazine while she is up and about and it's kind of nice. A lot of times she still has to be right there, you know, and I can't just sit to write a letter or pay the bills because she wants to do that stuff too, but she is starting. I'm starting to get a little bit of freedom back."

(2) *Conventional orientation.* At this level, a parent understands her or his child in terms of externally derived definitions and explanations of children (e.g., culture, tradition, "authority," age-related norms for children's development). Parenting is perceived as reasoning about such issues as the most correct way to, for example, toilet train or discipline children. Here, fulfilling one's role as predetermined by tradition is primary. This may be illustrated by the following statement (Thomas, 1996, p. 189): "For my three year-old, I have different expectations than for my one year-old. He is beginning to learn about rules so that I have expectations of him to be able to follow rules. As he gets older, you give them more boundaries and privileges. Perhaps use time-outs if necessary to get him to follow rules."

(3) *Subjective–individualistic orientation.* Here, a parent views her or his child as a unique individual who (differing from external definitions such as those embodied in norms) may now instead be understood through the parent–child relationship itself. Parents at this level broaden their reasoning about parenting and organize it instead around identifying and responding to the needs of this particular child. For example, one mother made the following statement (Thomas, 1996, p. 189): "I like to play with her toys and get involved in some of that imaginative play. She likes me to do that and I have found that a lot of fun. We sit and have wonderful conversations either in play or during the day. It is more fun now that she has started to develop her verbal skills more. She is so different from my son who would not tolerate sitting."

(4) *Analytic–systems orientation.* Here, a parent understands both herself or himself and her or his child as complex and changing psychological self-systems, which are embedded within interacting mutual systems that influence family, community, and global relations. The parent sees both her or his own and her or his child's development through the ongoing process of parenting (in which the parent finds ways to balance her or his own needs as well those of her or his child). For instance, one mother made the following statement (Thomas, 1969, p. 189): "Well, I guess it must be playing some role in the development of this human being. You know, taking responsibility for her is really satisfying, it really is. I think the responsibility of it all is not just food, clothing, and shelter, but all of the other aspects, whether it is her emotional development or physical development. That seems

somehow real freeing to me. I have that ability to respond to her and for me to develop too. I feel that she is really keyed into us and we into her. I still wrestle with that part of letting her go though. I think it is kind of a big picture transformation. It is real satisfying."

Both Newberger's and others' research has provided evidence of both the reliability and construct validity of parental awareness. For example, in developing a scoring manual, Newberger (1977) reported extremely high rates of interrater reliability. She (1980) also demonstrated that the continuum of parenting awareness levels meets the criteria for a cognitive–developmental stage sequence. Flick (1985) demonstrated that, in a sample of young mothers ranging in age from 15 to 20 years, level of parental awareness increases with age; Newberger (1980) reported similar findings in children between the ages of 8 and 16 years (e.g., modifying her interview to begin each question with "If you were a parent . . ."). Parental awareness has also been shown to be related to years of experience as a parent and not to be related to gender, race, or social status (Newberger, 1980; Newberger and Cook, 1983). Further, preliminary research on small samples suggested relations between parental awareness and parental behavior. That is, Newberger (1980) reported that, relative to normals, parents who had abused or neglected a child in their care scored significantly lower on parental awareness. Using a rural (preschool program for developmentally delayed children in Maine) rather than an urban (city hospital) sample, Cook (1979) reported that parents with a history of protective service involvement scored significantly lower on parental awareness than parents with no such involvement (cf. Flick, 1985; Flick and McSweeney, 1985).

Finally, preliminary evidence that parental awareness is responsive to intervention efforts has also been provided. First, Sandy (1982) reported a significant increase in parental awareness following a 12-week parent education program, which combined didactic presentation of child development information with group discussion of childrearing dilemmas. Later, Thomas (1996) combined Newberger's work on parental awareness with a second set of constructs widely reflected in the child development and parenting literature, namely, interpersonal interaction themes. Spanning perceptual, conceptual, motivational, and behavior systems, interpersonal interaction themes have been based on observations of parent–child interaction and have been shown to influence both child outcomes and parent–child relationships. The specific interpersonal interaction themes used by Thomas included sensitivity, responsiveness, reciprocity, and support.

Thus on the basis of research on both parental awareness and interpersonal interaction themes, Thomas developed a parent education program, namely, the Reflective Dialogue Parent Education Design (RDPED), with the following goals: (1) to help parents construct perspectives grounded in an accurate understanding of children's general and individual nature and of parent–child relationships; (2) to aid parents in the construction of interpersonal themes that center on sensitivity, responsiveness, reciprocity, and support; (3) to transfer parents' learning to different stages of children's development and to varied types of situations; and (4) to help parents become aware of their own perspectives and themes as well as the implications of these for their parenting practices. Among her findings, Thomas (1996) reported that (1) levels of parental awareness and interpersonal interaction themes are strongly related; and (2) following the parent education program (ten 90-minute weekly group sessions), parents exhibit lower levels of egoistic and conventional thinking and higher levels of individualistic and analytic thinking (as measured by preinterviews and postinterviews).

Both Sameroff's and Newberger's research made inroads into the more general problem of stages of parental development. They charted typical sequences in (cognitive) development and pointed out the relations between social behavior and underlying cognitive processes. Their work underpins the now voluminous literature on social cognitive–affective factors in parenting such as parental knowledge and expectations (Goodnow, in Vol. 3 of this *Handbook*), beliefs (Sigel and McGillicuddy-De Lisi, in Vol. 3 of this *Handbook*), and attributions (cf. Bugental and Happaney, in Vol. 3 of this *Handbook*). At the same time, their work may also be subject to some of the criticisms typically leveled against cognitive–developmental and/or stage theories more generally (e.g., Freud, 1935, 1938, 1963; Piaget, 1952a, 1952b, 1970a, 1970b). These critiques (see Gardner, 1982; Kaplan,

1966, 1983) have included the following: (1) the stages are not well-knit integrated wholes (so that it remains an open empirical issue as to whether parents use the same cognitive structure across different parenting situations); (2) progression through stages does not necessarily occur in an invariant and fixed sequence (e.g., Newberger, 1987, reported that individual parents' thinking reflects one level of awareness most frequently and adjacent levels some of the time; she has also documented that stress, unmet needs of their own, and/or other circumstances may cause parents' thinking in a particular instance or at a particular time to reflect lower levels of cognitive awareness than they are capable of expressing); (3) the stages are sometimes used as explanations (e.g., to name stages as causes, one must clearly establish what causes a child to function at a particular stage and, unfortunately, cognitive–developmentalists generally do not do this); (4) cognitive–developmental theories may place too much emphasis on intrinsic sources of motivation (e.g., the process of equilibration) and sometimes ignore important environmental influences (e.g., parental childrearing practices) as well as the sociohistorical context; (5) if stages lead to mature end states, then the inevitable (and perhaps erroneous) conclusion is that one stage is better than another (leading to the stigmatization of persons and of groups as less developed). Further, because parental awareness has been shown to relate to both age and years of parenting experience (e.g., Flick, 1985; Newberger and Cook, 1983), it is conceivable that these particular cognitive stages of parental development may well precede actual parenthood. Nonetheless, these theories have powerful implications for the study of stages of parental development more generally as well as for intervention efforts aimed at fostering parental development.

Stages of parenthood.   In contrast to theory and research on stage theories of other (e.g., cognitive, psychosocial) aspects of development, theory and research on stage theories of parental development are relatively new. There are several factors that may account for this phenomenon. First, from a practical standpoint, there has been a consistent increase in the number of live births since 1975 that has been attributed, at least in part, to the rise in the number of women currently of childbearing age born during the "baby boom" years of 1946 to 1964 (Lauer and Lauer, 1991). Coupled with the notion that this self-same cohort of adults characteristically claim, for a variety of reasons (e.g., including the need for dual incomes), that it is much harder to parent today than in the past (e.g., Jaffe, 1991), there has been a proliferation of cultural artifacts reflecting these societal trends (e.g., monthly magazines such as *Child*, *Parents*, and *Parenting*). Complementing society's practical interest in parental development, the confluence of several current theoretical strands within academic psychology led developmentalists to embrace parental development as a feasible area of study in and of itself. These theoretical strands included the lifespan perspective (e.g., Baltes, 1998), the ecological approach (e.g., Bronfenbrenner, 1986), and, perhaps most important, newer models of parent–child effects (e.g., Ambert, 1992; Bell, 1979; Collins, Maccoby, Steinberg, Hetherington, and Bornstein, 2000).

Against this backdrop and in contrast to the previously discussed stage theories of parents' cognitive development, Galinsky's (1981) work on stages of parenthood was based on Levinson's (1978, 1980, 1986, 1990, 1996) theory of adult development, which is considered more biopsychosocial or holistic in nature (cf. Sheehy, 1976, 1995). Thus, before Galinsky's theory is discussed in detail, Levinson's basic approach is briefly summarized. First, from biographical interviews (10 to 20 hours per participant) with 40 men (at the time of participation between 35 and 45 years of age, born between 1923 and 1924) divided among four occupational subgroups (hourly industry workers, business executives, university biologists, novelists) and information obtained from other sources, Levinson (1978, 1986) discussed adult life in terms of rhythms and shared patterns without invoking the concepts of goals or development.

Specifically, Levinson's (1986, p. 6) central concept was that of the life structure, which he defined as the "underlying pattern or design of a person's life at a given time." This (holistic) life structure was thought to include roles (sociocultural level) as well as the quality and patterns of one's relationships (interpersonal level), all filtered through one's temperament and personality (intrapersonal level). Because roles and relationships change, Levinson reasoned that life structures must change too;

thus he proposed that each adult creates a series of life structures at specific ages with transitional periods in between (during which the old life structure is reexamined and changed). That is, Levinson divided the lifespan into a series of broad eras, each lasting approximately 25 years, with a major transition between each era. Within each era, he proposed three periods, viz., the creation of an initial or entry life structure (novice phase); an intermediate readjustment of that life structure; and a last life structure created at the end of the era (culminating phase). He also proposed that each phase, transition, or era has a particular content, that is, a particular set of issues or tasks (cf. Havighurst, 1953). For instance, the midlife transition (at 40-45 years of age) has been thought to center around the growing awareness of one's mortality and the realization that the dreams of one's youth may never be actualized.

On the most general level, Levinson concluded that (1) there is a basic alternation for us all between stable life structures and transition periods (with each new life structure neither better nor more integrated than the previous life structure); and (2) this orderly pattern (including the basic tasks associated with each era and age) is shared by all people in all cultures. Although he was initially accused of gender parochialism, Levinson (1996) subsequently reported a comparable study of women, which concluded that women go through the same sequence of eras and periods at the same ages as men. Additional criticisms with applicability to Galinsky's work are subsequently presented.

Acknowledging the contributions of past and present psychoanalytically oriented researchers to her own thinking, Galinsky (1981) interviewed 228 parents with 396 children among them (from 10 to 40 children of each chronological year from *in utero* to 18 years). These parents included both mothers and fathers, parents from diverse groups (e.g., married, divorced, widowed, stepfamilies, adoptive families, foster families, guardians), and parents of all ages (ranging from adolescent to older parents with one or many children), races, ethnicities, religions, income levels, and regions of the country. From data collected through biographical interviews (cf. Levinson, 1978), she specifically proposed that parenthood progresses through a series of six stages (with relevant developmental tasks for parents):

(1) *Image-making stage.* Here, she has characterized the image-making stage (pregnancy until birth) as the time "when prospective parents begin to cull through, to form, and to re-form images of what's to come, of birth and parenthood" (p. 9). Parental tasks, for example, involve the parent preparing for a change in role, forming feelings for the baby, "reconciling the image of the child with the actual child" (p. 55), and preparing for a change in other important adult relationships.

(2) *Nurturing stage.* From birth until the child is approximately 2 years of age (when the child begins to say "no"), parents may experience a conflict between earlier expectations of what the child might be like and the actuality of parenthood. The major task of this stage is "becoming attached to the baby. . . . It took a couple of weeks until it wasn't like having an object in our home" (p. 74). In contrast to the initial state of symbiosis between mother and child, attachment "implies both emotional and physical separateness and connectedness" (p. 73). Here, parents assess their priorities, figuring out how much time they should devote to the baby and how much to other aspects of their lives.

(3) *Authority stage.* The central task of the authority stage (when the child is 2 to 5 years-old) concerns how parents handle "power," that is, how they accept the responsibility, communicate effectively, select and enforce limits, decide on how much to shield and protect the child, cope with conflicts with the child, and handle or avoid battles of the will. The authority issue is not restricted to children, however, but is also concerned with working out authority relationships with others (who deal with the child), including the other parent, grandparents, babysitters, teachers, neighbors, and the like.

(4) *Interpretive stage.* Here (when the child is 5 to 12 years-old) for parents "the major task is to interpret the world to their children, and that entails not only interpreting themselves to their children and interpreting and developing their children's self concepts, but also answering their questions, providing them access to the skills and information they need, and helping them form values" (p. 178).

(5) *Interdependent stage.* As the child reaches adolescence, the parent is faced with and must interact with a "new" child. All aspects of the prior relationship (e.g., communication) must be renegotiated and new issues (e.g., sexuality) addressed.

(6) *Departure stage.* As the adolescent gets older, the central task becomes that "of accepting one's grown child's separateness and individuality, while maintaining the connection . . ." (p. 307). "The 'old,' 'original,' family has changed, the children have grown, moved away, and the parents' roles have changed, and most parents search for new ways to say they are still a family" (p. 304). This stage is characterized by evaluations. "Parents evaluate their images of departure, when and how far they thought their child would go. They evaluate whether they've achieved the parent/grown child relationship they wanted as well as taking stock of their overall successes and failures" (p. 10).

What do these stages say about Galinsky's views of parenthood and of development? First, similar to Levinson (1978, 1986), Galinsky has not implied that all parents' lives are identical, but simply that an orderly pattern, including basic tasks associated with each stage, is shared by all parents at least within our culture. Second, also like Levinson, Galinsky has proposed that the stages follow one another and may be interrelated, but one stage is not of greater value than another nor does one represent a more advanced level of development than the others; thus the stages are assumed simply to be different. Third, although Galinsky's theory is inconsistent with other goal-directed theories of development that claim a higher endpoint (e.g., Freud, 1935; Piaget, 1970a), she has arguably integrated developmental notions within and across each stage. That is, she has assumed that all stages involve parents' ability to balance closeness to their child with an appropriate level of distance (or what has been termed self-world distancing; see Wapner and Demick, 1998, 1999, subsequent discussion).

Furthermore, one of Galinsky's most significant conclusions was that (Galinsky, 1981, pp. 7–8) "whenever parents describe a new event in the life of their family (an event as large as the birth of a child or as small as their child's reaction to a new toy), they used the words 'should' or 'supposed to' or 'expected.' I realized that parents had pictures in their minds of the way things were supposed to go, and of the way that they as parents and their children were supposed to act. I came to think of these pictures as images—because they were often fleeting, not fully conscious. This concept is similar to Bernice Neugarten's construct of 'the normal, expectable life cycle' and to Daniel Levinson's 'The Dream,' though I see parents having myriads of images, filtering in and out of their thoughts, as opposed to one dream." She has seen images as the adult legacy of children's play. That is, as we continue the lifelong process of imagining what lies ahead, images appear to us at times of transition; we also use them, she has reasoned, as measures of our success and failure as parents (e.g., [Galinsky, 1981, p. 8] "if an image has not been achieved in reality, it is seen as a loss and can cause anger and depression. If an image is realized, it brings joy").

Thus Galinsky appears to have acknowledged the possibility of development at points (irrespective of stage) at which parents modify an image to be more consistent with reality or modify their own behavior to reach toward an image (cf. Riegel, 1975). Such a position is similar to and different from that of Gould (1972). That is, both Galinsky and Gould have viewed development as potentially arising from conflict between images and actuality. However, whereas Gould stated that the image is usually a childhood one (involving a simple and beneficent world) that comes into conflict with a more rational, adult view of reality, Galinsky proposed that images stem not only from childhood, but also from adult experiences (particularly those related to parenthood). Furthermore, she went on to recommend the reconciling of images and reality almost as a self-administered therapeutic technique for the individual, the marital dyad, and the parent-child relationship alike. For example, as she has stated (Galinsky, 1981, p. 11), "When I find myself caught in a bind, everything seeming to cave in on me, I look for an underlying image. I ask myself, 'What am I expecting that's not coming true?' Then, when I uncover the image, I ask myself if it is a realistic one. If I decide it is, I look for constructive ways to achieve it; if it's not realistic, I try to replace it with a goal that's more workable."

Later, Unell and Wyckoff (2000) published the book *The Eight Seasons of Parenthood: How the Stages of Parenting Constantly Reshape Our Adult Identities.* From clinical interviews with several hundred parents ranging in age from 20 to 90 years, these authors elaborated a stage theory of parenthood, which bears a striking similarity to that of Galinsky. Specifically, they conceptualized stages of parenthood as consisting of three circles with various substages, indicated by the child's age and developmental milestones. For example, the first circle concerned *parenting young children*, which was divided into the following self-explanatory stages: *celebrity* (pregnancy); *sponge* (infancy); *family manager* (preschool years); *travel agent* (middle years); and *volcano dweller* (adolescence). The second circle involved *parenting adult children*, which was divided into the stages of *family remodeler* (the child leaves home to become independent) and *plateau parent* (independence). The third circle involved *being parented by children*; the only stage within this circle has been designated as *rebounder* (caring for a parent). The goal of this work appears to be different from that of Galinsky. That is, as family therapists, Unell and Wyckoff attempted to establish that parenthood is a predictable journey through adulthood and that parents can anticipate the impact that their children's development will have on them; in contrast, Galinsky's role as a developmentally oriented educator led her to adopt a more objective viewpoint. Against this backdrop, we now turn to an evaluation of Galinsky's research.

EVALUATION OF THEORY AND RESEARCH ON GALINSKY'S (1981) STAGES OF PARENTAL DEVELOPMENT

The analytic strategy for evaluating Galinsky's (1981) work on stages of parenthood is threefold. First, in light of the surprising lack of empirical attempts to validate her theory (although this may partly be related to the relatively recent advent of interest in lifespan development, e.g., Baltes, 1998, adult development, e.g., Levinson, 1978, and parenting, e.g., Ambert, 1992; Collins et al., 2000; Collins, Harris, and Susman, 1995), the stages are first reviewed against the backdrop of other social scientific research that has either supported or refuted her conclusions at each stage (cf. Wapner, 1993). Second, both theoretical and methodological critiques of this research are provided. Third, Galinsky's work in light of the changing demographics of contemporary American parents (cf. Milardo, 2001) are then reviewed. Finally, an alternative conceptualization of stages of parental development, namely, one based on my own holistic, developmental, systems-oriented approach to person-in-environment functioning across the lifespan, is then proposed.

Research Supporting Galinsky's Stages of Parenthood

Social scientific contributions to the parenting literature have generally supported Galinsky's notion of stages as well as of each particular stage. However, the support has primarily been theoretical rather than empirical in nature. That is, there have been surprisingly few empirical demonstrations of either the stages as a whole or of each stage individually (see subsequent discussion). For example, on the most general level (cf. Unell and Wyckoff, 2000), family sociologists have amassed a large body of research on the family life cycle (cf. Aldous, 1978). Specifically, they have argued that we can understand adult life in terms of movement through family roles (content or job description of social positions). Thus Duvall (1946, 1962) proposed eight stages of the family life cycle, each of which involves either adding or deleting some role or changing the content of a central role. The stages have been described as follows: stage 1, spousal role is added; 2, parental role is added; 3, oldest child is preschooler, parental role changes; 4, oldest child enters school, parental role changes; 5, onset of adolescence, parental role changes; 6, oldest child leaves home, parental role changes; 7, all children leave home, parental role changes; and 8, one or both spouses retire, role changes. These stages have been assumed to occur in a particular sequence and, at every stage, each set of roles shapes the experiences of the individuals within the stage. Furthermore, the theory has been considered adevelopmental insofar as no subsequent role or stage is assumed better, more complex, or more mature than any preceding role or stage. Thus this analysis has closely paralleled Galinsky's work on stages of parenthood and has been open to some of the same criticisms (see subsequent discussion).

Further, in line with Galinsky's general sentiment that parenthood is accompanied by profound changes in parents' sense of self (e.g., she described the transformative nature of parenthood whereby parents constantly put their children's needs first and thereby lose their sense of self only to find it and have it change again and again), a growing body of literature has begun to reinforce this sentiment (e.g., see Krasnow, 1997, who has described the woman's need, for similar reasons, to surrender to motherhood). In line with this, Schoen (1995) echoed aspects of Galinsky's thinking by including, within her influential volume on parent development, chapters concerning motherhood and fatherhood as equal opportunities for development, the spiritual nature of parenthood, the healing nature of parenthood, how parenthood can enrich our powers of self-expression, how parenthood can make a marriage grow, and the impact of parenthood on our self and world views.

With respect to the first of Galinsky's stages, viz., the image-making stage, considerable research has documented significant changes in aspects of parents' images of self at least over the transition to parenthood. As part of a larger study on changes in parents' experience of self, environment, and self-environment relations over the course of parenthood, Coltrera (1978) and Clark (2001) provided data on the powerful impact of first-time parenthood on parents' self-representation. Using a variation of Goodenough's Draw-a-Person Test (cf. Machover, 1949), these authors obtained findings such as the following (Wapner, 1978, pp. 21–22):

> That birth of the first child has an impact on the drawings of both husband and wife is almost self-evident. For the wife, the first spontaneous drawing of a person 3–4 weeks before birth is an adult male with moustache, etc.; in contrast, just before birth, the moustache is no longer present and the drawing has child-like boyish qualities. Does this representation reflect fusion of child-to-be-born and mother? After the birth of the child, the request to draw-a-person results in a representation where there is a dramatic shift to drawing a baby rather than an adult. The baby—conforming to actuality—is female. The second set of drawings, which are self-sex in this case, also undergo change, from a woman with a rounded middle, to a staid figure sitting and "waiting for birth" and finally, after the birth, to a woman with pronounced breasts and a flat stomach.
>
> The husband's drawings also show the impact of the transition: here, the major shift is from adult, toward representation of a child's body, especially in the third and fourth set of drawings, i.e., following birth. The third drawings, i.e., of husband, wife, and family also show the impact of the transition reaffirming the stress. One point worth noting is that the first three drawings by the wife all have mouths with a smile represented, while the fourth drawing has a mouth half downward in sadness and half upturned with a smile.

Galinsky's nurturing stage has gained support from the work of Mahler, Pine, and Bergman (1970, 1975), which considered mother–infant fusion as a prerequisite for the child's subsequent development of self. As Ainsworth and Wittig (1969) documented, the press for dependence and independence has been evident in the toddler's shifting between clinging to and running away from mother. The distinction has also been made between symbiosis or bonding and attachment. That is, symbiosis–bonding has been linked to the synchronization of the parent's and the child's behavior in which there is mutual gaze–response to gestures and noises and fusion of mother and child. In contrast, attachment (Galinsky, 1981, p. 73) "implies both emotional and physical separateness and connectedness." Finally, given the appropriate affectional tie on attachment, the child has been shown to enter an exploratory phase that is difficult for the parent to control; for instance, Ainsworth and Wittig (1969) documented that the mother is used a home base or anchor point from which to explore the world (cf. Shouela, Steinberg, Leveton, and Wapner, 1980).

Theoretical support for the remainder of Galinsky's stages has come from the field of developmental science. Support for the authority stage can be seen in the extensive body of research on the need for preschoolers to develop emotional regulation, that is, the ability to inhibit, enhance, maintain, and modulate emotional arousal to accomplish one's goals (e.g., Eisenberg et al., 1997). In this context, parents often need to set extremely clear limits on the "appropriate" expression of emotion. Support for the interpretive stage has been seen in school children's characteristic use of concrete operational thinking (Piaget, 1952a, 1952b) and in the increase in their self-doubt (Berger, 1994), both of which often necessitate parental interpretation and/or intervention. The existence of the interdependent stage has made sense in light of the myriad of physical, cognitive, and psychosocial changes that the adolescent experiences. Finally, the departure stage has made sense insofar as there is a voluminous literature on the phenomenon of the "empty nest syndrome" (e.g., Harkins, 1978; Sullivan, 1998), which has been called into question for current cohorts of parents (see Berger, 1994, for a comprehensive review of research in this area).

Theoretical and Methodological Critique

Galinsky's work on stages of parenthood, although widely accepted, has been subject to both theoretical and methodological criticisms. Methodologically, her use of autobiographical interviews (cf. Levinson, 1986) relied primarily on reconstruction and memory, which are not reliable. The method itself has been considered time consuming, expensive, and vulnerable to bias (on the part of both the participant and the interviewer) so that findings have often been difficult to replicate. In defense of the method, Levinson (1986) argued that it is one of the few psychological methods that allows the investigator to gain a sense of the complexity of a life course in the context of the everyday life environment; as Wapner and Demick (1998) have argued, however, data obtained from phenomenologically oriented methods (appropriate for the examination of individual experience) may still be subjected to systematic analysis without violation of any of the method's underlying assumptions (cf. Watkins, 1977). Furthermore, very few empirical investigations have attempted to verify the overall concept of stages of parental development as well as of the individual stages themselves. This may have been at least partly related to the notion that, because parenthood is assumed to have a profound impact on the parent's sense of self, interview methods might be more apt to capture changes in self-experience. However, as subsequently noted, our theoretical orientation has led to the development of experimental tasks and measures that capture such relevant concepts as self–other differentiation (ability of the individual to separate self from other), self–world distancing (degree to which the individual feels close to or remote from the environment), and developmental regression (degree to which the individual exhibits less developmentally advanced functioning), which all represent processes relevant to the study of parental development. At the least, Galinsky's work should continue to be verified through questionnaire studies that attempt to assess the roles of both potential mediator and moderator variables.

Several theoretical issues have also arisen from Galinsky's work. First, the concept of stages of parenthood has implied that the development of parents is of primary import, but the stages have nonetheless been characterized with respect to children (cf. stages of family life cycle). That is, even though each stage has been discussed with respect to the nature of the parent's tasks inherent within it, the stage itself has often been identified by the child's age and developmental tasks. In other words, the adult's tasks at each stage have almost been intuitive, that is, to deal with the child's developmental tasks at her or his various ages. Thus future work on stages of parental development would do well to focus exclusively on parents and to delineate their tasks and issues in a more precise and systematic manner. Second, Galinsky distinguished her work on stages of parenthood from family life cycle research on the basis that many parents have children of different ages and thus can be going through several stages concurrently; furthermore, her conception of stages has been adevelopmental and not directed toward a teleology. Under such circumstances, it has not been precisely clear as to how the concept of stages as applied to parenthood augments our understanding of either parenthood in general or of parental development more specifically. Third, Galinsky has identified several instances of common processes that cut across the various stages, with the most notable instance being that of parents' ongoing need to balance closeness with and distance from their children. This notion of self–other, or self–world, distancing has figured prominently within several grand developmental theories (e.g., psychoanalytic, organismic–developmental) and might also help capture some of the major tasks and issues involved in parental development. Thus re-framing parental development around major themes and issues cutting across stages (e.g., parents' treatment of sexuality across the child's development and not just at her or his adolescence) might advance the work in this area (see next major section). Fourth, the theory at it now stands has failed to take into account individual differences such as gender, ethnicity, socioeconomic status, and family type (e.g., married, divorced, step; see Hetherington and Stanley-Hagan, in Vol. 3 of this *Handbook*) in the sociocultural context (in which, e.g., adult children in the homes of midlife parents have become a more common occurrence and grandparenthood has typically become an important event in the lives of parents; see Smith and Drew, in Vol. 3 of this *Handbook*). This issue is elaborated in the next subsection.

The Changing American Parent

According to Milardo (2001), the last millennium has seen significant advances in family studies, particularly in the areas of theory development, the social ecology of marriage, families with young children, families in the middle and later years, the nature and determinants of marital satisfaction, family relationships of lesbians and gay men, marital processes and parental socialization in families of color, families in poverty, families in urban neighborhoods, and fatherhood more generally. How-ever, there is still the need to go further. Recent statistics (e.g., Teachman, Tedrow, and Crowder, 2001) have documented the changing demography of American families. Specifically, Teachman et al. (2001, p. 453) have noted that

> the declining prevalence of early marriage, increasing level of marital dissolution, and growing tendency to never marry, especially among some racial and ethnic groups, reflect changes in the relative economic prospects of men and women and support the conclusion that marriage is becoming less valued as a source of economic stability. These developments also imply that relatively more children are born outside of marriage, spend at least part of their childhood in a single-parent household, and endure multiple changes in family composition. Paralleling these trends have been sharp changes in the economic stability of families, characterized most notably by a growing importance of women's income and increasing economic inequality among American families.

Thus considerably less than half of the adults in the United States today follow the stages of the life cycle as outlined by Duvall (1962). Not everyone marries or has children; these adults, nonetheless, may still fulfill their need for generativity in the contexts of other relationships. Have these trends been captured in Galinsky's stages of parenthood? Further, those who marry frequently divorce, perhaps marrying again later or spending years as a single parent. Arguably, Duvall's as well as Galinsky's models may simply not be valid. Do the stages of parenthood as currently described by Galinsky hold for parents who live apart from their children? Do parents in nontraditional families follow the same stages of parenthood as those in traditional families? The answers to these and related questions have the potential to occupy researchers in the new millennium and advance our understanding of parental development within particular family configurations as well as of family processes more generally (cf. Demick and Wapner, 1992).

As one example, we now consider similarities and differences in adoptive versus biological parents (see, e.g., Brodzinsky and Pinderhughes, in Vol. 1 of this *Handbook*; Demick, in press; Suwalsky and Bornstein, 2000). To date, current research has suggested that there may be areas of similarities (e.g., Healy, Azar, and Demick, 2001, have reported no differences in basic attributional processes between the two groups concerning the causes of their own and other children's behavior) as well as areas of difference (e.g., Kirk, 1964, documented that adoptive parents *must* acknowledge that adoptive parenting is different from biological parenting). In particular, these differences have the potential to have an impact on parents' experience and action associated with our current conceptualization of stages of parental development.

In this case, inroads have been made into the general problem of the life cycle of adoptive families (e.g., Pavao, 1998; Rosenberg, 1992). Although these authors have acknowledged differences in the life cycle of adoptive families relative to biological ones (see also Patterson, 2001, in Vol. 3 of this *Handbook*, on gay and lesbian families), this preliminary research has been restricted by small sample sizes, issues associated with the analysis of data obtained predominantly from interview methods, and the use only of volunteer participants. Thus open empirical questions include the following. Relative to biological parents who usually have 9 months to prepare for the birth of a child, are there similarities or differences in the image-making processes of adoptive parents? Given that biological parents are constrained to some extent, do the image-making processes of adoptive parents carry more salience over the course of parenthood (e.g., prolonged discrepancy between the expectations and actuality of the child who was adopted)? In light of the general trend for parents to deal with their own sexuality when their children reach adolescence (e.g., see Buchholz, 2000), is sexuality more of an issue in adoptive parents (who reportedly are often concerned about the illegitimacy of their child or children)?

In line with this, recent reviews (e.g., McLoyd, Cauce, Takeuchi, and Wilson, 2001) have documented that marital and parental socialization processes in families of color are perhaps more complex than in white families. For example, there are racial and ethnic group differences in, for example, division of household labor, marital relations, children's adjustment to marital and family conflict, conceptions of masculinity, and the like. Thus, do these pervasive differences have implications for Galinsky's stage conceptualization of parenthood? That is, do parents of color go through similar or different stages of parental development than typical white, middle-socioeconomic parents? Do the issues of parents of color revolve around similar or dissimilar themes than those proposed by Galinsky? For example, if conceptions of masculinity lead to differing views of the parenting role, how do such conceptions have an impact on parents' development? Although one might speculate that Galinsky's stages need to be reexamined in light of racial and ethnic differences in behavior and experience, virtually no studies to date have focused on such issues. Thus these and related issues must be investigated in future research.

A HOLISTIC, DEVELOPMENTAL, SYSTEMS-ORIENTED APPROACH TO PARENTAL DEVELOPMENT

My and Wapner's holistic, developmental, systems-oriented approach to person-in-environment functioning across the lifespan is based on Werner's (1957; Werner and Kaplan, 1963) comparative–developmental theory. Both the original theory and my elaborated approach have been termed organismic (insofar as psychological part processes, e.g., cognition, affect, valuation, behavior, are considered in relation to the total context of human activity) and developmental (in that it provides a systematic principle governing developmental progression and regression so that living systems may be compared with respect to their formal, organizational features). For some time now, this approach has figured prominently within the areas of developmental psychology (e.g., Wapner and Demick, 1998), clinical psychology (e.g., Wapner and Demick, 1999), environmental psychology (e.g., Demick and Wapner, 1990; Wapner and Demick, in press-b), and personality psychology (e.g., Wapner and Demick, 2000).

My elaborated approach comprises a number of theoretical assumptions with powerful heuristic potential for the design and conduct of a wide variety of empirical studies (e.g., Dandonoli, Demick, and Wapner, 1990; Demick, 1993; Demick and Harkins, 1999; Demick et al., 1992; Demick, Hoffman, and Wapner, 1985; Demick, Ishii, and Inoue, 1997; Demick and Wapner, 1980; Silverstein and Demick, 1994; Toshima, Demick, Miyatani, Ishii, and Wapner, 1996; Wapner, Demick, and Redondo, 1990). Certain of these assumptions have definitive implications for the conceptualization of stages of parental development. Thus these assumptions are described and their implications for the study of parental development delineated.

On the most general level, my elaborated approach is

(1) *holistic*, insofar as we assume that the person-in-environment system is an integrated system, whose parts may be considered in relation to the functioning whole;

(2) *developmental*, insofar as we assume that progression and regression may be assessed against the ideal of development embodied in the *orthogenetic principle* (change from dedifferentiated to differentiated and hierarchically integrated person-in-environment functioning) and that development encompasses not only *ontogenesis*, but additional processes such as *phylogenesis* (e.g., adaptation manifest by different species), *microgenesis* (e.g., development of a percept or idea), *pathogenesis* (e.g., development of both functional and organic pathology), and *ethnogenesis* (e.g., changes during the history of humankind);

(3) *systems oriented*, insofar as we assume that the person-in-environment system includes three aspects of the *person* (*biological*, e.g., health; *intrapersonal*, e.g., stress; *sociocultural*, e.g., role) and three analogous aspects of the *environment* (*physical*, e.g., natural or built; *inter-organismic*, e.g., friends, relatives, pets; *sociocultural*, e.g., rules, laws of society).

Corollary notions include the assumptions of

(4) *transactionalism*: the person and the environment mutually define, and cannot be considered independent of, one another; similarly, the person-in-environment system's experience (consisting of cognitive, affective, and valuative processes) and action are inseparable and operate contemporaneously under normal conditions;

(5) *multiple modes of analysis*, including *structural analysis* (part–whole relations) and *dynamic analysis* (means–ends relations);

(6) *constructivism*: the person-in-environment system actively constructs or construes her or his experience of the environment;

(7) *multiple intentionality*: the person-in-environment system adopts different intentions with respect to self-world relations (i.e., toward self or the world out there);

(8) *directedness and planning*: the person-in-environment system is directed toward both long- and short-term goals related to the capacity to plan;

(9) *multiple worlds*: the person-in-environment system operates in different spheres of existence (e.g., home, work, recreation);

(10) preference for *process rather than achievement* analysis.

How do these assumptions help us conceptualize parental development across the lifespan? First, against the backdrop of our holistic assumptions, we advocate that a complete understanding of the development of parents-in-environments must include consideration of a wider range of variables (see Table 13.1) and their interrelations than has typically been the case. For example, some of the variables listed (e.g., gender differences in and contextual influences on aspects of parents' sociocultural functioning) have already received systematic attention in the literature. Others, however, still to be explored, have been identified through my holistic analysis. Furthermore, those previously examined have typically been studied in isolation, rather than in relation to one another. For example, Belsky's (1984) work on the determinants of parenting (which highlighted the personal–psychological well-being of parents, child characteristics, and contextual sources of stress and support and have implications for parental development) might be advanced through consideration of additional variables and their interrelations. Furthermore, relatively few theories and empirical studies have considered the role of values in parental functioning (the value of children to parents) and how these values interact with parents' cognitive, affective, and behavioral functioning (cf. Hoffman and Hoffman, 1973). In line with this, there have also been relatively few discussions of the extensive

TABLE 13.1
Variables Relevant to the Study of Parents-in-Environments (from Demick, 1999)

Person (× Environment)	*Environment (× Person)*
Biological/physical	*Physical*
Age	Environmental objects[a]
Sex	Physical locations[a]
Race[a]	
Physical health/stress[a]	
Modes of conception[a]	
Complications during pregnancy or delivery	
Psychological/intrapersonal	*Interpersonal*
Cognitive processes	Children
Decision making	Spouse (e.g., marital quality, stability)
Plans and expectations[a]	Family of origin
Meaning making[a]	Extended family
Cognitive style[a]	Friends
Affective processes	Co-workers
Motivation for parenthood	Daycare provider(s)[a]
Personality[a]	Neighbors[a]
Mental health/stress[a]	Child's teachers[a]
Valuative processes	General public
General values (e.g., family versus career; self versus other)[a]	Other social support networks
Life satisfaction	
Sociocultural	*Sociocultural*
Socioeconomic status (e.g., cost of children)[a]	Family developmental tasks
Religion[a]	Family history/themes
Politics[a]	Community[a]
Parental role	Society (e.g., media)
Spousal role	Legal[a]
Work role	Educational[a]
Gender role	Sociohistorical context
Leisure roles[a]	

[a]Not examined extensively in previous research.

reasons underlying why people want to become parents (cf. Wapner, 1993) and the ways in which these reasons have an impact on parents' overall functioning as well as the ways in which these reasons influence aspects of parents' development.

Likewise, my developmental assumptions have suggested that an analysis of parent-in-environment functioning might profit from a broader view of development than has typically been the case. In contrast to most professionals who restrict their view of development to ontogenesis, I view development more broadly as a mode of analysis of diverse aspects of person-in-environment functioning (which encompasses, e.g., ontogenesis, microgenesis, pathogenesis, phylogenesis, and ethnogenesis). Furthermore, components (person, environment), relations among components (e.g., means–ends), and part processes (e.g., cognition) of person-in-environment systems are assumed to be developmentally orderable in terms of the orthogenetic principle (Kaplan, 1966, 1983; Werner, 1957; Melito, 1985a, 1985b; Werner and Kaplan, 1956, 1963). The orthogenetic principle defines development in terms of the degree of organization attained by a system. The more differentiated and hierarchically integrated a system is, in terms of its parts and of its means and ends, the more highly developed it is said to be. Optimal development entails a differentiated and hierarchically integrated person-in-environment system with flexibility, freedom, self-mastery, and the capacity to shift from one mode of person-in-environment relation to another as required by goals, the demands of the situation, and the instrumentalities available (cf. Wapner and Demick, 1998).

The orthogenetic principle has also been specified with respect to a number of polarities, which at one extreme represent developmentally less advanced and, at the other, more advanced functioning (cf. Kaplan, 1966; Werner, 1957; Werner and Kaplan, 1963). These polarities, by use of examples relevant to parental development, are as follows:

(1) *Interfused to subordinated.* In interfused experience and action, goals and functions are not sharply differentiated, whereas in subordinated experience and action goals and functions are differentiated and hierarchized with drives and momentary motives subordinated to more long-term goals. For example, for the less developmentally advanced parent, always pleasing the child by granting her or his every wish is not differentiated from preparing the child for a realistic future. In contrast, the more developmentally advanced parent is able to differentiate and subordinate the former short-term goal to the latter long-term goal.

(2) *Syncretic to discrete.* Syncretic refers to the fusion or merging of multiple nondifferentiated mental phenomena, whereas discrete refers to mental contents, acts, meanings, and functions that represent unambiguous and specific things. For example, syncretic thinking is represented by the lack of differentiation between a parent's inner and outer experience; that is, the lack of separation of one's own feelings from that of one's child out-there (e.g., a parent in Newberger's, 1980, egoistic or Sameroff's, 1975a, symbiotic stage). Discrete is represented by a parent's accurately defining and distinguishing one's own feelings from those of one's child.

(3) *Diffuse to articulate.* Diffuse represents a relatively uniform, homogeneous structure with little differentiation of parts, whereas articulate refers to a structure for which differentiation of parts makes up the whole. For instance, diffuse is a structure represented by the law of *pars pro toto* (Werner, 1957); that is, the part has the quality of the whole, as is the case when a parent's judgment about a child is made on the basis of one brief experience. Articulate is represented by an experience in which distinguishable events make up the parent's whole impression of one's child, with each event contributing to and yet being distinguishable from the whole.

(4) *Rigid to flexible.* Rigid refers to behavior that is not readily flexible, whereas flexible refers to behavior that is plastic or readily changeable. Rigid is exemplified by a parent's perseveration, routine, and unchangeability in handling her or his child. In contrast, flexibility implies a parent's capacity to modify her or his transactions with the child depending on the context and the particular demands of a given situation.

(5) *Labile to stable.* Lability refers to the inconsistency and fluidity that accompanies changeability, whereas stability refers to unambiguity and consistency that co-occur with fixed properties. For example, lability may be seen in a parent's rapidly changing, inconsistent, fluid behavior with her or his child (e.g., use of words with many meanings, stimulus bound shifts of attention). In contrast, stability is represented by a parent's consistent action, which is underpinned by thinking that involves the precise definition of events, terms, or ideas.

Following from this conceptualization of developmental polarities, there has been a major difference in the concept of individual differences between my approach and many others. Whereas other approaches (e.g., learning theory, Piagetian theory) either interpret individual differences as manifest in different psychopathological states or simply as a source of error, we see individual differences as contributing to a differential developmental psychology that is complementary to a general developmental psychology (e.g., see Wapner and Demick, 1991, on cognitive style across the lifespan). Thus a developmental analysis of self-world relations by use of the orthogenetic principle may be applied to describe individual differences in a variety of content areas (here, parental development). For example, least developmentally advanced is the *dedifferentiated person-in-environment system state* (e.g., exemplified by the baby who is inseparable from her or his bottle and/or by the mother who is inseparable from her infant). Next are the *differentiated and isolated person-in-environment system state* (e.g., a parent who avoids participating in the activities of her or his child's school; knowing the consequences of being an abusive parent yet not being able to refrain from abusive action toward one's child) and the *differentiated and in conflict person-in-environment system state* (e.g., being in conflict with one's adolescent; being in conflict with her or his school's busing policy). Most advanced developmentally is the *differentiated and integrated person-in-environment system state* (e.g., a parent discriminates between being angry at her or his child and wanting to yet refraining from physically hurting her or him; a parent tolerates a grandparent spoiling her or his child because the parent values the relationships between grandparent and parent and between grandparent and grandchild).

The preceding discussion has revealed several implications of my approach that are relevant for the general study of parents-in-environments. However, what have these and related assumptions suggested about the specific study of stages of parental development? Relevant here is our ongoing work on critical person-in-environment transitions across the lifespan (e.g., Demick, 1996; Wapner and Demick, in press-b). First, use of the term critical is significant. Critical or dramatic transitions of the person-in-environment system—linked to changes in the person, in the environment, or in both—occur at all stages of the life cycle. Furthermore, because what is critical for one person is not necessarily critical for another, I have emphasized that "critical" must be experientially defined. This foreshadows my need to complement traditional quantitative methodologies with more qualitative ones (see subsequent discussion).

Every moment of life involves change, but our concern has been for those transitions in which a perturbation to the person-in-environment system is *experienced* as so potent that ongoing modes of transacting with the environment no longer suffice. Furthermore, a perturbation to the person-in-environment system may be initiated at the physical, intrapersonal, and/or sociocultural level of the person as well as the physical, inter-organismic, and/or sociocultural aspect of the environment (cf. Wapner and Demick, 1992, in press-b, in press-c). Such transitions are of great significance because, reverberating across all aspects of the system, they represent the occasion for progressive development, regressive change, or stasis (no change at all).

In light of the lack of extensive empirical data on the stages of parental development, Galinsky's (1981) notion that certain issues cut across all stages of parental development (e.g., self–other distancing; treatment of sexuality) and my assumptions about the nature of human functioning, I have preferred to reframe the issue of stages of parenthood as *developmental changes in the experience and action of parents over the course of bearing and rearing children* (cf. Demick, 2000c, Demick and Wapner, 1992). This reframing has been chosen for several reasons. First, this conceptualization may be more in line with the complexity of everyday life functioning. Related to the wide range of criticisms that have been leveled against stage theories of development coupled with the notion that developmentally ordered individual differences in self–world relationships (i.e., dedifferentiated, differentiated and isolated, differentiated and in conflict, differentiated and integrated) may characterize person-in-environment system states at any given moment in time and are thus malleable and potentially remediable, I have assumed that developmental changes in (cognitive, affective, and valuative) experience and action occur with greater frequency than stage theories have implied.

Second, relevant to parental stages, *it may be that, whenever there is a perturbation to the person-in-environment system (e.g., cognitive disequilibrium in a parent related to a child's behavior), the parent must reorganize her or his self–world relationship (e.g., to restore cognitive equilibrium). In this way, such developmental processes most probably occur with great frequency in transacting with one's children on a daily basis. Experiential accounts of parenthood attest to this notion as well as indicate that, although the particular issues posed by one's children may change from one moment to the next (even if some appear with great regularity), parental reactions do not necessarily change. That is, parents are constantly faced with restoring cognitive equilibrium (or equilibrium to the person-in-environment system) in a dialectical process that may feel similar every time that they are faced with a novel (or not so novel) stimulus from their children (cf. Holden and Ritchie, 1988). In my terms, parents are continually faced with attempting to return their differentiated and conflicted person-in-environment system state to a more differentiated and integrated one.*

Third, my conceptualization has uncovered problems worthy of empirical inquiry that have previously been unexamined. For example, my approach has suggested the following types of questions relevant to parental development. What are the relations among parents' cognitive, affective, valuative, and behavioral functioning as they bear and rear children? What roles do planning and values play in parental development? How do parents' specific experiences translate into action? How does the relation between parents' biological (e.g., sleep patterns, energy levels) and psychological functioning change over the course of parenthood? What impact do complications during pregnancy and/or delivery have on mothers', fathers', and children's subsequent functioning? Are there individual differences in the ways in which parents negotiate their various roles over the course of parental development? How do parents deal with the organization of their child's physical space (e.g., bedroom) over the course of parenthood? How do parents' relationships with their employers have an impact on their relationships with daycare providers? Are there individual differences in the ways in which parents deal with family developmental tasks and/or family history? These and other questions have been identified and elaborated in Demick (1999). Such questions—which stand in marked contrast to questions brought forth by stage theories of development—appear worthy of future empirical investigation and may ultimately lead us to a more comprehensive understanding of the complexity of parental development in the everyday life context.

Toward this end, a final word concerning methodology is offered. Because my approach has been wedded to the complementarity of explication (description) and causal explanation (conditions under which cause–effect relations occur), my preferred method of research has been to draw flexibly from both quantitative and qualitative methodologies, depending on the nature of the problem and the level of integration under scrutiny. With respect to quantitative methodologies, much of my empirical work on critical person-in-environment transitions across the lifespan has been aimed at documenting conditions facilitating developmental change. Here, I have identified the use of self–world distancing, anchor points, planning, triggers to action, and the phenomenon of *reculer pour mieux sauter* (draw back to leap) as examples of processes that may, in fact, facilitate developmental progression (see Wapner and Demick, 1998, in press-b). With respect to qualitative methodologies, the field has currently experienced a paradigm shift toward the use of, for example, narrative analysis (e.g., see Fiese, Hooker, Kotary, Schwagler, and Rimmer, 1995, on family stories in the early stages of parenthood). As I see it, these approaches taken together might profitably be used to understand developmental changes in parents' experience and action over the full course of bearing and rearing children.

CONCLUSIONS

Important inroads into the general problem of *stages of parental development* have been made. However, it is argued here that, toward a more complete understanding of what I have alternatively framed as *developmental changes in parents' experience and action over the course of bearing and rearing children*, additional research is clearly needed. For example, Galinsky's (1981) work on stages of parenthood may serve as a springboard from which these future attempts might proceed. Does subsequent research on larger samples verify the existence of her stages? Must these stages be qualified related to the important notion of individual differences (e.g., parent gender, religion, socioeconomic status)? Do they hold for nontraditional (e.g., adoptive) parents (cf. Demick, 2000a, 2000b; Golombok, 1999)? Can such a model be applied to childless individuals who fulfill their needs for generativity in alternative ways? Are organismic or contextual–transactional models of development more appropriate for the study of parenthood? Are there larger developmental changes in parents' experience (cognition, affect, valuation) and action over the course of parenthood? These and other questions have the potential to occupy family researchers for some time to come.

Finally, interest in parental development has not been lacking among lay persons and among professionals who transact with children and their families on a regular basis. Perhaps some of the surprising lack of empirical data on these issues has been related to the only recent interest of social scientists in lifespan development (e.g., Baltes, 1998), adult development (e.g., Levinson, 1978), and parenting (e.g., Collins et al., 1995, 2000). Nonetheless, there has been a proliferation of how-to books (e.g., Eisenberg, Murkoff, and Hathaway, 1984, 1989, 1994; Glenn and Nelson, 1988; Nagel, 1998; Unell and Wyckoff, 2000) and Internet websites (e.g., www.ParentStages.com) aimed at facilitating parental development. However, given the current state of theory and research in the area, such materials need to be reviewed cautiously by parents and professionals alike. It is hoped that this review will take one small step toward encouraging researchers to conduct additional systematic research on these and related problems.

REFERENCES

Ainsworth, M. D., and Wittig, B. A. (1969). Attachment and exploratory behavior of one-year-old children in a strange situation. In B. M. Foss (Ed.), *Determinants of infant behavior* (Vol. 4, pp. 111–136). London: Methuen.

Aldous, J. (1978). *Family careers: Developmental change in families.* New York: Wiley.

Ambert, A. (1992). *The effect of children on parents.* Binghamton, NY: Haworth.

Anthony, E. J., and Benedek, T. (Eds.). (1970). *Parenthood: Its psychology and psychopathology.* Boston: Little, Brown.

Antonucci, T. C., and Mikus, K. (1988). The power of parenthood: Personality and attitudinal changes during the transition to parenthood. In G. Y. Michaels and W. A. Goldberg (Eds.), *Transition to parenthood: Current theory and research* (pp. 62–84). New York: Cambridge University Press.

Azar, S. (1986). A framework for understanding child maltreatment: An integration of cognitive behavioural and developmental perspectives. *Canadian Journal of Behavioral Science, 18,* 304–355.

Azar, S. (1991, June). *The determinants of "maladaptive" parenting: Validation of a social cognitive model.* Paper presented at the New Directions in Child and Family Research: Shaping Head Start in the Nineties Conference, Arlington, VA.

Baltes, P. B. (1998). Theoretical propositions of life-span developmental psychology: On the dynamics between growth and decline. In M. P. Lawton and T. A. Salthouse (Eds.), *Essential papers on the psychology of aging* (pp. 86–123). New York: New York University Press.

Bell, R. Q. (1979). Parent, child, and reciprocal influences. *American Psychologist, 34,* 821–826.

Belsky, J. (1978). Three theoretical models of child abuse: A critical review. *International Journal of Child Abuse and Neglect, 2,* 37–49.

Belsky, J. (1984). The determinants of parenting: A process model. *Child Development, 55,* 83–96.

Belsky, J., and Pensky, E. (1988). Marital change across the transition to parenthood. *Marriage and Family Review, 12,* 133–156.

Benedek, T. (1959). Parenthood as a developmental phase: A contribution to the libido theory. *Journal of the American Psychoanalytic Association, 7,* 389–417.

Benedek, T. (1970). The family as a psychological field. In E. J. Anthony and T. Benedek (Eds.), *Parenthood: Its psychology and psychopathology* (pp. 109–136). Boston: Little, Brown.

Berger, K. S. (1994). *The developing person through the life span* (3rd ed.). New York: Worth.

Bibring, G. L., Dwyer, T. F., and Valenstein, A. F. (1961). A study of the psychological processes in pregnancy and of the earliest mother–child relationship. *Psychoanalytic Study of the Child, 16,* 9–24.

Bronfenbrenner, U. (1986). Ecology of the family as a context for human development: Research perspectives. *Developmental Psychology, 22,* 723–742.

Buchholz, E. S. (2000). Parenthood as a developmental stage. In L. Balter (Ed.), *Parenthood in America: An encyclopedia* (Vol. 2, pp. 440–442). Boulder: ABC-CLIO.

Chodorow, N. (1978). *The reproduction of mothering: Psychoanalysis and the sociology of gender.* Berkeley: University of California Press.

Clark, W. (2001). *Transition to parenthood: The experience and action of first-time parents.* Unpublished doctoral dissertation. Clark University, Worcester, MA.

Collins, W. A., Harris, M. L., and Susman, A. (1995). Parenting during middle childhood. In M. Bornstein (Ed.), *Handbook of parenting: Vol. 1. Children and parenting* (pp. 65–89). Mahwah, NJ: Lawrence Erlbaum Associates.

Collins, W. A., Maccoby, E. E., Steinberg, L., Hetherington, E. M., and Bornstein, M. H. (2000). Contemporary research on parenting: The case for nature and nurture. *American Psychologist, 55*(2), 1–15.

Coltrera, D. (1978). *Experiential aspects of the transition to parenthood.* Master's thesis proposal, Clark University, Worcester, MA.

Cook, S. (1979). *Parental conceptions of children and child-rearing: A study of rural Maine parents.* Unpublished master's thesis, Tufts University, Boston, MA.

Cowan, C. P., and Cowan, P. A. (1992). *When partners become parents.* New York: Basic Books.

Cowan, P. A., and Cowan, C. P. (1988). Changes in marriage during the transition to parenthood: Must we blame the baby? In G. Y. Michaels and W. A. Goldberg (Eds.), *The transition to parenthood: Current theory and research* (pp. 114–154). New York: Cambridge University Press.

Cowan, P. A., and Hetherington, M. (Eds.). (1991). *Family transitions.* Hillsdale, NJ: Lawrence Erlbaum Associates.

Dandonoli, P. P., Demick, J., and Wapner, S. (1990). Physical arrangement and age as determinants of environmental representation. *Children's Environments Quarterly, 7*(1), 28–38.

Demick, J. (1993). Adaptation of marital couples to open and closed adoption: A preliminary investigation. In J. Demick, K. Bursik, and R. DiBiase (Eds.), *Parental development* (pp. 175–201). Hillsdale, NJ: Lawrence Erlbaum Associates.

Demick, J. (1996). Life transitions as a paradigm for the study of adult development. In M. L. Commons, J. Demick, and C. Goldberg (Eds.), *Clinical approaches to adult development* (pp. 115–144). Norwood, NJ: Ablex.

Demick, J. (1999). Parental development: Problem, theory, method, and practice. In R. L. Mosher, D. J. Youngman, and J. M. Day (Eds.), *Human development across the life span: Educational and psychological applications* (pp. 177–199). Westport, CT: Praeger.

Demick, J. (2000a). In vitro fertilization. In L. Balter (Ed.), *Parenting in America: An encyclopedia* (Vol. 1, pp. 314–316). Boulder: ABC-CLIO.

Demick, J. (2000b). Infertility. In L. Balter (Ed.), *Parenting in America: An encyclopedia* (Vol. 1, pp. 325–326). Boulder: ABC-CLIO.

Demick, J. (2000c). Stages of parental development. In L. Balter (Ed.), *Parenting in America: An encyclopedia* (Vol. 2, pp. 436–438). Boulder: ABC-CLIO.

Demick, J. (2000d). Transition to parenthood. In L. Balter (Ed.), *Parenting in America: An encyclopedia* (Vol. 2, pp. 438–440). Boulder: ABC-CLIO.

Demick, J. (in press). "Roots that clutch": What adoption and foster care can tell us about adult development. In J. Demick and C. Andreoletti (Eds.), *Handbook of adult development.* New York: Kluwer Academic/Plenum.

Demick, J., and Azar, S. (2001). *A social cognitive-affective approach to adoption disruption.* Grant proposal submitted to the National Institute of Mental Health, Washington, DC.

Demick, J., Bursik, K., and DiBiase, R. (Eds.). (1993). *Parental development.* Hillsdale, NJ: Lawrence Erlbaum Associates.

Demick, J., and Harkins, D. (1999). Cognitive style and driving skills in adulthood: Implications for licensing of older adults. *International Association of Traffic Science and Safety (IATSS) Research, 23*(1), 1–16.

Demick, J., Hoffman, A., and Wapner, S. (1985). Residential context and environmental change as determinants of urban experience. *Children's Environments Quarterly, 5*(3), 54–62.

Demick, J., Inoue, W., Wapner, S., Ishii, S., Minami, H., Nishiyama, S., and Yamamoto, T. (1992). Cultural differences in impact of governmental legislation: Automobile safety belt usage. *Journal of Cross-Cultural Psychology, 23*, 468–487.

Demick, J., Ishii, S., and Inoue, W. (1997). Body and self experience: Japan versus USA. In S. Wapner, J. Demick, T. Yamamoto, and T. Takahashi (Eds.), *Handbook of Japan–United States environment–behavior research: Toward a transactional approach* (pp. 83–99). New York: Plenum.

Demick, J., and Wapner, S. (1980). Effects of environmental relocation upon members of a psychiatric therapeutic community. *Journal of Abnormal Psychology, 89*, 444–452.

Demick, J., and Wapner, S. (1988a). Children-in-environments: Physical, interpersonal, and sociocultural aspects. *Children's Environments Quarterly, 5*(3), 54–62.

Demick, J., and Wapner, S. (1988b). Open and closed adoption: A developmental conceptualization. *Family Process, 27*, 229–249.

Demick, J., and Wapner, S. (1990). Role of psychological science in promoting environmental quality. *American Psychologist, 45*, 631–632.

Demick, J., and Wapner, S. (1992). Transition to parenthood: Developmental changes in experience and action. In T. Yamamoto and S. Wapner (Eds.), *Developmental psychology of life transitions* (pp. 243–265). Tokyo: Kyodo Shuppan.

Deutsch, H. (1945). *The psychology of women: A psychoanalytic interpretation: Vol. 2. Motherhood.* New York: Grune and Stratton.

Duvall, E. M. (1946). Conceptions of parenthood. *American Journal of Sociology, 52*, 193–203.

Duvall, E. M. (1962). *Marriage and family development* (2nd ed.). Philadelphia: Lippincott.

Eisenberg, A., Murkoff, H. E., and Hathaway, S. E. (1984). *What to expect when you're expecting.* New York: Workman.

Eisenberg, A., Murkoff, H. E., and Hathaway, S. E. (1989). *What to expect the first year.* New York: Workman.

Eisenberg, A., Murkoff, H. E., and Hathaway, S. E. (1994). *What to expect: The toddler years.* New York: Workman.

Eisenberg, N., Fabes, R. A., Shepard, S. A., Murphy, B. C., Guthrie, I. K., Jones, S., Friedman, J., Poulin, R., and Maszk, P. (1997). Contemporaneous and longitudinal prediction of children's social functioning from regulation and emotionality. *Child Development, 68*, 642–664.

Emmerich, W. (1969). The parental role: A functional–cognitive approach. *Monographs of the Society for Research in Child Development, 34*, 1–71.

Erikson, E. H. (1950). *Childhood and society* (2nd ed.). New York: Norton.

Erikson, E. H. (1968). *Identity: Youth and crisis.* New York: Norton.

Erikson, E. H. (1982). *The life cycle completed.* New York: Norton.

Fedele, N. M., Golding, E. R., Grossman, F. K., and Pollack, W. S. (1988). Psychological issues in adjustment to first parenthood. In G. Y. Michaels and W. A. Goldberg (Eds.), *The transition to parenthood: Current theory and research* (pp. 85–113). Cambridge, England: Cambridge University Press.

Feldman, S. S., Biringen, Z. C., and Nash, S. C. (1981). Fluctuations of sex-related self-attributions as a function of stage of family life cycle. *Developmental Psychology, 17,* 24–35.

Fiese, B. H., Hooker, K. A., Kotary, L., Schwagler, J., and Rimmer, M. (1995). Family stories in the early stages of parenthood. *Journal of Marriage and the Family, 57,* 763–770.

Flavell, J. H. (1970). Cognitive changes in adulthood. In L. R. Goulet and P. B. Baltes (Eds.), *Life-span developmental psychology: Research and theory* (pp. 247–253). New York: Academic.

Flick, L. H. (1985, December). *The developmental nature of parental awareness in adolescent mothers.* Paper presented at the annual conference of the American Nurses Association, San Diego, CA.

Flick, L. H., and McSweeney, M. (1985, November). *Parental awareness: A social cognitive explanation of adolescent mother–child interaction.* Paper presented at the annual meeting of the American Public Health Association, Washington, DC.

Freud, S. (1935). *A general introduction to psychoanalysis* (Joan Riviare, Trans.). New York: Modern Library.

Freud, S. (1938). *The basic writings of Sigmund Freud* (A. A. Brill, Ed. and Trans.). New York: Modern Library.

Freud, S. (1963). *Three case histories.* New York: Collier. (Original work published 1918).

Galinsky, E. (1981). *Between generations: The six stages of parenthood.* New York: Berkeley.

Gardner, H. (1982). *Developmental psychology* (2nd ed.). Glenview, IL: Scott, Foresman, and Company.

Glenn, H. S., and Nelson, J. (1988). *Raising self-reliant children in a self-indulgent world.* Rocklin, CA: Prima.

Golombok, S. (1999). New family forms: Children raised in solo mother families, lesbian mother families, and in families created by assisted reproduction. In L. Balter and C. S. Tamis-LeMonda (Eds.), *Child psychology: A handbook of contemporary issues* (pp. 429–446). Philadelphia, PA: Taylor & Francis.

Gould, R. L. (1972). The phases of adult life: A study in developmental psychology. *American Journal of Psychiatry, 129,* 521–531.

Group for the Advancement of Psychiatry. (1975). *Joys and sorrows of parenthood.* New York: Scribner.

Gutmann, D. (1975). Parenthood: A key to the comparative study of the life cycle. In N. Datan and L. H. Ginsberg (Eds.), *Life span developmental psychology: Normative life crises* (pp. 167–184). New York: Academic.

Harkins, E. B. (1978). Effects of empty nest transition on self-report of psychological and physical well-being. *Journal of Marriage and the Family, 40,* 549–556.

Havighurst, R. (1953). *Human development and education.* New York: Longsmans, Green.

Healy, S., Azar, S., and Demick, J. (2001). *Do adoptive and biological parents differ in their attributions of children's behavior?* Manuscript in preparation.

Heinicke, C. M. (1984). Impact of pre-birth parent personality and marital functioning on family development: A framework and suggestions for further study. *Developmental Psychology, 20,* 1044–1053.

Heinicke, C. M. (1990). Towards generic principles of treating parents and children: Integrating psychotherapy with the school-aged child and early family intervention. *Journal of Consulting and Clinical Psychology, 58,* 713–719.

Hill, R., and Mattessich, P. (1979). Family development theory and life-span development. In P. B. Baltes and O. G. Brim (Eds.), *Life-span development and behavior* (Vol. 2, pp. 161–204). New York: Academic.

Hoffman, L. W., and Hoffman, M. L. (1973). The value of children to parents. In J. T. Fawcett (Ed.), *Psychological perspectives on population* (pp. 19–76). New York: Basic Books.

Holden, G. W., and Ritchie, K. L. (1988). Child rearing and the dialectics of parental intelligence. In J. Valsiner (Ed.), *Child development within culturally structured environments: Vol. 1. Parental cognition and adult-child interaction* (pp. 30–59). Norwood, NJ: Ablex.

Jaffe, M. L. (1991). *Understanding parenting.* New York: Brown.

Kaplan, B. (1966). The study of language in psychiatry. In S. Arieti (Ed.), *American handbook of psychiatry* (Vol. 3, pp. 659–668). New York: Basic Books.

Kaplan, B. (1983). A trio of trials. In R. Lerner (Ed.), *Developmental psychology: Historical and philosophical aspects* (pp. 185–228). Hillsdale, NJ: Lawrence Erlbaum Associates.

Kirk, D. H. (1964). *Shared fate.* New York: Free Press.

Kohlberg., L. (1969). Stage and sequence: The cognitive-developmental approach to socialization. In D. A. Goslin (Ed.), *Handbook of socialization theory and research* (pp. 347–408). Chicago: Rand McNally.

Kohlberg. L. (1981). *The philosophy of moral development.* New York: Harper & Row.

Krasnow, I. (1997). *Surrendering to motherhood.* New York: Hyperion.

Lauer, R. H., and Lauer, J. C. (1991). *Marriage and family: The quest for intimacy.* Dubuque, IA: Brown.

Leifer, M. (1980). *Psychological effects of motherhood: A study of first pregnancy.* New York: Praeger.

LeMasters, E. E. (1965). Parenthood as crisis. *Marriage and Family Living, 19,* 352–355.

Levinson, D. J. (1978). *The seasons of a man's life.* New York: Ballentine Books.

Levinson, D. J. (1980). Toward a conception of the adult life course. In N. J. Smesler and E. H. Erikson (Eds.), *Themes of work and love in adulthood* (pp. 265–290). Cambridge, MA: Harvard University Press.

Levinson, D. J. (1986). A conception of adult development. *American Psychologist, 41,* 3–13.

Levinson, D. J. (1990). A theory of life structure development in adulthood. In C. N. Alexander and E. J. Langer (Eds.), *Higher stages of human development* (pp. 35–34). New York: Oxford University Press.

Levinson, D. J. (1996). *The seasons of a woman's life.* New York: Knopf.

Loevinger, J. (1976). *Ego development: Conceptions and theories.* San Francisco: Jossey-Bass.

Machover, K. (1949). *Personality projection in the drawing of the human figure.* Springfield, IL: Thomas.

Mahler, M. S., Pine, F., and Bergman, A. (1970). The mother's reaction to her toddler's drive for individuation. In E. J. Anthony and T. Benedek (Eds.), *Parenthood: Its psychology and psychopathology* (pp. 257–274). Boston: Little, Brown.

Mahler, M. S., Pine, F., and Bergman, A. (1975). *The psychological birth of the human infant: Symbiosis and individuation.* New York: Basic Books.

McAdams, D. P., de St. Aubin, E., and Logan, R. L. (1993). Generativity among young, midlife, and older adults. *Psychology and Aging, 8,* 221–230.

McKenry, P. C., and Price, S. J. (Eds.). (2000). *Families and change: Coping with stressful events and transitions* (2nd ed.). Thousand Oaks, CA: Sage.

McLoyd, V. C., Cauce, A. M., Takeuchi, D., and Wilson, L. (2001). Marital processes and parental socialization in families of color: A decade review of research. In R. M. Milardo (Ed.), *Understanding families into the new millennium: A decade in review* (pp. 289–332). Minneapolis, MN: National Council on Family Relations.

Melito, R. (1985a). Adaptation in family systems: A developmental perspective. *Family Process, 24,* 89–100.

Melito, R. (1985b). Combining individual psychodynamics with structural family therapy. *Journal of Marital and Family Therapy, 14,* 29–43.

Michaels, G. Y., and Goldberg, W. A. (Eds.). (1988). *Transition to parenthood: Current theory and research.* New York: Cambridge University Press.

Milardo, R. M. (Ed.). (2001). *Understanding families into the new millennium: A decade in review.* Minneapolis, MN: National Council on Family Relations.

Nagel, G. (1998). *The Tao of parenting.* New York: Plume.

Newberger, C. M. (1977). *Parental conceptions of children and childrearing: A structural–developmental analysis.* Unpublished doctoral dissertation, Harvard University, Cambridge, MA.

Newberger, C. M. (1980). The cognitive structure of parenthood: Designing a descriptive measure. In R. L. Selman and R. Yando (Eds.), *Clinical–developmental psychology: New directions for child development, 7,* pp. 45–67. San Francisco: Jossey-Bass.

Newberger, C. M. (1987). Time, place, and parental awareness: A cognitive–developmental perspective on family adaptation and parental care. In J. B. Lancaster and R. J. Gelles (Eds.), *Child abuse and neglect: Biosocial dimensions* (pp. 233–251). New York: Aldine de Gruyter.

Newberger, C. M., and Cook, S. J. (1983). Parental awareness and child abuse: A cognitive–developmental analysis of urban and rural samples. *American Journal of Orthopsychiatry, 53,* 512–524.

Newberger, C. M., and White, K. M. (1989). Cognitive foundations for parental care. In D. Cicchetti and V. Carlson (Eds.), *Child maltreatment: Theory and research on the causes and consequences of child abuse and neglect* (pp. 303–316). New York: Cambridge University Press.

Patterson, C. J. (2001). Family relationships of lesbians and gay men. In R. M. Milardo (Ed.), *Understanding families into the new millennium: A decade in review* (pp. 271–288). Minneapolis, MN: National Council on Family Relations.

Pavao, J. M. (1998). *The family of adoption.* Boston: Beacon.

Piaget, J. (1952a). *The child's conception of number.* London: Routledge and Kegan Paul.

Piaget, J. (1952b). *The origins of intelligence in children* (Margaret Cook, Trans.). New York: International Universities Press.

Piaget, J. (1970a). *The child's conception of movement and speed* (G. E. T. Holloway and M. J. Mackenzie, Trans.). New York: Basic Books.

Piaget, J. (1970b). *The child's conception of time* (A. J. Pomerans, Trans.). New York: Basic Books.

Reber, A. S. (1995). *Dictionary of psychology* (2nd ed.). New York: Penguin.

Riegel, K. (1975). Adult life crises: A dialectical interpretation of development. In N. Datan and L. H. Ginsberg (Eds.), *Life-span developmental psychology: Normative life crises* (pp. 99–128). New York: Academic.

Rosenberg, E. B. (1992). *The adoption life cycle: The children and their families through the years.* New York: Free Press.

Rossi, A. S. (1971). The transition to parenthood. In A. S. Skolnick and J. H. Skolnick (Eds.), *Family in transition* (pp. 332–336). Boston: Little, Brown.

Sameroff, A. J. (1975a). Early influences on development: Fact or fancy? *Merill-Palmer Quarterly, 21,* 267–294.

Sameroff, A. J. (1975b, July). *The mother's construction of the child.* Paper presented at the meeting of the International Society of Behavioral Development, Guilford, England.

Sameroff, A. J. (1975c). Transactional models in early social relations. *Human Development, 18,* 65–79.

Sameroff, A. J., and Feil, L. A. (1985). Parental concepts of development. In I. E. Sigel (Ed.), *Parental belief systems: The psychological consequences for children* (pp. 83–105). Hillsdale, NJ: Lawrence Erlbaum Associates.

Sandy, L. (1982). *Teaching child development principles to parents: A cognitive–developmental approach.* Unpublished doctoral dissertation, Boston University, Boston, MA.

Schoen, E. (1995). *Growing with your child: Reflections on parental development.* New York: Doubleday.

Schouela, D. A., Steinberg, L. M., Leveton, L. B., and Wapner, S. (1980). Development of the cognitive organization of an environment. *Canadian Journal of Behavioural Science, 12*, 1–16.

Selman, R. L. (1980). *The growth of interpersonal understanding: Developmental and clinical analyses.* Orlando, FL: Academic.

Sheehy, G. (1976). *Passages: Predictable crises of adult life.* New York: Dutton.

Sheehy, G. (1995). *New passages: Mapping your life across time.* New York: Ballentine.

Silverstein, D., and Demick, J. (1994). Toward an organizational-relational model of open adoption. *Family Process, 33*, 111–124.

Sirignano, S., and Lachman, M. (1985). Personality change during the transition to parenthood: The role of perceived infant temperament. *Developmental Psychology, 21*, 558–567.

Sullivan, P. (1998, June). Empty nest syndrome: Starting a new phase of life. *Our Children: The National PTA Magazine, 23*(9), 32–33.

Suwalsky, J. T. D., and Bornstein, M. H. (2000). Adoptive family. In L. Balter (Ed.), *Parenthood in American: An encyclopedia* (pp. 20–22). Denver, CO: ABC-CLIO.

Teachman, J. D., Tedrow, L. M., and Crowder, K. D. (2001). The changing demography of America's families. In R. M. Milardo (Ed.), *Understanding families into the new millennium: A decade in review* (pp. 453–465). Minneapolis, MN: National Council on Family Relations.

Thomas, R. (1996). Reflective dialogue parent education design. *Family Relations, 45*, 189–201.

Toshima, T., Demick, J., Miyatani, M., Ishii, S., and Wapner, S. (1996). Cross-cultural differences in processes underlying sequential cognitive activity. *Japanese Psychological Research, 38*, 90–96.

Unell, B. C., and Wyckoff, J. L. (2000). *The eight seasons of parenthood: How the stages of parenting constantly reshape our adult identities.* New York: Random House.

Wapner, S. (1978). Some critical person-in-environment transitions. *Hiroshima Forum for Psychology, 5*, 3–20.

Wapner, S. (1993). Parental development: A holistic, developmental, systems-oriented perspective. In J. Demick, K. Bursik, and R. DiBiase (Eds.), *Parental development* (pp. 3–37). Hillsdale, NJ: Lawrence Erlbaum Associates.

Wapner, S., and Demick, J. (Eds.). (1991). *Field dependence–independence: Cognitive style across the life span.* Hillsdale, NJ: Lawrence Erlbaum Associates.

Wapner, S., and Demick, J. (1992). The organismic–developmental, systems approach to the study of critical person-in-environment transitions through the life span. In T. Yamamoto and S. Wapner (Eds.), *Developmental psychology of life transitions* (pp. 25–49). Tokyo: Kyodo Shuppan.

Wapner, S., and Demick, J. (1998). Developmental analysis: A holistic, developmental, systems-oriented perspective. In W. Damon (Series Ed.) and R. M. Lerner (Vol. Ed.), *Handbook of child psychology: Vol. 1. Theoretical models of human development* (5th ed., pp. 761–805). New York: Wiley.

Wapner, S., and Demick, J. (1999). Developmental theory and clinical practice: A holistic, developmental, systems-oriented approach. In W. K. Silverman and T. H. Ollendick (Eds.), *Developmental issues in the clinical treatment of children* (pp. 3–30). Boston: Allyn and Bacon.

Wapner, S., and Demick, J. (2000). Person-in-environment psychology: A holistic, developmental, systems-oriented perspective. In W. B. Walsh, K. H. Craik, and R. H. Price (Eds.), *Person–environment psychology: New directions and perspectives* (2nd ed., pp. 25–60). Mahwah, NJ: Lawrence Erlbaum Associates.

Wapner, S., and Demick, J. (in press-a). Adult development: The holistic, developmental, systems-oriented perspective. In J. Demick and C. Andreoletti (Eds.), *Handbook of adult development.* New York: Kluwer Academic/Plenum.

Wapner, S., and Demick, J. (in press-b). Critical person-in-environments across the life span: A holistic, developmental, systems-oriented program of research. In J. Valsiner (Ed.), *Differentiation and integration of a developmentalist: Heinz Werner's ideas in Europe and America.* New York: Kluwer Academic/Plenum.

Wapner, S., and Demick, J. (in press-c). The increasing contexts of context: Toward a more comprehensive study of environment–behavior relations. In R. B. Bechtel and A. Churchman (Eds.), *The new environmental psychology handbook.* New York: Wiley.

Wapner, S., Demick, J., and Redondo, J. P. (1990). Cherished possessions and adaptation of older people to nursing homes. *International Journal on Aging and Human Development, 31*, 299–315.

Watkins, M. (1977). *A phenomenological approach to organismic-developmental research.* Unpublished manuscript, Clark University, Worcester, MA.

Werner, H. (1957). *Comparative psychology of mental development.* New York: International Universities Press. (Rev. ed., originally published 1940)

Werner, H., and Kaplan, B. (1956). The developmental approach to cognition: Its relevance to the psychological interpretation of anthropological and ethnolinguistic data. *American Anthropologist, 58*, 866–880.

Werner, H., and Kaplan, B. (1963). *Symbol formation.* New York: Wiley.

14

Personality and Parenting

Jay Belsky
Birkbeck University of London
Naomi Barends
The Pennsylvania State University

INTRODUCTION

It is not uncommon for individuals to think of other people they know well or have recently met as being nasty or nice, conventional or open-minded, careful or sloppy, timid or adventurous. In point of fact, individual differences in personality manifest themselves in a wide range of behaviors and behavioral domains. These include, among other things, social relationships, including the parent–child relationship. Yet when it comes to thinking about mothers and fathers and the manner in which they parent, it seems that it is the exception rather than the rule to consider their personalities. Developmentalists seem more inclined, at least since the ecological revolution (Bronfenbrenner, 1979), to think in terms of parents' contexts—whether they are rich or poor, well or poorly educated, lacking or rich in social support, participating in satisfying work or experiencing unemployment. Perhaps this is because many believe that personalities are givens; they are not very subject to change. As a result, scholars, in particular those concerned with improving the lives of children and families, often focus on those aspects of children's experiences that they presume can be modified so as to promote healthy psychological and behavioral development.

What this point of view fails to acknowledge is how widespread the influence of parents' personalities may be, perhaps shaping not only maternal and paternal behavior, but the way in which adults function in these other contexts of their lives that many presume affect the way in which parents care for their offspring and, thereby, the child's development (Belsky, 1984). If this is the case, then personality may not only affect parenting directly, but indirectly as well. For example, it may influence the degree of social support a father secures or the occupational experiences that mothers have, which themselves can affect parenting. From this perspective, it should be clear why understanding personality is important to understanding parenting. It is for this reason that this chapter is devoted to exploring the relation between personality and parenting.

We begin by considering historical issues that have shaped the study of personality and parenting and then proceed to review issues central to the study of personality and parenting and the limited theory which guides this area of inquiry. With this foundation laid, we review empirical research before outlining future directions for research and drawing some conclusions.

HISTORICAL CONSIDERATIONS IN PERSONALITY AND PARENTING

Although until the past two decades there has been little empirical research into the relation between parental personality characteristics and their parenting behaviors, a review of the history of the field reveals some historical antecedents. In this section this historical context of work on personality and parenting is discussed, first by noting the earliest psychoanalytic writings on the topic, then by considering changes over the twentieth century in how personality was viewed in the field of psychology more generally, and, finally, by examining a most recent conceptualization of personality which goes by the name the Big Five.

Psychoanalytic Perspectives

Early speculation on the relation between parent personality and parenting behavior came primarily from psychoanalytic theorists. The main concern of these psychoanalysts was to propose theories of the development of personality structure. Moreover, they sought to understand ways in which such development could go astray in early childhood and result in psychopathology. Drawing from clinical experience, a central tenet of many of these theories was that the parent's personality determined the nature of parenting and the parent–child relationship, and in turn child development.

Attention was focused largely on pathological aspects of parental character and ways in which these factors gave rise to child psychopathology. For example, Anna Freud (1955/1970) discussed mothers who rejected their children, sometimes due to psychosis but more often because of neurotic conflicts. She wrote, "[the mother's] behavior toward the child is understood best when viewed in terms of her own conflicts" (p. 382). Spitz (1965/1970), too, wrote about maternal rejection as well as permissive and hostile parenting behavior, arguing that "the mother's personality acts as the disease-provoking agent" (p. 504) in the parent–child relationship. Levy (1943) stated that maternal overprotection stemmed from a lack of parental affection in mothers' own childhoods, which shaped their personalities and, in turn, their own childrearing behavior. Winnicott (1948/1975) also emphasized problematic aspects of the parent's personality, asserting that "the child lives within the circle of the parent's personality and . . . this circle has pathological features" (p. 93).

As Holden and Buck (in Vol. 3 of this *Handbook*) note, the common theme among these psychoanalytic theorists was that if parents' emotional needs had not been met during the course of their own development, then these unresolved needs would be reflected in their parenting behavior. Conversely, it was assumed that if parents had adaptive and flexible personalities, they would behave toward their children in growth-promoting ways. There was, however, little focus on ways in which personality characteristics within the normative range of functioning might determine parenting.

Although psychoanalytic theorizing served to stimulate the study of personality and development, a significant problem with the psychoanalytic movement was the lack of rigorous research. Clinical experience and case studies were the primary mode of knowledge generation and hypothesis testing (Westen and Gabbard, 1999). This situation severely limited the extent to which psychoanalytic ideas could continue to influence the study of developmental processes, and indeed, the field of psychology as a whole. Psychoanalysts' writings regarding the impact of parent personality on parenting and child development may continue to serve as hypothesis-generating material today (Cohler and Paul, in Vol. 3 of this *Handbook*) but by themselves remain insufficient as evidence for such processes.

The Personality–Situation Debate

A second historical thread relevant to the study of parental personality as a determinant of parenting was the state of personality psychology throughout the twentieth century. It is often said that the field of personality psychology truly coalesced with the publication of Allport's canonical text in 1937, which attempted to define and systematize the study of personality (Winter and Barenbaum, 1999). Allport surveyed the existing definitions of personality and the methods for studying it, and he argued that traits were the fundamental units of study for personality. He defined traits as neuropsychic systems with dynamic or motivational properties.

Following Allport's seminal delineation of the parameters for the study of personality, during the 1940s and 1950s there was tremendous emphasis on measurement and identification of important personality traits through factor-analytic methods (Winter and Barenbaum, 1999). As yet, though, there was little application to the study of the determinants of parenting behavior. In the 1960s, however, early pioneers in the field of developmental psychology began to conduct research on the relation between parental personality characteristics, sometimes assessed prenatally, and parenting behavior. Caldwell and her colleagues (Caldwell et al., 1963; Caldwell and Hersher, 1964, cited in Ainsworth, 1973) found that "polymatric" mothers who shared the care of their infants with one or more mother figures were rated prenatally as more hostile, dominant, and dependent than "monomatric" mothers who did not share their babies' care. Thus, personality measured prenatally appeared to influence the selection of patterns of infant care. Moss and his colleagues found that mothers who in prenatal interviews emphasized the warm, personal, and rewarding aspects of a baby, who accepted the feminine role, who were in frequent positive interaction with their own fathers, and who displayed more animation in their voices, were more responsive to and stimulating of their 3-week-old infants (Moss, Ryder, and Robson, 1967; Robson, Pedersen, and Moss, 1969). Manheimer (1963; cited in Clausen, 1966) noted that medically attended accidents occurred more frequently among children whose mothers were dissatisfied with their lives and had poor impulse control than among children of more satisfied and controlled mothers. Moreover, in regard to personality characteristics of abusive parents, enough research had been conducted by the early 1970s that Spinetta and Rigler (1972) concluded that abusive parents tended to be more aggressive, impulsive, immature, self-centered, tense, and self-critical than nonabusive parents.

Despite this early interest in parental personality characteristics and their effects on parenting behavior, the study of these issues was interrupted by important shifts within the field of personality psychology. Specifically, in 1968 with his publication of the innocuous-sounding *Personality and Assessment*, Walter Mischel made a devastating critique of personality psychology, claiming that the usefulness of broad personality traits was seriously overstated. In his review of the research literature, Mischel argued that personality variables, typically measured by paper-and-pencil tests and questionnaires, accounted for very little of the variance in human behavior. He further contended that these trait measures did not show the cross-situational consistency that was inherent to the very idea of personality traits. Moreover, he claimed that trait measures typically correlated no higher than 0.30 with behavioral outcomes, indicating that they could explain only 9% of the variance in human behavior. In consequence, Mischel advocated a social psychological perspective in which behavior was explained through differences in situations, not individual differences in traits. He championed what became later known as social-cognitive theory (Winter and Barenbaum, 1999). Mischel's critique created serious confusion and doubt in the personality psychology field for some time. Importantly for the subject of personality as a determinant of parenting, this took personality research off the developmental stage at a time when developmental psychology, and especially sophisticated observational studies of parenting and parent–child relations, were coming into their own.

Nonetheless, personality researchers did recover from Mischel's critiques (see Baumeister, 1999; Caspi, 1998; MacAdams, 1997; Winter and Barenbaum, 1999, for reviews). Several authors suggested that the prediction of behavior by traits could be improved through the use of moderator variables, such as the salience of the trait for the individual (Bem and Allen, 1974) or self-monitoring (Snyder, 1983). That is, rather than simply determining whether a trait always exerted an influence on functioning, the context in which it might be manifest needed to be considered. One would expect extraversion, a trait having to do with the experience of positive emotions, to shape behavior at a party more so than at a funeral, for example.

Others, like Ozer (1985), proposed that in situations where researchers are interested in the percent of variance in common by two variables, the unsquared correlation is a better estimate of the proportion of shared variance than the squared correlation. Thus a 0.30 correlation would signify 30% of the variance. Funder and Ozer (1983) examined effect sizes for several classic experiments in social psychology, finding that they were quite similar in size to the "personality coefficients" that Mischel derided. Moreover, in a pair of compelling papers, Epstein (1979a, 1979b) demonstrated that the low correlations noted by Mischel resulted from predicting one-shot behaviors from broad trait scales as well as measurement error. With better measures and aggregating behaviors over time, Epstein demonstrated that it was possible to obtain higher correlations between personality variables and behavioral outcomes than Mischel implied was the case. Thus, through numerous rebuttals to Mischel's critique, personality proponents once again found their footing after a period of serious confusion. This movement eventually allowed the study of individual differences in personality to move forward again toward the end of the 1970s and early 1980s.

The Big Five

A major part of this new movement was a surge of interest in the Big Five taxonomy of personality dimensions. The Big Five traits are typically labeled (a) extraversion or surgency, which describes individuals who are talkative, assertive, and energetic; (b) agreeableness, describing those who are good-natured, cooperative, and trustful; (c) conscientiousness, for individuals who tend to be orderly, responsible, and dependable; (d) neuroticism versus emotional stability, describing a tendency to be easily distressed; and (e) openness to experience or intellect, describing people who are imaginative and independent minded. The Big Five factors were identified first by Tupes and Christal (1961), who found through factor analytic techniques that long lists of personality variables compiled by Cattell (1943, 1945) could be reduced to five broadband personality factors. This five-factor structure has since been replicated in diverse samples and across numerous raters such as self-reports, peers, and clinicians (John and Srivastava, 1999).

Despite the relatively early identification of the Big Five, it was not until the mid 1980s that research in this area began to dramatically increase, with many researchers replicating the factor structure and developing new measures (John and Srivastava, 1999). Importantly for the issue of personality as a determinant of parenting, this widespread excitement regarding the Big Five brought personality back to the attention of social developmentalists focusing on family processes. Simultaneously, important theoretical models explicitly proposing that parental personality traits shaped parenting behavior were advanced (Belsky, 1984; Belsky, Hertzog, and Rovine, 1986; Belsky and Vondra, 1989; Heinicke, 1984). These models, which will be discussed later, stimulated research interest by providing a framework for this area.

CENTRAL ISSUES IN PERSONALITY AND PARENTING

Two major issues are discussed with respect to the study of parental personality and parenting. First, the general nature of predicting from personality traits to a behavioral domain is discussed. Second, more specific methodological issues with regard to personality measurement for personality and parenting research are explained.

Traits and the Prediction of Behavior

Traits refer to consistent patterns of directly observable behavior, or internal thoughts and feelings that must be either inferred by others or reported by the individual (Allport, 1937; MacKinnon, 1944). Johnson (1997) emphasized that traits can refer to any of these three domains of thoughts, feelings, or behavior, noting that too often psychologists limit their conceptualization of personality to only outer or inner phenomena. Often the inner traits are presumed to be the causes of the outer traits, in that emotions and cognitions are purported to generate behavioral consistencies (Johnson, 1997). It should be noted, however, that this is only one aspect of the larger domain of personality. For example, Wiggins (1997) argued that the structure of traits may well reside in a pattern of social rules that are mirrored in the structure of interpersonal behavior rather than within individuals. Although a full explanation of the metapsychology of the personality field is beyond the scope of this chapter, it should be noted that there are multiple ways of conceptualizing personality, and this diversity may shape the focus that personality and parenting researchers choose.

Another important issue to consider is what traits are purported to predict. The situationist challenge to the trait concept, led by Mischel (1968), argued that the trait concept is flawed because traits did not significantly predict cross-situational behavior, and that any consistency in behavior across situations is a function of the social context, not individual personality characteristics. As Johnson (1997) summarizes, however, trait theorists have responded by pointing out that (1) individuals need to have the trait of being responsive to situations, if situations are to reliably control behavior, (2) individuals respond differently to the same situation, implying the influence of personality, (3) behavioral inconsistency does not rule out inner consistency, as people may not have the situational opportunity to express inner dispositions, (4) having a trait does not mean that one's reactions are identical in every situation, and (5) having a trait implies reacting fairly consistently to the same situation, not to different situations.

The last two points are particularly informative for the study of parental personality as a determinant of parenting. Researchers should not expect that parental personality measures necessarily will predict a substantial proportion of the variance for parenting behavior that is measured in a single observation. Rather, personality is most likely to predict childrearing behavior that is measured across multiple situations. Furthermore, these situations must be similar to each other. Personality traits are not necessarily purported to predict parenting behavior across disparate childrearing contexts. Consistent with an interactionist perspective, individual traits and situational components both influence behavior.

Personality Measurement

Another central issue for the study of parental personality characteristics as determinants of parenting behavior is the measurement of personality. With the exception of Heinicke's delineation of domains of parental personality (in Vol. 3 of this *Handbook*) that are salient for parenting and child development, much of the research that has been conducted in this area so far lacks a systematic approach to the measurement of personality (Barends and Belsky, 2000). Typically, investigators have chosen one or two aspects of adult psychological functioning, such as self-esteem, locus of control, perspective-taking skills, or emotional distress, and tested links to parenting behavior and child outcome (see review below). Although these studies are helpful in beginning to establish that aspects of parents' psychological functioning are relevant to parents' abilities to engage in growth-promoting childrearing, a more comprehensive approach to the measurement of personality is warranted. The field of personality has itself moved toward formulating systematic taxonomies for personality traits as opposed to investigating single variables, and the empirical and theoretical work done in this vein should be brought to bear on the study of parenting determinants.

What are the prominent frameworks within personality research? As noted earlier, the Big Five taxonomy is one of the most influential ones today. The Big Five factors of neuroticism, extraversion, openness, agreeableness, and conscientiousness are conceptualized as broadband constructs, with each having lower level components, and they are meant to be primarily descriptive of regularly occurring behavior rather than explanatory or focused on inferred dynamic processes (John and Srivastava, 1999). Numerous measures of the Big Five have been developed, with the ones most commonly used today including the NEO Personality Inventory—Revised and its short form (Costa and McCrae, 1992), Goldberg's (1992) Trait Descriptive Adjectives, the Big Five Inventory (John, Donahue, and Kentle, 1991), and the Jackson Personality Inventory, which has been reconfigured into the Big Five (Paunonen and Jackson, 1996). These instruments, like proponents of the Big Five personality factors, differ slightly in their labeling of the factors, but all are very similar in terms of actual item content and thus what they are measuring. The Big Five taxonomy has been used to predict important outcomes for adolescents including delinquency, childhood psychopathology, and school performance (John, Caspi, Robins, Moffitt, and Stouthamer-Loeber, 1994; Robins, John, and Caspi, 1994), as well as adult outcome, such as job performance (Mount, Barrick, and Stewart, 1998), adult psychopathology (Wiggins and Pincus, 1989), and other patterns of behavior (for reviews, see Graziano and Eisenberg, 1997; Hogan and Ones, 1997; Watson and Clark, 1997). Because of its ability to predict various domains of functioning across a range of ages, the Big Five model of personality is a good candidate for the study of parental personality correlates with parental behavior.

Other Measurement Approaches

There are other important ways of measuring personality to consider as well. A major alternative to the Big Five is the measurement methodology arising from the tradition of interpersonal approaches to personality, which developed independently of the Big Five tradition. The structural model of the basic interpersonal system is comprised of two orthogonal dimensions which, when crossed, define a circular space (i.e., circumplex). The first dimension is that of dominance versus submission, and the second nurturance/friendliness versus lack of nurturance/hostility (e.g., Kiesler, 1983). Variables thus appear in a continuous manner around the circle, so there can be any combination along the two axes of dominance and nurturance. The two components have been found to converge with the Big Five factors of extraversion and agreeableness, respectively (McCrae and Costa, 1989). However, as Wiggins (1982) has argued, the interpersonal circumplex allows more fine-grained distinctions than the Big Five, and researchers examining parental personality and parenting might consider this difference in choosing a system. Moreover, the literature on interpersonal approaches to personality also has a more established tradition of using the predictive power afforded by studying how configurations of personality traits relate to behavioral outcomes, as this conceptualization is inherent in the circumplex model. Commonly used measures from the interpersonal tradition include Wiggins' (1995) Interpersonal Adjective Scales, and Benjamin's (1974, 1984, 1996) Structural Analysis of Social Behavior. The latter model has different axes than the circumplex described earlier (autonomy and affiliation), includes three foci of behavior (actions toward others, reactions to others, and self-directed actions), and can be operationalized using both self-report forms as well as observer-based coding. Thus it allows for a very detailed analysis of personality and behavior focusing on interpersonal dynamics that might be useful within the study of parent personality as a determinant of childrearing behavior.

   Other approaches to personality assessment are techniques derived from psychoanalytic perspectives. As Westen and Gabbard (1999) noted, psychoanalytic theory, with its focus on unconscious processes, ambivalence in affective and motivational processes, and mental representation of others, offers windows into human experience that are often not captured by theories and methods that focus only what individuals can easily self-report. Although empirical techniques used by researchers from a contemporary psychoanalytic perspective are too numerous to be fully reviewed here (see Westen and Gabbard, 1999), two are noteworthy. Blatt and his colleagues (Blatt, Auerbach, and Levy, 1997; Blatt, Wein, Chevron, and Quinlan, 1979; Levy, Blatt, and Shaver, 1998) developed a scale for assessing dimensions of object representations (mental representations of others) from free-response descriptions of significant others. This coding system assesses dimensions including the cognitive or conceptual level of mental representations, as well as qualitative themes such as affection, malevolence, idealization, and ambivalence. Another system for assessing mental representations via free responses was developed by Westen and colleagues (Westen, 1990, 1991; Westen, Lohr, Silk, Gold, and Kerber, 1990), who have used projective stories and descriptions of salient interpersonal interactions as the basis for their assessments. For both of these systems, their open-ended and low face-valid nature allow for a better assessment of mental representations, which are partially unconscious. These techniques could usefully be applied to understanding parent personality in relation to actual parenting behavior. For example, parents might provide a general description of their child or other significant figure, or a description of a salient interaction with that person, and the complexity and quality of the mental representations indicated by the description may have relation to childrearing behavior.

In sum, most of the literature on parental personality as a determinant of parenting has thus far been insufficiently systematic in its measurement of personality. Given that personality psychology has developed a number of comprehensive techniques from a variety of theoretical perspectives, these methods would be usefully applied to the study of personality and parenting.

THEORY IN PERSONALITY AND PARENTING

Traditionally, personality theorists have argued that individuals' traits constitute the primary determinants of behavior. The focus was largely internal, having to do with individual differences in thoughts, feelings, motivations, and so forth, which were conceived as located within the person. This emphasis on phenomena within the person was held by both psychoanalysts and early personality theorists, and was one reason why the study of personality fell out of favor in the 1970s. The 1960s and 1970s were decades of sweeping cultural change at a social level, with radical new movements that embraced values quite discrepant to earlier generations. This experience of broad social change in Western culture brought about a new fascination within psychology with the influence of culture and environment on human behavior in the early 1970s (MacAdams, 1997). The earlier focus on the individual's personality as the determinant of behavior was abandoned by many researchers in favor of attention to situations and context as the primary cause of behavior. This perspective was most strongly advanced by Mischel (1968), as discussed earlier.

Within the ranks of developmental psychologists, Bronfenbrenner (1979, 1986) was the strongest advocate for the role of situation and context in explaining individual behavior. From an ecological framework, he emphasized that the environment has multiple dimensions that interact with each other to shape child development. Bronfenbrenner outlined four major levels of the environment: the microsystem, the mesosystem, the exosystem, and the macrosystem. The microsystem describes the aspects of the environment that directly influence the child, such as family, school, church, and neighborhood. The mesosystem refers to the systems of relationships among the child's microsystems, such as the relationship between the parents and the child's teacher. The exosystem refers to social settings that can affect the child, but in which the child does not directly participate. This would include such factors as local government, the school board, and the parents' employers. Lastly, the macrosystem involves the entire culture and subculture in which the child lives, which influence the child through social beliefs and traditions. Although Bronfenbrenner noted that children influence their environments, his major emphasis was on the role of context. Thus Bronfenbrenner largely left individual differences out of his ecological model for human development, including the role of parent personality in shaping child outcome.

Despite this swing within the field away from individual differences to the polar opposite of almost exclusively contextual models, the pendulum eventually moved back to the middle through the development of models that integrate both aspects. Personality eventually came to be seen not only as a product of the environment, but also as a simultaneous determinant of the environment. In regard to the area of personality and parenting, two major conceptual models have been advanced suggesting that parent personality is an important determinant of parenting behavior, which in turn shapes child development (Belsky, 1984; Heinicke, 1984). Each of these models will be reviewed in turn.

Belsky's Process Model

Belsky (1984) proposed a process model of the determinants of parenting, which was derived from empirical work on the causes of child abuse. Belsky (1984; Belsky, Hertzog, and Rovine, 1986; Belsky and Vondra, 1989) noted that child maltreatment has been explained by three general perspectives: (1) the psychiatric model, emphasizing the role of problematic childrearing history and parental personality characteristics, (2) the child effects model, arguing that difficult child characteristics may elicit abusive treatment from parents, and (3) the sociological model, recognizing that social conditions such as poverty and unemployment stress parents and increase the likelihood that they will abuse their children. From this research basis focused on maltreating parents, Belsky (1984) offered a general model for the determinants of parenting. He argued that parenting is multiply determined by three general sources of influence, including (a) the parent's personality, or psychological resources, (b) the child's individual characteristics, and (c) contextual sources of stress and support, including marital relations, occupational experience, and the social network. Each of these domains was said to directly influence childrearing quality, and through parenting, child development. Of the three broad factors, Belsky (1984) argued that parent personality is the most important determinant. Moreover, Belsky (1984) proposed that parent personality is in turn directly shaped by parents' developmental histories and that the contextual factors of work, marital relations, and social support have relations of reciprocal influence with parent personality. Individual psychological resources of the parents were posited to have considerable influence on child development because in order for parents to behave in sensitive and responsive ways, they need to possess sufficient psychological maturity so as to be able to take the perspective of others, control impulses, feel secure in their own lives, and be able to find ways to have their needs met. Mature personality characteristics are especially important for parenting because parents must continue to be nurturant and firm even in response to frustrating child behavior. Belsky's (1984) model has served as the conceptual basis for a growing literature on the determinants of parenting, which will be reviewed later.

Heinicke's Framework

A second model for the influence of parent personality on parenting behavior was proposed by Heinicke (1984), who focused on prebirth parental characteristics in combination with marital functioning and family supports as determinants of later parenting. Assessment of parent personality and marital quality before the birth of the first child was suggested in recognition of the fact that children's behavior may affect parents' personality characteristics and marital relations. Heinicke (1984; in Vol. 3 of this *Handbook*) proposed that there are three major aspects of parent personality functioning: parents' adaptation competence, capacity for positive sustained relationships, and self-development. The first quality, adaptation competence, refers to the parent's efficient, calm, persistent, and flexible approach to problem solving. If parents are able to cope well with life issues before the birth of their children, it is more likely that they will be able to competently handle the demands of parenting. The second factor, capacity for positive sustained relationships, describes the parent's empathy and positive mutuality expressed in an ongoing relationship. Heinicke suggested that this has been measured both by parents' coherence and positive experience in regard to their own childhood and by sensitivity and warmth in current relationships. It was posited that if parents are able to develop and maintain positive relationships with others before the birth of their child, it is more likely that they will also be able to be nurturant and sensitive in parenting when their child is young. The third aspect of parental personality that Heinicke proposed to be an important determinant of parenting was the parent's self-development. Self-development was said to describe parents' ability to establish autonomy in relation to others and feel confident in themselves. Parents who are able to maintain self-esteem and appropriately individuated relationships with others were thought to function better in the parenting sphere. Support for Heinicke's (1984) framework for the association of prenatal parent personality and subsequent parenting has been provided by Heinicke (in Vol. 3 of this *Handbook*), who presents a comprehensive review of studies linking prebirth parental functioning to later parental responsiveness and adaptive infant development.

MODERN RESEARCH IN PERSONALITY AND PARENTING

In the section dealing with historical considerations, we noted that the earliest theorizing about personality and parenting was based on psychoanaltyic concepts such as neurotic conflicts and ego defenses (Freud, 1955/1970; Levy, 1943; Spitz, 1965/1970) and that research was clinical in character, often based on one or a few case studies. When more methodologically rigorous research on personality and parenting was initiated in the 1960s, it proved to be short lived, as Mischel's critique undermined a focus on personality in psychological inquiry in general, not just developmental psychology. It was not until the late 1970s and especially into the 1980s that more and more research linking personality and parenting was reported. But as we have noted, the personality constructs which were the focus of inquiry were not particularly well conceptualized, especially in terms of a theory of, or framework for studying, personality. Essentially, developmental psychologists simply selected one or a few instruments from the large number available, often on the basis of quite limited theorizing, and examined linkages between psychological characteristics of parents and the manner in which they treated their offspring. In consequence, the relevant empirical literature is littered with a host of diverse personality and personality-related constructs that makes reviewing the database a challenge. This is especially so because there are few investigations that are devoted principally to the question of personality and parenting. Indeed, much of the evidence to be cited comes from more complex investigations in which one or more personality variables are included among a large set of predictors aimed at explaining individual differences in parenting behavior. In light of this situation, the review of empirical findings to follow is organized as follows. First, we consider evidence linking parenting and adult psychological maturity and well-being, broadly conceived. Thereafter, we examine literature that can be organized in terms of the Big Five personality traits. Then, in a third subsection we select from a variety of diverse personality/psychological constructs two to focus on— self esteem and locus of control—that do not easily fall into the previous two subsections. Finally, we move beyond work linking personality to parenting and consider several noteworthy longitudinal studies that have examined longitudinal and even cross-generational linkages between personality, parenting, and child development. We will see, as we proceed through this entire review, that most research on personality and parenting focuses on mothers rather than fathers, and more often than not, mothers of infants rather than of older children. Most also focuses on American parents, and those of European American ancestry. Where studies diverge from this norm—by considering fathers or African Americans or parents from outside the United States—that will be indicated explicitly.

Psychological Maturity and Well-Being

If there is one core theoretical proposition that guides research on personality and parenting it is that psychologically healthier or more psychologically mature parents should care for their children in a more sensitive, responsive, authoritative (as opposed to authoritarian or permissive), and child-centered manner, whereas the opposite should be true of less psychological healthy or mature parents. This proposition itself is implicitly based on the premise that to parent in such a skilled and growth-promoting manner one needs to be able to decenter from the self, consider the world from the child's perspective, regulate one's emotions, especially negative affect, and thus be tolerant and patient with children rather than impulsive and excessively controlling or neglectful and detached (Belsky, 1984;

Heath, 1976). One challenge, of course, to testing such notions involves operationalizing the core psychological construct in question—psychological health or maturity. As will become apparent, a variety of strategies have been adopted. We begin by considering those that have relied on clinical interviews and an often complex coding system to assess psychological maturity before proceeding to consider approaches that have simply measured a variety of discrete psychological attributes and combined them in some manner considered, typically on an a priori basis, to reflect greater psychological health. To be noted at the outset is that very few of the investigations to be cited take into consideration the possibility that a parent's age may be related to psychological maturity or well-being when evaluating the effect of personality on parenting.

One approach that several teams of investigators have used is theoretically anchored in Loevinger's (1979; Hauser, 1976) theory of ego development, which conceptualizes individuals as varying along a series of nine sequential stages in the degree to which they are capable of conceptualizing themselves in relation to the world. At the most immature end of the framework is the "impulsive phase" where one's view of the world is concrete and egocentric, and at the opposite, most mature end are the "autonomous" and "integrated" phases, where one appreciates mutual interdependence as well as the need for autonomy, and begins to reconcile inner conflict. Using a sentence-completion methodology developed by Loevinger (1979), Levine, Garcia-Coll, and Oh (1984) found, in a study of adolescent and adult mothers of 8-month-old infants, that those women evincing greater psychological maturity within this theoretical and measurement scheme expressed more positive affect while interacting with their babies and spent greater amounts of time in mutual gaze during face-to-face interaction.

A second team of investigators who approached the measurement of psychological maturity from the same vantage point carried out a study of psychiatrically hospitalized and normal adolescents and their parents to determine whether parental ego development might influence parental verbal interaction and, thereby, the ego development of adolescent children. Consistent with theoretical expectations, Hauser, Powers, Noam, and Jacobson (1984) found that parental ego development predicted more supportive and encouraging—that is, "enabling" rather than "constraining"—remarks by both parent and teenager.

A team of Dutch investigators developed a measure to assess a parent's perspective taking that appears conceptually quite consonant with Loevinger's ego-development framework. On the basis of an in-depth interview about their children, Dekovic and Gerris (1992) characterized parents' psychological status in terms of one of four stages of perspective taking: egoistic, conventional, subjective child orientation, and mutual system. In an investigation of 113, two-parent families with a child between 6 and 11 years of age, they reported that more mature perspective taking was related to less restrictive control, more positive control, and more support being observed during a family puzzle-completion task in the case of mothers and fathers alike. Consistent with these findings, which are themselves quite similar to those reported above regarding "enabling" versus "constraining" verbal behavior on the part of parents, these Dutch investigators also found that the more immature parents' perspective taking, the more they endorsed authoritarian attitudes and values about childrearing. These findings were extended by Gerris, DeKovic, and Janssens (1997), who found, using the same sample, that more mature perspective taking fostered more child-oriented parenting and less authoritarian parental behavior (e.g., harsh discipline).

Also using a semistructured interview, this time to measure life adaptation, Grossman, Pollack, and Golding (1988) found that greater psychological maturity assessed prenatally predicted more warm and responsive fathering when children were 3 to 5 years of age. In this instance, life adaptation reflected the degree to which fathers successfully coped with major tasks in adulthood, including work and adulthood, managed relations with their own parents, and were free from debilitating physical and psychological symptoms. Similarly, Heinicke (1984) found that a prenatal interview designed to measure ego strength or the capacity to cope with the challenges of life predicted more positively emotional and responsive mothering when infants were 6 and 12 months of age.

One of the most sophisticated investigations which examined psychological maturity using a clinical interview was carried out by Benn (1985, 1986) in a study of low-risk, middle-income mothers, in which "psychological integration" was the focus of measurement. In the researcher's own words, psychological integration reflects the extent to which women are "warm and secure in their sense of self ... emotionally balanced and satisfied with themselves ... and enjoy intimacy with those important to them" (Benn, 1985, p.12). Not only did it prove to be the case, as expected, that infants of more psychologically integrated mothers were more likely to be securely attached to them by 1 year of age, but, when mother's psychological maturity was statistically controlled, the anticipated and discerned association between sensitive mothering and attachment security was substantially attenuated. This led Benn (1985, p.12) to conclude that "the characteristics of acceptance and sensitivity are overt manifestations of maternal integration which become associated with child development outcomes because of their own connection to this more underlying property of mothers."

In addition to reliance on clinical interview techniques to assess psychological maturity or health, investigators have also relied on a diverse set of measures of psychological functioning and then composited them, based on either conceptual or empirical (i.e., factor-analytic) grounds, in order to create indices of mental health or well-being. Using three of the Big Five constructs, the NICHD Early Child Care Research Network (2000) adopted this approach as part of its efforts to predict fathering behavior. Scores on extraversion and agreeableness were summed and from this total a father's score on neuroticism was subtracted. Men who scored higher on this composite index of psychological health were observed to be more sensitive when interacting with their 6-month-old infants and to engage in more caregiving activities with their 2- and 3-year-old children in this longitudinal study. When the same composite, this time reflecting maternal personality, was correlated with observational measures of maternal sensitivity at 6, 15, 24, and 36 months, a similar result emerged: greater maternal psychological health predicted greater maternal sensitivity at all four ages of measurement (unpublished data).

Three other investigations of mother–infant interaction have generated roughly similar results. In one, Belsky, Herzog, and Rovine (1986) observed that a composite index of well-being reflecting (high) self-esteem, (low) hostility, (low) emotional unresponsiveness, and (low) emotional instability predicted high levels of maternal stimulating engagement of the infant at 1, 3, and 9 months of age. Relatedly, Cox, Owen, Lewis, and Henderson (1989) found that two empirically derived summary factor scores based on measures of anxiety, depression, adjustment, locus of control, and ego development were effective in forecasting attitudes about both the infant and the parenting role, as well as observed warmth and sensitive responding in the case of mothers and fathers alike. Finally, in a study of high-risk mothers–infant dyads, Brunquell, Crichton, and Egeland (1981) reported that that lower levels of mental health, as reflected in a composite index composed of measures of anxiety, locus of control, aggression, succorance, suspicion and defendence, characterized mothers who abused and/or neglected their children over their first few years of life.

One final investigation meriting consideration in this section relies neither on clinical interview nor the compositing of individual measures to tap psychological well-being, but instead focuses on "ego resiliency," which can be defined as "the resourceful adaptation to changing circumstances," "flexible invocation of the available repertoire of problem-solving strategies," and "the ability to maintain integrated performance while under stress" (Block and Block, 1980, p. 48). Mothers who scored higher on ego resiliency evinced greater supportive presence and more structure and limit setting when interacting with their 15-month-old toddlers during a series of structured tasks than did mothers scoring lower on ego resiliency (van Bakel and Riksen-Walraven, 2000). Importantly, structural equation modeling revealed, consistent with Belsky's (1984) determinants of parenting model, that this effect was both direct and mediated by the effect of maternal personality on the quality of the parent's marriage.

Despite evidence that psychological well-being does not always predict parenting (Russell, 1997), it remains the case that, in the main, the data collected to date on psychological maturity and mental health in nonclinical samples reveals that psychological well-being is related to supportive, growth-promoting parenting. This seems true whether psychological health is measured by means of clinical interviews tapping multiple facets of a parents' psychological makeup (in general or with respect to parenting in particular) or by means of multiple measures that are composited on conceptual or empirical grounds. As it turns out, this will be a key story line that emerges continually as we proceed through this review of the empirical literature on personality and parenting.

The Big Five

Recall that the Big Five personality traits are neuroticism, extraversion, agreeableness, openness to experience, and concientiousness. As will become apparent shortly, these traits have not received any place near equivalent attention by developmental investigators. Neuroticism, in particular, has been the favored construct, even when not so labeled, and the amount of work on the other Big five traits pales by comparison.

Neuroticism. Neuroticism reflects adjustment versus emotional instability, and measures of neuroticism identify individuals prone to psychological distress, unrealistic ideas, excessive cravings or urges, and maladaptive coping responses. A person scoring high on this trait worries a lot, is nervous, emotional, insecure, and feels inadequate, whereas a person scoring low is calm, relaxed, unemotional, hardy, secure, and self-satisfied. Because factor analytic studies indicate that indices of the negative emotions of anxiety, hostility and depression all load on a single factor (Costa and McCrae, 1992)—whether measured as states or traits—some prefer to use the term negative affectivity rather than neuroticism (Tellegen, Watson, and Clark, 1999; Watson and Clark, 1984). The important point is less what this trait is called than what this trait reflects. And the fact that it reflects the proclivity or disposition to experience anxiety and hostility as well as depression raises important questions about the plethora of work carried out on depression and mothering within the field of developmental psychology over the past decade (Zahn-Waxler, Duggal, and Gruber, in Vol. 4 of this *Handbook*). In point of fact, one is forced to wonder whether studies in which only depression is measured report data pertaining only to depression and mothering or, instead, negative affectivity more generally—including anxiety and hostility. Until these other negative-emotion facets of neuroticism are examined in studies that also include measures of depression, it will be impossible to address this issue. Clearly, the lack of attention paid to hostility and anxiety relative to depression requires redress.

The fact that the empirical literature is the way it is means that much of the work to be considered in this section deals with depression. But because this is not a chapter concerned with psychopathology but rather with personality, consideration is restricted to research dealing with depression as measured as a continuous variable in nonclinical samples. We begin with investigations focussed on parents of infants and then proceed developmentally from that point forward.

As already indicated, during the infancy period depression has been the facet of neuroticism that has received the most empirical attention. Although the evidence is not without some inconsistency, there is repeated indication, even in nonclinical samples, that when mothers experience more versus less depression, they provide less sensitive care to their infants. This result emerged in the work of the NICHD Early Child Care Research Network (1999), in which depression was repeatedly measured in a sample of more than 1,000 mothers, as was maternal sensitivity, across the first 3 years of the child's life. Relatedly, Crockenberg (1987) reported in a study of teenage mothers that those experiencing more psychological distress engaged in more simple custodial and unstimulating care of their infants than other mothers. And when Zaslow, Pedersen, Cain, Suwalsky, and Kramer (1985) examined relations between mothers' feeling "blue" on eight or more days since the birth of their 4-month-old children and maternal behavior, they observed that increased depression predicted less smiling at, less speaking with, and less touching of the infant. In addition to undermining active involvement with the infant, negative affectivity may also promote negative and intrusive maternal behavior, as Diener and colleagues (1995; Goldstein, Diener, and Mangelsdorf, 1996) discovered on observing adolescent Latino mothers with their 3- to 24-month-old children.

During the preschool and middle childhood years similar results obtain. For example, in one investigation of rural African American and European American families with children, high levels of emotional distress (i.e., anxiety, depression, and irritability) among mothers was related to low levels of positive parenting (e.g., hugs and praise) and high levels of negative parenting (e.g., threats, slaps, and derogatory statements) during the course of structured parent–child interactions and also strong endorsement of authoritarian childrearing values (Conger, McCarthy, Yang, Lakey, and Kropp, 1984). When Zelkowitz (1982) studied poor African American and European American mothers of 5- to 7-year-old children, she further observed that high levels of anxiety and depression predicted high expectations for immediate compliance on the part of the child, but inconsistency in following up such demands when the child did not comply. Furthermore, high levels of psychological distress were associated with more hostile and dominating behavior, less reliance on reasoning and loss of privileges when disciplining the child, and more intensive demands for the child's involvement in household maintenance (Longfellow, Zelkowitz, and Saunders, 1982).

During the teenage years, neuroticism or negative affectivity continues to be associated with problematic parenting. Gondoli and Silverberg (1997) observed this relation when they studied mother–child interactions during a problem-solving discussion and on securing self-reports from mothers about their parenting practices. More specifically, mothers who experienced emotional distress (i.e., depression, anxiety, and low self-efficacy) were less accepting of their teen's behavior and were less supportive of the child's psychological autonomy. In a analysis of almost 1,000 mothers and fathers of 10- to 17-year-olds interviewed as part of a national survey, another team of investigators found that feeling sad, blue, tense, tired, and overwhelmed was related to parents not participating in activities with their children, though such negative affectivity proved unrelated to parental monitoring (Voydanoff and Donnelly, 1998). Finally, Conger, Conger, Elder, Lorenz, Simons, and Whitbeck (1992, 1993), Conger, Patterson, and Ge (1995), and Simons et al., (1993) have studied family interaction patterns in a large sample of Iowa farm families and discerned both direct and indirect effects of negative affectivity on maternal and paternal behavior. Not only did depression predict more harsh and inconsistent discipline on the part of both mothers and fathers (Conger et al., 1995; Simons et al., 1993) and less nurturant behavior by both parents when interacting with sons (Conger et al., 1992) though not daughters (Conger et al., 1993), in the case of both mothers and fathers with sons and daughters, elevated levels of depression predicted increased marital conflict and, thereby, lower levels of nurturant parenting (Conger et al., 1992, 1993). As noted earlier, such indirect pathways of influence of parent's general psychological functioning on their parenting are consistent with Belsky's (1984) process model of the determinants of parenting.

In sum, whether one considers research on infants, toddlers, preschoolers, school-age children, or adolescents, there is repeated evidence that high levels of depression, even in nonclinical samples, and of other facets of neuroticism, including anxiety and irritability/hostility, are related to less competent parenting. This effect can take the form of less active and involved parenting, as well as more negative, intrusive, and overcontrolling parenting.

Extraversion.   Extraversion reflects the quantity and intensity of interpersonal interaction, activity level, need for stimulation, and capacity for joy that characterize individuals. A person scoring high on extraversion is considered sociable, active, talkative, person oriented, optimistic, fun loving, and affectionate, whereas a low-scoring person is reserved, sober, unexuberant, aloof, task oriented, retiring, and quiet. One might anticipate, on the basis of this description, that extraverted individuals might function better as parents than less extraverted parents, if only because parenting is a social task involving another—though dependent—person. On the other hand, one might imagine that high levels of extraversion and especially of sociability might predispose one to be more interested in more social exchange than might be experienced by a parent, particularly one who remains home all day with children.

Although the database is by no means extensive, in general the evidence is supportive of the first prediction, namely that of a positive association between extraversion and sensitive, responsive, emotionally engaged, and stimulating parenting. True virtually to the definition of extraversion, Levy-Shiff and Israelasvilli (1988) found that Israeli men scoring high on this construct manifested more positive affect and engaged in more toy play and teaching when interacting with their 9-month-old infants in their homes than men scoring low on extraversion. Mangelsdorf, Gunnar, Kestenbaum, Lang, and Andreas (1990) detected similar personality–parenting associations when studying mothers of 9-month-old children. And Belsky, Crnic, and Woodworth (1995) essentially replicated both sets of results during the course of naturalistic home observations with a mother, father, and their 15- and 21-month-old toddlers. These investigators reported that mothers and fathers alike who were more extraverted expressed more positive affect toward their children and were more sensitive and cognitively stimulating when observed at home late in the afternoon and early in the evening. Finally, in a study of mothers, fathers, and their children up to 8 years of age, it was found that more extraverted parents reported engaging in more positive supportive parenting, such as displaying positive affection and encouraging independence (Losoya, Callor, Rowe, and Goldsmith, 1997). Apparently, the link between extraversion and positive parenting is not restricted to the infant–toddler period. To date, however, there are no studies linking this personality trait with parenting during the adolescent years.

Agreeableness. Agreeableness reflects one's interpersonal orientation along a continuum from compassion to antagonism in thoughts, feelings, and actions. A person scoring high on this trait is soft-hearted, good-natured, trusting, helpful, forgiving, gullible, and straightforward, whereas a person scoring low is cynical, rude, suspicious, uncooperative, vengeful, ruthless, irritable, and manipulative. Clearly, the basic prediction regarding parenting would be that more agreeable individuals would make better parents—at least as seen from the child's perspective. As it turns out, only four studies have examined the relation between this particular personality trait and parenting, two of which have just been mentioned. In the aforementioned toddler work by Belsky et al. (1995), higher levels of agreeableness predicted greater maternal (but not paternal) positive affect and sensitivity and lower levels of negative affect and intrusive–overcontrolling behavior. Consistent with these findings, Losoya et al. (1997) found in their study of parents with children as old as 8 that agreeableness was positively associated with supportive parenting and negatively associated with negatively controlling parenting. Kochanska, Clark, and Goldman (1997) recently reported that lower levels of agreeableness were related to more power-assertive and less responsive parenting in their study of young children, although in another study by this research team, only the agreeableness–responsiveness association was replicated (Clark, Kochanska, and Ready, 2000). Clearly, the evidence just reviewed is rather consistent with the hypothesis originally advanced.

As empathy appears to be a facet of agreeableness (Watson, Clark, and Harkness, 1994), work linking this construct with parenting bears considering in this section. Further, empathy appears to be a good candidate for a trait that would enhance parenting, given earlier observations about the need to decenter from self and consider the perspective of the child when seeking to provide sensitive, supportive care (see also Dix, 1992). In one relevant investigation, Kochanska (1997) found that highly empathic mothers were more able than less empathic ones to develop a mutually positive relationship with their young child. In another study, this one of nonparents, the role of empathy was also underscored, as those individuals scoring high on empathy evinced more affective responsiveness to infant signals as well as a stronger desire to pick up an infant when engaged in face-to-face interaction with a 5-month-old infant (Wiesenfeld, Whitman, and Malatesta, 1984). We see here, then, more evidence for a positive link between agreeableness, or at least one possible facet of this construct, and sensitive, supportive parenting.

Openness to Experience. The person who is open to experience tends to enjoy new experiences, have broad interests, and be very imaginative; in constrast, a person scoring low on this trait is down to earth, practical, traditional, and pretty much set in his or her ways. Predictions from this trait to parenting are less straightfoward than was the case with respect to the other Big five traits considered through this point. Only two investigations have explored this topic, with one showing that Israeli fathers who were more open to experience engaged in more basic caregiving of their infants than fathers less open to experience (Levy-Shiff and Isarelasvilli, 1988), perhaps because the father role itself is a new experience worth exploring for these highly open men. The other study found that openness was positively related to positive parenting for mothers and fathers alike (Losoya et al., 1997).

Conscientiousness. Conscientiousness reflects the extent to which a person is well organized and has high standards, always striving to achieve his or her goals. Thus, a person who scores low on conscientiousness is easygoing, not very well organized, tending toward carelessness, and not preferring to make plans. Once again, it is not exactly clear how this trait should relate to parental behavior, as it seems eminently possible that, however attractive high conscientious may appear—especially to an employer—it could prove too demanding to a child. At the same time, disorder and chaos, in contrast to organization, are typically not in children's best interests, so one could imagine low levels of conscientiousness also predicting parental behavior that might not be especially supportive of children's functioning. The aforementioned study by Losoya et al. (1997) that examined this trait in relation to the childrearing attitudes and practices of mothers and fathers with children under 8 years of age found conscientiousness to be positively related to supportive parenting and negatively related to negative, controlling parenting. Clark and associates (2000) chronicled similar relations when looking at mothers of toddlers, finding that more conscientious mothers are more responsive and less power assertive than less conscientious mothers. However limited, the evidence to date clearly suggests that conscientiousness and positive parenting go together.

Diverse Constructs

Beyond the Big Five, a number of personality-type constructs have been examined in the context of parenting in hopes of determining how parents' psychological makeup contributes to the manner in which they function in their parental role. Self-esteem is perhaps the most extensively studied characteristic other than those already discussed through this point. Thereafter comes locus of control, and from this point forward particular traits have fewer and fewer studies addressing their role in shaping parenting. Thus, this final substantive section of this empirical review of modern research on personality and parenting will focus exclusively on these two constructs, as the evidentiary basis for drawing firm conclusions about other personality-type constructs is simply too limited.

Self-esteem. Individuals high in self-esteem think well of themselves whereas those low in self-esteem think poorly of themselves. One might expect, therefore, for self-esteem to be related (negatively) to neuroticism or negative affectivity and (positively) to extraversion or positive affectivity. On this basis, it can be anticipated that high levels of self-esteem should predict more sensitive, supportive, stimulating, and growth-facilitative parenting. And this is exactly what a number of investigators have found—studying mothers of infants (Tronick, Cohn, and Shea, 1986), fathers of infants (Cowan and Cowan, 1983; Gamble and Belsky, 1984), parents of preschoolers from one- and two-parent households (Menaghan and Parcel, 1991), African American mothers of teenagers (Taylor, Roberts, and Jacobson, 1997), and European mothers mothers and fathers of teenagers (Small, 1988).

Locus of control. Locus of control reflects the extent to which an individual feels in control of his or her life. Persons who have an internal locus of control consider themselves, more or less, in control of their destiny. In contrast, persons who have an external locus of control regard events beyond their control as the principal shapers of their fate. Because an internalized sense of control is regarded as essential for mental health, it should be expected that locus of control predicts parenting, and this is exactly what the available evidence indicates. Mothers with an internal locus of control, in contrast to mothers with an external locus, have been found to interact with their 4- and 12-month-old infants in a more stimulating manner during bathing, dressing, and play (Schaeffer, Bauman,

Siegel, Hoskins, and Sanders, 1980), and with their preschoolers in a warmer, more accepting, and more helpful manner during a structured teaching task (Mondell and Tyler, 1981). Both and European America and African American mothers (McGroder, 2000; Stevens, 1988) and mothers in single- and two-parent households (Menaghan and Parcel, 1991) have been found to provide more stimulating, responsive, and less negatively controlling care to their preschoolers at home when they have a more internal locus of control.

PERSONALITY, PARENTING, AND CHILD DEVELOPMENT

The literature reviewed through this point underscores the fact that personality characteristics of adults are systematically related to the manner in which they parent. Although such information is of interest in its own right, to many developmentalists its significance lies in its implications for children's development. Then, if, as widely acknowledged (Collins, Maccoby, Steinberg, Hetherington, and Bornstein, 2000), parenting affects children's functioning and personality affects parenting, we might expect to find evidence that personality shapes parenting and, thereby, child development. In this section we consider, for illustrative purposes only, the results of a set of noteworthy studies that have explored this process of influence.

Drawing on data from the Berkeley Growth Study, Elder, Caspi and Downey (1986) were able to link personality to parenting and then to child development in a cycle that spanned several generations. They discovered, more specifically, that growing up in a home in which parents' personalities could be described as unstable (i.e., high negative affectivity/neuroticism) and in which parental care could be depicted as controlling, hostile, and lacking in affection led to the development of unstable personalities in the children as adults. This personal instability on the part of Berkeley parents, derived as it seemed to be from poor developmental experiences in their families of origin, was itself predictive of tension in their own marriages. Marital tension, in the face of another generation of personal instability, contributed to extreme and arbitrary discipline for the third generation of Berkeley children. And finally, exposure to such care resulted in the development of behavior problems in this third generation of children, who were predictive of undercontrolled behavior in adulthood. Thus, parenting difficulties, apparently originating from personality problems, seemed to leave a legacy of personal adjustment problems that were passed down through parenting from one generation to the next, testimony indeed for the role that personality plays as a determinant of parenting and, thus, an indirect influence on child development.

Confirmation of this pathway of influence is also evident in Engfer and Schneewind's (1982) cross-sectional study of the causes and consequences of harsh parental punishment. Relying upon self-report data provided by parents and children (8 to 14 years of age) from some 570 representative German families, these investigators sought to test, using path analytic techniques, a theoretical model of the determinants of child abuse. Results revealed, consistent with Belsky's (1984) model of the determinants of parenting, that, in the case of both mothers and fathers, unfavorable socialization experiences in parents' own childhoods were related to parental personality problems of irritability and nervous tension as well as family conflict (i.e., marital conflict). These personality problems, though their effect on parental anger proneness and helplessness, along with family conflict and a difficult, problem child, each contributed to the prediction of harsh parental punishment. Such childrearing was itself related to a "conduct disordered" personality on the part of the child, to preceived rejection, and, thereby, feelings of anxiety and helplessness by the child.

The final investigation to be considered linking parent personality to child development via parenting was carried out in the 1980s on a large number of Iowa farm families rearing adolescents and experiencing economic hardship due to a poor agricultural economy in the American Midwest. In this work, the index of parental negative affectivity or neuroticism tapped depression and was found to predict, in the case of both mothers and fathers, nurturant/involved parenting and, thereby, sons' adjustment problems, such that when depression was greater nurturance was lower and the latter predicted greater antisocial behavior on the part of children (Conger et al., 1992). In sum, then, these three investigations, carried out at different points in time and in rather different locales provide evidence that adult personality and psychological well-being predicts parenting and, thereby, children's functioning.

SUMMARY

This review of modern research on personality and parenting makes it clear that if one had to choose a parent to provide care for oneself, one's development would likely benefit from choosing a parent who is psychologically healthy and mature and, more specifically, low in neuroticism, high in extraversion and agreeableness, perhaps high in openness to experience and conscientiousness, as well as high in self-esteem and characterized by an internal locus of control. This is because these kinds of individuals have been repeatedly found to provide care that is more supportive, sensitive, responsive, and intellectually stimulating, almost irrespective of the child's age, though it must be acknowledged that with the exception perhaps of recent work on negative affectivity (i.e., neuroticism), most research on the role of personality in shaping parenting has been carried out on parents of younger rather than older children. It must be further acknowledged that virtually all the research cited has been conducted in the United States, except where otherwise indicated. This raises the question of whether the relations between peronality and parenting discerned in the literature to date hold across cultural contexts.

FUTURE DIRECTIONS IN THEORY AND RESEARCH
ON PERSONALITY AND PARENTING

These last comments make it clear that important future directions for theory and research on personality and parenting is to redress the disproportionate study of parents of infants and American parents, especially of European descent. The same goes for the relative neglect of fathers. And in a similar vein, there is a need for more work—and theorizing—about the role of the less studied Big Five constructs, especially conscientiousness and openness to experience, but agreeableness merits more attention as well. Beyond such obvious directions for future research, three others meriting consideration are discussed in this section, the first two dealing with mediators and moderators of personality–parenting associations, and the third dealing with comparative analyses of the role of personality in shaping parenting.

Mediators of Personality–Parenting Associations

It is one thing to observe that a parent's psychological makeup, that is, their personality and well-being, is predictive of their parenting; it is quite another to understand the mechanisms responsible for this relation. Two possibilities that have received some limited attention in the literature deserve more attention in the future. The first involves attributions; the second mood and emotion.

There is increasing appreciation in developmental research that attributions play an important role in close relationship processes, including in the parent–child relationship (Bugental and Happaney, in Vol. 3 of this *Handbook*). More specifically, models of social cognition that have been advanced in the marital, developmental, and social psychology literatures (e.g., Bradbury and Fincham, 1990; Dix Ruble, and Zambarano, 1989; Dodge, 1986) have been applied to the study of parenting (e.g., Bugental and Shennum, 1984). For example, it has been shown that parents who think their child is whining because he is tired are inclined to respond to the child in a manner quite different (i.e., sensitive) than when they believe the child is trying to manipulate them. Thus, Bugental and Shennum (1984) were able to show that mothers with more dysfunctional attributional styles responded to children in ways that maintained or enhanced the child's difficult behavior, a finding that was experimentally reproduced by Slep and O'Leary (1998) by manipulating parental attributions in a challenging situation. Relatedly, Johnston and Patenaude (1994) found that parents were more likely to regard oppositional–defiant child behavior as under the child's control than inattentive–overreactive behavior, and this accounted for why the former evoked more negative parental reactions than the latter.

The fact that such attributions predict much the same parenting behavior that personality characteristics also predict raises the possibility that one means by which personality shapes parenting is via attributions. Is it the case, as seems likely, for example, that it is neurotic rather than agreeable parents who are most likely to attribute negative intent to their young children when they misbehave? And if so, does this dynamic account for why these personality traits predict parenting in the ways that they do?

Because attributions themselves are linked to emotion, it is reasonable to wonder further about the role that emotion plays in mediating the effect of personality on parenting. After all, in the aforementioned experimental study by Slep and O'Leary (1998), the manipulation of mothers' attributions affected the degree to which they felt angry at their children. Emotion, of course, is central to the personality traits of neuroticism, also labeled negative affectivity, and extraversion, sometimes referred to in terms of positive affectivity.

Two studies to date have examined the mediating role of emotion in accounting for personality–parenting relations. In a German investigation of almost 300 families with 8- to 14-year-old sons, Engfer and Schneewind (1982) showed, via path analysis, that maternal irritability and nervousness (i.e., neuroticism) promoted the harsh punishment of their children via mother's proneness to anger. Belsky et al. (1995) tested and found some support for an "affect-specific" process, whereby personality affects mood, and thereby parenting, in their home-observational study of families rearing 15- and 21-month-old sons: Whereas extraversion, with its emphasis on the experience of positive emotions, predicted mothers' expressions of positive but not negative affect toward their toddlers, neuroticism, with its emphasis on the experience of negative emotions, predicted mother's expressions of negative but not positive affect. In light of these results and those concerning attributions, it seems appropriate to encourage further work examining the mediating role of attributions and emotion in accounting for some personality–parenting linkages, including the proposition that personaltiy→emotion→attribution→parenting.

Moderators of Personality–Parenting Associations

In the review of modern research on personality and parenting, all discussion focussed on the main effects of personality characteristics on parenting. Such a focus neglected the possibility that personality may play a differential role in shaping parenting depending on other factors. This is somewhat surprising, as central to Belsky's (1984) model of the determinants of parenting was the notion that parenting is multiply determined such that stressors and supports—including parental personality—interact to enhance or undermine a parent's capacity to provide growth-promoting care to the child. Future work should, therefore, focus on protective and potentiating factors and processes: what characteristics of parents, children, and families, for example, increase or decrease the probability that more neurotic and/or less agreeable parents will prove insensitive when it comes to caring for their infants or disciplining their older child? Another way of phrasing this question is "Under what conditions are particular personality attributes more or less important in explaining parental functioning?"

One team of investigators has specifically explored the issue of moderation recently. Focussing on the moderating role of infant temperament, Clark, Kochanska, and Ready (2000) found that highly extraverted mothers were substantially more likely to engage in power-assertive parenting when rearing more difficult, but not when rearing temperamentally easier, toddlers. On the basis of such an intriguing result, one begins to wonder how many of the findings reviewed earlier might be moderated by, among other things, children's temperament (Putnam, Sanson, and Rothbart, in Vol. 1

of this *Handbook*), the quality of parents' marriages (McHale, Khozan, Rotman, DeCourcey, and McConnell, in Vol. 3 of this *Handbook*), and parents' occupational experiences (Hoff, Laursen, and Tardif, in Vol. 2 of this *Handbook*). These are issues that future research should address.

The Comparative Influence of Personality on Parenting

With the exception of the immediately preceding discussion of moderating factors, this chapter has focussed on personality almost to the exclusion of other determinants of parenting implicated in Belsky's (1984) model of parenting. Belsky theorized that parental psychological attributes should be among the most influential in shaping parenting because they are likely to shape other forces that also contribute to parenting, including marital quality, occupation experiences, and social support. For the most part, investigators to date have not taken up the challenge to test this proposition, and this suggests that more work is called for in which the role of personality can be compared to other sources of influences on parenting. One team of investigators, however, was sufficiently impressed by the power of parental psychological characteristics to observe that "the enduring direct effects of psychological resources measured 6 and 7 years earlier (than measurements of parenting) are striking.... individual (psychological) resources may be as important as the current conditions that individuals experience in shaping family environments" (Menaghen and Parcel, 1991, p. 426–427).

There is also need for additional work examining the differential role played by a variety of psychological attributes of parents in predicting parenting. We can thus wonder not only about whether attributions, for example, mediate the effect of personality on parenting, but whether their relative power to predict parenting is greater than perhaps more "distal" personality constructs. One recent study by Barends and Belsky (2000) took up a related challenge by comparing the predictive power of three of the Big five personality traits (neuroticism, extraversion, and agreeableness) with that of mothers' working models of attachment as measured by the Adult Attachment Interview. Despite the fact that the latter has received much more attention than the former, it turned out that personality traits were far more predictive of mothering observed under naturalistic conditions in the home than was whether or not a mother's internal working model of attachment was autonomous, dismissive, or preoccupied.

There is also a need for more research comparing different personality traits so that greater insight can be achieved into the differential role of such traits in predicting different aspects of parenting. We have commented already on the need for depression researchers to move beyond this singular facet of neuroticism and examine the other negative affects of hostility and anxiety so that they can be compared with that of depression. The only investigation that has done this to our knowledge indicated that the effect of hostility on daily parenting hassles ($r = 0.48$) was twice the size of that of depression ($r = 0.24$), with the effect of anxiety falling in between (0.33, Crnic and Greenberg, 1985). Were this pattern characteristic of the differential importance of these three negative emotions in shaping parenting more generally—and we are not suggesting this to be the case—these findings would suggest that developmentalists' almost obsessive devotion to the study of depression may carry a sizeable intellectual cost. Ultimately, the point to be made is that our understanding of parenting would be enhanced were multiple aspects of neuroticism and of personality more generally studied in the same investigation so that greater insight could be achieved into the differential role of different personality characteristics in predicting different aspects of parenting.

CONCLUSIONS

In this chapter we have reviewed history and theory pertaining to the study of personality and parenting and examined the results of modern research in terms of general psychological health and the Big five. We have seen that for many years developmentalists ignored personality when it came to studying parenting, in large measure in reaction to Mischel's critique of the field of personality and also in response to the ascendance of ecological theory (Bronfenbrenner, 1979), which in emphasizing the role of social context in child development deemphasized the importance of individual differences in parents. We have seen further that, when it came to studying the role of personality in shaping parenting, developmentalists have at times seemed to select from a hodgepodge of available measurement instruments. Because many developmental investigators have not kept up with developments in the field of personality psychology, the power of the Big five to capture much of the variation in adult personality has simply not been sufficiently appreciated. Moreover, when it came to studying negative affectivity, developmentalists almost single-mindedly focussed on depression and have neglected the other negative emotion facets of neuroticism, hostility and anxiety. We noted that not only should this lacuna be redressed, but we highlighted other directions for future research. Presumably, in a decade's time, we should have increased our understanding of the moderators and mediators of personality–parenting associations and the role of personality in shaping parenting relative to other sources of influence.

REFERENCES

Ainsworth, M. D. S. (1973). The development of infant–mother attachment. In B. M. Caldwell and H. N. Ricciuti (Eds.), *Review of child development research: Vol. 3. Child development and social policy* (pp. 1–87). Chicago: University of Chicago.

Allport, G. W. (1937). *Personality: A psychological interpretation.* New York: Henry Holt.

Barends, N., and Belsky, J. (2000). *Adult attachment and parent personality as correlates of mothering in the second and third years.* Unpublished manuscript, Penn State University, University Park, PA.

Baumeister, R. F. (1999). On the interface between personality and social psychology. In L. A. Pervin and O. P. John (Eds.), *Handbook of personality: Theory and research* (2nd ed., pp. 367–378). New York: Guilford.

Belsky, J. (1984). The determinants of parenting. *Child Development, 55*, 83–96.

Belsky, J., Crnic, K., and Woodworth, S. (1995). Personality and parenting: Exploring the mediating role of transient mood and daily hassles. *Journal of Personality, 63*, 905–931.

Belsky, J., Hertzog, C., and Rovine, M. (1986). Causal analyses of multiple determinants of parenting: Empirical and method-ological advances. In M. E. Lamb, A. L. Brown, and B. Rogoff (Eds.), *Advances in developmental psychology* (Vol. 4, pp. 153–202). Hillsdale, NJ: Lawrence Erlbaum Associates.

Belsky, J., and Vondra, J. (1989). Lessons from child abuse: The determinants of parenting. In D. Cicchetti and V. Carlson (Eds.), *Child maltreatment: Theory and research in the causes and consequences of child abuse and neglect* (pp. 153–202). New York: Cambridge.

Bem, D. J., and Allen, A. (1974). On predicting some of the people some of the time: The search for cross-situational consistencies in behavior. *Psychological Review, 31*, 506–520.

Benjamin, L. S. (1974). Structural analysis of social behavior. *Psychological Review, 81*, 392–425.

Benjamin, L. S. (1984). Principles of prediction using structural analysis of social behavior. In A. Zucker, J. Aronoff, and J. Rubin (Eds.), *Personality and the prediction of behavior* (pp. 121–173). New York: Academic.

Benjamin, L. S. (1996). A clinician-friendly version of the interpersonal circumplex: Structural analysis of social behavior (SASB). *Journal of Personality Assessment, 66*, 248–266.

Benn, R. (1985, April). *Factors associated with security of attachment in dual career families.* Paper presented at the meeting of the Society for Research in Child Development, Toronto.

Benn, R. (1986). Factors promoting secure attachment relations between employed mothers and their sons. *Child Development, 57*, 1224–1231.

Blatt, S., Auerbach, J., and Levy, K. (1997). Mental representations in personality development, psychpathology, and the therapeutic process. *Review of General Psychology, 1*, 351–374.

Blatt, S., Wein,S., Chevron, E., and Quilan, D. (1979). Parental representations and depression in normal young adults. *Journal of Abnormal Psychology, 88*, 388–397.

Block, J. (1961/1978). The Q-sort method in personality assessment and psychiatric research. Palo Alto, CA: Consulting Psychology.

Block, J. H., and Block, J. (1980). The role of ego-control and ego-resiliency in the organization of behavior. In W. A. Collins (Ed.), *The Minnesota symposia on child psychology* (Vol. 13, pp. 39–101). Hillsdale, NJ: Lawrence Erlbaum Associates.

Bradbury, T., and Fincham, F. (1990). Attributions in marriage. *Psychological Bulletin, 107*, 3–33.

Bronfenbrenner, U. (1979). *The ecology of human development: Experiments by nature and design.* Cambridge, MA: Harvard University Press.

Bronfenbrenner, U. (1986). Ecology of the family as a context for human development: Research perspectives. *Developmental Psychology, 22,* 723–742.

Brunnquell, D., Crichton, L., and Egeland, B. (1981). Maternal personality and attitude toward disturbances of child-rearing. *Journal of Orthopsychiatry, 51,* 680–691.

Bugental, D., and Shennum, W. (1984). Difficult children as elicitors and targets of adult communication patterns. *Monographs of the Society for Research in Child Development, 49*(Serial No. 205).

Caldwell, B. M., and Hersher, L. (1964). Mother–infant interaction during the first year of life. *Merrill-Palmer Quarterly, 10,* 119–128.

Caldwell, B. M., Hersher, L., Lipton, E. L., Richmond, J. B., Stern, G. A., Eddy, E., Drachman, R., and Rothman, A. (1963). Mother–infant interaction in monomatric and polymatric families. *American Journal of Orthopsychiatry, 33,* 653–364.

Caspi, A. (1998). Personality development across the life course. In W. Damon (Series Ed.) and N. Eisenberg (Vol. Ed.), *Handbook of child psychology: Vol. 3. Social, emotional, and personality development* (5th ed., pp. 311–388). New York: Wiley.

Cattell, R. B. (1943). The description of personality: Basic traits resolved into clusters. *Journal of Abnormal and Social Psychology, 38,* 476–506.

Cattell, R. B. (1945). The principal trait clusters for describing personality. *Psychological Bulletin, 42,* 129–161.

Clark, L., Kochanska, G., and Ready, R. (2000). Mother's personality and its interaction with child temperament as predictors of parenting. *Journal of Personality and Social Psychology, 79,* 274–285.

Clausen, J. A. (1966). Family structure, socialization, and personality. In L. W. Hoffman and M. L. Hoffman (Eds.), *Review of child development research* (Vol. 2, pp. 1–54). New York: Plenum.

Collins, W. A., Maccoby, E. E., Steinberg, L., Hetherington, E.M., and Bornstein, M. (2000). Contemporary research on parenting. *American Psychologist, 55,* 1–15.

Conger, R., Conger, K., Elder, G., Lorenz, F., Simons, R., and Whitbeck, L. (1992). A family process model of economic hardship and adjustment of early adolescent boys. *Child Development, 63,* 526–541.

Conger, R., Conger, K., Elder, G., Lorenz, F., Simons, R., and Whitbeck, L. (1993). Family economic stress and adjustment of early adolescent girls. *Developmental Psychology, 29,* 206–219.

Conger, R., McCarty, J., Yang, R., Lahey, B., and Kropp, J. (1984). Perception of child, childrearing values, and emotional distress as mediating links between environmental stressors and observed maternal behavior. *Child Development, 54,* 2234–2247.

Conger, R., Patterson, G., and Ge, X. (1995). It takes two to replicate: A mediational model for the impact of parents' stress on adolescent adjustment. *Child Development, 66,* 80–97.

Costa, P. T., and McCrae, R. R. (1992). *NEO PI-R Professional manual.* Odessa, FL: Psychological Assessment Resources.

Cowan, C., and Cowan, P. (1983, August). *Men's involvement in the family.* Paper presented at the annual meeting of the American Psychological Association, New York.

Cox, M., Owen, M., Lewis, J., and Henderson, V. (1989). Marriage, adult adjustment, and early parenting. *Child Development, 60,* 1015–1024.

Crnic, K., and Greenberg, M. (1985, April). *Parenting daily hassles.* Paper presented at the meeting of the Society for Research in Child Development, Toronto.

Crockenberg, S. (1987). Support for adolescent mothers during the postnatal period. In C. Boukydis (Ed.), *Research on support for parents and infants in the postnatal period* (pp. 3–24). Norwood, NJ: Ablex.

Dekovic, M., and Gerris, J. (1992). Parental reasoning, complexity, social class and childrearing behaviors. *Journal of Marriage and the Family, 54,* 675–685.

Diener, M., Mangelsdorf, S., Contrerae, J., Hazelwood, L., and Rhodes, J. (1995, March). *Correlates of parenting competence among Latina adolescent mothers.* Paper presented at the meeting of the Society for Research in Child Development, Indianapolis, IN.

Dix, T. (1992). Parenting on behalf of the child. In I. Sigel and A. McGillicuddy-DeLisi (Eds.), *Parental belief systems* (pp. 319–346). Hillsdale, NJ: Lawrence Erlbaum Associates.

Dix, T., Ruble, D., and Zambarano, R. (1989). Mothers' implicit theories of discipline. *Child Development, 60,* 1373–1391.

Dodge, K. (1986). A social information processing model of social competence in children. In M. Perlmutter (Ed.), *The Minnesota symposia on child psychology* (Vol. 18, pp. 77–125). Hillsdale, NJ: Lawrence Erlbaum Associates.

Elder, G. H., Jr., Caspi, A., and Downey, G. (1986). Problem behavior and family relationships: Life course and intergenerational themes. In A. Sorensen, F. Weinert, and L. Sherrod (Eds.), *Human development: Interdsiciplinary perspetives* (pp. 293–340). Hillsdale, NJ: Lawrence Erlbaum Associates.

Engfer, A., and Schneewind, K. (1982). Causes and consequences of harsh parental punishment. *Child Abuse and Neglect, 6,* 129–139.

Epstein, S. (1979a). The stability of behavior: I. On predicting most of the people much of the time. *Journal of Personality and Social Psychology, 37,* 1097–1126.

Epstein, S. (1979b). The stability of behavior: II. Implications for psychological research. *American Psychologist, 35,* 790–806.

Freud, A. (1970). The concept of the rejecting mother. In E. J. Anthony and T. Benedek (Eds.), *Parenthood: Its psychology and psychopathology* (pp. 376–386). Boston: Little, Brown. (Original work published 1955.)

Funder, D. C., and Ozer, D. (1983). Behavior as a function of the situation. *Journal of Personality and Social Psychology, 44,* 17–112.

Gamble, W., and Belsky, J. (1984). *Stressors, support, and maternal personal resources as determinants of mothering.* Unpublished manuscript, Penn State University, University Park, PA.

Gerris, J., Dekovic, J., and Janssens, J. (1997). The relationship between social class and childrearing behaviors. *Journal of Marriage and the Family, 59,* 834–847.

Goldberg, L. R. (1992). The development of markers for the Big-Five factor structure. *Psychological Assessment, 4,* 26–42.

Goldstein, L., Diener, M., and Mangelsdorf, S. (1996). Maternal characterstics and social support across the transition to motherhood. *Journal of Family Psychology, 10,* 60–71.

Gondoli, D., and Silverberg, S. (1997). Maternal emotional distress and diminished responsiveness. *Developmental Psychology, 33,* 861–868.

Graziano, W. G., and Eisenberg, N. (1997). Agreeableness: A dimension of personality. In R. Hogan, J. A. Johnson, and S. R. Briggs (Eds.), *Handbook of personality psychology* (pp. 795–824). San Diego, CA: Academic.

Grossman, F., Pollack, W., and Golding, E. (1988). Fathers and children. *Developmental Psychology, 24,* 82–91.

Hauser, S. (1976). Loevinger's model and measure of ego development. *Psychological Bulletin, 33,* 928–955.

Hauser, S., Powers, S., Noam, G., and Jacobson, A. (1984). Familial contexts of adolescent ego development. *Child Development, 55,* 195–213.

Heath, D. (1976). Competent fathers. *Human Development, 19,* 26–39.

Heinicke, C. M. (1984). Impact of pre-birth parent personality and marital functioning on family development: A framework and suggestions for further study. *Developmental Psychology, 20,* 1044–1053.

Hogan, J., and Ones, D. S. (1997). Conscientiousness and integrity at work. In R. Hogan, J. A. Johnson, and S. R. Briggs (Eds.), *Handbook of personality psychology* (pp. 849–870). San Diego, CA: Academic.

John, O. P., Caspi, A., Robins, R., Moffitt, T. E., and Stouthamer-Loeber, M. (1994). The "Little Five": Exploring the nomological network of the five-factor model of personality in adolescent boys. *Child Development, 65,* 160–178.

John, O. P., Donahue, E. M., and Kentle, R. L. (1991). *The Big Five inventory—Versions 4a and 54.* Berkeley, CA: University of California, Berkeley, Institute of Personality and Social Research.

John, O. P., and Srivastava, S. (1999). The Big Five trait taxonomy: History, measurement, and theoretical perspectives. In L. A. Pervin and O. P. John (Eds.), *Handbook of personality: Theory and research* (2nd ed., pp. 102–138). New York: Guilford.

Johnson, J. A. (1997). Units of analysis for the description and explanation of personality. In R. Hogan, J. A., Johnson, and S. R. Briggs (Eds.), *Handbook of personality psychology* (pp. 73–93). San Diego, CA: Academic.

Johnston, C., and Patenaude, R. (1994). Parent attributions for inattentive–overeactive and oppositional–defiant child behaviors. *Cognitive Therapy and Research, 18,* 261–275.

Kiesler, D. J. (1983). The 1982 Interpersonal Circle: A taxonomy for complementarity in human transactions. *Psychological Review, 90,* 185–214.

Kochanska, G. (1997). Multiple pathways to conscience for children with different temperaments. *Developmental Psychology, 33,* 228–240.

Kochanska, G., Clark, L., and Goldman, M. (1997). Implications of mothers' personality for parenting and their young children's developmental outcomes. *Journal of Personality, 65,* 389–420.

Levine, L., Garcia-Coll, C., and Oh, W. (1984, April). *Determinants of mother–infant interaction in adolescent mothers.* Paper presented at the International Conference on Infant Studies, New York.

Levy, D. M. (1943). *Maternal overprotection.* New York: Columbia University Press.

Levy, K., Blatt, S., and Shaver, P. (1998). Attachment styles and parental representations. *Journal of Personality and Social Psychology, 74,* 407–419.

Levy-Shiff, R., and Israelashvili, R. (1988). Antecedents of fathering. *Developmental Psychology, 24,* 434–441.

Loevinger, J. (1979). *Scientific ways in the study of ego development.* Worcester, MA: Clark University Press.

Longfellow, C., Zelkowitz, P., and Saunders, E. (1982). The quality of mother–child relationships. In D. Belle (Eds.), *Lives in stress* (pp. 163–176). Beverly Hills, CA: Sage.

Losoya, S., Callor, S., Rowe, D., and Goldsmith, H. (1997). Origins of familial similarity in parenting. *Developmental Psychology, 33,* 1012–1023.

MacAdams, D. P. (1997). A conceptual history of personality psychology. In R. Hogan, J. A. Johnson, and S. R. Briggs (Eds.), *Handbook of personality psychology* (pp. 3–39). San Diego, CA: Academic.

MacKinnon, D. W. (1944). The stucture of personality. In J. McV. Hunt (Ed.), *Personality and the behavior disorders* (pp. 3–48). New York: Plenum.

Mangelsdorf, S., Gunnar, M., Kestenbaum, R., Lang, S., and Andreas, D. (1990). Infant proneness-to-distress temperament, maternal personality, and mother–infant attachment. *Child Development, 61,* 820–831.

Manheimer, D. (1963). *Progress report on research on children's accidents.* Unpublished manuscript.

McCrae, R. R., and Costa, P. T., Jr. (1985). Comparison of EPI and psychoticism scales with measures of the five-factor model of personality. *Personality and Individual Differences, 6,* 587–597.

McCrae, R. R., and Costa, P. T., Jr. (1989). The structure of interpersonal traits: Wiggins' circumplex and the five-factor model. *Journal of Personality and Social Psychology, 56,* 586–595.

McGroder, S. (2000). Parenting among low-income, African-American single mothers with preschool-age children. *Child Development, 71,* 752–71.

Menaghan, E., and Parcel, T. (1991). Determining children's home environments. *Journal of Marriage and the Family, 53,* 417–431.

Mischel, W. (1968). *Personality and assessment.* New York: Wiley.

Mondell, S., and Tyler, F. (1981). Parental competence and styles of problem solving/play behavior with children. *Developmental Psychology, 17,* 73–78.

Moss, H. A., Robson, K. S., and Pedersen, F. (1969). Determinants of maternal stimulations of infants. *Developmental Psychology, 1,* 239–246.

Moss, H. A., Ryder, R. G., and Robson, K. S. (1967). *The relationship between preparental variables assessed at the newlywed stage and later maternal behaviors.* Paper presented at the meeting of the Society for Research in Child Development, Chicago.

Mount, M. K., Barrick, M. R., and Stewart, G. L. (1998). Five-factor model of personality and performance in jobs involving interpersonal interactions. *Human performance, 11,* 145–165.

NICHD Early Child Care Research Network. (2000). Factors associated with fathers' caregiving activities and sensitivity. *Journal of Family Psychology, 14,* 200–219.

Ozer, D. J. (1985). Correlation and the coefficient of determination. *Psychological Bulletin, 97,* 307–315.

Paunonen, S., and Jackson, D. (1996). The Jackson Personality Inventory and the five-factor model of personality. *Journal of Research in Personality, 30,* 42–59.

Robins, R. W., John, O. P., and Caspi, A. (1994). Major dimensions of personality in early adolescence: The Big Five and beyond. In C. F. Halverson, J. A. Kohnstamm, and R. P. Martin (Eds.), *The developing structure of temperament and personality from infancy to adulthood* (pp. 267–291). Hillsdale, NJ: Lawrence Erlbaum Associates.

Robson, K. S., Pedersen, F. A., and Moss, H. A. (1969). Developmental observations of dyadic gazing in relation to the fear of strangers. *Child Development, 40,* 619–627.

Russell, A. (1997). Individual and family factors contributing to mothers' and fathers' positive parenting. *International Journal of Behavioral Development, 21,* 111–132.

Schaefer, E., Bauman, K., Siegel, E., Hosking, J., and Saunders, M. (1980). Mother–infant interaction. Unpublished paper, University of North Carolina, Chapel Hill.

Simons, R., Beaman, J., Conger, R., and Chao, W. (1993). Childhood experience, conceptions of parenting, and attitudes of spouse as determinants of parental behavior. *Journal of Marriage and the Family, 55,* 91–106.

Slep, A., and O'Leary, S. (1998). The effects of maternal attributions on parenting. *Journal of Family Psychology, 12,* 234–243.

Small, S. (1988). Parental self-esteem and its relationship to childrearing practices, parent–adolescent interaction, and adolescent behavior. *Journal of Marriage and the Family, 50,* 1063–1072.

Snyder, M. (1983). The influence of individuals on situations. *Journal of Personality, 51,* 497–516.

Spinetta, J. J., and Rigler, D. (1972). The child-abusing parent: A psychological review. *Psychological Bulletin, 77,* 296–304.

Spitz, R. (1970). The effect of personality disturbance in the mother on the well-being of her infant. In E. J. Anthony and T. Benedek (Eds.), *Parenthood: Its psychology and psychopathology* (pp. 503–524). Boston: Little, Brown. (Reprinted from *The first year of life: A psychoanalytic study of normal and deviant development of object relations,* 1965, New York: International Universities Press.

Stevens, J. (1988). Social support, locus of control, and parenting in three low-income groups of mothers. *Child Development, 59,* 635–642.

Taylor, R., Roberts, D., and Jacobson, L. (1997). Stressful life events, psychological well-being, and parenting in African American mothers. *Journal of Family Psychology, 11,* 436–446.

Tellegen, A., Watson, D., and Clark, L. (1999). On the dimensional and hierarchichal structure of affect. *Psychological Science, 10,* 297–303.

Tronick, E., Cohn, J., and Shea, E. (1986). The transfer of affect between mothers and infants. In T. Brazelton and M. Yogman (Eds.), *Affective development in infancy* (pp. 11–25). Norwood, NJ: Ablex.

Tupes, E. C., and Christal, R. C. (1961). *Recurrent personality factors based on trait ratings* (Tech. Rep.). Lackland Air Force Base, TX: U.S. Air Force.

Van Bakel, H., and Riksen-Walraven, J. (2000). *Determinants of parenting and development of 15-month-old infants.* Unpublished manuscript. University of Nijmegan, the Netherlands.

Voydanoff, P., and Donnelly, B. (1998). Parents' risk and protective factors as predictors of parental well-being and behavior. *Journal of Marriage and the Family, 60,* 344–355.

Watson, D., and Clark, L. A. (1984). Negative affectivity. *Psychological Bulletin, 95,* 465–490.

Watson, D., and Clark, L. A. (1997). Extraversion and its positive emotional core. In R. Hogan, J. A. Johnson, and S. R. Briggs (Eds.), *Handbook of personality psychology* (pp. 767–793). San Diego, CA: Academic.

Watson, D., Clark, L., and Harkness, A. (1994). Structures of personality and their relevance to psychopathology. *Journal of Abnormal Psychology, 103,* 18–31.

Westen, D. (1990). Psychoanalytic approaches to personaltiy. In L. Pervin (Ed.), *Handbook of personality: Theory and research* (pp. 21–65). New York: Guilford.

Westen, D. (1991). Social cognition and object relations. *Psychological Bulletin, 109,* 429–455.

Westen, D., and Gabbard, G. O. (1999). Psychoanalytic approaches to personality. In L. A. Pervin and O. P. John (Eds.), *Handbook of personality*: Theory and Research (2nd ed., pp. 57–101). New York: Guilford.

Westen, D., Lohr, N., Silk, K., Gold, L., and Kerber, K. (1990). Object relations and social cognition in borderlines, major depressives, and noromals: A TAT analysis. *Psychological Assessment, 2,* 355–364.

Wiesenfeld, A., Whitman, P., and Malatesta, C. (1984). Individual differences among adult women in sensitivity to infants. *Journal Personality and Social Psychology, 46,* 118–124.

Wiggins, J. S. (1982). Circumplex models of interpersonal behavior in clinical psychology. In P. C. Kendall and J. N. Butcher (Eds.), *Handbook of research methods in clinical psychology* (pp. 183–221). New York: Wiley.

Wiggins, J. S. (1995). *Interpersonal Adjective Scales: Professional manual.* Odessa, FL: Psychological Assessment Resources.

Wiggins, J. (1997). In defense of traits. In R. Hogan, J. Johnson, and S. Briggs (Eds.), *Handbook personality psychology* (pp. 95–141). San Diego, CA: Academic.

Wiggins, J. S., and Pincus, A. L. (1989). Conceptions of personality disorders and dimensions of personality. *Psychological Assessment, 1,* 305–316.

Winnicott, D. W. (1975). Reparation in respect of mother's organized defense against depression. *Through paediatrics to psycho-analysis.* New York: Basic. (Original work published 1948.)

Winter, D. G., and Barenbaum, N. B. (1999). History of modern personality theory and research. In L. A. Pervin and O. P. John (Eds.), *Handbook of personality: Theory and research* (2nd ed., pp. 3–30). New York: Guilford.

Zaslow, M., Pedersen, F., Cain, R., Suwalsky, J., and Kramer, E. (1985). Depressed mood in new fathers. *Genetic, Social, and General Psychology Monographs, 111,* 133–150.

Zelkowitz, P. (1982). Parenting philosophies and practices. In D. Belle (Ed.), *Lives in stress* (pp. 154–162). Beverly Hills, CA: Sage.

15

Parents' Knowledge and Expectations: Using What We Know

Jacqueline J. Goodnow
MacQuarie University

INTRODUCTION

This chapter on parents' knowledge and expectations revolves around two questions. The first asks: what do we know that is useful when we move from research into action: into advising parents or into planning or evaluating programs of parental "education" or "support"? The second takes the form: what gaps in our knowledge now become apparent?

The emphasis on action-oriented issues reflects a shift within developmental studies. There is now, for example, the journal *Parenting*, with the subtitle "Science and Practice." The term *developmental science* is also appearing as a term covering an aimed-for integration between research and action (e.g., Shonkoff, 2000; Shonkoff and Phillips, 2000). Increasingly, psychologists are being called upon to translate what they know into recommendations for action at a family or a policy level and into terms that make sense to others outside their own field.

For the present chapter, the emphasis on translations into practice involves a broadening in audience and perspective but not a complete breach with the past. The audience in mind now covers not only psychologists but also a variety of people who aim at understanding parents' viewpoints and, where needed, at promoting change: change in the way parents view their children or themselves, change in the way they go about the tasks of parenting or accessing community resources. That audience may now include physicians, nurses, teachers, social workers, and policy makers.

The sources drawn on have also been broadened. As in the chapter on this topic contained in the previous *Handbook*, these sources cover analyses of knowledge and expectations from anthropologists and sociologists as well as by psychologists. To them has now been added, however, more material from intervention programs aimed at changing parents' ideas and actions.

The shift toward asking about translations into action does not, however, mean a reduced interest in basic research on the way people think, especially research in relation to the nature and bases of change. Analyses of parents' ideas benefit by being linked to models and methods developed for the general analysis of ideas, whether held by parents or nonparents. That position is one to be found also in other chapters within this volume (e.g., Holden and Buck, in Vol. 3 of this *Handbook*).

The shift also does not mean that past research on parents' knowledge and expectations contains no interest in combining research and action. The study of parents' ideas has always contained the hope that knowing how these ideas are established, maintained, or changed would be useful when it comes to understanding differences among families or to proposals for action (e.g., Goodnow and Collins, 1990; Grusec, Rudy, and Martini, 1997; Sigel, McGillicuddy-De Lisi, and Goodnow, 1992). The goal of this chapter is to make that hope more explicit and to see how far it has been or could be realized.

The chapter is in six sections. The first introduces some changes in viewpoint in relation to parents' knowledge and expectations: changes that set the stage for some of the later sections. One of these changes has to do with the content of parents' knowledge and expectations. Increasingly, this content is seen as covering not only ideas about parenting and children but also ideas about the nature of the world that parents and children face. Another has to do with the ways in which parents' ideas are seen as established and sustained. The move is from an emphasis on ideas based only on parents' own experience to concepts handed on by others. The move is also from a view of information as willingly given and happily absorbed to an emphasis on more dynamic interactions between parents and advisers. Information is not always eagerly sought or willingly provided.

The second section recommends that any action or any analysis of actions start with the question: what are the goals of parents and advisers? Goals may be usefully considered as the pivots for many of our actions and feelings. Finding ways to describe the goals held by people with varying interests and to specify the nature of differences is then a crucial step in any form of action or analysis. It is also one that shows some useful changes in approach.

The third argues for the need to recognize that the information or advice that parents receive comes by way of a variety of routes and from multiple sources. It comes, for example, from a parent's own experience, a neighbor, relative, pediatrician, nurse, teacher, or social worker, from what is heard on the radio or seen in a book or magazine. At issue then are questions about the extent to which any particular source has credibility, the extent to which the several messages are compatible, and the areas where scarcity or silence still apply rather than an abundance or even a surfeit of information.

The fourth and fifth sections basically argue for the need to look carefully at the ways in which we regard matters such as "information processing" or "thinking." We do best, the argument runs, to start from positions that are now often found in general analyses of cognition. Knowledge and expectations, to boil down the recommendations, are matters of the heart as well as of the head. They are matters of mood, identity, and comfortable familiarity.

Knowledge and expectations involve also interpersonal relationships. They are matters of people as well as information. We would do well, then, to ask about the social aspects of asking or telling, the nature of the relationship between the people involved, and the nature of each person's image of the other. Such aspects are especially important when, as often happens, the advice or the program comes from a person of one background to a person from another, with differences in ethnicity and in socioeconomic status being frequent.

The last section takes up an issue that many providers of information and advice would often prefer not to address. This is the probable fate of what they provide. At issue in particular are concepts that might help advisers anticipate a variety of fates and tailor what they do accordingly. The section takes up the importance of information that has an "action tag" to it: a way of doing things rather than only "information about" a problem. Noted as well is the importance of timing. Information seems most readily attended to when it is provided shortly before it is needed: around transition points, for example, rather than well before or well after a bridge has been crossed. The section also summarizes what we know about the ways in which knowledge and expectations come to be revised and argues once more for the combination of data from research on the outcomes of intervention actions and research on the general nature of change in any set of ideas.

These several sections, it must be pointed out, provide no panacea—no simple set of steps—for any adviser to follow. They do, however, aim at casting some of what we know about the ways in which ideas are established and revised into a more useable shape for occasions when parents are given information or advice with the aim of influencing their knowledge and expectations.

A BRIEF HISTORY OF PARENTS' KNOWLEDGE

The study of parents' knowledge and expectations has displayed several changes over the last 5 years or so. This opening section introduces two of those changes. They are important both in themselves and because they set in train some further shifts described in later sections.

The Content of Parents' Knowledge and Expectations

For most developmentalists, the knowledge and expectations that first spring to mind have to do with what is thought about parenting and about children, with an emphasis on the latter. We ask, for example, what parents see themselves as responsible for or how they rate their capacity to influence events in comparison with the influence they see a child as having. We ask what kinds of timetables parents have in mind for children's development. When, for example, do parents think babies can follow with their eyes a moving target? When can children benefit from being read to? When can they be left alone in the house for a while? What do they think is the order in which children acquire various forms of language use? We ask also what methods parents see as most likely to be effective in achieving various goals—for example, the methods that help children to learn or to solve a problem, or the methods that make them most likely to accept a parent's request or directive.

These are by now well-travelled research areas, as three chapters in the first edition of this *Handbook* bring out (Goodnow, 1995; Holden, 1995; McGillicuddy-De Lisi and Sigel, 1995). We know less about what parents see as the nature of their settings and their sources of support. Do they, for example, see the neighborhood as helping them achieve their goals or as presenting hazards to their children? Do they see themselves as isolated or as having people they can turn to if need arises? What do they know about the availability of various sources of help, or ways to access these? About their rights or entitlements, and the ways in which they can act in order to turn these into reality?

Questions about parents' perceptions of the world outside the family are becoming more salient as the recognition arises that neighborhood and community conditions influence children's development, with parents' perceptions and coping strategies seen as one route by which this influence comes about (e.g., Furstenberg, Cook, Eccles, Elder, and Sameroff, 1998).

What do we gain by adding such questions to the ones we are most likely to ask? One gain is that they expand our sense of what to consider when we aim at changing parents' ideas. It is easy to believe that all we need to do is to alter a parent's ideas about what children are like or what children need in order to produce a different kind of child outcome. The ideas held about children may often need changing. Working only on that content, however, ignoring parents' ideas about the world that they and their children live in, is likely to take us only along part of the road.

A further gain is that we may begin to develop a different understanding of a parent's difficulties and a parent's actions. When an area is seen as physically unsafe, for example, parents may move toward isolating their children or attempting to build up neighborhood connections that help them know what their children are doing or can help when problems arise (Furstenberg et al., 1998). When an area is seen as containing values that undermine a parent's efforts to establish a particular view of the world, they may move toward "cocooning" a child or toward teaching them, in advance, defensive and discounting strategies (Goodnow, 1997).

Those examples are premised on the possibility of keeping a child away from danger or negative influences. In some neighborhoods, however, such moves may not be possible. In a "mixed" neighborhood, for example, it may not be possible to avoid encounters with racial discrimination. In such settings, it makes sense that African American parents adopt a variety of methods to instil in their children both a sense of pride in their own group and strategies for responding to direct denigration, varying their approach to fit the age of the child and the parent's own experience of discrimination (Hughes and Chen, 1999).

In effect, we may now well add perceptions of settings—from hazards to supports and possible strategic actions—to the range of content we usually consider when we start to think about parents' knowledge and expectations.

Influences on Parents' Knowledge and Expectations

It is easy to adopt an essentially private view of the way individuals come to hold the ideas they do. We see ourselves as mulling over the meanings of events, working toward a view of ourselves, others, and the world around us that makes some degree of sense. This private construction view of thinking was for some time the dominant view within analyses of children's thinking and adults' problem solving. We have come to recognize, however, the need to add other people to the picture.

To start with, developmentalists have come to recognize that many of the ideas we come to hold are taken over from others. We encounter them in a variety of ways: in the course of learning the names that others provide for objects or people, from hearing various kinds of narratives, from being caught up in everyday routines or practices. We may—in fact, we inevitably do—transform or reshape what we encounter, but the overall picture is far from one of individual invention or solitary construction (e.g., Miller and Goodnow, 1995; Shweder, 1982).

The same kind of shift in frame may well be applied to the ideas that parents hold. The ideas held about what mothers and fathers might contribute to childrearing, for example, may be influenced by a parent's own experience as a child or as a parent. They are influenced also, however, by encountering phrases such as "women and children" (Thorne, 1982), by narratives about parents, by the portrayals of mothers and fathers in the media, and by such everyday practices as the inclusion of fathers in childbirth classes or the facilities available for taking children to the toilet in public spaces. In these several ways, others provide us with ideas that are already prepackaged.

Once other people are added to the picture, attention can begin to turn toward the ways in which ideas are provided. Take, for example, answers to a parent's questions that take the form of saying, "It's just a phase, they will grow out of it." That kind of comment, Sameroff and Feil (1985) point out, leaves parents little wiser. It may also, several analysts of knowledge propose, express an interest in maintaining a monopoly of knowledge. Useful information then is not always willingly provided.

That kind of view of knowledge is more common in anthropology and sociology than in psychology (Bourdieu, 1979; Foucault, 1980). In these views, knowledge is regarded as a controlled commodity: owned by some and provided to others only under particular conditions. Those views have been translated into more familiar forms by some developmental scientists (e.g., Glick, 1985; Goodnow, 1990). The most direct way of giving them meaning, however, may be by a current proposal with regard to children "in care."

The proposal in question is one under discussion in Sydney (*Sydney Morning Herald*, July 17, 1999). This proposal comes at the end of a long and public debate about the extent to which a particular government department does in fact "care well" for children who are removed from a parent's care, primarily on the basis of neglect, abuse, or parental incompetence. The department has now come up with a proposal (labeled as tentative) that favors making a child's whereabouts unknown to the parent. The part of the proposal that arouses particular concern is the imposition of a fine on either a care provider or a child if they disclose a new address to the parent.

The proposal is one of several aimed at making it easier for foster parents to adopt children placed in their care and at "stabilizing" the child's relationship with the new carer providers. Those steps in turn are aimed at reducing the number of times that children move in and out of state care, or from one foster placement to another.

The ultimate aims may be praiseworthy. The specific proposals, however, make one very much aware that what parents know is not all a question of the efforts that they make. In this case, the department regards them as having neither the need to know nor the right to know. When we encounter such cases, the views of knowledge put forward by analysts such as Bourdieu (1979) and

Foucault (1980) no longer seem strange. These views can, in fact, illuminate a great deal of what happens between parents and their possible advisers.

It would be an error, however, to leave any impression of unwillingness as existing only on the side of people other than parents. Parents also may withhold information. They may as well be unwilling to learn new ways of looking at themselves, their children, or their settings, or to accept advice. The later sections of this chapter will pick up more material on this score. For the moment, however, the shift to be noted is a shift from knowledge as privately constructed and organized by individuals to the recognition that a great deal of that activity has a social basis and involves contributions of various kinds from various people.

WHAT ARE PARENTS AND ADVISERS SEEKING TO ACHIEVE?

Psychologists increasingly recognize that ideas, feelings, and actions revolve around the goals that people set for themselves and others. In relation to parents, that position has been especially argued by Dix (1991, 1992). Advisers to parents would have no difficulty accepting the general argument. What needs closer attention, however, is the extent to which people assume that goals are shared, easy to describe, and static.

Are Goals Shared?

One conclusion from a metareview of intervention efforts is that success is more likely when both the parents and those who seek to give advice agree that there is a problem, ideally the same problem (Olds et al., 1999).

At the same time, it is unlikely that goals are completely likely to be the same. A rising concern among policy makers and within intervention research, for example, has to do with the economic costs and benefits to the community of children or families receiving various kinds of assistance (e.g., Barnett, 2000; Greenwood, Modell, Rydell, and Chiesa, 1996; Haveman and Wolfe, 1984; Karoly et al., 1998). Keeping community costs under control or within a given budget is not likely to be a family's major concern.

Describing Goals and Differences in Goals

Psychologists are still seeking ways to specify the nature of differences between one goal and another, or between one person's goals and those of another individual. There are, however, several proposals that seem likely to be especially useful to people who seek to influence parents' knowledge and expectations:

(1) The same words may carry different meanings. Phrases such as "a happy child" or "a good job," for example, may vary in meaning from one parent to another or between parents and advisers. The differences most difficult to resolve may, in fact, be where people use the same terms and wrongly assume identical meanings. An example is Backett's (1982) analysis of partners who use terms such as "joint effort" or "fair" in describing their relative contributions to childrearing or the work of a household.

(2) Goals are best thought of as related to one another rather than in isolation. There may be trade-offs between goals. Goals may also form hierarchies. It might well be difficult, for example, to think about a child's level of happiness or adjustment until the child's physical needs and physical survival have been taken care of (LeVine, 1988). The actual hierarchies turn out to be not easy to establish. It nonetheless makes good sense to consider what parents see as a first and a later priority.

(3) Goals are not always accompanied by a knowledge of how to achieve them. Parental hopes and expectations, for example, are often not accompanied by an accurate knowledge of how to make them achievable. That kind of gap seems especially likely to happen when parents want their children to follow a path that lies outside the usual routes and the everyday knowledge of their social group.

That kind of point was made vividly some time ago by Jackson and Marsden (1966) in relation to blue-collar English parents who hoped to see their children go on to a university. These parents appreciated the need for a child to "do well" in school in the sense of a high overall score, summed across school subjects (a high "aggregate" or "grade point average"). What they did not know, and did not think to ask about, was the significance of some specific course requirements for the goals they had in mind. A lack of knowledge and confidence with regard to how to proceed appears also when parents regard "the school" as a solid wall, rather than as being made up of people who are differentially approachable and persuadable (Alexander and Entwisle, 1988). In both cases, effective action may take the form of supplying the know-how that parents lack, supplying what Bourdieu (1979) has called the "cultural capital" which is a major asset for middle-income, nonimmigrant parents.

(4) What happens when goals appear as not likely to be met? Parents' expectations often exceed their children's grasp. How do parents respond when difficulties appear? The interesting areas to explore, it has been proposed, are the forms of "stretch" (Rodman, 1963) that parents display. What are the acceptable substitutes, the acceptable compromises? What represents the bottom line (Goodnow, 1997) for parents? ("Any job that's decent," "Anything but working in the fields," "Any clean jobs," and "Just as long as they stay out of trouble" are examples of bottom lines).

Knowing about acceptable lines of action in the face of difficulties and points where compromise will be strongly resisted would clearly be useful when it comes to offering information or advice. That kind of knowledge offers as well a way of thinking about differences among parents.

One example of that possibility comes from the observations that prompted Rodman (1963) to think in terms of "value stretch." The major difference between middle-income parents and parents from other income groups, Rodman (1963) considered, lay not in their goals but in the way they responded when children began not to meet those goals. When the goal was achievement in school, for example, middle-income parents responded by sticking with the original goals as far as possible and searching for ways to make them still possible. Parents in lower-income groups tended more often to scale down their expectations about success in school.

A second example has to do with the timing of concern. When do parents begin to think that action might need to be taken? What happens, for example, when a child in the early grades of primary school performs around the average or below the average of the class? Parents in Japan, it turns out, describe themselves as being immediately concerned. Parents in the United States, in contrast, describe themselves as less concerned. Their concern would be more likely to start if in the following year the questionable performance continued (Chen and Uttal, 1988).

The bases of the difference are not clear. Compared with Japanese parents, U.S. parents may have a stronger belief in the possibilities of catching up, in the existence of "late bloomers," or in the accuracy of predictions from early performance. Whatever the bases of the difference, the result reinforces the value of considering not only what parents do when achieving their goals begins to seem in doubt but also when they begin to feel that difficulties might occur and the nature of their monitoring—their "temperature-taking"—to see how things are going (see also Crouter and Head, in Vol. 3 of this *Handbook*).

Changes in Researchers' and Advisers' Goals

The paragraphs above have all been written in terms of the nature of parents' goals. The proposals might as easily apply to the goals that researchers bring to attempts at influence. Researchers' goals, in fact, turn out to illustrate very nicely a further important feature of goals or expectations. This is the extent to which they are fluid, changing from one time to another.

The shifts I use as examples have to do with (1) a move from emphasizing academic skills to emphasizing social skills and the ability to regulate emotions, and (2) an increasing concern with economic costs and benefits.

The first large wave of intervention programs, for example, contained a heavy emphasis on school achievement. The need emphasized was a change in the academic skills that children brought to school. This academic bias is reflected in many of the program names (e.g., Head Start, Even Start, and Parents as Teachers). It is reflected also in the content of many programs (e.g., the emphasis on preliteracy, on learning the letters of the alphabet and recognizing numbers). Later waves of intervention efforts brought a stronger emphasis on children's social skills and their capacity to regulate emotional states, with particular attention in several programs to changing the occurrence and the persistence of unacceptable aggression. Examples are programs related to bullying (e.g., Olweus, 1994) and to early disruptive aggression (e.g., Tremblay, Pagani-Kurtz, Mâsse, Vitaro, and Pihe, 1995). The aims of researchers and of policy makers appear to have changed.

A further sign of change on the advisory side is an increasing emphasis on costs and saving for the community or the state. It is only in the later phases of the evaluation of the High/Scope program, for example, that we begin to see close attention to the savings to the state when children grow up without going on welfare or without getting arrested and—more positively—make commitments to a partner or to children (e.g., Schweinhart, Barnes, and Weikart, 1993).

The likelihood of welfare dependency and of involvement in delinquency is not limited to the High/Scope evaluations (see Barnett, 2000, on "the economics of early intervention programs," or Yoshigawa, 1994, 1995). Money costs and benefits have even drawn the attention of economists in the Rand corporation, with efforts directed toward building estimates and models to cover the cost of various programs—various forms of home visiting, for example—together with the financial benefits to the state of various outcomes (Greenwood et al., 1996; Karoly et al., 1998). In a world where funding for programs of any large scale is most likely to come from the state and where the state is most persuaded by economic rationalism, the goal of establishing the financial parameters of any effort seems likely to acquire more and more prominence.

What brings about such shifts is a matter for speculation. School achievement may be thought to be receiving adequate attention. The nature of the difficulties that children present may be seen as having changed. What we need to recognize as a starting point, however, is that a certain degree of fluidity when it comes to goals and the perception of problems characterizes both parents and advisers.

RECOGNIZING MULTIPLE ROUTES AND MULTIPLE VOICES IN PARENT KNOWLEDGE

This section is organized in "bottom-up" fashion. It begins with some observations on what parents know and then asks about implications for the way we consider changes in parents' knowledge and expectations.

The opening observation comes from a pediatrician working in a middle-income area. His current bane are parents who look up all the symptoms on the Web before they arrive with a child. Some even add the comment—after he has offered a diagnosis—that "you're right, Doctor. That's just what it said on the Web." His experience is a reminder that most parents have access to more than one source of information and that people give various degrees of credibility to various sources. Women who have not had children, for example, often lack credibility to mothers. Preschool teachers, likely to be regarded as "minders of children," often lack credibility when they speak about themselves as educators. We make a grave error if we begin to think of ourselves as the only source or as the most credible source for parents. It would be wiser always to ask: what is my credibility in this particular situation? Where do I rank in relation to other possible sources?

The second piece of data is more formal. It comes from observations of behavior over periods that span before and after the onset of formal campaigns for change: campaigns for having infants sleep on their back rather than on their stomachs, for example, for placing children in seat belts, or for not smoking, especially during pregnancy. Each of these formal campaigns has produced changes in parents' knowledge and actions. The changes began, however, before the onset of the formal campaigns (Powles, 2000).

Powles' explanation is that changes begin when information starts to appear in magazines or in informal talk. At this stage, however, the people most likely to make a change are the relatively well educated: the people who read magazines, talk about items they have read, or are alert to ways of "self-improvement." The data, Powles (2000) comments, point to information as coming from a variety of sources. They point also to the nature of the source as influencing the extent to which differences occur between people in one social group and in another. The differences are likely to be larger, Powles proposes, when the relevant information is in print sources or comes only from visits to a physician.

The third piece of data is a challenging and oddly neglected study by Frankel and Roer-Bornstein (1982). Here the parents of interest are mothers in two groups of recent immigrants to Israel. The sources of information for both are seen as twofold: the Israeli health system and the folk knowledge represented especially by the grandmothers in the group. Frankel and Roer-Bornstein asked the mothers in both groups about their understanding of events such as miscarriage or difficulties around the time of birth. The mothers in one group gave answers that were coherent and along the lines of those that members of the health system would give. The mothers in the second group gave answers that showed signs of confusion or misunderstanding. These mothers were also the more likely to make heavy use of the health system rather than turning to sources of folk knowledge. It was as if they had lost confidence in their own knowledge but had still not gained an understanding of the alternative.

The difference apparently reflects the degree of compatibility between the kinds of explanation offered by the health system and those contained in the folk knowledge. The first group accounted for events in predominantly physical terms. The particular explanations with which they started were often not accurate. The style of explanation, however, was similar to what was being offered by the health system. The old explanations needed some changing but the basic premises did not need to be altered. The second group accounted for events in predominantly animistic terms (e.g., the ill will of others or the presence of spirits). Now the basic premises needed to be altered: a demand that appears to have given rise to both confusion and a loss of confidence in the group's own approach.

The last piece of provocative data comes from another report of immigrant experience. In this case, the mothers were immigrants in Holland, predominantly from rural parts of Turkey and neighboring countries (Lans, van der Nijsten, and Pels, 2000). The new information they encountered was in the form of it being compulsory for all children—girls as well as boys—to attend school until a certain age. Schooling was now not a matter of choice, and the number of years required was greater than most children usually undertook in the parents' village of origin. Once again, the new information did not fall on a blank slate. In this case, the mothers who most quickly picked up and accepted the new set of expectations were mothers who had wanted more schooling for themselves and for their children. To their own voices they could now add the voice of the state, with the latter either adding credibility to their expectations or reducing the need for them to be individually persuasive.

Occasions of Lesser Availability

The data up to this point may give the impression that information rolls in from a variety of sources, with the critical questions having to do with issues of compatibility, competing voices, differential credibility, or ways of coping with a barrage of advice.

That, however, is not always the case: a point first noted in the opening section. Consider now some examples that expand the point:

(1) When a child has a disability, information about what to expect may not be readily available, either from formal sources or from looking to see what other children are doing (Barsch, 1968).

(2) When children are older, comparison benchmarks may be less available than they were when children were young. That comment is prompted especially by a report of parents in midlife (Ryff, Schmutte, and Lee, 1996). Now a parent's concern is often with asking: how have my children turned out? How well have I done?

The report by Ryff and her colleagues is a major break from the usual concentration on parents' knowledge and expectations with regard to young children. Parental expectations and evaluations clearly continue throughout life. The report is also a reminder that difficulties when it comes to informative comparisons are not limited to parents with a nonaverage child. The parents in this study often turned to their own lives for comparison ("Where was I at this point?"), in ways they would not have done when their children were younger and comparative judgments with other people's children were more easily made.

(3) The topic at issue may be an area of silence. Over a relatively short time, we have seen in the Western world the breaking of a number of silences: silences with regard to children born "out of wedlock," for example, or child abuse by parents, teachers, or clergy. We have seen also a turn toward mandatory reporting of suspected abuse by teachers or physicians, and expected reporting by neighbors. "Private family matters" are in many ways no longer so private.

There still remain, however, areas of relative silence: areas where information would only be disclosed to certain people or where great efforts would be made to keep knowledge restricted. "Secrets" still remain a part of life for parents and for society in general. We would do well, in interactions with the parents in any group, to try to anticipate the areas of probable silence on their part and the areas where disclosure is uncomfortable to ourselves.

(4) Information may be effectively unavailable because the provider misjudges the form in which it will be useful or preferred. That comment is prompted especially by a personal observation in a town where a "parent support program" was being implemented. Mothers of newborns were being given, while they were still in hospital, a pamphlet urging them to read to their children. Apart from the questionable timing, this was a group of mothers with low levels of literacy themselves. Print was not their preferred medium for information, and the pamphlet was probably quickly discarded.

That statement may seem to imply that we know a great deal about parents' preferences for the route by which information comes to them. In fact, we do not. We have, for example, still a great deal to learn about parents' preferences with regard to ultrasound, with some preferring not to make use of the procedure and some, while using it, preferring not to know if the child they are carrying is a girl or a boy (Gloger-Tippelt, Fischer-Winkler, Lichter-Roth, and Lukas, 1989). We also have a great deal to learn about parents' preferences—as against advisers' preferences—for information conveyed by print, video, or face-to-face talk with particular people. Overall, the choice of one medium rather than another for the provision of information and advice will need a great deal more data on preferences—by various people and for various topics—than we currently have.

KNOWLEDGE AND EXPECTATIONS ARE MATTERS OF BOTH HEAD AND HEART

When it comes to providing information and advice to parents, it is temptingly easy to assume that, as long as the information is clear, people will absorb it willingly and without difficulty. The history of work on cognition provides some salutary reminders that we may do well to consider some alternative possibilities.

The classic emphasis in studies of adult cognition, for example, was originally on the extent to which people displayed an accurate reproduction or synthesis of the information provided. With an increasing recognition of the importance of "motivated cognition" and "motivated strategies" (e.g., Showers and Cantor, 1985), interest increased in the extent to which people were motivated by other goals. To accuracy, for example, were added goals such as closure and structure, along with questions about the circumstances under which one goal or the other became paramount.

The addition of these goals helps make sense of some aspects to parents' knowledge and expectations. It has seemed surprising to many observers, for example, that parents so rapidly assign temperaments and potentials to their newborns, or even to their children while still in utero (e.g., Fischer and Fischer, 1963; Zeaman and Anders, 1987). Researchers who start from an interest in motivated cognition would see these swift judgments as motivated by a need for some degree of closure, some reduction of the uncertainty about what a child may be like.

Fischer and Fischer (1963) add the comment that the uncertainty may be especially high in cultural groups that assign to parents the task of "divining the potential" of each individual child and tailoring the environment accordingly. We still lack observations from other groups that would test this possibility. In the meantime, however, the goal of closure—prompted by a worrying uncertainty—fits the picture of parents' actions far better than the assumption of accuracy as always the main goal.

Where might a goal such as structure or order fit in the parental picture? The ideal thinker might be bothered by a lack of order or consistency in the ideas they hold. We have become aware, however, that a sizeable group of parents can live with what Palacios (1990) termed "paradoxical" ideas: with the belief, for example, that children need both stern discipline and a light hand. To use a different example, many can live happily with what appears to be a contradiction. They endorse the statement that household jobs and money should be quite separate matters. The money is "not for jobs". They also describe themselves as asking their children such questions as "Have you really earned your pocket money this week?" (Warton and Goodnow, 1995).

Beneath apparent discrepancies there may lie some unifying principles that need to be unearthed. An alternate possibility is that discrepancies are only bothersome and lead to effort under some circumstances. What is inside parents' heads, it could be said, is not particularly different from the general nature of society that many anthropologists and sociologists emphasize. Societies, they point out, are not monolithic structures in which one view of the world or one set of values is to be found. Instead, we live in a world where "multiplicity" is the social norm. There is more than one religion, one form of schooling, one form of medicine, one form of marriage, one kind of family (e.g., Strauss, 1992). Compartmentalization and a tolerance for inconsistency may just as easily become the norm within us, making any parental search for reconciling one idea with another or new information with the old a special circumstance rather than something we can take for granted (Goodnow and Warton, 1992).

Adding Issues of Mood, Comfort, and Identity

Within analyses of thinking in general, we have known for some time that mood affects the extent to which people seek or deal with information and advice. If the current state of affairs seems reasonably satisfactory (if there is, for example, no worrying discrepancy), then people are not likely to seek alternative explanations to those already in hand (e.g., Zanna and Cooper, 1978). The same kind of mood also makes it likely that people will accept information as it comes in, with few checks on its accuracy or validity. A similar point has been made with regard to parents. Parents are unlikely to seek new explanations for a child's health or behavior as long as things are going reasonably well. They can live quite happily with theories that range from the benefits of strict routines to the benefits of chicken soup (Sameroff and Feil, 1985).

Applicable to parents should also be proposals in the general area of cognition about the significance of comfortable ideas. The prime exposition of this argument remains Abelson's (1986), in an article with the summarizing title "Beliefs are Like Possessions." Like pieces of furniture or clothing, they come to be liked because they fit with one's sense of place, of identity, or history. Attempts by others to question or to impose new ideas may be responded to "as though one's appearance, taste, or judgment had been called into question" (Abelson, 1986, p. 23).

The discarding of such comfortable old shoes may then occur only under special circumstances. We have still a great deal to learn about the nature of those circumstances, both in general and in relation to parents. To date, one of the most intriguing proposals comes from Sameroff and Feil (1985). What counts, they propose, is the extent to which parents live in a culture that values what is new, that believes there is always a better way forward, and that parents have an obligation to be alert for the new and better way. Parents in the United States, Sameroff and Feil (1985) propose, live in such a culture to a far greater degree than do parents in cultures such as Mexico, with its stronger respect for tradition.

Proposals of this kind, however, have mostly to do with an individual's sense of personal identity. What also must matter is a parent's sense of social identity: the sense of belonging to a particular group and of being regarded by others as belonging to a particular social group (e.g., Tajfel, 1981; Turner, 1985). A change in ideas or expectations in relation to oneself or one's children can be a threat to social identity, leaving a parent open to being regarded by others as strange, as "trying to be better than you are," as abandoning one's original ethnic group or forgetting one's heritage.

We know very little about the circumstances under which a change in a parent's knowledge or expectations is seen by others as a positive "leading the way" or as a more negative "no longer one of us." We also know little about the consequences, for a parent's state of mind, of losing the sense of being part of a group.

Outside the area of parenting, there are some striking case studies of what it feels like to begin to question the ideas with which one grew up and to forfeit membership of an original group. An example is an autobiographical account of growing up within, and then leaving, a family and a community that followed a strictly orthodox form of Judaism (Benedikt and Lawrence, 1992). Similar accounts for parents are hard to find.

Perhaps the lack of direct parental data is not a major issue. For both the sense of loss and liberation when one social identity is lost and another perhaps gained, most of us can probably find parallels within our own experience. The recommendation seems warranted that, when we propose a change in parents' knowledge or expectations, we consider the implications for both change within a parent's head or heart and change in a parent's position within the groups that matter to them or that support them.

THE INTERPERSONAL ASPECTS OF INFORMATION AND ADVICE

Terms such as *information* or *advice* may make the process of search or provision seem impersonal. The reality is often one of an interaction between people who hold particular images of each other and of the way things should proceed.

The significance of relationship quality is increasingly recognized for interactions between parents and children (e.g., Collins, 1995; Collins, Gleason, and Sesma, 1997). The ways in which both interpret changes or challenges, for example, depend on the quality of the relationship: on the feeling of a long-term attachment and trust or, as in a study by Parpal and Maccoby (1985), on a shorter-term mood of reciprocity and willingness. Recognized also is the extent to which even interactions that seem directed toward task competence—competence in household tasks, for example—are for parents ways of conveying to children the kinds of contributions that are expected within a family relationship (Goodnow, 1996).

The same kinds of recognition need to be extended to interactions between parents and advisers. In fact, there is already at hand some data underlining the importance of the relationship established between a parent and a potential adviser. The data come from a study contrasting two approaches within a home visiting program for socially isolated, pregnant women. In one, the focus was on the provision of information and resources. In the other, the focus was on the relationship between the mother and the visitor, with the visitor functioning more as listener and therapist, responsive to the feelings of the other as well as to the more usual range of "needs." The latter approach had the stronger effect on the mother's depression and on her expectations about parenting (Booth, Mitchell, Barnard, and Spieker, 1989).

The ways in which the nature of an existing or hoped-for relationship can influence interactions could cover a broad territory. In this section, I concentrate on two aspects: (1) the particular features of asking and telling, and (2) occasions when parents and advice providers differ in background, with particular reference to differences in socioeconomic background and in ethnicity.

Asking and Telling

The initiative for face-to-face interactions may come about in a variety of ways. Suppose we start, however, with situations where a parent wants to know, for example, how a child is going in school, what to do about a perceived problem, or how to go about achieving a particular goal.

Taking such a step may seem straightforward. Asking, however, is often a delicate interpersonal situation. It takes confidence to approach an apparently faceless institution such as "the school" (Alexander and Entwisle, 1988). Parents may run the risk of appearing ignorant (Jackson and Marsden, 1966). They may need to find a delicate balance between seeming uninterested and appearing "pushy" (Barsch, 1968). In general, they may need to "know how," to be aware of what can be asked for and how this can be done. The appropriate forms of discourse when it comes to question asking can vary from group to group (Foucault, 1980), with the wrong forms leading to negative interpretations of the person asking.

To take a concrete example, Vietnamese parents in a section of Sydney were regarded by teachers as uninterested in their children's school progress, on the basis that they often did not appear on teacher–parent nights and, when they did, they did not ask questions. The parents were, in fact, intensely interested. They simply thought that the direct asking of questions showed a lack of respect for the teacher's authority and was an intrusion on the teacher's area of responsibility. On that basis, they sought their information in other ways (Duchesne, 1996).

On many occasions, however, parents do not make a direct request for information or advice. The decision is made by others that they are in need of the expertise that others could provide. What do we know that could be useful for such occasions? How parents respond to particular forms of proffered advice, it turns out, has not been given close consideration. We can, however, extrapolate from analyses of help, support, or advice offered to another group often seen as in need. These are people in the category of "elderly."

A case in point is a study that focused specifically on "unsolicited help, unasked-for advice" (Smith and Goodnow, 1999). This study constructed a list of 35 ways in which people might offer advice or help before it was asked for, ranging from help with a heavy bag to advice on finances, reminders about appointments, and suggestions on exercize, diet, housing, or friendships. People in three age groups (people in their twenties, forties, and seventies) were asked whether or not they had experienced such offers, whether they found the experience pleasant or unpleasant, and how they responded. The study yielded several findings that we might easily extend to the advice parents often receive:

(1) People in all three groups found these unsolicited offers more often unpleasant than pleasant.
(2) A great deal depended on the motive attributed to the person making the offer.
(3) The most frequent grounds for displeasure were the implication that one was incompetent and the sense that the offer had ignored a boundary surrounding what was private.
(4) The group reporting the most experience with unsolicited advice, and the greatest displeasure, was the youngest. Any group that is in the process of establishing its competence in the eyes of others, the results suggest, is especially sensitive to advice implying that its competence is suspect.

Differences in Background Between Parents and Advisers

It has been pointed out several times that most books of advice for parents and most "parent education" programs convey the impression that the parent lacks competence or needs improvement (e.g., Clarke-Stewart, 1978; Schlossman, 1976, 1978). That impression is all the more likely when the person seen as the target of advice is categorized not only as "a novice at parenting" but also as "poor" or as "immigrant."

The view from the adviser side, however, is only part of the picture. We need to add the view from the position of those being given advice. Increasingly, what is being expressed is their sense of incompetence on the part of would-be advisers. Advisers, it is pointed out, need to become more culturally aware, more culturally sensitive, more "culturally competent" (e.g., Garcia-Coll and Magnusson, 2000; Isaacs and Benjamin, 1991). As those phrases suggest, many of the objections to being treated incompetently are emerging from the groups often regarded as "ethnic" and as interested only in becoming assimilated as rapidly as possible. The same objections could also be made by people categorized as "the poor." The majority of calls for increases in advisers' social competence and sensitivity, however, are currently emerging from groups usually characterized as "culturally different."

What changes are needed for advisers to become more culturally competent? To start with, they may need to know more about the several ways in which particular cultural groups vary. We are now, for example, accumulating considerable evidence of the extent to which cultural groups may vary in their views about the course and the bases of child development, their definitions of maltreatment and of proper family relationships, their aspirations for their children and the methods of control or persuasion that they see as needed for those aspirations to be met (e.g., Bornstein, 1991; Greenfield and Suzuki, 1998; Harkness and Super, 1996; LeVine et al., 1994; Shweder et al., 1998).

Applicable to a variety of groups, however, are three aspects to our current understanding of what happens in interactions when people see each other as "different."

The first of these is the well-established tendency, on the part of all people, to assume what has been called *out-group homogeneity* (e.g., Turner, 1985). The group to which one belongs is perceived as made up of individuals who vary in a number of ways from one another. The out-group—"them"—is seen as consisting of people who are pretty much alike. To Europeans, for example, most "Chinese" look alike. To Chinese, most "Europeans" (the term often used for anyone outside Asia) look alike.

Breaking through the tendency to homogenize takes effort, experience, and the acknowledgment in the first place that this is the way we generally think about ourselves and others. Once that recognition occurs, we can become more attentive to the nature and the extent of within-group variability in the views that parents hold and in the nature of their experience and resources. That sensitivity is, for example, beginning to acquire some prominence in accounts of cultural differences in parents' views about the course of child development. Among parents in the United States and in Russia, for example, larger differences may appear between the middle-income and blue-collar levels within each national group than between the two national groups (Tudge, Hogan, Snezhjova, Kulakova, and Etz, 2000).

To shift for the moment from ethnicity, we can begin also to appreciate distinctions among parents or families often characterized only by their "poverty", their falling below a certain income level. We can appreciate, for example, arguments to the effect that being poor is not always a steady state. Family income can often vary considerably from one year to another (e.g., Duncan, 1988). We can also begin to appreciate distinctions between urban poor and rural poor, between working poor and nonworking poor, or between recently poor and long-term poor. It is among fathers who have become suddenly poor, for example, that explosive anger toward a partner or toward children seems especially likely to occur (Elder, Nguyen, and Caspi, 1985).

The second general aspect has to do with the nature of categorization. It is easy to assume that categories are fixed, reflecting some steady characteristics of the people in question (an assumption that has been proposed as the essence of stereotyping; Turner, 1985). It then comes as a surprise when we find parents who do not apply to themselves or their children the category names that we and others so confidently use. To take an Australian example, families that have for a long time been categorized as "Aboriginal" by non–Aboriginal Australians now often prefer to be referred to as "Koori" or, in some areas, as "Murray." The names are of their choice and are usually closer to the forms of identification they use with each other: namely by reference to the region of Australia their families come from or the people to whom they are related (Bourke and Bourke, 1995).

Social categories, we need to recognize, are fluid. They are constructions, varied to suit our changing purposes. They change not only from one historical period to another. They change also from one situation to another. No one in Sydney, for example, would speak of going to an "ethnic" restaurant. The term is too vague to be useful. The reference would be instead to eating Lebanese, Thai, Vietnamese, Indian, Sri Lankan, Chinese, with distinctions often made within such large categories as "Chinese." The same people might, however, describe a person as "ethnic," especially if their interactions with "ethnics" are limited or superficial (Goodnow, 1999).

The third general aspect to interactions between parents and advisers who vary in background has to do with the ways in which respect is indicated. I have already noted an occasion on which parents' respect for the authority of the teacher led to their being perceived as uninterested in their child's progress in school. Ways of indicating respect need also to be considered on the part of the adviser.

It is easy, however, to say that advisers need to respect the knowledge and position of parents. Less clear are the specific ways in which respect may be indicated and understood. The most useful theoretical source would appear to be the work of Giles and his colleagues on the several forms of accommodation we may make to others: accommodation in the form, for example, of language or the choice of where we meet (e.g., Giles, Coupland, and Coupland, 1991). The application of this body of research to parent–adviser interactions, however, has not yet been made.

THE PROBABLE FATE OF INFORMATION AND ADVICE

The evaluation of what happens to information or advice has become a major issue in relation to formal intervention programs (e.g., Shonkoff and Meisels, 2000). My concern here will not be with the results of those evaluations. Instead it will be with the processes that may lie between the occurrence of information or advice and an outcome for parents or children. These are processes that can help account for the off-and-on occurrence of effects. They are also processes worth anticipating before information or advice is provided.

Advisers may hope for several outcomes, for example, an effect on parents' knowledge and expectations, on parents' actions, on children's knowledge and expectations, or on children's actions. As the several chapters in the present and the previous *Handbook* make clear, all of these outcomes have received attention within studies of parents' ideas. I shall focus only on the first effect. The processes that influence whether it occurs or not, however, are also relevant to other outcomes.

Once again, the material often reflects changes in the way we regard thinking in general. The processes that emerge all moderate the view that people think, or should think, in an essentially scientific, rational, computer-like fashion. In this style, the information comes in. It is checked for accuracy, lined up against existing ideas, and then—if found accurate—used to adjust what was previously thought to be the case.

The earlier sections have already brought out some changes to this vision of how thinking proceeds, for example, the references to comfort, closure, and the reduction of uncertainty as goals that may override concerns with accuracy. This section presents some further changes in concept. In a sequence that roughly parallels what may happen to new information, it begins with the relevance of timing to whether new material is attended to or not. It then proceeds to cover some particular shifts in the way we regard the routes to acceptance or revision. It ends with what is often thought of as the last step in the incorporation of new information: the extension to actions.

The Significance of Timing

From studies of cognition, we can draw suggestions about when best to offer information or advice. One of those suggestions, already noted, has to do with taking note of the other person's mood at the time. More common are proposals to the effect that information and advice are most likely to be attended to when they are about to be needed or when ideas are still in the process of being established.

Advice with regard to pregnancy, birth, and the care of newborns provides an example of timing in relation to what is about to be needed. Parents-to-be seek information about pregnancy when they are in the early stages of pregnancy, and about life with a baby as they get close to delivery or to going home from hospital (Deutsch, Ruble, Fleming, Brooks-Gunn, and Stangor, 1988; Maccoby, Romney, Adams, and Maccoby, 1959). Mothers-to-be may even defer accepting information from their own body, in the form of movement of the fetus, until the results of ultrasound or amniocentesis confirm for them that they are carrying a child who is alive and well (Rothman, 1986).

Ruble's (1994) proposal with regard to schema formation looks less to the way external events unfold and more toward phases in the construction of ideas. She draws data from studies related to women's progressions through parenting, children's transitions through school grades, and experimental studies that require people to build ideas from new material. The general model is one of ideas displaying three phases: construction, consolidation, and integration. The description noted in the previous edition of the *Handbook* (Goodnow, 1995, p. 312) for the impact of each phase on the response to new information still holds:

> The first phase (construction) occurs at the point where the individual is about to enter, or has just entered, a new state: one in which the old categories and expectations may not apply. At this point, the individual is maximally open to new information and seeks it. The consolidation phase brings a drop in the breadth of interest in new information. The information sought is now more focused, designed to fill gaps in a picture that has already acquired some shape, At this point also, . . . inconsistent information may well be ignored or forgotten. In the third phase. . . . (integration), the ideas established in phase 2 are seen as becoming elaborated and linked to other ideas and to concepts of identity. . . . It is at this point that new information may be most actively avoided or resisted in order to maintain a course of action or a particular sense of identity.

It is important to distinguish this kind of view of timing from views that emphasize only the significance of early intervention on the basis of children being young. The target group in many formal intervention programs, for example, often consists of mothers who are expecting a baby or rearing a young child, frequently their first child. That choice could be made on the assumption that changing a young child will have long-term effects, perhaps even function like some form of inoculation or vaccination.

The same choice could be made, however, on the grounds that this is the point at which parents are most open to advice and information. These grounds, I suggest, are the more useful. We can, for example, now more easily think in terms of people as making transitions over the lifespan: from the birth of a child to the phases of "empty nest" or "revolving door." We can begin to be alert also to the continuing emergence of points of potential openness. The choice of timing and of message is not then one to be made once and for all. Instead, it needs to be made many times, with the need recurring for taking account of where a parent currently stands and with the opportunity recurring of tailoring when and what one offers for the new occasions that arise.

This is not to deny the importance of ages and phases with regard to children as well as parents. Once again, however, the more effective route is not to think only in terms of a child's age, with younger always regarded as the better choice for any intervention. One needs to think also in terms of where a child stands with regard to particular turning points. "Early" may then refer to the early stages of making a transition to primary school or high school, to involvement in various kinds of peer groups, to a shift from one kind of family structure to another. Points of transition and points of openness then become what one looks for over the lifespan rather than concentrating only on the early years of life (Developmental Crime Prevention Consortium, 1999).

A Stepwise Approach to the Processes Underlying Change

Whatever the kind of outcome hoped for, the direction usually sought is one that brings a parent's knowledge and expectations closer to an adviser's views. For that kind of change, it is worth keeping in mind the presence of two processes identified within analyses of whether and how children come to hold values that are similar to those of their parents.

The first process involves what people perceive the message to be. Is it, for example, heard accurately or not? The second has to do with the acceptance or rejection of the perceived message. A lack of congruence between parents and children may, for instance, come about because children hear a parental message accurately but reject it. It may also come about because they are happy to accept the message they hear, but this is not in fact the message parents intend.

This two-process approach to questions of congruence was first proposed by Furstenberg (1971), rediscovered independently by Cashmore and Goodnow (1985), added to by Goodnow (1992), and then substantially fleshed out by Grusec and Goodnow (1994). In Grusec and Goodnow's (1994) analysis, different circumstances could be influential for each process. Inaccurate perception, for example, could come about because the original message was poorly expressed or because the listener was not interested in listening carefully or not accustomed to doing so. In contrast, acceptance or rejection of the perceived message is seen as more likely to stem from whether or not people find that the message, if accepted, would lower their image of themselves, call for actions they would rather not take, or change their relationship to the other in ways they prefer to avoid.

To take a first example, consider adolescents' responses to a parent's message about the importance of being neat. Adolescents are clearly aware that this is the parental message. They often prefer, however, not to accept it (Cashmore and Goodnow, 1985).

An example of parents following a similar course is brought out by the comments of a nurse who works for an Aboriginal health service in the western desert section of Australia. Her advice is against children being allowed free access to items such as Coca-Cola. These items, she recommends, should be rationed. The message is clearly heard. It can be repeated accurately. Like many mothers, however, mothers in this area are deeply attached to the notion that it is "unkind" to deny children food that is available. For their children to regard them as "unkind" is a worse outcome than some possible long-term effect on the children's health.

Most then prefer to treat the nurse's message as "rubbish," as her odd idea about what is good for children (the fact that the nurse is vegetarian and the group favors meat probably helps the rejection). If mothers do accept the message that these items are not beneficial to children in more than small amounts, they still transform it in ways that avoid directly saying no to their children. They prefer, for example, to have the items become unavailable, either by forgetting to buy them, running out of money, or relying on the one store periodically having none to sell (J. Thwaites, personal communication, June 2000). In effect, the mothers' maintenance of their identity in relation to their children runs counter to any acceptance of this particular piece of advice about their children's health and the way to achieve it.

Beyond "Simple Revision"

The notion of there being at least two steps toward people holding similar or dissimilar ideas to those of their advisers is one move toward specifying how people respond to the information or advice that others offer. A second move is contained in proposals about the extent to which a change in ideas is in step with exposure to new pieces of information.

It is possible, for example, that people revise their ideas in what has been called a bookkeeping model (Weber and Crocker, 1983). Each new entry of information brings a corresponding change in what is recorded on the side of debit or credit, the side of "pro" or "con." More often, however, we seem to follow two other models. In one of these (a subtyping model), people add exceptions to the old ideas, leaving them intact. In the other (a conversion model), the old ideas remain intact for some time while the information builds up, followed by a sudden turnaround in position.

"That is a wonderful idea, but it wouldn't work for me," is one example of subtyping. Farber's (1983) description of the way parents change their perceptions of a severely handicapped child provide another. The differences in skill from most other children begin to be acknowledged but the child is still placed in the category of what is "normal," with the differences seen only as exceptions that do not call for any radical overhaul of perceptions and actions.

Farber (1983) offers also a description of moments of "conversion." When a child is severely handicapped, he notes, there comes a time when "the fiction of normality" (Farber, 1983, p. 114) has to be given up. It may, however, take some dramatic episodes for that to occur, rather than simply the slow accumulation of smaller bits of evidence.

Are there other shifts within studies of thinking that advisers to parents might find helpful when they ask about the processes involved in any possible change in parents' knowledge and expectations? One useful shift is toward the recognition of accessibility as a feature of ideas. There is a difference between an idea being present and its being "readily accessible," coming quickly to mind when a problem needs to be considered or some event needs to be given meaning (e.g., Higgins, King, and Mavin, 1982). The new ideas we present may become part of a parent's repertoire. They may not, however, come as quickly to mind as, say, the entrenched ideas about the balance of power between parent and child that Bugental and her colleagues see as often prompting child abuse (e.g., Bugental, Blue, and Cruzcosa, 1989).

A further noteworthy shift is a distinction between systematic and heuristic thinking. The latter term refers to the use of rules of thumb and handy approximations wherever possible. Systematic thinking may then be a default option, occurring only when the usual shortcuts do not work (cf. Eagley and Chaiken, 1993). We would do well not to expect systematic thinking as a regular way of proceeding by parents or by ourselves.

The last shift to be noted has to do with the *particular significance of actions*. Already noted has been Ruble's (1994) description of phases in openness to new information. Part of that description was a suggested resistance to new information once ideas came to be embedded in actions. With the exception that Ruble sees embedding in action as a late phase, her proposal fits well with those contained in emphases on what have been called cultural practices (e.g., Bourdieu, 1990; Goodnow, Miller, and Kessel, 1995). These are routine everyday actions that are perceived as part of a natural or moral order and that are followed by all or most members of a group (the shared quality contributes the adjective *cultural*).

Accounts of cultures in terms of practices occupy a dominant place within anthropological theory (Ortner, 1985). Their relevance to analyses of parents' knowledge and expectations lies especially in the arguments that (1) practices are likely to be a person's first introduction into an area (in effect, the beliefs follow from what we come to do), and (2) practices are likely to become unproblematic in the sense that they are often not thought about or are seen as not open to question.

In some cultures, for example, children do not sleep alone. They share a bed or a sleeping space with others. The suggestion that they should sleep alone may be immediately rejected as out of the question, as cruel. In other cultures, the suggestion that children might share their parents' bed is likely to be immediately rejected, this time not as cruel but as an intrusion on the parents' privacy and as a hazard to the child's proper development (Shweder, Arnett Jensen, and Goldstein, 1995).

To the several suggestions for what advisers might consider when they contemplate the probable or possible fate of what they offer, we may then add the suggestion that they first look at the routines already in place. If the new proposal can be fitted into a way of acting that is already routine and regarded as natural or right, the chances of success are greatly increased. If, on the other hand, the new proposal is difficult to fit into what is already routine or runs counter to what is regarded as natural or morally right, then some imaginative rethinking will be called for with regard to how the new idea might possibly become incorporated into parents' current patterns of action.

CONCLUSIONS

This chapter has been written with a particular audience in mind. This is an audience of people with a direct interest in the information or advice given to parents. Their interest may take a variety of forms, ranging from a first attempt to understand parents' positions to the face-to-face giving of advice and the more distant planning, proposing, or evaluating of programs designed to influence parents' knowledge and expectations.

The pervasive theme has been one of benefiting from proposals drawn from more than one discipline (more specifically, from anthropology, psychology, and sociology) and, within psychology, from several shifts in the way knowledge and expectations of any kind have come to be regarded.

Those several sources have served as a base for a number of recommendations. These began with the suggestion that we consider parents' views not only about children and parenting but also about the nature of the setting in which they live, for example, its hazards or the kinds of support and opportunity that it may offer. In a related recognition of the importance of the social context, the recommendation was offered that we keep in mind the extent to which knowledge and expectations are influenced by others. We often proceed, especially in research, as if the major influence on parents' ideas was a parent's own direct experience as a child or as a parent. In reality, many of the ideas that we and parents hold come from others.

The recommendation that followed had to do with considering the nature of the goals that either parents or advisers had in mind. The advice offered was that we ask always how much overlap there is between our goals and those of the people we advise. We would do well also to think about goals, no matter who holds them, in terms of priorities, possible substitutes, bottom lines, and possible forms of "stretch." Stretch, for example, may be easier to achieve than a complete change in goal.

That recommendation may make it sound as if only two people are involved in matters of information or advice. On the contrary, the recommendation that follows is based explicitly on the recognition that parents are exposed to a variety of sources of information. To function effectively as an adviser then calls for recognizing the presence of other sources of advice, asking how one's own credibility stacks up against that of other sources and giving thought to the presence of compatibility or dissonance among the several sources.

The shifts in position that have marked general analyses of thinking are especially apparent in the next set of recommendations. We would do well, these reanalyses recommend, to set aside any "cold" or computer-like images of thinking. The reality is one of ideas linked to people's sense of identity and to the comfortableness of familiar ideas. The reality is also one of any exchange of information—from parents to advisers or from advisers to parents—occurring within a relationship, within an interaction influenced by each person's image of the other's capacity and motives, of what each should contribute, of what each can ask for or speak about.

The quality of the existing or of the expected relationship, we have emphasized, is especially important when, as often occurs, a parent and an adviser come from different economic or cultural backgrounds. There is always a delicate tension between seeing parents as the experts with regard to their family and seeing them as in need of assistance. That tension needs all the more careful handling when there is a difference in background and a difference in assumptions about expertise or the need to change.

The final recommendation has dealt with the value of anticipating the probable or possible fate of the information or advice one has offered, and of considering in advance the kinds of circumstances and the kinds of processes that influence that fate.

Overall, these recommendations amount to no magic bullet for securing a successful outcome. They are instead considerations that hold promise as ways of improving the chances of success when we offer information or advice to parents with the goal of changing their knowledge and expectations.

ACKNOWLEDGMENTS

I owe a particular debt to people who have involved me in the analysis of several programs directed toward the improvement of children's lives, each containing a component directed toward changes in parents' knowledge and expectations. That involvement has been a major prompt toward the framing of this chapter in terms of the translation of research into practice. This debt is strongest to the consortium that produced the report "Pathways to Prevention: Developmental and Early Intervention Approaches to Crime Prevention" (1998): a consortium headed by Ross Homel and including, alphabetically, Judy Cashmore, Jacqueline Goodnow, Alan Hayes, Linda Gilmore, Jeanette Lawrence, Ian O'Connor, Marie Leech, Tony Vinson, and John Western.

REFERENCES

Abelson, R. P. (1986). Beliefs are like possessions. *Journal for the Theory of Social Behavior, 16*, 223–250.

Alexander, K. L., and Entwisle, D. R. (1988). Achievement in the first two years of school: Patterns and processes. *Monographs of the Society for Research in Child Development, 53* (Serial No. 218).

Backett, K. C. (1982). *Mothers and fathers: The development and negotiation of parental behaviour.* London: Macmillan.

Barnett, W. S. (2000). Economics of early childhood intervention. In J. P. Shonkoff and S. J. Meisels (Eds.), *Handbook of early childhood intervention* (2nd ed., pp. 589–612). New York: Cambridge University Press.

Barsch, R. (1968). *The parent of the handicapped child.* Springfield, IL: Thomas.

Benedikt, R., and Lawrence, J. A. (1992). Escape from orthodoxy: Choice points and psychological processes in one woman's journey to freedom. In P. Grimshaw, M. Campbell, and R. Fincher (Eds.), *Studies in gender* (pp. 220–234). Sydney: Allen & Unwin.

Bornstein, M. H. (Ed.). (1991). *Cultural approaches to parenting.* Hillsdale, NJ: Lawrence Erlbaum Associates.

Booth, C. L., Mitchell, S. K., Barnard, K. E., and Spieker, S. (1989). Development of maternal social skills in multiproblem families: Effects on the mother–child relationship. *Developmental Psychology, 25*, 403–412.

Bourdieu, P. (1979). *Distinction: A social critique of the judgment of taste.* London: Routledge and Kegan Paul.

Bourdieu, P. (1990). *The logic of practice.* Palo Alto, CA: Stanford University Press.

Bourke, E., and Bourke, C. (1995). Aboriginal families in Australia. In R. Hartley (Ed.), *Families and cultural diversity in Australia* (pp. 48–69). Sydney: Allen and Unwin.

Bugental, D. B., Blue, J., and Cruzcosa, M. (1989). Perceived control over caregiving outcomes: Implications for child abuse. *Developmental Psychology, 25*, 532–539.

Cashmore, J. A., and Goodnow, J. J. (1985). Agreement between generations: A two-process approach. *Child Development, 56*, 493–501.

Chen, C., and Uttal, D. H. (1988). Cultural values, parents' beliefs, and children's achievement in the United States and China. *Human Development, 31*, 351–358.

Clarke-Stewart, K. A. (1978). Popular primers for parents. *American Psychologist, 33*, 359–369.

Collins, W. A. (1995). Relationships and development: Family adaptation to individual change. In S. Shulman (Ed.), *Close relationships and socioemotional development* (pp. 129–155). New York: Ablex.

Collins, W. A., Gleason, T., and Sesma, A. Jr. (1997). Internalization, autonomy, and relationships: Development during adolescence. In J. E. Grusec and L. Kuczynski (Eds.), *Parenting strategies and children's internalization of values* (pp. 78–102). New York: Wiley.

Deutsch, F. M., Ruble, D. N., Fleming, A., Brooks-Gunn, J., and Stangor, C. S. (1988). Information seeking and maternal self-definition during the transition to motherhood. *Journal of Personality and Social Psychology, 5*, 420–431.

Developmental Crime Prevention Consortium. (1999). *Pathways to prevention: Developmental and early intervention approaches to crime in Australia.* Canberra, Australia: Attorney General's Department.

Dix, T. (1991). The affective organization of parenting: Adaptive and maladaptive processes. *Psychological Bulletin, 110*, 3–25.

Dix, T. (1992). Parenting on behalf of the child: Empathic goals in the regulation of responsive parenting. In I. E. Sigel, A. V. McGillicuddy-De Lisi, and J. J. Goodnow (Eds.), *Parental belief systems* (2nd ed., pp. 319–418). Hillsdale, NJ: Lawrence Erlbaum Associates.

Duchesne, S. (1996). *Parental beliefs and behaviours in relation to schooling.* Unpublished doctoral dissertation, Macquarie University, Sydney.

Duncan, G. J. (1988). The volatility of family income over the life course. In P. B. Baltes, D. Featherman, and R. M. Lerner (Eds.), *Life span development and behavior* (pp. 317–358). Hillsdale, NJ: Lawrence Erlbaum Associates.

Eagley, A. H., and Chaiken, S. (1993). *The psychology of attitudes.* New York: Harcourt Brace.

Elder, G. H. Jr., Nguyen, T. V., and Caspi, A. (1985). Linking family hardship to children's lives. *Child Development, 56*, 361–375.

Farber, B. (1983). Perceptions of crisis and related variables in the impact of a retarded child on the mother. *Journal of Health and Human Behavior, 1*, 108–118.

Fischer, J. L., and Fischer, A. (1963). The New Englanders of Orchardtown, U.S.A. In B. B. Whiting (Ed.), *Six cultures: Studies of child rearing* (Vol. 5, pp. 869–1010). New York: Wiley.

Foucault, M. (1980). *Power-knowledge: Selected interviews and other writings.* London: Brighton and Harvester Press.

Frankel, D. G., and Roer-Bornstein, D. (1982). Traditional and modern contributions to changing infant-rearing ideologies of two ethnic communities. *Monographs of the Society for Research in Child Development, 47* (Serial No. 196).

Furstenberg, F. F. (1971). The transmission of mobility orientation in the family. *Social Forces, 49,* 595–603.

Furstenberg, J. F., Cook, T. D., Eccles, J., Elder, G. H. Jr., and Sameroff, A. J. (1998). *Managing to make it: Urban families in high risk neighborhoods.* Chicago: University of Chicago Press.

Garcia-Coll, C., and Magnusson, K. (2000). Cultural differences as sources of developmental vulnerabilities and resources. In J. P. Shonkoff and S. J. Meisels (Eds.), *Handbook of early childhood intervention* (2nd ed., pp. 94–114). New York: Cambridge University Press.

Giles, H., Coupland, N., and Coupland, J. (1991). Accommodation theory: Communication, context, and consequence. In H. Giles, N. Coupland, and J. Coupland (Eds.), *Contexts of communication* (pp. 1–68). Cambridge, England: Cambridge University Press.

Glick, J. (1985). Culture and cognition revisited. In E. Neimark, R. De Lisi, and J. L. Newman (Eds.), *Moderators of competence* (pp. 99–116). Hillsdale, NJ: Lawrence Erlbaum Associates.

Gloger-Tippelt, G., Fischer-Winkler, G., Lichter-Roth, K., and Lukas, H.-G. (1989). Psychologische Verarbeitung spaeter Elternschaft. *Psychologie in Erziehung und Unterricht, 36,* 8–18.

Goodnow, J. J. (1990). Using sociology to extend psychological accounts of cognitive development. *Human Development, 33,* 81–197.

Goodnow, J. J. (1992). Parents' ideas, children's ideas: Correspondence and divergence. In I. Sigel, A. V. McGillicuddy-De Lisi, and J. J. Goodnow (Eds.), *Parental belief systems* (2nd ed., pp. 293–318). Hillsdale, NJ: Lawrence Erlbaum Associates.

Goodnow, J. J. (1995). Parents' knowledge and expectations. In M. H. Bornstein (Ed.), *Handbook of parenting* (1st ed., Vol. 3, pp. 277–304). Mahwah, NJ: Lawrence Erlbaum Associates.

Goodnow, J. J. (1996). From household practices to parents' ideas about work and interpersonal relationships. In S. Harkness and C. Super (Eds.), *Parental ethnotheories* (pp. 313–344). New York: Guilford.

Goodnow, J. J. (1997). Parenting and the transmission and internalization of values: From social-cultural perspectives to within-family analyses. In J. E. Grusec and L. Kuczynski (Eds.), *Parenting strategies and children's internalization of values* (pp. 333–361). New York: Wiley.

Goodnow, J. J. (1999). Ethnicity: Spotlight on person-context interactions. In J. M. Bowes and A. Hayes (Eds.), *Children, families, and communities* (pp. 40–57). Melbourne, Australia: Oxford University Press.

Goodnow, J. J., and Collins, W. A. (1990). *Development according to parents: The nature, sources, and consequences of parents' ideas.* Hillsdale, NJ: Lawrence Erlbaum Associates.

Goodnow, J. J., Miller, P. J., and Kessel, F. (1995). *Cultural practices as contexts for development.* San Francisco: Jossey-Bass.

Goodnow, J. J., and Warton, P. M. (1992). Contexts and cognitions: Taking a pluralist view. In P. Light and G. Butterworth (Eds.), *Context and cognition* (pp. 85–112). London: Harvester Wheatsheaf.

Greenfield, P. M., and Suzuki, L. K. (1998). Culture and human development: Implications for parenting, education, pediatrics and mental health. In W. Damon (Ed.), *Handbook of child psychology* (Vol. 4, pp. 1059–1109). New York: Wiley.

Greenwood, P. W., Model, K. E., Rydell, C. P., and Chiesa, J. (1996). *Diverting children from a life of crime: Measuring costs and benefits* (Rand Corp. Rep.). Santa Monica, CA: Rand.

Grusec, J. E., and Goodnow, J. J. (1994). The impact of parental discipline methods on the child's internalization of values: A reconceptualization of current points of view. *Developmental Psychology, 30,* 4–19.

Grusec, J. E., Rudy, D., and Martini, T. (1997). Parenting cognitions and child outcomes: An overview and implications for children's internalization of values. In J. E. Grusec and L. Kuczynski (Eds.), *Parenting strategies and children's internalization of values* (pp. 259–282). New York: Wiley.

Harkness, S., and Super, C. (Eds.). (1996). *Parents' cultural belief systems.* New York: Guilford.

Haveman, R., and Wolfe, B. (1984). *Succeeding generations: On the effect of investments in children.* New York: Russell Sage Foundation.

Higgins, E. T., King, G., and Mavin, G. H. (1982). Individual construct accessibility and subjective impressions and recall. *Journal of Personality and Social Psychology, 43,* 35–47.

Holden, G. W. (1995). Parental attitudes toward childrearing. In M. H. Bornstein (Ed.), *Handbook of parenting* (1st ed., Vol. 3, pp. 359–392). Mahwah, NJ: Lawrence Erlbaum Associates.

Hughes, D., and Chen, L. (1997). When and what parents tell children about race: An examination of race-related socialization in African American families. *Applied Developmental science, 1,* 200–214.

Isaacs, M. R., and Benjamin, M. P. (1991). *Toward a culturally competent system of care.* Washington, DC: Georgetown University Child Development Center.

Jackson, B., and Marsden, D. (1966). *Education and the working class.* Harmondsworth, England: Penguin.

Karoly, L. A., Greenwood, P. W., Everingham, S. S., Hoube, J., Kilburn, M. R., Rydell, C. P., Sanders, M., and Chiesa, J. (1998). *Investing in our children: What we know and don't know about the costs and benefits of early childhood intervention* (Rand Corp. Rep.). Santa Monica, CA: Rand.

Lans, J., van der Nijsten, C., and Pels, T. (2000). *Parenting and acculturation: Ethnotheories of Moroccan and Turkish mothers in the Netherlands*. In J. Gerris (Ed.), *The dynamics of parenting*. Leuven, Belgium: Garant.

LeVine, R. A. (1988). Human parental care: Universal goals, cultural strategies, individual behavior. In R. A. LeVine, P. M. Miller, and M. M. West (Eds.), *Parental behavior in diverse societies* (pp. 3–12). San Francisco: Jossey-Bass.

LeVine, R. A., Dixon, S., LeVine, S., Richman, A., Leiderman, P. H., Keefer, C. H., and Brazelton, T. B. (1994). *Child care and culture: Lessons from Africa*. Cambridge, England: Cambridge University Press.

Maccoby, N., Romney, A. K., Adams, J. S., and Maccoby, E. E. (1959). "Critical periods" in seeking and accepting information. *American Psychologist, 14*, 358.

McGillicuddy-De Lisi, A. V., and Sigel, I. E. (1995). Parental beliefs. In M. H. Bornstein (Ed.), *Handbook of parenting* (1st ed., Vol. 3, pp. 333–358). Mahwah, NJ: Lawrence Erlbaum Associates.

Miller, P. J., and Goodnow, J. J. (1995). Cultural practices: Towards an integration of culture and development. In J. J. Goodnow, P. J. Miller, and F. Kessel (Eds.), *Cultural practices as contexts for development* (pp. 5–16). San Francisco: Jossey-Bass.

Olds, D. L., Henderson, C. R., Kitzman, H., Eckenrode, J. J., Cole, R. E., and Tatelbaum, R. C. (1999). Prenatal and infancy home visitation by nurses: Recent findings. *The Future of Children, 9*, 44–65.

Olweus, D. (1994). Bullying at school: Long term outcomes for the victims and an effective school based intervention program. In L. R. Huesman (Ed.), *Aggressive behavior: Current perspectives* (pp. 97–130). New York: Plenum.

Ortner, S. (1985). Theory in anthropology since the sixties. *Comparative Studies in Society and History, 26*, 165–166.

Palacios, J. (1990). Parents' ideas about the development and education of their children: Answers to some questions. *International Journal of Behavioral Development, 13*, 137–155.

Parpal, M., and Maccoby, E. E. (1985). Maternal responsiveness and subsequent child compliance. *Child Development, 40*, 213–236.

Powles, W. (2000, July). *Healthier progress: Historical perspectives on the social determinants of health*. Paper presented at conference on the Social Origins of Health, Canberra, Australia.

Rodman, H. (1963). The lower-class value stretch. *Social Forces, 42*, 205–215.

Rothman, B. K. (1986). *The tentative pregnancy*. London: Pandora.

Ruble, D. N. (1994). A phase model of transitions: Cognitive and motivational consequences. In M. Zanna (Ed.), *Advances in Experimental Social Psychology, 26*, 163–214.

Ryff, C. D., Schmutte, P. S., and Lee, Y. H. (1996). How children turn out: Implications for parental self-evaluation. In C. D. Ryff and M. M. Seltzer (Eds.), *The parental experience in midlife* (pp. 383–422). Chicago: University of Chicago Press.

Sameroff, A. J., and Feil, L. A. (1985). Parental concepts of development. In I. E. Sigel (Ed.), *Parental belief systems* (pp. 83–105). Hillsdale, NJ: Lawrence Erlbaum Associates.

Schlossman, S. L. (1976). Before home start: Notes toward a history of parent education in America, 1897–1929. *Harvard Educational Review, 46*, 436–467.

Schlossman, S. L. (1978). The parent education game: The politics of child psychology in the 1970's. *Teachers College Record, 79*, 788–808.

Schweinhart, L. L., Barnes, H. V., and Weikart, D. P. (1993). *Significant benefits: The High/Scope Perry preschool study through age 27* (Monographs of the High/Scope Educational Research Foundation, No. 10). Ypsilanti, MI: High/Scope Press.

Shonkoff, J. P. (2000). Science, policy, and practice: Three cultures in search of a shared mission. *Child Development, 71*, 181–187.

Shonkoff, J. P., and Meisels, S. J. (Eds.). (2000). *Handbook of early childhood intervention* (2nd ed.). New York: Cambridge University Press.

Shonkoff, J. P., and Phillips, D. A. (Eds.). (2000). *From neurons to neighborhoods: The science of early childhood intervention*. Washington, DC: National Academy Press.

Showers, G. C., and Cantor, V. (1985). Social cognition: A look at motivated strategies. *Annual Review of Psychology, 36*, 275–305.

Shweder, R. A. (1982). Beyond self-constructed knowledge: the study of culture and morality. *Merrill-Palmer Quarterly, 28*, 41–69.

Shweder, R. A., Arnett Jensen, L., and Goldstein, W. M. (1995). Who sleeps by whom revisited: A method for extracting the moral goods in practice. In J. J. Goodnow, P. J. Miller, and F. Kessel (Eds.), *Cultural practices as contexts for development* (pp. 21–40). San Francisco: Jossey-Bass.

Shweder, R. A., Goodnow, J. J., Hatano, G., LeVine, R. A., Markus, H. R., and Miller, P. J. (1998). The cultural psychology of development: One mind, many mentalities. In W. Damon (Ed.), *Handbook of child development* (Vol. 1, pp. 865–938). New York: Wiley.

Sigel, I. E., McGillicuddy-De Lisi, A. V., and Goodnow, J. J. (Eds.). (1992). *Parental belief systems* (2nd ed.). Hillsdale, NJ: Lawrence Erlbaum Associates.

Smith, J., and Goodnow, J. J. (1999). Unasked-for support and unsolicited advice: Age and the quality of social experience. *Psychology and Aging, 14*, 108–121.

Strauss, C. (1992). Models and motives. In R. G. D'Andrade and C. Strauss (Eds.), *Human motives and cultural models* (pp. 1–20). New York: Cambridge University Press.

Tajfel, H. (1981). *Human groups and social categories.* Cambridge, England: Cambridge University Press.

Thorne, B. (1987). Re-visioning women and social change: Where are the children? *Gender and Society, 1,* 85–109.

Tremblay, R. E., Pagani-Kurtz, L., Mâsse, L. C., Vitaro, F., and Pihe, R. O. (1995). A bimodal preventive intervention for disruptive kindergarten boys: Its impact through mid-adolescence. *Journal of Consulting and Clinical Psychology, 63,* 560–568.

Tudge, J., Hogan, D. M., Snezhkova, I. A., Kulakova, N. N., and Etz, K. E. (2000). Parents' child-rearing values and beliefs in the United States and Russia: The impact of culture and social class. *Infant and Child Development, 9,* 105–122.

Turner, J. C. (1985). Social categorization and the self-concept: A social cognitive theory of group behavior. In E. J. Lawler (Ed.), *Advances in group processes* (Vol. 2, pp. 77–112). Greenwich, CT: JAI.

Warton, P. G., and Goodnow, J. J. (1995). For love or money: Parents' views of money in relation to children's household jobs. *International Journal of Behavioral Development, 8,* 235–250.

Weber, R., and Crocker, J. (1983). Cognitive processes in the revision of stereotypic beliefs. *Journal of Personality and Social Psychology, 45,* 961–977.

Yoshigawa, H. (1994). Prevention as cumulative protection: Effects of family support and education on chronic delinquency and its risks. *Psychological Bulletin, 115,* 28–54.

Yoshigawa, H. (1995). Long-term effects of early childhood programs on social outcomes and delinquency. *The Future of Children, 5,* 51–75.

Zanna, M. P., and Cooper, J. (1978). Dissonance and the attribution process. In J. Harvey, W. J. Ickes, and R. F. Kidd (Eds.), *New directions in attribution research* (Vol. 1, pp. 199–217). Hillsdale, NJ: Lawrence Erlbaum Associates.

Zeaman, C. H., and Anders, T. F. (1987). Subjectivity in parent–infant relationships: A discussion of internal working models. *Infant Mental Health Journal, 8,* 237–250.

16

Parental Monitoring and Knowledge of Children

Ann C. Crouter
Melissa R. Head
The Pennsylvania State University

INTRODUCTION

Over the last five decades, scholars from the fields of clinical and developmental science, criminology, family studies, and public health have become increasingly interested in a component of parenting typically referred to as parental monitoring, defined by Dishion and McMahon (1998, p. 61) as "a set of correlated parenting behaviors involving attention to and tracking of the child's whereabouts, activities, and adaptations." Interest in this potentially crucial facet of parent socialization has grown in response to consistent and robust findings that, from the preschool years through adolescence, low levels of parental monitoring are associated with high levels of problem behavior. But the gap between the conceptualization of parental monitoring and how researchers typically measure it has become difficult to ignore. Most measures of parental monitoring are really assessments of parental knowledge; researchers have made a crucial and, some would say, unwarranted assumption that parents acquire knowledge through tracking and surveillance. Recent research suggests, however, that parental knowledge develops in the context of a trusting parent–child relationship and has more to do with the child's willingness to confide in the parent than in the parent's ability to track and monitor the child (Stattin and Kerr, 2000). As Crouter, MacDermid, McHale, and Perry-Jenkins (1990, p. 656) have argued:

> Parents who are good monitors have made the effort to establish channels of communication with their child, and as a result of their relationships with the child, they are knowledgeable about the child's daily experiences. In order to be an effective monitor, however, parental interest is not enough: A child must be willing to share his or her experiences and activities with the parent. Seen in this light, parental monitoring is a relationship property.

In this chapter, we review research on parental monitoring in an attempt to articulate what parental monitoring really is and what it means in the lives of children and adolescents.

We focus on three primary areas: (1) definitions, historical roots, and measurement issues related to the concept of parental monitoring and its newly distinguished sibling concept: parental knowledge; (2) the association between parental monitoring and parental knowledge and a host of "problem behaviors" in childhood and adolescence; and, (3) the personal, relational, and contextual conditions that may facilitate or impede parental monitoring and knowledge. First, we attend to matters of definition and measurement to illuminate the gulf between common conceptualizations and operationalizations of parental monitoring. As we will show, researchers have typically not measured tracking and surveillance, the behaviors often associated with parental monitoring. Rather, they have focused on the presumed outcome of such behavior: parental knowledge about children's daily experiences. It is our hope that readers will consider the debate about what parental monitoring instruments are actually measuring as they review the remaining sections of the chapter. Second, we review the literature on the connections between low levels of parental monitoring or knowledge and children's psychosocial functioning, beginning with the preschool years and proceeding through middle childhood and adolescence, to establish that parental monitoring or knowledge is a strong and consistent correlate of a constellation of problem behaviors including conduct problems, delinquency, substance abuse, early sexual activity, and low school achievement. In the third section of the chapter, we consider the conditions that give rise to parental monitoring including the nature of the parent–child relationship, children's and parents' personal qualities, and the broader family ecology, specifically the marital relationship, divorce and remarriage, parents' and adolescents' employment circumstances, and poverty and economic strain. Understanding these antecedents will help us better conceptualize parental monitoring and knowledge. We conclude with recommendations for future research directions.

DEFINITIONS, HISTORICAL ROOTS, AND MEASUREMENT ISSUES IN PARENTAL MONITORING

In one of Shakespeare's most famous lines, Romeo asks plaintively, "What's in a name? That which we call a rose by any other name would smell as sweet." In social science, however, the names of constructs *are* important. Unquestioned, they take on a life of their own. The literature on parental monitoring is a case in point. In many studies, variables are labeled parental monitoring when, in fact, they are measuring something else. In Table 16.1, we provide a summary of how parental monitoring was measured in many of the studies cited in this chapter. The table highlights the considerable variability in the ways researchers have attempted to assess this construct and the frequent gulf between the label parental monitoring—with its connotation of parenting behaviors, such as tracking and surveillance—and the measurement strategies employed. In this section, we focus specifically on issues of definition and measurement, terrain that takes us back to some of the earliest work in this area.

As noted above, in a comprehensive review of the literature on parental monitoring, Dishion and McMahon (1998, p. 61) defined parental monitoring as "a set of correlated parenting behaviors involving attention to and tracking of the child's whereabouts, activities, and adaptations." This definition equates monitoring with a set of *parenting behaviors*; good monitors are seen as effective at tracking and surveillance. Moreover, the presumption seems to be that parents are acting deliberately (Kerr and Stattin, 2000). Anticipating the direction of some current research in the area, Dishion and McMahon (1998, p. 64) also noted that the foundation of parental monitoring is the quality of the parent–child relationship: "a positive parent–child relationship enhances parents' motivation to monitor their child and to use healthy behavior management practices." Here again, the parent is seen as the actor and the child the object of the parent's actions. As will unfold in this chapter, there is a movement afoot in some contemporary research to pay more attention to the child as an actor, emphasizing that parents cannot become or remain knowledgeable if their children fail to self-disclose (Stattin and Kerr, 2000) or if they deliberately lie, distort, or omit crucial information (Darling et al., under review).

TABLE 16.1
Measures of "Parental Monitoring" Used in Previous Studies

Study	Reporter	Measure of "parental monitoring"[1]
Ary, Duncan, Duncan, and Hops (1999)	Adolescent, parent	Disclosure (2)[2]; rules (1)
Biglan et al. (1990)	Parent	Obedience (1); supervision (1); perceived knowledge (1)
Bumpus (2000)	Adolescent, parent	Actual knowledge
Bumpus, Crouter, and McHale (1999)	Child, parent	Actual knowledge
Bumpus, Crouter, and McHale (2001)	Adolescent, parent	Actual knowledge
Chassin, Pillow, Curron, Molina, and Borrera (1993)	Parent	Perceived knowledge (3)
Chilcoat and Anthony (1996)	Child	Supervision (10)
Chilcoat, Anthony, and Dishion (1995)	Child	Supervision (10)
Crouter, Helms-Erikson, Updegroff, and McHale (1999)	Child, parent	Actual knowledge
Crouter et al. (1990)	Child, parent	Actual knowledge
Crouter, Manke, and McHale (1995)	Adolescent, parent	Actual knowledge
Crouter and McHale (1993)	Adolescent, parent	Actual knowledge
Darling, Cumsille, Hames, and Caldwell (under review)	Adolescent	Strategic disclosure (36)
Dishion, Capaldi, Spracklen, and Li (1995)	Adolescent, parent, interviewer	Adolescent: rules (6); parent: supervision (7); interviewer: supervision (1)
Dishion, Patterson, Stoolmiller, and Skinner (1991)	Adolescent, parent, interviewer	Child: perceived knowledge, availability, disclosure (5); parent: importance of knowing where child is (2); interviewer: supervision (1)
Fletcher, Darling, Steinberg, and Dornbusch(1995)	Adolescent	Strictness, supervision (9)
Forehand, Miller, Dutra, and Chance (1997)	Adolescent, parent	Perceived knowledge (4)
Glueck and Glueck (1950, 1662)	Adolescent, parent	Actual knowledge
Hirschi (1969)	Child	Perceived knowledge (2)
Kerr, Stattin, and Trost (1999)	Adolescent, parent	Perceived knowledge (9); disclosure (5); solicitation of knowledge (5); control (6)
Ladd and Golter (1988)	Parent	Monitoring peer contact
Manning (1990)	Parent	Rules
McCord (1979)	Interviewer	Supervision; expectations
Mekos, Hetherington, and Reiss (1996)	Adolescent, parent, observer	Perceived knowledge (13); attempted control (13); successful control (13); observer: knowledge, attempted and successful control
Meschke and Silbereisen (1997)	Adolescent	Disclosure (2)
Metzler, Noell, Biglan, Ary, and Smolkowski (1994)	Adolescent, parent	Adolescent: disclosure (1); rules (1); parent: supervision (4)
Mott, Crowe, Richardson, and Flay (1999)	Adolescent	Availability (2); control (1); perceived knowledge (1)
Otto and Atkinson (1997)	Adolescent	Availability (1); regulation (5); monitoring schoolwork (4)
Pagani, Boulerice, Vitaro, and Tremblay (1999)	Adolescent	Perceived knowledge (2); rules (4)
Pagani, Tremblay, Vitaro, Kerr, and McDuff (1998)	Adolescent	Perceived knowledge (2); punishment (5)

(Continued)

TABLE 16.1
(Continued)

Study	Reporter	Measure of "parental monitoring"[1]
Patterson (1982)	Adolescent, parent, interviewer	Child; perceived knowledge, time spent, disclosure (5); parent: importance of knowing where child is (2); interviewer: supervision (1)
Patterson and Dishion (1985)	Adolescent, parent, interviewer	Child: perceived knowledge, time spent, disclosure (5); parent: importance of knowing where child is (2); interviewer: supervision (1)
Patterson, Reid, and Dishion (1992)	Adolescent, parent, interviewer	Child: perceived knowledge, time spent, disclosure (5); parent: importance of knowing where child is (2); interviewer: supervision (1)
Patterson and Stouthamer-Loeber (1984)	Adolescent, parent, interviewer	Child: perceived knowledge, time spent, disclosure (5); parent: importance of knowing where child is (2); interviewer: supervision (1)
Pettit, Bates, Dodge, and Meece (1999)	Parent	Perceived knowledge, difficulty tracking, supervision by other adults (9)
Pettit, Laird, Dodge, Bates, and Criss (2001)	Adolescent, parent	Perceived knowledge (5 adolescent, 8 parent)
Romer et al. (1994)	Child	Perceived knowledge (6)
Sampson and Laub (1994)	Adolescent, parent	Actual knowledge
Shanahan, Elder, Burchinal, and Conger (1996)	Parent	Perceived knowledge (2)
Stattin and Kerr (2000)	Adolescent, parent	Perceived knowledge (9); disclosure (5); solicitation of knowledge (5); control (6)
Steinberg, Fletcher, and Darling (1994)	Adolescent	Perceived knowledge (5)
Waizenhofer and Buchanan (under review)	Adolescent, parent	Actual knowledge; parent: passive versus active supervision
White and Kaufman (1997)	Adolescent	Monitoring schoolwork
Wilson (1980)	Parent	Perceived knowledge, rules (4)

[1] Except for measures of actual knowledge and interviewer/observer ratings, all measures are close-ended survey items, and "disclosure" = child self-disclosure; "rules" = parental rules, requirements, or expectations; "supervision" = parental monitoring, tracking, surveillance; "availability" = presence or absence of parent.
[2] If known, the number of survey items about the construct are included in parentheses.

Early Research in Parental Monitoring

The historical roots of the parental monitoring construct can be found in early studies of delinquency (e.g., Glueck and Glueck, 1950; 1962; Hirschi, 1969; McCord, 1979; Patterson, 1982; Wilson, 1980). A common theme cutting across this literature is that parents of delinquent youths tend to have limited knowledge of their children's daily whereabouts, companions, and activities. Consider, for example, the Gluecks's (1950, 1962) ambitious, comparative study of 500 delinquent and nondelinquent male youth. In their book *Unraveling Juvenile Delinquency*, written over 50 years ago, Glueck and Glueck (1950) set the stage for much of the research on delinquency for the second half of the twentieth century, including work that emphasized parental monitoring. In a chapter entitled "The Boy in the Family," they considered the impact not only of family demographic characteristics, but also of family disruption, the affectional quality of mother–child and father–child relationships, parents' disciplinary attitudes and practices, and, most significant for our purposes, "awareness of leisure-time activities" (p. 130). They noted:

By and large, it is the impression of the home visitors that the parents of the delinquent boys were actually unaware of many of their activities. This deficiency is revealed in the lesser agreement between the parents and the delinquents than between the parents and the nondelinquents as to where the boys played (40.8%:79%), or how frequently they went to the movies (39.4%: 60.8%), or attended church (47.2%:69.8%). The delinquents' parents certainly knew far less, or were perhaps unwilling to admit what they actually knew, than the parents of the non-delinquents in regard to the bad habits of the boys (13.6%:66.4%).

Note that the Gluecks focused on parent–youth agreement about sons' activity patterns, not on parents' and sons' individual estimates of parental knowledge. Their approach would be adopted in a handful of future studies but veered away from in many others.

Thirty years later, in the late 1970s and 1980s, Patterson and his colleagues published a series of studies that highlighted the importance of parental monitoring in the etiology of delinquency. Hallmarks of this body of work include careful attention to measurement issues, adoption of a developmental orientation, ambitious longitudinal designs, and sensitivity to the complexity inherent in studying individuals within families. For example, Patterson and Stouthamer-Loeber (1984) focused on four family management practices and their associations with delinquency in seventh and tenth grade boys. Of the four management practices—monitoring, discipline, problem solving, and reinforcement—monitoring accounted for the most variance in adolescent boys' police contacts and in self-reported delinquency. Patterson and Stouthamer-Loeber (1984, p. 1305), like their predecessors, concluded: "It seems that parents of delinquents are indifferent trackers of their sons' whereabouts, the kind of companions they keep, or the type of activities in which they engage. Perhaps this omission constitutes an operational definition for what is meant by 'the unattached parent'."

This quote is interesting for two reasons. On the one hand, by invoking attachment language, Patterson and Stouthamer-Loeber (1984) infused the construct of parental monitoring with a relationship flavor. On the other hand, in equating low monitoring with indifferent tracking, they clearly conceptualized parental monitoring as a parenting behavior, not as a dyadic property of the parent–child relationship.

Measuring Parental Monitoring and Parental Knowledge

Patterson and Stouthamer-Loeber (1984) operationalized parental monitoring in a sophisticated way using a multimethod, multiple-reporter approach that triangulated "interview data from the mother, the child, the interviewer's impression, and a discrepancy score from daily reports of the child's activities" (p. 1300). In contrast, most studies of parental monitoring conducted over the last 20 years have relied on self-report data, usually from only one reporter. Sometimes children or adolescents are asked a series of questions about how much their parents really know about what they are doing and whom they are spending time with. In other studies, parents are asked to assess how much they really know about their offspring's activities, whereabouts, and companions. For example, Steinberg, Fletcher, and Darling (1994, p. 1061) asked high school students to respond to five questions: "How much do your parents REALLY know . . . Who your friends are? Where you go at night? How you spend your money? What you do with your free time? Where you are most afternoons after school?"

There are at least two problems with this approach: (1) children and parents may not be accurate judges of parents' knowledge and (2) these items do not tap tracking and surveillance. If children and parents were able to provide accurate estimates of how much parents really know about children's daily activities, whereabouts, and companions, their reports should be highly correlated with one another. This is typically not the case. In those few studies that include independent assessments of parental monitoring from parents and from youth, associations between family members' reports are only modestly related. For example, Pettit et al. (2001) reported a correlation of $r = .26$ for mothers and young adolescent offspring in a sample of over 400 families residing in Tennessee and Indiana. Similarly, Stattin and Kerr (2000) reported a correlation of $r = .38$ for parents and their 14-year-old offspring in their sample of over 700 families living in central Sweden. It is perhaps not surprising that parents' and adolescents' reports are not strongly related. Social desirability pressures may be experienced by some parents and some offspring, resulting in distorted estimates. In addition, questions are typically so general—and the time period they refer to is left so undefined—that parents and adolescents may mentally refer to very different previous events when completing the monitoring items. The fact that adolescents and parents do not strongly agree about how much parents know suggests that typical parental monitoring measures may tap something more subjective about the parent–adolescent relationship. But the biggest problem with typical measures of parental monitoring is that, even if parents and adolescents did see eye to eye on them, these questionnaires do not assess parents' actual activities directly. Instead, they typically measure the presumed outcome of parental tracking and surveillance—parental knowledge—providing no information about how parents acquire that knowledge.

Crouter and McHale and their colleagues have used a different measurement strategy, based on one element of Patterson and Stouthamer-Loeber's (1984) original approach: the use of parent–child discrepancy scores vis-à-vis reports on the child's daily activities (Bumpus et al., 2001; Crouter et al., 1990; Crouter et al., 1999; Crouter et al., 1995; Crouter and McHale, 1993; McHale, 1999). In a series of seven evening telephone interviews scheduled about 1 hour before the child or adolescent's bedtime, they ask the parent a set of questions about the child's experiences on that specific day (mothers and fathers both complete the same monitoring questions but on different nights). The questions focus around school-related issues, conduct, relationships, and leisure activities. A different set of questions is posed each night so that parents cannot prepare ahead for the call. After talking with the parent, the researchers ask the child the same questions. The item scores represent the "match" between parents' and children's answers to each question. Although they originally labeled their measure parental monitoring, Crouter and her colleagues (1999) now acknowledge that their measure does not assess parental tracking and surveillance and call theirs a measure of parental knowledge. A strength of their approach is that the measure is intrinsically dyadic, relying on information from both child and parent. Given its focus on specific, daily activities, rather than family members' general impressions, it reflects the daily, "hands on" connotation implied by the term *parental monitoring*. Drawbacks, however, are that the procedure assumes that the child is providing accurate information, when in fact this may not always be the case (Darling et al., under review), and it provides no data about how parents have acquired their information.

Parental monitoring has often been linked to parental supervision and control, and, indeed, in some studies researchers have folded parental monitoring items into a larger set of control-related issues. For example, Fletcher et al. (1995) employed a strictness–supervision scale that combined parental knowledge questions (e.g., "How much do your parents really know what you do in your free time?") with items about parental limit setting (e.g., "In a typical week, what is the latest you can stay out on school nights?"). Likewise, Mekos et al. (1996) combined parents' and adolescents' reports of parents' knowledge, parents' attempts to influence the child, and successful parental control, as well as observational ratings of these three phenomena in videotaped parent–adolescent interactions, into a global "monitoring/control" index.

Parental monitoring may reflect something different from parental control. Stattin and Kerr (2000) administered a traditional self-report measure of parental monitoring (e.g., "How much do your parents REALLY know about . . . ") and also assessed three possible mechanisms through which parents may acquire information about their children (p. 1075): (1) child self-disclosure (e.g., "Do you like to tell your parents about what you did and where you went during the evening?"); (2) parental solicitation (e.g., "How often do your parents ask you about what happened during your free time?"); and (3) parental control (e.g., "Must you ask your parents before you can make plans with friends about what you will do on a Saturday night?"). Child self-disclosure was the strongest correlate of parental monitoring: "... when "monitoring" is recognized as knowledge and we ask where parents have gotten that knowledge, we find that tracking or surveillance efforts, which are implied by the term monitoring and its previous interpretations, are less important than children's spontaneous sharing of information" (Stattin and Kerr, 2000, p. 1078).

Moreover, of the three sources of parental knowledge, child self-disclosure was most closely related to reports of delinquency; the more children self-disclosed to parents, the less problem behavior they engaged in and the less likely they were to have had contact with the police, leading Stattin and Kerr (2000, p.1080) to conclude that "... the link between "monitoring" and antisocial behavior exists, not because surveillance reduces antisocial behavior as has often been claimed, but because child disclosure is heavily represented in "monitoring," and children who talk openly to their parents tend to commit fewer antisocial acts."

Kerr and Stattin (2000), using a sample of Swedish youth living in urban environments, subsequently expanded on this finding by examining whether parental solicitation, parental control and/or child self-disclosure mediated the association between parents' knowledge and a wide range of indices of child adjustment, including school problems, depressed mood, failure expectations, and having friends who engage in deviant behavior. In no case did parental control or parental solicitation mediate the association, but the child's tendency to self-disclose consistently explained part or all of the association between perceived parental knowledge and adolescent adjustment. Interestingly, Kerr and Stattin (2000) is one of the few studies to systematically replicate results using both adolescents' and parents' perceptions of parental knowledge.

Stattin and Kerr (2000, p. 1081) also asked whether "child disclosure is just a proxy for good parent–child relationships." The results described above held up even when the researchers controlled for children's global perceptions of the closeness of their parent–child relationships or parents' global assessments of family closeness, leading Stattin and Kerr (2000) to conclude that parental monitoring is not just a proxy for good parent–child relationships and to argue that we need to pay far more attention to the correlates of child self-disclosure.

We may need to be more precise, however, about the specific dimensions of the parent–child relationship that underlie parental knowledge. Kerns, Aspelmeier, Gentzler, and Grabill (2001) examined two indicators of parent–child attachment—children's reports of security in the parent–child relationship and parents' reports of willingness to serve as an attachment figure for the child—in relation to parents' actual knowledge of their children's day to day experiences, assessed using the procedure developed by Crouter et al. (1990, previously discussed). Notably, the attachment-related items focused on specific issues such as the parent's responsivity and availability, the child's tendency to rely on that person during times of stress, and ease and interest in communication, more precise dimensions than overall assessments of relationship quality. Kerns et al. (2001) found that, for parents of sixth-grade children, mothers who were willing to serve as an attachment figure for the child knew more about their children's daily experiences, and fathers whose children saw them as secure attachment figures knew more about their offspring's daily experiences. These associations were not found, however, for parents of third-grade children.

Parental self-disclosure, parental control, and child self-disclosure are three routes to parental knowledge (Kerr and Stattin, 2000; Stattin and Kerr, 2000), but they are probably not the only routes. Researchers to date have failed to capture some of the subtle ways in which parents may acquire ongoing information about their children, ways not captured by the somewhat intrusive-sounding terms *tracking* and *surveillance*. Like social scientists, parents have a broader repertoire of tools than simply asking questions. Noticing and listening are two behaviors that deserve a closer look. Some parents may be very good at observing and attending to relevant details about their children: the slumping posture that may give away a bad day, the revealing tone of voice, or a sudden change in routine behavior. Noticing such clues may lead a sensitive parent to follow up either with the child or with another family member. Listening is another key parenting behavior that may be important. Children may self-disclose but feel that their mothers or fathers are too busy or distracted to pay close attention to what they are saying. Thus, noticing and listening may be two of the behaviors that children and adolescents are thinking about when they say their parents "really know" about their daily lives; for these children, saying that their parents "really know" may be the equivalent of saying that "their parents care" (N. Darling, personal communication, October 23, 2000).

As we have shown, there currently is no firm consensus on how to conceptualize parental monitoring, or even whether or not parental monitoring is the most accurate term for this construct. There is something, after all, in a name, and it is possible that, by referring to this phenomenon as parental monitoring, researchers in this field have been too quick to embrace the conclusion that parental knowledge is the equivalent of parental tracking and surveillance. In the remainder of this chapter, we review what is known about the effects of parental monitoring, as well as the conditions that give rise to variations in parents' levels of knowledge about their children's daily experiences. As we have done in Table 16.1, we will reserve the term *parental monitoring* for those few studies that appear to focus on parents' actual behavior. In describing other work, we will use the terms *actual parental knowledge*, *perceived parental knowledge*, or *child self-disclosure* in an effort to accurately capture the phenomena under study. This may mean that at times we use different terminology than the researchers in question. Throughout the review, we will occasionally remind the reader about the current debate about what parental monitoring means and, in doing so, attempt to move the field forward toward a coherent direction for future research.

LINKS BETWEEN PARENTAL MONITORING
AND CHILD PROBLEM BEHAVIOR

Parental monitoring has captured the interest of many parenting researchers because it has been found to be a consistent correlate of a range of problem behaviors including conduct problems and delinquency, substance use, early sexual activity, and poor school achievement. With the exception of a handful of studies focused on preschool children, the majority of studies in this area have focused on middle childhood and, especially, adolescence. To convey a flavor of the roles parental monitoring and parental knowledge may play in development, we organize our review chronologically, beginning with the preschool years and proceeding through middle childhood and adolescence.

Correlates of Parental Monitoring and Knowledge
During the Preschool Years

Although the concept of parental monitoring is applicable to families with preschool-age children, few studies have focused on this age group. Extant studies have been concerned primarily with safety issues and peer relationships.

Safety issues.   Studies of young children have focused primarily on issues of safety and injury prevention and, to a lesser extent, parents' monitoring of children's peer experiences. Dishion and McMahon (1998, p. 62) reviewed studies focused on child safety and injury prevention, noting that "low parental monitoring is associated with accidental poisonings . . . exposure to household safety hazards . . . , playground accidents . . . , and handling of hazardous substances in grocery stores." In these studies, low parental monitoring is akin to low supervision, and the boundaries between these constructs are blurred.

Peer relationships.   Monitoring preschool children's interactions with peers is one way in which parents may exert an indirect influence on their children's development. Ladd and Golter (1988), for example, focused on the ways in which parents initiated and monitored preschool-age children's contacts with peers and related them to children's social competence in and outside of school. Parents were telephoned on six different evenings and asked about their children's activities with peers that day. Parental monitoring of those peer experiences were coded as "(a) direct (i.e., parent[s] maintained a presence or participated in the children's activity; (b) indirect (i.e., parent[s] tended to oversee and were aware of the children's activity, but were not consistently present or involved in it), or (c) unmonitored (i.e., the children's activity appeared to be unsupervised)" (Ladd and Golter, 1988, p. 111). Results indicated that indirect parental monitoring was positively associated with social competence but that children whose parents maintained high levels of direct monitoring displayed less competence at school, as rated by their preschool teachers. Aware of the inherent difficulty in determining whether parenting affects child behavior or whether children's behavior causes parents to act in certain ways, Ladd and Golter (1988, p. 110) cautioned: "With young children, parental monitoring may be as much a cause of child competence as its consequence... whereas children who relate well with peers may elicit more indirect styles of supervision, those who have social difficulties may require close attention and, thus, more direct forms of parental monitoring."

Like Stattin and Kerr (2000), Ladd and Golter suggested that what the child is like may be a driving force behind parents' performance as monitors.

Parental Monitoring and Knowledge in Middle Childhood

The need to stay informed about children's activities and behaviors takes on special importance in middle childhood, when children's social orbits expand dramatically. As Collins, Harris, and Susman (1995, p. 67) explained, this wider social orbit and increasing independence have important implications for parenting:

> Six- to 12-year-olds experience a rapidly widening social world. Social networks expand significantly during middle childhood, incorporating extrafamilial adults and peers... Entry into school especially increases the number and kinds of developmental tasks and influences that children encounter. For parents, these experiences outside of the family often create additional burdens and responsibilities for monitoring children's activities and choices of companions at a distance.

Chilcoat and his colleagues are one of the few research teams to focus extensively on the implications of perceived parental knowledge during middle childhood (Chilcoat and Anthony, 1996; Chilcoat et al., 1995). Using an epidemiological sample of urban-dwelling elementary school students from low-income areas, Chilcoat and Anthony (1996) found that low levels of perceived parental knowledge at about age 8, operationalized with a 10-item measure completed by the child, were associated with a reduced probability that the child would abstain from drug use over the next several years. The protective effects of high perceived parental knowledge were especially pronounced through about age 10. Chilcoat and Anthony (1996, p. 95) noted that "Consistent with the hypothesis of a protective effect, there was a two-year delay in the onset of drug-taking for youths in the highest quartile of parent monitoring, compared with the experience of the least-monitored youths." They also found that, controlling for initial levels of perceived parental knowledge, decreases in perceived parental knowledge over time were associated with an increased risk of initiating use of marijuana, cocaine, and/or inhalants.

Associations between low levels of parental knowledge and problematic child outcomes are not confined to urban, low-income samples. Crouter et al. (1990) examined a sample of predominately European American 9- to 11-year-old children growing up in blue-collar and middle-income, two-parent households in small cities, towns, and rural areas. Operationalizing parental monitoring in terms of the "match" in parents' and children's responses to questions about daily activities (described above), they identified a group of children whose mothers' and fathers' actual knowledge scores were both relatively low compared with the rest of the sample. They found that boys with less knowledgeable parents performed less well in school than other children. In addition, the combination of low parental knowledge and growing up in a dual-earner family was linked to higher levels of conduct problems for boys.

Problem Behavior During Adolescence: The Role of Parental Knowledge and Monitoring

The lion's share of research on parental monitoring has focused on adolescence. Patterson (1988) proposed a multistage developmental process tracing the hypothetical route from ineffective parenting in early childhood to delinquency and substance abuse in late adolescence and early adulthood. In preadolescence, he argued, inadequate parenting practices, including low levels of parental monitoring, increase the likelihood that children will perform poorly in school and lack the social skills needed to be successful with peers. Poor school performance and social skill deficits in turn lead children to feel badly about themselves and to be rejected by peers. Low self-esteem and peer rejection subsequently increase the chances that, in adolescence—when active "niche-picking" (Scarr and McCartney, 1983) becomes an increasingly powerful engine of development—youth will gravitate toward deviant peer groups that promote substance use and delinquent behavior. At least one study has successfully tested this general model by focusing on a global construct of adolescent problem behavior that encompasses the full array of negative outcomes: antisocial behavior, high-risk sex, academic failure, and substance use (Ary et al., 1999). More typically, however, researchers have examined problem behaviors separately, reflecting the fragmentation of the field.

Conduct problems and delinquency.   Conduct problems and delinquency have been a major area of focus (Dishion et al., 1991; Forehand et al., 1997; Pagani et al., 1999; Pagani et al., 1998; Patterson and Dishion, 1985; Patterson and Stouthamer-Loeber, 1984; Pettit, Bates, Dodge, and Meece, 1999; Sampson and Laub, 1994; Stattin and Kerr, 2000). In a longitudinal study of young adolescent boys, for example, Dishion et al. (1991) reported that parental knowledge at age 10, assessed with a variant of the sophisticated multimeasure, multiple-reporter approach described above (see Patterson and Stouthamer-Loeber, 1984), was related to involvement with deviant peers at age 12 even when the child's own prior antisocial behavior was controlled. When the investigators added the stability of boys' involvement with antisocial peers to the model, however, parental knowledge dropped out as a predictor of peer antisocial behavior at age 12, suggesting that parental knowledge may exert its primary effects through reducing the chances that the child will become involved in a deviant peer group or that adolescents avoid disclosing their activities when they are involved with deviant peers.

The importance of parental monitoring or knowledge has been conceptualized in some research as a moderator, qualifying the association between family dynamics or contextual characteristics and child psychosocial functioning. Pettit et al. (1999), for example, found that, controlling for youth's behavior problems in sixth grade, unsupervised time with peers was associated with delinquency in seventh grade. Perceptions of parental knowledge moderated this association, particularly when children were living in neighborhoods low in safety and security. Pettit et al. (1999, pp. 776–777) concluded that "unsupervised self-care with peers, in the context of lack of monitoring and unsafe neighborhoods, does in fact forecast the development of externalizing problems." This finding makes sense if parental monitoring is equated with parents' active tracking and surveillance, but, importantly, it also makes sense if parental monitoring stands for a trusting, confiding parent–child relationship.

Substance Use

Low levels of parental knowledge have also been linked to higher levels of substance use in adolescence. Mott et al. (1999), for example, using survey data from over 2,000 urban and suburban ninth grade students, found that higher levels of perceived parental knowledge were associated with low levels of cigarette smoking. Steinberg et al. (1994) examined the connections between perceived parental knowledge and peer influences and self-reported substance use in a high school sample over the course of one year. Low levels of perceived parental knowledge at Time 1 predicted not only which nonusers would turn to substances over the year but which substance users would become *more* involved over time. As Steinberg et al. (1994, p. 1063) explained: "Strongly monitored adolescents are, in essence, doubly protected from substance use involvement: They have the protective benefits of effective socialization in the family and, because they themselves are less likely to begin using drugs, they are less likely to find themselves in situations in which they will be exposed to drug-using peers."

Dishion et al. (1995) took a somewhat different slant on the monitoring–peer group–substance use connection. They divided their sample of adolescent males into two groups, defined by high and low parental knowledge. The correlation between adolescents' substance use and their friends' substance use was modest for boys with knowledgeable parents and strongly positive for boys whose parents knew little about their daily experiences, suggesting either that boys whose parents are low in knowledge are more likely to conform to their peers or that they are more likely to seek out friends (or to be selected by peers) who share a similar substance use profile.

Sexual activity. Several studies have linked high levels of risky sexual activity to low levels of parental knowledge (Biglan et al., 1990; Meschke and Silbereisen, 1997; Metzler et al., 1994; Romer et al. 1994). For example, using a sample of over 300 children ages 9 to 15, living in urban housing projects, Romer et al. (1994; Romer et al. 1994) found that lower perceived parental knowledge, assessed via child self report, was correlated with higher levels of sexual activity. Similarly, Meschke and Silbereisen (1997), using a two-item adolescent self-report measure of parental knowledge, found that lower levels of perceived parental knowledge and higher levels of risky leisure activities were associated with earlier initiation of sexual experience in a sample of German 15- to 18-year-old adolescents.

School achievement. The results of studies focused on school achievement present a mixed picture. White and Kaufman (1997) analyzed data on recent immigrants in the High School and Beyond (HSB) study (for a description of the HSB, see *http://nces.ed.gov*). The HSB study surveyed over 50,000 high school sophomores and seniors in 1980 and conducted follow-up surveys with many of them in subsequent years. Using data from 1980 and 1982, and controlling for family socioeconomic status, White and Kaufman (1997) found that immigrant youth were less likely to drop out of school when parents supervised their schoolwork. Similarly, Crouter et al. (1990) reported that, when both mothers and fathers were relatively uninformed about their sons' daily experiences, sons performed less well in school; the association did not hold up for daughters, however. In contrast, Otto and Atkinson (1997) found a modest, negative association between parental monitoring of homework and adolescents' grades; the less well adolescents performed in school, the more parents supervised homework. This finding prompted them to speculate that "adolescents' poor academic performance may prompt parental monitoring of school work" (p. 85), again pointing to the possibility that parental monitoring may be as much the consequence as the cause of child behavior.

Having established that parental monitoring and parental knowledge are phenomena that have been consistently linked to a variety of problem behaviors in childhood and adolescence, we turn our attention to the conditions that give rise to monitoring and knowledge. Again, a close look at this literature reveals that most studies have focused on actual parental knowledge or family members' perceptions of knowledge, and not on the specific parenting behaviors connoted by "parental monitoring." As this literature comes into focus, it will be important to explicitly compare and contrast the antecedents of both parental knowledge and parental monitoring, ideally in the same study. Understanding the conditions that give rise to knowledge and monitoring may provide clues as to why parental knowledge and monitoring are apparently so important and how we can enhance this aspect of parent–child relationships.

ANTECEDENTS OF PARENTAL MONITORING AND KNOWLEDGE

Under what conditions are parents able to become and stay knowledgeable about children's and adolescents' daily activities, experiences, and companions? Like the literature on the determinants of parenting in general (Belsky, 1984), research on the determinants of parental monitoring and parental knowledge reveals that they are shaped by a variety of influences. The quality of the parent–child relationship is probably the most important and proximal correlate of parental monitoring and parental knowledge, as the ongoing debate about the meaning of parental monitoring illustrates. Thus, we begin our discussion of the antecedents of parental monitoring and knowledge with a closer look at the quality of the parent–child relationship. From there, we organize our review by moving from proximal to distal conditions. The most proximal correlates are the individual characteristics and dispositional qualities that children and parents bring to their relationships with one another. Children's qualities are particularly important to include in any conceptualization of the antecedents of parenting because they underscore the fact that, like the parent, the child is an actor who may, through his or her behavior, dispositional qualities, or other characteristics evoke, shape, and reinforce certain treatment from parents (Bronfenbrenner and Morris, 1998). From there, we examine the impact of marital quality, divorce and remarriage on parental monitoring and knowledge, as well as extrafamilial circumstances, including the demands of parents' and adolescents' employment circumstances and the broader socioeconomic milieu.

Quality of the Parent–Child Relationship

It is impossible to conceptualize the possible antecedents of parental monitoring or parental knowledge without acknowledging that the quality of the parent–child relationship is the fundamental platform that gives rise to them (Dishion and McMahon, 1998; Kerr et al., 1999; Stattin and Kerr, 2000). Not only does a warm, supportive relationship motivate the parent to stay informed (Dishion and McMahon, 1998), but it creates a context in which the child or adolescent can freely self-disclose to the parent (Kerr et al., 1999; Stattin and Kerr, 2000). Additional evidence for the relational roots of parental monitoring and knowledge can be found in a longitudinal study in which proactive, positive parenting, assessed before children entered kindergarten, predicted mothers' knowledge when the children reached adolescence, even when socioeconomic status and other background characteristics were held constant (Pettit et al., 2001). Furthermore, psychometric studies have pointed to the close interrelationship between indicators of parent–child relationship quality and measures of parental monitoring or knowledge (Patterson et al., 1992).

Kerr et al. (1999), delving into the meaning of parental knowledge for parent–adolescent relationships, found that knowledge of adolescent offspring's daily experiences was a strong correlate of parental trust in the child, stronger even than parents' knowledge of adolescents' feelings and concerns or knowledge of past delinquency. Kerr and her colleagues underscored the potential complexity of the processes involved, asking "whether the information itself is the important thing, or whether the willingness to share information makes an important contribution to trust, over and above the information in provides" (Kerr et al., 1999, p. 750). Likewise, they noted that the causal relationship between parental trust and child self-disclosure is unclear (Kerr et al., 1999, p. 750):

> It is reasonable to assume that the information disclosed by the child produces a certain level of parental trust, but it also could be true that trusting parents respond in such a way that children feel more free to disclose. Certainly, there is a history of parental reactions to information that a child would consider, either consciously or unconsciously, before deciding to disclose information about daily activities.

Darling et al. (under review) have focused on some of the conditions under which adolescents fully disclose, tell partial truths, and lie to their parents. Using self-report data from a volunteer sample of high school students, they began by ascertaining adolescents' perceptions of the extent to which they disagreed with their parents about a set of issues (e.g., "the type of TV shows or videos you watch . . . how much time you spend with your boyfriend/girlfriend," p. 15). Importantly, youth reported higher levels of agreement about these issues when they saw their parents as having a more authoritative parenting style (high on warmth and control) and when they themselves reported participating in lower levels of leisure activities disapproved of by their parents. Thus, high levels of agreement between parents and youth about adolescent activities and behaviors are inextricably linked to what the parent is like and what the adolescent is doing.

Youth reported that they would not fully disclose all information their parents would want to know for 68% of the issues involving parent–adolescent disagreement. Strategies of nondisclosure included avoiding the issue (25%), partial disclosure of some but not all information (47%), and lying (28%). Each strategy has a different set of correlates. For example, adolescents were more likely to report partial self-disclosure when the issue in question was important to them and less likely to do so when there was a rule about that particular issue in their family. Youth were less likely to opt for avoidance when they believed that their parents had legitimate authority over the issue in question. They were most likely to lie when they tended to be involved in leisure activities their parents disapproved of and when there was a rule in place about the specific issue they would lie about. Thus, adolescents appear to strategize about when and how to provide information to their parents. These findings underscore the fact that tracking and surveillance parenting strategies will certainly fail if offspring choose to withhold accurate information. They also point out that adolescents' participation in activities their parents disapprove of and adolescent–parent disagreement about issues set the stage for adolescents to become less than fully forthcoming to their parents about their behavior. Seen in this light, child and adolescent behavior is as much a cause as a consequence of differential patterns of parental monitoring and parental knowledge.

Many studies of parental monitoring or knowledge have examined possible antecedents without reference to the quality of the parent–child relationship. Thus, in the review that follows, some conditions are undoubtedly important because they directly facilitate or disrupt parents' acquisition of knowledge about their children's ongoing lives, whereas others probably make a difference indirectly via their general influence on the quality of parent–child relationships or on the child's willingness to confide in the parent. We will address these distinctions as we introduce the relevant material, working outward from proximal to distal sources of influence.

Children's Personal Qualities

Sex and age. Children's sex and age are two personal characteristics that have been found to be associated with parental knowledge. Although mothers tend to be considerably more knowledgeable than fathers overall (Crouter et al., 1990, 1999), parents' actual knowledge about specific children in a family depends in part on the sex of both the child and the parent (Crouter et al., 1999; Leaper, in Vol. 1 of this *Handbook*). Comparing mothers' and fathers' knowledge of their firstborn and secondborn school-age children's daily experiences, Crouter et al. (1999) found that, in general, mothers knew more about daughters and fathers about sons; these within-family differences were apparent in comparisons of families with opposite-sex versus same-sex offspring. Using the same data set, Bumpus (2000) found patterns suggestive of different routes to parental knowledge for sons and daughters. For daughters, a warm, accepting relationship, especially with their fathers, was associated with higher levels of actual knowledge for both mothers and fathers, whereas for sons, higher levels of time spent in joint activities with parents was predictive of parents' actual knowledge.

Children's age is also relevant. Crouter et al. (1999) found that both mothers and fathers tended to know more about their secondborns (8 years old on average) than their 11-year-old firstborn siblings. They also correlated age with parental knowledge separately for firstborns and secondborns. They found no associations for firstborns, perhaps due to restricted variance in age in their sample. For secondborns, however, parents were more informed about younger children than about older children, perhaps reflecting the fact that "as children move through middle childhood and become increasingly involved in contexts outside the family, it becomes harder for parents to know all the details of their daily lives" (Crouter et al., 1999, p. 256), a parent-centered explanation. The data may also reflect a tendency for children to be less forthcoming to their parents about what is going on as they make the transition to adolescence (Darling et al., under review), a child-centered perspective.

Temperament, personality, and dispositional qualities. Sex and age are two of the few immutable qualities in children that do not reflect prior parenting in any way. Children's temperaments, personalities, and dispositional qualities are also potentially important antecedents of parental monitoring or parental knowledge, but we must keep in mind that these qualities have been shaped in part by relationship history; they are not wholly independent phenomena (Putnam, Sanson, and Rothbart, in Vol. 1 of this *Handbook*). As noted, the child's tendency to self-disclose to the parent is a key determinant of how much parents know (Stattin and Kerr, 2000), particularly in adolescence when youth spend so much of their time out of the immediate purview of their parents. Some researchers have referred to other, similar qualities such as the "child's openness to socialization" (Bogenschneider, Small, and Tsay, 1997) or "the child's contribution to parental monitoring" (K. Kerns, personal communication, September 25, 2000; Kerns et al., 2001). Even as early as the preschool years, however, and certainly by middle childhood and adolescence, these so-called child qualities may reflect as much about the evolving qualities of the parent–child relationship as they do something intrinsic to the child.

In one of the few studies to consider the possible impact of children's temperamental qualities on parents' knowledge, Crouter et al. (1999) found different patterns for mothers and fathers. Fathers knew more about their firstborn and secondborn children when their older children were highly expressive and when their younger children were expressive and sociable. Crouter et al. (1999, p. 257) suggested that fathers may be "drawn to sociable and expressive children and pay more attention to their daily experiences" or, alternatively, that "these children [may] volunteer more information." In contrast, no associations between children's temperaments and parental knowledge were found for mothers, prompting Crouter and her colleagues (1999, p. 257) to conclude:

> Our data . . . suggest that fathers' knowledge about children is more influenced by their children's characteristics than is mothers'. This is consistent with the idea that parenting is more "scripted" for mothers than for fathers. . . . Given the optional nature of paternal involvement, fathers appear to "tune in" to their children's daily activities and experiences when their children's personal qualities predispose them to do so.

Parents' Personal Characteristics

It is unfortunate that so many studies fail to distinguish between maternal and paternal monitoring or knowledge. Much of what we know about parental monitoring blurs the identity of the parent by referring not to mothers and fathers, but to generic "parents." Perhaps as a result, parents' personal qualities have not received the attention they deserve.

Mothers and fathers. As noted above, the sex of the parent is important. When mothers and fathers in the same family are compared, mothers are considerably more knowledgeable about their children's daily lives than fathers are (Bumpus et al., 2001; Crouter et al., 1990, 1999; Waizenhofer and Buchanan, under review), reflecting a strong tendency in our culture for mothers to be more engaged in childrearing overall than fathers. Although studies rarely examine how parents have acquired their information, fathers are more likely to receive information about their youngsters' activities from their spouses than mothers are, whereas mothers are more likely to acquire their information via direct and indirect supervision of the child than fathers are (Waizenhofer and Buchanan, under review).

Education. Parents' educational level has been found to be a correlate of parental knowledge, especially for fathers. Better educated fathers know more about their children's daily experiences than their less educated counterparts; moreover, the tendency to be better informed about sons than about daughters is more pronounced in less-educated men (Crouter et al., 1999).

Gender role attitudes. In two separate studies on different samples, parents' attitudes about gender roles have been examined as possible antecedents of parental knowledge (Bumpus et al., 2001; Crouter et al., 1999). In both studies, mothers' gender role attitudes were linked to parents' knowledge. Fathers' gender role attitudes were not significantly related to parents' knowledge; the associations for fathers were similar to those of mothers but were not strong enough to reach conventional levels of statistical significance. Conceptualizing high levels of parental knowledge as low autonomy-granting in adolescence, Bumpus et al. (2001) reported that, in general, parents were less knowledgeable about postpubertal adolescent girls than about prepubertal daughters, signaling perhaps the growing independence of physically maturing daughters. This association was moderated, however, by mothers' gender role attitudes. In families in which mothers held less traditional attitudes about gender roles, parents knew less about postpubertal than prepubertal daughters, but in families in which mothers held more traditional attitudes about gender roles, parents maintained a high level of knowledge about daughters regardless of their pubertal status. This pattern may signify greater protectiveness toward daughters on the part of more traditional parents or a tendency for girls to have more trouble establishing autonomy in more traditional family contexts.

Crouter et al. (1999), in a study focused on school-age children, found that well-educated mothers with nontraditional gender role attitudes were generally quite knowledgeable about their children's daily experiences except when they had two sons. Puzzled by the finding, Crouter and her colleagues (1999, p. 257) noted: "Post hoc analyses failed to identify a confounding variable that might account for this finding. It is possible that better-educated mothers with less traditional sex role attitudes are especially interested in daughters and do not pay quite as much attention to their children's ongoing daily experiences when they have two sons."

Alternatively, families with older and younger sons may be very male-oriented environments in which fathers and sons pursue their own interests and activities, and mothers are left on the sidelines; in such circumstances, lower maternal knowledge may result.

Parents' problems. Parents sometimes bring their own psychological and substance-use problems to the parent–child relationship (Mayes and Truman, in Vol. 4 of this *Handbook*; Zahn-Waxler, Duggal, and Gruber, in Vol. 4 of this *Handbook*). Chassin et al. (1993) examined three possible pathways connecting parental alcoholism with adolescent substance use, one of which was perceived parental knowledge (assessed with three self-report items from parents). A strength of the study was that it assessed perceived parental knowledge, parents' lifetime alcoholism diagnosis, and parents' current alcohol consumption separately for mothers and fathers. Moreover, it controlled for parents' affective and antisocial personality disorder diagnoses which are not only correlates of alcoholism, but also potential sources of influence on adolescents' substance use. Alcoholic parents saw themselves as less knowledgeable about their adolescent offspring's daily activities and experiences, and lower levels of perceived parental knowledge in turn were related to higher levels of adolescent affiliation with drug-using peers and substance use. In contrast, parents' current alcohol consumption was not related to perceived parental knowledge or to adolescents' substance use. Chassin et al.'s (1993) explanations for why monitoring was linked to parents' lifetime clinical alcoholism diagnosis rather than to their current alcohol consumption emphasized the "cumulative effects" of lifetime alcoholism and what they may imply for parent–child relationships and reveal the complexity inherent in the study of parenting (Chassin et al., 1993, p. 15):

> Such a cumulative effect could be due to particular parental characteristics that are both associated with lifetime alcoholism and that also affect parenting (e.g., some type of gene–environment covariation). Alternatively, such an effect could be due to some cumulative impact of historical alcoholism on the parent-child relationship in which past parental alcoholism had a lingering negative impact on the parent's

ability to effectively control the child's behavior. Finally, it is possible that an acute mechanism does operate to influence parental monitoring but only above some threshold of " pathological" current parental alcohol consumption rather than through a linear relationship between parental alcohol consumption and parenting behavior.

Yet another possibility is that the legacy of the history of parental alcohol problems is child mistrust and a consequent reluctance to self-disclose to the parent.

Marriage, Divorce, and Remarriage

A diverse set of studies has focused on the possible implications of variations in family structure for how informed parents are about their children's daily activities and experiences.

Marital quality. A family systems perspective draws attention to the interrelations among different dyadic relationships in the family (Minuchin, 1988). Indeed, many studies point to the fact that strong marital ties undergird positive parenting (see review by Belsky, 1984; Grych, in Vol. 4 of this *Handbook*). Consistent with this picture, the quality of the marital relationship has been found to moderate the relation between parents' work stress and their actual knowledge about their children. For example, Bumpus et al. (1999) found that the combination of high paternal work demands (e.g., high levels of perceived work pressure and role overload and long work hours) and low levels of marital quality predicted lower levels of parental knowledge by both fathers and mothers. Paternal work demands were not associated with lower levels of knowledge, however, when the marital relationship was strong. Why might this be the case? Happier couples may be under less stress and therefore better able to pay close attention to their children's ongoing experiences, becoming more knowledgeable as a result: a parent-centered, tracking, and surveillance explanation. They may also spend more time in joint activities with their children, and knowledge about their children's experiences may arise through that joint interaction. Happier couples may also be perceived by their children as more open and easier to talk to, a line of reasoning that emphasizes children's self-disclosure as a route to parental knowledge. A final possibility is that happier couples communicate with one another regularly about their children's daily experiences with the result that each partner knows more than she or he would ordinarily know on her or his own.

Single parenthood, divorce, and remarriage. Growing up in a single-parent household or experiencing changes in family structure may make it more difficult for children's parents to stay informed about their children's experiences (Hetherington and Stanley-Hagan, in Vol. 3 of this *Handbook*). This may happen because parents in these stressful circumstances become distracted and self-absorbed and thus fail to keep track of their offspring effectively, or because children have more difficulty sustaining a close, confiding relationship with parents going through these difficult experiences. Pettit et al. (2001) reported that, holding constant the effects of socioeconomic status, single-parent mothers saw themselves as less knowledgeable than mothers in two-parent households. Using data from the Montreal Longitudinal Study, Pagani et al. (1998) examined the impact of family transitions on the development of boys' delinquency from kindergarten through about age 15. Controlling for teachers' ratings of the boys' disruptiveness in kindergarten in an effort to hold constant what the child was like prior to the family transitions in question, Pagani et al. (1998) detected a pronounced drop in perceived parental knowledge in early adolescence for boys whose custodial parent experienced remarriage during adolescence, especially when the remarriage occurred when the boy was between 12 and 14 years of age. The decrease over time in perceived knowledge for the boys who experienced remarriage during adolescence was significantly more pronounced than that of boys in families with marriages that remained intact. (The pattern for boys who experienced divorce but not remarriage fell in between.) For boys in the group that experienced their custodial parent's remarriage between ages 12 and 14, perceptions of parental supportiveness also dropped during this period. Tracking these drops in perceived parental knowledge and parental supportiveness, boys' delinquency and fighting behaviors increased over this period.

Mekos et al. (1996) examined problem behavior and parenting of two adolescent siblings in nondivorced and remarried families. Previous work had established that parental differential treatment of siblings is often a risk factor for children and youth, particularly for the child in the sibling pair who is disfavored (Dunn, Stocker, and Plomin, 1990; McHale, Crouter, McGuire, and Updegraff, 1995). Mekos et al. (1996), using a sample of over 500 same-sex adolescent sibling pairs, found that within-family differences in both problem behavior (i.e., alcohol use, marijuana use, and deviance) and parenting (e.g., parental monitoring/control) were most pronounced in remarried families in which the siblings did not share the same biological parent. Moreover, the association between mothers' differential monitoring/control of siblings and differences in siblings' problem behavior was stronger in families in which one sibling was the mother's stepchild; in these cases, stepchildren were monitored and controlled less than biological children. Similarly, the association between fathers' differential monitoring/control of siblings and differences in siblings' problem behavior was stronger in families in which one sibling was the father's stepchild. Differential monitoring/control was not associated with sibling differences in problem behavior, however, in nondivorced families or in families in which both siblings were the father's stepchildren.

In all cross-sectional studies of the relation between parental differential treatment of siblings and sibling differences in psychosocial outcomes, it is hard to know whether parental differential treatment is driving the differences in children's functioning, whether parents are reacting to preexisting differences in their two children, or whether both explanations hold. The Mekos et al. (1996) study, like almost all work in this field, leaves the direction of effect ambiguous. But the fact that the associations between differential monitoring/control and sibling differences were more pronounced in remarried contexts that contained both biological and stepchildren is intriguing. It may reflect the tumultuous nature of parent–adolescent relationships in blended, remarried households. It also suggests the possibility that biological and step-children in remarried contexts may be unusually sensitive and attuned to evidence of parents' differential treatment (Mekos et al., 1996).

Adolescents' and Parents' Work Circumstances

Only a handful of studies has examined the connections between adolescents' or parents' work circumstances and either parental monitoring or parents' knowledge about their children's daily experiences, whereabouts, and companions. For the most part, attention has focused on work hours, and the assumption has been that longer hours—on the part of either the adolescent or the parent— might detract from parents' abilities to keep track of their children's daily experiences.

Adolescents' work hours and earnings. In an analysis of data from respondents to the National Survey of Families and Households who were parents of 16- to 18-year-old adolescents, Manning (1990) found that the more hours adolescents worked, the less likely they were to be required to let their parents know where they were at all times. Relatedly, in a study of rural and urban adolescents, the more money adolescents earned on the job, the less mothers reported monitoring them (Shanahan et al., 1996). Youth working longer hours and earning more money, both powerful symbols of adult roles, may be signals to parents to lighten up on tracking and surveillance. Alternatively, busy employed adolescents may not have the time to engage their parents in conversation about their daily experiences and activities. It is also possible that working pulls adolescents into activities that parents are likely to disapprove of, such as drinking, substance use, and socializing with older peers, and that youth in such situations are less willing to fully disclose information to their parents (see Darling et al., under review).

Mothers' work hours. Mothers' work hours matter, too (Gottfried, Gottfried, and Bathurst, in Vol. 2 of this *Handbook*). In contrast to commonly voiced concerns that maternal employment is a possible risk factor for children, one study found that longer maternal work hours were not linked to lower levels of mothers' actual knowledge (Crouter et al., 1999). In fact, when mothers worked longer hours, fathers actually knew more about their school-age children's activities. As a result, children whose mothers worked longer hours had more knowledgeable parents overall than did children whose mothers worked fewer hours. Similarly, in a different sample, Crouter and McHale (1993) compared mothers' and fathers' knowledge across the seasons of a year from winter to summer to winter. This study, which emphasized the dynamic quality of mothers' participation in paid work, noted that fathers maintained their levels of actual knowledge in the summer when mothers' work hours remained high, whereas fathers decreased their levels of knowledge when their wives cut back their involvement in work during the summer months. Mothers may stay knowledgeable about their children regardless of whether they work longer or shorter hours because it is part of the "script" of what a good mother does. Fathers, in contrast, tend to be actively informed about their children's daily lives when their wives' work schedules call for them to play an active parenting role but then are more likely to step back and reduce their levels of knowledge when mothers are available to play the role of the primary parent. This scenario works for both interpretations of parental monitoring or parental knowledge—the tracking and surveillance view and the child self-disclosure view. In either case, fathers may calibrate their active involvement in parenting (and children may respond accordingly with self-disclosure) based on wives' work-related availability.

Work Demands and Stress

As noted above, Bumpus et al. (1999) reported that parents knew less about their children's daily experiences when fathers' experienced high levels of work demands and the marital relationship was less positive. Similarly, Bumpus (2000) found that the impact of high levels of negative work–family spillover (i.e., perceptions that their jobs were interfering with their family lives) on parental knowledge was mediated by marital quality and the quality of father–child relationships. Fathers reporting higher work–family spillover experienced less happy marriages, and less happily married parents were seen by parents and offspring as less warm and accepting. Fathers' warmth and acceptance was a positive predictor not only of fathers' own knowledge but also of mothers' knowledge. In contrast, no evidence of mediation was found for mothers. Mothers' spillover was related to a less positive marital relationship, which in turn predicted maternal warmth and acceptance, but maternal warmth and acceptance in turn was not linked either to mothers' own actual knowledge or to that of their husbands. Bumpus (2000) speculated that parental knowledge is more optional for fathers and hence appears only when the conditions are right, whereas mothers' role as the "parent in the know" is more scripted and hence less yoked to work circumstances or family dynamics.

Economic Hardship

The most distal set of antecedents of parental monitoring or knowledge in the extant literature pertains to the broader economic conditions in which families are embedded (Hoff, Laursen, and Tardif, in Vol. 2 of this *Handbook*). Several investigations have found that poverty and lower socioeconomic status are related to lower levels of perceived parental knowledge (Pagani et al., 1999; Pettit et al., 2001; Sampson and Laub, 1994). Sampson and Laub (1994), in a reanalysis of Glueck and Glueck's (1950, 1962) longitudinal data on delinquent and nondelinquent boys, reported that an index of family processes signaling informal social control, composed of three components—parent–child attachment, maternal supervision, and erratic/harsh discipline—mediated the effects of family poverty on adolescent delinquency. This association held true even when Sampson and Laub controlled for early childhood antisocial behavior, parental marital instability, and mothers' and fathers' criminality and drinking habits. In fact, in the complete model, there was no direct effect of early childhood antisocial behavior on adolescent delinquency. Sampson and Laub (1994, p. 538) interpreted this finding as evidence that "the correlation between childhood and adolescent delinquency is less an indication of a latent antisocial trait than a developmental process whereby delinquent children systematically undermine effective strategies of family social control, in turn increasing the odds of later delinquency." Noting that all of the families in the Gluecks's study resided in poor Boston neighborhoods during the Great Depression, Sampson and Laub (1994, p. 538) underscored the message that "strong family social controls may serve as an important buffer against structural disadvantage in the larger community."

In this section, we have reviewed research demonstrating some of the antecedents and correlates of parental monitoring and knowledge. At a more proximal level, mothers tend to know more than fathers and tend to acquire that knowledge more directly; mothers also tend to know more about their daughters and fathers tend to know more about sons. Greater expressivity and sociability in children is related to greater knowledge on the part of fathers, who may rely more on children's willingness to self-disclose than mothers do. Additionally, parents know more about younger than older children, reflecting the developmental path of autonomy. At more distal levels, parents' gender role attitudes, alcoholism, marital quality, and marital status, both mothers' and adolescents' work hours, adolescents' wages, and family economic status all serve to enhance or impede parents' acquisition of knowledge. Some of these antecedents may work directly to influence parental monitoring and knowledge; others, however, may operate indirectly via their impact on the most proximal correlate of parental monitoring and knowledge: the quality of the parent–child relationship. As we have seen, the dimensions of the parent–child relationship that appear to be important include trust, security, and ease of communication.

FUTURE DIRECTIONS IN PARENTAL MONITORING

As we look across the terrain of literature on parental monitoring and parental knowledge, we see three areas that deserve attention in the next generation of research and conceptualization. Those areas are (1) definitions and measurement, (2) studying families, and (3) prevention and intervention.

Definitions and Measurement

Our review of the extant literature on parental monitoring reveals a paradox. On the one hand, there is a voluminous literature documenting the relation between low levels of parental monitoring or parental knowledge, operationalized in a variety of ways, and problematic child and adolescent psychosocial functioning. Moreover, there is also considerable evidence about the individual, relational, and contextual conditions that give rise to "parental monitoring." The paradox is that researchers are only just beginning to ask the difficult questions about what our typical measures of parental monitoring are really measuring. Stattin and Kerr's (2000) work suggests that we must rethink our assumptions about "parental monitoring," including the assumption that parental monitoring can be equated with parenting behavior. Calling a construct parental monitoring does not make it so. Indeed, much of the literature is really focused on parents' or children's estimates of how much parents know about children's daily activities and experiences, and not on how parents acquired that supposed knowledge.

An important next step is to come to a consensus about the way we conceptualize and label constructs. There are at least three ways researchers have approached measuring the construct most refer to as parental monitoring. They include: (1) *perceived parental knowledge* (parents' or children's assessments of how much parents really know about the child's activities, whereabouts, and companions), (2) *parents' actual knowledge* (assessed by matching parents' and children's answers to questions about the child's daily experiences), and (3) *parental monitoring* (parenting behaviors such as tracking, surveillance, and supervision). Of these three phenomena, only the third can be accurately referred to as parenting; the first two tap presumed outcomes of parenting, but not parenting itself. Stattin and Kerr (2000) and others have suggested that we also need to pay more attention to what the child is contributing to the relationship. They suggest a fourth phenomenon for our list: (4) *child self-disclosure* (spontaneous instances in which the child provides information to the parent about the child's experiences that result in the parent becoming more knowledgeable about the child's daily life). Recall, however, that adolescent involvement in activities that parents disapprove of is a correlate of both parent–adolescent agreement about issues and adolescents' tendencies to fully disclose their activities in those areas (Darling et al., under review). Indeed, all four of these parental monitoring and knowledge constructs may develop not only in response to what the parent–child relationship is like but in response to what the child is up to and how likely the parent is to disapprove of those activities. In this domain of research, it is important that we recognize that children's behavior—and parents' real or imagined reactions to those behaviors—are as much cause as consequence of the unfolding patterns leading to parents' knowledge of their children's day-to-day activities.

Understanding these four constructs constitutes an ambitious goal for future research. We need to examine the associations among these four phenomena. How interrelated are they? What is the developmental trajectory of each phenomenon from the preschool years through adolescence? How interrelated are these trajectories? Conceivably, active tracking and surveillance may be adaptive in the early years but seen as intrusive by children as they develop. The ideal parent–child relationship may undergo a key transition in terms of the source of parents' knowledge about children's ongoing activities from parental tracking and surveillance to child self-disclosure. When and how this transition occurs and how it is related to quality of the parent–child relationship is exciting territory for the next generation of studies in this area.

The fact that adolescents' and parents' estimates of how much parents "really know" are only modestly related suggests that these phenomena may not in fact be highly intercorrelated, making it all the more important that researchers employ precise conceptualizations and terminology. A careful assessment of how each of these four perspectives on parental monitoring is related to child and adolescent problem behavior is also called for. Such an analysis may reveal that perceived parental knowledge is in fact the strongest correlate of child and adolescent problem behavior. If so, the next step is to rigorously identify the relation dynamics that give rise to these perceptions.

Studying Families

We call for the next generation of researchers to banish the "generic parent" and put in its place mothers and fathers. Only by paying equal attention to mothers and fathers will we begin to build a complete picture of how parental monitoring or knowledge takes shape in the context of the family. It is also important to go beyond examining mothers and fathers separately to ask questions about how one parent's circumstances shape the other parent's ability to become knowledgeable and to maintain that level of knowledge and behavior. There are hints of how these processes may work, but the picture is still very sketchy. Using our own findings as a jumping off point, we offer a series of research questions that push for the study of families and family processes. We know, for example, that fathers are more knowledgeable when their wives work more hours than when their wives work fewer hours (Crouter et al., 1999), but we do not know the mechanism whereby this happens. Do children confide more in their fathers when mothers work more hours? Or is the process a more incidental one in which fathers whose wives are still at work take on more of the caregiving, after-school supervision, and chauffeuring tasks and, in the process of carrying out these duties, pick up knowledge about their children's daily experiences? Do families in which mothers work longer hours place more controls and restrictions on their children that result in parents having a better idea of what their children are up to than other parents? Do longer maternal hours encourage parents to share their knowledge about their children's days between themselves more efficiently, with the result that fathers know more?

Similarly, we have documented that mothers tend to have higher levels of knowledge about daughters, and fathers tend to be more knowledgeable on a daily basis about sons (Crouter et al., 1999). But through what family dynamics does this sex-typed pattern arise? Does it happen because same-sex parents and offspring share more common interests, engage in more joint activities, or enjoy greater ease in communication than opposite-sex parent–child dyads do? Does it arise because parents believe that the same-sex child needs her or him, because mothers and fathers are better able to empathize with a child of the same sex, or some combination of these factors? Given that parents typically know more about the day-to-day activities of children of the same sex, what happens when this norm is violated? Is it particularly problematic for girls to have uninformed mothers and for boys to have fathers who are not knowledgeable? Is having one knowledgeable parent enough, or are the positive effects of parental knowledge cumulative such that children and adolescents fare best when both parents are informed?

Prevention and Intervention Programs

Until we are clear exactly what "parental monitoring" and "parental knowledge" are, it is premature to make pronouncements about the next steps for intervention and prevention programs. If child self-disclosure emerges as a more important correlate of "monitoring" than indices of parental tracking and surveillance, as Stattin and Kerr's (2000) provocative work suggests, we need to focus prevention programs around building trusting parent–child relationships that are facilitative of honest self-disclosure rather than around training parents to more effectively track their children's whereabouts and behavior.

It may also be the case that we need to think about parent monitoring differently depending on whether we are focused on normative samples or on "at-risk" samples. Work in the area of parental monitoring by the Oregon Social Learning Center (e.g., Dishion et al., 1991; Patterson and Stouthamer-Loeber, 1984) that has focused on samples of delinquent youth or children who share risk factors in this regard suggests that it may be profitable to think about different prevention or intervention strategies for different kinds of samples. Perhaps training parents of delinquents and parents of children facing multiple risk factors for delinquency to be more vigilant and more aware of their children's daily experiences will produce positive effects. People interested in facilitating parents' ongoing knowledge of their children's daily activities, whereabouts, and companions in normative samples, however, may be better advised to emphasize strengthening those features of the parent–child relationship that promote communication and child self-disclosure and minimizing parenting strategies that will be interpreted by the child as controlling or intrusive.

CONCLUSIONS

Social scientists have been interested in aspects of parental monitoring and parental knowledge for over 50 years. They have produced a sprawling body of research that makes a strong case for the importance of parental monitoring as a family process that may reduce children's and adolescents' involvement in a variety of problem behaviors. Lurking just under the surface of this body of work, however, is a messy reality of measurement limitations and mismatches between construct labels and operationalizations. Future generations of researchers need to be clear about whether they are measuring actual monitoring and supervision, parents' actual knowledge, parents' or children's perceptions of parents' knowledge, or children's self-disclosure. As we work with and learn more about these four conceptually interrelated constructs, we will learn more about how families work and how to help parents interact with their children more effectively.

ACKNOWLEDGMENTS

Ann Crouter's work on this chapter was facilitated by two grants from the National Institute of Child Health and Human Development, R01-HD32336, R01-HD29409, Ann C. Crouter and Susan M. McHale, coprincipal investigators. We are grateful to Matthew Bumpus, Nancy Darling,

Susan McHale, Margaret Kerr, and Håkan Stattin for conversations about parental monitoring and parental knowledge, as well as specific feedback on previous drafts of this chapter, and to Alice Saxion for her careful editing of this manuscript.

REFERENCES

Ary, D. V., Duncan, T. E., Duncan, S. C., and Hops, H. (1999). Adolescent problem behavior: The influence of parents and peers. *Behaviour Research and Therapy, 37,* 217–230.

Belsky, J. (1984). The determinants of parenting: A process model. *Child Development, 55,* 83–96.

Biglan, A., Metzler, C. W., Wirt, R., Ary, D., Noell, J., Ochs, L., French, C., and Hood, D. (1990). Social and behavioral factors associated with high-risk sexual behavior among adolescents. *Journal of Behavioral Medicine, 13,* 245–261.

Bogenschneider, K., Small, S. A., and Tsay, J. C. (1997). Child, parent, and contextual influences on perceived parenting competence among parents of adolescence. *Journal of Marriage and the Family, 59,* 345–362.

Bronfenbrenner, U., and Morris, P. A. (1998). The ecology of developmental processes. In W. Damon (Editor-in-Chief) and R. M. Lerner (Ed.), *Handbook of child psychology* (Vol. 1, pp. 993–1028). New York: Wiley.

Bumpus, M. F. (2000). *Mechanisms linking work-to-family spillover and parents' knowledge of their children's daily lives.* Unpublished doctoral dissertation, Penn State University, University Park, PA.

Bumpus, M. F., Crouter, A. C., and McHale, S. M. (1999). Work demands of dual-earner couples: Implications for parents' knowledge about children's daily lives in middle childhood. *Journal of Marriage and the Family, 61,* 465–475.

Bumpus, M. F., Crouter, A. C., and McHale, S. M. (2001). Parental autonomy-granting in adolescence: Exploring gender differences in context. *Developmental Psychology, 37,* 163–173.

Chassin, L., Pillow, D. R., Curran, P. J., Molina, B. S. G., and Barrera, M. (1993). Relation of parental alcoholism to early adolescent substance use: A test of three mediating mechanisms. *Journal of Abnormal Psychology, 102,* 3–19.

Chilcoat, H., and Anthony, J. C. (1996). Impact of parent monitoring on initiation of drug use through late childhood. *Journal of the American Academy of Child and Adolescent Psychiatry, 35,* 91–100.

Chilcoat, H., Anthony, J., and Dishion, T. J. (1995). Parent monitoring and the incidence of drub sampling in multiethnic urban children. *American Journal of Epidemiology, 141,* 25–31.

Collins, W. A., Harris, M. L., and Susman, A. (1995). Parenting during middle childhood. In M. Bornstein (Ed.), *Handbook of parenting* (1st ed., Vol. 1, pp. 65–89). Mahwah, NJ: Lawrence Erlbaum Associates.

Crouter, A. C., Helms-Erikson, H., Updegraff, K., and McHale, S. M. (1999). Conditions underlying parents' knowledge about children's daily lives in middle childhood: Between- and within-family comparisons. *Child Development, 70,* 246–259.

Crouter, A. C., MacDermid, S. M., McHale, S. M., and Perry-Jenkins, M. (1990). Parental monitoring and perceptions of children's school performance and conduct in dual- and single-earner families. *Developmental Psychology, 26,* 649–657.

Crouter, A. C., Manke, B. A., and McHale, S. M. (1995). The family context of gender intensification in early adolescence. *Child Development, 66,* 317–329.

Crouter, A. C., and McHale, S. M. (1993). Temporal rhythms in family life: Seasonal variation in the relation between parental work and family processes. *Developmental Psychology, 29,* 198–205.

Darling, N., Cumsille, P., Dowdy, B., and Caldwell, L. L. (under review). *Adolescents as active agents in the monitoring process: Disclosure strategies and motivations.*

Dishion, T. J., Capaldi, D., Spracklen, K. M., and Li, F. (1995). Peer ecology of male adolescent drug use. *Development and Psychopathology, 7,* 803–824.

Dishion, T. J., and McMahon, R. J. (1998). Parental monitoring and the prevention of child and adolescent problem behavior: A conceptual and empirical formulation. *Clinical Child and Family Psychology Review, 1,* 61–75.

Dishion, T. J., Patterson, G. R., Stoolmiller, M., and Skinner, M. L. (1991). Family, school, and behavioral antecedents to early adolescent involvement with antisocial peers. *Developmental Psychology, 27,* 172–180.

Dunn, J., Stocker, C., and Plomin, R. (1990). Nonshared experiences within the family: Correlates of behavioral problems in middle childhood. *Development and Psychopathology, 2,* 113–126.

Fletcher, A. C., Darling, N. E., Steinberg, L., and Dornbusch, S. M. (1995). The company they keep: Relation of adolescents' adjustment and behavior to their friends' perceptions of authoritative parenting in the social network. *Developmental Psychology, 31,* 300–310.

Forehand, R., Miller, K. S., Dutra, R., and Chance, M. W. (1997). Role of parenting in adolescent deviant behavior: Replication across and within two ethnic groups. *Journal of Consulting and Clinical Psychology, 65,* 1036–1041.

Glueck, S., and Glueck, E. (1950). *Unraveling juvenile delinquency.* Cambridge: Harvard University Press.

Glueck, S., and Glueck, E. (1962). *Family environment and delinquency.* Boston: Houghton Mifflin.

Hirschi, T. (1969). *Causes of delinquency.* Berkeley: University of California Press.

Kerns, K. A., Aspelmeier, J. E., Gentzler, A. L., and Grabill, C. M. (2001). Parent–child attachment and monitoring in middle childhood. *Journal of Family Psychology, 21,* 69–81.

Kerr, M., and Stattin, H. (2000). What parents know, how they know it, and several forms of adolescent adjustment: Further support for a reinterpretation of monitoring. *Developmental Psychology, 36*, 1–15.

Kerr, M., Stattin, H., and Trost, K. (1999). To know you is to trust you: Parents' trust is rooted in child disclosure of information. *Journal of Adolescence, 22*, 737–752.

Ladd, G. W., and Golter, B. S. (1988). Parents' management of preschooler's peer relations: Is it related to children's social competence? *Developmental Psychology, 24*, 109–117.

Manning, W. D. (1990). Parenting employed teenagers. *Youth and Society, 22*, 184–200.

McCord, J. (1979). Some child-rearing antecedents of criminal behavior in adult men. *Journal of Personality and Social Psychology, 37*, 1477–1486.

McHale, S. M., Crouter, A. C., McGuire, S. A., and Updegraff, K. A. (1995). Congruence between mothers' and fathers' differential treatment of siblings: Links with family relations and children's well-being. *Child Development, 66*, 116–128.

Mekos, D., Hetherington, E. M., and Reiss, D. (1996). Sibling differences in problem behavior and parental treatment in nondivorced and remarried families. *Child Development, 67*, 2148–2165.

Meschke, L. L., and Silbereisen, R. K. (1997). The influence of puberty, family processes, and leisure activities on the timing of first sexual experience. *Journal of Adolescence, 20*, 403–418.

Metzler, C. W., Noell, J., Biglan, A., Ary, D., and Smolkowski, K. (1994). The social context for risky sexual behavior among adolescents. *Journal of Behavioral Medicine, 17*, 419–438.

Minuchin, P. (1988). Relationships within the family: A systems perspective on development. In R. A. Hinde and J. Stevenson-Hinde (Eds.), *Relationships within families: Mutual influences*. Oxford, England: Clarendon.

Mott, J. A., Crowe, P. A., Richardson, J., and Flay, B. (1999). After-school supervision and adolescent cigarette smoking: Contributions of the settings and intensity of after-school self-care. *Journal of Behavioral Medicine, 22*, 35–58.

Otto, L. B., and Atkinson, M. P. (1997). Parental involvement and adolescent development. *Journal of Adolescent Research, 12*, 68–89.

Pagani, L., Boulerice, B., Vitaro, F., and Tremblay, R. E. (1999). Effects of poverty on academic failure and delinquency in boys: A change and process model approach. *Journal of Child Psychology and Psychiatry, 40*, 1209–1219.

Pagani, L., Tremblay, R. E., Vitaro, F., Kerr, M., and McDuff, P. (1998). The impact of family transition on the development of delinquency in adolescent boys: A 9-year longitudinal study. *Journal of Child Psychology and Psychiatry, 39*, 489–499.

Patterson, G. R. (1982). *Coercive family process*. Eugene, OR: Castalia.

Patterson, G. R. (1988). Family process: Loops, levels, and linkages. In N. Bolger, A. Caspi, G. Downey, and M. Moorehouse (Eds.), *Persons in context: Developmental processes*. New York: Cambridge University Press.

Patterson, G. R., and Dishion, T. J. (1985). Contributions of families and peers to delinquency. *Criminology, 23*, 63–79.

Patterson, G. R., Reid, J. B., and Dishion, T. J. (1992). *Antisocial boys*. Eugene, OR: Castalia.

Patterson, G. R., and Stouthamer-Loeber, M. (1984). The correlation of family management practices and delinquency. *Child Development, 55*, 1299–1307.

Pettit, G. S., Bates, J. E., Dodge, K. A., and Meece, D. W. (1999). The impact of after-school peer contact on early adolescent externalizing problems is moderated by parental monitoring, perceived neighborhood safety, and prior adjustment. *Child Development, 70*, 768–778.

Pettit, G. S., Laird, R. D., Dodge, K. A., Bates, J. E., and Criss, M. M. (2001). Antecedents and behavior-problem outcomes of parental monitoring and psychological control in early adolescence. *Child Development, 72*, 583–598.

Romer, D., Black, M., Ricardo, E., Feigelman, S., Kaljee, L., Galbraith, J., Nesbit, R., Hornik, R. C., and Stanton, B. (1994). Social influences on the sexual behavior of youth at risk for HIV exposure. *American Journal of Public Health, 84*, 977–985.

Sampson, R. J., and Laub, J. H. (1994). Urban poverty and the family context of delinquency: A new look at structure and process in a class study. *Child Development, 65*, 523–540.

Scarr, S., and McCartney, K. (1983). How people make their own environments: A theory of genotype-environment effects. *Child Development, 54*, 424–435.

Shanahan, M. J., Elder, G. H., Burchinal, M., and Conger, R. D. (1996). Adolescent paid labor and relationships with parents: Early work–family linkages. *Child Development, 67*, 2183–2200.

Stattin, H., and Kerr, M. (2000). Parental monitoring: A reinterpretation. *Child Development, 71*, 1072–1085.

Steinberg, L., Fletcher, A., and Darling, N. (1994). Parental monitoring and peer influences on adolescent substance use. *Pediatrics, 93*, 1060–1063.

Waizenhofer, R. N., and Buchanan, C. M. (under review). *Mothers' and fathers' knowledge and supervision of adolescents' daily activities*.

White, M. J., and Kaufman, G. (1997). Language usage, social capital, and school completion among immigrants and native-born ethnic groups. *Social Science Quarterly, 78*, 385–398.

Wilson, H. (1980). Parental supervision: A neglected aspect of delinquency. *British Journal of Criminology, 20*, 203–235.

17

Parent Beliefs Are Cognitions: The Dynamic Belief Systems Model

Irving E. Sigel
Educational Testing Service
Ann V. McGillicuddy-De Lisi
Lafayette College

INTRODUCTION

What parents believe about parenting is related to their own parenting and to virtually every aspect of children's developmental accomplishments. Moreover, parent beliefs extend to other facets of the family life environment (Miller, 1988).

We begin by acknowledging the emergence of a new look for "beliefs." As recently as five years ago, multiple perspectives on beliefs existed, and these ranged from quasi-philosophical conceptualizations to derivations from prior social psychological theories on attitudes, feelings, values, and beliefs (e.g., Baldwin, 1965; Goodnow, 1985; Heider, 1958; McGuire, 1999; Rokeach, 1980). At the same time, some scholars eschewed the very term *belief* because of the historical residue and vagaries that arise as a result of common, everyday meanings attached to such a label (Goodnow and Collins, 1990). Since that time, researchers, working from attribution approaches, information-processing models, constructivist perspectives, and transactional perspectives have embraced the notion that the core component of the belief construct is cognition. Parental beliefs are of interest because such cognitions are intrinsic to the exercising of parental responsibilities. Cognition about children and parenting is the new face of parent beliefs (Bugental, 1992).

The organization of this chapter follows a developmental sequence from the history of the study of parental beliefs to a proposed transformation of the previous Belief Complex (McGillicuddy-De Lisi and Sigel, 1995) to a dynamic belief systems model that takes into account what was learned from the research review. The historical section positions the study of beliefs in an historical context, a prelude to a review of empirical studies of parents' beliefs as sources of influence on children's cognitive development as instantiated in their childrearing practices and goals for their children. In this review the topics discussed will be limited to the effects of parents' beliefs on children's behaviors, academic achievement, and social and cognitive development. In addition, attention will be paid to parental practices relative to child management. Attention to cultural studies focusing on parental beliefs completes this section. After a brief summary and evaluation of most of the current research, the rationale for transforming the initial belief complex to a dynamic belief systems model for the study of parent beliefs is articulated. The final section is a concluding statement advocating the need for a comprehensive approach for the study of parent cognitions.

RECENT HISTORICAL BACKGROUND IN PARENTAL BELIEFS

Previously we set the study of parent beliefs in the context of three histories of beliefs about children (McGillicuddy-De Lisi and Sigel, 1995). These three histories were: (1) the history of Western philosophical thought as it has been applied to the meaning of life, the human's place in the world, and the nature of development; (2) the history that is shared by peoples within a culture and that is unique to particular cultures as each seeks to explain the nature of the child and optimize child outcomes (i.e., folk theories); and (3) the history of social science theory and method, which has influenced the course of formal articulated conceptions of human nature, behavior, and development. Rather than reiterate how each of these histories has contributed to current conceptualizations concerning the nature of beliefs about parenting and children, we refer the reader to McGillicuddy-De Lisi and Sigel (1995).

There have been three recent developments in the study of parental beliefs that theoreticians, researchers, and practitioners should be aware of in relation to interpretations of parental experiences. The first is the manner in which the current content of parent beliefs is derived from both assumptions rooted in traditions and in the changing landscape of contemporary interpretations of effective parenting. Clarke-Stewart (1998) noted that there is an ebb and flow to the themes about rearing children that shape the research, social policy, and political agenda in the United States. This is true in many cultures. However, history suggests that the fundamental psychological role that beliefs play remains consistent over generations. The content and focus of the belief systems and their instantiation in behaviors may change, but Clarke-Stewart's analysis suggests that beliefs regarding childrearing practices that influence how children develop are consistent with many of the tenets of parenting itself. We shall return to discuss the particular content that appears to have arisen in social science recently.

Although there has been an ebb and flow in the interest in empirical research on parent beliefs as presumed causative factors influencing the course of children's development, parent beliefs and values vis-à-vis childrearing are pervasive in discussions in various forms of popular and professional literature implicating the instantiation of parent beliefs of childrearing into practices and goals for children. An insightful analysis from an ethnological perspective helps to explain the basis for such concerns, as Eibl-Elbesfeldt (1989) writes: "with . . . the introduction of writing, a new, more powerful data bank becomes available to assist the memory enabling knowledge to be passed on without the presence of another society member. Thus accumulative culture develops" (p. 11). He argued that survival was served through the advent of books and the transmission of tradition, without the presence of the inventor, or even the understanding of the origins of many of these traditions, strategies, or techniques. He asserts that "They demonstrate effectively how much and in which ways our accumulating culture dominates human evolution. New ideas, theories, and inventions act like mutations in the biological realm, and they have to stand the test of selection. The problem to be solved is the survival in offspring and this is achieved by the elimination of mistakes." (p. 11). In this context, the schema of parents' beliefs about their role and responsibilities for the welfare of their children is held to be crucial.

Recognition of the salience of tradition and the deeply rooted beliefs that parents have regarding childrearing are related to the survival of the society through parenting practices. This viewpoint has led to the resurgence of the study of parent beliefs, particularly the interest in how traditions of societies and cultures reveal variations in beliefs about the nature of the child, childrearing goals, and parent beliefs about childrearing strategies (Harkness and Super, 1996). The vitality of beliefs as they function within particular societies or cultures, at times independently of philosophical analyses and at times in tandem with such reflections, is revealed in the research literature. The links between tradition and assumptions about children, parenting practices, and child behaviors, and in investigations that explore how beliefs vary with acculturation of immigrants, provide further evidence of the vitality of beliefs.

With the growth of research in cognitive science, children and adults have come to be viewed as naive theorists and/or active information processors. Bugental and Johnston (2000) asserted that over the past 15 years a major emergent focus has been the role of cognition in family life, when "the first official recognition of the centrality of cognitions within family interactions appeared in the edited volume by Sigel (in) 1985" (p. 316). There has been a shift from focus on behaviors and attitudes to a multilevel conceptualization of parents' cognitions that includes perceptions and descriptions, knowledge structures, and efficacy cognitions influencing children as well as family life in general. This shift is evident in the designation of beliefs as parent cognitions about children and parenting. Yet, each has placed cognition at the heart of her or his research and theoretical writings.

Subsuming beliefs in the broader conceptual space of cognitions raises the level of theoretical abstraction. It is argued by some that cognition is a superordinate construct and belief is a lower order construct. Bugental and Johnson (2000, p. 336) make such a case concisely when they write, "A general failure to consider the theoretical underpinnings of cognitive constructs [read by us as "belief" here] has led to limitations in the inferences that can be drawn from the empirical findings." They further argue that the empirical research on parent cognitions has focused on explicit cognitions: "The majority of the work in this field makes the assumption that such processes operate in a conscious mode" (p. 336). In this chapter we argue that the belief concept has a unique place in the cognitive domain but can also be on the unconscious or tacit level.

WHERE, WHEN, AND HOW BELIEFS MANIFEST THEIR INFLUENCE

It was clear from the research findings analyzed in a review of the literature on parenting (Collins, Maccoby, Steinberg, Hetherington, and Bornstein, 2000) that parents do have an impact on children's development, and that the nature of the relation between parents' behaviors and children's developmental accomplishments is complex. Although those reviews focused on parents' socialization behaviors rather than on the role of parent beliefs, a significant parallel in the literature on parental socialization practices and parental beliefs is apparent. The primary interest of developmental scientists who study parents is actually an interest in children rather than parents. They want to know not only what makes children smarter, better adjusted, more competent, and so forth, but also what role parents play in that developmental process, either by the way they interact with their children, directly or indirectly, through the ways they create environments for children, set goals, and contribute to their children's motivation, self-concepts, and even their genetics.

The number of studies devoted to such types of questions about beliefs reveals that most of the interest is in parental beliefs as sources of influence on the development of younger children. There is some information available concerning the origins and development of parental beliefs—not because of an intrinsic interest in adult cognitive development per se, but as a result of recognition that the parent affects child outcomes. We therefore will address the issue of where and when parent beliefs might manifest an influence by first considering child outcomes. The significant findings from research on parent beliefs are more often based on correlational studies rather than causal studies. However, there have been significant studies that can be construed as causal influences in early childhood, especially culturally based studies (Harkness and Super, 1996). One important contribution that this research literature has made is that what is labeled a belief does account for some of the variance in children's growth and development. A second contribution is more knowledge about cultural influences and the influences of acculturation processes, which are a result of increased attention to the content and processes of parent beliefs in a cultural context (see, e.g., Harkness and

Super, 1996; Rubin, 1998). The third contribution is a growing awareness that parents' beliefs about their own effectiveness as parents affect their parenting behaviors and influence the child's world. Selected research that illustrates knowledge in each area is reviewed in the three sections that follow.

Effects on Children's Development

A review of the research literature on parental beliefs reveals that the goal of many studies is to investigate the relation between parental beliefs and some specific aspect of children's behavior. By far, the major focus has been on effects of beliefs on children's cognitive development, with considerable emphasis on areas of academic achievement, especially mathematical and language achievement. Interest in children's social competence and child discipline is less than expected given the focus of American parents (in these areas of children's development). There is a small but growing literature on the role of parent beliefs on children's healthful behaviors. Our review is not necessarily exhaustive, but we have sampled studies that demonstrate the range of empirical information now available in the research literature.

Children's academic achievement and cognitive development. Andre, Whigham, Hendrickson, and Chambers (1999) found that parental beliefs about children's competencies in science appeared early, when children were 5 to 7 years old, and these beliefs were related to the children's views of their own competence in science, at least throughout the elementary school years. Parent beliefs and children's science performance were each consistent with gender stereotypes, favoring boys over girls in assessments of competencies. In studies of older children, similar relations between beliefs and child outcomes have also been observed. For example, Jacobs (1991) and Jacobs and Weisz (1994) reported that parent beliefs were influenced by gender stereotypes and that young adolescents, self-perceptions and grades in school were influenced more by these beliefs than by the children's prior performance in mathematics.

In a study of beliefs of U.S. parents of children who had been enrolled in Head Start, ethnic differences were found in the parents' beliefs about their own children's school abilities. In a pattern of findings that was similar to that observed by Andre et al. (1999) and Jacobs (1991) in their studies of academic achievement, parental beliefs were related to children's perceptions, which were in turn related to their achievement test scores in both reading and mathematics. Although there was variability in beliefs across different ethnic backgrounds of the parents, the parent belief–child belief–child outcome relation was observed across ethnic groups. In other studies of children who were enrolled in early Head Start programs, African American, Latin American, Asian American, and European American parents' beliefs have also been found to play a role in parenting effects and children's achievement (Galper, Wigfield, and Seefeldt, 1997; Mantzicopoulos, 1997).

Studies such as these show that, at a relatively young age, reliable relations between children's achievement test scores and classroom performance occur with parent beliefs. Although these findings are largely based on correlational designs, reports that children's subsequent achievement is predicted by parental beliefs rather than by children's prior performance or the children's own perceptions of their abilities have led investigators to conclude that parental beliefs have an influence on child outcomes in the academic areas of mathematics and science, at least during the years of elementary school (Cochran, 1988).

Achievement in language, reading, verbal skills, and communication ability has also been investigated in relation to parental beliefs. For example, Sonnenschein et al. (1997) asked parents of preschool and kindergarten children what they believed was the best way to help children learn to read. They found that parents who believed that reading should be presented as a fun activity with a high entertainment value had children who achieved higher scores on literacy tests than children of parents who believed that reading was a skill that needed to be taught and practiced. This study used a short-term longitudinal design in which parental beliefs reported when the children were 4 to 5 years old were predictive of children's later literacy performance.

Preschool children's oral language ability has also been found to relate to maternal beliefs. Donahue, Pearl, and Hertzog (1997) assessed mothers' beliefs about child development states and processes and observed the mothers and children on a referential communication task. These authors concluded that maternal beliefs were an important factor in children's performance because the mother's beliefs rather than the child's task performance predicted her behavior on the communication task.

Performance on achievement tests has also been related to measures of parent beliefs. In a short-term longitudinal study of African American 8- to 10-year-old children, Halle, Kurtz-Costes, and Mahoney (1997) found that children's achievement test scores at Time 1 and about 9 months later were predicted by parents' achievement-related beliefs (defined as expectations about educational achievement, beliefs about development of academic skills, and beliefs about one's child's abilities) even after Time 1 achievement in math was controlled.

Most of the recent studies relating parental beliefs and children's achievement have focused on young elementary school children. Frome and Eccles (1998) assessed parents' beliefs about their sixth graders' math and English abilities. Parent beliefs were predictive of children's beliefs about their own abilities and appear to mediate the relation that exists between the children's beliefs and the grades they earned in math and English. This suggests that the mediating influence of parental beliefs observed in younger children's achievement test scores is also operative at older ages and in relation to classroom grades.

Musun-Miller and Blevins-Knabe (1998) assessed adults' beliefs about how preschool children learn math and the role parents might play in the acquisition of math skills. Beliefs about mathematics and the importance of a parent's role in children's mathematical development were related to parents' behavior with their children around mathematical activities. When parents valued math and saw their role in their children's learning as important they engaged in more mathematical-related activities with their children. This suggests that the parents' teaching strategies might be enhanced in quantity or quality when beliefs suggest that the parents' behavior is a benefit for the child.

To summarize, there is considerable evidence suggesting that parental beliefs are related to children's academic achievement in science, math, and language. Most of the research has presumed that parental beliefs affect children's development through parental behaviors, either by fostering attitudes in the children through expectations, encouragement, and the like, or through interactions that create different learning environments for children within the context of the family. Some short-term longitudinal studies and some path analyses suggest that parental beliefs influence achievement or at least serve a mediating function. These relationships have been observed in several age groups, although for language and reading in particular the emphasis has been on preschool and young elementary school children. There is little information on the role of parental beliefs in relation to the academic achievement of adolescents, especially older adolescents during their high school years. More attention has been devoted to issues of gender, race, and ethnic factors in studies of the content and functioning of beliefs relative to children's achievement. The definition and measurement of beliefs continue to vary substantially across such investigations, with little effort directed at offering explanations as to why beliefs that are an internal, psychic component should have a direct effect on any child characteristic. Should the vehicle transporting the belief be identified?

Children's social development. The research literature reviewed prior to the publication of the first edition of the *Handbook on Parenting* acknowledged that some work (e.g., Bornstein, 1995; Rubin and Mills, 1992; Rubin, Mills, and Rose-Krasnor, 1989) was very promising in identifying connections between maternal beliefs and children's social behaviors. When Peet (1995) asked parents to report what sources of information they relied on with respect to their children's social development or cognitive development, parents found that their own intuition, religious beliefs, and childhood experiences were more important for guiding them in the areas of their children's social development than for cognitive development.

It is surprising that there has not been more emphasis on how parental beliefs relate to various aspects of children's social development, such as self-concept and identity, self-esteem, perspective taking, empathy, moral development, and social competence. However, Hastings and Rubin (1999) recently looked at the relation between maternal beliefs about the social behaviors of aggression and withdrawal in a 2-year longitudinal investigation of 2-year-old children. They report that many parents have different beliefs about the causes of children's aggressive and withdrawn behaviors, and, as a result, they have different beliefs about what childrearing strategies should be used with children with different behaviors. For example, many parents believe that aggressive behaviors are biologically based and aggression is intentional. Mothers' emotional reactions, parenting goals, and strategies for coping with aggressive and inhibited behaviors were elicited while observing their 2-year-old children interacting with an unfamiliar peer. Two years later, beliefs about aggressive and withdrawn behaviors from these mothers were assessed. The authors found that mothers' prior beliefs about authoritarian childrearing styles, their predictions about how they would feel and respond to children's negative social behaviors, their child's early aggressive behaviors, and their child's sex moderated the prediction of subsequent maternal beliefs. The authors suggested that a general belief system may "house" specific parental beliefs about children's negative social behaviors.

Working with different samples of children and their parents, Hinshaw, Zupan, Simmel, Nigg, and Melnick (1997) observed social interactions and simultaneously collected sociometric information about 9- to 10-year-old boys diagnosed as evidencing attention deficit hyperactivity disorder and a group of comparison boys. Even when other predictors were controlled, mothers' beliefs related to authoritative parenting strategies that were related to sociometric outcomes. In addition, mothers who reported confidence in their parenting roles, believed in encouraging independence, believed in setting limits and explaining the reasons behind their actions, and who derived pleasure from parenting had children who were more socially competent and positively regarded by their peers.

To briefly summarize the recent research literature on parental beliefs and children's social development, data suggest that beliefs are related to parents' behaviors with their children and exert some effects on children. However, the research in this area is sparse and does not address the range of personal–social competencies that comprise the social domain. It is interesting to note that much of the literature on personal–social development of children in relation to parental beliefs focuses on negative child behaviors (i.e., aggression and withdrawal or behavioral inhibition). The literature on children's cognitive development on the other hand has looked at positive outcomes in children, examining parental beliefs that are associated with academic achievement or cognitive skills.

The models and methods that characterize work in both of these domains are similar. Despite differences in conceptualization of beliefs, the general model is one of parental beliefs as a source of parental behaviors vis-à-vis the child, with an ultimate effect on child outcomes. Self-report methods abound, although observational data are sometimes offered, and the sources of information may include reports of "independent parties" such as teachers. Several longitudinal studies have provided evidence about the development of parental beliefs as well as information about the influence of beliefs on children.

Discipline and child behavior management.   There have been several studies of parents' beliefs about punishment. For example, Davis (1999) focused on parents who have used corporal punishment but were attempting to stop. He found that parents' desires to change their mode of punishment most often stemmed from a change in beliefs about the utility of corporal punishment. Relying on a different set of assumptions and methods, Durrant, Broberg, and Rose-Krasnor (1999) reported that mothers' reliance on punishment for preschool children was found to stem from a synergy of cultural norms regarding punishment, the parents' own history of discipline experiences as a child, beliefs about the role of punishment in controlling and teaching children, and their emotional responses to misbehaviors. This study differs from many other approaches to beliefs about punishment in the conceptualization of how cognitive, affective, personal, and cultural factors come together to influence behavior.

Mills (1999) suggested that many child management beliefs and behaviors are nonreflective. In a longitudinal study of mothers and daughters, the role of parental intentions and conscious awareness was investigated in studies of the relations among mothers' beliefs and behaviors and eventual social outcomes in their children. This study is informative in its focus on several questions about how intentions and consciousness are related to parent beliefs and to the issue of belief–behavior relationships.

Hastings and Grusec (1998) and Hastings and Coplan (1999) provided information about beliefs in relation to child management through demonstrations of the importance of parent goals when investigating the relation between beliefs and behaviors. For example, when parents focused on goals for themselves during actual interactions with their children, they experienced more negative affects and were more punitive than parents who had child- or relationship-centered goals. Grusec, Rudy, and Martini (1997) have analyzed the role of parenting cognitions in relation to control and discipline. In addition to knowledge, affective reactions, and relationship schemas, they suggest that goals (i.e., what parents hope to accomplish either in the short term or long term) have a direct link to parent behaviors. They note, for example, that beliefs about harsh, unidirectional discipline are associated with parent-centered goals and a negative view of the child in Western countries, but not in cultures that view the child as inherently good. Child outcomes as well appear to vary with these cultural differences. Research on goals suggests that goals may function as mediators or as moderators between beliefs and behaviors, especially in the context of child management situations. The role of goals will be discussed further in the final section of the chapter on the belief complex.

Health and physical well-being.   Children's health behaviors, especially preventive health behaviors such as washing one's hands before eating, diet and nutrition, and the like have recently been studied in relation to mothers' beliefs about health and beliefs about parenting. For example, Pebley, Hurtado, and Goldman (1999) studied mothers' views about causes of illness and symptoms of respiratory and gastrointestinal illnesses in rural Guatemala. Mothers' beliefs about the causes of illness suggested that there have been recent changes in their beliefs in the sense that references to problems with water and the importance of hygiene are included with other more traditional beliefs that are not based on biomedical explanations. This study and several others (Dawes and Cairns, 1998; Hupkens, Knibbe, van Otterloo, and Drop, 1998; Lees and Tinsley, 2000; Shonkoff, 2000) have focused on the role of beliefs in children's health that has important practical implications. Health practitioners are embracing the literature on parental beliefs because when mothers perceive that they do not have the ability to affect their children's health status (as in the case of external locus of control beliefs), their childrearing practices are not directed at instilling healthful behaviors. It is interesting to note that the majority of studies of beliefs about health behaviors draw links to cultural assumptions and practices that are most often cultures undergoing development and economic transformations.

Culture as a Window to Understanding the Origins and Development of Parents' Beliefs

We have noted that there is need for more information about where beliefs come from and why (McGillicuddy-De Lisi and Sigel, 1995). In particular, we asked how the beliefs come together in the parent's psyche, especially in relation to different cultural, racial, ethnic, social class, and gender experiences. Over the past five years, the research literature on children's academic and social competence has paid greater attention to racial, ethnic, social class, and gender issues. In addition, there has been a burgeoning of research on beliefs of parents from different cultural backgrounds and ethnic groups. At this point the results are largely descriptive. That is, some empirical work has been comparative, but it has not yet attended to some of the important questions regarding the role of culture and where beliefs come from in the manner sought by theoretical analyses of parental beliefs such as Valsiner's (1997) coconstructive model. Nevertheless, cultural factors seem to play an informative role, and it is not surprising that many of these descriptions of cultural differences are salient factors in the content of beliefs about children's learning, thinking, and social competence. In addition to comparisons across cultural groups, some research has focused on only one culture, but it has attempted to tie particular aspects of the cultural context to specific aspects of parental beliefs and to relate parental beliefs to child outcomes. Finally, one avenue of research has focused on how beliefs vary as acculturation occurs. Some findings from each of these three areas will be reviewed.

Research on parent beliefs within a particular culture. Beliefs of parents have been investigated in many cultures. For example, Hortacsu (1995) found that fourth-grade Turkish children's academic achievement was related to mothers' beliefs and fathers' beliefs about children and their development in different ways. Similarly, Li, Pan, Yi, and Xia (1997) reported that the beliefs of Chinese mothers concerning child development were related to the child's intellectual development. McBride-Chang and Chang (1998) investigated parent beliefs and children's school achievement among adolescent Hong Kong students. They reported that parents' beliefs about training their adolescent sons and daughters were not related to school achievement, although their self-reported parenting styles were correlated with the academic demand of the schools that children attended.

Zeitlin (1996) analyzed Yoruba parental beliefs about the nature of children in relation to traditional cosmological and religious beliefs in relation to practices that foster motor development, behavioral milestones, and feeding behavior. The Yoruba is a society in transition. It is a male-dominated society and beliefs about their children are traditionally set in a complex cosmology. Women are expected to be the primary caretakers. They have a preference for agile babies and spend a lot of time engaging them in play and motor development. Food is withheld from children so they will not grow up to be fat and lazy. To Western observers, the way food is allocated was considered child abuse if the children were not given extra food. There was a great premium on self-sufficiency. One unique task was to send children on errands as a way of disciplining them and helping them to learn locations. The problems facing the Yoruba are the shifting from an agricultural society to a modern Western-type society. Most of the beliefs and methods of childrearing originated in a rural agrarian society. Zeitlin asserts that "negotiating the transition from traditional to modern Yoruba parental theories is of more than theoretical importance" (p. 424). The reason is that their aspirations for their children are better education, urban living, and professional careers. As Zeitlin concludes, "The task of surviving in the world economic order now has placed the traditional village in a stage of ontological dissonance with the global village that requires global understanding and assistance to repair" (p. 425).

The findings of most research on parent-beliefs within particular societies or cultures suggest that belief systems that guide parents' childrearing practices are derived from their both general and specific aspects of the culture. Although the origins of these beliefs and the contents vary, there is considerable evidence that beliefs are endemic to the human condition.

Comparisons of beliefs across cultures. Parental expectations and parental beliefs concerning press for achievement that vary across different cultures or nationalities have been found to be related to higher levels of academic achievement in children. For example, Chao (1996) and Stevenson et al. (1990) have found cultural differences in parents' beliefs about the impact of their efforts on children's school achievement, and concomitant practices that appear to be expressions of this belief and the parent's value of high academic achievement. Measures of children's learning and achievement test scores have been related to these cultural differences in parental beliefs. In addition, cultural differences in maternal beliefs about the nature of children and child developmental processes that were shown to be derived from salient differences between two cultures were found to be correlated with children's school behavior. For example, children's positive and achievement-oriented classroom behaviors were found to be related to Tanzanian parental beliefs that Tanzanian children were dependent, and to beliefs in children's independence among U.S. parents (McGillicuddy-De Lisi and Subramanian, 1994).

The significance of the relation between culture and parent beliefs about children's social competence has been emphasized by Rubin (1998), who proposed that culture itself can be thought of as the beliefs, attitudes, and behaviors that characterize a group of people from one generation to the next. His analysis shows that cultural meanings for events and child behaviors lead to parental beliefs and childrearing practices. Investigators who have explored the relations of beliefs to children's personal–social behavior and skills have also looked to analyses of cultures in an effort to understand how such meanings are created by adults out of cultural, as well as personal experiences. For example, Chen et al. (1998) collected information from Chinese and Canadian mothers about behavioral inhibition, a term applied to children who show high levels of social wariness. These researchers proposed that parental beliefs exist within a larger context of cultural beliefs that provide the mechanism for making meaning out of children's behavior. In the case of behavioral inhibition, they made a compelling case that parents in China believe that such child behaviors indicate social competence as a result of emphasis on the development of self-restraint derived from Confucian and Taoist philosophies, and the cultural bases of maintaining social harmony and order.

In Canada, cultural beliefs are quite different: autonomy, individualism and social assertiveness are viewed as manifestations of increasing social maturity and competence. In both samples, mothers' beliefs, values, attitudes, and childrearing behaviors were assessed using a questionnaire, and observational measures of their 2-year-old children's inhibition were obtained. Results revealed that culturally mediated socialization beliefs led to different attitudes about behavioral inhibition. Furthermore, Canadian mothers were more likely to reject and punish inhibition behaviors, whereas Chinese mothers reported acceptance and lack of punitiveness.

These findings are consistent to those reported by Schneider, Attili, Vermigli, and Younger (1997), who assessed Italian and Canadian mothers' beliefs about their 7-year-old children's aggressive and withdrawn behaviors. Schneider et al. (1997) found that Canadian and Italian mothers would use moderate to high levels of power assertion when aggressive behaviors were involved, but lower levels of power assertion for social withdrawal. The Canadian mothers were more distressed by these problem behaviors, with no distinction for gender, in contrast to the Italian mothers, who differentiated their use of power for girls and for boys. Rubin (1998) has noted that culturally based belief systems that are used to assign meaning to children's behavior can result in strikingly different outcomes for children, even when the basis for children's behavior may be dispositional in a biological sense.

Differences between groups from different cultural backgrounds within a country. Roer-Strier and Rosenthal (1997) investigated Israeli- and Soviet-born immigrant mothers' beliefs about what constitutes an adaptive adult and examined their naive theories of development and developmental expectations. They found that definitions of adaptive adult and naive theories of development were related to country of origin. Soviet born mothers were more likely than Israeli mothers to believe that cognitive development can be accelerated and that preschoolers can control negative emotional behavior and understand social competition, and they were less likely to believe children could independently engage in problem solving. These beliefs were related to naive theories of development characteristic of the cultural background of the mothers. The authors assert that beliefs reflect the values of specific societies and serve as a guiding principle for childrearing goals.

The relation of parental beliefs and cultural background to children's performance in different areas of cognition has also been found to be important. For example, Savage and Gauvain (1998) assessed European American and Latino parents' beliefs about the development of 5- to 12-year-old children's planning abilities. Differences between European American and Latino parents' beliefs were consistent with cultural values for each group, and beliefs also varied with child age and gender in both groups. In addition, the authors found that the higher the level of acculturation of the Latino families, the more similar their beliefs about the development in general and their own child's actual behavior were to beliefs of European American parents. Level of acculturation was also related to opportunities children experienced for planning. They reported that children's planning behavior in a variety of different areas was related to parents' responses about developmental accomplishments of typical children in the area of planning.

Cote and Bornstein (2000), writing about the acculturation of U.S. mothers with Japanese or South American backgrounds in relation to their behavior in stimulating their infants' attention to the mother herself and to a physical object/event, suggested that parenting behaviors may become acculturated more rapidly than beliefs. This suggestion was based in part on the finding that observations of mothers' behaviors with their infants were not related to the mothers' self-reports of their own behaviors with their babies, which was taken as the measure of beliefs.

Although there appears to be considerable variability in the content of beliefs that are related to academic success in children across different groups, it is not clear how culture, parental beliefs, and children's cognitive abilities and school performance interact with one another to affect the lives of parents and children. However, particular content of parental beliefs does appear to be related to cultural assumptions about the nature of the child and norms concerning parents' roles in the schooling of their children.

The research of the anthropologically oriented psychologists such as Harkness and Super (1996) reported important differences among the groups they studied. The reason for this is primarily due to the differences in conceptualization of such basic issues as culture and its dynamic, pervasive influence. Culture is not grafted onto individuals, so terms such as cultural effects are not compatible with an anthropological model. Each individual in a society is an instantiation of her or his culture. In addition to differences in conceptualization, the anthropologically oriented psychologists use different methods, such as ethnology and field work within the culture, in contrast to the mainstream developmental psychologists, who employ distal measures such as questionnaires or formal assessment procedures such as psychological tests.

Each approach to the relation of culture to beliefs has contributed to the general knowledge bases of the role of culture, but usually superficially, assuming that an ethnic or racial label is adequate to acknowledge the cultural factor. Rarely is the rationale or justification for cultural or racial terms articulated. Rather, it is presumed. For example, most research with African American groups is based on color only. The question still remains, why should race be a more relevant variable than height, eye color, or hair color? The basic assumption is that "Blackness" is enough justification to consider people of color a group that has a unique culture with only rarely examining the culture. Ironically, this is also done with White study populations. The fact that European Americans differ in ethnicity or religious orientation is rarely considered as relevant (Hwang, Lamb, and Sigel, 1995). In most studies of parents, demographics such as social class, education, and occupational level are enough criteria for classifying study populations. Since skin color is genetically determined, there seems to be an assumption that this is sufficient to use as a proxy for culture. There are very few studies that have examined this presumption (Brody et al., 1994). In sum, the subtle, and hence nonobvious, cultural characteristics of research samples have been overlooked, thereby compromising the validity of many research studies on beliefs about childrearing.

The major development in the study of parent beliefs has been in the area of providing meaning to beliefs and through cultural perspectives. Of particular significance is the emphasis on intra- and intervariability in beliefs and comparisons of parental beliefs, practices, and child effects. These studies have enriched the database considerably and have had an impact on the conceptualization of the nature of beliefs and the processes through which they affect the lives of children.

Self-Efficacy

Parent effectiveness as parents. To this point the research review has focused on the consequences of parents' beliefs about their children's cognitive and social development, including their academic performance in school. Parents' beliefs about themselves as parents, their confidence in themselves as competent caretakers and role models, and their judgment as to their effectiveness as parents should be intimately related to how they function in the family context. Because of this consideration, the increasing body of research addressing parent qua parent characteristics will be the next topic to be addressed.

Markus, Cross, and Wurf (1990) report that feelings of competence as a parent is the second most common aspect of the "self" that is desired by adults. The work by Hastings and Rubin (1999) on mothers' beliefs about children's aggressive and withdrawn behavior that was previously summarized noted that mothers of inhibited or withdrawn children were more uncomfortable about their children's withdrawn behavior. The mothers suggested that somehow they themselves must be responsible for their children's negative social behavior. In short, they felt bad about their parenting.

Most often, research on parents' beliefs about their effectiveness is derived from Bandura's (1986) self-efficacy theory. Self-efficacy is applied to parent beliefs under the hypothesis that if parents feel competent they will behave in ways that are more effective with their children. We take the view that it is not necessary to justify an interest in parents' feelings of self-efficacy solely on the basis of their predictive power relative to child achievements or self-concepts, although those are certainly laudable outcomes. Parents' beliefs about their role as a parent are interesting in their own right as manifestations of adult cognitive development, and perhaps as influences in personal investment in that role. In this section we will first examine the literature on parents' feelings about their own effectiveness, which is presented most often as studies of parenting self-efficacy. We will then present some of the literature that has focused on beliefs as a source of parenting strategies and on beliefs that parents hold about the parenting role itself.

Coleman and Karraker (1998) recently reviewed the research literature on parents' feelings of self-efficacy. They summarized many studies that suggest mothers' beliefs about their capacity to effectively fulfill the parenting role are reliably related to specific parenting practices; parenting practices are then often related to positive child states and behaviors. Most often, parents' beliefs about their competence as parents have been connected directly to positive parenting behaviors and have been shown to be indirectly related to child achievements and behaviors. For example, Grolnick, Benjet, Kurowski, and Apostoleris (1997) asked mothers of children 8 to10 years old about their parenting beliefs and their school involvement. They reported that mothers with beliefs in their own self-efficacy as parents, and who believed that the parenting role included functioning as a teacher to their own child, were more likely to engage in cognitive activities with their children.

Brody, Flor, and Gibson (1999) also studied mothers' self-efficacy beliefs and found a complex relationship to parenting practices. They asked African American mothers of 6- to 9-year-old children about their parenting self-efficacy beliefs, childrearing goals, and childrearing practices. They also obtained measures of their children's academic and psychosocial competence. Parents' efficacy beliefs were related to their childrearing goals, which were in turn predictive of the mothers' childrearing practices. The mothers' childrearing practices were indirectly related to child academic and social competencies. Thus, in this study, self-efficacy beliefs of mothers were related to child outcomes, with childrearing goals and practices functioning as mediating variables.

Perozynski and Kramer's (1999) study of mothers' and fathers' beliefs about optimal ways to handle sibling conflicts included measures of the parents' feelings of confidence about their abilities to handle such conflicts. Mothers' and fathers' feelings of self-efficacy were not related to one another, suggesting that their sense of confidence was not due to the ease of managing their own children's behavior. Mothers felt more comfortable and effective than fathers did when handling conflicts using child-centered strategies, and mothers were equally comfortable using control strategies and child-centered strategies. Fathers reported a lower sense of efficacy with child-centered strategies than with control strategies. The parents' actual use of such strategies when monitoring sibling conflicts was consistent with these patterns of self-efficacy. In addition, these findings suggest that parents' sense of their effectiveness may play a role in their ability to select among different strategies and to manifest their beliefs in everyday discipline encounters with their children. For example, even when fathers reported that they believed a child-centered approach was optimal for resolving sibling conflicts (e.g., "help the children use words to express their feelings to each other"), they doubted their ability to effectively implement such strategies and were more likely to exhibit nonintervention or control strategies rather than use their preferred child-centered approach.

Wentzel (1998) found that parents who believed that intelligence was a malleable rather than a fixed ability also believed that they could affect their children's academic achievement directly through the parental role as teacher. They had higher educational aspirations for their children as a result of greater confidence in their ability to have an influence on the academic achievements of their children.

In a cross-cultural study of mothers' beliefs about self-efficacy, Bornstein et al. (1998) asked mothers of 20-month-old children from seven countries about their beliefs concerning their own parenting. They analyzed how mothers from each country conceived of the parent role, how they viewed children and childrearing, and what their childrearing goals were. This analysis of differences in cultural beliefs drove the predictions and analyses of the mothers' beliefs about their own parenting. When mothers believed their parenting practices affected outcomes for their children they were more likely to be active in promoting developmental achievements in their children. Regardless of the specific content of their beliefs, it appears that high levels of self-efficacy as a parent serve to engage the mother more fully and intensely in the parent role in the sense that their efforts and investment in parenting are greater.

Origins of a source of parenting beliefs and strategies.   Many researchers study beliefs because they hypothesize that the parents' assumptions and ideas about children and childrearing are a source of their behaviors with children and parenting. Haight, Parke, and Black's (1997) study of parental beliefs about toddlers' pretend play differs from more descriptive investigations of links between beliefs and child outcomes in several ways. Their interest in beliefs stems from a framework in which parents are seen as constructing meaning in social contexts. This includes a cultural milieu that provides social experiences to members of the community.

Such a developmental history also serves to frame the interpretation of their unique experiences with children and their own personal–social characteristics that shape beliefs. The authors focus on how the nature of beliefs led them to consider some questions beyond the level of describing relations of beliefs about pretend play. They addressed issues of motivational and affective dimensions of beliefs, questions about how beliefs in different areas relate to one another, and how beliefs about play relate to actual play behaviors with children for mothers and fathers. As a result, this study revealed that beliefs about play were related to the way in which mothers and fathers engaged in play. The beliefs and behaviors were shown to be consistent with cultural experiences that differ for mothers and fathers and were also linked to particular personal experiences and other beliefs, such as religious beliefs, in meaningful ways. Their analysis of variability in the connection between beliefs and behaviors was informed by theories of the role of cultural context on beliefs as well as consideration of how the domain investigated (e.g., pretend play versus reading) might be a factor in the construction of belief systems. This paper revealed much about the nature of parental beliefs and provided specific information about parents' beliefs concerning the cognitive and social functions of play.

The parenting role.   Many studies have been conducted that relate parental beliefs to other types of ideas that parents have about their children (see Goodnow in Vol. 3 of this *Handbook*). In recent years, considerable attention has been directed toward exploring the relation of parental beliefs to parental goals or aspirations for their children. For example, Wentzel (1998) suggested that parental beliefs, which included beliefs about the nature of children's intelligence, beliefs in parents' own abilities to serve as their children's teacher, and values regarding academic achievement were a source of parental goals. These goals were defined as aspirations for the child's academic achievements and served to organize the parent's behavior toward those ends. She assumed that these goals then directed parental behavior toward fostering particular child outcomes

Summary: Evaluation of Current Research on Parent Beliefs

The research findings we have reported show that beliefs often relate to parent behaviors, and especially to children's behaviors. Longitudinal studies have linked beliefs to developmental trajectories. The magnitude of the findings is often low, and the statistical significance is a function of the sample size. This is important in the study of beliefs because we are left with only a superficial understanding of the belief–outcome relation. (See Gigerenzer, 1993, for a discussion of the issues involved in statistical inference.) The more important lacuna in the research literature is a developed theory, which can guide future research as an explanatory basis to help understand why a parent's belief about achievement, for example, accounts for the obtained relationships.

An example of a study that does approach the investigation of beliefs in a more comprehensive way than most of those in the preceding review is by Mize, Petit, and Brown (1995). They report an analysis of the complexities of the belief construct. They were interested in identifying what factors influence children's social competence with peers. The problem was framed in terms of what parental actions play a role in their children's peer interactions. The authors presented a conceptualization that linked mothers' beliefs about the modifiability and importance of social skills to their beliefs about their own children's social competence with peers, and the strategies used in response to peer interaction problems. The interrelationship of three domains that interact is addressed, thereby filling out the belief model by moving away from a single belief dimension. Their findings extended our understanding of how beliefs interact with knowledge to influence the quality of supervision.

Although this study brought the belief issues into a larger context, it still presumed a unidirectional orientation, as if parents' influence is driven by parents' cognitions and are not interactive with the mother and child, each influencing the other. Sigel and Kim (1996) reported an example of how the child's behavior influences not only beliefs, but also immediate responses of the parent to the child's level of proficiency. For example, they found that the level of the child's language comprehension was a significant influence on the parent's inquiry strategies. Had Sigel and Kim (1996) not analyzed their data from the child's perspective, this finding would not have emerged.

A DYNAMIC BELIEF SYSTEMS MODEL

Why the transformation of the belief complex to a dynamic belief system? The move is based on a simple observation of the history of parenting: thoughts about children, as well as findings from current empirical analyses of the role of beliefs, have a long history in our study of parenting behaviors and parenting effects. Numerous research studies were reviewed in this chapter. We found that parents hold beliefs about virtually every facet of the parenting role and believe that they are sources of influence on the development of their children. Furthermore, we gained a glimpse into some of the inner workings of belief systems. However, in our search for deep-seated patterns that could potentially increase our understanding of the content, form, and function of beliefs for parents, we found that a clear conception of beliefs and theoretical explanations of how and why beliefs are effective are lacking.

Furthermore, the concept of belief is often confounded with attitudes, perceptions, beliefs, and even opinions, so that it is not clear what psychological construct is operating when parents report their "beliefs." The methods employed in most studies tend to be questionnaires that range from two to three questions to larger questionnaires or structured interviews. Little attention is paid to the structure of beliefs, either in theoretical or empirical form. There is now a considerable literature on beliefs, but much of it is superficial, poorly defined, and while often high in face validity, it is sorely lacking in providing information about construct and content validity. Almost any question one asks a parent about their children has been classified as a belief.

Finally, most studies have been designed for correlational analysis with few experimental approaches, and most are static snapshots of a parent's thoughts. Longitudinal studies are more convincing, but they also suffer from the lack of precision discussed above. We agree with McGuire (1999), who argued for a freer empirical approach that explores many routes with a greater reliance on thought experiments in the planning of research. We have to be more creative and move to mul-timethod studies if we are to understand the complexities of parenting and the role of beliefs in that process.

A grand theory of beliefs may be out of reach, and premature for the development of a full understanding of parent cognitions. Yet there is evidence that the search for shared meanings and findings among investigators from different fields within the social sciences arena has begun and is promising (e.g., Harkness and Super, 1996; Sigel, McGillicuddy-De Lisi, and Goodnow, 1992). These accomplishments, in conjunction with the great increase in knowledge about the content of beliefs that has been revealed over the past 5 years, give us cause for great optimism. However, the potential benefits will be realized only if the breadth of questions, approaches, and paradigms applied to investigations of parents' thinking about their children and their role in child development is amplified.

These are the issues and questions that emerged from our reading of the parent belief literature. We had the sense that there was a lack of embeddedness of beliefs into the real lives of families—families that are developing and in which each member is developing, each in multiple contexts. Beliefs, we came to realize, are core determinants of the way human nature unfolds. Beliefs are pervasive in all cultures and every sphere of life (e.g., parenting, scientific investigations, and domestic and international political decision making). Therefore, with some trepidation we offer a dynamic belief systems model as another paradigm by which to study beliefs. In our judgment, there has been a reality to the significance of beliefs in all societies from time immemorial. The proposed dynamic belief systems model is consistent with the emergence of interest in systems thinking (Thelen and Smith, 1994; Wachs, 2000).

The construction of a dynamic belief systems model has ecological validity that is absent from many recently published studies. The literature reveals relations between what parents believe about their parenting role, goals, values, ideas about health and educational practices, and so forth, at least within the early years of childhood in a variety of social contexts. From the point of view of applied behavior theory, and of psychologists interested in parenting, it is imperative that we now move forward to understand why people hold beliefs, what functions they serve, and their effects on parents, children, and families (Miller, 1995; Okagaki and Sternberg, 1991). The conclusion from this line of reasoning is that a reconfiguration of the initial belief complex is in order, a transformation which will be a greater approximation of the natural world than is evident from the existing methods of study.

Rejecting the modal logical positivist research tradition, a reasonable alternative is a holistic systematic approach that encompasses the complexity that characterizes the human mind. However, to avoid being grandiose at this stage, the model to be presented will be restricted to parental beliefs as but one major component of the parents' cognitive structure.

The Articulation of a Prototypic Model of Parent Beliefs

On the basis of a program of research, McGillicuddy-De Lisi and Sigel (1995) and Sigel (1985) have had occasion to observe that parental beliefs do not function as single variables having a particular relationship to some outcome, for example, the child's performance in school. Every belief is complex, comprised of a number of definable components that, in their totality, combine to lead to some type of instantiation. In the earlier version of this chapter (McGillicuddy-De Lisi and Sigel, 1995), a belief complex model was presented that identified eight dimensions considered to be intrinsic to the belief construct. Initially, each of these was considered as an independent variable, often with little consideration of the mutual influences among them.

On reflection, it was recognized that these components not only cannot function independently, and also cannot be experimentally controlled because the human mind just does not operate that way, in spite of the mechanistically minded psychologists who would reject the intrinsic dynamic nature of the living organism (Pepper, 1942/1970). These components form the basic elements in the proposed dynamic belief systems model.[1] They are listed below:

(1) Beliefs are knowledge based and are constructions of experience. The cognitive processes involved are assimilation and accommodation. (K)
(2) Beliefs are organized into categories of knowledge domains, each of which is bounded. The internal coherence of the domains may vary, and the boundaries may vary in permeability. (D)
(3) Beliefs may be held as absolutes or as probabilities. (A/P)
(4) Beliefs serve comparable functions for everyone irrespective of culture, although the content and experiential bases from which beliefs are constructed within a cultural milieu are different. (C)
(5) Beliefs are influenced by affect to varying degrees of intensity and quality of influence. (A)
(6) Beliefs are expressed in behaviors that may have one or more goals. (G)
(7) Beliefs vary in the degree to which they are valued (i.e., deemed important). (V)
(8) There is a subset of beliefs derived from core beliefs as to how and under what conditions to instantiate actions to express the core beliefs. These are praxis beliefs about how and in what form beliefs should be enacted. One important category of praxis beliefs is beliefs in one's ability to effectively generate and implement a parenting strategy, as well as other aspects of parenting self-efficacy. (SE)

Developing a Dynamic Belief Systems Model

Three topics will be addressed in this section: (1) an elaborated definition of *belief* to reflect the perspective, (2) organization of the beliefs on a hierarchically developmental system, and (3) a prototype of how the system can be instantiated.

"A belief is a mental form with a propositional content, that is, a formal structure of some complexity which encodes meaningful information that such and such is so and so. This is the sense in which a belief is a complex mental representation; with multiple functions depending which components are activated. These functions may involve one or more of the components from a content-encoding mental form to a cognitive or behavioral role, such a characterization fits the currently standard definition of belief" (Bogdan, 1986, p. 149). Bogdan (1986) continues to argue that this standard definition is incomplete (p. 149)

> because if belief is thought of as a function from content, then understanding the belief amounts to an understanding the nature of this function which in turn means understanding the constraints which shape it. What the standard notion of belief fails to identify and explain are precisely the condition, which shape the belief function, that is the conditions in which a content-encoding mental form comes to play a cognitive role and thus becomes a belief. This obviously becomes a very critical failure, for the very essence of belief, that of being a function from mental representation to causal role and behavior is left totally unexplained.

The model is situated in the cognitive domain, interacting with other systems of beliefs consistent with the goals of the dynamic belief systems model.

---

[1]There are two approaches to systems theory, dynamic systems theory and general systems theory. The former is reflected in the work of Thelen and Smith (1994) and the latter in the work of Von Bertalanffy (1968), in which total system are discussed with reference to developing self-organizing systems. The dynamics involved in this scenario reflect the complexity of the dynamic mind incorporating an array of cognitive, affective, and adaptive strategies functioning synergistically.

Further, these beliefs in their collectivity form the person's basic view of the physical, social, and psychological reality of attitudes, perceptions, and attributions. Beliefs are determinants of how we feels about objects, events, or persons, how we perceive and interpret others' actions, and how we project our own views on the extrinsic world. Beliefs form the substrate that defines the nature of attitudes, perceptions, and attributes. These latter psychological features derive from one's worldview. These beliefs form the basis for attitudes, attributions and perceptions related to the particular beliefs. Following through on the argument led to the consideration of dynamic belief systems model as analogous to the chaos metaphor that refers to inner mental states as active forces that are in constant dynamic movement (Robertson and Combs, 1996). The physical analogue is the atomic structure in which atoms moving around in space and bumping against one another are controlled by their positive or negative attractors, mutual attraction, or had more influence on movement than when they met one another as attractors. The belief components are now conceptualized as forces of interactive and mutual influence. Furthermore, there are an unknown number of belief domains that have different degrees of potency under particular conditions. For example, some parenting beliefs may be unaffected by parents' religious or political beliefs, while for others there is coherence between religious practice and childrearing. We argue that every belief is defined in its wholeness by one or more of the components described earlier.

THE DYNAMIC BELIEF SYSTEMS MODEL

This formulation is a preliminary effort to introduce the concept as a universal dynamic beliefs systems model. The goal is to transform the static belief complex into a dynamic belief systems model.

Sources of Beliefs

Beliefs evolve and the modes of their expression are all derived from idiosyncratic and nomothetic cultural experience because everyone is enmeshed in a culture that has shaped the content and the expression of everyone's beliefs. This analysis is consistent with the dynamic beliefs systems model. Other subsystems, which we will call noncognitive systems—biological, motoric-, kinesthetic, and coping mechanisms—are all involved and related to beliefs, enabling persons to live, move, and grow and develop in the world.

The act of expressing a belief is selected from a repertoire available to the parent as deemed relevant for the action to take now. The belief orients the individual to the event, and the actions employed emerge from a belief system dedicated to action. The quality of the action depends on the level of the individual's cognitive competence. Cognitive competence is defined in terms of a concrete–conceptual dimension. This should be thought of as analogous to executive functions that propel individuals to action, but this action is guided by the belief system. Cognitive competence is also influenced by personality characteristics such as emotional control, reflectivity, and flexibility.

The approach is applicable to every situation because there is the universal presence of core beliefs about actions as guided by the executive judgment of the situation and because the dynamic processes through which beliefs interact exist in every belief system. The belief is expressed in an act or several actions that can be identified. That is, the action can include utterance, gesture, tone of voice, "the look" (to quote one child), as well as physical behaviors. The dynamic action of belief is, however, inferred from such overt behavioral manifestations of beliefs. The belief actions or processes essentially become the basis of our dynamic interpretation. Beliefs function in the genre of a dynamic system. This contradicts other traditional unidimensional, unilinear approaches, for example, parent beliefs influence parent behaviors which influence child outcomes.

In our discussion of beliefs, we tended to focus on parent beliefs relative to positive outcomes for children, a state that reflects most of the empirical literature. There is a darker side to belief systems that is important to recognize, however. Although evil is not intended, certain beliefs regarding children can lead to behaviors that have negative consequences. For example, children are neglected, abused, moved from one family to another, pressured to behave in ways that are outside of their developmental or personal capabilities, or are left to fend for themselves or become responsible for others at a very young age, sometimes in part because of parents' beliefs (Howes and Cicchetti, (1993).

Beliefs can be distorted constructions of reality. In the political arena, we have seen Nazi beliefs about non-Aryans, white racist beliefs about African Americans, certain religious groups about other religious groups, and, of course, ultimate distortions of paranoid schizophrenic parents about their world. A dilemma in the study of beliefs is the issue of their veridicality. On the face of it, some belief systems are relatively clear-cut in their distortion. Nevertheless, there are those that pose judgment questions where the degree to which the belief system conforms to a shared social reality. We now enter into the realm of morals and ethics. For example, it has been reported that some parents believe that creating a restrictive environment is best for their children's cognitive and moral development (Bandura, 1986). Such beliefs are expressed in control strategies that are often commands, verbal demands for compliance, or threats of punishment for noncompliance. Often coupled with this orientation is a belief that corporal punishment is an effective way to deal with infractions or noncompliance.

Parents' evaluation of the effectiveness of their discipline practices in this scenario would be limited to the degree to which the child completed tasks, consistent with the parent's goals. If these strategies do not achieve effective results, the child is believed to be the source of the failure to accomplish the parenting goal, rather than a consideration of the inappropriateness of the parent's beliefs and practices (Howes and Cicchetti, 1993). What is often the case is that in spite of such failures of the belief, and in spite of failure of strategies as well, parent beliefs do not change. They remain because those beliefs and practices are related to other factors in the system, such as beliefs about the self in this very responsible role of childrearing. All of these factors speak to the multilevel significance of parental beliefs—and the importance of understanding them.

The Dynamic Belief Systems Model Explicated

As a first step, we propose an overarching generic, nested model. The comprehensive model is situated in the parent–child relationship within the family. The family environment is the primal socialization agency, with the parents as key agents of influence, at least during the early years. The parents, in their own socialization and acculturation, have developed a broad spectrum of beliefs about their world, including beliefs about themselves, and these beliefs function at different levels of awareness and are embedded within a micro social–political context (i.e., a family). The family, in turn, is nested in a broader network of communities (e.g., educational, political, social, and so forth), and further nested within a macrosocial context of the nation and the world. At every level there are constraints and affordances for belief-related activity. The type, awareness, and potency of influence will vary depending on the proximal relation to the social agents. For example, within one family the parent's beliefs about childrearing may be a product of mutually influential beliefs about the nature of development, parenting practices, values, goals, and the like among the members of the family. For other individuals, social institutions such as educational experiences, religious affiliation, or teaching may be more salient influences; in some contexts the child may be coequal in the belief action rather than a recipient of such action. These are conditions of distal influences. For the purposes of this presentation, the focus is on the proximal environment in the family. Thus, the parents or caregivers in the family context influence other family members as well as are influenced by them.

Level 1

Domain – Parenting

(Worldview)

Level II

Specific parent belief domain

| **Cognitive** | **Social-Moral** | **Interpersonal skills** | **Intrapersonal** |

Level III

Examples of specific beliefs within each Level II domain

Thinking	**Honesty**	**Getting along in**	**Emotional control**
Reasoning	Right from wrong	family, school	Self-awareness
Planning	Ethical	cooperation	
		Appropriate social	
		behavior	

Level IV

Praxis beliefs

(applicable to any specific belief or constellation of beliefs)

Inquiry strategies, direct instruction, suggestions, etc.

Level V

Modes of expression

Overt actions, e.g., inquiry, discipline, etc.

FIGURE 17.1. Dynamic belief system domain.

The environment can be organized into a "multilevel higher order structure with bidirectional patterns of influence both across and within levels . . . Five levels have been identified from the macrosystem to the microsystem each in descending order of proximal influence on the children's development" (Bronfenbrenner, 1979). At this point in the development of the model, the focus will be on environment, particularly the belief system.

The beliefs as a subsystem within the larger cognitive system can be organized in a hierarchically descending order, as described in Figure 17.1.

Level I refers to the dynamic belief system as a whole, which is an overarching category of beliefs that is, in a sense, a worldview. Level II contains cognitive belief domains, the focus of interest in this model. These categories have been identified by McGillicuddy and Sigel (1995). Within each of these areas are specific beliefs that are content specific. Level III refers to the content of specific beliefs for each Level II domain. Level IV refers to the how the particular beliefs are instantiated, that is, praxis beliefs. For example, Sigel (Sigel and Kim, 1996) found that a group of parents, who believed that children learn through thinking and reasoning, expressed this belief in different ways. Some used inquiry strategies, others used direct instruction, and still others used suggestions. When asked for the reasons for a particular practice, parents reported that different beliefs about how children should be encouraged to think and learn were due to different beliefs about the maturity level of the child or the child's comprehensions of instructions.

Every belief is presumed to include the eight enumerated components, which are listed in Table 17.1 These are: constructed knowledge (K), bounded knowledge domain (D), absolute/probabilistic nature (A/P), cultural tradition (C), affect (A), goals/intentionality (G), values (V), and praxis (P). Each of these dimensions varies in the degree of influence it exerts within the system.

The expression of a belief in any form is a product of the components that blend into a single action. Exactly how these dimensions play themselves out depends on the belief or beliefs in question. There are different degrees of influence. For example, a religious belief may activate the affective component in the course of a discussion between individuals from different religious perspectives (Thomas, 1988). The belief boundaries will vary in permeability, so that under some circumstances certain components will not be static. This is an individual difference issue.

Ideally, the various components will interact and this interaction can be expressed in an arithmetic equation or algorithm depicting how the dimensions enhance, diminish, or have no influence on a specific act (e.g., to illustrate, see the model depicted in Figure 17.2). The center of the diagram depicts a core set of beliefs about parenting and child development. Each of the segments reflects a different component as depicted in the legend, these components are dynamic, interacting in relationship to others (see dotted lines). For example, affect, value, and so forth. The smaller figure in the upper left depicts the dynamic movement in time as the belief function. This is expressed in the spiral, which denotes not a straight line, but a recursive potential.

Concretely stated, let us assume the parent believes the child can learn only by direct instruction. This belief is part of the praxis core system. The parent is also convinced that this is the only way a child can learn. Thus, based on her acclaimed knowledge of child development (K), she is further convinced that this is the only way and has strong feeling about it (A), and it is derived from her cultural tradition (C) and the value of it (V) because it will serve her goals or her child's (G) goals or both. These components are in a dynamic relationship within the system with relationship varying among them depending on exigencies of internal events. What is needed is a way of determining the differential influences of the components. The person's beliefs can be stated in a clear and convincing manner, as P (praxis belief). Another person may hold the same belief (same C) but with absolute certainty (different A/P), and might have a different view of her or his ability to instantiate or fairly represent that perspective (different P). Although the content of the belief might be identical, a different level of presentation of that belief could well be set in motion. A belief held strongly in relation to a praxis belief of high self-efficacy would likely also change affective features.

The differences in this setting may create a variety of actions within the belief system. As shown in Figure 17.3, the core belief may be shared with others in the culture or across cultures, but its expression may vary. The model that is developing is dynamic because these components are not static in influence. All of these components of the belief model function in a holistic, dynamic internal interactive system to influencing the quality of the mode of expression. The nature of the mode of expression, as well as time, place, and target of the actions, set up the quality of interaction with the target (Sigel, 1986). The next step is to examine the nature of the interaction, that is, the beginning of an investigation of actions in social contexts as sources of influence on how the dynamics within the system unfold.

CONCLUSIONS

In our search for understanding this complex set of relations, serious attention must be directed toward the research paradigms used to examine beliefs. There continues to be considerable controversy regarding the appropriateness of a dynamic system model for the study of these social and behavioral issues (Baker, 1987). The scheme presented in the foregoing is probably not without controversy. There is a considerable literature evaluating nonlinear approaches to the study of developmental change (e.g., Barton, 1994; Gottman and Rusche, 1993). A most comprehensive presentation of the theoretical and practical use of a dynamic belief systems approach is that of Wachs (2000), whose thorough analysis raises questions about the feasibility of the approach

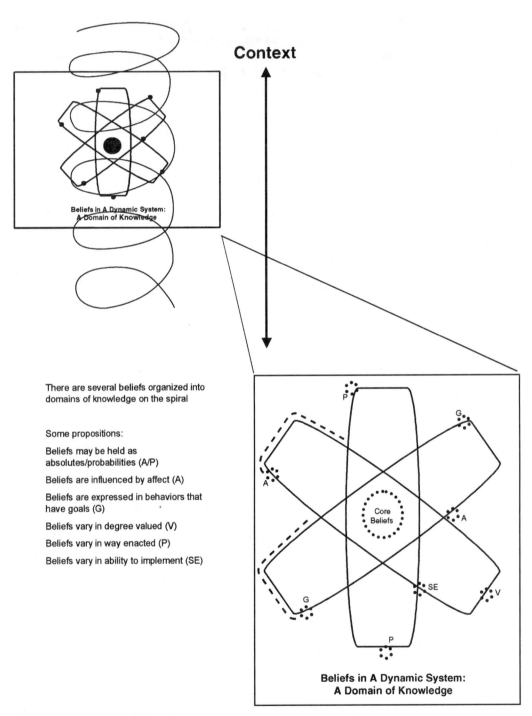

Context

There are several beliefs organized into domains of knowledge on the spiral

Some propositions:

Beliefs may be held as absolutes/probabilities (A/P)

Beliefs are influenced by affect (A)

Beliefs are expressed in behaviors that have goals (G)

Beliefs vary in degree valued (V)

Beliefs vary in way enacted (P)

Beliefs vary in ability to implement (SE)

**Beliefs in A Dynamic System:
A Domain of Knowledge**

FIGURE 17.2. Beliefs in a dynamic system.

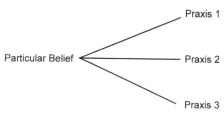

FIGURE 17.3. Belief system domain prototype.

advocated in this chapter. He demonstrates the inherent problems of fitting existing empirical data to a dynamic belief systems approach. The point of view offered here acknowledges the complexity of shifting from the current structural or linear and unidirectional research model, where the dynamic processes are not articulated or even considered. The argument for the consideration of the approach advocated in this chapter for experimenting with a dynamic beliefs systems model is based in its compatibility with a naturalistic view of human development (Thelen and Smith, 1994; Wachs, 2000).

An excellent summary of the perspective reported here is apparent in the following comment by Valsiner: "Parenting is . . . a heterogeneous phenomenon of bi-directional cultural transformations rather than a unidirectional and unitary guidance of children toward adulthood. Research questions that may become productive include those of the dynamic nature of the construction of belief orientations with actual actions" (Valsiner, 1997, p. 382).[2]

ACKNOWLEDGMENTS

The order of authorship was determined by our turn taking arrangements. The chapter is a product of a co-equal partnership. We wish to thank Linda Kozelski for her invaluable assistance in getting this manuscript in final form. Thanks also go to Carla Cooper for preparing Figure 17.2, Beliefs in a dynamic system and Ann McGillicuddy-De Lisi for the idea. Last, but not least, thanks to the editor of the volume for his careful and helpful editorial suggestions.

REFERENCES

Andre, T., Whigham, M., Hendrickson, A., and Chambers, S. (1999). Competency beliefs, positive affect, and gender stereotypes of elementary students and their parents about science versus other school subjects. *Journal of Research in Science Teaching, 36*, 719–747.

Baker, L. R. (1987). *Saving belief: A critique of physicalism.* Princeton, NJ: Princeton University Press.

Baldwin, A. (1965). A is happy—B is not. *Child Development, 36*, 583–600.

Bandura, A. (1986). The explanatory and predictive scope of self-efficacy theory. *Journal of Social and Clinical Psychology, 4*, 359–373.

Barton, S. (1994). Chaos, self-organization, and psychology. *American Psychologist, 49*, 5–14.

Bogdan, R. J. (1986). *Belief: Form, content and function.* Oxford, England: Clarendon Press.

Bornstein, M. H. (Ed.). (1995). *Handbook of parenting* (1st ed., Vols. 1–4). Hillsdale, NJ: Lawrence Erlbaum Associates.

Bornstein, M. C., Haynes, O. M., Azuma, H., Galperín, C., Maital, S., Ogino, M., Painter, K., Pascual, L., Pecheux, M.-G., Rahn, C., Toda, S., Venuti, P., Vyt, A., and Wright, B. (1998). A cross-national study of self-evaluations and attributions in parenting: Argentina, Belgium, France, Israel, Italy, Japan, and the United States. *Developmental Psychology, 34*, 662–676.

Brody, G. H., Flor, D. L., and Gibson, N. M. (1999). Linking maternal efficacy beliefs, developmental goals, parenting practices, and child competence in rural single-parent African American families. *Child Development, 70*, 1197–1208.

---

[2]The Valsiner approach is too extensive to summarize here in any detail. The interested reader is encouraged to read this stimulating chapter (Valsiner, 1997).

Brody, G. H., Stoneman, Z., Flor, D., McCrary, C., Hastings, L., and Conyers, O. (1994). Financial resources, parent psychological functioning, parent co-caregiving, and early adolescent competence in rural two-parent African-American families. *Child Development, 65*, 590–605.

Bronfenbrenner, U. (1979). *The ecology of human development: Experiments by nature and design.* Cambridge, MA: Harvard University Press.

Bugental, D. B. (1992). Affective and cognitive processes within threat-oriented family systems. In I. E. Sigel, A. V. McGillicuddy-De Lisi, and J. J. Goodnow (Eds.), *Parental belief systems: The psychological consequences for children* (2nd ed., pp. 219–248). Hillsdale, NJ: Lawrence Erlbaum Associates.

Bugental, D. B., and Johnston, C. (2000). Parental and child cognitions in the context of the family. *Annual Review of Psychology, 51*, 315–344.

Chao, R. K. (1996). Chinese and European American mothers' beliefs about the role of parenting in children's school success. *Journal of Cross-Cultural Psychology, 27*, 403–423.

Chen, X., Hastings, P. D., Rubin, K. H., Chen, H., Cen, G., and Stewart, S. L. (1998). Child-rearing attitudes and behavioral inhibition in Chinese and Canadian toddlers: A cross-cultural study. *Developmental Psychology, 34*, 677–686.

Clarke-Stewart, K. A. (1998). Historical shifts and underlying themes in ideas about rearing young children in the United States: Where have we been? Where are we going? *Early Development and Parenting, 7*, 101–117.

Cochran, M. (1988). Parental empowerment in family matters: Lessons learned from a research program. In I. Sigel (Series Ed.), and D. R. Powell (Vol. Ed.), *Advances in applied developmental psychology: Vol. 3. Parent education as early childhood intervention: Emerging directions in theory, research and practice* (pp. 23–50). Norwood, NJ: Ablex.

Coleman, P. K., and Karraker, K. H. (1998). Self-efficacy and parenting quality: Findings and future applications. *Developmental Review, 18*, 47–85.

Collins, W. A., Maccoby, E. E., Steinberg, L., Hetherington, E. M., and Bornstein, M. H. (2000). Contemporary research on parenting: The case for nature versus nurture. *American Psychologist, 55*, 218–232.

Cote, L. R., and Bornstein, M. H. (2000). Social and didactic parenting behaviors and beliefs among Japanese American and South American mothers of infants. *Infancy, 1*, 363–374.

Davis, P. W. (1999). Corporal punishment cessation: Social context and parents' experiences. *Journal of Interpersonal Violence, 14*, 492–510.

Dawes, A., and Cairns, E. (1998). The Machel Study: Dilemmas of cultural sensitivity and universal rights of children. *Peace and Conflict: Journal of Peace Psychology, 4*, 335–348.

Donahue, M. L., Pearl, R., and Herzog, A. (1997). Referential communication with preschoolers: Effects of children's syntax and mothers' beliefs. *Journal of Applied Developmental Psychology, 18*, 133–147.

Durrant, J. E., Broberg, A. G., and Rose-Krasnor, L. (1999). Predicting mother's use of physical punishment during mother–child conflicts in Sweden and Canada. In C. C. Piotrowski and P. D. Hastings (Eds.), *Conflict as a context for understanding maternal beliefs about child rearing and children's misbehavior* (pp. 25–41). San Francisco: Jossey-Bass. (*New Directions for Child and Adolescent Development,* No. 86).

Eibl-Elbesfeldt, I. (1989). *Human ethology.* Hawthorne, NY: De Gruyter.

Engle, P. L., Zeitlin, M., Medrano, Y., and Garcia, L. (1996). Growth consequences of low-income Nicaraguan mothers' theories about feeding 1-year olds. In S. Harkness and C. Super (Eds.), *Parents' cultural belief systems: Their origins, expressions, and consequences* (pp. 428–446). New York: Guilford.

Frome, P. M., and Eccles, J. S. (1998). Parents' influence on children's achievement-related perceptions. *Journal of Personality and Social Psychology, 74*, 435–452.

Galper, A., Wigfield, A., and Seefeldt, C. (1997). Head Start parents' beliefs about their children's abilities, task values, and performance on different activities. *Child Development, 68*, 897–907.

Gigerenzer, G. (1993). The superego, the ego, and the id in statistical reasoning. In G. Keren and C. Lewis (Eds.), *A handbook for data analysis in the behavioral sciences: Methodological issues* (pp. 311–339). Hillsdale, NJ: Lawrence Erlbaum Associates.

Goodnow, J. J. (1985). Change and variation in ideas about childhood and parenting. In I. E. Sigel (Ed.), *Parental belief systems: The psychological consequences for children* (pp. 235–271). Hillsdale, NJ: Lawrence Erlbaum Associates.

Goodnow, J. J., and Collins, W. A. (1990). *Development according to parents: The nature, sources, and consequences of parents' ideas.* Hillsdale, NJ: Lawrence Erlbaum Associates.

Gottman, J. M., and Rushe, R. H. (1993). The analysis of change: Issues, fallacies, and new ideas. *Journal of Consulting and Clinical Psychology, 61*, 907–910.

Grolnick, W. S., Benjet, C., Kurowski, C. O., and Apostoleris, N. H. (1997). Predictors of parent involvement in children's schooling. *Journal of Educational Psychology, 89*, 538–548.

Grusec, J. E., Rudy, D., and Martini, T. (1997). Parenting cognitions and child outcomes: An overview and implications for children's internalization of values. In J. E. Grusec and L. Kuczynski (Eds.), *Parenting and children's internalization of values: A handbook of contemporary theory* (pp. 259–282). New York: Wiley.

Haight, W. L., Parke, R. D., and Black, J. E. (1997). Mothers' and fathers' beliefs about and spontaneous participation in their toddlers' pretend play. *Merrill-Palmer Quarterly, 43*, 271–290.

Halle, T. G., Kurtz-Costes, B., and Mahoney, J. L. (1997). Family influences on school achievement in low-income, African American children. *Journal of Educational Psychology, 89,* 527–537.

Harkness, S., and Super, C. (Eds.). (1996). *Parents' cultural belief systems: Their origins, expressions, and consequences.* New York: Guilford.

Hastings, P. D., and Coplan, R. (1999). Conceptual and empirical links between children's social spheres: Relating maternal beliefs and preschoolers' behaviors with peers. In C. C. Piotrowski and P. D. Hastings (Eds.), *Conflict as a context for understanding maternal beliefs. New Directions for Child and Adolescent Development* (No. 86, pp. 25–41). San Francisco: Jossey-Bass.

Hastings, P. D., and Grusec, J. E. (1998). Parenting goals as organizers of responses to parent–child disagreement. *Developmental Psychology, 34,* 465–479.

Hastings, P., and Rubin, K. H. (1999). Predicting mothers' beliefs about preschool-aged children's social behavior: Evidence for maternal attitudes moderating child effects. *Child Development, 70,* 722–741.

Heider, F. (1958). *The psychology of interpersonal relations.* New York: Wiley.

Hinshaw, S. P., Zupan, B. A., Simmel, C., Nigg, J. T., and Melnick, S. (1997). Peer status in boys with and without attention-deficit hyperactivity disorder: Predictions from overt and covert antisocial behavior, social isolation, and authoritative parenting beliefs. *Child Development, 68,* 880–896.

Hortacsu, N. (1995). Parents' education levels, parents' beliefs, and child outcomes. *Journal of Genetic Psychology, 156,* 373–383.

Howes, P. W., and Cicchetti, D. (1993). A family/relational perspective on maltreating families: Parallel processes across systems and social policy implications. In I. Sigel (Series Ed.) and Cicchetti and S. T. Toth (Vol. Eds.), *Advances in applied developmental psychology: Vol. 8. Child abuse, child development and social policy* (pp. 149–299). Norwood, NJ: Ablex.

Hupkens, C. L. H., Knibbe, R. A., van Otterloo, A. H., and Drop, M. J. Class differences in the food rules mothers impose on their children: A cross-national study. *Social Science and Medicine, 47,* 1331–1339.

Hwang, C. P., Lamb, M. E., and Sigel, I. E. (Eds.). (1996). *Images of childhood.* Mahwah, NJ: Lawrence Erlbaum Associates.

Jacobs, J. E. (1991). Influence of gender stereotypes on parent and child mathematics attitudes. *Journal of Educational Psychology, 83,* 518–527.

Jacobs, J. E., and Weisz, V. (1994). Gender stereotypes: Implications for gifted education. *Roeper Review, 16,* 152–155.

Lees, N. B., and Tinsley, B. (2000). Maternal socialization of children's preventive health behavior: The role of maternal affect and teaching strategies. *Merrill-Palmer Quarterly, 46,* 632–652.

Li, L., Pan, L., Yi, J., and Xia, Y. (1997). Structure and influencing factors of parental belief of mothers of 2–6-year-old children. *Psychological Science (China), 20,* 243–247.

Mantzicopoulos, P. Y. (1997). The relationship of family variables to Head Start children's preacademic competence. *Early Education and Development, 8,* 357–375.

Markus, H., Cross, S., and Wurf, E. (1990). The role of the self-system in competence. In R. Sternberg and J. Kolligian (Eds.), *Competence considered* (pp. 205–226). New Haven, CT: Yale University Press.

McBride-Chang, C., and Chang, L. (1998). Adolescent–parent relations in Hong Kong: Parenting styles, emotional autonomy, and school achievement. *Journal of Genetic Psychology, 159,* 421–436.

McGillicuddy-De Lisi, A. V., and Sigel, I. E. (1995). Parental beliefs. In M. H. Bornstein (Ed.). *Handbook of parenting: Vol. 3. Status and social conditions of parenting* (pp. 333–358). Hillsdale, NJ: Lawrence Erlbaum Associates.

McGillicuddy-De Lisi, A. V., and Subramanian, S. (1994). Tanzanian and United States mothers' beliefs about parents' and teachers' roles in children knowledge acquisition. *International Journal of Behavioral Development, 17,* 209–237.

McGuire, W. J. (1999). *Constructing social psychology.* New York: Cambridge University Press.

Miller, S. A. (1988). Parents' beliefs about children's cognitive development. *Child Development, 59,* 259–285.

Miller, S. A. (1995). parents' attributions for their children's behavior. *Child Development, 66,* 1557–1584.

Mills, R. S. L. (1999). Exploring the effects of low power schemas in mothers. In C. C. Piotrowski and P. D. Hastings (Eds.), *Conflict as a context for understanding maternal beliefs about child rearing and children's misbehavior* (pp. 61–77). San Francisco: Jossey-Bass. (*New Directions for Child and Adolescent Development,* No. 86).

Mize, J., Pettit, G. S., and Brown, E. G. (1995). Mothers' Supervision of their children's peer play: Relations with beliefs, perceptions, and knowledge. *Developmental Psychology, 31,* 311–321.

Musun-Miller, L., and Blevins-Knabe, B. (1998). Adults' beliefs about children and mathematics: How important is it and how do children learn about it? *Early Development and Parenting, 7,* 191–202.

Okagaki, L., and Sternberg, R. J. (1991). *Directors of development: Influences on the development of children thinking.* Hillsdale, NJ: Lawrence Erlbaum Associates.

Pebley, A., Hurtado, E., and Goldman, N. (1999). Beliefs about children's illness. *Journal of Biosocial Science, 31,* 195–219.

Peet, S. H. (1995). Parental perceptions of the use of internal sources of information about children's development. *Early Education and Development, 6,* 145–154.

Pepper, S. C. (1970). *World hypotheses: A study in evidence.* Berkeley: University of California Press. (Original work published 1942.)

Perozynski, L., and Kramer, L. (1999). Parental beliefs about managing sibling conflict. *Developmental Psychology*, *35*, 489–499.

Robertson, R., and Combs A. (Eds.). (1996). *Chaos theory in psychology and the life sciences*. Mahwah, NJ: Lawrence Erlbaum Associates.

Roer-Strier, D., and Rosenthal, M. K. (1997, April). *Culture as context for child-rearing beliefs*. Paper presented at the biennial meeting of the Society for Research in Child Development, Albuquerque, NM.

Rokeach, M. (1980). Some unresolved issues in theories of beliefs, attitudes, and values. In H. E. Howe, Jr., and M. M. Page (Eds.), *Nebraska Symposium on Motivation, 1979* (pp. 261–304). Lincoln: University of Nebraska Press.

Rubin, K. H. (1998). Social and emotional development from a cultural perspective. *Developmental Psychology*, *34*, 611–615.

Rubin, K. H., and Mills, R. S. L. (1992). Parents' thoughts about children's socially adaptive and maladaptive behaviors: Stability, change, and individual differences. In I. E. Sigel, A. V. McGillicuddy-De Lisi, and J. J. Goodnow (Eds.), *Parental belief systems: The psychological consequences for children* (2nd ed., pp. 41–69). Hillsdale, NJ: Lawrence Erlbaum Associates.

Rubin, K. H., Mills, R. S. L., and Rose-Krasnor, L. (1989). Maternal beliefs and children's social competence. In B. Schneider, G. Attili, J. Nadel-Brulfert, and R. Weissberg (Eds.), *Social competence in developmental perspective* (pp. 313–331). Holland: Kluwer.

Savage, S. L., and Gauvain, M. (1998). Parental beliefs and children's everyday planning in European-American and Latino families. *Journal of Applied Developmental Psychology*, *19*, 319–340.

Schneider, B. H., Attili, G., Vermigli, P., and Younger, A. (1997). A comparison of middle-class English-Canadian and Italian mothers, beliefs about children's peer-directed aggression and social withdrawal. *International Journal of Behavioral Development*, *21*, 133–154.

Shonkoff, J. P. (2000). Science, policy, and practice: Three cultures in search of a shared mission. *Child Development*, *71*, 181–187.

Sigel, I. E. (1985). (Ed.). *Parental belief systems: The psychological consequences for children*. Hillsdale, NJ: Lawrence Erlbaum Associates.

Sigel, I. E. (1986). Reflections on the belief-behavior connection: Lessons learned from a research program on parental belief systems and teaching strategies. In R. D. Ashmore and D. M. Brodzinsky (Eds.), *Thinking about the family: Views of parents and children* (pp. 35–65). Hillsdale, NJ: Lawrence Erlbaum Associates.

Sigel, I. E., and Kim, M.-I. (1996). The answer depends on the question: A conceptual and methodological analysis of a parent belief–behavior interview regarding children's learning. In S. Harkness and C. M. Super (Eds.), *Parents' cultural belief systems: Their origins, expressions, and consequences* (pp. 83–120). New York: Guilford.

Sigel, I. E., McGillicuddy-De Lisi, A. V., and Goodnow, J. (Eds.). (1992). *Parental belief systems: The psychological consequences for children* (2nd ed.). Hillsdale, NJ: Lawrence Erlbaum Associates.

Sonnenschein, S., Baker, L., Serpell, R., Scher, D., Truitt, V. G., and Munsterman, K. (1997). Parental beliefs about ways to help children learn to read: The impact of an entertainment or a skills perspective. *Early Child Development and Care*, *127–128*, 111–118.

Stevenson, H. W., Lee, S., Chen, C., Stigler, J. W., Hsu, C., and Kitamura, S. (1990). *Monographs of the Society for Research in Child Development*, *55* (Serial No. 221).

Thelen, E., and Smith, L. B. (1994). *A dynamic systems approach to the development of cognition and action*. Cambridge, MA: MIT Press.

Thomas, D. L. (Ed.). (1988). *The religion and family connection: Social science perspectives*. Salt Lake City, UT: Brookcraft.

Valsiner, J. (1997). Co-construction of human development: Heterogeneity within parental belief orientations. In J. J. Grusec and L. Kuczynski (Eds.), *Parenting and children's internalization of values* (pp. 263–304). New York: Wiley.

Von Bertalanffy, L. (1968). *General systems theory*. New York: Braziller.

Wachs, T. D. (2000). *Necessary but not sufficient: The respective roles of single and multiple influences of individual development*. Washington, DC: American Psychological Association.

Wentzel, K. R. (1998). Parents' aspirations for children's educational attainments: Relations to parental beliefs and social address variables. *Merrill-Palmer Quarterly*, *44*, 20–37.

Zeitlin, M. (1996). My child is my crown: Yoruba parental theories and practices in early childhood. In S. Harkness and C. Super (Eds.), *Parents' cultural belief systems: Their origins, expressions, and consequences* (pp. 407–427). New York: Guilford.

18

Parental Attributions

Daphne Blunt Bugental
Keith Happaney
University of California, Santa Barbara

INTRODUCTION

Causal reasoning is a central component in the social life of humans. Our interactions with children (as with all our social interactions) are continuously influenced by our attributions concerning the reasons why they do things, the reasons why we ourselves do things, and the reasons why shared interactive events work out as they do. We speculate about the possible causes of events that have occurred in the past, ongoing events at the present time, and possible future events. In doing so, we facilitate our ability to understand, predict, and effectively function within relationships—including parent–child relationships.

Although many aspects of parenting relationships among humans are widely shared with non humans, attributional processes within social relationships are more distinctively human. Indeed, it may be that causal inference processes are only shared with our closest primate relatives (Boysen and Himes, 1999). Consideration of these higher level processes came to the fore late in the 1970s. Researchers had recently moved away from an exclusive focus on parent effects to include consideration of the role of child effects on parental practices (Bell, 1968). Within this new direction, it was soon recognized that child effects are qualified by the interpretation parents give to their children's actions (e.g., Bell, 1979; Sameroff, 1975).

Parents have the capacity to respond to identical social stimuli in different ways based on the causal inferences they draw. A crying infant, believed to be tired, may elicit parental sympathy and comforting efforts. The same infant behavior, if the child's needs have apparently been met, may elicit parental irritation or even anger. To some extent, parents rely on shared heuristics in drawing causal inferences about caregiving events; for example, explicit child disobedience accompanied by nonverbal cues suggesting defiance may be commonly seen as intentional in nature. At the same time, parents also show variability in the kinds of causal inferences they draw. In this chapter, we will consider the nature and reasons for variations in parental attributions across time, setting, and person.

We begin the chapter by considering the history of causal concepts in parenting relationships. This history extends past the specific field of parent–child relationships and borrows from the adult literature on attributional processes in general. We then move on to consider some questions about parental attributions that have received continuing or emergent empirical attention in this literature. Such questions include: Where do parental attributions come from? How do parental attributions affect adult responses during the course of their interactions with the young? How do parental attributions affect children's long-term social–emotional well-being? How do parental attributions foster or limit children's academic motivation and achievement? Finally, we consider some emerging questions and suggest possible directions for new research.

HISTORICAL PERSPECTIVES ON PARENTAL ATTRIBUTIONS

In reviewing the history of the study of parental attributions, we consider some of the key issues that have emerged. As a starting point, we consider the various ways in which "attributions" have been conceptualized and defined. We also consider differences in the types of research questions that have been stimulated by different theoretical perspectives. Finally, we give consideration to the increased attention that has been given to context or setting in the study of parental attributions.

What Is the Nature of Parental Attributions?

Although common usage is made of the term *parental attributions*, the construct of *attribution* itself has been used in rather different ways within different theoretical frameworks. From the standpoint of early attribution theory (as it evolved within the field of social cognition), attributions represent causal inferences made in response to the covariation of ongoing events. When theorists (e.g., Bandura, 1977) with a background in learning theory turned their attention to causal constructs, they focused on variations in causal thought as a function of the individual's experience; from this theoretical point of view, causal cognitions are learned. Causal inferences have also been conceptualized as knowledge structures or schemas; consistent with a social-information-processing approach, people may be thought of as building cognitive maps that serve to guide their relationships with others (Baldwin, 1992).

Attributions as on-line inference processes.   Initial discussion of attribution processes focused on generalities in causal inference. It asked why people, as a whole, analyze particular kinds of events as they do. Concern with naive causal cognitions has its origins in the early work of Heider (1944), as developed more completely by Kelley (1967). Kelley developed a theory that explored the ways in which social behavior is explained differently based on variations across time, situation, and person. The individual's understanding of social events follows from their use of covariation information. Thus, if Mary is typically disobedient with her mother (but not her father), and if other children in the family obey both parents, then it might be concluded that something is amiss in the dyadic relationship between Mary and her mother. Conversely, if Mary is disobedient with both parents (across context) but her siblings are obedient with both parents, it might be concluded that this behavior reflects "something about Mary."

Concern with attributional universals has been explored further in the work of Weiner (e.g., 1985, 1986). Weiner based his analyses on the use of three dimensions of causality: locus, stability, and controllability. In particular, he was concerned with the patterns of causal inference that contribute to perceptions of individual responsibility. Inferences regarding responsibility strongly influence the emotional reactions and behavioral responses shown to others—in particular for their misdeeds or mishaps (Weiner, 1993). So, for example, if a mother observes her capable 8-year-old son running into the street without looking, she might respond with anger and a disciplinary action. Suppose, on the other hand, a mother asked an older child to watch over an infant for a few minutes. If she then happened to look out the window and saw the infant crawl into the street, she might experience great fear and run after him but she would not punish him; instead, she might sternly rebuke the sibling she had placed in charge. In the first case, the mother's ire at a child is influenced by the fact that she saw him as responsible for his act (old enough to know better). In the second case, the mother's response followed from her belief that the infant was not yet capable of understanding the danger (and thus was not responsible).

Adults regularly make assumptions (sometimes unjustified) regarding the controllability of children's behavior—and thus the affective and behavioral responses they manifest. Although many instances of such reasoning seem quite obvious, the same reasoning processes in other settings seems more surprising. A classic example involves children who are overweight. Weight has traditionally been thought to be controllable; thus, the child who is overweight is easily seen as blameworthy (Weiner, Perry, and Magnusson, 1988). Although Weiner gave little initial attention to the role of attributions in parenting issues, his concepts were applied by others to these concerns. For example, Dix, Grusec, and their colleagues (e.g., Dix and Grusec, 1985; Dix, Ruble, Grusec, and Nixon, 1986) applied constructs from both Weiner and Kelley in their demonstration that parental attributions for children's behavior varied systematically as a function of children's age. In addition, Himelstein, Graham and Weiner (1991) demonstrated that parents reveal a different attributional pattern with secondborn than firstborn children as they acquire increased access to covariation information. Ultimately, the inferences that parents draw about their children's actions (how much the child can control their actions, how much they intended their actions) influence parents' affective responses and their socialization strategies (Grusec, Rudy, and Martini, 1997).

In general, on-line attributions have been conceptualized as involving "explicit" cognitions (Greenwald and Banaji, 1995). Within this framework, explicit attributional reasoning occurs as an effortful, conscious response to ongoing events. At the same time, Lazarus (1991) has proposed that certain kinds of explicit analytical processes (primary appraisal) may short-circuit awareness and thus may be conceptualized as essentially occurring "automatically." From this framework, potentially stressful events are initially appraised for their evaluative implications and their controllability. This theoretical framework has primarily been applied to non-normative parenting situations, for example, coping with the caregiving stresses associated with children's problematic behavior (as reviewed by Bugental and Johnston, 2000) or with children's special needs (e.g., Eiser and Haverman, 1992; Hodapp, in Vol. 1 of this *Handbook*). However, the same model is also applicable to the more common stresses that characterize normative caregiving experiences (e.g., Crnic and Low, in Vol. 5 of this *Handbook*; Levy-Shiff, Dimitrowsky, Shulman, and Har-Even, 1998).

Attributions as learned beliefs. Social cognitive learning theory directed attention to causal inference from a different perspective. That is, causal cognitions are thought to be acquired as a function of one's own personal experiences (and reinforcement history) and observations of the experiences of others. For example, children may learn that certain kinds of disobedience are followed by parental anger or punitive action. They may also acquire causal knowledge from the spoken attributions of others. For example, they may repeatedly hear certain kinds of causal statements from their parents. Learning theorists have introduced different kinds of constructs in the ways in which they have conceptualized such social knowledge. Here we think of Rotter, Bandura, and Seligman as individuals who have extended the basic premises of social learning theory in different ways.

Rotter (1966) directed attention to the stable ways in which we come to understand and manage life experiences as a function of our causal knowledge of the world. His view was a simple one, in that it focused on individual differences in placing causality (for all kinds of events) inside the person (I: internal locus) or outside the person (E: external locus). Although the construct proved useful (and inspired thousands of studies), it was also overly general (e.g., as noted by Seligman, 1992). It combines good and bad events, and it makes no distinctions between domains (e.g., social or academic outcomes).

Subsequently, other researchers solved one part of the problem by greater domain specificity. For example, a number of efforts were made to measure locus of control specifically for parenting events (e.g., Nowicki and Segal's measure of locus of control orientation, 1974). In addition, efforts were made to subdivide the unidimensional I–E construct into component factors (e.g., Levenson, 1973). However, limitations continued as a result of the combining of positive and negative outcomes.

Bandura (1989) developed an individual difference construct that reflected the kinds of learning experiences that lead one to think of oneself as high or low in self-efficacy. Self-efficacy is a composite construct that includes the belief that one has the requisite skills to execute particular response patterns that are necessary to the accomplishment of some desired goal. Although Bandura has not been centrally concerned with parents' self-efficacy, others have applied these notions to the parenting domain (e.g., Coleman and Karraker, 1997; Mash and Johnston, 1990; Teti and Gelfand, 1991). From Bandura's framework, it would be predicted that parents acquire a sense of high or low self-efficacy as a function of their experiences with their own children. The evidence for this prediction tends to provide a mixed picture. That is, parents are likely to show lower levels of perceived efficacy if they have had a history with "difficult" children; at the same time, low levels of parental self-efficacy may precede abusive parent–child interaction (Mash and Johnston, 1990). This mixed picture has often led parenting researchers to give joint consideration to the utility of self-efficacy constructs (with origins in adults' direct history as parents) and attributional constructs (with origins in adults' own childhood history; e.g., Grusec, Hastings, and Mammone, 1994).

Seligman and his colleagues have approached the issue of attributions from an integrative theoretical framework. They introduced the construct of attributional (or explanatory) style as a cognitive reformulation of the learned helplessness literature (Abramson, Seligman, and Teasdale, 1978). These investigators suggested that causal attributions serve as qualifiers of differential reactions to negative life events. That is, individuals respond very differently to the same events based on the ways in which they construe those events. Depression, ill health, and low achievement have all been found to be possible outcomes of negative life events, but primarily for those who invoke a pessimistic explanatory style (i.e., who see those events as due to internal, stable, and global causes; Burns and Seligman, 1989). Seligman and his colleagues focus attention on the benefits that follow from an optimistic explanatory style. Seligman has applied his attributional model to children (and the ways in which they may be innoculated against negative experiences by challenging a pessimistic explanatory style; e.g., Seligman, Reivich, Jaycox, and Gillham, 1995). Although he has not been directly concerned with the application of his measures or constructs to parenting outcomes, others have developed scales that do so (e.g., Donovan, Leavitt, and Walsh, 1997; Stratton and Swaffer, 1988).

Attributions as knowledge structures. Causal cognitions have also been approached as organized knowledge structures that serve as cognitive representations of past experience. Early in life, the child comes to organize the world into meaningful categories, scripts, and schemas (Nelson, 1993). Knowledge is acquired on the basis of the information to which they are exposed. From this standpoint, the parent brings to the relationship ready-made notions of the nature of children and the nature of parent–child relationships. Thus, parents may "know" that parent–child conflict is caused by willful child disobedience as a result of knowledge parents themselves acquired at a much earlier age. When conceptualized in this way, parental attributions represent memory-based cognitions—knowledge structures that provide a way of understanding and predicting caregiving events.

Internal working models of parent–child relationships (Bowlby, 1980; Bretherton, 1990) represent one type of knowledge structure. Notions of working models that have emerged with the attachment literature (Cummings and Cummings, in Vol. 5 of this *Handbook*) have a high conceptual overlap with notions of relationship schemas that have emerged within the social–psychological literature concerned with adult relationships (Baldwin, 1992). Among childhood attachment researchers, the individual is seen as developing an internal working model of parent–child relationships as a function of early experiences with primary caregivers. This model serves to organize the child's expectancies regarding relationship outcomes and the means by which such outcomes may be optimized. As pointed out by Goldberg, Grusec, and Jenkins (1999), such expectancies focus on reliability in obtaining comfort in response to distress. So, for example, one child may learn that her bids for comfort often bring maternal rejection (a causal sequence) and accommodates by reducing demands on her mother (avoidant attachment; Cassidy, 1994). Another child may learn that bids for comfort elicit positive maternal responses; this forms the basis for the child's acquisition of a secure working model of relationships. These models then carry forward to influence the kinds of attachment relationships individuals have with their own children (van IJzendoorn, 1995).

A number of researchers (e.g., Bugental, 1992; Grusec et al., 1997) have proposed that parental attributions can be conceptualized as stable knowledge structures that may be understood as schemas. When attributions are conceptualized in this way, use is often made of dimensions drawn from other frameworks, for example, Weiner's causal taxonomy (locus, stability, and controllability) in describing variations in parents' attributions. In their respective programs of research, Bugental, Dix, and Grusec were among the first to make use of Weiner's taxonomy in describing the role of causal thinking in parenting practices. Dix and Grusec (1985) developed and tested an attributional model of parental cognitions; within this model, they suggested that parents' affective reactions to children's behavior vary based on their belief that such behaviors are intentional, controllable, or dispositional, as opposed to being determined by developmental limitations or situational constraints. Bugental and Shennum (1984) focused on the extent to which parents' affective and behavioral responses to children's behavior differed, based on their perception that parents' own actions and those of their children were controllable.

Memory-based knowledge structures have typically been conceptualized as involving implicit processes. That is, they are activated automatically, do not involve effort, and operate outside of awareness (although the nature of such processes may become aware). Borrowing from Kelly's ideas of personal constructs, Bargh, Lombardi, and Higgins (1988) proposed that humans acquire schematic representations of the self and others, and that these representations—with repeated experience—become chronically accessible. As pointed out by Bargh and Chartrand (1999), contemporary psychology has a tendency to overestimate the extent to which people are fully aware of the rapidly changing kaleidoscope of their social lives. Much of our social-information-processing goes on nonconsciously and automatically. This is certainly true when individuals have competing demands on their attention, as is the case for much of busy family life (Papoušek and Papoušek, in Vol. 2 of this *Handbook*). Parents interact with children while watching TV, working on the computer, cooking a meal, driving a car, and so forth. Bugental, Lyon, Cortez, and Krantz (1997) assessed the ease with which parents accessed their cognitions about caregiving events when they were cognitively "busy." Parents were asked to make very fast judgments about their relationships with children under conditions that mimic the demands of real life (i.e., judgments were made when they were simultaneously engaged in a second task). When parents had a low-power schema in their relationships with their children (i.e., they saw their children as having more power than they did), they made judgments about power (e.g., "Who is bossier, you or your children?") very quickly. In other words, the thoughts of themselves as lacking power came to mind automatically and without effort. In contrast, other parents found this to be a less intuitive task (they were less likely to think of their relationship with their children in this way) and were considerably slowed when they had to make this kind of judgment while occupied with a second task.

When Do Parents Ask "Why" Questions?

In understanding the role of parental attributions in family life, it is important to consider when it is that such constructs are activated. Are parents just as likely to engage in causal reasoning under all circumstances, or are they selective in their demonstration of causal search processes? Are they more likely to search for the reasons for positive events? Negative events? Ambiguous events?

Causal analyses of negative events.   In general, human beings, are likely to engage in a search for causality in response to events that require some type of response, for example, events that are undesired or potentially threatening. As suggested by Pratto and John (1991), it is highly adaptive for organisms to direct attention automatically to undesired events that may pose a threat to the perceiver's well-being. In general, desired events are less likely to require explanation, as they do not suggest the need for some kind of change or remediation.

Causal analyses of ambiguous or novel events.   There is considerable evidence that causal appraisal regularly occurs in response to events that are ambiguous, novel, or unexpected (Hastie, 1984; Wong and Weiner, 1981). Because the individual's causal appraisal relies heavily on a memory search when the stimulus events themselves provide few cues as to their explanation, there is a high likelihood of individual differences in the causal appraisal of uncertain events. That is, the outcome of causal analyses in the face of an ambiguous or impoverished stimulus necessarily relies on causal hypotheses retrieved from the individual's own history. For example, parents who see themselves as "victims" within caregiving relationships might easily interpret a child's inattentiveness (an ambiguous behavior) as a challenge to their fragile sense of control; in contrast, parents with a stronger sense of control in the caregiving relationship might interpret the same event in a more benign fashion (e.g., the child is tired, sleepy, or preoccupied with something else).

There is emergent evidence both from Dodge and his colleagues (e.g., Nix, Pinderhughes, Dodge, Bates, and Pettit, 1999) and Bugental and her colleagues (e.g., Bugental, Lewis, Lin, Lyon, and Kopeikin, 2000) in support of the role of ambiguous events as elicitors of parental attributions. In a longitudinal study, Nix et al. (1999) assessed the relationship between parental attributions regarding their own children's ambiguous problem behaviors (depicted as hypothetical events in written vignettes) and their children's future aggression. Parents' hostile attributional style predicted children's later externalizing behavior. Bugental and her colleagues (2000) found that adults with a "low-power" attributional style (i.e., who believed that they had less power within caregiving relationships than did their children) responded distinctively only when children's response patterns were ambiguous. That is, the responses shown by "high-power" versus "low-power" adults were distinguishable only when a child "trainee" showed a problematic performance that was ambiguous (i.e., it was unclear whether a child's performance reflected lack of ability or deliberate resistance to the adult's training efforts). Adults with low perceived power only showed defensive response patterns (e.g., elevations in heart rate, affective inconsistencies, narrowing of attention, and increases in the use of force) when responding to a child whose behavior was undesired but motivationally ambiguous.

How Do Attributions Influence Parent–Child Interactions?

Interest in the role of attributions within parenting relationships emerged in the 1970s. Very early concerns with parents' causal thought approached the construct as a stable stylistic variable—very much like a diffuse personality trait. For example, early concerns with parents' locus of control explored linear relations between parents' generalized beliefs (internal vs. external locus of control) and the nature of their interactions with children (e.g., Nowicki and Segal, 1974). When developmentalists came to think of parenting processes as context sensitive, parental attributions were increasingly seen as operating in a contingent fashion (consistent with Mischel and Shoda's, 1995, "if: then" notion of context-dependent personality constructs). From this perspective, parental attributional processes are activated in response to relevant events in the caregiving environment and serve to moderate and/or mediate their reactions to those events. ("Moderators" represent third variables that "partition a focal independent variable into subgroups that establish its domains of maximal effectiveness in regard to a dependent variable." "Mediators" represent third variables that provide "the generative mechanism through which the focal independent variable is able to influence the dependent variables of interest," Baron and Kenny, 1986, p. 1173). Thus, the effects of children on their developmental outcomes are altered by the qualifying ("moderating") or intervening ("mediating") role of parental cognitions (e.g., Bell, 1979; Sameroff, 1975). In addition, parental attributions came to be understood as shaping and being shaped by their own individual history—a transactional process.

Along with awareness of these more complex dyadic effects came awareness of the interdependence of response systems within the individual. For example, questions arose about the relation between parents' attributions and their emotions. Are the effects of parental attributions mediated by their subsequent emotional reactions? Conversely, are the effects of parents' emotional states mediated by their subsequent attributional appraisals? For example, does a parent's negative affective state precede the judgment that a child has engaged in an intentional negative act, or does affect follow from the causal appraisal?

Implicit attributions. What sequential pattern one might expect depends on differences in type of attribution (i.e., implicit attributions that involve automatic retrieval of causal knowledge structures versus explicit attributions that involve slower "on-line" appraisal of ongoing events). If individuals are confronted with an ambiguous situation that requires a fast response, it is likely that they will directly retrieve a memory-dependent attribution relevant to this setting—an implicit attribution. Such attributional constructs are typically thought of as including both cognitive and affective components (sometimes referred to as affectively tagged schemas; Fiske and Pavelchak, 1986). Suppose, for example, that a parent has a negative attributional bias (either a low-power or "hostile" attributional bias) about the causes of a child's problem behavior. If a child engages in some undesired action, the "biased" parent will make the immediate ("automatic") interpretation that the child has misbehaved intentionally. This interpretation is likely to be directly associated with (or "tagged") with negative affect. Activation of an implicit attributional schema may also serve to automatically trigger motivational patterns (e.g., the activation of a "hostile" or low-power attributional schema will trigger the motive to exert high levels of power assertion). In short, the activation of negatively biased parental attributional schemas leads to schema-consistent patterns of parental thought, affect, and motivation.

Alternatively, of course, it may be that a parent's mood state (rather than a caregiving event) provides the starting point in an attributional sequence. So, for example, a negative mood state may serve to prime thoughts of the self as powerless (and foster continued or escalating levels of negative affect). Consistent with this notion, Reznick (1999) observed that maternal depression predicted judgments of negative infant intentionality.

Thus, an emotionally tagged caregiving schema may be primed either by caregiving events, mood, or causal ideation. However, in all cases, schema-relevant ideation and affect may be thought of as operating in concert. This conceptualization can account for the effects of parental mood on parental attributions (e.g., Dix, Reinhold, and Zambarano, 1990) or the effects of attributional priming on parental affect (e.g., Bugental et al., 1993).

Explicit attributions. If, on the other hand, we are thinking about parents' slower, on-line appraisal processes, a different sequence may ensue. From the standpoint of cognitive appraisal theory (e.g., Lazarus, 1991), the activation of emotions follows from at least some minimal evaluation of the significance of ongoing events. Empirical research, in turn, has shown that differential activation of explicit attributions leads to expected variations in subsequent affect (Neumann, 2000). For example, if a father becomes aware that his daughter regularly complies with her mother's requests but disregards his requests, this may precipitate resentment or some other negative affect. In such a case, the parent is processing covariation information in normative ways and responds affectively to the outcome of that appraisal.

Are Attributions Domain General or Are They Context and Domain Specific?

Questions have emerged with respect to the generality of parenting processes (including parental attributions) across domains or contexts. Does a parent draw the same causal inferences in all social settings? Is there anything special about attributions for parenting outcomes? Do parents engage in similar kinds of attributional processes even within different kinds of caregiving contexts? If, for example, a child challenges parents during a game, do parents draw the same kind of attributions as they would during a disciplinary encounter?

Early attention to parental attributions was quite general in terms of domains. Parents were asked about their generalized beliefs regarding the causes of life events—not the causes of caregiving events. As pointed out earlier, the assumption that we make the same kinds of attributions about all kinds of life experiences was increasingly questioned.

As the field advanced, greater recognition was given to the role of context in parenting (e.g., Bugental and Goodnow, 1998; Dix, 1992; Grusec and Goodnow, 1994). Contextual effects are relevant to parents' attributions as well as to their actions. For example, Dix (1992) proposed that parents operate in different ways based on the nature of their current goals. At some times, their responses to children will be based on their empathic concerns for the children's immediate welfare. At other times, their responses will be based on their socialization goals (i.e., the extent to which they are attempting to influence their children in ways that will facilitate their competence as adults). At still other times, parents' responses may involve their own personal goals, which at points will come into conflict with the goals of their young. Hastings and Grusec (1998) parsed parental goals in similar ways. They distinguished between parent-centered goals (organized around power assertion), relationship-centered goals (organized around warmth, negotiation, and cooperation), and child-centered goals (organized around reasoning processes).

Parents may vary in their attributions on the basis of other contingencies. For example, parents' attributions for children's misdeeds vary as a function of the seriousness of those misdeeds (Hastings and Coplan, 1999). Attributions may also differ as a function of qualifying events. So, for example, parents of (medicated) children with attention deficit hyperactivity disorder (ADHD) are less likely than other parents to see themselves as causal contributors to their children's behavior (Johnston et al., 1998).

The possibility that parents (and their young) activate different kinds of causal reasoning in different contexts is suggested by the work of Smetana (1995), Turiel (1983, 1998), and their colleagues concerning the different domains of social knowledge. Extending an early focus on children's understanding of these domains, Smetana (1997) suggested that such domain distinctions apply to parents' beliefs, goals, and practices. Thus, changes in parent–child interaction across the course of development involve declines in parental investment in certain domains (e.g., reduced control of the prudential or personal decisions of the young as they move into the adolescent years). It may be speculated that parental reasoning concerning the causes of parent–child conflict will also differ across these years (e.g., Hastings and Grusec, 1998).

Bugental (2000) proposed that social life can be conceptualized as reflecting five domains that are organized in distinctive ways and make use of different algorithms. Domains are defined as "bodies of knowledge that act as guides to partitioning the world and that facilitate the solving of recurring problems faced by organisms within that world" (p. 187). An algorithm is defined as "any effective procedure for solving a problem or accomplishing an end" (p. 187). The four domains that are potentially relevant to the relationship between parents and children (the fifth domain involves romantic relationships) are organized around:

(1) Proximity maintenance during late infancy with specific others in the service of safety (the attachment domain),
(2) Use and recognition of social dominance (the hierarchical power domain),
(3) Identification and defense of the lines that divide "us" and "them" in group coalitions (the coalitional group domain),
(4) Management of the reciprocal obligations and benefits that are involved in communal life (the reciprocity domain). (Bugental, 2000, p. 187)

Because of the shared nature of the goals or tasks implicit within each of these domains, the young show a high level of similarity in their acquisition of the algorithms that organize these different domains. At the same time, the architecture of the human brain allows a substantial level of flexibility in the ways in which these goals are implemented (as a result of our ability to simulate and consider alternative solutions to problems). For example, the cognitive organization of domains is adapted to reflect the individual's personal history or shared cultural history. Biological influences on these primary social domains also allow for a variety of ways of solving recurrent problems. So, for example, the proximity goals of attachment relationships can be "solved" by maintenance of contact via sight, sound, or touch. At the same time, the potential "tailoring" of domains to personal history, culture, or immediate context is not infinite. For example, Bugental suggested that dysfunctional parenting is most likely to occur when regulatory processes are mismatched to domains. Thus, if a parent responds to an infant's distress to separation (consistent with the algorithms of the attachment domain) with assertion in an effort to control the child, a domain mismatch occurs. One thinks here of the differential effectiveness of parents' positive responses to the "honest" cries of young infants (an effective means of reducing later crying) versus the ineffectiveness of parents' positive response to the strategic tantruming of a toddler (an ineffective means of reducing the child's later manifestations of such behavior; Hubbard and van IJzendoorn, 1991). As noted elsewhere, such domain mismatches are likely to have their origins in early experience; thus, the child who fails to establish a secure attachment bond is more likely to show an exaggerated investment in the power domain at later ages (e.g., Grusec and Mammone, 1995).

Summary

Concern with the topic of parental attributions owes much of its early history to other fields—social cognition theories, social-information-processing theory, and social-learning theory. Related concepts also evolved within attachment theory and the close relations literature. It was suggested that some of the apparent discrepancies in attributional processes may reflect differences in types of attributions measured. In addition, it was pointed out that attributional processes may vary across context or domain, and change as parental goals change. In short, parental cognitions are increasingly understood within a framework that includes consideration of parental motives.

CURRENT RESEARCH QUESTIONS IN PARENTAL ATTRIBUTIONS

At the present time, there are a number of research questions that have been subject to continuing interest or that are currently emerging as topics of interest. One topic concerns the origins of parental attributions. To what extent do they originate within adults' history as parents? To what extent do they originate in the adult's own past experiences in childhood? To what extent are they acquired as learned beliefs, either in the home environment or as shared cultural knowledge?

As a central topical concern, there is substantial literature that explores the effects of parental attributions on parents' own interpersonal response patterns (e.g., parenting tactics and socioemotional reactions) and children's subsequent response patterns (e.g., behavioral responses and emotional responses). In addition, there is continuing concern with the relationship between parental attributions and children's achievement motivation and performance in academic settings. Across topics, there is an increasing body of work that asks about differences in parental attributions reflecting culture and gender.

Where Do Parental Attributions Come From?

Although it is easily seen that parental attributions are drawn from information within the individual's history, questions can be raised concerning the relevant body of knowledge (about parent–child relationships). As one possibility, it may be that parental attributions are formed primarily on the basis of their direct proximal experiences with children in a caregiving relationship. The majority of research that has been concerned with the origins of parental attributions has followed this approach. Alternatively, it may be that parental attributions are primarily influenced by adults' distal history, for example, their early history with their own parents, or through cultural explanations about the nature of children and the nature of parenting.

Proximal influences. Early concern with parental cognitions focused on beliefs about the nature of children. Increasingly, attention turned to parents' beliefs concerning the reasons for children's behaviors. Why does my child misbehave? Why is my child having problems in school? Investigators have drawn conclusions regarding parental attributions for desired versus undesired child behavior, for the behaviors of girls versus boys, and for changes in child behavior across the course of development.

In 1995, Miller reviewed the literature on parents' attributions regarding their children's behavior. As has been noted in other reviews (e.g., Joiner and Wagner, 1996), most researchers have studied parents' causal appraisals of children's undesired behaviors. As anticipated, parents show different attributional patterns for children's positive versus negative social behaviors—biases that may be interpreted as child serving. That is, positive social behaviors are typically seen as due to something about the child (e.g., their personality), whereas negative behaviors of the same children are more typically seen as due to something about the situation. Subsequent research has supported the general findings reported in Miller's review. Positive (child-serving) parental biases have even been found to obtain even among parents of children who show behavior problems (e.g., Johnston, Reynolds, Freeman, and Geller, 1998); however, such biases are somewhat less in response to "difficult" than to "easy" children.

In addition, parents typically show self-serving biases in the attributions offered for children who behave in a desired fashion versus those who do not. For example, Himelstein et al. (1991) found that parents of gifted children were more likely to make attributions to caregiving practices than were the parents of children in special education classes. Similarly, Johnston and Freeman (1997) found that parents of ADHD children were more likely than other parents to attribute their children's misbehaviors to internal and stable, but uncontrollable, causes. Their attributions for their children's undesired behavior was consistent with a disease model. As a result, these parents were less likely to assume responsibility for their children's misbehaviors than were the parents of other children (a self-serving bias).

A similar attributional pattern has been found for the parents of special needs children (Hodapp, in Vol. 1 of this *Handbook*; Mickelson, Wroble, and Helgeson, 1999). Parents of children with Down's syndrome, autism, or developmental delays typically attribute their children's needs to situational factors that are outside their control (e.g., heredity, stress during pregnancy, fate, and God's will). Similarly, Bornstein, Haynes, and Painter (2000) found that mothers of deaf children were less likely than mothers of hearing children to engage in self-blame (internal attributions) for failure on parenting tasks. The utility of this attributional pattern (avoiding blame for negative parenting experiences with special needs children) is suggested by the fact that attributions to fate or God's will predict better child adjustment, whereas attributions to self or environment predict worse adjustment (Mickelson et al., 1999).

Considerable attention has been given to parents' shifting attributions as a function of child age. This line of thought was introduced by Dix et al. (1986) in their analysis of the changing ways in which parents interpret children's actions at different ages; with increased age, parents are more likely to believe that children's actions are intentional and controllable—and thus they are more responsible for their misbehaviors. Supporting this general notion, Reznick (1999) found that mothers attributed increasing intentionality to their infants with age. Although some researchers have failed to find such age changes in parental attributions, it is likely (as suggested by Miller, 1995) that discrepancies reflect differences in types of child behavior studied—with developmental changes in parental attributions more likely for child behaviors that are more controllable.

In addition, parents' attributions for children's behavior vary as a function of child gender (Cote and Azar, 1997; Hastings and Coplan, 1999). Gender-related attributions are a good example of causal analyses that reflect complex influences of direct experience and one's personal or cultural history. For example, the misbehavior of boys is more likely than the misbehavior of girls to be attributed to dispositional causes (Hastings and Coplan, 1999). As suggested by Hastings and Coplan, it is unclear whether these gender differences precede or follow experiences with children. That is, boys have repeatedly been found to be more aggressive and disobedient than girls (Maccoby and Jacklin, 1974); at the same time, there are cultural differences in gender expectations (Hofstede, 1998). Very reasonably, a transactional system is operating in which parental responses are influenced both by cultural beliefs and child behavior, and in turn come to influence child behavior.

Distal influences: Parents' own history as children. Despite evidence that parents' attributions are influenced by their experiences with their own children, there is also a great deal of evidence to suggest that they come to the parenting relationship with a well-established set of relevant beliefs. For example, Reznick (1999) found that (despite many uniformities in the ways in which mothers draw causal inferences about their own infants) there is a high overlap between maternal attributions for their own infants and their attributions for infants in general. Supporting the notion that attributions precede direct experience with children, the attributions of nonparental adults or prospective parents predict their responses to children just as well (if not better) than do the attributions of parental adults (Bugental, 1999; Lewis, Bugental, and Fleck, 1991).

Increasingly, researchers in this field have looked to parents' own childhood history as a major (and possible primary) source of influence on their attributions. The only secure way of determining the effects of early history on an adult's attributions as a parent would involve longitudinal research. At this point, this type of information is limited. As a result, it is necessary to rely primarily on suggestive evidence regarding plausible longitudinal relationships.

Grusec et al. (1994) suggested that parents' attributions about their own children are heavily dependent on their own history with their own parents. In testing this notion, Grusec and Mammone (1995) explored the relation between attachment history and parental attributions through the use of the Adult Attachment Interview (AAI: George, Kaplan, and Main, 1996). Although the AAI should not be interpreted as an inside track to actual attachment history, it does provide a defensible measure of the individual's updated working model of attachment relationships. For example, attachment patterns revealed by mothers on the AAI provide an excellent predictor of their own children's attachment pattern as measured by the Strange Situation (van IJzendoorn, 1995). It is interesting to learn that women who showed a dismissive pattern of attachment on the AAI showed a pattern of low perceived power on the Parent Attribution Test; that is, they attributed high power to children and low power to self. In addition, mothers who scored as "preoccupied" on the AAI revealed an exaggerated sense of their own power on the Parent Attribution Test (very high attributed power to self, low attributed power to the child). It may be that early problems in establishing a secure attachment relationship foster reliance on power-based interactions.

From a different theoretical perspective, Haines, Metalsky, Cardamone, and Joiner (1999) have explored the childhood origins of a pessimistic attributional style. They concluded that either an insecure attachment history or a history of parental abuse serves as a predictor of a pessimistic attributional style. They suggested that young children's tendency to blame themselves for negative events—paired with very negative life experiences—combine to foster this pattern. They also suggested that the simpler, less differentiated self-image of younger children may lead children's negative self-view to have a very broad impact on many kinds of relationships, not just the parent–child relationship. Negative experiences outside the home may, in turn, serve to provide further support for the child's pessimistic attributional style.

Distal influences: Parental tuition or modeling. A number of recent efforts have been made to track the intergenerational continuity of attributional patterns. Typically, this involves determining the relation between adults' attributions, as measured by adult scales, and children's attributions, as measured by scales designed for younger ages. At this point, primary support has been shown for the relation between mothers' and children's causal attributions (Burks and Parke, 1996; Seligman et al., 1984).

In considering the transmission of power attributions, there would be reason to anticipate either complementary relations (parents with high perceived power would have children with low perceived power) or matched relations (parents with high perceived power would have children with high perceived power). Bugental and Martorell (1999) assessed the relations between parents' attributions for caregiving outcomes on the PAT and children's attributions for caregiving outcomes (tested within a picture story format and implemented with 6- to 10-year old children). They found support for a matching relation, with the strongest association being between mothers and sons. Additional support for this pattern of matched attributions between mothers and sons is provided by the findings of MacKinnon and her colleagues (1992, 1994); these investigators, within a longitudinal design, showed a linkage between mother's and sons' hostile attributional biases.

Distal influences: Cultural effects.   Over the last few decades, there has been a steady body of work exploring differences across cultures in parents' caregiving beliefs and practices (e.g., Goodnow, 1997). Parental attributions may be learned from general cultural sources—the ways in which families are depicted in the media (including implicit attributions regarding the reasons for successful and unsuccessful parenting outcomes) and common folklore passed on within families regarding the effects of different kinds of parental practices or concerning the nature of children themselves and what makes them do the things they do. From this perspective, parents' ideas are acquired, negotiated, and transmitted across generations as part of their active involvement in the rules and values of their cultural group.

Most of the systematic research on cultural differences has focused on what may be thought of as typical family relationships. Bornstein and his colleagues (1998) conducted a study in seven different countries (Argentina, Belgium, France, Israel, Italy, Japan, and the United States). Primiparous mothers of toddlers were asked (among other things) their attributions regarding the causes of success and failure on a series of parenting tasks (bathing, comforting, playing, teaching, communicating, disciplining, and dressing), using the Parent Attribution Questionnaire (PAQ; MacPhee, Seybold, as cited in Fritz; Sirignano and Lachman, 1985). Specifically, mothers were queried regarding the importance of their own ability, mood, and effort as well as the importance of task difficulty and child behavior. As anticipated, there were a number of differences across cultures. Three examples provide an idea of the range observed. Italian mothers attributed much importance to their own ability and effort as sources of influence on caregiving success; in contrast, they attributed little importance to children's behavior. This finding only partially supports the prevalent notion that Italian mothers believe that child development unfolds naturally and is little influenced by parental intervention. The authors concluded that Italian mothers may be attributing the emotional well-being of their children to themselves—consistent with the strong emphasis on protection and warmth within *la famiglia*. As expected, Japanese mothers downplayed the importance of their own ability (consistent with cultural self-presentation norms). However, they attributed high importance to children's behavior as a causal determiner of success; According to this view, a "good child" is critical to positive caregiving outcomes. Mothers in the United States attributed high importance both to themselves and to children as causal influences on success but not on failure. This reflects a basically optimistic position with regard to caregiving outcomes.

Within the United States, Reznick (1999) found that Latin American mothers were less likely than European American or African American mothers to attribute intentionality to infants. Reznick also found differences in the judged intentionality of infant actions by mothers' with different levels of education. Mothers with higher levels of education (in comparison with less educated mothers) were unwilling to judge infants' negative actions as intentional or to see them as able to carry out spiteful or mean acts.

Parents are exposed to cultural knowledge about atypical as well as typical children. Such knowledge includes implicit attributions concerning the basis of "difference." For example, children who are physically or cognitively disabled are viewed in different ways in different cultures. In some cultures, children's disabilities are accepted as just another type of individual difference; indeed, such cultures may not even have words to describe the concept of "disability" or "handicap" (e.g., as is true for many Native American cultures; Connors and Donnellan, 1993). Traditional folk beliefs have been found to be more common among Latino than Anglo families (e.g., belief in "susto," the notion that a child's frightening experience may cause a chronic illness; Mardiros, 1989).

Members of different cultures not only differ in their attributions regarding the cause of children's disabilities, they also make different attributions regarding the future implications of those disabilities. That is, they differ in the causal role they project for the child's later outcomes. In the United States, disabilities are standardly interpreted in terms of the level of risk they pose for the child's later outcomes, and attempted resolutions follow a technological approach to relevant service delivery (Kalyanpur and Harry, 1999). In other cultures, disability may be viewed as having positive or spiritual implications (e.g., Kisanji, 1995). Ultimately, variations in the ways in which families understand and explain children's physical and medical challenges strongly influence how they cope with them (Garwick, Kohrman, Titus, Wolman, and Blum, 1999).

A number of researchers have asked about the ways in which effective parenting is viewed in different cultures. That is, they have asked parents for their causal beliefs about the consequences of different parental practices and their beliefs about the practices that are most likely to produce children that fulfill their expectations. As one example, there are substantial differences across cultures in the extent to which punitive control tactics are believed to be effective. For example, Durrant, Broberg, and Rose-Krasnor (1999) assessed differences between parents in Canada (where parental use of spanking is sanctioned) and Sweden (where parental use of spanking is prohibited by law) in their use of spanking and their beliefs about its effectiveness. As might be expected, substantial differences arose in the use of spanking in the two countries. For example, 45% of Canadian mothers said they would use physical punishment in some circumstances, whereas only 15% of Swedish mothers said they would do so. More important to our concerns, parents in the two countries showed large differences in the extent to which they believed that spanking had desirable consequences (e.g., agreement with such statements as "Sometimes a spank is the best way to get my child to listen"). A secure interpretation of these findings is somewhat constrained, of course, by possible cultural differences in willingness to provide honest responses.

Palacios and Moreno (1996) pointed out the importance of attending to educational differences a qualifying factor—across cultures—in parental beliefs about the effects of different parental practices. That is, parents with higher levels of education and exposure to contemporary parenting information are more likely to believe that positive caregiving outcomes follow from effortful activity, both on the part of parents and on the part of children. In contrast, parents from lower educational backgrounds and more rural areas are less likely to believe that effortful activity will influence a child's outcomes. Instead, they are more likely to attribute causality to biological factors—children "are the way they are." From this standpoint, parents are more likely to believe that the best they can do is to contain their children's unruly behavior with strict discipline.

Just as the effects of parental education cross national boundaries, the effects of religious beliefs are ubiquitous. So, for example, conservative Protestant parents are more likely than those of other religions to believe that parental use of corporal punishment is an effective means of preventing future transgressions (Gershoff, Miller, and Holden, 1999).

How Do Parental Attributions Affect Parent–Child Interactions?

Parental attributions about children begin before they are even born and may have profound effects on parents' very earliest relationships with their children. Lieberman (1999, pp. 739–740) provided an informative anecdotal example of this process:

> While she [the mother] was pregnant, she imagined her baby as demanding and devouring every bit of energy she had, leaving her empty and depleted. When her daughter was 2 days old, she commented: "She is pretty, but she is very greedy." . . . [interpreting] her baby daughter's healthy appetite as a sign

of voraciousness and worried that there would not be enough nourishment available for the two of them. . . . [T]his attribution of greediness had a rather straightforward behavioral expression. The mother let the baby cry for 30 to 40 minutes if the crying occurred while the mother was eating.

Parental attributions and parental responses.   As one research strategy, parental attributions have been studied for their direct effects on parental practices, physiological responses, processing of social information, and emotional reactions. Dix et al. (1986) argued that parents' attributions about their children's social behavior (and misbehavior) would influence the ways in which they responded (both affectively and behaviorally) to those children. The focus of this program was on the consequences of attributions parents made concerning children's behavior. For example, Dix, Ruble, and Zambarano (1989) found that parents increasingly saw power-assertive strategies as a reasonable choice when children knowingly violated rules and were fully capable of complying with them. Supporting these correlational findings, Slep and O'Leary (1998) found that parents demonstrated a harsher style of interaction with their children if they had been experimentally induced to believe that their children were misbehaving intentionally.

A number of research programs have focused on the consequences of parents' attributions about their own control. Parental attributional patterns that reflect a generalized lack of perceived control (as parents) have generally been found to be associated with less-effective parenting. Beginning at birth, parents who believe that their infants' perinatal problems are outside their control do not adapt as well as do those who see such problems as controllable (Tennen, Affleck, and Gershman, 1986). In general, parents who believe they lack control are more likely to engage in harsh parenting practices (e.g., Janssens, 1994) and to show a lack of positive affect (e.g., Carton, Nowicki, and Balser, 1996). Paralleling these findings (employing self-efficacy rather than direct attributional measures), Bondy and Mash (1997) found that a coercive parenting style is more common among parents who are low in self-efficacy.

Some investigators have taken a third dyadic, approach to parental attributions, focusing on parents' attributions of their own control in comparison with the perceived control of children. In an early study, Bugental and Shennum (1984) found that parents with low perceived power (relative to their children) are highly reactive to child behaviors and settings that have implications for their ability to exert control or dominance within the relationship. For example, with unresponsive children, parents show (1) physiological mobilization (elevations in motoric activation, elevations in heart rate; e.g., Bugental et al., 2000), (2) inconsistent or negative affect (e.g., Bugental, Blue, and Lewis, 1990; Bugental, and Happaney, 2000), and (3) reduced social-information-processing ability (Bugental, Brown, and Reiss, 1996). However, the assertiveness of their response is contingent on the possibility of successfully exercising control. For example, parents show a highly assertive tone of voice when the setting allows them control and a highly unassertive tone of voice when such control is absent (Bugental and Lewis, 1998).

When confronted with children's misdeeds (an event that poses a potential threat to control), parents who make low-power attributions either show a highly assertive or highly submissive response, dependent on other contextual factors. For example, Mills (1999) found that low-power women use negative control tactics (guilt induction and love withdrawal) with fearful children but not with fearless children. Such reactivity is very different from the chameleon-like, interpersonal mimicry that tends to characterize people who are highly empathic (Chartrand and Bargh, 1999). Rather than being "tuned in" to children, those parents with low perceived power appear to be particularly inept in interpreting children's intentions and in making fine-grained distinctions between types of child behavior (e.g., Lovejoy, Polewko, and Harrison, 1996; Milner and Foody, 1994). Their responses appear to reflect exploitation of the immediate situation in ways that optimize control. As suggested by Rudy and Grusec (1999), this response pattern may reflect a "minimization" strategy (Taylor, 1991). That is, low-power parents exploit situations they believe they can control, and disengage from situations they cannot control. This interpretation is consistent with the findings that low-power mothers are also more likely to show a dismissive attachment style (Grusec and Mammone, 1995). It is likely that a dismissive style in adults, like an avoidantly attached style in infants (Spangler and Grossman, 1993), hides a high level of unexpressed distress.

Although most attention has been directed to the effects of mothers' perceived lack of control or power, a literature has emerged showing the negative effects of overestimated or "illusory" control. Consistent with this perspective, Donovan, Leavitt, and Walsh (1990, 1997) observed that mothers who overestimate their power (i.e., who make an unrealistic judgment regarding their ability to terminate an infant's cries) easily showed learned helplessness in their later reactions to infant cries that they could not terminate. In addition, mothers showed distinctive autonomic and affective responses—revealing elevations in heart rate and increases in depression. They also showed a low ability to distinguish between the cries of "difficult" versus "easy" infants (cries that differed in pitch properties). In many ways, the responses of mothers who overestimate their control parallel the responses of mothers who underestimate their control. It may be that exaggerated perceptions of control (in either direction) suggest a focus on competition for power, an emphasis that has negative implications for parent–child relationships.

Parental attributions and child responses. To a more limited extent, parents' attributions have been studied with respect to their implications for children's immediate reactions, including (1) their behavioral compliance, (2) their physiological reactivity, (3) their social information-processing, and (4) their emotional responses. In general, the children of parents who perceive themselves as lacking control in the parenting relationship are likely to be low in behavioral compliance. For example, Roberts, Joe, and Rowe-Halbert (1992) found that clinic-referred "oppositional" children were more likely to show resistive behavior with parents who had an external locus of control than with parents who had an internal locus of control.

Donovan et al. (2000) extended their research concerned with the responses of mothers who overestimate their control to ask how children respond to such mothers. Mothers with a high illusion of control were very likely to make use of power-assertive control strategies. However, children were defiant with mothers who made very low estimates of their control as well as with mothers who overestimated their control. This suggests the possibility that optimal attributions are those in which parental power is seen as moderate rather than either extremely high or low.

In much of this research it is difficult to determine whether children's more negative reactions to parents follow from or precede parents' lack of perceived control. In an effort to unscramble direction of effects, Bugental, Lyon, Lin, McGrath, and Bimbela (1999) observed the reactions of children to videotaped "teachers" who were either (1) unrelated mothers selected on the basis of their perceived power (high versus low) or (2) an unrelated actress portraying an interactional style characteristic of high-versus low-power mothers. Children (6- to 10-year olds) responded to low-power women—or to a woman showing a low-power response style—in distinctive ways. They showed low levels of autonomic orienting (reflecting attentional disengagement). Consistent with such disengagement, they also showed relatively poor performance on a cognitively demanding task.

How Do Parental Attributions Affect Children's Long-Term Social–Emotional Welfare?

A considerable body of research has been concerned with the long-term effects of parental attributions on children's social–emotional welfare. Such concerns have been organized primarily around the implications of parental attributions for child maltreatment and children's aggression.

Implications for child maltreatment. A consistent linkage has been observed between parents' attributional biases and their harshness or maltreatment of the young (Azar, in Vol. 4 of this *Handbook*). Most of this work has relied on correlational assessment of the association between parental practices and parental attributions, with attendant problems in determining the direction of effects. To the extent these findings reveal causality, parents who either attribute defiant intentions to children or who see themselves as lacking power are more likely to be harsh or abusive (Bradley and Peters, 1991; Silvester, Bentovim, Stratton, and Hanks, 1995; Smith and O'Leary, 1995; Stratton and Swaffer, 1988).

Although much of this body of work has explored the main effects of parental attributions on their maltreatment of the young, some research has studied the moderating effects of attributions. When a moderator model is tested, it typically reveals that parents who show maltreatment-promoting attributions are more likely to maltreat children who may be interpreted as difficult or demanding. For example, Bugental (2000) found that infants who show risk patterns at birth (low Apgar scores or prematurity) were more subject to subsequent abuse by parents with low perceived power.

Implications for child aggression. Just as considerable attention has been directed to the implications of parental attributions for parents' aggressive practices, systematic attention has also been given to the implications of parental attributions for the aggressive behaviors of their children. For example, Nix et al. (1999) conducted a longitudinal investigation from which they concluded that mothers' hostile attributional biases (as assessed in response to ambiguous problem behaviors of children) predicted children's externalizing behaviors at home and at school. Parents' harsh disciplinary style served to partially mediate this relation. MacKinnon et al. (1992, 1994) conducted a longitudinal study exploring the effects of attributions on aggression in the family. Specifically, they assessed the role of maternal attributions—along with child attributions—as predictors of aggressive interactions between mother and child. As anticipated, the most aggressive dyads included the combination of mothers who revealed hostile attributions when paired with sons who showed the same attributional pattern.

How Do Parental Attributions Foster or Limit Children's Long-Term Academic Motivation and Achievement?

One of the earliest interests in parental attributions concerned their influence on children's motivation and achievement in school. This interest has continued, and expanded to include extensive concerns with the ways in which differences in parental attributions differ by sex of child, sex of parent, and across culture.

General effects. Weiner's (1985) theoretical concepts of attributional processes have been highly influential in this area of research. Even when investigators do not directly cite Weiner, the attributional constructs they employ typically have their origins in his work. That is, central attention has been directed to the extent to which parents attribute their children's academic success or failure to causes that are stable or unstable, internal or external, and controllable or uncontrollable (by the child).

Interest in parental attributions for children's academic outcomes follows from the assumptions that such causal beliefs ultimately come to influence children's academic motivation and achievement. Supporting this general notion, a number of investigators have demonstrated that parents' belief in controllable causes (e.g., child effort) is likely to predict their children's academic success, whereas parents' belief in uncontrollable causes (e.g., luck) is likely to predict children's underachievement (e.g., O'Sullivan and Howe, 1996).

It is sometimes assumed that the higher levels of achievement shown by the children of "effort-attributing" parents results from the greater investment such parents make in fostering their children's academic pursuits. However, the simple presence of a correlation between parental attributions and child achievement does not itself imply causality. Increasing attention needs to be paid to variables that may mediate the parent attribution–child performance relation. For example, Georgiou (1999) used structural equation modeling to determine the role of different kinds of parental involvement within this relation. Within an elementary school population, those parents who attributed high importance to their own role were more likely to be both (1) highly invested in developing children's academic interests (e.g., encouraging the child to read for pleasure and (2) highly controlling (e.g., controlling children's TV viewing time). In addition, parental attributions to their children's effort (but not their control activities) also served to predict parental investment in developing their children's academic ability. Further research is needed, however, to establish whether parental investment in developing children's interests actually serves to mediate the relationship between parental attributions and children's achievement.

Gender variations.   Eccles, Freedman-Doan, Frome, and Jacobs (2000) spearheaded an interest in the effects of parents' cognitions about the ability of their sons and daughters. They directed particular attention to the effects of parental cognitions on gender-stereotyped activities (e.g., math and sports). Based on their perceptions regarding the abilities of their sons versus their daughters, parents make different attributions for their children's performance. Parents' gender-biased attributions, in turn, influence children's self-perceptions and activity choices.

The assessment of parental attributions for children's school-related outcomes has typically been limited to mothers. Cote and Azar (1997) extended our knowledge on this topic by assessing differences between mothers and fathers in attributions for the academic and social outcomes (in school) of their sons and daughters (across the course of development). Complex interactions were found between gender of parent and gender of child. For example, mothers of sons were more likely than mothers of daughters to ask the reasons for any academic failure and to encourage them to try harder. In contrast, fathers were more likely than mothers to directly involve themselves with the academic and social problems of their daughters (e.g., talking to teachers on their behalf). These differences have implications for the implicit attributions made by fathers and mothers for the outcomes of their sons and daughters (and the corresponding attributions that are likely for children themselves).

Cultural variations.   Attention to cultural differences in parental attributions for their children's academic outcomes has centered on Asian versus Western cultures (Stevenson et al., 1990; Tuss, Zimmer, and Ho, 1995). For example, Stevenson et al. (1990) assessed differences in parental attributions in for their children's academic outcomes in the United States, Japan, and China. Parents in Asian countries typically believe that school performance is determined by effort, an attribution that assigns value to their children "trying harder" as a means of doing better in school. In contrast, parents in Western countries are more likely to believe that school performance is determined by ability, an attributional pattern that is less suggestive of ways that children might improve their performance. At the same time, there are indications that Asian parents do not verbalize their attributions concerning the role of effort; instead, there appears to be a mutual understanding between parents and children that children should and will exert high levels of effort in accomplishing academic goals (e.g., Bembechat, Graham, and Jimenez, 1999). This shared expectation (that children will exert academic effort) should be distinguished from the optimistic beliefs about the value of education held by African American and Latin American parents in the United States (e.g., Stevenson et al., 1990). The first view focuses on a (shared) expectation of children themselves, and the second view focuses on expectations of educational institutions.

Summary

Current research on parental attributions has produced several consistent themes. One theme relates to their origins. Although parental attributions appear to be updated as a result of later experience, they appear to be strongly influenced by adults' own early history, both within their own family and within their culture. In the social–emotional domain, particular attention has been directed to the relationship between parental attributions and harsh or abusive parenting tactics; a consistent picture has emerged in which parents with a blame-oriented attributional style are more likely to demonstrate harsh or abusive tactics, in particular with children who pose a perceived source of threat.

Such parental attributions (and resultant parenting tactics) also foster the likelihood of subsequent child aggressiveness and other types of antisocial behavior.

Concern with the role of parental attributions on children's academic achievement motivation and performance has directed particular interest to variations across gender (in particular, child gender) and culture. Parents show consistent differences across these child and cultural, differences which, in turn, may influence children's motivational patterns and, ultimately, their performance. Little information is currently available, however, concerning the events that mediate the relationship between parental attributions and child achievement.

FUTURE DIRECTIONS IN THE STUDY OF PARENTAL ATTRIBUTIONS

In considering future directions in the study of parental attributions, we need to consider the gaps in our existing knowledge, the adequacy of the methods we use, and the application of our findings. In doing so, we necessarily move across disciplinary boundaries. Parenting research has always benefitted by considering theory from other fields by expanding and refining the ways in which we study parenting processes, and by considering the utility of our knowledge for children and families.

New Research Questions

Along with the many continuing issues in this field (e.g., concern with parenting contexts or domains, or concern with the origins of parents' attributions), there are also some issues that represent relatively new concerns. Two of these pose some particularly intriguing possibilities.

Attributions versus expectations. Past research has focused on the role of parental attributions about past or hypothetical events; that is, researchers have typically asked parents about their perception of the causes of caregiving events that actually occurred or might occur. In general, such processes have been found to be more predictive of undesired than desired caregiving outcomes. That is, parents who make certain kinds of attributions are more likely to engage in harsh or ineffective parental practices and to have children who show deficits in their emotional responses, social behaviors, and/or achievement motives. Less attention has been given to parents' expectations or to the extent to which parents' causal reasoning necessarily predicts their expectations. Thus, for example, two parents may both believe that child effort predicts positive outcomes (if children make an effort to behave in a socially positive way, they are likely to succeed in doing so; if they study hard, they will succeed in school). At the same time, one of these parents may expect that their child will actually make an effort, whereas another parent may question the extent to which their child will do so. Differences in child behavior may then follow as a result of parental expectations.

In reviewing this literature, there have been some very tentative indications that optimal parenting may be more associated with positive expectations than with attributions. Indeed, if positive events are expected, causal appraisal serves little function. Let's take a case in point. As noted earlier, Asian families have often been observed to hold optimistic expectations for children's social and academic behavior. Bempechat et al. (1999) pointed out that Asian parents invest little effort in attempting to influence children to behave in responsible ways—they simply expect such behavior as a given. Further work is needed to determine the differential effects of expectations versus the attributions on parenting practices. Optimistic beliefs may preclude the need for attributional activity (typically directed to explaining undesired or ambiguous events). Alternatively, of course, it may be that certain kind of attributions serve as necessary but not sufficient condition for positive caregiving outcomes. Thus, for example, parents' beliefs that child effort is predictive of positive outcomes may be a necessary but not a sufficient condition for positive outcomes.

In the future, parenting researchers may do well to follow the emerging debate within the close relationships literature. Within this area (focused primarily on adult relationships), consideration has been increasingly directed to the conceptual boundaries between expectations and attributions, and the extent to which life outcomes are affected by these two processes (Carver et al., 2000; Folkman and Moskowitz, 2000). For example, Carver and his colleagues suggested that expectations may be more important processes than attributions in fostering positive life outcomes. Within this research, there has been considerable support for the advantages of optimistic beliefs for future outcomes, with a focus on social and health outcomes (Murray and Holmes, 1997; Scheier and Carver, 1993). These ideas have also been framed in terms of the advantages of "positive illusions" (Taylor, Kemeny, Reed, Bower, and Gruenewald, 2000). Those individuals who have a "trust" and anticipation that good events will happen ultimately are more likely to act in ways that increase the probability that desired events will indeed occur. That is, "optimism," or "positive illusion," serves to foster self-fulfilling prophecies. Within these changing conceptions, there has also been a shift to "positive psychology," that is, to the processes (including attributional processes) that foster "well-being" and "thriving" (e.g., Peterson, 2000; Seligman and Csikszentimihalyi, 2000).

Parental attributions and mediating processes.   There has been increasing use of moderator models in studying the effects of attributions. For example, researchers have assessed the role of parental attributions as qualifiers of the relation between child characteristics and parenting strategies. Thus, those parents who attribute high blame to children may be particularly likely to use punitive tactics with an apparently unresponsive child. At this point, models are needed that not only provide a role for attributional moderators but that also consider the route through which those attributions produce their effects. For example, is the relation between parental blame and use of punitive tactics mediated by anger? By retributional motives?

As one important omission, little attention has been given to the role of stress-related physiological processes as mediator variables. For example, there is evidence that parents with low perceived power are (1) more likely to maltreat their children, (2) show high autonomic mobilization to caregiving threat, and (3) show social-information-processing deficits in response to threat. However, the relevant mediating role of autonomic processes has not been fully demonstrated. It may be that greater attention should be given to other physiological indications of stress (e.g., increased production of cortisol—a response that has potential implications for the social and cognitive processes of parents and their young). That is, overactivation of the hypothalamic–pituitary–adrenal (HPA) axis and resultant bombardment of the hippocampus with cortisol has negative consequences for both cognitive and social functioning (e.g., Bremner and Narayan, 1998). Thus, the effects found as a function of biased cognitions (e.g., attentional narrowing and memory deficits) may to some extent be mediated by associated hormonal reactivity. So, for example, children with low levels of perceived control show elevated levels of cortisol in response to stress (Granger, Weisz, and Kauneckis, 1994), and a similar pattern has been found for mothers with low perceived control (Bugental, 1999). Thus, it will be profitable to further explore the mediating role of hormonal processes within conflictual family relationships (Margolin and Gordis, 2000).

Methodological and Sampling Issues

Within the future of parental attribution research, our knowledge will be enhanced by redress of some continuing methodological limitations. Of the many issues that might be identified, several deserve particular attention. The first issue concerns problems with shared method variance. The most commonly seen problem of this type involves reliance on parental self-report as both an independent and a dependent measure. As a result, negative (or positive) biases may come to simultaneously influence both (1) what parents have to say about causality and (2) what they have to say about their children's behavior.

Exclusive reliance on self-report measures also creates simultaneous problems with managed self-presentations; parents may easily be motivated to present themselves and their children in a favorable light. Such limitations have long been known in the assessment of parental beliefs (e.g., Becker and Krug, 1965; Holden and Edwards, 1989). To avoid such problems, investigators need to routinely direct attention to issues of social desirability of measures (Bugental, Johnston, New, and Silvester, 1998). That is, we can place greater faith in what parents tell us if their responses are not easily managed. For example, attributions are more likely to reveal more spontaneous, implicit cognitions if they are assessed in naturalistic circumstances (e.g., when the individual's attention is constrained by the presence of other ongoing activities). As one possible method for accomplishing this goal, attributions can be assessed during discourse (e.g., the Leeds Attributional Coding System; Stratton, Head, Hanks, and Munton, 1986). Spontaneously produced attributional statements during a stressful conversation, although not completely free from self-management, are more likely to be revealing of the speaker's implicit attributions.

Another associated problem involves reliance on correlational research. Although new fields of inquiry benefit from correlational analyses in an effort to determine possible relations (hypothesis generation), there comes a point when attention is better directed to hypothesis testing and the use of methods that allow causal inference. Causal modeling provides a first step in this direction, although with the clear caveat that such methods only support the possibility of causality but do not prove such causality. Ultimately, a full test of causality requires the use of experimental methods. In parental attribution research, this involves the experimental manipulation of (1) the kinds of caregiving stimuli to which parents are exposed, (2) the mediating events believed to serve as causal links in the attribution–behavior association (e.g., elevated levels of affect or arousal), and (3) parental attributions themselves (within intervention research).

As another type of limitation, research on parental attributions continues to focus on European American mothers in the United States. There also continues to be a paucity of research concerned with gender differences in parental attributions (as noted in Bugental and Johnston, 2000). As research on fathers increases, it has become increasingly apparent that gender differences are often observed in the attributions mothers and fathers make for child and caregiving outcomes. In addition, there is still a continuing need for exploration of cultural differences in parental attributions. Although there have been a few large-scale studies concerned (directly or indirectly) with cultural differences in parental attributions (e.g., Bornstein et al., 1998; Stevenson et al., 1990), more work of this type is needed. Finally, more attention needs to be directed to parental attributions for children with special needs (e.g., chronically ill children or children with disabilities).

Application Issues: Programs Focused on Altering Parental Attributions

Increasing attention has been given to issues of change in parents' attributions. There is a twofold motivation for such efforts. From a clinical standpoint, it can reasonably be argued that, if parents' attributions foster caregiving problems, alteration in those attributions should serve to reduce or prevent those problems (e.g., Johnston, 1996). From the standpoint of basic research, it can be seen that experimental alteration of parents' attributions also allows a direct test of the causal implications of parental attributions.

Bugental (1999) demonstrated that an attributionally based prevention program may serve to prevent later instances of child maltreatment. In a longitudinal design, at-risk parents (e.g., from low-education, low-income, and high-stress backgrounds) were randomly assigned to different prevention activities prior to the birth of a child: (1) an attributionally augmented home visitation program, (2) a standard "healthy families" home visitation program (Duggan, McFarlane, Windham, and Rohde, 1999), or (3) referral to other currently available community services. The attributional intervention focused on reducing parents' tendency to assign personal blame to self or others as causes of difficult caregiving events and facilitating their problem-focused orientation. The lowest level of physical child abuse at the end of one year was found for parents in attributionally augmented home visitation (4%) in comparison with standard home visitation (20%) or community referral (36%). The highest level of benefit was shown for those children at the highest level of risk (e.g., children who experienced birth complications or early illness).

Across programs, one of the advantages of a cognitive intervention is the possibility of making "automatic" processes more easily accessible to awareness. As Rudy and Grusec (1999, p. 87) suggested, "If coercive parenting is more conscious, ambiguous misbehaviors on the part of the child will be less likely to be automatically interpreted negatively." If parents' existing attributional biases become more accessible, opportunities increase for more flexible problem solving. Such interventions may serve to facilitate a new "correction" process in which parents engage in data-based appraisal processes before immediately invoking old, overlearned explanations and parental responses based on those explanations.

CONCLUSIONS

Over the last 30 years, the theoretical framing of parental attributions has changed in ways that reflect advances in both social cognitive psychology and social developmental psychology. We have become more aware of distinctions in the ways in which cognitive processes work—sometimes operating as unaware, automatic, implicit processes and sometimes as aware, effortful, explicit processes. We have also directed greater attention to the ways that attributional processes moderate parent–child relationships, and we have an enhanced understanding of the circumstances that are most likely to foster attributional activity. Although early work in this field focused on explicit attributional processes, increasing importance has been given to the role of parental attributions as implicit processes. During the course of family life, parental attributions regularly operate below the level of awareness but, nonetheless, act as a running guide to parents' interpretations of ongoing events, their emotional responses to those events, and their parenting practices.

The basic ways in which parental attributions play out during the course of interaction have been studied with increasing recognition of context or domain. Rather than being seen as stable personality constructs that exert a uniform influence on parenting practices, parental attributions are more regularly seen as constructs that are accessed differentially with different children and in different caregiving settings. As an easy example, the kinds of parental attributions that foster optimal academic outcomes differ from those that foster optimal social–emotional outcomes. There are also differences in the kinds of attributions that parents make concerning children's prosocial actions versus their misdeeds. However, a broader range of child or caregiving events needs to be considered in the study of parental attributions. As noted by others (e.g., Grusec et al., 1997), there has been a tendency to focus on parental attributions for children's misdeeds. Such research has strong implications for parents' selection of disciplinary strategies. In future work it will be useful to learn more about parents' attributions for other types of child variables. For example, we need to know more about parents' attributions for the causes and consequences of children's medical conditions, physical disabilities, or temperament problems.

Continuing questions in this field include concern with the origins of parental attributions along with the short-term and long-term effects of parental attributions. Parental attributions are influenced by direct proximal experiences with one's own children, but they are also strongly influenced by parents' distal personal and cultural history. Attachment history has emerged as an important early influence on later attributions for the parenting relationship.

There are several important gaps in the study of parental attributions. We need more information about the extent to which parental attributions and expectations serve as overlapping or independent contributors to parental practices. More systematic attention should be directed to mediating processes in the relation between parental attributions and child and family outcomes. That is, what is the route through which parental attributions come to produce their effects? To what extent do parental attributions influence parents' and children's behavior? Their affective and physiological responses to caregiving events? The ways in which they process ongoing information? Finally, increased effort need to be given to fostering optimal parental attributions—either as part of parent training or family intervention efforts. In this way, our knowledge can be directed to promoting long-term benefits to children and families.

ACKNOWLEDGMENTS

We would like to express our appreciation to Joan Grusec for her very thoughtful comments on this chapter. Funding from National Science Foundation Grant BMS9021221 and National Institute of Mental Health Grant RO1 MH 19095 provided partial funding for this project.

REFERENCES

Abramson, L. Y., Seligman, M. E. P., and Teasdale, J. D. (1978). Learned helplessness in humans: Critique and reformulation. *Journal of Abnormal Psychology, 87*, 49–74.

Baldwin, M. W. (1992). Relational schemas and the processing of social information. *Psychological Bulletin, 112*, 461–484.

Bandura, A. (1977). Self-efficacy: Toward a unifying theory of behavior theory of behavior change. *Psychological Review, 84*, 191–215.

Bandura, A. (1989). Regulation of cognitive processes through perceived self-efficacy. *Developmental Psychology, 25*, 729–735.

Bargh, J. A., and Chartrand, T. L. (1999). The unbearable automaticity of being. *American Psychologist, 54*, 462–479.

Bargh, J. A., Lombardi, W. J., and Higgins, E. T. (1988). Automaticity of chronically accessible constructs in person × situation effects on person perception: It's just a matter of time. *Journal of Personality and Social Psychology, 55*, 599–605.

Baron, R. M., and Kenny, D. A. (1986). The moderator–mediator variable distinction in social psychological research: Conceptual, strategic, and statistical considerations. *Journal of Personality and Social Psychology, 6*, 1173–1182.

Becker, W. C., and Krug, R. S. (1965). Parent Attitude Research Instrument: A research review. *Child Development, 36*, 329–365.

Bell, R. Q. (1968). A reinterpretation of the direction of effects in studies of socialization. *Psychological Review, 75*, 81–95.

Bell, R. Q. (1979). Parent, child, and reciprocal influences. *American Psychologist, 34*, 821–826.

Bempechat, J., Graham, S. E., and Jimenez, N. V. (1999). The socialization of achievement in poor and minority students. *Journal of Cross-Cultural Psychology, 30*, 139–158.

Bondy, E. M., and Mash, E. J. (1997, April). *Parenting efficacy, perceived control over caregiving failure, and mothers' reactions to preschool children's misbehavior.* Paper presented at the biennial meetings of the Society for Research in Child Development, Washington, DC.

Bornstein, M. H., Haynes, O. M., Azuma, H., Galperin, C., Maital, S., Ogino, M., Painter, K., Pascual, L., Pêcheux, Marie-Germaine, Rahn, C., Toda, S., Venuti, P., Vyt, A., and Wright, B. (1998). A cross-national study of self-evaluations and attributions in parenting: Argentina, Belgium, France, Israel, Italy, Japan, and the United States. *Developmental Psychology, 34*, 662–676.

Bornstein, M. H., Haynes, O. M., and Painter, K. M. (2000). *Parenting beliefs and behaviors in mother/child dyads of varying hearing status.* Unpublished mauscript, National Institute of Child Health and Human Development.

Bowlby, J. (1980). *Attribution and loss: Vol. 3. Loss.* New York: Basic Books.

Boysen, S., and Himes, G. T. (1999). Current issues and emerging theories in animal cognition. *Annual Review of Psychology, 50*, 683–705.

Bradley, E. J., and Peters, R. D. (1991). Physically abusive and nonabusive mothers' perceptions of parenting and child behavior. *American Journal of Orthopsychiatry, 61*, 455–460.

Bremner, J., and Narayan, M. (1998). The effect of stress on memory and the hippocampus throughout the life cycle: Implications for childhood development and aging. *Development and Psychopathology, 10*, 871–885.

Bretherton, I. (1990). Open communication and internal working models: Their role in the development of attachment relationships. In R. A. Thompson (Ed.), *Socioemotional development: Nebraska Symposium on Motivation, 1988* (pp. 57–113). Lincoln: University of Nebraska Press.

Bugental, D. B. (1992). Affective and cognitive processes within threat-oriented family systems. In I. E. Sigel, A. V. McGillicuddy-DeLisi, and J. Goodnow (Eds.), *Parental belief systems: The psychological and affective consequences for children* (pp. 219–248). New York: Lawrence Erlbaum Associates.

Bugental, D. B. (1999, October). *Power-oriented cognitions as predictors of family violence*. Paper presented at the meeting of the Society for Experimental Social Psychology, St. Louis, MO.

Bugental, D. B. (2000). Acquisition of the algorithms of social life: A domain-based approach. *Psychological Bulletin, 126*, 187–219.

Bugental, D. B., Blue, J., Cortez, V., Fleck, K., Kopeikin, H., Lewis, J., and Lyon, J. (1993). Social cognitions as organizers of autonomic and affective responses to social challenge. *Journal of Personality and Social Psychology, 64*, 94–103.

Bugental, D. B., Blue, J. B., and Lewis, J. (1990). Caregiver cognitions as moderators of affective reactions to "difficult" children. *Developmental Psychology, 26*, 631–638.

Bugental, D. B., Brown, M., and Reiss, C. (1996). Cognitive representations of power in caregiving relationships: Biasing effects on interpersonal interaction and information-processing. *Journal of Family Psychology, 10*, 397–407.

Bugental, D. B., and Goodnow, J. G. (1998). Socialization processes. In W. Damon (Series Ed.) and N. Eisenberg (Vol. Ed.), *Handbook of child psychology: Vol. 3. Social, emotional, and personality development* (5th ed., pp. 389–462). New York: Wiley.

Bugental, D. B., and Happaney, K. (2000). Parent–child interaction as a power contest. *Journal of Applied Developmental Psychology, 21*, 267–282.

Bugental, D. B., and Johnston, C. (2000). Parental and child cognitions in the context of the family. *Annual Review of Psychology, 51*, 315–344.

Bugental, D. B., Johnston, C., New, M., and Silvester, J. (1998). Measuring parental attributions: Conceptual and methodological issues. *Journal of Family Psychology, 12*, 459–480.

Bugental, D. B., and Lewis, J. (1998). Interpersonal power repair in response to threats to control from dependent others. In M. Kofta, G. Weary, and G. Sedek (Eds.), *Personal control in action: Cognitive and motivational mechanisms* (pp. 341–362). New York: Plenum.

Bugental, D. B., Lewis, J. C., Lin, E., Lyon, J., and Kopeikin, H. (2000). In charge but not in control: The management of authority-based relationships by those with low perceived power. *Developmental Psychology, 35*, 1367–1378.

Bugental, D. B., Lyon, J. E., Cortez, V., and Krantz, J. (1997). Who's the boss? Accessibility of dominance ideation among individuals with low perceptions of interpersonal power. *Journal of Personality and Social Psychology, 72*, 1297–1309.

Bugental, D. B., Lyon, J. E., Lin, E., McGrath, E. G., and Bimbela, A. (1999). Children "tune out" in response to the ambiguous communication style of powerless adults. *Child Development, 70*, 214–230.

Bugental, D. B., and Martorell, G. (1999). Competition between friends: The joint influence of self, friends, and parents. *Journal of Family Psychology, 13*, 1–14.

Bugental, D. B., and Shennum, W. A. (1984). "Difficult" children as elicitors and targets of adult communication patterns: an attributional–behavioral transactional analysis. *Monographs of the Society for Research in Child Development, 49*, pp. 1–70.

Burks, V. S., and Parke, R. D. (1996). Parent and child representations of social relationships: Linkages between families and peers. *Merrill-Palmer Quarterly, 42*, 358–378.

Burns, M. O., and Seligman, M. E. (1989). Explanatory style across the life span: Evidence of stability over the years. *Journal of Personality and Social Psychology, 56*, 471–477.

Carton, J. S., Nowicki, S., Jr., and Balser, G. M. (1996). An observational study of antecedents of locus of control of reinforcement. *International Journal of Behavioral Development, 19*, 161–175.

Carver, C. S., Harris, S. D., Lehman, J. M., Durel, L. A., Antoni, M. H., Spencer, S. M., and Pozo-Kaderman, D. (2000). How important is the perception of personal control? Studies of early stage breast cancer patients. *Personality and Social Psychology Bulletin, 26*, 139–149.

Cassidy, J. (1994). Emotion regulation: Influences of attachment relationships. *Monographs of the Society for Research in Child Development, 59*, pp. 228–283.

Chartrand, T. L., and Bargh, J. (1999). The chameleon effect: The perception–behavior link and social interaction. *Journal of Personality and Social Psychology, 76*, 893–910.

Coleman, P. K., and Karraker, K. H. (1997). Self-efficacy and parenting quality: Findings and future applications. *Developmental Review, 18*, 48–85.

Connors, J. L., and Donnellan, A. M. (1993). Citizenship and culture: The role of disabled people in Navajo society. *Disability, Handicap and Society, 8*, 265–280.

Cote, L. R., and Azar, S. T. (1997). Child age, parent and child gender, and domain differences in parents' attributions and responses to children's outcomes. *Sex Roles, 36*, 23–50.

Dix, T. H. (1992). Parenting on behalf of the child: Empathic goals in the regulation of responsive parenting. In I. E. Sigel, A. V. McGillicuddy-DeLisi, and J. J. Goodnow (Eds.), *Parental belief systems: The psychological consequences for children* (Vol. 2, pp. 319–346). Hillsdale, NJ: Lawrence Erlbaum Associates.

Dix, T., and Grusec, J. (1985). Parent attribution processes in the socialization of children. In I. E. Sigel (Ed.), *Parental belief systems* (pp. 201–233). Hillsdale, NJ: Lawrence Erlbaum Associates.

Dix, T., and Reinhold, D. P., and Zambarano, R. J. (1990). Mothers' judgments in moments of anger. *Merrill-Palmer Quarterly, 36*, 465–486.

Dix, T., Ruble, D., Grusec, J., and Nixon, S. (1986). Social cognition in parents: Inferential and affective reactions to children of three age levels. *Child Development, 57,* 879–894.

Dix, T., Ruble, D. N., and Zambarano, R. J. (1989). Mothers' implicit theories of discipline: Child effects, parent effects and the attribution process. *Child Development, 60,* 1373–1391.

Donovan, W. L., Leavitt, L. A., and Walsh, R. O. (1990). Maternal self-efficacy: Illusory control and its effect on susceptibility to learned helplessness. *Child Development, 61,* 1638–1647.

Donovan, W. L., Leavitt, L. A., and Walsh, R. O. (1997). Cognitive set and coping strategy affect mother's sensitivity to infant cries: A signal-processing approach. *Child Development, 68,* 760–762.

Donovan, W. L., Leavitt, L. A., and Walsh, R. O. (2000). Maternal illusory control predicts socialization strategies and toddler compliance. *Developmental Psychology, 36,* 402–411.

Duggan, A. K., McFarlane, E. C., Windham, A. M., and Rohde, C. A. (1999). *Evaluation of Hawaii's Healthy Start program. Future of Children, 9,* 66–90.

Durrant, J. E., Broberg, A. G., and Rose-Krasnor, L. (1999). In C. C. Piotrowski and P. D. Hastings (Eds.), *Conflict as a context for understanding maternal beliefs about child rearing and children's misbehavior* (pp. 25–42). San Francisco: Jossey-Bass.

Eccles, J. S., Freedman-Doan, C., Frome, P., and Jacobs, J. (2000). Gender-role socialization in the family: A longitudinal approach. In T. Eckes and H. M. Trautner (Eds.), *The developmental social psychology of gender.* Mahwah, NJ: Lawrence Erlbaum Associates.

Eiser, C., and Havermans, T. (1992). Mothers' and fathers' coping with chronic childhood disease. *Psychology and Health, 7,* 249–257.

Fiske, S. T., and Pavelchak, M. A. (1986). *Category-based versus piecemeal-based affective responses: Developments in schema-triggered affect.* In R. M. Sorrentino and E. T. Higgins (Eds.), *Handbook of motivation and cognition: Foundations of social behavior* (pp. 167–203). New York: Guilford.

Folkman, S., and Moskowitz, J. T. (2000). The context matters. *Personality and Social Psychology Bulletin, 26,* 50–51.

Garwick, A. W., Kohrman, C. H., Titus, J. C., Wolman, C., and Blum, R. W. (1999). Variations in families' explanations of childhood chronic conditions: A cross-cultural perspective. In H. I. McCubbin, E. A. Thompson, A. I. Thompson, and J. A. Futrell (Eds.), *The dynamics of resilient families* (pp. 165–203). Thousand Oaks, CA: Sage.

George, C., Kaplan, N., and Main, M. (1996). *Adult Attachment Interview.* Unpublished protocol, Department of Psychology, University of California, Berkeley.

Georgiou, S. N. (1999). Parental attributions as predictors of involvement and influences on child achievement. *British Journal of Educational Psychology, 69,* 409–429.

Gershoff, E. T., Miller, P. D., and Holden, G. W. (1999). Parenting influences form the pulpit: religious affiliation as a determinant of parental corporal punishment. *Journal of Family Psychology, 13,* 307–320.

Goldberg, S., Grusec, J. E., and Jenkins, J. M. (1999). Confidence in protection: Arguments for a narrow definition of attachment. *Journal of Family Psychology, 13,* 475–483.

Goodnow, J. J. (1997). Parenting and the transmission and internalization of values: from social–cultural perspectives to within-family analyses. In J. E. Grusec and L. Kuczynski (Eds.), *Parenting and children's internalization of values* (pp. 331–361). New York: Wiley.

Granger, D. A., Weisz, J. R., and Kauneckis, D. (1994). Neuroendocrine reactivity, internalizing behavior problems, and control-related cognitions in clinic-referred children and adolescents. *Journal of Abnormal Psychology, 103,* 267–276.

Greenwald, A. G., and Banaji, M. R. (1995). Implicit social cognition: Attitudes, self-esteem, and stereotypes. *Psychological Review, 102,* 4–27.

Grusec, J. E., and Goodnow, J. J. (1994). Impact of parental discipline methods on the child's internalization of values: A reconceptualization of current points of view. *Developmental Psychology, 30,* 4–19.

Grusec, J. E., Hastings, P., and Mammone, N. (1994). Parenting cognitions and relationship schemas. In J. G. Smetana (Ed.), *Beliefs about parenting: Origins and developmental implications* (pp. 5–19). San Francisco: Jossey-Bass.

Grusec, J. E., and Mammone, N. (1995). Features and sources of parents' attributions about themselves and their children. In N. Eisenberg (Ed.), *Social development: Review of personality and social psychology* (Vol. 15, pp. 49–73). Thousand Oaks, CA: Sage.

Grusec, J. E., Rudy, D. D., and Martini, T. (1997). Parenting cognitions and child outcomes: An overview and implications for children's internalization of values. In J. E. Grusec and L. Kuczynski (Eds.). *Parenting and children's internalizations of values: A handbook of contemporary theory* (pp. 259–282). New York: Wiley.

Haines, B. A., Metalsky, G. I., Cardamone, A. L., and Joiner, T. (1999). Interpersonal and cognitive pathways into the origins of attributional style: A developmental perspective. In T. Joiner and J. C. Coyne (Eds.), *The interactional nature of depression* (pp. 65–92). Washington, DC: American Psychological Association.

Hastie, R. (1984). Causes and effects of causal attribution. *Journal of Personality and Social Psychology, 46,* 44–56.

Hastings, P. D., and Coplan, R. (1999). Conceptual and empirical links between children's social spheres: Relating maternal beliefs and preschoolers' behaviors with peers. In C. C. Piotrowski and P. D. Hastings (Eds.), *Conflict as a context for understanding maternal beliefs about child rearing and children's misbehavior* (pp. 43–59). San Francisco: Jossey-Bass.

Hastings, P., and Grusec, J. E. (1998). Parenting goals as organizers of responses to parent–child disagreement. *Developmental Psychology, 34*, 465–479.

Heider, F. (1944). Social perception and phenomenal causality. *Psychological Review, 51*, 358–374.

Himelstein, S., Graham, S., and Weiner, B. (1991). An attributional analysis of maternal beliefs about the importance of child-rearing practices. *Child Development, 62*, 301–310.

Hofstede, G. (1998). The cultural construction of gender. In G. Hofstede (Ed.), *Masculinity and femininity: The taboo dimension of national cultures* (pp. 77–105). Thousand Oaks, CA: Sage.

Holden, G. W., and Edwards, L. A. (1989). Parental attitudes toward childrearing: Instruments, issues, and implications. *Psychological Bulletin, 106*, 29–58.

Hubbard, F. O. A., and Van IJzendoorn, M. H. (1991). Maternal unresponsiveness and infant crying across the first 9 months: A naturalistic longitudinal study. *Infant Behavior and Development, 14*, 229–312.

Janssens, J. M. A. M. (1994). Authoritarian child rearing, parental locus of control, and the child's behaviour style. *International Journal of Behavioral Development, 17*, 485–501.

Johnston, C. (1996). Addressing parent cognitions in interventions with families of disruptive children. In K. S. Dobson and K. D. Craig (Eds.), *Advances in cognitive–behavioral therapy* (Vol. 2, pp. 193–209). Thousand Oaks, CA: Sage.

Johnston, C., and Freeman, W. (1997). Attributions for child behavior inparents of children without behavior disorders and children with Attention Deficit–Hyperactivity Disorder. *Journal of Consulting and Clinical Psychology, 65*, 636–645.

Johnston, C., Reynolds, S., Freeman, W. S., and Geller, J. (1998). Assessing parent attributions for child behavior using open-ended questions. *Journal of Consulting and Clinical Psychology, 27*, 87–97.

Joiner, T. E., Jr., and Wagner, K. D. (1996). Parental, child-centered attributions and outcome: A meta-analytic review with conceptual and methodological implications. *Journal of Abnormal Child Psychology, 24*, 37–52.

Kalyanpur, M., and Harry, B. (1999). *Culture in special education.* Baltimore: Brookes.

Kelley, H. H. (1967). Attribution theory in social psychology. *Nebraska Symposium on Motivation, 15*, 197–238.

Kisanji, J. (1995). Interface between culture and disability in the Tanzanian context: I. *International Journal of Disability, Development and Education, 42*, 93–108.

Lazarus, R. S. (1991). Progress on a cognitive–motivational–relational theory of emotion. *American Psychologist, 46*, 819–834.

Levenson, H. (1973). Perceived parental antecedents of internal powerful others, and chance locus of control orientations. *Developmental Psychology, 9*, 260–265.

Levy-Shiff, R., Dimitrowsky, L., Shulman, S., and Har-Even, D. (1998). Cognitive appraisals, coping strategies, and supportive resources as correlates of parenting and infant development. *Developmental Psychology, 34*, 1417–1427.

Lewis, J. C., Bugental, D. B., and Fleck, K. (1991). Beliefs as moderators of reactions to computer-simulated responsive and unresponsive children. *Social Cognition, 9*, 277–293.

Lieberman, A. (1999). Negative maternal attributions: Effects on toddlers' sense of self. *Psychoanalytic Inquiry, 19*, 737–756.

Lovejoy, M. C., Polewko, J., and Harrison, B. (1996). Adult perceptions of interpersonal control and reactions to disruptive child behaviors. *Social Cognition, 14*, 227–245.

Maccoby, E. E., and Jacklin, C. N. (1974). *The psychology of sex differences.* Stanford, CA: Stanford University Press.

MacKinnon, C. E., Lewis, C., Lamb, M. E., Arbuckle, B., Baradaran, L. P., and Volling, B. L. (1992). The relationship between biased maternal and filial attributions and the aggressiveness of their interactions. *Developmental Psychopathology, 4*, 403–415.

MacKinnon, C. E., Volling, B. L., Lamb, M. E., Dechman, K., Rabiner, D., and Curtner, M. E. (1994). A cross-contextual analysis of boys' social competence from family to school. *Developmental Psychology, 30*, 325–333.

Mardiros, M. (1989). Conception of childhood disability among Mexican-American parents. *Medical Anthropology, 12*, 55–68.

Margolin, G., and Gordis, E. B. (2000). The effects of family and community violence on children. *Annual Review of Psychology, 51*, 445–479,

Mash, E., and Johnston, C. (1990). Determinants of parenting stress: Illustrations from families of hyperactive children and families of physically abused children. *Journal of Clinical Child Psychology, 19*, 313–328.

Mickelson, K. D., Wroble, M., and Helgeson, V. S. (1999). "Why my child?": Parental attributions for children's special needs. *Journal of Applied Social Psychology, 29*, 1263–1292.

Miller, S. A. (1995). Parental attributions for their children's behavior. *Child Development, 66*, 1557–1584.

Mills, R. S. L. (1999). Exploring the effects of low power schemas in mothers. In P. D. Hastings and C. C. Piotrowski (Eds.), *New directions for child development: Maternal beliefs about child-rearing and children's misbehavior: The causes and effects of beliefs in conflict situations* (pp. 61–78). San Francisco: Jossey-Bass.

Milner, J. S., and Foody, R. (1994). The impact of mitigating information on attributions for positive and negative child behavior by adults at low and high risk for child-abusive behavior. *Journal of Social and Clinical Psychology, 13*, 335–351.

Mischel, W., and Shoda, Y. (1995). A cognitive–affective-system theory of personality: Reconceptualizing situations, dispositions, dynamics, and invariance in personality structure. *Psychological Review, 102*, 246–268.

Murray, S. L., and Holmes, J. G. (1997). A leap of faith? Positive illusions in romantic relationships. *Personality and Social Psychology Bulletin, 23*, 586–604.

Nelson, K. (1993). Events, narratives, memory: What develops? In C. A. Nelson (Ed.), *Memory and affect in development. Minnesota symposia on child psychology* (Vol. 26, pp. 1–24). Hillsdale, NJ: Lawrence Erlbaum Associates.

Neumann, R. (2000). The causal influences of attributions on emotions: A procedural priming approach. *Psychological Science, 11*, 179–182.

Nix, R. L., Pinderhughes, E. E., Dodge, K. A., Bates, J. E., and Pettit, G. S. (1999). Do parents' hostile attribution tendencies function as self-fulfilling prophecies? An empirical examination of aggressive transactions. *Child Development, 70*, 896–909.

Nowicki, S., and Segal, W. (1974). Perceived parental characteristics, locus of control orientation, and behavioral correlates of locus of control. *Developmental Psychology, 10*, 33–37.

O'Sullivan, J. T., and Howe, M. L. (1996). Causal attributions and reading achievement: Individual differences in low-income families. *Contemporary Educational Psychology, 21*, 363–387.

Palacios, J., and Moreno, M. C. (1996). Parents' and adolescents' ideas on children, origins and transmission of intracultural diversity. In S. Harkness and C. M. Super (Eds.), *Parents' cultural belief systems: Their origins, expressions, and consequences* (pp. 215–253). New York: Guilford.

Peterson, C. (2000). The future of optimism. *American Psychologist, 55*, 44–55.

Pratto, F., and John, O. P. (1991). Automatic vigilance: The attention-grabbing power of negative social information. *Journal of Personality and Social Psychology, 61*, 380–391.

Reznick, J. S. (1999). Influences on maternal attribution of infant intentionality. In P. D. Zelazo, J. W. Astington, and D. R. Olson (Eds.), *Developing theories of intention: Social understanding and self-control* (pp. 243–367). Mahwah, NJ: Lawrence Erlbaum Associates.

Roberts, M. W., Joe, V. C., and Rowe-Halbert, A. (1992). Oppositional child behavior and parental locus of control. *Journal of Clinical Child Psychology, 21*, 170–177.

Rotter, J. B. (1966). Generalized expectancies for internal versus external control of reinforcement. *Psychological Monographs, 80*.

Rudy, D. D., and Grusec, J. E. (1999). Parenting cognitions and parent–child conflict: Current issues and future directions. In P. D. Hastings and C. C. Piotrowski (Eds.), *New directions for child development: Maternal beliefs about child-rearing and children's misbehavior: The causes and effects of beliefs in conflict situations* (pp. 79–90). San Francisco: Jossey-Bass.

Sameroff, A. (1975). Transactional models in early social relations. *Human Development, 18*, 65–79.

Scheier, M. F., and Carver, C. S. (1993). On the power of positive thinking: The benefits of being optimistic. *Current Directions in Psychological Science, 2*, 26–30.

Seligman, M. E. P. (1992). Power and powerlessness: Comments on "Cognates of personal control." *Applied and Preventive Psychology, 1*, 119–120.

Seligman, M. E. P., and Csikszentmihaly, M. (2000). Positive psychology: An introduction. *American Psychologist, 55*, 5–14.

Seligman, M. E. P., Peterson, C., Kaslow, N. J., Tanenbaum, R. L., Alloy, L. B., and Abramson, L. Y. (1984). Attribution style and depressive symptoms among children. *Journal of Abnormal Psychology, 93*, 235–238.

Seligman, M. E. P., Reivich, K., Jaycox, L., and Gillham, J. (1995). *The optimistic child.* Boston: Houghton Mifflin.

Sidanius, J., and Pratto, F. (1999). *Social dominance: An intergroup theory of social hierarchy and oppression.* New York: Cambridge University Press.

Silvester, J., Bentovim, A., Stratton, P., and Hanks, H. G. (1995). I. Using spoken attributions to classify abusive families. *Child Abuse and Neglect, 19*, 1221–1232.

Sirignano, S. W., and Lachman, M. E. (1985). Personality change during the transition to parenthood: The role of perceived infant temperament. *Developmental Psychology, 21*, 558–567.

Slep, A. M. S., and O'Leary, S. G. (1998). The effects of maternal attributions on parenting: an experimental analysis. *Journal of Family Psychology, 12*, 234–243.

Smetana, J. G. (1995). Morality in context: Abstractions, ambiguities, and applications. In R. Vasta (Ed.), *Annals of child development* (Vol. 10, pp. 83–130). London: Kingsely.

Smetana, J. G. (1997). Parenting and the development of social knowledge reconceptualized: A social domain analysis. In J. E. Grusec and L. Kuczynski (Eds.), *Parenting and the internalization of values* (pp. 162–192). New York: Wiley.

Smith, A. M., and O'Leary, S. G. (1995). Attributions and arousal as predictors of maternal discipline. *Cognitive Therapy and Research, 19*, 459–471.

Spangler, G., and Grossman, K. E. (1993). Biobehavioral organization in securely and insecurely attached infants. *Child Development, 64*, 1439–1450.

Stevenson, H. W., Chen, C., and Uttal, D. H. (1990). Beliefs and achievement: A study of Black, White, and Hispanic children. *Child Development, 61*, 508–523.

Stevenson, H. W., Lee, S., Chen, C., Stigler, J. W., Hsu, C. C., and Kitamura, S. (1990). Contexts of achievement: A study of American, Chinese, and Japanese children. *Monographs of the Society for Research in Child Development, 55*.

Stratton, P., Head, D., Hanks, H. G., and Munton, A. G. (1986). Coding causal beliefs in natural discourse. *British Journal of Social Psychology, 25*, 299–313.

Stratton, P., and Swaffer, R. (1988). Maternal causal beliefs for abused and handicapped children. *Journal of Reproductive and Infant Psychology, 6*, 201–216.

Taylor, S. E. (1991). Asymmetrical effects of positive and negative events: The mobilization–minimization hypothesis. *Psychological Bulletin, 110*, 67–85.

Taylor, S. E., Kemeny, M. E., Reed, G. M., Bower, J. E., and Gruenewald, T. L. (2000). Psychological resources, positive illusions, and health. *American Psychologist, 55*, 99–109.

Tennen, H., Affleck, G., and Gershman, K. (1986). Self-blame among parents with perinatal complications. The role of self-protective outcomes. *Journal of Personality and Social Psychology, 50*, 690–696.

Teti, D. M., and Gelfand, D. M. (1991). Behavioral competence among mothers of infants in the first year: The mediational role of maternal self-efficacy. *Child Development, 62*, 918–929.

Turiel, E. (1983). *The development of social knowledge: Morality and convention.* Cambridge, England: Cambridge University Press.

Turiel, E. (1998). Moral development. In W. Damon (Series Ed.) and N. Eisenberg (Vol. Ed.), *Handbook of child psychology: Volume 3. Social, emotional, and personality development* (pp. 863–932). New York: Wiley.

Tuss, P., Zimmer, J., and Ho, H. (1995). Causal attributions of underachieving fourth grade students in China, Japan, and the United States. *Journal of Cross-Cultural Psychology, 26*, 408–425.

Van IJzendoorn, M. H. (1995). Adult attachment representations, parental responsiveness, and infant attachment: A meta-analysis on the predictive validity of the Adult Attachment Interview. *Psychological Bulletin, 117*, 387–403.

Weiner, B. (1985). An attributional theory of achievement motivation. *Psychological Review, 92*, 548–573.

Weiner, B. (1986). *An attributional theory of motivation and emotion.* New York: Springer-Verlag.

Weiner, B. (1993). A theory of perceived responsibility and social motivation. *American Psychologist, 48*, 957–965.

Weiner, B., Perry, R., and Magnusson, J. (1988). An attributional analysis of reactions to stigmas. *Journal of Personality and Social Psychology, 55*, 738–748.

Wong, P., and Weiner, B. (1981). When do people ask "why" questions, and the heuristics of attributional search. *Journal of Personality and Social Psychology, 19*, 650–681.

19

Parental Attitudes Toward Childrearing

George W. Holden
M. Jeanell Buck
University of Texas at Austin

INTRODUCTION

For much of the twentieth century, childrearing attitudes enjoyed the role of being the preeminent parenting construct. Researchers in the first half of that century believed that attitudes of parents held the key for unraveling the mystery of human development. How could childrearing attitudes reveal so much? Early investigators believed that childrearing attitudes determined parental behavior as well as more subtle family nuances such as the emotional climate (Darling and Steinberg, 1993). In turn, parental behavior was thought to determine child outcome in a unidirectional way (Holden, 1997). Consequently, the key for understanding development, it was believed in the 1930s through the 1950s, was to focus on childrearing attitudes.

What exactly is this psychological construct that was believed to be so powerful? Attitudes are a component of social cognition that refers to a tendency, internal state, or explicit evaluations of an "attitude object" (Eagly, 1992). This internal state biases or predisposes an individual toward reacting favorably or unfavorably to the entity or object. Although attitudes are closely related to other aspects of social cognition, such as knowledge and beliefs, attributions, expectations, and perceptions, attitudes represent a distinct class of thoughts. In the task of childrearing, it is reasonable to assume that parents do indeed develop attitudes about such considerations as breastfeeding, "spoiling" an infant, use of corporal punishment, parental involvement, and a wide range of other topics. Therefore, it follows that attitudes should hold considerable importance in parenting as these thoughts presumably guide how parents think and rear their children.

Although childrearing attitudes continue to be widely investigated, over the past two decades they have been dethroned from their once lofty research perch. Researchers now have a more realistic understanding of what attitudes can and cannot reveal. But at the same time, childrearing attitudes are undergoing an identity crisis. Their stature as a fundamental childrearing construct has been chipped away by the oft-cited recognition of methodological problems, the uncertain relation they hold to behavior, and the apparent promise of new social cognition constructs.

This chapter will examine the rise, current status, and future of childrearing attitudes. The review begins with a brief history of research into childrearing attitudes, followed by a summary of the childrearing attitude research in the 1990s. Their current status will then be evaluated. The final section of the chapter outlines several directions for future research.

THE RISE OF CHILDREARING ATTITUDES

The notion of attitudes was one of the first psychological constructs to attract widespread appeal. According to the *Oxford English Dictionary* (1933), Herbert Spencer was the first psychologist to use the term *attitude* in his book *First Principles*, originally published in 1862. When discussing the conflict between science and religion, he wrote, "Arriving at correct judgements on disputed questions, much depends on the attitude of mind we preserve while listening to, or taking part in, the controversy ... " (Spencer, 1896, p. 4). The construct rapidly gained popularity and became incorporated into the work of prominent American theorists, including James Mark Baldwin, John Dewey, William James, and George Herbert Mead. Experimental psychologists in the Wurzburg school, in Germany, pioneered the study of attitudes in the laboratory by using reaction time measurements. By the 1920s, social and experimental psychologists in the United States were investigating a wide variety of attitudes, such as attitudes toward crime, sexual practices, pacifism, and people from different nationalities or racial groups (e.g., Thurstone, 1931).

Investigations into parental childrearing attitudes were present almost at the beginning of American psychology. Sears (1899), in collaboration with G. Stanley Hall, developed a questionnaire to assess 486 adults' opinions about punishment for children. Questions concerned topics such as the purpose of punishment, punishable and nonpunishable offenses, and opinions about "breaking the will." The results consisted of lists of responses and some quotes from parents; no descriptive statistics were included. For example, Sears reported that attitudes toward misbehaviors regarded as most punishable were those perceived as intentional, persistent, or due to repeated carelessness.

The first systematic study of parents published in North America focused on assessing parental attitudes. In her Columbia University dissertation, Laws (1927) recruited 50 mothers enrolled in a parent education class. Each mother filled out four different "tests" concerning their childrearing attitudes. A total of 346 questions assessed attitudes toward particular childrearing practices (e.g., breastfeeding, spanking, and nagging), attitudes toward interacting with their children (e.g., affectionate, calm, and critical), perceptions of their children's current behavior (e.g., sleeps quietly at night or teases playmates), and attitudes toward 56 nouns or verbs associated with parenting (e.g., authority, cooperation, noise, and coddling). Among the descriptive results, she found that most of the mothers thought that they should never ridicule (90%) or humiliate (82%) the child, nor should they keep the child "tied to apron strings" (78%) or "throw cold water" on the child's enthusiasms (80%). Laws recognized a number of limitations with the approach (e.g., multiple interpretation of items, inclusion of abstract concepts, and multiple determinants of attitudes) but nevertheless concluded that "It is practicable to develop relatively objective means of rating the attitudes and practices of parents ... " (p. 32).

The early proponents of the study of parents' childrearing attitudes pledged that merely by uncovering childrearing attitudes the secret of children's development would be revealed. For example, one early advocate accurately recognized that attitudes were "impalpable and intangible" but also they were of key importance for "fashioning the lives of our children" (Glueck, 1927, pp. 3–4). Attitudes began to be considered of key importance for revealing the "destiny" of children.

Psychiatrists were particularly excited about the construct. They saw attitudes as largely unconscious in nature with potent outcomes. Richards (1926, p. 226) opined the "common parental attitudes that do a great deal of damage in the way of warping the development of children." Another psychiatrist predicted "How successfully a given individual will traverse the path from the asocial and amoral state of infancy to an adequately socialized adulthood . . . will depend more on the character and wisdom and attitudes of his parents than on anything else" (Glueck, 1928, p. 741). Before long, attitudes ascended into first place among determinants of children's development. Attitudes were more important than childrearing behavior because they transcended behavior. "Parental attitudes must be of paramount importance because the very young child is exposed to them continually, and the attitudes themselves are relatively fixed and constant" (Pearson, 1931, p. 290).

The assessment—and influence—of attitudes continued to grow rapidly during the 1930s. One pioneer was John Stogdill, who developed four parent attitude questionnaires designed to assess parents' attitudes toward undesirable child behavior, parental control, and the effect of parental practices on children (Stogdill, 1931, 1934, 1936a, 1936b). Before long, investigators were exploring various other childrearing attitudes. Studies assessed such topics as attitudes toward pregnancy (Despres, 1937), sex education (Ackerley, 1935), self-reliance in children (Ojemann, 1935), and independence in children (Koch, Dentler, Dysart, and Streit, 1934). These investigators set the stage for making childrearing attitudes a fundamental construct in the study of parent–child relationships. By the 1940s, researchers were focusing their attention on the parents and parental attitudes. Efforts at diagnosing problematic parent–child relationships centered on the parents. The logic was expressed as follows (Field, 1940, p. 293):

> We recognize more and more that we are dealing with problem environments and problem parents rather than problem children. . . . The parents' experiences, their attitudes and behavior, influence the character and behavior of the children, who in turn carry over these attitudes into their later lives, their marital adjustments and in relation to their own families. Thus a vicious circle is created.

Childrearing attitudes, as a psychological construct, reached their apex in the 1950s. The significance of parental attitudes was so well accepted that the following statement could be made: "The importance of parental attitudes in the development of personal and social behavior is one of the *basic tenets* in the fields of child development and parent education" (Burchinal, Hawkes, and Gardner, 1957, p. 65, italics added).

Given these and other pronouncements about the importance of parental attitudes, researchers from a variety of backgrounds with wide ranging interests joined the childrearing attitudes bandwagon. Investigations into clinical, community, counseling, cross-cultural, educational, personality, school, and social psychology all adopted parental attitudes as an essential construct. Childrearing attitudes were used both as independent and dependent variables to quantify the social environment, study interindividual family differences, identify differences between groups of individuals, screen individuals at risk for maladaptive parenting, assess the effects of intervention programs, examine parental correlates of child pathology, and address a wide range of other research questions.

In addition to the psychological research, the other major rootstock of interest in attitudes derived from Freud's psychoanalytic theory. Freud saw attitudes, stemming from the unconscious, as the source of love, rejection, and many other proclivities toward children. Although Freud devoted few words to parents' attitudes and their effects on children (e.g., Freud, 1936), his disciples including Jones (1923), Horney (1933), and Ribble (1943) each gave prominent attention to parental attitudes.

Writings regarding childrearing attitudes through the first half of the last century made frequent references to or included discussions of the relation between the unconscious and childrearing attitudes (see review by Brody, 1956; Cohler, Grunebaum, Weiss, Hartman, and Gallant, 1976). For example, Horney (1933) believed that unconscious emotional reactions to one's own parents could impact one's conscious childrearing attitudes. Middlemore (1941) argued that mothers' attitude toward breastfeeding was determined chiefly by unconscious infantile oral fantasies. And a final example was published in 1953: Coleman, Kris, and Provence (1953) argued that unconscious parental conflicts were a key instigator of change in parental attitudes. However, with the waning of Freudian influence, discussion of unconscious influences on attitudes all but disappeared.

The major legacy of the psychoanalytic theory to parental childrearing attitudes has been in the area of parental overprotection. The basic premise was that the normal "attitude" of the parent is one of affection. However, if the parents' emotional needs had not been met at some point in their development, then parents would carry these unresolved needs into their childrearing behavior. These needs were then thought to appear in the form of overprotection or rejection of the child, according to the psychiatrist Levy (1943, p. 3):

> It is generally accepted that the most potent of all influences on social behavior is derived from the primary social experience with the mother. If a mother maintains toward the child a consistent attitude of, let us say, indifference and hostility, the assumption is made that the child's personality is greatly affected thereby. His outlook on life, his attitude toward people, his entire psychic well-being, and his destiny are presumed to be altered by the maternal attitude. . . . If human behavior is influenced so markedly by maternal attitudes, then surely the most important study of man as a social being is a study of his mother's influence on his early life.

The study of maternal overprotection—defined as the prolonging of infantile care through excessive control—was believed to be caused by one of several different possible reasons. Most prominent of these antecedents was rejection by one's own parents. Subsequently, the concept of overprotection was supplanted by the conceptually simpler constructs of acceptance and rejection. Interest in the causes and consequences of parental acceptance or rejection has continued steadily since the 1930s; by now over 800 studies have been published on the topic (Rohner, 1986).

The study of overprotection and rejection led the way for a variety of other childrearing attitudinal "excesses" to be investigated. Childrearing attitudes of anxiety, authority, indulgence, perfectionism, permissiveness, responsibility, solicitude, and strictness all began to receive attention in the 1930s (see reviews by Bakwin and Bakwin, 1942; Symonds, 1949). This work resulted in a new clinical orientation for parents called attitude therapy, designed to modify errant parental attitudes (Garrett, 1936).

The model of parental childrearing attitudes shared by the psychologists and psychiatrists was simplistic yet held a powerful appeal. Once you understood the core philosophy that guides a parent's childrearing you could then understand both parental behavior and the child's development. The unidirectional, deterministic relation can be diagrammed as:

Parental Attitudes $\longrightarrow$ Parental Behavior $\longrightarrow$ Child Outcome

Admittedly, not all of the early psychologists accepted such a simple model of development. Some researchers recognized that parental attitudes did not necessarily reflect behavior but could be better conceived of as filters that indirectly affected parental behavior. Nevertheless, parental attitudes were often considered to be a useful proxy of a child's home environment (e.g., Francis and Fillmore, 1934; Updegraff, 1939). Whatever way someone chose to view parental attitudes, the common denominator was the great importance attached to the construct. Consequently, the assessment of a wide variety of childrearing attitudes became the popular focus of parenting research.

Childrearing attitudes occupied prominent roles in all the classic childrearing studies from the 1940s through the early 1970s (e.g., Baldwin, Kalhorn, and Breese, 1945; Baumrind, 1971; Sears, Maccoby, and Levin, 1957; Sears, Rau, and Alpert, 1965). Sears and his colleagues (1957, p. 470) concluded that "The pattern of any mother's child-rearing practices and attitudes is as individual as her fingerprints."

Those and other classic studies helped to establish childrearing attitudes as an indispensable and fundamental variable for the study of childrearing. Those studies represented the green light to expand the inventory of attitudes studied. Indeed the range of attitudes assessed is impressive. By

TABLE 19.1
Alphabetical Listing of the Childrearing Attitudes Assessed in the Literature

Acceptance	Early maturity demands	Physical punishment
Achievement	Effect of parent on child	Play
Actual and ideal parenting	Efficacy	Pleasure, arousal
Adaptive attitudes	Emotional needs	Possessiveness
Adolescent mothers	Employment orientation	Protectiveness
Affection	Encouragement of independence	Providing sex information
Aggravation	Exclusive maternal care	Punishments and rewards
Aggression	Expressing affect	Punitiveness
Amount of independence		
Anxiety	Feeding	Racial–social awareness
Approval	Flexibility	Reaction to deviant behavior
Approval of control/freedom	Frustration	Reasoning
Assertiveness		Rejection
Authoritarian parenting	Goals	Rejection of pregnancy and mother
Authoritarianism		Responsibility
Authority	Home practices	Responsiveness
Autocratic orientation	Hostility	Restrictive, mixed, analytical, and
Autonomy in children		neutral parenting
	Ignoring	Restrictiveness
Belief in fate	Importance of a father	Rigidity
	Importance of various	Role of socioeconomic status
Categorical thinking	influences on child's	
Causation	social competence	Same and cross-sexed behavior
Child abuse proneness	Indulgence	Self-reliance in children
Child centeredness	parenting skills	Sibling relations
Communication		Strict discipline
Conformity	Malicious intent	
Consistency of parenting	Manifest rejection	Teaching and learning
Control	Marital conflict	Traditional orientation
Control toward child's emotionality	Maternal adjustment	
and expressiveness		Understanding
Coping	Need for approval	Undesirable child behavior
Creativity	Neglect	Use of fear for child control
Cultural differences	Nontraditional parenting	
	Nurturance	Warmth
Democratic orientation	Obedience	Weaning
Determinism	Objectivity	Worry
Developmental importance of	Oral activities	
parent on child actions	Overinvolvement	
Directiveness	Overprotection	
Discipline	Perfectionism	
Dominance	Permissive parenting	
	Permissiveness	

our count, almost 100 different attitudes are quantifiable by one or more instruments. These range from acceptance to worry (see Table 19.1 for an alphabetic listing). These attitudes can be sorted into three categories: (1) attitudes that primarily focus on the parents' characteristics or orientation toward their own children (e.g., acceptance, coping, and rejection), (2) attitudes that focus on perceptions of their children or the children's development (e.g., achievement, obedience, and sibling relations), and (3) attitudes that concern parents' views about environmental influences on development (e.g., employment orientation, importance of father, and marital conflict). Fifty-four percent of the attitudes assess qualities or characteristics of the parent, 37% focus on orientations toward the child or the child's development, and the remaining attitudes concern parental orientations toward developmental influences.

CHANGING ATTITUDES TOWARD CHILDREARING ATTITUDES

Despite the popularity of attitudes in developmental research, signs of dissatisfaction with the construct had been mounting, primarily in the area of the attitude–behavior link. Early warnings were first heard back in the late 1950s when Gordon (1957) and then others (e.g., Zunich, 1962) were unable to find links between attitudes and behavior. Despite the importance of the issue, Holden and Edwards (1989) found only a dozen studies that provided data on the link. And those studies can readily be faulted on such grounds as inadequate samples of participants and behavior or limited assessments of vague, global attitudes. Despite the limitations of the database, what evidence was available did not provide compelling evidence that attitudes were closely affiliated with behavior.

Additional concern about the dubious nature of the attitude–behavior link was sounded by Radke-Yarrow and her colleagues (Radke-Yarrow, Campell, and Burton, 1968) when their thorough and systematic examination of the associations between childrearing variables and child outcomes was unsuccessful. They observed: "In general, we have to conclude that studies of childrearing . . . have not done very well in delivering up the secrets of socialization processes . . . . The reasons for this failure of findings to add up in convincing fashion seem to be many—many of which are methodological in nature" (p. 151).

Social psychology, the intellectual home of attitude research, has also been home base to many critiques of the construct of attitudes (e.g., Campbell, 1963; Festinger, 1964). One critique that galvanized much negative opinion was published by Wicker (1969). He reviewed 42 studies and concluded that little support could be found for the idea that stable attitudes influence overt behavior. Wicker's analysis was "superficial" (Eagly and Chaiken, 1993, p. 156) but influential. It served to stimulate considerable new work in the area of attitude–behavior relations. At the same time, it did considerable damage to the concept of attitudes as many social scientists took that review as the final word and the death blow to attitudes.

Nevertheless, childrearing attitude research in developmental science continued largely oblivious to the ongoing debate about the utility of attitudes in social psychology. If developmentalists had been more widely read they might have been tempted to abandon the construct. Instead, parenting researchers continued studying childrearing attitudes largely the same way it had been done since the 1940s. That maintenance of the status quo led to a critique of childrearing attitudes by Holden and Edwards (1989). They analyzed the quality of the more than 100 instruments intended to assess parental attitudes. A range of methodological and conceptual problems were identified. Among those problems were basic questionnaire design issues (e.g., vague words, phrasing in the third person, lack of situational specificity, use of "double-barreled" questions), problematic conceptual underpinnings (outmoded concepts, attitudes as unidirectional and preexisting, attitudes as deterministic of behavior), and lack of reliability and validity data. They concluded that given the many problems inherent in most of the childrearing attitude instruments, they should be abandoned in favor of more sophisticated instruments.

To gauge whether attitudes toward childrearing attitudes have indeed changed, we examined the number of publications that included the construct. We considered this analysis to provide a rough indication of researchers' attitude toward childrearing attitudes. Yearly publication citations were counted (using the key word *childrearing attitudes* and limited to publications in English) in *Psychological Abstracts* from 1960s and 1970s and PsychInfo from the 1980s and 1990s. The average number of articles or dissertations per year concerning childrearing attitudes was then computed for each decade, and these averages are displayed in Figure 19.1. The average rate for the 1960s was 7.5, jumped up to 26 for the 1970s, and continued to rise to a high of 39.8 for the 1980s. The 1990s saw a decrease to an annual average of 28.8. (The dramatic increase in the average from the 1960s to the 1970s is in part real but in part an artifact of new indexing procedures at *Psychological Abstracts*; many more journals were included in the abstracts beginning in 1970.)

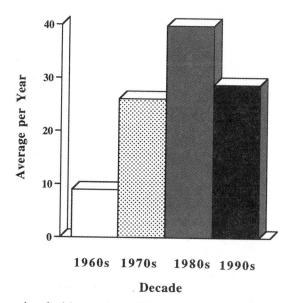

FIGURE 19.1. Average number of articles containing childrearing attitudes published per year per decade.

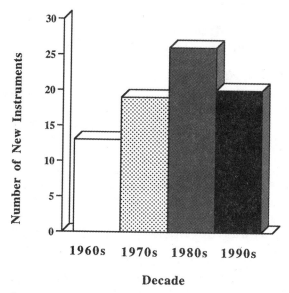

FIGURE 19.2. Number of new childrearing attitude instruments published per decade.

Another index of the status of childrearing attitudes is the number of new attitude instruments created during a particular time span. Using the data from Holden and Edwards (1989), the most prolific years for new attitude instruments were the 1980s, when 26 new instruments were published in just a 7 year period (1980 to 1986; see Figure 19.2). In contrast, according to Dix and Gershoff (2000), only 20 new instruments that focused exclusively, or in part, on childrearing attitudes were published in the final decade of the century. These new instruments address a range of new as well as seasoned attitudes, including foster parenting, corporal punishment, childbearing, supervising children, and the degree of liking children.

TABLE 19.2
Childrearing Attitude Topics: 1990–2000

Topics	# of Articles
Adolescent mothers	13
Child abuse	3
Child outcomes	13
Cross-cultural issues	61
Gender issues	7
Intergenerational transmission	10
Miscellaneous	7
Nontraditional family structure	9
Parent characteristics	7
Parent education	9
Parental functioning	11
Physical discipline	7
Reviews/new conceptualization	9
Special-needs children	14

CURRENT STATUS OF RESEARCH ON CHILDREARING ATTITUDES

Given this continued work, albeit at a decreased volume, what have childrearing attitudes revealed about parenting and child development? To summarize the work over the last decade, we used the data from the PsychInfo search described above. Despite the downward trend in the frequency of papers published that included childrearing attitudes as a keyword, an ample number of articles were found. A total of 181 articles were published over the past decade related to childrearing attitudes.[1] We then sorted those articles into topics. Although some articles could be multiply categorized, the sort was based on the primary focus of the article. Fourteen categories emerged and are listed in Table 19.2.

It is instructive to examine the frequency with which different topics were addressed. The single most active category was ethnic and cross-cultural studies, with a total of 61 articles. Bornstein (1991) identified many of the reasons why cross-cultural parenting studies are popular. These include satisfying basic curiosity, testing environmental influences on development, and getting a fresh perspective on development. Whatever reason motivated them, researchers have been able to readily identify a variety of attitudinal differences across countries or cultures. The next three most popular categories had far fewer entries. The categories of adolescent mothers, child outcomes, and special-needs children (e.g., those with handicaps or chronic illness) each had 13 or 14 articles. The next eight categories had between seven and eleven exemplars. These included the functioning of parents (e.g., predictors of satisfaction and attributions), reviews or conceptualizations of parenting, intergenerational transmission of parenting, nontraditional family structure (fathers as primary caregivers and homosexual parents), parent education, gender issues, parent characteristics, and discipline. Excluding cross-cultural investigations into child abuse, only three articles addressed childrearing attitudes in abusive parents.

Compared with prior attitude research summarized in Holden (1995), fewer studies focused on such topics as maternal adjustment, maternal employment, children's intelligence and achievement, and fathers. Sustained research attention was seen in such areas as cross-cultural studies, discipline, adolescent mothers, gender issues, intergenerational transmission of parenting, parent education, and children's outcomes. In the past decade, more research attention has been initiated into the applied

---

[1] To limit the search to a manageable number, we used the key words *childrearing attitudes, mothers' attitudes*, and *fathers' attitudes*. We did not include *parental attitudes*, which would have increased the number of references to an unmanageable number.

topics of special needs children such as those with sickle cell disease (e.g., Schuman, Armstrong, Pegelow, and Routh, 1993) and nontraditional parents such as immigrant parents (e.g., Gorman, 1998).

Three of the central questions concerning childrearing attitudes are: What are the determinants of attitudes? How do attitudes relate to childrearing behavior and, in turn, child outcome? Do attitudes change and if so, how? New information about those questions that has been learned over the past decade will be reviewed below.

Influences on Attitudes

Just as the determinants of parental behavior come from a variety of sources (Holden, 1997), there is increasing evidence that childrearing attitudes are also multiply determined. For example, as Palacios (1990) found when he investigated influences on Spanish parents' childrearing attitudes, systematic effects could be attributed to parents' gender, their level of education, the number of children that they had, and whether they lived in an urban or rural setting. In contrast to Palacios' study, most of the work that examined influences on attitudes focused on one of three topics. As indicated above, cross-cultural attitude studies have been popular. A second topic is cross-national studies, or studies that look at socioeconomic group or subgroup differences. One new type of attitudinal influence appeared at least occasionally in the 1990s—child effects. Those studies focused on how parental attitudes are impacted by children's characteristics or behavior. Findings from studies into each of those three types of determinants are discussed further below.

Cross-cultural comparisons.   The single largest category of childrearing attitudes concerned cultural influences. A variety of culture-based attitudes has been assessed, as the examples below indicate. One of the most fundamental attitudes concerns the centrality of children for a fulfilled life. Out of this attitude comes lifestyle decisions, level of involvement in childrearing, and perhaps the degree of child-centeredness that parents exhibit. This attitude was examined cross-culturally by Jones and Brayfield (1997) in 6,679 adults in six Western European countries (Austria, Great Britain, Ireland, Italy, Netherlands, and West Germany). Results revealed that Italians and Austrians held the most favorable attitudes toward the centrality of children. Adults in West Germany, Ireland, and Great Britain had slightly below average attitudes toward the centrality of children, and Dutch adults had the least favorable attitudes. In general, women and men with more egalitarian views had less favorable attitudes toward the centrality of children, as well as younger people in general. Not surprisingly, parents, in comparison to nonparents, held more favorable views about the necessity of children for a happy life. It was also found that parents who maintained religious affiliations had more positive attitudes toward children than other parents.

Bornstein et al. (1996) studied parenting attitudes and other social cognitions (i.e., beliefs, self-perceptions, and expectations) in three countries (Argentina, France, and the United States). Among their findings was that American mothers emphasized the importance of limit setting more than Argentine and French mothers. It was surprising that Argentine mothers had less positive attitudes toward limit setting than American mothers, given the Argentines tended to support an authoritarian parenting style (Bornstein et al., 1996).

In a subsequent study, Bornstein et al. (1998) extended the research on cross-cultural parenting attitudes by adding four additional countries (Belgium, Israel, Italy, and Japan) to the earlier three countries. In all seven countries, mothers considered the child's behavior as an important factor when considering child outcomes, but they also recognized that their own parenting abilities would play a key role if parenting fails. At the same time, some of the cross-national differences were quite remarkable. Argentine mothers had little faith in their parenting abilities and thought that they would succeed at parenting only when the task was not difficult. In contrast, Israeli mothers found parenting to be relatively easy and uncomplicated. French mothers did not consider effort to be very important when it comes to parenting success. They also had negative attitudes toward parent training, preferring to rely on intuition. The views of Japanese mothers contrasted starkly. Their attitude reflected the view that success in parenting was accomplished through effort rather than through their own abilities. Italian mothers took an interactionist viewpoint: effective childrearing was due to the effort of the parent as well as the difficulty of the task.

Attitudes about the role children play in their own development have also been shown to reflect cultural-specific constructs. Parents in Nso of northwest Cameroon believe that their children are largely responsible for their own learning and, consequently, need little formal instruction (Nsamenang and Lamb, 1995). According to Nso parents' attitudes, observational learning accounts for most of how children become educated and socialized. Through this process they then learn their role in society, and only then begin to act in the appropriate way.

Parental attitudes have also been investigated in order to examine culture-specific views of child maltreatment. For example, a study was conducted in Bangladesh to investigate the high rate of abandoned babies. It was concluded that the widespread negative attitude toward unwed mothers was the likely reason that up to 50% of abandoned babies came from single mothers (Wilson, 1999). The Republic of Palau, a small cluster of islands in the northern Pacific ocean, is home to some childrearing practices that are unusual by American standards. When a parent needs to go somewhere, 2- to 3-year-old children may have their legs tied to a post until the parent returns. Children are spanked with a *skobang* broom, which may break the skin and leave scratch marks and bruises. Collier, McClure, Collier, Otto, and Polloi (1999) found that Palau teachers considered intentional or severe injuries as abusive (e.g., placing a hand on open flame or throwing a child against the wall), but other behaviors such as putting a leash on a toddler's leg or telling a child to go find another home to live in were viewed as normal and acceptable practices. These findings were then used to create an organization to monitor child maltreatment.

Subculture comparisons. Many studies in the last ten years focused on the influence of subculture, ethnic, or racial group on childrearing attitudes within the same country. For example, Brody, Flor, and Gibson (1999) looked at the relation between perceived family resources, efficacy beliefs, and parental attitudes in rural single-parent African American families. They found that a mother's perception of adequate finances was related to beliefs in the efficacy of parenting. This belief in the efficacy of their parenting led to more endorsement and positive attitudes toward educational goals, respect for others in the community, and concern for others.

The childrearing attitudes of Chinese immigrants have been examined with great interest due to the academic success of Asian American students. Gorman (1998) found that although Chinese parents are known for their authoritarian parenting, several differences emerged between their attitudes and European American authoritarian attitudes. Immigrant Chinese mothers reportedly provided guidance to children through subtle comments and suggestion rather than using a direct confrontation. They also felt, when parents and children disagree, children should be free to make up their own minds. Support was found for Chinese immigrant mothers favoring authoritarian attitudes, but they reportedly adopted nonauthoritarian practices to socialize their children. In contrast to immigrant Chinese mothers, Jewish immigrant parents from the former Soviet Union endorsed very strict authoritarian attitudes (Shor, 1999). Along those lines, many of these parents had positive attitudes toward the use of physical punishment for male children.

Social and political orientations such a liberalism versus conservatism also are associated with childrearing attitudes. In one study, parents with a liberal orientation were found to have positive attitudes toward the importance of guidance, but with an emphasis on promoting independence in the child (Eisenman and Sirgo, 1991). In contrast, politically conservative parents valued and endorsed guidance, control, and, when the situation calls for it, physical punishment. Similarly, parents with an orientation toward religious fundamentalism (often associated with a conservative orientation) endorsed values such as obedience and corporal punishment rather than autonomy, and those attitudes were predictive of the childrearing practices they used (Danso, Hunsberger, and Pratt, 1997).

Floyd and Saitzyk (1992) found evidence that social class did play a role in shaping childrearing attitudes for parents of children with mild or moderate mental retardation. They reported that high socioeconomic status parents valued traits such as self-direction and personal growth, independent of whether or not their children were mentally handicapped. This provides additional support for Kohn's (1979) thesis that socioeconomic status influences parental values, which in turn influences parental behavior. Specifically, Kohn argued that parental occupation and "life situation" lead parents to hold particular childrearing values. Parents from higher socioeconomic status groups value such characteristics as being responsible, taking initiative, and showing independence. Parents from lower socioeconomic groups were theorized to value obedience, conformity, and self-control. Also in line with Kohn's theory, Floyd and Saitzyk hypothesized that lower socioeconomic status parents would value traits such as control and conformity, but little support for this was found.

Child effects on parental attitudes. Over the past decade, some attention has been directed to children's influence on their parents' attitudes. This topic is noteworthy because it approaches childrearing attitudes from the "child effects" or "two-way" effects perspective (Bugental and Goodnow, 1998). This is in stark contrast to the traditional view of childrearing attitudes as originating in the parent. However, most of the studies that illustrate child effects on attitudes rely solely on group differences to provide evidence.

Researchers studying the relation between child gender and parental attitudes have documented a gender-based child effect on attitudes toward maternal employment. Downey, Jackson, and Powell (1994) found that the more sons a mother had, the more negative her attitudes were toward maternal employment and the more positive her attitudes were toward obedience. This effect held even when controlling for demographic variables (i.e., education and income). The authors concluded that parenting attitudes are "developed through maternal experiences in the family. In turn, these experiences are shaped by the sex composition of the progeny" (p. 44).

Perhaps the strongest evidence for child effects on attitudes comes from a study of self-reports of within-subject change on attitudes (Holden, Thompson, Zambarano, and Marshall, 1997). More than 100 mothers were interviewed to assess influences on their attitudes toward corporal punishment. The open-ended interview collected reports about their current attitudes as well as retrospective reports about their attitudes before they became parents. The correlation between those two temporally divergent attitudes was only $r(106) = .31$, $p < .001$. A majority of the mothers reported that their attitudes had changed since becoming a parent: 36% revealed they had grown less in favor of corporal punishment, in contrast to 30% who indicated they had grown more in favor of the disciplinary practice. For the 71 mothers who changed views, most (75%) reported the reason for the change lay with the child's reaction to spanking or the child's characteristics. Other reasons included pressure from husbands' or friends, reading new information, taking a parenting class, or observing "out-of-control" children.

Parental attitudes toward childrearing have also been shown to be affected by child characteristics such as special needs (Meadow-Orlans, in Vol. 4 of this Handbook). The effect on caregiving practices and attitudes of having a child with chronic illness such as sickle cell disease provides a good example. Noll, McKellop, Vannatta, and Kalinyak (1998) compared medical professionals' reports of childrearing practices and attitudes of parents with children diagnosed with sickle cell disease to the parents' self-reported childrearing attitudes. The medical professionals perceived the sickle cell disease parents as more protective, worried, and less effective with discipline. Although sickle cell disease parents reported that they worried more about their children's health, they did not endorse more protective attitudes nor complain of discipline problems.

Other determinants. In addition to cross-cultural, subculture comparisons, and child effects, several other influences on attitudes received attention in the past decade. Intergenerational transmission of attitudes continued to attract attention, as demonstrated by Kendler's (1996) large multigenerational twin study. He found evidence that childrearing attitudes, derived from the parent's family of origin, influenced parental behavior in addition to genetically influenced parental temperamental characteristics. Specifically, parental attitudes of protectiveness and authoritarianism, compared with warmth, appeared to be more influenced by one's experience in family of origin. Another determinant that received more attention than in previous decades was that of religious beliefs. Several teams of investigators have studied the role of religious beliefs as a determinant of childrearing attitudes and also linked them to behavioral intentions. Evidence for connections between religious beliefs and childrearing attitudes have been found by Ellison, Bartowski, and Segal (1996), Danso et al. (1997), and Gershoff, Miller, and Holden (1999).

Ellison et al. (1996), analyzing a national data sample, found that parents with conservative scriptural beliefs (i.e., "The Bible is God's word and everything happened or will happen exactly as it says") reportedly engaged in more physical punishment than parents with less conservative theological views. Gershoff et al. (1999) found that parents who labeled themselves as "conservative Protestants" (i.e., Baptists and Pentecostal) differed from "mainline Protestants" (Episcopalians, Lutherans, Methodists, and Presbyterians), Roman Catholics, and parents with no religious affiliation on several variables. Conservative Protestants reported a greater frequency of spanking or slapping their 3-year-old children as well as held more positive attitudes about corporal punishment than the other groups.

Do Attitudes Change?

A second central issue about the nature of childrearing attitudes concerns the question of whether they are stable or subject to change. Ironically, stability is a shifty concept, as there are several types of stability and no uniform terminology (Cairns, 1979). One form of stability, sometimes labeled *absolute stability* or *continuity*, refers to whether or not the same attitude, behavior, or construct occurs within a group of individuals in the same magnitude at two or more points in time. The second form of stability, which has been called *interindividual consistency*, concerns whether an individual maintains his or her relative rank across time within a group with respect to the construct in question (Holden and Miller, 1999).

For a graphic example of these two types of stability, consider a parent's attitude toward nudity in children. Most parents may permit some display of nudity when their offspring are infants or toddlers, but as they grow older this attitude changes dramatically. Before long, parents begin modesty training. Within a few years, parents hold a completely different attitude about their children's display of nudity. Here there is discontinuity, or little absolute stability, with regard to that attitude. Alternatively, one can expect more rank-order stability over time with regard to such attitudes as parental involvement in childrearing, the importance of fathers, or children's need for strict discipline. As these examples make clear, these two forms of stability are conceptually and statistically independent (see Bornstein and Suess, 2000).

Most of the research attention to change in attitudes has been limited to interindividual consistency. Certainly, the early researchers into childrearing attitudes assumed that a parent's attitudes were largely fixed and unchanging (e.g., Pearson, 1931). Indeed, in a review of the stability and change in childrearing, Holden and Miller (1999) found several studies providing evidence for enduring parental attitudes. For example, Hock reported that attitudes toward maternal investment in motherhood role are relatively stable over 6 years ($r = .48$, Hock, 1988, cited in Hock and DeMeis, 1990). Similarly, Buck, Holden, and Stickels (2000), in a longitudinal study of attitudes toward corporal punishment, found in a sample of more than 100 parents that childrearing attitudes measured when their children were 6 months old were significantly correlated ($r[110] = .59$, $p < .01$) with the same attitude when their children were 48 months old. So evidence for interindividual consistency can be found.

At the same time, variability or change in a parent's childrearing attitudes can occur for various reasons. As the section above on child effects indicates, behavior or characteristics of the child can promote change in the *absolute stability* of attitudes, reflecting group change as a function of developmental change. But change or variation in an individual's childrearing attitudes can also be found across children and across situations (Holden and Miller, 1999). For example, parents may hold strict disciplinary attitudes for one child but are more relaxed with another child. Or the parent may consider physical punishment of children inappropriate in public and should only be practiced

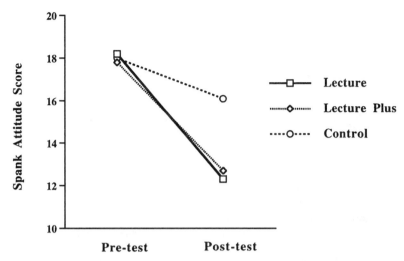

FIGURE 19.3. Change in spank-attitude scores.

in the home. However, to date, very little empirical attention has been devoted to examining change in childrearing attitudes.

The capacity to modify attitudes is especially important in the area of childrearing, where problematic or even dysfunctional attitudes may negatively impact children's development. Graziano and Diament (1992), in a review of the literature about parent behavioral (modification) training, found such programs were indeed effective for changes in behavior and attitudes. Similarly, Harrison (1997) reported that a 6-week parent education program was effective in promoting a significant and positive change in incarcerated fathers' attitudes. The largest effort to change parental attitudes of the 1990s was conducted by Cudaback, Dickinson, and Wiggins (1990). They mailed parenting education booklets to parents in 10 states, and more than 2,200 parents returned questionnaires about their reactions to the booklets. Parents reported attitudinal (as well as behavioral changes) as a result of the home-learning program.

Stickels (1999) conducted a true experiment in an effort to change adults' attitudes toward corporal punishment. She hypothesized that if adults heard a lecture about the negative, long-term outcomes of corporal punishment they would modify their views. Toward that end she randomly assigned adults into one of three groups: Lecture, Lecture Plus Essay (to consolidate what they had heard in the lecture), or Control. To guard against demand characteristics, initial attitudes toward corporal punishment were collected in a pretest situation several months prior to the lecture. The lecture was ostensibly about family violence, but in the Lecture and Lecture Plus Essay condition, a 5-minute mini-lecture on corporal punishment was edited onto the video. Following the video, participants completed a questionnaire. Embedded among the questions were the three pretest attitude questions regarding corporal punishment. As shown in Figure 19.3, there was a significant decrease how positive corporal punishment was viewed by the participants in the two lecture conditions, but not in the control condition. Consequently, this study provides experimental evidence that childrearing attitudes can be modified with relatively brief interventions.

How Are Attitudes Related to Parental Behavior and Child Outcomes?

Ultimately, the most important implication of parental attitudes concerns how they relate to children's outcomes. Presumably, the mechanism is through childrearing practices. As Darling and Steinberg (1993, p. 488) pointed out, "Behavior is determined and made meaningful by attitudes, but attitudes are expressed through behavior". Although parental attitude research has been long critiqued for its lack of correspondence with behavior, there have been several reports over the past decade relating attitudes to observed or reported behavior.

To test the links between attitude toward physical punishment and reported spanking behavior, Holden, Coleman, and Schmidt (1995) called 39 mothers each night for two weeks. During those nightly phone interviews, reports of physical punishment as well as other disciplinary techniques that had occurred that day were collected. Those reports were then aggregated and correlated with a 10-item Attitude Toward Spanking survey. Maternal attitudes toward spanking correlated significantly with the daily reports of spanking, $r(37) = .54$, $p < .001$. Furthermore, the correlation coefficient between attitudes toward spanking and aggregated maternal reports of how often they spanked in the past week was even higher, $r(37) = .73$, $p < .001$. This study provides strong evidence that circumscribed childrearing attitudes can indeed be associated with specific behaviors.

An attitude–behavior link was also found by Corral-Verdugo, Frias-Armenta, Romero, and Munoz (1995). They investigated the relation between attitudes about punishment and documented physical abuse with sample of Mexican mothers. The abusive mothers endorsed attitudes concerning the beneficial effects of punishment at significantly higher rates than a nonabusive comparison group. This study provides more evidence about the correspondence between maternal attitudes and their childrearing behavior in the disciplinary domain. However, additional research is needed to address the strength of the link in other domains.

Going beyond attitude–behavior associations to relating childrearing attitudes to child outcomes has occupied the attention of several researchers over the past decade. Maternal childrearing attitudes were found to relate to cognitive as well as social outcomes in children. Andersson, Sommerfelt, Sonnander, and Ahlsten (1996) discovered that nurturing childrearing attitudes in mothers were associated with better cognitive abilities in Scandinavian boys. Pahdi and Dash (1994) studied the relation between parental attitudes and adolescent competence. They found that parental attitudes of encouragement, verbalization of ideas, and firmness of parental authority were significantly correlated with ratings of children's competence. In addition, more competent children had parents who held positive attitudes toward home and school cooperation.

Brody et al. (1999) examined single mothers' childrearing attitudes (labeled as developmental goals). They found the goals (such as importance of being respectful and well behaved) were related significantly but indirectly to children's psychosocial competence. These attitudes were related to mothers' efficacy beliefs as well as to a set of behaviors labeled competence promoting parenting. In turn, those behaviors were found to be statistically associated with children's self-regulation.

Yamasaki (1990) was interested in assessing whether the family climate differed for different types of children. Toward that end, he studied the parental attitudes of Japanese children exhibiting Type A behaviors. Type A children are those who tend to be time urgent, competitive, and aggressive, whereas Type B children are the opposite. He found an interaction between gender of children and of parents. Mothers of boys with Type A behaviors reported lower levels of childrearing anxiety and affection toward their children than mothers of Type B boys. The attitudes of fathers with Type A sons showed similar results. Mothers of girls with Type A behaviors had less anxiety about their daughters than mothers of Type B girls, but fathers showed no significant group differences. The results were interpreted as showing that parents' attitudes influence the development of their children's activity level, although it was not a longitudinal study.

One study that did use a longitudinal design was the 9-year prospective study of 386 children by Katainen, Raikkonen, and Keltikangas-Jarvinen (1998). They used structural modeling analyses to discover that maternal childrearing attitudes as well as constitutional factors contributed to the development of temperament. They found that mothers of girls, with attitudes low in disciplinary control, had girls with low levels of negative emotionality. In contrast, mothers of boys with positive attitudes toward strict control had boys who were low in sociability but high in negative emotion.

Efforts to link parental attitudes with child outcomes are not always significant; undoubtedly many failed attempts never get published. One exception was by Potgieter (1992), who studied the effect of parental attitudes on childhood leadership ability. He was unable to detect any difference between the attitudes of the parents of leaders compared with the parents of followers.

Another approach to investigating the association between childrearing attitudes and child outcomes was pursued by Deal, Halverson, and Wampler (1999). They examined a finding first published by Block, Block, and Morrison (1981) indicating that the more similar the mother and father are in terms of childrearing attitudes, the better their child's outcome. However, Deal et al. (1999) hypothesized and found support for the view that what drives this relation is not parents' attitudinal similarity, per se, but rather their adherence to normative attitudes of the culture. Hence, any two parents sharing greater similarity in the standard cultural views of child development are socializing their children into socially accepted behavior. Not surprisingly, those children are considered as functioning more competently in the culture.

Summary

Contemporary research studies on childrearing attitudes have built on prior attitudinal research and continued to address a rich variety of topics. The single most actively researched topic concerned differences—as well as similarities—among cultural groups. These types of studies have served to reveal more clearly how group membership can be associated with particular childrearing attitudes. Surprisingly, one group that has continued to receive inadequate attention is fathers. Despite the "discovery" of fathers in the late 1970s (e.g., Lamb, 1976), over the past decade very few attitudinal studies included fathers. Although several studies assessing the attitudes of fathers were found, not enough such studies were located to create a separate topic category. One encouraging trend is that the view of childrearing attitudes as static and unchanging has begun to be challenged over the past decade. However, the most important area of attitudinal research, studies addressing childrearing attitude–behavior–child outcome links, has been limited. Little progress has been made in understanding those associations.

EVALUATION OF THE CURRENT STATUS OF PARENTAL ATTITUDE RESEARCH: AN IDENTITY CRISIS?

As is evident by the number of publications in the 1990s as well as their breadth, childrearing attitudes continue to enjoy considerable research attention. But despite the proliferation of new scientific journals springing up over the past decade, there has not been a steady increase in the publication of childrearing attitude studies. In fact, the lower annual average of childrearing articles depicted in Figure 19.1 indicates an inauspicious trend that is likely to intensify over the next decade. Such a trend is also echoed in the number of new attitude instruments that were developed during the 1990s, as indicated in Figure 19.2, shown earlier.

Yet a third indication of the decline of childrearing attitudes can be found in other indices. In contrast to earlier editions of *The Handbook of Child Psychology*, there were no entries related to childrearing attitudes in the index of the most recent edition (Damon, 1998). Childrearing attitudes are in decline and, it can be predicted, will continue to fall in an increasingly steep slope unless several central issues are addressed. The three problems are turf erosion, the attitude–behavior split, and dearth of theory.

Turf Erosion

The almost sacred turf of childrearing attitudes is facing threats from several sides. It appears that many investigators have forgotten the meaning of the attitude construct. Or, more accurately, there has always been some confusion about the nature of childrearing attitudes. Attitude instruments historically have contained a hodgepodge of items, with any one childrearing attitude questionniare often including self- and other perceptions, attributions, knowledge, beliefs, belief systems, values, goals, behavioral intentions, and behavioral reports (Holden and Edwards, 1989). Today, attitudes are at-risk of losing their identity to other "newer" social cognition constructs that, as relatively fresh, appear to offer more promise than one that has been around for more than three fourths of a century. These newer model constructs include attributions, beliefs, expectations, knowledge, ideas, and understandings. As evidence for this point, the index of the first edition of the *Handbook of Parenting* (Bornstein, 1995) contained 34 entries under the section on parental attitudes, but almost as many (32 entries) for "parent's beliefs."

Attitudes, as discussed at the beginning of the chapter, refer to an internal state that biases or predisposes an individual to react favorably or unfavorably toward an entity, or "attitude object." Attitudes are unique and distinct from other social cognition concepts because they represent the hypothetical construct of a tendency, internal state, or explicit evaluations (Eagly, 1992). The statements "Breastfeeding an infant is good," "Strict discipline is necessary for children's development," or "The Internet is useful educational tool for children" represent attitudes. Therefore, attitudes build on beliefs (knowledge) or ideas and are a function of them because these affective evaluations are based on understanding of the children, parenting, and the world.

So what is the difference between attitudes and some of the other social cognition constructs? As Eagly (1992, p. 693) defined it, an attitude is a "psychological tendency that is expressed by evaluating a particular entity with some degree of favor or disfavor." In contrast, beliefs are knowledge (or understandings) or ideas that are accepted as true (McGillicuddy-DeLisi and Sigel, 1995; Sigel, 1985). Consequently, attitudes are based on knowledge or ideas, but go beyond that information by evaluating it. Thus, attitudes represent childrearing opinions—whether they be about children's TV viewing, supervision, or disciplinary practices. Knowledge is a subclass of ideas that are about the present and future (including expectations but not reconstructions of the past) and related to information or evidence of some kind (Goodnow, 1995, p. 305). Bacon and Ashmore (1986, p. 10) inadvertently illustrated how these concepts can get muddied:

> Affect and belief systems ... are structured sets of knowledge, more or less affectively charged. By knowledge we do not mean "facts" or even simple verbal or verbalizable information. Rather, we see affect and belief systems as compose of any cognitive or affective distinctions or discriminations made by the parent.

Although the distinctiveness of attitudes needs to be maintained, at the same time it is important to recognize the role of attitudes in the context of parental thinking. As indicated above, attitudes are a function of beliefs. Attitudes are also closely related to some of these other constructs, such as expectations. Holden and his colleagues (Holden, Miller, and Harris, 1999) found that parents with positive attitudes toward physical punishment differed systematically on some of their outcome expectancies. Specifically, mothers and fathers of 3-year-old children who had positive attitudes toward spanking and reported that they spanked at least weekly expected that spanking would result in good short- (e.g., immediate compliance) and long-term outcomes (e.g., appropriate socialization) for their children. Thus, both positive attitudes and behavior were found to be associated with outcome expectancies. It may be that such expectancies are the primary "drivers" of positive attitudes toward spanking, although this proposition awaits further research.

To preserve the turf of attitudes, it is important to identify their boundaries. Attitudes come into play most often in deliberative situations that are illustrated by the expectancy-value models such as the Theory of Reasoned Action, developed by Fishbein and Ajzen (1975). According to expectancy-value models, attitudes develop from beliefs about an attitude object. Each belief links the behavior to a certain outcome. Because those outcomes are valued positively or negatively, an attitude can be acquired automatically (Ajzen, 1991). In expectancy-value models, attitudes are not the direct cause of behavior, but they influence the intention to act. However, parental thinking and behavior can also be guided by affective, unintentional, automatic, or nonconscious processes (Bargh, 1997;

Bugental and Goodnow, 1998; Goodnow, 1995). In sum, the turf of attitudes needs to be shored up by carefully specifying what attitudes are, what they can account for, when they come into play, and when they do not.

Attitude–Behavior Split

The second fundamental problem that burdens childrearing attitudes is its reputation of having failed to predict observed parent behavior. Hence, attitudes have been discredited by some as useless or little more meaningful than an intellectual exercise. Other researchers believe that parental attitudes can provide a way to tap into parenting style, a quality that is distinct from parenting practices (Darling and Steinberg, 1993). Clearly, dismissive arguments about attitudes are undeserved and premature, as they neither reflect the extensive research on the topic nor the fact that the relation is an extremely complex issue that requires both good theory and careful empirical study (Eagly and Chaiken, 1993).

A full discussion of this issue is worthy of nothing less than a book, but three general points will be made. First, the assessment of childrearing attitudes has been problematic. Second, the conceptual basis on which attitude instruments have been constructed is often faulty. Third, behavioral assessments have their own problems that often go unrecognized. Each of these points will briefly be considered below.

As discussed in Holden and Edwards (1989), researchers have committed a variety of errors in their efforts to assess attitudes. Many of the problems reside in the development of the attitude questionnaires. The major problems associated with questionnaires are with item and response scale composition, and unknown or weak psychometric properties.

Each item in an attitude survey must be carefully crafted (Schwartz, 1999). But all too often there are glaring errors, including ambiguous wording, double-barreled or dual questions, and a lack of contextual information (Converse and Presser, 1986). Another common problem is the use of the third-person format (e.g., "A good mother should protect her child from life's little difficulties"). The problem is that a parent does not know how to respond to such items. Other sources of confusion can come from outdated terms or concepts, double negatives, and questions about childrearing issues that the respondent has not yet experienced.

There are often problems with the Likert-type response scales as well. Vague probability terms, such as "sometimes" or "occasionally" are common, as is the mismatch between the item and the response scale making it unclear what it means to moderately agree with that item. Response sets include acquiescence set (agreeing with oppositely worded statements), the opposition set (disagreeing with all statements), or the extreme set (selecting extreme responses). Although there are ways of dealing with these response sets, such as reversing a certain percentage of items, such precautions are not commonly taken.

The psychometric properties of attitude instruments are often problematic. Reliability information may not be tested or it may be low. For example, only 45% of 83 attitude questionnaires reviewed reported internal consistency data, and 25% had test–retest data (Holden and Edwards, 1989). The median internal consistency of instruments using Cronbach's coefficient alpha is more often than not below the recommended 0.80 level for research purposes. Evidence for validity is even more limited. Only about half of the attitude instruments have any supporting validity data, and what is available is typically limited at best and sometimes of dubious quality.

Besides problems with assessing attitudes, there are fundamental questions about the conceptual nature of attitudes. Most childrearing attitude instruments reflect an underlying conceptualization of attitudes as preexisting, unchanging, unidimensional, and deterministic of parenting behavior. Each of these assumptions is problematic and generally unsupported (see Holden, 1995). For instance, it is presumed that parents develop and hold a wide range of childrearing attitudes before their children are born. However, it is likely that some attitudes develop in reaction to their children's behavior (e.g., Holden et al., 1997). As was discussed above, there is also evidence that attitudes are not necessarily stable. As Stolz (1967, p. 278) wrote, based on her analysis of her interviews concerning parental attitudes, "Parents operate within a milieu of psychological pressures." The pressures can result from competing ideas of short- and long-term goals, conflicts between attitudes, or the competing needs of different individuals. To reduce those psychological pressures into one unidimensional attitude score is problematic. Finally, there is evidence that attitudes may not determine behavior. Given that behavior is multiply determined, it is unlikely that childrearing attitudes alone (even if they were perfectly assessed) could determine behavior. McCillicuddy-DeLisi and Sigel (1995) as well as Goodnow (1995) have argued that researchers need to work much harder to discover the links between parental social cognition and behavior. This can be accomplished by, in part, contextualizing attitudes, avoiding global attitudes, assessing behaviors that would reflect the attitudes studied, and aggregating parental behaviors.

A third basic point concerning the attitude–behavior issue is that all of the blame for the lack of correspondence cannot be saddled on the attitude side of the equation. The assessment of behavior is beset with traps. If one relies on behavioral self-reports, such data can be flawed (Schwarz, 1999). Systematic observations of behavior are time consuming and complex (Bakeman and Gottman, 1997). Behavior is situationally specific, and any one sample of behavior can be highly discrepant with another. The situation has strong influences on parenting, as Miller, Shim, and Holden (1998) found when observing the same mothers in the home, the park, and the laboratory. They found that the type of setting systematically elicited different maternal behavior. In the home, where the mothers had a competing demand of preparing lunch, mothers were less attentive, less affectionate, and used more prohibitions. In the park, mothers were more attentive and directive. In the laboratory, mothers were both attentive and showed positive affect. To arrive at a representative sample of childrearing behavior, aggregated observations within the same situation are required, but almost never done (see Wachs, 1987).

Third, although attitudes can relate to behavior, they need not. One would expect a relatively high degree of correspondence when behavior is intentional and goal oriented (Ajzen, 1991) or the result of a "cool" regulatory system (Metcalfe and Mischel, 1999). But behavior can also be guided by unintentional, automatic, nonconscious, or "hot" processes (e.g., Bargh, 1997; Bugental and Goodnow, 1998; Metcalfe and Mischel, 1999). Under these conditions, one would not expect the same degree of association between childrearing attitudes and behavior.

The fact that parenting is by definition an interactive task with a child makes it necessary to consider the child's potential influence on parental behavior and attitudes. So empirical efforts to document the childrearing attitude–behavior link need to be prudent and well thought out. Most have not been. Finally, it should be kept in mind the needed match between levels of specificity. It is most likely that specific attitudes may correspond to specific behaviors. But it is unlikely that specific attitudes will relate to more molar behavior or that global attitudes will correspond to specific behaviors.

Dearth of Theory

On the one hand, parental attitudes (or a proxy for them) continue to occupy a prominent role in theorizing about child development. Models of child outcomes, such as parental influences on their children's motivation and achievement (Eccles, Wigfield, and Schiefele, 1998), are based on decades of research and rely heavily on parental attitudes and other exemplars of social cognition (e.g., beliefs, values, and goals). But most childrearing attitude research is conducted in the absence of a theory or even theoretical influences. Social psychologists have been diligently investigating the nature of attitudes and developing new theoretical models supported by empirical tests (Eagly and Chaiken, 1993). In particular, two characteristics of attitudes are particularly critical for understanding the conditions under which parental attitudes are likely to influence childrearing behavior: attitude strength and implicit attitudes.

The single most important characteristic of an attitude (after its valence) is its strength. Attitude strength has been defined and operationalized in different ways. Consider two parents who hold the same positive (or negative) attitudes toward breastfeeding, corporal punishment for defiant disobedience, boys playing with toy guns, or attendance at a child's sporting events. What differentiates the mother who may espouse a positive attitude but have a weak attitude–behavior link with the other mother whose behavior is in line with her attitudes? The property of attitude strength is thought to help account for the difference between these two attitude–behavior links (Eagly and Chaiken, 1993).

Attitude strength has been conceptualized in various ways. Some researchers have argued that strength is a function of the structure of the attitude. That is, if an attitude has an extensive and coherent set of intra-attitudinal associations, then that attitude is likely to be stronger (Petty and Krosnick, 1995; Visser and Krosnick, 1998). For example, if a mother knows that infant breastfeeding is linked to a number of positive health outcomes in both the infant and mother, then she is more likely to act in a way consistent with her attitude.

Fazio (1995) has adopted another approach to attitude strength—that of attitude accessibility. The accessibility of an attitude refers to how easily the attitude is activated when encountering the attitude object. If a parent believes strongly that defiant disobedience must be dealt with firmly and swiftly, then that attitude will be activated when such behavior is perceived.

A third approach to attitude strength focuses on the interattitudinal characteristics of an attitude. Here, the more consistent the attitude is with other attitudes and values, then the more likely it is to be behaviorally expressed (Eagly and Chaiken, 1993). A mother who is concerned about all the manifestations of violence in our society is unlikely to purchase a toy gun for her toddler. A final example of how attitude strength has been conceptualized focuses on the individual's perception of the important of a particular attitude. Abelson has labeled this dimension of attitudes "conviction." If a father holds dear the notion that a "good father" always attends his child's athletic events, and it is important to the father's self image that he be a "good father," then such an attitude is likely to be acted upon.

Other than attitude strength, the other development related to attitudes that holds promise for understanding childrearing attitudes is the notion of implicit attitudes. To date, almost all the research into attitudes has focused on explicit attitudes or attitudes that are accessible to self-reports and introspection. In contrast, implicit attitudes are automatically activated without the individual's awareness and generally cannot be accurately identified by introspection (Greenwald and Banaji, 1995). But like explicit attitudes, they are based on past experience and can mediate favorable or unfavorable feelings, thoughts, or behavior.

Greenwald and his colleagues have developed a procedure to assess these attitudes (the Implicit Association Test) by manipulating the level of association between two paired items and then measuring response time (Greenwald, McGhee, and Schwartz, 1998). This procedure provides an alternative to the evaluative semantic priming technique that has been used previously (e.g., Bargh, Chaiken, Govender, and Pratto, 1992; Fazio, Sanbonmatsu, Powell, and Kardes, 1986). In the priming method, target words are classified based on the word's evaluative meaning. Target words are immediately preceded by a prime word that is to be ignored. By looking at the response latencies to classify the target words following the prime, the variations in response latencies are used to measure automatic evaluations of the prime category.

Unfortunately, childrearing attitude researchers have largely ignored these conceptual and theoretical advances in their studies of parent–child relationships. While social psychologists have been making steady, if "uneven" progress in the study of attitudes (Eagly, 1992), the same cannot be said of the research into childrearing attitudes. The quality and sophistication of research into childrearing attitudes has not developed appreciably from what was being done perhaps 30 years ago. Goodnow's (1988) plea for developmental researchers to pay more attention to the work of social psychologists has gone largely unheeded.

How serious are the problems of turf erosion, the attitude–behavior gulf, and dearth of theory for the future of childrearing attitudes? These are potent challenges that, if left unanswered, can spell doom for the construct. Alternatively, these current problems can be addressed by careful and more thoughtful analyses of childrearing attitudes. Toward that end, we propose that researchers into parenting attitudes focus on three areas for future research.

CHILDREARING ATTITUDE RESEARCH IN THE NEXT DECADE

Putting Attitudes in Context

The greatest need for research into childrearing attitudes is to recognize their distinctive role in social cognition. This means to map out what indeed are attitudes in contrast to other aspects of social cognition, such as perceptions, expectations, or attributions. Clarifying what attitudes are operating in conjunction with what ideas would help to reveal the associations between different social cognition constructs, how they relate to behavior, and in turn impact the socialization process.

Recognizing the distinctiveness of childrearing attitudes also means appreciating the context specific nature of attitudes. Although values are global evaluations of what is important to an individual, attitudes, and especially childrearing attitudes, are based in the context and the developmental history of a particular child. Schwarz (1999), an expert in questionnaire construction, concluded that "attitude measurement is subject to pronounced context effects" (p. 103). He provided an easy suggestion for researchers to begin to reveal contextual dependency: include a context manipulation in the design of the study or questionnaire. For example, to investigate the extent to which attitudes are affected by the context, one could assess attitudes in two or more situations. If that manipulation were put into effect, along with Plomin's suggestion of including assessments of siblings (Plomin, 1994), and the attitude domain was narrowly defined, we would have a much clearer understanding of the context-specific as well as child-specific nature of attitudes.

Another key contextual question is when are particular attitudes activated? Long-held attitudes may be overridden by strong emotion or "hot cognition" as Metcalfe and Mischel (1999) argued.

Investigating Implicit Attitudes

Perhaps the most exciting new direction in attitude research is the work by social psychologists investigating implicit attitudes (Greenwald et al., 2000; Greenwald et al., 1998). Over the past few years several papers have been published arguing that people can hold dual attitudes about the same attitude object. Individuals may be aware of their explicit attitudes but can be simultaneously unaware of implicit ones. According to Wilson, Lindsey, and Schooler (2000), some evaluations occur automatically (i.e., implicit attitudes). Other attitudes require more capacity and motivation to retrieve, and may vary according to different situations and levels of information (i.e., explicit attitudes). At times these two types of attitudes may conflict, such as attitudes about race, or in the case of parenting, attitudes about discipline or expressing negative emotion.

Although the idea of implicit attitudes is controversial partly due to methodological concerns with one of the current procedures used to assess them (e.g., Brendl, Markman, and Messner, in press), the concept is pregnant with applications for childrearing attitudes. Given it is likely that certain attitudes develop early in life based on childrearing experiences the child receives, such as attitudes toward parental warmth or rejection, physical punishment and other forms of violence in the family (see Holden and Zambarano, 1992), or displays of emotion (Halberstadt, Crisp, and Eaton, 1999). However, as children mature they may develop new and explicit attitudes based on new experiences, information, or associations.

There are a number of intriguing research questions one can ask about the development of implicit attitudes. The initial question is whether implicit attitudes actually exist. If so, how are they formed? Several distinctions concerning the development of dual attitudes have been proposed. One way to form dual attitudes is through "independent systems." Here two different evaluations can be formed independently. Take the case of spanking attitudes. It is possible for a parent to have developed early in life an implicit attitude that condones spanking in certain situations (e.g., when child is in danger of bodily harm; Holden et al., 1995). However, later in life—perhaps in high school or college—the individual may develop a new, explicit attitude that spanking is an unacceptable form of discipline. When that parent is placed into a situation which activates the implicit response system (e.g., the child runs into the street endangering themselves), their automatic response, in line with their implicit attitude, may be to spank.

A second way the two types of attitudes may develop has been dubbed motivated overriding (Wilson et al., 2000). Here, the individual is fully aware of an implicit attitude but finds it unacceptable. People are motivated to develop or employ a different type of explicit attitude, but the implicit attitude lingers. Consider the attitude toward expressing affection. If a mother had early, negative experiences of affection with her family of origin through sexual abuse or rejection, then she may be aware of this negative implicit attitude. However, she may also recognize that such an attitude is not conducive to her child's healthy development, and thus attempts to override this propensity.

Research is clearly warranted into the investigation of implicit childrearing attitudes. Although the best way to measure implicit attitudes has yet to be determined (e.g., Brendl et al., in press), the approach has considerable promise. Attitudes created in childhood or through cultural ideals may be expressed through implicit attitudes because they are formed early in life and are less influenced by outside information. Perhaps more exciting is the possibility that such attitudes may provide an avenue to re-address the questions posed by early attitude researchers as to the role of the unconscious may play with childrearing attitudes and behavior (e.g., Richards, 1926; Cohler et al., 1976). Finally, it is likely such work could also inform us much about the attitude and behavior link, the final suggestion for future work.

Renewing Efforts to Link Attitudes and Behavior

Ultimately, the power of the construct of childrearing attitudes lies in its link to parenting behavior. The two directions suggested above both have clear implications for better revealing that link. By achieving a better understanding of the social cognition mileau within which attitudes operate, we will have a clearer vision of when attitudes should relate to behavior. Assessing implicit as well as explicit attitudes should also result in a better understanding of the links between attitudes and behavior. Dual attitudes created through independent systems or motivated overriding may allow implicit attitudes to guide behavior through their influence on automatic associations and responses.

Investigating implicit attitude accessibility and strength may help to reveal the linkages between parental attitude and behavior. Fazio and his colleagues (Fazio, Ledbetter, and Towles-Schwen, 2000) have shown that having accessible attitudes eases the decision-making process by providing a predetermined attitude. If both parents possess positive attitudes toward immediate child obedience but one parent has an accessible attitude and the other does not, the parent with the more accessible attitude will be more likely to have an attitude–behavior correspondence. The same considerations and distinctions may be true for attitude strength.

Whether or not a parent researcher elects to investigate implicit attitudes in conjunction with understanding how attitudes relate to behavior, it is essential that the investigation represent a diligent and concerted effort. The problem is that it is too easy and expedient for researchers to throw a parenting attitude measure into a study and then see if they can extract a significant finding or two. Perhaps a drastic approach is necessary. Perhaps it is time for journal editors to publish policy statements indicating that all attitude measures must be backed up with one or more behavioral measures—whether it be self-reports, reports from others, or systematic observations. Such a policy would provide the needed onus on researchers to consider behavioral variables and to refocus attention on the attitude–behavior link.

CONCLUSIONS

Over the past decade, childrearing attitudes have continued to enjoy considerable research attention. However, we detected evidence for a diminished status in the construct by counting, across decades, the number of publications that included childrearing attitudes. This decreased standing is likely the consequence, in part, of unrealistic expectations for attitudes. Promises about childrearing attitudes made in the first half of the twentieth century were not borne out in the second half.

Despite the decrease in frequency of childrearing attitude publications, the last decade of the twenieth century saw sustained research attention devoted to childrearing attitudes. Studies addressed a numerous attitudes and a rich variety of topics. Cross-cultural studies were the most popular followed by investigations into the attitudes of parents of special-needs children, adolescent mothers, and how attitudes are related to children's outcomes. The research over the past decade provided some new information concerning three fundamental childrearing attitude issues. These questions concern the source of the attitudes, the extent they can be modified, and how they relate to behavior and children's outcomes. Although some progress was made in better understanding the origins of childrearing attitudes, particularly with regard to cross-cultural research, inadequate attention has been devoted to the latter two questions.

In some ways, parental attitude research can be characterized as being in an identity crisis. The construct is no longer regarded as the panacea many early researchers believed that it was. This awareness has contributed to turf erosion. Other components of social cognition, such as beliefs and attributions, have encroached on the domain once occupied by attitudes. This is largely a healthy development, as attitudes were often an intellectual catchment area for a variety of social cognition constructs. However, it is important to clarify what are attitudes and what are the other social cognition constructs. Other "newer" topics are beginning to attract more attention, but that does not mean they should replace attitudes.

Another cause of the identity crisis is the attitude–behavior split. In an example of throwing the baby out with the bathwater, attitudes have all to often been rejected due to the apparent lack of relation to behavior. But as discussed above, such a reaction is premature and fails to recognize some fundamental issues involved. Problems with attitude measurement, attitude conceptualization, as well as behavioral assessments can all account for the tenuous evidence linking attitudes and behavior.

A third source of the identity crisis is due to the lack of attention that has been devoted to theory with regard to childrearing attitudes. Although social psychologists have been making progress in better understanding the nature and expression of attitudes, little work has been done either linking these ideas to childrearing attitudes or identifying independent theories.

The next decade promises to be a watershed for the construct. If research continues on the same path, it will only result in a continued downward spiral. Instead, renewed efforts are needed to breathe new life into the construct. Along those lines, three suggestions are made. First, greater attention must be paid to contextual nature of attitudes. It is likely that attitudes are often at the mercy of the situation and particular child. Systematic efforts to reveal those qualities are needed. Second, a potentially exciting and fertile area to investigate childrearing attitudes is implicit attitudes. Such attitudes may well be established early in life. Cross-sectional and longitudinal studies are needed to explore this new domain of attitude research. The third recommendation concerns the need for renewed efforts to discover the links between attitudes, other social cognition components, and parenting behavior. Such work could help to reveal the relations between cognition, emotion, and behavior. It would also lead to a better understanding of the sources of automatic versus deliberative behavior.

Over the next 10 years will childrearing attitudes continue their downward spiral? Or will this type of research be rejuvenated with renewed attention and sophisticated theory-driven research? It is up to researchers to adopt a renewed commitment to understanding childrearing attitudes and parenting behavior. Only such an effort will enable attitudes regain their identity.

REFERENCES

Ackerley, L. A. (1935). The information and attitudes regarding child development possessed by parents of elementary school children. In G. D. Stoddard (Ed.), *University of Iowa studies: Studies in child welfare: Vol. 10. Researchers in parent education* (pp. 113–167). Iowa City: University of Iowa Press.

Ajzen, I. (1991). The theory of planned behavior. *Organizational Behavior and Human Decision Processes, 50*, 179–211.

Allport, G. (1935). Attitudes. In C. Murchison (Ed.), *A handbook of social psychology* (pp. 798–844). Worcester, MA: Clark University Press.

Andersson, H. W., Sommerfelt, K., Sonnander, K., and Ahlsten, G. (1996). Maternal child-rearing attitudes, IQ, and socio-economic status as related to cognitive abilities of five-year-old children. *Psychological Reports, 79*, 3–14.

Bacon, M. K., and Ashmore, R. D. (1986). A consideration of the cognitive activities of parents and their role in the socialization process. In R. D. Ashmore and D. M. Brodzinsky (Eds.), *Thinking about the family: Views of parents and children* (pp. 3–33). Hillsdale, NJ: Lawrence Erlbaum Associates.

Bakeman, R., and Gottman, J. (1997). Observing interaction: An introduction to sequential analysis (2nd ed.). New York: Cambridge University Press.

Bakwin, R. M., and Bakwin, H. (1942). *Psychologic care during infancy and childhood.* New York: Appleton-Century.

Baldwin, A. L., Kalhorn, J., and Breese, F. (1945). Patterns of parent behavior. *Psychological Monographs, 58,* (Whole No. 268).

Bargh, J. A. (1997). The automaticity of everyday life. In R. S. Wyer, Jr. (Ed.), The *automaticity of everyday life: Vol. 10. Advances in social cognition* (pp. 1–61). Mahwah, NJ: Lawrence Earlbaum Associates.

Bargh, J. A., Chaiken, S., Govender, R., and Pratto, F. (1992). The generality of the automatic attitude activation effect. *Journal of Personality and Social Psychology, 62,* 893–912.

Baumrind, D. (1971). Current patterns of parental authority. *Developmental Psychology Monographs, 4* (Pt. 2).

Block, J. H., Block, J., and Morrison, A. (1981). Parental agreement–disagreement on child-rearing orientations and gender-related personality correlates in children. *Child Development, 52,* 965–974.

Bornstein, M. H. (1991). (Ed.). *Cultural appoaches to parenting.* Hillsdale, NJ: Lawrence Erlbaum Associates.

Bornstein, M. H. (1995). (Ed.). *Handbook of parenting.* Mahwah, NJ: Lawrence Erlbaum Associates.

Bornstein, M. H, Haynes, O. M., Azuma, H., Galperín, C., Maital, S., Ogino, M., Painter, K., Pascual, L., Pêcheux, M., Rahn, C., Toda, S., Venuti, P., Vyt, A., and Wright, B. (1998). A cross-national study of self-evaluations and attributions in parenting: Argentina, Belgium, France, Israel, Italy, Japan, and the United States. *Developmental Psychology, 34,* 662–676.

Bornstein, M. H., and Suess, P. E. (2000). Child and mother cardiac vagal tone: Continuity, stability, and concordance across the first 5 years. *Developmental Psychology, 36,* 54–65.

Bornstein, M. H., Tamis-LeMonda, C. S., Pascual, L., Haynes, O. M., Painter, K. M., Galperin, C. Z., and Pêcheux, M. (1996). Ideas about parenting in Argentina, France, and the United States. *International Journal of Behavioral Development, 19,* 347–367.

Brendl, C. M., Markman, A. B., and Messner, C. (in press). How do indirect measures of evaluation work? Evaluating the inference of prejudice in the Implicit Association Test. *Journal of Personality and Social Psychology.*

Brody, G. H., Flor, D. L., and Gibson, N. M. (1999). Linking maternal efficacy beliefs, developmental goals, parenting practices, and child competence in rural single-parent African American families. *Child Development, 70,* 1197–1208.

Brody, S. (1956). *Patterns of mothering.* New York: International Universities Press.

Buck, M. J., Holden, G. W., and Stickels, A. C. (2000). *A longitudinal study of the onset and stability of parental reports of disciplinary practices.* Manuscript in preparation, University of Texas at Austin.

Bugental, D. B., and Goodnow, J. J. (1998). Socialization processes. In W. Damon (Series Ed.) and N. Eisenberg (Vol. Ed.), *Handbook of child psychology: Vol. 3. Social, emotional, and personality development* (pp. 389–462). New York: Wiley.

Burchinal, L. G., Hawkes, G. R., and Gardener, B. (1957). The relationship between parental acceptance and adjustment of children. *Child Development, 28,* 65–77.

Cairns, R. B. (1979). *Social development: The origins and plasticity of interchanges.* San Francisco: Freeman.

Campbell, D. T. (1963). Social attitudes and other acquired behavioral dispositions. In S. Koch (Ed.), *Psychology: A study of a science* (Vol. 6, pp. 94–172). New York: McGraw-Hill.

Cohler, B. J., Grunebaum, H. U., Weiss, J. L., Hartman, C. R., and Gallant, D. H. (1976). Child care attitudes and adaptation to the maternal role among mentally ill and well mothers. *American Journal of Orthopsychiatry, 46,* 123–134.

Coleman, R. W., Kris, E., and Provence, S. (1953). The study of variations of early parental attitudes. *The Psychoanalytic Study of the Child, 8,* 20–47.

Collier, A. F., McClure, F. H., Collier, J., Otto, C., and Polloi, A. (1999). Culture-specific views of child maltreatment and parenting styles in a Pacific-island community. *Child Abuse and Neglect, 23,* 229–244.

Converse, J. M., and Presser, S. (1986). *Survey questions: Handcrafting the standardized questionnaire.* Beverly Hills, CA: Sage.

Corral-Verdugo, V., Frias-Armenta, M., Romero, M., and Munoz, A. (1995). Validity of a scale measuring beliefs regarding the "positive" effects of punishing children: A study of Mexican mothers. *Child Abuse and Neglect, 19,* 669–679.

Cudaback, D. J., Dickinson, N. S., and Wiggins, E. S. (1990). Parent education by mail. *Families in Society, 71,* 172–175.

Damon, W. (Ed.). (1998). *Handbook of child psychology.* New York: Wiley.

Danso, H., Hunsberger, B., and Pratt, M. (1997). The role of parental religious fundamentalism and right-wing authoritarianism in child-rearing goals and practices. *Journal for the Scientific Study of Religion, 36,* 496–511.

Darling, N., and Steinberg, L. (1993). Parenting style as context: An integrative model. *Psychological Bulletin, 113,* 487–496.

Deal, J. E., Halverson, C. F., Jr., and Wampler, K. S. (1999). Parental similarity on child-rearing orientations: Effects of stereotype similarity. *Journal of Social and Personal Relationships, 16,* 87–102.

Despres, M. A. (1937). Favorable and unfavorable attitudes toward pregnancy in primiparae. *Journal of Genetic Psychology, 51,* 241–254.

Dix, T., and Gershoff, E. T. (2000). Measuring parent–child relations. In J. Touliatos, B. Perlmutter, and G. W. Holden (Eds.), *Handbook of family measurement techniques: Vol. 2. Abstracts.* Newbury Park, CA: Sage.

Downey, D. B., Jackson, P. B., and Powell, B. (1994). Sons versus daughters: Sex composition of children and maternal views on socialization. *Sociological Quarterly, 35,* 33–50.

Eagly, A. H. (1992). Uneven progress: Social psychology and the study of attitudes. *Journal of Personality and Social Psychology, 63,* 693–710.

Eagly, A. H., and Chaiken, S. (1993). *The psychology of attitudes.* New York: Harcourt Brace Jovanovich.

Eccles, J. S., Wigfield, A., and Schiefele, U. (1998). Motivation to succeed. In W. Damon (Series Ed.) and N. Eisenberg (Vol. Ed.), *Handbook of child psychology: Vol. 3. Social, emotional, and personality development* (pp. 1017–1095). New York: Wiley.

Eisenman, R., and Sirgo, H. B. (1991). Liberals versus conservatives: Personality, child-rearing attitudes, and birth order/sex differences. *Bulletin of the Psychonomic Society, 29,* 240–242.

Ellison, C. G., Bartowksi, J. P., and Segal, M. L. (1996). Conservative Protestantism and the parental use of corporal punishment. *Social Forces, 74,* 1003–1028.

Fazio, R. H. (1995). Attitudes as object-evaluation associations: Determinants, consequences, and correlates of attitude accessibility. In R. E. Petty and J. A. Krosnick (Eds.), *Attitude strength: Antecedents and consequences* (pp. 247–282). Hillsdale, NJ: Lawrence Erlbaum Associates.

Fazio, R. H., Ledbetter, J. E., and Towles-Schwen, T. (2000). On the costs of accessible attitudes: Detecting that the attitude object has changed. *Journal of Personality and Social Psychology, 78,* 197–210.

Fazio, R. H., and Powell, M. C. (1997). On the value of knowing one's likes and dislikes: Attitude accessibility, stress, and health in college. *Psychological Science, 8,* 430–436.

Fazio, R. H., Sanbonmatsu, D. M., Powell, M. C., and Kardes, F. R. (1986). On the automatic activation of attitudes. *Journal of Personality and Social Psychology, 50,* 229–238.

Festinger, L. (1964). *Conflict, decision, and dissonance.* Stanford, CA: Stanford University Press.

Field, M. (1940). Maternal attitudes found in twenty-five cases of children with behavior primary disorders. *American Journal of Orthopsychiatry, 10,* 293–311.

Fishbein, M., and Ajzen, I. (1975). *Beliefs, attitudes, intention, and behavior: An introduction to theory and research.* Reading, MA: Addison-Wesley.

Floyd, F. J., and Saitzyk, A. R. (1992). Social class and parenting children with mild and moderate mental retardation. *Journal of Pediatric Psychology, 17,* 607–631.

Francis, K. V., and Fillmore, E. A. (1934). The influence of environment upon the personality of children. *University of Iowa Studies in Child Welfare, 9,* 1–71.

Freud, S. (1936). *The problem of anxiety.* New York: Norton.

Garner, P. W. (1996). Does hearing a lecture on attachment affect students' attitudes about "spoiling" infants? *College Student Journal, 30,* 168–172.

Garrett, A. (1936). Attitude therapy. In E. R. Gorves and P. Blanchard (Eds.), *Readings in mental hygiene* (pp. 36–40). New York: Holt.

Gershoff, E. T., Miller, P. C., and Holden, G. W. (1999). Parenting influences from the pulpit: Religious affiliation as a determinant of parental corporal punishment. *Journal of Family Psychology, 13,* 307–320.

Glueck, B. (1927). Concerning parental attitudes. *Child Study, 4,* 3–11.

Glueck, B. (1928). The significance of parental attitudes for the destiny of the individual. *Mental Hygiene, 12,* 722–741.

Goodnow, J. J. (1988). Parents' ideas, actions, and feelings: Models and methods from developmental and social psychology. *Child Development, 59,* 286–320.

Goodnow, J. J. (1995). Parents' knowledge and expectations. In M. H. Borstein (Ed.), *Handbook of parenting: Vol. 3. Status and social conditions of parenting* (pp. 305–332). Mahwah, NJ: Lawrence Erlbaum Associates.

Gordon, J. E. (1957). The validity of Shoben's Parent Attitude Survey. *Journal of Clinical Psychology, 13,* 151–158.

Gorman, J. C. (1998). Parenting attitudes and practices of immigrant Chinese mothers of adolescents. *Family Relations: Interdisciplinary Journal of Applied Family Studies, 47,* 73–80.

Graziano, A. M., and Diament, D. M. (1992). Parent behavioral training: An examination of the paradigm. *Behavior Modification, 16,* 3–28.

Greenwald, A. G., Banaji, M. R. (1995). Implicit social cognition: Attitudes, self-esteem, and stereotypes. *Psychological Review, 102,* 4–27.

Greenwald, A. G., Banaji, M. R., Rudman, L. A., Farnham, S. D., Nosek, B. A., and Rosier, M. (2000). In J. P. Forgas (Ed.), *Feeling and thinking: The role of affect in social cognition* (pp. 308–330). New York: Cambridge University Press.

Greenwald, A. G., McGhee, D. E., and Schwartz, J. L. K. (1998). Measuring individual difference in implicit cognition. *Journal of Personality and Social Psychology, 74,* 1464–1480.

Halberstadt, A. G., Crisp, V. W., and Eaton, K. (1999). Family expressiveness: A retrospective and new directions for research. In P. Philippot, R. S. Feldman, and E. Coats (Eds.), *The social context of nonverbal behavior: Studies in emotion and social interaction* (pp. 109–155). New York: Cambridge University Press.

Harrison, K. (1997). Parental training for incarcerated fathers: Effects on attitudes, self-esteem, and children's self perceptions. *Journal of Social Psychology, 137,* 588–593.

Hock, E., and DeMeis, D. K. (1990). Depression in mothers of infants: The role of maternal employment. *Developmental Psychology, 26,* 285–291.

Holden, G. W. (1995). Parental attitudes toward childrearing. In M. H. Borstein (Ed.), *Handbook of parenting: Vol. 3. Status and social conditions of parenting* (pp. 359–392). Mahwah, NJ: Lawrence Erlbaum Associates.

Holden, G. W. (1997). *Parents and the dynamics of child rearing.* Boulder, CO: Westview.

Holden, G. W., Coleman, S. M., and Schmidt, K. L. (1995). Why 3-year-old children get spanked: Parent and child determinants as reported by college-educated mothers. *Merrill-Palmer Quarterly, 41,* 431–452.

Holden, G. W., and Edwards, J. (1989). Parental attitudes toward child rearing: Instruments, issues, and implications. *Psychological Bulletin, 106,* 29–58.

Holden, G. W., and Miller, P. C. (1999). Enduring and different: A meta-analysis of the similarity in parents' childrearing. *Psychological Bulletin, 125,* 223–254.

Holden, G. W., Miller, P. C., and Harris, S. D. (1999). The instrumental side of corporal punishment: Parents' reported practices and outcome expectancies. *Journal of Marriage and the Family, 61,* 908–919.

Holden, G. W., Thompson, E. E., Zambarano, R. J., and Marshall, L. A. (1997). Child effects as a source of change in maternal attitudes toward corporal punishment. *Journal of Social and Personal Relationships, 14,* 481–490.

Holden, G. W., and Zambarano, R. J. (1992). Passing the rod: Similarities between parents and their young children in orientations toward physical punishment. In I. E. Sigel, A. V. McGillicuddy-DeLisi, and J. J. Goodnow (Eds.), *Parental beliefs systems: The psychological consequences for children* (2nd ed.). Hillsdale, NJ: Lawrence Erlbaum Associates.

Horney, K. (1933). Maternal conflicts. *American Journal of Orthopsychiatry, 3,* 455–463.

Jones, E. (1923). The phantasy of the reversal of generations. *Papers on psycho-analysis* (pp. 674–379). New York: Wood.

Jones, R. K., and Brayfield, A. (1997). Life's greatest joy? European attitudes toward the centrality of children. *Social Forces, 75,* 1239–1270.

Katainen, S., Raikkonen, K., and Keltikangas-Jarvinen, L. (1998). Development of temperament: Childhood temperament and the mother's childrearing attitudes as predictors of adolescent temperament in a 9-yr follow-up study. *Journal of Research on Adolescence, 8,* 485–509.

Kendler, K. S. (1996). Parenting: A genetic-epidemiologic perspective. *American Journal of Psychiatry, 153,* 11–20.

Koch, H. L., Dentler, M., Dysart, B., and Streit, H. (1934). A scale for measuring attitude toward the question of children's freedom. *Child Development, 60,* 56–63.

Kohn, M. L. (1979). The effects of social class on parental values and practices. In D. Reiss and H. Hoffman (Eds.), *The American family: Dying or developing* (pp. 45–68). New York: Plenum.

Lamb, M. E. (Ed.). (1976). *The role of the father in child development.* New York: Wiley.

Laws, G. (1927). *Parent–child relationships.* New York: Columbia University Press.

Levy, D. (1943). *Maternal overprotection.* New York: Columbia University Press.

Matthews, B., and Beaujot, R. (1997). Gender orientations and family strategies. *Canadian Review of Sociology and Anthropology, 34,* 415–428.

McGillicuddy-De Lisi, A. V., and Sigel, I. E. (1995). Parental beliefs. In M. H. Bornstein (Ed.), *Handbook of parenting: Vol. 3. Status and social conditions of parenting* (pp. 333–358). Mahwah, NJ: Lawrence Erlbaum Associates.

Metcalfe, J., and Mischel, W. (1999). A hot/cool-system analysis of delay of gratification: Dynamics of willpower. *Psychological Review, 106,* 3–19.

Middlemore, M. P. (1941). *The nursing couple.* London: Hamish Hamilton.

Miller, P. C., Shim, J. E., and Holden, G. W. (1998). Immediate contextual influences on maternal behavior: Environmental affordances and demands. *Journal of Environmental Psychology, 18,* 387–398.

Murray, J. A. H., Bradley, H., Craigie, W. A., and Onions, C. T. (1993). *The Oxford English Dictionary.* New York: Oxford University Press.

Noll, R., McKellop, J. M., Vannatta, K., and Kalinyak, K. (1998). Child-rearing practices of primary caregivers of children with sickle cell disease: The perspective of professionals and caregivers. *Journal of Pediatric Psychology, 23,* 131–140.

Nsamenang, A. B., and Lamb, M. E. (1995). The force of beliefs: How the parental values of the Nso of northwest Cameroon shape children's progress toward adult models. *Journal of Applied Developmental Psychology, 16*, 613–627.

Ojemann, R. H. (1935). The measurement of attitude toward self-reliance. In G. D. Stoddard (Ed.), *University of Iowa studies: Studies in child welfare: Vol. 10. Researchers in parent education* (pp. 101–111). Iowa City: University of Iowa Press.

Padhi, J., and Dash, A. S. (1994). The relation of parental attitudes to adolescence competence. *Psycho-Lingua, 24*, 33–42.

Palacios, J. (1990). Parents' ideas about the development and education of their children: Answers to some questions. *International Journal of Behavioral Development, 13*, 137–155.

Pearson, G. H. (1931). Some early factors in the formation of personality. *American Journal of Orthopsychiatry, 1*, 284–291.

Petty, R. E., and Krosnick, J. A. (Eds.). (1995). *Attitude strength: Antecedents and consequences.* Mahwah, NJ: Lawrence Erlbaum Associates.

Plomin, R. (1994). Nature, nurture, and social development. *Social Development, 3*, 37–53.

Potgieter, J. R. (1992). Relationship between child-rearing attitudes and sport leadership. *Psychological Reports, 71* (Pt. 1), 1023–1026.

Radke-Yarrow, M., Campbell, J. D., and Burton, R. V. (1968). *Child rearing: An inquiry into research and methods.* San Francisco: Jossey-Bass.

Ribble, M. A. (1943). *The rights of infants: Early psychological needs and their satisfaction.* New York: Columbia University Press.

Richards, E. L. (1926). Practical aspects of parental love. *Mental Hygiene, 10*, 225–241.

Rohner, R. P. (1986). *The warmth dimension: Foundations of parental acceptance–rejection theory.* Beverly Hill, CA: Sage.

Schuman, W. B., Armstrong, F. D., Pegelow, C. H., and Routh, D. K. (1993). Enhanced parenting knowledge and skills in mothers of preschool children with sickle cell disease. *Journal of Pediatric Psychology, 18*, 575–591.

Schwarz, N. (1999). Self reports: How the questions shape the answers. *American Psychologist, 54*, 93–105.

Sears, C. H. (1899). Home and school punishments. *Pedagogic Seminary, 6*, 159–187.

Sears, R. R., Maccoby, E. E., and Levin, H. (1957). *Patterns of childrearing.* Evanston, IL: Row Peterson.

Sears, R. R., Rau, L., and Alpert, R. (1965). *Identification and child rearing.* Stanford, CA: Stanford University Press.

Shor, R. (1999). Inappropriate child rearing practices as perceived by Jewish immigrant parents from the former Soviet Union. *Child Abuse and Neglect, 23*, 487–499.

Sigel, I. E. (Ed.) (1985). *Parental belief systems: The psychological consequences for children.* Hillsdale, NJ: Lawrence Erlbaum Associates.

Spencer, H. (1896). *First principles* (4th ed.). New York: Appleton.

Stickels, A. C. (1999). *Changing attitudes toward spanking children: An application of the Elaboration Likelihood Model.* Unpublished master's thesis, University of Texas at Austin.

Stogdill, R. M. (1931). Parental attitudes and mental-hygiene standards. *Mental Hygiene, 15*, 813–827.

Stogdill, R. M. (1934). Attitudes of parents toward parental behavior. *Journal of Abnormal and Social Psychology, 29*, 293–297.

Stogdill, R. M. (1936a). Experiments in the measurement of attitudes toward children: 1899–1935. *Child Development, 7*, 31–36.

Stogdill, R. M. (1936b). The measurement of attitudes toward parental control and the social adjustments of children. *Journal of Applied Psychology, 20*, 359–367.

Stolz, L. M. (1967). *Influences on parent behavior.* Stanford, CA: Stanford University.

Symonds, P. M. (1949). *The dynamics of parent-child relaitonships.* New York: Columbia University Press.

Thurstone, L. L. (1931). The measurement of social attitudes. *Journal of Abnormal and Social Psychology, 26*, 249–269.

Updegraff, R. (1939). Recent approaches to the study of the preschool child: Vol. 3. Influence of parental attitudes upon child behavior. *Journal of Consulting Psychology, 3*, 34–36.

Visser, P. S., and Krosnick, J. A. (1998). Development of attitude strength over the life cycle: Surge and decline. *Journal of Personality and Social Psychology, 75*, 1389–1410.

Wachs, T. D. (1987). Short-term stability of aggregated and nonaggregated measures of parental behavior. *Child Development, 58*, 796–797.

Wicker, A. W. (1969). Attitudes versus actions: The relationship of verbal and overt behavioral responses to attitude objects. *Journal of Social Issues, 25*, 41–78.

Wilson, M. (1999). "Take this child": Why women abandon their infants in Bangladesh. *Journal of Comparative Family Studies, 30*, 687–702.

Wilson, T. D., Lindsey, S., and Schooler, T. Y. (2000). A model of dual attitudes. *Psychological Review, 107*, 101–126.

Yamasaki, K. (1990). Parental child-rearing attitudes associated with Type A behaviors in children. *Psychological Reports, 67*, 235–239.

Zuckerman, M., Oltean, M., and Monashkin, I. (1958). The parental attitudes of mothers of schizophrenics. *Journal of Consulting Psychology, 22*, 307–310.

Zunich, M. (1962). Relationship between maternal behavior and attitudes toward children. *Journal of Genetic Psychology, 100*, 155–165.

20

Psychoanalysis and Parenthood

Bertram J. Cohler
Susan Paul
University of Chicago

INTRODUCTION

Parenthood is both one of the most central of adult social roles and also a subjective experience endowed with particular meanings fashioned over a lifetime. Although a couple may anticipate and plan for the first birth and the transition to parenthood, evidence from studies of the transition to parenthood suggests that prospective parents cannot fully anticipate the significance of caring for the baby (Bibring, 1959). Furthermore, as the psychoanalyst Therese Benedek (1973) observed, once a woman or man has become a parent, one is a parent as long as there is memory; Benedek also suggests that even following the years of active parenting, mothers and fathers continue to feel particular responsibility and affection for their offspring. Across the course of life, parents continue to induct their offspring into new roles through forward socialization just as offspring continue through backward socialization to influence parental conceptions of self and management of such adult roles as being parents of yong adults. This process of continued reciprocal socialization across the course of adult life is experienced by both parents and offspring in ways shaped by their own conceptions of self, their unique life history and accompanying memories and hopes, and living in a particular time and place.

In this chapter we consider parenthood across the course of adult life from the dual perspective of psychoanalysis and the contemporary social context of adult lives in the United States. While acknowledging the many satisfactions of being a parent, parents in contemporary society all too often experience feelings of role strain, overload, and conflict (Cohler, 1985). More than four decades ago, an ethnographic and comparative cross-cultural study showed that parenthood was a greater source of both anxiety and hostility for American parents as contrasted with those in the six other cultures around the world for whom comparative data were available (Fischer and Fischer, 1963; Minturn and Lambert, 1964). This anxiety regarding being a competent parent is also reflected in the preoccupation of parents in our society with guides and primers regarding childcare and with feelings of responsibility for how children "turn out" as adults (Clarke-Stewart, 1978; Ryff, Schmutte, and Lee, 1996).

In this chapter we first consider those aspects of psychoanalytic thinking that are particularly germane to the study of parenthood, and then we review particular psychoanalytic contributions to the study of parenthood. We then consider several areas in which psychoanalytic perspectives have been used in the systematic study of parenthood. Perhaps the best known of these contributions has concerned study of pregnancy and the meaning for prospective parents (particularly mothers) of the transition to parenthood. Additional areas in which psychoanalysis has made a contribution to the study of parenthood that are discussed in this chapter include both understanding the basis of parental contributions to the quality of the child's attachments to others and also the study of the father's role in the family. The chapter concludes with a discussion of additional areas in which psychoanalysis can make a contribution to the study of parenthood, including parenthood within lesbian and gay families, parenting, the lives of families living in the midst of social disadvantage, and the study of family life following divorce.

PSYCHOANALYSIS AS A PERSPECTIVE
FOR THE STUDY OF PARENTHOOD

Psychoanalysis is among the most complex and often misunderstood perspectives on the study of social life and personal development. Referring both to a method for the study of wish or intent and also a method of intervention among those experiencing distress in the conduct of their life, psychoanalysis was a term used by the Viennese physician Sigmund Freud (1856–1939) for a method of observation founded on study of associations that his patients made between thoughts that occurred to them and that were then both the subject of communications to Freud and also realized through action and the daily round. As a result of listening carefully to these communications, Freud was able both to assist his analysands in understanding the significance of their own life experiences and to help analysands realize enhanced personal vitality through recognition of an inevitable conflict between the experience of desire founded initially in the child's caregiving experiences within the family, but necessarily remaining out of conscious awareness as a consequence of taboos imposed by social reality, but symbolically enacted as hysterical symptoms.

As a result of Freud's careful clinical observation with his first analysands, he was prompted to develop a comprehensive statement of mental life. In the introduction to *The Interpretation of Dreams* (Freud, 1900/1958), editor and translator James Strachey (1958) noted that, in his early psychoanalytic study, Freud observed the compulsion both among his analysands and himself to connect ideas coming to mind or "associations." Apparently meaningless ideas made sense as a train of thought to which both he and his analysands were able to attach meanings. Freud's emphasis on wish or intent, revealed through the meanings that his analysands attributed to relationships, including that with Freud himself, together with the realization that cultural context provides the template within which these meanings are organized (Chodorow, 1999; Geertz, 1973, 1974; Kakar, 1995; Obeysekere, 1990), represents the foundation of psychoanalysis as a method of study in the human sciences. Freud's focus on careful listening to the pattern of the analysand's associations and the meanings made of these associations provided a method of study relevant not only in the clinical context but also in the study of the meanings that we make of all aspects of our lives, including the experience of parenthood (Cohler and deBoer, 1996; Friedman, 2000; Hoffman, 1996, 1998; Schafer 1980, 1981, 1992).

Freud had recognized the importance of understanding the meanings that we make of our experiences with others in the family even before his father's death in October, 1896. However, in the aftermath of this loss, Freud recognized both his feelings of sadness and also accompanying feelings of joy and relief that he traced to what he saw as an inevitable rivalry between fathers and sons beginning in early childhood but reverberating across the course of life (Gay, 1988). Freud (1900/1958, 1910/1957a, 1910/1957b) saw in Sophocles' drama of *Oedipus the King* an example of this powerful wish that inevitably arises within the family of early childhood when the little boy first realizes that there is a rival for his mother's attentions (Rudnytsky, 1987). Ideally, over time, the little boy resolves these feelings of rivalry by seeking to become like his father and going out into the world to find a woman for himself like his remembered mother of early childhood. For the little girl, Freud saw the problem as symmetrical: Although the little boy was able to maintain his relationship with his primary caregiver and take his father as a rival, for the little girl, caregiver and rival were the same, leading to lifelong struggle between these two generations of women within the family.

Freud described his own self-exploration in the wake of his father's death (Anzieu, 1986; Gay, 1988) as a psychoanalysis, marking the beginning of what has since become a unique means of inquiry regarding wish and intent in mental life (Anzieu, 1986). Ross observed that, already within a week of the first anniversary of his father's death, Freud had written to his Berlin correspondent Wilhelm Fliess of the parallel between his feelings regarding his father and Oedipus' deed in slaying his father. An early result of his self-analysis, he reports to Fliess (Freud, 1897–1904, p. 272) that "... a single idea of general value dawned on me. I have found, in my own case too, [the phenomenon of] being in love with my mother and jealous of my father, and I now consider it a universal event in early childhood...." This observation, fundamental for the subsequent elaboration of psycho-analysis as a human science, focuses on the part of the son in this drama. What Freud neglected to consider was not only the callous act on the part of Laius, abandoning his infant son because of his own needs and fears, but more generally the problem of parents whose own preoccupations are placed before the best interests of the child. Ross (1982a) observed that Freud neglected Laius' active role in the events leading up to their final and fateful confrontation. Issues of incest and taboo haunt the House of Atreus from its origins in the bad parenting reflected in the birth of Dionysus, heir of Zeus and the human Semele, abandoned by his god–father and denied his own legitimacy as a god.

Freud's self-analysis and the field of study that it inspired have presented three problems in using psychoanalysis in the study of parenthood: In the first place, beginning with Freud's own self-analysis, psychoanalysis has been a psychology of offspring struggling with feelings about the remembered parents of early childhood. In the second place, Freud's great discovery of his self–analysis, that of ambivalent feelings toward parents, was based on the study of sons rather than daughters. In the third place, as a result of his own scientific education and the spirit of the times, Freud emphasized the importance of the experience of early childhood as formative for adult personality. In this model, there was little effort to portray personality development across the adult years as other than the continuing repetition of unresolved childhood conflicts. Experiences distinctive of the adult years were of little significance in understanding intention and action.

Freud viewed psychoanalysis as a means for offspring struggling with feelings about parents specifically sons struggling with feelings about fathers. Freud "discovered" in his self-analysis con-flicting and ambivalent feelings toward his father's death. Although he had deeply loved his father, he also he recognized that he had regarded his father as a lifelong rival and was in some ways also relieved by his father's death. Freud described the little boy's desire for his mother a fundamental or "nuclear wish" and the resulting conflict between his wish for intimacy with his mother and his rivalry with his father for his mother's attention a fundamental or "nuclear conflict."

Freud postulated that the little boy harbored wishes for an intimate relationship with his mother based on earliest experiences of caregiving, but that sometime in the second or third year of life, the little boy became aware of his father as a rival and that the ground was laid for rivalry that the little boy could not win (Freud, 1910/1957a, 1910/1957b). Anxiety leading to the formation of psychological symptoms such as obsessions was the consequence of realizing that this could be a dangerous situation in which the little boy feared he could suffer physical harm (castration) at the hands of his presumably competitive and vengeful father." Freud (1910/1957b) subsequently term-ed this nuclear conflict the Oedipus complex in deference to his then-colleague Carl Jung. However, as popularly understood, this latter term does not fully reflect the intensity and psychic pain of the boy's intense struggle with these issues of intimacy and rivalry implicit in the concept of conflict that Freud (1909/1995a) so clearly showed in his report on the analysis of a 3-year-old boy.

Freud presumed that the parental relationship is accorded particular significance within the Western bourgeois family, reflected in the household pattern in which parents generally sleep separately from children. He presumed that this priority that accorded with the parent's relationship with each other, apart from offspring, was a universal phenomenon present in all cultures. Understood in contemporary terms, it might be more accurate to suggest that every culture recognizes that there are some relationships within the family that are accorded particular status. However, it is not necessarily the case that other cultures similarly privilege the intimate relationship of wife and husband and mother and father, which is characteristic of our own culture (Kakar, 1995; Obeysekere, 1990).

Because the wish to be rid of father and have mother for oneself was both socially and personally unacceptable, it remained out of conscious awareness through the force of repression emerging with the transition to middle childhood. However, because this nuclear wish has force and direction, it continues to seek satisfaction lifelong, a compromise between wish and personal and social reality, disguised as dreams, so-called "unintended" actions, psychoneurotic symptoms, enacted in and through the quality of relationships with others, and even leading to such humanistic activities as art, literature, and music. In this formulation, it is the son who wishes, fears, and regrets; the person of the father has little significance, apart from the meaning imparted by the son's experiencing his father.

Ross (1984), struggling with his own feelings about being both a father and a son, has portrayed the dilemma posed by the neglect by the father Laius in Sophocles' epochal statement in Western culture regarding the motives of the father. Ross wondered what kind of a father would want to abandon his firstborn son; Weiss (1985) and Ross (1984) have both noted that the curse placed on Laius that led him to abandon his infant son was a result of a pederastic act with the son of a neighboring king while teaching him to drive a chariot. Weiss maintained that Laius loved boys and did not want to marry, that Jocasta tricked him into the union that led to Oedipus' birth by getting Laius drunk. Weiss (1985) observed that each parent was so preoccupied with his and her own needs that those of the son were sacrificed. However, as both Mahl (1982) and Ross (1982a) observed, Freud later focused on the feelings of fathers regarding sons, referring to his own jealousy of the youth of his sons even while he was growing older. Further, in the *Three Essays on Sexuality*, Freud (1905/1953a) noted the phenomenon of jealousy of middle-aged mothers, perhaps entering menopause, just as their daughter were in the first bloom of adolescence.

The tale of Oedipus focuses on parental preoccupation as the foundation for failure to consider the best interests of offspring. In large part, psychoanalysis has been a psychology of sons' (and daughters') struggles to resolve conflict experienced with their own parents. Parents are implicated as the source of their children's distress. Michels (1993) noted that most of the early clinical findings providing the basis for psychoanalytic study were from the analysis of childless young adults; parents were seen from the perspective of the analysand, rather than in terms of parents' own experiences. As a consequence, psychoanalysis had difficulty developing a psychology parenthood. This problem was compounded by Freud's focus on the emergence and resolution of the nuclear conflict marking the transition from early to middle childhood with little interest in personality development across adulthood.

Viewed from a larger perspective, reconsideration of the meaning of the story of Oedipus in terms of parental neglect poses the question of the the significance of the parents' own psychology, found both on social and personal circumstances, in providing care for offspring across the course of life. In a similar manner, the psychoanalyst Blos (1985) noted that issues posed by the nuclear conflict emerge only after the child's attainment of psychological autonomy from the mother in infancy; once this struggle is experienced, its repercussions continue across the course of life, influencing the son's own experiences as a father.

A second problem is posed for the psychoanalytic study of parenthood, beyond that of psychoanalysis as a psychology of offspring rather than that of parents, was founded on Freud's portrayal of his own ambivalent feelings as a son. It is ironic that nearly all of Freud's early analysands were women. In his early writing Freud (1900/1958) regarded the little girl's struggles with her conflicting feelings first as symmetrical to the problem posed for the little boy. Particularly as emerged in Freud's later writing (Freud's, 1925/1959, 1933/1964), the little boy's sense of morality developed as a consequence of his fear of his father's possible retaliation in the form of genital mutilation for the little boy's desire for an intimate relationship with his mother. This capacity for oversight and possible self-punishment should such wishes be enacted, even in symbolic form, was clearly lacking among girls. Freud presumed that because girls did not face the danger of such mutilation, believing such mutilation had already been realized by a jealous mother as an explanation for their lack of male genitals, there was little impetus for the development of a moral sense founded among boys and based on prohibition as the outcome of the fear of genital mutilation.

As psychoanalysis has shifted from a theory of personality development based on mental conflict to a relational psychology characteristic of much of contemporary psychoanalytic developmental study, it has been possible to enlarge our understanding of gender, sexuality, and development to include the reality of variation in life circumstances as factors involved in the understanding that girls and boys and women and men have of the significance of both gender and psychological development. It is only within the past two decades that psychoanalysis has begun to clarify issues related to psychological development in girls (Chasseguet-Smirgel, 1970) and the related problem of gender differences in the development of a moral sense (Chodorow, 1978, 1989, 1994, 1999; Gilligan, 1983, 1990). Chodorow (1999) emphasized the extent to which, based on shared understandings of bodies and fantasies about body and self, women and men maintain particular stories about their sexuality and their sense of right and wrong, feelings of loyalty and love, desire, guilt, remorse, or regrets regarding the presently remembered past.

In the third place, following an epigenetic model (Freud, 1905/1953a) in which later outcomes were presumed to originate in earlier structures (Gay, 1988; Sulloway, 1979), Freud paid more attention to origins than to outcomes. Implicitly adopting Darwin's perspective on evolution (Ritvo, 1990), Freud worked backward from present psychological symptoms to remembered and reconstructed events of early childhood. At the same time, he recognized that postdiction is much easier and more certain than prediction in the study of lives (Freud, 1920/1955b). Much of subsequent psychoanalytic study followed in this tradition of epigenetic study from Abraham's (1924) first elaboration of the epigenetic model to Erikson's (1951) effort to extend this model to the adult years. Early psychoanalytic contributions to the study of parenthood continued in this tradition of epigenetic study (Benedek, 1959; Bibring, 1959; Deutsch, 1945). Benedek (1970d) did note the importance of studying parenthood across the course of life, because adults remained parents as long as they retained memory. Colarusso and Nemiroff (1979) showed the significance of a psychoanalytic understanding of adult lives that recognized psychological development beyond childhood.

Reviews such as those of Wood, Traupmann, and Hay (1984) and Blieszner, Mancini, and Marek (1996) showed the importance of understanding the meaning of parenthood for parents. Despite these contributions, much of the psychoanalytic focus on the study of parenthood has been on the role of the parent's own childhood experiences on their response to parenthood or to the complex issues of the adolescent boy and his father (Blos, 1985), understood in terms of the father's own oedipal issues without sufficient recognition of the father's present place in the course of life and his experiences of himself in dealing with such particularly salient issues of adult lives as work and aging.

HISTORICAL CONSIDERATIONS IN THE PSYCHOANALYTIC STUDY OF PARENTHOOD

Freud (1900/1958, 1915/1957d, 1915/1957e, 1916–1917/1963, 1923/1961a, 1933/1964) postulated a topographic model of the mind, founded on the assumption that mental life was arrayed as levels of awareness ranging from out of awareness and capable of entering into awareness ("unconscious") to the realm of the potentially knowable ("preconscious") to conscious awareness ("consciousness") (Rapaport and Gill, 1959). Freud maintained that there was an inevitable conflict between the nuclear or fundamental wish of the preschool epoch, portrayed as the desire for diffuse and exclusive pleasure and intimacy with the parent of the other gender and internalized taboo against acknowledgment of this wish whose expression would be prohibited by society. Freud maintained that the nuclear wish has force and direction, always seeking satisfaction, albeit outside of even potential awareness. Awareness guards against explicit expression of this wish, even though one's wish may be admitted into conscious awareness in a disguised manner. Attaching itself to some apparently innocuous aspect of daily life, but associatively connected in some way with the wish, a compromise is struck between the wish and personal–social reality in which there may be some partial discharge of the wish symbolically expressed in the form of dreams, so-called unintended actions and slips of the tongue, psychoneurotic symptoms (hysteria, phobias, obsessions and compulsions), socially approved artistic expressions, and relationships with others.

Precisely because this wish stemming from the family romance of childhood conflicts with personal and social reality, Freud's model of the mind may be portrayed as a conflict psychology, a drive psychology, or an instinct psychology. There is some contradiction between Freud's focus on the events of the preschool years as critical for personality development and his recognition of the importance of the caregiver–infant tie as the foundation for later personality development. On the one hand, Freud is little interested in events before the point, in the child's third to fifth year of life, when the boy's competies for his mother's affection and imagines fear of his father's reprisal, which ultimately lead both to repression of this childhood conflict and also to the search for a mate outside the family. On the other hand, Freud emphasizes the importance for the child's later personality development of the quality of love and affection experienced from the boy's or the girl's mother in the tie to caregiver of earliest childhood. Freud's (1905/1953a) model of epigenetic development stresses that the inevitability of the child's later capacity for loving others is founded on such a close tie with the caregiver of earliest infancy. This epigenetic model provided the foundation for significant changes in the psychoanalytic models of development, focusing on the child's experience of caregiving the epoch before emergence of the nuclear conflict over the preschool years.

In an effort to account for altruism and the developmental of a moral sense, Freud (1923/1961a, 1933/1964) posed a revised, structural model for psychoanalysis. This revised model posed three macrosystems: ego or I, superego or observing I, and id or it. In this reformulation of his earlier topographic model of levels of consciousness, mental life was seen as a horse with three riders, an it, seeing to direct activity in the service of satisfaction of the nuclear wish, the I or ego whose origins were in the it and that searched the external world for means of satisfying the it or id, and the observing I or superego whose task it was to keep tabs on the potentially delinquent ego or I, also the source of satisfaction living up to ideals and standards (Schafer, 1960).

Sigmund Freud occupied a unique place within psychoanalysis. As founder of a new and influential perspective on the psychology of mental life with broad implications for study of personal and social life, through the force of both his person and his writing, his was the dominant voice, not only until his death in 1939, but for much of the time until it was overtaken by dramatic changes in social and intellectual life in the period 1965 to 1975. These changes have been important in a changing psychoanalytic understanding of both the motivation for parenthood and the study of parenthood across the adult years. Much of this change is exemplified by Pine's (1988, 1990) portrayal of the four psychologies of psychoanalysis—drive, ego, object relations, and self—and the review by Lerner and Ehrlich (1992) of changes taking place in psychoanalysis, from the structural (conflict) models focusing on the interplay of the three macrosystems of ego or I, id or it, and observing I or superego systems of Freud (1923/1961a, 1933/1964) to the self, and child developmental perspectives in the period following the end of the Second World War to the present time. Pine (1988, 1990) suggested that each of these perspectives on psychoanalysis assumes the necessity of a compromise between an intention or desire that is generally unacceptable in social life and the expectations of orderly social life. As a result, each of these approaches found in some aspect of Freud's work share a concern with the manner for resolving the problem of satisfying wish or desire within the constraints imposed by social life.

The first modification of Freud's drive psychology or "ego psychology" focused on the person's psychological adaptation to the environment (Hartmann, 1939/1958). Two other perspectives in psychoanalysis, object relations and self, have received much greater attention in the contemporary psychoanalytic literature and have particular relevance in understanding psychoanalytic contributions to the study of parenthood. The object relations perspective represents the reformulation of a position initially elaborated by Freud (1905/1953a) that the drive has an origin (the body), an aim (satisfaction), and an object (that which would satisfy the drive). Freud saw this drive as plastic, satisfied in a variety of ways depending on both constitutional and developmental factors. Some persons seek satisfaction in something other than an intimate relation with women or men, preferring objects such as a shoe fetish, or as a result of being looked at or looking and others in sexual intimacies; the term "person relation" might have been less awkward, recognizing that the object of desire might be a person of either gender and that such alternative modes of satisfaction as fetish are based on experiences both in childhood and across the adult years.

Having discovered the significance of the son's experienced rivalry with his father, together with the emergence and resolution of fantasies regarding both own wishes and father's presumed retaliation, Freud was little interested in events in childhood predating this drama marking the transition from early to middle childhood. However, Freud (1905/1953a) did recognize that, to the extent that the son could not resolve this intrapsychic conflict, the son retreated from this encounter, seeking satisfaction in terms more typical of the toddler epoch than that of the preschool child. Drive satisfaction was said to be attained in the manner most characteristic of children not yet encountering this nuclear conflict, with relationships with others inevitably also characteristic of this retreat from the psychic conflict of the preschool epoch.

Since Freud's signal contributions, psychoanalysis has moved away from a focus on wish, drive, and conflict to focus on accompanying object–person relationships and accompanying focus on psychological needs arising in connection with caregiving outcomes from the period of infancy and early childhood, as contrasted with wishes arising in connection with the emergence and resolution of the nuclear conflict and the prototypical neurosis founded on anxiety and the appearance of psychological symptoms such as hysteria or obsessions as a means of protection or defense against awareness of the nuclear wish appearing across the preschool years (Akhtar, 1994; A. Freud, 1965). The term object relation in its contemporary meaning was first adopted by Balint (1935) in an important paper focusing on the epoch in early childhood in which the child first learns the experience of satisfaction from person relations in the early caregiver–child tie. Balint focused on the life of those for whom this earliest experience had been less than satisfying and the implications of this disappointment for subsequent relationships with others. Winnicott (1960a, 1960b), first a pediatrician and then a psychoanalyst, followed in the tradition pioneered by Balint, portraying the dilemma of the infant whose mother is emotionally unavailable, restating essentially the same issue of the caregiver not experienced by the baby as good enough as experienced by the baby.

This focus on the periods of infancy and toddlerhood was given additional impetus with the emergence of systematic study of early childhood in the years following the Second World War. Spitz (1945, 1946) reported that, in foundling homes, Children who were given even minimal care were able to survive but those infants who were neglected failed to thrive. Reports such as that by Spitz, together with burgeoning research in developmental science, had such an impact on clinical psychoanalytic activity that, by 1961, it had become the dominant model for making sense of personal experience (Gitelson, 1962). Preeminent in this shift was the psychoanalyst John Bowlby (1969, 1973, 1980, 1982, 1988), who pointed to the importance for the child's personality development of the quality of attachment with her or his caregiver, and the psychoanalyst Margaret Mahler and her colleagues (Mahler, Pine, and Bergman, 1975), who highlighted the significance of the child's experience of both attachment and, later, emergence of sense of separateness from the caregiver of early infancy.

Guntrip (1961) and Mitchell (Mitchell, 1988; Mitchell and Black, 1995) each elaborated on the theme of the importance for psychological development of the child's earliest experiences with others, or object relations, first elaborated from Freud's earlier work by Balint (1935), for the course of adult experience of others. As systematized by Mitchell (1988), who articulated what has come to be known as the relational perspective, much of the variation in the adult's capacity for sustaining intimate ties with others is founded in the first years of life, particularly in those instances in which the child experiences caregiving as "not good enough" (Winnicott, 1960b, pp. 145–146); a deficit is constructed for the later capacity for empathy with others and for establishing appropriate mature ties across the adult years.

The relational perspective is principally a deficit theory; for relational theorists, focus is much more on what might go "wrong" in development than in explaining positive contributions of the child's experience of caregiving, except as the absence of deficit. Furthermore, psychoanalytic explanations of both childhood and adult personality rely primarily on the child's development and experience of caregiving in infancy and early childhood in explaining the course of adult lives (Lerner and Ehrlich, 1992). Cohler and deBoer (1996), Colarusso and Nemiroff (1979), Galatzer-Levy and Cohler (1993), Kagan (1980, 1998), and Nemiroff and Colarusso (1990) all have critiqued this perspective regarding the course of development as solely determined within the first years of life. These authors question the assumption that psychological development in the first years of life can serve as a template for understanding adult development. Rather, these authors suggest that the nuclear conflict of early to middle childhood may be the first of several important transformations in the sense of time and memory across the course of life. Further, these authors suggest that, although the meaning of relationships across the course of life may be influenced by events of early childhood, life changes across adolescence and the adult years also influence the experience of self and others.

Another critique of the relational perspective is that psychoanalysis ceases to focus on the psychological experience of others and becomes instead a two-person psychology (Gill, 1994), emphasizing a real relationship rather than meanings made of this relationship. Even if important for the technique of clinical psychoanalysis, it may be questioned whether this two-person psychology moves away from Freud's fundamental concern with the experienced other rather than a social psychology of relationships (Kohut, 1971). Although still reflecting the bias within psychoanalysis regarding the first years of life as formative for later psychological development, psychology of the self, as initially formulated by Kohut (1971, 1972, 1977, 1985), focuses on the development of a sense of personal continuity and integrity across the course of life. Kohut (1977) suggested that the realization of self as vital and effective was a domain of personality separate from capacity for relationships with others. Psychology of the self maintained that it is difficult to realize satisfying relationships when we are preoccupied with the effort to maintain self-regard.

Still presuming concern with the young child's experience of caregiving as the foundation for psychological development across the course of life, Kohut and his colleagues emphasized that initially the child does not differentiate between self and caregiver (Cohler, 1980); to the extent that the caregiver fails to be "good enough" (Winnicott, 1960b, pp. 145–146) for that child, this failure is experienced less as the preparatory step for later deficits in relatedness than as the beginning of a sense of self as unable to manage states of increased tension and to modify grandiose ambitions needed to prop up an enfeebled self. Kohut and his colleagues maintained that others become important as they are used either to provide missing self-sustenance or to complement efforts after maintaining a sense of integrity and vitality across the course of life (Wolf, 1980, 1994). As Wolf (1994, pp. 81–82) observed, " The need for selfobject experiences is not confined to early years but self object responses in a variety of forms are needed throughout the life span . . . the need for selfobject responses is always present, waxing and waning with the ups and downs of the strength and vulnerability of the self. . . . the universal need of any self to be affirmed as significant."

Although Kohut and Wolf presume that the evoked or experienced other is a valuable asset at any point of creative challenge or time of difficulty, through oldest age, Basch (1985) maintained that concern with the manner in which others are used as a source of support and self-sustenance is laid down in early childhood and that adults should no longer need to rely on an evoked other as a source of solace and support. Consistent both with Freud's (1927/1961b, 1930/1961c) view that humankind should outgrow such infantile dependence and with the view of Mahler et al. (1975) that at approximately the age of 4 years the child should have attained autonomy from reliance on a caregiver, Basch's view regarded the concept of an evoked or experienced other as an attribute of earliest childhood development that is characteristically of little significance for adults having realized emotional maturity. Basch maintained that continued reliance on others as a source of emotional sustenance is present only among those unable to sustain personal vitality.

The contributions of Wolf (1980, 1994) and Colarusso and Nemiroff (1979) are distinctive in psychoanalysis for their explicit concern with the course of adult lives. These more recent contributions view psychosocial issues of adult lives, including parenthood, as influenced by the course of both currently recalled childhood experiences and also by adult experiences. This concern with self and personal narrative goes well beyond Erikson's (1963) effort to understand adult lives within a more mechanistic epigenetic perspective. This discussion of changes in psychoanalytic understanding of the course of personality development beyond the direct influence of the childhood years reflects changes taking place in this perspective for the study of adult lives (Cohler and deBoer, 1996; Lerner and Ehrlich, 1992; Mitchell and Black, 1995). Influenced by significant changes more generally in the humanities and social sciences across the past four decades, psychoanalysis has reconsidered Freud's portrayal of psychological development. At the same time, recent discussion of adult lives from a psychoanalytic perspective has expanded on Freud's fundamental observation that our thoughts and feelings are determined by wish and intent, not necessarily in conscious awareness. However, these thoughts and feelings can be discerned through a study of the connections between the meanings that we make of our experience. These meanings have been fashioned over a lifetime and also change over the course of life as the outcome of particular life changes within a template of shared meanings provided by social and historical context (Chodorow, 1999).

This fundamental assumption of meanings founded on lived experience and determining wish and intent reflects the distinctive contribution of psychoanalysis to the study of parenthood and other adult roles. Finally, it should be noted that, although Freud's conflict psychology is a psychology of sons mourning the loss of the father, fathers have largely been excluded from psychoanalytic discussion of parenthood. Although edited collections such as those of Cath, Gurwitt and Ross (1982) and Cath, Gurwitt, and Ginsburg (1989) have sought to correct this imbalance, which maintained that the important aspect in studying psychoanalysis was motherhood. There has been much less psychoanalytic study of fatherhood than of motherhood.

PARENTAL PERSONALITY DEVELOPMENT
AND THE PARENTING PROCESS

Discussion of the historical background of the psychoanalytic study of lives highlights two problems in applying this perspective to the study of parenthood as an adult experience. The dilemma that psychoanalysis has been a psychology of offspring, particularly of sons, poses particular problems as offspring become parents responsible for the care of another rather than being cared for. The further dilemma that psychoanalysis has made at best limited progress in understanding the psychological development of women adds to the problem in discussing motivation for parenthood among women. Freud (1925/1959, 1931/1961d) considered the wish for a baby as a fundamental aspect of female sexuality. Wyatt (1967) suggested that the motivation for parenthood may be more complex than Freud acknowledged. Rejecting Freud's claim of an instinct for parenthood, he noted that social forces and a lifetime of experiences with others codetermine the motivation for parenthood. Wyatt noted the singular importance of experiences of early childhood as a determinant of attitudes regarding the decision to be a parent. Should a little girl observe that her own mother is ambivalent about caring for her, this experience of childhood is likely to affect her own attitude toward becoming a parent. Wyatt chided his colleagues for assuming one single and sovereign motive for motherhood. He observed that both little girls and little boys wish for a child of their own, which may reflect part identification with the child's own parents enacted anew as children later become parents themselves. Wyatt maintained that parenthood provides a new identity, one that is both personally and socially validated.

The classical position regarding psychoanalysis and parenthood was stated by Deutsch (1945, p. 14) who made the following observation:

> Every mother brings into [motherhood] certain emotional factors and conflicts, that is, a certain psychodynamic background partly determined by her life situation, partly by her inner disposition due to her whole psychological development. From this, we can understand that while the beginning of motherhood poses the most mature task of femininity, it will also tend to revive all the infantile conceptions of pregnancy and motherhood and childhood emotional reactions.

Although providing the guiding hypothesis for much of psychoanalytic study of parenthood to the present time, Deutsch (1945) discussed the motivation for motherhood very much within the scope of Freud's initial discussion of the psychology of women, emphasizing penis envy and the significance of childbirth as a means of compensating for the disappointment at having a vagina. The desire for a child is in this view a means for a woman of gaining the long-sought penis (Kestenberg, 1956). Langer's (1992) effort to include social context in understanding the problems posed for women as mothers in the postwar epoch was also founded on Freud's drive psychology and supporting his limited understanding of women's lives. Even Langer's more socially aware discussion of motherhood, founded largely on Melanie Klein's (1932, 1935) assumptions regarding envy and aggression among young children, appears somewhat limited when viewed in terms of such contemporary contributions as that of Chodorow (1999).

Although the dilemma currently confronting psychoanalysis of abandoning Freud's initial conflict or drive perspective, which emphasizes wish or intent, in favor of a psychology based on developmentally founded needs arising from vicissitudes of caregiving, both posed problems for understanding motivation and meaning regarding the role of becoming and being a parent. In view of this later problem, it is ironic that the two most important contributions to the psychoanalytic study of parenthood have been posed by two female psychoanalysts originally a part of the European psychoanalytic community before their immigration to the United States following the rise of National Socialism in Germany in the late 1930s.

Parenthood as a Developmental Phase: The Work of Therese Benedek

In this discussion we focus on more specifically psychoanalytic research from a normative context, and more generally on psychodynamic issues among "ordinary devoted parents," rather than among those identified as showing psychiatric distress. Benedek's (1959) initial contribution was phrased in terms of Freud's psychology of psychological conflict founded on the compromise between the nuclear wish that seeks satisfaction and the opposition of social reality that leads to some satisfaction of the nuclear wish in terms of such disguised means as dreams, slips of the tongue, psychoneurotic symptoms, artistic productions, and endowment of others with one's own wishes or "transferences." At the same time, the scope of Benedek's contribution went well beyond Freud's epigenetic psychology. In her statement of parenthood as a developmental phase of the libido, Benedek (1959) sought to extend Freud's (1905/1953a) epigenetic theory (Hartmann and Kris, 1945), as later revised by Abraham (1924) and Erikson (1963), yet taking into account the reality that parent and child reciprocally influence each other across the course of life (Parens, 1975). Benedek viewed parenthood as an emergent adult role, the response to which is largely colored by the experience of the early childhood years. At the same time, caring for the baby leads to maternal psychological change (in this formative essay, Benedek focused primarily on mother rather than father, which follows from her previous extensive study of the woman's psychophysiology). Benedek framed her discussion in terms of drive theory, maintaining that, through initial caregiving in meeting the baby's needs, the infant becomes attached to the mother. At the same time, this caregiving is important for the mother herself. Optimally responsive caregiving provides the baby with a sense of self-confidence and the mother with increasing self-confidence. However, this experience of caregiving presumes that the mother is able to feel comfortable with the provision of such basic care.

Benedek's view of the importance of caregiving for the baby follows the postwar emphasis in psychoanalysis on the "diatrophic bond" (Gitelson, 1962) between mother and child, which stressed the importance for the baby's development of personal integrity of good enough care or care as experienced by the baby as satisfying (Winnicott, 1956, 1960a). What is significant about Benedek's discussion is that she also focuses on the impact of caregiving for the mother, including the emergence of the ability to receive enjoyment and enhanced self-confidence from caring for her baby. As Benedek (1959, p. 383) observes, "the oral-dependent needs of the child as well as the psychologic processes which evolve from them have been well studied. The mother's receptive needs from the child, however, are not easily recognized in their healthy manifestations except through psychoanalysis."

Benedek maintained that, to the extent that the mother herself had experienced unresolved issues related to feeding and caregiving stemming from her own presently experienced childhood years, she will find it additionally difficult to respond appropriately to the baby's demands. Her own pleasures and pains as an infant are stimulated once again by the act of caregiving. As a result of unresolved conflict regarding childcare, the mother may either overprotect the baby through continuing needs of her own for such care or, alternatively, may enact anew her feelings of deprivation through her failure to respond appropriately to the baby's needs. Benedek (1959, p. 384) further observes that "... motherliness involves the repetition and working through of the primary, oral conflicts with the mother's own mother, the healthy normal processes of mothering allows for resolution of those conflicts ... [t]hus motherhood facilitates the psychosexual development toward completion."

This discussion of the mother–baby tie as an interaction that is psychologically significant for baby and mother alike leads to Benedek's (1959, p. 385) statement of her position:

> I propose that not only with and as a result of the physiologic symbiosis of pregnancy and the oral phase of development, but in each "critical period" the child revives in the parent his related developmental conflicts. This brings about either pathologic manifestations in the parent, or by resolution of the conflict it achieves a new level of integration in the parent. In turn, the child reaches each "critical period" with a repetition of the transactional processes which lead anew to the integration of the drive experience with the related object and self-representations.

This formulation remains the basis of much of the discussion of parenthood from a psychoanalytic perspective (Parens, 1975). Benedek then extends this perspective to the study of fatherhood, noting that for a father the baby represents primarily an extension of his own hopes and fears, to be realized through his child; she does note that, to the extent that fathers are able to care for the baby, they realize some enhanced sense of self-esteem. However, Benedek (1959, p. 388) also extends her perspective to include the father who, like the mother, "repeats with each child, in a different way, the steps of his own development, and under fortunate circumstances achieves further resolution of his conflicts."

Although phrased in terms of Freud's (1905/1953a) epigenetic theory of the development, focusing on the vicissitudes of satisfaction of infant needs for later life, Benedek's discussion was implicitly posed in relational terms, concerned with the experience of each participant for the parent–child exchange, and Benedek also recognized the importance of this process for the development of self and the capacity for empathy for the baby and for a continued sense of positive self-esteem for mothers and fathers able to provide good care. Again, recognizing Freud's (1923/1961a, 1933/1964) structural theory, including the observing I or superego, Benedek was concerned with the impact of parenting for the reciprocal identifications of child with parent and parent with child. Finally, in reflecting on her contribution, Benedek (1959) noted the importance of both biology and culture in determining the interplay of parent and child. She also extended her discussion to include the active phase of parenthood as a whole until the time the now-adult offspring leave home to begin a new life beyond the family of origin.

With the child's sexual maturity often coinciding with parental middle age, parents inevitably want the best for their children but their own revived conflicts may help or hinder the child's ability to move on, to find a mate, and to become a parent; Benedek maintained that there is a biological need for parents to survive through their children's own children. However, echoing Freud's (1905/1953a) discussion, Benedek suggested that mothers have greater difficulty than fathers in maintaining an appropriate relationship with adult offspring. Benedek maintained that the adult child's marriage and, somewhat later, advent of parenthood, was particularly likely to revive the mother's unconscious identification with her adult child that is reflected in the effort to be involved in every aspect of the adult offspring's life. This continued identification is reflected in the particularly complex lifelong tie between older mothers and their young adult to middle-aged daughters (Cohler, 1987; Cohler and Grunebaum, 1981).

Following the publication of the initial essay in 1959, Benedek pursued the significance of her observation regarding the determinants of parental experience and the impact of this experience on the parent–child tie from infancy to the course of life as a whole. Benedek (1973, p. 407) observed that, as long as there is memory of past experiences, parenthood is timeless and parents are always parents: "parenthood ends when memory is lost and intrapsychic images fade out." Collaborating with the psychoanalyst E. J. Anthony, she published a collection of papers extending her conception to parenthood across the adult life course well beyond her earlier concern with the psychobiological factors emerging in the early mother–child interaction (Benedek, 1970d). In a series of papers (Benedek, 1970a, 1970b, 1970c, 1970d), remarkable for their dual focus on the psychological experience of parenthood and the complexities of parenthood as an adult role, Benedek makes clear both that parenthood is timeless and also that parents and children are continually negotiating anew their relationship with each other. Benedek sought to move beyond study phrasing the parent–offspring interaction as pathological to considering the impact of the expanding worlds of children and their parents on parental understanding of themselves as parents. In this series of papers, she (1970a, 1970e) distinguished among (1) "total parenthood", while the child is still young, the time when children are in school, through adolescence, (2) a middle phase of parenthood as offspring become adults, marry, and have children of their own, and (3) grandparenthood, as older parents become involved in perpetuating the lineage.

Benedek (1970e) noted that, as children enter school, parents begin to feel exposed; the child's success in school and community becomes a test of the parent's own success in providing for children earlier in life. She also observed that parents of school-age children wish to hang on to the past when they knew everything about the child. She believed that parents become apprehensive when children begin school and enter into a world beyond the family. At the same time, parents also identify with their children's school successes and failures. The child's sexuality may pose particular problems for women less comfortable with their own womanliness and, particularly as children become adolescents, live again their own adolescence through that of their offspring. Benedek (1970d) observed that fathers may have similar difficulties, not infrequently jealous of their son's virility. This identification with the lives of offspring, particularly daughters, increases as the daughter becomes an adult, marries, and has children of her own. Often, instead of relaxing their influence over their daughter's life, mothers may become increasingly intrusive. The arrival of grandchildren may intensify this identification, realizing enhanced sense of self-esteem from bestowing the status of parent on their offspring and ensuring that grandchildren are able to carry on family traditions. Freed from the demands of total parenthood when their own children were young, grandparents are able to enjoy their grandchildren in ways in which they could not enjoy their own children.

From Pregnancy to Parenthood: Grete Bibring and the Concept of "Crisis" Points in Development

The psychoanalyst Bibring (1959) and her colleagues (Bibring, Dwyer, Huntington, and Valenstein, 1961a, 1961b) also considered the psychological significance of parenthood. Although Benedek's work was largely theoretical, her research group tried to anchor their formulation in findings from the study of women across the course of pregnancy. Bibring noted the spate of studies attributing personality and adjustment among offspring to presumed aspects of mothering, but she also noted that these studies did not consider the reality that observed parental distress may already be reactive to the child's own disturbance. To study the origins of maternal distress reported in so many studies of parents caring for young children, Bibring and her colleagues recruited a group of 15 women who were about to become first-time mothers and who were willing to participate in a course of psychoanalytic investigation designed to aid in understanding maternal personality before the first birth. Pregnancy was understood as a period of crisis involving both somatic and psychological changes. Bibring's presumption in this study was similar to that of Benedek, endorsing both Freud's (1905/1953a) epigenetic psychology and Erikson's (1963) extension of Freud's formulations across the adult years, although presuming the careful psychobiological study that had first encouraged Benedek's exploration of the psychodynamics of parenthood. Bibring (1959, p. 116) made the following observation:

> In pregnancy, as in puberty and menopause, new and increased libidinal tasks confront the individual, leading to the revival and simultaneous emergence of unsettled conflicts from earlier developmental phases and to the loosening of partial or inadequate solutions of the past . . . the outcome of this crisis is of the greatest significance for the mastery of the thus initiated phase (maturity in puberty, aging menopause and motherhood in pregnancy). However, it is well known that these crises are equally the testing ground of psychological health, and we find that under unfavorable conditions they tend toward more or less severe neurotic solutions.

This perspective was well demonstrated in the Boston pregnancy study; Bibring et al. (1961a, 1961b) reported that the women in their study repeated a mode of relating to others, such as pronounced dependency on others, that was most characteristic of their own earlier life. This tendency was particularly pronounced after women felt the first signs of life in their fetus. At the same time, the developmentally relevant challenge of becoming a parent forced new solutions to their lack of "good enough care" from them (Winnicott, 1960a) and recollected parental emotional preoccupation that they had experienced during their own childhood. Furthermore, the crisis of transition to parenthood was not completed until after delivery and in the immediate postpartum epoch.

Maternal personality maturation, following the backward shift to earlier modes of satisfaction during pregnancy, was followed by new maturational steps as women kept pace with their babies' development. Daughters were reported to be better able to realize psychological independence from their own mothers following the advent of parenthood. There has been much more limited psychoanalytically informed study of the impact of becoming a parent on the father. However, Liebman and Abell (2000) have suggested that expectant parenthood leads men to resolve their relationship with their own father in ways more satisfying than they had experienced as young children, including continuing efforts to resolve once again the psychological conflict of affection for their mother and fear of their father's reprisal for having this desire.

Ghosts in the Nursery: The Contributions of Selma Fraiberg and Daniel Stern

Whereas Benedek and Bibring and her colleagues had relied on Freud's epigenetic perspective, as modified by Abraham (1924) and Erikson (1963) in explaining the impact of parents' experienced early childhood as a determinant of response to the baby, Fraiberg, Adelson, and Shapiro (1975) restated this perspective in terms more consonant with ego–psychological perspectives in psychoanalysis. Fraiberg et al. (1975, p. 100), observing that "in every nursery there are ghosts," maintained that, although there is some variation in the extent to which parents' own experiences of being parented interfere in the baby's care, a detailed presentation of two case studies of work with mothers showed that parents use strategies founded on a continuing affective haunting experience of an aggressive parent of their own childhood (A. Freud, 1936/1966) in their relationship with their own children. In these instances, the past is repeated rather than remembered and resolved. Fraiberg et al. observed that parents keep the psychological pain of their own childhood alive and suggested that parents experience this pain anew with the advent of parenthood and as they care for their own young children.

Stern (1985, 1995) extended the paradigm for understanding the impact of the mother's receipt of care during her own childhood initially developed by Fraiberg et al. (1975) in his description of "the motherhood constellation." The mother's own subjective experience of caregiving is founded both in experiences with her own parents from earliest childhood and also with other significant persons in her life to the present time, such as her husband (representations of interactions that have been generalized or RIGs). These evoked or essential others (Galatzer-Levy and Cohler, 1993) or RIGS as formulated by Stern (1985) are meanings that are made of relationships with others based on the generalization of interactions repeated with particular significant persons over relatively long periods of time. Stern suggested that RIGS of mother and father provide a template for a mother's interactions with her own children. The child, in turn, forms a similar representation based on generalization of interactions over time, which then provides the template for the child's own understanding of self and others across the course of life.

Stern (1985) maintained that it is not enough to show that parental representations of childhood experiences influence the present relationship with the child. The child must experience this enactment of the parental past, and there must be evidence in the child's response to the parent that the child has experienced this "ghost" of the parent's own childhood currently represented in their relationship through recording of a brief parent–child interaction sequence and the parent's experience of this sequence directly following the observation. Stern used the mother's narrative of her experience during this video-recorded interaction as the basis for understanding both her experience of caring for her child, founded on her own experience being parented, and also as a means for evaluating the child's response to caregiving.

Self Psychological Perspectives on Parenthood

In his discussion of the motivation for parenthood, Wyatt (1967) questioned views focused on presumed instinctual–biological psychoanalytic perspectives and particularly those that viewed the wish for a baby as simply another means of a woman's effort to resolve her disappointment that she did not have a penis. Wyatt called attention to the significance of the motive for parenthood as an expression of the adult self, noting that there is an "inner duality" in which motivation for parenthood both evokes anew early life experiences within an adult's own parental family and also resolves feelings associated with remembered dissatisfactions with an adult's own parental care as the adult becomes a parent. The advent of parenthood becomes a means for fostering integration of experiences of a lifetime crystalized in this new role. Wyatt's discussion and his critique of the motivation for parenthood in terms of a woman's conflict regarding her sexuality anticipated a more recent discussion of parenthood as an expression of the adult self (Kohut, 1971, 1977; Kohut and Wolf, 1978).

Freud (1914/1957c) discussed the origins of self-regard and the importance of this sense of personal integrity for both well-being and psychopathology. He suggested that parental love and concern was an expression of the parent's own self-love now transformed into the care for another. Freud (1914/1953b) noted in his essay on narcissism that parents need to view their child as the essence of perfection, renewing the sense of heightened self-regard that they had since been forced to renounce when confronted with reality. From this perspective, parental love is little more than self-regard reborn, although identifying the child's own attainments with what parents had desired for themselves. For Manzano, Espasa, and Zilkha (1999), this investment in the child represents a problem, but for those working within the tradition of psychology of the self, to the extent that parents both experienced positive morale and also enjoyed enhanced self-regard from what they had experienced as emotionally attuned caregiving, this experience of parental attuned caregiving provides for an enhanced sense of personal integrity as offspring become parents themselves. Again, these authors focused on problems in which parental anxiety interferes with being able to remain empathetically attuned, but with parents enacting unresolved struggles anew with their children, the terms narcissism and presumptive self-love too often have negative connotations in psychoanalysis.

Kohut (1971, 1977) and Kohut and Wolf (1978) extended Freud's (1914/1953b) discussion in his essay on narcissism in an effort to provide a complementary developmental process to that provided by Freud's drive or conflict theory, and they have suggested that it is difficult to care for another unless able to realize self-love or self-regard. In contrast to separation–individuation theorists (Mahler et al., 1975), Kohut suggested that the baby experiences care provided by parents not as something external and separate from self, with a problematic attachment the outcome of this struggle to realize psychological autonomy, but rather as an integral aspect of the baby's own self-experience (Cohler, 1980). To the extent that such care is not good enough in terms of the child's own needs, the child develops an enfeebled sense of self. Lacking personal vitality and integrity, the child, and later the adult, feels unable to modulate wishes and desires, experiences increased psychological tension, and ultimately experiences a sense of depletion and despair.

Over time, parental caregiving activities become part of the child's experience of self and others and, with attainment of adulthood, the basis for experiencing oneself as caregiver in the parental role. To the extent that the baby experiences parental concerns and actions as affirming nascent efforts after mastery and as modulating tension states, the child can develop the skills necessary to modulate ambitions and talents in terms of that which is both personally satisfying and that may be realistically attained. Certainly parents relive their own ambitions anew through their children, albeit in a modulated and transformed manner expressed as empathy and attunement to the baby's needs and, later, to each aspect of the child's development. Although parents may wish for unbounded success for their offspring, they are generally realistic regarding that which their children might realize. Elson (1985) stressed the reciprocal nature of parent and offspring experiences of each other. Clearly, a baby easy to care for and alive to the world, responsive to caregiving and vigorous, makes fewer demands for caregiving on the part of mother and father.

To the extent that one or both parents experienced some failure of parental empathic response to their nascent efforts at mastery during their own early childhood, parents would experience some limitations in their ability to provide caregiving that is good enough for the baby's needs. Furthermore, as Elson (1985) observed, each parent must able to empathetically respond to the needs of the other in order to facilitate caregiving. For the father, this often means supporting his wife's caregiving activities. Elson (1985) viewed this as a clarification of the position of Benedek and Bibring regarding the role of the personal past in determining the manner of response to parenthood. If parents fail each other as partners in caregiving, this failure may be experienced by the child as a failure in his or her own ability to modulate tension states and, later in childhood and adulthood, as a deficit in the capacity to remain empathetic with others or to feel a continued sense of personal integrity and vitality.

This self psychological perspective on parenthood was also explored by Ornstein and Ornstein (1985). Sharing with Elson (1985) an appreciation for the findings of developmental study that had shown both the competence of infants and the reciprocal nature of influences in the parent–child relationship, the Ornsteins stressed the extent to which parenting, the active caregiving for offspring, is characterized by parent–child mutuality in which each adapts to characteristics of the other, as a "self–self–object unit." For the child, self and experienced caregiving are experienced as one. For the child, appropriate, well-modulated parental response supports the development of a sense of personal vitality and integrity; for the parents, the ability to respond empathetically to the baby leads to baby's development of an enhanced sense of personal vitality and self-confidence. The Ornsteins emphasize that parents and offspring each use the other psychologically to enhance this sense of personal integrity or self-regard. Following Kohut's self psychological perspective in psychoanalysis, to the extent that the child feels appreciated and affirmed by caregiving, the child is able to develop a sense of self as competent and, feeling positive self-regard, is later able to reach out empathically to others.

Much of both psychoanalytic and systematic observational study of children has shown the functions that parents serve for children, but there has been much less focus on the significance of childcare for the parents' own adult selves. Again, consistent with the point of view advanced by Emde (1983), Colarusso and Nemiroff (1979), Nemiroff and Colarousso (1990), and Galatzer-Levy and Cohler (1993), it is important to understand the impact of childcare for the adult self. From the moment of conception, parental hopes and expectations provide the basis for parental concern for the child, facilitating the child's own development of a firm sense of self. As the child grows and develops particular talents and skills, the child's developing abilities are ever important for parents who both join in affirming the child's growth and maturation and realize newly enhanced self-regard from participating with the child. Although in the extreme instance parents may "live" through their child's accomplishments, within families parents take pleasure in the attainments of their offspring, from the first smile and the development of motor activities and language through later attainments in school and community.

Parents thus receive affirmation for their parenting through their caregiving; parenting is a valued aspect of adult lives. The intrusiveness and parental preoccupations that interfere in appropriate, empathetic responses unique to each point in the child's own development are understood as a deficit in the parent's own personality stemming from experienced empathetic failure in the parent's own earlier life and may interfere with the child's emotional development. Parents may view their child as an extension of self, becoming overly involved, or else may distance themselves from their child out of a fear of loss of self in the intimacy of caregiving. Ornstein and Ornstein (1985) share Winnicott's (1956) view that in the average devoted family parents are able to continue to provide developmentally appropriate responses reciprocal to the child's developmental gains and to support the child through inevitable everyday disappointments and frustrations.

Finally, the Ornsteins called attention to the importance of the continued experience of each generation of the other through the adult years. Even following the end of active parenting, each generation provides sustaining functions for the other through mutual empathetic resonance with both the disappointments and problems of everyday life, including such significant life changes as the unexpected death of a spouse in either generation, job loss, or serious illness in another family member. Each generation seeks continued validation and support across the course of life, and each generation provides empathetic support for the other. Parents and offspring continue to need and to use each other in ways appropriate for point in the life course through the parents' own oldest age.

RESEARCH ON PARENTAL PERSONALITY AND OFFSPRING DEVELOPMENT

Research in psychoanalysis remains somewhat problematic; much of the formal research concerned the study of the efficacy of clinical psychoanalytic intervention to relieve personal distress (Galatzer-Levy, Bachrach, Skolnikoff, Waldron, and Levy, 2000; Miller, Luborsky, Barber, Docherty, 1993; Shapiro and Emde, 1995). Grünbaum (1993) questioned the value of this research based on case studies that rely on a patient's verbal reports and the analyst's subjective judgment of the meaning of these verbal reports by using presumably circular reasoning, patient verbal accounts that are liable to suggestion, and theoretical commitments. Much of this critique applies to all research that relies on life-history accounts. In response, psychoanalysis has made available, as has other research in which narratives are used (Mishler, 1990; Spence, 1994), the evidence used in formulating assumptions regarding meanings and in the study of particular lives.

Expecting Parents and the Transition to Parenthood

Much of both classical and contemporary study of parenthood from a psychoanalytic perspective has focused on parental preparation for parenthood, particularly the meaning for the prospective mother of pregnancy and parturition (Bradley, 2000). There has been much discussion of the psychology of pregnancy and childbirth over the past half-century. Much of this study has been concerned with the onset of psychiatric illness in the period just before or following childbirth (Cohen, 1966; Grunebaum, Weiss, Cohler, Gallant, and Hartman, 1982; Melges, 1968; Miller, 1999; Yalom, Lunde, Moos, and Hamburg, 1968). The first systematic study was Bibring's (1959) formulation regarding pregnancy as a crisis or turning point in a woman's life, similar to both puberty and menopause, that requires new and different solutions for lifelong adaptation and leads under favorable conditions to enhanced adjustment or, under less optimal circumstances, to the failure to move forward in the course of adult development. Bibring and her colleagues wondered what the impact might be of the profound psychological changes assumed to take place during pregnancy on the mother's attitudes toward her newborn. In particular, to the extent that a woman avoids coming to terms with her pregnancy and is unable to face the reality of parturition, a woman may be less sensitive to her baby's needs and less able to be a responsive mother.

A related question concerns the extent to which pregnancy as a maturational crisis differs from other such transformations across the course of life (Rossi, 1968). Pregnancy includes both a woman's loving relationship with her husband together with her effort to make sense of physiological and psychological changes; this inward-looking experience may lead the pregnant woman to focus more intensely on herself and these changes than she did before pregnancy. First, there is the expectation that a woman will be able to experience the fetus as a part of herself and then, with "quickening," to tolerate the disruption in this merger of self and baby, accepting the baby as both part of herself yet also separate; from birth onward the baby represents part of herself, and yet she must also love the baby as a separate being. At the same time she reproduces herself, she is also reproducing a child who will from birth onward also be loved as a separate being. Finally, there is the task of recognizing that, from birth onward, the woman adopts a new identity and responsibility as a mother and also changes her relationship with her own mother. Any of these related aspects of the psychophysiological challenge of pregnancy can pose an obstacle to the mother's ability to provide caregiving that is attuned to the child's needs and to permit the child to develop a sense of self as psychologically separate from the mother.

From a study of 15 women, generally highly educated and articulate, volunteering for the study that included detailed, repeated interviews based on the model of the psychoanalytic interview (including two women who agreed to participate in a recorded research psychoanalysis across the course of the study), Bibring et al. (1961a, 1961b) reported that, across pregnancy, they found signs of conflict and a return to psychologically earlier modes of dealing with the woman's own needs related to food and other aspects of bodily functioning. Much of this change took place in the time after the women first felt sings of life. However, women who were highly rational and organized showed less such return to concern with body and eating, becoming ever more rational and well organized, anticipating and trying to carefully plan every aspect of pregnancy and the postpartum period.

One of the distinctive aspects of this research was a careful specification of issues to be studied and the related effort to translate concepts from clinical psychoanalysis into terms that could be reliably rated, including means used to deal with conflicts taking place across the period of pregnancy, a number of semistructured (projective) techniques, and rating sheets used in interviews with the patient and her husband (little information was provided regarding findings with fathers). These measures were developed on a pilot group of more than 50 mothers. The original research plan was for women to be interviewed up through the first postpartum year. Tragically, this systematic psychoanalytic research study of pregnancy and parenthood never came to fruition.

Three other psychoanalytically influenced accounts of pregnancy among women pregnant with their first baby have been reported (Ballou, 1978; Breen, 1975; Leifer, 1980). Breen (1975) studied a group of 60 first-time mothers and reported that those women most able to admit to concern about being able to care for the baby also reported coping better with providing care for their infants. Extending her earlier discussion, Birksted-Breen (2000) reported that women inevitably feel mixed feelings about becoming parents but all too often have noone to talk with about their concerns. Following the psychoanalytic theory advanced by Klein (1932, 1935), Birksted-Breen stressed the problems posed for the pregnant woman feeling both love and hate toward the baby growing inside her and the anxiety that accompanies recognition of these ambivalent feelings. Birksted-Breen (2000) also noted that pregnancy may lead a woman to feel pulled back to her relationship with her own mother during her own childhood. Pregnant women may then believe that their childbirth experiences must inevitably be like those reported by their own mother and may confuse their own body with their mother's body.

Relying on the relational perspective in psychoanalysis, concerned with the manner in which we experience and make meaning of others, Ballou (1978) studied a group of 12 pregnant women in a university community who were willing to volunteer in a study relying on clinical ratings of semistructured (projective) tests and participation in detailed clinically informed interviews including reports of dreams. Clinically experienced raters examined protocols for a woman's characteristic ways of getting along with her husband and parents, sense of self, and overall style of relating to others. Women were interviewed during each trimester of pregnancy and again 6 weeks and 3 months postpartum. Independent ratings of the mother–baby relationship were made during the postpartum period.

From the discussion of a number of themes emerging in the interviews and tests, Ballou (1978) reported that, across the course of pregnancy, women were able to make peace with their earlier feelings of resentment and anger regarding their relationship with their own mother. Consistent with the concept of "ghosts in the nursery" of Fraiberg et al. (1975), an important determinant of the mother's response to her own baby was her relationship with her own mother; Ballou (1978) reported that women tended to repeat with their infant their relationship with their own mother. Consistent with Bibring's (1959) clinical observation that pregnancy leads to disruptions in the ways in which a woman understands herself and others, the principal concern of Ballou (1978) was with the impact of pregnancy on these ways of understanding self and others. Themes of both autonomy and dependency emerged anew during pregnancy. Women who had been able to work out the complexities of their relationship with their mother and father and with others showed a better adjustment across the period of their pregnancy.

Relationships with their husbands proved more complex for these women; husbands found it difficult to be nurturant with their wives, together with showing enhanced anxiety regarding the integrity of both their own body and that of their wives over the course of the wife's pregnancy. Finally, although the women dealt in quite different ways with issues of the baby's coming separateness after childbirth, repeating an issue also considered by Bibring et al. (1961a), observation of mother–child interaction at 3 months postpartum suggested that these women were able to foster reciprocity with the baby as a separate person.

A study similar in design to that of Ballou was reported by Leifer (1980). A group of 19 women volunteers within a university community, all in their first trimester of pregnancy with their first child, was interviewed at each trimester of pregnancy and again approximately 2 months postpartum. In general, these women reported greater worry and dissatisfaction with the process of pregnancy, including changes in physical appearance and physical symptoms *after* rather than during pregnancy. Indeed, these women also reported lowered sense of well-being in the postpartum period, along with increased concerns and fatigue. Many women felt overwhelmed by the transition to parenthood and socially isolated even as they became preoccupied with the baby. Most women even felt some regret at becoming a parent. These women did not consider themselves sick during pregnancy but did report enhanced symptoms during the first and the third trimesters; the second trimester was marked by the greatest sense of physical and emotional well-being.

Women worked during pregnancy to develop more realistic attitudes toward their marriage (husbands were reported to experience their wife's pregnancy with enhanced stress and concern) and in anticipating parenthood. Across the period of pregnancy, women developed increased feelings for the baby, together with fantasies and expectations regarding the advent of parenthood. By 7 months postpartum, moods returned to normal in approximately two thirds of the women who were actively struggling to strengthen their relationship with their baby and continuing ambivalence regarding the process of becoming a parent; most women reported their husbands to be of little assistance and, most often, actively working to build their careers. Consistent with Gutmann's (1975, 1987) claim that the impact of the advent of parenthood is to lead to stereotyped enactment of gender roles, women became particularly focused on the baby while their husbands became preoccupied with issues of providing for the family.

Most mothers of girls expressed some initial disappointment that they had not given birth to boys; by 7 months postpartum mothers of girls appeared to be protecting themselves against remembering this initial disappointment. Women worried about rearing a boy who would be appropriately masculine. Finally, women whose babies were somewhat less responsive to their care felt an enhanced sense of disappointment that their baby was not more responsive. Still, most women felt an enhanced sense of womanliness at having born a child. At the same time that they were able to take great pride in their achievement and in finally realizing social maturity, these women struggled across the first months of parenthood at managing role conflict, strain, and overload. As Cohler (1985) noted, virtually all studies of the transition to parenthood similarly report a drop in morale with the advent of parenthood that begins to shift as all children finally begin school and mothers realized increased personal freedom during the day. As Leifer (1980, 230) observed, ". . . seven women who have achieved a mature level of personality integration, satisfying marriages, and stable identities, and who enjoy caring for their infants, nevertheless experience considerable stress on being confronted with the life changes associated with motherhood."

These two detailed studies of response to pregnancy and parturition among small groups of well-educated women, who volunteered for an extensive interview study provide thoughtful observations that support larger and more detailed social psychological studies such as those of Shereshefsky and Yarrow (1973), Grossman, Eichler, and Winickoff (1980), Entwisle and Doering (1981), and Cowan and Cowan (1992), as well as Michaels' and Goldberg's (1988) edited collection, and Heinicke (in Vol. 3 of this *Handbook*), together with the large literature on the transition to parenthood in the sociological tradition (Cohler, 1985; Cohler and Grunebaum, 1981; LeMasters, 1970; Walker, 1999). Perhaps most striking of these studies is that of Cowan and Cowan (1992), who followed up nearly 100 expectant parent couples and a group of nonparent couples volunteering for the study in Northern California over a period of more than a decade.

Adopting a family systems perspective, including the family's relationships with both other kindred and the larger community, the Cowans highlighted the problem that the transition from couplehood to parenthood is a difficult one; parents' satisfaction with their marriage, work, and ties with their own family have much to do with maintaining closeness after becoming parents and in continuing to support each other. Such particularly troublesome issues for expectant parents after becoming parents is the assignment of childcare responsibilities. Echoing the psychoanalytic perspective of Fraiberg et al. (1975), the Cowans (1992, p. 204) noted that parents must be on guard not to repeat with their own children problems experienced in their own growing up.

Parents' Remembered Childhood Experiences and the Adjustment of Their Young Children

A second area in which psychoanalysis has made significant contributions to the study of parenthood concerns the complex relationship of parenting and such aspects of early childhood adjustment as the child's evidence of being able to form a secure attachment. As already noted, ours is a culture that presumes that the child's psychological development depends very much on the quality of parenting provided in the first years of life. Presuming that, as Wordsworth (1807/1984) stated, "the child is the father of the man," to the extent that parents have been able to offer the average expectable environment, children will be able to overcome the challenges to development across the first years of life (Hartmann, 1939/1958; Robertson, 1962; Winnicott, 1960a). Subtle variations in childcare may have less of an influence than is often supposed; it is those long-term, malignant patterns of maladaptation with the family that might have a negative impact on the child's development (Stern, 1985, 1989).

Mahler and the separation–individuation paradigm. Although Freud's model of the development of the mind placed great emphasis on the parental care of infants, contemporary psychoanalysis has singled out the second year of life as the critical one for the child's development. The first discussion of this period (Mahler et al., 1975) was as an extension, by analogy, to work with children whose coping ability was severely limited by personal distress. Mahler (1968) described her work with a group of infants who lacked communication abilities and suffered from a syndrome known as "infantile autism." Generalizing from this earlier study of a small group of infants with unusual limitations in coping ability, Mahler et al. (1975) maintained that the infant was born without relatedness and only gradually developed a tie to caregivers (primarily the mother) across the first months of life, leading to a merger of mother and self.

Over the course of the second year of life, the toddler struggled with the first emergence of sense of separateness from mother—reflected in darting and shadowing—as the toddler makes the first hesitant moves away from mother, only to return to the safety of the mother's lap and "emotional refueling." This so-called practicing subphase foreshadows the child's growing awareness of both the possibilities and the dangers of being separate from the mother reflected in an anxious, hesitant, ambivalent effort to move psychologically away from the mother toward greater psychological autonomy, which Mahler et al. term the subphase of "rapprochement" on the way to realization of complete psychological independence and object constancy, or the ability to maintain a sense of relatedness with the mother apart from her physical presence during the third to fourth year of life.

This portrayal of the child's development of a sense of psychological autonomy focuses very much on the child's struggle to realize a sense of separateness rather than on attributes of the mother that might foster or interfere with this effort. Mahler presumed that the mother is emotionally available to the child during this critical developmental period of the second year of life and is able to foster that sense of psychological separateness that later leads to the sustained experience of a reliable caregiver, which is important during those times of increased tension and sense of vulnerability, and to the ability to use without overuse those caregiving others available in later life. However, among those children unable to realize this sense of separateness when attaining adulthood and parenthood, this earlier intrapsychic struggle may interfere in fostering a sense of separateness among those children's own offspring and in fostering those childrens' own sense of separateness.

Kramer, Byerly, and Akhtar (1997) suggested that parents who themselves had difficulty in realizing a sense of psychological autonomy with their own parents show problems in fostering psychological autonomy among their offspring; these parents may interfere with their children's development of friends and any life outside the binding relationship with the mother, unable to foster this sense of separateness. In this portrayal of the mother who psychologically (and socially) prevents her children from developing real-world connections outside the family, Mahler et al. reflected the ideal within our own culture that independence and autonomy are desirable aspects of personal adjustment and that interdependence and sense of connectedness with other family members pose a problem.

This perspective is elaborated in Stierlin's (1974) discussion of parents who either use their offspring as their "delegates" in managing the reality outside the family, sending their offspring into the world to realize the successes and goals they believe they never attained, or binding their adolescents so closely to them that the adolescent is unable to leave home. Blos (1967, 1985) also noted that issues of separation and individuation are evoked anew within the family of the adolescent. Ideally, the adolescent has the psychological autonomy, able to separate from parents and manage adulthood. For Blos, adolescence poses problems for both young people and their parents, but also provides an opportunity for the resolution anew of the crisis of the nuclear neurosis as a young man is able to find a mate similar in many respects to his mother. Furthermore, discussions of the separation–individuation paradigm posed by Mahler et al. (1975), initially focused on the meanings made of relationships, subtly shift to interpersonal characteristics.

Attachment theory and the systematic study of "ghosts in the nursery."   Mahler et al. initially observed mother–child pairs in a clinical research setting. Providing evidence for their theory of psychological development over the course of past two decades, this developmental perspective has been less influential as an intellectual focus for research. In part, the particular assumptions of Mahler's approach, founding normal developmental study on observations originally made with troubled children, and the use of clinical terms for these normal developmental processes have been a source of concern. Furthermore, the emergence of both relational and self psychological perspectives for understanding development across the first years of life has questioned whether focus on issues of separation and emergence of psychological autonomy adequately reflect the emergence of a stable sense of self and ability to realize satisfying relationships with others across the childhood years (Fonagy, 1995, 1999, 2000; Main, 1995, 2000; Wolf, 1994).

For these theorists, portraying the process of emergence of a sense of psychological autonomy among children later destined to become parents, much of the emphasis is placed on the relationship between mother and toddler in the second year of life. A similar perspective is provided by theorists focusing on emergence of the child's experience of "attachment" to caregivers (Cummings and Cummings, in Vol. 5 of this *Handbook*). This perspective on the caregiver's contribution to the child's capacity for relatedness was influenced by Bowlby's (1969, 1973) clinical study of the formation of affectional bonds or attachment in earliest infancy, which focused on the emotional impact of mourning and loss in childhood on personality development across the course of life and the adaptive potential of attachment in a social evolutionary context. Concern with the manner in which the baby develops the capacity for relating to others and for forming a secure sense of self is shared among psychoanalytic theorists of development across the course of life. Consistent with both cultural accounts of development and psychoanalytic study, this capacity for relatedness and self-regard is determined in large part by caregiver attributes, particularly the mother's ability to foster a sense of psychological separateness while being able to resonate with the emotional states of others and to use intimacy as a source of comfort and satisfaction across the course of life.

There is an obvious connection between Bowlby's formulation, expressed in his concern with the baby's realization of a secure experience of the availability and comfort of the caregiver through representation of this caregiving that is stable over time and similar concern within psychoanalysis regarding representations of caregiving that are psychologically sustaining. Fonagy (1999) has reviewed the points of convergence and divergence between the two developmental traditions of psychoanalysis and attachment theory. Reviewing the contributions of Anna Freud (1965) in the elaboration of a developmental scheme, Mahler et al., object relations theorists, and such psycho-analytically informed developmental theorists as Stern (1985, 1989, 2000), Fonagy's (1999) review highlighted the theoretical congruence between the concept of attachment and a secure working base for the child's attachment to others and the role of facilitating caregiver.

As Fonagy notes, few psychoanalytic propositions have been submitted to systematic tests (and indeed there is considerable question whether this natural science model is in any way relevant to psychoanalytic study). Moreover, whereas psychoanalysis focuses primarily on incongruities in development and problems in realizing a secure sense of caregiver as an aspect of one's own self-regard, the attachment perspective focuses on the realization of developmental continuities. These two perspectives share a common concern with a developmental perspective in personality devel-opment focused on the caregiver–infant tie. Furthermore, attachment theory focuses on both the contribution of the parent to the child's personality development and on attributes of the parent's own personality that are related to the child's personality development. Indeed, Fonagy (1999) ex-plicitly acknowledged the concern of Fraiberg et al. (1975) with the "ghost in the nursery" as a guiding presumption of attachment perspectives.

Much of the focus in studies that used the Strange Situation experimental paradigm developed by Ainsworth and her colleagues (Ainsworth, Blehar, Waters, and Wall, 1978; Cassidy and Shaver, 1999; Cummings and Cummings, in Vol. 5 of this *Handbook*) to evaluate the security of the child's attachment to parents has concerned some attribute of caregivers such as variation in childcare arrangements, differences in maternal adjustment, or variations in socioeconomic disadvantage (primarily of mothers) that might be associated with individual differences in the baby's response that lead to placement of the baby within one of the four categories of response to separation and reunion. Based on this attachment paradigm, there has been an effort to systematically portray the mother's own contribution to the formation of attachment bonds with her baby in terms of the mother's own style of attachment founded on recollection of experiences with others within the psychoanalytic relational paradigm.

From more than a decade of research based on the attachment paradigm (Bretherton and Munholland, 1999), Main and her colleagues (Main, 1985; Main, Kaplan, and Cassidy, 1985) created an Adult Attachment Interview (AAI). Their classification of caregiver security, founded on a person's own parental family, is based primarily on the coherence reflected within a narrative analysis of a caregiver's memories of care within his or her own parental family (Hesse, 1999; Hesse and Main, 2000; Main, 1995, 2000). As Bretherton and Munholland (1999, p. 105) observed, "What appears to count, in terms of transmitting patterns of relating from parents to children, is a parent's ability to produce a coherently organized account of his or her own childhood attachment experiences as currently remembered and interpreted."

One obvious focus of studies that use approaches such as the AAI was as a means for studying the guiding "hypothesis" of psychoanalytic study of parenthood, that the nature of parental response to the tasks of parenthood is determined by the parents' own experience of being parented across the years of early childhood. Indeed, it was the apparent relationship between classification of adult attachment styles among parents and classification of response to the Strange Situation that provided initial support for the use of this measure. As Main (1995, p. 211) observed, "parents who are coherent, consistent, and plausible in describing and evaluating their own attachment histories, whether favorable or unfavorable, have infants whose response to them in this semistressful situation is judged secure." This finding of an association between parental narration and offspring classification in the Strange Situation was statistically significant at well beyond chance levels.

Influenced by the classic report of Fraiberg et al. (1975), Fonagy, Steele, Moran, Steele, and Higgitt (1993) used the AAI in a study involving 100 mothers and fathers preparing for the birth of their first child. Prospective parents were interviewed with the AAI, and their children were later studied in the Strange Situation paradigm at the age 1 year and again at 18 months. Fonagy et al. reported that not only did the AAI predict the child's response to separation and reunion, but also there was an association between mothers whose narratives were classified as secure–autonomous, dismissing–detached, or entangled–preoccupied and infant response: 78% of mothers rated as secure–autonomous had children who at 1 year of age showed a secure attachment; 72% of infants of mothers classified as other than secure were classified as not showing a secure response to maternal separation and reunion.

Fonagy et al. (1993, p. 969) observed that "... the ghost haunting the nursery, as predicted by Fraiberg, *is* more likely to appear when the parents' defensive stance is apparently formidable ... among parents of infants manifesting avoidance on reunion, defensive strategies ... were far more marked in accounts of childhood relationships." The important determinant of the child's response in the Strange Situation paradigm was the mother's AAI classification rather than that of the father. Mothers who are unable to recognize and acknowledge their own feelings are less able to respond empathically to their baby's cues; even young infants learn to respond in ways directed in part by maternal style of managing relationships with others.

Maternal capacity for self-reflection, measured by a scale of parental ability to reflect on both their own motives and those of both their own parents and their children, showed a modest relation to security of infant attachment. Fonagy et al. maintained that the capacity for "mentalizing" or self-reflection is of critical importance in the provision of childcare. Indeed, if care has been good enough (Winnicott, 1960a), the child develops this capacity for self-reflection; realization of this empathic state is difficult if a secure caregiver–infant attachment bond has not developed. Furthermore, the child's own ability to engage in such self-reflection depends in large part on the child's parents' own capacity for self-reflection; following Main's (1991) suggestion, Fonagy and his colleagues (Fonagy, 1999) maintained that the mother's own capacity for reflective self-awareness depends on having experienced a caregiver during childhood who was able to provide such self-reflection (Fonagy et al., 1993, 1995).

The AAI is a particularly controversial means for studying parents' contribution to childcare, both because of the presumption that parental childhood experiences directly affect such aspects of adult life as childrearing, and also because of the presumption that parents are able to recall in some accurate way their own experiences across the childhood years. Main and her associates maintained that present maternal attachment classifications, founded in the parent's own childhood experiences, are coded on the basis of the coherence and structure of the account rather than specific content of the account. Therefore the AAI does not depend on accuracy of accounts of the past. Rather, following from the topographic point of view in psychoanalysis in which forces out of awareness are presumed to influence attention (Rapaport, 1960), the telling of the narrative is interrupted by intrusions founded on past conflict.

Main and her colleagues presumed that any disruption that is present or evident in the parent's own narrative has its origins in a remembered past. The study of autobiographical memory appears to challenge that assumption (Brenneis, 1997; Conway, 1996; Fitzgerald, 1996; Singer and Salovey, 1993; Thompson, Skowronski, Larsen, and Betz, 1996). This area of study suggests that memories are constructed anew across the course of life. From this constructionist perspective, memories of the past change across the course of life as a result of life changes and social and historical change. Memories of childhood caregiving reported by adults may not correspond either with childhood experiences or with memories of caregiving reported at other points across the adult years. Stern (1995) also challenged the assumption underlying the AAI. He suggested that the mother brings to each encounter with her baby not only an internal working model (Bowlby, 1969) or representation of her own mother as caregiver, but also working models of her husband and other present and past significant persons in her own life. Stern suggested that the AAI more closely reflects the mother's own present relationship with her mother than the remembered childhood relationship. Cohler and deBoer (1996), Kagan (1998), and Stern (1985, 1995) all questioned the assumption that there are particular sensitive periods for personality development in early childhood that might directly influence such adult personality attributes as attachment styles.

Affect expressed in the AAI interview is as easily understood in terms of recent experiences that may have little to do with either a personal past or childcare as in some cloudy recollection of emotion from childhood. Some events are remembered more clearly than others; across the course of life, adults are always rewriting the story of their personal past. This life writing represents a continued reintegration of a currently recollected past that may bear little relation to a past as it "really" existed. Present coherence of the narrative may as easily be affected by the stresses and strains of adult life as by a shadowy past. Main and Hesse (1990) suggested that maternal experience of early childhood loss had an adverse impact in helping their 1-year-old children to realize a secure attachment, leading the infants to be classified as disorganized–disoriented. This classification is presumed to reflect the lasting impact of severe parental childhood trauma.

This report, although based on a very small group of mothers experiencing such loss, provided support for the basic hypothesis of the ghost (of the parental past) in the nursery. That some parents are rejecting, leading to disruption in childcare, is clear. That such interference may be attributed to parental trauma stemming from childhood may be less clear. Brenneis (1997) has shown that there is little support for any premise that adults are able to recall their childhood past with any degree of accuracy. Furthermore, parents are not even able to recall with accuracy recent events in the lives of their own children (Mednick and Schaffer, 1963; Robbins, 1963; Wenar, 1961; Yarrow, Campbell, and Burton, 1968), let alone remember aspects of their own childhood. Challenging assumptions presumed to be central both to social learning theory and to relational perspectives in psychoanalysis, Kagan (1998, p. 105) suggested there is little reason to assume that events of early childhood necessarily have a greater impact on adult experience of self and others than do events taking place decades later.

Fatherhood and Psychoanalytic Study of The Parental Role

To date, and most clearly evident in studies within the attachment tradition, the study of parenthood has presumed study of the mother's personality, life experiences, and impact on the child's development. Indeed, few other cultures around the world presume either that specific aspects of childcare have a major impact on adult lives or that mothers bear the primary responsibility in determining adult adjustment (Fischer and Fischer, 1963; Minturn and Lambert, 1964). As Blos (1985) observed, it is ironic, considering the emphasis that Freud placed on the little boy's experience of the father, evidence founded on his construction of psychoanalysis as a psychology of the son mourning the loss of his father and the ambivalence consequent in such mourning (Freud, 1917/1957f), so evident in Freud's study of a preschool-age boy (Freud, 1909/1955a), that much of psychoanalytic study of parenthood has focused on the role of the mother.

Striking in Freud's account is the involvement evident in the father's care of his little son, Hans, who was suffering a phobia resolved through psychoanalytic intervention by means of the father. Even while the family was on summer holiday, staying in a suburb of Vienna, with Han's father going to work in the city during the week, his father carefully followed Han's development (although Ross,1989, questions the extent to which his father fostered in Hans the desire to be a father himself someday). This theme of the importance of the father for the child's development remains a theme in contemporary discussions of fatherhood (Dowd, 2000; Lamb, 1997; Marsiglio, Amato, Day, and Lamb, 2000; Parke, 1996, in Vol. 3 of this *Handbook*). Again, Benedek (1970d) was keenly aware of the father's role in childcare and of the importance of studying the family in terms of Burgess' (1926) description of the family as the unity of interacting personalities.

In her discussion of fatherhood, Benedek (1970d) stressed the significance of the father's role as family provider. Gutmann (1975, 1987) suggested that, with the transition to parenthood, new parents experienced an "emergency" that led them to emphasize socially stereotyped definitions of gender roles within the family, with the husband–father the provider and the wife–mother providing nurturance. Over the past two decades, there has been considerable discussion regarding the father's role within the family. Much of this discussion has been critical of traditional gender-role socialization in which the father is relegated to the position of breadwinner with little day-to-day involvement in the child's development (Dowd, 2000; Lamb, 1997; Parke, 1996). Indeed, Chodorow (1978) suggested that if mothers and fathers really coparented their young children, it might be possible to change the understanding that these offspring would have when they became parents. Gutmann (1975, 1987) maintained that traditional gender-role socialization is intrinsic to adult development across cultures and is a function of the meaning that parenthood has for fathers and mothers.

Clearly influenced by reports of the father's contributions to the child's development (Lamb, 1997; Parke, 1996, in Vol. 3 of this *Handbook*), the psychoanalytic study of fatherhood has wrestled issues regarding renewed focus on the role of the father within the family that have has been fostered by social change and its impact on the family across the past three decades. Cath et al. (1982, 1989) posed alternatives to the presumption of the father's role within the family as the distant, somewhat autocratic parent whose stern presence is necessary for the little boy to develop a strong moral sense. They stress the importance of warm caregiving by each parent as essential for the well-being of both daughters and sons. At the same time, much of the psychoanalytic literature on fatherhood views the father's role within the family in the socially scripted manner of provider and "instrumental" as contrasted with "emotional" socializing agent within the family (Parsons, 1955).

For example, both Galenson and Roiphe (1982) and Pacella (1989), using the paradigm of symbiosis–individuation (Mahler et al., 1975), emphasized the significance of the father–daughter tie for the resolution of the daughter's tie to her mother, shifting and diluting the symbiotic pull of the little girl to her mother and fostering both psychological autonomy and self-esteem. Pacella (1989) noted that the father is not involved in the child's experience of ambivalence of the child portrayed by Mahler et al. (1975) as the rapprochement child who seeks emotional reassurance from her or his caregiver. However, the father is important for the child in the rapprochement stage since able to foster psychological autonomy and enhanced sense of reality of the world beyond the family in both sons and daughters and provides a basis of positive gender identity for boy, pulling the little boy towards the father and for little girls, pushing the little girl towards her mother. Galenson and Roiphe (1982) noted that, although their study revealed marked variation in the time that fathers spent with their young children, the important factor in the father's contribution to the child's development was the mother's expectation regarding what role she wanted her husband to play in the child's life. The father–child relationship must be understood in terms of the mother–child tie.

Galenson and Roiphe (1982) reported one detailed case study that showed that the mother's own disappointment in the failure to realize an erotic tie with her own father during her childhood was repeated in the manner in which she encouraged her toddler-aged daughter to relate to her husband. Particularly during the period when her daughter was approximately 18 months old and throughout the second year, the result was that her daughter turned almost exclusively to her father, and the mother received unconscious satisfaction of unresolved wishes from her own childhood in identifying with her daughter as father and daughter formed a close tie. The mother's effort to resolve her own disappointment with the failure of the father–daughter tie during her own childhood and the effort to resolve this issue anew through identification with her daughter's tie to her husband was at the cost of the daughter's own development of a feminine identity and consequent loss of the vitality that the authors observed in the little girl across the first year and a half of life. However, Tessman (1989) suggested that both a daughter's capacity for love (erotic excitement) and for work (endeavor excitement) is significantly influenced by her tie to her father. The little girl's ability to feel excitement in later relationships with men depends on her father's ability to respond positively to her bids for affection in early childhood.

Tessman (1989) also noted that the little girl's relationship with her mother is important in understanding the father–daughter tie. The mother's own capacity for erotic excitement is important if the daughter is to realize that such happiness can exist. When a group of women scientists was studied, those realizing exceptional achievements across the adult years showed more positive childhood and adult ties with their own fathers, but in ways that were typically feminine. This study suffers from the obvious problems both of retrospective bias, as women were reporting on currently remembered aspects of childhood, and also of presuming that a more "characteristic" feminine role was more appropriate for women. Ross (1982b) and Liebman and Abell (2000), extending the position initially provided by Blos (1967), suggested that the father is critical in fostering in his son those instrumental skills that permit the son to move out beyond the parental family and to find a marital partner. Problems emerge when fathers are either overcontrolling, perhaps seeking to resolve unfulfilled expectations and disappointments through the son's achievements, or ignore their sons. Herzog (1982) and Liebman and Abell (2000) observed that the father is important in fostering the boy's appropriate "core" gender identity. Fathers are important in helping their boys to learn an appropriate capacity for modulating aggressive and residual competitive feelings first emerging in the oedipal struggle of the preschool years (Blos, 1967). In a similar manner, Sarnoff (1982) stressed the particular importance of the father in supporting the self-esteem and school achievements of both daughters and sons, fostering such ego skills as memory and tolerance of ambiguity.

Psychoanalytic writers stress the father–offspring relationship (primarily with sons) as critical for adult development. Following Blos (1967) and Stierlin (1974), Esman (1982) noted the importance of the father's ability to foster enhanced psychological autonomy across the years of adolescence (Anthony, 1970): the boy's idealization of his father and the ability of both father and son to deal with the inevitable deidealizations that follow from the son's immersion in the world outside the family and the development of a more realistic picture of the father's strengths and problems at work and at home. Esman is among the few writers on the father–son relationship during adolescence to focus on the father's experience of this process of the "second individuation" phase (following the paradigm discussed by Mahler et al., 1975). As the son struggles with the issue of a more realistic understanding of his father's strengths and weaknesses, the father may experience enhanced sense of threat, further challenged by his son's newfound sexual maturity and rebelliousness. Esman offers the hope that, through empathetic understanding of his son's struggles, the father at midlife may have yet another opportunity to resolve for himself issues of potency and authority that were the inheritance of his struggle with his own father within the multigenerational family.

There has been much less discussion of the father's contribution to the family of adulthood than to the development of offspring through the first two decades of life. All too often, the manner in which the father resolved his relationships with his own father is viewed as presaging both the father's relationship with his offspring and in dealing with the larger world across the adult years. Colarusso and Nemiroff (1979) and Nemiroff and Colarusso (1990) considered the interplay of personal development in adulthood as the nexus within which adults experience and respond to relationships with others. Both expected role changes of adult life such as retirement and those unexpected changes such as loss of work or serious illness or death of spouse or children inevitably alter the relationship of fathers and their adult offspring. Sons and daughters need their parents as sources of affirmation and support across the adult years. Fathers (and mothers) preoccupied by their own grief and disappointment may find it difficult to reach out to their adult offspring struggling with such life changes as marriage and the advent of parenthood, as well as both successes and problems at work.

NEXT DIRECTIONS IN THE PSYCHOANALYTIC STUDY OF PARENTHOOD

Psychoanalysis is a field of study in which the focus on meanings that we make of the world about us, jointly constructed by shared meanings prevalent in culture and particular life experiences, influences both wish and action. This human science emphasis on meanings, including those understood through empathy or vicarious introspection in the study of experience, is unique as a method for providing additional perspectives on issues in parenting in contemporary society (Kohut, 1971, 1985), such as in the study of parenthood and sexual orientation, the psychological problems posed for parents living in poverty, and the impact of divorce on parents.

The meaning of parenthood for lesbians and gay men. The rapid social transformations of the past three decades have led to dramatic changes in every aspect of gay male and lesbian life, including family formation, which is no longer open only to those gay men and lesbians who choose to marry heterosexually (Cohler and Galatzer-Levy, 2000). Patterson (1996, 2000, in Vol. 3 of this *Handbook*) has shown that there are many routes into parenthood among gay men and lesbians and that gay and lesbian parenthood can begin at different points in the life course of both parents and children. Findings reviewed by Patterson (2000, in Vol. 3 of this *Handbook*) suggest that lesbian mothers and gay fathers may both be more child centered than their same-gender heterosexual counterparts and particularly emotionally available for their offspring. Furthermore, divorced lesbian mothers are more likely to be living with a partner (and able to provide both support and assistance with caregiving) than are divorced heterosexual mothers.

There has been little study of the motivation for parenthood among lesbians and particularly gay men in the manner undertaken by Wyatt (1967) more generally for parenthood. There has been a much less systematic study of gay fathers than of lesbian mothers. To date, there have been two primary routes into gay fatherhood: Fathers may have shared or sole custody of children following divorce or they may adopt. In general, gay fathers have found it much more difficult to retain custody following divorce compared with lesbian mothers (Falk, 1989; Patterson, 1996). Indeed, far fewer gay fathers than lesbian mothers share a household with their children (Bigner and Bozett, 1990). Gay fathers are typically more concerned about the impact of their sexual orientation on the development of their children and are less likely than lesbian mothers to see possible benefits for offspring, such as increased tolerance for diversity (Harris and Turner, 1985).

In a comparison of divorced gay fathers and divorced and married heterosexual fathers, Bigner and Jacobsen (1989) and Dunne (in press) found few differences in motivation for becoming parents, although gay fathers noted that societal expectations and pressures to assume this quintessential adult role made realization of the parental role even more significant for them than among heterosexual counterparts who had not had to overcome social barriers in caring for their children. Bigner and Jacobsen (1989) report that gay fathers were more committed than straight paternal counterparts to providing ongoing care and more motivated to maintain close ties with children. Recognizing that the comparison group contained both married and divorced men, it may well be that divorce enhances such motivation irrespective of sexual orientation.

Isay (1986, 1996) suggested that, among at least some boys later identifying as gay, the boy struggling with the resolution of the nuclear neurosis of early childhood develops an erotic tie to the father rather than to the mother. The father, sensing this same-gender attraction, may be frightened of this attraction and withdraw from his son, leaving the little boy feeling this absence and perhaps resentful regarding his father's effort to create emotional distance. Later, as these gay men become fathers, this unresolved issue from childhood may be experienced anew with their own sons (Dunne, in press). However, anecdotal reports suggest that gay men may be particularly motivated to provide warm and empathic care for their offspring (Dunne, in press). Rather than hindering the ability to respond empathically, perhaps in an effort to resolve childhood disappointments, these men are determined to be particularly involved in their sons' lives. These gay men are particularly motivated to be parents. Many gay men have suffered an ambiguous loss (Boss, 1999) during their own childhood as a result of their fathers' own confused and troubling emotional withdrawal in response to the gay sons' emerging gay identity (Isay, 1986, 1996). As fathers, these men appear determined to provide support for their own sons that they felt missing in their own childhood. At the same time, this very determination may pose problems as the adolescent sons of these gay fathers seek the autonomy and interdependence associated with adolescence. These questions can be resolved only through a longer-term psychoanalytically informed study of gay fathers and their sons.

Psychoanalytic Perspectives on Parenthood and the Socially Disadvantaged Family and Community

Among the most pressing social problems confronting families in contemporary urban society is that of families living in the midst of urban poverty and suffering the impact of social stigma, stereotyping, and poverty. These are often families in which mothers and their young children live together in crowded conditions in deteriorating and dangerous public housing projects in which physical violence is all too common (Bell and Jenkins, 1993; Mahron, 1993). A study of these families living in abject urban poverty and often in the midst of an unresponsive community that turns away from care for the most disadvantaged families may provide additional information regarding the complex interplay of social context and meanings of parenthood for these parents who have grown up in the midst of social disadvantage.

Although many parents are able to overcome this impact of stigma and social advantage and provide continuity in childcare, other parents become overwhelmed and depleted by the demands of childcare while at the same time maintaining precarious personal balance. Osofsky, Wewers, Hann, and Fick (1993) and Kilpatrick and Williams (1997) suggested that psychiatric symptoms reported by parents and offspring living within these socially disadvantaged communities most often resemble posttraumatic stress disorder, shown in fears for personal safety, avoidance of memories connected with violence, inability to fall asleep, protective armor of violent actions, and lack of concern for the welfare of others. Understood from a psychoanalytic perspective, parents who live in a world experienced as overwhelming may experience feelings of personal depletion and fragmentation and may find it difficult to remain empathetically attuned to the needs of offspring.

Sensation seeking, such as through substance abuse, may provide at least some feeling of being alive in a world otherwise felt as psychologically dead (Galatzer-Levy, 1993, Mahron, 1993). The sensation seeking that is so often associated with violence in our urban society (Galatzer-Levy, 1993) may be viewed as arising from a personally adaptive effort to maintain a sense of being psychologically alive rather than alternatively from a feeling an overwhelming and deadening sense of personal depletion and depression. From earliest childhood, many parents living in the midst of poverty were cared for by parents and other adults who were so personally overwhelmed and depressed that they were unable to provide that empathetic concern that is so essential for the development of a sense of self (Cohler, 1980; Kohut, 1977; Kohut and Wolf, 1978). Having grown up with the experience of personal depletion leading to impending fragmentation relieved only by the sensation seeking and the feeling of being alive that arises from involvement in violence, these parents have few emotional resources available for responding to their own children. Psychoanalytic perspectives on parenthood, focusing on the parent's own experience of caregiving and its motivation, may be particularly relevant in understanding the interplay of social disadvantage and poverty and in working to improve the lives of parents and children alike (Pavenstedt, 1967).

Divorce and the Psychodynamics of Parenthood

Over the course of the postwar period, there has been a dramatic increase in the proportion of marriages ending in divorce (Glick and Lin, 1986). Although this statistic is somewhat inflated by the tendency of some people to successively marry and divorce, it has had a lasting impact on the lives of both parents and offspring. Although there has been much study of the impact of parental divorce on offspring (Buchanan, Maccoby and Dornbusch, 1996; Hetherington and Clingempeel, 1992; Hetherington and Stanley-Hagan, in Vol. 3 of this *Handbook*; Maccoby and Mnookin, 1992; Wallerstein and Blakeslee, 1989, 2000; Wallerstein and Kelly, 1980; Wallerstein, Lewis, and Blakeslee, 2000) there has been much less study of the impact of divorce on the parent's own life-story and of the personal meaning of this life change for the future among divorcing mothers and fathers. For example, much of the problem posed for offspring is the consequence of marital conflict before divorce; following divorce, breakup of the household and often complex custody arrangements not necessarily in the best interest of the child, problems posed for the child depend on the capacity of parents to maintain the "parenting alliance" (Cohen and Weissman, 1985), together with the quality of the postdivorce family situation for each of the divorcing parents. There is little information regarding the manner in which parents experience custody arrangements as an important factor in fostering the parenting alliance.

Wallerstein and her colleagues (Wallerstein and Blakeslee, 1989; Wallerstein, Lewis, and Blakeslee, 2000) believe that families of divorce maintain particular vulnerability over time. Offspring of divorced parents, often later becoming parents themselves, experienced their family life before parental divorce in much more positive terms than did their parents (although this portrayal of the family situation before divorce may be colored by the offspring's wish that family life had been close). Offspring of divorced parents were much less likely than their parents to feel that the impact of the divorce had been favorable. Wallerstein's work supports that of other studies that it is the quality of the parenting alliance that is critical for the child's adjustment following divorce.

Wallerstein followed up her group of divorcing families at 10- and 25-year intervals (Wallerstein and Blakeslee, 1989; Wallerstein, Lewis and Blakeslee, 2000). In the 25-year restudy, Wallerstein and her colleagues estimated that one fourth of currently young to middle-age adults have experienced parental divorce and that the aftermath of the divorce may be felt across a lifetime. In seeking to understand this lasting adverse impact, Wallerstein, Lewis, and Blakeslee (2000) noted that mothers generally have custody of the children and are overwhelmed by financial obligations and needing to be both parents.

This postdivorce world is lonely for parents and offspring alike and includes the chaos for the household of custody, the child's movement between two different households, lovers coming and going, and parental feelings of depression and resulting emotional unavailability for their children. Reviewing the findings from the report by Hetherington and Clingempeel (1992), Maccoby (1992) reviewed evidence showing that divorced mothers find it difficult to maintain the authority of two parents; adolescent offspring in these families report enhanced conflict with their mothers regarding such typical adolescent issues as daily routine and use of control and punishment. It would be interesting to know of the mother's own experience of these issues as a parent of an adolescent and of the impact of this responsibility in terms of the psychodynamics of parenthood for adolescents (Anthony, 1970; Benedek, 1970e).

Wallerstein and Blakeslee (2000, p. 299) observed that ". . . it's in adulthood that children of divorce suffer the most. The impact of divorce hits them most cruelly as they go in search of love, sexual intimacy and commitment." Wallerstein, Lewis, and Blakeslee (2000) claimed that children raised in divorced or remarried families are less well adjusted as adults than those raised in intact families. Even the most resilient of these children experience the long-term impact of parentification; other children experience enhanced vulnerabilities because of parental personal and emotional absence from the day-to-day tasks of childcare.

As particularly relevant for the present discussion, Wallerstein, Lewis, and Blakeslee (2000) maintained that the impact of parental divorce is felt anew as these offspring themselves become parents. They maintain that they lack good role models for becoming marital partners and parents. Further, they lack continuing support from their own parents, particularly their fathers, as they confront the expectable tasks of adulthood. Wallerstein, Lewis, and Blakeslee (2000) claim that these adult children of divorce remain lonely and single or, if parents, fail to protect their own children. However, Wallerstein and her colleagues are less specific regarding the different impacts of parental divorce on the experience of parenting for men and for women, on offspring of divorce, and on their becoming parents. Further, in much of the study, focus was on the experience of divorce for the mother's parenting. As is characteristic of much of the literature on parenthood, there is much less attention paid to the determinants of the father's experience of divorce and capacity for continued concern with the best interests of the child within the parenting alliance.

CONCLUSIONS

Psychoanalysis began as the effort by a son to grieve his father's death and the "discovery" of ambivalent feelings when confronted with this loss. To a large extent, psychoanalysis has continued as a son's psychology and a man's psychology. Freud's own fascination with the drama *Oedipus the King* focused on the son's triadic relationship with a disappointing and neglecting father concerned with his own pleasure at the cost of his son, the accidental slaying, and the intimate union with his mother. Although Sophocles provided Freud with abundant evidence for understanding the psychology of the son, there was little evidence regarding the experience of either mother or father. Particularly intriguing is the question of Jocasta's own motive in fostering this incestuous union. Presumably knowing Oedipus' true identity, her own experience of parenthood remains veiled. This legacy of a son's psychology has posed problems for the realization of a psychoanalytic study of parenthood. To a very large extent, psychoanalysis has focused on the development of boys rather than on that of girls and has focused on either the mother–son or the father–son relationship of the preschool years.

Further, Freud's own archeological model of personality development, in keeping with the science of the late nineteenth century, stressed beginnings without considering the transformations taking place across adolescence and adulthood through the later years, which posed new challenges for maintenance of a sense of personal integrity and vitality. Finally, much of psychoanalytic understanding has emerged from the consulting room, based on the detailed accounts of analysands.

Generalization to the world beyond the consulting room poses both an additional challenge but also a new opportunity for increasing psychoanalytic understanding.

Following the framework proposed by Benedek (1959), Bibring (1959), Elson (1985), Ornstein and Ornstein (1985), and particularly Fraiberg et al. (1975), there are ghosts (of the parental past) in the nursery, but these ghosts are a function not just within the parental childhood past, but of a currently remembered past in an ever-changing life story across the course of childhood, adolescence, and adulthood (Cohler and deBoer, 1996; Colarusso and Nemiroff; 1979). It is in the parent's own continuing life story of a currently remembered past, experienced present, and anticipated future that the parent's response to caregiving is formed, both concerning offspring and also understanding of the parenting experience for onself at a particular point in the course of life. To the extent that parents feel burdened by such personal and social problems as marital conflict and separation, early off-time parenthood and poverty, the capacity to respond empathetically to offspring and to maintain a focus on generativity is bound to be compromised. One of the tasks of subsequent psychoanalytic study of parenthood is to study the manner in which these problems affect parental understanding of self and the ability to realize the many complex demands of parenthood in contemporary society.

REFERENCES

Abraham, K. (1924). A short study of the development of the libido, viewed in the light of mental disorders. In *Selected papers of Karl Abraham, M.D* (pp. 418–501). London: Hogarth.

Ainsworth, M. S., Blehar, M. C., Waters, E., and Wall, S. (1978). *Patterns of attachment: A psychological study of the strange situation*. Hillsdale, NJ: Lawrence Erlbaum Associates.

Akhtar, S. (1994). Needs, disruptions, and the return of ego instincts: Some explicit and implicit aspects of self psychology: Discussion of Wolf's chapter "Selfobject experiences: Development, psychopathology, and treatment." In S. Kramer and S. Akhtar (Eds.), *Mahler and Kohut: Perspectives on development, psychopathology, and technique* (pp. 99–116). Northvale, NJ: Aronson.

Anthony, E. J. (1970). The reaction of parents to adolescents and their behavior. In E. Anthony and T. Benedek (Eds.), *Parenthood: Its psychology and psychopathology* (pp. 307–324). Boston: Little, Brown.

Anzieu, D. (1986). Freud's self-analysis (P. Graham, Trans.). London: Hogarth/Institute of Psychoanalysis.

Balint, M. (1935). Critical notes on the theory of the pregenital organizations of the libido. In *Primary love and psychoanalytic technique* (pp. 49–72). New York: Liveright.

Ballou, J. (1978). *The psychology of pregnancy*. Lexington, MA: Lexington Books/Heath.

Basch, M. (1985). Some clinical and theoretical implications of infant research. In D. Silver (Ed.), *Commentaries on Joseph Lichtenberg's psychoanalysis and infant research: Vol. 5. Psychoanalytic inquiry* (pp. 509–516). Hillsdale, NJ: Analytic.

Bell, C. C., and Jenkins, E. J. (1993). Community violence and children on Chicago's Southside. *Psychiatry, 56*, 46–54.

Benedek, T. (1959). Parenthood as a developmental phase. In *Psychoanalytic investigations: Selected papers* (pp. 377–401). New York: Quadrangle/New York Times Book Company.

Benedek, T. (1970a). The family as a psychologic field. In E. Anthony and T. Benedek (Eds.), *Parenthood: Its psychology and psychopathology* (pp. 109–136). Boston: Little, Brown.

Benedek, T. (1970b). The psychobiology of pregnancy of pregnancy. In E. Anthony and T. Benedek (Eds.), *Parenthood: Its psychology and psychopathology* (pp. 137–152). Boston: Little, Brown.

Benedek, T. (1970c). Motherhood and nurturing. In E. Anthony and T. Benedek (Eds.), *Parenthood: Its psychology and psychopathology* (pp. 153–166). Boston: Little, Brown.

Benedek, T. (1970d). Fatherhood and providing. In E. Anthony and T. Benedek (Eds.), *Parenthood: Its psychology and psychopathology* (pp. 167–184). Boston: Little, Brown.

Benedek, T. (1970e). Parenthood during the life-cycle. In E. Anthony and T. Benedek (Eds.), *Parenthood: Its psychology and psychopathology* (pp. 185–208). Boston: Little, Brown.

Benedek, T. (1973). Discussion of parenthood as a developmental phase. In *Psychoanalytic investigations: Selected papers* (pp. 401–407). New York: Quadrangle/New York Times Book Company.

Bibring, G. (1959). Some considerations of the psychological processes in pregnancy. *Psychoanalytic Study of the Child, 14*, 113–121.

Bibring, G. L., Dwyer, T., F., Huntington, D., and Valenstein, A. F. (1961a). A study of the psychological processes in pregnancy and of the earliest mother-child relationship. I: Some propositions and comments. *Psychoanalytic Study of the Child, XVI*, 9–24.

Bibring, G. L., Dwyer, T. F., Huntington, D., and Valenstein, A. F. (1961b). A study of the psychological processes in pregnancy and of the earliest mother-child relationship. II: Methodological considerations. *Psychoanalytic Study of the Child, XVI*, 9–24.

Bigner, J., and Bozett, F. (1990). Parenting by gay fathers. In F. W. Bozett and M. B. Sussman (Eds.), *Homosexuality and family relations* (pp. 155–176). New York: Haworth/Harrington Park.

Bigner, J., and Jacobsen, R. (1989). The value of children to gay and heterosexual fathers. In F. W. Bozett (Ed.), *Homosexuality and the family* (pp. 163–172). New York: Harrington Park.

Birksted-Breen, D. (2000). The experience of having a baby: A developmental view. In J. Raphael-Leff (Ed.), *'Spilt milk' perinatal loss and breakdown* (pp. 17–27). London: Institute of Psychoanalysis.

Blieszner, R., Mancini, J. A., and Marek, L. I. (1996). Looking back and looking ahead: Life-course unfolding of parenthood. In C. D. Ryff and M. M. Seltzer (Eds.), *The parental experience in midlife* (pp. 607–637). Chicago: University of Chicago Press.

Blos, P. (1967). The second individuation process of adolescence. *Psychoanalytic Study of the Child, 12*, 162–186.

Blos, P. (1985). *Son and father*. New York: Free Press/Macmillan.

Boss, P. (1999). *Ambiguous loss: Learning to live with unresolved grief*. Cambridge, MA: Harvard University Press.

Bowlby, J. (1969). *Attachment and loss: Vol. 1. Attachment*. New York: Basic Books.

Bowlby, J. (1973). *Attachment and loss: Vol. 2. Separation, anxiety and anger*. New York: Basic Books.

Bowlby, J. (1980). *Attachment and loss: Vol. 3. Loss, sadness and depression*. New York: Basic Books.

Bowlby, J. (1982). Attachment and loss: Retrospect and prospect. *American Journal of Orthopsychiatry, 52*, 664–678.

Bowlby, J. (1988). Developmental psychiatry comes of age. *American Journal of Psychiatry, 145*, 1–10.

Bradley, E. (2000). Pregnancy and the internal world. In J. Raphael-Leff (Ed.), *'Spilt milk' perinatal loss and breakdown* (pp. 28–38). London: Institute of Psychoanalysis.

Breen, D. (1975). *The birth of a first child*. London: Tavistock.

Brenneis, C. B. (1997). *Recovered memories of trauma: Transferring the present to the past*. Madison, CT: International Universities Press.

Bretherton, I., and Munholland, K. A. (1999). Internal working models in attachment relationships: A construct revisited. In J. Cassidy and P. R. Shaver (Eds.), *Handbook of adult attachment: Theory, research, and clinical applications* (pp. 89–114). New York: Guilford.

Buchanan, C. M., Maccoby, E. E., and Dornbusch, S. (1996). *Adolescents after divorce*. Cambridge, MA: Harvard University Press.

Burgess, E. (1926). The family as unity of interacting personalities, *Family, 7*, 3–9.

Cassidy, J., and Shaver, P. R. (Eds.). (1999). *Handbook of adult attachment: Theory, research, and clinical applications*. New York: Guilford.

Cath, S. H., Gurwitt, A., and Gunsberg, L. (Eds.). (1989). *Fathers and their families*. Hillsdale, NJ: Analytic.

Cath, S. H., Gurwitt, A. R., and Ross, J. M. (Eds.). (1982). *Father and child: Development and clinical perspectives*. Boston: Little, Brown.

Chasseguet-Smirgel, J. (1970). *Female sexuality: New psychoanalytic views*. London: Karnac Books.

Chodorow, N. (1978). *The reproduction of mothering*. Berkeley: University of California Press.

Chodorow, N. (1989). *Feminism and psychoanalytic theory*. New Haven, CT: Yale University Press.

Chodorow, N. (1994). *Femininities, masculinities, sexualities: Freud and beyond*. Lexington: University Press of Kentucky.

Chodorow, N. (1999). *The power of feelings: Personal meaning in psychoanalysis, gender and culture*. New Haven, CT: Yale University Press.

Clarke-Stewart, A. (1978). Popular primers for parents. *American Psychologist, 33*, 359–369.

Cohen, M. B. (1966). Personal identity and sexual identity, *Psychiatry, 29*, 1–12.

Cohen, R., and Weissman, S. (1985). The parenting alliance. In R. Cohen, B. Cohler, and S. Weissman (Eds.), *Parenthood: A psychodynamic perspective* (pp. 119–147). New York: Guilford.

Cohler, B. (1980). Developmental perspectives on the psychology of self in early childhood. In A. Goldberg (Ed.), *Advances in self psychology* (pp. 69–115). New York: International Universities Press.

Cohler, B. (1985). Parenthood, psychopathology and childcare. In R. Cohen, B. Cohler, and S. Weissman (Eds.), *Parenthood: A psychodynamic perspective* (pp. 119–148). New York: Guilford.

Cohler, B. (1987). The adult daughter–mother relationship: Perspectives from life-course family study and psychoanalysis. *Journal of Geriatric Psychiatry, 21*, 51–72.

Cohler, B., and deBoer, D. (1996). Psychoanalysis and the study of adult lives. In J. M. Masling and R. F. Bornstein (Eds.), *Psychoanalytic perspectives on developmental psychology* (pp. 151–220). Washington, DC: American Psychological Association.

Cohler, B. J., and Galatzer-Levy, R. M. (2000). *The course of gay and lesbian lives: Social and psychoanalytic perspectives*. Chicago: University of Chicago Press.

Cohler, B., and Grunebaum, H. (1981). *Mothers, grandmothers and daughters: Personality and child care in three generation families*. New York: Wiley-Interscience.

Colarusso, C. A., and Nemiroff, R. A. (1979). Some observations about the psychoanalytic theory of adult development. *International Journal of Psychoanalysis, 60*, 59–71.

Conway, M. A. (1996). Autobiographical knowledge and autobiographical memories. In D. C. Rubin (Ed.). *Remembering our past: Studies in autobiographical memory* (pp. 67–93). New York: Cambridge University Press.

Cowan, C. P., and Cowan, P. A. (1992). *When partners become parents: The big life change for couples.* New York: Basic Books.

Deutsch, H. (1945). *The psychology of women* (Vol. 2). New York: Grune and Stratton.

Dowd, N. (2000). *Redefining fatherhood.* New York: New York University Press.

Dunne, G. A. (in press). The lady vanishes ? Reflection on the experience of married and divorced non-heterosexual dads. *Journal of Sexualities.*

Elson, M. (1985). Parenthood and the transformations of narcissism. In R. S. Cohen, B. J. Cohler, and S. H. Weissman (Eds.), *Parenthood: A psychodynamic perspective* (pp. 297–314). New York: Guilford.

Emde, R. (1983). The representational self and its affective core. *Psychoanalytic Study of the Child, 38*, 165–192.

Entwisle, D., and Doering, S. (1981). *The first birth: A family turning point.* Baltimore: Johns Hopkins University Press.

Erikson, E. H. (1963). *Childhood and society* (2nd ed.). New York: Norton.

Esman, A. (1982). Fathers and adolescent sons. In S. H. Cath, A. R. Gurwitt, and J. M. Ross, (Eds.), *Father and child: Development and clinical perspectives* (pp. 265–274). Boston: Little, Brown.

Falk, P. (1989). Lesbian mothers: Psychosocial assumptions in family law. *American Psychologist, 44*, 941–947.

Fischer, J., and Fischer, A. (1963). The New Englanders of Orchard Town. In B. Whiting (Ed.), *Six cultures: Studies of childrearing* (pp. 869–1010). New York: Wiley.

Fitzgerald, J. M. (1996). Intersecting meanings of reminiscence in adult development and aging. In D. C. Rubin (Ed.), *Remembering our past: Studies in autobiographical memory* (pp. 360–383). New York: Cambridge University Press.

Fonagy, P. (1995). Psychoanalytic and empirical approaches to developmental psychopathology: An object relations perspective. In T. Shapiro, and R. N. Emde (Eds.), *Research in psychoanalysis: Process, development, outcome* (pp. 245–260). Madison, CT: International Universities Press.

Fonagy, P. (1999). Psychoanalytic theory from the viewpoint of attachment theory and research. In J. Cassidy and P. R. Shaver (Eds.), *Handbook of adult attachment: Theory, research, and clinical applications* (pp. 595–624). New York: Guilford.

Fonagy, P. (2000). *Attachment theory and psychoanalysis.* New York: Other Press.

Fonagy, P., Steele, M., Moran, G., Steele, H., and Higgitt, A. (1993). Measuring the ghost in the nursery: An empirical study of the relation between parents' mental representations of childhood experience and their infants' security of attachment. *Journal of the American Psychoanalytic Association, 41*, 957–989.

Fonagy, P., Steele, M., Steele, H., Leigh, T., Kennedy , R., Madiun, G., and Target, M. (1995). Attachment, the reflective self, and borderline states. In S. Goldberg, R. Muir, and J. Kerr (Eds.), *Attachment theory: Social, developmental and clinical perspectives* (pp. 233–278). Hillsdale, NJ: Analytic.

Fraiberg, S., Adelson, E., and Shapiro V. (1975). Ghosts in the nursery: A psychoanalytic approach to the problem of impaired infant–mother relationships. In. L. Fraiberg (Ed.), *Selected writings of Selma Fraiberg* (pp. 100–136). Columbus: Ohio State University Press.

Freud, A. (1936/1966). *The ego and the mechanisms of defense* (rev. ed.). New York: International Universities Press.

Freud, A. (1965). *Normality and pathology in childhood: Assessments of development.* New York: International Universities Press.

Freud, S. (1897–1904). *The complete letters of Sigmund Freud to Wilhelm Fliess, 1887–1904,* J. Masson (Ed.). Cambridge, MA: Harvard University Press.

Freud, S. (1953a). Three essays on the theory of sexuality. In J. Strachey (Ed. and Trans.), *The standard edition of the complete psychological works of Sigmund Freud* (Vol. 7, pp. 13–243). London: Hogarth. (Original work published 1905).

Freud, S. (1953b). Some reflections on schoolboy psychology. In J. Strachey (Ed. and Trans.), *The standard edition of the complete psychological works of Sigmund Freud* (Vol. 13, pp. 241–244). London: Hogarth.(Original work published 1914).

Freud, S. (1955a). Analysis of a phobia in a five-year-old boy. In J. Strachey (Ed. and Trans.), *The standard edition of the complete psychological works of Sigmund Freud* (Vol. 10, pp. 5–147). London: Hogarth.(Original work published 1909).

Freud, S. (1955b). The psychogenesis of a case of homosexuality in a woman. In J. Strachey (Ed. and Trans.), *The standard edition of the complete psychological works of Sigmund Freud* (Vol. 18, pp. 147–172). London: Hogarth.(Original work published 1920).

Freud, S. (1957a). Five lectures on psychoanalysis (The Clark Lectures). In J. Strachey (Ed. and Trans.), *The standard edition of the complete psychological works of Sigmund Freud* (Vol. 11, pp. 9–58). London: Hogarth.(Original work published 1910).

Freud, S. (1957b) A special type of object choice made by men (Contributions to the psychology of love—I). In J. Strachey (Ed. and Trans.), *The standard edition of the complete psychological works of Sigmund Freud* (Vol. 11, pp. 163–175). London: Hogarth. (Original work published 1910).

Freud, S. (1957c). On narcissism: An introduction. In J. Strachey (Ed. and Trans.), *The standard edition of the complete psychological works of Sigmund Freud* (Vol. 14, pp. 73–102). London: Hogarth. (Original work published 1914).

Freud, S. (1957d). The unconscious. In J. Strachey (Ed. and Trans.), *The standard edition of the complete psychological works of Sigmund Freud* (Vol. 14, pp. 159–216). London: Hogarth. (Original work published 1915).

Freud, S. (1957e). Repression. In J. Strachey (Ed. and Trans.), *The standard edition of the complete psychological works of Sigmund Freud* (Vol. 14, pp. 141–158). London: Hogarth. (Original work published 1915).

Freud, S. (1957f). Mourning and melancholia. In J. Strachey (Ed. and Trans.), *The standard edition of the complete psychological works of Sigmund Freud* (Vol. 14, pp. 237–258). London: Hogarth.(Original work published 1917).

Freud, S. (1958). The interpretation of dreams. In J. Strachey (Ed. and Trans.), *The standard edition of the complete psychological works of Sigmund Freud* (Vols. 4–5). London: Hogarth. (Original work published 1900).

Freud, S. (1959). Some psychical consequences of the anatomical distinction between the sexes. In J. Strachey (Ed. and Trans.), *The standard edition of the complete psychological works of Sigmund Freud* (Vol. 20, pp. 173–179). London: Hogarth. (Original work published 1925).

Freud, S. (1961a). The ego and the id. In J. Strachey (Ed. and Trans.), *The standard edition of the complete psychological works of Sigmund Freud* (Vol. 19, pp. 12–59). London: Hogarth. (Original work published 1923).

Freud, S. (1961b). The future of an illusion. In J. Strachey (Ed. and Trans.), *The standard edition of the complete psychological works of Sigmund Freud* (Vol. 21, pp. 5–58). London: Hogarth. (Original work published 1927).

Freud, S. (1961c). Civilization and its discontents. In J. Strachey (Ed. and Trans.), *The standard edition of the complete psychological works of Sigmund Freud* (Vol. 21, pp. 59–145). London: Hogarth. (Original work published 1930).

Freud, S. (1961d). Female sexuality. In J. Strachey (Ed. and Trans.), *The standard edition of the complete psychological works of Sigmund Freud* (Vol. 21, pp. 225–243). London: Hogarth. (Original work published 1931).

Freud, S. (1963). Introductory lectures on psychoanalysis. In J. Strachey (Ed. and Trans.), *The standard edition of the complete psychological works of Sigmund Freud* (Vols. 15 and 16). London: Hogarth.(Original work published 1916–1917).

Freud, S. (1964). New introductory lectures on psycho-analysis. In J. Strachey (Ed. and Trans.), *The standard edition of the complete psychological works of Sigmund Freud* (Vol. 22, pp. 5–182). London: Hogarth. (Original work published 1933).

Friedman, L. (2000). Are minds objects or dramas. In D. K. Silverman and D. L. Wolitzky (Eds.), *Changing conceptions of psychoanalysis: The legacy of Merton M. Gill* (pp. 145–170). Hillsdale, NJ: Analytic.

Galatzer-Levy, R. (1993). Adolescent violence and the adolescent self. *Adolescent Psychiatry, 19*, 418–441.

Galatzer-Levy, R., and Cohler, B. (1993). *The essential other.* New York: Basic Books.

Galatzer-Levy, R. M., Bachrach, H., Skolnikoff, A., Waldron, S., and Levy, R. G. (2000). *Does psychoanalysis work?* New Haven, CT: Yale University Press.

Galenson, E., and Roiphe, H. (1982). The preoedipal relationship of a father, mother and daughter. In S. H. Cath, A. R. Gurwitt, and J. M. Ross (Eds.), *Father and child: Development and clinical perspectives* (pp. 151–162). Boston: Little, Brown.

Gay, P. (1988). *Freud: A life for our time.* New York: Norton.

Geertz, C. (1973). Thick description: Toward an interpretive theory of culture. In *The interpretation of cultures* (pp. 3–30). New York: Basic Books.

Geertz, C. (1974). 'From the native's point of view:' On the nature of anthropological understanding. In *Local knowledge: Further essays in interpretive anthropology* (pp. 55–72). New York: Basic Books.

Gill, M. (1994). *Psychoanalysis in transition: A personal view.* Hillsdale, NJ: Analytic.

Gilligan, C. (1983). *In a different voice.* Cambridge, MA: Harvard University Press.

Gilligan, C. (1990). Remapping the moral domain: New images of the self in relationship. In C. Zanardi (Ed.), *Essential papers on the psychology of women* (pp. 480–496). New York: New York University Press.

Gitelson, M. (1962). On the curative factors in the first phase of analysis. In *Psychoanalysis: Science and profession* (pp. 311–341). New York: International Universities Press.

Glick, P. C., and Lin, S. (1986). Recent changes in divorce and remarriage. *Journal of Marriage and the Family, 48*, 737–747.

Grossman, F., Eichler, L., Winickoff, S., and Associates. (1980). *Pregnancy, birth and parenthood.* San Francisco: Jossey-Bass.

Grünbaum, A. (1993). *Validation in the clinical theory of psychoanalysis* (Psychological Issues, Monograph 61). Madison, CT: International Universities Press.

Grunebaum, H. U., Weiss, J. L., Cohler, B. J., Gallant D., and Hartman, C. (1982). *Mentally ill mothers and their children* (2nd ed.). Chicago: University of Chicago Press.

Guntrip, H. (1961). *Personality structure and human interaction.* New York: Basic Books.

Gutmann, D. (1975). Parenthood: A comparative key to the life-cycle. In N. Datan and L. Ginsberg (Eds.), *Life-span developmental psychology: Normative crises* (pp. 167–184). New York: Academic.

Gutmann, D. (1987). *Reclaimed powers: Toward a psychology of men and women in later life.* New York: Basic Books.

Harris, M., and Turner, P. (1985/1986). Gay and lesbian parents. *Journal of Homosexuality, 12*, 101–131.

Hartmann, H. (1958). *Ego-psychology and the problem of adaptation.* (D. Rapaport, Trans.). New York: International Universities Press. (Original work published 1939).

Hartmann, H., and Kris, E. (1945). The genetic approach in psychoanalysis. *Psychoanalytic Study of the Child, 1,* 1–29.

Herzog, J. M. (1982). On father hunger: The father's role in the modulation of aggressive drive and fantasy. In S. H. Cath, A. R. Gurwitt, and J. M. Ross, (Eds.), *Father and child: Development and clinical perspectives* (pp. 163–174). Boston: Little, Brown.

Hesse, E. (1999). The adult attachment interview: Historical and current perspectives. In J. Cassidy and P. R. Shaver (Eds.), *Handbook of adult attachment: Theory, research, and clinical applications* (pp. 395–433). New York: Guilford.

Hesse, E., and Main, M. (2000). Disorganized infant, child, and adult attachment: Collapse in behavioral and attentional strategies. *Journal of the American Psychoanalytic Association, 48,* 1097–1128.

Hetherington, E. M., and Clingempeel, W. G. (1992). Coping with marital transitions: A family systems perspective. *Psychological Monographs, 57* (Whole numbers 2–3).

Hoffman, I. (1996). Merton M. Gill: A study in theory development in psychoanalysis. *Psychoanalytic Dialogues, 6,* 5–53.

Hoffman, I. (1998). *Ritual and spontaneity in the psychoanalytic process.* Hillsdale, NJ: Analytic.

Isay, R. (1986). The development of sexual identity in homosexual men. *Psychoanalytic Study of the Child, 41,* 467–489.

Isay, R. (1996). *Becoming gay: The journey to self-acceptance.* New York: Pantheon.

Kakar, S. (1995). Clinical work and the cultural imagination, *Psychoanalytic Quarterly, LXIV,* 265–281.

Kagan, J. (1980). Perspectives on continuity. In O. G. Brim Jr. and J. Kagan (Eds.), *Constancy and change in human development* (pp. 26–74). Cambridge, MA: Harvard University Press.

Kagan, J. (1998). *Three seductive ideas.* Cambridge, MA: Harvard University Press.

Kestenberg, J. (1956). On the development of maternal feelings in early childhood—Observations and reflections. *Psychoanalytic Study of the Child, 11,* 257–291.

Kilpatrick, K. L., and Williams, L. M. (1997). Post-traumatic stress disorder in child witnesses to domestic violence. *American Journal of Orthopsychiatry, 67,* 639–644.

Klein, M. (1932). *The psychoanalysis of children.* London: Hogarth.

Klein, M. (1935). A contribution to the psychogenesis of manic-depressive states. In *Love, guilt and reparation, and other works, 1927–1945* (pp. 262–289). New York: Delacorte.

Kohut, H. (1971). *The analysis of the self.* New York: International Universities Press.

Kohut, H. (1972). Thoughts on narcissism and narcissistic rage. In P. Ornstein (Ed.), *The search for the self* (Vol. 2, pp. 615–658). New York: International Universities Press.

Kohut, H. (1977). *The restoration of the self.* New York: International Universities Press.

Kohut, H. (1985). Self psychology and the sciences of man. In C. Strozier (Ed.), *Self psychology and the humanities: Reflections on a new psychoanalytic approach by Heinz Kohut* (pp. 73–94). New York: Norton.

Kohut, H., and Wolf, E. (1978). The disorders of the self and their treatment: An outline. *International Journal of Psychoanalysis, 59,* 413–425.

Kramer, S., Byerly, L. J., and Akhtar, S. (1997). Growing together, growing apart, growing up, growing down. In S. Akhtar and S. Kramer (Eds.), *The seasons of life: Separation–individuation perspectives* (pp. 1–22). Northvale, NJ: Aronson.

Lamb, M. (Ed.). (1997). *The role of the father in child development* (Rev. ed.). New York: Wiley.

Langer, M. (1992). *Motherhood and sexuality.* New York: Guilford.

Leifer, M. (1980). *Psychological effects of motherhood: A study of first pregnancy.* New York: Praeger.

LeMasters, E. E. (1970). *Parents in modern America.* Homewood, IL: Dorsey.

Lerner, H. D., and Ehrlich, J. (1992). Psychodynamic models. In V. B. Van Hasselt and M. Herson (Eds.), *Handbook of social development: A lifespan perspective* (pp. 51–79). New York: Plenum.

Liebman, S. J., and Abell, S. (2000). The forgotten parent no more: A psychoanalytic reconsideration of fatherhood. *Psychoanalytic Psychology, 17,* 88–105.

Maccoby, E. (1992). Family structure and childrens's adjustment: Is quality of parenting the major mediator. In E. M. Hetherington and W. G. Clingempell (Eds.), Coping with marital transitions: A family systems perspective. *Psychological Monographs, 57* (Whole numbers 2–3, pp. 230–238).

Maccoby, E. E., and Mnookin, R. H. (1992). *Dividing the child: Social and legal dilemmas of custody.* Cambridge, MA: Harvard University Press.

Mahl, G. F. (1982). Father–son themes in Freud's self-analysis. In S. H. Cath, A. R. Gurwitt, and J. M. Ross, (Eds.), *Father and child: Development and clinical perspectives* (pp. 33–64). Boston: Little, Brown.

Mahler, M. (1968). *On human symbiosis and the vicissitudes of individuation. Vol. 1. Infantile psychosis.* New York: International Universities Press.

Mahler, M., Pine, F., and Bergman, A. (1975). *The psychological birth of a human infant.* New York: Basic Books.

Mahron, R. (1993). Rage without content. In. A. Goldberg (Ed.), *The widening scope of self psychology: Progress in self-psychology* (Vol. 9, pp. 129–141). Hillsdale, NJ: Analytic.

Main, M. (1985, April). *An adult attachment classification system.* Paper presented at the biannual meetings of the Society for Research in Child Development, Toronto, Ontario, Canada.

Main, M. (1991). Metacognitive knowledge, metacognitive monitoring, and singular (coherent) vs. multiple (incoherent) models of attachment: Findings and directions for future research. In C. M. Parkes, J. Stevenson-Hinde, and P. Marris (Eds.), *Attachment across the life cycle* (pp. 127–159). London: Routledge.

Main, M. (1995). Discourse, prediction, and recent studies in attachment: Implications for psychoanalysis. In T. Shapiro and R. N. Emde (Eds.), *Research in psychoanalysis: Process, development, outcome* (pp. 209–244). Madison, CT: International Universities Press.

Main, M. (2000). The organized categories of infant, child, and adult attachment: Flexible vs. inflexible attention under attachment-related stress. *Journal of the American Psychoanalytic Association, 48,* 1055–1096.

Main, M., and Hesse, E. (1990). Parents' unresolved traumatic experiences are related to infant disorganized attachment status: Is frightened and/or frightening parental behavior the linking mechanism. In M. T. Greenberg, D. Cicchetti, and E. M. Cummings (Eds.), *Attachment in the preschool years: Theory, research, and intervention* (pp. 161–182). Chicago: University of Chicago Press.

Main, M., Kaplan, N., and Cassidy, J. (1985). Security in infancy, childhood and adulthood: A move to the level of representation. *Monographs of the Society for Research in Child Development, 60* (1–2, Serial 209).

Manzano, J., Espasa, F. P., and Zilkha, N. (1999). The narcissistic scenarios of parenthood. *International Journal of Psychoanalysis, 80,* 465–476.

Marsiglio, W., Amato, W., Day, R. D., and Lamb, M. E. (2000). Scholarship on fatherhood in the 1990s and beyond. *Journal of Marriage and the Family, 62,* 1173–1191.

Mednick, S., and Schaeffer, J. (1963). Mothers' retrospective reports in childrearing research. *American Journal of Orthopsychiatry, 33,* 457–461.

Melges, F. T. (1968). Post-partum psychiatric syndromes. *Psychosomatic Medicine, 30,* 95–106.

Michaels, G. Y., and Goldberg, W. A. (1988). *The transition to parenthood: Current theory and research.* New York: Cambridge University Press.

Michels, R. (1993). Adulthood. In G. H. Pollock and S. I. Greenspan (Eds.), *The course of life: Vol. V. Early adulthood* (pp. 1–14). Madison, CT: International Universities Press.

Miller, L. J. (Ed.). (1999). *Postpartum mood disorders.* Washington, DC: American Psychiatric Press.

Miller, N., Luborksy, L., Barber, J. P., and Docherty, J. P. (Eds.). (1993). *Psychodynamic treatment research: A handbook for clinical practice.* New York: Basic Books.

Minturn, L., and Lambert, W. (1964). *Mothers of six culture: Antecedents of child rearing.* New York: Wiley.

Mishler, E. (1990). Validation: The social construction of knowledge—A brief for inquiry-guided research. *Harvard Educational Review, 60,* 415–442.

Mitchell, S. (1988). *Relational concepts in psychoanalysis: An integration.* Cambridge, MA: Harvard University Press.

Mitchell, S. A., and Black, M. J. (1995). *Freud and beyond: A history of modern psychoanalytic thought.* New York: Basic Books.

Nemiroff, R. A., and Colarusso, C. A. (1990). Frontiers of adult development in theory and practice. In R. Nemiroff and C. Colarusso (Eds.), *New dimensions in adult development* (pp. 97–124). New York: Basic Books.

Obeyesekere, G. (1990). *The work of culture.* Chicago: University of Chicago Press.

Ornstein, A., and Ornstein, P. H. (1985). Parenting as a function of the adult self. In E. J. Anthony and G. H. Pollock (Eds.), *Parental influences in health and disease* (pp. 183–234). Boston: Little, Brown.

Osofsky, J., Wewers, S., Hann, D. M., and Fick, A. C. (1993). Chronic community violence: What is happening to our children. *Psychiatry, 56,* 36–45.

Pacella, B. (1989). Paternal influence in early child development. In S. H. Cath, A. Gurwitt, and L. Gunsberg (Eds.), *Fathers and their families* (pp. 225–240). Hillsdale, NJ: Analytic.

Parens, H. (1975). Parenthood as a developmental phase. *Journal of the American Psychoanalytic Association, 23,* 154–165.

Parke, R. (1996). *Fatherhood.* Cambridge, MA: Harvard University Press.

Parsons, T. (1955). Family structure and the socialization of the child. In T. Parsons and F. Bales (Eds.), *Family, socialization and interaction processes* (pp. 35–131). New York: Free Press/Macmillan.

Patterson, C. (1996). Lesbian and gay parents and their children. In R. C. Savin-Williams and K. M. Cohen (Eds.), *The lives of lesbians, gays, and bisexuals: Children to adults* (pp. 274–304). Fort Worth, TX: Harcourt, Brace.

Patterson, C. J. (2000). Family relationships of lesbians and gay men. *Journal of Marriage and the Family, 62,* 1052–1069.

Pavenstedt, E. (Ed.). (1967). *The drifters: Children of disorganized lower-class families.* Boston: Little, Brown.

Pine, F. (1988). The four psychologies of psychoanalysis and their place in clinical work. *Journal of the American Psychoanalytic Association, 36,* 571–596.

Pine, F. (1990). *Drive, ego, object, and self: A synthesis for clinical work.* New York: Basic Books.

Rapaport, D. (1960). On the psychoanalytic theory of motivation. In M. M. Gill (Ed.), *The collected papers of David Rapaport* (pp. 853–915). New York: Basic Books.

Rapaport, D., and M. Gill. (1959). The points-of-view and assumptions of metapyschology. *International Journal of Psychoanalysis, 40,* 153–162.

Ritvo, L. B. (1990). *Darwin's influence on Freud: A tale of two sciences.* New Haven, CT: Yale University Press.

Robbins, L. C. (1963). The accuracy of parental recall of aspects of child development and of childrearing practices. *Journal of Abnormal and Social Psychology, 66,* 261–270.

Robertson, J. (1962). Mothering as an influence on early development. *Psychoanalytic Study of the Child, 17,* 245–264.

Ross, J. M. (1982a). Oedipus revisited: Laius and the "Laius complex." *Psychoanalytic Study of the Child, 37,* 169–200.

Ross, J. M. (1982b). Mentorship in middle childhood. In S. H. Cath, A. R. Gurwitt, and J. M. Ross, (Eds.), *Father and child: Development and clinical perspectives* (pp. 243–252). Boston: Little, Brown.

Ross, J. M. (1984/1989). The darker side of fatherhood: Clinical and developmental ramifications of the "Laius motif." In. G. H. Pollock and J. M. Ross (Eds.), *The Oedipus papers* (pp. 389–417). Madison, CT: International Universities Press.

Ross, J. M. (1989). The riddle of little Hans. In S. H. Cath, A. Gurwitt, and L. Gunsberg (Eds.), *Fathers and their families.* (pp. 267–283). Hillsdale NJ: Analytic.

Rossi, A. (1968). Transition to parenthood. *Journal of Marriage and the Family, 30,* 26–39.

Rudnytsky, P. (1987). *Freud and Oedipus.* New York: Columbia University Press.

Ryff, C. D., Schmutte, P. S., and Lee, Y. H. (1996). How children turn out: Implications for parental self-evaluation. In. C. D. Ryff and M. M. Seltzer (Eds.), *The parental experience in midlife* (pp. 383–422). Chicago: University of Chicago Press.

Sarnoff, C. (1982). The father's role in latency. In. S. H. Cath, A. R. Gurwitt, and J. M. Ross (Eds.), *Father and child: Development and clinical perspectives* (pp. 253–264). Boston: Little, Brown.

Schafer, R. (1960). The loving and beloved superego in Freud's structural theory. *Psychoanalytic Study of the Child, 15,* 163–188.

Schafer, R. (1980). Narration in the psychoanalytic dialogue. *Critical Inquiry, 7,* 29–53.

Schafer, R. (1981). *Narrative actions in psychoanalysis* (Vol. XIV of the Heinz Werner Lecture Series). Worcester, MA: Clark University Press.

Schafer, R. (1992). *Retelling a life: Narration and dialogue in psychoanalysis.* New York: Basic Books.

Shapiro, T., and Emde, R. N. (1995). *Research in psychoanalysis: Process, development, outcome.* Madison, CT: International Universities Press.

Shereshefsky, P., and Yarrow, L. (1973). *Psychological aspects of a first pregnancy and early post-natal adaptation.* New York: Raven.

Singer, J. A., and Salovey, P. (1993). *The remembered self: Emotion and memory in personality.* New York: Free Press.

Spence, D. P. (1994). *The rhetorical voice of psychoanalysis: Displacement of evidence by theory.* Cambridge, MA: Harvard University Press.

Spitz, R. (1945). Hospitalism: An inquiry into the genesis of psychiatric conditions in early childhood. *Psychoanalytic Study of the Child, 1,* 53–72.

Spitz, R. (1946). Anaclitic depression. *Psychoanalytic Study of the Child, 2,* 313–342.

Stern, D. (1985). *The interpersonal world of the infant: A view from psychoanalysis and developmental psychology.* New York: Basic Books.

Stern, D. (1989). The representation of relational patterns: Developmental considerations. In A. Sameroff and R. Emde (Eds.), *Relationship disturbances in early childhood: A developmental approach* (pp. 53–69). New York: Basic Books.

Stern, D. (1995). *The motherhood constellation: A unified view of parent-infant psychotherapy.* New York: Basic Books.

Stern, D. (2000). The relevance of empirical infant research to psychoanalytic theory and practice. In J. Sandler, A.-M. Sandler, and R. Davies (Eds.), *Clinical and observational psychoanalytic research: Roots of a controversy* (pp. 73–90). London: Karnac Books.

Stierlin, H. (1974). *Separating parents and adolescents: A perspective on running away, schizophrenia and waywardness.* New York: Quadrangle Books.

Strachey, J. (1958). Editor's introduction. In *The standard edition of the complete psychological works of Sigmund Freud* (Vol. 4, pp. xi–xxii). London: Hogarth.

Sulloway, F. (1979). *Freud: Biologist of the mind.* New York: Basic Books.

Tessman, L. H. (1989). Fathers and daughters: Early tones, later echoes. In S. H. Cath, A. Gurwitt, and L. Gunsberg (Eds.), *Fathers and their families* (pp. 197–223). Hillsdale, NJ: Analytic.

Thompson, C. P., Skowronski, J. J., Larsen, S. F., and Betz, A. L. (1996). *Autobiographical memory: Remembering what and remembering when.* Hillsdale, NJ: Lawrence Erlbaum Associates.

Walker, A. (1999). Gender and family relationships. In M. Sussman, S. K. Steinmetz, and G. W. Patterson (Eds.), *Handbook of Marriage and the Family* (2nd ed., pp. 439–474). New York: Plenum.

Wallerstein, J., and Blakeslee, S. (1989). *Second chances: men, women, and children a decade after divorce.* New York: Ticknor and Fields.

Wallerstein, J., Lewis, J. M., and Blakeslee, S. (2000). *The unexpected legacy of divorce: A twenty-five year landmark study.* New York: Hyperion Books.

Wallerstein, J., and Kelly, J. (1980). *Surviving the breakup*. New York: Basic Books.

Werner, C. (1961). The reliability of mothers' histories. *Child Development, 32*, 491–500.

Weiss, S. (1985). How culture influences the interpretation of the Oedipus myth. In G. H. Pollock and J. M. Ross (Eds.), *The Oedipus papers* (pp. 373–385). Madison, CT: International Universities Press.

Winnicott, D. W. (1956). Primary parental preoccupation. In D. W. Winnicott (Ed.), *Collected papers: Through paediatrics to psychoanalysis* (pp. 300–305). New York: Basic Books.

Winnicott, D. W. (1960a). The theory of the parent–infant relationship. *International Journal of Psychoanalysis, 41*, 585–595.

Winnicott, D. W. (1960b). Ego distortion in terms of the true and false self. In *The maturational process and the facilitating environment* (pp. 140–152). New York: International Universities Press.

Wolf, E. (1980). On the developmental line of selfobject relations. In A. Goldberg (Ed.), *Advances in self-psychology* (pp. 117–130). Madison, CT: International Universities Press.

Wolf, E. (1994). Selfobject experiences: Development, psychopathology, and treatment. In S. Kramer and S. Akhtar (Eds.), *Mahler and Kohut: Perspectives on development, psychopathology, and technique* (pp. 67–76). Northvale, NJ: Aronson.

Wood, V., Traupmann, J., and Hay, J. (1984). Motherhood in the middle years: Women and their adult children. In G. Baruch and J. Brooks-Gunn (Eds.), *Women in midlife* (pp. 227–244). New York: Plenum.

Wordsworth, W. (1984). My heart leaps up when I behold. In *William Wordsworth: A critical edition of the major works* (p. 246). Oxford, England: Oxford University Press. (Original work published 1807).

Wyatt, F. (1967). Clinical notes on the motives of reproduction. *Journal of Social Issues, 23*, 29–56.

Yalom, I., Lunde, D., Moos, R., and Hamburg, D. (1968). Post-partum "blues" syndrome: A description and related variables. *Archives of General Psychiatry, 18*, 16–27.

Yarrow, M. R., Campbell, J. D., and Burton, R. V. (1968). *Child rearing: An inquiry into research and methods*. San Francisco: Jossey-Bass.

Author Index

Elias, J., **II**, 68, *95*
Elias, M. F., **II**, 274, *277*
Elicker, J., **I**, 87, *96*, 388, *412*; **III**, 232, 233, 234, *245*;
    IV, 164, *176*; **V**, 271, 272, *303*, *401*
Elins, J. L., **I**, 178, 180, *188*; **III**, 98, 99, *106*
Eliot, L., **IV**, 195, *198*
Elkind, D., **V**, 213, *216*
Ella, S., **II**, 288, *310*
Eller, C., **II**, 349, 353, *375*
Elliot, G. L., **III**, 120, *139*
Elliott, K., **V**, 397, *400*
Ellis, B. H., **V**, 60, 80, *84*
Ellis, B. J., **II**, 24, 27; **III**, 305, *312*; **IV**, 304, *321*
Ellis, C., **V**, 337, *346*
Ellis, J. W., **III**, 308, *311*
Ellis, L. K., **I**, 257, *275*
Ellis, S., **III**, 273, *281*, *284*
Ellison, C. G., **III**, 548, *560*
Ellison, R. C., **V**, 319, *327*
Ellwood, D. T., **II**, 222, *229*; **III**, 179, 200, 201, *203*, *213*
Elmen, J. D., **I**, 90, *100*, 123, *133*; **V**, 90, 93, 100, 105, *110*, 156, *167*
Elmen, J. E., **V**, 59, *88*
Elmer, E., **IV**, 301, *324*
El-Sheikh, M., **III**, 42, *65*, 82, *102*; **IV**, 230, 245, *254*
Elshtain, J. B., **III**, 288, *314*
Elson, M., **III**, 577, 592, *594*
Elstein, A. S., **V**, 448, *461*
Elster, A., **IV**, 51, *56*
Elster, A. B., **III**, 41, 44, *68*, 191, *209*; **IV**, 311, *321*
Elwood, D., **IV**, 98, *116*
Elwood, R. W., **II**, 164, 165, *175*
Ely, R., **I**, 196, 197, *220*
Emans, S. J., **III**, 199, *206*
Emanuele, N. V., **II**, 40, *55*
Ember, C. R., **I**, 206, *218*; **III**, 37, *73*, 268, *281*
Emde, R. N., **I**, 11, 12, 16, 20, *33*, *38*, *41*, 48, 58, *67*, 195, 199, *216*, 365, 369, *378*, *381*; **II**, 157, *174*; **III**, 6, *23*, 191, *212*, 578, *594*, *598*; **IV**, 162, *176*, 208, 209, 215, 217, 221, *224*, 248, *254*; **V**, 48, *56*, 64, *84*, 95, *109*, 112, *137*, 255, *265*
Emerick, R., **I**, 171, *187*
Emerson, P. E., **V**, 37, *57*
Emery, R. E., **I**, 78, 89, *96*, 316, 319, *326*, 404, *412*; **II**, 332, *341*; **III**, 79, 84, 88, *102*, *107*, 196, *207*, 295, 296, 305, 306, 308, 309, *312*; **IV**, 207, *224*, 228, 229, 249, *254*, 368, *385*; **V**, 22, *31*
Emes, C. E., **V**, 351, 352, *370*
Emhart, C. B., **IV**, *354*
Emick, M. A., **III**, 161, *167*
Emig, C. A., **II**, 221, 222, *229*
Emler, N. P., **I**, 206, *218*
Emmerich, W., **I**, 82, *96*; **III**, 392, *410*
Emmons, D. W., **V**, 448, *459*

Emory, E., **IV**, 301, *325*
Encyclopedia Britannica, **IV**, 95, *118*
Endriga, M. C., **I**, 390, *413*
Endsley, R., **V**, 376, *400*
Endsley, R. C., **V**, 382, 393, *401*
Engel, I., **V**, 127, *137*
Engel, W. L., **V**, 444, *457*
Engels, F., **V**, 19, *31*
Engelsmann, F., **III**, 227, 230, 235, 238, 239, 241, *246*
Engfer, A., **I**, 407, *412*; **III**, 340, 343, *357*, 430, 432, *435*; **IV**, 184, *198*, 207, 209, 210, 211, 213, 214, 215, *224*; **V**, 74, *84*
Engle, P., **II**, 285, *309*
Engle, P. L., **II**, 222, *226*; **III**, *506*
English, D. J., **IV**, 367, *385*
English, J. B., **II**, 76, *94*
Englund, M., **I**, 87, 96, *100*, 388, *412*; **IV**, 164, *176*; **V**, 271, 272, *303*
Enkin, M., **I**, 6, *35*
Enns, L. R., **I**, 204, *218*
Enns, R., **I**, 269, *274*
Ensminger, M. E., **III**, 93, *104*, 132, *138*, 157, 161, *170*, 195, *209*
Entman, S. S., **V**, 454, 455, *458*, *459*
Entwisle, D. R., **I**, 90, *94*, *96*; **II**, 234, *248*; **III**, 98, *102*, 444, 450, *457*, 581, *594*
Epperson, A., **II**, 300, *310*
Epperson, M. J., **III**, 146, 150, *167*
Epstein, J. L., **I**, 76, 90, *96*; **IV**, 82, *88*
Epstein, J. N., **V**, 364, *373*
Epstein, N., **III**, 305, *312*
Epstein, S., **III**, 418, *435*
Equal Education for All Handicapped Children Act, **IV**, § 1219.1, **IV**, 265, *286*
ERA Study Team, **I**, 302, 306; **IV**, 185, 189, 190, 192, *198*, *199*, *200*, *201*
Erasmus, C. J., **V**, 14, *31*
Erb, K., **III**, 340, *360*
Erchak, G. M., **III**, 37, *73*
Erdley, C. A., **I**, 78, *96*
Erel, O., **III**, 42, *66*, 79, *102*, 227, 228, 229, *245*; **IV**, 203, 205, 213, 220, *224*, 233, *254*
Erera, P. I., **I**, 320, *326*; **III**, 78, 94, 95, 96, *102*, *103*
Erera-Weatherley, P. I., **III**, 95, *103*
ERIC Digest, **V**, 366, *370*
Erickson, M., **I**, 356, 360, *378*; **III**, 342, 343, *357*
Erickson, M. F., **I**, 390, *412*; **II**, 142, *177*; **III**, 366, 373, 376, *388*; **IV**, 163, *176*, 371, 378, *385*; **V**, 271, 272, *303*
Erickson, M. T., **I**, 241, *251*; **III**, 236, *244*
Ericson, M. C., **II**, 233, *248*
Ericson, P. M., **V**, 361, *370*
Ericsson, K. A., **V**, 186, *192*
Erikson, E. H., **I**, 7, 29, *36*, 48, *67*, *218*; **III**, 54, *66*, 391, *410*, 567, 571, 572, 575, *594*; **IV**, 136, *148*, 266, 269, *286*; **V**, 225, *238*
Erikson, M., **I**, 367, *378*; **III**, 35, *65*

Erikson, M. T., **V**, 340, *346*
Erikson, S., **IV**, 339, *353*
Eriksson, P. S., **IV**, 195, *198*
Erin, J. N., **IV**, 264, 265, *286*
Erkut, S., **IV**, 32, *45*
Erlich, S. H., **IV**, 308, *321*
Erman, A., **II**, 352, *375*
Ernest, L., **III**, 155, *167*
Ernst, C., **I**, 166, 167, 168, 169, 170, 171, 172, *185*; **III**, 277, *281*
Ernst, J. M., **II**, 148, *174*
Eron, L. D., **I**, 398, 399, 400, *412*, *414*; **III**, 160, *169*; **IV**, 311, *322*; **V**, 128, 133, *138*
Erskine, M. S., **II**, 52, *55*
Erting, C. J., **I**, 26, *36*; **II**, 194, *199*; **IV**, 264, 272, 273, *286*, *289*
Ervin, F., **IV**, 334, *357*
Erwin, L. J., **IV**, 27, *44*
Esau, A. M. L., **I**, 291, *307*
Escalona, S., **V**, 335, *344*
Escalona, S. A., **I**, 256, *274*
Escalona, S. K., **IV**, 405, *408*
Escamilla-Mondanaro, J., **IV**, 337, *354*
Escovar, J. I., **IV**, 8, *17*
Eskilson, A., **I**, 211, *218*
Esman, A., **III**, 587, *594*
Espasa, F. P., **III**, 576, *597*
Espinosa, M., **II**, 285, *312*; **IV**, 332, *352*, *355*
Espinosa, M. P., **V**, 285, *304*
Esser, G., **IV**, 300, *323*
Esterberg, K. G., **II**, 333, *343*
Estes, D., **III**, 225, *250*
Estroff, D. B., **I**, 335, *350*
Etaugh, A., **I**, 59, *67*
Etaugh, C., **I**, 59, *67*, 191, 193, 194, 205, *219*; **II**, 208, 211, 222, *226*
Ethridge, T., **I**, 59, *70*
Etienne, R., **II**, 347, *375*
Etz, K. E., **II**, 237, *252*; **III**, 451, *460*
Eugster, A., **III**, 340, *357*
Euler, H. A., **II**, 18, *27*; **III**, 144, *167*
Evans, A. D., **IV**, 266, *286*
Evans, B., **I**, 332, 333, *353*
Evans, D. E., **I**, 257, *275*
Evans, D. W., **I**, 366, *379*
Evans, E., **I**, 119, *128*
Evans, G., **II**, 78, *88*
Evans, G. W., **II**, 239, *248*, 282, 285, 287, 288, 290, 292, 297, *308*, *309*
Evans, J. A. S., **II**, 369, 373, *375*
Evans, M. E. E., **IV**, 36, *46*
Evans, R. I., **V**, 315, *325*
Everingham, S. S., **III**, 443, 445, *458*
Everitt, B. J., **II**, 76, 80, *89*
Everitt, L., **III**, 7, *22*
Evoniuk, G. E., **II**, 84, *89*
Ewell, K. K., **V**, 293, *309*
Ewert, B., **I**, 197, *224*
Ewigman, B., **II**, 293, *312*
Ewing, C. P., **V**, 475, *483*
Ewing, M. E., **I**, 208, *222*
Ex, C. T. G. M., **II**, 213, *226*
Exum, C., **II**, 355, 357, *375*

Mitchell, P., **IV**, 166, *179*
Mitchell, R., **V**, 252, *266*
Mitchell, S., **I**, 61, *66*; **III**, 569, 570, *597*
Mitchell, S. A., **III**, 569, 571, *597*
Mitchell, S. K., **III**, 16, *22*, 449, *457*; **IV**, 110, *116*
Mitchell, V. F., **V**, 448, *458*
Mitchell-Keman, C., **IV**, 51, *58*
Mithen, S., **II**, 16, *29*
Mittelman, M. S., **I**, 154, *159*
Mittler, P., **I**, 228, 242, 243, *252*
Miyahara, H., **I**, 9, *38*
Miyake, K., **II**, 330, 332, *343*; **V**, 161, *166*
Miyashita, H., **I**, 9, *38*
Miyatani, M., **III**, 403, *413*
Miyazaki, K., **II**, 78, *93*
Mize, J., **I**, 201, 204, 205, *222*, 397, 398, *415*; **III**, 58, *69*, 497, *507*; **IV**, 234, *257*; **V**, 269, 272, 273, 275, 276, 277, 279, 281, 291, 292, 293, 295, 296, *305*, *306*, *307*, *308*
Mizouguchi, Y., **II**, 16, *26*
Mnookin, R. H., **I**, 117, *131*, 314, 318, *327*; **III**, 292, 293, 294, 295, 296, 297, 309, *313*, 590, *596*; **V**, 20, 21, 22, 25, *32*, *33*, 470, 472, 473, *484*
Mo. Ann. Stat. § 452.340.5, **V**, 472, *484*
Mobley, C. E., **IV**, 264, *288*
Mobley, L., **I**, 174, 175, *187*
Mobley, L. A., **III**, 264, *284*
Model, K. E., **III**, 443, 445, *458*; **V**, 60, *85*
Modell, J., **II**, 320, *341*; **III**, 28, *66*, 183, *210*
Moe, N., **III**, 340, *360*
Moely, B. E., **II**, 147, 155, 160, *173*
Moen, P., **II**, 221, *229*
Moffat, S. D., **II**, 78, *93*
Moffitt, T. E., **I**, 268, *273*; **III**, 420, *436*; **IV**, 166, *175*
Moger, W. H. B., **II**, 165, *174*
Mogi, E., **II**, 78, *93*
Mogilner, M. B., **I**, 337, *352*
Mohay, H., **IV**, 273, *290*
Mohnot, S. M., **II**, 114, *137*
Mohr, P. J., **V**, 361, *371*
Moilanen, I., **I**, 236, *252*
Moldestad, M., **IV**, 334, *353*
Molina, B. S. G., **III**, 463, 475, *482*
Molina, G., **III**, 175, *213*
Molina, V. A., **IV**, 347, *354*
Molitor, A., **I**, 334, *350*; **II**, 153, *175*
Molitor, A. E., **I**, 334, *353*
Moll, L. C., **III**, 274, *283*
Moll, L. S., **IV**, 2, 14, *19*
Molnar, G. E., **IV**, 265, *290*
Molteno, C., **IV**, 319, *321*
Moltz, H., **II**, 37, 38, 41, *57*, 65, 70, *93*, 95
Monahan, S. C., **I**, 180, *187*
Monashkin, I., **III**, *562*
Monbeck, M. E., **IV**, 262, *290*
Mondanaro, J. E., **IV**, 337, *356*
Mondell, S., **III**, 430, *437*
Moneta, G., **I**, 107, 115, *130*
Monica, C., **III**, 82, *103*
Monkhouse, E., **II**, 150, *180*

Monroe, G. N., **IV**, 275, *290*
Monsour, M., **II**, 301, *312*
Montagner, H., **II**, 158, 160, *180*
Montalvo, B., **III**, 83, *105*
Montare, A., **V**, 97, *108*
Montemayor, R., **I**, 21, *39*, 114, 115, 116, 117, *131*; **III**, 32, *69*
Montfort, V., **III**, 89, 90, *103*
Montgomery, A., **I**, 150, 151, *159*
Montgomery, R. J. V., **I**, 154, *159*
Mont-Reynaud, R., **I**, 125, *128*; **IV**, 69, *88*
Montvilo, R. K., **I**, 75, *98*
Moody, C. A., **IV**, 347, *354*
Moon, R. Y., **V**, 445, *460*
Mooney, A., **III**, 239, *249*
Moore, **III**, 202, *210*
Moore, C., **I**, 10, *39*; **II**, 84, *93*; **V**, 160, *164*, 272, 273, *301*
Moore, C. L., **II**, 71, *93*
Moore, E., **I**, 292, *307*
Moore, G., **I**, 395, 398, *411*; **V**, 49, *54*
Moore, G. A., **I**, *39*
Moore, G. T., **II**, 292, *312*
Moore, J. B., **I**, 334, *353*
Moore, K. A., **III**, 122, *138*, 173, 174, 177, 178, 180, 183, 189, 191, 192, 200, 201, *210*, *214*; **IV**, 37, *45*, 103, 104, 107, 114, 118, *119*, *120*
Moore, L. L., **V**, 319, *327*
Moore, M., **V**, 330, *345*
Moore, M. K., **I**, *39*; **III**, 263, 264, 270, *283*
Moore, T. R., **IV**, 340, *356*
Moore, Y., **III**, 159, *166*
Moorehouse, M. J., **II**, 222, *228*
Moores, D. F., **IV**, 265, 279, *290*
Moorman, M., **V**, 356, *373*
Moos, B., **V**, 259, *266*
Moos, B. S., **II**, 220, *228*
Moos, R. H., **I**, 404, *410*; **II**, 220, *228*; **III**, 380, *388*, 579, *599*; **V**, 259, *266*, 282, 284, *301*, *304*, 335, 338, 340, *344*, *348*
Moran, G. S., **I**, 199, *225*, 343, *353*; **III**, 377, *387*, 584, 585, *594*; **IV**, 165, *179*; **V**, 493, *506*
Moran, P. B., **III**, 323, 325, 326, *336*
Morash, D., **I**, 201, *216*
Mordkowitz, E., **IV**, 83, *91*
Moreland, S., **I**, 313, 318, 324, *326*
Morelli, G. A., **I**, 31, *39*; **II**, 144, *181*, 273, 279, 299, *313*, 332, *343*; **IV**, 271, *290*; **V**, 161, *166*, 233, *239*
Morelock, M. J., **V**, 195, 198, 205, 211, *217*
Moreno, M. C., **III**, 521, *534*
Moretto, D., **II**, 67, 76, *89*, *93*
Morgan, D., **V**, 252, *265*
Morgan, E. R., **V**, 202, *218*
Morgan, G. A., **V**, 228, *239*
Morgan, H. D., **II**, 68, 69, 71, 74, 76, 82, 84, *89*, *93*, *175*
Morgan, J., **I**, 297, 299, *309*
Morgan, J. N., **IV**, 98, *118*
Morgan, L., **IV**, 55, *57*
Morgan, L. A., **I**, 143, 146, *159*

Morgan, M., **IV**, 269, *290*; **V**, 354, 363, 366, *370*, *372*
Morgan, M. C., **III**, 199, *207*
Morgan, P., **III**, 122, 133, *137*, 175, 178, 180, 182, 183, 186, 187, 188, 189, 190, 195, *207*
Morgan, R. R., **V**, 127, *141*
Morgan, S. B., **I**, 366, *380*
Morgan, S. P., **II**, 291, 296, *310*
Morgan-Lopez, A., **IV**, 22, 24, 32, 39, *42*, *45*
Morikawa, H., **II**, 145, *175*
Morison, P., **I**, 405, *415*
Morison, S. J., **I**, 288, 302, *306*; **IV**, 185, 189, 190, *198*
Morisset, C. E., **I**, 198, *222*; **III**, 15, 17, *24*; **IV**, *407*
Morland, J., **IV**, 54, *58*
Morley, D., **V**, 368, *372*
Morrell, **II**, 76, *93*
Morrell, J. I., **II**, 40, 41, 45, *53*, *54*, *55*, 76, 77, *88*, *89*, *93*; **IV**, 347, *358*
Morris, A. J., **IV**, 347, *356*
Morris, A. S., **I**, 123, *133*
Morris, C., **II**, 349, *375*; **V**, 446, *460*
Morris, C. A., **I**, 362, *380*
Morris, D., **II**, 100, *137*
Morris, J. T., **I**, 204, 205, *223*
Morris, M. J., **V**, 453, *458*
Morris, N., **II**, 164, *176*
Morris, P., **V**, 338, *345*
Morris, P. A., **I**, 51, *66*, 192, *217*; **II**, 316, 317, 318, 326, 327, 328, 329, *340*; **III**, 27, *64*, 201, *211*, 472, *482*
Morris, S. C., **I**, 75, *99*
Morrisett, C., **III**, 191, *211*
Morrisett, C., **III**, 191, *211*
Morrison, A., **I**, 404, *410*; **III**, 84, 85, *101*, 551, *559*; **IV**, 229, 230, 232, 249, 250, *253*
Morrison, D. R., **III**, 173, 174, 177, 178, 180, 183, 189, 191, 200, *206*, *210*, 290, 291, 292, 305, 306, 307, *311*, *314*, *315*
Morrison, G. M., **IV**, 28, *44*
Morrison, G. S., **I**, 46, *69*
Morrison, J. R., **IV**, 310, *323*
Morrissette, P. J., **I**, 316, 324, *326*
Morrissy, J. R., **V**, 315, *326*
Morrongiello, B. A., **I**, 56, *69*
Morrow, J., **I**, 258, *276*
Morrow, L. M., **IV**, 36, *44*
Morrow, R. D., **IV**, 72, *91*
Morse, A. C., **II**, 67, *92*
Mortensen, N., **I**, 116, 125, *128*
Mortimer, J., **II**, 211, 221, *228*
Morton, E. S., **II**, 190, *200*
Morycz, R., **I**, 149, 150, 152, *160*
Mosbacher, D., **III**, 319, 324, 328, *336*
Mosby, L. A., **V**, 17, *33*
Moscov, S., **III**, 385, *387*
Moselle, K., **V**, 13, *30*
Moses, K. L., **IV**, 264, *290*
Mosher, D. L., **IV**, 31, *46*
Mosher, W., **III**, 173, *211*
Mosher, W. D., **I**, 286, *309*

Mosier, C., **I**, 53, *69*; **III**, 256, 260, 274, *281*, *284*; **IV**, 24, 30, *44*; **V**, 223, 231, *238*, *239*
Mosko, S., **II**, 274, *279*
Moskowitz, D. W., **III**, 229, *249*
Moskowitz, J. T., **III**, 527, *532*
Mosley, J., **III**, 56, *69*
Moss Iaukea, K. A., **I**, 286, *306*
Moss, E., **III**, 227, *251*
Moss, H., **II**, 144, *178*; **III**, 373, *388*
Moss, H. A., **I**, 169, 180, *186*, 190, 195, 222, 401, *413*; **II**, 148, 164, *178*, *179*; **III**, 417, *437*
Moss, H. B., **IV**, 310, *321*
Moss, P., **III**, 222, *249*, 256, *283*
Most, R. K., **V**, 225, 229, *237*
Mota, M. T., **II**, 49, *57*, 165, *178*
Mott, F. L., **III**, 29, 44, *69*, 122, *138*, 180, 189, 191, 194, *205*, *210*; **IV**, 103, *120*
Mott, J. A., **III**, 463, 470, *483*
Motti, F., **IV**, 234, 246, *258*
Mould, L., **IV**, 274, *284*
Mount, M. K., **III**, 420, *437*
Mounts, N. S., **I**, 90, *100*, 107, 119, 122, 123, 124, 125, *130*, *131*, *133*, 204, 205, 212, *217*, *223*, 397, 399, 400, *414*; **II**, 244, *252*, 293, *308*, 330, *343*; **III**, 30, *69*, 290, *314*; **IV**, 75, 78, *92*, 157, 158, 159, *178*, *180*; **V**, 59, *88*, 90, 93, 100, 105, *110*, 155, 156, 160, *166*, *167*, 286, 293, 295, *306*
Mouradian, V. E., **V**, 130, *141*
Mouskhelishvili, A., **II**, 11, *28*
Moussa, W., **II**, 298, *314*
Mowbray, C. T., **IV**, 298, *324*
Mowery, J. L., **IV**, 330, 345, *357*
Mowl, G. E., **IV**, 261, 278, *290*
Mowrer, O. H., **I**, 398, *412*
Moynihan, D., **IV**, 4, *19*
Moyse, A., **II**, 158, 160, *180*
Mrazek, D. A., **I**, 59, *68*
MTA Cooperative Group, **IV**, 402, *409*
Mucklow, B. M., **III**, 322, *337*
Mudar, P. J., **IV**, 330, 337, 342, 345, *356*
Mueller, B., **III**, 227, *250*
Mueller, B. A., **II**, 294, *312*
Mueller, E., **V**, 287, *306*
Mueller, E. C., **I**, 48, 50, *69*
Mueller, R. A., **I**, 211, *217*
Mueller, R. F., **IV**, 271, *289*
Muenchow, S., **IV**, 398, *410*
Mufson, L., **III**, 159, *172*
Muhesen, S., **II**, 16, *26*
Muir, D., **II**, 159, *180*
Mukai, D., **II**, 274, *279*
Mukai, T., **V**, 322, *327*
Mukhopadhyay, R., **III**, 97, *102*
Mukopadhyay, T., **V**, 351, 352, 356, 359, 363, *371*
Mulaik, S. A., **I**, 173, *186*
Mulhall, P., **I**, 119, *128*
Mulhern, R. K. B., **V**, 317, *327*
Mullally, P. R., **I**, 231, 244, *253*

Mullan, J. T., **I**, 136, 140, 151, 152, *157*, *159*
Mullaney, H. A., **V**, 321, *328*
Mullatini, L., **III**, 97, *105*
Muller, E., **II**, 156, *178*
Mulligan, G. M., **III**, 85, *100*
Mullin, C. H., **III**, 122, 123, 124, *138*
Mullins, L. L., **V**, 282, *306*
Mullis, A. K., **III**, *139*
Mullis, R. L., **III**, *139*
Mullooly, J. P., **V**, 444, *458*
Mumma, G. H., **IV**, 234, *257*
Mumme, D. L., **V**, 47, *55*
Mundform, D. J., **IV**, 38, *40*, 109, *117*; **II**, 294, *308*
Mundy, P., **I**, 367, *379*
Mundy-Castle, A. C., **III**, 258, 267, *283*
Munholland, K. A., **III**, 584, *593*; **V**, 48, *54*
Munir, K., **IV**, 310, *320*
Munn, P., **I**, 202, 204, *218*; **III**, 272, *280*
Munoz, A., **III**, 550, *560*
Munroe, R. H., **II**, 261, *279*
Munroe, R. L., **II**, 261, *279*
Muns, S., **II**, 41, *60*, 65, *97*
Munsterman, K., **III**, 488, *508*
Munton, A. G., **III**, 528, *535*
Murata, Y., **II**, 78, *88*
Murdoch, T., **II**, 165, *174*
Murdock, G. P., **I**, 3, *40*
Murkoff, H. E., **I**, 63, *67*; **III**, 409, *410*
Murphey, D. A., **I**, 16, *40*
Murphy, B., **I**, 347, *353*; **V**, 96, 105, *108*
Murphy, B. C., **III**, 401, *410*; **V**, 47, *55*, 116, 120, 125, 128, *136*, *141*, 276, *303*
Murphy, C., **III**, 84, 85, 91, *104*
Murphy, C. C., **IV**, 398, *410*
Murphy, C. M., **I**, 404, *413*; **IV**, 228, *256*
Murphy, D. L., **I**, 64, *381*
Murphy, G., **II**, 284, *311*
Murphy, J. K., **II**, 301, *312*
Murphy, J. R., **V**, 444, *460*
Murphy, J. V., **V**, 70, *83*
Murphy, K., **V**, 355, 361, 362, 363, *373*
Murphy, K. C., **I**, 84, *101*
Murphy, P. R., **II**, 165, *174*
Murphy, S., **III**, 270, *283*
Murphy, S. L., **I**, 136, *158*
Murphy, S. O., **III**, 265, 266, 270, *283*
Murphy-Cowan, T., **III**, 160, *169*
Murray, A., **II**, 155, *178*
Murray, B. A., **V**, 453, *460*
Murray, C., **III**, 328, *336*, 344, 346, 349, 351, 352, 354, *357*, *358*; **IV**, 53, 54, *57*
Murray, C. A., **V**, 190, *193*
Murray, C. B., **I**, 211, *222*
Murray, H., **III**, 232, 237, *248*; **V**, 376, *403*
Murray, J., **IV**, 244, *253*, 340, 341, *353*
Murray, J. A. H., **III**, *561*
Murray, K., **I**, 59, *68*; **IV**, 164, 167, 168, *177*; **V**, 47, *56*
Murray, K. T., **III**, 5, 17, *24*; **IV**, 168, 172, *177*; **V**, 120, *139*
Murray, L., **I**, 5, *40*, 195, *222*; **II**, 317, *343*; **IV**, 305, 309, 319, *321*, *323*, *325*
Murray, R., **IV**, 182, 185, 188, *201*

Murray, R. B., **III**, 151, *170*
Murray, S. L., **III**, 527, *534*
Murry, T., **II**, 156, *178*
Mushin, D., **III**, 341, 349, *358*, *359*
Musick, J., **II**, 292, *310*
Musick, J. S., **III**, 161, 164, *170*
Musiol, I., **II**, 78, *94*
Musselman, C., **IV**, 264, *290*
Mussen, P., **IV**, 77, *93*; **V**, 112, 120, *140*
Musto, D., **IV**, 331, *356*
Musun-Miller, L., **III**, 489, *507*
Mutzell, S., **IV**, 333, 334, *356*
Muxem, A., **V**, 347
Muzio, C., **III**, 96, *105*
Mydral, G., **IV**, 53, *57*
Myer, D. J., **III**, 156, *170*
Myers, B., **I**, 59, *70*; **IV**, 52, *56*
Myers, B. J., **I**, 336, 340, 341, *351*, *353*; **III**, 146, 150, 164, *167*, *170*; **IV**, 346, *354*
Myers, D. E., **III**, 173, 174, 177, 178, 180, 183, 194, 196, 200, *209*, *210*
Myers, J. E., **III**, 154, *170*
Myers, L., **III**, 225, 227, 233, 235, *247*
Myers, R. A., **I**, 284, *306*
Myers, R. L., **IV**, 230, 234, 250, *254*
Myers, S., **I**, 195, 199, *216*; **IV**, 51, *56*
Myhal, N., **II**, 65, 66, 67, 75, *89*
Myklebust, H., **IV**, 267, 268, *290*
Myowa-Yamakoshi, M., **II**, 104, 107, *132*
Myrianthopoulos, N. C., **I**, 342, *252*

N

N. H. Rev. Stat. Ann. § 546-A: 2, **V**, 471, *484*
N. J. Rev. Stat. § 2A: 4A-76, **V**, 479, *484*
Nabors, L. A., **III**, 230, 238, 240, *245*
Nachmias, M., **I**, 390, *415*; **II**, 142, *177*; **V**, 96, *109*
Nachtigall, R., **III**, 352, 353, *359*
Nadel, J., **I**, 10, *40*
Nadelman, L., **I**, 175, *187*
Nader, P. R., **IV**, 35, *41*; **V**, 319, 324, *325*, *326*, *327*
Nadler, R., **II**, 100, 105, 128, *137*
Nadler, R. D., **II**, 101, 106, 110, 123, *137*, *139*
Naerde, A., **V**, 256, *266*
Nagano-Nakamura, K. N., **IV**, 72, *91*
Nagel, G., **III**, 409, *412*
Nagel, S. K., **II**, 211, *227*
Nagi, S. Z., **IV**, 276, *290*
Nagle, K. J., **I**, 196, *223*; **V**, 230, *239*
Nagle, R. J., **III**, 225, *244*
Nagler, S., **IV**, 302, *323*
Nahas, Z., **II**, 169, *178*
Naiman, S., **II**, 157, *174*
Nair, R. C., **I**, 368, *376*
Naito, M., **III**, 264, 276, *284*
Najbauer, J., **II**, 84, *93*
Najman, J. M., **IV**, 299, 319, *324*
Nakamura, K., **II**, 237, *252*
Nakashima, K., **II**, 40, *59*
Nakstad, P., **V**, 315, *328*

Subject Index